D1252366

The Cambridge Dictionary of Modern World History

In a world where we take for granted the ability to communicate instantly across vast distances and time, world history has come of age. We increasingly reflect on history from a position which no longer privileges Europe or the West, and from a global perspective which ranges from the Pacific Rim to the Balkans, and from Latin America to the Middle East. Compiled by an international team of contributors, area editors and general editors, *The Cambridge Dictionary of Modern World History* provides a much needed guide to the main global events, personalities and themes from the eighteenth century to the present. Major themes of war, politics, society and religion are covered, alongside more recent subjects within the discipline; from globalization and the environment to transnational social movements and human rights. This is an essential new work of reference not only for scholars and students but also for the general public.

Chris Cook is a former Senior Research Officer and head of the Modern Archives Survey at the London School of Economics and Political Science. He has combined the careers of academic historian and distinguished compiler of reference works. His many publications include the *Dictionary of Historical Terms* (1998), the European Political Facts series and the standard *Short History of the Liberal Party* (2010). With John Stevenson he has co-edited the Routledge Historical Companions as well as co-authoring *The Slump* (2009), a major study of Britain in the 1930s.

John Stevenson is a former Reader and Fellow of Worcester College, University of Oxford. He has published widely on British, European and world history, including works on both political and social history. His publications include *A History of Europe* (2005), *The Routledge Companion to World History since 1914* (2005, with Chris Cook), *A History of British Elections since 1688* (2014, with Chris Cook) and *William Cobbett: Romanticism and Enlightenment* (2015, edited with J. Grande). He is currently editing a volume of English historical documents for the period 1914–57.

The

Cambridge Dictionary of

MODERN WORLD HISTORY

Edited by

CHRIS COOK

and

JOHN STEVENSON

CAMBRIDGE
UNIVERSITY PRESS

CAMBRIDGE
UNIVERSITY PRESS

University Printing House, Cambridge CB2 8BS, United Kingdom

One Liberty Plaza, 20th Floor, New York, NY 10006, USA

477 Williamstown Road, Port Melbourne, VIC 3207, Australia

314–321, 3rd Floor, Plot 3, Splendor Forum, Jasola District Centre, New Delhi – 110025, India

79 Anson Road, #06–04/06, Singapore 079906

Cambridge University Press is part of the University of Cambridge.

It furthers the University's mission by disseminating knowledge in the pursuit of education, learning, and research at the highest international levels of excellence.

www.cambridge.org
Information on this title: www.cambridge.org/9780521847711
DOI: 10.1017/9780511842740

Cambridge University Press 2018

First published 2018

Printed in the United Kingdom by Clays, St Ives plc

A catalogue record for this publication is available from the British Library.

Library of Congress Cataloging-in-Publication Data
Names: Cook, Chris, 1945– editor. | Stevenson, John, 1946– editor.
Title: The Cambridge dictionary of modern world history / edited by Chris Cook
and John Stevenson.
Description: Cambridge, United Kingdom ; New York, NY : Cambridge University Press, [2018] |
Includes bibliographical references and index.
Identifiers: LCCN 2017033140 | ISBN 9780521847711 (alk. paper)
Subjects: LCSH: History, Modern – Dictionaries.
Classification: LCC D209 .C18 2017 | DDC 909.003–dc23
LC record available at https://lccn.loc.gov/2017033140

ISBN 978-0-521-84771-1 Hardback

Contents

Contributors

Calvin H. Allen, Jr, Cemil Aydin, William Beezley, Jonathan Bell, Magnus T. Bernhardsson, Carlos Brando, Winnifred R. Brown-Glaude, David Buisseret, Trevor Burnard, Brian Caton, Pratik Chakrabarti, Aryendra Chakravartty, Lily Chang, Elizabeth Clapp, Peter Coates, Frank Cogliano, George Conyne, Philip Cook, R. Douglas Cope, Graham Cornwell, Martin Crawford, Robert Crews, Gareth Davies, Carmen De Michele, Elizabeth Dillenburg, Rod Duncan, Xavier Duran, Martin Durham, Howard Eissenstat, Felipe Tamega Fernandes, Jonathan Goldstein, Pablo Gomez, Leonard Gordon, Harry Harmer, Robert Harrison, Timothy Hawkins, Michael Heale, Gad Heuman, Brian Holden Reid, Nadine Hunt, Emma Hunter, Steve Jacobson, Rhodri Jeffreys-Jones, Andrew Johnstone, Tim Keirn, John Killick, Peter F. Klaren, Deep Kanta Lahiri Choudhury, George Lewis, Toby Lincoln, Peter Ling, Brian Loveman, Julie MacArthur, Lisa Maguire, Bertie Mandelblatt, Robert Mason, James McClellan, John McNeill, Martin Meenagh, Ranald Michie, David Milne, Farina Mir, Rana Mitter, Ryoko Nakano, Phillip Naylor, Kendrick Oliver, Kenneth Owen, Sebastian Page, Fabio Parasecoli, Albert L. Park, Graham Pitts, Marshall Poe, Mridu Rai, Monica Rankin, Donald Ratcliffe, Vera Blinn Reber, Christoph Rosenmüller, Haimanti Roy, John Saillant, Friedrich Schuler, Daniel Scroop, Alex Seago, Ronald E. Seavoy, James Seelye, Jr, Jay Sexton, Verene Shepherd, Jeffrey Shumway, Julia Stephens, John Stevenson, John Thornton, Robert Travers, Stephen Tuck, Knut S. Vikør, Adrian Webb, Emily West, Mark White, Merry Wiesner-Hanks, Gary Williams, Wasana Wongsurawat, Khodr Zaarour and Chitralekha Zutshi.

Editors' Preface

World history has come of age in recent years. Today, we live in an interrelated and mobile environment where we take for granted the ability to communicate instantly across the world. Accordingly, history has gone global as we increasingly reflect on history from a position which no longer privileges Europe or the West. The coverage of the *Cambridge Dictionary of Modern World History* is by definition worldwide, from the Pacific Rim to the Balkans and from Latin America to the Middle East. Its themes range widely from political issues such as civil rights, feminism and revolution to cultural areas such as cinema and romanticism. The great world religions, Buddhism, Islam, Hinduism and Christianity, are fully represented, as are more major secular currents of thought from the Enlightenment to democracy and neoliberalism. Within the many entries dealing with individual nation states, countries and geographical regions the *Dictionary* considers issues in a global context such as agriculture, energy, exploration, health and disease, imperialism and decolonization, industrialization, migration, state formation, the transport revolution and the concept of globalization itself.

World history does not fall into neat categories and much of the traditional periodization historians use is Eurocentric or fits into an outdated model of the 'rise of the West'. Historians have shown us that globalization has a long history, that intercontinental contacts existed even in the distant past, possibly as far back as the Bronze Age or earlier, and historians have highlighted the significance of the so-called 'Silk Road', which provided a route for contact between Asia and Europe long before the trans-oceanic voyages of European explorers and traders. These began at the end of the fifteenth century with the first transatlantic voyages and the circumnavigation of the globe in the early sixteenth century led by a European, Ferdinand Magellan. From that period onwards, the impact of Europe on the wider world became a significant feature in global history. It was the Spanish who invaded and conquered the Latin American empires of the Aztecs and Incas rather than the other way round, and Portuguese seafarers who voyaged into the Indian Ocean, the China Seas and the Pacific rather than the reverse. No Polynesian war canoe sailed into the Lagoon of Venice when Cook charted the Pacific; no Chinese junk sailed through the Dover Straits when Dutch and Portuguese merchants and missionaries were navigating those of Malacca. The interventions of Europeans in Latin America, Africa and the Indian Ocean accelerated through the sixteenth and seventeenth centuries, making decisive steps towards the emergence of an increasingly globalized world.

When, then, did 'modern' history begin? For more than half a century historians have become familiar with the term *early modern* to describe a period approximately from the fifteenth century to the eighteenth in which fundamental changes occurred which acted as precursors to the 'modern' world, including the beginnings of the scientific revolution, the development of printing, the so-called 'military revolution' and the emergence of powerful nation states in Europe which, as stated, were already having an increasingly influential impact upon the rest of the world. The eighteenth century – the approximate starting point for this volume – can be seen as the realization of these developments on an increasingly global scale. Not only were European empires well established in Central and Latin America; interventions in North America, Africa and the Indian subcontinent were beginning to have critical impacts in these regions and upon their indigenous rulers. Something like a worldwide trading network was being established on the initiative of Europeans and having increasingly transformative effects.

Transformative but not one-way, as the fertile notions of the *Columbian exchange* and *orientalism* remind us. Two-way exchanges of goods, peoples and ideas had a long history but became greater as the world grew smaller. Gunpowder and printing, invented in China, were taken up in Europe and utilized to transform power relations and the world of ideas. Potatoes, sugar and tobacco flowed from the Americas to influence the diets and well-being of the whole world, while millions of pieces of Chinese porcelain and countless crates of tea were shipped westwards to Europe, paid for by western merchants with silver mined in Potosi in Peru and opium from India. The Atlantic slave trade moved as many as 10 million people from Africa to the Americas, while the nineteenth century saw tens of millions of migrants from Europe travelling to almost every part of the globe. From the eighteenth century there was an intensification of commercial and economic relationships in which almost every corner of the world was involved.

From the eighteenth century industrialization provided a fresh impetus, enhancing the commerce and power of those states which most rapidly adapted to it. Coal, cotton, iron and manufactured goods flowed from the mines and factories of the first industrial nations, dominating trade in a new range of products and revolutionizing lives. The rise of mechanized production and commercial society, the transport revolution and rapid urbanization created a new world whose repercussions are still being felt. During the course of the nineteenth century steam-powered machines working night and day produced textiles and other goods in unprecedented quantities, railway engines travelled at speeds never before achieved, and steel structures such as the Eiffel Tower were the first to rise higher than the wonders of the ancient world. By the early twentieth century world cities such as London, New York and Tokyo were the largest the world had ever seen, but they in turn would be eclipsed by the mega-cities of the twenty-first. There would be no turning back from the economic transformation which began three centuries ago, as scientific and technological advances propelled unheralded developments from space exploration to the

Internet. But the transformations were not solely economic. The birth of the 'modern' world owed at least as much to the eighteenth-century Enlightenment and the revolutionary impact of concepts of democratic and human rights, socialism, feminism and the sovereignty of peoples, ideas which resonate down to our own day.

The 'rise of the West' had a geopolitical reality – by the time of World War I a handful of 'great powers' politically and economically controlled the greater part of the world in formal or informal empires – but so did its decline. Within fifty years the 'Great Empires' had been largely dismantled, creating a world of nearly two hundred nation states. Fresh geopolitical divisions, such as the Cold War, were dismantled in their turn, a bipolar rivalry of the United States and the Soviet Union replaced by a multiplicity of new examples of collaboration and cooperation, tension and conflict. To this end as far as possible, the *Dictionary* brings world history right up to date to the early twenty-first century, including events such as the Arab Spring, conflicts in Islam and the rise of new global economic powers. It tries too, to focus on the larger themes which are more deeply embedded and evolve more slowly. In doing so, it attempts to present a rounded reference work to the history of the modern world.

In compiling the *Dictionary* we have incurred many debts. The many area editors and contributors are acknowledged separately, but particular thanks are due to Victoria Grant for her work at the beginning and Dr H. Harmer, Dr M. Meenagh, Dr P. Thompson and Dr A. Webb for their invaluable assistance in bringing the work to a conclusion. Victoria Parrin assisted greatly with the production and our copy-editor Hilary Hammond considerably improved the original text. To our editor, Michael Watson, we owe a considerable debt of gratitude for his patient support during its lengthy completion. Great thanks are also due to Sandra Byford and Linda Hollingworth for their invaluable assistance with the typing.

THE DICTIONARY

A

Abako

Founded in 1950 in Leopoldville, now Kinshasa, as a cultural organization concerned with the Kikongo language. In 1954 **Joseph Kasavubu** took over its leadership and on 23 August 1956 he responded to A. A. J. van Bilsen's blueprint for the gradual decolonization of the **Belgian Congo** over thirty years by demanding immediate independence. In contrast to the unitary nationalism of **Patrice Lumumba**'s Mouvement Nationale Congolese (MNC), Abako was committed to a federal solution recognizing ethnic identities.

Abbas, Ferhat (1899–1985)

Algerian nationalist, son of a Muslim civil servant. Initially favoured the assimilation of the 'native element' (the Arab population) in French society and the abolition of colonialism through the emancipation of his fellow Muslims as French citizens, but rebuffed by the French in 1938. Responded by founding the Union Populaire Algérienne seeking equal rights for Arabs and French. His *Manifesto of the Algerian People*, proclaimed 10 February 1943, called for self-determination and a constitution conferring equality on all Algerian citizens. A May addendum urging sovereignty was presented to the French in June, but rejected. Abbas responded by jointly organizing the Amis du Manifeste et de la Liberté (AML – Friends of the Manifesto and Liberty) proposing an Algerian autonomous republic federated with **France**. Sentenced to a year's imprisonment and the AML suppressed, he continued vainly to advocate cooperation. He escaped to join the **Front de Libération Nationale** (FLN) and became president of the Algerian Republic's first provisional government in 1958. He was president of the Algerian Constituent Assembly in 1962. Opposed to **Ben Bella**'s revolutionary approach, he was placed under house arrest in 1964–5.

Abbas I, Khedive of Egypt (1813–1854)

Khedive (viceroy) of Ottoman Egypt, 1848–54. Distrustful of European influences, he rejected the reforms introduced by his grandfather and predecessor, Muhammad 'Ali Pasha, viceroy, 1805–48. He reduced government spending and the military and the number of military and public schools, and halted the construction of the Delta Dam and opposed the French plans for a **Suez Canal**. Nevertheless, he allowed the British to build the **Alexandria** to Cairo railway; they responded by helping him in his dispute with the Turkish Ottoman government about the application in Egypt of westernizing reforms. He dispatched an expeditionary force to help the Turks in the **Crimean War**, 1853, and abolished the state trade monopolies which were contrary to Ottoman treaties with the European powers. He reduced the burden on the poor of taxation, compulsory labour and military conscription, but was strangled by two of his servants.

Abbas II, Khedive of Egypt (1874–1944)

Last khedive (viceroy) of Ottoman Egypt (1892–1914) and a nationalist opponent of British power there. Encouraged by the popular nationalist hostility to growing British influence, he initially attempted to rule independently of the British agent and consul general, Lord **Cromer**, and appointed an anti-British prime minister, but Cromer responded to criticism of the efficiency of British troops by curtailing the khedive's freedom of action. Financially supported the pan-Islamic and anti-British daily paper, *al-Mu'ayyad*, he rejected the nationalist demands for constitutional government in 1906. He endorsed the formation of the National Party of **Mustafa Kamil** in opposition to the moderate nationalist Ummah Party preferred by the British, 1907, but the National Party leaders were exiled or imprisoned and the khedive's authority further curtailed by the British consul general, Lord **Kitchener**, 1912–14. Urged the Egyptians and Sudanese to support the Central Powers by fighting the British, 1914, but **Egypt** was declared a British protectorate, 18 December 1914, and Abbas II was deposed and exiled the next day.

'Abd al-Aziz ibn 'Abd al-Rahman Al Sa'ud (1880–1953)

Commonly known as Ibn Sa'ud, founder and first king of the Kingdom of **Saudi Arabia**. 'Abd al-Aziz was born in Riyadh at the time of the collapse of the second Saudi state in Najd. He remained in Riyadh while his father served as the Al Rashid-appointed emir of the city until 'Abd al-Rahman staged an unsuccessful revolt in 1890–1. While 'Abd al-Rahman sought refuge in the desert, 'Abd al-Aziz joined other family members in **Bahrain**. In 1893, 'Abd al-Rahman found protection in Kuwait. 'Abd al-Aziz joined his father and became a protégé of Sheikh Mubarak Al Sabah, the new ruler of **Kuwait**. 'Abd al-Aziz joined with Sheikh Mubarak in several raids against their joint enemy the Al Rashid, and in 1900 he staged an unsuccessful effort to retake Riyadh. However, in 1902, he and a small band of followers returned to Riyadh and expelled the Rashidis, thereby setting the stage for a renewed Saudi state. During the next decade 'Abd al-Aziz consolidated his control over central Arabia by beginning to settle nomadic populations and using the tenets of Wahhabi Islam as state ideology against Ottoman and Rashidi external threats. By 1912 he had begun forming the settled Bedouin populations into a military organization known as the Ikhwan (Brothers). They became a highly loyal and devoutly religious mobile fighting force, and during the next fifteen years he conquered al-Hasa from the **Ottoman Empire** (1913), Jabal Shamar from the Al Rashid (1921), and the Hijaz from Sharif Husayn (1925). But as expansion ceased and changes deemed innovations by conservative Ikhwan entered the state, they became disruptive, sabotaging projects such as telegraph lines and launching unauthorized raids into **Jordan**, **Kuwait** and **Iraq**. Grievance turned to revolt in 1928, but 'Abd al-Aziz defeated the Ikhwan and destroyed their settlements.

With the slowing of expansion and suppression of the Ikhwan, he turned his attention to consolidation of his newly formed kingdom. In September 1932 he merged all his territories and proclaimed the Kingdom of **Saudi Arabia**. One of his first acts as king was to award an oil concession to Standard of California (which operated as **Aramco**) in 1933. He then finalized the territories of the kingdom as a brief war with **Yemen** in 1934 led to the annexation of Asir. **World War II** was quiet for Saudi Arabia, although 'Abd al-Aziz's February 1945 meeting with American president **Harry Truman** brought the Saudi king world attention. The discovery and export of oil following the war also alleviated the kingdom's poverty. New-found wealth, much of which went directly to members of the royal family, placed increasing social and economic pressures on the aging king. 'Abd al-Aziz's final years saw modest political reforms with the creation of government ministries in 1951 and a council of ministers in 1952, but also greater social upheaval with a strike of Aramco workers in 1953.

'Abd al-Karim al-Kattabi (1882–1963)

'Abd al-Karim al-Kattabi led an anti-colonial struggle against Spanish imperalism in the Rif Mountains of Morocco from 1920 to 1926. 'Abd al-Karim served as a judge in the Islamic court of his tribe, the Ait Waryaghar, and later in the Spanish colonial administration before unifying tribal groups of the Rif in rebellion against Spanish occupation. He experienced great success at first and by 1921 controlled most of northern **Morocco** under the Rif Republic. His success concerned the French authorities to the south, and the French and Spanish eventually amassed an army of 500,000 troops to crush the Rifian forces. 'Abd al-Karim surrendered in 1926 and was exiled to Reunion, where he remained until 1947. He eventually settled in Cairo, where he became an outspoken advocate of Arab independence movements. His military and political success against the Spanish served as a blueprint for anti-colonial guerrilla movements around the world.

'Abd al-Qadir ibn Muhyi al-Din, 'al-Jaza'ari' (1808–1883)

Hero of the Algerian resistance. The son of a leading Sufi religious leader, 'Abd al-Qadir was asked to lead resistance to the French invasion of western **Algeria** in 1830. Showing great organizational and military talent, he was able to unify the tribes against a French force that was still limited. Alternating between periods of combat and several ceasefires with the French, he set up a modernizing small state in the interior of western and central Algeria in 1834–9, but the expansion of the French forces drove him on the defensive from the early 1840s, and to guerrilla warfare. Finally, he had to seek refuge in Morocco, but under French pressure Sultan **'Abd al-Rahman** pushed him back to Algeria where he surrendered in 1847. He retired to Damascus, gaining fame for his religious writings.

'Abd al-Rahman ibn Hisham, 'Moulay' (1778–1859)

Moroccan sultan, 1822–59. The first modernizing sultan of **Morocco**, 'Abd al-Rahman tried to develop trade and economy while strengthening central authority. He gave priority to establishing a modern army in the face of the growing challenge from the European powers. The war in neighbouring **Algeria** meant he lost the conflict with the French, and he had to accept increasing European influence over his country.

'Abd al-Rahman al-Jabarti (1753–1825)

Egyptian scholar and historian, born in the Nile Delta region, who lived for most of his life in Cairo. He received an Islamic education at **Al-Azhar University**, where he also taught, and began keeping a detailed monthly chronicle of **Egypt**'s history as he witnessed it. His entries include detailed accounts of **Napoleon**'s invasion and **Mehmet Ali**'s seizure of power, and the work is regarded as one of the most detailed accounts from an Egyptian perspective.

Abdülhamid II, Ottoman Sultan (r. 1876–1909)

Sultan Abdülhamid II assumed power in the **Ottoman Empire** at a time of military, economic and political upheaval. In 1876 he replaced his brother Murad, who had succeeded their uncle, **Abdülaziz**, but he reigned for less than one year. Remembered as a political reactionary, Abdülhamid II suspended the first Ottoman parliament in 1878, barely more than a year after its inception. Although an apparent enemy of political liberalization, Abdülhamid II oversaw a quickening of reforms in diverse arenas such as infrastructure, education and military affairs. Under his reign, the **Ottoman Empire** suffered a string of military defeats resulting in significant loss of territory and a mass influx of refugees. The spectre of territorial loss and even the potential break-up of the empire loomed throughout his reign. The **Young Turks** revolt in July 1908 forced him to restore the constitution, and he was deposed the following year, accused of sponsoring a counter-coup.

Abdülaziz, Ottoman Sultan (r. 1861–1876)

After succeeding his older brother Abdülmecid as sultan and caliph, Abdülaziz continued the **Tanzimat** reforms of his predecessor. Under Abdülaziz, a powerful clique of bureaucrats pursued wide-ranging administrative modernization. No place was given to opposition political movements, however. A broad coalition of forces, religious and secular, supported a coup to depose him in 1876 after military defeats in Bosnia and **Bulgaria**. Days later, Abdülaziz was found dead in disputed circumstances.

Abdullah, Emir of Transjordan and King of Jordan (1882–1951)

Abdullah, the second son of Sharif Hussein of Mecca, participated in the **Arab revolt** of 1916 along with his younger brother Faisal. Before the war, he had represented Mecca in the Ottoman Parliament. His family, the **Hashemites**, who trace their lineage to the family of the Prophet, controlled the holiest sites of **Islam** until 1919 when they lost hold of Mecca and Medina to their rivals the Saudi family (at the time also British clients). Thus deprived of their zone of influence in the Hijaz, the Hashemites received recompense with other territories from the British. Abdullah became the of Emir of Transjordan, which proved a more resilient entity than his brother Faisal's Arab kingdom, based in Damascus. Abdullah received the title of king when Transjordan won independence in 1946 and subsequently oversaw the addition of the West Bank and **Jerusalem** to its territory in 1950. Whilst visiting the Al-Aqsa Mosque a year later, Abdullah was killed by a Palestinian nationalist. After the brief reign of his eldest son Talal, Abdullah's grandson **Hussein** became king in 1953, ruling until his death in 1999.

Abdullah, Sheikh Muhammad (1905–1982)

A leading politician and founder of the Jammu and Kashmir National Conference. In the 1930s and 1940s Abdullah organized protests against the Maharaja of Kashmir. In 1947 he helped orchestrate the accession of **Kashmir** to **India** and became the new state's prime minister, but was later imprisoned due to his efforts to defend Kashmiri autonomy. After a negotiated settlement, he served as Chief Minister of Kashmir from 1974 until his death. He is known as the Lion of Kashmir.

Abdülmecid, Ottoman Sultan (1839–1861)

Succeeding his father, **Mahmud II**, after the latter's death in 1839, Abdülmecid's reign is closely associated with the **Tanzimat**, a programme of reform which aimed to modernize the **Ottoman Empire**. Abdülmecid ascended the throne at the age of 16. He was sympathetic to the goal of modernization and the two most important documents associated with the Tanzimat reforms, the Gulhane Edict

(1839) and the Hatt-ı Humayun (1856), were both promulgated during his reign. Like other nineteenth-century monarchs, Abdülmecid was increasingly tasked to serve as a living symbol of the empire, while day-to-day decisions were made by the bureaucracy. As such, he made a number of public tours of Ottoman provinces. During his reign, the **Ottoman Empire** became increasingly dependent on French and British support and allied with them against **Russia** during the **Crimean War**. He died of tuberculosis at age 38.

Abeokuta

A town in modern-day **Nigeria** founded around 1825 by refugees from the civil war that was spreading through the old **Oyo** Empire as a result of constitutional crisis, jihadist invasions from the north, and interventions from **Dahomey** and other neighbouring polities. In the 1850s Abeokuta was the scene of serious attempts by European and American missionaries and abolitionists to create a centre of 'legitimate trade' in commodities other than slaves, of which cotton was one of the most prominent. It also became a cultural centre for new Yoruba–Christian culture including the publication of an early Yoruba newspaper. Dahomey frequently attacked the city, but each time it was successfully defended. At the end of the nineteenth century it was incorporated into the British colony of Nigeria. More recently it was the home of a number of prominent Nigerians including novelist Wole Soyinka, musician Fela Kuti and President Olusegun Obasanjo.

Abkhazia

– see **Georgia**.

abolition of slavery

Slavery existed in antiquity; it exists, although formally outlawed, in the present. For millennia, slavery was legal and few attempts were made to make it illegal. The long-standing relationship between law and slavery began to break down in the second half of the eighteenth century, with the emergence in western Europe, first in **Britain** and then in **France** and the **Netherlands**, of organized anti-slavery movements. The crucial factors encouraging the growth of such groups were **Enlightenment** doctrines that suggested slavery was both immoral and despite claims to the contrary, uneconomical, as well as the intensification of evangelical Protestantism in Britain, especially in the aftermath of the Seven Years War (1756–63). Evangelicals came to believe that the holding of slaves was a sin. The movement to abolish slavery started slowly. It began first among **Quakers** and later took root among Anglicans such as **William Wilberforce**. Even so, up until the mid 1780s anti-slavery advocates remained a minority in Britain.

The movement to abolish slavery began in the Americas during the **American Revolution**, when northern mainland colonies acted upon revolutionary ideas of freedom to end slavery in New England and to embark upon gradual emancipation schemes in Pennsylvania and New York. The most significant steps towards its abolition came in the mid 1780s in Britain, when abolitionist societies embarked upon enormously popular campaigns to end the Atlantic Slave Trade. In 1787 the London Committee for Effecting the Abolition of the Slave Trade was formed. Its activities enjoyed unusual public success and if the **French Revolution** had not intervened to make its leaders scared of any reform, then the slave trade to the Americas might have been abolished as early as 1792. The outbreak of the **Haitian Revolution** in 1791 and war with France as well as opposition from planters delayed the abolition of the **slave trade** in the **British Empire** until 1807. In the meantime, slave rebels in Haiti (previously Saint-Domingue) achieved their freedom in the only successful slave revolt in modern history. France granted slaves their freedom in 1794 and although this offer was rescinded by **Napoleon Bonaparte** in his attempted reconquest of Haiti, slavery was effectively ended in the largest slave colony in the Americas well before France was finally defeated in 1815. The abolition of the slave trade in the West Indies was a body blow to the economy of those islands, and although planters delayed full abolition for another generation, anti-slavery sentiment was strong enough in the metropolis for the abolition of slavery to occur by 1838. Matters were different in the **United States**, where a growing plantation economy, a self-sustaining slave population and a powerful and politically dominant planter class prevented abolitionists' demands until planters were defeated in a bloody civil war. Slavery was abolished in the United States in 1862 and made effectual with the Confederate defeat in 1865. The last places to abolish slavery in the Americas were in the Spanish Caribbean (**Cuba** abolished slavery in 1886) and in **Brazil** (slavery abolished in 1888).

abolitionism, abolitionist

Broadly understood, a movement that for a century from the **American Revolution** called for an end to the transatlantic **slave trade** and subsequently for the **abolition of slavery** itself. Abolitionism was a predominantly Anglo-American phenomenon, drawing much of its moral inspiration from evangelical Protestantism and mobilizing public opinion through means such as the press, petitions and non-governmental associations, all of which were comparatively lacking in countries with more authoritarian government and weaker civil society.

The late eighteenth century witnessed the convergence of religious, especially **Quaker**, objections to slavery with **Enlightenment** critiques of the inefficiency of unfree labour, the institution's assault on individual liberty, and the affront to **republicanism** embodied in dependence on the toil of others. Abolitionists focused on the transatlantic trade, since it represented a continued evil whereas slavery was an inherited one. In Britain, developments such as the *Somersett* case (1772) and the establishment of the Society for Effecting the Abolition of the Slave Trade (1787) proved false starts in the light of conservative reaction arising from the **American** and **French Revolutions**, but Parliament became confident enough of the stability of the British West Indies to bow to public pressure to pass **William Wilberforce**'s long-mooted Slave Trade Act (1807). Popular abolitionism re-emerged in the 1820s and turned towards the institution itself, resulting in the **Emancipation Act** (1833) and then a successful attempt to truncate the period of apprenticeship for former slaves that the same had laid down. Up until this point, British abolitionism had evinced remarkable structural integrity, but the movement began to split over whether to spread the struggle worldwide, over continued **protectionism** for uncompetitive British West Indian sugar versus support for a policy of **free trade**, and over Britain's ability and right to suppress an inexhaustibly resilient international slave trade. By 1850 the public was weary of abolitionist idealism, and the movement itself was disheartened.

In the **United States**, abolitionism threatened a domestic rather than a colonial institution, but one that also existed under the protections of a federal system. Early anti-slavery comprised legislative measures towards gradual emancipation or more in the north, and a spate of private manumissions everywhere. It also looked to non-extension into the territories and to broad economic trends to undermine the institution without infringing on slaveholders' property rights. Congress prohibited the slave trade with effect from 1808, but to little fanfare; the cause of anti-slavery was essentially dormant until after the **American War of 1812**, when the formation of

the **American Colonization Society** and the debates culminating in the **Missouri Compromise** revived it. White abolitionists followed **African American** opinion and the example of abolition in the **British Empire** to found the American Anti-Slavery Society in 1833, rejecting colonization, gradualism and compensation in favour of immediatism. 'Abolitionism' now became synonymous with this narrower, radical stance, as opposed to the moderate emancipationism that continued to hold a wider but comparatively subdued and unorganized appeal. **William Lloyd Garrison**'s feminism and anti-clericalism alienated many fellow abolitionists, who founded a break-away society that was also more favourable to participation in mainstream politics. The political abolitionists tended to join the **Liberty Party** and the **Free Soil Party** and to regard an unamended **American Constitution** as sufficient to abolish slavery; **Frederick Douglass** would move to their ideological camp. **Sectional conflict** bolstered northern political anti-slavery of the lowest common denominator, but abolitionists proper remained unpopular until the **American Civil War**, which ended slavery.

It is hard to link the economic motivation of abolitionists to anything other than vague pieties about the superiority of free labour that actually became difficult to maintain in the face of insatiable market demand for slaves. Abolitionists' tendency towards factionalism also carries a hint of the depth of their conviction. The corollary of acknowledging their sincerity is to realize that only in the British and Brazilian cases can we really attribute the end of slavery to widespread abolitionist sentiment more than to the dislocation brought about by war, rebellion and **slave revolts**, or to elite decision-making, or to external diplomatic pressure – though admittedly, this was almost always British in provenance, thus attesting to the indirect importance of abolitionism.

The persistence of various forms of slavery and human trafficking has recently produced a resurgence of abolitionist organizations.

Aborigines, Australian

The word *aborigine* is derived from the Latin for 'from the origin or the beginning'. Though applied to indigenous (First Nations) peoples in other countries from as early as 1789, it was used to describe all the indigenous peoples of the Australian continent and its nearby islands other than those from the Torres Strait Islands, who are considered a distinct ethnic group. Arriving forty to fifty thousand years ago from South East Asia, it has been estimated that at the time of European settlement, the aboriginal population was in the vicinity of three-quarters of a million. This included some seven hundred different groups, speaking more than two hundred distinct languages, largely subsisting on hunting, gathering and techniques which exploited the differing environments found in Australia, including the harshest conditions of the interior. European arrival precipitated profound change in the fortunes of the aboriginal peoples, who faced dispossession, disease, violence and cultural assimilation by missionaries and governmental paternalism. The Tasmanian aborigines were completely wiped out by the 1870s and in 1933 the total aboriginal population was estimated at only 66,000. A growing assertion of aboriginal rights from 1945 led to gradual improvements and greater recognition of the sophistication and integrity of the indigenous culture, such as aboriginal art. In 1967 aborigines were accorded full citizenship for the first time and in 1992 the High Court ruled in the Mabo decision that Australia was not 'empty' when Europeans arrived, allowing aboriginal claims to land based on prior occupancy. As much as 10 per cent of land now has aboriginal freehold title, but a proposal to recognize the aborigines in the constitution as Australia's 'first people' was heavily defeated in a referendum. In 2000 the Council for Aboriginal Reconciliation delivered a document of reconciliation to the Australian government, but issues concerning aboriginal welfare and endemic social problems, such as poverty, alcoholism, crime and family break-up, remain. The current population is estimated at approximately a quarter of a million.

abortion

The elimination of the state of pregnancy by deliberate means before birth. Abortion is a highly controversial issue and has become, as technology and feminism have advanced, a touchstone of western political debates. Many religions view the elimination of any post-conception matter, whether zygotic, blasttocytic or a foetus, as a grave sin. Such people are associated with the 'right to life' arguments predicated upon the admission of the unborn, with potential to be human, to the right of protection. Not all 'right to life' proponents are religious, and many allow for a period between conception and the development of the foetus in which abortion should be legal and offered as a cure for a condition. Others allow for the consequences of a full-term pregnancy in the aftermath of rape, incest or life-threatening illness

to justify early abortion. Some believe that individual human dignity is undermined by abortion, and point to the examples of totalitarian states in which abortion was widespread and effectively in use on demand to prove their point.

Such 'right to life' groups are frequently contrasted with 'pro-choice' groups. These latter, based around feminist convictions of female freedom to choose, scientific views of the viability of the foetus or a wish to individuate control of the reproductive cycle, uphold the provision of abortion as a medical procedure and a legal right. Opinions vary as to whether all abortions, or early abortions, should be legal, and many within the 'pro-choice' camp reject the notion that the foetus is an entity in its own right, preferring the idea that it is a part of a woman until birth.

Abortion and infanticide are as old as recorded history. However, with the emergence of state-backed schemes of medical provision or insurance, and new technologies which allow for relatively safe abortion procedures, the number of acknowledged abortions rose very significantly in the later twentieth century. The entry of women into the workforce in the 1960s and 1970s, and the sexual revolution of the same period, coincided with an increased debate over the value of life and the role of women in society which often became emotional and confrontational. This was particularly true in the **United States**. It tended to divide political parties and their supporters from each other, and also to alienate Roman Catholics, evangelicals and other religious groups from participation in the political process. The emergence of abortion on demand, termination for disability, physical characteristics or sex, in-vitro fertilization and stem cell research, ultrasound pictures of children in the womb, as well as partial birth abortions, complicated the issue enormously, and no satisfactory legal or political resolution was ever found which could calm either side. By 2010, in the overwhelming number of countries, abortion was legal, but there were few in which it was wholly accepted.

absolutism

Absolutism in the period since 1700 was claimed in its purest form by Louis XIV of **France** (1638–1715) when he declared 'L'état, c'est moi' ('I am the state'). The monarch actually enshrined the state, and there was an echo of that approach in 1940 when General **Charles de Gaulle** called on the **Free French** to rally to him personally in London after the fall of France. Nevertheless, absolutism was the norm almost everywhere in Europe, except **Britain**, in the eighteenth century. It did not, however, mean quite the same thing everywhere. In Russian **tsarism**, law had no meaning other than the will of the autocrat. At the other extreme, in Prussia, **Frederick the Great** fully recognized that however great his power, it could only be exercised within the limits set by the law. On the other hand, the monarch was 'like the soul of a state' and thus his rule had to be personal. He could not delegate his responsibilities to ministers, who were likely to be selfish or represent factions. Moreover, he had to sacrifice his own personal interests and feelings, and arbitrariness was precluded by the obligations of his position. Only such personal rule could give the unity and consistency essential to successful policy making and execution. Such an austere and reasoned justification of absolutism was, however, the exception. Louis XIV's successors in France believed in autocracy essentially 'because it was there'. Even in 1815, the rabid royalists maintained that France could have only one constitution: 'What the king wants, the law wants.' Moreover, few monarchs had either the ability or the energy to rule in the Frederician manner. They needed strong ministers.

History was also running against royal absolutism, partly as a result of the success of constitutional monarchy in Britain after 1688. The abolition of parliamentary government and the assertion of royal power by Gustav III of **Sweden** in 1772 was followed by his assassination twenty years later, although absolutism was not abolished in Denmark until 1849. The attempt of **Charles X** of France to revert to Bourbon autocracy collapsed in 1830. **Franz Josef** ruled as neo-absolute Emperor of Austria, 1841–59, although with influential advisers, but defeat in **Italy** brought the period to an end. Twentieth-century royal absolutism has been confined to the **Balkans**, where King Alexander established a royal dictatorship in 1929 to combat national divisions in what was to be **Yugoslavia**, and King Boris III became effectively Bulgarian dictator in 1938.

Absolutism can also be extended as a term to describe the rule of **Napoleon**, particularly after his self-coronation as Emperor in 1804, although it was always qualified by reliance on his family and advisers, such as Talleyrand, in a way that **Frederick the Great**'s rule had not been. It can perhaps be extended also to the fascist dictators, notably **Hitler**, **Mussolini** and **Franco**, whose ideology made them the leader (*Führer*, *Duce*, *Caudillo*) or the head from whom all power flows, and to **Lenin** and **Stalin**, who donned the mantle of tsarist absolutism. From a different perspective, the **papacy** must be deemed a form of absolutism, particularly after the declaration of papal infallibility in 1870.

Abu Dhabi

Largest of the seven emirates comprising the former Trucial States and current **United Arab Emirates** (UAE). Under the Nahayyan family of the Bani Yas tribe, Abu Dhabi emerged in the late eighteenth century around oasis settlements in Liwa and al-'Ayn (Buraimi) and the coastal town of Abu Dhabi. The sheikhdom became part of the Trucial system beginning in 1820 and a British protectorate in 1892. The discovery of oil in 1958 brought wealth but little economic development under Sheikh Shakhbut ibn Sultan Al Nahayyan. He deposed his brother in 1966 and initiated a comprehensive economic development programme. A long-standing border dispute with **Saudi Arabia**, thought resolved in 1974, has resurfaced. Abu Dhabi became a charter member of the UAE upon the termination of the British protectorate in December 1971, and its ruler, Sheikh Khalifah ibn Zaid Al Nahayyan, served as president of the federation.

Abu Nidal (1937–2002)

Born Sabri Khalil al-Banna in 1937, al-Banna adopted the moniker Abu Nidal, which means 'Father of the Struggle' in Arabic. He was the founder of the Palestinian group **Fatah**, which is commonly referred to as the Abu Nidal Organization. Palestinian by birth, Nidal's childhood is not well known and confused further by his frequent embellishment of his own past. Receiving little to no official schooling after the third grade, Nidal taught himself. Joining the **Ba'ath Party** around the age of 18, he formed his own division of the group: the Palestinian Secret Organization – at the time he was residing in **Saudi Arabia**. The Saudi government refused to shelter the organization and deported Nidal to **Palestine**. Nidal and **Yasser Arafat** worked hand in hand within the Palestinian organization Fatah, but had a bitter falling out. Nidal and his Fatah followers have taken credit for numerous violent attacks, many involving hijackings and bombings.

Abyssinia

– *see* **Ethiopia**.

Abyssinian crisis

A crisis in the period before **World War II** originating in 1928 but only reaching crisis point in 1935. Abyssinia (now **Ethiopia**) was undermined and attacked by Fascist **Italy**, which was eager to build a 'New Roman Empire' and dominate the area from north Africa to the Indian ocean via **Libya**, **Eritrea** and Somaliland. During a one-year campaign ostensibly to resolve 'border issues', Italian troops looted holy cities and employed chemical weapons against an Ethiopian army of Emperor **Haile Selassie I**, in some cases armed with bows and arrows. When details of Italian aggression were brought to the **League of Nations**, economic sanctions were imposed on Italy. However, these were minimal and not capable of being implemented in the face of Italian defiance and Franco-British inaction; and the **USA** did not participate, not being a member of the League. The crisis is often seen as laying the groundwork for Nazi militarism and encouraging **Adolf Hitler** in his defiance of the **Treaty of Versailles**. The Italian Empire in East Africa lasted until 1941.

Achebe, Chinua (Albert Chinualumogu Achebe) (1930–2013)

Nigerian writer, dealing notably with the clash between western values and those of African traditional society. An academic and publisher, among his novels are *Things Fall Apart* (1958), *No Longer at Ease* (1960), *Arrow of God* (1964) and *Anthills of The Savannah* (1987). He also published short stories, poetry and essays. Achebe supported Biafra's independence effort during the 1967–70 war and moved permanently to the United States in 1990.

Acheh

Acheh (modern Aceh) was an important sultanate and centre of Islamic commerce and trade in the early modern period. It was based in Northern Sumatra but had a trade power extending to the Malay lands. Comparisons with medieval Venice are not wholly fanciful. It was allied with the **Dutch East India Company** and the **Ottoman Empire** against the Portuguese, but never gave itself wholly to either. It built a key role for itself as a purveyor of pepper since it sat astride an important trade route, and as such the **British Empire** declared it a possession whilst ceding it to the Dutch in 1824. This formed part of a complex relationship in which the British treated the Dutch as proxies who could keep other states out. Pirate pressure in the 1870s, which led to the Acheh

War, exposed Dutch dependence on the British. The war ended in 1903, and Aceh then enjoyed a period of calm until Japanese occupation galvanized an anti-Dutch, but also anti-Japanese, Islamic nationalism in the territory known as the Ulama. This proved problematic when Aceh was incorporated with promises of autonomy into independent **Indonesia**, and led to a great rebellion between 1953 and 1959. Aceh was reincorporated into Indonesia in 1959, but the discovery and exploitation of large mineral resources by the Indonesian government and American companies reignited rebellion in 1976. This was suppressed but not eliminated, and over time Indonesian military commitment to Aceh grew (often alongside human rights violations). It was only the tsunami of 2004, which functioned as a disastrous outside pressure, that forced peace agreements on the area. Aceh is now a semi-autonomous territory of Indonesia once again.

Acheson, Dean (1893–1971)

According to the title of his memoir, Dean Acheson was 'present at the creation' of America's enduring cold war strategy. As Undersecretary of State (1945–9) and Secretary of State (1949–53) through the Truman administration, Acheson played a key role in the creation of the **Truman Doctrine**, the **Marshall Plan**, **NATO** and the **World Bank**, and supported military intervention in the Korean War. Following **Eisenhower**'s assumption of the presidency, Acheson continued to advise presidents on foreign policy until his death.

Achille Lauro hijacking

– *see* **Palestine Liberation Organization (PLO)**.

Adams, John (1735–1826)

A native of Braintree, Massachusetts, Adams graduated from Harvard and established himself as a Boston lawyer. An early critic of British taxation in the colonies, he defended the British soldiers tried for murder as a result of the **Boston Massacre**. He represented Massachusetts in the **Continental Congress**, serving on the committee which drafted the **American Declaration of Independence** in 1776. During the War of Independence Adams served in Congress, represented the **United States** in **France** and the **Netherlands**, and was the primary author of the Massachusetts Constitution of 1780. After the war he was the first American ambassador to Britain. He served two terms as **George Washington**'s vice president before being elected president in 1796. During his presidency

Franco-American relations deteriorated to the point where the two nations waged a 'quasi-war' at sea. In anticipation of a declaration of war against France, the Federalists in Congress adopted the **Alien and Sedition Acts** which limited civil liberties. These acts undermined the popularity of the Federalists and Adams was defeated by **Thomas Jefferson** in the election of 1800. Adams enjoyed a long retirement, living to see his son, **John Quincy Adams**, elected president in 1824.

Adams, Sam (1722–1803)

Born in Boston, Sam Adams was educated at Boston Latin and Harvard College. He was the most important advocate of colonial rights in Boston, helping to organize the resistance to British rule from the **Stamp Act** crisis to the **Boston Tea Party**. He represented Massachusetts in the **Continental Congress** and was an early advocate of independence. He signed the **American Declaration of Independence** in 1776, and served as governor of Massachusetts between 1793 and 1797. He was second cousin to **John Adams**.

Aden

Port city in the Gulf of Aden in **Yemen**, former British crown colony (1937–63) and capital of the People's Republic of South Yemen (1963–90). Following British occupation in 1839, Aden rose to commercial and strategic importance as a coal depot and military base serving the southern access to the **Suez Canal**. It became one of the world's busiest ports following the 1954 opening of the Aden Refinery, but traffic declined during the closure of the Suez Canal (1967–75). Construction of new terminals in the late 1980s and the 1999 commissioning of the Aden Container Terminal revitalized the port. Plans to upgrade the ageing refinery have been under discussion since the late 1990s. A resumption of the port's strategic importance came in 1999 when the US Navy contracted its use as a refuelling station. However, on 12 October 2000 terrorists associated with **al-Qaida** attacked the USS *Cole* during a refuelling stop. In the Yemen Civil War after 2014, Aden was again a battleground.

Adrianople, Treaty of

The treaty signed on 14 September 1829 (also known as the Treaty of Edirne) was imposed by **Russia** on the **Ottoman Empire**, ending the war of 1828–9 in which Russian troops had advanced into the Balkans, north-east Anatolia and the **Caucasus** in a conflict provoked by the Greek independence struggle. The treaty significantly weakened the Ottoman Empire's position in the Balkans while fortifying that of Russia. **Turkey** agreed to the opening of the Straits of the Dardanelles to free passage for commercial shipping, guaranteed autonomy that had previously been promised to **Serbia** and pledged autonomy to **Greece**, recognized the autonomy of the principalities of Moldavia and Wallachia (placing them under Russian supervision until Turkey paid an indemnity), ceded islands at the mouth of the Danube and a coastal strip of the Caucasus on the Black Sea to Russia, and recognized Russian sovereignty over **Georgia** and other Caucasian principalities.

aerial warfare

The use in war of primarily airborne (as opposed to thrown) devices, craft or weapons followed swiftly on from the development of heavier-than-air flight at the start of the twentieth century, though balloons had been used as observation posts in the nineteenth century. Air war developed in four rough phases. The first phase involved the development of craft which could reliably be used to launch reconnaissance missions, bombing runs and attacks on opposing infantries or air forces. During this phase airships and aeroplanes competed until the relative vulnerability of airships (they were slow, large and inflammable) was revealed towards the end of **World War I**. It was also during this phase that technical problems with aeroplanes, such as the need to coordinate machine guns with propellers, the development of parachutes and seatbelts as safety devices and the specifics of aircraft construction, were addressed.

By the 1930s a second phase had begun, in which problems of air power were recharacterized by dedicated branches of the armed forces rather than as part of an army or navy issue. States developed the capacity to build long-range, heavy bombers, which were seen as an ultimate weapon, alongside fast, enclosed and manoeuvrable fighter aircraft that could be used against other fighters or against infantry. This phase of air warfare also involved the creation of paratroop regiments and tactics to deliver well-trained soldiers in great numbers via parachute behind or to the flanks of enemy lines. By the end of **World War II** the development of ballistic missile technology (launched from fixed or mobile land platforms or eventually from submarines) competed with the growth of helicopters, long-range nuclear bombing patrols, radar and anti-aircraft missiles as well as surveillance craft for money and a place in the strategies and tactical manuals of great powers. Oddly, despite the diffusion of technology, the expense of this phase and the tight control on materiel, parts and training maintained by the superpowers prevented large-scale use of air power by new or emerging powers, and the civil wars and conflicts of 1950s–1980s were not marked by the decisive use of air power; indeed, during the **Vietnam War**, its limitations were fully exposed.

Finally, a new phase began in the 1990s with the development of pilotless technology – 'drones' – which could monitor battlefields, drop ordnance and coordinate with intelligence operations to assassinate or destroy individuals or small groups of opponents whilst not exposing the powers using it to any obstacles or immediate retaliation. This phase, which could be said to have begun with the laser-guided, satellite-aided 'smart bombs' and cruise technology of the **Gulf War**, continued through the development of 'stealth weapons' and culminated in the drone technology of the 'war on terror' in the early twenty-first century. Today, air power is also linked with space-based satellites and mapping systems, although the 1968 Outer Space Treaty and the Arms Limitation Treaties of the 1970s effectively stopped the development of fully space-based weapons systems for defensive or aggressive purposes.

affirmative action (American)

The 1964 Civil Rights Act banned job discrimination. Affirmative action refers to efforts to ensure that minorities (and women) are not denied equal access to education, employment and career advancement. President **Lyndon Johnson**'s September 1964 executive order required government contractors to take 'affirmative action' to avoid discrimination and to document their policies. President **Richard Nixon**'s 1969 Philadelphia Plan referred to definite goals in relation to minority hiring and to timetables to achieve these goals. Test cases established that under-representation of minorities was proof of discrimination unless institutions could demonstrate that affirmative action had been taken. In the *Bakke* case (1978), however, the Supreme Court ruled that rigid admission quotas were unconstitutional as they denied equal protection to whites. Conservative critics in the 1980s railed against preferential treatment. In 2003 the court accepted race as one factor among many in university admissions but only in the interest of diversity, not equality.

Afghan Wars

A set of three conflicts, also called Anglo-Afghan Wars, fought between British Indian armies against Pashtun rulers or pretenders, primarily in the eastern regions of **Afghanistan**. In the first (1839–42), the **East India Company** sought to reinstate Shah Shuja as emir, yet ultimately his rival Dost Muhammad Khan reunified Afghanistan and negotiated a peace agreement with the Company in 1855. Russian expansion into central Asia and a British desire to make Afghanistan a protectorate led to the second war (1878–80). After a brief period of direct British rule in 1879, Abdur Rahman Khan brokered a deal with the British and their Pashtun and Tajik opponents, thereby permitting his reunification of Afghanistan. Since Britain did not grant independence in exchange for his father's unpopular neutrality during **World War I**, Emir Amanullah declared a war of independence in 1919. Despite victories against Afghan forces, Britain granted independence and ended the Afghan government's subsidy.

Afghani, Jamal al-Din al- (1839–1897)

Probably born in Persia (modern-day **Iran**), he claimed to be born in **Afghanistan** to hide his Shi'ite roots. He is regarded as the founder of Islamic modernism. He travelled widely in his youth, but spent many of his productive years in **Egypt** where he wrote and developed his ideas that the Islamic world should unite against European imperialism. Although a believer in pan-Islam and the recipient of a traditional Muslim education, Afghani was not strongly religious and did not believe that Islamic unity had to rest on traditional jurisprudence. Rather, he favoured a constitutional system. His involvement in politics led to his extradition from Egypt and arrest in the **Ottoman Empire** for an alleged plot against the Shah of Iran. He spent his time there organizing a foundation to resist British imperialism and to reconcile Sunni and Shia Islam. He was buried in Afghanistan following his death.

Afghanistan

Afghanistan lies between central and south Asia, sharing borders with **Pakistan, Iran, China**, Tajikistan, Uzbekistan and Turkmenistan. Forty per cent of its population in 2014 were thought to be 14 years of age or younger. The modern Afghan state emerged in the early nineteenth century around Kabul, where a dynasty claiming succession from **Ahmad Shah Durrani** (r. 1747–3) governed a kingdom that sat astride an important trade corridor. The term *Afghanistan* began to appear regularly on maps and in diplomatic correspondence around mid-century; however, its borders were fixed later. Following decades of struggle among claimants to the throne and British interventions in the two Anglo-Afghan Wars (1838–42 and 1878–80), the current territorial limits of Afghanistan took shape under Emir Abdur Rahman (r. 1880–1901), who forcefully consolidated Kabul's control. The kingdom served as a buffer between the Russian and British empires, though the emir (and subsequent Afghan rulers) would periodically claim the loyalties of the Pashtun tribes beyond the eastern border, the Durand Line of 1893. Britain retained control of Afghan foreign relations, while the emir received a subsidy. In 1919 a third Anglo-Afghan War, launched by **Amanullah** (r. 1919–29), earned complete independence.

The Afghan monarchy initiated a series of modernizing measures, drawing support from a small though cosmopolitan elite that was increasingly educated abroad. Amanullah promulgated a constitution in 1923 and introduced reforms to improve the status of women and expand education. **Nadir Shah** (r. 1929–33) oversaw state-directed modernization focused on military and educational institutions and solicited the advice of international experts. Military trainers, engineers, doctors and teachers from **Turkey**, **Germany** and elsewhere were attached to key institutions. Under Zahir Shah (r. 1933–73) great power involvement increased, as Germany, **Italy**, **Japan**, the **Soviet Union** and Britain competed for influence over the Afghan elite and access to this strategic territory. Kabul remained neutral during **World War II** but continued to solicit financial and other assistance from several states. During the **Cold War** the Americans and Soviets emerged as the largest suppliers of aid for large infrastructural projects such as dams, roads and airports. The Afghans also sought to draw the powers into their conflict with Pakistan over the disputed borderland that many nationalists insisted should be an independent 'Pashtunistan'. The 1964 constitution broadened press and other freedoms, allowing a spectrum of underground political opinion ranging from Maoists to Islamists to emerge. This period of intense ideological ferment forms the backdrop to **Muhammad Daud**'s coup against the monarchy in 1973 and ultimately to the communist coup against the republic in 1978 and a period of civil war that persists to the present.

Popular resistance to the communists' violent modernizing agenda prompted Soviet intervention in December 1979. The **mujahideen**, in turn, received support from the US, Pakistan, Iran, **China**, **Saudi Arabia** and others. Their inability to govern contributed to the appearance of the **Taliban**, a movement whose human rights record made it a pariah and who clashed with US following the attacks of 11 September 2001. American and **NATO** forces dispersed the Taliban, but despite multiple elections and billions of dollars in aid they failed to bring stability or security to the country after more than a decade of fighting.

Afghanistan, Russian invasion of

On 27 December 1979 the USSR moved troops into Afghanistan in order to forestall the collapse of the Marxist regime which had taken control in Kabul in 1978 and install their preferred leader, Barbrak Karmal. Anticipating a brief intervention as in **Czechoslovakia** in 1968, Russian airborne forces seized Kabul, killing the current leader of the People's Democratic Party of Afghanistan, while four divisions of Russian troops crossed the border. Faced with the disintegration of an Afghan Army loyal to the previous ruler, overwhelming international condemnation and growing resistance, the Soviets were forced to massively reinforce their presence in the face of an increasingly bitter conflict, in order to maintain supply lines and control the major cities. The conflict precipitated the largest refugee crisis hitherto as over 5 million refugees sought safety in **Pakistan** and **Iran**. The breadth and skill of the Afghan resistance expressed through the idiom of **jihad** and carried out by **mujahideen** supported by the **USA** and **Saudi Arabia** furnishing aid through Pakistan, produced a bloody ten-year war. Soviet control of the cities and vital routes was nullified by almost total loss of support in the countryside and the vulnerability of its supply columns to guerrilla attack. Mujahideen groups fighting as independent units were often forced on to the defensive by Soviet air power, but the supply of sophisticated anti-aircraft missiles such as the Stinger began to compromise even this Soviet advantage. Continuing heavy losses and diplomatic exposure forced the Soviets to consider withdrawing by 1986, a process finally achieved by Premier **Gorbachev** following talks in Geneva in April 1988 which agreed a phased withdrawal of all 100,000 Soviet troops by February 1989. Following their removal, the Soviet-sponsored replacement of Karmal, **Ahmadzai Najibullah**, sought to establish a government of 'national reconciliation'. Soviet casualties numbered 64,000, with over 10,000 dead; Afghan casualties, civilian and military, certainly numbered hundreds of thousands. Aimed to achieve a degree of stability, Soviet intervention contributed to greater turmoil in the region and served as a major stimulus to radical jihad and new aggressive Islamic groups such as the **Taliban** and **al-Qaida**.

AFL-CIO

The American Federation of Labor (AFL) and the Congress of Industrial Organizations (CIO), representing respectively the craft and industrial union traditions in the **USA**, merged in 1955 to form the AFL-CIO. It represents and lobbies for affiliated unions, and also attempts to lead and mediate between them; nearly all mainstream unions have joined it. Among the largest, in 1955, were the United Auto Workers, and in 2000, the Service Employees International Union (SEIU). Jimmy Hoffa's corrupt Teamsters' Union (IBT) was temporarily excluded. In 2005, after many years of union decline, the new and more aggressive Change to Win organization captured several leading AFL-CIO unions. **Globalization**, the shift from smoke stack to service industries, government opposition, cheap immigrant labour and occasional scandals had reduced union membership from 20 per cent of the workforce in 1983 to 15.6 million or 12.5 per cent of the workforce in 2005. The long-term future of labour organization in the USA is unclear.

Aflaq, Michel (1910–1989)

Syrian political intellectual; co-founder of the **Ba'ath Party** (*ba'arth* in Arabic means 'resurrection' or 'renaissance'). Born into a Greek Orthodox family in French-mandated Syria, Aflaq studied in Paris, returning home to become a teacher. In 1942 he and Salah al-Bitar (1912–80) established the Arab Ba'ath movement, a synthesis of secular pan-Arab nationalism and socialism. Aflaq became the party's leader in 1947. Forced into exile in **Lebanon** by **Syria**'s military dictatorship in 1952, he and al-Bitar cooperated with the Arab Socialist Party, amalgamating the two parties following the overthrow of the Syrian regime in 1954. The party supported the 1958 merger of Syria and **Egypt** in a short-lived **United Arab Republic** (UAR). Following the UAR's collapse in 1961, Aflaq sought a revival but was exiled from Syria in 1966 following a coup by right-wing Ba'athists, moving to Lebanon, **Iraq** (where he became nominal Secretary General of the country's Ba'ath Party in 1968) and **France**.

Africa

Africa is the world's second largest continent and home to over a billion people; it is also an idea. Speaking at the All-African People's Conference in 1958, the prime minister of the newly independent state of **Ghana**, **Kwame Nkrumah**, proclaimed that the mid twentieth century was Africa's century and that national independence was only a first step towards the ultimate goal of a United States of Africa. No such political entity which we can call 'Africa' has come into existence yet, but since 1700 'Africa' has come to describe not only a continental land mass but also a shared experience of modern world history, defined in terms of global economic, political and intellectual change.

Africa and the changing world economy

In 1450 African economies participated in a number of overlapping trading systems across the Sahara and the Indian Ocean and within the continent. After this date, however, western Africa was increasingly drawn into a new trading system, that of the Atlantic world. While initial demand was for gold and other natural resources such as copper, hides and skins, as the plantation economy of **Brazil** and the Caribbean developed, so demand for slaves increased. The **slave trade** reached its height in the eighteenth century before starting to decline after 1807. It is estimated that approximately 10 million men, women and children were exported from Africa to the New World between the 1440s and the last slaving voyage of 1867. The slave trade created a large African diaspora in the New World. It also reoriented western African economies towards the export of people, with consequences for the economic, political and demographic history of the region. The precise nature of those consequences, and specifically the question of whether the roots of Africa's 'underdevelopment' lie in the period of the Atlantic slave trade, continue to be debated.

Africa and the world political system

As the world economy shifted towards the industrialized countries of **Europe** and North America, Africa increasingly came to be seen as a source of raw materials, opening the way for significant political change. In the late nineteenth century the continent was divided into colonial states. Colonial partition took place in the context of the 'new imperialism' of the late nineteenth century, when new and existing colonial powers engaged in a rush to secure colonies. While trade and the search for raw materials drove the partition, the language used was that of a 'civilizing mission', and for the half-century which followed, most of Africa, with the exceptions of **Ethiopia** and Liberia, was ruled by European colonial powers.

The establishment of colonial states marked a significant structural change. Africa was a continent of plentiful land and sparse population, and political centralization tended to be concentrated in areas where geography and the quality of the soil permitted high population density. Elsewhere state-building was made difficult by the existence of an 'exit option': reluctant subjects could simply leave and find new polities elsewhere. From the 1880s, a uniform state structure was imposed as colonial regimes sought to extract taxes and labour and build state institutions. Yet projecting power remained difficult, and colonial states had to establish uneasy alliances to create and maintain it. By the 1950s, many of these alliances were breaking down as new anti-colonial coalitions emerged. In developing their critiques of colonialism, new political actors drew on religious ideas, **pan-Africanism** and anti-imperialism.

intellectual change

The period after 1800 saw a rapid expansion of **Islam** and Christianity in Africa, and by the early twenty-first century the majority of Africa's population described themselves as Muslim or Christian. The expansion of both religions after 1800 was tied to wider changes including Islamic revival, the abolition of the slave trade and the growth of European power in Africa. In northern Nigeria, 'Uthman dan Fodio's jihad established the **Sokoto Caliphate** in which education, particularly of women, ensured that Islamic ideas achieved a wider social reach than they had in the past. In Yorubaland, freed slaves who had been converted to Christianity in **Sierra Leone** arrived as missionaries to spread Christianity.

Religion helped to connect Africans to global networks and provided a shared language in which to debate Africa's present and imagine its future. The African and African-American intellectuals of the mid-nineteenth-century 'Black Atlantic', men such as **Africanus Horton**, Samuel Ajayi Crowther and **Edward Blyden**, were inspired by the horrors of the slave trade to build a new future in Africa, one in which, they believed, Africa would be 'saved' by the twin powers of education and Christianity. In the process, they helped to imagine an entity called 'Africa', and established the roots of pan-African thought of the twentieth century.

A series of **pan-African congresses** were held in the interwar period, but the pan-African congress held in Manchester in 1945 was the first to call for African independence. It was dominated by a new

generation of political leaders from Africa, many of whom would go on to lead their countries after independence. It tapped into a growing sense, inspired by the 1941 **Atlantic Charter**, that imperialism was illegitimate and that everyone had a right to national self-determination. Over the next twenty years the African continent was transformed from a continent of colonial states into a continent of independent states, though with some exceptions the state boundaries imposed in the late nineteenth century remained the same.

Africa since independence

Many of the hopes expressed at independence were disappointed in the decades which followed. Economic growth was steady in the 1960s but stalled as the world economy was shaken in the 1970s. State-building proved as hard for post-colonial leaders as it had been for their predecessors. Life expectancy fell at the end of the century as the **AIDS** crisis took hold. But while a mood of 'Afro-pessimism' descended on some, others began the new century inspired by the hopes which new technologies and new modes of political engagement offered.

African Americans

Africans were first brought to the American colonies in the 1620s as slaves. Bondage became entrenched in Southern society, but not in the North, where slavery was abolished in the revolutionary era. By the eve of the **American Civil War** there were approximately 4 million African Americans living under slavery in the Southern States. All those enslaved were emancipated at the end of the civil war through the passing of the Thirteenth Amendment of 1865, and during the era of **Reconstruction** there were hopes that a more equal system of race relations would emerge in the South. However, the **Compromise of 1877** was followed by the emergence of a system of **Jim Crow** segregation which ensured that black and white remained apart. Many African Americans therefore chose to leave the south and partake in the **Great Migration** to the cities of the North. Segregation was overturned in the 1950s and 1960s by the efforts of those participating in the **Civil Rights movement**.

African National Congress (ANC)

The leading political party in **South Africa**, established in 1912 under the leadership of Congregationalist priest John Lube (1871–1946) as the South African Native National Congress to organize peaceful protests against mounting discrimination by white government and society. Renamed the African National Congress in 1923, the ANC remained a largely ineffective pressure group under a Christian black elite working to persuade whites to moderate discrimination. There were also divisions over how far to cooperate with the Communist Party. In 1944 younger radicals, including **Nelson Mandela** (1918–2013), Oliver Tambo (1917–93) and Walter Sisulu (1912–2003), formed the ANC Young League to press for a more activist stance. With the institution of **apartheid** by the National Party government elected in 1948, the ANC was prominent in organizing protests and passive resistance, launching the Defiance Campaign in 1952, while remaining non-violent. Increasingly taking on the complexion of a mass movement, the ANC developed links with the Communist Party and formed a Congress Alliance with the South African Indian Congress, the Coloured People's Association and the Congress of Trade Unions. The ANC Freedom Charter set out the goal of black majority rule. The ANC was banned following the 1960 **Sharpeville Massacre** and in 1961 adopted a strategy of violence against economic targets, setting up Umkhonto we Sizwe (Spear of the Nation) under Mandela's leadership in alliance with the Communist Party. As government repression intensified, the ANC was weakened by the imprisonment of leading figures following the 1963–4 Rivonia trial. Tambo reorganized the ANC in exile during the 1970s and support was boosted in the wake of the 1976 Soweto uprising. Bolstered by training camps in **Angola, Mozambique** and **Tanzania**, the ANC resumed the armed struggle in 1978. As white businessmen recognized the implications of international condemnation of apartheid, and the relatively liberal F. D. de Klerk became South African president, discussions began with the ANC on the country's future. The ANC was legalized in 1990, Mandela released from prison and the apartheid structures dismantled. In 1994 the ANC won the first multiracial elections, taking 12.5 million votes, 63 per cent of the total. Mandela became president as the ANC took on a moderate, business-friendly posture, disappointing radical black supporters with the apparent slow progress in improving their conditions. Nevertheless, under the successive leadership of Mandela, Thabo Mbeki (1942–) and Jacob Zuma (1942–), the ANC remains the dominant force in South African politics.

African slave trade
– see **slave trade**.

African socialism
– see **Ujamaa**.

African Union
Established as the Organization of African Unity (OAU) by charter in Addis Ababa, **Ethiopia**, by thirty-two independent African states on 25 May 1963. A further twenty-two states subsequently joined, **South Africa** not until 1994 and South Sudan most recently. The OAU had as its central aims acting as the collective voice of **Africa** and promoting the continent's unity and solidarity, coordinating efforts to improve living standards, defending the independence and territorial integrity of member states and assisting in eradicating the remaining elements of colonialism from Africa. The OAU established a Liberation Committee to assist independence movements, which ceased functioning in 1994. The organization agreed from the outset that national frontiers drawn up by European powers in the era of colonialism would remain largely unaltered. Following the Abuja Treaty establishing the African Economic Community in May 1994, the body became known as the OAU/AEC. The organization was superseded by the African Union on 9 July 2002.

Afrika Korps
The Deutsches Afrika Korps (DAK) was a force of two divisions sent by **Hitler** in February 1941 under the command of Erwin Rommel to shore up the Italian forces who had suffered severe reverses against the British in North Africa. Under his dashing leadership it scored victories against the British, seizing Tobruk and pushing them back to the Egyptian frontier, where it was eventually halted and then defeated at the battles of **El Alamein**. By then the Afrika Korps was a component of a much larger Italian–German force which was forced into a long, fighting retreat to **Tunisia** where it was eventually forced to surrender as part of a total of 238,000 Axis soldiers trapped by Anglo-American armies advancing from both east and west. The Afrika Korps, and its commander Rommel, achieved distinction for their formidable fighting qualities and leadership, usually against numerically superior opposition.

Afrikaaners
The term used for the descendants of Dutch settlers in southern Africa. Dutch settlers first arrived at the Cape of Good Hope in 1652. The term *Afrikaaner* was first used in the early eighteenth century and gradually replaced the

term **Boer**, which was primarily attached to the rural Dutch settler population. When the British took control of the **Cape Colony** in 1809, Dutch settlers left en masse in the **Great Trek** of the 1830s, which led to the establishment of three Afrikaaner states: **Orange Free State**, **Natal** and the **Transvaal**. After two wars, the Afrikaaner states and British colonies integrated into the Union of **South Africa** in 1910. Afrikaans, the language spoken by Dutch settlers, developed largely from Dutch but also included Malay, Bantu, Portuguese, French and Khoi linguistic influences. The growth of Afrikaaner nationalism in the interwar period led to the establishment of the **apartheid**, or 'separateness' government in 1948. White minority rule in South Africa came to an end after the first multiracial elections in 1994.

Afrocentrism

A cultural and political movement that attempts to counter the impact of Eurocentrism and white racism, encouraging black pride on the basis of a revisionist interpretation of history (or 'pseudo-history') placing **Africa** rather than **Europe** at the centre of the development of modern civilization. Molefi Kete Asante (formerly Arthur Lee Smith Jr) (1942–) made one of the earliest uses of the term in 1980 in *Afrocentricity: The Theory of Social Change*. George James (dates unknown) claimed in *Stolen Legacy* (1954) that Ancient Greek philosophy was in reality a development of the Egyptians, who were black Africans, and that Europeans had appropriated African technologies and ideas. Cheikh Anta Diop (1923–86) argued similarly in *The African Origin of Civilization: Myth or Reality* (1974), as has Martin Bernal (1937–) in *Black Athena: The Afroasiatic Roots of Classical Civilization* (1987–2006). Afrocentrism is also influenced by the ideas of **Marcus Garvey** (1887–1940).

Aga Khan

The leader of the Khoja Ismaili community, a Shia sect of Islam concentrated in south Asia but with a large diaspora. The Shah of Iran bestowed the title Aga Khan on the leader of the Ismailis in 1818. After rising against the shah, the Aga Khan and his followers fled to **Afghanistan** and settled in Bombay in 1845. The third Aga Khan, Sultan Muhammad Shah (1877–1957), co-founded the **Muslim League** in 1906.

Agadir Crisis

– *see* **Moroccan Crisis, 1911**.

Agaja (*c.* 1673–1740)

King of **Dahomey** (1708–32). The fifth king on traditional lists of rulers. Little is known of Agaja's early reign, and it appears that the country was divided by a complex civil war for several years. However, Agaja, having managed to overcome his opposition embarked on a campaign of expansion, first taking the coastal state of Allada, which had been Dahomey's nominal overlord for at least two generations, in 1724. Although Allada fell, its rulers managed to evade capture and established a rival dynasty at Porto Novo in the east, in the marshy coastal district. These rulers would be a constant thorn in the side of Dahomey for most of the century that followed. After his victory over Allada, Agaja launched an attack on Whydah, another small coastal state, in 1727, this time taking captive a number of European merchants from trading factories in the region. One such merchant, Bullfinch Lamb, subsequently wrote a description of the war and also delivered a letter which Agaja sent to the King of England. He apparently sent similar letters announcing himself and describing his conquests to the French factor, and perhaps also to the Portuguese. As was the case with Allada, the leaders of Whydah also managed to flee Dahomey's armies and formed a rival dynasty at Little Popo, in the coastal region. Dahomey was also troubled to the east by raiding armies of a renegade general from Akwamu on the neighbouring Gold Coast, which were able to retreat to the coast and thereby avoid serious combat. Agaja was never able to secure the coast primarily because he lacked the naval power to attack the rival dynasties in the swampy lagoon district. Although he managed to create a fleet under the leadership of a puppet dynasty he created in Allada, this navy was unable to tip the balance in his favour. Historians have debated Agaja's motives for his coastal campaigns, some suggesting that he did so to stop the disintegration of social order caused by the **slave trade** that local European merchants encouraged, while others contend that in fact he sought to gain a coastal outlet in order to sell the slaves he captured in war. In his letter to the King of England, Agaja noted his fondness for gunpowder weapons, claiming that he had almost entirely stopping using traditional weapons, and his dependency on these imported weapons may have played a role in his decisions about war and the slave trade. Indeed, as historians agree, Agaja eventually became a major dealer in slaves. Dahomey's expansion to the coast upset the balance of power in the region, and as a result the powerful inland kingdom of **Oyo** intervened, sending in a large cavalry contingent in 1728. For the next twenty years Oyo regularly raided Dahomey, and although unable to annex the country they forced Agaja's successor Tegbessou to pay tribute beginning in 1747.

Agha Muhammad Khan (1742–1797)

Turkmen founder of Iran's **Qajar dynasty**. Castrated at the age of 6 at the behest of 'Adil Shah in a vain attempt to prevent his becoming a political rival, he effectively became governor of Azerbaijan province in 1757 and chief of the Qajar Qavanlu clan in 1758. Captured by a rival tribal chieftain in 1762, he was a political hostage in Shiraz until he escaped in 1779, fleeing to Astarabad, the centre of Qavanlu power. His reign can effectively be dated from this time, but he had to defeat a number of rivals including Lotf 'Ali Khan, the last member of the Zand dynasty. He reasserted Iranian rule over **Armenia** and reconquered **Georgia**, capturing and sacking Tbilisi and massacring the population in 1795. He reconquered Khorasan, torturing the blind ruler, Shah Rokh, **Nadir Shah**'s grandson, to death, and was formally crowned *shahanshah* (king of kings) in 1796. He sought to deter rebellion by policies of deliberate cruelty, but was assassinated by two of his servants.

agrarian ideal (USA)

'God made the country, and man made the town', an aphorism of the eighteenth-century British poet, Thomas Cowper, has particular resonance in American culture. **Thomas Jefferson** expressed this notion of rural and agricultural superiority most famously in *Notes on the State of Virginia* (1784): 'Those who labour in the earth are the chosen people of God, if ever he had a chosen people, whose breasts he has made his peculiar deposit for substantial and genuine virtue.' Agrarianism generated a conviction that the future of American democracy and American exceptionalism itself were tied to territorial expansion that would keep at bay the European fate of congestion, stark inequalities of wealth and social strife. Agrarian spokesmen repeatedly articulated this belief in 'cultivation' over 'manufacture', notably **William Jennings Bryan**'s 1896 'Cross of Gold' speech. The agrarian ideal's nemesis was the rise of agribusiness, evoked in John Steinbeck's novel *The Grapes of Wrath* (1939).

Agrarian Reform Law (Chinese)

The Agrarian Reform Law was passed on 28 June 1951 in response to the extension of land reform into the more developed parts of central and southern China after 1949. The law offered some protection to richer farmers, leaving them enough land for subsistence, and allowed them to carry on commercial activities. However, many still suffered criticism and re-education through labour. When land reform ended in 1953, 45 per cent of all farmland had been redistributed.

agricultural revolution

– *see also* **agriculture; economic development**.

Transformation in agricultural techniques and productivity that occurred between the mid sixteenth and late nineteenth century and transformed economic and social life first in Britain and later throughout **Europe** and the **United States**. New techniques and innovations in farming facilitated the transformations associated with the agricultural revolution by making more effective use of land and labour. Enclosure of open fields accelerated the shift from the medieval tradition of common lands and tenant farmers to the more modern system of large-scale farming done by farm labourers. While the process of enclosure began at the end of the Middle Ages, it accelerated and became more universal in the mid eighteenth century with the passage of parliamentary legislation. The process of enclosure accompanied the extension of arable farm land, facilitated by the clearing of woodland and the drainage of fens. The introduction of fertilizers further improved agricultural output. New machinery – including the Rotherham plough, seed drills and threshing machines – made farming more efficient and reduced labour input. New crops, particularly clover and turnips, improved product quality and land output. In addition to crop improvements, new methods in selective breeding created more profitable animals. Such changes in techniques and productivity initiated widespread social and economic transformations. New technology and larger farms required different managerial techniques. The agricultural revolution provided pre-conditions necessary for **industrialization**. More efficient output and the disappearance of traditional agrarian life meant people lost their livelihoods, leading to a change from agricultural to industrial occupations. Moreover, by enabling farmers to successfully feed the growing population in Britain, the agricultural revolution facilitated a greater demand for manufactured goods.

The agricultural revolution was not confined to Britain; other European nations experienced a transformation in agricultural techniques. Like

Britain, the **Netherlands** served as an early site of the revolution. By the mid seventeenth century the Dutch practised enclosure and crop rotation and increased arable land through the drainage of marshes. Dutch overseas trade stimulated demand for agricultural goods. While religious warfare devastated **Germany** in the early modern era and hindered its agricultural growth, reform in the nineteenth century led an increase in productivity. Similarly, transportation difficulties, warfare and taxation reduced productivity and innovation in **Spain**, **France** and **Italy**. However, by the mid nineteenth century mechanization and foreign competition encouraged the modernization of agricultural techniques. In **Russia**, leaders hoped the **emancipation of serfs** in 1861 would stimulate economic development. However, Russia still trailed behind other countries until the interwar years of the twentieth century, when the introduction of new technology improved farm production.

The agricultural revolution remains a prolific area of historiographical debate, with understandings of the changes continuing to evolve. While original scholarship conceptualized the revolution as rapid changes occurring between 1750 and 1850, historians have increasingly emphasized a more gradual process of change and the need for a longer historical perspective. Although the chronology and significance of the changes remain central areas of debate, historians have also questioned basic understandings and definitions. Instead of defining the agricultural revolution as a single unitary phenomenon, recent scholarship has expanded traditional definitions to include a broader and more multi-dimensional understanding of the transformation. Agricultural changes outside Europe and the United States are considered under **economic development** rather than as part of the agricultural revolution.

agriculture

Whilst agriculture has been the major economic activity of the majority of the world's population over the past three centuries, it has occupied relatively fewer people with the onset of **economic development**, **industrialization** and **urbanization**. In 1700 a considerable proportion of the world's population was still dependent upon subsistence agriculture for its livelihood. Famine was an ever-present threat and was still a real possibility even in western Europe, for example in **France**, in the last decades of Louis XIV's reign (1638–1715), with acute excess mortality brought about by harvest failure. The commercialization of agriculture,

however, already existed in many areas of the world producing commodity crops and surpluses to feed urban centres and for export. During the centuries that followed agriculture became increasingly commerialized and a higher proportion of the global population became dependent on it to provide foodstuffs which it did not produce itself. Population growth, industrialization and urbanization could have dramatic effects, as shown in the earliest industrial societies. In the early eighteenth century the **United Kingdom** was an exporter of grain; by 1900 it was dependent on imports for an estimated eighty per cent of its food requirements. By the early twenty-first century the most intensively urbanized societies, such as western **Europe**, **Japan** and the **United States**, had a relatively small proportion of the population engaged in agriculture and the majority of their populations were dependent on foodstuffs produced whether domestically or imported from abroad.

Even those with still substantial populations engaged in agriculture, such as **India**, **China**, **Mexico**, **Brazil** and **Nigeria**, sustain huge urban populations dependent on domestic and foreign agriculture for their existence. In many parts of the world subsistence agriculture remains the norm, though often now existing alongside commodity production and highly developed forms of agri-business depending on levels of economic development. The transition of agriculture from subsistence to commercial production is often seen as the first priority of economic development. There are a number of reasons. First, assured food surpluses are essential to feed factory and building/infrastructure workers and teachers and technicians. Second, assured food surpluses are a source of political stability because the latter is required to sustain industrialization. Third, in the initial stages of economic development most of the food to feed wage labourers must be produced by domestic cultivators in order that capital can be invested in infrastructure projects and teaching literacy rather than spent on imported food.

These conditions do not necessarily occur automatically. In 1967 the economist Nicholas Kaldor observed that one of the principal reasons why peasant nations failed to develop was the backwardness and stagnation of agriculture, arguing that the rate at which non-agricultural employment increases depends on the rate of growth of marketed food supplies. He raised two crucial questions about agricultural change. First, why was it peasant societies failed to commercialize agriculture, and, second, what policies and conditions assisted the commercialization of agriculture in industrializing nations.

contemporary subsistence agriculture

Policies prescribed by development economists assume that requisite surpluses will automatically flow from peasant villages because economic policies will motivate peasants to increase food production for market sale in order to increase their money incomes. They prescribe economic policies because they observe monetized peasant societies producing limited amounts of exchange commodities (sheets of raw rubber, beans, cocoa nuts, kilos of coffee, kilos of rice) for market sale. These commodities are usually of indifferent quality and in limited amounts. The production of exchange commodities is not commercial production. Peasant households produce exchange commodities to acquire target sums of money that are used to purchase a limited number and variety of manufactured items (textiles, edged tools, cooking pots, plastic buckets). Economists assume that peasants will increase the production of marketable commodities if the right economic policies are implemented. This often does not happen. After target sums of money are acquired, peasants may cease labouring to produce more commodities for market sale. According to most development economists, the right policies are a complex mix of new technologies and government initiatives. Among these are: access to **green revolution** (GR) technologies, institutional credit to purchase GR inputs, instruction so that peasants can properly apply GR technologies, and anonymous markets that pay fair market prices for food and commodities produced by peasants. Development economists assume that GR technologies and good planning will motivate peasants to increase per capita food production for market sale, but often do not recognize the revolutionary difference between subsistence and commercial motivation. The social good of peasant villages is an acceptable level of subsistence welfare. This is summarized by the subsistence compromise, 'peasants attempt to grow enough food to last until the next harvest with the minimum expenditure of labour, on the assumption that every year will be a normal crop year'. Peasants know that every year is not normal but they willingly accept the risk of hunger in poor crop years and privation in consecutive poor crop years if, on average, they can minimize the labour of cultivation. Peasants cherish the customary laws that govern village labour expenditure because they preserve the enjoyment of maximum amounts of indolence (leisure). Peasants believe

that indolence is the proper use of time. Javanese peasants (Indonesia) summarize this aspiration with the word *cukupan* ('enough'): a large enough rice harvest to last until the next harvest, grown with minimal amounts of labour. There is a fundamental difference in sources of welfare security between city households and monetized peasant households. City households require money incomes to purchase all their food, shelter and clothing. This requires continuous paid labour. This labour is unnecessary in peasant villages. In poor crop years both housing and a minimal subsistence diet are assured and all purchases can be deferred.

Moreover, peasants have sources of welfare security other than incomes. The principal one is communal land tenure. Communal tenure divides village land into equalized cultivation units that are allocated to households that qualify as residents. In other words, the welfare of peasant households depends on control of land use; and access to land use is guaranteed by communal tenure. As population increases, cultivation units are reallocated into smaller but equal-sized units to satisfy the subsistence needs of new families. After reallocation, all village households must marginally increase labour expenditure; however, intensification of cultivation does not occur until more households must be fed from the same area of land. Observed from a different perspective, peasants believe that a fixed amount of annual labour will produce subsistence-sized harvests in normal crop years. The customary law that upholds communal tenure also enforces a communal obligation on all village households. In poor crop years harvests must be shared among households. All households may experience serious hunger, but no household starves, and subsistence labour norms are preserved until the return of normal crop years. As long as a household has a claim to land use, much of the labour cultivation can be transferred to dependants so that adults escape a high percentage of agricultural labour. The principal way of transferring labour is high birth rates. All peasant societies have high birth rates because a high percentage of agricultural labour can be transferred to children beginning at very young ages. This is in contrast to commercial cultures that have low birth rates because it is expensive to raise children to maturity when all food, shelter, clothing and literacy must be purchased. In male-dominant peasant societies large amounts of agricultural labour are also transferred to women because they have a dependent status.

Monetized peasant societies must have places to spend their money or money is worthless. Most peasant village have storekeepers who carry a limited variety of items in a small inventory. They are often strangers: Chinese in **Indonesia**, Indians in East Africa and Lebanese in West Africa. Storekeepers have no claim to land use. They are, therefore by necessity, commercially motivated. They must also be literate in order to keep accounts. Literacy is the basic commercial skill and storekeepers perform this function for illiterate peasants when they market exchange commodities and supply them with desired manufactured items. Storekeepers extend personal credit money on account to peasant households so they can acquire desired items. The credit extended by storekeepers is repaid when a peasant household sells a small amount of an exchange commodity to the storekeeper. The cost of personal credit is very high, but peasants get the items they want when they need them. Selling to repay personal credit is not selling on an anonymous market. Peasants are highly ambivalent about using GR inputs that must be purchased with money. They do not usually use available technology unless population increases force them to produce more food from the same area of land. They are also highly ambivalent about using institutional credit to get higher prices on anonymous markets because institutional credit requires literacy. For illiterate peasants, using institutional credit is a very complex transaction, and therefore they use storekeeper credit because here illiteracy is not a barrier.

commercial agriculture

Commercial agriculture in **Europe** began with commodities. The two most important were grapes for making wine and olives for pressing into oil. Owners of vineyards and olive groves used paid labour to cultivate and harvest grapes and olives. Paid labour was supervised in order to extract a full day of labour from workers. During the seventeenth century commodity cultivation was established on vacant ground in the Americas and was fully operational by 1700. Commodity crops, however, were not food crops. Commercial cultivation of food crops had a different origin. European landowners had to end communal tenure so that supervised paid labour could be applied to the cultivation of food grains. In England, communal tenure was called copyhold tenure; it existed in several forms under variant names in all the nations in western Europe. Before cultivation of food crops could be commercialized, feudal landowners had to extinguish

communal tenure. This required a social revolution that often generated large amounts of opposition. Commerializing food production usually meant ending communal tenure and putting management of their estates in the hands of farmers. Landowners in England and the **Netherlands** used every legal strategy to replace communal tenure with freehold tenure, often simply enforcing landlord freehold rights of clearance and enclosure. Freehold tenure was used to curtail or extinguish communal uses which could not be upheld in law and management increasingly entrusted to farmers and tenants who would maximize rent and output, often through innovative techniques. They did not need to specialize in food grains but whatever was likely to command the highest prices, for example in the Scottish Highlands, clearing subsistence crofters for extensive cattle and sheep ranching.

The earliest European settlements in Central and **Latin America** tended to mirror agricultural practices in Europe or adapt agriculture to the needs of the conquerors. Spanish monarchs were largely indifferent to the possibility of commercializing food production in the former native empires because of their primary concern with the extraction of precious metals. As a result they supported the status quo of subsistence cultivation in the **Spanish Empire** and peasant immigrants from the Iberian Peninsula tended to carry subsistence labour norms with them. In England, the Netherlands and other parts of Europe an increasing number of commercial cultivators emerged in the sixteenth and seventeenth centuries. In Protestant Europe many were able to buy up confiscated monastic lands, farming it as landowners or tenants with total control over the sale of their crops. Growing cities and towns became dependent on agricultural production for their growth, with large populations, such as those of the Dutch cities, London and Paris, becoming dependent on extensive supply networks of foodstuffs over sub-regions, in the cast of the Dutch, as far away as the Baltic for supplies of grain. These 'engines of growth' stimulated agricultural enterprise, innovation and specialization. The Dutch pioneered intensive agriculture with land relamation, the development of root crops to feed overwintered animals, and the use of crops such as clover to replenish soils under systems of crop rotation. Taken further in the British Isles, with selective animal breeding and the first farm machinery, such as seed drills, the techniques of the **agricultural revolution** soon spread to the rest of the continent and to the developing colonial empires. These empires had their impact in bringing new subsistence crops to Europe, such as the potato and maize, permitting some parts of Europe to combine subsistence peasant agriculture alongside cash crop cultivation. Prior to the mid nineteenth century and the development of more rapid forms of transportation for bulk commodities such as grain, Europe was able to sustain a very substantial increase in population through increased indigenous agricultural improvement and more productive subsistence food crops such as the potato. Where commercial production of wines, olive oil and citrus fruit developed in the Mediterranean, much of the rural population remained supported by peasant sharecropping and wage labour. Similarly, commercial grain production in the Baltic and in southern Russia and the **Ukraine**, often based on unfree serf labour, existed alongside subsistence agriculture for much of the population.

When the first settlers from Europe emigrated to North America, commercial cultivation was initially subsidiary to mere subsistence, but they brought cultivation implements and livestock with them and quickly developed sufficient commercial agriculture to support the first towns and cities. Initially work was often supplied by indentured labour, contracted to work for a set period. Labourers freed from indentures and new migrants fuelled the development of both commercial and near subsistence farming in the early North American colonies. But labour for the most lucrative crops for export to Europe, such as tobacco, was never in sufficient supply locally, giving rise to the **slave trade** and a system of extensive plantation cultivation for export using African labour. Initially used for tobacco and rice cultivation, the eighteenth century saw the development of cotton as a cash crop using plantation slave labour.

In the Caribbean, the huge demand for sugar from the seventeenth century saw the extensive development of highly commercialized plantation production, with the importation of millions of African slaves. **Cuba**, **Jamaica** and St Dominique became the world's largest sugar producers in the eighteenth century, while the system of sugar production using slave labour spread extensively through the tropical European colonies in Latin America and **Brazil**. Between 1600 and 1870 it is estimated that over 4 million slaves were imported into the Caribbean, nearly 5 million into Latin America and nearly half a million into North America, primarily to serve as agricultural labour. With the ending of slavery in the nineteenth century labour was imported from other parts of the world to maintain production.

global food production in the nineteenth and twentieth centuries

During the nineteenth century industrializing Europe required foodstuffs for expanding populations. It became available through the large areas of land opened up for cultivation in the **United States**, **Canada**, **Argentina**, Australasia and the Ukraine, often through the displacement of existing populations. From the mid nineteenth century steamships and railways allowed the rapid movement of goods from producing areas far inland, such as the American Midwest, to ports and on to Europe.

Refrigeration and canning permitted meat, fish and fruit to be brought halfway around the world for consumption in Europe and the cities of the eastern seaboard of the United States. Allied with the mechanization of cultivation such as the use of horse-drawn reaper-binders and threshing machines, grain cultivation could overcome potential problems of labour shortages in places such as the American prairies, while other areas such as Argentina and **New Zealand** concentrated on products such as beef and lamb which required less labour to produce. The abundance of new supplies, in turn, forced European producers both to increase efficiency through the use of machinery, better plant and animal breeding and the use of chemical fertilizers and to specialize in crops which could still command high value, such as bacon and sausage, dairy produce, soft fruit and high-quality wines. Nonetheless, falling prices for bulk agricultural produce in the latter half of the nineteenth century forced European rural workers off the land and swelled migration to Europe's cities and emigration abroad. Many of the nineteenth- and early twentieth-century emigrants from Europe to the Americas and Australasia were Irish, German, Italian and eastern European rural workers forced abroad by poverty and land hunger.

Where colonial governments had control over indigenous populations, new commodity crops were introduced for peasant cultivation. Amongst them were rubber trees, peanuts and cocoa beans. Additionally, vacant land was used for plantations of commodity crops. Amongst them were coffee, tea, oil palms, rubber trees and sisal as well as sugar, cotton and tobacco. At a later date pineapples and bananas became plantation crops. Colonial acquisition in the nineteenth century was similar to what happened in the Americas in the seventeenth and eighteenth centuries. Land was available for plantation agriculture but indigenous peasants refused to become supervised paid labourers. The solution was indentured servants, especially for sugarcane cultivation on the islands of **Trinidad**, **Mauritius** and **Fiji**, and in Natal, South Africa. They were also used in **Malaysia** and Sumatra to cultivate sugarcane and other plantation crops. The indentured servants came from south India and south China where famines forced migration for survival.

Incipient attempts by colonial governments to commercialize food production went into abeyance or disappeared after colonial independence (1948–70). Post-colonial governing elites had different priorities, except in Malaysia. When it became clear about 1965 that endemic hunger could become a permanent condition in most postcolonial nations, private philanthropic organizations aided by the governments of the United States and western Europe funded thirteen international crop research institutes. The first of these was the International Rice Research Institute established in the **Philippine Republic** in 1960. Similar institutions were established in other nations for wheat, maize, potatoes, sorghum and millet. These institutes and other scientific advances proved successful in plant breeding to increase yields, providing cultivators used commercial seeds, artificial fertilizers and pesticides, and were prepared to devote more time, often with training, in cultivating their crops. This has sometimes met with innate resistance from peasant cultivators unwilling to incur risks such as indebtedness in purchasing the commercial inputs required or the loss of a harvest through using unfamiliar techniques. Governments too, have proved reluctant to overcome peasant resistance to change where it might destabilize fragile post-colonial regimes.

However, a number of examples have shown that with political action as well as new techniques, agriculture can be transformed from near subsistence to much higher levels of production. In western Europe, the example of **Ireland** showed how changes in land tenure assisted the commercialization of peasant proprietorship in the seventy or so years that followed the **Irish famine** of the 1840s in which over a million people died and at least another million were forced into emigration. An agriculture based on a small number of landowners producing export crops, but with a large mass of subsistence peasant proprietors, many living on tiny plots, was transformed with the emergence of a larger class of tenant farmers as famine eased the predominant land hunger. In addition, the British government purchased the estates of absentee landowners and introduced schemes for tenants to buy out their landlords on easy terms backed by government loans. By 1914 Ireland was transformed from a country of large landlords and poverty-stricken peasants to one of larger tenants and freehold farmers, pursuing a more viable commercial agriculture based on dairying and stock-rearing.

In the twentieth century, at the other end of Europe, the new Soviet regime after the 1917 revolution inherited a mixture of highly commercialized extensive farming combined with an undercapitalized and backward peasant sector. Following the Soviet expropriation of all landholding, initial experiments with peasant proprietorship were abandoned for collectivization from the end of the 1920s. At a cost of enormous upheaval, short-term losses of output and consequent famine, Soviet agriculture was modernized and provided the surplus production necessary to support a rapid programme of industrialization under **Stalin**. The statist model of collective agriculture continued during the Soviet era, bringing vast new areas under cultivation. After the break-up of the **Soviet Union** in 1989–91, the return of land to private ownership permitted Russia and the now independent Ukraine to commercialize agriculture, allowing them to export grain by the early twenty-first century. Similarly, the Communist model was adopted following the **Chinese Revolution of 1949** with the expropriation of landlords and the introduction of collective farms. Subject to wayward policies under **Mao Zedong**, agricultural output suffered severe disruption producing serious famine, but under subsequent leaders Chinese agriculture proved capable of sustaining population growth and the modernization of the economy. Latterly, under more relaxed ideological control a flourishing commercial agriculture has developed.

Agriculture remains fundamental to the world economy and the feeding of the huge urban populations that have developed in an industrialized world, and those which remain dependent on agriculture for their livelihoods, whether as subsistence cultivators or engaged in commercial production. Only a portion of the world's land surface is suitable for agriculture and even with modern farming techniques, concerns about world supplies remain. A growing world population, an increasing percentage of which is urban, climate change affecting some food producing areas, and the loss of agricultural land to urban development suggest that the amount of agricultural land available per head will decline significantly by 2050. Moreover, growing affluence means that an increasing amount of land is being used to produce meat and other cash crops at the expense of subsistence crops. Although widespread famine had been largely kept at bay in the twentieth century through an often skeletal transport infrastructure and food aid made available through the **United Nations** and aid agencies such as **Oxfam**, Save the Children Fund and Cafod, the threat of it remains real in areas such as sub-Saharan Africa, and malnutrition is still endemic in many parts of the world, including the poorest urban areas.

Aguinaldo, Emilio (1869–1964)

Founder of the **Philippine Republic**. Aguinaldo was an anti-Spanish nationalist who became prominent in the revolutionary government of 1896–7, of which he was president. He was exiled, allied himself with the **USA**, and returned in 1898–1900. Despite attempts to become independent of the United States, he was forced to swear allegiance to US power, which caused him to retire. He attempted to stage a comeback in the 1935 presidential elections, but lost. He survived the Japanese occupation and liberation, despite accusations of collaboration, and lived out his remaining years as a member of the Council of State.

Ahmad Shah Durrani (1722–1773)

Ahmad Shah Durrani founded the Durrani dynasty that ruled **Afghanistan** from 1747 to 1978. He was born into a Pashtun family belonging to the Abdali tribe that had served Safavid rulers and one of their successors, Nadir Shah (r. 1736–47), whom he accompanied as an officer on campaigns against the Mughals in **India**. Upon Nadir's assassination in 1747, Ahmad asserted his own claim to kingship, assuming the title of shah and engineering a ceremony at which other Afghan notables offered their assent. Ahmad Shah adopted the honorific 'Pearl of Pearls' (*Durr-i Durran*), and his tribe, the Abdalis, became 'Durranis'. Drawing on the legacy and institutions of Nadir Shah, he established an empire at Kandahar that eventually stretched to **Iran** in the west, the Amu River in the north, the Indian Ocean in the south and northern India in the east. In the twentieth century Afghan nationalists would portray him as the father of the Afghan nation.

Ahmadu Bello

– *see* **Bello, Muhammad**.

Ahmed, Saiyid of Rae Bareilly (1786–1831)

A charismatic spiritual teacher and folk hero who led a jihad against the Sikh kingdom. Saiyid Ahmed called for religious reform based on direct consultation of the Qur'an and Hadith. Although bearing some similarity to Arabian Wahhabis, Saiyid Ahmed maintained deep connections to Sufi spiritual practices. In 1826 he started an armed struggle against the Sikh rulers in the region around Peshawar, but died in battle.

aid

– *see* **economic development**.

AIDS

Acquired immune deficiency syndrome; a term for the illnesses associated with the human immunodeficiency virus which emerged on the scientific record at some point in the mid twentieth century. AIDS became one of the major health challenges facing humanity, particularly in **Africa**, by the 1990s. Transmitted via bodily fluids and initially concentrated in homosexual and drug-using populations, it swiftly mutated and became a pandemic. In southern Africa in particular, it ravaged communities and devastated the most productive sections and age groups of Australafrica, particularly since it developed an ability to migrate to babies in the womb, and through sexual intercourse not employing barrier contraception. The illness raised questions of social cohesion, public policy and the status of women, and responses to it were essentially palliative and extremely expensive. Though by the twenty-first century it had become a manageable illness through the use of retroviral medicines in the richer world, the lack of such drugs and the lack of a medical infrastructure to deliver them to patients ensured that AIDS in Africa and the third world remained a social and economic challenge.

airships

– *see* **transportation**.

air travel

– *see* **transportation**.

Akali Dal

An organization created in 1921 to mobilize Sikh masses towards the achievement of a legal instrument guaranteeing the ownership of *gurudwaras* (temples), the Akali Dal became a formal political party after the passage of the Gurudwara Reform Act of 1925. It became factionalized between 1985 and 1995, and its largest faction since then has formed state governments in **Punjab** and allied with the Bharatiya Janata Party at the centre.

Alabama Dispute

An Anglo-American diplomatic controversy regarding the illegal construction in neutral British shipyards of warships for the Confederacy, including the *Alabama*, during the **American Civil War**. These Confederate ships inflicted great damage, both directly and indirectly (through increased insurance premiums), on the US merchant marine. The oft-tortuous diplomatic negotiations led to the Treaty of Washington (1871) and the Geneva Arbitration (1872), which awarded the **United States** 15 million dollars. This settlement began an Anglo-American rapprochement that would culminate later in the century.

Alam II, Shah (1728–1806)

Mughal ruler. Shah Alam II's reign as emperor (1761–1805) witnessed a dramatic decline in Mughal sovereign power. Most famously, he, along with his allies the Nawabs of Awadh and Bengal, lost the Battle of Buxar of 1764. Thus, in 1765 he was forced to grant the *diwani* (right to the revenues) of the rich province of **Bengal** to the victorious **East India Company**, a concession which vastly strengthened British resources and enabled the further conquest of India.

Alamo

– *see* **Texan War of Independence**.

Alaska

US Secretary of State William H. Seward purchased this vast territory in the western Arctic of North America from **Russia** in 1867 at the bargain price of 7.2 million dollars. Critics dubbed the territory an 'ice-box' and labelled the move 'Seward's folly', though the Senate ultimately extended its approval to the purchase. Seward viewed Alaska as a 'drawbridge' to **Asia** in the context of his programme of commercial expansion. Eventually, Alaska, home to many tribes of native peoples and a source of great natural resources, would become the forty-ninth state in 1958.

Alawi dynasty (Morocco)

The Alawis are the ruling dynasty of Morocco, coming to power in the late seventeenth century. As *shurafa*, they claim descent from the Prophet Muhammad. The dynasty traces its roots back to a sharif who migrated from Arabia to Sijilmasa in south-eastern Morocco in the thirteenth century. The Alawis rose to prominence centuries later when another descendant, Ali al-Sharif, led a jihad against Portuguese settlements on the Moroccan coast in the 1430s. The failure of previous dynasties and tribal groups to expel the Christian invaders opened the door for resistance campaigns led by *shurafa*, who were thought to possess spiritual charisma and blessing because of their saintly lineage. The line gradually gained in prestige, benefiting from military prowess and from their position in the Tafilalet oases astride important caravan routes. The Alawis under Rashid emerged victorious during a bloody civil war that followed the collapse of the Saudi dynasty. By 1669, the Alawites controlled Fez and Marrakesh. Rashid died in 1672, but his brother Ismail consolidated Alawite rule throughout the country. Pre-colonial Alawi rule was marked by varying degrees of central control by the sultan's state enterprise, or the *makhzan*. During his fifty-year reign, Ismail centralized the military and taxation, while state capacity diminished during the reigns of Abdallah and Soulayman. The Alawis put a premium on sharifian descent, rebuilding the sanctuary of Idris II (the seventh-century sharifian founder of Fez) and emphasizing their spiritual authority in addition to their temporal power. The current constitution of Morocco declares the eldest son of the Alawis the 'Commander of the Faithful', and the king still presides over important religious ceremonies on holidays such as Eid al-Adha.

The French established colonial rule over Morocco in 1912 through the Treaty of Fes, signed by the Alawi sultan himself. The treaty left the sultan in power but his role was largely symbolic. A coup in the years before the French invasion pitted two Alawi brothers against each other; the French handpicked a third, Moulay Youssef, to be sultan. After his death in 1927, the French again selected a successor, Mohammed V, who was only 18 when he took the throne. Expecting him to be compliant, he skilfully negotiated between the nationalists and the French regime. Ultimately, the nationalist movement rallied around the figure of the sultan, especially during his brief exile in 1953, and put him at the centre of their claims for independence. Mohammed V became the first modern king of the dynasty in 1957. He died suddenly in 1961, leaving his son, **Hassan II**, to succeed him. Hassan ruled for thirty-eight years, withstanding two major coup attempts in the early 1970s, and controversially occupying the former Spanish Sahara territory which is still disputed. He courted powerful allies in **France** and the **United States** while relying on the traditional symbolism of his position as Commander of the

Faithful and repression of political opponents. He, too, died suddenly in 1999, and his 35-year-old son, Mohammed VI, began a long rule.

Alawis (Syria)

A clannish and secretive sect of **Shi'ite Islam** found mainly in **Syria** and dating back to the ninth and tenth centuries, since when it has been widely persecuted as heretical. It is distinctive in its deification of 'Ali, its treating of the five duties of Islamic practice as symbolic and the eclecticism of its beliefs. Concentrated in the Lattakia region and around Homs and Hama, it was favoured by the French as a warlike group which would counterbalance the majority **Sunnis** in a deliberate policy of divide and rule after the declaration of the **mandate** over Syria. The Alawite district was declared autonomous under French protection and administered separately from Syria in 1922–42. Encouraged to join the police and the army, Alawis have come to dominate the Syrian state, although comprising only 11 per cent of the population. They are sometimes seen by other minorities as a defence against Sunni domination, and have been in power since the coup of 1970 by Lieutenant General Hafez al-Assad, father of President Bashar al-Assad. They provided the backbone of his support in the **Syrian Civil War**.

Al-Azhar University

The world's prime centre of **Sunni** Muslim and Arabic learning, founded in Cairo, AD 970, and focused on the mosque of that name. The core subjects have remained Islamic law (**sharia**), Islamic thought and the Arabic language, but philosophy was reinstated in the nineteenth century at the instigation of the educational reformer, Jamal ad-Din al-Afghani. Social sciences were added at a supplementary campus in Nasr City in the twentieth century. There is a further branch of the University at Tanta in the Nile Delta. The University in Cairo is organized in fourteen faculties for men and five for women, who have been admitted since 1962. The scholars of Al-Azhar have been given the power to elect the Grand Mufti, the leading arbiter of faith across the Islamic world, and elected Dr Shokri Ibrahim Abdel Karim, a professor of Islamic jurisprudence, as Egypt's nineteenth Grand Mufti in February 2013. Professor Karim is perceived as a moderate and is not a member of the **Muslim Brotherhood**. His predecessors had been directly appointed by the Egyptian president.

Albania

An integral part of the **Ottoman Empire** in the **Balkans** from the fifteenth century until declared independent by Treaty of London in 1913. Under strong Italian economic and political influence in the interwar years, it was proclaimed an Italian protectorate with the Italian king as monarch in 1939. Occupied Kosovo region of **Serbia**, 1941. Liberated itself under communist leadership, 1944. Annexation by **Yugoslavia** urged by **Soviet Union**, 1948. Broke off economic relations with Yugoslavia following **Tito**'s rupture with **Stalin** later that year. Member of **Comecon**, 1949, and **Warsaw Pact**, 1955–68. It accused the Soviet Union of 'revisionism' and developed closer links with **China** in 1961; the Soviet Union subsequently broke off diplomatic relations. Broke with China, 1978. Reopened to the world and opposition parties permitted, 1991. Non-Communist government formed, 1992, but Albania remained subject to economic, judicial and political malpractice. A national state of emergency was declared in 1997. It is presently seeking membership of the **European Union**.

alcohol

Alcohol is an organic compound which, in the form of diluted ethanol, is found in ascending percentages in beverages such as beers, wines and spirits or liquor. It is a natural product of fermentation, but in its manufactured form has featured very heavily in the development of European and American society. Wine, for instance, has come to have a definitive association with Mediterranean and especially French culture, as has beer for **Germany** and other northern European countries. Special laws and defences have been developed around the effects of intoxication which alcohol produces, and significant attempts have been made to restrict or tax the chemical. Between 1919 and 1933 the **USA** attempted to prohibit non-medical use of alcohol completely, but the effort is largely seen as a failure which induced the expansion of illegal organizations. The consumption of alcohol for leisure purposes is banned in Islamic culture, and its tendency to lower inhibitions of all sorts has been from time to time associated by moralists with cultural decline, revolutionary belligerence, crime and illicit sexual behaviour. Nevertheless, alcohol remains at the core of the plurality of western social and leisure activity in many cultures.

Al-e Ahmad, Jalal (1923–1968)

Iranian intellectual. Born in **Tehran**, he graduated from teaching college in 1946, breaking with his religious family. Studied at Tehran University.

Joined the **Tudeh Party** after World War II but distanced himself from it for its pro-Soviet line in the late 1940s. Supported Dr **Mossadegh** and helped found the Toilers' Party, a component of the National Front. Imprisoned for several years after the shah's restoration, in 1953. A noted writer and translator from the French of Camus, Gide and Sartre, he is best known for his 1962 essay *Gharbzadegi* (usually translated as 'Weststruckness'), which is critical of western civilization and technology and argues that the beginning of western 'economic and existential victories over the East' was the decline of such traditional Iranian industries as carpet weaving. Such an analysis was readily endorsed by **Ayatollah Khomeini** and then by the other leaders of the **Iranian Revolution, 1978–9**. Al-e Ahmad was thus one of the numerous Iranian intellectuals prior to 1979 who, while remaining left-wing, advocated authenticity, religion and a return to the self rather than the shah's Aryan nationalism, modernization and development.

Alexander I, Tsar (1777–1825)

Russian monarch, 1801–25. Succeeded his father Paul I after the latter's death in a palace coup. Initially relatively (but largely ineffectually) liberal in domestic policy, Alexander became increasingly reactionary after the discovery of a revolutionary conspiracy against him in 1818. His expansive foreign policy secured much of the **Caucasus** for **Russia** in conflicts with Persia in 1804–15, Bessarabia from the **Ottoman Empire** in 1806–12, and **Finland** from **Sweden** in 1808–9. In 1805 Russia joined the War of the Third Coalition against **France** but was forced to make peace at Tilsit in 1807. With **Napoleon**'s invasion of 1812, Russia rejoined the alliance and Alexander led his army into Paris in 1814. In 1815 he instigated a conservative Christian 'Holy Alliance' with the emperors of **Austria** and **Prussia**. Alexander's death in 1825 was shrouded in mystery and he was rumoured to have fled to become a hermit in Siberia.

Alexander II, Tsar (1818–1881)

Russian monarch, 1855–81. Succeeding to the throne during the 1854–6 **Crimean War**, Alexander ascribed **Russia**'s defeat to the country's backwardness, initiating a programme of reform and encouraging industrial development. The 1861 Emancipation Proclamation abolishing serfdom was followed by local government reform (including the establishment of *zemstva* – district and provincial councils – in 1864), improvements

in the legal system, expansion of secondary and university education, and military modernization, with the introduction of universal conscription. National unrest in Poland and an attempt on Alexander's life in 1866 ended this reforming phase. The return to despotism was accompanied by pan-Slavic advance into the **Balkans**, threatening **Turkey**, and a Russian expansion into central Asia. Growing radical agitation at home led to assassination attempts in 1879 and 1880 and – at the moment Alexander appeared prepared to consider limited constitutional reform – his death in a bomb attack by 'People's Will' in 1881.

Alexandria (al-Iskandariya)

Egypt's largest port and second largest city. A traditionally cosmopolitan city, one of its best-known sons was the poet K. P. Cavafy (1863–1933), perhaps the only writer in modern Greek to have a true international reputation. The city is also an intellectual centre: the Institut founded by **Napoleon** in Cairo in 1798 was reopened there in 1859, while the State University was opened in 1942. Also the seat of the Coptic patriarchate with authority over the Coptic Christians of Egypt, and more tenuously over those of **Ethiopia**. Bombarded by the British in 1882, in an attempt to quell the anti-British nationalist sentiment associated with **Ahmad Urabi Pasha al-Misri**. The burning of the city caused a resentment lasting till 1956 and the **Suez Crisis**, when many European residents left. Alexandria saw the attempted assassination of President **Nasser** by the **Muslim Brotherhood** on 26 October 1954, and his declaration of the nationalization of the Suez Canal on 26 July 1956.

Alexandria Protocol (1945)

– *see* **Arab League**.

Alfonsín, Raúl (1927–2009)

A lawyer and Radical Party politician, as president of **Argentina** (1983–9) Alfonsín had to govern after seven years of brutal military rule (1976–83). His government prosecuted and convicted numerous military commanders for **human rights** abuses committed during the dictatorship. Faced with hyperinflation and further military uprisings, he stepped down from office a few months early in 1989. Nonetheless, Argentines widely respect Alfonsín as the leader who redemocratized their country.

Algeciras, Conference of

An assembly held at Algeciras, **Spain**, from 16 January to 7 April 1906 arising from the 1905

Moroccan crisis, called at German insistence and involving the major European powers and the United States, with President **Theodore Roosevelt** as mediator. The crisis arose over **Germany**'s attempt to test the 1904 Anglo-French **Entente Cordiale** and to undermine French prestige by protesting against the recognition of French ambitions in **Morocco**. Initial German proposals put to the conference were rejected by ten votes to three and it soon became clear that **Britain** and **France** were working in close cooperation. The conference agreed that a Swiss inspector-general would command the Moroccan police but the force would come under joint French–Spanish supervision while France would maintain order on the Algerian–Moroccan frontier. The outcome of the conference signified the growing strength of Anglo-French relations since 1904 and represented a chastening diplomatic setback for Germany.

Algeria (al-Jazairiya)

A region with little historical identity, nominally part of the **Ottoman Empire** but effectively under the control of the **Barbary Pirates** prior to the French invasion of 1830. Their resistance was largely broken by 1847, and the region was heavily settled by the French and declared part of metropolitan France in 1881, but the peaceful agitation for Muslim emancipation as French citizens, associated with **Ferhat Abbas**, was rebuffed. Rebellion by the **Front de Libération Nationale** (FLN) was organized by **Ben Bella** from 1954 onwards, and torture was widely used in the savage **Algerian War of Independence** until a ceasefire in 1962. Radical socialist policies prevailed until deposition of Ben Bella by Colonel **Boumédienne** in 1965, after which there was an alliance of the FLN and the army and a socialist approach to the economy with many admirers in the developing world. Islamist rioting took place after 1985 and a multiparty constitution took effect from 1989. This was abrogated when the success of the fundamentalist Islamic Salvation Front (FIS) in the 1991 elections was aborted by the army, ushering in a brutal civil war. Power was retained by the FLN under President Abdelaziz Bouteflika in successive elections after 1999 after an estimated 150,000 deaths in the conflict.

Algerian War of Independence

Initially part inspired by the harsh French repression of a Muslim uprising in Setif in May 1945, which radicalized **Ben Bella** and other future Algerian nationalist leaders. Effectively started with the campaign of ambushes and sabotage launched, November 1954, by the **Front de Libération Nationale** (FLN) organized by Ben Bella and other nationalist exiles in **Cairo**. **Nasser**'s political and material support for the rebellion helped persuade **France** to attack **Egypt** during the 1956 **Suez Crisis**. The French response was more extreme than in **Morocco** and **Tunisia** where there were comparable liberation movements, mainly because the European settler population was proportionately very much larger and much of the country had officially been part of metropolitan France since 1881. Moreover, many Muslims had been extensively Gallicized. Those on both sides, however, who like **Ferhat Abbas** sought the full integration of Algeria in the French political system with complete Muslim equality of rights, always failed to persuade either the Arab nationalists or the French authorities, who responded with increasingly severe repression, the point of no return being the Special Powers Act of 1956. Guy Mollet, the prime minister humbled in the Suez Crisis, sought to restore his standing by putting 350,000 French troops at the disposal of Generals Salan and Massu, a number which was to rise to 500,000. Nevertheless, the number of guerrillas increased from about 5,000 in mid 1955 to some 20,000 by the end of 1956, remaining at that level for some three years prior to a rapid decline. During that time the French resettled about 2 million Algerian peasants, sometimes in supervised 'model' villages but more often in concentration camps. The suppression of rural guerrilla warfare resulted in a renewed concentration on urban warfare, notably the Battle of Algiers, in January 1957, won only militarily by the French. The use of torture by French forces was so extensive that even the Algiers police chief, who had himself been tortured by the Nazis, resigned in protest.

The war moreover proved destabilizing in France itself. The weak Fourth Republic collapsed in May 1958, in the face of mutiny in the army and the hostility of the settler community and its mainland supporters, who all demanded the return to power of **General de Gaulle**, who they assumed would be an ally. His then intentions are actually unclear, with his declaration in Algiers, 4 June 1958, that 'Je vous ai compris' ('I have understood you') a masterpiece of political ambiguity. His initial determination that the French must make themselves 'masters of the battlefield' was balanced by the opening of peace negotiations with the FLN, which outraged his erstwhile settler supporters. His hand was increasingly forced. Army officers of the Organisation Armée Secrète (OAS) (Secret Army Organization), founded to fight all supporters of Algerian independence, seized power in Algiers in April 1961 and briefly threatened Paris. Bomb attacks and assassinations followed, with some 12,000 victims and an attempt on de Gaulle's life in September 1961. Paris itself suffered violent unrest in February 1962, but de Gaulle remained in control and a ceasefire agreement was signed by the Algerian government-in-exile and France in Evian, March 1962, leading to independence on 1 July 1962. More than a million European settlers promptly left **Algeria**.

Al-Hajj Umar Tall (c. 1797–1864)

A pre-colonial Senegalese religious reformer and political leader educated in Futa Toro and Mecca. In 1848 after moving to Futa Jallon (modern Guinea) he formed an army and launched a jihad and built an empire over much of modern **Senegal** and **Mali**. He resisted French attempts to conquer the Senegal valley while trying to conquer the Niger valley, and this was continued after his death by his son **Ahmadu Seku**.

Al-Husayni, Hajj Amin, Mufti of Jerusalem (c. 1897–1974)

Al-Husayni was Mufti of Jerusalem, an Islamic religious figure, from 1921 to 1937, under the British **mandate** after **World War I**. Al-Husayni was the son of the Mufti of Jerusalem. In 1922, he was appointed to the newly created position of President of the Supreme Muslim Council and simultaneously appointed the Mufti of Jerusalem upon his predecessor's death. Al-Husayni was a known conservative and revolutionary, who had in the two years prior to his appointment been convicted of violent radical opposition to the growing Jewish settlements and the idea of a Jewish independent state in **Palestine** at the expense of Arabs and Muslims. This agenda was not softened by his political and religious appointments. Involved in uprisings against British rule, the mufti actively called for violence against Jewish expansion. In 1929 he instigated an attack on Jews to demonstrate his opposition to the mandate. With the rise of Nazi Germany, he extended his hand to the German regime. He expressed his solidarity with Nazi Germany and sought **Germany**'s support in expelling Jews from Palestine. As a result, he was removed from office by the British mandate leadership in 1939. Both **Yasser Arafat** and **Saddam Hussein** are said to have looked to the Mufti of Jerusalem as a hero for his radical Arab nationalist ideals, and he was co-opted by the **Palestine Liberation Organization** (PLO) as a hero

for Arab and Palestinian nationalism Al-Husayni's nationalist ideals formed the basis for the PLO's charter, and long after his death, the former mufti continues to affect the political and religious tone of the Palestinian government.

Al-Husri, Sati´ (1882–1968)

Educator and influential and prolific proponent of pan-Arab nationalism. Born to a Syrian family of Ottoman officials in **Yemen** and educated in Istanbul, al-Husri was heavily influenced by German romantic nationalists in his articulation of Arab nationalism. When **Faisal I** became king of **Iraq** in 1921, he appointed al-Husri director general of education in Iraq. Al-Husri developed a highly centralized curriculum that promoted pan-Arabism. This curricular focus on Arabism alienated many Iraqi Kurds and Shi´i. He also served as director of antiquities in Iraq (1934–41) and established the Museum of Arab Antiquities. Expelled from Iraq in 1941 for his role in the al-Gaylani coup, al-Husri settled in **Egypt** where he became the first director of the Institute of Higher Arab Studies and published a number of works on Arab nationalism such as *Ma Hiya al-Qawmiya?* (*What is Nationalism?*) (1963).

Ali, Maulana Muhammad (1878–1931) and Ali, Maulana Shaukat (1873–1938)

Together led the Indian **Khilafat movement**. The brothers attended the Muhammadan Anglo-Oriental College in Aligarh. A talented orator and essayist, Muhammad Ali founded an English paper *Comrade* in 1911 followed by an influential anti-British Urdu newspaper *Hamdard* in 1912. After the defeat of the Ottoman Empire at the end of War World I, the brothers spearheaded protests against the partition of Ottoman territories and called on the British to recognize the Ottoman emperor as the *khalifa* or leader of the Islamic community. They forged a partnership with **Gandhi**, eventually uniting the Khilafat movement with the **Non-Cooperation movement**, and were repeatedly imprisoned by the British. In 1923 Muhammad Ali served as president of the **Indian National Congress**, but growing discontent with the leadership's failure to accommodate Muslim interests led both brothers to break with Congress in 1928.

Ali, Muhammad (1942–2016)

Born Cassius Marcellus Clay Jr in Louisville, Kentucky, he was winner of the Light Heavyweight gold at the 1960 Olympics and World Heavyweight champion in 1964. He converted to Islam in 1964 and changed his name. Threatened with imprisonment for refusing the draft in 1967 and stripped of titles, he had comeback fights with George Foreman in Zaire (1974) and Joe Frazier in Manila (1975); he retired from boxing in 1981. In 1984 he announced he was suffering from Parkinson's disease. Chosen to light the Olympic Flame in Atlanta in 1996, he was named UN Messenger of Peace in 1998 and received the Presidential Medal of Freedom in 2005.

Ali Bey al-Kabir (1728–1773)

An Egyptian soldier and leader, born to a monk family in **Georgia** (**Caucasus**). Kidnapped as a young child by Turkish soldiers, he was taken to Cairo and integrated into the Ottoman administration of **Egypt**. His administrative skill caused him to be promoted rapidly and in 1760 he became the *sheikh al-balad*, the local administrator of Egypt under the Ottoman governor. In 1768 Ali Bey deposed the Ottoman governor of Egypt and assumed the role of governor. Although he did not formally renounce his subordination to the **Ottoman Empire**, he stopped paying tribute to Istanbul and struck his own coinage, thus rendering the country effectively independent. In 1770 he expanded his rule into **Syria** and Arabia. A local rebellion in Syria, led by Abu al-Dhahab, forced Ali Bey to abandon his claims in Syria. Al-Dhahab turned on Ali Bey, and eventually killed him in Cairo.

Alien and Sedition Acts

After the election of **John Adams** as president of the **United States** in 1796, Franco-American relations deteriorated because Adams and his Federalist Party were opposed to the **French Revolution**. Negotiations between France and the United States broke down in the spring of 1798 (*see* **XYZ Affair**) and the Federalist-dominated Congress adopted a series of measures during the summer in anticipation of a declaration of war. These acts extended the period of time that immigrants would have to reside in the country before they could vote from five to fourteen years; and prohibited writing, speaking or publishing anything deemed 'false, scandalous, or malicious' about the government or its officers. Ten newspaper editors, all from the opposition Republican Party, were convicted under the Sedition Act. These acts represented the first challenge to civil liberties during wartime in American history. The Republican legislatures of Virginia and Kentucky adopted resolutions,

written by **James Madison** and **Thomas Jefferson** respectively, condemning the legislation and calling for its nullification (*see* **Kentucky and Virginia Resolutions**).

Aligarh

A city in the Indian state of Uttar Pradesh, located approximately 90 miles south-east of New Delhi. Aligarh takes its name from a nearby fort. Its historical significance stems from its connection to Muslim modernism. Aligarh was the site of the Muhammadan Anglo-Oriental College, established by Sir Sayyid Ahmad Khan in 1877. The college, which became the Aligarh Muslim University in 1920, continues to be an important educational institution.

Al-Ikhwan al-Muslimun

– *see* **Muslim Brothers**.

Aliyah

The immigration of Jews from the Diaspora to **Israel**. Literally, the Hebrew word for 'ascent' as opposed to *yerida*, meaning 'descent', describing emigration from Israel. Essentially a metaphysical description, but also recognizing the higher altitude of Israel than of **Egypt** or of ancient Babylonia, now southern Iraq. An abstract ideal of the Jewish faith since the ejection of the Jews from **Palestine** by the Romans, but not a concrete objective before **Zionism** and the first Zionist Congress, 1897, which declared in its Basel Programme that 'Zionism strives to create for the Jewish people a home in Palestine secured by public law.' Pre-Zionist settlement in Palestine had been token in the Middle Ages but reached a few thousand in the early nineteenth century. It has enjoyed legal force since the enactment by the state of Israel, founded in 1948, of its Law of Return, which guarantees to any Jew, or eligible non-Jew, the right to assisted immigration and settlement in Israel, as well as Israeli citizenship. An eligible non-Jew is defined as a child and a grandchild of a Jew, the spouse of a Jew, the spouse of a child of a Jew and the spouse of a grandchild of a Jew. *Aliyah* is seen by more religious Jews as the fulfilment of God's biblical promise and even as a divine commandment. For some, it is associated with the coming of the Jewish Messiah who will return world Jewry to the land of Israel under theocratic rule. For a no doubt larger number, *Aliyah* has essentially represented an alternative to intolerable discrimination in the home country.

Zionists recognize five waves of *Aliyah* (Hebrew plural *Aliyot*). In the first, dated 1882–1903, some

35,000 Jews emigrated into what was then the south-western part of the Ottoman province of Syria. Most came from the **Russian Empire** but a minority from Yemen. In the second, 1904–14, a further 40,000 immigrants arrived, again mainly from the Russian Empire, but strongly influenced by socialist ideals, leading to the establishment of the first *kibbutz* (communal farm), Degonia Alef, 1909. The number of Jewish immigrants and their aspirations were, however, already provoking Arab hostility and the first self-defence organizations also appeared. The third *Aliyah*, 1919–23, subsequent to the **Balfour Declaration**, saw the arrival of a further 40,000 Jewish immigrants, again primarily from the Russian Empire, including many trained agriculturalists. The fourth *Aliyah*, 1924–9, brought a further 82,000, particularly from re-established **Poland** and **Hungary**. For the first time, many were middle class, and some 23,000 ultimately left. The fifth *Aliyah*, lasting until **World War II** and reflecting the growth in European, particularly German, anti-Semitism, saw the arrival of a further 250,000, the majority from eastern Europe but also many highly qualified professionals from **Germany**. The attempt by the British to respect the rights of the Arabs by restricting further Jewish immigration after 1933 was met by a major growth in *Aliyah Bet* (illegal immigration) by at least a further 110,000 Jews.

The practice of numbering *aliyot* ceased on Israeli statehood, 1948, but immigration continued, peaking at nearly 250,000 in 1949. The total number of immigrants between 1882 and 2012 is put at nearly 3,631,000, of which some 768,000 have come from the Arab world.

Al-Jabarti, 'Abd al-Rahman (1753–1825)

Egyptian scholar and chronicler. An ethnic Somali about whose life little is known. Born in either the Nile Delta or Cairo, his family can be traced back to the al-Jabart region in Zeila, in modern Somalia. Al-Jabarti studied to become a *sheikh* (religious leader) at **Al-Azhar University**, where he commenced the work for which he is remembered, *Aja'ib al-athar fi al-tarajim wal-akhbar*, a monthly chronicle of events in Cairo, usually known in the English-speaking world as *History of Egypt*. This work is widely valued because it includes eye-witness accounts of **Napoleon**'s Egyptian Expedition (1798–1801) and the seizure of power, in 1805, by the ethnic Albanian adventurer, **Muhammad 'Ali**, who was to found Egypt's ruling dynasty until the **Egyptian Revolution** of 1952.

The section of his chronicle dealing with the French expedition and occupation has been published separately in English as *Napoleon in Egypt*.

Allada

A small state on the coast of modern-day Benin that flourished between the sixteenth and eighteenth centuries. It appears in the early seventeenth century to have controlled the coast and some distance into the interior and to have had a centralized government. In 1724 the army of **Dahomey**, one of its former subjects, attacked and destroyed the capital of Allada, but the rulers fled to Porto Novo and established a rival dynasty.

Allenby, Edmund Henry Hynman (1861–1936)

British army officer and conqueror of Palestine. After training at the British Military College at Sandhurst, he commanded British cavalry operations in the **Boer War** (1899–1902). From 1910 until 1914 he was Inspector General of British Cavalry, and in **World War I** he first commanded British cavalry in France, then in June 1917 was sent to Cairo as commander of the British Expeditionary Force. In October 1917 he launched an offensive against the Ottoman defensive line in **Palestine**. British troops were rebuffed at **Gaza**. Deceiving the enemy into thinking he would launch another frontal attack, he took Beersheba instead (31 October), thus forcing the Ottomans to withdraw from Gaza and leading to the capture of Jaffa and Jerusalem (9 December). He entered the Holy City on foot and was greeted by the population as their liberator.

The transfer of a large part of his troops to France in the spring of 1918 prevented Allenby from continuing his advance in Palestine. In September 1918 troops transferred from Mesopotamia and **India** crossed into Palestine from **Jordan**. Having secretly transferred the bulk of his forces (some 35,000 men) to the orange groves north of Jaffa, he broke through on the night of 18/19 September. The 38th and 39th Battalions of the Royal Fusiliers, also known as the Jewish Legion (see **Vladimir Jabotinsky**, **David Ben-Gurion**), took part in this manoeuvre. Allenby reached Nazareth via Megiddo before the Ottomans realized what was happening. Their escape route blocked, tens of thousands of Ottoman troops were taken prisoner. He captured Damascus and Aleppo and forced the **Ottoman Empire** out of the war on 30 October. Allenby then became military governor of the conquered territory. In recognition for his services he was promoted to the rank of Field Marshal and elevated to the peerage as Viscount Allenby of Megiddo and Felixstowe. He also received a parliamentary grant of 50,000 pounds.

Of massive build and forceful personality, he was known to his troops as 'The Bull' or 'Bloody Bull'. As commander of the British Expeditionary Forces and as military governor of Palestine, Allenby was non-committal toward Zionist aspirations, doubting the wisdom of British policy concerning a Jewish national home. In 1918 he was present at the laying of the foundation stone for the Hebrew University of Jerusalem on Mount Scopus. At a 1925 inaugural banquet of the university, he expressed what seemed to be a sympathetic understanding of **Zionism**. For his efforts in liberating **Jerusalem** from the Ottomans, many streets in **Israel** are named in his honour.

Allende Gossens, Salvador Isabelino (1908–1973)

Chilean politician. First involved in radical politics as a medical student, Allende was one of the founders in 1933 of the Chilean Socialist Party, an anti-Communist Marxist party. Elected to the Chamber of Deputies in 1937, he served as Health Minister, 1939–41. A senator, 1945–70, Allende unsuccessfully stood for president in 1952, 1958 and 1964. In 1970 he became the world's first democratically elected Marxist president, heading a Popular Unity government and inheriting an economy in crisis. A programme of wealth redistribution including price controls, nationalization of the copper industry and the banks and collectivization of land antagonized business interests and the **United States** government. **Central Intelligence Agency** encouragement of senior officers to overthrow Allende culminated in a military coup led by General **Augusto Pinochet** on 11 September 1973, Pinochet replacing Allende as president following his death in fighting around the presidential palace.

Alliance for Progress (USA)

The policy of economic assistance for Latin America adopted by **United States** President **John F. Kennedy** in response to the **Cuban Revolution**. Inspired by a proposal of Brazilian President **Juscelino Kubitschek**, an inter-American conference in Montevideo, **Uruguay** (August 1961) adopted the charter for the alliance. The US committed 20 billion dollars in loans and aid over ten years, with much larger amounts required from Latin American governments. As part of the alliance, the US pressurized

Latin American governments to adopt agrarian reforms to counter the appeals of the Cuban Revolution. From 1961 to 1967 US military training and counter-insurgency programmes paralleled the Alliance for Progress, often becoming indistinguishable from the alliance itself. Most of the economic goals were not achieved, but counter-insurgency prevented more revolutions on the Cuban model. The permanent committee of the **Organization of American States** (OAS) assigned to implement the alliance was disbanded in 1973.

Allied Control Commission

This term describes commissions of the victors after both world wars, but is more commonly used for the second. The **World War I** body is often known as the Inter-Allied Control Commission, functioning until 1927 to enforce the decision to disarm **Germany**. After **World War II** commissions were established for each defeated state (Germany, **Austria**, **Italy**, **Japan**, **Bulgaria**, **Romania**, **Hungary** and **Finland**), sometimes called Allied Commissions. They overcame internal frictions and managed to create some order until peace treaties could be signed and regular governments established. The commissions were ended during or before 1951 except for Austria (1955) and Germany (1991).

al-Qaida (al-Qaeda)

Group, meaning `the Base', founded by **Osama bin Laden** in **Afghanistan**, dedicated to fighting against the West 'occupying Islamic sacred land in Palestine and the Arabian Peninsula'. It functions as a network of terrorists rather than a structured organization, mounting attacks on US embassies in **Kenya** and **Tanzania**, the USS *Cole* in Aden harbour, and the attacks on the World Trade Centre, New York, and the Pentagon, Washington in September 2001. The last prompted the invasion of Afghanistan under a UN mandate, scattering the **al-Qaida** network. It survived the death of bin Laden in **Pakistan** in 2011, continuing to operate in north Africa, **Iraq** and other parts of the **Middle East**.

Al Sabah (ruling family of Kuwait)

– *see* **Sabah, Al**.

Alsace and Lorraine

French-ruled areas on the borders of **France** and **Germany**. Most of Alsace and part of Lorraine was incorporated into the second German Reich in

1871. Their recovery was a French war aim in 1914, and their possession was controversial in Germany, which ran them as an autonomous imperial territory frontier. At Versailles in 1919, France demanded the areas – which had a distinctive Franco-German culture – 'back'. Alsace was, for a matter of weeks, a soviet-style republic following the defeat of Germany. The regional capital, Strasbourg, became the seat of several European institutions to demonstrate Franco-German amity after **World War II**.

Al-Said, Nuri (1888–1958)

Major Iraqi politician and prime minister during the **Hashemite** Monarchy. Born in Baghdad of a humble **Sunni** background and educated at a military academy in Istanbul, he served in the Ottoman Army during World War I. When **Faisal I** became King of **Iraq** in 1921, Al-Said started his close association with the Hashemite monarchy. Throughout his political career he worked towards maintaining a friendly relationship with the British much to the chagrin of other Iraqi nationalists. Yet Al-Said was reluctant to execute policies that could possibly prompt British intervention in Iraq. He first became prime minister in 1930 and would hold that office on seven different occasions (1930–2, 1938–40, 1941–4, 1946–7, 1949, 1950–2, 1954–7 and 1958). He was particularly close to the regent 'Abd al-Ilah and together they dominated Iraqi politics from 1941 to 1958. In the time of Cold War politics, they were instrumental in maintaining Iraq's pro-western stance seen most visibly in Iraq's membership in the pro-western military alliance, the Central Treaty Organization, also known as the **Baghdad Pact**.

During his first period as prime minister, Al-Said was largely responsible for executing the 1930 Anglo-Iraqi Treaty. His second and third stints were more decisive, with war clouds gathering over **Europe**. In 1940 he resigned after he failed to persuade his cabinet to declare war on **Germany** or to break off diplomatic relations with **Italy**. After the 1941 Rashid Ali coup and the resultant British occupation, Al-Said once again became prime minister and strengthened the government's relationship with Britain and the position of the monarchy. After the war he was central to the establishment of the **Arab League**. The League's charter, influenced by Al-Said, enshrined the independent sovereignty of member states and only made rhetorical references to pan-Arabism. The Iraqi Army did participate in the 1948 war against the newly established Israel. After the Arab loss, Al-Said sought to minimize the damage it would do to the Iraqi government by a series of proposals and formal enquiries into the army's performance. He threatened to expel the entire Iraqi Jewish community if Palestinian refugees were not given the right to return to their homes. Subsequently, he proposed a population exchange but eventually the Iraqi government passed legislation that allowed Iraqi Jews to renounce their Iraqi citizenship and nearly all Iraqi Jews left Iraq. Though Iraq was deriving more revenue from its oil, al-Said's economic policies largely benefited the landed and commercial elite. He was one of the main architects of the Iraq Development Board that would oversee development projects funded by Iraq's oil wealth. In the mid 1950s, he was the 'strong man' of Iraqi society and he felt that political parties were unnecessary and that all political factions should work in one organization to benefit Iraq as defined by him. Among many Iraqis, especially in the military ranks, Al-Said had become too corrupt, powerful and out of touch. In the 1958 revolution, Al-Said tried to flee disguised as a woman but was found, shot dead and buried; the next day a mob disinterred his body, mutilated it and dragged the corpse through the streets of Baghdad.

Amadu, Seku (1775–1844)

A religious leader in the middle Niger region. Born into the Fulbe ethnic group, he studied in the **Middle East** and absorbed some of the revolutionary ideas of Usuman dan Fodio, who would lead an Islamic jihad in the Hausa region (modern-day Nigeria). In 1810 he began the jihad which would overthrow the ruling dynasty of Massina, and made it the headquarters of his own movement, establishing a headquarters at Hamdallahi. His movement was violently resisted not just in Massina but also by Massina's overlord, the King of Segu, and as a result by 1818 his forces had overthrown them, establishing a substantial empire along the Niger River. The Massina kingdom was a theocracy, ruled by a committee of religious leaders who demanded an uncompromising acceptance of the sharia, or Islamic law.

Amal

Lebanese politico-military movement. An acronym, meaning 'hope', for Afwaj al-Muqawmat al-Lubnaniyya (Lebanese Resistance Brigades). Founded in 1975 as the military wing of Harakat al-Mahrumin (Movement of the Disinherited), an essentially secular political movement founded by Musa as-Sadr in 1974, with the objectives of securing more influence for the **Shi'ites**, traditionally **Lebanon**'s weakest political grouping, and a higher allocation of resources to the Shi'ite dominated south. Grew with the support of Syria when **Israel**'s invasion of south Lebanon, 1982, created 300,000 internal refugees.

At its peak the militia numbered some 14,000 men but split, 1982, when the deputy leader, Husayn al-Masawi, founded Islamic Amal, allied to and supported by **Iran**, which was ultimately absorbed into **Hezbollah**. The weakened mainstream Amal under Nabih Berri remained allied to **Syria** and participated in the Lebanese Civil War when, together with the **Druze** Progressive Socialist Party, it attacked al-Murabitun, the main Lebanese **Sunni** militia which was the close ally of the **Palestine Liberation Organization (PLO)**, 1985. Fought the Palestinians for control of the Sabra, Shatila and Burj el-Barajneh refugee camps, May 1985 and May 1986. Worsted by Hezbollah in further fighting, 1988–9. It has since remained a political force supportive of a Syrian presence.

Amanullah, Emir (1892–1960)

Amanullah ruled **Afghanistan** from 1919 to 1929. He ascended the throne following the murder of his father, Emir Habibullah, and initiated a campaign to free Afghanistan of its dependence upon the **British Empire**. As a result of his leading role in waging the third Anglo-Afghan War (May–June 1919) and gaining Afghan independence, he assumed the honorific title *ghazi* (holy warrior). Early in his reign, he voiced support for pan-Islamic causes: many Indian Muslims looked to him as the figure who would resurrect the institution of the caliphate after the Ottoman defeat, and he gave refuge to anti-Soviet rebels in northern Afghanistan. He subsequently launched an ambitious programme of reform in which he was joined by Queen Soraya, the daughter of the modernist intellectual Mahmud Tarzi. Reforms relating to education and marriage aimed at improving the status of women in particular, but they also provoked clerical and tribal resistance. Rebels forced him into exile after a controversial tour of **Europe** in 1928.

Amazons of Dahomey

Although female guards were reported at the **Dahomey** palace in the early eighteenth century, it was not until the early nineteenth century that armed women became a regular unit in **Dahomey**'s army. They were increasingly used as shock troops in Dahomey's campaigns, and often received the best equipment, being the first to obtain machine guns and modern artillery. They were decimated in the wars against **France** that resulted in Dahomey's defeat in 1894.

Ambakistas

A merchant group in nineteenth-century colonial Angola originating from the small Portuguese outpost of Ambaca (founded 1617). In the nineteenth century most Ambakistas were mixed-race descendants of Portuguese men and African women. Many were literate, knowledgeable of both Portuguese and African culture, and possessed protection from the Portuguese government. They pioneered Portuguese commerce into the interior of **Angola**, especially following the end of the external slave trade, founding colonies throughout central Africa.

America First Committee

In the summer of 1940 conservative opponents of American involvement in **World War II** launched the America First Committee. While seeking to exclude supporters of the Nazi regime, the organization was often portrayed as pro-Hitler and in late 1941 one of its leading figures, the aviator Charles Lindbergh, accused Jews of being a leading force in the drive to war. Soon after, the Japanese attacked **Pearl Harbor** and opposition to American intervention collapsed.

American Civil War (1861–1865)

The greatest war fought between the fall of **Napoleon** and 1914 resulted from a fundamental disagreement between North and South over the place of slavery in the Union. It was detonated by the South's refusal to accept the election of **Abraham Lincoln** in 1860, the secession of the slave states, and in April 1861 the bombardment of Fort Sumter. Despite the Northern defeat at First **Bull Run**, by the spring of 1862 the Federals had won a series of victories at Forts Henry and Donelson, **Shiloh**, and occupied Nashville, Memphis, New Orleans and important lodgements on the North Carolina coast. The likelihood of a brief war and an easy Northern victory was swept away by Confederate triumphs in the Seven Days Battles and at Second Bull Run. The Confederacy mounted an improvised counteroffensive by entering Maryland and Kentucky, incursions brought to an end by Antietam and Perryville respectively. Following Antietam, the preliminary Emancipation Proclamation freed all slaves in Confederate-held territory, and transformed the war from a limited conflict designed to restore the Union into a crusade resolved to destroy the slave system; moreover, 186,000 black soldiers were recruited into the Union Army. The Southern victory at **Fredericksburg** and the drawn battle at Murfreesboro did not radically alter the stalemate at the end of the year. The year 1863 would prove to be the decisive turning point. It began well for the South with success in the First Vicksburg Campaign, at Chancellorsville, and the invasion of Pennsylvania. However, in July Vicksburg fell and Southern arms were defeated at **Gettysburg**. A Union advance in East Tennessee was halted at Chickamauga, but this Confederate success only prepared the way for humiliating defeat at Chattanooga, which exposed the Deep South to invasion.

The 1864 campaign witnessed an attempt by **Ulysses S. Grant** to launch a simultaneous offensive on all fronts. The most important thrusts were aimed at Richmond and Atlanta. That in Virginia ended in disappointing stalemate after the ferocious battles of the Wilderness, Spotsylvania, Cold Harbor, the Crossing of the James River and the Siege of Petersburg. The equally remorseless campaign in Georgia was rewarded by the seizure of Atlanta. This success combined with the taking of Mobile, Alabama, and Philip H. Sheridan's victories in the Shenandoah Valley propelled the re-election of Lincoln in November, and the maintenance of a strategy that brooked no compromise with the South. The final Southern collapse was precipitate. **William T. Sherman**'s marches through Georgia and the Carolinas revealed the Confederacy's fragility. In December 1864 the Army of Tennessee was annihilated, and its premier field force, the Army of Northern Virginia, abandoned Richmond and capitulated on 9 April 1865. On 26 April the remnants of Confederate forces surrendered to Sherman at Durham Station, and so too in May did isolated detachments in the Trans-Mississippi.

The Civil War had momentous consequences. Where in 1860 the slave states held 30 per cent of total American wealth, by 1870 this had slumped to 12 per cent. The issue of secession had been settled conclusively and slavery extirpated. All this cost 620,000 American lives, 360,000 Union and 260,000 Confederate.

American Colonization Society

An organization established in 1816 to promote the voluntary resettlement of free **African Americans** outside the **United States**. Its offer to remove manumitted slaves to **Liberia** held some appeal for conservative emancipationists in the upper south and northern moderates and churchmen, but its ambiguous mission incurred both pro-slavery and **abolitionist** hostility from an early date. Never that successful, the turbulent 1850s rekindled interest in the ACS's middling anti-slavery solution, but the **American Civil War** rendered it obsolete.

American Constitution

The American Constitution was debated at the Philadelphia Convention of 1787, and came into effect following the ratification of New Hampshire on 21 June 1788. The Constitutional Convention was called owing to a number of difficulties which faced the **USA** under the Articles of Confederation. Most problems revolved around the absence of any central power to enforce national laws. Many delegates also mistrusted state governments, which were acting in ways that seemed to threaten property rights and economic stability.

The first priority of the Constitutional Convention was to establish a national government with clear coercive powers held at the centre. This was achieved by making federal law trump state law in all areas of conflict. This principle is also established in the 'checks and balances' of the three governmental branches, in which governmental powers are shared among the legislature, executive and judiciary to prevent any one branch exercising tyrannical power. This also meant all checks on power were held at the federal level; it insulated national government from the interposition of individual states. The creation of the Supreme Court in the Constitution, and particularly the development of the doctrine of 'judicial review' in the nineteenth century, helped increase the power of the national government, as it allowed citizens the right to appeal against state laws they considered unconstitutional.

Representation caused one of the largest debates at the convention; delegates from large states wanted representation to be proportional to the population, whereas small states wanted each state to have equal voice. Eventually, compromise was reached with the House of Representatives being elected according to state population, and each state given two senators in the upper chamber. (Senators were largely appointed by state legislatures until the passage of the 17th Amendment in 1913.) As the 'popular' chamber, money bills can only be originated from the House of Representatives; the Senate is responsible for ratifying treaties, and confirming executive appointments.

The executive branch was given extensive power in the Constitution. Though some delegates feared entrusting too much power to one man, the convention decided that one President would be elected for four-year terms. As some delegates mistrusted the public's ability to accurately judge the merits of candidates for the office, the President would be elected by a convoluted and indirect system known as the Electoral College. Voters in each state would choose 'electors' who would then cast their own votes for President and Vice President. The President was made Commander-in-Chief of the military, had power to conduct foreign policy (with the exception of declaring war), and the right to appoint judicial officers and Cabinet advisers.

The Constitution has been amended twenty-seven times since its ratification, most notably in 1791 with the passage of the first ten amendments as the Bill of Rights. The next most notable period of amendment followed the end of the civil war, with the 13th, 14th and 15th Amendments abolishing slavery, granting citizenship to all born within the United States, and guaranteeing the right to vote.

American Declaration of Independence

On 2 July 1776 the second **Continental Congress** voted to declare Britain's rebellious thirteen colonies independent. Between July 2 and July 4 Congress considered and amended a draft Declaration of Independence which had been written by a committee consisting of **Benjamin Franklin**, **John Adams**, Roger Sherman, Robert Livingston and **Thomas Jefferson**. Jefferson was the primary author of the draft submitted to Congress. The declaration began with a preamble which asserted, 'We hold these truths to be self-evident, that all men are created equal, that they are endowed by their Creator with certain unalienable Rights, that among these are Life, Liberty and the pursuit of Happiness.' The declaration then enumerated a series of crimes and transgressions which **George III** had allegedly committed in an effort to undermine American liberties. Congress altered Jefferson's draft considerably, eliminating a condemnation of the Atlantic **slave trade** and making stylistic changes. The final version of the declaration, which established the **United States** as a republic, was adopted on 4 July 1776.

American exceptionalism

The term is generally used to suggest that the **United States** is different in its essential character to other countries. It has sometimes been argued that the United States is unique, even a model nation, possessed of superior political and economic systems and perhaps of moral virtue, with the capacity to offer hope to the peoples of other lands. The notion has been variously traced to the country's Puritan origins, to its history as a nation of immigrants, to the republican ideas of the **American Revolution**, to the impact of an expanding frontier, and to other experiences. In historical writing, a major focus has been on the possible exceptional circumstances in which the labour movement has functioned, arguably disadvantaged by the absence of the kind of class structures associated with Europe. In 1906 the German sociologist Werner Sombart famously triggered the debate by asking 'Why is there no socialism in the United States?'

American Federation of Labor (AFL)

– *see* **AFL-CIO**.

Founded 1886 as a federation of national labour organizations. Under its first president, Samuel Gompers, it concentrated on organizing craft unions not unskilled workers, and on demands for economic benefits, using strikes and boycotts. It avoided association with radical politics and enjoyed steady growth. In the early twentieth century it survived the anti-union stance of courts and employers, eventually joining with its rival Congress of Industrial Organizations (CIO) in 1955.

American Indians

– *see* **Native Americans**.

American Party

An 1850s **nativist** party in the **United States** that emerged from secret organizations, hence its adherents' alternative name, 'Know Nothings'. Northern support won its presidential candidate **Millard Fillmore** 22 per cent of the vote in 1856, but it then split over slavery. Its treatment is often that of a stepping-stone between the **Whig** and **Republican** parties of the second and third **American party systems**, and as a vehicle of anti-**Democratic** sentiment in a South lacking balanced partisan competition by this point.

American party systems

The **federalism** of the **American Constitution** allows remarkable inclusiveness under just two major party labels. The mechanisms for both congressional and presidential elections also inhibit third parties, whose agendas the dominant pair often absorb. Changing issues, political philosophies and voting blocs can however produce 'realignment'. During the first party system (1790s–1820s), the northern, mercantile **Federalist Party** lost its ground to the southern, agrarian Democratic Republicans. An **Era of Good Feelings** gave way to a nationally competitive second system of the **Whig** and **Democratic** parties (1830s–1850s), which contested federal involvement in the economy. **Sectional conflict** and the **American Civil War** pitted **Republicans** against Democrats over race, **Reconstruction**, economic issues and monetary issues in a third system (1854–96). 'Free Silver' and overlap with the **Populists** undermined a previously competitive Democratic Party for a fourth system (1896–1932) of Republican hegemony tempered by its **progressivism**. Conversely, the **New Deal** coalition made the fifth system (1932–68) one of Democratic domination; the fragmentation of the same has defined the current, sixth system of Republican and Democratic periods of dominance.

American Revolution (c. 1763–1789)

The American Revolution generally refers to the period of political, constitutional and social change that led to the creation of the **United States**. It usually includes the period prior to the War of Independence, the war itself and the period of constitutional change after the conflict (though some scholars favour a broader chronology and others sometimes apply the term to the war only). In the late eighteenth century a political dispute between Britain and thirteen of its colonies in mainland North America escalated to the point where the colonies declared themselves independent in 1776. The rebellious colonists and the British fought a lengthy war between 1775 and 1783. Eventually, with French assistance, the rebels compelled the British to accept American independence. With the rebel victory in the War of Independence the Americans undertook a prolonged period of constitutional change. They adopted a series of constitutions – both at state and national levels – each of which sought to institute republican principles in the new republic. The period of constitutional change began in 1776 with the adoption of the **Declaration of Independence** and ended in 1789 with the ratification of the federal Constitution.

In the aftermath of its victory in the **Seven Years War** (known in its American incarnation as the **French and Indian War**), Britain was faced with a substantial deficit. In response to this, Parliament sought to introduce direct taxes in the colonies. In the face of sustained colonial protests organized by groups such as the **Sons of Liberty** a crisis in British–American relations ensued. Parliament asserted its right to govern and tax the colonies as it saw fit while the colonists stipulated that they should not have to pay taxes to which they had not given their assent. Eventually the narrow dispute about taxation evolved into a larger constitutional question regarding sovereignty. Britain was obliged to send troops to America to uphold its authority and American resistance hardened. By early 1775, with British rule in danger of breaking down completely and American **militias** preparing for war, the crisis seemed likely to enter a new phase. This occurred when British forces and rebel troops fought in Massachusetts. These conflicts inaugurated the American War of Independence, which lasted for eight years. Having declared independence in 1776 the rebels sought foreign assistance which the French provided, first covertly and then by means of a formal alliance after the rebel victory at **Saratoga**. Although Britain enjoyed substantial military advantages it did not prevail in the war, which was primarily a political struggle. After independence was won in 1783 the newly independent Americans focused on creating republican governments to address the fundamental constitutional issues raised by their tax protests a generation before. Eventually they agreed to create a federated republic which was a collection of equal state republics enjoying parity within the union. Like most such upheavals, the American Revolution had substantial unforeseen consequences as its libertarian and egalitarian ideology, expressed in the **Declaration of Independence**, led socially marginal groups such as women and **African Americans** to demand greater rights within the new republic. These demands were only partially fulfilled as evidenced by the abolition of slavery in the northern states but its retention in the south.

American War of 1812

This conflict between the **United States** and **Great Britain** occurred in the wider context of the **Napoleonic Wars**. The struggle between Britain and France led both nations to disregard the neutral rights of American ships on the high seas. British actions, including restrictions placed on neutral trading in the 1807 Orders in Council and the practice of impressment (in which alleged deserters from the Royal Navy, often American citizens, were impressed into service), were particularly injurious to the United States. **Thomas Jefferson**'s efforts to use economic retaliation in the Embargo Act of 1807 failed to change British policy. The United States declared war in 1812. The conflict was militarily indecisive. Though the

British repelled the US invasion of **Canada**, the Americans fared well in the naval conflict and scored a symbolic victory at the Battle of New Orleans. The Treaty of Ghent (December 1814) and the Battle of New Orleans (January 1815) concluded the conflict. The treaty did little to address the maritime issues that had caused the war.

Amethyst Incident (1949)

The HMS *Amethyst*, a British frigate, was fired at by Communist Chinese forces in August 1949 while sailing up the Yangtze River to deliver supplies to the British community in Nanjing. Seventeen sailors were killed and the ship was trapped for fourteen weeks before being able to complete its mission. Although the reason behind the temporary detention of the *Amethyst* remains unclear, it is thought that the action was an assertion of Chinese sovereignty over international waters.

Amin al-Husayni

– *see* **Hajj Amin al-Husayni, Grand Mufti of Jerusalem**.

Amin Dada, Idi (*c.* 1925–2003)

Ugandan soldier and president. Amin joined the King's African Rifles, a British colonial regiment, in 1946 and became commander of **Uganda**'s post-independence army with the rank of major general. In 1971 he overthrew President **Milton Obote** and won initial backing from **Libya**, the **Soviet Union**, **Israel**, **South Africa** and the **United Kingdom**, where he was seen as sympathetic to British interests. Amin headed a regime rife with corruption, repression and gross abuse of human rights. In 1972, as part of his effort to 'Africanize' the country's economy, he expelled the Ugandan Asian population, much of which settled in Britain. Chairman of the **Organization of African Unity** in 1975–6, Amin faced mounting resistance at home. His attempt in 1978 to seize Kagera province from **Tanzania** provoked war, Uganda's defeat and Amin's overthrow. He fled first to Libya, settling finally in **Saudi Arabia**, where he died.

Amin, Qasim (1863–1908)

Egyptian reformer. Born, **Alexandria**, to a wealthy Ottoman Turkish father, who was the commander of Khedive Isma'il Pasha's army, and an aristocratic Egyptian mother related to Muhammad 'Ali. He received a Europeanized education in Cairo and then attended the University of Montpellier, 1881–5. Appointed an advocate in the **Mixed Courts**, 1885. A judge in the national courts,

1891. One of those reformers who believed that the proper response to the political eclipse of **Islam** was to favour modernization and absorb progressive western ideas into the religion. He was, therefore, a founder of **Egypt**'s first secular university, now Cairo University. A friend of **Sa'ad Zaghlul** and Muhammad 'Abduh, the associate of **Rashid Rida**, similarly stigmatizing blind traditionalism. Particularly remembered as a member of the Nahda (Awakening) movement and for his advocacy of female equality, which he insisted was the true teaching of the Qur'an, arguing that women's 'slavery' to Egyptian men was the cause of Egypt's weakness.

Amir-e Kabir (1807–1852)

Reformist Iranian chief minister. Real name Mirza Taqi Khan. Of humble origins, but joined the bureaucracy becoming financial supervisor of the army in **Azerbaijan**, 1835. Observed Russian power when in St Petersburg. A member of the commission delimiting the Ottoman–Iranian frontier. Chief tutor, 1847, and chief minister and 'great prince' (*amir-e kabir*), 1848, to **Nasir od-Din Shah Qajar**, whose sister he married. Forcefully suppressed unrest. Introduced radical reform to balance the budget, curbing corruption and extravagance. Replaced tax farming with direct collection and overhauled all administration. Encouraged agriculture and industry and introduced vaccination. Founded **Iran**'s first modern educational institution, the Skills House (Dar al-Fonun), the genesis of the later Tehran University. Sought to curb the political power of the *ulama* and suppressed Babism (later Baha'i) as a threat to the state, but protected other religious minorities. Resented by the court, whose privileges he had attacked, and opposed by European powers, whose influence he had reduced. Exiled in 1851, he was murdered on the shah's orders a year later.

Amnesty International

Founded by an English lawyer Peter Benenson who, in consultation with Eric Baker and other writers, academics and lawyers, wrote the article 'The Forgotten Prisoners' in the *Observer* newspaper on 18 May 1961. The article brought attention to violations, by governments, of articles 18 and 19 of the **Universal Declaration of Human Rights**. Amnesty International (AI) is a non-partisan organization embodying a worldwide movement of people who campaign for internationally recognized human rights.

Amritsar Massacre (1919)

On 13 April 1919 Brigadier General Reginald Dyer ordered riflemen of the British Indian Army to fire on an unarmed crowd gathered (in defiance of British emergency regulations) in an enclosed square in the Punjab city of Amritsar. Official figures suggested that 379 people died and over 1,200 were wounded; unofficial estimates ran much higher. The massacre attracted worldwide press coverage, outraged Indian opinion, and stimulated the growth of anti-colonial nationalism. While British authorities blamed Dyer's bad judgement, the massacre became a symbol of the brutal violence of colonial rule.

anarchism

A political philosophy and practice that considers the development of the free individual is best secured in a society based on voluntary cooperation rather than the coercive authority of the state and the monopolistic private ownership of land and industry. Anarchism had a presence in the twentieth-century international labour movement, notably in the form of anarcho-syndicalism, but little lasting influence. While the concept of a stateless society has a long history, Pierre-Joseph Proudhon (1809–65) was the first to use the term *anarchist* in a positive sense, advocating overcoming the state and capitalism through the establishment of workers' cooperatives and federations of autonomous communes. Some of his supporters were active in the 1871 Paris Commune. Michael Bakunin (1814–76) argued for a spontaneous revolutionary overthrow of the state (and religious authority) and the establishment of collectivism, taking the means of production under popular control. The International Working Men's Association (the First International) was riven by disputes between rival followers of Bakunin's libertarianism and the authoritarian socialism of **Karl Marx** (1818–83), leading to the creation of a short-lived Anarchist International, which found its support predominantly in **Spain**, **Italy**, **Switzerland** and **Belgium**. The anarchist communism of Peter Kropotkin (1842–1921), who saw a general strike as the means of overthrowing the state and capitalism, envisaged a society based on mutual aid and the immediate principle of from each according to their abilities, to each according to their needs.

Anarchist encouragement of labour militancy rather than parliamentary activity in the late nineteenth century aroused increasing repression in **France**, Spain and the **United States**, where four anarchists were executed in Chicago in 1887 for alleged participation in the Haymarket bombing.

A turn to 'propaganda by deed' by individual anarchists manifested itself in a series of assassinations, including those of King Umberto I of Italy, Empress Elizabeth of Austria, President Carnot of France and President **McKinley** of the United States, creating a lasting popular image of anarchism as **terrorism**. Anarchists participated in the 1917 **Russian Revolution**, many initially as supporters of the Bolsheviks but soon as opponents of their authoritarian methods. An anarchist communist peasant army in the **Ukraine** led by Nestor Makhno (1888–1934) fought both the Bolsheviks and their 'White' adversaries.

Anarchism's most significant twentieth-century presence was in Italy, Spain and, to a lesser extent, **Latin America** and the United States, where the **Industrial Workers of the World** had an anarcho-syndicalist tendency. In Italy, anarchists were prominent in the 1920 factory occupation movement. In Spain, the anarcho-syndicalist Confederación Nacional del Trabajo (CNT, National Confederation of Labour), established in 1910, had a million members at the outbreak in 1936 of the **Spanish Civil War**. CNT activists, together with those of the Federación Anarquista Ibérica (FAI, Iberian Anarchist Federation), developed industrial self-management and agricultural collectivization in the Republican zone on anarchist principles. Paradoxically, prominent FAI members became ministers in the government. There was a revival of interest in anarchism in the student–worker militancy of the 1960s and again in the **anti-globalization movement** of the late twentieth century onwards.

Ancien Régime

The name accorded to the form of government and culture which operated in **France** before 1789. This was based around an absolutist king located in Versailles, to which regional and national nobility had to pay court personally, at least three dozen different administrative divisions, with different economic rules and parliaments, the rule of royal intendants, bishops, dukes and princes, the virtual exclusion of the bourgeois and ordinary people from all but taxation and military service, and a web of canon and ordinary law in which some 140 bishops and archbishops, as well as cardinals and monks, acknowledged the role of the king as co-powerful with the pope. Society was further organized into three estates, corresponding to the clergy, nobility and commoners in order of primacy, but the French kings refrained from bringing all three groups together in a parliament of the whole realm, known as an Estates-General, to advise, hear petitions and legislate, after 1614. When forced to constitute such a body by financial crisis and administrative problems in 1789, **Louis XVI** quickly found that the Third Estate ran out of control, and constituted itself as the National Assembly. This act, above all others, began the French Revolution.

Andrada e Silva, José Bonifacio de (1763–1838)

Brazilian naturalist and statesman. Born in Santos, São Paulo, José Bonifacio was educated at Coimbra University, **Portugal**, studied modern science in northern Europe and held government offices in Portugal. Talented and self-confident, he returned to Brazil in 1819 and entered the provisional government of São Paulo in 1820. He became chief minister of prince regent Dom Pedro and encouraged him to remain as emperor of an independent **Brazil**. A monarchist who initially supported independence reluctantly, José Bonifacio engineered substantial power for the new emperor, but in 1823 was dismissed, along with his also politically active brothers, joined the opposition to the Portuguese faction at court, and was soon exiled. Returning to Brazil in 1829, he became guardian of **Pedro II** after his father abdicated in 1831. Ousted in late 1833, he went into permanent retirement.

Anglican Communion

– *see* **Protestantism**.

Anglo-Boer War

– *see* **Boer War**.

Anglo-Egyptian Treaty, 1936

– *see also* **Montreux Convention**.

The treaty giving **Egypt** sovereignty, stimulated by the Abyssinian crisis and signed in London, 1936. Although nominally independent since 28 February 1922, Egypt had been under British occupation for some fifty years (*see* **Muhammad Tawfiq**). The associated twenty-year military alliance nevertheless permitted **Great Britain** to impose martial law and censorship in Egypt in circumstances of international emergency, to station up to 10,000 British troops and 400 pilots in the Canal Zone until the Egyptians could protect the area, and to retain its **Alexandria** naval base for up to eight years. The British imperial title of high

commissioner was replaced by the international diplomatic title of ambassador. The associated 1937 international Montreux Convention specified that, after transitional periods, the Capitulations and the **Mixed Courts** were to be abolished, making foreigners subject to Egyptian law. The treaty became somewhat academic during **World War II**, with 36,000 British troops being stationed in Egypt in 1940 and Egypt being technically neutral throughout the war although the monarchy protected British interests. A Canal Zone agreement was negotiated between the British and Colonel **Nasser** prior to the **Suez Crisis**.

Anglo-Iranian Oil Company (AIOC)

Nationalized by the Iranian government of Dr **Mossadegh**, pursuant to its declaration of intent of 20 March 1951. The Iranian government took control of the British-owned company's oil refineries at Abadan, then the largest in the world, 2 May 1951, as well as of its assets. Widely hated by the Iranian public as an autocratic company and perceived as having passed under British control through commercial trickery. It was 51 per cent owned by the British government, it habitually made payments to the British Treasury several times greater than it did to **Iran** and did not show its accounts to the Iranian government. It behaved like a colonial power in Khuzistan province and paid low wages to its Iranian employees. The 4,500 British around the oil fields were totally segregated from Iranian society. Moreover, the company's negotiating stance was widely criticized even by British insiders. Despite serious consideration being given by the British Labour government to military intervention, the option was not pursued. Absorbed into British Petroleum (BP), it was a party to the 1954 consortium agreement.

Anglo-Japanese Alliance

With a shared concern over a possibility of Russian advancement to the south, **Japan** and **Britain** reached a strategic agreement in 1902 to assist one another in defending their special interests in **China** and **Korea**. In the **Russo-Japanese War** (1904–5), Japan benefited from this alliance, which deterred **France** from assisting **Russia**. It was renewed twice, first in 1905, when Britain approved Korea as a Japanese protectorate, and second, in 1911. Under the Anglo-Japanese Alliance, Japan joined **World War I** on the side of the Allies. Britain did not seek to extend the alliance in 1921, in deference to the Anglo-American relationship. By then, Russia was no longer a threat to British interests; the United States and industrialized Japan were intensifying their confrontation in the Asia–Pacific area. The Anglo-Japanese Alliance Treaty was officially terminated in 1923 by the Four-Power Pacific Treaty.

Angola

Former Portuguese colony in south-west Africa, a centre of the seventeenth- and eighteenth-century Atlantic **slave trade**. The country's borders were fixed at the 1885 Berlin conference and, with indigenous opposition overcome, land was distributed to white settlers. As anti-colonial resistance resumed, the Popular Movement for the Liberation of Angola (MPLA) was formed in 1956, followed by the National Liberation Front of Angola (FNLA, 1961) and the National Union for the Complete Independence of Angola (FNLA, 1966). Angola gained independence with the MPLA's António Agostinho Neto (1922–79) as president in 1975, but civil war broke out between the three liberation movements, with the Soviet- and Cuban-backed MPLA running a predominantly socialist economy until 1990, when market reforms were introduced. Despite a fragile peace agreement in 1988, clashes continued until 2002. The country is predominantly Christian, with an economy based on oil (contributing over 50 per cent of state revenue), diamonds and subsistence agriculture. President José Eduardo dos Santos served as president for over three decades after 1979.

Animal Rights movement

The modern Animal Rights movement arose from the confluence of four trends in western society in the last third of the twentieth century. One was the movement amongst philosophers, particularly in Oxford in the late 1960s and early 1970s, to establish a moral status for some animals based upon their potentially sentient condition. A second, transatlantic strand (which became popular with law departments) was that a moral duty was owed by humans to animals neither to exploit, nor inflict suffering upon animals because of the consequences for both species. A third strand emerged from the reaction against vivisection in laboratories, driven by pictures of distressed or apparently suffering creatures and by outrage at the reasons for the testing of cosmetic and non-essential products on animals. A fourth anarchist and 'activist' strand, driven to release animals from laboratories and holding pens from whence they might be moved and killed for fur or other rewards, also arose. The movement gained great popularity, inspiring a spectrum of legal and illegal activities, vegetarian and vegan lifestyle choices, and anti-suffering laws, but caused great controversy amongst those who questioned extreme tactics, disliked the equivalence of children or the disabled with animals, or who balanced animal testing against the search for safe life-saving or life-enhancing pharmaceutical products for humans.

Annales

A school of historical studies and a collection of techniques associated with **France** in general and **Marc Bloch**, Lucien Febvre, **Fernand Braudel** and Jacques Le Goff (inter alia) in particular. Centred on a journal of varying titles which began as *Annales d'Histoire économique et sociale* in 1929, the school emphasized the importance of 'total history' and 'history from below' in the early modern and post-feudal world. It directed historians, beginning with medievalists, to economic and social history, to the study of how culture and 'mentalité' interact with language to create the reality that most people believe in. Although stretching across a very wide variety of fields, the school emphasized the importance of understanding how documents and written works were constructed, and also sought to integrate the subsequent understandings with social scientific methods drawn from psychology, economics and sociology. It deliberately rejected a 'traditional' history of famous men, battles, political events and diplomacy, and in doing so probably helped reclaim history for the study of ordinary lives and cultures. The school was much more popular in France, **Italy** and **Poland** than in the English-speaking world.

Annan, Kofi Atta (1938–)

Ghanaian Secretary General of the **United Nations**, 1997–2006. Director of Administrative Management Services, then of Budget, in the United Nations, New York, 1984–7; Assistant Secretary General, Human Resources Management, UN, 1987–90; Controller, Programme Planning, Budget and Finance, 1990–2; Under-Secretary General, 1993–5; and Department of Peacekeeping and UN Special Envoy to the former **Yugoslavia**, 1995–6. He shared the Nobel Peace Prize with the United Nations in 2001. He declared the 2003 American and British invasion of **Iraq**, without a second UN resolution for military intervention, illegal in 2004.

Antarctic

– *see* **Arctic and Antarctic**.

Anthropocene era

Term used by environmentalists and environmental historians to reflect the impact of the human species on the planet by marking it as a distinct epoch in its history akin to a geological period. It highlights the distinctive effects of *Homo sapiens* in particular upon other species, the natural environment and the climate. The role of human beings in exterminating whole species, including possibly other branches of the hominid family at an early stage of evolutionary development, and endangering others became increasingly recognized during the twentieth century. Archaeology provides evidence of species which once coexisted with humans, such as the mammoth and the auroch, or wild ox, while some species have been hunted almost to the point of extinction within historic times, such as the North American bison and many maritime species, particularly whales. Crowding out by human population growth, especially from the twentieth century, has been identified by both botanists and naturalists for the extinction of many species of flora and insects, amplified by commercialized agriculture, deforestation and the use of pesticides. Large-scale environmental degradation has been seen as a direct result of human intervention, reshaping the natural world in potentially catastrophic ways because of their effects upon the climate. A variety of threats have emerged in which the human role in **climate change** has been identified and solutions sought in limiting some of the more damaging effects of human activity, such as carbon emissions and nuclear testing. Efforts have also been made from the mid twentieth century to conserve and protect endangered species of flora, fauna and wildlife.

anti-clericalism

In Europe and Latin America a set of postures and activities dedicated to opposing the existence, influence or institutional power of religious organizations, anti-clericalism has historically been associated with revolutionary, freemasonic and anti-Catholic movements, though it has also been manifest in Islamic countries. It is almost impossible to identify any one cause or support group for the movement. In French history, for instance, many peasant groups were opposed to religious foundations on the basis that tithes and taxes taken by monasteries in the form of food or goods were depriving farmers of their living, whereas many intellectuals viewed the Church as a force for obscurantist superstition and an obstacle to the Age of Reason. On the other hand, the Austro-Hungarian rulers, and in particular Joseph II, saw

the Church as a supranational body which threatened central national control, and in consequence required national seminaries and barred direct communication between the papal curia and Habsburg bishops.

Like the French intellectuals, Communists in **Spain** or the **Soviet Union** clove to the proposition that destructive de-Christianization was necessary for the advancement of society, and in consequence despoiled monuments and graves, dug up saints, created their own cults, and in some cases destroyed or secularized historic cathedrals whilst banning membership of the clergy. In **Mexico**, anti-clericalism was institutionalized in the constitution, attempts were made to remove the Church from education, to license priests but to remove their political rights, and generally to suppress Catholicism in public life. This policy was pursued to the point of civil war, on the basis that the Church was associated with large landowners and anti-revolutionary forces in the face of peasant rebellion and secular nationalism. Similarly, the Peronist movement in **Argentina** was associated with attacks upon churches and priests, but mostly because of the perceived obstacle the Church posed to devotion to the nation and its government, rather than on any basis of social justice.

Countries which are or were predominantly Protestant have manifested slightly different forms of anti-clericalism. In Britain, **Canada** and the **United States**, for instance, anti-clerical riots, attacks upon churches and arson against perceived eruptions of 'catholic' art or architecture such as Brompton cemetery in the 1850s, or the protests against papal visits in the twentieth and twenty-first centuries, have been more common than formal anti-clerical policies. However, many historians have noted a perceived tendency in the media and political life of such countries to promote criticisms of the Church and priests as consensus, for example, on issues such as contraception, abortion, priestly celibacy or the historic excesses of the Spanish Inquisition or the Crusades. The basic difficulty which states based upon any ideology, whether liberal, socialist, nationalist or fascist, have had with the Church and clergy is that clerics have traditionally sought to bear witness to a higher and absolute morality, and to inculcate in the young a form of reasoning which imbues social values and ethics with a religious sensibility. This runs contrary to the idea that the spiritual and temporal division which churches uphold should be not confused with the religious and secular dividing line which many liberals see, or with the 'true consciousness' which nationalists, socialists and fascists think contrasts with what they dismiss as religious superstition. This has been as true of Asian anti-Buddhist regimes as of Iranian anti-clerical liberals, but has been particularly manifest in violence against the Catholic faith because of its supranational independence and historic catechism.

Anti-Comintern Pact

The pact signed in 1936 by **Germany** and **Japan** as part of the series of international alliances that led up to **World War II**. Under its terms, the two countries would consult with each other if either was attacked by the **Soviet Union**. **Italy** joined the pact in 1937 and **Spain** joined in 1939. However, the pact was marked by mutual distrust from its earliest days, and neither Japan nor Germany ever made it a major part of their strategy during World War II.

anti-Confucian campaign (China)

Also known as the anti-Lin Biao campaign, this took place in China in 1974 and was an attack on the moderate leader of the Chinese Communist Party, **Zhou Enlai**, by radicals in the party. By Lin Biao's death in 1971, the most radical phase of the **Cultural Revolution** had ended. **Mao Zedong** had reacted to the chaos of the **Red Guards** by allowing Zhou Enlai to rehabilitate moderates in the party, including **Deng Xiaoping**. Jiang Qing and other radicals reacted to this with a campaign in 1974 that criticized Confucians for their respect for elders and praised legalist scholars who had advocated the rule of law. This was an attack on Zhou Enlai for rehabilitating moderates and a warning that China was moving away from policies of class struggle that had defined the Cultural Revolution. The campaign was short-lived, and in June 1974 Zhou Enlai was admitted to hospital with cancer. He died two years later.

Antietam, campaign and Battle of (4–19 September 1862)

Events of the **American Civil War**. In response to **Robert E. Lee**'s invasion of Maryland, by 11 September **George B. McClellan** had advanced with knowledge of Confederate dispositions thanks to the discovery of the 'Lost Order'. After his setback at South Mountain on 14 September, Lee rallied behind Antietam Creek. On 17 September, McClellan attacked clumsily, enabling Lee to drive each corps back separately. Lee withdrew two days later, and the

preliminary **Emancipation Proclamation** followed on 23 September. Twenty-five thousand men fell on this, the bloodiest day of the American Civil War.

Anti-Fascist People's Freedom League

The Anti-Fascist People's Freedom League (AFPFL) was the product of a union of communism, socialism and nationalism in **Burma** in 1944. It quickly evolved into the leading party of the new Burmese state. It was associated most closely with the Burmese patriot leader against the Japanese, Aung San, and later U Nu. The league, which contained multiple parties and groups, was often fissile, but managed to negotiate British recognition as the leading national group whilst dropping the Communist Party between 1947 and 1948. Under U Nu, it remained in occasionally punctuated power from independence in 1948 until 1962, evolving rightwards. It was essentially destroyed in the **Ne Win** coup of 1962.

Anti-federalists

The term commonly used to describe opponents of the ratification of the **American Constitution** (1787–8), though they never used this term themselves. Although Anti-federalists espoused a broad range of political and constitutional opinions, they were broadly united by opposition to the concentration of power given to the federal government. Their chief concerns included the small number of representatives in Congress, and the fear that the power given to the office of the president, would lead to 'executive tyranny'. Others also worried that concentrating the ultimate power of taxation and military force in the federal government would end up destroying state governments (which Anti-federalists saw as the most effective check and balance against federal government). Many Anti-federalists campaigned for a bill of rights to be added to the Constitution, to help demonstrate that proponents of the new constitution paid sufficient attention to popular liberties.

anti-globalization

– *see also* **capitalism; multinational corporations**.

The concentration of economic power represented by global capitalism and the rise of the multinational corporation has never gone unchallenged. As early as 1848 **Marx** and **Engels** were highlighting in the *Communist Manifesto* the uncontrolled power of the new productive forces, and communism and socialism have always sought since either to control outright or to influence the exercise of economic power. **Nationalization** was by definition anti-global. The right also has often sought to safeguard a functioning market economy by prohibiting cartels and anti-competitive practices. The title of Dr E. F. Schumacher's 1973 *Small is Beautiful* encapsulates the more recent perception that the trend towards size and specialization is actually inefficient and inhumane and a cause of environmental pollution. His answer was the communal ownership of much smaller working units and the local satisfaction of local need, a call taken up by environmentalists and Green movements. The young, in particular, also often sense the aggressiveness of international business and the concomitant cultural imperialism dubbed *Cocacolaization*, and fear its ability to dominate government and bend international regulation to its advantage. Anti-globalization sentiment played a part in many populist protests in the second decade of the twenty-first century.

Antigua

Antigua (and the neighbouring island of Barbuda) comprise a small state in the Lesser Antilles, which is a member of the British **Commonwealth**. In 2015 it had a population of around 81,000 and a per capita income of over 18,000 US dollars. Tourism is its major industry. Settled by English settlers from nearby **St Kitts** in 1632, its early history was dominated by slavery and sugar. It gained independence from Britain in 1981.

anti-imperialism, East Asian

– see also **Pan-Asianism**.

Anti-Imperialism in East Asia was an ideology and a movement that developed in response to western and Japanese **imperialism** starting in the nineteenth century. The rhetoric of anti-imperialism assumed diverse forms as intellectuals, government officials and civilians struggled with the discursive and material ruptures caused by western powers and **Japan**'s drive for hegemony in East Asia.

Western imperialism in East Asia grew significantly during the nineteenth century as western countries sought to expand their economic and political influence and domination in the global capitalist market. Prompted by economic motives, beliefs of racial superiority and **social Darwinism**, western governments used military power and violence to achieve favourable economic positions in **Asia**. **China**, for example, became the site of economic competition between western powers. Between 1839 and 1842, **Great Britain**

strengthened its power in China through the **Opium War** and the Treaty of Nanjing, which was an unequal treaty that awarded numerous political and economic concessions including **Hong Kong** to the British. Using gunboats, the **United States** brokered its own unequal treaties with Japan from 1853 to 1858. With western powers having already gained control over nearly 85 per cent of the earth's land surface by 1914, Asian countries were unable to shield themselves from western imperialism.

In the late nineteenth century the threat of western imperialism forced individuals and groups in East Asian countries to think of ways to maintain and bolster their national sovereignty. The discourse of the nation state and a 'western-style' model of economic, political and social development captured the popular imagination. Starting with the Meiji *Ishin* (Revolution) in 1868, Japanese leaders embarked on a path of modern development that featured western-style reforms, transforming the country into a powerful nation state. In its pursuit to become modern, Japan itself became a strong imperial power that threatened its immediate neighbours. Responding to both western and Japanese imperialism, Chinese and Koreans also turned to the western model of modern development in order to protect their country's sovereignty. However, **Korea** lost its independence to Japan in 1910 while China continuously faced the threat of losing its independence to Japan or western countries after the fall of the royal monarchy in 1911.

At the everyday level, anti-imperialist sentiment manifested itself through movements and protests. The 1898 **Boxer Rebellion** in China featured both protests against western imperialism and violence against westerners residing in the country. The 1919 March 1st movement in Korea was a large-scale mass protest against Japanese colonial rule, while people in China continually attacked Japanese and western interference in Chinese national affairs. Anti-imperialist discourse and movements by the 1930s, however, largely featured anti-western sentiments. Many critics and citizens in Korea, Japan and China saw western imperialism as a drive to not only politically and economically control Asia, but also to extinguish Asian identities and practices. By the late 1930s, intellectuals and political figures in Japan, China and Korea became inspired by pan-Asian ideologies and called for an armed struggle against western imperialism. For them, **World War II** represented a war to put an end to western dominance in Asia.

Antimasonic Party

This party operated in the northern United States between 1827 and 1834, in protest against the supposed dominance of public office by Freemasons. It became a key element of opposition to the Jacksonian Democrats, winning considerable influence in New York, Pennsylvania (till 1839) and parts of New England, and securing laws against extra-constitutional oaths. In 1832 its presidential candidate, William Wirt, carried Vermont, but soon thereafter the party lost most of its members to the new **Whig Party**.

anti-Semitism

The name given to a distinctive, virulent and long-standing ethnic and political prejudice against Jewish people. Anti-Semitism as an organizing political principle emerged in **Austria–Hungary** in the mid nineteenth century, but in truth had roots deep in Christian and Islamic civilization. Communal attacks upon, and the physical confinement or isolation of, Jewish communities have been a recurrent feature of Christian society. Though the term *Semitic* applies to peoples other than Jews, it has come to characterize Jewish people in particular. Anti-Semites hold that Jewish people are uniquely bad on three grounds. Racially, Jews have been associated with the death of Jesus Christ, with banking, and with successful urban service industries. These are either accidents of history or a consequence of the isolation of Jews within ghettoes in the Middle Ages. Secondly, anti-Semites have held that, because of a highly stable tradition of in-group marriage and rabbinic priesthood, Jewish people are both racially more pure and somehow at the same time a racial threat to other people. This prejudice perhaps reflects a fear of the resilience and indefatigability of Jewish communities in the face of persecution over thousands of years and a national culture of survival against the odds. A third sort of anti-Semitism emerged in the late twentieth century and focused on the idea that Jewish people would not only owe their highest loyalty, regardless of the state they were a citizen of, to the state of **Israel**, but would cooperate as part of a formal and informal community of aid towards that state in defiance of international law and the rights of Palestinians. This particular form of anti-Semitism tended to focus on the importance of the Jewish lobby in American politics and questioned the patriotism of many Jews. It is a new development since it focuses so strongly on the state of Israel, which did not exist before 1948.

Anti-Semitism has been a successful vehicle for the motivation of large crowds and totalitarian movements in the modern period. The Nazi Party and **Adolf Hitler** took hatred of the Jews as their central position, linking that group to both Bolshevik Communism in the **USSR** and capitalism in the West. This fixation eventually resulted in the **Holocaust** and the destruction of 6 million of Europe's Jews in death camps after 1941. The **Russian Empire** before 1917 had been a centre of anti-Semitic state-sponsored violence, named **pogroms**; these had resulted in oppression in and mass emigrations from Russian-occupied **Poland** in the nineteenth century. The Russian Empire had also sponsored forgeries aimed at stirring up hatred of Jews, such as the 'protocols of the elders of Zion'. This latter document, rehashing claims of Jewish child cannibalism, plans to manipulate and dominate the world and various immoralities, was to continue as a basic text of anti-Semitism into the twenty-first century. Russian anti-Semitism transferred to the USSR, despite the Jewishness of some of its founders. **Stalin** was marked by anti-Semitism and at the time of his death in 1953 was preparing a campaign against 'Jewish doctors'. His death did not eliminate anti-Semitism in the USSR, which saw increasing pressure on Jewish people, and accusations of anti-patriotic **Zionism** amongst scientists and professionals reach a peak in the 1970s. This led to a reaction amongst friends of the Jews in the West, and Soviet encouragement of emigration of Russian Jews to Israel.

The third centre of anti-Semitism in recent history has been the **Middle East**. Hatred and suspicion of Jews has not generally characterized Islamic history; unbelievers had mostly been tolerated within Muslim countries before the late twentieth century. However, the potential of demagogue-inspired populist agitation and the historically tested lies of anti-Semitism proved irresistible as an organizing and rallying tool to those fundamentalists who wished to accommodate and benefit from the anger of young male populations at Israeli military victories after 1967 and the challenges of modernization and secularization. Anti-Semitism of this latter sort, supported by those who associate Jewish identity with pro-American and Israeli views they oppose in the West, is growing.

Anti-Slavery movement

– *see* **abolitionism**.

Anti-Slavery Squadron

As a result of the Abolition of the Slave Trade Act of 1807, **Great Britain** committed itself to suppressing the **slave trade** from the African coast, and for the next two decades the British government negotiated reciprocal treaties with European governments to abolish the trade. To this end, the Royal Navy commissioned a squadron of ships to patrol the areas north of the Equator (the abolition was only extended south of the Equator in 1839). These ships were to intercept suspected slavers on the high seas and inspect them. If found to be carrying slaves, their goods were to be confiscated, although the slaves themselves were not returned to the port from which they had embarked, but taken to **Sierra Leone**, a British colony. The squadron was supported by British consular offices, for example, in Fernando Po, whose own actions would eventually assist in establishing a British colonial presence in **Africa**.

antitrust laws (American)

Antitrust laws including the Sherman Act (1887), Clayton Act (1914) and Federal Trade Commission Act (1914) were passed by Congress to curb the power of large business combinations known as 'trusts' that had emerged during the late nineteenth century. Their effectiveness was reduced by clumsy drafting and, more fundamentally, by a conflict between a desire to break the trusts up into smaller units and a desire to control them more rigorously.

Antoinette, Marie (1755–1793)

French monarch born Maria Antonia Josepha Johanna von Habsburg-Lothringen. Austrian-born, she married Louis-Auguste, the French Dauphin in 1770, becoming queen when he ascended the throne as **Louis XVI** in 1774. Increasingly unpopular throughout his reign and an opponent of reform following the fall of the Bastille in 1789, she was deposed with Louis and imprisoned in 1792. In 1793 she was tried and convicted of treason and guillotined following Louis' execution.

Anzac

A term referring to the combination of British imperial forces drawn from **Australia**, **New Zealand** and **Canada**, often alongside British soldiers or under British leadership, in **World War I**. Anzac forces earned a high reputation for bravery on the Western Front, but will forever be associated with the futile and bloody assault at **Gallipoli** in 1915 against Ottoman and German forces. The operation was botched because of poor coordination, and the massive casualties which resulted dealt a lasting blow to British imperial unity, which was particularly remembered in Australia.

Aotorea

– *see* **New Zealand**.

apartheid

– *see also* **Bantustans**.

From the Afrikaans 'apartness', apartheid – introduced by the National Party in **South Africa** – was institutionalized racial discrimination intended to preserve white domination. The main legislative measures were: the 1949 Immorality Act banning interracial sexual relations; the 1950 Population Registration Act, registering the population on a racial basis; the 1950 Group Areas Act, separating housing areas; the 1951 Native Building Workers Act, restricting skilled work to whites; the 1952 Natives (Abolition of Passes and Co-ordination of Documents) Act, enforcing passes for the black population; the 1953 Reservation of Separate Amenities Act, separating transport and public facilities; the 1953 Native Labour (Settlement of Disputes) Act, outlawing strikes by black workers; and the 1953 Bantu Education Act and the 1959 Extension of University Education Act, segregating education. The 1971 Bantu Homelands Constitution Act forced the black population to take citizenship of spuriously independent 'homelands'. President Frederick de Klerk announced apartheid's abandonment in 1991.

Appeasement

A policy of settling the demands of potentially violent foreign antagonists by agreeing to and thus 'appeasing' their demands for territory, status or armaments. It is particularly associated with **Neville Chamberlain** and the Anglo-French policy towards **Hitler** and **Mussolini**, but was also evident in **Winston Churchill**'s treatment of imperial Japanese expansion in 1926, and of British attitudes to the IRA in the 1920s and 1930s. Critical features were the idea that antagonists might be able to play on legitimate grievance, that military confrontation was too costly or difficult, and that world opinion would fairly assess concessions as strengthening the side that made them and exert pressure on anyone who demanded more once their grievances had been settled not to do so. The policy collapsed after its apotheosis at Munich in 1938, when democratic **Czechoslovakia** was partitioned for the Dictators by the democracies.

Appiah, Kwame (1954–)

Ghanaian-British-American philosopher, cultural theorist and novelist. Born in London, Appiah was raised in Kumasi by his father, the prominent lawyer and opposition leader Joe Emmanuel Appiah. After earning a PhD in Philosophy at the University of Cambridge, Appiah taught at Yale, Harvard and Princeton. In 1992 his collection of critical essays, *In My Father's House*, won the Herskovitz Prize for African Studies. His writings focus on ethics and morality, race and identity, and a strong critique of **Afrocentrism**.

APRA (Alianza Popular Revolutionaria Americana)

A continent-wide movement founded by **Victor Raul Haya de la Torre** in Mexico in 1923. It called for the formation of a broad-based popular alliance in **Latin America** in opposition to the expansion of US imperialism. It also advocated Latin American political unity, internationalization of the Panama Canal, the nationalization of lands and industry and the solidarity of all oppressed people and classes in the world. Haya envisioned APRA as the basis for new national reform parties in the region, the first of which he organized in **Peru** in 1929 as the first mass-based political party in Peruvian history. As Haya had envisioned, APRA became the model for a number of similar nationalist parties throughout Latin America during the 1930s and 1940s and went on to become the most important and enduring political party in Peru for nearly a century.

Aquino, Benigno (1932–1983)

Filipino senator, 1967–72, and a leading opponent of the corrupt regime of President **Ferdinand Marcos**. He was imprisoned from 1972 to 1980, and was assassinated in Manila in 1983, at which point the role of opposition leadership passed to his wife, **'Cory' Aquino**.

Aquino, Corazón 'Cory' Sumulong (1933–2009)

The widow of opposition leader **Benigno Aquino**, as a self-styled 'plain housewife' without political experience she became president of the Philippines in late February 1986. This followed a 'people power' revolution which ousted President **Ferdinand Marcos**, following his apparent victory in a fraudulent election earlier in the month. Cory Aquino oversaw the promulgation of the 1987 constitution limiting the power of the presidency and reintroducing a bi-cameral parliament. She

supported human rights and survived several coup attempts before her term expired in 1992.

Arabism

– *see* **Arab nationalism**.

Arab–Israeli conflict

The Arab–Israeli conflict concerns the historic tensions between the Arab peoples and the Jewish community in **Palestine**, the region of independent Jewish rule conquered by the Romans in AD 70 but with a continuous Jewish presence ever since then. It has religious, economic, ethnic, political and territorial aspects. The modern conflict began with the rise of **Zionism** and Arab nationalism in the mid nineteenth century and intensified with the rebirth of State of Israel in 1948. Territory regarded by the Jewish people as their historical homeland is also regarded by Arabs as their ancestral home. Starting as a political and nationalist conflict over competing territorial ambitions following the defeat of the **Ottoman Empire** in **World War I**, it has recently involved a more localized conflict specfically between Israelis and Palestinian Arabs.

mid nineteenth century to 1948

Theodor Herzl's 1896 manifesto, *The Jewish State*, led to the creation of a modern political Zionist movement. The ferocity of pogroms in **Russia** prompted large numbers of Jews to seek refuge in **Palestine** between 1882–1904 (the first **Aliyah**) and 1904–14 (the second Aliyah). By the early twentieth century, lands for collective farms, known as *kibbutzim*, were purchased, as was the first entirely Jewish city in modern times, Tel Aviv. The promise of liberation from the Ottomans led many Jews and Arabs to support the Entente powers during **World War I**. The Ottomans were defeated by the British army under General **Allenby** which invaded Palestine in 1917. That year the British government issued the **Balfour Declaration**, viewing favourably 'the establishment in Palestine of a national home for the Jewish people', a stipulation that was subsequently incorporated into the British mandate for Palestine, endorsed by the **League of Nations** but rejected by Arab leaders. Jewish immigration peaked soon after the Nazis came to power in **Germany**. Jewish policies of purchasing land greatly angered some within the Palestinian Arab community. This resentment led to outbreaks of violence. In March 1920 a first violent incident occurred at Tel Hai. Later that year riots broke out in **Jerusalem** and **Hebron**. **Winston Churchill**'s 1922 White Paper tried to reassure the Arab population, denying that the creation of a Jewish state was the intention of the Balfour Declaration. By 1936 escalating tensions led to a full-blown 1936–9 **Arab revolt**, which was directed against both the British and the Jewish community of Palestine.

In response to Arab pressure, British mandate authorities greatly reduced the number of Jewish immigrants to Palestine. These restrictions remained in place until the end of the mandate. On 29 November 1947 the **United Nations** General Assembly accepted a 'two state solution' by 33 votes to 13 with 10 abstentions. The Arab states rejected this partition. The Jews, desperate for a homeland for their brethren made homeless by **Hitler**, accepted the partition even though Jerusalem was excluded from the Jewish state. Beginning with an Arab attack on 30 November on a Jewish bus heading for Petach Tikva, Arab and Jewish Palestinians battled openly to control strategic positions in the region.

On 14 May 1948, with the bulk of the British Army long since departed, **Israel** declared its independence. The next day, the armies of **Egypt**, **Lebanon**, **Syria**, **Jordan** and **Iraq** invaded in an attempt to strangle the Jewish state at its birth. The fledgling Israeli Defense Force took huge casualties but was able to repel this invasion. By March 1949, with the conquest of Elath, Israel controlled the bulk of the Palestine mandate west of the River Jordan. A total of 713,000 Palestinian Arabs fled their original lands to become refugees. Arab Palestinians today constitute approximately 20 per cent of Israel's population. Israel's War of Independence ended with the signing of 1949 Armistice Agreements between Israel and each of its Arab neighbours.

1948–1967

In 1948 Egypt closed the **Suez Canal** to Israeli shipping, in contravention of the Constantinople Convention of 1888, and in 1950 it blockaded the Straits of Tiran. Many argued that both acts violated the 1949 Armistice Agreements. On 26 July 1956 Egypt nationalized the Suez Canal Company. Israel responded on 29 October by invading the Sinai peninsula with British and French support. During the Suez war, Israel captured the **Gaza Strip** and the Sinai peninsula. The **United States**, the **USSR** and the **United Nations** soon pressured Israel into withdrawing from the territories. The canal remained closed to Israel but the Tiran Straits were opened. A United Nations Emergency Force (UNEF) was deployed on the Egyptian side of the border.

Israel's June 1967 **Six Day War** was the result of escalating tensions after the Suez conflict. Israel fought with Syria over water resources in the Golan Heights and had border clashes with Jordan and Egypt, especially after the founding in 1964 of the **Palestine Liberation Organization (PLO)**. (In its charter, the PLO committed to the 'liberation of Palestine [which] will destroy the Zionist and imperialist presence'.) On 19 May Egypt expelled the UNEF observers, deployed 100,000 soldiers in the Sinai peninsula, and again closed the Straits of Tiran to Israeli shipping, cutting off Israel's critical oil supply from Iran. Jordan signed a defence pact with Egypt. Egyptian units massed on Israel's southern border. On 5 June Israel launched a pre-emptive attack on Egypt. The Israeli Air Force (IAF) destroyed most of the Egyptian Air Force on the ground and then turned east to destroy the Jordanian, Syrian and Iraqi air forces. This strike was the crucial element in Israel's victory. At war's end, Israel had gained control of the Sinai peninsula, the Gaza Strip, the **West Bank**, eastern Jerusalem and the **Golan Heights**. On 19 June 1967 Israel offered total withdrawal from Sinai and the Golan in return for peace with Egypt. The proposal was rejected at the end of August 1967, when Arab leaders met in Khartoum and reached a consensus that there should be no recognition, peace and/or negotiations with Israel.

Israel and Egypt, Jordan, Syria and Iraq after 1967

In 1969 Egypt initiated a war of attrition across the closed Suez waterway, with the goal of exhausting Israel into surrendering the Sinai peninsula. The war ended inconclusively on 7 August 1970. Egyptian leader **Gamal Abdul Nasser** died of a heart attack several weeks later. On 6 October 1973 Syria and Egypt staged a surprise attack on Israel on Yom Kippur, the holiest day of the Jewish calendar. The Israeli military were caught off guard and took three days to fully mobilize. US President **Richard Nixon** and Secretary of State **Henry Kissinger** sent Israel emergency military aid. When Israel had turned the tide of war, the USSR threatened military intervention. The United States, wary of nuclear war, secured a ceasefire. Kissinger subsequently negotiated a separation of forces and interim agreements between Israel and Egypt and Syria.

Following the **Camp David One** agreements of 1978, in March 1979 Israel and Egypt signed a full peace treaty. Under its terms, Israel returned the

Sinai peninsula to Egypt. The Gaza Strip remained under Israeli control. The agreement also provided for the free passage of Israeli ships through the Suez Canal and recognition of the Strait of Tiran and the Gulf of Aqaba as international waterways. In October 1994 Israel and Jordan signed a full peace treaty which ended hostilities and established full diplomatic relations.

Israel and **Iraq** have been implacable foes since 1948. Iraq sent its troops to participate in the 1948 Arab–Israeli War and backed Egypt and Syria in the **Six Day War** in 1967 and the Yom Kippur War in 1973. In June 1981 Israel destroyed a newly built Iraqi nuclear facility. During the **Gulf War** in 1991, Iraq fired thirty-nine Scud missiles into Israel, in the hopes of uniting the Arab world against the coalition which sought to liberate Kuwait. At the behest of the United States, Israel did not respond to this provocation in order to prevent a greater outbreak of war.

Israel and the Palestinians, 1970–2000

In 1970, following an extended civil war, **King Hussein** expelled the PLO from Jordan (*see* **Black September**). The PLO resettled in **Lebanon**, from which it staged raids into Israel. In 1981 Syria, allied with the PLO, positioned missiles in Lebanon. In June 1982 Israel invaded Lebanon and on 17 May 1983 Israel and Lebanon signed an 'end to the state of war' agreement. However, Syria pressured President Amin Gemayel into nullifying the pact in March 1984. By 1985, Israeli forces withdrew to a 15-kilometre wide southern strip of Lebanon, following which the conflict continued on a lower scale, with relatively low casualties on both sides. In 1993 and 1996 Israel launched major operations against the Iranian-backed Shi'ite militia of **Hezbollah**, which had become an emergent threat. In 2000, as part of a greater plan for a peace agreement with Syria, Israel abandoned the security zone in southern Lebanon. In 2006, as a response to a Hezbollah cross-border raid, Israel launched air strikes on Hezbollah strongholds in southern Lebanon, starting the 2006 Lebanon War. The war lasted for thirty-four days and resulted in the creation of a buffer zone in southern Lebanon and the deployment of Lebanese troops south of the Litani River for the first time since the 1960s. Hezbollah withdrew its fighters from the border areas, and Israel eventually turned over its occupied areas in Lebanon to UN peacekeepers. Both sides declared victory.

The 1970s were marked by a large number of major international terrorist attacks, including the massacres at Lod Airport and the Munich Olympics in 1972 and the taking of hostages at Entebbe in 1976. In December 1987 the First **Intifada**, a mass Palestinian uprising against Israeli rule in the Palestinian Territories, began in the Jabalia refugee camp and quickly spread throughout Gaza, the West Bank and east Jerusalem. Stone-throwing by youths against the Israel Defense Forces brought the intifada international attention. The PLO, which until then had not been recognized as the leader of the Palestinian people by Israel, was invited to peace negotiations after it recognized Israel and renounced terrorism. In December 1991 Israel met publicly in Madrid with Palestinian representatives who were technically part of a Jordanian delegation. In September 1993 Israel and the PLO signed the **Oslo Accords**, known as the Declaration of Principles or Oslo I; in side letters, Israel recognized the PLO as the legitimate representative of the Palestinian people while the PLO recognized the right of the state of Israel to exist and renounced terrorism, violence and its desire for the destruction of Israel. The Oslo II agreement was signed in 1995 and detailed the division of the West Bank into areas A, B and C. Area A was land under full Palestinian civilian control; here Palestinians were also responsible for internal security.

2000–2016

After the failure of the Barak–Arafat–Clinton Camp David summit in July 2000, when Israel presented a series of proposals and failed to receive a counter-proposal, the Palestinians resumed terror attacks on civilian targets in the Second **Intifada**, and Israel was forced to rethink its relationship and policies towards them. The Israeli Army launched Operation Defensive Shield, the largest military operation it had conducted since the Six Day War. Israel expanded its security apparatus around the West Bank, establishing a complicated system of roadblocks, fences and checkpoints around major Palestinian areas to deter violence and protect Israeli settlements. However, since 2008 the IDF has slowly transferred authority to Palestinian security forces. Israeli Prime Minister Ariel Sharon began a policy of unilateral withdrawal from the Gaza Strip in 2003. This policy was fully implemented in August 2005. Sharon's announcement to disengage from Gaza came as a tremendous shock to critics on the left and the right. In June 2006 **Hamas** militants infiltrated an army post near the Israeli side of the Gaza Strip and abducted Israeli soldier Gilad Shalit, who was released in exchange for over a thousand prisoners in 2011. In July 2006 Hezbollah fighters crossed the border from

Lebanon into Israel, attacked and killed eight Israeli soldiers and abducted two others as hostages, setting off the 2006 Lebanon War, which caused much destruction in Lebanon. A UN-sponsored ceasefire took effect on 14 August that year, officially ending the conflict.

In June 2007 Hamas seized control of the Gaza Strip after a violent civil war with rival **Fatah**. Israel placed restrictions on its border with Gaza and ended economic cooperation with the Palestinian leadership based there. Israel maintains the economic blockade is necessary to limit Palestinian rocket attacks from Gaza and to prevent Hamas from smuggling advanced rockets and weapons capable of hitting its cities. A fragile six-month truce between Hamas and Israel expired on 19 December 2008; attempts at extending the truce failed amid accusations of breaches from both sides. Following the expiration, Israel launched a raid on a tunnel suspected of being used to kidnap Israeli soldiers, which killed several Hamas fighters. Following this, Hamas resumed rocket and mortar attacks on Israeli cities, most notably firing over sixty rockets on 24 December. On 27 December, Israel launched Operation Cast Lead against Hamas, a manoeuvre which lasted until January 2009. Numerous human rights organizations accused Israel and Hamas of committing war crimes.

Despite on–off negotiations, the Arab–Israeli conflict still remains deadlocked over the questions of borders, security issues, the fate of Palestinian refugees, settlement blocs, normalization of relations and an end-of-conflict clause in any final status agreements.

Arab League (League of Arab States – LAS) (al-Jami'a al-Arabiyah)

Regional organization of Arab states in the Middle East. First delineated in the 'Alexandria Protocol', which was the fruit of an Arab conference in **Alexandria** in autumn 1944. The protocol argued that neither a unitary state nor a federation could be realized but only a league of sovereign states, and a covenant establishing such a league was signed in Cairo by representatives of **Egypt, Iraq, Lebanon, Saudi Arabia, Syria**, Transjordan (now **Jordan**) and **Yemen**, 22 March 1945. Neither Syria nor Transjordan was formally independent at the date of signature. **Libya** joined, 1953; the **Sudan**, 1956; **Morocco** and **Tunisia**, 1958; **Kuwait**, 1961; **Algeria**, 1962; **Bahrain, Oman, Qatar** and the **United Arab Emirates**, 1971; **Mauritania**, 1973; **Somalia**, 1974; **Palestine Liberation Organization**

(PLO) for **Palestine**, 1976; Djibouti, 1977; and Comoros, 1993. Comoros, Djibouti and Somalia are only Arab by association, and Palestine is not sovereign. The objectives of the league as defined in 1945 were to strengthen and coordinate the political, cultural, economic and social programmes of member states and to provide mediation in disputes both between member states and with third parties. An agreement signed on 13 April 1950 added joint defence and economic cooperation, including the coordination of military activities.

The league operates through a council in which each member state has one vote, a range of committees and a permanent secretariat, together with twenty-two specialist agencies. The council, which is charged with mediation, may meet in any Arab capital. The political committee comprises the foreign ministers of the Arab states. The permanent secretariat is based in Cairo and its secretary general enjoys full diplomatic status and the rights of an observer at the **United Nations**. The Arab League also has its own flag, with its seal superimposed on a dark green background.

The Arab League organized the first Arab petroleum congress, 1959, and created the Arab League Educational, Cultural and Scientific Organization (ALECSO) in 1964. The Arab Common Market, which is open to all league member states and on which agreement was reached on 13 August 1964, became operative as of 1 January 1965 and the agreement signed by Egypt, Iraq, Jordan and Syria. It provides for the progressive abolition of customs duties on agricultural goods and natural resources and, at a slower rate, on industrial goods. It also envisages the free movement of capital and labour, the establishment of common external tariffs and the elaboration of a common foreign economic policy.

The Arab League's success in promoting political coordination has been chequered. The admission to membership of the Palestine Liberation Organization as the representative of all Palestinians was opposed by Jordan in 1964, and Egypt was suspended from membership for signing the peace treaty with Israel in 1979–89, and the league's headquarters moved to Tunis accordingly until 1990. The response to the Iraqi invasion of **Kuwait** was highly divisive, with only half the membership (Bahrain, Djibouti, Egypt, Kuwait, Lebanon, Morocco, Qatar, Saudi Arabia, Somalia, Syria and the United Arab Emirates) endorsing the stationing of foreign, particularly US, troops in Saudi Arabia. Syria was suspended from membership as a result of its civil war.

Arab Legion

Also known as Al Jeish al-Arabi (the Arab Army), a British-led and trained force in Transjordan in British-mandated **Palestine** (and subsequently the Kingdom of Jordan) established in 1923 by Captain (later Lieutenant Colonel) Frederick Peake ('Peake Pasha', 1886–1970) to maintain internal order. The Arab Legion expanded in 1936 in response to the **Arab revolt** against British rule in Palestine. Lieutenant General John Bagot Glubb ('Glubb Pasha', 1897–1986) succeeded Peake as commander in 1939. In **World War II** an enlarged and well-equipped Arab Legion participated in the successful Allied campaigns in Iraq in April 1941 and in Syria in June 1941. Following the end of the British mandate the legion was in action against Israeli forces in the 1948–9 Arab–Israeli War, securing the West Bank and capturing the Jewish Quarter of Jerusalem Old City in May 1948. It became the Jordan Arab Army following Glubb's dismissal in March 1956.

Arab nationalism

The pattern of evolution of Arab nationalism has been more complex than that of most nationalisms for two broad reasons. First, it has sought liberation from not one but a succession of colonial or dominant powers – not just the Turks, as was the prime Balkan experience, but also the British, the French and, more marginally, the Italians and even the Spaniards, and lastly, but by no means least, from the Israelis and from a pervasive, albeit sometimes inconsistent, US influence. Second, Arab nationalism has shared Arabs' own, sometimes difficult, intellectual quest for authenticity and identity in the modern world.

Four competing and sometimes contradictory currents can be distinguished in the quest for an authentic nationalist identity that is relevant to the whole Arab world. The first is identification with **Islam**. A succession of thinkers from **Rashid Rida** onwards has seen the renewal of Islamic heritage as key to the anti-colonial struggle, but such an identification poses its own difficulties. Rida himself, like **Qasim Amin**, envisaged an Islam renewed by the incorporation of many western concepts, but Rida also envisaged the unification of the Muslim community (*umma*) through a true caliph who would guide Muslim governments. The radical, but highly influential, **Sayyid Qutb** went further, arguing that all Muslim governments were heretical by definition because they were a violation of Allah's sovereignty over his creation. Such Islamic suspicion of, even hostility to, western concepts of national governance is further complicated by the call of many reformers, including Rida and Qutb, for a return to the perceived purity of early Islam and the full implementation of **sharia** law. Sharia, however, is anathema to many Muslims, particularly in **Turkey** but also in Arab countries such as **Egypt** and **Algeria**, where western ideas have struck deep roots, who see it as reactionary and regressive. It is also obviously the case that the Islamic world stretches far beyond the Arab world. On the other hand, Arabic is the language of the Qur'an, which is in some senses a particularly Arab possession. Moreover, the emergence of the **Muslim Brotherhood** as a political force during the Arab Spring of 2011–12 and, even more, the declaration of the establishment of a caliphate by the self-styled Islamic State of Iraq and ash-Sham (**ISIS**) on 29 June 2014 are a reminder that 'religious nationalism' is a potent competitor to more orthodox concepts of nationalism in the Arab world.

The second current is the secular pan-Arab nationalism of which Colonel **Nasser** remains the most successful exponent. Its leading theorist, however, was the Syrian, **Michel Aflaq**, who founded the **Ba'ath Party** (Harakat al-Ba'ath-al-Arabi – Movement for Arab Rebirth) in **Syria** in 1940. Although himself a Greek Orthodox Christian, he promoted a secular Arab nationalism with a socialist tendency, while stressing the importance of Islam for Arab solidarity. His new party appealed to young intellectuals and army officers and in particular to the Alawite community. Colonel Nasser's subsequent secular pan-Arabism achieved a number of successes at the time, including the **United Arab Republic** of Egypt and Syria, the projected union of Egypt and the **Sudan** and, arguably, even the monarchical union of **Iraq** and **Jordan**. It built on the common heritage of the Arabic language and the artificiality of many inter-Arab frontiers, it embraced the modern world, and it generated wild enthusiasm. Its achievements, however, evaporated after Nasser's death and it remains, at best, in abeyance. Perhaps it did not allow sufficiently for the Arabs' sense of common Islamic identity, perhaps it was overly associated with a particular interpretation of socialism, perhaps it did not succeed in providing the social welfare net achieved by the Muslim Brotherhood, perhaps it was undermined by its failure to combat the expansion of **Israel**, perhaps local and personal interests were just too strong to permit the cultivation of a common pan-Arab nationality.

51

The third current is the persistance of tribal structures in many Arab states, which compete for allegiance with the nation state. They are a permanent feature of both Lebanese and Syrian politics. If a regime is overthrown, particularly with foreign assistance as in **Libya** in 2011, tribal interests may become paramount, especially if there is access to a valuable resource such as **oil**. The resulting fiefdoms exercise power but are remote from any normal definition of 'nation'. Libya, **Western Sahara** and **Yemen** all face this challenge.

The fourth current is the loyalty felt towards existing Arab states, some, like Egypt, ancient entities, others twentieth-century creations. This current has proved as problematic as the other currents. Did Egypt's identity, for example, lie in its pharaonic past, as **Taha Hussein** argued, or in its Islamic past, as mainstream thinkers alleged? Or does it lie in its ability to forge a new future along modern secular lines as Turkey had done under **Atatürk**?

Arab nationalism first gained practical expression in the clashes between the Arabs and the Turks in the decades before 1914 and in the revolt against the British, who had effectively replaced the Turks, in Egypt, in 1882. It was intensified by the Arab revolt against the **Ottoman Empire** in Arabia during **World War I** but only succeeded in liberating North Yemen and the putative Saudi Arabia. The other Arab lands of the former empire had either already become European colonies or protectorates or passed under British or French control in the guise of **League of Nations mandates**. Arab nationalist sentiment was, however, recognized by the grant of formal independence to Egypt, 1922, Iraq, 1932, and Syria and **Lebanon**, 1944. Arab interests were nevertheless widely discounted. Syria resented the 1939 French transfer to Turkey of the half-Turkish- and half-Arab-inhabited province of Alexandretta (Turkish Hatay) in a vain attempt to bring neutral Turkey on to the allied side immediately prior to **World War II**. Of much greater import was the British acceptance of Jewish settlement in mandated Palestine, which culminated in the 1948 proclamation of the state of Israel.

Arab nationalism entered a new phase with the **Egyptian Revolution of 1952** and the subsequent emergence of Colonel Nasser as its leader. Egypt acquired true independence and Nasser humiliated both Britain and France in the 1956 **Suez Crisis**. British domination of Iraq was terminated by the military *coup d'état* of 1958. Arab nationalism in the form of pan-Arabism became internationally prominent by allying itself successfully with the wider causes of colonial liberation and non-alignment. The brutal **Algerian War of Independence** finally resulted in Algerian independence in 1962.

Despite such achievements, Arab nationalism has not proved a cohesive force in even the mid term. The numerous hereditary rulers feared Saddam Hussein's secular expansionist Iraq as they had feared Nasser's Egypt, and in the **Gulf War (1990–1)** could again rely on western support, now under United States leadership. The most religiously and socially conservative of the Arab states, Saudi Arabia, is the intimate ally of the US in fighting, in countries like the Yemen, the Islamic extremism of **al-Qaida**, which its own fundamentalism has helped to create. The military in Egypt, with the benefit of lavish US military aid, cooperate in the harassment of the elected but radical **Hamas** administration of **Gaza**, despite Egypt's alleged sympathy for the Palestinian cause. The Islamic cleavage between **Sunni** and **Shia** is yet another source of division. Above all, Arab nationalism has failed to trump individual state interests and inspire a common determination over time to prioritize Palestinian interests, leaving it to the Palestinians themselves to pursue their claim to statehood through the **United Nations** and its agencies in the face of Israeli and US opposition.

Arab revolt (World War I)

– see also **Lawrence, Thomas Edward**.

The so-called Arab revolt was the fruit of negotiations between **Husayn ibn Ali**, the Sharif of Mecca, and the British High Commissioner for Egypt, Sir Henry McMahon. Their negotiations, now known as the Husayn–McMahon correspondence, formed the basis for an alliance between the Sharif and Britain that would constitute 'the Arab Revolt' as well as the foundation for Arab claims of sovereignty after **World War I**. For Husayn ibn Ali, an ambitious local Ottoman notable who spoke fluent Ottoman Turkish, the negotiations seemed to promise the possibility of an Arab empire, delivered to him by the British. The British, on the other hand, saw in Husayn the possibility of countering the Ottomans' claims to leadership of the Muslim world through their title of caliph, a means of breaking the deadlock that they suffered in the **Dardanelles**, the hope of awakening popular resistance to Ottoman rule in its Arab provinces, and the possibility that Britain would be able to serve as 'patron' to the Arabs after the war. Debates about what exactly was promised by the

British to Husayn, along with the apparent contradictions between these negotiations and those with France in the **Sykes–Picot Agreement** (1916) and the Zionists (culminating in the **Balfour Declaration**, 1917) laid the basis for some of the fundamental diplomatic debates of the post-war era.

Some Arab troops fought directly under the British flag under the command of **Edmund Allenby**, but most fought as irregulars under the command of Husayn's son, **Faisal**. British and French military advisers helped to train and direct the revolt. The most famous of these was **T. E. Lawrence**, who joined the revolt in October 1916. For most of the war, the Arab revolt concentrated on attacking convoys, outposts and, especially, the Hejaz railway. As the war came to a close and Ottoman control dissolved, the revolt gained troops and became increasingly ambitious in its targets, gaining control of **Aqaba** in 1917 and entering **Damascus** in 1918. Nonetheless, its main military contribution to the British war effort was weakening Ottoman supply routes, providing intelligence and tying down Ottoman troops.

Despite the mythology, the Arab revolt was not a general uprising of the Arabs against the **Ottoman Empire** and, indeed, it seems that most Arab subjects were loyal to the empire until it became clear that it would not survive the war. The revolt did not dramatically alter the outcome of the war or the post-war structures that would define the Middle East. Its real significance lies elsewhere. Firstly, it created an alliance between Husayn's family (the **Hashemites**) and the British, which would help determine the ruling dynasties of **Iraq** (until 1958) and Jordan (to the present). Secondly and perhaps more importantly, it bestowed on nascent Arab states a memory of resistance to Ottoman rule that would prove fundamental to reframing their histories in nationalist Arab terms.

Arab revolt (Palestine) (1936–1939)

During the Arab disturbances in **Palestine** in 1936–9 both British and Jews were attacked. The first phase of the revolt, lead by Jerusalem Mufti Hajj **Amin al-Husayni**, consisted of a general strike from April through October 1936. Iraqi reinforcements under Fawzi al-Kawukji also participated in the disturbances and were suppressed by the British Army. A second phase of the revolt lasted from summer 1937 to 1939. It began with the murder of a British district commissioner and was ultimately suppressed by British Captain Orde C. Wingate's special night squads.

The general strike closed the port of Jaffa and prompted the opening of the port of Tel Aviv. The **Peel Commission** report of 1937 recommended partitioning Palestine into Jewish, Arab and British zones but did little to allay Arab fears over the creation of a Jewish state in Palestine. Only the British White Paper of 1939, which promised to reduce Jewish immigration to Palestine to a trickle, lead to a temporary cessation of Arab resistance. The situation would flare up again immediately following the United Nations' passage of its 29 November 1947 partition plan.

Arab Spring

The wave of revolutionary protest which swept much of the Arab world following the self-immolation of a 26-year-old fruit seller, Mohamed Bouazizi, in the Tunisian town of Sidi Bouzid in December 2010. His desperation at the confiscation of his cart by council officials, after his refusal to pay them bribes, inspired demands for jobs, food and social justice and for the substitution of democracy for corrupt dictatorship, which rapidly spread from **Tunisia** to **Egypt**, **Libya**, **Bahrain**, **Syria** and **Yemen**, with aftershocks elsewhere. The public mood may also have been conditioned by the well-publicized American neoconservative message that democracy would bring peace and prosperity to the **Middle East**. There was often the hope of foreign intervention.

The initial results were spectacular. Tunisia's President Zine El Abidine Ben Ali fled, Egypt's President **Husni Mubarak** was ousted and arrested, Libya's Colonel **Gaddafi** was killed and Yemen's President Saleh later resigned. The momentum, however, was not maintained. The Arab Spring's vaunted use of new technology to mobilize protest was no substitute for discipline and leadership, and could not compensate for its inchoate objectives. Foreign intervention meant flows of money from the Gulf to the **Sunni** rebels against the Alawite regime in Syria and like flows from **Iran** and **Russia** to sustain the regime. Saudi troops quashed Bahrain's pro-democracy protests by the **Shi'ite** majority. Britain and France gave aerial support to the ousting of Colonel Gaddafi, but little else. In Libya and Yemen, the ending of autocracy brought widespread anarchy, and Egypt soon returned to military rule. Only Tunisia may have made the democratic transition, although it is challenged by poverty and unemployment, with graduate joblessness across the country soaring to 70 per cent by 2016. Ominously, anarchy and war have facilitated the emergence of fundamentalist Islamic groups, notably **ISIS**, of singular ruthlessness.

Arafat, Yasser (1929–2004)

Mohammed Abdel-Raouf Arafat as Qudwa al-Hussaeini, as Arafat was named at birth, was born in Cairo into a Palestinian–Egyptian family but was moved to live with relatives in **Jerusalem** after his mother's death when he was 5 years old. Arafat returned to **Egypt** a few years later to live with his father and siblings. A participant in the Palestinian resistance to Israeli occupation of the Palestinian Territories, he offered aid to the cause in a number of ways, including smuggling weapons from Egypt to **Palestine**, and fought with a resistance force in **Gaza** for a time. After studying intermittently at the University of Faud I in Cairo, he graduated in 1956 with a degree in engineering. While working as an engineer, he emersed himself in political activism. To this end, he cofounded al-Fatah in 1958. The group advocated the liberation of Arab lands from Israeli occupation of Palestine and published a magazine to this aim the following year. In 1964 Arafat began to focus on his political aims, mainly the struggle against the Israeli occupation. A fringe group at its inception, **Fatah** came to prominence after the defeat of the **Palestinian Liberation Organization (PLO)** in the **Six Day War** in 1967. Joining with the PLO, Fatah took over the running of the organization, with Arafat at its helm.

Arafat became, during the 1970s, the recognized, and legitimized, leader of the Palestinian people on the local and international stage. During this decade, under his leadership the PLO attempted to shrug off its violent image by condemning and distancing itself from the violent resistance movements which were offshoots of the organization. After a speech at the **United Nations** in 1974, Arafat began to make concessions and work within an international framework for the larger goals of a Palestinian state. Significantly, in 1988 he led the PLO in accepting UN Resolution 242, which called for recognition of the state of Israel, sending shock waves through the more radical factions. He survived this seeming betrayal of the radical aims of the PLO (factions within the PLO had been calling for the creation of an independent Palestinian state and doing away with Israel). On 18 November 1988 Arafat proclaimed the independent State of Palestine, and in 1989 he was elected its first president. Key to the signing of the peace treaty between Palestine and Israel in 1993, the **Oslo Accords**, as they came to be known, are his major life accomplishment. For his role, Arafat

was awarded the Nobel Peace Prize in 1994. Erratic and controversial in the following years, he was increasingly isolated and seemingly lacked complete control. He died after a brief illness in 1994, and is buried in Muqata in Ramallah.

Aramco

The Arabian American Oil Company began in 1933 as the California Arabian Standard Oil Company (CASOC) when Standard of California (SOCAL) was awarded a sixty-year oil concession in **Saudi Arabia**'s Eastern Province. The Texas Oil Company (TEXACO) partnered with SOCAL the following year, and SOCAL both discovered and began exporting oil in 1938. Field development slowed during **World War II**, but the company, renamed ARAMCO in 1944, opened the Ras Tanura refinery in 1945. Then in 1948 Standard of New Jersey (EXXON) and Socony-Vacuum Oil Company (Mobil) completed the consortium. In 1973, in the wake of the Arab oil embargo, the Saudi government assumed a 25 per cent interest in ARAMCO. The company became fully Saudi owned in 1980 and was renamed the Saudi Arabian Oil Company or Saudi Aramco in 1988. Saudi Aramco, the largest oil company in the world, is responsible for all aspects of the petroleum business in Saudi Arabia.

Araucanians

This historical term describes the Hulliche, Pihunche and Mapuche, indigenous populations who inhabited **Chile** from Coquimbo to Chiloé. Expanding into **Argentina** in the eighteenth century, they were unified by a common language, an exogamous kinship system and shared cultural and religious beliefs. Although nominally part of the Inca Empire, the Mapuche, the largest group, resisted Spanish/Chilean conquest until 1883. Today numbering 1 million, Araucanians include assimilated urbanites and reservation inhabitants who farm in southern Chile.

Arbenz Guzmán, Jacobo (1913–1971)

As a junior military officer, Arbenz became a leader in the 1944 popular uprisings that removed Guatemalan dictator Jorge Ubico and inaugurated ten years of democratic government. Elected president of **Guatemala** in 1950, he launched social and economic reforms targeting the **United Fruit Company**. Concerned about leftist influence in Central America, the **United States** overthrew Arbenz in a CIA-orchestrated coup in 1954 that precipitated four decades of political and social turmoil in Guatemala.

Arctic and Antarctic

Despite the attraction of the Arctic periphery to fur traders from at least the sixteenth century and a series of unsuccessful attempts to find a sea passage (the Northwest Passage) from the Atlantic to the Pacific, the Arctic remained essentially unexplored until the Norwegian Roald Amundsen succeeded in sailing from east to west in 1903–6 and the American Robert E. Peary reached the North Pole in 1909.

The Arctic has achieved a new significance with the advance of global warming, which appears to be running at double the speed there than in the rest of the world and could make it free of summer ice by as early as 2040. The Russian vessel *Akademik Fyodorov* became the first to reach the Pole without an ice breaker in 2005. This is making the exploitation of the region's resources a realistic possibility, and the eight countries bordering it have all submitted competing national claims to ownership of the continental shelf. Both **Russia** and Denmark have claimed the Pole itself. Drilling for oil in the Arctic has raised major environmental concerns.

Although Antarctica has witnessed comparable pressures they have been restrained by its extreme conditions, and scientific interests have, as yet, remained paramount.

Argentina

The world's eighth largest nation occupies 1,719,265 square kilometres of southern South America. The 2011 population was nearly 42 million of which 97 per cent were literate and Caucasian, 92 per cent Catholic and 92 per cent urban. In 1580 Spaniards settled at Buenos Aires. Incorporated in the Viceroyalty of the Rio de la Plata in 1776, Argentina declared independence on 9 July 1816. By the 1880s the indigenous population was largely exterminated. Italians and Spaniards populated the nation, prospering with the export of meat and wheat. Despite substantial natural resources, twentieth-century Argentina suffered persistent economic crises and military interventions. The labour and welfare policies of **Eva** and **Juan Perón** (1946–55) ended in military control, the so-called Dirty War, 1976–83, hyperinflation, corruption, mounting external debt, capital flight and unemployment. Since 2003 export agriculture, diversified industries and a dominant service sector have to some extent improved, but the economy urgently needs reform. Argentina participates in Mercosur, UN peacekeeping operations, and claims the Malvinas Islands.

Arias Sánchez, Oscar (1940–)

While president of **Costa Rica** (1986–90), Arias Sánchez received the Nobel Peace Prize for diplomatic efforts, culminating in the Esquipulas II Accords that ended the civil wars raging in Central America during the 1980s. Remaining active in international peace projects and Costa Rican politics, in 2005 he established the Arias Foundation for Peace and Human Progress and in 2006 won a second term as president.

Arif, 'Abd al-Salam (1921–1966) and Arif, 'Abd al-Rahman (1916–2007)

The Arif brothers were prominent in Iraqi politics in the 1950s and 1960s. 'Abd al-Salam was a leader of a dissident faction within the Iraqi military that along with the **Ba'ath Party** toppled Abdul Karim Qassem's government in 1963; he became president of **Iraq** until his death in a helicopter crash in 1966. Fellow military officer 'Abd al-Rahman succeeded him as president until 1968. 'Abd al-Salam participated in a series of talks with Egyptian President **Nasser** to explore whether the two countries could work towards a full political union, but this never materialized. In order to facilitate such a pan-Arab union, Arif nationalized, via the 1964 nationalization laws, most banks and several big manufacturing firms. During 'Abd al-Rahman's short rule, Iraq's foreign policy shifted towards the socialist bloc. His government was overthrown by a Ba'ath Party faction in just two years and he was exiled to **Turkey**.

aristocracy

Aristocracy comes from the Greek word meaning 'the rule of an elite'. In Europe, that was traditionally defined by bloodlines of nobility conferred by monarchs or inherited directly. Traditionally, the aristocracies of Europe were the military elite, inheriting a duty to provide armed service to the state and often expecting to fulfil the major roles in government. Where laws of inheritance were not clearly defined, they also provided a pool out of which monarchs were chosen and several monarchical lines were effectively derived from successful seizures of power which established royal dynasties. During the early modern period, different traditions had emerged. In some countries, such as the Italian city-states, nobility was less important as a source of legitimate rule compared with large merchant or ruling non-noble dynasties, such as the Borgias or Medicis. In what was to become the **United Kingdom**, non-noble gentry and merchant elites shared power with a small noble class of less than two hundred families. In pre-Revolutionary **France**, by contrast, the nobility comprised 400,000 people out of a population of over 20 million. Relatively large noble classes also existed in Spain, central Europe and Italy.

The degree of power exercised by the noble classes also varied enormously. They remained a major support for the autocracy in **Russia** until the mid nineteenth century when economic development and technocratic reform began to undermine their position, and the Bolshevik Revolution and ensuing civil war destroyed their position entirely. In France, their political power was broken by the Revolution of 1789, though they remained influential in conservative politics during the nineteenth century. In a newly unified **Germany**, aristocratic influence remained important in the armed forces, though increasingly subject to meritocratic influence. In the United Kingdom, the aristocracy retained political power through the House of Lords, not entirely yielded until the twentieth century, and they continued to dominate cabinets until the mid nineteenth century. Many aristocracies in western Europe were able to retain considerable wealth into the twentieth century through successful entrepreneurship, investment and agricultural improvement. The break-up of large estates, often with compensation, as in the case of Ireland or some Scandinavian countries, permitted aristocracies to survive and diversify economically. Communist control in eastern Europe after 1945 virtually eliminated the old aristocratic caste.

Attempts to read the term *aristocracy* across other cultures is common but not particularly informative. The Brahmin caste in Hindu society could be considered a form of aristocracy, but derives from a different tradition to that of western Europe, with a specific religious dimension lacking in European aristocracy. Similarly, the Chinese mandarinates might have possessed aspects of aristocratic exclusiveness, but it did not conform in any precise way with European models which were in themselves highly varied. Generally, the term *aristocratic* is often used loosely to refer to exclusive elites in other cultures even if their delineation owes little to European precedents based on bloodlines and heredity.

Armenia

A republic in the South Caucasus. It shares borders with **Azerbaijan**, **Georgia**, **Iran** and **Turkey**. A modern Armenian state first emerged in May 1918 amid the collapse of the **Russian Empire** and Turkish and British occupations of the region. Centred around Erevan, the new state was led by the Dashnaktsutiun, a party founded in 1890 in Russia to mobilize the diaspora for the nationalist cause. In December 1920 the Soviet Army ended Armenian independence. Under the Bolsheviks, Armenia became part of the **Union of Soviet Socialist Republics (USSR)**, first within a Transcaucasian federated republic in 1922, and then as a separate republic which became the focus of migration from the diaspora and the nationalization of government and culture. In 1988 the launching of protests challenging Azerbaijani control of the Armenian-majority territory of **Nagorno-Karabakh** and a devastating earthquake fuelled the anti-Soviet nationalist movement. Since 1991 independent Armenia has been beset by economic crises as well as by conflict with Turkey and war with Azerbaijan.

Armenian genocide

Reform within the **Ottoman Empire** in the late nineteenth century produced violent sectarian tension culminating in massacres of the Anatolian Armenian population in 1894–6 and 1909. State-sponsored violence against Armenian populations reached its climax during **World War I** when the Ottoman Empire became free from Russian, British and French influence. Those powers had fashioned themselves as protectors of the Armenian population, contributing to the (false) impression that most Armenians were a traitorous fifth column. The **Young Turk** administration seized the opportunity presented by the war to remove the empire's Armenian population. Claiming isolated military action against Ottoman forces by Armenian irregulars as a pretext, the Ottoman government ordered the mass deportation of Armenian civilians on 24 April 1915. The death of more than a million men, women and children ensued. Whilst scholars with Turkish nationalist commitments still reject the label *genocide*, the fact that the Armenian population of Anatolia all but disappeared during World War I is indisputable.

arms control

A concept introduced by the 1919 **Treaty of Versailles** which sought unsuccessfully to restrict Germany's armaments. An elusive and sporadically successful objective of US and Soviet policy after **World War II**, driven by the mutual acquisition of the **atomic bomb** and then the hydrogen bomb. Successes include the Test-Ban Treaty, 1963, which barred the signatories (Britain, the **Soviet Union** and **United States**) from carrying out nuclear tests in the atmosphere, underwater or in space (but not underground); the ABM (Anti-Ballistic Missile) and **SALT I** (Strategic Arms Limitation I) Treaties, 1972, between the Soviet Union and US, which limited missiles and strategic systems for five years; the **SALT II** Treaty, 1979, which imposed further limits (US ratification of the latter was suspended after the Soviet invasion of Afghanistan, although the US undertook to adhere to it); and the INF (**Intermediate Nuclear Forces**) Treaty, 1987, a disarmament agreement limited to some 4 per cent of nuclear weaponry.

Articles of Confederation (USA)

The Articles of Confederation served as the first Constitution of the United States, before the adoption of the Federal Constitution in 1788. Drafted primarily by John Dickinson, the Articles provided for a 'firm league of friendship' between the thirteen states, in which a national legislature would be responsible for foreign and defence policy. Each state, however, retained all powers not expressly granted to the national government. The government consequently struggled to execute its responsibilities effectively, as the Articles granted no central judicial or executive power to enforce treaties or other national laws. The Articles, moreover, made no provision for national taxation, and thus deprived the government of the ability to reliably manage its responsibilities, including paying off the foreign debt. These perceived weaknesses helped lead to the call for a convention discussing amendments, held in Philadelphia in 1787, which resulted in the adoption of an entirely new constitution.

Artigas, José Gervasio (1764–1850)

Born in Montevideo, Artigas was a gaucho leader serving in the military when he emerged to head an independence movement in the Banda Oriental (**Uruguay**). He defeated the royalist troops at Las Piedras on 18 May 1811, but a Portuguese army from **Brazil** soon forced him to lead about 16,000 supporters into Entre Ríos. Returning to the Banda Oriental in 1812, he convoked a congress, served as its president, and broke with Buenos Aires. Victory in 1815 achieved independence from **Spain**. Artigas promised to liberate slaves fighting for him. His land reform and decentralized constitution resonated with rural peasants but disconcerted merchants and landholders. The elite supported the return of the Portuguese in 1817. Defeated in 1819, Artigas in 1820 withdrew into permanent exile in **Paraguay**. Posthumously he became a national hero to Uruguayans, who attained independence from Brazil in 1828.

arts

– *see* **culture**.

Aruba/Bonaire/Curaçao (Dutch Caribbean)

Known as the ABC islands, Aruba, Bonaire and Curaçao are three Dutch islands in the Caribbean, located north of **Venezuela**. These three Leeward islands were part of the Netherlands Antilles until 1986, when Aruba seceded and became a separate, autonomous member of the Kingdom of the **Netherlands**. Bonaire and Curaçao have a governor named by the Dutch crown, while Aruba is an independent territory within this country. The local language is Papiamentu.

Arusha Declaration

President **Julius Nyerere**'s declaration in Arusha, northern Tanzania, on 5 February 1967 of his vision of an African socialism – **ujamaa** – and self-reliance with a programme based on the collective ownership of the means of production by farmers and workers rather than the centralized Soviet model. At its heart lay a 'villagization' project drawing dispersed family smallholdings into locally administered villages as a means of developing a self-sufficient economy. As Nyerere saw it, ujamaa villages were intended to be socialist organizations created by the people and governed by those who lived and worked in them. Although there were some achievements, particularly in primary education, bureaucratization and corruption made the programme unpopular. The adoption of a Basic Industrial Strategy in 1974 marked a shift away from an emphasis on rural development and the policy was largely abandoned in the 1980s.

Arya Samaj

A socio-religious Hindu reform organization founded by Dayananda Saraswati in 1875. The larger reform agenda of the *Samaj* combined opposition to Hindu practices such as idolatry, polytheism, child marriage, taboos against widow remarriage and foreign travel, with an assertion of Hindu supremacy over other religious faiths based on Vedic infallibility. It advocated and practised new rituals of *shuddhi* (purification) of non-Hindus and lower castes. Its members came from trading castes based in **Punjab** and western Uttar Pradesh.

Ashanti

A powerful kingdom located in modern-day **Ghana**, Ashanti emerged from a federation in the early eighteenth century, its first king Osei Tutu having conquered the surrounding area. In the second half of the eighteenth century Ashanti became more centralized, forming a bureaucracy from among its most loyal families and constructing a road network through which its armies were able to deploy quickly to put down rebellion. Ashanti was involved in the slave trade for most of the eighteenth century, selling the captives from many wars to Dutch, Danish and English merchants on the coast. Its attempts to take over Fante in 1807 led to war with **Great Britain**, who guaranteed the independence of Ashanti's great rival coastal state. Early in the nineteenth century Ashanti gradually abandoned the slave trade in favour of other exports, notably gold and increasingly cocoa. Further wars with Great Britain resulted in the country's conquest in 1896 and annexation to the Gold Coast Colony.

Asia

The idea of Asia in the modern geographical and political sense emerged in the eighteenth century under the influence of globalization and imperialism. The definition of Asia is a contested term. However, the concepts of East Asia, South Asia and South East Asia have become widely accepted. The name *Asia* originated in classical antiquity, when it referred to the region sometimes now termed West Asia, although the terms Middle and Near East are more often found today for this area. As West Asia is more separated in its political and cultural interactions than the other parts of Asia, it is less centrally included in this definition.

In the early modern era there were distinct spheres of political and cultural interaction across the Asian continent. Among the most important were the Persian Empire, the Arabic-speaking countries of the **Middle East**, the **Russian Empire**, the Indian subcontinent and the East Asian 'sino-sphere', in which Confucian culture was an important influence. These societies had significant trading and cultural relationships with each other, both across the land mass of the Eurasian continent but also by sea across the Indian Ocean and into the Pacific. However, their political relationships were broadly speaking separate and distinct, and were not defined by a conscious 'Asian' identity that differentiated them from Europe. While Europeans defined societies as 'Asian' or 'Asiatic', the inhabitants of the region itself did not identify themselves in those terms.

Circumstances began to change in the eighteenth and nineteenth centuries. Increasing British domination of **India** in the eighteenth century also brought about a change in the economic relationship between different parts of Asia, for example, the growing of opium in Bengal, in eastern India, which from the early nineteenth century was exported to **China**. While there had always been significant trade within Asia, the arrival of European imperialism, particularly from the mid nineteenth century, brought commerce into a more globalized and militarized context. The nineteenth century saw the position of Asia rapidly altered by the impact of the western empires. After the Uprising of 1857, India was placed under more formal British colonial government. The **Opium Wars** that began in 1839 saw China's government constrained by a series of treaties that demanded trade and territorial concessions to the western powers. **Japan**, which had been relatively isolated, was forced to open up under Russian and American pressure in the 1850s. By the late nineteenth century there were further colonial conquests in the region from **Manchuria** in the north (**Russia**) to **Vietnam** in the south (**France**).

A highly significant turning point in the idea of Asia as a meaningful entity was the emergence of Japan as a regional power. The **Meiji restoration** of 1868 led to fast and comprehensive modernization of Japanese society. As part of this, Japanese thinkers began to perceive of themselves as in some way separate from the continent that surrounded them. The thinker Fukuzawa Yukichi advocated the idea of *Datsu-A, Nyu-O* ('leaving Asia, entering Europe') as the best way to cement Japanese progress. The European example perhaps most enthusiastically taken up by the Japanese was the drive to empire: by the turn of the twentieth century, Japan had taken **Taiwan** as a colony and had effective control of **Korea** (which it colonized in 1910).

Yet within a couple of decades there was increasing wariness in Japan about the wisdom of embracing western models too closely. Instead, many thinkers began to consider what Japan had in common with its neighbours, rather than their differences. One of the most important expressions of this idea came from the Japanese thinker Okakura Kakuzo, who wrote the book *Ideals of the East* (1904) which began with the line 'Asia is one', and argued for a 'spiritual' East which would stand in contrast with the more materialistic West. This idea became the basis of the ideology of **pan-Asianism**.

The year of publication of Okakura's book also saw another turning point: Japanese victory in the

Russo-Japanese War of 1904–5. This was the first occasion that an Asian power had defeated a European power in war, and was a source of inspiration to anti-imperialist activists across the continent, including a young **Nehru** in India. Even though Japan's victory led to further imperial conquests of its own in **Manchuria**, it also gave weight to pan-Asian ideas that European dominance was not inevitable. Pan-Asian ideas were popular among Japanese and Indian thinkers during the 1910s to 1930s, notably with the great Indian polymath **Rabindranath Tagore**. They were less popular in China, where they were associated with Japanese imperialism on Chinese territory.

Conflicting ideas of Asia came to a head during **World War II**. By this point, Japanese pan-Asianism had metastasized into an ideology of imperial conquest. The invasions of Manchuria in 1931, China in 1937, and much of South East Asia in 1941–2 were underpinned by a rhetoric of liberation from European colonial domination, which was proved hollow by the brutal regimes installed by the Japanese in their newly conquered territories. However, the Allied powers struggled to find a powerful language of liberation to oppose Japan's pan-Asian ideas, largely because **Britain** was ambivalent about how far it was willing to grant its Asian colonies independence after the war. Opportunities for intra-Asian ideas of liberation were not fully exploited: the Indian independence movement and the Chinese war of resistance against Japan were not very extensively coordinated even though the relevant leaders (**Chiang Kai-shek**, Nehru and **Gandhi**) had some sympathy for each other's causes.

The post-war era saw significant decolonization in Asia. However, ideas of collective Asian identity became blurred into a wider idea of Afro-Asian solidarity symbolized most strongly by the **Bandung conference** of 1954. Greater coordination was made different by the different positions of the three major regional powers: India failed to project much of an idea of itself beyond South Asia, **Mao Zedong**'s China sought a international revolutionary role that alienated it from liberal powers in the region, and Japan's regional role was largely defined by the **United States**. These differences between the powers have remained relevant even into the post-Cold War era. In retrospect, the 1910s–1930s looks like the high point for the potency of a wider collective 'Asian' identity.

Assad, Hafez al- (1930–2000)

Hafez al-Assad was born on 6 October 1930 in a western province of **Syria**, the country of which he would become president. Assad was born into an Alawite family. The Alawites are a minority religious and ethnic group/sect which claims ties to Shia Islam. Assad graduated in 1955 from the Syrian Military Academy and joined the air force. He became a member of the **Ba'ath** Arab Socialist Party in 1946, not long before the party gained control of the Syrian government in 1953. As a member of the party, and upon attaining the rank of general in the Syrian air force, he rose through the party ranks. The party faced many internal divisions, and in 1966 Assad helped to put an end to these as the party's Secretary General. For his role in unifying the party, he was promoted to Minister of Defence. In 1967 Syria lost the Golan Heights to **Israel**. This was a major blow to national moral and a setback for al-Assad. He also held the title of Prime Minister from 1970 to 1971. Through a referendum in March 1971 he became president of the Syrian Arab Republic.

His presidency was marked by a cult of personality. Under Assad's regime, Soviet-backed infrastructure projects flourished, creating popular support for Assad and his government. In 1976 he sent troops into **Lebanon** to intervene in the civil war there. Syrian forces remained in Lebanon and influenced politics for many years after. Perhaps an attempt at gaining control of the neighbouring nation, Assad was accused of trying to destabilize Lebanon and seeking to control it politically and militarily. Although denying any wrongdoing, he kept the troops in Lebanon. His regime was accused of contributing to the violence and political murders that took place in Lebanon. In 1982 the Syrian Army pushed Israeli forces out of Lebanon, thus bolstering Assad's image as a strong leader across the Arab world. Assad was remembered for his ability to unite Syria, a feat that had eluded the nation for many years prior to his presidency. After his death his son Bashar al-Assad took over the presidency, but the rising in 2011 against his role led to the **Syrian Civil War**.

Assam

State located in north-eastern India, defined primarily by the Brahmaputra watershed before its southern turn into **Bangladesh**. Ahom and other princely territories were gradually added to the Bengal Presidency in the early nineteenth century, and after Indian independence smaller states were gradually created from portions of Assam. Although famed for tea, Assam produces significant rice, timber and mineral resources. Immigration from Bangladesh and uneven development have fuelled ethnic conflict.

Assembly of Notables (1866–1879) (Egypt)

Inaugurated by two khedival decrees, 22 October 1866. The first established an assembly of seventy-five members, indirectly elected for a three-year term, to be known as the Majlis shura al-nuwwab (Consultative Assembly). It also included an eighteen-article fundamental law (*la'iha asasiyya*) laying down the assembly's functions and electoral arrangements. The second decree comprised an organization law (*la'iha nizamiyya*) governing the assembly's procedures. The Assembly of Notables first met on 25 November 1866.

Endowed with no real legislative function, since the ruler regarded his authority as absolute, it was created by Khedive Isma'il to associate the country's notables, mainly the village sheikhs and headmen, with his financial policies and his consequent diplomatic moves to thwart foreign intervention. The merchant and artisan classes were, therefore, barely represented. Its sessions saw the beginnings of criticism of the ruler's financial recklessness and of the pressure for a greater share in power, which would subsequently mature into pressure for constitutionalism. The assembly was suspended by Khedive Isma'il in the crisis of March–April 1879, although its members continued to meet privately.

Assignats

The currency issued by the French revolutionary authorities from 1790 and eventually replaced by the Napoleonic franc in 1801. Assignats represented a move on the part of a self-styled 'new' French state towards paper money and away from the gold-and silver-based debt of the past. Issued by the constituent assembly of the new republic after the revolution, they in fact became hyperinflated quite quickly because of a tendency to increase the amount of paper in circulation without maintaining its value on the part of the authorities. The associated fluctuations and massive rises in the prices of goods and the encouragement to local clandestine barter that resulted was one of the chief causes of instability within Revolutionary France, if disguised by the revolutionary wars. When **Napoleon I** came to power, he moved swiftly to abolish assignats and replace them with a more stable currency.

Asturias

An area of north-western **Spain** known for its radicalism, coal industry and status as the principality of the heir to the Spanish throne. A 1934 revolt by coalminers in Asturias was famously suppressed with notable brutality by **Franco**, during which over a thousand miners were killed and more taken captive. This in turn led to it becoming a republican bastion during the **Spanish Civil War**. Asturias is also notable in being a cradle of the Reconquista, as it was never part of Islamic Spain, and also of the Spanish Enlightenment.

Aswan Dam

The Aswan High Dam in **Egypt** (as distinct from the Low Dam built by Britain in the late nineteenth century). **Britain** and the **United States** agreed in 1955 to make loans to enable Egypt to construct an additional dam to control Nile flooding and generate electricity, a project of President **Gamal Abdel Nasser**, after whom a resulting lake was to be named. In 1956 the US withdrew its offer after Egypt recognized the People's Republic of **China**. Britain soon followed suit. President Nasser responded by nationalizing the Suez Canal, declaring that operating revenues would be used to finance the dam project and setting off the 1956 **Suez Crisis**. Egypt turned to the **Soviet Union** for aid. Construction of the dam, which began in 1960, took a decade to complete. The work necessitated the relocation of 90,000 people and the movement of the Nubian temples at Abu-Simbel.

Atatürk, Mustafa Kemal (1881–1938)

A successful Ottoman military officer during **World War I**, Mustafa Kemal (Atatürk) became the leading figure in the Turkish nationalist movement after the war, and after the creation of the **Republic of Turkey** in 1923, became that country's first president, until his death in 1938. His role in shaping modern Turkey is unparalleled and his imprint on Turkish national culture is evident to this day. Mustafa was born to a Turkish-speaking, Muslim family in Ottoman controlled Thessalonica. He took the additional name, Kemal, during his school years, and, with the passage of a law requiring surnames in 1934, Mustafa Kemal was granted the family name Atatürk, or Father of the Turks, by the Turkish National Assembly. Kemal's early career was shaped both by his responsibilities as a young military officer and by his relation to the revolutionary Committee for Union and Progress (CUP). He served first in Damascus, but, presumably because of support from the CUP, was transferred to the Third Army headquarters in Macedonia in 1907, where he continued his CUP activities. He played a minor role in the 1908 Constitutional Revolution, continuing to serve as a regular military officer in **Albania** and, in the Italo-Turkish War of 1911, in Tripoli.

Kemal's reputation as a commander began to gain wide public attention during World War I, when he played a key role in the defence of **Gallipoli**. Throughout the rest of the war, he burnished his reputation further as he rose to the rank of brigadier. He was not widely known, but he had a strong reputation among the Ottoman officers' corps as a patriot, as critical of the wartime leadership of the CUP and as a winning general.

In 1919, apparently as part of a wider CUP conspiracy to re-establish itself after defeat, Mustafa Kemal was ordered to Eastern Anatolia, ostensibly to oversee the disarmament of the Ninth Army. Instead, landing in Samsun, on 19 May, he connected with other nationalist officers and began the organization of a national resistance to occupation and the developing terms of **Treaty of Sèvres** (1920). In a complicated campaign of warfare and diplomacy traditionally referred to as the Turkish War of Independence, Kemal was able to weld a unified army in Anatolia, which defeated both the Democratic Republic of **Armenia** and **Greece**. In 1923 these successes were ratified in the **Treaty of Lausanne**, which gave international recognition to an independent **Turkish Republic**.

In a broad programme of social transformation known as the Turkish Revolution, Kemal attempted to secularize and westernize the country. Resistance to centralization, as in the Sheikh Said Rebellion (1925) or in Dersim (1937–8), was dealt with using overwhelming force. The caliphate was abandoned, the alphabet was changed from Arabic to Latin script, new sartorial and public practices were established, all with the goal of creating a homogeneous and secular national culture. From 1923 until his death in 1938, Mustafa Kemal was the single most important figure within the Turkish Republic.

Atlanta Campaign (4 May–2 September 1864)

In one of the decisive campaigns of the latter phase of the **American Civil War**, **William T. Sherman** succeeded in manoeuvring Confederate forces out of strong, entrenched positions before Resaca and Allatoona. Engagements followed at Dallas, New Hope Church, Kennesaw Mountain and Kolb's Farm. After he crossed the Chattahoochee River, the Confederates attacked Sherman at Peach Tree Creek and before Atlanta. Sherman advanced around its western outskirts to cut the railway links, throwing back Confederate stabs at Ezra

Church and Jonesboro. On 1–2 September Atlanta fell, ensuring the re-election of **Abraham Lincoln** in November 1864.

Atlantic, Battle of

– *see* **World War II**.

Atlantic Charter (1941)

A statement of war aims agreed in August 1941 by President **Franklin Roosevelt** of the **United States** and Prime Minister **Winston Churchill** of **Great Britain** after a secret meeting in the mid-Atlantic to discuss the then neutral United States' role in opposing the fascist powers. The eight-point plan for a post-war world included the renunciation of territorial expansion, the self-determination and self-government of subjugated peoples, free trade, an international commitment to economic security for all, freedom from fear of international aggression, freedom of travel and the future abandonment of the use of force as an instrument of foreign policy, both voluntarily and through the forcible disarmament of aggressor states. The continued commitment of the British to the maintenance of their empire and the post-war drift in the United States towards a foreign policy dominated by anti-communism undermined many of the aims of the charter.

Atlantic history

A term that most often refers to the scholarly approach of integrating the study of **Europe**, **Africa** and the Americas. Its practitioners explore the links and complex relationships between the peoples, goods and ideas that comprised the integrated system of the 'Atlantic world'. Though Atlantic history is often periodized as 1500–1800, many historians employ the concept and approach to the study of the nineteenth and twentieth centuries. Atlantic history is often characterized by an interdisciplinary approach, with the traditional methods of historians accompanied by economics, anthropology, demography, medical science and literary theory, to name but a few.

atomic bomb

First tested successfully at Alamogordo, New **Mexico**, on 16 July 1945 and dropped by the **United States** on Hiroshima, 6 August, and Nagasaki, 9 August 1945, killing some 70,000 and 35,000 people respectively. **Japan** capitulated, 15 August; the bomb may have shortened the war by up to two years. US President **Truman** said of Hiroshima at the time 'This is the greatest thing in history', but few then appreciated the dangers of nuclear contamination or foresaw proliferation. In fact the **Soviet Union** exploded its own bomb in August 1949, followed by Britain (October 1952), **France** (February 1960) and **China** (October 1964). The atomic bomb has, however, been overtaken by the hydrogen bomb exploded by the US in November 1952, the Soviet Union in August 1953, and China in June 1967.

The **Nuclear Nonproliferation Treaty**, 1968, forbids countries with nuclear weapons from helping others to acquire them, but was never signed by **India, Pakistan, Israel, South Africa, Brazil** or **Argentina**. India exploded its own bomb, May 1974; Pakistan and **North Korea** have followed, and **Iran** may do so. Israel is a known but unacknowledged nuclear power.

Atomic Energy Commission

The civilian agency established by the US government in 1946 to regulate and develop the country's nuclear energy programme in the wake of the atomic attacks on **Japan** that ended **World War II**. The **Cold War** stymied plans for the **United Nations** to gain international control of atomic power. The first chair of the American AEC was David Lilienthal, former head of the Tennessee Valley Authority. The commission was abolished in 1974.

Auchinleck, Claude (1884–1981)

A British general who served as commander-in-chief of the Indian Army, 1943 to 1947, Auchinleck had long experience in **India**. During **World War II** he served as commander of British forces in the **Middle East**, but his lack of success against the Germans led to his dismissal. He was appointed commander-in-chief of the Indian Army and served under Viceroys Wavell and **Mountbatten**. He was largely responsible for the division of the Indian Army between the new nations of India and **Pakistan** in 1947.

Auschwitz

Site of probably the most infamous of the Nazi concentration camps, now Oświęcim, Poland. Strictly, an annihilation camp (*Vernichtungslager*), it is estimated that 1.5 million people were gassed or died there of ill-treatment. The great majority of the victims were Jewish, but many thousands of gypsies and other opponents of the Nazis were also killed. Tension arose during the 1990s over the 'moral ownership' of the site. The preserved camp was declared a UNESCO World Heritage site in 1979.

Austerlitz, Battle of

Also known as the Battle of the Three Emperors, a decisive clash in Moravia (now the Czech Republic) on 2 December 1805 between a 73,000-strong French Army commanded by **Napoleon** and Tsar **Alexander I**'s Russian–Austrian Army of 86,000. Napoleon's victory shattered the Third Coalition, **Austria** agreeing to peace at Pressburg on 23 December, effectively ending the Holy Roman Empire and enabling the establishment in 1806 of the French-dominated Confederation of the Rhine.

Australia

Officially known as the Commonwealth of Australia, the country is located in the southern hemisphere and is comprised of a mainland of the world's smallest continent and a number of islands in the Southern, Indian and Pacific Oceans. The country's area totals 7,686,850 square kilometres, out of which the land mass comprises 7,617,930 square kilometres and water 68,920 square kilometres. Australia is separated from Asia by the Arafura and Timor seas. Its name is derived from the Latin *Australis*, meaning 'of the South'. Aboriginal settlers arrived on its mainland about 40,000 years before the first Europeans began exploration in the seventeenth century. Before 1770, when Captain **James Cook** took possession in the name of **Great Britain**, no formal territorial claims had been made – the first official settlement dates to 26 January 1788, when the Colony of New South Wales was established by Captain Arthur Phillip. In the late eighteenth and nineteenth centuries five other colonies (Queensland, South Australia, Tasmania, Victoria, Western Australia) were created, which later federated into the Commonwealth of Australia in 1901. Two territories were later established: the Australian Capital Territory and the Northern Territory. The Commonwealth of Australia is a constitutional monarchy with a parliamentary system of government. Queen Elizabeth II is Queen of Australia but is nominally represented by the Governor General at federal level and by the governors at state level. Despite the powers given to the Governor General by the constitution, they act only under the advice of the Prime Minister. In practice, formal ties to the UK have diminished over the years, especially after the passing of the Australia Act in 1986 (ending any British role in the governance of Australian States and judicial appeals to the United Kingdom Privy Council). In 1999 the Australian public rejected a move towards a republic. Australia is a prosperous country with a per capita GDP slightly higher than that of the United Kingdom, **Germany** and **France** in terms of purchasing power parity. Moreover, the country was third in the United Nations' Human Development Index for 2005. Indeed, it took advantage of its natural resources to rapidly develop agricultural and manufacturing industries and to make a major contribution to the British effort in **World Wars I** and **II**. In recent decades, partly due to reforms carried out in the 1980s, Australia registered one of the highest growth rates among OECD countries.

Austria

The German-speaking central European political and cultural core of the Habsburg Austrian Empire, Austria only became a nation state under the **Treaty of Versailles** in 1919, which forbade union with **Germany**. The country was effectively rendered nationally bankrupt by the collapse of Vienna's Kreditanstalt Bank in 1931. It was a **corporate** but not fascist state under Dr Dolfuss, who was assassinated by Austrian Nazis in 1934, the same year civil war raged between the Clericals and the Socialists. The country was united with Germany in the *Anschluss*, with wide popular support, in 1938. The capital, Vienna, remained the great centre of European cultural and scientific life which it had been under the **Austro-Hungarian Empire** until that time. In 1945 it was under four-power occupation until a separate government was restored. It became independent under the Austrian State Treaty, 1955, which imposed permanent neutrality and forbade any return of the Habsburg dynasty. Austria joined the **European Union** in 1995.

Austria–Hungary, Austro-Hungarian Empire

Evolved from the territorial possessions of the Austrian house of **Habsburg** in central Europe dating back to the Middle Ages and including the modern Austria and Czech Republic. The territory of modern **Hungary** came under Habsburg rule with the defeat of the Turks and the conclusion of the Treaty of Karlovic (1699), as did southern **Poland** (Galicia), including Krakow, with the partition of Poland by **Austria**, **Prussia** and **Russia**, 1772–95. The Habsburgs ruled, however, as Holy Roman Emperors until that empire's nominal existence was swept away by **Napoleon**, and the Austrian Empire only came into formal existence in 1804. The defence of the ascendancy of Roman Catholic Christianity nevertheless continued to be seen as an imperial obligation.

The empire's chief minister, Count **Metternich**, was the architect of the new European order created by the **Congress of Vienna**, 1815, but his restoration of autocratic conservatism was increasingly challenged over the following decades by the twin forces of liberalism and nationalism, particularly in **Hungary** and **Italy**. Austria's position as leader of the German states was lost with its defeat in the Austro-Prussian War, 1866, and subsequent expulsion from the German Confederation. The Austrian emperor, Franz Joseph, responded by coming to terms with Hungary, which had been growing in importance as a centre of commerce and industry. The compromise (*Ausgleich*) of 1867 officially created Austria–Hungary, a 'common monarchy' of emperor, court and ministers of foreign affairs and war, but without a prime minister or cabinet. Hungary became fully autonomous internally with the emperor as its king. Although the emperor remained supreme, Austria–Hungary recognized civil rights, freedom of belief and an independent judiciary. The empire proved unable or unwilling, however, to widen the compromise to incorporate its other ethnic groups in a federal or confederal structure. The tide of nationalism demanded outright independence for the Czechs, the re-establishment of partitioned Poland and the recognition of the claims of a number of other ethnic groups; demands which the empire found ever harder to withstand.

It was this consciousness of growing weakness which led the empire in 1908 to try to enhance its prestige by annexing Bosnia, provoking the **Bosnian crisis**. In practice, however, the annexation only fuelled southern (Yugo-)slav national sentiment, with the assassination of Crown Prince Franz Ferdinand by a Bosnian Serb in Sarajevo in June 1914 as a disastrous consequence. The subsequent declaration of war on **Serbia** by Austria–Hungary activated the system of great power alliances, unleashing **World War I**. Despite defeating Serbia, 1915, Austria–Hungary had to sign an armistice with the Allies, November 1918, knowing that its Croat, Czech, Hungarian, Romanian, Slovak and Slovene citizens had already proclaimed their independence. The Poles followed within days. Emperor Karl, on the throne only since 1916, abdicated as king of Hungary the same month. The Treaties of Saint-Germain between the Allies and Austria, 1919, and of Trianon between the Allies and Hungary, 1920, recognized the independence of the newly proclaimed states and brought the history of Austria–Hungary to a close.

autarky

From Greek meaning 'self-sufficiency', autarky describes an economy closed to international trade, or an ecosystem not affected by influences from outside and reliant entirely on its own resources. Autarky is advocated to maintain cultural traditions and local economies. Modern examples of pure autarky are **North Korea** and **Bhutan**. Other countries have pursued autarky temporarily, for political reasons or to balance the flows of imports and exports (e.g. the **United States** during 1808). A form of autarky, combined with territorial expansionism, is **mercantilism**. In the seventeenth and eighteenth centuries empires practised mercantilism by impeding trade with countries outside the empire. International trade theory indicates there is no economic basis for preferring autarky to international trade.

automobiles

– see **transportation**.

Awadh

Among the richest northern provinces of the **Mughal Empire**. In the early eighteenth century its governor, Saadat Khan, took advantage of factional conflict in Delhi and the politically weakened emperor to combine military and revenue powers formerly kept separated. He thus established an autonomous kingdom with its capital in Lucknow and set himself at the head of a new dynasty. Awadh disappeared as an independent polity when the English **East India Company** annexed it in 1856.

Awami League

Formed first as the Awami Muslim League Party in 1949, it became the Awami League under the leadership of **H. S. Suhrawardy**. The latter joined in a coalition with the parties of Fazlul Huq and Maulana Bhasani to defeat the **Muslim League** in the 1954 elections. After the death of Suhrawardy, Sheikh **Mujibur Rahman** led the party to victory in the 1970 elections in **Pakistan**. The military and political leaders of Pakistan, almost all of whom were from the western wing of the country, carried out a military crackdown to prevent the Awami League from coming to power in Pakistan. Its leaders were imprisoned and a war between Bengali guerrillas and the Pakistan Army ensued. After **India** entered the war on the side of the Bengalis, Pakistan capitulated and the independent nation of **Bangladesh** was formed with Awami League leadership. The party has continued to play an important role in the politics of Bangladesh ever since.

It long stood for a secular nation and presently is the more secular of the two major parties in the country.

Awolowo, Obafemi (1909–1987)

Nigerian politician, chief and opposition leader. Recognized as one of the founding fathers of **Nigeria** and leader of the **Yoruba**, Awolowo began his political career as a journalist, trade unionist and leader of the youth movement in late colonial Nigeria. As head of the **Action Group**, he advocated federalism and universal education. From 1952 to 1959 he served as the first premier of the Western Region under Nigeria's parliamentary system and became the official leader of the opposition at independence. In 1963 he was arrested and tried for treason. General **Yakuba Gowon**'s military government, which took power after the *coup d'état* of 1996, pardoned Awolowo and appointed him Federal Commissioner of Finance. Awolowo wrote several important tracts on federalism, democracy and socialism, including *Thoughts on the Nigerian Constitution*, written while he was imprisoned.

Axis

An agreement of mutual defence and insurance signed between **Benito Mussolini**, Duce of **Italy**, and **Adolf Hitler**, Fuhrer of **Germany**, in 1936. The actual phrase was that of the Italian dictator, and implied a new ruling 'axis' on which Europe could move. The Axis later included **Japan**, **Hungary** and **Romania**, as well as several other fascist and fascist-aligned countries. It was intended to underpin and execute a 'new order' in world affairs typified by violence, racism, *machtpolitik* and the personal rule of the dictators. As a term, it was popularized by the propaganda efforts of **Britain** and the **United States** during **World War II**. The Allies intended to irrevocably link its members both together and to the name of lawless imperialism and criminality, the better to bring about their ultimate and unconditional defeat. In art and culture, the term refers to the combination of modernism, homoeroticism, stylized architecture, fascist couture and the distorted remains of art deco and Bauhaus styles that made up Fascist expression.

Ayatollah

The highest level of Iranian **Shi'ite** cleric, the Persian-language title being derived from the Arabic *ayatu Allah* (sign of Allah) reflecting the Shi'ite interpretation of the Qur'an that human beings can be seen as signs of Allah. Those bearing the title are expert in the study of Islamic jurisprudence, ethics and philosophy, and are usually teachers. They can be women, and most teach in Shi'ite seminaries (*hawzas*). The most significant ayatollahs can be awarded the distinction of *ayatollah uzma* (Grand ayatollah or Great sign of Allah), of which there were over sixty worldwide in 2017, principally in the holy cities of an-Najaf, **Iraq**, and Qom (Qum), **Iran**. Such leading scholars do not necessarily hold the same views on political, social and religious issues.

Ayodhya

Town in Indian state of Uttar Pradesh, said to be the birthplace of epic hero deity Rama. Rashtriya Swayamsevak Sangh and **Bharatiya Janata Party** activists in the 1980s revived claims that a sixteenth-century mosque (the Babri Masjid) had been built on the site of a Rama temple, and the same activists destroyed the mosque on 6 December 1992. Because no temple has been built on the mosque site, it remains central to Hindu nationalist discourse.

Ayub Khan, Mohammed (1907–1974)

As commander-in-chief of **Pakistan**'s army, Mohammad Ayub Khan served as the chief martial law administrator after a military-orchestrated coup in 1958. He soon declared himself president as well, and retained power until 1969. In 1960 he established the 'Basic Democracies' system, a thin democratic veneer for his military regime. Public outrage over the absence of universal adult suffrage eventually challenged his hold on power, pushing him to resign in early 1969.

Azad, Abu`l-Kalam (1888–1958)

A religious scholar and politician, renowned for his advocacy of a free and undivided **India**. After gaining prominence as a nationalist journalist and publisher of the paper *al-Hilal*, Azad became a leading member of the Indian **Khilafat movement**. In 1923 he was elected president of the **Indian National Congress**, and served as president again from 1940 to 1946. After India's independence, he became India's first Minister of Education.

Azerbaijan

Azerbaijan (population around 10 million) is a country in the South Caucasus bordering the Caspian Sea, **Russia**, **Iran**, **Armenia**, **Georgia** and **Turkey**. Amid the collapse of the tsarist empire, in April 1918 Azeri nationalists proclaimed Azerbajian, carved out of oil-rich Baku and neighbouring provinces, to be part of an independent Transcaucasian Federation (joined by Georgia and Armenia). When this collapsed a month later, nationalist leaders declared an 'Azerbaijani Democratic Republic', which fell until August 1919 under Ottoman and British occupation. The **Red Army** established Soviet rule in April 1920. It was incorporated into the USSR as part of the Transcaucasian Soviet Federative Socialist Republic in December 1922. From the late 1980s, tensions with Armenia over **Nagorno-Karabakh**, an Armenian-majority enclave, have dominated regional politics. Displacing over a million refugees and claiming tens of thousands of lives, fighting between Armenian separatists and Azeri forces intensified following the Soviet collapse in 1991 and continued until a ceasefire in 1994. Oil and gas exports and the authoritarian rule of the Aliyev family have been persistent features of the independence era.

Azhari, Ismail al- (1902–1969)

A Sudanese politician, Ismail al-Azhari served as **Sudan**'s first prime minister and later as president. Born in Omdurman, he studied at Gordon Memorial College and the American University in Beirut. He became involved in Sudanese nationalist politics in 1931 with the establishment of the Graduates' Congress Party (GCP). Azhari co-founded the Ashigga Party in 1943, which favoured cooperation with **Egypt** over **Great Britain**. Under the umbrella National Unionist Party, Ashigga and similar groups selected him as prime minister in 1954. He held this position for the remainder of the self-rule period and the early months of Sudanese independence. Forced out in July 1956 after a vote of no confidence, he remained involved in politics until his election as president in 1965. He served until his government was overthrown by a military coup in May 1969, and died a few months later in custody.

Aziz, Shah Abdul (1745–1824)

A religious scholar and teacher in Delhi. The son of famous reformer **Shah Waliullah**, he was a distinguished scholar of Hadith, acquiring a large circle of disciples and issuing influential fatwas, especially on subjects related to the advent of British rule. A subtle pragmatist, he urged his co-religionists to adjust to the times, declaring it legal under present circumstances to receive interest, learn English and take employment with the British.

B

Ba'ath Party

A leading political party in **Syria** and **Iraq**, the Arab Ba'ath Socialist Party, as it is officially known, combined two strands of thought that had been most influential among Arab intellectuals in the interwar years: pan-Arabism and radical social change. The Ba'ath (resurrection) Party was founded in Damascus in 1947 by Salah al-Din al-Bitar, a Sunni Muslim, **Michel Aflaq**, an Orthodox Christian, and the followers of Zaki al-Arsuzi, an Alawite. Under the slogan 'Unity, Freedom, Socialism', the Ba'ath had a revolutionary agenda seeking to bring about a complete transformation of Arab societies. Ba'athi socialism was not based on western thinkers but was explicitly defined as Arab socialism which, the Ba'athists maintained, had its origins with the prophet Muhammad. Their political vision was predicated on the belief in the existence of one Arab nation and that this Arab nation has the natural right to live in one large state. This pan-Arab state would restore Arab dignity and put an end to social inequality and class exploitation and be better equipped to resist foreign imperialism.

Soon the party's platform attracted followers from beyond Syria. In 1958 members of the Syrian Ba'ath Party approached Egyptian President **Gamal Abdel Nasser** about forming a union which eventually became the **United Arab Republic** (1958–61). This new republic was dominated by Egypt and the Syrian Ba'athists played only minor roles. After the dissolution of the United Arab Republic in 1961, a significant power struggle emerged within the party both between the civilian and military members, on the one hand, and between Iraqis and Syrians, on the other. At its 1963 congress a split also emerged between those who wanted to take the party further to the left, especially in its economic policies, which leading ideologue Michel Aflaq was dissatisfied with. In 1963 the Ba'ath party carried out a *coup d'état* in **Syria**. One of the leaders of this coup was **Hafiz al-Assad**, a commander in the

Syrian air force, who became Secretary of Defence. This new government instituted a social agenda that was inspired by Ba'athism. It nationalized more than a hundred companies and expropriated and redistributed agricultural lands held by the landowning elite. At the same time, in **Iraq**, the Ba'ath Party became the leading political party in government after the Arif brothers successively became presidents. In 1970 al-Assad was able to consolidate his power and became president of Syria, and similiarly in 1979 **Saddam Hussein**, also a member of the Ba'ath Party, became president of Iraq.

Ironically for a party committed to positive social change and Arab unity, the Ba'ath Party in Iraq and Syria were bitter rivals and fervently nationalistic. The party served as a vehicle to preserve brutal and oppressive authoritarian military regimes and the perpetuation of a small elite, rather than as a redistributer of wealth and eradicator of social inequality. During the 1970s and 1980s the party rhetoric became hollow and meaningless. The Ba'ath oppressed its citizens and held them hostage. Ba'ath party rule in Iraq came to an end in 2003 but continued in Syria following the death of al-Assad, when his son Bashar became president in 2000.

Baghdad Pact

An anti-communist military alliance, also known as the Central Treaty Organization. Created in 1955, it was part of the US **Cold War** policy of containment to develop a network of interlocking alliances across Asia to serve as a barrier to Soviet expansion. The member states consisted of **Iraq**, **Turkey**, **Iran**, **Pakistan** and the **United Kingdom**. The **United States** was not formally part of the alliance but was a member of its military committee. Initially the alliance was based in the Iraqi capital Baghdad. Leading Arab nationalists such as Egyptian President **Gamal Abdel Nasser** criticized the alliance for being an instrument of American imperialism. After the 1958 coup that overthrew Iraq's Hashemite monarchy, Iraq withdrew from the alliance and the headquarters were moved to Ankara, Turkey, until the alliance was dissolved in 1979 just after the **Iranian Revolution**.

Bahadur Shah Zafar (1775–1862)

Bahadur Shah Zafar, ascending the throne in 1837, was the last Mughal emperor of India. While his real talents lay in calligraphy and Urdu poetry, in 1857 the reluctant 82-year-old was made a symbolic leader of the **Indian mutiny and revolt** against the English **East India Company**. After the British crushed the rebellion in 1858, Bahadur Shah was exiled to Rangoon where he died in abject circumstances, heartbroken and destitute.

Bahamas

The Bahamas consist of about 700 islands, only thirty of which are inhabited, stretching about 600 miles east south-east from the Florida Strait. Christopher Columbus landed on one of them in 1492, when they were inhabited by Lucayan Indians; after that, their position on the homebound route for Spanish vessels made them an ideal base for pirates. The emergence of the **United States** led to other dangerous activities; they served as a base for blockade-runners during the **American Civil War**, and were used by liquor-smugglers during the era of **Prohibition**. Today the islands are an independent nation within the British **Commonwealth**, with a population of about 300,000, many of whom live in the capital, Nassau, on New Providence.

Bahia

A state in north-eastern **Brazil**, 564,830,859 square kilometres in size, and with a multiracial population. Heavily dependent on sugar production using black slavery during the colonial period, its economy stagnated through most of the nineteenth century. Cacao became its major export from 1907 into the 1930s. Agriculture, commerce, industry and tourism now underpin its economy.

Bahrain

Small Muslim Arab kingdom located in the Arabian Gulf, ruled by the Al Khalifah family since 1783, with its capital at Manamah. A number of islands comprise the country, and various disputes with neighbouring **Qatar** plagued relations between the two countries until their resolution by the International Court of Justice in 2001. **Iran** has also laid claim to the islands based on historic occupation. Bahrain was the first Gulf state to begin exporting oil in 1932, and oil wealth provided for steady economic development. Politically the emirate was a British protectorate beginning in 1892 and became independent on 15 August 1971. Amir Hamad ibn Isa Al Khalifa introduced wide-ranging political reforms following his succession in March 1999 and proclaimed the kingdom in 2002. Bahrain's major political issue is the dispute between the Sunni Al Khalifah ruling family and the demands of the Shi'ite majority population for greater political participation (which resulted in widespread protests after the **Arab Spring**).

Balaguer Ricardo, Joaquín (1907–2002)

Born in Navarrete, Dominican Republic, Balaguer was a writer, diplomat and government official during General **Rafael Leonidas Trujillo**'s rule. President after Hector Trujillo's resignation in 1960, Balaguer was ousted by the military in 1962 and left the country. Subsequently elected president in 1966, 1970 and 1974, he returned to office in 1986 and served until 1996. Cronyism and political repression helped him to stay in office.

balance of power

A theory of European state relations associated particularly with English foreign policy between 1533 and 1918, the Treaties of Westphalia in 1618 and **Utrecht** in 1713, and **Klemens von Metternich**, but actually of longer standing. It held that European security could only be guaranteed by an antagonistic balance of empires within the continent, so that no one state or empire was ever allowed to dominate or aspire to dominate **Europe**. The theory called for states, and especially plenipotential foreign ministers, to ruthlessly patrol their interests, sometimes in secret, and to associate with whatever ally was necessary to contain an otherwise dominant bloc; this sometimes led to a logic of geographical alliances, sometimes to a sympathy of liberal or autocratic states, sometimes to guarantees of mutual assistance in the event of a war. The system was extremely strained by the emergence of the German Second Reich after 1871, which presented a power which could potentially have dominated all except the **United Kingdom** on its own. In response, by 1905 the balance of power hardened into one in which two great alliances emerged, with Britain, **France** and **Russia** on one side, and Germany, **Italy** and **Austria–Hungary** on the other. This system degenerated, because of the Balkan crisis of 1911–14, into **World War I**, which swept away or severely weakened the empires which had practised it by 1918, and which introduced the **League of Nations** system. Later, **Henry Kissinger** – whose doctoral thesis had been concerned with Metternich and the balance of power – tried to apply the idea to 'trilateral diplomacy' by introducing the People's Republic of **China** into America's global cold war competition with the **Soviet Union**, on the American side. The metaphor of a balance of power is often used by neorealist political scientists to explain environments in which multiple states which are potential or actual rivals seek to secure a way of living together without necessarily embracing trade or international law.

Balewa, Abubakar Tafawa (1912–1966)

First prime minister of independent **Nigeria**. Born in northern Nigeria to a Muslim family, he was trained as a teacher and studied at London University. He served in the colonial government and founded the Northern People's Congress, which as part of a coalition won elections prior to independence in 1960. He was chosen as prime minister and was re-elected in 1964, but was overthrown and killed in a military coup two years later.

Balfour Declaration

Official British declaration of sympathy with Zionist aspirations which Foreign Secretary Arthur Balfour addressed to Lionel Walter Rothschild, honorary president of Great Britain's Zionist Federation, on 2 November 1917. The British government viewed with favour 'the establishment in Palestine of a national home for the Jewish people'. The declaration was an official foreign policy statement of the British War Cabinet. It was national policy in the sense that it represented the views of all three British political parties. It had international status since **Britain**'s principal allies – **France**, **Italy**, **Russia** and the **United States** – had all given it their prior approval. **China**, **Japan** and **Siam** would subsequently approve.

The origins of the Balfour Declaration can be traced back to Herbert Samuel, the only Jewish member of Asquith's cabinet. After the Ottomans went to war with Britain on 5 November 1914, Samuel stressed that Britain and the Jews held common interests in detaching **Palestine** from the **Ottoman Empire**. Britain should therefore encourage Zionist aspirations. **Chaim Weizmann**, the major figure within the Zionist movement promoting such a declaration, at first worked independently of Samuel. Weizmann was a major scientific contributor to the British war effort and was admired and recognized by **Lloyd George** when he was British Minister of Munitions. In November 1916 Lloyd George became prime minister. Because of the pressures

of the war effort he, Weizmann, Samuel and Balfour were all inclined to support some sort of British pledge in favour of the Zionist cause. Furthermore, after the democratic revolution in Russia in March 1917 and the overthrow of tsardom, British leaders hoped that their support for Zionism might win over Russian Jews and help keep Russia in the war. The same logic applied to winning over American Jews after the United States entered the war on Britain's side in April 1917. Balfour stressed the international value of the declaration when he won the British War Cabinet's endorsement of it on 31 October 1917. The Allied conference at San Remo, Italy, on 24 April 1920 approved the incorporation of the Balfour Declaration into the **Mandate** for Palestine, which the **League of Nations** conferred on Britain on 24 July 1922. A struggle over its implementation then ensued, lasting until Britain returned the mandate to the League's successor organization, the **United Nations**, in the autumn of 1947.

Balkan Wars

The First Balkan War broke out, October 1912, when **Bulgaria, Greece**, Montenegro and **Serbia** asserted their national claims over **Turkey**'s remaining Balkan empire. The Turkish armies were defeated within a month. The resulting peace conference, involving all the Great Powers, reached agreement on independence for **Albania**, declared independent by the Treaty of London, May 1913. The other provisions of the treaty were soon overtaken by Bulgarian resentment at the Serbian occupation of the whole of Macedonia and the Greek seizure of Salonica (Thessaloniki) and much of the Aegean coast. Bulgaria launched the Second Balkan War, June 1913, but was soon defeated by Greece and Serbia, joined by **Romania**, which wanted the Dobrudja. The ensuing Treaty of Bucharest, August 1913, awarded Bulgaria only a narrow strip of Macedonia and eastern Thrace, while Greece and Serbia kept their gains. Romania secured the Dobrudja and Turkey retained Edirne (Adrianople).

Balkans

Culturally divided since the second half of the first millennium between the Orthodox south and the Roman Catholic north, and, with the exception of small Montenegro (Crna Gora), part of the **Ottoman Empire** from, in general, the fourteenth and fifteenth centuries until the seventeenth in the far north and the early twentieth in parts of the south. Significant conversion to **Islam** under the Turks only in **Bosnia–Hercegovina** and in **Albania**, the latter being Europe's sole predominantly Islamic state. Albanians were prominent in the Ottoman Empire's administration in the eighteenth and nineteenth centuries and the khedives of **Egypt** were of ethnic Albanian stock. Predominantly Slav in population, but Greek to the south, Albanian to the south-west, Romanian to the east and Hungarian on the northern perimeter. The Balkan nationalisms resurfaced progressively throughout the nineteenth century, as Turkish authority weakened, and defined themselves to no small degree by their anti-Islamic and anti-Turkish character. **Serbia** rebelled first, 1804, gaining recognized autonomy, 1829. **Greece** was the first to gain full independence, 1830. Moldavia and Wallachia, the core of modern **Romania**, gained autonomy, 1856, and **Bulgaria** followed, 1878. The full independence of Romania and Serbia recognized, 1878, and of Bulgaria, 1908. Albania formally independent, 1912.

The weakening of Turkish power in the south was mirrored by the less pronounced weakening of Austro-Hungarian power in the north, provoking the tension between **Austria–Hungary** and Serbia over the political vacuum of Bosnia, which culminated first in the 1908 **Bosnian crisis** and then in the events triggering **World War I**. The nineteenth-century Balkan nationalisms received little positive help from the Great Powers, who were always concerned about the possible impact on their own empires and tended to favour dealing with a single authority to facilitate their own schemes for economic development. Retaining the balance of power between themselves over such sensitive issues as the control of **Constantinople** (Istanbul) was the prime consideration. Nationalism in the Balkans, however, was always problematic and remains so. Ethnic groups were everywhere intermingled, and large areas had either no obvious national identity or multiple ones. Near identical ethnic and linguistic groups like the Serbs and Croats were divided by culture, history and religion. The **Balkan Wars**, 1912–13, were a predictable consequence, as were the undeclared interwar conflicts between Bulgaria and **Yugoslavia** over Macedonia and between **Hungary** and Romania over **Transylvania**.

Most Balkan states were under authoritarian control in the interwar period, followed in many cases by Communist rule, after **World War II**, with the notable exception of Greece, which joined **NATO**. Bulgaria and Romania remained in the Soviet bloc, while Yugoslavia and Albania followed forms of one-party communist rule independent of the **Soviet Union**.

From 1990 the Balkans were convulsed by the collapse of Soviet communism and by the break-up of Yugoslavia following the death of **Tito** and the ensuing bitter ethnic and religious conflict. Out of these two developments emerged a multiplicity of new states and the adoption, with various degrees of success, of multiparty rule, though often compromised or invalidated by problems of corruption. Some states have joined the **European Union** and others are candidate members in which the EU has sought to promote liberal democracy as a key to future membership. There is also a residue of ethnic and national bitterness in areas affected by human rights abuses following the break-up of Yugoslavia.

Balta Liman, Commercial Convention of (1838)

In search of new markets for manufactured goods, the British government seized on a political crisis in the **Ottoman Empire** to demand a commercial treaty favourable to their interests. Egyptian ruler **Mehmet Ali**'s invasion (1832) had left the Ottoman Empire reeling. In need of British support the *Porte* was in dire need of allies to help extricate the Egyptian forces from **Syria** and agreed to open their economy completely to British traders by signing the commercial convention at Balta Liman. Thereafter, the Ottoman inability to protect their manufacturing hampered the development of industry in the empire.

Baltic states

A name generally applied to Estonia, Latvia and Lithuania, as well as occasionally **Finland**, because of their shared history and proximity to the Baltic Sea. Estonia, Latvia and Lithuania gained independence from the **Russian Empire** in 1918, though they had previously enjoyed long histories, with Lithuania in particular having been a great medieval power. This first experience of independence, however, was undermined by **World War II**, in which many took the side of Nazi **Germany** against the **Soviet Union**; after 1945 the states were absorbed once more into a Russian-dominated entity, the **USSR**, subsisting as Soviet republics before mass peaceful rebellion and secession between 1989 and 1991. They then petitioned for, and thirteen years later were accepted into, full membership of the **European Union** and **NATO**. 'The Baltics', with small populations, have been typified ever since by

Atlanticist politics, low tax, pro-business policies and openness to the outside world.

Bandaranaike, Sirimavo (1916–2000)

Prime Minister of **Sri Lanka**, 1960–5, 1970–7 and 1994–2000. After her 1940 marriage to S. W. R. D. Bandaranaike (Prime Minister of Ceylon, 1956–9), she bore three children. On her husband's assassination she inherited the leadership of the Sri Lankan Freedom Party and became the first female elected prime minister in 1960. Under her leadership, the SLFP government continued implementation of socialist economic policies, diplomatic neutrality and state promotion of Sinhalese language and Buddhism.

bandits

Marxist historian Eric Hobsbawm invented the term 'social bandits' in his 1969 book *Bandits*. He used poems and ballads to construct the social image of individuals living in rural societies but involved in robbing and pillage. Hobsbawm suggested bandits should be understood in their social and historical contexts, where they are seen as heroes fighting for freedom and justice, inspiring social resistance, and are often sustained by local communities. Bandits express primitive forms of rebellion and appear spontaneously and sporadically in many societies. Hobsbawm's thesis was criticized on the grounds that it depicted ideals more than realities, and that bandits are simply predatory criminals.

Bandung conference (1955)

The first international conference held on 17 April 1955 by independent Asian and African states at Bandung in Java, **Indonesia**. It brought together twenty-nine states and called for world peace and the neutrality of lesser developed countries during the period of the **Cold War** in an effort to promote economic and cultural cooperation. The conference promoted the non-alignment movement and led to the adoption of five principal tenets: non-aggression, respect for sovereignty, non-interference in internal affairs, equality and peaceful co-existence. However, the deterioration of relations between **India** and **China** subsequently limited the impact of the movement and the significance of the conference.

Banerjea, Surendranath (1848–1926)

A leader of Indian nationalism from **Bengal**, Banerjea passed the Indian Civil Service exam, but was cast out of the service and turned to educational activity and nationalist agitation. He helped found the Indian Association and the **Indian National Congress**. A moderate in the nationalist movement, he joined the nationalists in the Swadeshi movement but opposed the extremists' means of action. Near the end of his life he was a minister of the Bengal government in the 1920s.

Bangladesh

An independent nation formed from East Pakistan, or the east wing of the nation of **Pakistan**. When the British left **India** in 1947, they divided India into two nations and Pakistan into a nation of two wings, one to the west of India, one to its east. Relations between the two parts of Pakistan became ever more strained when politicians in the eastern wing representing the **Awami League** won all the seats in the east in the 1970 elections. A military crackdown prevented these Bengali politicians from taking power, but after a civil war and then Indian military intervention, East Pakistan became the new nation of Bangladesh. A densely populated nation, it has experienced frequent military coups and then military rule during its more than three decades of existence. Mostly Muslim, it also has a significant Hindu minority. There is a growing radical Islamic movement. Most of the country is low-lying land cross cut by rivers and subject to natural disasters.

Bani-Sadr, Abolhassan (1933–)

First president of the Islamic Republic of **Iran**. Born to an ayatollah who was close to **Ruhollah Khomeini**. He studied economics at the University of Tehran, and was a leader of the student movement against the Shah in the early 1960s. He fled to **France** to study economics at the Sorbonne, obtaining a doctorate. An adviser to the exiled Khomeini in Paris, he returned with him to Iran in February 1979, to become Deputy Minister and then Minister of Finance. A member of the Revolutionary Council, he was Foreign Minister in November 1979. He was elected president of the Islamic Republic in January 1980 and was briefly commander-in-chief in the **Iran–Iraq War** (June 1981).

A Muslim democrat rather than an Islamist, he was opposed to the Islamist Mohammad Ali Raja'i as his prime minister, and seen as a rival by clerics such as Rafsanjani and Khameini. He disagreed with the prolongation of the **Tehran Embassy hostage crisis**. Impeached by the *majli*, 21 June 1981, he was dismissed by Khomeini, who also ordered his arrest for conspiracy and treason. He fled to France, where he was granted political asylum. He formed the National Council of Resistance against the government and was its chairman until 1984.

Bank of the United States, First

The First Bank of the United States, located in Philadelphia, Pennsylvania, was a critical part of Treasury Secretary **Alexander Hamilton**'s plan for creating a modern financial system in the new republic. Agrarian interests opposed the bank, which they believed unreasonably favoured mercantile and commercial interests. Supporters argued, however, that it would guarantee stability for the new nation by encouraging rich Americans to take a financial stake in the success of the new government.

Bank of the United States, Second

Congress chartered the Second Bank for twenty years in 1816, after five years of financial chaos. Essentially a commercial bank with some public responsibilities, it pursued irresponsible policies until Nicholas Biddle, president from 1822, conducted it more like a modern central bank and as a restraining force on state banks. In 1832 President **Andrew Jackson** vetoed a recharter bill on constitutional grounds, and in 1833 withdrew all federal monies. The ensuing political protests could not prevent the national bank from expiring in 1836.

banking

A process vital to capitalism in which banks serve as secure stores of money for investors, a clearing system for transactions and the originators of credit while allowing economic agents to leverage their assets. At different times, banks have been organized in diverse ways. For example, from the late medieval until the early modern period banking was associated with families and religious orders, and was based upon the unlimited liability of the owners. Generally, this form of banking was connected with the need of kings and princes to borrow money, or of shipowners to finance trade. It was made very difficult by defaults, the lack of real bills of exchange, and a prohibition on interest which led to complicated dual-purchase arrangements. Very few family banking concerns survived into the modern period. By the nineteenth century joint stock banks allowed industrialists to leverage their capital and future projections of return against loans at interest, and encouraged the transfer by landowners of economic rent into capital through mechanisms such as mortgages. These had evolved from the joint stock model of central banks, which allowed

for the emergence of bond-based national debts, through monopolies, to the appearance of private organizations.

Around the turn of the twentieth century banks transmuted into merchant banks, which carried on sophisticated financial activity at risk, often with unlimited liability, and retail banks, which allowed ordinary savers the opportunity to gain access to long-term finance for house purchases, career development or consumption. In addition, a 'shadow finance' industry, concerned with providing funds to allow the purchase of goods from particular stores or manufacturers, such as automobile makers, arose. Also during the twentieth century, central banks were created in every country which generally issued paper currency backed only by their own guarantee, or by a nominal commitment to gold. The combination of these developments led governments to restrict or prohibit the interaction of banks open to customers and banks which operated in the financial markets from the 1930s until the 1990s. When electronic technology and globalization made this impossible to maintain, walls between institutions were removed.

By the early twenty-first century a new, global banking environment had thus emerged. It did not matter whether banks emerged in an oligopoly environment which provided a variety of 'free' services, as in **Britain**, or in highly competitive markets, as in the United States. Instead, all were under huge pressure to deliver returns, finance mortgages and maintain credit. The combination of these globalized pressures with the development of derivatives and insurance systems based around highly sophisticated electronic technology was a key factor in the near collapse of the western banking system in 2008. The system was saved by massive and coordinated government intervention, through subsidies, low or negative interest rates on currencies from central banks and bond purchases by government institutions, at the cost of a debt transfer to state budgets.

The crisis of 2008 gave rise to intense examination of banking. Though global trade and currency imbalances, as well as a rebalancing of the world economy from the Atlantic to the Pacific countries had also been to blame, works by theorists such as Hyman Minsky suggested that reckless lending by banks which had to maintain the appearance of lending growth were culpable. Others turned to the idea that banks had forced individuals to leverage all potential asset values – economic rent – and thus had departed from industrial investment, creating a cycle of outsourcing and job and manufacturing transfer which was not in the long-run interest of hitherto rich societies. A few pointed to **Marx**'s prediction about monopoly finance eventually leading to economic crisis, as well as to the perceived ethical failings of bankers who had been previously operating according to largely amoral individualism. Regardless, the crisis was not satisfactorily 'solved' in any state; the effect of accumulated government and personal debt on aggregate demand was at least enough to prevent the monetary and fiscal bank relief measures from creating an immediate hyperinflation.

Banna, Hassan al- (1906–1949)

Egyptian founder of the **Muslim Brotherhood**. Born in Mahmudiyya in the Nile delta, where his father, Sheikh Ahmad al-Banna, was an imam and a mosque teacher following the puritanical Hanbali school of **sharia** law, whose well-regarded work on the Hanbali school had brought relationships with the Islamic scholars of Cairo. Experienced an upbringing marked by a strong emphasis on Islamic values and the interpretations of the Hanbali school, but also influenced by **Rashid Rida**'s journal, *al-Manar*, the Salafism of Muhammad 'Abduh and Sufism, joining the Hassafiyyah order at the age of 15. Had already been a demonstrator, publisher of political pamphlets and founder of youth reform societies during the **Egyptian Revolution of 1919**. Moved to Cairo, 1923, where, against his father's wishes, he attended the Dar al-Ulum, which trained teachers in modern subjects, for four years, but also built on his father's connections to meet the leading Islamic scholars of the time and to become associated with the Islamic Society for Nobility of Islamic Morals and the Young Men's Muslim Association. Shocked by the social secularization and the abandonment of **Islam** by the young of Cairo, he concluded that the young must be re-educated to resist the influence of the West. He graduated in 1927 to become an Arabic language teacher in Isma'iliya, then the Egyptian town most exposed to European influences. This confirmed him in his hostility to British colonialism and suspicion of western concepts. Active as a preacher and teacher of adults, who sought to reinvigorate Islamic civilization and shared the conviction of Muhammad 'Abduh and Rashid Rida that the answer was to return to the perceived purity of early Islam, but dissented from their analysis that stagnation and traditionalism were the principal barrier and argued that the true enemies were western cultural, political imperialism and **secularism**, not least as espoused by the **Wafd** within Egypt.

Banna founded the Muslim Brotherhood in Isma'iliya in March 1928. Its motto was 'Allah is our purpose, the Prophet our leader, the Qur'an our constitution, **jihad** our way, and dying for Allah's cause our supreme objective.' By 1939 the Brotherhood had 500,000 active members across the Arab world, reflecting Banna's organizational genius as well as his ideological fervour. He endowed the Brotherhood with sophisticated governance structures anchored in pre-existing social networks, and its members enjoyed material, psychological and social support. These open activities were partnered by a network of underground cells which stole weapons and planned violence, and reflected Banna's belief that contemporary Islam was misguided in its interpretation of jihad as being primarily about the duty of battle with the inner devil rather than about the violent war against the enemies of Islam. His parallel emphasis as a Salafi on the restoration of the lost caliphate as an immediate political goal has, however, been dismissed as political expediency by some Salafis. Banna established links with Nazi Germany as a natural ally against both the British and Jewish Zionists in **Palestine**, but was also attracted by its worship of violence and cult of death and martyrdom. The Brotherhood's underground network surfaced after **World War II** with a series of bombings and assassinations, culminating in that of the prime minister, Mahmoud el-Noqrashi Pasha, in December 1948. Although Banna had condemned the assassination, he was assassinated himself three months later, almost certainly by government agents.

Bantustans

Ten areas in **South Africa** and ten in South African-administered South West Africa (now **Namibia**) set aside for the black population under **apartheid** in 1962, the white minority allocating 81 per cent of cultivable land to themselves and 19 per cent to the black majority. Effectively black reservations, they were renamed 'homelands' in 1968 and a number were granted a spurious independence, though none gained international recognition. The homelands were abolished in 1994 after the fall of apartheid.

Barbados

Barbados is an island in the Lesser Antilles. Independent from **Britain** since 1966, its major historical significance is as the place which first developed and perfected the sugar–slavery complex that brought great wealth to a small number of English planters and great misery to thousands of enslaved Africans who formed the majority of the workforce. Slavery was abolished in 1838.

Barbary pirates

An umbrella description for the Muslim pirates based along the North African (Barbary) coast from **Libya** to **Morocco**, who were active for centuries until the nineteenth, and at their most powerful in the seventeenth when those of **Algeria** and **Tunisia** joined forces, holding 30,000 captives in Algiers alone in 1650. The pirate captains of the cities of Algiers and Tunis were a distinct social class whose vessels were fitted out by wealthy backers who claimed 10 per cent of the proceeds in return. Provincial sultans under the Ottomans were no less ready to encourage piracy for its valuable revenue. Piracy inevitably came into conflict with the expanding commercial interests of the western powers during the nineteenth century. Although there was warfare between those of Libya and the **United States**, piracy had become focused on Algeria, and first the British tried to crush it twice after 1815 and then the French terminated it by occupying Algeria in 1830.

Baring, Sir Evelyn

– *see* **Cromer, Earl of**.

Barnum, Phineas Taylor (1810–1891)

This Connecticut native entered show business in the mid 1830s. His American Museum (1842) on Broadway offered freak shows and much publicized 'humbugs' (hoaxes) to both the delight and disappointment of millions. He came out of semi-retirement in 1871 to establish his globetrotting circus, 'the Greatest Show on Earth', and fitfully collaborated from 1881 with rival James Bailey. A Republican who served in the legislature of Connecticut and a conscientious mayor of Bridgeport, election to the US Congress eluded him.

Barth, Heinrich (1821–1865)

German explorer of West Africa. On British commission, Barth crossed the Sahara from **Libya** to Lake Chad in 1850. He spent five years travelling in western **Sudan**, from Timbuktu to Borno and Adamawa (Northern Nigeria and **Cameroon**), visiting the Muslim states (including the **Sokoto Caliphate**) and collecting historical as well as anthropological and geographic information. His travel narrative remains one of our most important sources for the period.

Barton, Clara (1821–1912)

Founder of the American Red Cross. A teacher and civil servant in her early career, at the outbreak of the **American Civil War** she collected and distributed medical supplies to hospitals and camps; later she became a nurse and started a missing persons agency. After the war she became involved with the International **Red Cross** and lobbied for American ratification of the **Geneva Treaty**. In 1881 she organized the American Association of the Red Cross (chartered 1893), in whose humanitarian efforts she was fully involved until her death.

Barzani, Mustafa (1903–1979)

One of the most prominent **Kurdish nationalists** of the twentieth century. Born in Ottoman Mosul to a locally prominent family, Barzani was a leading figure in Kurdish activism in interwar **Iraq** and led a Kurdish insurrection in 1941. In 1946 he joined the short-lived Mahabad Republic, serving as its field marshal until the republic collapsed early the next year. It was during this period that he helped to create the Kurdistan Democratic Party (KDP) of Iraq, which he would lead until his death. After the collapse of the Mahabad Republic he fled to the **Soviet Union** where he lived in exile until 1958, when he was allowed to return to Iraq. By 1961 he was once more agitating for Kurdish independence, with a full-scale insurrection breaking out in 1974. Iraq quickly crushed the rebellion and, in 1975, Barzani was again forced into exile, first in **Iran**, and then in the **United States**.

Basques

A distinctive ethnic and linguistic group, long settled along the Atlantic coast of **France** and **Spain** and known to themselves as the *Euskadi*. Frequently in conflict with the central government of Spain, the Spanish Basques developed a strong sense of national identity and growing self-confidence with the industrial development of northern Spain. They formed the Partido Nacionalista Vasco (PNV) which under its leader José Antonio Aquirre (1904–60) grew into a mass movement during the 1930s demanding complete autonomy within the Spanish Republic, but with a Catholic-orientated Christian Democratic agenda. Following the outbreak of the **Spanish Civil War**, most Basques sided with the Republic against **Franco**, setting up a Basque Republic of Euzkadi with Aquirre as president. The Basque country was the scene of the terror bombing of the historic Basque capital of **Guernica** in April 1937 and was finally overrun by Nationalist forces in June 1937, forcing

Aquirre into exile. After his victory, Franco suppressed the Basque language and removed all autonomy, forcing Basque nationalism underground. It developed a terrorist wing Euzkadi ta Askatasuna (ETA) from 1959, carrying out several hundred assassinations, including the Spanish prime minister in 1973. Following Franco's death and the return of democracy, the Basque country was granted substantial autonomy by statute in 1979, though ETA continued its terror campaign for complete independence. Its political wing obtained only a minority of seats in the Basque parliament, its continued terrorism alienating support as the region prospered with EU membership. Successive failed ceasefires and the banning of its political wing, Herri Batasuna, in 2002 showed that ETA has not disappeared entirely, though the majority of the Basque region does not support it. However, in 2011 a definitive ceasefire was proclaimed by ETA.

Basutoland
– *see* **Lesotho**.

Batavian Republic
Netherlands republic established on 19 January 1795 which, though imposed by the occupying French to supersede the United Provinces of the **Netherlands**, nonetheless proved popular. *Batavi* derives from a Germanic tribe that resisted Roman occupation, adopted by the Dutch as their mythological ancestors. The republic adopted a formal democratic constitution in 1798. In 1805 it became the Batavian Commonwealth, replaced in 1806 by the Kingdom of Holland under **Napoleon**'s brother Louis Bonaparte.

Batista, Fulgencio (1901–1973)
Fulgencio Batista y Zaldívar governed **Cuba** twice: the first time quite effectively in 1933–44 after organizing the 'sergeants' revolt' and replacing Carlos Manuel de Céspedes. During his second regime (1952–9) he ruled as a dictator, jailing alleged foes and enriching himself and his associates. He controlled Congress, the press and the universities, until the revolutionary forces of **Fidel Castro** successfully attacked the regime in 1958, whereupon Battista fled Cuba and went into exile on the **Dominican Republic**.

Battle of Britain
– *see* **Britain, Battle of**.

Bavarian Succession, War of (1778–1779)
A short and relatively bloodless conflict from July 1778 to May 1779 between **Austria** and a Prussian–Saxon alliance over the disputed succession to the Duchy of Bavaria. The war, also known as the 'Potato War' because Prussian troops passed their time picking potatoes, ended with the Peace of Tetschen, by which the duchy remained with Charles IV Theodore, Prussia gained Ansbach and Bayreuth, and Austria a strip on the border with Bavaria.

Bay of Pigs (1961)
On 17 April 1961 fifteen hundred American CIA-trained Cuban exiles landed at the Bay of Pigs in **Cuba**. The objective was to trigger an uprising that would overthrow **Fidel Castro**. However, without air cover and outnumbered by Cuban forces, the exiles were quickly defeated and captured. Operation Pluto has been described as the 'perfect failure' of American intelligence and military and political intervention.

Bayar, Mahmut Celal (1883–1986)
A prominent Turkish nationalist who is particularly associated with economic liberals in the early **Turkish Republic**. He joined the Union and Progress Party after the **Young Turk Revolution** of 1908, and was elected to the Ottoman parliament in 1919. He soon joined the nationalist resistance, under the leadership of **Mustafa Kemal**, and fled to Ankara in 1920. In 1921 he became Economy Minister for the nationalist government and served as an adviser to the Turkish delegation at the **Lausanne Treaty** negotiations. Serving alternately as Economy Minister and Public Works Minister, he was instrumental in developing state industries and banks. In 1934, with the promulgation of the surname law, he took the family name Bayar. In 1937 he became prime minister of Turkey, serving until 1939. In 1945 Bayar became one of the founders of the Democrat Party, which won the first fully free elections in 1950. He served as president of the republic from 1950 to 1960, when the government was deposed in a *coup d'état*. He was released from prison in 1964.

BBC
The British Broadcasting Corporation, established in 1922 but chartered in 1927 as a public corporation funded by a flat-charge tax now based upon ownership of any apparatus that can receive television signals, known as the 'TV licence'. The BBC was precluded from carrying commercial advertising on its electronic services and charged with a mission to 'entertain, educate and explain'. It is governed by a royal charter, renewed by Parliament every ten years, and is independent of government, under the control of a board of

trustees. The BBC broadcasts on radio and television worldwide, commissions a wide range of television programmes, and has a lucrative operation in sales of programmes to foreign stations and the public. It was the model for a number of other public broadcasters across the former **British Empire**, but has no peer in its domination of domestic news, digital channels and funding arrangements. For many years it drove electronic culture and was the major force in commissioning new art on television and radio despite the establishment of commercial rivals in 1955.

Bechuanaland
– see **Botswana**.

Bedouin
– see **nomadism**.

Begin, Menachem (1923–1992)
Zionist leader and prime minister of **Israel**, 1977–83. Under the guidance of his mentor **Vladimir Jabotinsky**, Begin rose to command the Betar (Zionist Revisionist) movement in his native **Poland**. At the outbreak of **World War II** he escaped to the **USSR**, where he was jailed for Zionist activities. After **Stalin**'s 1941 pact with Polish Prime Minister Władysław Sikorsky, Begin was released from jail, joined General Władysław Anders' Free Polish Army, and, with that army, made his way via **Iran** to **Palestine**. There he left the army and, in 1943–8, commanded the Revisionist underground anti-British army, the **Irgun Zvai Leumi**. Begin approved the Irgun's 22 July 1946 demolition of the British Army headquarters in Jerusalem's King David Hotel, which, despite the warning that had been given, resulted in the deaths of ninety-one Jews, Arabs and English nationals. Equally controversial, in Israel's 1948 War of Independence, the Irgun under Begin's command participated in fighting at the Arab village of Deir Yassin, which resulted in heavy Arab civilian casualties.

As a member of the Israeli Knesset (parliament) from 1948 to 1983, Begin led the **Likud** party in opposition to **Ben–Gurion**'s **Mapai** (Labour) Party. Begin successfully urged the lifting of military rule and the establishment of civilian rule in many Israeli–Arab regions of the country. Military rule enabled those areas to repeatedly vote Labor. In 1952 he lead violent demonstrations against Israel's acceptance of reparations payments from **Germany**. Because of his participation he was barred from the Knesset for several months. On the eve of the June 1967 war Mapai Prime Minister Levy Eskhol brought Begin into the National Unity government as Minister Without Portfolio. He served in that capacity until 1970, urging Jewish settlement in newly acquired territories in Judea and Samaria. Begin became prime minister after Likud defeated Mapai in the 1977 national elections. He continued to press for settlement in all parts of the Land of Israel, free and compulsory higher education and liberalization of the economy from the socialism favoured by Mapai.

Begin's greatest foreign policy achievement was the peace treaty he negotiated with Egypt at **Camp David One** (1978). Beginning in 1979, he authorized clandestine Israeli contacts with the **China** of **Deng Xiaoping**, who shared a visceral hatred for the Soviets. In 1992 these contacts blossomed into full Sino-Israeli diplomatic relations. In 1981 Begin authorized Israel's destruction of **Iraq**'s nuclear bomb factory, and in August 1982 he launched Operation Peace for Galilee in **Lebanon**, a war which aimed to destroy bases of the **Palestine Liberation Organization**. That protracted conflict, the death of his beloved wife Eliza in November 1982, and personal illness caused Begin to resign office on 28 August 1983. He was succeeded by **Yitzhak Shamir**. Begin died in 1992 and was buried on Jerusalem's Mount of Olives next to two of his comrades who had committed suicide while in British custody. The Begin Cultural Centre in Jerusalem and many streets in Israel perpetuate his memory.

Behanzin (1844–1906)
King of **Dahomey** from 1889 to 1894 who ruled in an environment of crisis with **France**. He sought to play France off against other European powers in order to protect his power and influence, and modernized his army with German machine guns and modern artillery. In 1890 he attacked the French coastal port of Coutonou but was repulsed. In 1894 the French in alliance with the rival kingdom of Weme attacked and defeated him, forcing him into exile in **Algeria**.

Beirut
– see also **Lebanon**.

The capital of the **Lebanon**, situated on the Mediterranean coast, with an important port. The city was historically controlled by various powers and had a distinctly cosmopolitan population and atmosphere when it became the major urban centre of the independent Lebanon after

1946. The outbreak of fighting between Muslim and various non-Muslim groups in the Lebanon from 1975 was fought out in Beirut by rival militias over the next fifteen years, inflicting huge damage. West Beirut was virtually destroyed in 1982 when **Israel** launched an attack on **PLO** bases in the city, forcing their withdrawal. A ceasefire in 1989 brought a measure of peace and the revival of the city's strong cultural life and economy.

Belarus

A state bordered by **Poland**, **Russia** and the **Ukraine**, amongst others, formerly known as Byelorussia and 'White Ruthenia'. Belarus was first acquired for Russia from the Duchy of Poland by Catherine the Great, was lost to **Germany** in **World War I**, returned to Russia as a Soviet Republic and then lost again in 1940. As a consequence of invasion, it lost over 2 million people, including its historic Jewish population. Upon liberation, it was reincorporated into the **USSR**, where it remained until 1991. Belarus remained close to Russia after that date, engaging in a plan for an economic and monetary union within the **Commonwealth of Independent States (CIS)**. Under its long-serving authoritarian ruler, President Lukashenko, the country is sometimes called Europe's last dictatorship.

Belgian Congo
– *see* **Belgian Empire**.

Belgian Empire

Unique in that it effectively extended to just one territory, the **Congo**, and that it belonged initially not to the Belgian state but to the King of the Belgians personally, Leopold II being recognized as the sovereign head of the Congo Free State by the Berlin Conference of 1884–5. Joseph Conrad's *Heart of Darkness* memorably evokes the Congo of that time. Leopold's rule was characterized by forced labour, torture and massacre. It was annexed by Belgium as the Belgian Congo in 1908. The small territories of **Burundi** and **Rwanda**, formerly part of German East Africa, also came to **Belgium** as a **League of Nations** mandate in 1919, gaining independence in 1962. The Congo became a valuable possession in the mid twentieth century with the discovery of rich deposits of uranium, and the demise of the empire on the declaration of Congolese independence in 1960 was followed by the active participation of Belgian interests in promoting the secession of the uranium-rich province of Katanga.

Belgium

A state established after the southern regions of the **Netherlands** revolted in 1830. To many observers, Belgium represented a buffer to the ambitions of **France** and the German states, and to the possibility that one state might eventually dominate the coastline of **Europe** as **Napoleon** had done. This was in part why its security was initially guaranteed by **Britain**, until 1914. In fact, Belgium contained historic Flemish and German areas as well as a regional capital, Brussels. It was initially a constitutional monarchy, but in 1870 its king, Leopold, discovered that he could also function as the owner of a private company, which proceeded to colonize the **Congo** in Africa. This colonial enterprise, during which Leopold became 'Proprietor' of the Congo, made Belgium the eighth richest country in the world, but also brought it great shame because of the treatment of native Hutu and Tutsi groups, amongst others, and the condemnation of other imperial powers. In 1914 the invasion of Belgium by German troops became the official trigger for British entry into **World War I**, and the state became an occupied area. This situation was accompanied by reports of great brutality during the occupation, and 'gallant little Belgium' became a rallying call and image for western recruitment of soldiers to the war. Upon liberation, the country was devastated, but rebuilt and fed by a largely American effort coordinated by **Herbert Hoover**, who was later to become president of the **United States**. Belgium was again occupied by **Germany** in 1940, and this time subject to the removal and murder of large numbers of its Jewish population as well as the enslavement of many of its citizens. Belgium had, however, developed its own Flemish-, German- and French-speaking fascist movements in the interwar period, and some associated closely with the Nazi Third Reich while others, especially in the Catholic south, looked to **Mussolini** and **Franco** for inspiration.

At the close of **World War II**, Belgium was again liberated, this time by British and American armies, and a federal but monarchical government again developed. The Belgian authorities quickly pooled their financial and monetary sovereignty with the Netherlands and Luxembourg to create an economic entity referred to as 'Benelux', a precursor of the European Community. The Belgian capital, Brussels, also became the European seat of **NATO**, and a capital of international organizations such as the European Community and the later **European Union**. This, combined with a reputation for safe but surreal public culture (René Magritte was a famous son), allowed Belgium to avoid any painful confrontation with its past until the emergence of Flemish nationalism and national paedophile scandals associated with Catholic politicians and policemen in the late twentieth century. Belgium abandoned its empire in the Congo in 1962, thus inaugurating an era of intermittent warfare which would eventually encompass millions of deaths, and, as the twenty-first century began, seemed unsure of its continuing existence as a functioning nation, with threats of break-up often held off by the twin features of the monarchy and political and economic investment from the European Union.

Belize (British Honduras)

Belize, on the north-east coast of **Central America**, is an independent member of the British **Commonwealth**, having gained independence in 1981. It was a centre of Mayan civilization and from the sixteenth century a Spanish colony before becoming the British colony of British Honduras in the late eighteenth century. Formerly devoted to the production of slave-worked mahogany, it is now known for its tourism, agriculture and oil.

Bello, Muhammad (Ahmadu Bello) (d. 1837)

Second ruler of the **Sokoto Caliphate** and son of its founder Usuman dan Fodio, who retired in his favour in 1815. Muhammad Bello ruled until his death in 1837. During his rule, the Sokoto Caliphate continued the jihad warfare instituted by its founder and extended its domains far to the south, into the country of the Yoruba and in support of other jihads organized by Muslims in other states in the vicinity.

Bello faced considerable resistance to his rule by rival families of the loosely organized caliphate, notably by 'Abd al-Salam. He was able to hold on to power largely by distributing land taken in the continuing military operations to his followers, and by placating his rivals. During his reign the caliphate became a highly cultured and luxurious state. Bello was an accomplished jurist and writer, who composed an important history of the lands that would become central Nigeria.

Ben Bella, Ahmed (1918–2012)

Leader of the Algerian independence movement. He served in **World War II** in the French Army, and returned to **Algeria** to form the **Front de Libération Nationale (FLN)**. A major leader in the Algerian Revolution which began in 1954, he was arrested in 1956 and released in 1962 following independence. He entered politics, becoming president in 1963. He was ousted in a military coup in 1965, and eventually went into exile in Europe.

Ben-Gurion, David (1886–1973)

Zionist leader and first prime minister of **Israel**. As an early Labour Zionist, Ben-Gurion opposed the idea of **Uganda** as a possible homeland for the Jews. He migrated to **Palestine** in 1906 and was in the forefront of making Hebrew rather than Yiddish the dominant language of Palestine's Jewish Labour movement. At the outbreak of **World War I** he was exiled to **Egypt**, where he met Zionist Revisionist leader **Vladimir Jabotinsky**. In 1918, believing that siding with the British would be the best way to oust the Turks from Palestine, he joined Jabotinsky's Jewish Legion within the regular British Army.

Ben-Gurion was the founder of Israel's General Federation of Labour (**Histadrut**) and was its secretary general from 1921 to 1935. In 1930 he helped found the Labour Party (**Mapai**). From the 1920s he was a political centrist, believing that settlement work 'without the Communists and without the Revisionists' was the best way to achieve Zionist objectives. Unlike the Revisionists, he favoured the **Peel Commission**'s 1937 proposal to partition Palestine into Arab, Jewish and British zones. He felt that even a Jewish mini-state was acceptable as a much needed haven for refugees from **Hitler**. He vigorously opposed the British White Paper of 1939, which reduced Jewish immigration to Palestine to a trickle and envisaged a Palestinian state with an Arab majority. After Britain's entry into the war against Hitler, he nevertheless supported Jewish recruitment into a Jewish Brigade and other units within the British Army, believing that that was the best way to protect the Jews of Palestine from Hitler.

During the war Ben-Gurion also vigorously sought American support for a post-war, independent Jewish state. He was successful in winning over many adherents of America's traditionally anti-Zionist Reform movement. He also laid the groundwork for clandestine arms shipments to the **Haganah** and for its work smuggling Jewish refugees into Palestine. He bitterly opposed Britain's post-war reaffirmation of the White Paper and helped oust **Chaim Weizmann** from the Zionist leadership because of Weizmann's support for further negotiations with Britain. After the United Nations' 1947 vote partitioning Palestine into Arab and Jewish states, and upon the departure of the last British troops from Palestine on 14 May 1948, Ben-Gurion proclaimed Israeli independence in Tel Aviv on 15 May 1948.

Ben-Gurion served as Israeli Prime Minister and Defence Minister in 1948–53, a period in which Israel won much international recognition, and again in 1955–63. He was reconciled with Weizmann, who became Israel's first president. Seeing Egypt as the greatest existential threat to the fledgling Jewish state, Ben-Gurion led Israel alongside Britain and **France** into the October 1956 Sinai campaign. In addition to strengthening ties with the United States, he favoured economic ties with **Germany**, incurring the wrath of Revisionist leader **Menachem Begin**. Ben-Gurion also developed extensive military ties with France, which became Israel's major foreign armourer up until the June 1967 **Six Day War**. By then Ben-Gurion was still in the Knesset but largely irrelevant to Israeli politics. In 1970 he retired to his kibbutz in the Negev, believing that the future of the Jewish state 'resides in the south'. There he founded a teachers' college and scientific research institute which evolved into one of Israel's major universities – it was named in his honour upon his death. The graves of Ben-Gurion and his wife Paula overlook the vast Rimon crater of the Negev desert. Tel Aviv's international airport and numerous streets within Israel also perpetuate the memory of this major architect of the reborn Jewish state.

Bengal

Bengal is a cultural area in eastern India that has also been, with changing boundaries, an administrative unit within various Indian empires at least since the sixteenth century. In 1947 it was divided at the time of the partition of India into the state of West Bengal in India and East Pakistan, now the independent nation of **Bangladesh**. Bengalis are those who speak the Bengali language, largely derived from Sanskrit; they number more than 200 million. Many in Bangladesh now prefer to be called Bangladeshis, not Bengalis. Although most are residents of West Bengal and Bangladesh, many others have emigrated to foreign countries, including **Great Britain**, **Canada** and the **United States**. Once they have become citizens or permanent residents of those other countries and speak English or other foreign languages, they may no longer be called Bengalis. Many who are bilingual continue to identify, in some important ways, with the land of their origin.

Benin

Formerly known as the Republic of **Dahomey**, the country was occupied by France in 1894, becoming part of French West Africa in 1904, and granted limited self-government in 1957. Full independence came in 1960 under President Hubert Maga (1916–2000). His overthrow in 1963 started a period of political instability with civil and military governments alternating in quick succession. In 1972 an army officer, Mathieu Ahmed Kérékou (1933–2015), became president, and in 1974 he declared the renamed People's Republic of Benin a Marxist–Leninist state. Kérékou abandoned socialism in 1980, accepting **International Monetary Fund**-imposed economic marketization and, subsequently, political liberalization. Nicéphone Soglo (1935–) was elected president in 1991, but Kérékou returned in 1996, remaining in office until 2006. Former banker Thomas Boni Yaya (1951–) was elected in 2006 and again in 2011 on a programme of growth and anti-corruption. The country is mixed Christian and Muslim, with an economy based on subsistence agriculture and cotton production.

Bennett, James Gordon (1795–1872)

A poor immigrant from Scotland, Bennett founded the *New York Herald* in 1835, and made this daily penny press the world's largest circulation newspaper and himself the first newspaper millionaire. He introduced the sensational reporting of police trials, society scandals and sporting events, and dramatized more traditional political and commercial news. His news-gathering service embraced **Europe** and reached the battlefield during the **American Civil War**. His editorial stance was usually Democratic, pro-slavery and Negrophobe, but its inconsistency and eccentricity considerably reduced its influence.

Bentham, Jeremy (1748–1832)

Jeremy Bentham developed the political and philosophical credo of utilitarianism, in which the greatest benefit of the greatest number is paramount. Utilitarianism embodies equality between persons, as each counts for one, and no more than one, in the calculation of optimum utility. Bentham concluded that poor relief, rehabilitation of offenders and democratic reform were all sanctioned by the principle of utilitarianism. His utilitarianism exerted a profound intellectual influence over Victorian liberalism, and remains important to contemporary Anglo-American liberal politics.

Bentinck, Lord William (1774–1839)

A liberal aristocrat who tried to reform the bloated military government of British **India**. After serving as a soldier and diplomat in Europe, he was appointed governor of Madras (1803–7), but then recalled after a mutiny of Indian troops at Vellore (1806). As British envoy in Sicily and commander-in-chief in the Mediterranean (1811–15), he promoted Italian nationalism and parliamentary government. Having run up large debts in draining his fenland estates, he became governor general of India (1828–35,) where he cultivated a new style of imperial liberalism. His flagship reforms, notably the abolition of *sati* (*suttee*) or widow-burning (1829), his sponsorship of English-language education for Indians and attempts to involve more Indians in lower-level administrative jobs have sometimes been portrayed as a decisive moment of 'modernization' in India. However, Bentinck's overriding goal was cutting government costs, and a major trade depression severely blunted his schemes for imperial uplift.

Berlin airlift (1948–1949)

The response of the western Allies to the Soviet blockade of land routes to Berlin starting on 24 June 1948, itself a reaction to the currency reform in the western zones of **Germany**. The airlift, launched on 26 June, lasted until the lifting of the blockade on 12 May 1949 and carried 1.7 million tons of supplies, mainly to Berlin's Tempelhof airport. The airlift did much to soften German hostility to the western Allies.

Berlin Wall

Rapidly erected by East German troops from 13 August 1961 under the direct supervision of Erich Honecker (1912–1994) to prevent the flow of East Germans to West Berlin. It completed the 1952 'Iron Curtain' between East and West Germany, and was motivated by alarm at the cost of the flow to the East German economy. The only true crossing point was 'Checkpoint Charlie' on *Friedrichstrasse*. The wall was opened on 9 November 1989. Only token lengths of the concrete wall remain.

Berlin–Baghdad Railway

In 1899 the German-financed Baghdad Railway Company won an **Ottoman Empire** concession to construct a railway link from **Constantinople** to the Persian Gulf. As a line already operated from the German to the Ottoman capital, the project was dubbed the Berlin–Baghdad Railway. Construction began in 1903 but Russia and Britain soon expressed concerns over a possible threat to their interests in Persia. Britain was also troubled by the railway's proximity to **Iraq**, where oil was discovered in 1912. These issues were largely resolved diplomatically by 1914. On the outbreak of **World War I** much of the project remained unfinished and hostilities in the region delayed further progress. The **Treaty of Versailles** (1919) cancelled German rights in the railway. Work recommenced under British and French control in the 1930s and the first train ran along the 1,600-kilometre (990-mile) route through **Turkey**, **Syria** and Iraq in 1940.

Berlusconi, Silvio (1936–)

Italian prime minister, 1994–5, 2001–6 and 2008–11. Berlusconi was a transformative figure in Italian politics; a media mogul, football club owner and nightclub singer, he had risen to pre-eminence via the foundation of a new party, Forza Italia, which promoted pro-business, low tax policies and conservative social policies. He became the third longest-serving prime minister (and one of the richest men) in Italian history, but was a polarizing figure, constantly surrounded by allegations of personal promiscuity and business impropriety. He faced hostility from Italian opinion formers, the Catholic Church and rival media interests, but maintained a core of personal popularity until the Italian financial crisis of 2011.

Bermudas

The Bermudas consist of seven main islands, about 750 miles east of Cape Hatteras. With very little cultivable land, they were always important as a maritime base. The British settled them in the early seventeenth century, and the Royal Navy built a substantial base there in the nineteenth century; Confederate blockade runners used them in the 1860s, as did liquor smugglers during the era of **Prohibition**. Today they serve as a centre of tourism and international finance, with 60,0000 inhabitants who are members of the British **Commonwealth**.

Bernadotte, Jean Baptiste Jules (1763–1844)

French soldier; king of **Sweden** and **Norway**. French by birth, Bernadotte rose from the ranks to become marshal of France under **Napoleon Bonaparte** in 1804. In 1810 he was elected heir to the Swedish crown and, adopted by Charles XIII, turned against Bonaparte and came to the throne in 1818 as Karl XIV Johan of Sweden and Karl III Johan of Norway, which he had seized from Denmark in 1814.

Besant, Annie (née Wood) (1847–1933)

British writer, activist and Theosophist. Following the collapse of her marriage in 1874, Besant joined the National Secular Society, becoming an associate of Charles Bradlaugh. A prominent Social Democratic Federation and Fabian Society speaker and a campaigner for birth control and women's suffrage, Besant subsequently joined the Theosophical Society, becoming president in 1908. Moving to India, she supported the home rule movement and was elected **Indian National Congress** president in 1917.

Bharatiya Janata Party (BJP)

Federal-level political party (created 1980) with formal and informal ties to Rashtriya Swayamsevak Sangh (RSS), Vishva Hindu Parishad (VHP) and other Hindu nationalist organizations. Preceded in electoral politics by the Jana Sangh (1951–77), which had limited electoral success in the 1970s. The BJP gained in popularity in Hindi-speaking states in the early 1980s. This popularity resulted in the formation of BJP-led governments in Uttar Pradesh and other states between 1989 and 1991, at precisely the moment when scandal and defections weakened both the **Congress** (I) and **Janata Party** coalitions. The BJP government in Uttar Pradesh stood by as a mob destroyed the Babri Masjid in **Ayodhya** in 1992, sparking communal violence across northern India. It capitalized on discontent with the Congress-led central government in the mid 1990s, resulting in BJP-led coalition governments in 1996 and 1999–2004. In 2014 it won a landslide general election victory under Narendra Modi.

Bhopal Incident (1984) (India)

A gas leak at the Union Carbide pesticide plant in Bhopal, **India**, on 2/3 December 1984, that killed an estimated 3,500 people within days and up to 15,000 since, the world's worst industrial accident to date. The victims received slow and minimal compensation, with Union Carbide making an interim payment in 1990 and a final settlement of 470 million dollars in 1999. In 2010 seven former Union Carbide employees were convicted of causing death by negligence.

Bhutan

Himalayan kingdom in north-eastern South Asia, bordered by **Tibet** to the north, West Bengal to the south-west and **Assam** to the south-east. Spurs of the Lesser Himalayas have promoted political and economic segmentation for most of Bhutan's history. Ethnic Tibetans began to displace Assamese influence in the seventh century, resulting in increased intellectual and commercial traffic with Tibet. However, Tibetan immigrants into Bhutan founded new Buddhist sects and fought numerous wars against Tibetan invaders through the seventeenth century. Bhutanese expansion in the eighteenth century into Sikkim, Kuch Bihar and neighbouring Assamese tracts met the ambitions of the **East India Company**, and a durable treaty was reached in 1865. After two decades of support from the British against Tibet, local strongman Ugyen Wangchuk established a hereditary monarchy over Bhutan in 1907. His successors gradually reduced the powers of the monarchy in favour of, ultimately, a constitutional parliamentary democracy in 2008.

Bhutto, Benazir (1953–2007)

Politician who served as prime minister of **Pakistan** in 1988–90 and 1993–6. Daughter of former Prime Minister **Zulfiqar Ali Bhutto** (1971–9), she came to political prominence in the 1980s as an opponent of military dictator General **Zia ul-Haq**. Upon Zia's death in 1988, Bhutto's Pakistan Peoples Party joined a coalition government which she headed. In 1999 Bhutto went into self-imposed exile after being convicted of corruption by a Pakistani court. She was assassinated in December 2007 after her return to contest the 2008 general election.

Bhutto, Zulfiqar Ali (1928–1979)

President of **Pakistan**, 1971–3, and prime minister of Pakistan, 1973–7. Bhutto's political career began in the late 1950s in the military regime of **Mohammad Ayub Khan**, whom he served as both Commerce and Defence Minister. He broke with the regime after the **Indo-Pakistan War of 1965** and in 1967 established the Pakistan Peoples Party (PPP). In the national elections of 1970, the PPP fared well, though not as well as the **Awami League**. The military prevented the Awami League from forming a government, almost surely with Bhutto's collusion, leading to Pakistan's civil war and the creation of **Bangladesh** in 1971. After the civil war Bhutto took power in Pakistan. He promulgated a new constitution (1973), nationalized industries, undertook moderate land reforms, worked assiduously to concentrate power in the central government's hands, and instituted a process of Islamization. In 1977 he was unseated in a military coup. He was tried and convicted of political corruption, and received the death sentence, which was subsequently carried out.

Biafran War (1967–1970)

A major conflict which threatened to tear **Nigeria** apart. On 30 May 1967 the military governor of the Eastern Region, Colonel Ojukwu, declared the Ibo homeland an independent sovereign state under the name of the Republic of Biafra. Troops of the Nigerian Federal Army attacked across the northern border of Biafra on 7 July 1967. The Biafrans invaded the neighbouring Mid-West Region on 9 August 1967. The Federal Army recaptured Biafra on 22 September 1967, and Port Harcourt fell on 20 May 1968. Supply shortages and starvation finally led to the collapse of Biafran resistance after a four-pronged federal attack in December 1969. The Biafran Army surrendered on 15 January 1970. New threats to Nigerian territorial integrity have arisen with the Boko Haram uprising in the north, while Biafran separatism has now re-emerged.

Biennio Rosso (1919–1920) (Italy)

The Bienno Rosso, or 'two red years', is the period of social and political turbulence in Italy from 1919 to 1920. Against a background of inflation and soaring unemployment, workers occupied factories and peasants the land, mounting insurrectionary strikes and forming workers' councils and militias, as trade union, Anarchist and Socialist membership grew and Italy came close to revolution. Middle-class fear encouraged reaction from the right, the rise of Fascism and **Benito Mussolini**'s March on Rome in 1922.

Big Stick Policy (USA)

'Speak softly and carry a big stick', an expression used by **Theodore Roosevelt** (United States president, 1901–9) to describe his preferred method in pursuing foreign and domestic policy. Roosevelt claimed the term was a West African proverb and an early use came when he pressed Congress to authorize naval expansion to underpin America's diplomacy, notably in **Latin America**. He subsequently used it to describe his action against industrial monopolies and trusts.

Biko, Steve (1947–1977)

South African black consciousness leader. Born in Natal, expelled from high school for activism, Biko became a medical student, co-founding the South African Students Organization in 1968. He became president in 1972 of the subsequently outlawed Black People's Convention, a black consciousness umbrella organization. Subject to a banning order in 1972 and frequently arrested, Biko's murder by police following his arrest in August 1977 made him a martyr of the anti-apartheid struggle.

Bill of Rights (USA)

The Bill of Rights comprises the first ten amendments to the US Constitution. First proposed as a list of seventeen amendments by **James Madison** in 1789, twelve were sent to the states for ratification, of which ten received approval by December 1791. These amendments included guarantees of a free press, free speech, freedom of assembly, the right to bear arms, the right to trial by jury and a ban on cruel or unusual punishment. Some Federalists feared a Bill of Rights could place too many restrictions on a government still seeking to establish its authority. Many states, however, had ratified the constitution while suggesting the immediate addition of a Bill of Rights; Madison saw it as a necessary measure to convince those sceptical of the new constitution that the federal government would be responsive to their concerns.

Bin Laden, Osama (1957–2011)

One of the founders of **al-Qaida**. He was born in 1957 into a wealthy Saudi family with Yemeni ties. Bin Laden had no formal Islamic training. At King Abdul Aziz University, he was exposed to **Muslim Brotherhood** intellectuals in exile. After the Soviet invasion of **Afghanistan** in 1979, he followed one of them, 'Abd Allah 'Azzam (1941–89), to **Pakistan**, embracing his call for Muslims to see the Afghan **jihad** as an individual obligation and global struggle. There he mixed with radicals who interpreted the Soviet defeat as the beginning of a militant tide against 'infidel' governments everywhere. He focused initially on the Saudi government during the first **Gulf War** and in 1996 declared war on the US. From exile in **Sudan** and Afghanistan, he oversaw an al-Qaida network that carried out attacks on American embassies in **Kenya** and **Tanzania** in 1998 and against New York and Washington in 2001. Bin Laden carefully crafted the persona of a humble ascetic and explained his actions as a defence of Muslims and humanity in general. American special forces killed him in Abbottabad, Pakistan, in 2011.

birth control
– see also **Pill, the**.

In the eighteenth century birth control in the modern sense appears to have been non-existent, and the most frequent way of limiting family size to have been simply to abandon unwanted children. They were left in some numbers on doorsteps or convenient alcoves, where many no doubt did not survive. More than 4,000 of the more fortunate were left at London's Foundling Hospital alone between 1741 and 1760. The first real evidence for some form of positive family planning in **Europe** is from nineteenth-century **France** where the peasantry started to marry later, seemingly so as to reduce the number of heirs amongst whom property would have to be shared. More generally, from about 1875 onwards women in the developed world started to have notably fewer children, stimulated in the cities, perhaps, by the desire for the higher standard of living possible with fewer children to support, which the growing range of consumer goods made increasingly attractive. For humbler families, growing prohibitions on the use of child labour made children an even heavier economic burden than before. It was, though, a period in which physical sex was normally never spoken or written about, and the practical means of control must be conjectural. Coitus interruptus, confining intercourse to times of the month when fertility was expected to be lower, non-penetrative sex, and simple abstinence must all have played a part, as did abortion, although it was normally illegal.

Those pioneering women who openly advocated birth control, in the contemporary sense of having full intercourse but avoiding pregnancy through the use of an artificial barrier to conception, were sent to prison in **Britain** until just before **World War I**, and deprived of their children. The war, however, introduced major change with millions of soldiers using the condom. Marie Stopes (1880–1958) promoted contraception in *Married Love*, published in Britain in 1918, and opened her first eponymous clinic in 1921. A Dutchman invented a diaphragm for women (hence the 'Dutch cap') in 1919, and the first practical IUD (the 'coil') appeared in 1929. It has been estimated from imperfect sources that in the period between the two world wars one man in ten in Britain used a condom regularly, but only a handful of upper-class women the diaphragm. Coitus interruptus may have been normal in up to 70 per cent of marriages. Condoms, however, were long sold surreptitiously and only became widely available in the 1950s, and the pill, invented by Carl Djerassi in the 1950s and introduced for married women only in Britain, 1961, gave the woman direct and easy control of her own pregnancies for

the first time. The pill came to be seen as a symbol of **feminist** empowerment, and like the other forms of birth control, including sterilization and, more recently, the 'morning after' pill, contributed to the loosening of the ties between sex, marriage and procreation which is a marked characteristic of modern European society. Partly for such reasons, birth control was always viewed with suspicion by the churches and by the Roman Catholic Church in particular, which has continued to argue in addition that use of the condom is sinful because it kills incipient life. Although widely ignored by western Catholics, it is a teaching which is believed to have contributed both to many unwanted births elsewhere and to the spread of **AIDS**. The most radical form of birth control, abortion, remains controversial in western Europe but was widely used in the former Soviet bloc, and continues to be so. For example, **Russia** in 2010 recorded 1·2 million abortions, as against 1·7 million actual births.

Bismarck, Otto Eduard Leopold von (1815–1898)

Prussian ambassador; minister president, 1862; chancellor of the North German Confederation, 1867; Reich chancellor of **Germany**, 1871–90. Bismarck was a Prussian reactionary who concluded that the only way to control liberal nationalism was to create a conservative German federation to contain it. To that end, he displaced **Austria** as a leading state in the German Confederation by military means at Koninggratz in 1866, then formed a North German Confederation centred around **Prussia**. The economic integration of the German lands followed. In 1871 the opportunity offered by victory in the **Franco-Prussian War** was exploited to proclaim at Versailles a Second German Reich, of which Bismarck became chancellor and foreign minister. He used his position to launch what was meant to be a unifying *kulturkampf* against Catholics, bought off working-class votes with militarist welfarism, and ran a 'reptile fund' which provided intelligence from the bribed functionaries of half of Europe. Bismarck is recognized for running a superb foreign policy based around the idea of the use of treaties agreed by congresses to elevate the position of Germany without unleashing general European war. He also tolerated the election of liberals and socialists to the imperial parliament, the Reichstag, and the apparent existence of independent newspapers, while keeping them all under his own control. In reality, he built a state around himself, and when he was dismissed as chancellor in 1890, it did not take long for imbalances between the military and democratic elements within Germany, and European alliances outside, to mesh with the character of Kaiser Wilhelm II and Germany's economic growth to create the conditions for disaster in 1914.

Black Hand

Nationalist secret society formed in 1911 in reaction to the Austro-Hungarian occupation of **Bosnia–Hercegovina**. Led by Colonel Dragutin Dimitrijevic, the Serbian army general staff intelligence chief, the society's objective was establishment of a Greater **Serbia**. The assassination of heir to the Austro-Hungarian throne Archduke Franz Ferdinand by Black Hand member Gavrilo Princip in Sarajevo on 28 June 1914 provoked an Austrian attack on Serbia, leading to **World War I**. Serbia outlawed the society in 1916.

Black Legend

The Black Legend holds that Spaniards are uniquely and inherently cruel, avaricious, treacherous and intolerant. In large part, this myth reflected the resentment that other Europeans felt towards **Spain**'s growing power in the late fifteenth and sixteenth centuries. During the **Enlightenment**, anti-Hispanic discourse gradually changed in emphasis: Spain came to be seen less as a threat and more as a cautionary example – a nation in decline precisely because of its well-known negative traits. For example, the Inquisition was not just vicious and unjust; its obscurantism actively impeded Spain's intellectual and cultural progress. Spanish American patriots deftly combined these themes of immorality and backwardness, accusing Spain of degrading the Indians, denying the Creoles a voice in government and keeping the region underdeveloped. They could thus present their independence movements as redemptive. However, most western observers believed that the newly founded nations continued to suffer from the unfavourable racial, cultural and religious effects of their colonial heritage. They needed the protection or tutelage of more advanced powers – a view that underwrote both the **United States'** participation in the Spanish–American War and its **'big stick'** diplomacy in Central America and the Caribbean. Yet while Hispanophobia demonstrated great persistence, countervailing views had always existed, especially in Spain itself. The twentieth century witnessed a re-evaluation and the development of better informed and more balanced perspectives on Hispanic colonization.

As a result, the Black Legend has little resonance in modern scholarly discussions.

Black Muslims
– *see* **Nation of Islam**.

Black Power (USA)

In June 1966 Stokely Carmichael, head of the Student Non-violent Coordinating Committee, led Mississippi followers in chanting 'We want Black Power!' Widely reported, the slogan symbolized the rejection of the non-violent integrationist position that had previously dominated national civil rights coverage. In reality, there had always been **African Americans** who were more interested in collective advancement than in interracial brotherhood, and even more who endorsed armed self-defence. Carmichael believed African-American economic, political and cultural solidarity could generate Black Power in the same way that Irish or Jewish American solidarity gave those groups leverage. Whites reacted to Black Power against a backdrop of ghetto uprisings and the emergence of groups such as the Black Panthers whose rhetoric continued **Malcolm X**'s angry defiance. Sharing Black Power's goals, **Martin Luther King** lamented its harmful effects: a white backlash that underpinned a conservative political resurgence and black suffering as ghetto clashes exacerbated inner-city deprivation.

Black September Organization (BSO)

The name of this Palestinian paramilitary group derives from a conflict which began on 16 September 1970, when King **Hussein of Jordan** declared military rule in response to a Palestinian attempt to seize his kingdom. Hussein's crackdown resulted in the deaths or expulsion of thousands of Palestinians from Jordan. A small cell of the **Palestine Liberation Organization (PLO)** determined to take revenge upon King Hussein and the Jordanian Army. BSO actions included the 28 November 1971 retaliatory assassination of Jordanian Prime Minister Wasfi al-Tal and the 1972 massacre of Israeli athletes at the Munich Olympic Games. The PLO closed BSO down in September 1973, calculating that no more good would come from this type of terrorism. Instead, the PLO concentrated on anti-Israel activities in the **West Bank**, the Gaza Strip and **Israel** proper. BSO was partially responsible for the creation of the permanent and professional counter-terrorism forces of major European countries, such as **France**'s Groupe d'intervention de la Gendarmerie Nationale (GIGN).

Black Ships
– *see* **Perry, Commodore Matthew Calbraith**.

Blitzkrieg
A term for a style of warfare first employed by the Third Reich in its European campaigns of 1939–40 which defeated **Poland** and **France**. Elements of Blitzkrieg were tested in the **Spanish Civil War**. Blitzkrieg (literally 'lightning' war) involves a combination of very rapid light infantry, fast man-eouvre around enemy defences and the coordinated use of air power and light tanks against enemy columns. The central idea is to shock, divide and then consume a larger enemy before it has had time to react, and bears some similarity to nineteenth-century cavalry war. The great dangers with Blitzkrieg stem from its rapidity and advance; that supply lines are lost or cut, and that an enemy resorts to a strategy of strategic retreat or insurgency against a foe which is initially successful. When added to rocket and missile artillery in the second half of the twentieth century, Blitzkrieg seemed to offer a model of quick advance. When stalled however, Blitzkrieg becomes a trap for the side which employed it, as happened to the Nazis at **Stalingrad**, since it cannot overcome a determined entrenched foe which can bear superior losses on its own territory, and nor can it deal with guerrilla activity.

Bloch, Marc (1886–1944)
Founder of the **Annales** school. The son of a professor of ancient history, Bloch was educated in Paris, Leipzig and Berlin, and was a medieval historian. He published *French Rural History* in 1931 and *Feudal Society* in 1939, and founded the important history journal *Annales*. He is known for his innovative work in comparative social and economic history and for his resistance during the German occupation. He was executed by the Nazis in June 1944.

Blood River, Battle of
– *see* **Great Trek**.

Bloody Sunday (1905)
Massacre of unarmed demonstrators who had marched on the Winter Palace of Tsar **Nicholas II** in St Petersburg on 22 January 1905 (old style 9 January) to present a petition seeking relief of their conditions, universal suffrage and an end to the war with Japan. The march was led by Father Georgi Gapon (1870–1906), who had formed an Assembly of Russian Workers. The deaths of over a hundred people triggered the 1905 Russian Revolution.

Bloody Sunday (1972)
The name given to civil disturbances in which fourteen members of the **Northern Ireland** public were shot by British forces in Londonderry, Northern Ireland on 30 January during civil rights demonstrations. Small sections of a peaceful crowd of around 10,000, who were marching through the city, became agitated and began to throw small items at troops who manned a barrier in front of the crowd, whilst declaring support for the IRA. The First Batallion Parachute Regiment was then ordered through the barricade. Controversy has raged ever since, resulting in the longest judicial inquiry in British history, as to whether the Paras were ordered by the government to open fire or came under fire, or opened fire independently. The events poisoned community relations in Northern Ireland for the rest of the Northern Ireland 'Troubles'.

Blum, Leon (1872–1950)
The first Socialist premier of **France**, and the first Jewish one. Although himself a centrist, he was from time to time forced to rely on Communist support, partly because of the depth of the right's anti-Semitic distaste for him. When combined with his essential moderation (he had entered politics because of the **Dreyfus affair** and was a socialist theoretician rather than a firebrand) and the tumultuous times in which he lived, his periods as prime minister tended to be short. His first regime fell because he attempted neutrality in the **Spanish Civil War**, his second because he aided the Spanish Communists with large amounts of materiel. He refused to support the **Vichy** regime and spent **World War II** in German concentration camps, narrowly avoiding death. In 1945 he was released by the Allies and returned to serve as premier between December 1946 and January 1947 at the head of a centrist alliance.

Blyden, Edward Wilmont (1832–1912)
A writer and political activist born in the Virgin Islands, who travelled to **Liberia** in 1851 when no US university would admit him because of his race. Blyden taught classics at Liberia college and began publishing pamphlets and writing in newspapers on the value of **pan-Africanism**. He is known especially for *Christianity, Islam and the Negro Race* (1887). He opposed colonialism and worked for a union of **Sierra Leone** and Liberia to model a regeneration for all **Africa**.

Blücher, Gebhard Leberecht von (later Prince of Wahlstaat) (1742–1819)

A field marshal of **Prussia**. He was originally a soldier in the Swedish Army, but converted to the cause of **Frederick the Great** following capture in 1760. His temperament caused the Prussian forces, who did not doubt his courage or ferocity, to ease him from the army and into farming. Recalled during the French Revolutionary Wars, he distinguished himself as a francophobe, and retired again in 1806. He was recalled again in the final stage of the wars against **Napoleon**. The arrival of Blücher and his 50,000 troops at **Waterloo** at the last moment is widely credited as the key to the allied victory.

boat people

Vietnamese refugees who escaped from **Vietnam** after North Vietnamese Communist forces captured Saigon in 1975. The name refers to the fact that most of them fled Vietnam by sea and spent long periods in boats while searching for asylum. Initially, they were taken into refugee camps in **Hong Kong** and South East Asia. Eventually, most were relocated to **Australia**, **Canada**, **France** and the **United States**.

Boer War, First (1880–1881)

Conflict of 1880–1 between the **Boers** of the Transvaal and the **British Empire**. **Great Britain** annexed the Transvaal Boer Republic in 1877. In December 1880 the Boers proclaimed their independence. General Sir George Colley, leading British troops from Natal, was defeated and killed at Majuba Hill on 27 December 1881. The British government decided on withdrawal and signed an armistice on 6 March 1881. Peace was concluded by the Convention of Pretoria on 5 April 1881, granting the Boers independence under British suzerainty.

Boer War, Second (1899–1902)

Conflict of 1899–1902 between Britain and the South African **Boer** republics of Transvaal and the Orange Free State over Britain's objective to annex the republics. The Boers had initial successes from October 1899, overcoming British forces at Magersfontein and Stormberg, and besieging Ladysmith, Mafeking and Kimberley. The war's complexion changed with the arrival of British reinforcements under Lords Roberts and **Kitchener**, the relief of the besieged towns, the Boer defeat at Paardeburg in February 1900 and British occupation of the republics. The Boers turned to a guerrilla campaign, harrying British

forces. Kitchener responded with punitive attacks on Boer farms and properties and the establishment of concentration camps in which thousands died. Having refused a British peace offer in March 1901, Boer leaders accepted the Treaty of Vereeniging in May 1902, Britain annexing the Transvaal and Orange Free State with a guarantee of local autonomy.

Boers

Term applied to the rural, non-British white Calvinist settlers, mainly Dutch, but also including Flemish, German and French Protestants in **South Africa** who migrated from the Cape to the interior, establishing virtually independent states and clashing with native powers such as the **Zulus** and eventually with the British in the **First** and **Second Boer War**s. With the decline of farming in the economic structure of South Africa, the term *Boer* was replaced by the linguistic and ethnic term *Afrikaaner*.

Bohemia

An historic region in central Europe that comprises the modern Czech Republic. Although Bohemia served as constituent state of the Habsburg Empire from 1526, the centralization of Habsburg rule in 1749 led to the loss of Bohemia's administrative autonomy. Despite aggressive Germanization, Bohemian cultural nationalism remained strong. During the **Revolutions of 1848**, Prague served as a centre of revolutionary activity with Czech nationalists advocating liberal political reforms and autonomy. The formation of the **Austro-Hungarian Empire** in 1867 frustrated Czech ambitions for greater independence and a tripartite monarchy, leading to the growth of extremist nationalism. With the collapse of Austria–Hungary at the end of **World War I**, Bohemia gained independence and became the core of the new state of **Czechoslovakia**. In 1939 **Germany** annexed the historic lands of Bohemia and established the German Protectorate of Bohemia and Moravia. During the **Cold War**, Bohemia became part of the Czechoslovak Socialist Republic until 1993, when, along with Moravia, it became the Czech Republic.

Bolívar, Simón (1783–1830)

Born into an aristocratic family in Caracas, Bolívar completed his largely autodidactic education in Europe. He read widely in political philosophy and returned to **Venezuela** convinced that its independence was inevitable. By early 1810 it appeared that **France** would soon complete its takeover of

Spain. In response, leading citizens of Caracas established a junta on 19 April 1810, to rule until Ferdinand returned to the throne. From that time Bolívar, a republican, actively worked for the liberation of the future countries of Venezuela, **Colombia**, **Panama**, **Ecuador**, **Peru** and **Bolivia**. The course was difficult. Repeatedly Bolívar, known as 'the Liberator' from 1813, was plagued by rivals within the republican cause as well as by royalist forces. Despite defeats, however, neither his dedication to independence from Spain nor his transnational vision was in doubt. Although Spain sent a large army to Venezuela following Ferdinand's restoration to the throne in 1814, Bolívar and his allies helped to prevent their enemies' military successes from also becoming political victories. Bolívar dealt successfully with rivals in the 1810s and was able to resurrect the cause of independence from the plains of the Orinoco in Venezuela's interior. There he benefited from the arrival of surplus weapons and ammunition from **Britain** in addition to numerous young adventurers. Meeting the forces led by General Francisco de Paula Santander, the combined armies crossed the Andes and defeated the royalists at Boyacá, thus opening the way to Bogotá and independence for New Granada. A congress at Angostura celebrated the victory in 1819 by creating the Republic of **Colombia**, incorporating Venezuela, New Granada and the Kingdom of Quito, a combination known to historians as **Gran Colombia**, despite the awkward reality that none of the component parts was yet completely independent.

In 1821 the Liberator was back in Caracas. His lieutenant, Antonio José de Sucre, freed Ecuador in 1822, and in the same year José de San Martín, whose arrival in Peru had forced Lima to declare independence in 1821, met the Liberator and then resigned as 'Protector' of Peru, leaving the interior of Peru and Charcas for Bolívar and Sucre to free in 1824 and 1825. Bolívar spent most of his remaining life trying to achieve transnational unity among the newly independent states and stability within them. He failed due to regional sentiments, personal ambitions, fiscal woes, social divisions and political differences. The most important leader in the wars of independence in Spanish America, he was more a political theorist than a practitioner, despite his many offices. He perceived the difficulties that the new states faced and believed only a strong executive could surmount them. Although a republican, he proposed a lifetime president who could select his successor as the supreme executive for Bolivia. By Bolívar's death, Colombia had broken into its three constituent states: Venezuela, New Granada and Ecuador. His famous lament in 1830 encapsulates his frustration with independent states he had helped to create: 'Those who served the Revolution have ploughed the sea.'

Bolivarian Revolution
– *see* **Venezuela**.

Bolivia, Republic of
Marked by geographic fragmentation and extreme climates, South America's sixth largest country spans the high Andes in the west, the Amazon Rain Forest in the east and the dry, sparsely populated Chaco lowlands in the south, but lacks navigable rivers and access to the Pacific. The population is divided between a small, dominant Spanish-mestizo population and an indigenous majority, the latter located in rural areas in the *altiplano* in small, impoverished communities. A mountain of silver at Potosí dominated the colonial economy. After independence from **Spain** in 1821, extreme political instability marked by 190 regime changes and a great divide in income distribution became hallmarks of South America's poorest country. Only in 1994 did the state officially recognize the 'multi-ethnic and plural-cultural' nature of Bolivian society, overturning the country's centuries-old socio-political hierarchy to create a more genuinely democratic polity. Evo Morales, elected in January 2006, became Bolivia's first indigenous president.

Bolshevism
Bolshevism was born from the 1903 division in the Russian Social Democratic Labour Party. **Vladimir Lenin**'s Bolshevik (majority) faction wished to restrict party membership to professional active revolutionaries, while the Mensheviks (minority) wished to extend membership to non-active supporters and sympathizers. Under Lenin's leadership, the Bolsheviks gained control of **Russia** following the 1917 revolution. Bolshevism became characterized by authoritarian 'democratic centralism', world revolution and intolerance of political opposition. **Stalin**'s Bolshevism rejected world revolution, and associated the movement with political violence and oppression.

Bonny
A town in the Niger Delta in existence in the seventeenth century. A slave port during much of the eighteenth century, it became the base of **Jaja**, a former slave who became rich from the palm oil trade that followed the abolition of the **slave**

trade. Jaja's migration to Opobo as a result of internal strife in 1867 led to a significant decline, though the town recovered during the colonial period after British occupation.

Boone, Daniel (1734–1820)

Born in the proverbial log cabin in backwoods Pennsylvania, Boone was the young American nation's most influential and celebrated frontiersman. Hunter, trapper, fighter of native Indians, politician, land speculator and slave owner, his most notable achievement was the opening of the trans-Appalachian West to colonization by blazing the `Wilderness Road' across the mountains into central Kentucky (1775). The prototypical pioneer, he became legendary within his own lifetime and his fame was perpetuated through movies and television shows.

Bophutatswana
– see Bantustans.

Borges, Jorge Luis (1899–1986)

Born in Buenos Aires, Borges became a world-renowned writer whose short stories, essays and poems reflected life in Buenos Aires, Argentina, travels in Europe and readings in world literature, mathematics, theology and philosophy. He created fantasies about life and death that stimulated development of science fiction and magic realism. In 1923 his first book of poems introduced him to the Buenos Aires literary scene and led to the founding of several literary magazines. Out of favour during the Perón years, Borges subsequently became director of the National Library and a professor at the University of Buenos Aires. He received the National Prize for Literature and in 1961 the Prix Formentor. His short stories collected as Ficciones (1944), El Aleph (1949) and El Hacedor (1960) are writers' models. He also wrote poetry, essays (Otras inquisiciones, 1952), screenplays, literary criticism, edited anthologies and translated works into Spanish.

Bosch Gaviño, Juan (1909–2001)

A critic of the Dominican Republic's dictator Rafael Trujillo, Bosch helped found the Dominican Revolutionary Party (PRD) while in exile. A leftist reformer, he won the first post-Trujillo presidential elections in 1961. The Dominican military overthrew him in September 1963 and a US military invasion in 1965 ended his supporters' efforts to return him to office. Bosch remained active in Dominican politics, often as a presidential candidate, into the 1990s.

Bose, Sarat Chandra (1889–1950)

Indian nationalist leader, barrister and elder brother of Subhas Bose, he joined the Calcutta High Court Bar and the then nationalist movement after World War I. Active in Calcutta city government and the Indian National Congress, he was leader of the opposition in the Bengal Legislative Assembly from 1937, served several long terms of imprisonment, and was a minister in the (Indian) interim government in 1946. Leaving Congress in 1948, he was a socialist opposition leader in free India at the time of his death.

Bose, Subhas Chandra (1897–1945)

A charismatic and controversial Indian nationalist leader from Bengal, Bose studied at Presidency College, Calcutta, but was expelled for participating in an attack on an English professor alleged to have insulted Indians. Resuming his studies at Scottish Churches College, he graduated as World War I ended and went to Great Britain to study at Cambridge University and take the Indian Civil Service exam. He finished fourth in the competition in 1921, but resigned to join the national movement and returned to Calcutta, where he became a trusted protégé of C. R. Das, leader of the nationalists in Bengal. Bose became chief executive officer of the Calcutta Corporation or city government but shortly afterwards was gaoled for allegedly using funds to smuggle arms. During his imprisonment, mostly in Burma, Das died. On his return to Calcutta in 1927, Bose became a leader of younger Indian nationalists and was elected mayor of Calcutta. In and out of prison, he, along with Jawarharlal Nehru, pressured Gandhi to move more rapidly to a declaration of independence as nationalist India's goal. Bose declared himself a socialist, but his activities were curtailed by repeated imprisonments and ill health. During the mid 1930s he was in Europe as an unofficial ambassador for nationalist India. He returned to India in 1936, was imprisoned and then released, and was chosen by Gandhi as president of the Indian National Congress for 1938. A year later, he challenged Gandhi and stood in an election for a second term. He defeated Gandhi's candidate, but resigned shortly afterwards when the Gandhian majority in the working committee of Congress would not assist him in running the organization. Bose formed the Forward Bloc, a grouping within Congress, and was still intimately involved with Congress work.

Imprisoned in 1940 after war broke out in Europe, he was released and decided he had to work outside India for its liberation from British rule, believing the British would never leave India without an armed struggle. He emerged in **Germany** in the spring of 1941 after his 'great escape' from Calcutta. In **Europe** he organized the Free India Centre and the Indian Legion, the latter formed from Indian army prisoners. Dissatisfied with the possibilities available to him in Europe, Bose was finally allowed to travel to South East Asia and **Japan** in 1943 via German and Japanese submarines. In Tokyo he met Prime Minster Tojo, and in South East Asia formed the provisional government of Azad Hind, or Free India. He also reorganized the **Indian National Army** (INA), which invaded India along with a much larger Japanese force in 1944. After serious defeats, the Japanese and INA retreated to **Burma** and **Singapore**. Trying to escape to **Manchuria**, Bose was badly burned in a plane crash in **Taiwan** in mid August 1945, just as the war ended. Many Indians refused to believe that he had died, but parliamentary commissions in 1956 and 1970 and reports of British intelligence reaffirmed the details of his death. The British Raj put officers of the INA on trial in 1945 for treason in Delhi. Three were convicted but released soon after because of nationwide demonstrations in their favour. The unrest created by the trial and news about the INA contributed to unrest in India and to the British decision to grant its independence.

Bosnia–Herzegovina

From the late fifteenth century the area making up modern Bosnia–Herzegovina was part of the **Ottoman Empire**, and this is what gave rise to the ethnic and religious mix that still exists today. Following failed revolts against Ottoman rule, Bosnia–Herzegovina came under Austro-Hungarian administration as a result of the 1878 Treaty of Berlin and in 1908 the area was annexed. The Austro-Hungarian Empire collapsed in 1918 and Bosnia–Herzegovina joined the Kingdom of Serbs, Croats and Slovenes, later **Yugoslavia**. Occupied by pro-Axis **Croatia** in 1941–5, Bosnia–Herzegovina formed part of the Socialist Federal Republic of Yugoslavia in 1945–91. With the break-up of Yugoslavia and independence in 1992, ethnic and religious tensions intensified, producing bitter conflict between shifting alliances involving Croat, Serb and Muslim nationalists, each with irreconcilable objectives. The 1995 Dayton Peace Accords secured agreement on a multi-ethnic central government, with a second layer made up of a Bosniak–Bosnian Croat Federation and a Bosnian-Serb Republika Srpska, initially supervised by an externally appointed Office of the High Representative. Individuals accused of war crimes during the conflict were subsequently tried at an International Criminal Tribunal at The Hague. Bosnia–Herzegovina has applied for EU membership.

Bosnian Crisis (1908)

Triggered, 1908, by **Austria–Hungary**'s annexation of the formerly Turkish Bosnia–Herzegovina, which it had administered since 1878. The provinces had been seen by **Serbia** as the natural extension of its nation state but by Austria–Hungary as an opportunity to enhance its prestige. Although recognized by the other Great Powers, the annexation created a south Slav problem and heightened the tensions between Austria–Hungary and **Russia**, in particular, which contributed to the outbreak of **World War I**.

Bosphorus

A strategic waterway connecting the Black Sea with the Sea of Marmara, modern Istanbul sits on its shores. In the nineteenth century **Russia** coveted control of the strait which connected its warm water ports in the Black Sea with the Mediterranean. The **Ottoman Empire** retained control of the Bosphorus until its defeat in November 1918, and the **Republic of Turkey** did not gain the right to militarize the strait until 1936.

Boston Massacre (1770) (USA)

On 5 March 1770 British soldiers in Boston, Massachusetts, were confronted by an angry mob. The troops had been sent to Boston to enforce unpopular customs duties created by the 1767 **Townshend Acts**. Their presence depressed wages and violent conflicts between the soldiers and Bostonians occurred frequently. The crowd threw snowballs, bricks and debris at the soldiers, who fired their weapons killing five Americans and wounding five more. Although most of the soldiers were acquitted when tried for murder, the incident hardened the opposition of many Americans to British rule.

Boston Tea Party (1773) (USA)

A protest on 6 December 1773 when sixty members of the **Sons of Liberty** in Boston, Massachusetts, boarded three merchant ships and destroyed 342 chests of East India Company tea with a value of 10,000 pounds. The protest was undertaken in response to a revised duty introduced by the Tea Act adopted by Parliament in May 1773. The Tea Act actually lowered the duty on tea, but it called attention to the tax which had remained after the repeal of the

Townshend Acts in 1770. Other protests took place in New York, Philadelphia and Charleston; however, that in Boston was the most violent and dramatic. In response to the Boston Tea Party, Parliament adopted the 1774 Coercive Acts to punish the people of Boston in particular and Massachusetts more generally for their opposition over the previous decade. These inflicted political and economic sanctions on the city and colony until restitution was made for the destroyed tea. The Boston Tea Party set in motion the final sequence of events culminating in the outbreak of war between the rebellious colonists and British forces in April 1775.

Boumedienne, Houari (1927–1978)

Algerian military leader and president. Born Mohamed Boukharouba in Guelma, 'Houari Boumedienne' was his *nom de guerre*. Boumedienne received a French and Arabic education and joined the Armée de Libération Nationale (ALN) in 1955. He subsequently became chief of staff of the external ALN positioned along Algeria's Moroccan and Tunisian frontiers. After Algeria became independent in July 1962, Boumedienne supported Ahmed Ben Bella but deposed him in June 1965. Austere and authoritarian, Boumedienne initiated socialist state-building plans featuring industrialization. In particular, he nationalized French hydrocarbon concessions in February 1971. He also inaugurated cultural and agrarian revolutions. Under him, Algeria championed third world interests by promoting an equitable global distribution of wealth. Algeria also supported pan-Arabism and national liberation movements, such as Western Sahara's Polisario. The National Charter and Constitution of 1976 reflected his political and socialist vision. He died from a rare blood disease.

Bourguiba, Habib (1901–2000)

Tunisian national leader and president, 1957–87. Having studied law in France, Bourguiba was frustrated by the limits placed on Tunisians in the French protectorate system. He joined the Destour nationalists but broke out in 1934 to form the more radical Neo-Destour Party. A mass movement, this forced the French to partial concessions, but Bourguiba insisted on full independence, which France conceded in 1956. The following year Tunisia became a republic and Bourguiba was president. Neutralizing his rivals, he made Tunisia a one-party state with himself as president-for-life, initially with general approval. In the 1960s and 1970s he steered his country between socialism and capitalism, but was strongly modernist and secular. In the 1980s an economic downturn, together with old age and health problems, made his rule more erratic, and he was removed from office by prime minister Ben Ali in 1987.

bovine spongiform encephalopathy (BSE)

Bovine spongiform encephalopathy, popularly 'mad cow disease', has been recognized in cattle for centuries, but a very serious outbreak started in the United Kingdom in 1986. Attributed to infected animal remains in feed, it was controlled by a controversial policy of mass slaughter rather than by the innoculation favoured elsewhere in Europe. The consumption of infected beef products can lead to the transfer of the disease to humans, where it is known as variant Creutzfeld-Jakob disease (CJD).

Boxer uprising (1900) (China)

The Boxer uprising was a peasant rebellion in northern China in 1900 that was used by the Empress Dowager Cixi as an opportunity to declare war on foreign powers. In 1899 flooding and drought led to the formation of rebel bands known as Boxers United in Righteousness, after the martial arts the groups practised. The rebels attacked missionaries and adopted the slogan 'Support the Qing and destroy the foreign.' By June 1900, the Boxers had reached Beijing and turned back a contingent of 2,100 troops sent from Tianjin to protect the foreign legations in the city. Cixi then declared war on the foreign powers, and the legations were besieged. An eight-nation alliance broke the siege, and the Boxer Protocol was signed in September 1901, which ended the war. China agreed to pay an indemnity of 450 million taels and have foreign troops stationed in Beijing and Tianjin for two years.

Brahmo Samaj

The Brahmo Samaj was a Hindu reform movement organized by Rammohun Roy in 1828 aimed at a purification and better understanding of Hindu traditions. In time, the Brahmos became separated from the orthodox Hindu fold, rejected the worship of images, designed their own forms of worship and frequently married within their own community. After the death of Roy, it was reorganized by Debendranath Tagore. In the later decades of the nineteenth century it split twice, but continued into the twentieth century as an important reform group with branches not only in Bengal but also across northern India.

Braudel, Fernand (1902–1985)

Born in Luméville-en-Ornois, **France**, Braudel studied under the supervision of Lucien Febvre and became a leading figure of the **Annales** school of history and editor of *Annales* in 1956. Awarded several honorary doctorates by the world's most prestigious universities and elected member of the French Academy, among his major works are *The Mediterranean and the Mediterranean World in the Age of Philip II* (1949) and *Capitalism and Material Life, 1400–1800* (3 volumes, 1967–79). He died in Haute-Savoie, France.

Brazil, Federative Republic of

The fifth largest country in the world, Brazil encompasses 5,289,089 square kilometres (3,286,488 square miles) and shares boundaries with every South American country except **Chile** and **Ecuador**. It extends approximately 4,345 kilometres (2,700 miles) from north to south and the same distance from east to west. The Amazon river basin, located primarily in Brazil, is drained by the **Amazon River** that originates in **Peru**. Brazil emerged from Portuguese control when Pedro, son of the Portuguese ruler, declared its independence in 1822, announcing himself emperor and ruling until 1831. His son, **Pedro II**, ruled until 1889 when he was overthrown and Brazil declared a republic. A boom in rubber production attracted increasing numbers of immigrants, boosting the wealth of the country as a whole. It participated on the side of the Allies in **World War I**, but the interwar depression hit it hard, leading to the intervention of the military and the suspension of the republic in 1937 under **Getulio Vargas**, who ruled as effective dictator until he was deposed in 1945. In 1946 a new democratic constitution was introduced permitting Vargas to return as president from 1950 to 1954. Political and financial difficulties meant that military rule was an ever-present threat, though the country continued to attract immigration and forge ahead economically with a new capital built at Brasilia in 1960, opening up the interior with the completion of the Trans-Amazonian Highway in 1973 and a huge hydroelectric scheme on the Parana River in 1982. By 1975 its population had passed 100 million, doubling since 1950.

After a coup in 1964 and military rule until 1985, Brazil returned to democracy and civilian government. A new constitution in 1988 established the Federative Republic of Brazil with twenty-six semi-autonomous states and the federal district.

The document established citizens' rights, divided the federal government into executive, legislative and judicial branches, authorized direct presidential elections every four years and shifted greater tax revenues from the federal government to states and municipalities. The success of President **Fernando Henrique Cardoso**'s *Real* Plan to end hyper-inflation enabled the national government to pursue recentralized authority. The *Real* Plan championed by **Cardoso** as finance minister in 1994 dramatically reduced inflation and brought his election as president. Although re-elected, his second term was marked by devaluation of the *real* and limited economic growth. Successor **Luiz Inácio Lula da Silva** built on Cardoso's efforts to reduce Brazil's debt, restrain inflation and promote economic growth. He also succeeded in elevating the country to being a recognized participant in major international meetings of the world's leading economic powers. Brazil has the estimated seventh largest economy in the world with substantial sectors in agriculture, mining, manufacturing and services. Its biggest trading partners are **China**, the **United States** and **Argentina**. Major offshore oil deposits and successful ethanol production have reduced dependence on imported petroleum products and the economy has grown rapidly since the government's success in dealing with debt and inflation. In 1990 the federal government began to privatize state companies. A decade later it tightened fiscal control over all levels of government. Brazil's census population of 191 million in 2010 made it the fifth most populous country in the world. The largest city, São Paulo, had a population of 20 million; over 85 per cent of the population lives in urban areas. Persons claiming at least partial African descent are nearly as numerous as those who consider themselves white.

Brazzaville conference

The Brazzaville conference, or Conférence Africaine Française, was initiated by the Comité Français de la Libération Nationale under General **de Gaulle** and held in January–February 1944. It had as its goal the construction of a new reformist French colonial policy. The conference rejected self-determination for **France**'s colonies, but promised a number of reforms including constitutional reform and increased political representation, the abolition of forced labour, investment in social services and a new penal code.

Brest-Litovsk, Treaty of

Signed by **Germany** and **Russia**, 3 March 1918, following Bolshevik Russia's unilateral termination of hostilities at **Lenin**'s direction, 26 November 1917. Russia lost **Poland**, **Lithuania** and much of Latvia, and had to evacuate the remainder of Latvia, Estonia and **Finland** and parts of the **Caucasus**, as well as recognize the anti-Bolshevik Ukrainian government. Largely overtaken by the German collapse of November 1918, the treaty's actual beneficiaries were not the Germans but the new national movements.

Bretton Woods conference

The United Nations Monetary and Financial Conference, commonly known as the Bretton Woods conference, was held from 1 July to 22 July 1944, during **World War II**. The purpose of the meeting was to establish financial arrangements for the post-war world. More than 730 delegates from all forty-five Allied nations met at Bretton Woods, New Hampshire. They agreed to set up the International Bank for Reconstruction and Development, the General Agreement on Tariffs and Trade (GATT) and the **International Monetary Fund** (IMF), to regulate the international monetary and financial system after the conclusion of World War II. The Bretton Woods system for exchange rate management remained in place until the early 1970s.

Brezhnev, Leonid (1906–1982)

General secretary of the Communist Party of the **USSR** and Soviet leader, 1964–82. Leonid Brezhnev is often associated with 'stagnation' and indolence, and his long geriatric decline in office is sometimes taken as indicative of the decline of the USSR. Nevertheless, Brezhnev was relatively popular as Soviet leader; though he was a principal player in the removal of **Nikita Khrushchev**, he is associated with **détente**, strategic arms limitation, the **Helsinki Agreement** and numerous summits with American leaders. He was in charge when the decision to invade **Afghanistan** was taken in the USSR, and is also associated with the idea of Soviet space competition with the **USA** by the production of Soviet technology on exactly American lines.

BRICS

– *see* **economic development**.

Britain

– *see* **United Kingdom**.

Britain, Battle of

– *see* **World War II**.

British Empire

– *see also* **Commonwealth; decolonization**.

The largely unsystematized, uncodified and occasionally changing territories dominated by Great Britain from around 1707 to around 1960 represented the greatest empire by physical size and population in recorded history. However, the British Empire as such was never one thing. At the time of its largest extent, between 1919 and 1941, it was already a loosening collection of colonies, territories, Dominions, dependencies and condominia, and its focus had shifted twice, from the American colonies to the rubble of the **Mughal Empire** in **India** in the 1770s, and then from the Indian Ocean to **Africa** in the 1880s. The Empire (as it was known) was largely expanded by autonomous chartered companies such as the **East India Company**, which maintained their own paramilitaries, until the 1850s, or by individuals such as Sir **Cecil Rhodes** and Sir **Stamford Raffles**. It was not until 1858 that formal control by the central government was extended across India, for example. British banks and shadow finance bodies dominated South American states such as **Argentina** without any military presence or formal involvement in governance at all.

Within the Empire, a small volunteer army was complemented by a huge and dominating Royal Navy. Control of the oceans was in tune with the fact that very early, loose, mercantile policies had been displaced by free trade in the history of the entity. The Empire functioned as a safety valve for a state which, after 1688, never experienced revolution but which blended the appearance of conservatism with the adoption of liberal values. For instance, **Britain** exported large numbers of its own skilled population, prisoners and discontented radicals to the Empire whilst maintaining the sovereignty of a unitary parliament, containing representatives from the home islands and members of a British-based House of Lords. This fact alone is possibly an explanation for Britain's lack of revolutions. Nevertheless, when given the chance to share power with colonial parliaments, in 1775–81, 1880–1900 or post 1920, the British preferred to grant functional or real independence and maintain their home system over federation or confederacy. Indeed, the dissolution of the Empire, between 1946 and 1980, though not without fatalities, has been viewed as a far better managed process than that of others, such as the French, Portugese or Spanish ends of empire.

In this curious entity, the unifying factors were largely economic and cultural. The Crown (elevated to imperial status by Benjamin Disraeli in 1876), the English language, common law and a gold-backed pound sterling as currency generally helped hold the Empire together, as did a remarkably strong and modernized aristocracy at home. The Empire delivered cheap food to the working classes, opportunities for service in colonial or corporate bureaucracies to the middle classes, the risk and reward of science- and engineering-based business for those engaged in industry, and service in colonial government for the upper middle classes and minor aristocracy. Formal office-holding at the expense of taxpayers was however minimized, and for most of its history, imperial administration was carried out by fewer than 5,000 people in London and across the world.

Many scholars have also identified a racial consensus within the Empire, in which, over time, white Anglo-Protestant civilization was valued and prioritized over all others. At home, newspapers, political culture and public opinion upheld the value of ritual and hierarchy, leading some scholars to suggest that the local princes, kings, chiefs, tribes and aristocracies which the British tended to govern through or to leave in place illustrated the 'ornamentalism' and governance through display of the Empire. The preponderance of evidence, however, shows that it was extraordinarily difficult, and illicit, for people of any colour other than white to progress within imperial structures, and that even within these bars, open racism, anti-Irish, anti-Catholic and anti-Semitic feelings were extraordinarily easy to provoke. The Empire was associated with many of the worst moments in history, such as the slave trade, the Bengal and Irish famines, the scramble for Africa, the attempted genocide of aboriginal cultures and peoples in Oceania and North America, and Indian partition. However, it was also associated with the abolition of the slave trade and slavery, the promotion of national self-governance within Africa, the Indian subcontinent and Native America, and ultimately with war against far more destructive and openly racist powers such as **Germany**, **Italy** and **Japan**, the colonial records of whom were almost wholly bleak.

Given its administrative diversity and weakness, and the tendency of the British until the twentieth century to avoid European wars and entanglements, modern scholarship has often turned to the question of why the British thought that they had a unified empire at all. This has produced works focused on the way public schools, which trained the staff of the imperial civil services, military and politics, appropriated the image and language of the western Roman Empire for the state created by the union of Scotland with England and Wales in 1707. Others point to the fact that celebration of the Empire largely began as it passed its zenith and entered obvious decline, in the early and mid twentieth century. The interests of postcolonial thinkers and leaders in blaming a unified empire for their problems has also contributed to the image of the Empire, as has the largely post-imperial presentation of it in film, popular literature and television. In recent years, a remarkable strain in American neoconservative thought has also sought to uphold the idea of an 'Anglosphere' in which the great democracies of **Canada**, India, **Australia** and Britain, as part of a wider post-imperial cultural community, join in a 'League of Democracy'. It stands in contrast to the strains within Britain itself, which, shorn of real imperial power by the mid 1960s, began to experience nationalist movements within Scotland and Wales which paralleled the previous Irish one and which envisaged the break-up of the British state.

The **United Kingdom** today maintains a small number of colonies and territories. These are largely held over from the past, though some are of strategic value, such as **Gibraltar** in **Spain** and Diego Garcia in the Indian Ocean. Others, such as Bermuda, have become part of a shadow network of tax havens and financial centres which emerged almost as soon as the formal empire fell, and which have maintained the influence of English commercial law and the City of London in the modern world. A few, such as the Falkland Islands, hold out the hope of mineral wealth and global presence. Her Majesty the Queen is still queen of sixteen countries, including Australia, Canada and **New Zealand**, and the **Commonwealth** is perhaps the epitome of influential international organizations outside the **United Nations** system. It is therefore very likely that as the years pass, new historical perspectives on the British Empire and its continuing legacy will emerge.

British Honduras
– *see* **Belize**.

British South Africa Company (BSAC)
Enterprise established under Royal Charter in 1889 by **Cecil Rhodes** (1853–1902) to exercise commercial and quasi-government rights in southern **Africa** after the British government had declined to become directly involved in exploitation of

regional resources. BSAC was empowered to set up political administration and security forces in the areas coming under its remit, nominally with the agreement of local rulers. This meant, in practice, that Rhodes and his colleagues worked through BSAC to exploit African land, mineral resources and labour for the company's benefit. The company governed Southern Rhodesia (now **Zimbabwe**) from 1894 and Northern Rhodesia (now **Zambia**) from 1890, until the British Colonial Office took control in 1923, BSAC retaining valuable mineral rights. BSAC maladministration in Matabeleland provoked rebellion in 1896, which required British military intervention to quell. Company attempts to secure influence in **Mozambique** were thwarted by the 1891 Anglo-Portuguese Convention.

Brown v. Board of Education (USA)

In May 1954 the Supreme Court declared that racially segregated schools were inherently unequal and so the *Plessy* doctrine of 'separate but equal' (1896) was overturned. The subsequent legal dismantling of *de jure* segregation relied on the *Brown* decision. However, Southern whites criticized the ruling as policy-making, breaching the separation of powers in American governance. Public hostility to bussing and increased residential segregation have frustrated efforts to enforce *Brown*. Resegregated minority–majority schools are now commonplace.

Brown, John (1800–1859)

White militant abolitionist synonymous with a failed attempt at fomenting slave rebellion in the **United States**. In one of the key events ensuing from the **Kansas–Nebraska Act**, Brown butchered five pro-slavery men in the Pottawatomie massacre (1856). He then seized the federal arsenal at Harpers Ferry, Virginia, in October 1859. Besieged, captured and hanged following an unapologetic defence, Brown's sanctification in the North infuriated a South already paranoid over slave insurrections, in turn hastening **secession** and the **American Civil War**.

Bruce, James (1730–1794)

A Scottish diplomat and scholar. Sent to Algiers in 1762 as a consul, Bruce embarked on extensive travels in **Egypt**, the Red Sea, **Ethiopia**, the Nile valley and then back to England in 1774. During his travels he collected many ancient Ethiopian manuscripts and wrote a voluminous account of Egypt, Ethiopia and the Nile valley, published in 1790. Although not fully recognized, Bruce's work

is important for the study of the history of northeast Africa.

Brunei

A sultanate on the north of the island of Borneo, bordering the South China Sea. By the nineteenth century the former Bruneian Empire was in decline, weakened by internal division and encroaching European colonial ambitions. In 1841 Sultan Omar Ali Saifuddien II (1799–1852) gave the British adventurer James Brooke (1803–68) control of Sarawak as 'White Rajah' for restoring him to power following an uprising. British influence was extended with the cession in 1846 of Labuan Island and in 1888 Brunei became a British protectorate. Oil extraction began in 1929, beginning the area's industrial development. Occupied by **Japan** during **World War II**, Brunei's subsequent economic progress was rapid but political evolution was chequered. The sultan is an absolute monarch under the 1959 constitution, despite notionally democratic amendment. Brunei gained independence in 1984 under Sultan Omar Ali Saifuddien III (1914–86). The country is predominantly Muslim and in 2014 became the first South East Asian state to adopt **sharia law**.

Brutus, Dennis (1924–2009)

A South African poet, graduate of the Universities of Fort Hare and Witswatersrand. As a political activist, Brutus was instrumental in gaining international support for anti-**apartheid** actions outside of **South Africa** as a part of the Anti-Colored Affairs Department. He was arrested in 1963 as a result, and imprisoned. He fled the country and eventually won refugee status in the **United States**, where he taught literature at various universities.

Bryan, William Jennings (1860–1925)

A lawyer practising in Lincoln, Nebraska, Bryan served in Congress from 1891 to 1895. He ran unsuccessfully as a Democratic candidate for the presidency in 1896, 1900 and 1908 but, in doing so, helped to turn the party from a strict adherence to minimal government to a more interventionist progressive programme. Appointed secretary of state by **Woodrow Wilson**, he resigned in 1915 over the *Lusitania* controversy. In later life Bryan became associated with the campaign to prohibit the teaching of evolution in schools.

BSE

– *see* **bovine spongiform encephalopathy (BSE)**.

Buchanan, James (1791–1868)

Lawyer, Pennsylvanian state and national politician, and fifteenth president of the **United States** (1857–61). Despite an impressive Washington portfolio (House, 1821–31; Senate, 1834–45; secretary of state, 1845–9), it was essentially Buchanan's distance from domestic debates over slavery as **Franklin Pierce**'s minister to Britain that garnered him the 1856 **Democratic** nomination. Although he came to power amidst prior **sectional conflict**, Buchanan nevertheless enjoys a consistently low reputation for his part in developments that would culminate in the **American Civil War**. His apparent complicity in the **Dred Scott** ruling (1857), and attempts to admit Kansas as a slave state in defiance of the 'popular sovereignty' envisaged in the **Kansas–Nebraska Act**, belied his claims to stand above such controversy. Buchanan's strict construction of the **American Constitution** was favourable in practice to the South and in 1860–1 he refused to resist **secession** even as he denied its legality. Allegations of executive corruption and a recession (1857) also marred his term.

Buddhism

Known to its adherents as the *Dharma*, a Sanskrit word conveying the concepts of truth, law, doctrine and the 'right and proper'. The predominant faith of Bhutan, Burma (**Myanmar**), Cambodia (**Kampuchea**), **Laos**, **Mongolia**, **Sri Lanka**, **Thailand** and **Vietnam**, and of the Chinese region of **Tibet** and the Indian state of Sikkim. There is a very large community in **Japan**, where it overlaps with Shintoism, and in **Singapore**, where it overlaps with **Taoism**. The size of the community in **China** itself, where again it overlaps with Taoism, is unknown but may well be significant. There are also lesser communities in **Indonesia** and **Malaysia**. Although the faith originated in **India**, it has largely died out there except in the border state of Sikkim. There may currently be some 410 million adherents worldwide.

Founded by the Nepalese prince Siddhattha Gotama, known as the Buddha or 'Enlightened One', in the sixth century BC, it is the oldest of the world's great faiths after Hinduism, from which it sprang. Buddhism ignores the question of whether a God or gods exist but believes in reincarnation. Unlike Muhammad but like Jesus, the Buddha left no writings of his own, and the first written record of his teachings based on oral tradition dates from some four hundred years after his death. He was essentially moved by the problem of human suffering and after long meditation came to believe in

'four noble truths' which could release humanity from suffering. The first was that all living was itself suffering; the second, that all suffering was caused by desire; the third, that suffering ceased when desire was eradicated; and the fourth, that suffering could be destroyed by following the 'noble eightfold path'. The steps along that path were: right views; right thought; right plain and truthful speech; right conduct, including abstinence from illicit sex, the taking of alcohol or drugs, the taking of any life and theft; right livelihood which harmed no one; right positive effort; right awareness of the here and now; and, finally, right meditation. Right meditation would inculcate an attitude of mind beyond thinking and reasoning which would enable the meditator to escape from the physical body. Buddhism is, therefore, no more a rationalist than it is a theistic system. The more man followed that eightfold path in his succession of reincarnated lives, the sooner he would achieve the ultimate goal of *nirvana* (extinguishment, as of a candle), whereby he lost the illusion of his own separate identity and merged into universal life. The meaning of *nirvana* could not be conveyed in words, but was something 'unborn, unbecome, unmade, unconditioned'.

Although Buddhism eschewed the Indian tradition of ascetic self-torture, its philosophical asceticism and pessimistic attitude to the nature of ordinary life almost inevitably produced a parallel popular Buddhism incorporating deities, the concept of a heavenly afterlife and the veneration of relics. The Temple of the Tooth, in Kandy, Sri Lanka, containing the alleged tooth of the Buddha, is perhaps the most familiar example of the latter. Contemporary Buddhism falls into two broad categories. The purest tradition is the *Theravada* (the doctrine of the elders) of south Asia, while China and Japan follow the *Mahayana* (great vehicle) school. *Mahayana* followers called it the 'great vehicle' to emphasize its wider appeal than the purer school derived from the *Theravada*, which they dubbed *Hinayana* or 'lesser vehicle'. The *Lamaism* of Tibet and Mongolia is a highly distinctive, and some would say decadent, variety of the *Mahayana*, marked by a high degree of ritualism and the role of the **Dalai Lama** as effectively both king and high priest.

Although Buddhism is amongst the most pacific of faiths and has largely escaped the deadly internal conflicts of Christianity and **Islam**, it has nonetheless become associated at times with nationalist, political and social movements of a similarly violent kind. Of nowhere is this truer than the country with the oldest continuous Buddhist tradition in the world, Sri Lanka. The development of armed organizations by the essentially secular **Tamil** separatist movement in the 1970s provoked in its turn a strong Sinhalese backlash in the form of a nationalist ideology based on Buddhism and an 'Aryan' concept of racial superiority rooted in the Indo-European identity of the Sinhalese language. This took its most extreme form in the Janata Vimukthi Peramuna (JVP), which evolved out of a left-leaning essentially youthful insurrection against the socio-political establishment into a militant terrorist organization based mainly in the countryside and promoting a violent Sinhalese-Buddhist racist chauvinism.

A far less extreme but not dissimilar evolution appeared in Buddhist Burma (Myanmar) after 2012, where the Muslim minority population of Rakhine (Arakan) is not acknowledged as Burmese by the authorities. Perhaps 180 people died in intercommunal bloodshed and a further 125,000 were displaced. Mosques were demolished and Muslim neighbourhoods flattened with the seeming connivance of the central government. Violence against Muslim communities spread to other parts of Burma in March 2013, with Buddhist monks being detained for armed rioting in Mektila. Nevertheless, Buddhism played a much more pacific role in South Vietnam, where Buddhist monks immolated themselves, May 1963, in protest against the dictatorial rule of the Roman Catholic Ngo Dinh Diem. Moreover, they could only suffer from afar when the extremist Muslim Taliban destroyed the giant figure of the Buddha at the Afghan World Heritage site at Bamiyan.

Living Buddhism, as distinct from heritage, has, however, been under the greatest pressure in the Chinese region of Tibet, where the long-held official Communist line was that Tibetan backwardness was due to centuries of Buddhist rule and that progress could only be made by eliminating religion from people's lives. The suppression of a revolt in 1959 led to the flight of the Dalai Lama and, with the additional stimulus of the Chinese Cultural Revolution of the 1960s, to the damaging or destruction of perhaps two thousand monasteries and their contents. With the changed Chinese policy of the 1980s, many are, however, being rebuilt along traditional lines, the monks encouraged by their cyclical rather than linear sense of the nature of existence.

buffalo

The buffalo (American bison) was the American West's largest animal and the most significant to both indigenous peoples and settlers. Tribal economies revolved around products from this (also spiritually central) keystone species. Populations estimated at 60–100 million in the 1850s had dwindled to mere hundreds by 1890 through recreational hunting and unsustainable exploitation for robes, meat and hides. Rescued by conservationists, it is currently enjoying a modest revival (350,000), but mostly on ranches as livestock.

'Buffalo Bill', Cody, William Frederick (1846–1917)

Frontiersman and entertainer who served as a US cavalry scout during the **American Civil War** and Plains conflict with **Native Americans**, among other things. Celebrated in prolific 'dime novels', Cody and his genuine accomplishments were always inseparable from his legend. He put on shows from 1872, notably his touring 'Wild West' from 1883. Cody adapted as the Old West that he personified essentially disappeared, taking an interest in conservation, early western films and a ruinous irrigation scheme. A pioneer aviator, he was killed in a flying accident.

Buganda

A pre-colonial African kingdom located in modern-day **Uganda**. Founded in the late eighteenth century from the previous kingdom of Bunyoro, it became the most important of the interlacustrine kingdoms in the nineteenth century, especially under Mutesa I (r. 1856–1884) who sought to westernize the kingdom. It allied with **Britain** in making the conquest of Uganda and was absorbed into that colony as a semi-automous region under its own ruler and parliament, the *Katikiro*.

Bulgaria

An integral part of the **Ottoman Empire** in the Balkans from the fourteenth century. Declared autonomous by Treaty of Berlin, 1878. United with Eastern Rumelia, 1885, and declared full independence, 1908. A participant in the **Balkan Wars**, 1912–13. An ally of the central powers in **World War I** and obliged to cede land to **Yugoslavia** and **Greece** in the Treaty of Neuilly, 1919. Bulgaria signed the **Axis** Pact in 1941, declaring war on America and Britain but not the **Soviet Union**. It attempted to withdraw from **World War II** in August 1944, proclaiming neutrality in the German–Soviet war, a position which led to a Soviet declaration of war and occupation by 1945. Peace treaty with the Allies, February 1947. A People's Republic, 1947–90, a member of **Comecon**, 1949–90, and of the **Warsaw Pact**, 1955–91. The leading role of the **Communist** Party terminated, 1990, but the reformed successor Bulgarian Socialist Party (BSP) remains politically significant. Bulgaria became a member of the **European Union** in 2007.

Bull Run, Battles of (21 July 1861; 29–30 August 1862) (USA)

These Confederate victories were significant in the **American Civil War** because Manassas Junction formed a vital logistical staging post in any Union assault on the Confederate capital, Richmond, Virginia. In the first, Irvin McDowell's attempt to outflank the Confederate was left disintegrated once troops were rushed to the threatened sector. In the second, two corps of **Robert E. Lee**'s Army of Northern Virginia separated and rejoined on the battlefield to crush John Pope's Union Army of Virginia in a 'nutcracker'.

Bunmei Kaika movement (Japan)

Early **Meiji** period movement which aimed to enhance modernization under the banner of 'Civilization and Enlightenment' (Bunmei Kaika). The **Meiji restoration** created a new direction for a modern Japan, including political reforms to abolish feudal structures, and promoting educational reform. The Bunmei Kaika movement was initiated by Meiji intellectuals, most notably, Nakamura Masanao (Keiu) and Fukuzawa Yukichi. Nakamura's translation of Samuel Smiles' *Self-Help* (*Saikoku Rishi Hen*) emphasized individual ability and self-respect. Fukuzawa's widely read manuscript, *Gakumon no Susume* (*On the Encouragement of Learning*) fostered popular enthusiasm for education. This intellectual elite established the Meiji Sixth Year Society (Meirokusha) as an arena for discussing the advancement of modernization in Japan, and published *Meiroku Zasshi* (*Journal of the Japanese Enlightenment*) in 1874 for the purpose of education. The association, confronted by a government that had created a modern state, voluntarily dissolved itself after the press laws forbade criticism of the government

Bunyoro

An ancient kingdom in modern-day **Uganda** founded probably around 1500 but reaching prominence in the early eighteenth century. Its domination extended over much of the area between the East African Great Lakes. In the early nineteenth century, thanks to internal divisions within the country, several of its constituent units, such as **Buganda** and Toro, became independent leaving only a much smaller state. It was conquered by the British in 1899 and incorporated into Uganda.

Burckhardt, Jacob Christoph (1818–1897)

Swiss historian and author of important works on the Italian Renaissance and on ancient Greek civilization. One of the first supporters of art history and cultural history as academic disciplines, he emphasized the importance of art both in its own right and as a primary source for historical study. Opposed **Hegel**'s dialectic method and Auguste Comte's positivism, as well as the nineteenth century's conception of history as the study of politics alone.

Burgos, laws of

Promulgated on December 1512, this largely ineffective group of laws was aimed to regulate Spanish colonists' behaviour towards Indians in the New World. Answering to complaints from Spanish missionaries regarding the mistreatment of Indians in places such as Hispaniola, the laws sought to rein in abuses of indigenous peoples and promote their conversion to Catholicism. The laws also created the *encomienda* system under which groups of Indians were assigned to Spanish *encomenderos* for work, mostly in gold mines, and religious instruction.

Burke, Edmund (1729–1797)

Irish-born Whig politician who campaigned for the right of a parliamentarian to act as a representative, and not a delegate, of his constituents. Burke sought to compromise with the American colonial revolutionaries and campaigned against **Warren Hastings** over corruption in British **India**, but in his *Reflections on the Revolution in France* (1790) he repudiated revolutionary politics. Burke argued that political principles were derived from traditional historical practice, and not rational idealism. His conservatism informs contemporary objections to rationalism and ideology in politics. Often seen as one of the founders of conservative ideology.

Burkina Faso

Upper Volta until 1983, this west African country was occupied by **France** in 1898. Indigenous resistance continued until 1904. The territory was incorporated into French West Africa in 1919 and gained independence in 1960. The authoritarian rule of President Maurice Yaméogo (1921–93) provoked instability and in 1966 he was overthrown by Sangoulé Lamizana (1916–2005). Political parties were banned, but in 1977 Lamizana introduced a new constitution and was democratically elected in 1978. He was ousted in a military coup, Thomas Sankara (1950–) taking power in 1983 with a reform programme. In 1987 Sankara was assassinated in a coup led by Blaise Compaoré (1951–), who followed policies less threatening to the elites. He was elected president in 1991, 1998 and 2005 but ousted by the military in 2014. Civilian government was restored under Michel Kafando (1943–). Burkina Faso has few natural resources and the bulk of its predominantly Muslim population (60 per cent; Christians 20 per cent) undertake subsistence farming.

Burma
– see **Myanmar**.

Burmese Campaign (1942–1945)
Major campaign of **World War II**. **Burma** was invaded by Japanese forces in January 1942, forcing the weak British forces to withdraw, abandoning Rangoon and undertaking a long retreat to **India**. Their retreat was aided by the intervention of Chinese forces under the command of the American General Stilwell (1883–1946), who aimed to keep open the land link to **China**, the Burma Road. An attempted British counter-attack in the Arakan in December 1942 was decisively defeated by May 1943. British morale, however, was bolstered by the start of Chindit, guerrilla-style operations behind Japanese lines led by the charismatic Orde Wingate (1904–44). Under General William Slim (1891–1970), the British forces also developed techniques of air supply and learned to adapt better to local conditions. A second campaign in the Arakan in early 1944 proved more successful in challenging Japanese superiority in jungle fighting. A Japanese offensive against Imphal and Kohima, mounted in January 1944 by the Fifteenth Army led by General Mutaguchi, aimed to open the road to India. Imphal was successfully defended in a three-month siege from early April and an epic defence of Kohima led to the retreat and destruction of the Fifteenth Army with over 50,000 dead and loss of all their equipment. Meanwhile, Stilwell's American-led Chinese forces were eroding Japanese positions in northern

Burma. During 1945 Slim's Fourteenth Army brilliantly outmanoeuvred the Japanese in central Burma, capturing Mandalay on 2 May, with a separate operation destroying the Japanese Twenty-Eighth Army in the Arakan. The fighting in Burma constituted one of the greatest defeats of the Japanese forces in World War II.

Burton, Richard Francis (1821–90)
British adventurer who travelled widely in Asia (particularly **India**, where he served for a time as an official), **Europe**, **Africa** and the Americas. A man of great intellect who could speak forty languages and was competent in a number of scientific fields, he is best known for a translation of the *Arabian Nights* and his detailed descriptions of East Africa as well as the Kingdom of **Dahomey** and the mouth of the Congo River.

Burundi
Heir to the sixteenth-century Burundian kingdom, this landlocked central African country was incorporated into German East Africa in 1890. In 1919 it became a League of Nations **mandate** under Belgium, which continued the practice of minority Tutsi landowners dominating the majority peasant Hutu. The country gained independence as a constitutional monarchy under King Mwami Mwambutsa IV (1912–77) in 1962. He was deposed in 1966, Michel Micombero (1940–83) becoming president. There were outbreaks of violence between the Tutsi and Hutu in 1965, 1972 and 1988. In 1976 Jean-Baptiste Bagaza (1946–) ousted Micombero, instituting a one-party state in 1981. Bagaza was overthrown in 1987 by Pierre Buyoya (1949–) and in 1993 Melchior Ndadaye (1953–93) was elected the first Hutu president. His murder provoked a civil war in which over 150,000 died between 1993 and 2005. Following a peace brokered by South African President **Nelson Mandela**, Hutu Pierre Nkurunziza (1963–) became president. Burundi is predominantly Christian, with a small Muslim minority. Over 90 per cent of the population is engaged in agriculture.

Bush, George Herbert Walker (1924–)
US president. Following periods as chairman of the Republican National Committee and director of the **Central Intelligence Agency**, in 1980 George Herbert Bush was chosen as **Ronald Reagan**'s running mate. After serving two terms as vice president, in 1988 he was the successful Republican nominee for president. His presidency

was particularly associated with foreign policy, ranging from the collapse of the **Soviet Union** to the invasion of **Panama**, and in 1991 Bush responded to the Iraqi invasion of **Kuwait** by launching and quickly winning the first **Gulf War**. Despite this success, however, he was unable to retain sufficient support either from the electorate or his own party. Accused of being unable to deal with America's worsening economy, he was defeated in the 1992 presidential election by the Democratic candidate, **Bill Clinton**. Following Clinton's two terms, George H. W. Bush's son, **George W. Bush**, won the 2000 presidential election.

Bush, George W. (1946–)

US president, 2001–9, the son of President **George H. W. Bush**. Elected Republican governor of Texas in 1994, Bush's first election as president was controversial; initially there was no clear winner and the election was resolved by the Supreme Court in Bush's favour. The **al-Qaida** attacks of September 11th, 2001 on the **United States** led to the administration's 'war on terror', which meant war in **Afghanistan** and later in **Iraq**. Though US and allied forces quickly overthrew the incumbent regimes, which helped Bush secure re-election, it proved impossible to establish stable governments in those countries and casualties mounted. Domestically, the presidency was marked by large tax cuts and a huge federal budget deficit. The Bush administration was criticized for its response in 2005 to Hurricane Katrina, which destroyed much of New Orleans, and its reputation was further damaged by the turmoil in the US financial system in 2007–8.

Bustani, Butrus al- (1819–1883)

Arab literary scholar who sought to reinvigorate Arab culture through his encyclopedia and dictionary. The former, in six volumes, with its echoes of the French *Encyclopédie* of a century earlier, sought to enshrine the fruits of western civilization and science in the hope that they would stimulate contemporary Arab culture, and it was partnered by his dictionary which sought to render the Arabic language a more effective and flexible instrument for expressing those western concepts. His conviction of the need for cultural reinvigoration, which was paralleled in **India** and other regions of **Asia**, was expounded in the political and literary magazine he founded, 1870, entitled *al-Jinan* (*The Shield*). Himself a Christian, he sought also to develop toleration and trust between the mutually suspicious religions and religious groups characterizing the **Lebanon** of his time, then part of Ottoman **Syria**.

Buthelezi, Mangosuthu Gatsa (1928–)

South African politician and **Zulu** leader. Educated at Fort Harare University and Natal University and a member of the **African National Congress (ANC)**, he assumed his position as hereditary chief of the Buthelezi clan in 1953. Buthelezi worked for the Department of Native Affairs from 1951, becoming Zulu Territorial Authority chief executive in 1970 and KwaZulu legislative assembly chief executive councillor in 1972. As chief minister of the KwaZulu 'homeland' from 1976, he rejected the government's spurious description of independence. In 1975 he revived the Zulu cultural movement Inkatha as the Inkatha Freedom Party (covertly financed by the government) and opposed ANC guerrilla action and international sanctions as means of combatting the **apartheid** system. Thousands died in violent clashes between Inkatha and ANC supporters. Buthelezi was home affairs minister in 1994–2004 in the post-apartheid government, but declined an offer of the post of Deputy President.

C

Cabildo

A city council in colonial Spanish America, modelled on Castilian precedent. *Cabildos* typically consisted of six to twelve *regidores* or aldermen (originally appointed by the king or viceroy) who yearly selected two *alcaldes ordinarios* or magistrates. From the late sixteenth century on, local elites began purchasing offices and passing them on to their heirs; these councils therefore became the one governing institution consistently dominated by Creoles. They had wide scope in urban affairs, collecting taxes, regulating markets, distributing land, maintaining infrastructure, exercising police power and representing the city to royal authorities.

Cabinda

– *see* **Angola**.

Cabinet mission (Indian)

In March 1946 British Prime Minister Clement Attlee sent a three-man mission to India to discuss terms for independence. Its plan envisaged a three-tiered federation in which most powers would vest in a middle level of provinces grouped in three, with two comprising the Muslim-majority provinces of the north-east and north-west and the third the remaining Hindu-majority provinces. The central government would control only defence, foreign affairs and communications. The last hope for a united independent India ended when the **Indian National Congress**, objecting to compulsory grouping and the weak centre, rejected the proposal.

Cairo conferences

Conferences of 22–6 November and 2–7 December 1943 between America's President **Roosevelt** and Britain's Prime Minister **Winston Churchill**, separated by the Tehran conference with the Soviet leader, **Joseph Stalin**. The first conference declared, with China's leader, General **Chiang Kai-shek**, the objective of taking away from **Japan** all the territories it had acquired since 1914 and restoring Korean independence. It also discussed Allied plans for the **Normandy landings**. The second conference sought unsuccessfully to persuade **Turkey**'s President **Ismet Inönü** to bring Turkey into the war on the Allied side. President Roosevelt also announced to Churchill his choice of General **Dwight D. Eisenhower** as supreme Allied commander for the Normandy landings.

Calcutta (Kolkata)

One of the great cities of India, it was first a commercial centre from the end of the seventeenth century, growing to become the commercial, transport, administrative and cultural hub of eastern India. The British chose it as the capital of their Indian empire in the second half of the eighteenth century and it remained that until 1912. At the same time it became the centre of Bengali culture and educational activity, which still thrives. Built on swampy land on the bank of the Hughli River, a branch of the Ganges, it was a great port until the 1950s when the silting up of the river drove trade downstream to other ports. It remains the capital of the state of West Bengal and has revived economically in recent decades, including improvements in transportation (a metro or subway running north and south through the centre, a second bridge across the Hughli and new flyovers and access roads). The city has been expanding into the suburbs with the building of new housing colonies and efforts to attract new industry including technology firms. Its official name is now Kolkata.

Calhoun, John Caldwell (1782–1850)

Later renowned as the great defender of slavery, Calhoun began his political career as an energetic nationalist, both as Congressman from South Carolina (1811–17) and as **Monroe**'s secretary of war (1817–25). Then in his anxiety to protect slavery, as vice president (1825–32) he moved with his state toward a defensive sectionalism and developed the doctrine of **nullification** that South Carolina adopted when it threatened to obstruct the collection of import duties in December 1832. Moving to the US Senate (1832–43), political isolation forced him to accept an unsatisfactory compromise tariff. As **John Tyler**'s secretary of state (1844–5), he worked for the annexation of **Texas**, but back in the Senate (1845–50) he opposed further annexations from **Mexico**. He then sought to unify the South behind states rights and the expansion of slavery, insisting in effect on a right of veto for the South, and resisted the Compromise of 1850 up until his death.

caliphate
– *see* **Islam**.

Cambodia
– *see* **Kampuchea**.

Cameroon
Involved by the Portuguese and Dutch in the **slave trade**, the area became the German west African colony of Kamerun in 1884. In 1919 **Britain** and **France** divided it as **League of Nations** mandated territories. Both became independent in 1960 under President Ahmadou Ahidjo (1929–89) and reunited in 1961. In 1966 Ahidjo's Cameroon National Union became the sole legal party. Paul Biya (1933–) succeeded Ahidjo in 1982; he restored multiparty politics in 1990 and in 1992 was returned in an election boycotted by the opposition. The English-speaking Southern Cameroons National Council, meanwhile, advocated secession of Ambazonia. Biya was re-elected in 1997, 2004 and 2011. A border dispute with **Nigeria** over the oil-rich Bakassi peninsula was settled in 2006 and in 2014 Cameroon allied with neighbouring **Chad** to confront the Islamist Boko Haram. Cameroon's economy is based on agriculture, oil and mining, and is 70 per cent Christian, with a 20 per cent Muslim minority.

Camp David One (1978)
In 1977 newly elected Israeli Prime Minister **Menachem Begin** set about trying to negotiate peace with **Egypt**, a goal which had eluded all previous Israeli governments. Early in his administration Begin convinced United States President **Jimmy Carter** and Romanian President **Nicolae Ceaușescu** to serve as intermediaries in **Israel**'s quest for Egyptian negotiations. These contacts bore fruit with Egyptian President **Anwar Sadat**'s 19–21 November 1977 visit to **Jerusalem** and address to Israel's parliament (the Knesset). Subsequent Israeli–Egyptian negotiations at Ismailya, Cairo, London and Washington became bogged down over the future status of the Palestinians and interpretations of the United Nations' 1967 resolution 242, which called for

Israeli withdrawal from 'territories' (not all territories) occupied during the June 1967 war. In August 1978, in an attempt to break the deadlock, United States President Jimmy Carter invited Begin and Sadat to meet him in the comparative seclusion of the presidential retreat at Camp David, Maryland.

The conference produced Camp David One, a series of agreements which were signed on 17 November. Israel would withdraw from Sinai, the peninsula would be demilitarized, Egypt would terminate its economic boycott of the Jewish state, and Israel would enjoy full freedom of navigation through the **Suez Canal** as well as the Straits of Tiran, a *causus belli* in June 1967. Egypt would enjoy the freedom of overland passage between the Sinai and **Jordan**. The future of the **West Bank** and **Gaza** would be determined in negotiations between Israel, Jordan, Egypt and the Palestinians. Ultimately the Israeli Army would withdraw and be replaced by a freely elected self-governing authority. A peace treaty was also envisaged between Israel and Jordan.

For their role in negotiating Camp David One, Begin and Sadat shared the December 1978 Nobel Peace Prize. The Knesset approved the accords by a vote of 84 in favour, 19 against, and 17 abstentions. Opponents included two staunch members of Begin's own party, Foreign Minister Arens and Knesset speaker and future prime minister **Yitzhak Shamir**. Most of the opposition Labour Party voted in favour. On 26 March 1979 an Egyptian–Israeli peace treaty was signed on the White House lawn, to be followed five years later by a treaty with Jordan. Israel completed its withdrawal from Sinai in April 1982, although negotiations dragged on for many years over the status of the Taba resort on the Egyptian–Israeli border. The International Court of Justice ultimately awarded the resort to Egypt.

Camp David Two (2000)
Between 11 and 20 July 2000 United States President **William Clinton**, Israeli Prime Minister Ehud Barak and Palestinian Authority Chairman **Yasser Arafat** met at Camp David, Maryland, the presidential retreat, to follow up on the 1978 **Camp David One** and 1993 **Oslo Accords**. Their goal was to produce a final status agreement ending the Israeli–Palestinian conflict. Major disagreements arose almost immediately over territory, Jerusalem, refugees and Israeli security concerns. Palestinian negotiators indicated they wanted full Palestinian sovereignty over the entire **West Bank** and **Gaza** Strip, although they would consider a one-to-one land swap with **Israel**. The parties

also disageed over the Israeli proposal to annex areas which would lead to a cantonization of the West Bank into blocs creating, for example, barriers between Nablus and Jenin with Ramallah. The Palestinians demanded complete sovereignty over East Jerusalem and its holy sites, in particular, the Al-Aqsa Mosque and the Dome of the Rock, a site holy in both Islam and Judaism. Israel proposed that the Palestinians be granted 'custodianship', though not sovereignty, on the Temple Mount, with Israel retaining control over the Western Wall. With respect to Arab refugees' 'right' to return, the Palestinians demanded full implementation of the right of return, meaning that each refugee would be granted the option of returning to his or her home, with property restored, or accept compensation instead. Israel rejected this, fearing that the sheer number of refugees would demographically overwhelm the country. With respect to security, Israel demanded that a Palestinian state be demilitarized, with the exception of its paramilitary security forces, and that it dismantle terrorist groups and declare the conflict over. Israel also wanted water resources in the West Bank to be shared by both sides and to remain under Israeli management. Arafat and the Palestinians never presented a formal counter-offer to the detailed Israeli proposals, which were rejected out of hand. Both sides blamed the other for the failure of the talks.

Campaign for Nuclear Disarmament (CND)

A campaigning organization conceived in England in 1957 and inaugurated in February 1958 with a mass public meeting, which peaked between 1962 and 1963. Through annual marches to the Aldermaston Atomic Weapons Research Establishment, the acquisition of cultural, political and public supporters, a national membership structure after 1966 and a 'long march' through the Labour and Liberal parties, CND came close to committing British governments to unilateral nuclear disarmament and the abandonment of nuclear power in the 1970s and 1980s. It declined rapidly as a force towards the end of the **Cold War**, and was a frequent target of the right-wing and intelligence interests in British politics.

Canada

Although the first humans in the Americas may have arrived via Siberia more than 50,000 years ago, ice impeded settlement of all bar the westernmost part of Canada until c. 10,000 BC. Despite a brief Norse presence in Newfoundland,

and fishing and exploration of the area from the 1500s, European colonization only commenced in earnest under the French in the early seventeenth century. New France eked out a living from the **fur trade**, incurring the hostility of the English Hudson's Bay Company (1670). The eighteenth century brought a series of **French and Indian Wars** in which **Britain**, France and their **Native American** (First Nation) allies contested control of North America. The last of these (1754–63) pitted the million or more inhabitants of the thirteen colonies that later became the **United States** against New France's 70,000, producing a decisive British victory.

The **Peace of Paris** (1763) ceded most of French North America to Britain, engendering a century of attempts to reconcile the needs of imperial policymakers with the wants of the essentially alien populace of the new province of **Quebec**. The **American Revolution** transformed the source of British strength on the continent to one of weakness; the United States invaded Canada in 1775 and in the **American War of 1812**. Domestically, Britain sought an elusive framework that suited both francophones, accustomed to **Roman Catholicism** and civil law, and an influx of **Loyalists** who demanded representative government and land-ownership by common law. The former were concentrated in the east ('Lower Canada', now southern Quebec) while the latter increasingly migrated to the west ('Upper Canada', now southern Ontario), so Parliament divided Quebec in the Constitutional Act (1791). Most subsequent immigration was that of American farmers somewhat amenable to **republicanism**, who brought about an anglophone majority in Canada by the mid nineteenth century.

Discontent over the oligarchic basis of the 1791 arrangement and other complaints saw both parts of Canada rebel in 1837. In response, Britain created the United Province (1840) but did not delegate 'responsible government' until the British North America Act (1867), drafted in the light of Anglo-American tensions arising from the **American Civil War**. The Act divided power between Ottawa and the provinces, and confirmed Quebec and Ontario's constitutional rights, which finally freed the latent impulse for westward expansion of its potential to upset the internal Anglo-French balance. British Columbia joined the Confederation in 1871 and the intermediate prairies had all achieved provincial status by 1905. Canada entered the twentieth century bullishly as an expanding rail network exploited its timber and mineral wealth.

Entering **World War I** by dint of its place in the **British Empire**, the Canadian war effort and military actions such as those at Vimy Ridge heightened a sense of nationalism already apparent in pre-war frustration at Canada's inability to treat with foreign powers. Britain abolished Westminster's supremacy over the parliaments of the imperial dominions in 1931. Canada's separate, independent declaration of war in 1939 intimated no detachment from **World War II** operations. The **Cold War** and the emergence of the US as a superpower confirmed Canada's move away from the British sphere of influence, albeit as much towards internationalism as a bilateral relationship with Washington, though **NAFTA** has cemented that connection too. Canada has also been an active member of **NATO**.

At home, unprecedented post-war prosperity enabled the social programmes of Prime Minister Lester Pearson (1963–8) and his Liberal Party, until recently the dominant force in politics. Burgeoning Québecois separatism forced his charismatic successor Pierre Trudeau (1968–79, 1980–4) to address fundamental questions of Canadian nationality with the 1982 'patriation' of the constitution and an official commitment to bilingualism. Yet the 1990s still witnessed Quebec voters coming close to reclaiming 'sovereignty', and saw more assertive jurisdictional claims by the First Nations. National identity evidently remains as complicated as ever, but recent elections have hinged more on economic concerns.

canals
– *see* **transportation**.

Candomblé
Originating in **Nigeria**, this Afro-Brazilian religion gained a following in north-eastern Brazil, perhaps in the eighteenth century, but definitely by the early nineteenth century. The exportation of Yoruba slaves from West Africa to **Brazil** increased in the years after the fall of the Yoruba capital at Oyo about 1837 until the end of the Brazilian slave trade in 1850. The slaves brought with them religious practices based upon a harmonious relationship between humans and natural forces, both creations of a single god, Olodumare. The religion included the use of deities (*orixás*; orishas) or important intermediaries between humans and God, a relationship that devotees equated to that between humans

and Catholic saints; each town had its own principal orisha. Devotees in Brazil were long forced to practice their religion in secret because of the opposition of the Catholic Church and government harassment. Supporters now practice their faith openly.

Canning, Charles (1812–1862)
Governor general of **India**, 1856–7, and viceroy of India, 1858–62. The mutinies and uprisings of '1857' tested him. Dubbed 'Clemency Canning' by the English press for his attitude towards indiscriminate atrocities against Indians, it serves him as a tribute. **East India Company**'s rule ended and Crown rule began (1858) with him as the viceroy. He established universities in Calcutta, Bombay and Madras, curbed the excesses of indigo planters and introduced the Criminal Procedure Code (1861).

Canning, Stratford (1789–1880)
A British diplomat who served in the **Ottoman Empire**, at the **Vienna Congress**, and in the **United States**, along with a number of lesser posts. His primary importance was in representing British interests in the Ottoman Empire where he became remarkably well connected and influential. In 1812, during the height of the **Napoleonic Wars**, he brokered the **Treaty of Bucharest**, which ensured peace between the Ottoman Empire and **Russia** and allowed the latter to redeploy its forces against **France**. Canning had close ties with key figures within the Ottoman bureaucracy and played a fundamental role in developing a de facto Anglo-Ottoman alliance through most of the nineteenth century. His influence also helped to shape some of the liberal qualities of the **Tanzimat**, the Ottoman reform movement of 1839–76. Many historians argue that his influence on the Ottomans emboldened them to resist Russian demands in 1853, which in turn served as one of the causes of the **Crimean War**.

Canton system
A system of trade which developed between Chinese and foreign merchants in the southern China city of Guangzhou (Canton). From 1759 to 1842 all foreign trade coming into **China** had to be conducted with authorized Chinese merchants in Guangzhou, where they were subject to Chinese law and other restrictions. British merchants' complaints grew during the early nineteenth century and China was forced to abolish the system after Britain's victory in the first **Opium War**.

Cape Coast Castle

A trading fort/post first erected on the Gold Coast by the Swedish Africa Company in 1653. It passed into English hands in 1664 and became the centre for operations by the Royal Africa Company on the Africa coast, which was at times used to house slaves awaiting export. In 1844 it became the seat of government for the British Gold Coast until the capital was moved to Accra in the colonial period.

Cape Colony

A province of Southern South Africa, established by the Dutch East India Company in 1652. After defeating the native Hottentots, the colonists expanded north and east of Cape Town. When the **Netherlands** fell to **Napoleon** in 1795 the British occupied it and finally made it a colony in 1814. It remained under British rule until 1910, when it merged into the Union of **South Africa**.

capital punishment

The execution of a convicted criminal has a long history and has traditionally been upheld as providing a mixture of exemplary punishment, deterrence, retribution and social protection for the community which practises it. Challenges to its use came with the **Enlightenment** in the writings of Cesare Beccaria (1735–93), advocating moderate punishments to induce reform in criminals, and opposition from writers such as **Voltaire** to cruel forms of capital punishment as degrading both to the sufferer and to society at large. `Cruel and unusual' punishments were outlawed in the **American Constitution** and some enlightened rulers, such as **Joseph II**, abolished it in their realms. Theories of reformative penal policy and the use of alternatives, such as transportation, imprisonment and lesser punishment led in many European countries to the elimination of capital punishment for many crimes, reducing those in Great Britain from over 200 capital offences in 1800 to a handful by 1850. More humane forms of capital punishment, such as the guillotine, shooting and `long-drop' hanging, and the end of public execution as a spectacle became the norm in nineteenth-century Europe and America, though they were not always extended to colonial territories. Western attitudes towards capital punishment were absorbed by many modernizing regimes such as **Japan** and some ex-colonial states. Wholesale abolition of capital punishment has remained politically controversial, some states having abolished its use as a violation of human rights during the twentieth century, whereas it is largely accepted as part of the justice system of countries such as the **United States**, **China**, **Iran**, India, **Indonesia** and **South Korea**. Death sentences can be executed through a variety of means, with hanging, shooting, gassing, electrocution and the administration of poison being the most common, though beheading by sword is practised in some Arabic countries. Many believe that the extended period between sentencing and execution, which can be drawn out if judicial appeals are allowed, is an associated form of torture as the exact time of imminent death and the hope of relief are held out of the reach of the condemned.

Almost one hundred countries have abolished the death penalty, and a further number have not used it for such a long period that it might be considered extremely rare. The arguments against it range from the pragmatic (that criminal justice systems cannot be shown to have convicted the right person consistently over time, through the moral (that it is wrong to take life) to the sociolegal (that it institutionalizes cruel and unusual punishment which is often deployed against people of diminished capacity). Capital punishment has also been criticized on the grounds that it does not achieve its traditional goals, as it rarely deters, and embodies vengeance. Utilitarians have also argued that the existence of execution as a punishment brutalizes society and places a special burden on minorities, who have a greater tendency to be charged, convicted and sentenced as a percentage of criminals than the distribution of crime in society would suggest. Religious objectors also point to the possibility of rehabilitation. Despite these arguments, the death penalty remains popular and has often been treated as a leitmotif of political viability by candidates for office who run on a strong `anti-crime' platform. Opposition to the death penalty was a catalyst for the creation of several international non-governmental organizations, the most prominent of which was **Amnesty International**. It has also become the settled position of most European lawyers and legal establishments, to the point where states which contemplate or actually practise it, such as **Turkey** and **Russia**, can be barred from European institutions as either members or observers. The United Nations General Assembly has also passed several (non-binding) resolutions against the death penalty, and has overwhelmingly voted against motions in favour of the practice.

capitalism

Capitalism is a term that first emerged in the seventeenth century to describe a type of business and production system which had been in operation in parts of Europe for several centuries beforehand.

The system is based upon the price mechanism, the accumulation and trade of private alienable assets, and the conversion by private owners of profits into personal wealth. It is most commonly associated with the free market in which demand and supply meet and provides price information which allocates, indicates and incentivises economic resources and production without the need for any social coordination or government intervention. In this form of classical capitalism, all that government needs to do is guarantee contract, protect the legal institution of private property and maintain confidence in the money supply. Anarcho-capitalists and libertarians would go further, suggesting that capitalists are more than able to defend themselves and to establish and choose between private systems of money at different rates of interest and exchange.

Capitalism is a term with many iterations and almost as many critics. Most of the dispute about the system centres around the precise roles of the state and society within it. For mercantilists, capitalism is and always was a state-led and state-sanctioned system of resource and labour exploitation, in which the authorities either carry out, licence or guarantee particular enterprises which return the bulk of their earnings to the government through income flows and positive trade balances. In this context, modern and early modern colonies, imperialism, chartered companies and even the licensed form of piracy known as 'privateering' have been seen as 'capitalist' creations. Such perspectives have also overlapped with those who argue that 'crony capitalism', 'market socialism', 'corporate welfare' and nationalized industries are features of modern society, describing the common nexus of trading corporations of great wealth and compromised or captured policymakers and regulators. Such a system sits in contrast to one based on small businesses, consumer sovereignty and absolute private property.

Marxists introduced the idea that capitalism is a stage in human development with a clear pathology, beginning in the accumulation of capital through the expropriation of the value labour adds to production, continuing through technological development and business takeovers and ending in state-sanctioned monopolies. In such an analysis, capitalism would eventually lead to two processes that would in combination prove fatal to the system. One process would encourage resource competition between states as monopolies became centralized drivers of policy, leading in **Lenin**'s analysis to a global war which would destroy the system. A second process would so enhance

technology that workers would be increasingly exploited for decreasing income, leading to alienation and revolt. Both, Marxists argued, would result in a new system of communal property and government-allocated distribution known as 'communism'.

Market socialists and distributists agreed in part with this analysis, but argued for government action and regulation to protect small business, expand and protect property ownership and break up large monopolies whilst guaranteeing a minimum level of welfare through state insurance or benefits. These policies, they argued, would prevent collapse and spur social and technological development. Similarly, Keynesians argued that capitalism could be managed through government choices in fiscal policy, leading to stable and progressive growth and the redistribution of income to benefit all. Many classical capitalists argued that such interference with the market as market socialists, distributists and Keynesians supported would in effect reduce welfare, by sustaining unviable industries and replacing the price mechanism with flawed political choices, and some tended to denounce all such measures as 'socialism'. This was especially true in the countries of the western hemisphere and amongst a particular section of the global English-speaking community. In continental Europe, managed forms of capitalism proved far more popular, whether on a socialist or a 'Christian Democratic', communal and distributist basis.

Styles of capitalism have developed alongside forms of business, accounting procedures, legal and political views of the individual and the nature of the resources available, as well as the capacity of workers to protect their contribution to the production process. For instance, the modern corporation, which tends to be based upon the divorce of ownership and control, requires the idea of the limited liability of owners and the idea of share ownership to function fully. This in turn implies a legal system of protection for property rights which in themselves are not possessed of any physical, alienable existence, and the idea that risk should be borne by the buyer and lender. In turn, this implies a system of interest, which in many societies has been complicated by religious restrictions on usury. In addition, large corporations distinguish between owners, managers, directors and workers, each of whom may have different duties and relationships. Some systems have blended all four, such as cooperative-based capitalism, the European model of mandatory worker-directors, and the private limited company in which directors are owners and managers, but these blended models have tended to reach limits to their development which share-based, public limited companies do not encounter. Similarly, the idea of profit would be primitive without tradeable systems of exchange, and double-entry book-keeping, the latter having emerged in Venice in the early part of the last millennium. Ecological analysts have also pointed out that capitalism and the sort of societies it sponsors and helps to create need to be seen in terms of the energy system used. Coal-based systems give priority to the management of workers as producers, for example, whereas oil has hitherto created states in which the vast majority are consumers and where the economies of scale offered by large companies can be trumped by the innovation of smaller ones, which have access through cheap electricity to information resources, flexible production and research opportunities.

Though many have railed against capitalism in general, most forms have proved much more durable than alternatives such as communism, fascism or feudalism. During the latter era of **globalization**, complaints have arisen over the integration of domestic markets into global ones, the lack of a global regulator for capitalism, the power and irresponsibility of finance and resource depletion. However, it is noticeable that the period in which capitalism 'went global' has seen the greatest expansion of population, living standards, technology and scientific innovation in human history. Many analysts would argue (even if they did not believe that periodic shocks and recessions were a good feature of capitalism, because they produced 'creative destruction') that the system in one form or another will be a mainstay of the human future.

capitulations

In the sixteenth century the **Ottoman Empire** began to distribute concessions granted to foreign powers as a method of encouraging trade and a political tool to manipulate the players in European rivalries. As the balance of power tilted against the Ottoman Empire beginning in the late eighteenth century, the capitulations became an avenue for aggressive European economic and political penetration of the Ottoman Empire. When European productive capacity outstripped that of Ottoman manufacturers after the industrial revolution, the ability of untaxed foreign traders to outcompete local traders proved to be a critical disadvantage in the development of local production.

Because the Ottoman Empire suffered a relative loss of political power to European nations in the late eighteenth century, the capitulations became

a primary conduit for Europeans to undermine Ottoman autonomy. While still theoretically subject to renewal, capitulations increasingly provided rights that European nations demanded and which the empire was reluctantly obliged to grant. **Russia** demanded to be recognized as protector of the whole Greek Orthodox population of the empire in 1774. The primary abuse in this regard was the extension of *berats*, which granted extraterritoriality to Ottoman citizens. Once having gained the privileges of a foreign national, these Ottoman citizens could enjoy significant tax advantages compared to local competitors in importing and exporting goods. In exchange for receiving British support in extricating **Muhammad Ali** from **Syria** in 1838, the British forced the empire to guarantee its privileges in perpetuity and negotiated improved tariff rates and an exemption from the internal transit levy. Other nations could claim the same privileges under 'most favoured nation status'. Subsequently, the Ottoman government could do little to protect its economy. **France** and Britain, especially, became responsible for the construction of most of the empire's modern infrastructure, giving them enormous influence over the empire's economic life. In declaring war against the Entente in November 1914, the empire abolished all foreign concessions.

Capitulations outlasted the Ottoman Empire in its former province of **Egypt** where mixed courts, established in the nineteenth century, continued to exempt foreign citizens from prosecution by Egyptian courts until 1949. The **Montreux Convention**, concluded in 1937, set a twelve-year time limit for their abrogation. Another Montreux Convention (of 1936) had abolished the final concessions guaranteeing foreign powers navigation rights in the Turkish Straits.

Cárdenas (del Río), Lázaro (1895–1970)

Born in Jiquilpan, Michoacán, he was president of Mexico, 1934–40. Revolutionary veteran and governor of Michoacán, his presidential administration is regarded as the apogee of the **Mexican Revolution** because of commitment to land reform, workers' rights and socialist education. Proclaimed a national hero for achieving economic independence by expropriating foreign-owned petroleum companies in 1938, he broke **Plutarco E. Calles**'s hold on the official party and reorganized it as the Mexican Revolutionary Party (PRM). He achieved popular support because of his nation-wide presidential campaign visits, once a week free telegram service for requests or complaints to the president, political use of the radio and his association with mariachi music. He supported the Spanish Republicans, welcomed Spanish refugees including orphans, and had an active diplomatic campaign in **Latin America**, called the *Buen Vecino* (Good Neighbour) programme. His son Cuauhtemoc Cárdenas held office as mayor of Mexico City but lost a presidential campaign in 1994.

Cardoso, Fernando Henrique (1931–)

Brought up in São Paulo, **Brazil**, he was an academic who served in the Senate and as finance minister, devising a neoliberal economic plan that ended Brazil's hyper-inflation, stabilized the economy and brought him two terms as president, from 1995 to 2002. He privatized government-held enterprises, encouraged foreign capital, increased the national debt and successfully improved school attendance. He left the Brazilian economy poised for growth but the government still facing structural fiscal problems.

Caribbean Basin Initiative

The Caribbean Basin Initiative (CBI) is a broad programme intended to facilitate economic development and export diversification through private sector initiatives in Central American and Caribbean economies. Shaped by three US trade acts: the Caribbean Basin Economic Recovery Act of 1983, the Caribbean Basin Economic Recovery Expansion Act of 1990 and the Caribbean Basin Trade Partnership Act of 2000, the CBI provides beneficiary countries with duty-free access to the US market for most goods.

CARICOM

The Caribbean Community is a regional grouping of British Commonwealth Caribbean states **Antigua**, **Barbados**, **Belize**, Dominica, **Grenada**, **Guyana**, **Jamaica**, Montserrat, **St Kitts-Nevis**, **Anguilla**, St Lucia, St Vincent, **Trinidad and Tobago**. In addition, non-Commonwealth countries **Haiti** and Surinam are members. The initial grouping was formed by a treaty which came into force on 1 August 1973. It was conceived as a stage in the movement towards regional cooperation and integration in the Caribbean after the failure of the experiment with federation.

CARICOM's objectives are to achieve improved standards of living and work; full employment of labour; accelerated, coordinated and sustained economic development; expansion of trade and economic relations; enhanced levels of international competitiveness; organization for increased production and productivity; greater economic leverage and effectiveness of member states in dealing with non-member states; enhanced coordination of member states' foreign policies; and enhanced functional cooperation.

Carlism

A Spanish conservative movement which upheld the claims of the line descended from Don Carlos (1788–1855), brother of King Ferdinand VII, as opposed to those of the Houses of Bourbon, Bourbon-Parma, Habsburg and Parma. Between 1833 and 1876 the movement appeared both in politics and in three major Spanish domestic wars, as supporters attempted to carve out territory and ultimately to overcome the state. It declined, was revived after the **Spanish–American War**, and then boosted again during **World War I** and especially the **Spanish Civil War**. During the latter period, the movement (and some 100,000 troops) were uneasily united with the dictatorship of Francisco Franco and his Falange Party, before Carlist claims were displaced and apparently subsumed in the Bourbon restoration of **Juan Carlos I** in 1975.

Carlowitz, Treaty of (1699)

Treaty which brought the conflict between the Ottoman Empire and the European Holy League after 1683 to a close and established Austrian power in east central Europe for two centuries. Following the defeat of his last major northwards assault by the Austrians at the Battle of Zenta in 1697, the Ottoman Sultan Mustafa II accepted negotiations. The ensuing peace conference at Carlowitz (Karlowitz – now Sremski Karlovci, Serbia) between the Turks and the Holy League of **Austria, Poland, Russia** and Venice in 1698 resulted in the Treaty of 26 January 1699. Constituent treaties between **Turkey** and Austria, **Poland** and Venice, respectively, transferred **Hungary**, other than the Banat, **Transylvania, Croatia** and **Slovenia**, from Turkey to Austria, the Peloponnese (now **Greece**) and Dalmatia (now **Croatia**) to Venice, and Podolia and part of the **Ukraine** to Poland, which nevertheless surrendered Moldavia (now **Romania**). The Russians concluded only a two-year armistice, which ended with the 1700 Treaty of Constantinople transferring Azov to Russia.

Carlsbad decrees

Repressive measures agreed by representatives of states of the German Confederation at a conference convened by Prince **Klemens von Metternich** at Carlsbad (now Karlovy Vary, Czech Republic) on 6–13 August 1819. The decrees, which came into effect in September and remained in force until the

1848 revolutions, were intended to counter liberal and nationalist aspirations (particularly among students), and included press censorship, the banning of political meetings and close supervision of university education.

Carlyle, Thomas (1795–1891)

Thomas Carlyle studied mathematics at the University of Edinburgh before becoming a schoolteacher. Initially liberal, he became a conservative author of history books and a writer of epigraphs and letters. He was highly influential in Victorian England, both in the inspiration of social reform and in the promotion of the idea of the heroic individual in history as a prime mover of events. His works have been credited as helping the development of satire, romanticism, socialism and fascism, but largely fell out of favour when the Victorian era ended ten years after his death.

Carnegie, Andrew (1835–1911)

Born in Dunfermline, Scotland, Carnegie migrated to the **United States** in 1848. After gathering managerial experience working for the Pennsylvania Railroad and capital from a series of well-chosen investments, he formed the Carnegie Steel Company in 1872. Carnegie ruthlessly applied the most advanced technologies to cut costs and rapidly expanded his business until, at the time of his retirement in 1901, his was the largest steel company in America. Much of his wealth was applied to educational and other philanthropic enterprises.

Carranza, Venustiano (1859–1920)

Born in Coahuila, Carranza became a Mexican revolutionary in 1910 and First Chief of the Constitutionalists with the 1913 assassination of President **Francisco I. Madero**. His commanders defeated usurper **Victoriano Huerta**, but turned on each other with **Alvaro Obregon** defeating **Pancho Villa** and **Emiliano Zapata** in 1915. Carranza became president, 1916–20, and summoned the convention that wrote the revolutionary constitution of 1917. He survived international provocations, but died by assassination.

Cartagena

A port city that Spaniards founded in 1533 on the Caribbean coast of present-day **Colombia**. As European settlers began to settle in the highlands, it became the entry point for imported goods and served as a terminus of the fleet system from the 1560s to 1739, as well as a centre for contraband. It became one of the few strongly fortified

locations in the Indies. Today, it is a popular tourist destination.

Carter, James Earl (1924–)

Thirty-ninth president of the **United States**, 1977–81. Born in Plains, Georgia, he served in the navy before inheriting his father's peanut business. He served in the Georgia State Senate during 1962–6 and as governor from 1970 to 1974. In 1976 he won the Democratic nomination for president as a centrist southerner who could unite a fractious country reeling from the impact of the **Vietnam War** and social upheaval at home. He narrowly defeated incumbent Republican Gerald Ford in the general election. In office he faced major crises at home and abroad: poor economic growth and high inflation, the Soviet invasion of **Afghanistan** and the fall of the Shah of Iran in 1979, and the seizure of US hostages in Teheran in 1979–80. He oversaw the attainment of the peace accord between **Egypt** and **Israel** at **Camp David** in 1978.

cartography

– *see* **exploration**.

Casablanca conference

A World War II summit meeting in 1943 between US President **Franklin Roosevelt** and British Prime Minister **Winston Churchill**, who decided to follow the North African campaign with an invasion of Sicily and then **Italy**, rather than **France**. To prove to the **Soviet Union** that the absence of a second front did not mean a lack of military commitment, Roosevelt controversially announced that the Allies would demand the 'unconditional surrender' of the Axis powers.

caste

System of social stratification in Hindu society in which status is determined by birth and occupation. The groupings are ordered hierarchically by concepts of religious purity or spirituality in which the Brahmin, originally the priestly class, claimed highest status, with the `untouchables' (or Dalit) the lowest who did the most unpleasant and servile tasks. Caste was sufficiently prevalent to provide the dominant form of social differentiation in many parts of the Indian subcontinent, with ideas of pollution and taboo separating social groups and dominating the allocation of occupations and marriage patterns. It was officially abolished in the Constitution of Independent India in 1951 but has remained a powerful social feature, with attempts to outlaw caste discrimination or provide positive discrimination to lower castes by reserving posts or places in higher education provoking sometimes violent opposition.

Castro Ruz, Fidel (1926–2016)

A charismatic revolutionary leader of **Cuba** for nearly fifty years, Castro assumed power in 1959. As a Cuban nationalist and anti-imperialist, he alienated the **United States**, ended the domination of the Cuban elite, drove much of the middle class into exile and suppressed political dissent. He embraced the **Soviet Union**, which provided both weaponry and economic assistance until its own collapse in 1991, became the leader of the reorganized **Communist Party** of Cuba in 1965, turned the country into a communist state and tried to spread communism abroad. Under Castro, Cuba achieved an infant mortality rate lower than that of the US and a marginally higher literacy rate. Its economy, however, continued to rely on sugar exports and its infrastructure was failing. Medical problems led Castro to turn over the presidency to his brother Raúl on an interim basis in 2006 and permanently in 2008.

Catalans

The people of Catalonia, north-eastern Spain, with its capital in Barcelona. Their separatist movement originated in the seventeenth century, but was suppressed in 1714 by Philip V, who abolished both Catalan autonomy and constitution. Separatism re-emerged in the 1850s with the deliberate revival of the Catalan language, itself closely related to Spanish and the Occitane of southern France. Autonomy was supported by the Church in 1876, and some home rule was granted in 1913, but revoked in 1925. A Catalan Republic was declared by the left-wing Esquerra Republicana in 1931, but compromise autonomy was negotiated, 1932. The republic was the focus of resistance to **Franco** in the **Spanish Civil War**, with Barcelona not falling until 1939. All autonomy was then abolished. Following restoration of Spanish democracy, limited autonomy was granted in 1977, and full autonomy in 1979. Even greater autonomy was granted by Catalan charter in 2006. It is unclear whether this will be sufficient to defuse the growing pressure from the richest and most industrialized part of Spain for total independence.

Catherine the Great (1729–1796)

Born Sophie von Anhalt-Zerbst. she was Empress Consort of All the Russias, 1761–2, and Empress of All the Russias, 1762–96. Catherine was one of the greatest female leaders in history. Under her rule, which began after a *coup d'etat* against her husband, Peter III, **Russia** became an enlightened despotism. Catherine attempted to modernize laws, expand Russian borders, develop the arts and sciences, and generally to make Russia a great power. In this effort she succeeded. Under her, agriculture, trade and infrastructure were built up, as was education. She inflicted very heavy defeats on the **Ottoman Empire** in the two Russo-Turkish wars, annexed most of the **Ukraine**, Crimea and Black Sea, and partitioned **Poland**. Catherine was also famous for her tendency to promote and dismiss her lovers to and from major jobs in the empire, the most famous of whom were Grigory Orlov (with whom she had a son) and Prince Grigory Potemkin, whom she may have secretly married.

Cattle Kingdom (USA)

After the **American Civil War**, cattle-raising boomed on the grazing frontier opened up by the retreat of the buffalo and the American Indians. A cattleman's empire soon dominated the Great Plains' landscapes, economies and politics from Texas north to Montana. Though synonymous with western US history, the kingdom's demise was as swift as its rise. By the late 1880s, extreme weather, overstocking, overgrazing and competition from sheepherders and homesteaders closed the open range integral to the Kingdom's success.

Caucasus

A mountainous area between **Asia** and **Europe** flanked by the Black and Caspian Seas. Dominated by the Persian Empire for much of its history, the region came under Russian control in the nineteenth century, notably through the 1817–64 Caucasian Wars. After the 1917 Revolution the area was briefly unified and then divided as Azerbaijani, Armenian and Georgian republics. In 1922 it was reunited under Soviet control as the Transcaucasian Socialist Federative Soviet Republic, until dissolution in 1936, when the former republics were restored. With the collapse of the Soviet Union in 1991 **Azerbaijan**, **Armenia** and **Georgia** became independent states. Territorial disputes led to a series of conflicts involving the independent states and those parts of the Caucasus that remained part of the Russian Federation. These included the 1988–94 Nagorno–Karabakh War, the 1989–91 Ossetian–Ingush War, the 1992–3 Abkhazia War, the **Chechen conflict** of 1994–6 and 1999–2009, and the 2008 South Ossetia War.

caudillo

An authoritarian leader who gains power when central authority is weak. Most common in Latin America since independence, *caudillos* rely on unconditional supporter loyalty, charisma, wealth, military power and more recently nationalism, rigged elections and constitutional changes. They manifest individual styles, such as folk (**Juan Manuel de Rosas**, who ruled **Argentina**, 1829–52); military (Antonio López de Santa Anna, **Mexico**, various years, 1833–55; and modernizing (**Porfirio Díaz**, Mexico, 1876–80, 1884–1911; and **Augusto Pinochet, Chile**, 1973–90).

Cavour, Count Camilo Benso di (1810–1861)

Piedmontese statesman and leading figure in Italian unification. A pragmatic reformer and exceptional diplomat, Cavour founded the Italian Liberal Party and the influential newspaper, *Il Risorgimento*. From 1852 to 1861 he was prime minister of Piedmont-Sardinia and focused on expanding its influence and status. He gained international attention in the Crimean War and successfully led Piedmont during the second Italian War of Independence. In 1861 he became the first prime minister of the Kingdom of Italy, but died three months later.

Cayman Islands

The three Cayman Islands lie about 290 kilometres north-west of **Jamaica**. Christopher Columbus saw them in 1503, and in due course they would become important as a source for turtles. The British occupied them in the late seventeenth century, sometimes as a result of wrecks on their dangerous eastern reefs. Their inhabitants have long been known as pirates and perhaps wreckers. Today the Cayman Islands, a crown colony in the British Commonwealth, has about 30,000 inhabitants, mostly engaged in tourism and international finance.

Ceauşescu, Nicolae (1918–1989)

First Secretary of the Romanian Communist Party, 1965–89, and president of **Romania**, 1967–89. He followed his mentor, Gheorghe Gheorgiu-Dej, in developing nationalistic policies to compensate for the **Communist** Party's low historic base, and opposed both the **Warsaw Pact**'s invasion of **Czechoslovakia** and the Soviet invasion of **Afghanistan**. Feted by the West in the 1970s, but ultimately lost domestic support as a result of his extreme economic policies. Summarily tried and shot in the 1989 uprising, along with his wife.

Ceded Islands

During the colonial period, European countries were always competing for territories. Many wars were fought to gain lands in the Americas, with peace treaties being signed to agree on war spoils. The previously French islands acquired beginning with the 1763 Paris Peace Treaty and continuing through the first part of the nineteenth century were collectively known as the Ceded Islands and represented the British Empire's first major Caribbean acquisition in a century. The southernmost island in the group is Tobago; it is separated by a 32-kilometre sea passage from Trinidad. Grenada also became British, along with more than a hundred small islands called the Grenadines. St Vincent and Dominica too transferred from one imperial power to the other. The Ceded Islands yielded substantial revenue to the Crown. They also provided a field of activity for white adventurers and coloured labourers, while adding to the British Empire's plantation base.

Cemal Pasha (1872–1922)

Cemal Pasha served as a member of the Committee of Union and Progress triumvirate that governed the **Ottoman Empire** in its final years. During **World War I** he ruled the Ottoman Empire's Syrian provinces. Reviled in the Arab world as 'the Butcher' (*al-Saffah*) for his heavy-handed policies against political opponents, Cemal also participated in organizing the Armenian massacres. After the Ottoman defeat, he fled first to **Afghanistan**, then to Georgia. Armenian nationalists assassinated him in Tblisi in 1922.

Central African Republic

Landlocked central African state which became the French colony of Ubangi Shari in 1894. The country gained independence in 1960 under David Dacko (1930–2003), who was deposed in 1966 by Jean-Bédel Bokassa (1921–96). Bokassa declared himself President for Life and then Emperor Bokassa I in 1977. French troops ousted him in 1979, restoring Dacko to office. Dacko was overthrown two years later by General André Kolingba (1936–2010), who remained dependent on French assistance. In 1993 Ange-Félix Patassé (1937–2011) became the first freely elected president. He was re-elected in 1999 but as disorder became endemic, he was replaced by François Bozizé (1946–), who himself was dismissed by the army in 2013. Michel Djotodia (1949–), the first Muslim to become president, sought deployment of a United Nations peacekeeping force in an increasingly chaotic situation. The Republic is predominantly Christian, with a small Muslim minority. The economy is based on subsistence agriculture, forestry and diamond mining.

Central America

The modern nations of **Guatemala**, **Belize**, **El Salvador**, **Honduras**, **Nicaragua**, **Costa Rica** and **Panama** exist on an isthmus that connects North America to South America. A volcanic mountain chain extending from the north-west to the south-east along the Pacific coast dominates the region's geography. Extensive tropical lowlands and dense jungle, in contrast, characterize the Caribbean coast. The majority of the region's diverse population is of mixed ancestry and lives in the more temperate mountain valleys along the Pacific. Large numbers of indigenous groups remain, especially in the Guatemalan highlands, as well as smaller numbers of Caribbean tribes.

Before European colonization, western Central America was the centre of classical Maya civilization. Under Spanish rule, the region failed to develop an export economy to compete with **Mexico** or **Peru**. Despite its strategic importance, the colony languished until after independence from **Spain** in 1821. Although briefly joined to Mexico, the new states soon established the Central American Federation, which survived for fifteen years before dissolving into five constituent parts (Belize, as British Honduras, remained a British colony into the twentieth century, while Panama remained a province of Colombia until 1902). By 1900, coffee and bananas linked the region to the global economy. Following the 1898 **Spanish–American War** and construction of the **Panama Canal**, Central America came within the sphere of influence of an expanding US empire in the Caribbean. Multiple US interventions followed as Panama and Nicaragua became de facto US protectorates and US multinational corporations, such as the **United Fruit Company**, assumed informal political and economic hegemony across the isthmus.

In the first half of the twentieth century Central American society witnessed three major challenges that reverberated for decades. An uprising against the US occupation of Nicaragua in the 1920s expelled American troops but created a power vacuum filled by Anastasio Somoza (1896–1956), whose family dominated the country until the Sandinista Revolution of 1979. A brutal crackdown against a peasant uprising in El Salvador in 1932 ushered in decades of military-led government and inspired the revolutionary movement which

splintered Salvadoran society in the civil war of the 1980s. A progressive revolution in Guatemala in 1944 overthrew an entrenched dictatorship and launched a decade of social reforms. However, US concerns over communist influence and protests from the United Fruit Company led to a **CIA**-sponsored coup in 1954, an event which also precipitated the rise of military dictatorships and revolutionary movements that fought for power in Guatemala through the 1980s. The only significant exception to this pattern was Costa Rica, which sustained its commitment to a civil democracy following a short revolution in 1948. This history of conflict adversely affected the political, social and economic development of Central America. The nations of the isthmus remain among the poorest in the hemisphere. While the wars that defined the past half-century have ended, the region continues to struggle with endemic poverty, corruption, politicized militaries and US intervention, as the 1989 Panama invasion demonstrates, as well as new sources of instability, such as drug cartels.

Central Intelligence Agency (CIA)

The National Security Act of 1947 created the CIA to help the **United States** counter Soviet expansionism. The director of the CIA also served as the director of central intelligence (DCI), with authority over the whole of the intelligence community. The agency's main function was its oversight of the 'Soviet estimate', an assessment of the military threat emanating from Moscow. Its subsidiary function was 'covert operations', attempts to influence world affairs through secret propaganda and 'dirty tricks'. A congressional investigation in 1975 and later the end of the Cold War diminished the prestige and mission of the CIA, and in 2004 the Intelligence Reform and Terrorism Prevention Act subordinated it to a newly created office, that of the Director of National Intelligence.

Central Powers (World War I)

One of the two main alliances of **World War I**, the Central Powers consisted of **Germany**, **Austria–Hungary**, the **Ottoman Empire** and **Bulgaria**. At the core of the system was the relationship between Germany and Austria–Hungary. **Russia** also represented an immediate threat to the **Austro-Hungarian Empire** because of the latter's support for nationalist movements in the **Balkans** (*see* **pan-Slavism**). An alliance between Austria–Hungary and Germany, largely to counter Russia, was formalized in 1879. The value of Austria–Hungary to Germany became even more prominent after the development of the Franco-Russian Alliance in 1894. Although Germany was arguably the most powerful military force in continental Europe, it now viewed Austria–Hungary's survival as intertwined with its own. This sense of existential threat helped to create the crisis which developed after the assassination of Archduke Francis Ferdinand on 28 June 1914. Austria–Hungary was determined to use the assassination to counter perceived Serbian support for Serbian nationalists at home and Germany, for its part, was determined to counter Russian influence in the Balkans. Relations between Germany and the Ottoman Empire had been developing for a number of decades. The alliance which developed between them was the result of the Ottoman long-standing tensions with **Russia** and the Ottoman elite's sense that **World War I** represented a tremendous opportunity to renew the empire. Nonetheless, they strung out negotiations with the Germans for some time in the hopes of getting the best possible deal. The Ottomans signed a secret treaty with Germany in August 1914, but only formally entered the war in October, after the transfer of three German cruisers to the Ottoman Navy, and their subsequent shelling of Russian ports on the Black Sea.

Like the Ottoman Empire, Bulgaria also hoped that participation in World War I would provide the opportunity to reverse recent losses and aggrandize its position. In particular, the Bulgarians hoped to make territorial gains at the expense of their neighbours, to whom they had lost territory during the **Balkan Wars**. After remaining neutral for more than a year, Bulgaria definitively entered into the alliance in September 1915.

Despite the remarkable hardships of the war, the alliance survived almost to its end. Bulgaria was the first to sign an armistice, in September 1918. The Ottomans followed suit on 30 October 1918. Within weeks, both Austria–Hungary (4 November) and Germany (11 November) followed. The former allies fared poorly in the treaties which emerged from the **Paris Peace Conference**. Austria–Hungary and the Ottoman Empire were dissolved and broken into a series of smaller, national states. In the case of former Ottoman territories, many of these new national states remained under direct European control through the mandate system. Bulgaria lost territory to **Greece**, **Romania** and the new state of **Yugoslavia**. Germany suffered immense territorial losses and the occupation of the industrially vital Ruhr basin. All suffered political instability and economic crisis. To this must be added the human

costs, with Germany and Austria–Hungary suffering approximately 7 million casualties each during the war. Bulgaria, which had a pre-war population of about 5 million, lost more than 80,000 soldiers. Hundreds of thousands of civilians died of starvation and malnutrition. The Ottoman case was the worse because civilians were often targeted in the warfare. More than 750,000 Ottoman soldiers are estimated to have died during the war. Numbers of civilian dead are highly disputed, but more than 2 million and perhaps as many as 5 million Ottoman civilians died during the war from violence, disease and malnutrition. This number includes approximately 1 million Armenians and other eastern Christian populations that were targeted by the Ottoman state during the **Armenian massacres**.

Central Treaty Organization
– *see* **Baghdad Pact**.

Çesme, Battle of (Chesme, Chesma)
The battle of 1770 in the Aegean Sea off Çesme near Chios, between the respective fleets in the **Russo-Turkish War, 1768–74**. The result was the total annihilation of the Ottoman fleet, attributable to no small degree to the Turkish surprise that the Russians had been able to reach Ottoman Greece by sailing from the Baltic to the Mediterranean through the Strait of Gibraltar. The battle terminated **Turkey**'s hope of remaining mistress of the Black Sea, which it had dominated since 1453.

Céspedes y Borja del Castillo, Carlos Manuel (1819–1874)
Born in **Cuba** to a wealthy plantation family, Céspedes studied law in Spain and then initiated the Ten Years War in 1868 by starting a movement of independence that also called for universal suffrage and freedom for slaves. He led the insurrectionary government and sought annexation by the **United States**. Deposed in 1873, he was apparently killed by Spanish forces in a minor engagement.

Cetewayo (c. 1826–1884)
The last of the major **Zulu** rulers. Cetewayo became king in 1872 and re-established Zulu military power. Initially viewed by the British as a counterweight to the **Boers**, he was subsequently seen as threatening British Natal, leading to the **Zulu War**. In 1879 he overcame a British force at Isanhlwana but was defeated at Ulundi, captured, deposed and imprisoned. He was restored to the

throne in 1883 but was ousted in a Zulu civil war and is believed to have been poisoned.

Ceuta
– *see* **Spanish Empire**.

Ceylon
– *see* **Sri Lanka**.

Ch'ing dynasty
– *see* **Qing dynasty**.

Chaco War
The Gran Chaco that separated **Bolivia** and **Paraguay** for more than a century after their independence was a flat and largely roadless wilderness with few non-Indian inhabitants. The countries failed to agree on a border between them and Bolivia, having lost to **Chile** its access to the Pacific Ocean as a result of the **War of the Pacific** (1879–83), saw an alternative in the Paraguay River located across the Chaco as a route leading to the Atlantic. Preliminary skirmishes in the 1920s escalated in 1932 to what, with some 100,000 deaths, became South America's bloodiest twentieth-century war. Although much smaller in territory and population, Paraguay proved victorious as the result of a much superior logistical infrastructure, better generals and access to arms, and neighbouring states that allowed food, weapons and other needed supplies to reach its army. Peace in 1938 gave Paraguay control of the entire Chaco region.

Chad
A landlocked central African state which **France** took over a decade to subdue before absorption into French Equatorial Africa in 1913. The country gained independence in 1960 under President François Tombalbaye (1918–75). He banned opposition parties in 1962 and his favouring of the Christian south over the Muslim north provoked civil war in 1966–8 in which his regime was only saved by French intervention. Tombalbaye was assassinated in 1975. Northern forces backed by **Libya** and the French-supported Hissène Habré (1936–) competed for power. Habré became president of a country in turmoil in 1982. Idriss Déby (1952–), at the head of the Patriotic Salvation movement, ousted Habré in 1990. Elected president in 1996, Déby was faced by continuing resistance in the north and east. He was re-elected in 2006 and narrowly survived a coup attempt in 2013. Chad has a majority Muslim population, with a large Christian minority, and an economy based on agriculture and oil.

Chamberlain, Neville (1869–1940)
Also known as Arthur Neville Chamberlain. British businessman and politician who held the roles of Postmaster General, Minister of Health, Chancellor of the Exchequer, Leader of the Conservative Party, Prime Minister of the **United Kingdom** and Lord President of the Council. Chamberlain was the half-brother of Austen Chamberlain and the son of Joseph Chamberlain. Neville Chamberlain dominated British politics for most of the 1930s and enjoyed an ascendancy within the Conservative Party, pursuing his themes of small, directed governance, thrift and appeasement as well as looser self-governance for the **British Empire**. He was an opponent of **Winston Churchill**. Chamberlain sought to appease the European dictators by conceding to their territorial demands and encouraging them in their anti-communism, believing that they would either be unable to gain support once their demands had been met for further aggression or become engulfed in the anti-communist struggle. Horrified by **World War I**, he sought to avoid war and entrap dictators in agreements, sometimes by means of personal diplomacy such as his trip to Munich in 1938 where he agreed to the partition of democratic **Czechoslovakia** in a four-power deal involving **France**, **Italy** and Nazi Germany. His policy ultimately failed, and though he remained as prime minister after the outbreak of war in September 1939, he was forced from office by the refusal of other parties to serve under him in a coalition after the Norway campaign of 1940. He was replaced as prime minister by Winston Churchill, but remained in the British Cabinet and as leader of the Conservative Party and Lord President of the Privy Council until his death.

Chamorro, Violeta (Barrios de) (1929–)
Widow and political heir of Pedro Joaquín Chamorro, an outspoken anti-Somoza activist whose 1978 assassination helped precipitate the Sandinista Revolution in **Nicaragua**. Chamorro led a coalition of fourteen parties (UNO) against the Sandinistas in the 1990 national elections. Following her upset victory as president, Chamorro governed as a moderate during a difficult transition period, prioritizing national reconciliation efforts and neoliberal economic policies before handing power to her successor in 1997.

Chancellorsville, Campaign and Battle of (29 April–5 May 1863) (USA)
During the **American Civil War** the Union commander, Joseph Hooker, intended to advance around **Robert E. Lee**'s left and strike him in the

rear, either by mastering Confederate communications or by cooperating with a substantial force left at Fredericksburg. He did not expect to be outflanked himself, as occurred on 2 May, when Stonewall Jackson smashed his right before falling wounded. Lee then turned east to destroy the Union wing advancing from Fredericksburg that had just escaped. Psychologically beaten, Hooker abandoned his offensive and withdrew back across the Rappahannock River.

Charles III (1716–1788)

King of Spain, 1759–88, and of Naples, as Charles VII, 1734–59. An absolute ruler, but an '**enlightened despot**' who sought to restore **Spain**'s status as a leading European power. Opened the Spanish Empire to commerce and reformed its administration, but lost Florida after war with Britain in 1762. He secured from the papacy the complete suppression of the Society of Jesus (Jesuits) in 1773, and curtailed the powers of the Inquisition in Spain as an affront to his authority.

Charles IV (1748–1819)

King of Spain, 1788–1808, Charles responded to the French Revolution's radicalization by naming favourite Manuel Godoy first minister. Spaniards blamed him for Spain's fiscal problems, its loss of Santo Domingo to France, and their alliance against Britain. Following **Napoleon**'s invasion of **Spain** in 1807, Charles was forced to demit to son Ferdinand VII in March 1808. Their subsequent abdications to Napoleon caused a political crisis. Charles died in exile.

Charles X (1757–1836)

Younger brother of **Louis XVIII**, succeeding him as king of France in 1824. Personally scarred by his experience as an émigré from the **French Revolution**, his government generated opposition by pursuing policies which were politically and religiously reactionary as well as unconstitutional. His resistance to the Charter and constitutional monarchy led to his overthrow in the Parisian insurrection of the 'Three Glorious Days' of July 1830 and the accession of **Louis Philippe**.

Charles XII (1682–1718)

King of Sweden, and the first and last to be born to **absolutism**. He initially resisted the expansionary ambitions of **Peter the Great** and the coalition of Denmark, Saxony and **Russia** which attacked **Sweden** in the spring of 1700, launching the **Great Northern War**. He eliminated Denmark, spring 1700, and defeated Peter at Narva (Estonia),

November 1700. He defeated the army of Augustus II, elector of Saxony and king of Poland, in 1701; invaded Saxony, 1706, to install Stanislaw Leszczynski as king of Poland and his ally for attacking Russia; invaded Russia, 1707, but was defeated at the Battle of Poltava (Ukraine) in 1709, whereafter he fled to **Turkey**. He returned to Swedish Pomerania in 1714 and sought unsuccessfully to restore Swedish power by diplomatic means. He was killed while invading **Norway** in 1718. A Protestant monarch with a strong sense of duty; nevertheless, his death marked the end of Sweden's status as a great power.

Charter 77

A document drafted in the mid 1970s but dating from January 1977 in **Czechoslovakia**. Charter 77 was a petition which attempted to hold the Czechoslovak communist government to the human rights standards promulgated in its constitution and agreed to by representatives of the Soviet bloc at the Helsinki conference of 1975 (*see* **Helsinki Agreement**) and as part of the **United Nations**. Though it attracted only a few hundred signatures initially, these belonged to critical figures such as its co-author Václev Havel (1936–2011), drawn from the cultural, political and intellectual underground, and it became a focal point for opposition to the communist government both within Czechoslovakia and the West. It was a rallying point in the 1989 revolution, and has also been a model for civic reformers in the **Britain, Belarus** and **China**.

Chateaubriand, François-René, Vicomte de (1768–1848)

French diplomat and Romantic writer of the extreme right, who exalted the Gothic in his *Génie du Christianisme* (1802) against the Revolution. A refugee in London, 1793–1800. His novel *Atala* (1801), inspired by a visit to the **United States** in 1791, is a notable contribution to the French literary and philosophical tradition of the 'noble savage'. Ambassador to Berlin, 1821, and to London, 1822. As foreign minister he restored French prestige by persuading **Austria, Prussia** and **Russia** to allow a French Army to suppress antimonarchical rebellion in **Spain**.

Chattanooga, campaign and Battle of (21 September–27 November 1863) (USA)

During the **American Civil War** Union forces were besieged in Chattanooga after their defeat at Chickamauga. **Ulysses S. Grant** accepted command of the western theatre and called reinforcements to his aid. Two corps under Joseph Hooker also were sent from Virginia. The siege was lifted by taking Brown's Ferry. Thereupon Hooker assaulted Lookout Mountain while **W. T. Sherman** failed to land the decisive blow on the Union left at Missionary Ridge. An unauthorized attack on its centre by the Army of the Cumberland brought an overwhelming victory.

Chattopadhyay, Bankimchandra (1838–1894)

Through an outstanding career in the service to the British Raj, Chattopadhyay rose to deputy magistrate. His other career was as the first important Indian novelist, writing in Bengali. His most famous work, entitled *Anandamath* (*Temple of Bliss*) (1882), is concerned with an order of nationalistic sannyasins or monks in the later eighteenth century who struggle to revive degraded **India** from Muslim exploiters and also have their eye on dealing with the British who are waiting to take the place of the Muslims.

Chavez y Ramírez, Carlos (1899–1978)

A prominent Mexican composer and conductor, he helped to found the Symphony Orchestra of Mexico in 1928, which he led until 1948. He subsequently composed numerous commissioned works including operas and ballet scores and conducted widely in **Europe** and the **United States**. His early compositions emphasized native themes. His efforts extended appreciation of music in **Mexico** and the indigenous contribution to it.

Chechnya

A land in the north **Caucasus** historically typified by the resistance of a loose affiliation of Chechen clans to domination by **Turkey**, **Persia** or **Russia**. By 1858, Russian and Cossack groups had gained control of the Chechen lands, which Islamicized in resistance; Russians then moved to completely dominate Chechnya, alter the ethnic balance in the lands, and generally to develop oil and railway resources. In the twentieth century, after a period of confusion, Chechnya coexisted with and within Russia as an autonomous unit with no right to leave, before breaking out again in the **Chechnya–Russia conflict** from the 1990s, when Chechen nationalists attempted to establish a sovereign state.

Chechnya–Russia conflict

The name given to the rebellions and attempted independence of **Chechnya** against **Russia** between 1991 and 2009. The period covers two wars

(1991–6), a period of independent but compromised self-rule between 1996 and 1999, and a Russian 'counter-terrorist' operation which eventually resulted in Russian reassertion of control over the Chechen regime in 2009. The conflict began when the Chechen authorities, unlike eighty-seven other Russian districts and autonomous republics, refused to sign a new Federation Treaty on the fall of the **Soviet Union** in 1992. Reports followed of violence against Ukrainians, Russians and Armenians in the republic, and during a period of civil war Russian troops were gradually drawn into what became an all-out intervention against the mountain land in 1994. This failed, leading to a peace treaty in 1996, the outbreak of new violence and an attempted Islamic republic associated with terrorism in 1999, and a further devastating war before the Russians installed a stable regime a decade later.

Cheik Anta Diop (1923–1986)

Senegalese scientist and writer who was famous for his advocacy of the black identity of ancient **Egypt** and its direct connection to his own Wolof people. Originally a physicist, he submitted his controversial ideas as a thesis to the University of Paris; it was published in 1955. An influential historian in **Senegal**, he was selected as head of the national university, which was named after him following his death.

Cheka

The acronym of the All-Russian Extraordinary Commission for Combating Counter-Revolution and Sabotage (VCHEKA, or 'CHEKA) organized by **Lenin** and Felix Dzerzhinsky in November 1917 and a precursor to the replacement OGPU (1922), NKVD (1934) and **KGB** (1954). Cheka became a feared and vicious Bolshevik secret police, perpetrating terror, clandestine intelligence operations and surveillance in a way that ensured **Lenin**, **Stalin** and the Soviet Politbureau had a very firm grip on the Russian people, as well as a potent sword with which to dispatch political opponents. Cheka also ran the initial prison camps which eventually made up the Soviet **Gulag** camps.

chemical weapons

The use of toxic chemical substances in war has a long history. The first use of gas warfare possibly dates back to the fifth century BC when Spartans besieging the Athenians used sulphur to incapacitate their enemies by noxious smoke. Traditional chemical warfare burned and ignited secondary fires. For centuries turpentine, tallow, rosin, sulphur and antimony were delivered in shells during sieges. Yet, the real lethal power of chemical warfare peaked during **World War I**, when the Germans released chlorine gas against French and British troops killing thousands by asphyxiation and injuring thousands more. Allied forces responded by filling shells with phosgene and mustard gas. Gas masks reduced the effectiveness of gas warfare. Mutual deterrence prevented the use, if not further development, of chemical weapons during **World War II**. The US used defoliants, such as Agent Orange, and incendiaries, such as Napalm, in the **Vietnam** and **Korean Wars**. Chemical weapons were also used by **Saddam Hussein** to suppress internal rebellion and by the Assad regime in the **Syrian Civil War** against opponents.

Chernobyl

The world's worst nuclear disaster occurred in 1986 in the **Ukraine**, then part of the **Soviet Union**. Although directly attributable to human error, the Chernobyl disaster was facilitated, in western expert opinion, by safety deficiencies in the early design of the reactor. The **European Union** made the phasing out of comparable reactors at Ignolina in Lithuania and Kozloduy in **Bulgaria** a precondition of those countries' EU membership. The number of deaths and disabilities from radiation is uncertain but substantial.

Chiang Ching-kuo (1910–1988)

Chiang Ching-kuo was the son of Nationalist leader **Chiang Kai-shek** and president of the Republic of China on **Taiwan** from 1979 to 1988. He spent much of his early life in **Russia**, but returned to **China** in 1937. After the Nationalists retreated to Taiwan in 1949, Chiang held various positions in the military and civil bureaucracies. While president, he allowed more Taiwanese to enter the government, improved relations with the **USA** and repealed martial law in 1987.

Chiang Kai-shek (1887–1975)

Chiang Kai-shek was leader of the Nationalist Party in **China** and then president of the Republic of China on **Taiwan**. He studied in **Japan** and joined **Sun Yat-sen**'s Revolutionary Alliance in 1908. After participating in the **Chinese Revolution of 1911**, he fled to Japan and only returned in 1923, when he was appointed head of the Whampoa Academy in Guangzhou. In 1926 he launched the **Northern Expedition** to unify China. He married Soong Mei-ling, who became his secretary and interpreter. He continued attacks on Communist base areas until the outbreak of war with the Japanese in 1937

forced him to agree to a second United Front between the Nationalists and the Communists. Defeat by the Communists in the civil war forced Chiang to flee to Taiwan, where he established the Republic of China. He imposed martial law on the island, but implemented a series of successful economic reforms.

Chicanos

The term is used for Mexican-Americans (*Chicanas* is the feminine), particularly those of Mexican ancestry born in the **United States** (rather than Mexicans living there.) Its origins are unclear but it was in use within the Chicano community no later than the 1930s, although sometimes with a derogatory connotation. It became widely used in the United States in the 1970s and has, generally, lost any specific connotation. There continue to be different usages.

Chikunda

A local name for African slaves that were recruited to defend and work on Portuguese-held territories in the Zambezi valley. Following the introduction of the Prazo system of land control in the Zambezi, in the seventeenth century, the Chikunda went on to become famous as traders and soldiers, especially in the eighteenth- and nineteenth-century trade of east central Africa. When the Prazo system ended, the Chikunda were recognized as a distinct ethnic group.

childhood

A word that refers to the period of life between infancy and adolescence, extending from ages 1–2 to 12–13. The early years of childhood are marked by rapid advances in symbolic thought, logic, memory, emotional awareness, empathy, moral sense and a sense of identity, including sexual identity. In 1962 Philippe Aries published *Centuries of Childhood*, suggesting that in medieval times children were not given much attention as they were dependants and likely to die. Once they reached a certain physical strength they were considered to be adults, indicating that the idea of childhood did not exist. Aries' work suffered from methodological shortcomings, and the research it triggered has focused on important changes in childhood experienced over the nineteenth century as documented in sources such as British parliamentary papers, child labour legislation, the reconceptualization of juvenile delinquency, the introduction of compulsory schooling, raising age of consent for girls and development of medicine for children. This has led to substantial changes in attitudes towards childhood and to its 'sacralization', as children cease to be wage earners and become pupils. Governmental organizations are now accepted as legitimate regulators of family life. Recent research into parent–child relationships has been stimulated by psychology and sociology.

Chile
– *see also* **Allende Gossens, Salvador Isabelino**; **Pinochet, Augusto**.

Officially known as the Republic of Chile, the country is located in South America and extends some 4,185 kilometres (2,600 miles) from the northernmost city of Arica, past the Strait of Magellan and on beyond the world's southernmost town, Puerto Williams. Since 1888, Chile also includes Easter Island, located in the middle of the Pacific Ocean 2,700 kilometers from Chile's coast. The country's area totals 757,000 sqare kilometres (292,000 square miles) and borders the Pacific Ocean on the west, **Peru** and **Bolivia** to the north and north-east, and **Argentina** to the east. The country's major urban centres – Santiago, Valparaíso-Viña del Mar and Concepción-Talcahuano – and the regional capitals, from Arica south to Puerto Montt, sit on one of the world's most geologically active regions and have suffered repeated earthquake damage. Spanish is Chile's official language. Mapudungun (Mapuche people), Rapa Nui (Eastern Islanders), Aymara and Quechua (Inca and related) are also spoken by indigenous minorities. Chilean authors offer various theories on the origin of the name *Chile*, including the Aymara word *Chilli* ('where the world ends') and the Quechua word *Chiri* (cold land), among many others. By the mid seventeenth century most indigenous groups north of the Maule River had been subjugated, but the Araucanians (Mapuche) south of the Biobío resisted throughout the colonial era (1535–1818) and were not definitively conquered until the 1880s. Despite several short civil wars (1828–30, 1851 and 1859) Chile was considered the most politically stable country in nineteenth-century **Latin America**.

Chile is a constitutional republic with a bicameral legislature (a senate and a chamber of deputies) and an elected president. According to the 1980 constitution, as amended, the president may not be immediately re-elected. For administrative purposes the country is divided into regions and provinces for which the president appoints intendants and governors. Municipal governments are autonomous, with elected mayors and councils, but their authority is defined in the national constitution. In 1973 a military coup ousted the elected president, Salvador Allende, and a military government remained in power until 1990. Since then, elected civilian governments have governed Chile. In 2010 Chile's population was estimated at 17 million, concentrated in the central valley. The Santiago metropolitan region was home to 40 per cent of the country's population and more than 86 per cent of Chileans lived in urban areas. According to the census, less than 5 per cent is identified as indigenous, though those of mixed European and indigenous ancestry (*mestizos*) form a majority of the population. Immigrants from other western hemisphere countries, Europe and the Middle East have also settled in Chile. The country's economy is the most 'open' in Latin America, with exports accounting for 40 per cent of GDP. Mining (especially copper) accounts for over 50 per cent of the value of exports. Other leading exports include fruit, wine, forest products, fish and shellfish. The UN Human Development Report (2010) ranked Chile 45 on the list, the highest in Latin America, but notes that income inequality persists at levels found in **Paraguay**, **Guatemala**, **Honduras** and **Colombia**.

Chilembwe, John (1871–1915)
African minister and rebellion leader in the British colony of **Nyasaland** (now **Malawi**). An early Christian convert, Chilembwe studied at a seminary in the **United States** and was ordained a Baptist minister. A famine in 1913, harsh labour conditions and conscription during **World War I** prompted him to launch an anti-colonial rebellion in January 1915. Colonial officials killed him and hundreds of his followers in later reprisals. Chilembwe also had connections with the millennial and anti-colonial **Watchtower** movement.

China
– *see also* **Hong Kong**.

late imperial period
During much of the Ming (1368–1644) and earlier part of the Qing (1644–1912) dynasties, China was a prosperous and confident society. A highly commercialized economy was combined with a mass print culture, as books and artwork became much easier to reproduce. In the eighteenth century the Qing expanded westwards into central Asia, greatly increasing the amount of territory under imperial rule. The growth of new world crops allowed greater areas of land to be settled, and China's population doubled in the eighteenth century from around 150 to 300 million. However, the expansion in size was not matched by a growth in

the size of the bureaucracy or tax revenues, storing up problems for later on.

fall of the Qing

From the early nineteenth century, opium was grown in large amounts in the new **British Empire** in eastern India, and it was steadily exported to China, leading to mass consumption and addiction. Qing officials confronted the British over the issue, leading to the **Opium War** of 1839–42. China lost, and was forced to grant a series of territorial and trade concessions to foreigners, many of which endured for a century. At the same time, internal crises began to destroy the Qing. The **Taiping War** (1856–64) saw an alternative, pseudo-Christian regime, challenge the Qing. Although it was defeated, its legacy was to leave significant military power in the hands of local armies rather than the central government. An agricultural crisis also exacerbated droughts and famines, stimulating uprisings such as the **Boxer** crisis of 1900, when the Qing encouraged peasant rebels to attack foreigners and Christians. Although the dynasty instituted wide-ranging reforms in the years after 1902, their grip on power had slipped. In 1911 an uprising against the dynasty in the southern city of Wuhan sparked a national crisis leading to the formation of a republic and the abdication of the emperor in early 1912.

crisis of the republic

The new republic quickly fell under the influence of militarists, most notably Yuan Shikai, who was president from 1912 to 1916. China was in practice split into semi-autonomous regions. Meanwhile, western imperialist powers and **Japan** continued to maintain their privileged positions within China. A key moment occurred on 4 May 1919 when student protesters marched through Beijing to protest at clauses in the **Treaty of Versailles** which were unfair to China. The **May Fourth** incident became symbolic of a wider trend that looked to 'science and democracy' to save China, largely rejecting its traditional past. As part of that movement, the **Chinese Communist Party** (CCP) was formed in 1921. Under Soviet influence, in 1923 the fledgling CCP allied with the Nationalists (**Kuomintang**) under **Sun Yat-sen**, with both parties intent on fomenting a nationalist revolution. Sun died in early 1925, but just a few months later anti-imperialist demonstrations starting on 30 May in Shanghai, and spreading across China, proved a trigger for the parties to move. The **Northern Expedition** of Nationalists and Communists conquered much of central China in 1926–7.

However, the new Nationalist leader, **Chiang Kai-shek**, had become suspicious of CCP intentions and organized a brutal massacre of Communists in Shanghai in 1927, thereby breaking the united front between the parties.

Nationalist government

The Communists spent most of the period from 1927 to 1937 in rural exile. This allowed Chiang to establish his Nationalist government of China at Nanjing in 1928. Chiang's government was essentially a military dictatorship, and was marked by significant corruption and abuses of human rights. It also paid little attention to distress in China's rural areas. However, it had significant successes to its credit, including improvements in China's industrial and transport infrastructure and advances in its international status, such as the restitution of tariff autonomy. It began discreet preparations for war against Japan after the invasion of **Manchuria** in 1931, but most of its visible military strength was used to attack the Communists, forcing them on the **Long March** from central China to the north-west in 1934–5. However, the increasing threat of Japanese invasion after 1935 meant that Chiang was forced to divert attention from the CCP to forming another united front, this time against Japan, in late 1936.

war against Japan

On 7 July 1937 an unplanned incident between Chinese and Japanese soldiers stationed near Beijing led within weeks to all-out war. A Japanese invasion took most of the cities in eastern China and forced Chiang's government to retreat to the inland city of Chongqing. During the years 1937–45 the Nationalists and CCP maintained an uneasy united front against Japan, fighting alone until the entry of the Allies after Pearl Harbor in 1941. China remained a secondary front for the Allies, however, leading to the disintegration of Chiang's government, which was struck by a series of military and economic crises. A civil war followed in 1946–9, ending with the rout of the weakened Nationalists by the CCP.

Mao's China and reform

The period 1949–76 is associated with the rule of CCP chairman, **Mao Zedong**. The first decade of Mao's rule was marked by the mass redistribution of land to poor peasants, as well as cooperation with the **USSR**. An experiment in **collectivization** of farming and swift industrialization, the **Great Leap Forward** (1958–62), was a disaster leading to a famine that killed over 20 million people. In the early 1960s ideological disagreements led to a split with the USSR. By 1966, Mao became convinced that the CCP itself had become bureaucratic and ossified, and launched the **Cultural Revolution**, a movement in which China's youth was encouraged to rebel against their elders and the party itself. The movement led to massive violence and destruction, but was not officially ended until after Mao's death in 1976. In the early 1970s, Mao decided to open up links with the **USA**, leading to the visit of President Richard Nixon to Beijing in 1972. From 1978 to 1997 Chinese politics was dominated by the veteran leader **Deng Xiaoping**, who introduced market policies to China, reversing most of Mao's intentions, and turning China into one of the world's fastest-growing economies, but a society that also became less and less equal. The two decades since 1997 have seen continued impressive economic growth.

China Lobby

In the 1930s and 1940s the Chinese Nationalist government was engaged in a civil war with the country's Communist Party. Following the Nationalists' defeat in 1949, American conservatives organized what was known as the China Lobby against recognition of the People's Republic of China. While for many years meeting with considerable success, the lobby was ultimately confounded by Richard Nixon's 1972 visit to China and the US's subsequent recognition of the People's Republic.

Chinese Exclusion Act (1882) (USA)

This was passed by President Chester A. Arthur in 1882. The Act excluded all Chinese immigrants except those who could claim Chinese-American parentage and some skilled professionals. Nativist pressure for exclusion had grown on the west coast, as exemplified by Dennis Kearney's 'Workingmen's Party', which had some political successes in California in 1879. Anti-Chinese sentiment then became a national issue, and the 1882 Act was periodically renewed until 1943 when it was finally abolished.

Chinese Revolution (1911)

This event marked the overthrow of the **Qing dynasty** and the end of two thousand years of imperial rule in China. The latter decades of the Qing saw internal rebellion, foreign threats, and then in the twentieth century, attacks by revolutionaries such as **Sun Yat-sen**. In 1911 a plan for nationalizing railways sparked protests in Sichuan over concerns about the end of provincial

autonomy. A planned uprising on 16 October in Hankou was discovered, and on 10 October Sun's supporters attacked the governor general's office in Wuchang. The revolution spread, and by the end of November fifteen of twenty-four provinces had broken away from the Qing. Sun Yat-sen was appointed the first president of the provisional government of China on 1 January 1912, although he was replaced soon after by Yuan Shikai, who secured the abdication of the last Manchu emperor, Puyi.

Chinese Revolution (1927)

– see also **Northern Expedition**.

This refers to the unification of **China** by the Nationalist Party from 1926 to 1928 and the establishment of a government in Nanjing. In 1926 the National Revolutionary Army, an alliance of Communists and Nationalists led by **Chiang Kai-shek**, launched the **Northern Expedition**, which in one year overran south and central China. Success split the **Kuomintang**, with the left wing of the party under **Wang Jingwei** establishing a government in Wuhan and expelling Chiang from the party because of his purge of Communists in Shanghai in April 1927. After an abortive attempt to launch their own military campaign, and instructions from **Stalin** ordering the Communists to seize control of the Kuomintang, Wang Jingwei purged the remaining Communists and Chiang was allowed to return to the Nationalist Party. In 1928 he renewed the push northwards, and took Beijing on 8 June. The Nationalist government was established in Nanjing on 10 October 1928.

Chinese Revolution (1949)

This is the term given to the founding of the People's Republic of China (PRC) in 1949. After the surrender of the Japanese in 1945, **China** was divided into two areas. The Communists controlled the countryside in the north, while **Chiang Kai-shek**'s Nationalist government was based in the cities of the lower Yangtze delta. Open civil war broke out, and Nationalist forces had initial success in 1946 and 1947, when they recaptured all the major Chinese cities except Harbin. However, Communist use of guerrilla tactics proved successful and Chiang's forces were pushed out of **Manchuria** by Lin Biao, who then took Beijing and Tianjin in January 1949. Meanwhile, the Communists were victorious in fighting in northern Shandong. By May 1949 they had taken all the major cities in the lower Yangtze delta, and Chiang fled to Taiwan. On 1 October 1949 **Mao Zedong** announced the founding of the People's Republic of China in Tiananmen Square in Beijing.

Chiquita Brands International

The current incarnation of the powerful multinational corporation, **United Fruit Company**, Chiquita Brands remains a major producer and distributor of fruit and vegetable products from Central America, the Caribbean and northern South America. Like its predecessor, Chiquita has stimulated controversy in the region. Since 1985, efforts to reform its banana cultivation and land use practices have conflicted with persistent allegations of labour abuses, environmental pollution, bribery and protection payments to Colombian guerrillas and paramilitaries.

Chirac, Jacques (1932–)

Mayor of Paris, 1977–95; Prime Minister of France, 1974–6 and 1986–8; President of France, 1995–2008. Chirac was known from very early in his career as a 'bulldozer' who got things done, and was instrumental in the rise of neo-Gaullism in **France**. This idea brought together traditional conservative nationalism with more liberal economic policies, including tax cuts and privatization. Chirac ran twice for president, in 1981 and 1988, and was defeated on both occasions before ultimately winning as a result of the consolidation of voters against his National Front opponent in 1995. In office, Chirac refused to join in the **Iraq War**, proposed a global tax on capital flows, and promoted a distinctive defence of French culture which was defined against **Islam**, in favour of European integration and underpinned by the nuclear deterrent. Chirac was convicted in 2011 on two counts of corruption whilst in office, and was given a suspended sentence.

Chônin culture

Chônin, meaning 'townsfolk', refers to the groups, primarily merchants, who shaped the urban culture of late Tokugawa-era (1603–1868) **Japan**. Associated in particular with the city of Edo (modern Tokyo), *chônin* were regarded in traditional Japanese social hierarchies as being below the warrior class (*samurai*). However, they produced a vibrant culture of their own, including major drama, painting styles (such as the genre known as *ukiyo-e*, or pictures of the 'floating world' or pleasure quarters of the city), and were responsible for the development of a sophisticated consumer culture.

Chosŏn dynasty

– *see also* **Korea** and **Confucianism**.

The Chosŏn was the longest-lasting Korean royal dynasty, dating from 1392 to 1910. Founded by Yi Song-gye, it featured neo-Confucianism as the ruling ideology that shaped political, economic, social and cultural structures in society. A balance of power existed between the royal court and the Yangban class – the landed gentry whose sons also typically served as bureaucrats – through an agrarian bureaucratic structure while a patriarchal social hierarchy system limited the autonomy and power of women who had enjoyed many privileges in the previous matriarchal dynasty. Under King Sejong in the fifteenth century, Chosŏn society experienced a flourishing of cultural developments, especially with the invention of Han'gŭl – the Korean written alphabet. By the late nineteenth century internal problems and foreign imperialism threatened the survival of the Chosŏn state. **Japan**'s annexation of **Korea** in 1910 officially ended the dynasty.

Christian Democracy

The term has its origins in Pope Leo XIII's 1891 papal encyclical *Rerum Novarum*. This encyclical implored Roman Catholics to organize and participate with the nascent democracies of Europe. The Roman Church expressed concern at the growth of atheistic communism, greater material inequality and the extension of the state's influence deeper into the fabric of social life. During the early twentieth century Christian Democracy developed as a less exclusively Roman Catholic movement as Christian Democratic political parties drew in supporters from various Christian denominations. Christian Democratic parties resisted the increased jurisdiction of the state, particularly at the service of radical political ideologies. This rather conservative attitude to government was however combined with a strong commitment to social justice through redistributive welfare reform. Following **World War II**, Christian democratic parties became powerful and popular parties of government in Europe, and to a lesser extent in **Chile**, **Venezuela** and **El Salvador**.

Christian Right

In the late 1970s evangelical Christians in the **USA** mobilized against what they saw as government hostility to religion and opposition to family values. While much of their concern has centred on **abortion** and the rise of the **gay rights** movement, the Christian Right has also been involved in such issues as opposition to the **Sandinista** regime in **Nicaragua** and support for the state of **Israel**. Initially particularly associated with the **Moral Majority**, more recently leading roles have been played by the Christian Coalition and Focus on the Family. Strongly supportive of President **Ronald Reagan** in the 1980s and **George W. Bush** more recently, the Christian Right has been a key force in Republican electoral victories. Nonetheless, it has often expressed discontent with Republican priorities.

Christian Socialism

Christian Socialism teaches that the social injustices of poverty, oppression and exploitation are also sins against God. English Christian Socialism flourished in the mid nineteenth century, led by former Chartists F. D. Maurice, Charles Kingsley and John Malcolm Ludlow. These men opposed the social and economic consequences of laissez-faire capitalism and promoted economic cooperation as a Christian alternative to the capitalist competitive mode of production. The notion of a society and economy as a Kingdom of God in which equality, freedom and justice prevail motivated these early Christian Socialists. Whilst this movement declined by the late 1850s, many members and leaders of the growing Labour movement were motivated by a similar Christian conviction, and the Christian Socialist Movement continues to play an active role in the British Labour Party. Similar Christian Socialist movements grew in France and Germany during the late nineteenth century. The Society of Christian Socialists was founded in America in 1889, and influenced the Social Gospel movement in the early twentieth century.

Christianity

– *see* **Catholicism; Orthodoxy; Protestantism.**

Churchill, Winston (1872–1965)

British politician and statesman, Churchill's career was enviable and legendary almost from the outset. He was born to an Anglo-American marriage of Jenny Jerome, an American society beauty, and a scion of the Marlborough family, Randolph Churchill, a successful Conservative politician, at the Marlborough family home, Blenheim Palace in Oxfordshire. Unhappy at school, he joined the army, participating in one of the last imperial cavalry charges against the **Mahdi's** followers in the Sudanese campaign of 1896. Writing up his experiences and showing an early talent for self-publicity and journalism, he escaped Boer captivity during the second Boer War and launched a political career. A Member of Parliament for four different constituencies, and switching allegiance between parties, he was a dynamic trade secretary, then home secretary in a reforming Liberal government, before becoming a young First Lord of the Admiralty by the outbreak of war in 1914, controlling the largest navy in the world. He was forced to resign following the disastrous **Gallipoli campaign** in 1915, serving for a period in **France** as a front-line officer on the Western Front. He returned to government before the war's end, serving in post-war governments, and as Chancellor of the Exchequer controversially returned Britain to the **gold standard** in 1925. Losing office in 1929 and beset by financial problems, he became a prolific author and journalist. His taste for journalism and the company of adventurers led to his isolation from more sober Conservative leaders such as Baldwin and **Neville Chamberlain** during the 1930s, increased by what was seen as his maverick opposition to concessions on Indian independence, support for Edward VIII in the Abdication crisis of 1936 and his vehement opposition to the **appeasement** of the European dictators.

When war broke out in 1939, Chamberlain was forced to return him to the Cabinet and the Admiralty and on Chamberlain's resignation in May 1940, Churchill became head of a coalition government, not without some disquiet on the part of the Conservative majority in the House of Commons. As prime minister he saw **Britain** through the fall of France, the invasion scare of 1940, the **Battle of Britain** and bombing campaign, and the Blitz on London and other British cities. Resolute in refusing to make peace with **Hitler** after the fall of France, probably his most significant decision, he rallied the country through stirring speeches. Abroad, he courted **Roosevelt's** support and obtained crucial American aid via 'lend-lease', encouraging American entry into the war, and made an alliance with the **Soviet Union** when Hitler invaded in July 1941. He gathered the exiled remnants of the European democracies in the United Kingdom, including the **Free French** under **Charles de Gaulle** and exile governments from **Poland**, **Norway** and Holland, amongst others. With **Stalin** and Roosevelt he held out for the total defeat of Adolf Hitler and 'unconditional surrender' and saw his efforts as part of an historic 'English-speaking' defence of liberty, though keen to support as much of Britain's imperial influence as possible. His influence to shape the post-war world, however, was increasingly compromised by American and Soviet power. At home, he delegated domestic policy, overseeing the passing of wartime legislation and plans that led to the creation of a **welfare state**.

His surprise defeat by Labour in 1945 did not bring about his resignation from the leadership of the Conservative Party, while his influential 'iron curtain' speech in 1946 heralded the **Cold War**. His historical writing earned him a Nobel Prize in literature and he returned as prime minister in 1951, developing Britain's nuclear deterrent, refashioning the British Empire as the **Commonwealth**, and at home presiding over the end of post-war austerity and growing prosperity. Having survived two strokes, he was forced from the premiership by Anthony Eden in April 1955 and lived another ten years. His funeral, in 1965, staged one year after he left Parliament, was one of the great ceremonies of British history and is often described as the 'unofficial end of the British Empire'. Since his death, he has become a celebrated figure, especially in the USA, held to typify liberty, defiance, determination in war, and magnanimity, as much as for his cigars, drinking and rakish but ultimately moral outlook on life. He was married to Clementine Hozier in 1903, to whom he was devoted, and fathered a son and a daughter who followed him into public life with much less success.

Científicos

This 1870s generation of Mexican politicians inspired by French positivist Auguste Comte and sponsored by dictator **Porfirio Díaz** (1876–1910) sought to remake their nation through economic development by applying modern European and US scientific ideals. Although they entirely dismissed native American culture, they deepened the secularization of education and supported railway construction, oil production, mining and banking with European and US financial and technical involvement. José Limantour was their most prominent representative.

cinema

Cinema has become one of the most widespread forms of popular entertainment since the development of 'moving pictures' at the end of the nineteenth century. Initially shown in a variety of venues, the development of purpose-built cinema houses made it one of the most important leisure activities alongside mass spectator sport. Latterly, cinema films have become at least as commonly available via television and personal computers. Film 'stars', both past and present, and film genres

such as musicals, thrillers, westerns, horror and sci-fi have become reference points of modern culture.

From the Greek work for 'movement', the term *cinema* was originally a contraction of *cinematograph* and evolved into an all-encompassing term referring to motion pictures as a whole. The Lumière brothers are credited with inventing the first projection machine (1895) using electronically driven equipment and celluloid film. By **World War I** a range of films were being made including dramas, fantasy, comedy and epics, featuring stage and music hall performers such as Sarah Bernhardt. Although most films were 'shorts', such as the Keystone Cops series from 1913, some longer multiple-reel films such as the Italian *Quo Vadis* (1913) appeared. There was considerable cross-fertilization of performers and genres between Europe and North America in the early years, so that in 1914 half of all films shown in New York were European. The growth of the American industry was assisted by the opportunities for large studio lots, attractive desert and canyon scenery, and abundant good weather offered by the first Hollywood studios set up in California from 1913. Cinema was quickly taken up elsewhere with the first films produced in Bombay and **Japan** by the outbreak of World War I. The Great War demonstrated that film could be used for political propaganda, with British government-sponsored films such as *The Battle of the Somme* (1916) and *The Battle of the Ancre* (1916) representing something of the realities of modern warfare to large audiences. The propaganda role of film was also seized on very quickly by the new Soviet government in the **USSR** to bring the Bolshevik message to a largely illiterate population. It laid the basis for a strong state-sponsored Soviet film industry, producing in the works of Sergei Eisenstein and his successors a series of powerful propaganda films, such as *Battleship Potemkin* (1925) and *October* (1927).

With over 10,000 cinemas and a huge audience of tens of millions each week by 1914, the **United States** took advantage of wartime disruption to dominate commercial film-making between the two world wars. The first Hollywood stars, such as Charlie Chaplin, Mary Pickford and Rudolph Valentino, emerged during the silent era and reached audiences worldwide. As a commercial entertainment, however, cinema was dramatically enhanced by the introduction of 'talkies' from the late 1920s and the development of colour from the 1930s. Hollywood became increasingly dominant in the production and distribution of commercial films such as the elaborate musicals of Busby Berkeley and blockbuster productions such as *Gone With the Wind* (1939). But although the Hollywood 'big five' studios dominated, producing some of the most popular films ever made, national cinemas also developed rapidly. Japan produced even more films than Hollywood on the eve of **World War II**, at over 500 a year, while **India**, **France**, **Germany** and the **United Kingdom** produced over a hundred films each. The 1940s boosted the importance of American film production, though there was a notable output of propaganda, newsreel and feature films in Germany, the United Kingdom, **Italy** and the **Soviet Union** during World War II.

Cinema audiences peaked after 1945 with a new generation of stars such as Marilyn Monroe and Marlon Brando reaching audiences of tens of millions each week. But in North America, Japan and **Europe** cinema faced increasing competition from television. British cinema admissions fell by three-quarters between 1945 and 1960; in America they more than halved between 1960 and 1972 as family audiences switched from cinema-going to television watching. The studios responded with highly successful blockbuster 'epics' and musicals such as *Ben Hur* (1959) and *The Sound of Music* (1965), and fresh technological advances such as wide-screen 'cinemascope' and experiments with 3-D. The late twentieth century saw crisis and revival. The spread of television saw cinema audiences plummet, widespread closure of cinemas and the end of many famous Hollywood studios. Individual films and genres, such as the Bond films and Star Wars series, continued to do well, and 'art' cinema attracted status through prizes awarded at regular film festivals in Cannes (from 1939), Berlin, Venice and, latterly, Sundance. The creation of multi-screen 'multiplex' cinemas, attracting a variety of audiences to smaller auditoriums, and the translation of film to video, DVD and television reinvigorated cinema. Live cinema audiences revived in the early twenty-first century alongside the increasingly widespread transmission of film in other media.

CIS

– *see* **Russian Empire**.

Civil Disobedience movement (India)

Launched in early 1930 by **Mohandas K. Gandhi**, the Civil Disobedience movement in **India** incorporated the demands of no-tax and no-revenue campaigns and a boycott of British goods and institutions and mobilized large numbers of Indian men and women. It began with Gandhi and his followers marching from Sabarmati Ashram to the western coast and symbolically defying the taxation on salt. Although Gandhi had urged for non-violent demonstrations, in places such as Punjab and Bengal the movement aligned itself with the violence of revolutionary nationalists. The largely economic struggle also gained communal complexity as in some places Muslim peasants rose against Hindu moneylenders. The Gandhi–Irwin Pact of 1931 signalled the end of the first phase of the movement. Gandhi called for a resumption of Civil Disobedience in 1932 after the failure of the second Round Table conference. By 1934 the colonial state was able to subdue both violent revolutionaries and non-violent protestors.

civil rights movement (USA)

In the **United States** historians initially adopted this name for the waves of protest by **African Americans** and white liberals for racial reform in the period 1954–68. Scholars quickly revised this chronology in recognition of the fact that black protest was an important historical phenomenon well before 1954. Protest activities that fed into the classic phase of the movement have been traced back at least to the formation of the National Association for the Advancement of Colored People (NAACP) in 1908 and much more fully into the decades of the 1930s and 1940s. Historians distinguish between a 'freedom struggle' that can encompass everything from the fight against slavery to contemporary battles against racism, and a civil rights movement which marked a particular phase and focus of that struggle. As the name suggests, the focus of the movement in the 1950s and 1960s was on constitutional rights that had been presumed to be assured to African Americans by the post-civil war constitutional amendments: the 14th Amendment which guaranteed equal legal protection to all citizens and the 15th Amendment which protected the right to vote. The southern states, in the 1890–1910 period in particular, had largely erased these rights by legally instituting segregated public accommodation and education and by establishing a deeply prejudicial voter registration and primary election system. In 1954 the NAACP's long-running legal campaign culminated in a Supreme Court decision that overturned the principle that segregated facilities could be equal though separate. More importantly, the following year the citizens of Montgomery successfully challenged legally required bus segregation through a year-long boycott as well as litigation. The boycott leader **Martin Luther King Jr** captured the headlines by advocating a non-violent response to white attacks. In 1957 he organized the Southern Christian Leadership conference to orchestrate and promote non-violent protest in the region.

The protest campaign against segregated facilities continued in the late 1950s and in February 1960 the South was swept by a wave of sit-ins at department store lunch counters beginning in Greensboro, North Carolina. Often run alongside a consumer boycott, the sit-ins combined the economic pressure of a boycott with the public spectacle of police and vigilante brutality against non-violent protesters. Downtown businesses worried over the loss of trade and nationally Americans were appalled by photographs that captured the gulf between the democratic creed of American life and its everyday practices. Various preconditions favoured the civil rights movement's non-violent strategy. The South's political role within the **Democratic Party** had weakened, which ensured that Democratic and Republican presidential candidates were as interested in the urban black vote outside of the South as in the Southern white vote between 1948 and 1968. The **Cold War** ensured that every president from Truman to Johnson was concerned by hostile world reaction to publicised racial violence. Television brought images of that violence into respectable homes both in America and overseas. Finally, the southern economy itself was changing profoundly from a land of cotton to a sunbelt of modern industries. This diminished the need for unskilled black labour and increased the quest for outside investors and experts whose willingness to relocate to the South was reduced by images of violent inter-communal strife.

During the **Kennedy** administration (1961–3), actions such as violent white reactions against the Freedom Rides in the summer of 1961, the riots at the University of Mississippi in 1962 and the demonstrations in Birmingham and elsewhere in 1963 induced the federal government to intervene. By the summer of 1963, President Kennedy had announced that he would introduce a civil rights bill to address African American grievances and the March on Washington had shown that the movement had generated mass interracial support behind Dr King's dream of an America that lived up to 'the fullness of its creed'. The Kennedy assassination (in Dallas, a Southern town) added further momentum for reform and despite dogged Southern resistance in Congress, a wide-ranging

Civil Rights Act, which banned racial segregation in public accommodation and discrimination in employment, was passed in July 1964.

White segregationist violence continued to alienate public opinion. During the Mississippi Freedom Summer of 1964, three voter registration workers, two of whom were white Jewish volunteers from New York, were murdered. Similarly, the Selma campaign of 1965, which King organized to increase the pressure for further legislation to secure federal protection of black voting rights, saw three further deaths, two white and one black, at the hands of white vigilantes and state troopers. The nation's revulsion at the televised scenes of police violence ensured that President **Lyndon Johnson** received a standing ovation when in a televised speech to Congress in support of voting rights he embraced the movement by declaring their struggle to be the nation's, and adding: 'And we shall overcome.'

While the national organizations involved in the movement had largely agreed to target segregation and disenfranchisement, there were well-established divisions and local differences. African Americans in the North knew that the de facto segregation that confined them to ghettos and poor jobs was as real as the legal segregation they fought in the South. By 1965 their anger was evident in protests against police brutality, school segregation and job and housing discrimination. Moderate groups such as the NAACP were strengthened by the new legislation and were crucial to its implementation. But victories that immediately benefited a token black middle class did not express the frustration of poorer blacks whose feelings were better articulated by separatist groups such as the Black Panther Party. Groups that had previously worked in the South, such as the Student Non-violent Coordinating Committee, similarly adopted the slogan '**Black Power**' and expelled whites. At the time of his assassination in April 1968, Dr King was largely unable to hold together a cohesive civil rights movement. Official repression suppressed the separatist wing of the movement while its moderates concentrated on electoral politics and enforcement of new legal guarantees.

Civil Service Commission (USA)

After the **American Civil War**, a number of elite reformers, concerned about the abuses associated with patronage politics, called for a reformed civil service in which appointment and promotion would be based on merit rather than political favouritism. In 1883 Congress created a Civil

Service Commission with power to set regulations and administer examinations for a reformed civil service. Over time successive presidents expanded the number of posts covered by civil service rules, and the commission's authority correspondingly increased.

Cixi (1835–1908)

Cixi was de facto ruler of **China** for much of the latter half of the nineteenth century. Originally, a concubine of Emperor Xianfeng, after his death in 1861 she became empress dowager and co-regent to the emperors Tongzhi and then Guangxu. She ruled with the help of eunuchs, and in 1898 staged a coup against Guangxu, which halted the hundred days' reform. Two years later, during the **Boxer uprising**, she declared war on foreign powers, a war which China lost.

classicism

The cultural movement characteristic of the seventeenth and eighteenth centuries in **Europe** which found its inspiration in the world of classical Greece and Rome. It represented a rejection of the medieval, denigrated as 'Gothic' and perceived as irrational and superstitious, and was a striving for light, rationality and order, qualities which its proponents found in the classical world and believed to be the bedrock of civilization. The movement was dominant in different countries and arts at slightly different times and remained influential long into the nineteenth century and even the twentieth.

It can be traced back to the Renaissance, which spread out from **Italy** from the fourteenth century and flowered in much of Europe in the sixteenth. The classical Greek language was rediscovered and Latin became the international language of scholars such as Erasmus of Rotterdam, and not just of churchmen. By the end of the seventeenth century the influence of classicism was all powerful. Inigo Jones (1573–1652) and Sir Christopher Wren (1632–1723) had brought classical forms to English architecture, not least in Wren's St Paul's Cathedral in London. The eighteenth century, however, was to be the classical century par excellence in the arts across Europe. The music of Haydn and Mozart in **Austria**, and the building of St Petersburg in **Russia** and of Bath in England, are but a few of its greatest achievements. Nevertheless, classicism had evolved. Under the inspiration of the Counter-Reformation, earlier austerity had given way to the controlled emotionalism and love of decoration of the Baroque, and the even more extravagant rococo, of central

Europe. The underlying structural discipline, however, remained.

The impact of classicism on philosophy and politics was, in the longer term, destabilizing. The new rationalism sat uneasily with traditional Christianity, particularly Roman Catholicism, and **Diderot** (1713–84) and **Voltaire** (1694–1778) in **France** questioned and sometimes ridiculed faith with devastating effect. In **Germany** G. E. Lessing (1729–81) likewise called for the application of reason in religious matters. Rationalism also helped to undermine the aura of royalty, and although Voltaire leaned to **enlightened despotism**, his influence on the **French Revolution** of 1789 was potent. On the other hand, the discipline and regularity of classicism, particularly French classicism, had a strong appeal for autocrats. The **palace of Versailles**, built for Louis XIV of France (1638–1715), directly inspired **Peter the Great**'s palace of Peterhof (Petrodvorets) outside St Petersburg. The urban planning of Paris, Schinkel's (1781–1841) Berlin and **Mussolini**'s Rome all reflect the same impulse, as does the Madeleine in Paris, 1804–49. Classicism lacked empathy with the imaginative and irrational dimensions of human nature, and the immense popularity of Goethe's *Werther* (1774) announced the Romantic reaction which was to dominate the nineteenth century. Nevertheless, the music of Beethoven and Schubert, however Romantic in spirit, remained classical in form, and Jane Austen (1775–1817) must be considered England's greatest classical writer. Classicism probably remained strongest in municipal architecture, where it dominated until the beginning of the twentieth century, and in urban planning, notably Haussmann's Paris. Neoclassicism lasted in a pared-down guise until **World War II** and the Municipal Buildings, Norwich, 1938, are perhaps its last great achievement.

Clausewitz, Karl von (1780–1831)

Prussian general and major military theorist who had an important role in the military reforms which helped to defeat **Napoleon**. Trained in the Berlin War Academy, he saw service in the wars against revolutionary **France** and soon began to consider the need for reform of the Prussian Army. Captured by the French in 1806, following **Prussia**'s defeat he assisted in reform of high command and infantry tactics. Offended by Prussia's treaty with Napoleon in 1811, he served with the Russian forces in 1812 but rejoined the Prussian armies for the final defeat of **Napoleon**. As director of the staff college in Berlin, he developed his views on warfare, which were published posthumously in 1832–3 as *On War*. His most famous dictum, `War is the continuation of policy by other means', proved immensely influential but was only part of his sophisticated analysis of good strategy and the operational characteristics of warfare under almost any circumstances.

Clay, Henry (1777–1852)

Later renowned as 'the great compromiser', this dynamic and eloquent Kentucky lawyer entered Congress in 1812 as a War Hawk and immediately became speaker, transforming the office during his tenure (1812–21 and 1823–5). He served on the peace delegation at Ghent in 1814, supported 'Negro' colonization, pressed for recognition of Latin American independence and helped produce the **Missouri Compromise**. Advocating the 'American System' – a programme of protective **tariffs** and federally financed roads and canals – Clay ran unsuccessfully for president in 1824 but then backed **John Quincy Adams** and served as Secretary of State (1825–9). Entering the Senate in 1831, he led the opposition to Andrew Jackson, fruitlessly ran against his re-election in 1832, engineered the compromise that ended the Nullification crisis, and laid down the principles underlying the new **Whig Party**. As Whig leader in the Senate, he came into conflict with President **Tyler** after 1841 and narrowly lost the 1844 election. Finally, in 1850 he helped to engineer yet another compromise over slavery.

Clayton–Bulwer Treaty (1850)

In this settlement the **United States** and **Great Britain** agreed to halt expansion in Central America and to internationalize an envisaged isthmian canal (planned, at this point, in **Nicaragua**). Many opponents of the treaty, members of the Democratic Party, argued that the terms violated the **Monroe Doctrine**. Subsequent American statesmen would seek to disavow the treaty, succeeding ultimately in the Hay–Pauncefote agreements of 1900–1 which allowed the United States to unilaterally construct and fortify the canal (soon to be built in Panama).

Cleveland, Stephen Grover (1837–1908)

Twenty-second and twenty-fourth president of the **United States**, 1885–9 and 1893–7. A lawyer from Buffalo, New York, Cleveland was elected as a Democrat to the posts of sheriff of Erie County, mayor of Buffalo and governor of New York, where his record of economical administration and political independence attracted bipartisan support.

Nominated for the presidency in 1884, he narrowly defeated Republican James G. Blaine. As president, he continued to promote economy in government, vetoing a large number of internal improvement and pension bills, and in 1887 launched a vigorous attack on the protective tariff. Elected to the presidency again in 1892, his second term was overshadowed by the depression that began shortly after his inauguration. To this, Cleveland, as a believer in minimal government, offered little response, turning aside demands for public works projects and free coinage of silver. As a result, in 1896 the so-called 'Silver Democrats' captured the party and nominated **William Jennings Bryan** on a platform that explicitly repudiated most of his policies. Though an honest and courageous politician, Cleveland proved unable to adjust his political principles to changing circumstances.

climate change

– see also **energy**.

Climate change is a comprehensive term for the phenomenon of global warming and the extremes of weather, including droughts, floods and hurricanes, associated with it. Few scientists now dispute the evidence for the reality of global warming, but some do still question the belief of the majority that it is attributable to human agency, primarily through the burning of fossil fuels but to a much lesser extent through intensive stock-rearing practices. The former generates carbon dioxide (CO_2) and the latter methane. The concentration in the atmosphere of these two substances, together with some other much rarer gases, is believed to create the 'greenhouse effect', as it is popularly known, hence the name 'greenhouse gases'. Higher concentrations of greenhouse gases in the upper atmosphere effectively prevent the reflection back of the sun's rays into space and warm the globe below.

Fossil fuels include coal, oil and gas, and the Inter-governmental Panel on Climate Change (IPCC) believes that by 2050 the proportion of carbon dioxide in the upper atmosphere will have doubled since the beginning of the Industrial Revolution. Global concentrations are rapidly increasing as the developed world uses ever more energy and the developing world follows its pattern of growth. During 2006, **China** was opening new coal-fired power stations at fortnightly intervals. In 1990, however, the IPCC estimated that a reduction of 60 per cent in emission levels was required then, if the climate were to enjoy a stable equilibrium. By 2000 that estimate had risen to 70 per cent.

Estimates of the impact of climate change vary considerably depending on the rate of warming, which is now put at a minimum of 2°C and a maximum of 4·5 °C every century. At the higher end of the range, sea levels would have risen by up to a metre, making some island states uninhabitable and putting extensive areas of low-lying land across the world at serious risk of inundation. Equally large areas would have become desert, putting 400 million people at risk of starvation. Some scientists fear, however, that climate change could develop its own momentum, resulting in even more rapid and dramatic change. Global warming would be accompanied by an increase in extreme weather patterns and there is considerable evidence that this is happening. The reinsurance giant, Munich Re, calculated in 1998 that the number of natural disasters had increased threefold over the preceding twenty-five years.

It is difficult, though, to be precise even about trends in different parts of the world. A warmer global climate, for example, could lead to a diversion of the Gulf Stream, which would actually make north-west Europe colder. It is also difficult to say for certain that any particular disaster has been caused by global warming, only that it is the sort of disaster which global warming will make more likely to occur. The devastation of New Orleans by Hurricane Katrina in 2005 is a case in point. The increasing frequency of the El Niño phenomenon, however, whereby the large area of water off South East Asia associated with the monsoon is displaced eastwards towards the Pacific seaboard, causing drought in **Australia** and parts of **Indonesia** but catastrophic storms in western Latin America, is almost certainly attributable to global warming.

Clinton, William Jefferson (1946–)

Invariably known as 'Bill' Clinton, US president between 1993 and 2001. Born in 1946 to a modest background, Clinton was educated at Oxford and Yale and was elected Democratic governor of Arkansas in 1978. A political centrist or 'New Democrat' and consummate campaigner, he won the White House for the Democrats in 1992 and 1996, though never secured a majority of the popular vote and faced opposition majorities in Congress for most of his presidency. As president in the immediate post-**Cold War** era he promoted free trade and democracy on the foreign front and fiscal conservatism domestically, bringing the US budget into surplus in 1998 after decades of deficits. Following from his affair with a White House intern, Monica Lewinsky, he was impeached on charges of perjury and obstruction of justice, though he was acquitted by the Senate in 1999. He left the White House with high approval ratings, a booming economy and a more or less peaceable world. His wife, Hillary Clinton, became in 2016 the first ever woman to lead a major party White House bid.

Clive, Robert (1725–1774)

The first Baron Clive of Plassey was among the most controversial of the so-called British 'nabobs', who laid the foundations of the **British Empire** in India, accumulating huge personal profits in the process. Employed as a 'writer' by the **East India Company** in 1744, Clive soon switched to a military command, participating in a series of famous victories against the French in South India. Later he played a leading role in the conquest of Bengal after 1757, serving as the company governor in the region (1757–60 and 1765–7). Clive's massive fortune from trade and 'gifts' from Indian rulers, combined with his authoritarian style of government, attracted plentiful criticism among other company servants and British politicians. He defended his record in memorable speeches in Parliament in 1772–3, while consolidating his position as a major landowner, MP and power broker. Frequently dogged by illness and depression, he died possibly from an overdose of opium.

cloning

The processes whereby genetically identical copies, clones, can be made of living matter. Clones occur naturally, however, in those plants and bacteria which propagate themselves by asexual reproduction. The most famous artificial cloning was in 1996 when Scottish researchers succeeded, after 276 attempts, in producing Dolly the lamb from the mature or somatic udder cell of a 6-year-old sheep. The technique employed was to combine an empty egg with a somatic cell, which was allowed to develop into an early embryo in the test tube before implantation in the womb of a surrogate mother. Once born, Dolly was the clone of the donor sheep. Cloned animals do not, however, necessarily look identical because genes are not the only factor in appearance. Although cloning has considerable medical potential, many people have moral and religious reservations concerning its possible implications. Cloning of a complete human or other primate would appear possible but is technically more difficult than for a cow or sheep.

Club of Rome

– *see* **population**.

Cokwe

An ethnic group in eastern **Angola** who rose to prominence in the middle and late nineteenth century as one of the pre-eminent trading groups in the period following the end of the slave trade. They were especially active in the rubber trade. Commercial colonies of Cokwe were spread all over central Africa and became involved in the local politics of the region, including intervention in civil war in the Lunda Empire, which fell as a result.

Cold War

A global conflict between forces arranged alongside the **USSR** on one side and the **USA** on the other. The term was coined by **George Kennan** in 1947 to suggest the nature of the confrontation between broadly capitalist liberal democracy and socialist systems in the period after the world wars and the invention of the atomic bomb. Given the emergence of hundreds of new states into the world after the dissolution or fall of empires and the rejection of the racism that the Axis elevated as an organizing principle, the two sides had to attract new states and economic resources to their side whilst propagating their philosophies. The means that presented themselves were 'proxy' wars, intelligence activities, competition in space exploration, the arts, sport and scientific discovery, accompanied by clandestine but destructive confrontations in the third world. The Cold War also represented the need of the two sides to respond to the weakness of European empires whilst conscious of the possibility from 1953 that their nuclear arsenals could easily destroy each other and possibly all life on earth.

The Cold War moved through several phases and some historians have even located it in the mutual suspicion of the USA and Russia as rising powers in 1900. Most date its beginning from the general American institutional and popular perception of communist expansionism and hostility bound up with the end of the **Yalta** settlement and the withdrawal of an exhausted **Britain** from **Greece** in the face of communist agitation. President **Truman** took the latter event as a cue to proclaim the **Truman Doctrine** that the USA would aid the cause of nationalists and established governments against communism everywhere. Very many politicians and citizens in the USA became concerned about domestic subversion by agents of what they saw as a global communist conspiracy during the Red Scare of 1947. This attitude was reinforced by the secretiveness, aggression and domestic policies of **Joseph Stalin**, who was portrayed as a tyrant after **World War II** despite his image as Uncle Joe in that conflict. This phase of the Cold War heightened with the collapse of eastern European governments into communist regimes, the **Berlin airlift**, the Chinese communist revolution in 1949 and the Soviet acquisition, partly through spying, of the hydrogen bomb in 1953. Propagandistic abuse and clandestine activities on both sides were accompanied by active preparation of the citizenries of the East and West for war. Though the death of Stalin cooled this move towards a 'hot war' somewhat in 1953, the national security structures which had been created in form or name – such as **NATO**, the **CIA** and the American National Security Council and Department of Defense in the West, and the **KGB** in the East – ensured the maintenance of institutional hostility and suspicion. A 'thaw' began in 1955 with the rise of **Nikita Khrushchev**, who seemed committed to a more peaceful and demonstrative competition, but this was again reversed. Western and eastern interests began clashing in the decolonizing Arab world over energy resources, in space over satellite and space technology (and the accompanying ballistic missile potential of rocketry) and in the third world, where Soviets and Americans attempted to sponsor ideologically favourable movements to power. In this early competition the USSR (which strictly controlled information disseminated about itself, unlike the West) won many more victories than the West.

With the rise of **Richard Nixon** and the election of **John Kennedy** in the USA in 1960, the Cold War entered a new and even more dangerous phase. Kennedy favoured covert operations, special forces, ideological challenge and activity on all fronts, and combined his American idealism with an initial hard line towards communism in **Cuba**, eastern Europe and Berlin, and **Vietnam**. When Khrushchev responded at the 1961 Vienna summit with violent rhetoric of his own, the two men directed a worldwide competition that led to the **Cuban Missile Crisis** of October 1962. Broadly, this attempt by the USSR to place offensive ballistic missiles 144 kilometres (90 miles) from the American coast in a communist state opposed unreservedly by the USA created an international crisis. During the thirteen days of the crisis, the world came close to nuclear destruction. It was only the personal diplomacy of the two men through 'side channels' which allowed them to pull away from the brink in an agreement that was seen as a victory for the USA. Kennedy nevertheless pressed on with attempts to overcome perceived Soviet leads in space by calling for a national effort to place men on the Moon, and to peacefully coexist and compete. He also provided American assistance to decolonized anti-communist Vietnam, and maintained a hard line on the Soviet occupation of Berlin, which was ensured by the creation of the **Berlin Wall** between East Berlin and the western sector.

There is some evidence that Kennedy was considering an offer of détente by the time of his death in 1963; but his replacement by **Lyndon Johnson** and the fall of Nikita Khrushchev at the hands of **Leonid Breznev** and others a year later stalled any such process. The USA became engulfed in the **Vietnam War**, and the USSR became concerned about the possibly violent defection of its allies in **China** and eastern Europe from the communist bloc. By the time Richard Nixon came to power in 1968, both sides had moved from any capacity or wish to wage new military conflicts and towards a sober appreciation of the thermo-nuclear stakes. In addition, Nixon and his associate **Henry Kissinger** became enthusiastic about a diplomatic coup that would see the People's Republic of **China** either neutralized or functioning as a western ally, an aim they achieved by 1972. A period of détente thus began, in which the two sides sought via summit meetings of leaders, negotiations and international agreement to draw back from the brink and yet to build up their military production of strategic weapons. By 1979, inflation driven by increased oil prices and economic competition from new sources such as the European community and Japan (both of which also contributed to western markets and technology) had weakened both anyway, but the Soviets more than the USA.

A final phase of the Cold War began in 1979–81. This was inaugurated by the election of the anti-communists, American President **Ronald Reagan**, British Prime Minister **Margaret Thatcher** and of the Polish Karol Wojtyla as Pope **John Paul II**. The three leaders, though not in a coordinated fashion, drove the Soviets into a new and ruinous competition to develop arms, symbols of scientific progress, and ideological arguments to maintain their grip on eastern Europe and the third world. This competition effectively bankrupted the Soviets, struggling in the **Afghan War** and attempting to maintain their self-confidence in the face of nationalist and religious uprisings and new technologies. The Soviet leadership was also ageing, if not decrepit, and unable to improve productivity or morale within USSR, and with the failure of the **Virgin Lands campaign** over a decade earlier, effectively unable to feed its own population.

The consequence was not the breakdown into hard-line leadership and war feared by some, but instead the rise of **Mikhail Gorbachev**. Gorbachev engaged the West in an extended and ultimately effective dialogue to end the Cold War, as well as attempting to restructure the USSR and the Eastern bloc through his policies of glasnost and perestroika. However, in the face of a massive western economic expansion and internal strains, he in fact accelerated the collapse of communism, first in **Poland**, then across eastern Europe, and then, ultimately in 1991 in the USSR itself. The Cold War ended with western triumph and the emergence of China and **India** as new and growing world economic powers, and the total military primacy of a heavily indebted USA, which now had to face new economic and ideological competition from within its own self-proclaimed 'free world' bloc, as well as the sometimes unpleasant diplomatic and geo-political backwash of the Cold War alliances it had formed in the **Middle East** and South America.

collaboration
– *see also* **Vichy France**.
To collaborate is to work together for a common purpose, but the term emerged during the Napoleonic Wars as a term for illegal or illegitimate cooperation with an occupying or enemy power. The word gained new currency during the twentieth century as a term of abuse for those governments and willing accomplices who worked with Nazi Germany during its campaign of expansion. It was also applied to those non-Germans who participated in the **Holocaust**. Following the war, formal charges of treason, as well as participation in war crimes, were preferred against various defendants, and convictions were secured though a wider class of individuals than those arraigned were marked with the term.

collective security
A term that evolved after **World War I** for the principle of reinsurance in international affairs, by which states guaranteed by treaty to remain neutral in disputes or to collectively uphold the peace of **Europe**. In the form of the **League of Nations, NATO** and the **United Nations Organization** it was elaborated so that states could join an organization in which they had an obligation to aid others in

distress by treating an attack on any member as an attack on all. In 2001, Article 5 of the NATO treaty was invoked to this end following the September 11th attacks on the **USA**.

collectivization

The deliberate takeover by the state of the agricultural sector in order to create collective farms. The policy was conceived as one which would increase productivity, free workers for industrial work, feed those transferring to urban areas and produce a grain surplus which could, via export, offer both capital and collateral for industrialization. It is most associated with **Joseph Stalin** in the **Soviet Union** between 1927–34, and with **Mao Zedong** in **China** before 1970. Though carried out differently in the **USSR** and the People's Republic of China, the consequences were of the policy was dispropriation, coercion and ultimately mass famine in both countries.

Collectivization took place in two phases in the USSR. The first, in 1927–9, was associated with the consolidation of Stalinist power and 'dekulakization'. It involved the removal of peasant communal power and an end to the **New Economic Policy**, and its replacement with the construction of a series of new agro-towns and settlements of varying size through a mixture of fiat and targeted terror. This process slowed and was consolidated in the early 1930s, before increasing again to a point at which lying about production became institutionalized and starvation became a weapon of policy. This led to the Holodomor, or Ukrainian famine. In China, law and the activity of the people's courts led to the same end over a longer and arguably more thorough process, which was built into the development of the people's court system after 1949. It accelerated during the Great Leap Forward engineered by Chairman Mao in the 1960s. Estimates vary, but it is thought that some 1.5 to 3 million were killed or forced into suicide by the policy in China, while up to 20 million more may have starved to death. This was partly an effect of climate, but also because labour was diverted and food exported.

In the longer term, the policy of collectivization set back the development of the Soviet economy and led to attempts to develop land from above, such as the Virgin Lands campaign, which emerged on the back of permanently damaged production and the lack of a profit incentive in rural areas for production. These policies, in their turn, failed, and left the USSR, which contained some of the most fertile land in the world, requiring food aid by the 1970s. Dependence on American and western grain credits can be seen as highly relevant to détente and the move to a human rights culture, or at least the signature of treaties indicating such a move, as well as to perestroika and glasnost in later years. In China, the Communist Party retained control of rural areas but the policy of development through trade and 'capitalism with Chinese characteristics' was given a significant boost, as China found that food security came to depend on trade with Asia and the West.

Collins, Michael (1890–1922)

Irish revolutionary leader. Collins joined the Irish Republican Brotherhood in 1909, participating in the 1916 **Easter Rising**. Elected to the British Parliament in 1918, he sat instead in the 1919 Dáil Éireann (Assembly of Ireland) in Dublin and was appointed finance minister. Irish Republican Army commander in the War of Independence against **Britain**, Collins negotiated and signed the 1921 treaty establishing the Irish Free State. He was assassinated in the civil war that followed.

Collor de Mello, Fernando (1949–)

Born in Brazil into a wealthy and politically active family, Collor de Mello served as governor of the state of Algoas before winning the presidency in 1989, despite being a political outsider. The first popularly elected president since 1964, he ruled during a difficult period of foreign debt and hyperinflation. Accused of corruption, he resigned when facing impeachment in 1992 but was impeached nonetheless.

Colombia

A country of massive Andean ranges, river valleys and extensive lowlands that reach the Pacific and Caribbean coasts, Colombia has a diverse population of over 45 million, three-quarters of whom are urban. The capital, Bogotá, is home to more than 8 million. Liberal and Conservative parties emerged following the dissolution of **Gran Colombia** to dominate Colombian politics, although civil war has been recurrent. Under US pressure, **Panama** declared its independence in 1903. By 1890 coffee had replaced gold as Colombia's leading export; it reached over 80 per cent of total exports in the 1950s before declining. Legal and illegal drugs, especially cocaine, soon afterward became the country's most important export. The assassination of Liberal Jorge Eliécer Gaitán in 1948 sparked enormous riots in Bogotá and political violence until 1964. Conflicts between the government, drug cartels, guerrilla groups and paramilitary units have blighted the country. In June 2016 an agreement was signed to end the 52-year conflict with FARC (the left-wing guerrillas), but a referendum rejected the deal.

colonialism
– see **imperialism**.

Columbian Exchange

Coined by historian Alfred Crosby (1972), the Columbian Exchange refers to the biological exchange between the hemispheres that resulted from maritime trade, migration and colonial expansion in the centuries after Columbus' voyages. While initially the exchange of microbes, fauna and flora was transatlantic in nature, by the mid eighteenth century such biological interactions also resulted from transpacific maritime connections. The microbial exchange between the Americas and Afro-Eurasia was for the most part one-sided. With relatively dispersed populations, Amerindian populations prior to contact hosted syphilis and tick- and lice-born diseases such as spotted fever and typhus, but had no immunity to viruses associated with the 'crowd diseases' found in Afro-Eurasia. Smallpox, measles, mumps, diphtheria and yellow fever had evolved within denser populations, and often from pathogens amongst domestic mammal herds, to become highly infectious human diseases. Europeans and Africans bought these diseases to the Americas; the resulting illness devastated Amerindian populations that lacked resistance. In addition, parasites from Africa (most notably malaria) contributed to both Amerindian and European mortality in the Americas. Infectious disease weakened Amerindian polities and diminished potential labour supplies, leading to the development of the transatlantic slave trade.

The movement of Afro-Eurasian mammals to the Americas dominated the diffusion of fauna in the Columbian Exchange. Prior to contact, Amerindians domesticated few animals. Europeans, and to a lesser extent Africans, brought varieties of cattle, goats, horses, pigs and sheep to the Americas. Voracious herbivores, these domesticated and feral beasts radically transformed the local ecology and were a source of tension between Europeans and Amerindian communities. Some Amerindians successfully incorporated these animals within their economies; the Comanche in North America developed equestrian economies and polities based on the hunting of bison. Others, such as the Navajo, developed pastoralism, based on sheep breeding and wool production.

The movement of flora involved more mutual exchange between the hemispheres. A number of American tubers achieved global historical importance. The potato grew in poor soils and provided more calories per acre than Eurasian grains. Potatoes were easily prepared without the need for milling or baking; they also became useful as animal feed and replaced fallow in crop rotations. The potato sustained population growth in Europe and supported Russian eastward migration to Siberia and the Pacific. Potatoes found their way to northern India where the **East India Company** promoted their planting. Potatoes and sweet potatoes found their way to East Asia with the establishment of transpacific trade. Manioc was another American tuber that became an important crop in much of sub-Saharan Africa. Other Amerindian crops, including beans, cocoa, maize, peanuts and peppers, had global significance. Maize in particular was cultivated widely in Afro-Eurasia as it thrived in a variety of environments and stored easily.

The Columbian Exchange dramatically differentiated hemispheric demographic patterns. American plants generally supported Afro-Eurasian population growth, while the diseases of the latter devastated the population of Amerindians. The Columbian Exchange, in conjunction with the expansion of commercialized food production, also radically shifted the locations of plant and animal species. Today, **China**, **India** and **Russia** are the largest producers of the American potato, while North and South Americans raise the largest numbers of Eurasian cattle.

Combination Laws

Legislation of the British Parliament in 1799 and 1800, a period of industrial agitation, banning workers from organizing collectively to press for improved conditions. Employers were similarly banned from organization. In practice they were little used and trade unions grew. Repeal in 1824 was followed by an outbreak of strikes and a new Combination Act in 1825 allowed trade unions but severely limited their members' rights.

Comecon

The commercial and economic organization to coordinate economic development and mutual trade, established by the **Soviet Union**, **Albania**, **Bulgaria**, **Czechoslovakia**, **Hungary**, **Poland** and **Romania**, January 1949, partly to discourage the spread of Titoism. The **German Democratic Republic** (East Germany) joined in October 1950. Comecon promoted from 1956 a national 'division of work', but also joint investment projects and multilateral projects including the 'Mir' electric grid operative throughout Comecon by 1967 and the 'Druzhba' oil pipeline operational by 1964. Integration, however, never reached the level achieved by the **European Union** and the exchange of substandard products just to meet quotas was an ongoing problem. Comecon came to an end with the collapse of the Soviet bloc and the reorientation of much trade towards the European Union.

comfort women

It is estimated that between 80,000 and 200,000 women provided or were forced to provide sex labour in Japanese military brothels during **World War II**. The majority were Koreans, Japanese and Chinese. **Japan** officially recognized its moral, not legal, responsibility for comfort women in 1992 when the direct involvement of the military was proved by official documents. In 1995 the Asia Women's Fund was established to serve as a semi-official body to compensate former comfort women.

Comintern

The Third or **Communist** International, established by **Lenin** in the summer of 1919 to help give central direction to the anticipated worldwide Bolshevik revolutions. All the Bolshevik leaders participated, but for all their hopes and the fears of their opponents the impact of its activities was minimal. In practice, the Comintern's foundation confirmed and deepened the cleavage between communists and socialists. It was wound up by **Stalin** in 1943, to improve relations with the western Allies.

Committee of Union and Progress
– *see* **Young Turks**.

Commonwealth

The Commonwealth of Nations is an international association of over fifty free and independent states. It emerged from the **British Empire** in piecemeal fashion, beginning with the need to coordinate governmental policies between the various self-governing regions and Dominions of the British Empire in the 1880s. Between 1926 and 1931 the formal equality of **Britain** and dominions such as **Canada**, **New Zealand**, **Australia**, Newfoundland and **South Africa** was acknowledged, and following **World War II**, in the London Declaration of 1949, the Commonwealth became a fully post-imperial body. Though Her Majesty the Queen is the head of the organization, it contains monarchies and republics, and is

dedicated to democracy, civil society and the rule of law. The Singapore declaration of 1971 emphasized this point, committing the league in addition to liberal principles of free trade, equality of opportunity and anti-racism. Member citizens generally enjoy privileges, such as the vote, in each others' countries, and Commonwealth states have high commissions rather than embassies between them. The Commonwealth is an important international forum, and sponsors regular meetings of heads of government, as well as making attempts to secure and enhance good governance in some of the world's poorest countries. As with many international bodies, the union is divided, with a secretariat, an educational network and a civil society foundation disbursing money, technical assistance and ideas between member states. The Commonwealth also sponsors a quadrennial international sporting competition, the Commonwealth Games, which is second only to the Olympic Games as an international sporting event.

British views of the Commonwealth and its role in national life have from time to time changed. A persistent theme has been confusion at the refusal of the body to accept automatic British leadership, or any historic debt to the UK. This has been expressed in abandoned policies to use the Commonwealth as a coordinating body for a League of Nations or United Nations military alliance, to exert nuclear power on the world stage, and to promote British post-imperial interests in a forum other than **NATO** or the **European Community**. Though it is clear that Queen Elizabeth has viewed the global community offered by the Commonwealth as a vital feature of her reign, successive British politicians, beginning in the 1960s, have tended to commit Britain to Europe through tariff or governance arrangements in ways which have alienated the body. In addition, though the established dominions have been a source of British emigration for some time, immigration from the non-white countries of the Commonwealth to Britain between the 1950s and 1970s changed the demography and politics of the UK profoundly and not always to the approval of some sections of UK society. A few former parts of the empire, such as **Burma** and the Republic of **Ireland**, did not join the Commonwealth.

communal societies

Settlements founded by utopian reformers who have deemed separation from the outside world the best means of undertaking a given social experiment. Their ideological basis generally rests on religious egalitarianism or artisan socialism where all perform useful jobs without capitalist competition. The most striking examples originated in the mid-nineteenth-century **United States**, including Welshman **Robert Owen**'s New Harmony, Indiana, and John Humphrey Noyes' Oneida Community in upstate New York. They were generally short-lived as communitarian idealism turned into divisive conformism or authoritarianism; their sexual and racial mores could also incur external hostility.

Commune (Paris)

The radical democratic municipal authority that administered Paris for two months from 26 March 1871 in the wake of **France**'s defeat by **Prussia**, the government having fled to Versailles. The Commune – a short-lived but emblematic experiment that gained mass working-class support – proclaimed widespread economic, social and political reforms, separating church from state, establishing workers' cooperatives and instituting female suffrage. Government troops defeated it on 28 May, executing many thousands of Parisians.

communications

The history of communications is best understood as the invention and assimilation of a series of successive media tools: writing, printing, audio-visual (A/V) technologies and networked digital technologies. As is the case with other major technologies, new media tools were 'pulled' rather than 'pushed' into existence and widespread use. The pattern of pulling and accumulation can clearly be seen in the history of modern printing. The technologies necessary to print words are very old. They can be seen in seals, stamps and ink, among the oldest human communicative tools. The Romans used moveable type to print words on pipes; the ancient Chinese used wooden moveable type to print on paper; the Koreans used metal moveable type in the early fifteenth century. Presses – i.e. for grapes – were known in medieval Europe. Yet modern printing was not invented until 1450, when the German goldsmith Johannes Gutenberg put together the first press with metal, moveable type. His invention was a huge success. It spread throughout Europe with remarkable speed, not because it was so wonderfully new but because it fulfilled rising demand for reading material within a population that was increasingly literate. Hand-copying text on vellum was expensive; printing text on paper was – after the technology was sufficiently finely tuned and widespread – comparatively cheap. Throughout the early modern period, printing drove the price of text down and thereby made it available to larger groups of literate people (and those who enjoyed listening to them read). With the advent of steam-powered presses and pulp paper in the nineteenth century, it became economically feasible to print true ephemera – such as mass circulation newspapers – in titanic quantities. At the same time, literacy rates spiked, thanks largely to state-mandated and funded primary education. The era of mass literature and mass literacy was born. Of course, readers did not stop talking. After all, they had something new to talk about – what they had read.

The same pattern of pulling and accumulation is seen in rise of A/V media technologies. The ideas that stand behind photography – the pinhole camera effect and the photochemical effect – were in circulation in Europe as early as the seventeenth century. No one put them together before Nicéphore Niépce in the 1830s. Commercial photography took off very quickly thereafter. The first sound-recording device on record – the 'phonoautograph' – was invented by Edouard-Leon Scott in 1857. Sound-recordings, however, were not brought to market before Thomas Edison's 'phonograph' cylinders in the 1880s and Emile Berliner's 'gramophone' disks in the 1890s. The precursors to motion pictures – the flip book, the Zoetrope – were in circulation decades before Eadweard Muybridge began his experiments with 'serial photography' in the late 1870s. It wasn't until the late 1890s, however, that Edison and the Lumière brothers succeeded in commercializing film, and it was decades after that before movies assumed their modern form. There are too many good candidates for the title 'inventor of radio' to pick a winner, though it is certain that the technology was in the air by the 1890s at the latest. Guglielmo Marconi was granted a patent for 'wireless' in 1896, but he sold it for ship-to-shore communications. Commercial radio was not born until the 1920s. As with radio, several people 'discovered' television in the 1920s. But the first commercial broadcasts were not made until the 1930s and the technology was not widely adopted until the 1950s. By the mid twentieth century the media landscape looked very different than it had a century before: the middle classes were taking 'snapshots', going to 'movie palaces', listening to 'disc jockeys' and settling in every evening for 'prime time'. Naturally, listeners and viewers didn't stop talking and reading. A/V media gave them something new to talk about around the water cooler ('Who killed JR?') and to read about in the TV guide.

Finally, the history of the Internet shows much the same pull and accumulation pattern as that of writing and A/V technologies. The Internet is not so much a technology (though it is that) as an idea, and a very old one at that. The notion that all important human knowledge should and could be made available to everyone is at least as old as the Scientific Revolution. It stands behind the sixteenth-century *Kunstkammer* (the processor of the museum), the seventeenth-century scientific society, the eighteenth-century *Encylcopédie*, the nineteenth-century research library, and technologist Vannevar Bush's fanciful though prophetic 1945 essay 'How We May Think'. Scientists, then, knew what the Internet would do; the trouble was, they didn't have the technology to do it. That technology was provided by the US Department of Defense and allied universities. Both were interested – for different reasons – in creating a robust network of computers capable of transmitting masses of data instantaneously. In 1969 they created such a network – ARPANET – using a much older technology, telephone lines. The Inter-network – a network of networks – wasn't formed until some fifteen years later; it, too, ran on the back of the older telephone network. The Internet, as we know it today, however, emerged only after Tim Berners Lee created the World Wide Web in 1990 and Marc Andreessen created the first popular web browser in 1993. Since the Internet could do almost everything printing and A/V could do but better and cheaper, it spread around the world very quickly. Many pundits predict that the Internet will destroy 'legacy' media such as traditional print and A/V. They almost certainly overstate their case. Just as people continue to talk to one another in the age of the Internet, they will continue to read printed text and consume traditional A/V, at least for the foreseeable future.

communism

Communism as a philosophy is rooted in the writings of two Germans, **Karl Marx** (1818–83) and **Friedrich Engels** (1820–95), and in particular their joint work, *The Communist Manifesto*, 1848, and Marx's own mammoth study *Das Kapital* (*Capital*), 1867. Marx and Engels were, however, part of the wider radical movement which had briefly and unsuccessfully come to the fore in the European revolutions of 1848. *The Communist Manifesto* was a dramatic appeal to the proletariat, the working class, to revolt, and concluded with the famous call best known in English as 'Workers of the world unite, you have nothing to lose but your chains!'

The first phrase of the call was to adorn the coat of arms of the later **Soviet Union**. Marx was revolutionary at the time in claiming that it was the style of production which shaped society rather than the other way round, an analysis which has passed into mainstream economics. It was more significant, in his view, that society was feudal or capitalist than that it was French or German: 'The working men have no country' as *The Communist Manifesto* put it. He also believed that there was an essential conflict between the interests of those who had capital, the 'bourgeoisie', and the workers – the class struggle – and that the workers were historically destined to win and overthrow the power of capital. Marx was, however, an organizer as well as a writer, and for some years until 1872 he ran the International – a loose association of radicals, extending to anarchists, democrats and trade unionists, who were united in their belief that the class struggle was inseparable from the international solidarity of the radical left.

The workers' movement of the nineteenth century did not draw any distinction between communism and socialism, and the Social Democratic Party of Germany (SPD) (1869–75) was both the world's first socialist party and directly inspired by Marxism. The distinction which slowly emerged had both ideological and social roots. Socially, the homogeneous labouring poor of the first half of the nineteenth century were tending to separate into the aspiring artisan, on the one hand, and the labourer, on the other – the famous English distinction between the 'respectable' and the 'unrespectable'. Ideologically, those who favoured gradualism and a measure of accommodation with the middle classes, the future socialists, were diverging from those who favoured direct revolutionary action, the future communists. This was, however, far from clear at the time and was only marginally applicable to Britain where socialism had low church and trade union rather than Marxist roots. It was formally recognized with enormous future impact in Russia when the Social Democratic Party split between the majority revolutionary 'Bolsheviks' and the minority gradualist 'Mensheviks' in 1903.

It was Russian Bolshevik leader **Lenin** who was to provide the final strand in the emergence of orthodox communism. His 1905 pamphlet, *Chto dyelat'?* (*What is to be done?*), argued for the creation of a disciplined and united party which would form the vanguard of the revolutionary struggle. Lenin was openly contemptuous of liberal democracy and trade unionism, which he saw as at best a distraction from, and at worst a betrayal of, the task of securing power for the working class. Although Marxism–Leninism was to become communist orthodoxy, it contrasted with the ideals of his rival, **Rosa Luxemburg**, who urged democracy and the spontaneous expression of revolutionary fervour.

World War I changed the situation profoundly. The international solidarity of the working class foundered utterly when the Social Democratic members of the German Reichstag, with the exception of **Karl Liebknecht**, voted in favour of war credits. The British and German working classes were as national in their loyalties as the heads of state who led them, first cousins though those monarchs were. Rosa Luxemburg protested in vain. In **Russia**, the military collapse of 1917 led to the establishment of Bolshevik power and the establishment of the **USSR** in 1923.

This was not what the Bolsheviks had anticipated. Revolution was to have started in **Germany**, because it had the most politically conscious working class, and then spread worldwide, with backward Russia as a marginal player. The **Comintern** established for the purpose was disappointed. Attempts to ferment revolution by Kurt Eisner in Bavaria, Karl Liebknecht and Rosa Luxemburg in Berlin and **Béla Kun** in **Hungary**, 1919, were all quickly suppressed, and discontent elsewhere did not lead to revolution. Worst of all from the communist perspective, the attempted German revolutions were violently suppressed by a Social Democrat chancellor in cooperation with the army. The resulting bitterness between communist and social democrat was to contribute to the assumption of power by **Hitler** in 1933. The Soviet Union turned in on itself and under Lenin's successor, **Stalin**, pursued 'socialism in one country', adopting policies such as central planning which were to define state socialism but were not part of the original communist agenda. The internationalism of communism was interpreted by Stalin as a duty on communists everywhere to defend the Soviet Union as the world's first communist state.

World War II proved to be more extensively, if not more deeply, revolutionary than the World War I. Soviet influence after the 1945 victory led to the fusion of communist and socialist parties across central and eastern Europe and to the wide establishment there of 'people's democracies' and the 'dictatorship of the proletariat' – in practice, rule by a communist party oligarchy practising Leninist democratic centralism which put all real power in the hands of the party's first or general secretary.

Communist rule achieved much in education, health and welfare, and greatly increased living standards, but never succeeded in matching those of the liberal West. It collapsed in **Europe**, 1989–91, as a result of inefficient and unbalanced economic development, disproportionate military expenditure and a denial of civil rights which its citizens would no longer accept. Its last hope of genuine political reform had been lost with the suppression of the **Prague Spring** in 1968. It remains to be seen whether such Marxist successor parties as Germany's Party of Democratic Socialism (PDS), now part of the Left, would be able to combine original democratic, egalitarian and humanist ideals with the exercise of real power. World War II proved to be as revolutionary in **Asia** as in Europe, although communist power was not established in **China** until 1949 and **Vietnam** until 1962. China in recent decades has pioneered the adoption of market relationships within a framework of Communist Party control, which has proved outstandingly successful to date, at least in economic terms. Communism has been highly influential at times in **Latin America** also, notably in **Chile**, **Nicaragua** and **Venezuela**, but only in **Cuba** has it exercised lasting power. The results are controversial.

Communist Party of China

The Chinese Communist Party (CCP) came to power in China in 1949 after defeating the Nationalists in a civil war, and still rules the country today. It was founded in Shanghai in July 1921. In 1922 its members joined the **Kuomintang**, but they were purged by **Chiang Kai-shek** in 1927, and took refuge in rural Jiangxi. During this period, **Mao Zedong**'s ideas of peasant revolution came to the fore and he was elected head of the CCP in 1935. Mao further consolidated his position at the seventh National Party Congress in Yenan in 1945, where he was confirmed as head of the Politburo, and Mao thought was designated as the correct party line. By this time the CCP had 1.2 million members and controlled an area containing 90 million people.

With the end of the second Sino-Japanese War in 1945, full-scale civil war between the CCP and the Nationalists broke out. On 1 October 1949 Mao proclaimed the founding of the People's Republic of China (PRC). The CCP initiated a series of policies to consolidate power, which included land reform, a marriage law giving women the right of divorce and an alliance of peasants, workers and other classes known as New Democracy. In 1954 the CCP passed its constitution which established the institutions of governance that still remain today. State authority rests in the National People's Congress, with the Chinese People's Political Consultative Conference composed of elected delegates from the provincial congresses acting as a supervisory body. The CCP has a National Party Congress, with the Central Committee working under this. Its powers are exercised by the Politburo, which has a standing committee of leaders who manage the day-to-day affairs of the party and government.

Although Mao remained head of the CCP until his death in 1976, he wasn't unopposed. The failure of the **Great Leap Forward** forced him to step down as chairman of the PRC in 1959, and over the course of the following two years Liu Shaoqi, Deng Xiaoping and other moderates initiated limited economic reform. Concerned that he was losing control of the party, Mao supported his wife Jiang Qing and a group of radicals known as the **Gang of Four**, who began a purge of the CCP during the **Cultural Revolution**. Although its worst excesses were curbed in 1968, the turmoil continued until Mao's death.

After Mao's death, **Deng Xiaoping** mobilized support in the party and was able to gain power. In 1978 he proposed the policies that have formed the basis of China's modernization. These have brought about great economic and social change, but little political reform. Power passed relatively smoothly from Deng Xiaoping to Jiang Zemin and then to Hu Jintao, who is the current secretary of the party and president of the PRC. Protest movements, internal corruption and issues associated with China's modernization have posed significant problems for the CCP, although it remains firmly in control of China. With a membership of some 60 million in 2000, the CCP is the largest political organization anywhere in the world.

Communist Party of Cuba

With roots dating back to the 1920s, a merger with **Fidel Castro**'s 26th of July movement (M-26-7) in 1961 and subsequent reorganizations, the Communist Party of Cuba assumed a Soviet form in 1965 and became the only legal political party in Cuba. After 1965 Fidel and his brother Raúl, who is now president of Cuba, dominated the party. The 25-member Politburo selected by the Party Congress determines party and thus the state's policy.

Communist Party of Indonesia

The Indonesian Communist movement was established by Dutch Socialists in 1914, and became a vehicle for educated members of the Indonesian native classes to resist imperial rule and assert modernizing principles without regard to religion. It initially organized in a clandestine fashion, infiltrating organizations such as Sarekat Islam, before emerging as a fully fledged Party in 1920; even the name PKI was not finalized until 1921. A failed revolt in 1926 led to suppression until 1945. Over the course of the next twenty years the party rose to become the biggest in the world, before being crushed by military and nationalist forces under General Suharto, who blamed it for what appeared to be an attempted coup in 1965. Subsequently, party members were killed, blacklisted or exiled, and the movement did not rise again.

Communist Party of North Vietnam

The Communist Party of North Vietnam was founded by **Ho Chi Minh** and fellow Vietnamese exiles in **Hong Kong** in February 1930. It was a merger of two rival Vietnamese Communist forces, the Indochinese Communist Party and the Communist Party of Annam. After the first plenum, the name of the party was changed to the Communist Party of Indochina, according to **Comintern** policy. In 1945 the party was temporarily dissolved while its activities were folded into that of the Common Front for National Liberation, the **Viet Minh**. The party was refounded in 1951 as the Vietnamese Workers' Party. It became an important driving force in establishing socialist society in North Vietnam and carrying out revolution and liberation in South Vietnam. After the reunification of **Vietnam**, the party was again renamed, this time as the Communist Party of Vietnam. It is the current ruling party as well as the only legal political party in the country.

Compromise of 1850 (USA)

These measures passed by the US Congress apparently settled the issues that had embittered sectional argument in the preceding four years. The debate over the status of slavery in the lands acquired from Mexico in 1848 resulted in the immediate admission of California as a free state, and the division of the remainder into two territories, New Mexico and Utah, with the status of slavery to be decided by the settlers who went there. The boundaries of New Mexico were confirmed, to the detriment of Texas, but Congress took over Texas' huge state debts. A new Fugitive Slave Act removed state discretion over implementation, but Congress prohibited the trading of slaves in the District of Columbia while confirming the continuation of slavery there. These measures did not pass as a single compromise package but as a series of separate measures, each with a different basis of sectional support. Dispute over the meaning of these provisions would embitter relations to the outbreak of civil war.

Compromise of 1877 (USA)

The outcome of the closely contested American presidential election of 1876 turned on the results from Florida, Louisiana and South Carolina, where the Democrats had engaged in systematic intimidation of black voters and the Republicans in systematic fraud. It was resolved by an understanding that the Democrats would acquiesce in the inauguration of the Republican presidential candidate, **Rutherford B. Hayes**, and Republicans in the inauguration of Democratic candidates for governor. The Compromise of 1877 is usually seen as marking the end of **Reconstruction**.

computing

– see also **information technology**.

Used traditionally as a synonym for counting and calculation, 'computing' is now connected to the operation and usage of computing machines (hardware). Computer software (also called programmes) enables a computer to perform specific tasks, including word processing, emailing, statistical calculations and information storage. Modern computers manipulate data according to instructions or programmes. They work with memory cells that store binary numbers in bytes (groups of eight), each of which represents 256 different numbers. To store larger numbers, several bytes are used. A computer may store any kind of information in its memory so long as it can be translated into numerical form.

concentration camps

– see also **Auschwitz**.

The idea of concentrating military enemies or potential civilian insurgents in camps emerged in the US wars against native Americans and Filipinos in the late nineteenth century, but also on the Spanish side in **Cuba** during the **Spanish–American War**. It altered again with the British practice, during the **Second Boer War** in South Africa, of interning and geographically controlling civilian populations so as to identify and eliminate paramilitary or guerrilla opponents. As a practice of racial displacement and segregation, German administrators in South-West Africa before and during the Great War also employed concentration camps, often as much to eliminate native peoples as to remove them from their land.

However, the idea was transferred to the sphere of criminal justice during the 1920s and 1930s, when it blended with fashionable eugenic ideas in portions of the psychiatric community. New theories of deviance gave rise to the idea that certain classes of criminals, as well as homosexuals and political subversives, could not be dealt with by normal means but should instead be concentrated together and subjected to regimes of physical discipline and character building so as to overcome what were seen as problems rooted in a lack of psychological control. In contrast, other theories of race also encouraged the isolation of deviant groups as a way of removing the danger of decline or corruption from society. This idea was seized upon both by social reformers and National Socialists in Germany. The latter moved to create a concentration camp for political opponents in Dachau in 1933, as part of a wider system which was to complement the Nazi structure of totalitarian social control.

Dachau, under the control of Theodor Eicke and the SS, became the model for a series of prison camps which Heinrich Himmler began to establish after taking overall control of the camp programme in 1934. The techniques of transportation, prison construction, administration and imprisonment learned from the concentration camp system would be expanded to the extermination camps of the German government in Poland, as part of the **Holocaust**. Concentration camps thus came to symbolize something similar to the **gulag** network of penal and construction camps which sprang up in the Soviet Union under **Joseph Stalin**, and which were associated with later communist regimes such as that of North Korea. However, by the late 1930s German concentration camps were also being used as the base for unethical and debased experimentation in human body tolerances of cold, pressure and heat as well as for genetic research. The camps illustrate how easily a security establishment armed with scientific justifications, an idea of racial hygiene or eugenics, and the political debasement of a class of human beings from full human dignity can lead to a professionalized system of control and destruction of human life which moves easily from the marginal to the general.

concordats

A concordat is the name given to the style of legal agreement favoured by the Holy See (sometimes referred to in error as the Vatican) and another sovereign state. It corresponds roughly to a treaty in international law. Concordats have been employed as a means of establishing religious structures and privileges in foreign countries, and the rights of states vis-à-vis the Church, since 1107. They often cover matters such as tax status or the exemption of the clergy from particular laws. The most famous, or infamous, of modern concordats have included the 1933 agreement between the **Hitler** regime and the Church in **Germany**, and the 1929 Lateran Accords which established the status of the Vatican City State on the basis of an agreement with the **Mussolini** government. In 2003 the Church and Israel concluded the first of what the Vatican hoped was a series of agreements which might ultimately lead to an enhanced role for the Church in the government of a neutralized Jerusalem. As late as 2009, concordats still caused controversy, when Brazil signed one recognizing the introduction of Catholic education into the nominally secular Brazilian education system.

Confederate States of America

A slaveholding republic formed out of the secession from the Federal Union in 1860–1 of eleven Southern states. The Confederate States of America initially comprised the lower South states of South Carolina, Mississippi, Florida, Alabama, Georgia, Louisiana and Texas. In February 1861 delegates met in Montgomery, Alabama, to write a constitution and elect a provisional government. For president, the Confederate founding fathers chose a leading Mississippi planter-politician, Jefferson Davis, and for vice president, Alexander Stephens of Georgia. The Confederate Constitution (there were provisional and permanent versions) closely resembled its Federal counterpart; it diverged mainly in its affirmation of the 'sovereign and independent character' of the states, in its express protection of slavery and in restricting the executive to a single six-year term. Notwithstanding the republic's states rights origins, the right of secession was not included. After hostilities began in April 1861, four more states, from the upper South, joined the Confederacy: Virginia, Arkansas, Tennessee and North Carolina. Shortly afterwards the Confederacy moved its capital from Montgomery to Richmond, Virginia, a decision partly dictated by Richmond's position as the South's leading industrial centre.

The history of the Confederate States is inseparable from that of the **American Civil War**. From the outset the new republic was forced into a military defence of its independence, an effort that ultimately failed. The doctrine of states rights was especially vulnerable to wartime exigencies, and the actions of the Davis government in areas such

as conscription (first enforced in April 1862) proved highly contentious. States rights' opposition to Confederate nationalism, notably from Georgia's Governor Joseph Brown, although frustrated by Congress and the courts, helped undermine Jefferson Davis's authority. Although the Confederacy failed to develop a two-party system, political resistance to the war intensified after the 1863 congressional elections, with mounting calls for peace coming from influential figures such as the North Carolina editor William W. Holden.

Numerous factors were responsible for the Confederacy's failure. At its core, the Confederate States existed to sustain a particular way of life in which slavery, as an economic and racial system, loomed large. But that system proved the republic's Achilles heel, with slaves finding innumerable ways, including escape to Union lines and, after 1863, enlistment in the Northern armies, to subvert their masters' cause. Confederate diplomacy, relying heavily upon the coercive power of 'King Cotton', proved incapable of persuading **Britain** and **France** to intervene on the slaveholders' behalf. Economically, the South was disadvantaged by its overwhelmingly agricultural character. Although the Confederacy made impressive strides in surmounting its military-industrial deficiencies, ultimately it failed to compete with the better resourced, equipped and populated North. As fighting persisted into its third and fourth years, inflation and mounting food shortages exacerbated popular disillusionment and class resentments grew. One consequence was the increased level of desertion from the Confederate armies. The surrender of General **Robert E. Lee**'s much depleted Army of Northern Virginia on 9 April 1865 effectively brought the war – and the Confederate States of America – to an end.

Confederación Nacional del Trabajo

National Confederation of Labour (CNT), an anarcho-syndicalist union federation established in **Spain** in 1910. Outlawed under the 1923–31 dictatorship, by 1936 the CNT had a million members, predominantly in Catalonia. Allied to the Federación Anarquista Ibérica (FAI, Iberian Anarchist Federation), CNT militias resisted the July 1936 military rising and members were prominent in developing agricultural collectivization and industrial self-management in the Republican zone. Banned following the 1939 Nationalist victory, the CNT survived in exile.

Confucianism
– *see also* **Chosŏn dynasty**.

Confucianism is a philosophical and religious system founded by Confucius (551–449 BC). It gained many followers throughout Asia and had a profound impact on political, cultural and economic developments in **Korea**, **Japan** and **China**. Confucian morals and ethics today continue to influence social and cultural practices throughout Asia.

Confucius developed his ideas during the late Zhou period in China when continuous conflict and warfare beset everyday life although intellectual development flourished. In this environment, Confucius designed a philosophical system to cultivate proper thought and actions through the pursuit of a moral and ethical life. According to him, *jen* (goodness, benevolence or love) represented the most virtuous quality of individuals. To unfold this perfect state, Confucius stressed that people should follow *li* (ritual norms), *zhong* (loyalty to one's true nature), *shu* (reciprocity) and *xiao* (filial piety), which were practices that embodied proper virtue. By realizing *jen* through rituals and customs, Confucius believed humanity would be in accord with the will of Heaven and order and stability would therefore exist in society.

Confucius wrote little, and so the responsibilities to articulate and spread his ideas fell to future Confucian scholars, including Mencius (372–289 BC). The principles of Confucianism consequently were continuously reinterpreted. Through the work of Chu Hsi (1130–1200), Confucianism underwent a dramatic transformation that culminated with the birth of neo-Confucianism. As the principal force of the universe that endowed it with goodness, Ultimate Reality (*T'ai-chi*), according to Chu Hsi, consisted of *li* (principle) and *ch'i* (material force). Differences in individual *ch'i* prevented people from experiencing and being unified with Ultimate Reality. Chu Hsi argued that individuals should transform their *ch'i* through a moral lifestyle and education. Many scholars have argued that Chu Hsi supplied a metaphysical system for Confucianism and thus turned it into a formal religion.

As a religious and philosophical system that featured rules, rites and rituals for a vibrant moral and ethical life, Confucianism significantly influenced the political, economic, social and cultural structures in countries where it had gained popularity. During the **Chosŏn dynasty** in Korea, for example, the royal court instituted neo-Confucianism as its reigning political ideology. All laws, practices and rituals embodied the principles of neo-Confucianism, such as the social hierarchy system, examination systems and rituals to venerate ancestors. Because neo-Confucianism emphasized the male over the female, Chosŏn laws deprived many women of social and economic rights that they had enjoyed in earlier periods of history. Through customs and traditions, neo-Confucianism continues to play a strong role in shaping morals, ethics and daily life in North and South Korea, especially in the area of gender relations.

Congo, Belgian
– *see* **Belgium Empire**.

Congo, Democratic Republic of
From the fourteenth to the nineteenth centuries the territory of the Congo (Kongo) kingdom. The area now comprising the Democratic Republic of **Congo** was recognized at the 1885 Congress of Berlin as the personal property of the Belgian King Leopold II. His ruthless exploitation of the country's people and resources prompted its annexation by the Belgian government in 1908. Neglected by Belgium, the wholly unprepared colony gained independence as the Republic of Congo in June 1960 under President **Joseph Kasavubu** (c. 1910–69) and Prime Minister Patrice Lumumba (1925–61). In July the mineral-rich Katanga Province seceded under **Moise Tshombe** (1919–69) and the country entered a period of instability. In 1964 Kasavubu and Tshombe, who had become prime minister of the reunited Congo, were overthrown in a coup led by the western-backed **Joseph Mobutu** (1930–97). Mobutu renamed the country Zaire and himself Mobutu Sese Seko in 1971. Under growing internal and external pressure, Mobutu reluctantly allowed the formation of rival political parties in 1990 but was ousted in 1997 by **Laurent-Désiré Kabila** (1939–2001), who gave the country its present name. Congo found itself at the centre of a brutal regional war over resources involving Rwanda, **Uganda**, **Angola**, **Chad**, **Namibia** and **Zimbabwe**, combined with internal conflict with predominantly Tutsi rebels who seized the east of the country. Kabila was assassinated in 2001 and succeeded by his son Joseph (1971–), who became the country's first democratically elected president in 2006. He was re-elected in 2011 and the protracted conflict with Tutsi rebels ended in 2013. To date, Congo has never seen a peaceful transfer of power.

Congress of Berlin

At the Congress of Berlin, convened on 13 July 1878, European powers forced **Russia** to temper its territorial gains made during the Russo-Ottoman War (1877–8). The scale of the Russian victory, and the seizure of territory in the Balkans in particular, had upset the balance of power in **Europe**. An initial agreement, the Treaty of **San Stefano** (3 March 1878), had envisioned a 'Greater Bulgaria' under Russian suzerainty. That state was to incorporate (Ottoman) Thrace's Aegean coast, giving Russia direct access to the Mediterranean, an outcome that was unacceptable to the Great Powers. According to the revision of San Stefano signed at Berlin, **Serbia**, **Romania** and Montenegro all became independent. **Bosnia–Hercegovina** came under Austro-Hungarian control while Great Britain gained **Cyprus** in return for helping keep Thrace and Albania under Ottoman control. Ottoman losses (some 20 per cent of its population and some of its most productive land) enshrined by the treaty, were nevertheless significant.

Congress of Industrial Organizations (CIO) (USA)

The Congress of Industrial Organizations was formed in 1935 to represent workers in the heavy new mass production industries such as coal, steel and autos which the conservative craft organized American Federation of Labour (AFL) had ignored. It grew rapidly in the late 1930s, amid bitter struggles, and both organizations flourished during the wartime boom. The CIO merged with the AFL in 1955 as the more combative founders died and the sharper ideological and organizational differences softened.

Congress of Racial Equality (CORE) (USA)

Founded in Chicago in 1942, CORE pioneered the use of Gandhian non-violence against **segregation**. The 1961 Freedom Rides gave it a national reputation and funding to participate in Southern voter registration efforts. Three CORE members were murdered during the 1964 Mississippi Freedom Summer. By then, many CORE chapters had all-black leadership to promote community empowerment and this explains CORE's rapid embrace of **Black Power** tactics in 1966, urging African-American economic cooperation and political independence.

Congress of Vienna

An important international conference held in 1814–15 that established a balance of power within Europe. The congress reflected a desire for stability, conservativism and pragmatism following the **French Revolution** and **Napoleonic Wars**. Chaired by **Austria**'s **Klemens von Metternich**, the meeting involved complex negotiations between representatives of the major European powers: Viscount Robert Castlereagh of England, Charles Maurice de Talleyrand-Périgord of **France**, Tsar **Alexander I** of **Russia** and Prince Karl August von Hardenburg of **Prussia**. Members reinstated legitimate monarchs and modified European boundaries to establish barriers against French aggression. The conference restored France's pre-revolutionary borders, united **Belgium** and Holland, granted independence to **Switzerland**, returned most of **Italy**'s principalities, partitioned **Poland**, and allocated territories to **Britain**, Prussia, Austria and Russia. Leaders from the four main powers agreed to meet periodically and continue the Quadruple Alliance. Although the alliance later collapsed, the Congress of Vienna transformed traditional diplomacy and helped ensure an extended period of peace and stability that essentially lasted until **World War I**.

Congress System

International system that originated with the **Congress of Vienna** in 1815 and shaped European diplomacy in the early nineteenth century. The four major European powers of the Quadruple Alliance – **Austria**, **Britain**, **Prussia** and **Russia** – agreed to meet periodically to preserve the agreements of the Congress of Vienna and maintain a balance of power. In 1818, **France** joined the agreement at the Congress of Aix-la-Chapelle, creating the Quintuple Alliance. Rivalries, conflicting interests and pressures of nationalism and liberalism complicated agreement and led to its breakdown. In 1823, the Congress System effectively ended with the withdrawal of Britain over differences concerning intervention in the Iberian revolts. Despite its limitations, the system marked the birth of the European state system and acted as a precursor to the **League of Nations** and **United Nations**. It initiated a prolonged period of international peace and stability that essentially remained until **World War I**.

conscientious objection

A ground for refusal to participate in military service or activity on the basis that such service runs against the conscience of the individual because its nature or consequences are against the individual's moral or religious outlook. It has historically been associated with Protestant, Quaker and Mennonite Christianity, and as such was recognized in the laws of the **United States**, the **United Kingdom** and the **Russian Empire** in the eighteenth and nineteenth centuries. However, the term came to great prominence after 1916, when the British military draft allowed for individuals to appear before a tribunal to object to service in **World War I**. Conscientious objection is now generally but not universally recognized as a human right, which can be based on secular grounds, though some states draw distinctions between absolute objection to war and selective objection to particular wars or orders. Many states require alternative civilian service from objectors. The importance of the term has largely declined in inverse proportion to the rise of volunteer armies.

Constantinople

Constantinople was the capital of the **Ottoman Empire** between 1459 and 1923. British forces occupied the city after World War I, relinquishing control after the Turkish nationalist victory in 1923. The Turkish Republic established its capital at Ankara in central Anatolia and insisted that the former capital of the Ottoman Empire be referred to in all languages by its Turkish name, Istanbul. Before the fall of the Ottoman Empire, the city was Istanbul in Turkish, while other languages retained the Roman name. At the turn of the twentieth century, Constantinople was home to 1 million inhabitants. Although the seat of the Islamic Caliphate, its diverse citizenry was perhaps only half Muslim. The city's Christian population, mostly Greek Orthodox and Armenian, dwindled after the fall of the Ottoman Empire. A sharp rise in urbanization after **World War II** saw the construction of informal settlements (*gecekondus*) inhabited by waves of immigrants arriving from eastern Anatolia.

Constitution of 1876 (Ottoman Empire)

Signed by Sultan Abdulhamit II shortly after his accession in a year of diplomatic, financial and political crisis, which had seen a mass demonstration by theological students and the deposition of the two preceding sultans. Drafted by a constitutional commission under Midhat Pasa (1855–1912), a known reformer, it bowed to the demands of both students and Young Ottoman reformers but confirmed the prime authority of the sultan both as head of state and as caliph of **Islam**, who even enjoyed the right to suspend the constitution itself. The grand vizier was to be no more than first among equals in the Council of Ministers. Parliament was divided into a Chamber of Deputies and a Chamber of Notables, and the Council of State remained a supreme court with responsibility for drafting bills. All Ottoman citizens were declared equal. The liberalism of the constitution was, however, soon negated by Sultan Abdulhamit's autocratic style of rule. Parliament was simply suspended for thirty years after 1878.

Constitution of 1979 (Islamic Republic of Iran)

The Constitution of the Islamic Republic was approved by a national referendum in December 1979. Supreme authority is vested in the Spiritual Leader (*wahi faqih*), the position being first filled by **Ayatollah Ruhollah Khomeini** until his death in 1989. His successors were elected. The president, who is the head of the executive, is popularly elected but may not serve for more than two four-year terms. The president appoints the cabinet subject to the approval of the Islamic Consultative Assembly (*Majlis*). The Assembly, which has 270 members, is directly elected on a non-party basis for a four-year term by all citizens aged 15 or over, with five seats being reserved for religious minorities. Although voting is secret, electors must write the name of their preferred candidate themselves as the ballot paper is not printed. All legislation, however, is subject to approval by the Council of Guardians whose duty it is to ensure that it accords with both the Islamic code and the constitution. Six of its twelve members are appointed by the Spiritual Leader and six by the judiciary.

constitutional amendments, American

The **American Constitution** allowed for its own amendment, provided that two-thirds of each house of Congress (or a constitutional convention) and three-quarters of the states agreed. The process was used immediately to create a bill of rights: the first ten amendments (1791) mostly provided guarantees for individual liberties. The tenth and the eleventh (1798), protected the position of the states, while the twelfth (1804) adjusted the procedure for electing the president and vice president. Thereafter no further amendments occurred until 1913 – except in the wake of the civil war. The thirteenth amendment (1865) abolished slavery; the fourteenth most importantly guaranteed equal civil rights to all born (or naturalized) in the United States; the fifteenth amendment prohibited states from refusing the vote on the grounds of 'race, colour, or previous condition of servitude'.

The interpretation and enforcement of these last two would long be contested, but ultimately they opened the way to the equal rights movements of the twentieth century.

consumerism

The mass consumption of goods and services beyond levels needed to satisfy basic needs is said to be a defining feature of developed contemporary societies and the main aspiration of the developing world. There is no historical equivalent to the extraordinarily high levels of consumption achieved by modern developed economies, compared to pre-modern societies, but traits of consumerism have prevailed since ancient times as the privilege of political and economic elites. Their jewellery, tapestries, artworks, clothing and exotic food stuffs represent anticipation of modern consumerism.

Sumptuary laws designed to restrict consumption constitute valuable evidence as to what sort of goods and services were luxuries and considered by governments as excess forms of consumption. The Locrian Code (seventh century BC) in Greece stated that 'no woman should be allowed more than one maid to follow her, wear jewels of gold about her, or be seen in one of those effeminate robes'. The Roman *Sumtuariae Leges* prevented unnecessary expense in banquets and dress, sixteenth-century legislation in France decreed that only princes should eat turbot and wear velvet or gold lace. Such restrictions on consumption usually covered clothing, personal services, jewellery and food.

Although absence of sumptuary laws might well have constrained consumerism, demand in pre-modern societies has structural foundations. Agrarian economies maintained populations close to subsistence levels of consumption and the scale of economic surpluses necessary to spend on non-basic commodities could not be sustained. Pre-modern economies were dominated by peasants whose purchasing power was meagre. In addition, religions and dominant value systems tended to discourage consumerism. Buddhism scorned material possessions, Christianity portrayed a life of poverty as exemplary, and Hinduism postponed worldly desires to other lives, while Confucianism equated the good life with the acquisition of knowledge and virtue rather than material possessions.

Thus, the rise of consumerism in modern economies has benefited from gradual secularization and the adaptability of religions to allow for material progress. Nevertheless consumerism owes its extension to increases in agricultural productivity and the mechanization of industry that drastically reduced the costs of manufactured goods and raised the overall purchasing power of the urban masses. Sustained and drastic falls in transportation costs facilitated the expansion of regional and international trade, which further reduced prices and widened the range of goods available to shoppers. It is the conjunction of these forces that brought about the decisive transformation from minority consumerism of pre-modern societies into the mass-based indiscriminate consumption of developed economies with high incomes and standards of living.

Continental Congress (USA)

The First Continental Congress met at Carpenters' Hall in Philadelphia in September 1774 to discuss an inter-colonial response to the Intolerable Acts. Delegates agreed to enter into a 'Continental Association' enforcing a non-importation and non-exportation agreement, designed to bring economic pressure on Great Britain. The second Continental Congress, which convened in Philadelphia from 1775, found itself charged with managing the war effort following the outbreak of the Revolutionary War. Early efforts focused on establishing the Continental Army, including writing a 'Declaration on the Causes and Necessity of Taking Up Arms', whilst simultaneously attempting to negotiate reconciliation with Great Britain through the 'Olive Branch Petition'. Its most famous act was approving the resolution on Independence from Great Britain on 2 July 1776, after a month of tense debate. The Congress was also responsible for the drafting of the **Articles of Confederation**.

Continental System

The name given to the protectionist economic bloc established by the 1806 Berlin Decree of **Napoleon Bonaparte**, which lasted until 1814. The aim of the system was to draw western Europe behind **France** so as to deny to **Britain** the ports and commerce of the continent. However, the effect was to cause inflation and disruption to industry, and the complication of relationships with neutral nations. Indirectly, the blockade led to smuggling, the Peninsular campaign, and the disastrous invasion of **Russia**, which much reduced the Napoleonic forces by 1812–13. Britain itself retained naval supremacy and, though its economy was temporarily if severely damaged, it did develop new markets and coped both with unemployment in its industrial north and war with the neutral **USA** in 1812. It was therefore Britain which emerged to preside over the defeat of Napoleon in 1814–15, rather than vice versa.

contraband

– see also **smuggling**.

Contraband refers to goods that were illegally traded or smuggled, generally across a state border or other boundary. The attribution of the status of contraband to a traded good or category of traded goods in the modern world depended on the presence of a number of elements: first, legal frameworks governing the trade in goods between states, and which most often imposed a tax or tariff; second, borders across which trade took place and which were the site of the control of trade by representatives of the state, such as customs officials; and, third, the willingness of individuals to undertake and manage this illegal trade in order to avoid the customs tax. One consequence of the increasing globalization of legal regimes governing trade after 1700 was the higher proportion of traded goods that fell afoul of new laws, and which, therefore, became contraband. Indeed, there was no category of good that could not *become* contraband when modifications were introduced to the legal regime that defined its status, and contraband tended to be the goods of highest value in a given social or economic context. Bullion, slaves, textiles, porcelain and opium were all goods that circulated the globe both legally and as contraband as their value rose after 1700.

Even in the clear presence of laws, borders and smugglers, however, the contraband status of a traded good was ambiguous and changeable. Goods could quickly move from being legally traded to being illegally traded because of changes in trade policy, for instance; and the deliberate substitution of the national or imperial provenance of merchandize by smugglers could transform what is in essence contraband into a legally traded good. An example of the latter phenomenon is the relabelling of barrels of sugar as French or English so that they could be freely traded amongst colonies of the same empire in the Atlantic world of the eighteenth century, when intra-imperial trade was forbidden. The question of border crossing could also be complicated; in metropolitan France, the distillation of sugar syrups into rum (and the trade in such rum from French Caribbean colonies to **France**) was decreed illegal in 1713, so all subsequent cargoes seized by French officials were considered contraband, although they crossed no state boundary.

The transformation of goods into contraband when traded illegally across a border depended on the existence of two sets of legal frameworks, those of the origin of the goods and those of the destination of the goods. Therefore, it was possible and even common for merchandize to be legally traded goods by the regulatory bodies of the place of origin, and considered as contraband by the regulatory bodies of the destination, or vice versa, and for these statuses to change as the laws themselves changed. For example, in 1763 after the Seven Years War, bowing to the pressure of colonists, the French allowed the import of selected non-French goods into the French colonies of the Caribbean, where they had previously been disallowed. In many cases, these goods came from British colonies, often in North America, where these trades were still illegal, so that while the goods were British contraband, French colonists broke no French law by purchasing or trading for them.

contraception

– see **birth control**.

Contras, Nicaraguan

The Contras (an abbreviation of the Spanish for counter-revolutionary) were armed groups that fought the Sandinista National Liberation Front government after the 1979 Nicaraguan Revolution. The **United States** controversially provided substantial funding to the right-wing Contras, directly and indirectly, in an effort to overthrow the **Sandinistas**. The end of American funding, international pressure and a Central American peace plan (proposed by the Costa Rican president) led the Contras into a negotiated solution with the Sandinistas in 1988. Following the Sandinista defeat in 1990 presidential elections, the Contras were disbanded.

Cook, James (1728–1779)

English explorer, navigator and cartographer born in 1728. Captain of the Royal Navy and fellow of the Royal Academy, Cook sailed three legendary voyages between 1768 and 1779. On his first trip, after successfully observing the transit of Venus across the Sun at Tahiti, Cook set out to find Terra Australis, a continental land mass then believed to exist in the southern hemisphere. En route, he charted all of **New Zealand**, navigated Queensland's Great Barrier Reef and claimed New South Wales for the British Crown. On his second voyage he circumnavigated the **Antarctic**, charting Tonga and Easter Island, discovering New

Caledonia and other minor islands, and confirmed the real status of Terra Australis. His last expedition, an attempt to find a passage around Alaska or Siberia connecting the Pacific to the Atlantic, proved fruitless. On his return to **Hawaii** in 1779, Cook died at the hands of local people.

Coolidge, Calvin (1872–1933)

Thirtieth president of the **United States**, 1923–9. Originally from Plymouth, Vermont, he built his political career in Massachusetts, where he served as a Republican in the state legislature (1912–15), as lieutenant governor (1916–18) and governor (1918). Elected vice president in 1920, he became president when Warren Harding died of a heart attack. Coolidge was a business conservative who favoured low taxes, small government and a limited role for the United States in foreign affairs.

Coolie labour

A term used to describe South and East Asian immigrants to the Caribbean in the years after slavery ended. Their numbers were considerable: nearly 250,000 went to British Guyana, almost 150,000 to Trinidad and over 36,000 to **Jamaica**. Coolies came to the Caribbean as indentured labourers; in general, they agreed to a five-year indenture. During that time, they could not leave their employer or refuse to do the work that had been assigned. After their five-year indenture ended, these labourers could choose other employers but they were not entitled to free passage back to **India** until after they had worked for ten years in the colony. Though the nature of the indenture was harsh and the punishments severe, the overwhelming majority of coolies remained in the Caribbean. Asian migrants of this type formed the basis of a free peasantry that helped to diversify the region's economy by producing rice and other food crops.

Co-operative movement

An organization that exists for commercial or charitable purposes, in which those who work are also owners, retailers or consumers of their product. Such organizations are often associated with mutualism, and have appeared since the Industrial Revolution in most sectors of the economy with varying degrees of success (although co-operatives per se have existed for much longer). The modern movement has been traced to east Scotland in the 1760s, though the consensus acknowledges the network of weavers and consumers who pooled resources and obtained products they could not otherwise have afforded in Rochdale in 1844 as the model of modern co-operatives in the United Kingdom. Elsewhere, the Mondragon corporation in Spain, which is a confederation of highly successful worker-owned businesses, embodies distributist Catholic principles, and credit unions have appeared worldwide, especially in poor areas, as mutual societies which operate on depositor-owner lines. Though not requiring members to espouse political outlooks, co-operatives have been associated with social justice and socialist movements, and in some countries they sponsor political parties. In **Britain**, the Co-operative Party has existed since 1917, and is in a permanent alliance with the Labour Party, with its own separate organization and annual conference.

corn

The archaic English word *corn* referred to any small grain, typically wheat, rye or barley; this meaning continued to see wide use in Europe through the nineteenth century. On the east coast of North America in the early seventeenth century, English colonists applied the word to the Amerindian staple, maize, and absorbed it into their diets. It shifted its meaning accordingly in subsequent centuries, and now, in English, it applies exclusively to maize. Maize was one of the main crops to be transmitted through the **Columbian Exchange** from the Americas to Europe.

Corn Laws

– *see* **laissez-faire**.

Cornwallis, Charles (1738–1805)

An aristocrat with impeccable social connections, Charles Cornwallis was educated at Eton and Cambridge. He served as junior officer during the **Seven Years War**. During the **American Revolution** he rose to command British forces in the South. He achieved successes over the rebels at the battles of Camden and Guilford Court House before capitulating to a combined Franco-American force at **Yorktown** in October 1781, which effectively ended the American War of Independence. He later served with distinction in India and Ireland.

corporate state

The term *corporatism* is derived from the Latin word for the body and saw the state as an organism like the human body in which each part had an allotted function and was under the leadership of the head. Parallels were drawn with the traditional family in which husband and wife had different roles and in which there was an accepted generational and functional hierarchy. It was as bad for the state to harbour elements unwilling to play their allotted role as it was for the body to harbour malignant organisms. Corporatism attracted many who sought a sense of belonging, of continuity and tradition in the insecure European world bequeathed by **World War I**. It strongly influenced, but was not identical to, **fascism** and reached its philosophical peak with the papal encyclical, *Quadragesimo Anno*, of 1931. Corporate states, of which **Italy** and **Austria** were amongst the first, were characterized by hierarchical and syndicalist patterns of organization in all spheres.

Cortázar, Julio (1914–1984)

Acclaimed Argentine writer and key participant of the 'boom' in Latin American literature after **World War II**, Cortázar is best known for short stories and innovative novels. Opposed to Perónism, Cortázar moved permanently to France in 1951 where he worked as a translator for the **United Nations** and produced some of his finest works. His writing became more politicized during the **Cold War**, when he supported various revolutionary movements in **Latin America**.

Cossacks

A group of people of ultimately nomadic origin who functioned from the seventeenth century as a Ukrainian border population of soldiers and settlers. Following hostilities between Poles and Cossacks, the Cossacks elected a ruler, the Hetman, effectively a ruler in his own right until the office was suppressed in 1722. Memories of independence led to their support for the Pugachov rising against **Catherine the Great**, but its suppression led to them reverting to their former role as an important military force, employed in wars against the Ottoman Turks and against **Napoleon** when they formed a feared light cavalry force, scouting, foraging and harassing alongside regular forces. During the nineteenth century the Cossack territories remained administratively separate under the Russian Ministry of War, with the Don Army territory being by far the most important. In return for economic privileges, the Cossacks were pledged to military service and acted as an internal security force, helping to suppress the Russian Revolution of 1905. Although there was growing support for greater compensation for their services and recognition of their claims to autonomy, 300,000 Cossacks out of a population of 4 million served in the Russian armies by 1917. Short-lived Cossack republics emerged during the turmoil which followed the Russian Revolution, and many chose to fight with the **White Russian** forces during the ensuing civil war, or go into exile after their defeat. Although some had cooperated with the Bolsheviks in return for promises of autonomy, the Cossack areas were incorporated into the **Soviet Union** by 1920. Cossack traditions survived under the Soviet regime, though they were devastated by Ukrainian famines, **collectivization** and purges of the interwar years. Cossack regiments of cavalry were still employed by the Soviet Army during **World War II**, but Cossack populations now largely inhabit the **Ukraine** and other independent states that emerged following the break-up of the Soviet Union in 1991.

Costa Rica

Once largely isolated from the forces that shaped the rest of Latin America, Costa Rica, in **Central America**, attained complete independence by 1838 and quickly became an early centre of coffee cultivation. Heightened national pride accompanied this economic boom after the decisive 1856 defeat of filibuster William Walker in neighbouring **Nicaragua**. The banana trade then encouraged Caribbean economic development. The country's liberal elite, unlike their neighbours, demonstrated by 1900 their commitment to democratic principles such as civilian rule, institutional transfer of power and public education. Although divisive civil war in 1948 threatened this progressive tradition, the subsequent rise of **José Figueres** and the National Liberation Party (PLN) ensured that Costa Rica would remain a model of institutional stability and social development in Latin America despite the ideological divisions and economic unrest that marked the Cold War and its aftermath.

Côte d'Ivoire

– *see* **Ivory Coast**.

cotton

An agricultural commodity best grown in subtropical climates, cotton is the basis of many finished goods, most notably textiles. Though cultivated since ancient times, technological innovation in the late eighteenth century – namely the 1793 'cotton gin' (which separated the seed from the fibre) and the industrialization of textile manufacturing (especially in **Great Britain**) – led to a boom in production of the commodity, which was soon referred to as 'white gold'. Cotton production in the early and mid nineteenth century fuelled the expansion of slavery in the southern **United**

States. Disruptions in American production during the civil war years led to an increase elsewhere, especially **Egypt** and **India**. Overproduction in the late nineteenth and early twentieth centuries depressed prices and trapped impoverished small farmers in 'sharecropping' arrangements. In recent years subsidies to cotton farmers in the United States have led to trade conflict with African and South American producers, and stimulated global campaigns for 'fair trade'.

counter-culture

A widespread movement that emerged to counter the political establishment and dominant cultural norms of the **Cold War** era. Initially characterized by sexual liberation, psychedelic drug use, communitarian experiments and Timothy Leary's exhortation to 'tune in, turn on, and drop out', counter-culture's exponents became increasingly politicized. In the **United States**, that revolved around opposition to the **Vietnam War** and continued racial segregation, while in the **United Kingdom** and elsewhere in **Europe** demonstrations against nuclear weapons and opposition to the Vietnam War broadened out into wider opposition to the political establishment in 1968.

counter-revolution

– *see* **revolution**.

Crazy Horse (*c*. 1840–1877)

Iconic **Native American** warrior. He won his spurs during the Oglala Lakota's mid-1860s war against white incursions into Wyoming and Montana. Unlike other tribal leaders, he rejected the Fort Laramie Treaty (1868) and allied with the northern Cheyenne when the **United States** ordered outstanding Lakota to reservations in 1875. Hunted over a harsh winter after his victory over Custer at **Little Bighorn**, he surrendered in 1877 but was fatally bayoneted in a mishandled attempt to imprison him.

Creole

The word *creole* or *criollo*, of uncertain origin, has had many meanings, but essentially applies to a person or thing reared in the New World. Thus people might have distinguished between African(-born) and creole slaves during the eighteenth century, or even between European and creole vegetation. In the course of the resistance movements in Spanish America during the nineteenth century, the opposing parties were often known as *criollos* and *peninsulares*, the former finding that the latter,

from Spain, often seemed to enjoy undue privilege and power.

Creolization

Cultural creolization is a very important and increasingly significant factor in twenty-first-century cultural globalization. Originally conceived by the anthropologist Ulf Hannerz, the idea of cultural creolization has its roots in Creole languages and cultures that evolved in the slavery-based economies and social structures of the Caribbean and **Latin America**. Like Creole languages, Creole cultures are intrinstically of mixed origins, however this mixing involves much more than a simple relationship between a dominant cultural 'centre' and a submissive colonized 'periphery'. The process of cultural creolization instead involves a highly creative, and typically subtly subversive, cultural interplay in the creation of radically original cultural forms. The process of cultural creolization has much in common with the concept of the 'Black Atlantic', a term coined by the cultural studies scholar Paul Gilroy to describe the process of identity formation of peoples of African descent on both sides of the Atlantic as a being one of constant subversive exchange which transcends 'both the structures of the nation state and the constraints of ethnicity and national particularity'.

The origins and development of New Orleans jazz provides an excellent example of the processes of cultural creolization. Described by the Austrian cultural historian Reinholt Wagnleitner as 'the classical music of globalization', the creolized roots of jazz facilitated its evolution, adoption and adaptation by a multitude of global practitioners. These processes of global cultural creolization and the dynamics of the 'Black Atlantic' are also evident in musical genres such as Cuban son, Brazilian samba, Trinidadian calypso and, more recently, in the case of hip hop. The product of a creolized fusion of Jamaican, African American, Puerto Rican and West German musical influences, hip hop was a creative response to the poverty, deprivation and violence of the poorer boroughs of New York City during the mid 1970s. By the early twenty-first century hip hop has exponents in virtually every nation on the planet and has also helped revolutionize the aesthetics and production techniques of global popular music – processes facilitated by the hybridized, subversive creole aesthetic which lies at the heart of the genre.

Another way in which local cultures creatively adapt and adopt global cultural flows without succumbing to McDonaldized cultural homogenization is via the process of cultural indigenization.

This occurs when local and national cultures capture global influences and in the process change them into cultural forms compatible with local and national traditions. A prime example of this can be seen in 'Bollywood', the Hindi-language film industry based in Mumbai, one of the largest film industries in the world. A large number of Bollywood films indigenize Hollywood genres, particularly musicals, fusing them with traditional cultural forms such as ancient Indian epics and Sanskrit dramas. Exemplifying the cultural impact of the contemporary 'ethnoscapes' to which Appadurai refers, the global film industry in the early twenty-first century has seen the global success of several Bollywood-style films aimed at a global market.

Musical genres such as jazz, reggae and hip hop, products of the creolized cultures of the Caribbean, have themselves become indigenized into a wide range of local and national cultures. This process of musical indigenization often involves the subtle incorporation of political messages – as witnessed, for example, by the very important role played by jazz and rock music in the cultural resistance to authoritarian communist regimes in eastern and central Europe during the final decades of the twentieth century or by the role played by local rap music as 'under the radar' communication in the **Arab Spring** of 2011. The Japanese concept of *Nihonjinron* also involves the domestication of global cultural flows in its re-emphasis of the uniqueness and distinctiveness of Japanese culture.

Although it is typical of newly independent ex-colonies, the cultural strategy of reinvention and rediscovery has been widely practised as a form of resistance to the forces of cultural homogenization. The desire to reinvent and rediscover national cultural identities was a widespread feature of post-colonial societies, and was a process often implemented by law and official government policies. An archetypal example of cultural reinvention and rediscovery was the policy of *authenticité* which became the official ideology of the **Mobutu** regime in Zaire (now the **Democratic Republic of Congo**) during the 1960s and 1970s. Inspired by **Mao Zedong**'s Cultural Revolution in **China**, *authenticité* was an attempt to reinvent and rediscover the rich cultural heritage of this vast central African nation while avoiding the pitfalls of tribalism and regionalism. The policy was clearly manifested in many aspects of Zairian culture including language (where colonial French gave way to local Lingala) and in music where the genre known as *soukous* reinvented, rediscovered and

re-Africanized the sounds of the 'Black Atlantic', in particular, the music of Afro-Cuba. Partly due to the increasing economic importance of the tourist industry, the strategy of reinvention and rediscovery has now entered the cultural mainstream of virtually every relatively affluent nation on the planet in numerous manifestations, including the revival of interest in local music, dance, art, craft and of organic, regional 'slow' food and drink. This revival of interest in cultural localism highlights a crucial dichotomy between 'locals' and 'cosmopolitans'. Since the Enlightenment left-liberal intellectuals have sought to move beyond what Marx and Engels referred to as 'the idiocy of rural life' and towards a cosmopolitan culture. Although the desire to move beyond the confines of local, regional and national identities and towards an acceptance of a multifaceted cultural outlook continues to be thoroughly despised by nationalists, fascists and fundamentalists, the widespread embrace of global cultural cosmopolitanism seems our best bet of avoiding a constant repetition of the genocidal horrors of the last two hundred years of world history.

crime

– *see also* **criminal justice**.

Crime is an activity of which the state disapproves on behalf of society and against which it provides a sanction, usually involving the deprivation of life or liberty. This distinguishes an offence from a civil wrong, which is usually a matter for the individuals or groups involved to resolve, possibly through a financial process centred on civil courts. In the West, Roman and Germanic societies typically focused on civil wrongs done to the head of a family, which the families involved could resolve through money reparations as well as equivalent sanctions. Emperors and later Christians, on the other hand, preferred that a version of Justice corresponding to that of an impartial secular power invade this largely private sphere, the better to secure order and allegiance in complex societies. This transition was never quite completed in the Islamic world, which inherited the idea that families could and should interpret justice, although this was mediated through the revelation of that religion that justice was based on the will of the Deity. Common law systems were very much influenced by Christianity to the point that they broke a crime into two essential elements, the guilty act and the more serious 'guilty intention', and developed graduated punishments accordingly. At the same time, 'minor' offences of unsanctioned conduct or trivial crimes that were essentially regulatory emerged, leading to the distinction in the English-speaking world between serious 'felonies' and trivial 'misdemeanours'.

By contrast with common law systems, the European continent was much more influenced by Roman traditions. This led to a greater influence for the opinions of a judge on the process of trial, and to a tendency to relate law not to cases but to the application of legal codes. At the same time, continental systems tended to view canon law and state law as contiguous parts of the same system, and the development of criminal concepts was much more associated with the growth and jurisprudence of the Church than in the British Isles. In central and eastern Europe, the enlightened despots saw the development of clear legal codes as a way of strengthening and legitimizing their power, and many, such as the Russian Empress **Catherine the Great** cultivated reputations as law givers in whom the justice of God abided, whilst at the same time appealing to those further west who believed in rational order rather than freedom as the central aim of a civilized society.

From the seventeenth century onwards the emergence of more complex urban societies, the decline of feudalism in western Europe and **Japan**, and the development of scientific and secular concepts of society led to the expansion of criminal law into the protection of property. In England, this process led after 1688 to the massive expansion of execution and transportation for property crimes. Across Europe, public executions to demonstrate the power of the state over the individual grew coterminously with the emergence of the trial and secular legal professions. This gave rise to the formalized study of law, and almost immediately to the ongoing search for law reform. Around the Atlantic, states sought to establish commissions to clarify law, develop codes and generally eliminate anomalies. At the same time, the emergence of sociology sought justifications for criminal law. These ranged from arguments based on the nature of the state and the need for command, through the idea that deviation from social norms should be identified and punished by judges interpreting precedent, to Marxist analyses of crime as those things which threatened the prevailing socio-economic regime. In the twentieth century complex behavioural and relativistic sociological interpretations of crime meshed with a `new social history' of deviance.

The issue of penal reform and capital punishment is closely connected with that of crime.

The **Enlightenment**, with its emphasis on individual rights and the intrinsic worth of human beings, encouraged the link. For instance, Cesare Beccaria (1738–94) suggested in his 1762 work, *Crime and Punishment*, that police forces and prisons were much preferable to sporadic and savage demonstrations of dominance and punishment, or to overly punitive sanctions. This suggestion was taken up by the enlightened despots, and penal reformers such as John Howard and Elizabeth Fry. Others reformers, such **Jeremy Bentham**, emphasized prison design, the use of silent systems and solitary confinement to 'reset' prisoners away from bad influences, and the utility of forced labour. This trend continued into the twentieth century with the experiments in youth rehabilitation such as 'borstals', and in the evolution of prison design to mesh humane treatment with the reduction of rioting and despair.

The development of policing also led to the elevation of forensic science and detective skills in the public and police mind. This was in part because the solution of crimes moved from 'thief taking' to the accumulation of evidence for a separate trial procedure, which again was separated from sentencing by the separation of police, juries and judges. At some point in the nineteenth century or early twentieth, it thus became common to refer to individual crimes as 'cases', implying use of taxonomic or therapeutic language on the part of the police. By the late twentieth century and early twenty-first, the development of global societies and complicated urban problems saw the invasion of more and more aspects of life by the state in the name of public safety. Thus, laws against **drugs**, which had their roots in late nineteenth-century moral reform, reached an apogee; the state sought to regulate sexuality, the family, clothing and religion in the name of security; and terrorism, immigration and the environment, as well as the needs of the authorities to maintain the tax base, saw crime, policing and punishment expand dramatically. The boundaries between civil and criminal matters began to merge under the technology of surveillance, the challenge of radical **Islam** and the example of public and individual control by newly rich non-democratic regimes. This process, which crystallized during the post-2001 'war on terror', is ongoing. It was at one point thought that western modes of criminal trial would, through international institutions and the structures left behind by decolonization, displace autochthonous ones and thence achieve universality. This was a particular hope of post-colonial rulers in Africa. There is some evidence of this process, but in the twenty-first century it would be more justified to characterize it as in large part an aspiration rather than a reality.

Crimean War

Often called the first modern war, this conflict pitted Russian forces against the Ottoman, British and French imperial armies. While battles ranged from modern-day **Romania** to the **Caucasus** during 1853–6, the most significant action took place on the Crimean peninsula. Thus, the conflict became known as the Crimean War in English. After a protracted siege, allied forces conquered Sevastopol, Crimea's main port, forcing a Russian surrender. In the lead up to war, **Russia** had sought increased influence in the **Ottoman Empire** and in particular over its Greek Orthodox populations. Russia retaliated against Sultan **Abdülmecid**'s refusal of Tsar Nicholas' demands in that regard by capturing the Ottoman Empire's Danubian provinces Moldovia and Wallachia (contemporary Romania) in July 1853. In October of that year the Ottoman Empire declared war and counterattacked in the **Balkans** and the Caucasus. Many diplomats in **France**, **Britain** and **Austria** hoped for a diplomatic resolution. However, the Ottoman government sought to draw France and Britain into the armed conflict and left a portion of their fleet vulnerable to Russian attack. Exploding shells, used for the first time in history, rained down on Ottoman ships docked at Sinope, only a hundred miles from the base of the Russian Black Sea fleet docked at the Crimean port of Sevastapol. In response, British and French forces mobilized to confront Russia.

Even before British and French forces could fully engage with the Russians, the Ottoman Army had routed the Russian forces, expelling them from the Danubian provinces. Meanwhile, France and Britain had mobilized almost 100,000 troops and transported them to the war theatre. Their governments were loath to bring them back without engaging their Russian adversary. Allied powers chose Sevastopol as their target in the hope of destroying Russian naval power in the Black Sea and thereby eliminating the Russian naval threat to the Ottoman Empire. In September 1854 Anglo-French and Ottoman forces scored a significant victory over the Russians at Alma. Had they pressed their gains, Sevastopol might have fallen and the British could have returned home without having missed the winter uniforms they had not brought, planning for a quick victory. Instead, disorganization led to them digging in for prolonged trench

warfare. For the first time in history, war correspondents transmitted the appalling human cost to readers at home. Ultimately, the allies' recourse to industrial production to provision their forces extended beyond Russia's ability to sustain their war effort. Sevastopol fell a year after Alma, on 13 September 1855. A peace agreement was signed in Paris the following March.

Even if the Ottoman Empire saw the Russian threat in the Black Sea diminish, having relied on Britain and France to defeat Russia left them more beholden to those powers. Subsequently, British pressure helped advance destabilizing reforms. In Russia, too, the war's legacy was increased momentum for reform: the institution of serfdom often appeared as the explanation for Russia's failure to match the economic and military might of France and Britain. Defeat engendered a mistrust of the European powers and consequent intensification of the pan-Slavic movements. Russia rectified their losses during the **Russo-Ottoman War** (1877–8).

criminal justice

Time has dramatically changed the body of law that defines criminal offences, regulates apprehension, charging and the trial of suspects, and fixes the penalties for and modes of treatment of convicted offenders. It is widely accepted that in ancient civilizations the most common approach in criminal law was to conceive of crime as an act which was morally wrong and the chief purpose of any criminal sanction was retributive; that is, to make the offender give retribution for the harm done and to expiate his or her moral guilt. Retributive justice revolved around the principle of proportionate punishment; matching the infliction of pain and loss caused by the offender. Expressions such as 'eye for eye, tooth for a tooth' and 'let the punishment fit the crime' first materialized in ancient Mesopotamia, and in *circa* 1760 BC, the Hammurabi Code enumerated the various crimes and respective punishments and settlements they entailed. The ruling principle, the *Lex Talionis* (Law of Retaliation), displayed plenty of symbolism. For theft, punishment could mean cutting off a hand; perjury, the amputation of a tongue; and loss of ears for slaves denying their masters. The death penalty was freely awarded for illegal trading, false claims on property, incest, burglary, seduction of a daughter-in-law, rape and manslaughter. The code did not provide opportunity for justification and granted out punishment to an offender's family, especially his sons. Modern conceptions of the due process of law were clearly alien to retributive criminal justice.

A key feature of ancient criminal justice present in Judaism and Christianity was the pervasiveness of religion in nearly all aspects of the criminal process. A worldview that placed man in relationship to God, and in which God was the only legitimate source of justice, established the foundations for legal action. Thus, not only was divine law eternal, just and immutable; it was coupled with a troublesome condition that rendered justice susceptible to grave abuse when the role of the judiciary was exercised by the clergy. Classical Roman law exhibited stark contrasts to those legal traditions. First, God had no say in legal matters; laws were made by humans and could be no higher than man himself; that is, laws were relative, and hence flexible. Second, a professional and distinct class of jurists played by the rules of well-drafted legal statutes. Third, Roman law was more practical and efficient, since it basically looked for a *mala prohibitia*, the technical violation of law, so easing prosecution.

Modern criminal justice borrows heavily from the Romans, but was also influenced by the **Enlightenment**. Beccaria, **Voltaire**, **Montesquieu** and Feuerbach advanced a rationalistic and pragmatic approach to criminal justice seeking the prevention of crime, the reform of the offender and the public scrutiny of the process. They also emphasized the certainty of the punishment rather than its severity. **Rousseau** and others brought forward the sacrosanct status of basic and inalienable rights to all humans, which led the way to the contemporary due process of law.

Cripps Mission

In March 1942, under US pressure and as the Japanese advanced close to **India**'s borders, **Winston Churchill** sent Stafford Cripps, a Labour member of his cabinet, to broker nationalist support for **Britain**'s war effort. However, Churchill intended the mission to fail. Though offering dominion status, not only did it disregard Indian demands for an immediate handover of key central ministries such as defence; its provision allowing provinces to opt out of the Indian union was rejected by the **Indian National Congress**. By August 1942 suspicion of British insincerity fuelled the **Quit India movement**.

Croatia

A Hungarian territory of the **Austro-Hungarian Empire** until 1918 when incorporated in the Triunine Kingdom of the Serbs, Croats and Slovenes, later **Yugoslavia**. Unsuccessfully sought autonomy in the new kingdom, but declared independent by the Germans, 1941, with boundaries drawn to include Bosnia. Its fascist puppet government was infamous for its viciousness. A constituent republic of federal Yugoslavia, 1945–91, it was independent again in 1991, and in 1995 it expelled some 300,000 Serbs from Krajina and Slavonia with tacit American assistance. Croatia joined the **European Union** in 2013.

Crockett, Davy (1786–1836)

This ill-educated Tennessee frontiersman served in Congress in 1827–31 and 1833–5, splitting with President Jackson over land policy and Indian removal. Already the subject of exaggerated newspaper articles, he wrote an autobiography in 1834 that manipulated his reputation as an honest country boy. When his presidential hopes collapsed in 1835, he migrated to rebellious **Texas**. Joining the defence of the Alamo mission against the invading Mexicans, he was captured and executed, though myth portrayed this folk hero as cut down while still fighting with an empty rifle.

Cromer, 1st Earl of (1841–1917)

British imperial administrator. Born Evelyn Baring, he was commissioned into the Royal Artillery in 1858. He acted as private secretary to his cousin, Lord Northbrook, Viceroy of India, 1872–6, before his appointment as English Commissioner on the Egyptian Debt in 1877. Two years later he became British Controller General in **Egypt**, supervising the country's confused finances. He gained supreme power in 1883 with his selection as British agent and consul general (as well as minister plenipotentiary), effectively ruler of Egypt under a 'Veiled Protectorate', holding the post until his retirement in 1907. During his period in office, Cromer's military reforms secured the reconquest of the **Sudan** in 1896–9, while his administrative, financial and agricultural restructuring consolidated the prosperity of the local elites. Cromer advocated closer relations with **France** and pressed for creation of the 1904 **Entente Cordiale**. He presided over the Dardanelles Commission in 1916–17.

Crowther, Samuel Ajayi (*c.* 1806–1891)

Born in the Yoruba region of today's Nigeria, he was captured by Muslims during the Oyo Civil War and sold as a slave. Redeemed in Sierra Leone, he became a member of the Anglican Church in 1825 and subsequently a missionary to Abeokuta in his home region in 1843. He produced a number of

Yoruba religious texts and eventually rose to be a bishop in the Anglican Church.

Cuba, Republic of

Granted ostensible independence from **Spain** in 1902, Cuba experienced repeated US intervention, political instability and military dictatorship. On 1 January 1959 the 26th of July movement (M-26-7) led by **Fidel Castro** overthrew dictator **Fulgencio Batista** in a revolution from which thousands of prosperous Cubans fled. The Communist Party of Cuba quickly gained a central role in government. Soon excoriated by the **United States**, the new Cuba increased literacy, improved medical care and the status of women, and sought to become a leader among developing countries. A US-imposed embargo in 1960 drove Cuba to accept economic support from the **Soviet Union** until its collapse. As sugar harvests failed and prices dropped, Cuba successfully developed international tourism for foreign exchange. In 2008 Fidel Castro turned over power to his brother Raúl, but Cuba's conflictive relationship with the United States remained until an easing of diplomatic relations by President **Obama** in 2015. However, this policy was reversed by President Trump in 2017.

Cuban Missile Crisis

The Cuban Missile crisis began 15 October 1962 when an American U2 spyplane revealed that the **Soviet Union** was placing nuclear weapons in Cuba. The Soviet Union and Cuba had different reasons for this risky deployment. Cuban President **Fidel Castro** was pleased to host the missiles as a deterrent to a possible American invasion (the **United States** had directed the **Bay of Pigs** invasion of April 1961). For Soviet Premier **Nikita Khrushchev**, deploying nuclear weapons to Cuba, just 145 kilometres from Florida, meant doubling his nation's strategic arsenal and countering the US deployment of fifteen Jupiter Intermediate Range Ballistic Missiles to **Turkey** in 1961.

President **John F. Kennedy** convened the Executive Committee of the National Security Council (Excomm) on 16 October to explore the US response. The ensuing discussion identified three potential options: air strikes to destroy the missiles already in place; invasion of Cuba; and a naval blockade of Cuba to prevent Soviet ships holding nuclear cargo from entering port. The Joint Chiefs of Staff advised immediate air strikes and a full-scale invasion. Kennedy's secretary of defense, **Robert S. McNamara**, believed that a blockade, or quarantine, was the option best suited to compelling Soviet withdrawal

without precipitating war. After presiding over wide-ranging discussions, Kennedy concluded that quarantine was the option least likely to provoke nuclear hostilities. On 22 October he delivered a televised address announcing the discovery of the Soviet missiles and outlining the American response.

In addition to the public diplomacy, an important secret channel was opened between Attorney General **Robert F. Kennedy** and Soviet Ambassador to the US, Anatoly Dobrynin. Through this, Kennedy gave private assurances that if the Soviet Union desisted from its attempt to establish a nuclear bridgehead in the western hemisphere, the United States would agree to respect Cuba's sovereignty and 'voluntarily' withdraw its ageing Jupiter missiles from Turkey. This offer was communicated to Khrushchev, who responded positively in a personal letter of 26 October, indicating interest in a quid pro quo deal on the lines suggested.

A more belligerent message from Khrushchev, denouncing America's aggressive tactics, arrived the next day. Faced with mixed signals, Kennedy arrived at a disarmingly simple solution: he responded positively to the more constructive letter and ignored the other. The crisis was resolved on 28 October, when Khrushchev made a public announcement on Moscow radio declaring that the missiles would be returned to the Soviet Union. In return, Kennedy made a public pledge to respect Cuba's independence, renounced the use of warfare as a means to oust Castro, and secretly arranged for the removal of the American missiles from Turkey.

The Cuban Missile Crisis was the closest the two superpowers came to a nuclear exchange during the **Cold War**. While the climb-down was publicly humiliating for Khrushchev – his apparent acquiescence to US pressure led to his eventual removal – his actions effectively safeguarded Cuba's independence and led to a major US concession on the Jupiter missiles. Most historians accord John F. Kennedy significant plaudits for his deft management of the crisis, focusing particularly on his wide range of consultation and his facing down of more reckless voices.

Cuban Revolution

After Cuban dictator **Fulgencio Batista** succeeded with his second coup, a revolutionary circle formed in Havana. On 26 July 1953, Fidel Castro led 119 revolutionary rebels in a failed attack on the strategically important Moncada army barracks in Santiago de Cuba. The army caught fifty-five men, who were tortured and executed. Castro managed to escape to the nearby mountains, but was later captured and sentenced to fifteen years of imprisonment While in jail he wrote his political manifesto, *History Will Absolve Me*, defending his part in the assault. In 1955 Batista became president through fraudulent elections. He freed all political prisoners, including Castro, who then went to **Mexico** in order to prepare another revolutionary attack. Meanwhile, the teacher Frank País secretly organized the resistance of the 26th of July movement (M-26–7) in Havana. José Antonio Echevarría became the leader of the Directorio Revolutionario (DR), which was established by students of the University of Havana. In December 1956 Castro and eighty-one rebels landed with the small yacht *Granma* at Playa Las Coloradas, where Batista's army almost captured them. But Fidel and eleven other survivors, including his brother Raúl, the Argentine doctor Ernesto Che Guevara and others were able to escape into the Sierra Maestra mountains. The M-26–7 leader Cecilia Sánchez helped them by sending supplies for their guerrilla fight. They quickly gained support both in Cuba and abroad. On 13 March 1957 a group of university students tried to assassinate Batista and attacked the Presidential Palace in Havana, but most were killed in the attempt. In retaliation, Batista executed everyone potentially connected to the attack. The following year the **United States** imposed an arms embargo on Cuba. Many military commanders joined the revolutionary movement. Fulgencio Batista left the country on 1 January 1959, taking 40 million US dollars in government funds with him. A day later, Castro entered Santiago de Cuba, while Guevara, Cienfuegos and 800 of their followers arrived in Havana.

The M-26–7 had no previous experience in government, but it was able to gain the support of many peasants, workers and students. The Communist Party of Cuba, established in 1925, took over, making Cuba the first socialist state in the Americas. Manuel Urrutia, a former judge who defended the M-26–7 prisoners, became the first president, while Castro was named prime minister. The new regime reduced living costs, tried to abolish racial discrimination, achieved better health care and education, collectivized farmland and established a planned economy similar to eastern European socialist states. The First Agrarian Reform nationalized large private property and businesses, many of them owned by US companies. This led to drastic measures by the US government, such as a trade embargo and the support of the

unsuccessful invasion by Cuban exiles at the **Bay of Pigs** in April 1961. Meanwhile, Castro maintained a close economic relationship with the **Soviet Union**, as US opponents regularly did during the **Cold War**. Expropriation drove many middle- and upper-class Cubans into exile, mainly to nearby Florida. Decreasing productivity was counterbalanced by generous Soviet subsidies. Many Latin American intellectuals regarded the Cuban Revolution as a role model, as it represented a successful nationalist movement in the face of Cold War politics.

cultural diffusion

Cultural diffusion refers to how cultural items, such as ideas, religious practices and languages, spread from one culture to another. While the process has occurred since ancient times, the intensity of cultural diffusion increased after the **Columbian Exchange** initiated in 1492. European encounters with the Americas led to increased interaction between **Europe**, **Asia**, **Africa** and the Americas. By the late nineteenth century the world was largely integrated into a global system, allowing cultural diffusion to be more regular, even expected. Cultural diffusion often involved another process: syncretic adaptation. The latter term suggests, for New World cultures, how cultures changed through processes of interaction. In some cases, extensive syncretism, in which many cultural forms coexisted, led to the original cultural forms being largely supplanted by new cultural tendencies, which were a mixture of several different cultures without one culture being predominant. An example of this is the indigenous American adaptation of Catholicism in Latin America. While this religion in Latin America is no less Roman Catholic than western European Catholicism, Latin American Catholicism is distinctive in its emphasis on characteristics of the faith that reminded Native American adherents of the religious practices that they had held before they converted to Christianity.

Cultural diffusion is not always voluntary or positive. It can occur when one dominant political culture forces its cultural norms on cultures that it deemed politically inferior. **Alcohol** use in New World societies is but one example of cultural diffusion. Rum was used by European traders in North America, and in Polynesia, as a means of increasing trade. The result of using alcohol as a trade good in societies without experience in alcohol consumption was to disrupt customary social and cultural patterns in highly negative ways. Nor is cultural diffusion always complete. Few dominant cultures effectively stopped less strong cultures from distorting cultural forms to suit their own practices, even when such adaptations were strongly discountenanced. European clothing, for example, was adopted around the world in the nineteenth and twentieth centuries as the appropriate form of dress. Nevertheless, how clothing was adopted did not always meet the standards of decorum and presentation that Europeans expected.

Cultural diffusion is also associated with the notion of cultural hearths. These hearths were places where particular cultural forms were first formulated and perfected. The success of cultural forms in cultural hearths led other places to adopt and often adapt these cultural practices in ways that reflected on the power of cultural hearths to influence other places. **Barbados** could be considered one such cultural hearth. Its development in the mid seventeenth century of a highly successful type of commoditized slavery was copied by plantation societies throughout plantation America and the West Indies. In this way, a plantation culture rooted in slavery diffused across the Americas, yet the original form as it was practised in Barbados remained distinct from each of the places to which it spread.

Cultural Revolution (China)

The Cultural Revolution was begun by **Mao Zedong**'s wife, Jiang Qing, with the support of Mao in 1966, and lasted for ten years. It began with a purge on moderate party members during which the radicals Jiang Qing, Zhang Chunqiao, Yao Wenyuan and Wang Hongwen, who were known as the **Gang of Four**, gained ascendency. In August an estimated 11 million students attended eight large political demonstrations of **Red Guards** in Tiananmen Square in Beijing. Following this, Red Guards throughout the country vandalized schools, temples and old historical sites and beat people they accused of being bourgeois and anti-revolutionary. By 1968, factionalism in the Red Guards threatened China's stability, and they were disbanded by Mao. After this, the Cultural Revolution was institutionalized, with people made to study political thought in factory work units and communes in the countryside. It ended with Mao's death, in 1976, and the arrest of the Gang of Four.

culture

Since the late 1960s theories of culture and the practice of cultural analysis have assumed an increasingly prominent role in history and the social sciences. This academic development, sometimes referred to as 'the cultural turn', has paralleled the increasing importance of cultural issues in the political sphere. During the same period in the political life of many nations issues of cultural identity and debates about the pros and cons of cultural assimilation, cultural pluralism or multiculturalism have taken centre stage. As Raymond Williams pointed out in *Keywords* (1976), 'culture is one of the two or three most complicated words in the English language' – partly because of its 'intricate development in several European languages' but mainly because it has come to be used for important concepts 'in several distinct intellectual disciplines and in several distinct and incompatible systems of thought'. Although the earliest uses of the word *culture* referred to the tending of crops and animals (as is continued in the noun *agriculture*), its uses were gradually extended by analogy and metaphor to other, more abstract realms of human endeavour and experience. Beginning in the early eighteenth century, culture began to be used, particularly in **France** during the **Enlightenment**, as a term to denote a general process of intellectual, spiritual and aesthetic development and refinement.

The meaning of the term *culture* or *cultures* as shared and negotiated systems of meaning that people learn and put into practice in specific social contexts can be traced back to the work of Johann Gottfried von Herder in the 1770s. An ardent nationalist and patriot, Herder objected to the idea of universal cultural values and focused instead upon the ways in which language and what we now refer to as 'cultural traditions' such as folk music, dance, cuisine, art and craft help determine and bind together 'national cultures'. Herder's conception of a culture therefore refers to a particular 'way of life' – whether of a people, a period or a group – and can be regarded a precursor to the anthropological understanding of the term.

This value-neutral conception contrasts sharply with the modern European idea of culture that took shape from the mid nineteenth century onwards. Referring specifically to intellectual endeavour – particularly to artistic activity in the fields of painting, sculpture, literature, theatre, music and architecture – this conception of culture was self-consciously elitist in its advocacy of the ideal of individual human refinement and its distinction between what Matthew Arnold referred to as 'Culture' and its antithesis, 'Anarchy'. Championed by mid-twentieth century critics such as the Cambridge academic F. R. Leavis and contributors to his influential journal *Scrutiny*, it was this definition of culture as 'the best that has been thought and said in the world' that became the dominant trope for the study of English literature. From the late 1950s onwards the academic hegemony of this stance was challenged from a variety of positions. In France, the work of the **Annales** school led by **Fernand Braudel** and Emmanuel Le Roy Ladurie championed the study of history from the point of view of *mentalités* – an attempt to understand the feelings of common people. In Italy, the work of Carlo Ginsberg emphasized micro-history and the analysis of clues and common myths. This shift of interest to 'history from below' built the foundations of the discipline that became known as cultural studies. Employing a combination of sociological and anthropological methodologies and Marxist, semiotic and feminist theoretical approaches, cultural studies scholars turned their attention away from 'high culture' and towards working-class cultures and subcultures and to forms of contemporary popular culture such as film, television and pop music, which were either ignored or despised by existing studies. The idea that culture is socially constructed and is an arena of competing and conflicting forces resulting from structural power relations in society is a fundamental assumption of cultural studies – as is the idea that oppressed and marginalized social groups employ cultural strategies as forms of resistance to what the Marxist philosopher Antonio Gramsci termed the cultural hegemony of the dominant class.

Through the influence of key twentieth-century theorists such as Gramsci and Michel Foucault the discipline of cultural history has often shared a similar perspective to cultural studies. Although the relationship between the two disciplines is complex, both cultural historians and cultural studies scholars typically employ anthropological definitions of culture in their analyses of the cultural aspects of historical experience, and share the idea that the culture of a group or a class is its particular and distinctive 'way of life'. Also, as in the case of contemporary cultural studies, the focus of much current research in cultural history has been modified and influenced by the concept of an emerging cosmopolitan global culture and by the processes of cultural globalization.

Global culture can be understood as being distinct from national cultures. As Stuart Hall has pointed out, global culture has no equivalent to the shared memories of 'ethnic cores' (national myths, legends, customs, heroes, events) providing identities for nations and their peoples. Although 'global events' such as the 9/11 attacks on the **United States** may mark the beginning of a new idea of global culture in the twenty-first century, there are currently few global stories and memories which can compete with the emotional ability that national cultures possess to create a sense of shared meaning and solidarity. Global culture is therefore primarily media-driven. It is relatively free of strong connections with time and place and is essentially 'deterritoralized'. Anthropologist Ulf Hannerz emphasizes that the global culture that emerged in the late twentieth century is different to other cultures that previously moved around the world because it is synonymous with and dependent upon technology (satellite television or the Internet). The virtual omnipresence of media-generated global culture in the twenty-first century has resulted in a situation in which increasing interconnectivity between local and national cultures has led to the creation of cultures 'without anchorage in any one territory' and to increasing numbers of global 'cosmopolitans' with cultural allegiances to several territories.

Globalization is one of the most frequently used terms in twenty-first century academic discourse. Definitions of the term abound, but all share certain key components, particularly references to what can be described as 'complex connectivity' and 'time/space compression' – the rapidly accelerating and ever more complex networks of interconnections and interdependences that characterize modern life. The emphases of scholarly work on globalization is usually determined by whether or not the author's focus is political, economic or cultural, but the idea that globalization is defined by worldwide 'networks', 'flows' and 'interconnections' of capital, goods, people, knowledge, images, sounds and so on, is what unifies definitions of globalization – whether they are written by scholars of cultural history, cultural studies, anthropology, sociology, international relations or business and management studies. As John Tomlinson points out in *Globalization and Culture* (1999), 'Globalization lies at the heart of modern culture; cultural practices lie at the heart of globalization.' This is an important claim as it maintains that globalization cannot be properly understood unless its processes are grasped through the conceptual framework of culture. Similarly, it is implied that the cultural 'deterritorialization' or 'disembedding' central to the globalization process is changing the fabric of everyday cultural experience all over the world.

Cultural globalization is not new, of course. Closely aligned to colonialism and **imperialism**, it has involved the diffusion of ideas and other symbolic products across the globe since the sixteenth century. The majority of global cultural flows during the early stages of globalization tended to originate from dominant colonial powers – the global dissemination of Catholicism, or of the Portuguese, Spanish, English and French languages are examples. The attraction of Europeans to the delights of tobacco, cocoa, coffee, tea (and to stronger, more sinister stimulants such as hashish, opium and cocaine) paralleled their growing enthusiasms from the mid eighteenth century onwards for Chinese textiles and porcelain, Indian spices, African garden plants and the tattoos of sailors who had ventured to the 'South Seas'. European diets were changed fundamentally by the introduction of formerly unknown staples such as sugar, potatoes, tomatoes and peppers, and by luxury foods such as chocolate. At the same time, cultures of resistance, such as the Andalucian *gitano* culture of *flamenco* dance and music, developed from hybridized fusions of the cultural traditions of those oppressed by religious and nationalistic monoculturalism.

During the eighteenth and nineteenth centuries, as colonialism matured into its imperial phase, Romantic poets such as Byron and Coleridge were inspired by the cultures of what was loosely referred to as the 'Orient'. The cultures of the colonized (or, probably more accurately, what the artists in the colonizing countries imagined these cultures to be) began to influence the art and design practices that defined the refined taste of the bourgeois elite – as evidenced, for example, in Britain from the early to the late nineteenth century by John Nash's Indian-inspired Royal Pavilion in Brighton, by the Arab fantasies of the Victorian artist Lord Leighton or by the Chinese- and Japanese-influenced Liberty prints on sale in London from the mid 1870s. The *japonisme* that was so fashionable in Europe during the 1880s and 1890s was particularly influential on the development of Art Nouveau, while development of the Cubist avant-garde – as evidenced in Picasso's seminal *Demoiselles d'Avignon* (1907) – was heavily influenced by the African art on display in contemporary Parisian museums.

Despite Nazi and Stalinist attempts to crush it in the 1930s and 1940s, the trend towards global cultural hybridization continued throughout the twentieth century and became a definitive characteristic of anti-establishment counter-culture from the late 1950s onwards. For those western European, Australasian and North American beatniks and hippies who gathered in Istanbul in the mid 1960s to begin their 'magic bus' journey to

Nepal, an interest in Zen Buddhism, haiku poems, Aztec myth, Hindu mandalas and the Maharishi Mahesh Yogi provided an obligatory accompaniment to the *raga*-influenced sounds of The Beatles' *Revolver* LP.

It is obvious that cultural globalization is not new, but twenty-first-century cultural globalization can be distinguished from earlier forms by its sheer speed, ever more complex connectivity and the rapid change in cultural relationships between what was once the colonial/imperial global 'centre' and the formerly colonized 'periphery'. Indeed, just as economic and political globalization are bringing the future of the traditional nation state into question, so the rapidity of contemporary cultural globalization is having a major impact upon the meaning and viability of distinctive national or local cultures. Particularly since the mid 1960s, national and local cultures have been determined by 'reverse cultural flows' from the former global 'periphery' to the ex-colonial 'centre'.

During the latter half of the twentieth century debates about cultural globalization tended to be dominated by advocates of the cultural imperialism thesis. Indeed, it could be argued that the theory of cultural imperialism was the earliest theory of cultural globalization – casting the process as a key aspect of western imperialism involving the increasing hegemony of dominant cultures – particularly after 1945 by the mass media's diffusion of the values, consumption patterns and lifestyles of the United States of America and its allies. The central propositions of the cultural imperialism thesis – that certain dominant cultures threaten to eliminate those which are more vulnerable – is straightforward. However, as John Tomlinson has pointed out, the cultural imperialism thesis actually involves a number of fairly discrete discourses of domination including the domination of the United States over Europe, 'the West over the rest of the world', of the imperial 'core' over the formerly colonized 'periphery', of the modern world over fast-disappearing traditional societies, and of capitalism over more or less everything else.

production and consumption

For the sake of clarity it is useful to differentiate between debates that concentrate on the cultural effects of the production of the 'cultural industries' and those debates focusing on aspects of cultural consumption and the growth of global consumerism. Indeed, a major weakness of the cultural imperialism thesis, and one of the main reasons why the thesis is less popular today than it was during the latter decades of the twentieth century, is that its advocates tend to assume that the global spread of the cultural products of multinational corporations and the acceleration of global consumerism and consumer lifestyles will inevitably result in a global capitalist monoculture dominated by the United States. Such Cocacolaization theories often ignore the complex and unpredictable character of cultural appropriation and tend to infer that the worldwide presence of standardized cultural goods necessarily results in standardized cultural and ideological effects.

Contemporary analyses of cultural globalization that focus on cultural consumerism tend towards a general optimism or pessimism. Pessimistic accounts are typically strongly influenced by the classical sociological theories of **Karl Marx** and Max Weber in their view of individuals being shaped by socio-economic forces beyond their control. For example, during the 1940s Frankfurt school sociologists Adorno and Horkheimer built upon Marx's idea of commodity fetishism to argue that the mid-twentieth-century Fordist system of mass production obliged businesses to fuel consumers' desire for new goods via strategies of planned obsolescence. The modern global advertising industry plays a key role in promoting the relentless fetishization of the commodities ever-increasing numbers of global consumers are persuaded to buy as capitalism (to quote Marx and Engels in *Communist Manifesto* (1848)) 'batters down all Chinese walls'. In order to appeal to a mass global market, the meanings employed in consumer culture need to be direct and simple, a process that erodes distinctions both between national and local cultures and between 'high' and 'low' culture in western societies. According to this school of thought, the end result of this process is the creation of an anodyne, stupefying global capitalist monoculture that threatens to extinguish the rich cultural ecology of the planet.

A more recent, and even more pessimistic, view of the relationship between cultural globalization and consumerism can be seen in the work of the French cultural theorist Jean Baudrillard, who argues that the 'use value' of global consumer brands has been largely supplanted by their fetishistic 'sign value' through which ever-growing numbers of global consumers balefully attempt to create spiritual meanings and cultural identities. Baudrillard's bleak vision is of a universal global capitalist monoculture in which genuine cultural distinctiveness and identity is replaced everywhere by the fake 'simulacra' of

shopping malls, theme parks, reality TV shows, computer games and tabloid celebrities. For Baudrillard, the future of global culture can be experienced today in simulated environments such as Disney World, Las Vegas resort hotels or the Happy Valley-style theme parks springing up throughout modern China.

Similarly bleak are those perspectives of cultural globalization based upon Max Weber's dystopian sociological theories of rationalization and bureaucratization. Arguing that the principles of the fast-food restaurant are coming to dominate ever-increasing sectors of American society as well as the rest of the world, George Ritzer's McDonaldization theory emphasizes that the four key ingredients underpinning the global success of the fast-food chain (and numerous other global businesses that follow the same formula) are efficiency, calculability, predictability and control. Although McDonalds adapts a little to national cultures in its attempt to appeal to local consumers, the ultimate effect of the McDonaldization process is the creation of a global monoculture in which, to use Ritzer's terminology, diverse and rich local, regional and national cultures that were once based on 'something' are being displaced by a bland, shallow Americanized capitalist global 'nothing'. An ever more sophisticated McDonaldized system now promises global consumers a combination of 'fun-filled' entertainment and self-fulfilment while, in reality, the genuine and traditional sources of human happiness – strong family ties, stable and cohesive communities and secure and fulfilling employment – become increasingly difficult to maintain and protect.

In contrast to these bleakly pessimistic views of global culture and cultural dissemination, perspectives of global culture and cultural consumption influenced by anthropological thought tend to be more nuanced and optimistic. Pierre Bourdieu, for example, emphasizes the dynamic role of individual 'agency' in the creation of cultural meaning. Bourdieu's concept of *habitus* – the cultural strategies and consumption patterns employed by various social subgroups in order to create a sense of autonomous cultural space – can be usefully applied to a broader understanding of patterns of global culture in which an emphasis upon the creative interpretation of global cultural flows by local actors is a key component. This focus upon the dynamic cultural interaction between the local and the global – a process Roland Robertson has termed *glocalization* – contrasts sharply with an orthodox sociological focus upon 'macro' socio-economic forces and the homogenizing cultural tendencies of global capitalism.

The fact that cultural globalization is an extremely complex, multidimensional process is brilliantly conceptualized by the anthropologist Arjun Appadurai. Appadurai invites us to think of the world in terms of a map or a landscape of competing and contrasting 'scapes' – or flows of people, technology, money, images and ideas. He points out that these 'ethnoscapes', 'finanscapes', 'technoscapes', 'mediascapes' and 'ideoscapes' – which move at different speeds but also strongly influence one another – create a turbulent, chaotic sea of global cultural influences and flows which is very different from any conception of global cultural homogenization. This conception of global culture as being essentially 'rhizomic', and determined by multidirectional, unpredictable flows of influence has largely replaced the older 'centre and periphery' or 'hub and spokes' conception characteristic of the cultural imperialism thesis. The more optimistic contemporary conceptions of cultural globalization tend therefore to focus upon the different ways in which local cultures respond creatively to global cultural flows.

Curaçao

A small, semi-arid island located off **Venezuela**'s northern coast that was discovered by the Spanish explorer Alonso de Ojeda in 1499. Spanish labour demands soon destroyed its only resource, the indigenous Arawak population, and the nominal colony languished until the Dutch West India Company conquered the island in 1634, and made it a strategic component of the growing Dutch empire in the Caribbean. For two centuries Curaçao flourished as the centre of the Dutch slave trade, but its economic value withered with the rise of the Abolitionist movement in the nineteenth century. Currently an autonomous territory of the Netherlands, Curaçao, with its capital Willemstad, was from 1954 to 2010 the administrative centre of the Netherlands Antilles, the now dissolved, self-governing confederation of the Dutch Windward and Leeward Islands. With a population of around 150,000 of mostly mixed African ancestry, it survives largely on profits from tourism and petroleum refining.

Curie, Marie Sklodowska (1867–1934)

The first great woman scientist, born in Warsaw in then Russian **Poland**. She married Pierre Curie, with whom she discovered radium and shared the Nobel Prize in physics in 1903. Awarded the Nobel Prize in chemistry, 1911, she was appointed to the International Commission on Intellectual Co-operation by the Council of the League of Nations. She died as a result of earlier exposure to radioactivity in her research. Her daughter, Irène Joliot-Curie, also shared a Nobel Prize with her husband: that for chemistry, in 1935.

Curzon, George Nathaniel (1859–1925)

Viceroy of India, 1899–1905; British Foreign Secretary, 1919–24. Curzon was one of the imperialist triad, along with Cromer in Egypt and Milner in South Africa. For Curzon, India's larger formal and informal empire was crucial to the survival of the British Empire. He saw himself as the supreme authority in India, an equal to the head of the India Office, and to the British prime minister, thus earning himself enemies. His partition of Bengal (1905–11) launched the **Swadeshi** and Boycott movement: **Aurobindo Ghose** demanded complete independence for India. Curzon resigned and returned to the political wilderness until his appointment as the Conservative government's foreign secretary, though he played an important role in the War Cabinet (1916–19). He hoped for the premiership but died a disappointed man. His viceregal tenure saw the zenith of British imperialism and witnessed the birth of a more aggressive nationalism in India.

Custer, General George (1839–1876)

United States cavalry officer famous for an eponymous 'last stand'. A mixture of staff duty, unexpectedly impressive combat performance and flamboyant self-promotion during the **American Civil War** saw Custer a general by the age of 23. Transferred to the northern plains following postwar anti-Cheyenne operations around Kansas, his Seventh Cavalry led an expedition that discovered gold in the Black Hills in 1874. The ensuing gold rush provoked a **Native American** war in which Custer's recklessness caught up with him at **Little Bighorn**.

Cyprus 'Emergency'

– *see* **Cyprus**.

Cyprus

Cyprus was conquered by the **Ottoman Empire** in 1570. During the Ottoman period it became more ethnically and religiously diverse, and by 1874 the island had a population of 44,000 mostly Turkish-speaking Muslims and 100,000 mostly Greek-speaking Orthodox Christians. In 1870 the Ottomans turned over administration of the island to the British as the price of British support at the San Stefano conference. **Turkey** relinquished claims to the island at the Lausanne conference (1923) and **Britain** declared the island a crown colony in 1925. However, unrest against colonial rule erupted after **World War II** and Cyprus won independence in 1960. Intercommunal violence between Greek and Turkish Cypriots increased after independence and the **United Nations** sent peacekeepers to the island in 1964. In 1974 a *coup d'état* against the government of Archbishop **Makarios**, supported by the Greek government, seemed likely to result in a union between Cyprus and **Greece**. Instead, Turkey invaded the island, occupying the north and unilaterally declaring a Turkish Republic of Northern Cyprus in 1983. Despite lack of international recognition and repeated efforts by the UN and other bodies to broker a peace deal, attempts at reunifying the island have so far been unsuccessful.

Czechoslovakia

Recognized by the Treaty of Saint-Germain, 1919, which brought together for the first time the closely related Czechs, Slovaks and Ruthenes. The Czech territories had been the medieval kingdom of **Bohemia**, under Habsburg rule, 1526–1918; **Slovakia** and Ruthenia had been Hungarian territories within the Habsburg **Austro-Hungarian Empire**. A formal democracy in the interwar years, but torn by tensions between its constituent peoples including the Sudeten Germans. It ceded the **Sudetenland** under the Munich Agreement, September 1938. Slovakia remained independent with German support but Ruthenia was occupied by **Hungary**, and the Czech provinces of Bohemia and Moravia absorbed into the Greater German Reich, March 1939. Reconstituted, 1945, bar Ruthenia, which was absorbed into the Soviet Ukraine. A People's Republic, 1948–68, Czechoslovakia became a federal socialist republic in 1969–89. A member of **Comecon**, 1949–90, and of **Warsaw Pact**, 1955–91. In 1968 it was invaded by Warsaw Pact forces who wished to suppress the **Prague Spring**. Czechoslovakia was voluntarily dissolved into the Czech Republic and Slovakia from 1 January 1993, a separation which became known as the Velvet Divorce.

D

Daesh
– see **ISIS**.

Dahomey
– see **Benin**.
An important pre-colonial kingdom in modern-day **Benin**. The kingdom was probably founded in the late seventeenth century as a break-away interior province of the earlier coastal kingdom of **Allada**. King Agaja (1708–32) greatly expanded the kingdom, taking over parts of the coast (Allada and Whydah), but Dahomean kings never won complete control of it and were forced to pay tribute to the inland kingdom of Oyo in 1747 following a series of military campaigns. Dahomey's wars on the coast and with Mahi in the interior supplied thousands of slaves to European buyers. In the nineteenth century, as the slave trade waned, Dahomey turned to producing palm oil on royal plantations. In the later nineteenth century European powers, especially **France**, began to encroach on Dahomey's interests and to protect its enemies. Wars between France and Dahomey in 1890 and 1894 resulted in the annexation of the kingdom to the French colony of Dahomey.

Daimio
A feudal lord in the Japanese warrior class who owned a land territory (domain) with governing authority. Their origin is in the tenth century, but it was in the Tokugawa period that daimios, whose domains occupied three quarters of **Japan**, were used for a centralized system of indirect control. Whilst daimios retained their administrative structures and managed fiscal systems and armies, they were required to pay homage to the shogun in alternate years and leave a family member as a hostage in Edo.

Dalai Lama
Regarded as the spiritual head of Tibetan Buddhism. The first was the founder of a monastery in **Tibet** and his successors were regarded as his reincarnations, who like himself were manifestations of the bodhisattva *Avalokitesvara*. When a Dalai Lama dies his soul is believed to pass into the body of an infant, born forty-nine days later. The present Dalai Lama temporarily fled to India in 1959 after a failed revolt against the Chinese government. He has been in exile ever since.

Dalhousie, 1st Marquess of, James Andrew Broun-Ramsay (1812–1860)
The governor general of **India** and governor of **Bengal**, 1848–54. He was a controversial figure and an aggressive annexationist whose Doctrine of Lapse de-recognized adoption by Indian rulers in the absence of legitimate male heirs, thereby extending British rule to several parts of India. Dalhousie's second Anglo-Sikh War resulted in the fall of the Sikh kingdom (1849), the second Anglo-Burmese War, again on a minor pretext, annexed southern **Burma** to British India (1853), the charge of 'misgovernance' attached **Awadh** (1856), and began an engagement with tribes on the north-western frontier. He also introduced railway and telegraphs, and by 1856 Peshawar was linked to **Calcutta** and 4,500 miles of telegraph existed. But this reflected his vision of India as *tabula rasa* by following extremely linear routes. After his departure, the **Indian Mutiny** broke out, and history holds his policies at least partly responsible.

Dalits
– see **caste**.

Damascus
Damascus (Arabic: Dimashq) is the capital city of the modern state of **Syria**. It is widely considered to be the city with the longest continuous habitation in the world. Fourth-century tablets mention it by name and prehistoric evidence has been found which points to even longer habitation of the area. Damascus sits at the foot of the Anti-Lebanon Mountains in an oasis in the Syrian Desert. The River Barada runs through it. It boasts a large population, estimated at about 2 million, and is also the communication, administrative and financial centre of the nation. The genesis of

Damascus as the Syrian capital dates back to 1941, and again after the Syrian government became independent from the **United Arab Republic** in 1961. It was the scene of bitter fighting in the **Syrian Civil War**.

dams

Dams have been used from the earliest times to control floods and provide irrigation. They were also essential in providing the `head' of water required to power water wheels for a variety of processes such as flour milling and ore crushing, and for driving early water-driven industrial machinery. Dam building on a large scale was triggered by the Industrial Revolution, with the need to provide large urban populations with a water supply, leading to the creation of large reservoirs in upland areas in which substantial dams were used to create often extensive man-made lakes. By the late nineteenth century they were also being used to generate hydro-electric power, especially in countries such as Norway, where hydro-electric power now supplies almost 100 per cent of the energy requirement. Large dams came to play a significant part in **economic development**. The Tennessee Valley Authority in the **United States**, established in 1933, controlled the Tennessee and Cumberland Rivers with a series of dams which also provided hydro-electric power as a means of regenerating a poor region. The project, like the Hoover Dam in Arizona, which developed a large area of the semi-arid south-west, was characteristic of the US **New Deal** era. In the Soviet Union, **Stalin** inaugurated several major schemes including the Dnieper River dam as symbols of socialist planning. After **World War II**, dams came to play a significant role in third world development, notable examples being the **Aswan Dam** (1971) on the Nile in Egypt, the Kariba Dam (1959) on the Zambesi, and the giant Chinese Three Gorges project (1994–2011), which aimed to provide two-fifths of China's electricity needs. In recent years these large projects have drawn increasing criticism on environmental grounds and for forcing some countries down a path of expensive large-scale projects inappropriate for their economies.

Danish West Indies

The islands of St Thomas, St John and St Croix represent the former Danish West Indies. The colonial capitals included Charlotte Amalie in St Thomas and Christiansted in St Croix. In the 1670s the Danish West India and Guinea Company as well as Danish colonists settled on St Thomas. In the 1700s the company and the Danes expanded their colonial efforts to St John and St Croix. The three islands attracted European nationals from Scandinavia, **Britain**, **France** and elsewhere. Inhabitants focused their efforts on producing sugar, but also carried on a smuggling trade with neighbouring Caribbean colonies and the thirteen North American colonies. The production of sugar led to an increase of enslaved peoples arriving on the island from West Africa to work on plantations. Slavery was abolished in 1848. In 1917 the Danish archipelago was sold to the **United States** (US) and became known as the US Virgin Islands.

Danton, Georges Jacques (1759–1794)

French revolutionary. A lawyer, Danton became a leading orator and founder of the Cordeliers (the Society of the Friends of the Rights of Man and of the Citizen). Elected justice minister, he organized the overthrow of **Louis XVI** in 1792. From April to July 1793 Danton presided over the ruling Committee of Public Safety. Attempting subsequently to act as a moderating influence, he was accused of conspiring against the government and executed.

Danubian Principalities

The principalities of Moldavia and Wallachia emerged in the thirteenth century and came under **Ottoman Empire** suzerainty from the fifteenth century. Russian occupation in 1829–34 weakened **Turkey**'s hold. **Russia** reoccupied the principalities in 1853 during tension that led to the **Crimean War** the following year. Occupied by **Austria** with the agreement of Russia and Turkey in 1854–7, Moldavia and Wallachia united in 1859 to establish **Romania**, the independence of which was recognized in 1878.

Danzig (also Gdansk)

A port city at the mouth of the Vistula, Polish until Prussian annexation in 1793. Inhabited largely by Germans, Danzig was placed under **League of Nations** administration by the 1919 **Versailles Treaty** to allow **Poland** access to the Baltic, a cause for German (and particularly Nazi) agitation. Restored to Poland in 1945, Danzig was the scene of anti-Communist riots in 1970 and the birthplace of the **Solidarity** trade union federation in 1980.

Daoism

Daoism is a collective term that refers to a variety of indigenous Chinese religious practices dating from China's earliest history. While the term's meaning has changed greatly over the centuries, many associate it with ideas in the Chinese classic *Daodejing* (*The Classic of the Way*) such as harmony with nature and inaction. Daoism is not a formal religious affiliation, and therefore its number of adherents is hard to categorize. It also existed in conjunction with Buddhist religious practice and Confucian ethical norms for much of Chinese history, although the **Qing dynasty** (1644–1911) was suspicious of Daoism. However, most Chinese would have come into contact with Daoist folk religion over the centuries, and attempts by secular Nationalist and Communist governments to eliminate it in the twentieth century attest to its continuing power. Daoism is now an officially approved religion in **China**, but the authorities keep a careful watch on any attempt by Daoist practitioners to subvert state doctrines.

D'Arcy Concession (1901)

– see also **Anglo-Iranian Oil Company**.

The concession for oil exploration and exploitation in **Iran** granted by **Muzaffar od-Din Shah Qajar**, 1901, which led to the discovery of oil, 1908, and the formation of the Anglo-Persian, later **Anglo-Iranian Oil Company** (APOC, AIOC), 51 per cent of whose shares were owned by the British government. Subject to lengthy but fruitless attempts by Iran to renegotiate in the late 1920s and early 1930s until the company's announcement that its payment to Iran in 1932 would be one quarter of that in 1931 led Reza Shah to cancel the concession. Britain responded by referring the dispute to the **League of Nations**, and following further negotiations a new agreement was concluded in 1933. Although its terms were more favourable to Iran than previously, it extended the concession period by a further thirty years. The extension was highly unpopular and, although Reza Shah had tried to resist it, it was widely believed in Iran that he had been a willing party to a conspiracy.

Dardanelles

– see also **Straits Question**.

The Dardanelles are the narrowest and most easily defensible position controlling access from the Mediterranean to the Sea of Marmara, and the **Bosphorus** and Black Sea beyond. Russian policy in the nineteenth and early twentieth centuries aimed to seize control of the waterway in order to gain unfettered Mediterranean access to its Black Sea fleet. During **World War I**, **France** and **Britain** launched their ill-fated **Gallipoli campaign** (1915–16) to seize control of the straits.

Dardanelles campaign

– see **Gallipoli campaign**.

Darfur

A predominantly semi-arid region in western **Sudan**, an independent and powerful sultanate from the seventeenth century until internal conflicts opened the way for Anglo-Egyptian dominance in 1875. In 1916, concerned that Darfur might fall under Ottoman influence (or that the French might move into the area from the west), Britain incorporated it into the Sudan, where it suffered economic neglect, a process continuing after the Sudan became independent in 1956. Comprising a mixed though mainly Muslim population, black African accusations that the central government was discriminating in favour of the Arab population mounted, particularly in the wake of famine in the 1980s. Non-Arab groups launched an uprising in 2003 which the government countered with an Arab militia, the Janjaweed, leading to charges of genocide as the humanitarian crisis intensified. In 2006 the Darfur Peace Agreement was concluded, but the conflict still simmers. In 2009 the International Criminal Court issued a warrant against President Bashir of Sudan for alleged war crimes.

Darío, Rubén (1867–1916)

A Nicaraguan-born writer and diplomat, Darío revolutionized Spanish-language poetry in the late nineteenth century by breaking with classical forms and fostering the literary movement known as *modernismo* (Modernism). He achieved influence as a journalist and speaker and was instrumental in promoting a strong sense of Latin-American identity and pride in Hispanic culture in the face of growing US influence in **Central America** and the Caribbean Basin following the 1898 **Spanish–American War**.

Darwin, Charles (1809–1882)

– see also **Darwinism**.

British scientist popularly associated with the theory of Evolution, towards which he made a vital originating contribution. Darwin studied at Edinburgh and Cambridge before embarking on a five-year voyage of exploration on board HMS *Beagle* in 1831. His observations of finches on the Galapagos Islands during this voyage, and the inferences he drew from collated fossils and other observations, led him to a theory of natural selection in 1838, two years after his return to England. This theory held that random mutations of living things would, from time to time, prove useful in particular environments and convey an advantage over non-mutants expressed in terms of propagation and population growth in the future. A combination of fear, other work and due scientific process kept Darwin from propounding this theory in full until he did so in collaboration with Alfred Russell Wallace in 1858. Fear arose from the controversy and intellectual consequences of the application of the theory to humans, whom Darwin intuitively understood were a species of mutated ape, at a time of intense Christian religiosity. He published widely on plant and animal diversification, evolution and sexual selection, and died an agnostic. His name was subsequently attached to ideas of guided or progressive evolution, eugenics and competition which had little or nothing to do with his original insights.

Darwinism

Darwinism is a term that originally referred only to the ideas of Charles Darwin concerning evolution and natural selection, but now refers to evolution more broadly, or other ideas not directly associated with the work of Darwin. The term is generally applied by creationists as a pejorative for 'evolutionary biology' contrasted with its use by evolutionary scientists simply to refer to Darwin's work. Darwinism may also refer to a specific strand within evolutionary biology dealing with the mechanism of natural selection as opposed to evolutionary processes that were unknown in Darwin's day, such as genetic drift and gene flow. Darwin was born on 12 February 1809 into a moderately wealthy family in Shrewsbury, England. His father, Robert, had the largest medical practice outside London at the time and his mother, Susannah Wedgwood, was from a family of wealthy pottery manufacturers. After quitting medical studies in Edinburgh, Charles Darwin moved to Cambridge University to study theology. It was there that he became acquainted with the scientific ideas of the geologist Adam Sedgwick and the naturalist John Henslow. Apparently, influenced by Sedgwick and Henslow, Darwin rejected the concept of biological evolution at first, in spite of the fact that he had been exposed to the ideas of Lamarck about evolution while he was a student in Edinburgh. Soon after graduation in Theology in 1831, John Henslow secured Darwin a berth on a British Navy mapping expedition that was going around the world on what would ultimately become a five-year long voyage. They sailed two days after Christmas in 1831 aboard the survey ship HMS *Beagle* with Darwin acting as an unpaid naturalist and gentleman companion for the aristocratic captain, Robert Fitzroy.

His intellectual preparation along with research during the voyage were critical in leading Darwin to accept evolution. But especially important to the development of his ideas was the five-week visit to the Galapagos Islands in the eastern Pacific Ocean, where he began to understand evolution, and which became the basis for his famous book, *On the Origin of Species by Means of Natural Selection, or the Preservation of Favoured Races in the Struggle for Life* (*The Origin of Species*), published 24 November 1859. Darwin's underlying idea of natural selection stated that in a world of stable populations where each individual must struggle to survive, those with the 'best' characteristics would be more likely to survive, and would pass on desirable characteristics to their offspring. These advantageous characteristics, in turn, would be inherited by following generations, and become increasingly dominant among populations. The theory and the convincing evidence that evolution occurs were very threatening to many Christians insofar as they believed that people were created by God in His image. For them, the idea that there could have been anatomically different prehistoric humans was inconceivable. Moreover, present-day Creationists believe that the biblical account in Genesis accurately describes the origins of the world and humanity, explicitly rejecting Darwin's theory.

Das, Chitta Ranjan (1870–1925)

An important Indian nationalist leader from **Bengal**, Das was a barrister at the Calcutta High Court who was successful in civil and political cases and who identified with the Extremist faction. He emerged in 1919 as the leader of the Bengal Provincial Congress and was a key figure nationally. He opposed, then supported **Gandhi**'s Non-Cooperation movement and when it was called off in 1922, Das, along with **Motilal Nehru**, organized the Swarajya Party to stand for election under the 1919 reforms and oppose the British Raj from within the legislative councils.

Daud, Muhammad (1909–1978)

Prime minister of **Afghanistan**, 1953–63; president of Afghanistan, 1973–8. Born and educated in Kabul and in **France**, he began his career in the early 1930s as a general and provincial governor. After appointments to various ministerial posts, Daud became prime minister. His government aggressively challenged **Pakistan** over the right of self-determination for Pashtuns. Daud's advocacy on behalf of 'Pashtunistan' drew the **United States** into a mediating role. Border closures forced Kabul to expand commercial ties with the **USSR**, with which Daud had close military contacts. He launched a five-year plan for economic development in 1956 and pushed for the unveiling of elite women in 1959. In 1973 he led Soviet-trained officers and leftist allies in a coup against his cousin Muhammad Zahir Shah and declared a republic. His programme of authoritarian modernization ended in April 1978 when forces led by the Marxist People's Democratic Party of Afghanistan seized power, murdering Daud and his family.

Davis, Jefferson (1808–1889)

First and only president of the **Confederate States of America**, 1861–5. Raised in Mississippi, Davis interrupted his congressional career (**Democratic Party**, House, 1845–6; Senate, 1847–51 and 1857–61) with service in the **Mexican–American War**, an unsuccessful gubernatorial campaign against the **Compromise of 1850**, and as **Franklin Pierce**'s secretary of war. A slaveholder who aspired to a model plantation of benign paternalism, Davis thought **secession** impolitic during the crisis of 1860–1 but counted it among **states' rights**. The Confederate convention provisionally elected him president in February 1861, a position confirmed later that year. Plunged into fighting the **American Civil War**, Davis evinced traits of political vindictiveness, military micromanagement and underappreciation of the western theatre, and had little of his counterpart **Abraham Lincoln**'s popular touch. Yet harsh personal assessments risk reductionism and abuse of hindsight in attributing Southern defeat to an individual. An 1865–7 imprisonment did not produce the desired treason trial, and Davis later defended the Confederate cause in his memoirs instead.

Dawes Act (USA)

A misguided law that allotted reservation land to individual **Native Americans** (1887). Paternalistic reformers wanted to break tribal, nomadic society by replicating European-style farming; those Native Americans who accepted the offer also received **United States** citizenship. It only passed Congress once amended to allow the public sale of unclaimed stakes, and the resulting speculation had placed three-fifths of 1887 reservation land in white hands by 1934. The Dawes Act demoralized and swindled Native Americans, who did not adapt to such agriculture.

Dawes Plan (USA)

The Dawes Plan was a temporarily successful American programme to revive **Germany** after **World War I**. Following German refusal to pay **reparations** and the punitive French occupation of the Ruhr in 1923, Anglo-American financiers organized large American loans to Germany on condition France evacuated its troops. These loans stabilized the mark, revived the German economy, financed reparations and softened Franco-German relations. Tragically, the opportunity for long-term amelioration was undermined by the **Wall Street Crash** in 1929.

Dayan, Moshe (1915–1981)

Israeli military commander and politician. Born in Ottoman-ruled **Palestine**, Dayan was imprisoned by the British authorities for two years in 1939 for membership of the Jewish **Haganah** militia. On his release he fought for the Allies against the Vichy French in **Lebanon** and **Syria**. He rose to military prominence in the 1948 Arab–Israeli War, becoming military commander of Jerusalem, and from 1953–8 was chief of staff of the Israeli Defence Forces (IDF), commanding the Israeli Army in Sinai during the 1956 Suez War. Entering politics on his retirement from the IDF, Dayan served as Agriculture Minister in 1960–4 and was appointed Defence Minister shortly before the 1967 **Six Day War**, a position he continued to hold until after the 1973 **Yom Kippur War**. As foreign minister in the Likud government in 1977–9, he played a central part in formulating the **Camp David** Accords that secured peace with Egypt.

Dayanand Saraswati (1824–1883)

Dayanand Saraswati was born in Kathiawar, Gujarat, into a well-to-do Brahmin family. He established the Hindu reform organization **Arya Samaj** in 1875, the same year he authored *Satyartha Prakhash* (*The Light of Truth*) in which he considered the Vedas to be the only authentic source for all Hindu rituals and beliefs. Dayanand opposed existing Hindu practices such as idolatry, polytheism, child marriage, prohibitions against widow remarriage and foreign travel.

De Gaulle, Charles (1890–1970)

A soldier and statesman of **France** who rose to the rank of general via action in **World War I** and with a Polish division in the **Russian Civil War**. De Gaulle, an advocate of dynamic defensive strategies including tank warfare, served in the Battle of France with distinction before escaping to England in 1940 to lead the **Free French**. He was de facto prime minister of the French provisional government between 1944 and 1946, before retiring to his home in Colombey-les-deux-Églises. From there he was recalled in 1958 to lead the **Fourth Republic** in the Algerian Crisis. He founded the Fifth Republic in 1958 and became its first president. He was confirmed in that role by popular election in 1962, and held office until 1969. During that time he worked to conquer inflation, bring France and West Germany together, build up the European Economic Community as a customs union, and moved to exclude the British from EEC structures. He also negotiated the end of French rule in **Algeria**, created the Gaullist nationalist movement, and separated France from **NATO**. Surviving the disturbances of 1968, he resigned on losing a referendum on decentralization in 1969, and died after completing his memoirs.

De Valera, Eamon (1882–1975)

Mathematician, Irish revolutionary, prime minister and president of **Ireland**. The New York-born de Valera was raised in Ireland from the age of 2, and through the Irish language movement was inducted into the Irish Volunteers, and then the Irish Republican Brotherhood. He escaped a death sentence for his part in the 1916 Rising, was imprisoned, given amnesty and became a **Sinn Fein** Member of Parliament. He raised money in the **USA**, was reimprisoned, escaped and eventually became leader of an Irish cabinet which assembled in Dublin and declared him, after a time, head of state and president of the Republic. From this position, he moved **Michael Collins** to negotiate an agreement with **David Lloyd George**, which established the Irish Free State, then resigned and attacked the treaty. He was imprisoned by the Irish forces, was released, and rose again through Fianna Fáil to the Irish premiership. In 1937 he took advantage of the Abdication crisis to make Ireland a republic in all but name, becoming fully so in 1949. He kept Ireland neutral during **World War II**, turning down an offer to reintegrate Northern Ireland with the republic from **Winston Churchill**, and even sent condolences on **Hitler**'s death to the German embassy in 1945. He was Taoiseach again in 1951–4 and 1957–9, reinforcing the Catholic and agricultural nature of the state. In 1959 he became president of Ireland; he was re-elected in 1966 and retired in 1973. He was honoured by **Israel** and the United States as well as many Catholic and British luminaries across the world.

Decembrist Conspiracy

An unsuccessful attempt in December 1825 by liberal army officers in St Petersburg (the Northern Society) and members of the nobility in southern Russia (the Southern Society) to overthrow the newly installed Tsar **Nicholas I** and establish a constitutional monarchy that would modernize Russia, though the ultimate aims were confused. Five conspirators were executed and over a hundred exiled to Siberia. Confirmed in his absolutist beliefs, Nicholas established a secret police in 1826.

decolonization

Decolonization has been one of the major transforming forces of the past two and a half centuries, creating new nation states out of the colonial empires which were being formed from the early modern period. The **American Declaration of Independence** of 1776 marked one of the first and most major of the disruptions of the early colonial empires. Resulting from a developing crisis of British imperial authority with some of its north American colonies over taxation and colonial representation, the American colonists utilized ideas drawn from British constitutional struggles in the seventeenth century and the ideas of the **Enlightenment** to formulate a justification for revolt. Calling on the idea of `no taxation without representation', the American War of Independence also emphasized the `rights' of individuals and their justification as a `people' to govern themselves. This latter concept was given fresh emphasis with the **French Revolution** of 1789 with its call for subject `peoples' to rise against despotic rulers. These appeals to liberal nationalism had powerful long-term effects within **Europe** upon national groups who found themselves controlled by foreign powers, leading to `national' struggles by Poles, Italians, Finns, Irish and many others, which would often take decades to realize. They also affected European colonies across the Atlantic.

The first European colony to achieve independence after the **United States** was the former French colony of **Haiti** on the island of Hispaniola following a slave revolt and civil war led by **Toussaint L'Ouverture**. It achieved independence for the western half of the island of Hispaniola in 1804, though the eastern half, Santo Domingo, remained under intermittent control of Haiti, **France** and **Spain** for another half-century until it achieved independence as the **Dominican Republic** in 1865. **Napoleon**'s invasion of **Spain** and **Portugal** in 1808 provided the catalyst for their Central and

Latin American colonies to begin to free themselves. A Mexican war of independence began in 1810 which culminated in decisive Spanish defeat in 1821. The struggle for independence in Spanish Latin America was led from the north by the Venezuelan **Símon Bolívar** and from the south by the Argentine **José de San Martín**. As a result, following a series of armed conflicts, all the former Spanish colonies obtained independence by the mid 1820s. **Brazil**, a Portuguese colony, saw a less violent separation. The Portuguese Braganza dynasty had established itself in Brazil after Napoleon invaded the Iberian peninsula. When the Portuguese king returned to **Portugal** following the defeat of the French, his son Pedro remained in Brazil, becoming sovereign of an independent Brazil in 1822. Other European colonies were ceded as part of diplomatic and commercial negotiation. In the **Louisiana Purchase**, Napoleon sold to the United States in 1803 the extensive French colonial possessions between the Mississippi River and the Rocky Mountains for 15 million dollars. The former Spanish colonial territories of Florida were incorporated into the United States partly by annexation in 1812 and the rest by treaty in 1819, becoming the twenty-seventh state of the United States in 1845.

Although many former colonies had become independent by the first half of the nineteenth century, substantial colonial empires remained and were being added to throughout the century. **Great Britain** retained extensive colonial possessions in Canada, the **West Indies** and Australasia, and extended its imperial possessions in **Africa**. British control over the Indian subcontinent was extended and consolidated even as some of the 'white' possessions, notably **Canada** and **Australia**, were being offered a degree of self-government as a half-way house to virtual complete independence. The **French Empire** was extended into North Africa with the colonization of **Algeria**, **Morocco** and Saharan West Africa. Portugal and **Spain** still retained large parts of their former colonial territories, while the **Ottoman Empire** still embraced large areas of the **Middle East** and would do so until **World War I**. Also amongst the older empires, the Dutch controlled the East Indies, comprising modern **Indonesia**. The end of the nineteenth century witnessed further colonization as the **scramble for Africa** saw virtually the whole of the continent divided up between the older imperial powers and new entrants such as **Germany** and **Italy**, who sought to establish colonial empires as part of their Great Power status. Similarly, the United States and other powers completed the

colonization of Pacific islands such as **Hawaii**, annexed by the USA in 1898. The United States also annexed the **Philippines** following the **Spanish–American War** in 1898, though future independence was promised following a large-scale insurrection which cost almost 250,000 lives.

At the end of World War I the largest European empires, those of Britain and France, reached their greatest extent by taking over former German colonies and large parts of the Ottoman Empire as **mandates**. In 1926 there were eighty colonies and dependencies of the European states and the United States, comprising one-third of the population and land areas of the world. The seven west European countries – Britain, France, Spain, Holland, Portugal, **Belgium** and Italy – controlled colonies with populations of approximately 700 million people.

The renewed process of decolonization began when the British white colonies were given virtual self-government as dominions. In 1931 the Statute of Westminster established the basis of the **Commonwealth**, consisting of independent countries owing allegiance to the British Crown, with legislatures on an equal footing to Britain. Colonial rule in Africa and **Asia** was expected to continue, however. Colonial revolts in **Morocco**, **Libya**, **Syria** and elsewhere were suppressed, while aggressive powers such as Italy and **Japan** were actively engaged in enlarging their colonial possessions, seen in Italy's conquest of **Ethiopia** and the creation of an enlarged East African empire and Japan's conquest of **Manchuria**. But the interwar years also witnessed the rise of nationalist agitation in India led by **Mahatma Gandhi** and **Mohammed Jinnah** for complete independence from Britain.

With **World War II**, the pace of decolonization quickened. The overrunning of the European empires in the Far East by Japan and new strains placed upon imperial countries transformed the situation. Britain had accepted eventual self-government for India by the India Act of 1935, but World War II made it an imminent reality. Britain's post-war weakness could not sustain opposition to a growing tide of Indian and Pakistani nationalism which culminated in Indian independence on 15 August 1947. In the Far East, the Dutch attempted to retain hold of their colonies in the Dutch East Indies, but in December 1949 accepted their independence. France sought to maintain her colonies by policies of integration and assimilation. At the **Brazzaville conference** in 1944 they were offered incorporation into a French Union with representatives elected to the French

National Assembly. Taken up by some African states, the policy was overtaken by the communist insurrection in **Vietnam** which brought about the **Indo-China War** of 1946–54. After France's shattering defeat at **Dien Bien Phu** in 1954, the French presence in South East Asia was ended by the **Geneva Agreement**. Elsewhere, France, like Britain, vacated the Middle East. France left Syria and **Lebanon** by 1945, Britain left **Palestine** in 1947 and the Suez Canal in 1956. North Africa proved a more stubborn problem. Tunisian independence was granted in 1956, but the **Algerian War of Independence** proved a protracted nightmare for France and Algeria alike – it was not settled until 1962. Britain, too, fought campaigns to slow down the pace of decolonization. The **Mau Mau revolt** in Africa in 1952–60 cost 11,000 lives and the communist insurgency in Malaya was only officially defeated in 1960.

Meanwhile, a first wave of black African colonies obtained independence in the 1950s. The Gold Coast (**Ghana**) became independent in 1957, followed by **Nigeria** in 1960. When British Prime Minister Harold Macmillan gave his `Wind of Change' speech in **South Africa** in February 1960, he was speaking amidst the rapid dismantling of the European empires. More than fifteen states achieved independence from Britain and France in that one year alone. By the 1960s decolonization had become an avalanche. Belgium vacated the **Congo** in June 1960, plunging it into temporary chaos and requiring **United Nations** intervention. Of the largest European empires, only those of Portugal held out fighting protracted guerrilla wars in **Angola**, **Mozambique** and Guinea-Bissau until an army coup in Portugal in April 1974 ended Portuguese resistance to independence. The white Rhodesian government resisted black majority rule by declaring a white-rule **Unilateral Declaration of Independence** (UDI), but eventually was forced to a settlement in 1980 at Lancaster House, London, after a protracted guerrilla war.

The United States honoured its commitment to the **Philippines** in 1946 and granted it full independence. **Hawaii** was made the fiftieth state of the Union in 1950. The United States was influential in supporting colonial independence, having strongly supported national self-determination as early as 1919 at the peace conference following the Great War and reaffirming the principle in the **Atlantic Charter** of 1942, but during the **Cold War** found itself sometimes opposing communist-backed nationalist movements, as in Vietnam. Although never formally colonized, the **Chinese Revolution of 1949** sought to expel foreign

influence, notably Japanese annexation of Manchuria, foreign `concessions' in China, and reclaim **Hong Kong** from British control, achieved by agreement in 1997.

Several conflicts of decolonization remain unresolved, notably British possession of the Falkland Islands, which occasioned a war in 1982 with **Argentina**; and the issue of Palestinian nationhood and that of the state of **Israel**, which emerged from the wreckage of the former Ottoman Empire and the redrawing of boundaries in former colonial territories elsewhere in the Middle East. There are still a few relatively small territories under colonial rule, such as **French Guiana** and **Ceuta** (Spain).

The decolonizing process has attracted various interpretations. An initial tendency to focus on the nationalist movements and their leaders has given way to studies of the pressures on decision makers in the imperial countries. Economic and military weaknesses, the inability to sustain colonial rule in the face of opposition, and an ideological climate which was unsympathetic to imperialism have all been put forward. Attention has shifted towards **neocolonialism**, forms of economic control and dependency, such as debt relationships and aid, which have survived independence and even increased as new states sought to modernize.

An important effect of decolonization was its potential to upset domestic politics in the home countries. In fact, decolonization was often hastened to prevent burdens of colonial defence becoming insupportable. India and Suez were the most visible occasions when Britain was faced with the reality of its powerlessness to engage in colonial actions. For France, Dien Bien Phu and the Algerian War marked the end of colonial ambitions and caused great political turmoil. Portugal was brought to revolution in 1974 by the strain of continuing colonial wars. For former colonies, the legacy of colonialism remains complex, particularly for the multiplicity of states formed since 1945 whose borders, rationale and institutions are essentially artificial creations of the colonial era. While many have adjusted to this new reality as viable states, others remain in a state of post-colonial flux with borders and identities still being arbitrated by force, contingency and external pressures.

deforestation

The loss of forest cover as a result of logging, either to produce valuable timber, usually for export, or to clear land for agricultural use, or indeed both. Deforestation is environmentally significant because it leads to a reduction in biodiversity and reduces the natural 'carbon sink' of photosynthesis: the absorption of carbon dioxide (CO_2) and the emission of oxygen by growing vegetation. Deforestation thereby accelerates **climate change**, particularly as it is concentrated in the world's tropical regions where photosynthesis is at its most rapid. There is, however, reason to believe that forest cover has now started to increase in the more temperate continents of North America and particularly **Europe**, but also in **China**.

Deir Yassin Massacre

– see also **Arab–Israeli Conflict**.

The Deir Yassin massacre took place on 9 April 1948, when some 120 paramilitary fighters from **Menachem Begin**'s Irgun Zvai Leumi (or Etzel) and **Yitzhak Shamir**'s Lohamei Herut Israel (or Lehi) attacked Deir Yassin, an Arab village of roughly 600 people near Jerusalem. The village commanded the heights above the Tel Aviv–Jerusalem highway. The assault occurred as Jewish militias sought to relieve the blockade of **Jerusalem** during the civil war that preceded the end of British rule in **Palestine**. The death toll from the fighting was 107 Arab villagers and 4 Jewish militiamen. Stories of atrocities in Deir Yassin helped trigger the 1948 exodus of many Arabs from Jewish-held areas of Palestine. The leadership of the **Haganah** – the Jewish community's official military force – and the area's two chief rabbis condemned the killings. The **Jewish Agency** sent Jordan's King **Abdullah** a letter of apology, which he rebuffed. The narrative of Deir Yassin was used by various parties to attack each other – by the Arabs to besmirch Palestine's Jewish community and subsequently **Israel**, and by the Haganah to accuse the Irgun and Lehi of violating the Jewish principle of purity of arms, thus blackening Israel's name around the world. The event strengthened the resolve of five Arab governments to attack the fledgling Jewish state, which they did five weeks later.

deism

A philosophical conviction that while a supreme being exists and acted as the 'first cause' of creation, this being plays no direct part in human affairs and leaves the universe to function on natural laws comprehensible through observation and reason. Deists reject revealed religion and holy texts. Deism rose to prominence in the eighteenth century and **Voltaire**, **Adam Smith**, **Napoleon Bonaparte**, **Thomas Paine**, **Thomas Jefferson** and **George Washington** are thought to have been among its adherents.

Delhi

One of the oldest continuously inhabited cities in the world, Delhi has a long history of settlements, such as Indraprastha, that can be dated to approximately two and a half millennia ago. In 1206 Delhi became the centre of an expansive sultanate established by Muhammad Ghuri, which lasted until 1526 when it was displaced by the **Mughal Empire**. The third Mughal emperor shifted the capital to neighbouring Agra, but Delhi became the imperial centre once more when Shah Jahan (r. 1628–58) built the fortress city of Shahjahanabad. While formal control passed to the English **East India Company** in 1803, the British preferred to govern India from their old base in **Calcutta**. In 1912, following nationalist agitation in protest at the partition of **Bengal**, the British decided to shift the capital away from Calcutta, with its volatile political climate, to a new city they constructed adjacent to Mughal Delhi. In 1947 New Delhi became the capital of the independent republic of India.

Demerara

Demerara is one of three counties of **Guyana**, which is located on the north-eastern coast of South America. Originally a Dutch colony, it was captured by the British in 1796 and remained in its possession until 1814 when Britain purchased it along with two other colonies, Berbice and Essequibo, and united them to form the colony of British Guiana. In 1966 British Guiana gained its independence and renamed itself Guyana. Today, Demerara accommodates Guyana's capital, Georgetown.

Demirel, Süleyman (1924–2015)

One of the dominant Turkish politicians of the late twentieth century, Demirel joined the Justice Party in 1961, quickly taking leadership and leading it to victory in 1965. He served in a series of governments thereafter, but after the 1980 *coup d'état* he was banned from public office by the Turkish military. In 1987 he returned to public life as the chairman of the True Path Party. In 1993 he once again became prime minister and served as president of **Turkey** in 1993–2000. Demirel's political persona was marked by a capacity to make bargains and, capitalizing on his provincial roots, populist flair. He is typically associated with centre-right politics in Turkey: pro-West, nationalistic and pro-market. Like a number of politicians of that era, Demirel was intrigued by the possibilities of ties with new Turkic states in the **Caucasus** and central Asia after the collapse of the **Soviet Union**, and worked to develop ties between Turkey and these countries.

democracy

– see also **suffragettes; women's rights, American**.
The literal meaning of the word *democracy* is `the rule of the people'. By the early twenty-first century most states in the world described themselves as democratic in that their citizens have an opportunity to cast a vote to determine their government, but not all would be described as effective multiparty democracies in practice. Although the idea itself has ancient origins, it only became a significant feature with the **Enlightenment** when the idea of individuals having a right to a say in their own government was derived from the general idea of **human rights**. The authors of the **American Constitution** and writers such as **Thomas Paine** articulated the idea of universal political rights, though even in the early **United States** voting rights were limited, excluding women, those without property and slaves. **Jean-Jacques Rousseau** articulated the concept of `sovereignty of the people', emphasizing that the only legitimate source of political authority lay with them, leading to a more radical implementation of democratic ideas by the French **Jacobins**, who introduced universal manhood suffrage during their brief period of rule under **Robespierre**.

Representative democracy with some form of constitution, representative institutions and the franchise for at least some sections of the population, remained the aim of western **liberalism** through the nineteenth century, fostering protest movements, revolts and revolutions in both **Europe** and **Latin America**. The use of plebiscites by **Napoleon I** and **Napoleon III** provided only a limited means of offering an element of democratic accountability, and even those states which had representative institutions, such as the United States and the **United Kingdom**, restricted the number of people who could exercise the vote through property or educational qualifications, as well as confining the vote to men. Even countries which introduced at least nominal universal manhood suffrage, such as imperial Germany, restricted the power of representative institutions over executive decisions concerning military matters and foreign policy. Complete universal manhood suffrage was practised in only a small minority of states even by 1900, and no representative institutions of any kind existed in imperial Russia until 1905.

Women were totally excluded from the franchise of most European states and federal elections in the United States until after **World War I**. The first places to give women the vote were some of the American states and **New Zealand**, which adopted equal suffrage for men and women in 1893. During the twentieth century extensions of the franchise and the introduction of representative institutions became the norm in most of Europe, the United States, **Japan** and the British Dominions. However, the first communist state, the **Soviet Union**, rejected western-style democracy to become a `one party' state, but with elections for Communist Party candidates. Similarly, having achieved the status of the largest party in the Reichstag, the Nazis after 1933 abolished all other parties. Nominally democratic constitutions in many of the new states in Europe, created as a result of World War I, collapsed into dictatorship during the **Great Depression**, along with long-established states such as **Italy**, **Spain** and **Portugal**. Military-dominated governments in **China** and Japan and dictatorships in many Latin American countries reduced active democracies to a handful of states by the outbreak of **World War II**.

A new chapter was opened in 1941 with the **Atlantic Charter** agreed between **Winston Churchill** and **Franklin Roosevelt** as a declaration of war aims which set out support for democracy and freely chosen governments. These principles were enshrined in the charter of the **United Nations** signed in June 1945. Most of the post-colonial states created after 1945 adopted democratic constitutions, such as **India**, creating in that case the most populous democracy in the world. Elsewhere, however, communist-style single party governments were adopted, as in North Vietnam and the east European states that fell under Soviet control after 1945. The aspiration to democratic government continued to animate political movements in the post-war period, as seen in movements such as **Solidarity**, which undermined communist government in eastern Europe in the years preceding the fall of the Berlin Wall and the break-up of the Soviet Union. Those events led to a new round of democratic constitutions being created in eastern **Europe**, **Russia**, the **Ukraine** and some of the republics of the former Soviet Union. Latterly, the **Arab Spring** sought to democratize autocratic regimes in North Africa and the **Middle East** but with limited success. Other movements have sought to correct the deficiencies of existing democracies, such as the **civil rights** movement in the United States, primarily seeking to ensure the voting rights of minority groups.

The extension of democratic rights to women formed a major feature of the twentieth century, although women did not achieve the vote even in some European countries until after World War II and are still denied equal voting rights in some Islamic countries, notably Saudi Arabia.

Democracy Wall (China)

In 1978 students and intellectuals placed posters expressing their political views on a wall located in the Xidan district of Beijing. This practice was permitted by the Communist Party because the views expressed were critical of the recently ended **Cultural Revolution**, and therefore gave momentum to the rise to power of the reformist leader Deng Xiaoping. The placing of posters was forbidden in April 1979 after concerns grew within the leadership about the increasingly strong grievances expressed in the posters, particularly in favour of faster democratization.

Democratic Party (American)

One of the two main political parties of the **United States**, opposed in modern times by the **Republican Party**. Its origins lie in the Democratic-Republicans marshalled by **Thomas Jefferson** and **James Madison** in the 1790s to oppose the **Federalist Party**, and it was called the Democratic Republican Party until 1828. The collapse of the Federalists left the Democrats as a loose consensus defending states rights, supporting labour and small farmers, and pro-territorial expansion. Opposition to the moral prescriptiveness represented in the American **Whig Party** attracted the support of immigrant groups in the north, especially the Irish. Pro-slavery and expansionist, the pre-civil war party dominated the presidency and the Senate and, up to 1841, also the House of Representatives. Divided over slavery and secession, they entered a long period of opposition after the **American Civil War** with support concentrated in the former Confederate states and the immigrant districts of northern cities; only two Democrats sat in the White House between 1860 and 1933, though under **William Jennings Bryan** and **Woodrow Wilson** the party became more committed to government regulation of the economy. **Franklin Roosevelt**'s victory and the New Deal era initiated a period of Democratic Party hegemony until the 1950s. Under **John F. Kennedy** and **Lyndon Johnson** the party added increasing minority support through **civil rights** and welfare legislation. In turn, some southern and mid-west voters deserted the party. The elections of **Clinton** and **Obama** confirmed the Democrat's appeal to minority groups, poorer

voters and women. However, the party was shaken by the victory of **Donald Trump**, a right-wing Republican, over Hillary Clinton in 2016.

Deng Xiaoping (1904–1997)

Deng Xiaoping was one of three key figures who shaped modern **China** (along with **Mao Zedong** and **Chiang Kai-shek**). A native of Sichuan province, Deng took part in the **Long March** of 1934–5, and over the years rose in the Chinese Communist hierarchy. In 1966, during the Cultural Revolution, he was declared to be the 'second most important figure taking the capitalist road' (after state president Liu Shaoqi), and was dismissed from the Politburo. He was restored to the leadership between 1973 and 1976, then purged again in Mao Zedong's final days. Between 1976 and 1978 he outmanoeuvred Mao's chosen successor, Hua Guofeng, and effectively became China's most powerful politician. The Party Congress in 1978 saw Deng take forward the 'Four Modernizations'. The reforms led to the conversion of China from a socialist command economy to a marketized corporatist economy, in which the state significantly reduced its role. Deng strove to balance political liberalization with continued Party control, but in 1989 he responded to worker and student occupation of Tiananmen Square in the centre of Beijing by sending in troops who killed hundreds, possibly thousands, of non-violent protestors. In 1992, however, aged 88, he made a well-publicized tour of southern China to stress that economic reform would continue.

Deoband

A Muslim reform movement that began in India in the late nineteenth century and continues to influence Muslim affairs in **India**, **Pakistan** and **Afghanistan**, in particular. It started with the establishment of a school to train clerics – the Dar-ul-Uloom – in the Indian city of Deoband in 1867. The movement emphasized scripture over custom (often seen as Hindu 'accretions'), and saw the revitalization of the Indian Muslim community as rooted in individual piety.

Depression

– *see* **Great Depression**.

Derozio, Henry Louis Vivian (1809–1831)

An author, poet and teacher. He studied at the Hindu College (later the Presidency College) in Kolkata (**Calcutta**), 1826–31, and was an Eurasian who considered himself an Indian. He inspired the radical Young Bengal movement, and his poems include 'My Native Land'. The Hindu College dismissed him, and elite society threatened by the loss of racial and Brahmanical purity, condemned the movement's promise of a composite culture adhering to equality and rationality, which was to be racially unsegregated. Isolated, he died of cholera aged 22.

Desai, Bhulabhai (1877–1946)

An important Congress leader from Gujerat from 1930 to his death. He rose from poverty to become an advocate before the Bombay High Court. At **Gandhi**'s request, he assisted in the Bardoli inquiry in 1921–2 and gained a favourable outcome for the peasants. Early on a member of the Liberal Party, Desai shifted to the Congress in 1930 and was the leader of the Congress group in the Imperial Legislative Assembly, 1935–9. Although in ill health, he was also noted for his brilliant defence of **Indian National Army** officers on trial for treason in 1945.

Desai, Morarji (1896–1995)

A member of the **Indian National Congress** and later the **Janata Party**, Desai was prime minister of **India**, 1977–9, as part of a governing coalition unseating the Congress in the federal elections following the conclusion of the Emergency in 1975–7. An unwillingness of the coalition partners to devise and implement a cohesive political programme led to a loss of popular support and defections, and Desai resigned to avoid a no-confidence vote.

desegregation (USA)

In 1948 President **Harry Truman** ordered the racial desegregation of the US armed forces. Legal efforts to desegregate education lead to the ***Brown*** decision (1954). Mass protests against segregation from 1955 to 1964 in the form of boycotts, Freedom Rides, marches, sit-ins and even wade-ins at segregated beaches epitomized the **civil rights movement**'s non-violent strategy. Reflecting governmental concern during the **Cold War** at international reaction to these protests, the 1964 Civil Rights Act banned segregated public accommodations.

Dessalines, Jean Jacques (c. 1758–1806)

Hailed today as one of Haiti's founding fathers, Dessalines is believed to have been born Jean-Jacques Duclos on a plantation in the Plaine du Nord in Cormier (north of Haiti). In his early thirties he was purchased by a free black man named Dessalines and became Jean Jacques Dessalines. In 1791 Dessalines joined the slave uprising that evolved into the **Haitian Revolution** and became the principal lieutenant of **Toussaint Louverture**. After Toussaint's capture by the French, Dessalines became general-in-chief of the revolution and led his army to victory over the French Army of **Napoleon Bonaparte**. On 1 January 1804 Dessalines proclaimed the independence of Saint-Domingue, renamed it Haiti (its original Taino name meaning 'mountainous land'), and declared himself governor general for life. The following September he adopted the title Emperor Jacques I. Dessalines ruled the republic with an iron fist and was subsequently assassinated in a revolt at Pont-Rouge.

détente

A policy of the superpowers during the **Cold War** predicated upon dialogue, peaceful competition, non-military cooperation and communication between the two hostile blocs of the Cold War, and in particular the **USA** and **USSR**. Détente was envisaged by the **Kennedy** and **Khrushchev** administrations but their separate termination in 1963–4 precluded any moves towards accommodation, and had to wait for **Richard Nixon** and **Henry Kissinger** to revive the idea after 1969. The policy resulted in treaties on strategic arms limitation (**SALT I**), a convention on biological weapons, cooperation in space policy (after the race to the Moon had effectively been won by the USA) and the **Helsinki Agreement** on human rights, which had a dissolving effect on Soviet political confidence. Détente lasted some eleven years until the Soviet invasion of **Afghanistan** and the rise of a new generation of anti-communist leaders in the West, during which time the Soviet economy entered a state of stagnation, the People's Republic of **China** left the Sino-Soviet communist bloc and associated with the West, and increasing tensions between eastern European populations and their governments burst through into the Solidarity movement and internal reform by **Gorbachev** eventually led to the collapse of Soviet communism.

Dhaka

Dhaka is one of the world's fastest-growing cities. During the seventeenth century it flourished as the capital of the Mughal province of **Bengal** and was a centre of textile trading and production. Under British rule it receded in importance. In 1947 Dhaka became the capital of East Pakistan, and in 1971, after battling for independence, it became the capital of the new state of **Bangladesh**.

Diagne, Blaise (1872–1934)

Senegalese politician. Born in Gorée, **Senegal**, Diagne joined the French customs service after studying in **France**, serving throughout French West Africa. In 1914 he became the first black African elected to the French National Assembly. In 1916 he convinced French parliament to pass the 'Loi Blaise Diagne' granting full citizenship to all residents of the 'Four Communes' in **Senegal**. Daigne continued to work for the French military and labour office for the colonies and served as mayor of Dakar from 1920 until his death.

diaspora

– *see* **migration**.

Díaz, Porfirio (1830–1915)

Winning popularity for his role in stopping the French Army's advance at Puebla on 5 May 1872, Díaz, born in Oaxaca, **Mexico**, opposed **Benito Juaréz**'s abuse of office. Gaining the presidency through support for his 1876 Plan of Tuxtepec, he ushered in more than three decades of fraudulent dictatorial politics. He headed a regime that modernized parts of Mexico's economy, but was deeply unjust in social matters. He governed with changing authoritarian political coalitions and repressed indigenous traditions, and divided leading economic sectors by nationality (oil: **Great Britain**; mining: **USA**; commerce and hardware: **France** and **Germany**; finances: France), but ended direct foreign occupation. His new federal police gave a false impression of security and stability. A 1910 violent rebellion in northern Mexico led by **Pancho Villa** and **Francisco I. Madero** and in Morelos by **Emiliano Zapata** forced him into exile in 1911. He died in Paris.

Diderot, Denis (1713–1784)

Diderot was the editor of the *Encyclopédie*, the dictionary of the arts and sciences of the **Enlightenment** movement which championed the authority of reason in opposition to received religious and monarchical authority. Diderot's atheism and political radicalism earned him a period in gaol and an official, if ineffectual, ban on the publication of the *Encyclopédie*. **Voltaire**, **Montesquieu** and **Rousseau** were amongst the contributors to the work that influenced the intellectual and political ferment of pre-revolutionary **France** and **Europe**.

Diem, Ngo Dinh (1901–1963)

President of the Republic of **Vietnam**, 1955–63. His regime was independent but received much support from and was heavily influenced by the **United States**. Diem pursued violently anti-Communist and strongly pro-Catholic policies. In 1963 the Buddhist monk Thich Quang Duc set himself on fire in protest against the government. Subsequently, the government was overthrown in a military coup and Diem was captured and executed.

Dien Bien Phu

A former French military base in North Vietnam, the site of the last major battle between French forces and the **Viet Minh** in **Indochina**. Dien Bien Phu was established as a French stronghold in November 1953. After being under siege for several months, it was bombarded into submission on 7 May 1954. The devastating defeat at Dien Bien Phu led **France** to pull out all military forces and relinquish control of Indochina.

Dingiswayo (c.1780–c.1817)

Born Godongwana or Ngodongwa, little is definitively known about the life of this head of the Mthethwa clan of the Bantu people in what is now KwaZulu-Natal province of **South Africa**. Exiled after a dispute with his father, the Mthethwa chief Jobe, he was impressed by Portuguese military methods and returned to depose his brother Mawewe in 1807. Dingiswayo developed alliances between the Zulus and trading relations with the Portuguese, strengthening the army by adopting European techniques and discipline. He mentored **Shaka**, who would go on to become the most prominent Zulu leader. Dingiswayo successfully expanded the confederation of Nguni kingdoms through raids and conquest. He was believed to have been killed by Zwide, chief of the rival Ndwande clan, in the opening stages of what became known as the **mfecane**, the period of warfare among the peoples of south-eastern Africa.

Dinshaway Incident (1906)

– *see also* **Cromer, Earl of**.
The incident in the Egyptian village of Dinshaway (Dinshwai) in which a British officer was killed. The brutal sentences passed on the Egyptian peasants involved (four hangings for assault) prompted public outrage both in **Egypt** and in the British House of Commons, and prompted the new Liberal government, elected in 1906 under Sir Henry Campbell-Bannerman, to adopt a more conciliatory approach towards Egypt than had been favoured by Lord Cromer, technically British plenipotentiary agent and consul general in Egypt but actually its ruler since 1883 under what had become known as the 'veiled protectorate'.

Although Lord Cromer had been on home leave at the time and not directly involved in the sentences, he was in deteriorating health and, sensing that change was coming, resigned in 1907.

direct rule

The method of administration used by **France**, **Belgium**, **Portugal** and **Germany** in their African colonies in the nineteenth and twentieth centuries, and – to a lesser extent – by **Britain** in **India**. A highly centralized method of governing – French colonies, for example, were controlled from Paris and Portuguese colonies integrated into Portugal – direct rule was filtered through appointed rather than traditional chiefs, negating pre-existing political mechanisms or indigenous power structures. Direct rule was predicated on an attempt at assimilating the colonies' populations into European attitudes and ways of life, in the eyes of the colonial powers bringing them up to European standards. Britain, by contrast, favoured control through indirect rule (advocated by Lord **Lugard**), allowing local traditional rulers to maintain a nominal internal authority as a means of managing the wider population, with all major decisions ultimately in the hands of colonial officials acting in Britain's interest. More narrowly, the term applied in the United Kingdom to the government of **Northern Ireland** from Westminster which replaced the devolved Stormont administration in 1972 following the breakdown of public order and sectarian conflict. Direct rule came to an end in 1999, when a devolved Assembly assumed power, but on occasions it has had to be reinstated.

Directory

The name given to the executive government of **France** between 1795 and 1799, in which a presidency of five people drawn from a bicameral legislature directed the affairs of the French Republic. One of the directors was replaced annually to ensure regeneration and continuity. Although relatively stable, the Directory presided over a France split by the **Terror**, which it ended, and was increasingly dependent upon the support of military leaders, at the forefront of which was **Napoleon Bonaparte**. Its legitimacy was badly damaged by a coup in 1797. The institution itself was formally removed and replaced with a consulate in Napoleon's coup of 18 Brumaire two years later.

Disney, Walt (1901–1966)

An animator in **Hollywood** by 1923, his studio launched cartoons featuring Mickey Mouse in 1928, proving a popular success and earning the first of twenty-two Academy Awards in 1932. Disney expanded into television and regular film after **World War II**. He disliked trade unions and cooperated with the investigations of alleged communist influence in Hollywood. In the 1960s he presided over a vast entertainment and communications empire that included the vast California amusement park, Disneyland, founded in 1955.

Disraeli, Benjamin (1804–1881)

Benjamin Disraeli (after 1878 Lord Beaconsfield) was ethnically Jewish, though a member of the Anglican Church. He was leader of the British Conservative Party from 1868 until 1881, and prime minister in 1867–8 and 1874–80. He is associated with Tory Democracy and One Nation politics, which were both communitarian attempts to associate conservatism with the skilled working class and social reform under a patriotic banner marked by royal and imperialist symbolism. Disraeli, a former barrister's clerk and a member of Lincoln's Inn, began his political career as an anti-Peelite protectionist Tory. This was not only a matter of conviction but of political sense, because it insulated him from the charge, as an outsider, that he associated with political radicalism. Via a combination of political and personal rebuffs, he became an antagonist of Sir Robert Peel but moved into the parliamentary leadership of the Conservative Party in the House of Commons after Peel's fall, under Lord Derby. A budget-balancing chancellor, Disraeli was instrumental in passing the Reform Act of 1867 which expanded the electoral franchise in the **United Kingdom** to most propertied men, and which therefore inaugurated an era of relative democracy. He took full leadership and the premiership in 1868, but lost the 1868 election to **William Gladstone**, in his opposition to whom both were defined. Despite winning fewer votes than Gladstone's Liberal Party in the 1874 election, the Conservatives won in the House of Commons and Disraeli became prime minister. In this capacity he pursued a policy of isolationist self-interest in foreign affairs which won the respect of **Otto von Bismarck**, expanded British settlement of **Africa**, and awarded Queen **Victoria**, who liked him immensely, the title of Queen-Empress of India.

Disraeli also pursued social reform as part of a vision set out in his pre-leadership novels *Sybil* and *Coningsby*. He thought of Britain as an organic community torn by industrial development and urbanization and endangered by the existence of a domestic society divided into two separate groups, workers and capitalists, in such a fashion as to create two nations. He pursued food and drug acts, factory reform, the expansion of government inspection of working conditions, the expansion of artisan housing and popular patriotism as potential solutions. All of these policies had the happy dual effect of winning skilled working-class voters to the Conservative Party and undermining the Liberals. Disraeli was elevated to the House of Lords in 1878, from where he continued to govern until losing the 1880 election to Gladstone. He held on for another year, but then died. In his personal life, he had an apparently happy marriage to an older and wealthier woman, Sarah, who survived him, but no children. Disraeli was viewed as the most important influence on the Conservative Party until the rise of the monetarists and Thatcherites in the last third of the twentieth century.

dissidents

A term particularly used in the mid to late twentieth century by liberal regimes of those in communist or totalitarian states who were persecuted for thinking differently from the government. After the **USSR** committed itself to human rights with the **Helsinki Agreement** in 1975, the existence of internal exiles and convicts whose only crime was their deviation from the communist party 'line' was a serious embarrassment to the Soviet Union, and the term is still used for freethinkers in **China**, **Cuba** and **North Korea**, many of whom are in exile.

DNA

Deoxyribonucleic acid (DNA) is the genetic material that contains the instructions for the development and function of all living things. All known cellular life and some viruses contain DNA. The main role of DNA in a cell is the long-term storage of information needed to direct protein synthesis and replication. A molecule of DNA consists of two chains or strands composed of a large number of chemical compounds, called nucleotides, tied in a chain. These chains are arranged like a right-handed spiral, called a double helix, which is held together by hydrogen bonds between the bases (adenine, cytosine, guanine and thymine) attached to the two strands. The description of the structure of DNA was first published in 1953 by an American biochemist, James D. Watson, and a British biophysicist, Francis Crick, who were awarded the Nobel Prize in physiology and medicine in 1962. The discovery opened the way for a new era in biological science with profound implications for medicine, and for human, animal and plant research. It led to the mapping of the genome, the genetic information about organisms, and the development of genetic engineering to speed up the production of new strains of genetically modified (GM) crops, the **cloning** of animals (first achieved with Dolly the sheep in 1997) and the identification of the genes which cause particular diseases.

dollar diplomacy

A foreign policy associated with the administration of President **William H. Taft** (1909–13) who told Congress (1912): 'The diplomacy of the present administration has sought to respond to modern ideas of commercial intercourse. This policy has been characterized as substituting dollars for bullets.' Taft sought to expand US investments abroad, open new markets for American products and create financial stability, especially in the Caribbean, **Central America** and **China**. Secretary of State Philander C. Knox strongly promoted American business interests in **Latin America** and **Asia**. In order to secure governments favourable to US investors and national interest, US diplomats and military officers actively intervened in the domestic affairs of Caribbean and Central American nations, overthrew 'irresponsible' governments, created customs house receiverships to ensure repayment of loans, and eventually sent American marines to shore up client governments, as in **Nicaragua**. In Latin America these policies increased resentment towards the **United States**.

Dominican Republic

A Caribbean nation that shares the island of Hispaniola with **Haiti**. The location of Spain's earliest permanent settlements in the Americas, the Dominican Republic experienced a problematic transition from plantation colony to independent nation in the nineteenth century that initiated various problems that have plagued its subsequent history. Haitian rule (1822–44) was followed by civil war, a failed search for foreign protection marked by a brief restoration of Spanish rule (1861–5), and the dictatorship of General Ulises Heureaux (1882–99). After the **Spanish–American War**, the Dominican Republic experienced repeated US interventions, including an extended military occupation (1916–24). This status as a US protectorate continued until General **Rafael Trujillo** launched his long dictatorship (1930–61). Since his death, the Dominican Republic has struggled to build a stable political culture, free itself from foreign intervention and address the pervasive poverty that afflicts the majority of its population.

Domino Theory

During a news conference in April 1954, US President **Dwight Eisenhower**, reflecting on the potential consequences of French defeat at **Dien Bien Phu** by Vietnamese communists and nationalists, invoked what he called the 'falling domino' principle: 'You have a row of dominoes set up, you knock over the first one, and what will happen to the last one is the certainty that it will go over very quickly.' His theory was highly influential through the **Cold War**: Presidents **John F. Kennedy** and **Lyndon B. Johnson** both invoked it to justify increased US military support for South Vietnam. While Eisenhower had South East Asia in mind, subsequent presidents believed in its universal applicability: **Ronald Reagan** cited it to justify interventionist policies in **Central America**. Some believe that, following America's withdrawal from **Vietnam**, the fall of **Cambodia**, **Laos** and South Vietnam to communism vindicates it. Others believe that the post-1973 independence of **Thailand**, **Indonesia** and **India** prove the theory unfounded.

Douglass, Frederick (1817–1895)

Frederick Douglass was the son of an enslaved woman and an unknown white man. Born a slave, he escaped in 1838 and began promoting abolition from 1841 as an agent for the Massachusetts Anti-Slavery Society. His best-selling book *Narrative of his Life*, published in 1845 and his abolitionist newspaper the *Northern Star*, founded in Rochester in 1847, became major forces in the campaign against slavery. He advised **Abraham Lincoln** and during the **American Civil War** helped to recruit **African Americans** into the Union forces. He held a number of government positions, ending his career as US consul general to Haiti.

Dreadnought

The name for a revolutionary class of large battleships taken from the British HMS *Dreadnought*, launched in 1906. 'Big gun' ships with their turrets ranged fore and aft, heavily armoured and capable of high speed through the use of steam turbines, they rendered all previous classes of ships obsolete. A bold move by the Royal Navy, it simultaneously removed **Britain**'s existing numerical advantage in naval vessels and prompted a furious naval race with **Germany** in which only ships of the new type counted. The American Navy quickly built its own ships of the type, followed by the other major powers, such as **Japan**, **Russia** and **France**. Secondary powers, such as **Turkey** and **Austria–Hungary** also built or purchased dreadnought-class ships before the Great War. The only engagement fought between Dreadnought class battle fleets was at Jutland in 1916, though the result yielded no change in the status quo. Nevertheless, the Dreadnought design became the basis for all battleships subsequently constructed, up to and during **World War II**.

Dred Scott case (USA)

An infamous 1857 ruling of the **United States** Supreme Court. With good precedent, the slave Dred Scott claimed freedom through former residence in a free state and territory. Yet Chief Justice Roger B. Taney used the case to tackle contentious sectional issues in the South's favour. Showing disregard for the **American Constitution**'s comity clause, he ruled that **African Americans** could not be US citizens, and that Congress had never been allowed to prohibit slavery in the territories, thus rendering the **Missouri Compromise** unconstitutional. Taney had hoped to remove the **Republican Party**'s key plank, the non-extension of slavery, but the apparent complicity of **James Buchanan** and two Northern justices only bolstered Republican accusations against a 'slave power'. The ruling against territorial prohibition undermined the **Democratic Party**'s 'popular sovereignty' formula in the **Kansas–Nebraska Act**. Despite sincere internal attempts to reconcile it with *Dred Scott*, notably Stephen Douglas's 'Freeport Doctrine', the Democrats split in 1860 over the protection of territorial slavery.

Dresden, bombing of (1945)

Dresden suffered, 13–14 April 1945 and after, the gravest bombing of **Europe** in **World War II**. Eight hundred British and American aircraft created a firestorm which virtually destroyed the 'Florence of the North' to scant military purpose. The city was packed with refugees and the death toll was put by the Allies at 30,000, by the German Red Cross at 60,000, and by some others at more than 100,000. The true tally can never be known. Restoration and reconstruction of the historic city has continued to the present day.

Dreyfus affair (1894–1899) (France)

A scandal involving Alfred Dreyfus (1859–1935), a Jewish army officer who was accused, tried and convicted of passing information to the Germans. Having been sentenced to life imprisonment on Devil's Island, he was found innocent and later exonerated by a second trial in 1899 which proved that many of the documents used to convict him had been forgeries. It became apparent that the authorities had used Dreyfus as a scapegoat to cover up the activities of a Major Esterhazy. During the time taken to convince the authorities of the need for a second trial, many accusations were made, including Zola's letter 'J'accuse', that anti-Semitism of the authorities and the army had ensured Dreyfus' conviction and delayed his retrial. The 'Dreyfusard' and 'anti-Dreyfusard' camps revealed many of the divisions in the **Third Republic**, though they were never as clear-cut as sometimes suggested. After much pressure Dreyfus was retried, pardoned and the verdict finally overturned in 1906.

drug trafficking

Psychoactive substances have been traded for at least as long as there is an historical record. The first world conference on opium traffic at The Hague in 1912 marked the beginning of a concerted international effort to control illegal drugs. Traffic of cannabis and cocaine between **Central** and **South America**, and **Europe** and the **United States** exploded during the 1970s and 1980s. Answering to this swell in drug trade and demand, in 1971 the United States government launched its 'war on drugs'. This and other efforts in drug trafficking control have been controversial. With approximately 5 per cent of the world population using illicit drugs on an annual basis as of 2009, the production of cocaine, heroin and cannabis in Central and South America has remained stable or increased since the 1960s. Similarly, the centuries-old commerce of cannabis and opium derivates between African and Asian producers and the markets of western and, increasingly, eastern Europe has continued to grow, making this a global phenomenon.

drugs

The extent to which drugs were used for recreational rather than medical purposes in the eighteenth and nineteenth centuries is difficult to assess, but references to laudanum, or opium, in the fiction of Wilkie Collins and Charles Dickens, and de Quincey's *Confessions of an English Opium-eater*, all suggest that they were widely used in wealthier and more artistic circles. Public and political responses have always been divided. Many countries, including the **UK**, have favoured total legal prohibition, others led by the **Netherlands** have preferred decriminalization of use, albeit with some quantitative restrictions. Prohibitionists emphasize the danger to life of even such common drugs as Ecstasy, the potential consequences of recourse to mind-changing substances, and the

agony of withdrawal symptoms, but have to accept that drug use has flourished under prohibition. The Dutch approach has made drugs a public health rather than a criminal issue and appears to have stabilized usage, but is inconsistent in that drug production and supply remain illegal and a nexus for organized crime.

'drugs, war on'

In 1880 the **United States** and **China** agreed to prohibit the movement of opium between the two countries and, since then, a succession of laws has attempted to suppress the consumption of an array of narcotic drugs. The abuse of substances such as marijuana and crack cocaine has been at the root of problems ranging from mental and physical breakdown to serious and organized crime. In a speech in 1971, President **Richard Nixon** coined the phrase 'war on drugs'; in 1973 the Drug Enforcement Agency came into being, and by 2005 over 45 billion dollars annually was being spent on suppression. Allegations that the CIA was trading in drugs in order to fund illegal undercover operations tarnished the suppressive effort. Critics compared the effects of the war on drugs with those alleged in the case of alcohol **prohibition** (1919–33), namely rises in consumption, prices and therefore corruption.

Drum

A South African lifestyle magazine. Founded by Bob Crisp and Jim Bailey in 1951, *Drum* originally took a paternalistic approach to African tribal life. The publication quickly shifted its focus to the vibrant cultural life in black urban townships. The height of the magazine's influence came between the Defiance campaign in 1952 and the 1960 Sharpeville massacre. Important writers such as Lewis Nkosi and William Bloke Modisane began their careers writing for *Drum*.

Druze

A highly secretive Middle Eastern religious group whose doctrines are ultimately derived from Isma'ilite teachings with an eclectic admixture of Jewish, Christian, Gnostic, Neoplatonic and Iranian elements. Isma'ilism was an offshoot of **Shi'ite Islam**, but claimed heretically to combine the best of **Islam**, **Judaism** and **Christianity**. There are some 250,000 Druze in **Lebanon**, where they represent some 7 per cent of the population; 100,000 in **Syria**, mainly in the Jabal ad-Duruz; 125,000 in **Israel** and 20,000 in **Jordan**, together with a further 100,000 outside the **Middle East**. Founded in Cairo in 1017, the Druze, known to themselves as the *muwahhidun* (monotheists), have proved intensely cohesive, rejecting both conversion either from or to their religion and intermarriage. Their religious system is kept secret both from outsiders and from most of their own number, with only a small group of initiates known as the *uqqal* (knowers) being allowed to participate in religious services and to know the secrets of the Druze teachings (*hikmah*). They await the return of their divine saviour, Caliph Hakim of Egypt, who mysteriously disappeared in 1021.

At periodic intervals the Druze have played a significant political role. A separatist movement was already active among the Druze of Ottoman Syria, inclusive of **Palestine**, at the end of the eighteenth century, and **Napoleon** sought the aid of the Shihab family's feudal leadership, 1799, in his campaign against Syria. A period of social conflict, 1840–60, culminated in the 1860 Lebanese Civil War between the Maronite Christian independence movement, which had Roman Catholic and French support, and the Ottoman Turks and the Druze, the latter allying themselves with the British and allowing entry to Protestant missionaries. French intervention, because restrained by **Britain**, resulted not in Maronite independence but in Lebanese autonomy within the **Ottoman Empire** under a Christian governor, which lasted till 1914. The Druze, however, rebelled against the Ottoman Empire in the Syrian province of Hauran, 1909, opposing both taxation and conscription into the Ottoman Army. By 1910 the Turks had suppressed the rebellion, with the deaths of 2,000 Druze and the execution of their leaders. They were then the driving force behind the **Syrian revolt of 1925–7**, and have had variable relations with different Syrian regimes since independence. They were actively attacked by President Adib Shishakli, 1949–54, who was assassinated by a Druze in Brazil in 1954 for his bombardment of the Jabal ad-Duruz. They provided a number of the military officers under the subsequent Baathist regime, however.

They were intimately involved in the Lebanese Civil War of 1974–90 when most Druze primarily supported the Progressive Socialist Party (PSP) created by their leader, Kamal Jumblatt, in opposition to the primarily Maronite Christian Lebanese Front. The PSP initially supported the **Palestine Liberation Organization (PLO)** but in 1985 joined **Amal** in fighting the main Lebanese **Sunni** militia, which was the close ally of the PLO, for control of the Sabra, Shatila and Burj al-Barajneh refugee camps in Beirut. They became embroiled in the

Syrian Civil War, many supporting the regime of President Assad.

The 125,000 Druze in Israel are Arabic-speaking citizens who are drafted into military service like the Jewish majority and are assimilated into public life in general.

Dubai

A member state of the **United Arab Emirates** (UAE) ruled by the Al Maktum dynasty. Dubai became an independent sheikhdom in 1833, part of the Trucial States in 1853, a British protectorate in 1892 and a member of the UAE in 1971. During the twentieth century the port rose to prominence as a smuggling and then legitimate commercial centre in the Arabian Gulf region and internationally. Dubai also became a minor oil exporter in 1969.

Du Bois, William Edward Burghardt (1868–1963)

The first **African American** to be awarded a Harvard PhD, Du Bois authored *The Philadelphia Negro* (1899) and *The Souls of Black Folk* (1903), and criticized Booker T. Washington, the leading African American of the day, for being too accommodating to whites. He helped found the National Association for the Advancement of Colored People (1909) and edited its journal until 1934. He died in **Ghana**, where he had recently migrated, having been appointed editor of the *Encyclopaedia Africana* and become a member of the Communist Party.

Dulles, John Foster (1888–1959)

A Wall Street lawyer descended from a line of American diplomats, Dulles served as secretary of state in the **Eisenhower** administration. In the 1952 election campaign he condemned President **Truman**'s 'containment' campaign as timid, and called for the 'rollback' of international communism. Perceived as a strident and forceful Cold Warrior, he was nevertheless a faithful servant of Eisenhower's policies, and under his management America enjoyed six years of relative peace.

Duma

The lower house of the modern Russian Federal Assembly, otherwise known as *Gosudartsvennaya Duma* (the State Assembly). In abeyance during the Soviet period. The preceding imperial Duma was inaugurated, based on some historic precedents, by Tsar **Nicholas II** in response to the 1905 revolution. It met May–July 1906, March–June 1907, November 1907–June 1912 and November 1912–March 1917, but only exercised significant power at the end, when it set up its Provisional Committee which formed the first provisional government and accepted the tsar's abdication in 1917.

Dumbarton Oaks conference

At the Dumbarton Oaks conference in 1944, **Britain, China, Russia** and the **USA** agreed the **United Nations** would be comprised of a General Assembly, open to all 'peace-loving' nations, a Security Council (UNSC) including the four great powers plus **France**, an International Court of Justice, and a Secretariat, led by a Secretary General. The UNSC could raise troops to settle disputes, but could only act with substantial unanimity. The UN was formally established at San Francisco in 1945.

Dunkirk

A name given both to a battle between allied British and French troops and the German armed forces between 26 May and 4 June 1940, which resulted in a German victory, and the largely successful evacuation of the allied forces to England via a flotilla of naval, merchant and fishing ships which rescued almost 340,000 soldiers from the beaches and port shortly afterwards. The Battle of Dunkirk was an example of the success of **Blitzkrieg**, and ensured that there was to be no repeat of the trench warfare of **World War I**. It also opened the way to Paris, and heralded the fall of France. The reasons why the German forces halted are difficult to discern and have proved to be the basis of much conjecture. The evacuation, on the other hand, was hailed by **Winston Churchill** as a miracle and was a considerable boost to the morale of the United Kingdom, with the 'Dunkirk Spirit' invoked thereafter as testimony to the power of hope and improvization in the most apparently dire of circumstances.

Dupleix, Joseph François, Marquis de (1697–1763)

Joseph François Dupleix, appointed governor of the Compagnie des Indes in 1742, extended French power in **India** at the cost of the British through the 'game of nabobism'. Offering the services of French troops to one of the contenders in succession disputes that beset Indian states, he obtained extensive economic concessions. However, without the wholehearted support of the metropolitan government, the French company lost out to its English rival in the contest for the mastery of India. In 1754 Dupleix was recalled to France in disgrace.

Dutch East India Company

The Dutch East India Company (Verenigde Oostindische Compagnie) (VOC) was a Dutch vehicle for trade, imperialism and discovery. It was chartered in 1602 and lasted until 1800. Amongst other things, it was the first multinational, share-based monopoly, and the first of a series of European companies to act with quasi-state powers of war, taxation and administration in Asia. The VOC grew rich on the spice trade, but also engaged in gold and silver arbitrage. Anglo-Dutch Wars, resistance to trade in **China** and **Japan**, and the decline of the Dutch Republic by the 1790s led to its gradual collapse. The company was also undermined, however, by its complex division of manager-shareholders and non-manager stock owners, and by its administrative responsibilities. The latter led the VOC to maintain large fleets, backed by a network of military outposts, because politically connected managers saw this as the natural form of expansion and as good for themselves. However, the declining class of initially dominant trader-managers, often of lower social standing, could do nothing about declining productivity, sunk cost or the promotion of a range of Asian commodities which carried low profit margins. In addition, the company depended upon a stream of officers from Europe, who were increasingly subject to illness and epidemic in the eighteenth century, and upon local information, which forced ships through headquarters in Jakarta rather than allowing direct multiple routes to Europe. When faced with European disruption, American competition and falling dividends, the company simply could not cope. Its assets were ultimately passed (via the **Congress of Vienna**) to the Dutch East Indies, and form most of modern **Indonesia**.

Dutch East Indies
– *see* **Indonesia**.

Dutch Empire

The Dutch Empire, like the British and French Empires, originated in the acquisitions and settlements of the sixteenth and seventeenth centuries. Ceylon (**Sri Lanka**) was captured from the Portuguese in the mid seventeenth century but had to be surrendered to the British, 1796, during the **Napoleonic Wars**. The Cape of Good Hope had to be surrendered similarly, but the large-scale movement (*Vetrek*) of the Dutch settlers (**Boers**) into what became the Orange Free State and the Transvaal, 1836, was a Boer, not a Dutch imperial, initiative. **Guyana** was settled by the Dutch West

India Company, 1620, but it also was largely ceded to Britain as British Guiana, 1814, leaving only Dutch Guiana (**Surinam**). The Caribbean islands of Saba and St Eustatius were acquired by the Dutch, 1632, and of Curaçao, Bonaire and Aruba, 1634, and the southern part of St Maarten, 1648. By far the largest Dutch imperial possession, however, was always what is now **Indonesia**. The Netherlands East India Company ran the territory as the Netherlands East Indies, 1602–1798, but it became a colony run by the Dutch government in 1814, under Japanese occupation, 1941–45, during **World War II**.

The period of Dutch rule was characterized by the protection of local customary law and its application by the indigenous authorities, with the consequence that the western-educated administrative elite was small. The evolution of an independence movement was, however, greatly facilitated by the adoption of *Bahasa Indonesia*, a form of coastal Malay written in the Latin alphabet, as a lingua franca, 1928. The Japanese occupiers actively promoted the language and banned the use of Dutch. They also supported both the secular Indonesian nationalists and the Muslim organizations, establishing a Muslim council, and raised an Indonesian national army with 6,000 Japanese-trained officers. Independence was proclaimed 17 August 1945, two days after the Japanese surrender.

The Dutch, who did not recognize the proclamation, sought to reassert control and launched military action, 26 July 1946, seeking to establish a federal state within a union under the Queen of the Netherlands, but were finally forced to give way under international pressure. Power was formally transferred, 27 December 1949. The Dutch, however, refused to relinquish Western New Guinea until 1961, when it was handed over to the **United Nations**, who immediately transferred it to Indonesia, as Irian Jaya.

Elsewhere, Surinam became independent on 25 November 1975. The Caribbean islands were part of the Dutch West Indies from 1828, and formed the Netherlands Antilles, 1845. Granted internal self-government, 29 December 1954, as an integral part of the Kingdom of the **Netherlands**. Aruba was constitutionally separated from the Netherlands Antilles, 1 January 1986, but earlier references to ultimate independence were deleted at Aruba's request, June 1990. In November 1993 Curaçao voted in a referendum to remain part of the Netherlands Antilles, and since 2010 it has been an antonomous country within the Kingdom of the Netherlands.

Dutch Guiana
– *see* **Surinam**.

Dutch learning (Japan)
Modern knowledge of western science and technology was brought by the Dutch to Dejima, Nagasaki Harbour, which was the only trading post open to **Europe** under the policy of national isolation enacted during the Tokugawa period. Books brought by the Dutch emissaries were translated into Japanese, especially in the fields of science, anatomy and Dutch medicine. Shogun Tokugawa Yoshimune gave approval for Franz von Siebold to disseminate Dutch learning to experts in Japan. The early exposure to Dutch learning shaped **Japan**'s flexible attitude to modernization.

Dutch West India Company
– *see also* **Dutch Empire**.

In 1621 the Dutch West India Company (WIC) was chartered and given its monopoly to trade in Africa and the Americas. In the seventeenth century the WIC dominated Dutch commerce in the Atlantic, including the **slave trade**. The company governed colonial settlements in **Brazil**, the Caribbean and North America, and maintained trading factories on the African coast. Facing financial difficulty in the eighteenth century, the Dutch government bought the shares of the WIC in 1791 and took control of the company's colonies.

Duvaliers ('Papa Doc' and 'Baby Doc') (1907–71 and 1951–)
François Duvalier, nickname 'Papa Doc', was elected president of **Haiti** in 1957. With the support of his secret police, the Tontons Macoutes, he imposed an authoritarian regime, promoting himself as the embodiment of the Haitian nation. Despite diplomatic isolation, Haiti remained stable but chronically underdeveloped. On his death, political power was transferred to his son 'Baby Doc', who promised reform, but was forced by increasing social unrest to flee the country in 1986. Attempts at democratization and reform followed, though the country remains one of the poorest in the world.

E

Earth Day

Either the equinox heralding the start of spring in the northern hemisphere and autumn in the southern, or 22 April each year as the anniversary of demonstrations first held across the **United States** in 1970 in favour of environmental reform. Jointly organized by Wisconsin Senator Gaylord Nelson and Denis Hayes, the first Earth Day involved an estimated 20 million people. Large-scale anniversaries organized by Hayes in 1990 and 2000 involved participants in 141 and 184 nations respectively.

East India Company (English)

In December 1600 Queen Elizabeth I granted a charter awarding exclusive trading rights to a new company of London merchants trading into the East Indies. This grant followed decades of fitful and largely unsuccessful efforts by English traders to challenge the Portuguese and the Dutch for access to the valuable commerce of the Indian Ocean. The company's finance was initially limited to a series of terminable investments until 1657, when its stock was made permanent. Thus, the company came to resemble a modern joint-stock corporation, financed by shareholder investors who elected twenty-four 'committees' (after 1709, styled as directors) to manage the company's affairs.

Dutch commercial and naval strength limited the English company's opportunities in the spice trade of South East Asia, so directors focused their efforts on building up fortified 'presidencies' at Madras (1639), Bombay (1668) and **Calcutta** (1690). Convoys of armed East Indiamen (ships) sailed to a vast network of company ports from St Helena in the Atlantic to Bengkulu on the island of Sumatra, exchanging silver exported from **Europe** for Asian spices, saltpetre and textiles. After a period of fierce competition with a rival 'new' **East India Company** chartered by Parliament in 1698, the old and new companies merged in 1709. The resulting 'United Company' became a major pillar of British national finance, through loans to the state, customs revenues and dividends to shareholders. In the 1740s global warfare between the British and French empires spread to the Indian Ocean, while the decline of the **Mughal Empire** created a period of political conflict and opportunity in India. Drawing on royal naval forces and on locally recruited soldiers, company officials in **India** moved both to block French commercial expansion and also to conquer coastal territories. The conquest of the rich province of **Bengal** between 1757 and 1765 enabled British traders to expand their lucrative 'private' stake in Asian commerce, while the company consolidated its grip on exports of cotton and silk textiles to Europe, diverting new revenues from territorial taxes into commercial investments. The company's trade in tea from **China** also grew rapidly at the end of the eighteenth century, financed by exports of opium and silver from India, and fuelled by the expanding purchasing power of British consumers.

Driven close to bankruptcy in the 1770s and 1780s by military costs in India, the company survived a series of parliamentary inquiries, though after 1784 the British state established a 'Board of Control' to supervise the company's government of Indian territories. British conquests in India grew relentlessly in the early nineteenth century, while the company evolved into a branch of British imperial administration, a process hastened by the loss of its trade monopolies with India (1813) and China (1833) after pressure from free-traders. Considered by modern historians as a pioneering **multinational corporation**, an agent of **globalization** and a harbinger of modern European imperialism, the company was finally abolished after the **Indian mutiny** of 1857.

East Pakistan

– *see* **Bangladesh**.

East Timor (Timor Este)

A Portuguese possession from the sixteenth century and declared an overseas province of **Portugal** in 1930, East Timor has a mixed and largely Roman Catholic Portuguese-Malay population. An isolated nationalist uprising was suppressed in 1959. It was occupied by the Indonesian Army and annexed by **Indonesia** as its twenty-seventh province with the support of the **United States** and **Australia** in July 1976, following the emergence of the allegedly communist Frente Revolucionaria do Timor Leste Independente (FRETILIN) in the wake of Portuguese abandonment of its former colony, 1975. Guerrilla warfare ensued. Two prominent East Timorese leaders, Bishop Carlos Belo and José Ramos Horta, were awarded the Nobel Peace Prize in 1996. Timorese militias opposed to independence and sponsored by the Indonesian Army conducted a reign of terror in 1998–9, while 98 per cent of the electorate voted for independence in a referendum under UN auspices on 30 August 1999. Order was restored by a UN-backed Australian peacekeeping force, and a UN transitional administration established in October 1999. Perhaps 100,000 had been killed since 1976. Independence was achieved on 19 May 2002.

Easter Rising (Ireland)

Seminal event in the Irish independence struggle against Britain, undertaken by the Irish Volunteers (under Patrick Pearse) and James Connolly's Irish Citizen Army, led by the Irish Republican Brotherhood. On 24 April 1916 rebels seized the Dublin General Post Office and proclaimed a republic. With many Irish serving in the British forces against **Germany**, the rising lacked support but the execution of the leaders following their surrender on 30 April won sympathy for the cause.

Eastern Question

The name given to the complex of diplomatic issues arising from the decline of the **Ottoman Empire** in the nineteenth and early twentieth centuries, and the rivalry between the European Great Powers to ensure that the new pattern of nation states accorded with their own strategic interests. For the British this meant naval control of the Mediterranean, particularly after the opening of the Suez Canal. For the French it meant the extension of their new North African empire. For the Russians it meant the security of their Black Sea coastline and control at **Constantinople** (Istanbul). For the Austrians it meant the insulation of their multinational empire from the nationalist sentiment of the Balkan Slavs. For the Italians it meant securing a toehold on North Africa in either **Tunisia** or **Libya**. Every power, however, except perhaps **Russia**, whose ambitions extended to partitioning **Turkey**, had an interest in the survival of the Ottoman Empire and all sought to preserve the European balance of power.

The Eastern Question came to the fore on five occasions. On the first, the British, French and Russians all supported the Greek cause in the War of Independence, jointly defeating the Turks and Egyptians at the naval **Battle of Navarino**, 1827. The weakened Ottoman Sultan, **Mahmud II**, was nevertheless subsequently able to secure Russian, but not British, help against **Egypt**'s Muhammad 'Ali and to conclude the Treaty of **Unkiar Skelessi**, 1833, whose secret article raising the **Straits Question** then alarmed the British. The French, meanwhile, were supportive of Muhammad 'Ali in Egypt. On the second, the British, French and Turks were ranged against Russia in the **Crimean War**, 1854–6, provoked by Russia's occupation of Moldavia and Wallachia, May 1853, pursuant to its claim to a protectorate over Turkey's Orthodox subjects tenuously based on the Treaty of Kutchuk Kainardji, which had terminated the **Russo-Turkish War of 1768–74**. Although the Russians withdrew, the victorious British and French demanded the neutralization of the Black Sea and the Turks had to recognize the autonomy of Moldavia and Wallachia. On the third, the interests of **Austria** and Russia were opposed during the Balkan crisis of 1875–78, triggered by the rejection of Turkish rule by first **Bosnia–Hercegovina** and then **Bulgaria**. Partly inspired by pan-Slav sentiment, Russia declared war on Turkey, 1877, and won the autonomy of Bulgaria by the Treaty of San Stefano, 1878, but was checked by a Turko-British agreement whereby **Britain** acquired **Cyprus** in return for a guarantee to protect Asian Turkey against Russia. At the Congress of Berlin that year, moreover, Russia had to accept the exclusion of Turkish Macedonia from Bulgaria and the transfer of Bosnia–Herzegovina to the Austro-Hungarian Empire. These were the seeds of further crises. In 1908, **Austria–Hungary** created the fourth occasion by annexing Bosnia outright, relying on the support of **Germany**, and the Eastern Question arose for the fifth time in the **Balkan Wars**, 1912–13, when the Balkan states, having ousted the Turks from Macedonia and Thrace, for the first time made their own peace, that of Bucharest, 1913, without submitting it to the rival Great Powers who were unwilling to go to war themselves. **Italy**, meanwhile, secured **Libya** from the Turks.

The Eastern Question was finally overtaken in 1914, when Great Power rivalry ushered in **World War I**.

Ecevit, Bülent (1925–2006)

Bülent Ecevit was perhaps the most important figure of the left in Turkish politics from the late twentieth century. Entering Parliament in 1957, he began working to redefine the Republican People's Party (RPP) as a party of the centre left and, in 1972, he replaced **Ismet Inonu** as party chairman. In the fragmented political environment of the 1970s Ecevit's RPP was often part of coalitions and, in 1975, constituted a minority government. In 1974 he led the coalition government which initiated the Turkish invasion of **Cyprus**. Banned from politics following the military coup of 1980, Ecevit founded the Democratic Left Party (DLP) in 1987 and returned to Parliament in 1991. The DLP was part of a number of coalition governments in the 1990s, and following the capture of PKK leader Abdullah Öcalan in 1999, captured a plurality of votes. Soon, however, ill health and an economic crisis had sapped his popularity and the DLP received less than 2 per cent of the vote in the 2002 elections. Ecevit retired from political life in the aftermath.

economic cycles

The term *economic (business) cycles* refers to the ups (recovery and prosperity) and downs (contraction and recession) of economic activity experienced by a whole economy. Some economists prefer not to use the word *cycle*, which connotes similar and persistent increments, but to simply refer to particular and supposedly unique swings in levels of economic activity. During the nineteenth century business cycles were not thought of as cycles at all but rather as 'crises' interrupting the smooth development of an economy.

Economists began to develop the theory that these fluctuations were regular in form and formation. Stanley Jevons and Clemens Juglar developed explanations based on changes in climate. Nikolai Kondratiev described the evolution of modern economies in the form of long waves that include the Industrial Revolution in the first wave, while the second wave is associated with the appearance and spread of the railways. These waves developed from forces within the economic system, as innovations. Joseph Schumpeter in his 1990s work *Business Cycles* followed this tradition and summarized the literature by defining five different economic cycles: seasonal (1 year), Kitchin (3 years), Juglar (9–10 years), Kuznets (15–20 years) and Kondratiev (48–60 years). He represented business cycles as interconnections flowing from all five types of cycles. Entrepreneurs who by investing to transform inventions into innovations over-invest and then pull back are the core mechanism of his theory of cycles in economic growth.

A more empirically based approach was developed by Wesley C. Mitchell, who in 1920 founded the National Bureau of Economic Research to measure and analyze business cycles. His students improved on the tools and concepts to measure aggregate economic activity. Simon Kuznets produced national accounts for that purpose. The rise of **Keynesian** economics focused on the role of demand and the potential for policy interventions to stabilize economic cycles. Keynesianism suggested that small positive changes in expected future demand can lead to substantial investment. But if investors anticipate that demand will shrink, they will cut back and demand *will* shrink, in a self-fulfilling anticipation. Fiscal policy may counter the movements of aggregate demand and stabilize aggregate economic activity.

In the late twentieth century several alternative hypotheses on the origin of economic cycles have appeared. Finn Kydland and Edward Prescott focused on short- and long-term economic fluctuations arising from random changes in technology. Others explored the possibility that democratic political processes are at the centre of cycles. Political economists and economic cycles are connected because it is difficult to achieve growth and full employment, on the one hand, and low inflation, on the other hand, and parties are elected to implement policies that reverse those of the previous governments. For example, party A implements pro-growth policies, generates inflation, is voted out of office and replaced by party B implementing anti-inflationary policies generating high unemployment and so on. Other theories on policy changes within governments suggest that governments normally take over economies in a state of disequilibrium, have to stabilize them through contractionary policies with little growth, and then develop expansionary policies increasing growth, but generate disequilibrium by the end of their term in power.

economic development

Economic development is the replacement of subsistence institutions and subsistence social values with commercial institutions and commercial social values. In practical terms, it means that households are forced to measure their welfare by money incomes earned by continuous paid labour. Economic development is primarily a political process because peasants performing subsistence labour norms must be induced to perform commercial labour norms. Most peasants will not do this voluntarily. What are the inducements to get peasants to perform continuous paid labour? They are political and their success ultimately depends on some variety of coercion. The usual form is money taxation. In *Toward a Theory of Economic Growth* (1954), Simon Kuznets summarized thus: 'The transition period can be described as periods of controlled social and economic revolution.' In other words, economic development (commercialization of culture) is a revolutionary political process. Economic policies are secondary, as in the term *political economy*. In many instances it is difficult to detect the effectiveness of commercializing policies. There is, however, one sure measure: birth rate. In all commercial cultures births are limited by contraception, abortion, delayed marriages or high rates of celibacy. Religious teachings have diminishing effects on birth rates in commercial cultures because children are expensive to raise to maturity. All food, shelter and clothing must be purchased by money earned by continuous paid labour. Race, climate, geography and religious teachings are less relevant as determining factors. Even at low levels of commercialization, birth rates will decline to near replacement rates. Birth rates are the only sure measure of commercial cultures.

The process of economic development can be described and analyzed under four headings: (1) political policies of central governments, (2) production of assured food surpluses, (3) literacy and (4) industrialization. Economic development in the modern sense began in the city-states of Italy during the fourteenth century (Renaissance) and moved to northern Europe in the sixteenth and seventeenth centuries, especially to the Netherlands and England, and then to the rest of the world in the eighteenth, nineteenth and twentieth centuries.

political policies

What were the policies that commercialized culture in western European nations? The first was the energetic encouragement of maritime trade by central governments, usually monarchies. This was the easy part. The second was reducing the power of feudal landholders and motivating them to extinguish communal land tenure on their estates. This was the hard part. At the beginning of the commercializing process in western Europe, central governments had to reduce the power of feudal landholders because the subsistence status quo preserved their power base. It was not until feudal landholders were deprived of political power that economic development could be put on a sustaining basis. Central governments (usually monarchies) had to have the coercive powers necessary to sustain economic development.

The power of central governments was in the form of a bureaucracy and a police force capable of collecting money taxes, plus an army as a reservoir of force. These coercive institutions had to be completely controlled by central governments. In the nineteenth century, when industrial nations acquired overseas colonies governed by tribal and feudal institutions, colonial governors faced a similar problem of governance. These principalities had commercial sectors located in cities, but they had an ambiguous status. Emperors and other feudal governors often stripped merchants of assets by predatory taxation when they needed funds for war. More often than not, this occurred when commercial sectors were dominated by immigrant communities: Jews, Chinese, Indians, Armenians and Lebanese. In other words, commercial wealth was not protected by law, nor were there policies to stimulate capital accumulation. Colonial governance was welcomed by merchants in feudal and tribal cultures because the first purpose of colonization was to increase commerce by putting governing policies and taxation on a predictable basis.

agriculture

Governments committed to economic development must make the production of an assured food surplus a top priority because food must be available to feed urban residents employed in commerce and industry. This means commercializing food production. Some contemporary nations, for example **Saudi Arabia**, **Nigeria** and **Angola**, are able to postpone this by food purchases because they have large oil revenues. Some nations in Europe began the process of commercializing agriculture in the sixteenth century. By 1700 England and the **Netherlands** had large sectors of commercial food production. Commercializing food production in the rest of Europe was a slow process that was not complete until the twentieth century. Commercialization could not begin as long as communal tenure controlled land use because this gave peasants control of their labour expenditures. As long as they controlled labour expenditures they would produce only subsistence amounts of food. When landholders attempted to coerce more labour from peasant tenants in order to increase the amount of marketed food, peasants often rebelled. Peasant rebellions were endemic in western Europe during the centuries it took to end communal tenure; therefore, ending communal tenure must be a first priority of governments that actively attempt economic development.

What tenure will induce cultivators to produce assured food surpluses? Put another way, what tenures are available to replace communal tenure? Foremost is freehold tenure. Freehold tenure requires agricultural land, like city land, to have surveyed boundaries so that money taxes can be levied on it. The money to pay the taxes is the responsibility of the household that cultivates the land. Cultivating households must produce sufficiently large harvests to sell for sufficient money to pay the tax. Money taxation and tenure change are different sides of the same coin. Money taxation forces cultivating households to labour longer hours to increase food production to pay taxes (or rent) or be evicted from their holding. In other words, freehold tenure linked to money taxation helps induce the production of assured food surpluses. Other commercial tenures are leasehold and collective. In 1700 feudal landholders in **Europe** paid two types of taxes to the Crown: a labour tax and a money tax. The labour tax had two parts. Peasants were mobilized as foot soldiers and corvée labourers who helped build megaprojects such as castles, bridge embankments and roads. Their labour was no different from the corvée labourers who built pyramids in **Egypt** and **Mexico** and religious temples at Karnak and Tikal. Corvée labour (and slave labour), however, is unskilled and has minimal possibility of learning the commercial skills that accompany paid labour, money taxation and literacy. The money tax that feudal landholders paid to the Crown was on their estates as a whole. The money tax did not come from taxing individual peasant holdings because peasant holdings were in widely scattered strips that were held in communal tenure. Feudal landholders assented to communal tenure because they received a customary share of the harvest from each peasant household. When the landholder's share was sold it provided the money to pay the money tax to the Crown. The money tax was paid at irregular intervals when the monarch assembled feudal landholders in a parliament (or similar representative institution), where they decided how much to pay the Crown. Money taxes were usually used to finance war; otherwise, European monarchs governed with money derived from their feudal estates and taxation of commerce.

Governing elites of post-colonial nations seldom attempt to extinguish communal tenure on the estates of feudal landholders or on tribal land where customary law protects communal tenure. These governments avoid revolutionizing land tenure because armed peasant resistance is often strong enough to destabilize fragile governments.

The governing elites of post-colonial nations know this but development economists do not understand the risks of commercializing land tenure for peasant societies..

Development economists prescribe land reform (without calling it tenure change) as part of a package of polices to increase agricultural productivity. They gloss over how it can be accomplished. Instead, they concentrate their analysis on good planning of economic policies because they believe good planning will automatically motivate peasants to become producers of assured food surpluses to avoid hunger in poor crop years. Tenure change disappears from their analysis and assured food surpluses are never produced. Nor do development economists recognize that most members of governing elites of post-colonial nations have a different priority: becoming rich. Increasing national wealth by undertaking the politically risky policy of enforcing tenure changes in agricultural land has a very low priority. Post-colonial nations are, therefore, continually vulnerable to food deficits. This is still most obvious in sub-Saharan Africa

maritime commerce

In the fifteenth, sixteenth and seventeenth centuries European monarchies wanted increased money revenues for warfare and to reduce the power of feudal landholders. The source of this revenue was maritime commerce because taxes on maritime commerce were the exclusive property of monarchs. It was, therefore, in the interests of monarchs to encourage maritime trade. Merchants welcomed encouragement from monarchs if they could provide protection. Merchants and monarchs became partners in producing new commercial wealth. The assumption that motivated this partnership was that new markets would be monopolized by a nation's merchants and the Crown would protect this monopoly and derive revenue accordingly. By 1700 some European monarchs made the expansion of maritime commerce a policy that equalled policies of dynastic ambitions, territorial expansion in Europe and religious conformity. In this process both domestic and maritime merchants exerted continual pressure on monarchies to make promotion and protection of commerce the primary purpose of governance. As producers of new wealth, merchants wanted to be consulted about policies they believed would promote (or impede) wealth creation. Feudal landholders usually objected to the pretensions of merchants to share governance because they claimed that landholders were the proper persons to define policies that protected the national interest. It usually required revolutions to elevate commercial policies to the principal purpose of governance. From the seventeenth century onwards these revolutions occurred in western Europe. In the process, landholders who actively managed their land to maximize production of food grains or food products such as cheese and meat, or commodities such as wool and hops, joined the new political order. Like merchants, they measured their welfare and political influence by money incomes. For them, land became a capital asset, not a hereditary entitlement to govern. In summary, the revolutionary governments established in the Netherlands and England in the seventeenth century and in **France** in the eighteenth century governed in the interests of commerce.

By 1700, western European nations had established the roots of the global economy of the twenty-first century. The roots went in two directions: east to the Indian Ocean and **China** and west to the Americas. In the east, superior naval power from cannons mounted on ships forced indigenous rulers to accept European export merchants as permanent residents in coastal enclaves. Wherever possible, European merchants paid less than market prices for commodities they exported to Europe. They were never fully successful, but superior naval power allowed European merchants to dominate long-distance commerce. The best examples of European dominance of long-distance commerce were the enclaves of export merchants at Goa, Bombay, **Calcutta**, Madras, Colombo, Malacca, Macao, Nagasaki and Jakarta. Profits from this trade helped propel the economic development of European nations. In the Americas, colonies of European cultivators were established in Virginia, Massachusetts Bay, **Cuba**, **Brazil** and **Argentina**. Their purpose was to produce commodities that had an instant market in Europe. Principal among these were sugar, tobacco, cotton and ship timbers, but the most sought-after commodity was precious metals from Mexico and **Peru**. All paid high taxes to the Crown when they landed in Europe.

transportation

The huge improvements in ship design that sustained maritime commerce to the Indian Ocean and America did not happen for inland transportation in European nations until the eighteenth century. These improvements were canals, bridges and roads to carry wagons. They were coincident with the accelerated commercialization of culture, especially agriculture. A revolution in inland transportation similar to the revolution in ship design did not occur until the nineteenth century. It was railways. It is difficult to overestimate the impact of railways on the economies of nations that built them, because they speeded the movement of people and commodities at vastly reduced costs. At the same time they were an enormous stimulus to coal mining, smelting of iron ores and experimenting with engineering designs to apply steam power to other uses. Foremost among the new applications were marine engines that propelled iron-hulled ships.

literacy

Literacy is the basic commercial skill and is second only to producing assured food surpluses for sustaining commercial cultures. There are two classes of literacy. The first is functional literacy in peasant villages. It is the literacy of storekeepers, and is sufficient to write a series of numbers and do simple arithmetic computations that count the production of commodities by client households, and keep records of money of account for illiterate peasant households. The second is knowledge-acquiring literacy, which is required by persons who staff bureaucracies, clerks in urban businesses, or persons who operate transportation and communication networks. Likewise, persons who operate technically complex machinery such as windmills to grind grain, saw logs or pump water; or in order to earn profits in changing commercial environments, where persons must be able to learn skills beyond functional literacy. In practical terms, knowledge-acquiring literacy means that persons must be able to read printed instructions and understand technical vocabularies. Establishing schools to teach functional literacy in peasant villages is an initial step in commercializing food production. In most villages it is a tentative step because most parents keep their children out of classrooms most of the time after age 8 or 9 because they value their labour more than literacy. From the point of view of parents, illiteracy glues their children to the village community where large amounts of labour are transferred to them at young ages because peasant children are born to labour.

Economists often prescribe education like they prescribe land reform, as one of the essential policies of economic development. Their prescription assumes that the education needs of peasants and urban residents are the same. This assumption allows them to plug education into algebraic equations, but their econometric models say little about where scarce resources should be allocated, who should be taught, and what should be taught. Using city curriculums to teach literacy in peasant villages is likely to retard literacy acquisition because the knowledge students are supposed to learn has little relation to subsistence reality where peasant households have no reading material. Any knowledge-acquiring literacy learned by peasant children is soon forgotten.

technology

Three of the principal technologies of the industrial revolution of the nineteenth century were blast furnaces to smelt iron ores, furnaces to convert iron into steel, and high-pressure steam engines. Iron smelting became a small-scale industrial skill in the sixteenth century when foundries were established to cast iron cannons for mounting on ships. Making sufficient iron to cast cannons was expensive. The first technical innovation to lower the cost of smelting iron ores was using coke instead of charcoal. This was first done in 1709. The next metallurgical innovation was producing iron and steel on an industrial scale. In the eighteenth century the technology of making steel was an artisan skill. It was expensive and steel had limited usage. Among its most important uses were making muskets and swords. Steel became cheap after 1855 when Henry Bessemer in England invented a new furnace. It mass-produced pure iron to which alloys were added to produce steel. Steel became cheap. After Bessemer's invention steel rapidly replaced iron in most applications because of its superior strength.

This was especially true for railways. Railways were not new in the nineteenth century. In the eighteenth century wooden rails carried coal wagons from mine mouths to riverside piers where it was dumped into ships' holds. The wagons were pulled by horses. Wooden rails needed continual replacement, even when iron straps were nailed on them. When George Stephenson's steam locomotive demonstrated that it could pull a passenger train in 1829, it moved on iron rails. When cheap steel became available, steel rails replaced iron rails because they were more durable and much stronger.

A parallel technology was boiler construction. James Watt perfected a high-pressure steam engine in 1775. Its first use was to drain water from mines but it was soon harnessed to power factory machinery. When boilers were made from steel, steam engines could contain much higher pressures and their efficiency increased. When steel boilers were used to power railway locomotives, they pulled more cars with each car carrying heavier loads. Similar innovations in steam power were applied to steel-hulled ships and to power-manufacturing machinery.

industrialization

Many models of economic development require peasants to migrate from villages to cities in order to be employed as wage labourers in commerce and industry, especially industry. Industry takes precedence because it can create huge amounts of new wealth in a short time because urban migration supplied the labour to industrialize European nations. It did, but not initially. Industrialization in Europe began at rural sites where mechanical power was transmitted from water wheels to machinery that manufactured artisan items in new ways. Foremost among these items were textiles. The mechanization of spinning thread and weaving cotton and woollen textiles began in the mid eighteenth century and underwent rapid technological improvement. At the same time, power to operate textile machinery became more efficient when water turbines replaced water wheels and iron replaced wood in machinery construction. Machines made with iron were stronger and allowed higher operating speeds. Finally, textile manufacturing moved from rural water power sites to cities where looms were powered by steam engines. What occurred in textile manufacturing occurred for many consumer items: pottery, shoes, edged tools of all varieties; plus capital goods such as boilers, steam-powered pumps and machinery applied to cultivation.

But economic development need not evolve into industrialization. Denmark and **Ireland** made the transition to commercial cultures without industrializing. Denmark is governed in the interests of farmers who supply western European nations with huge amounts of high-quality food. Ireland is governed in the interests of yeomen cultivators who produce smaller amounts of food for export. Both nations have undergone economic development but remain primarily agricultural; nonetheless, both Danish and Irish cultivators measure their social security by money incomes. By the mid nineteenth century the Industrial Revolution produced unimaginable amounts of new wealth. It also produced the ability of nations with industrial sectors to project their power worldwide in order to enter new markets and acquire new sources of raw materials to sustain industrialization. Many of the needed raw materials would come from colonies.

colonization in the nineteenth century

After the end of the **Napoleonic Wars** (1815), England, France, **Germany**, **Japan** and the **United States** acquired colonies by conquest, protectorates and trade treaties. Governing elites in subsistence cultures were powerless to reject participation in the commerce thrust on them by imperial armies. Five policies guided colonial governance but enforcement was variable. The three most important were: (1) commodities produced in the colonies had to be marketed in the imperial nation; (2) imports into the colonies had to come from the imperial nation; and (3) colonial commerce had to be carried in ships owned by merchants of the imperial nation. Two other policies were optional: (1) only citizens of the imperial nation could be export merchants; and (2) all commodity exports were conducted by a monopoly corporation. After colonies were acquired, governance and commerce had to be extended into the interior. The first step was ending internecine warfare (feudal and tribal). All other changes that followed from the imposition of peace were designed to create a modern commercial sector that had safe trade routes from port cities to interior locations. The end of internecine warfare was followed by pervasive monetization. Monetization existed in most subsistence cultures before colonial governance, but it was not uniform and the variety of items available for purchase was limited. The Industrial Revolution provided an abundance of cheap manufactured items to replace artisan-made items. Edged steel tools, iron pots and machine-made textiles were clearly superior in utility and durability to clay pots, edged iron tools made by village smiths and textiles woven on hand-looms. Manufactured products were readily available if peasants had money. The money needed to purchase them came from commodity crops introduced by colonial governors. These commodities had an instant market in Europe. Among them were coffee, tea, cocoa, peanuts, tobacco, cotton, jute and rubber. At the same time, plantations were established on vacant land to grow these same crops, plus oil palms and sisal. These commodities paid export taxes and this revenue paid the costs of establishing governing institutions designed to increase the size of the commercial sector and protect it from internal disruptions.

What were the institutions established by colonial governance? Foremost was a central government dedicated to creating a commercial sector and enlarging it as quickly as possible. This was done by organizing a bureaucracy, a police force and a school system to teach knowledge-acquiring literacy. The school system was often a partnership with Christian missionaries. One of the first improvements in infrastructure was building docks where ships could be loaded from the shore instead of by barges while they were anchored in a bay. Equally visible were roads and railways into the interior. The power and permanency of colonial governance was confirmed by monumental building that housed hospitals, bureaucrats and mercantile businesses; and by new cities plaited with square grids of streets. Complementing the visible monuments of colonial governance were invisible public health investments. Hidden pipes carried potable water and sanitary sewage; and vaccinations and new medicines were available to all persons who had money to pay for them. A key policy in colonial governance was teaching a European language, especially English and French. Learning a European language was eagerly grasped by persons who wanted to escape a fixed status in a feudal or tribal social order. Fluency in a European language was necessary for employment in the commercial sector centred in cities; it was the opportunity to join the new social order where merit was rewarded. Such persons became bureaucrats, policemen, recruits in the colonial army and employees who operated railways and telegraph systems, drove and maintained trucks and, after 1920, operated electricity-generating facilities that supplied port cities with power and light.

When imperial governments transferred power to post-colonial governing elites, all of the ingredients of economic development were in place for them to participate in the rapidly expanding global economy. Economic development had already begun. This was the positive legacy of colonial governance. The continuation of economic development, however, depended on the willingness of post-colonial governing elites to mobilize the available political resources and use them to enforce commercializing policies. They had to intensify the policies they had inherited from colonial governance if economic development was to continue. The governing elites of most post-colonial nations have not done this, especially in food production. Except for commercial sectors in cities, subsistence institutions continue to protect subsistence labour norms and subsistence food production in peasant villages. All the economic prescriptions of development economists will not change this as long as post-colonial governing elites refuse to enforce the requisite political policies.

economic history

A branch of historical studies concerned with the development of economies and their broader effects. Analysis of economic processes at large developed from the **Enlightenment** and was further boosted by the growth of commerce and industry from the late eighteenth century. A study of the effects of economic transformation was central to the work of **Karl Marx** and an increasing number of commentators on the **Industrial Revolution**, as well as on changes in agricultural conditions. Early compilers of statistical data such as J. E. Thorold Rogers and Sir William Beveridge began to provide a basis for the evaluation of historical movements in population, output, prices and wages. Controversies over the causes of industrialization and the consequences of rural, urban and industrial change provided a major impetus to economic history and the founding of specialist journals and societies. In France, the **Annales** school of historians emphasized the broad geographical and economic factors underpinning human societies, prioritizing them over short-term, contingent political and diplomatic history. From the 1970s, the so-called `New Economic History' employed greater quantitative and econometric analysis, reflecting changes in economics. Highly technical studies of such issues as the economics of slavery and counter-factual analysis of the impact of the railways tended to move economic history out of the mainstream of historical studies, though other specialisms such as business history, transport history and financial history have continued to develop.

Ecuador, Republic of

The second smallest country in South America is geographically divided (into the Andean highlands, the Pacific coast, the Amazonian rainforest and the Galapagos Islands) and ethnically diverse, with Indians comprising around 40 per cent of the population. These divisions and sharp class cleavages have posed formidable obstacles to national unity and economic and political development since independence in 1830. A predominantly rural country, three principal export commodities – cacao, bananas and oil – have, at different times, shaped Ecuador's economy while extreme volatility has characterized its politics. Since independence, Ecuador has had twenty-one different constitutions and only twenty presidents have completed terms in office. During the twentieth

century alone the military seized power no less than thirteen times, and in the period 1996–2003 the country had six different presidents.

ecumenicism

– *see also* **Roman Catholicism; Methodism**.

The essentially modern movement to promote a greater sense of common purpose within the numerous, historically often hostile, denominations of the Christian Church. Its greatest formal achievement has been the establishment in Amsterdam in 1948 of the World Council of Churches representing 147 churches from forty-four countries, the fruit of the work of a provisional committee created in Utrecht, **Netherlands**, in 1938. The number of churches had risen by 1996 to over 300 from more than a hundred countries, including Protestant, Anglican, Orthodox, Old Catholic and Pentecostal denominations. The Roman Catholic Church remains outside, although closer contacts gained momentum under Pope Francis. Progress towards formal denominational unions has proved much more elusive although the three earlier Methodist sects united in London as the Methodist Church in 1932. Attempts to reunite the Anglican and Methodist Churches, however, failed in 1969 and 1972, but a joint 'covenant' to prepare for unity is under negotiation. Also in England, the Presbyterian and Congregationalist Churches merged to form the United Reformed Church in 1972. Of wider historical significance has been the thawing in personal relations between the Roman Catholic and Protestant Churches since the Second Vatican Council, 1962–5, at both parish and leadership levels. Doctrinal divisions over abortion, contraception, homosexuality and women priests, however, have deepened.

Edison, Thomas Alva (1847–1931)

A prolific American inventor who made substantial improvements in early electrics, telegraphy and telephony, and who created the phonograph (1877) and the hitherto elusive commercially viable light bulb (1879). Edison's creativity had peaked by the early 1880s and he notoriously overestimated the benefits of electrical transmission by direct current, but by establishing the first professional research laboratory he secured himself wealth as well as renown while his peers frequently achieved neither.

Edo

Modern Tokyo, established by the first shogun, Tokugawa Ieyasu, as the capital of **Japan** in 1603.

Whilst Edo was built as the administrative centre of the Tokugawa shogunate, it also became a hub of urban development and mass culture. All *daimyo* were required to journey to Edo to pay homage to the shogun as well as to send family members to Edo as hostages. At the end of the Tokugawa period, it was renamed Tokyo in 1868.

education

A process by which persons are exposed both to bodies of accumulated knowledge and to cognitive skills by means of which they can develop themselves and fit into their societies. The roots of modern education are multiple and various. Most societies have in some way developed a body of learning which has been passed down. Ancient Greece provided, for example, a tradition of the elite academy of philosophy which developed the idea of 'reason' as leading to the highest virtue. Roman elites, similarly, valued the transmission of processes which indicated social refinement. East Asia developed a state-based tradition in order to provide a clerical class to administer various regimes, under the influence of the scholar Confucius. Christianity, particularly of the monastic type from the sixth century or so onwards, melded Jewish, Greek and Roman academic 'schools' with clerical skills in the service of the church and state. As **Islam** expanded, particularly into Persian, Indian and central Asian lands, as well as the former Byzantine Empire, it too developed urban centres of learning to which people would travel, and along with the church, encouraged the growth of early science.

However, three critical historical events changed the terms of what had been a largely elite-driven set of procedures. The Renaissance, Reformation and **Enlightenment** brought to bear the idea that individuals could and should be taught via technologies such as books and writing to follow standardized arguments and procedures. The expansion and competition of states and military technologies after the fifteenth century also encouraged the development of skills and talents in a standard way. Finally, the idea, in **Europe**, of the individual – an awakened, self-interested and reasoning creature with a conscience who was not automatically associated with any one group, class or faith – emerged in the eighteenth century and encouraged the idea of schooling from youth to inculcate reason. This idea meshed with the need of modern industrial societies for basic literacy and numeracy, given the collapse of feudal structures and the rise of money and of large urban societies in which networks based on local intelligence and the

memory of favours could not cope. To this was added the idea of 'development', both intellectual and emotional, that was associated with the ideas of **John Locke**, **Jean-Jacques Rousseau** and other Enlightenment figures. This held that children should be 'liberated' in such a way that they could grow into their natural reason and goodness. Educational pioneers such as Johann Pestalozzi (1746–1827) and Friedrich Froebel (1782–1852) built upon these ideas and developed child-centred educational schemes which reached a peak with the ideas of Maria Montessori (1870–1952). At the same time, less radical liberals believed that the gradual decline of child labour in the nineteenth century allowed for a period of inculcation and training which would see the emergence of independent men and women. Churches and regimes, in reaction, saw the point of creating their own versions of 'schools' and curricula so as to train children in loyalty to them. Out of all these pressures, the idea of universal public education was born.

Attention should be paid, however, to the ways in which local religious and political cultures affected the growth of mass education. In Massachussetts from the seventeenth century, for example, education was predicated on the idea that it would allow for better Protestants in the future. Many English schools a century later, however, were supported by factory owners on the basis that the schools would provide more obedient and productive workers. In **France** and Scotland, public education was supported as a way of developing social mobility and encouraging the growth of a reasoning and innovative commonwealth. The rich, and those selected for higher education, still enjoyed a parallel system based around universities of Greco-Roman culture, or military schooling in mathematics and ballistics. It was also true, as the European economy expanded, that both competitive examination for a global civil and diplomatic service in the empires and later-life education after the accumulation of personal money in trade characterized what many would see as 'education' too. There was never any one 'system' of instruction.

By the late nineteenth century the question of mass education had become impossible to ignore in any society. In the West and western offshoots, education was seen as vital to the suffrage, which had been gradually expanded. In central and eastern Europe, a powerful drive began to embrace economic growth, which required the widespread dissemination of literacy, numeracy and engineering skills as well as the growth of law-governed economic systems. The European empires based claims of cultural superiority, propaganda and growth on the training of those they ruled in metropolitan languages and culture, and in East Asia the collation of books and western culture with Confucian and modernizing ideas encouraged the growth of education systems. This led to powerful literacy campaigns which eventually extended to a network of basic schools across the planet.

During the period of decolonization, nationalists embraced the matrix created by imperial education and replaced metropolitan languages, cultures and symbols with local ones, which at the same time elevated nationalist middle classes and idealists. The superpowers commenced programmes of rival instruction for newly decolonized elites, both 'in country' and through programmes of scholarship and support at institutions such as Moscow University. Powerful competition for the allegiance of teachers and education ministers, and thus for the hearts of their charges, arose via exchange programmes and the provision of educational materials. This process was eagerly embraced by the **United Nations** as well as other international bodies as a way of expanding their role in the developing world. Women's education, which had generally lagged behind that of men across the planet, gained greater priority from the late nineteenth century, with equal access to primary and secondary education for women in many countries. By the end of the twentieth century the UN could characterize the extension of education to women across the world as a form of empowerment equivalent to the direct induction of economic growth or the relief of famine, as well as a matter of human rights. Such a facility had also proved vital to the extension of economic productivity.

Education thus moved away from a matter of elitism through liberal individualism and the satisfaction of the needs of industry, the military, the state and organized religions, to a matter of general empowerment and integration. This was helped by the development during the twentieth century of standardized educational programmes worldwide, and by the example of primary, secondary, tertiary and lifelong learning as centres of profit, economic growth and civilizational vitality.

Edwards, Jonathan (1703–1758)

The foremost philosopher and theologian of New England Puritanism and an instigator of the first **Great Awakening**. Combining religious intensity with a sweeping intellectual rigour, he argued that all consciousness derived from the divine

will; he defended original sin and salvation by faith, not works. Doctrinal controversy over eligibility for communion lost him his pulpit in Northampton, Massachusetts, in 1750 for a harsher frontier posting. He died shortly after assuming the presidency of what would become Princeton.

Egypt (Misr)

By far the most populous Arab state. Part of the **Ottoman Empire**, 1517–1914, but autonomous under Khedive (Viceroy) **Mehmet Ali** in the first half of the nineteenth century. **Napoleon**'s attempted acquisition was defeated by the British at the Battle of the Nile, 1798. It was British-dominated after 1882 and a British protectorate, 1914–22. An independent monarchy, 1922–53, although British influence remained decisive. Egypt became a republic after the **1952 Revolution**, and British influence ended by the time of the 1956 **Suez Crisis**. Attacked by **Israel** in 1956 and 1967, Egypt then attacked Israel in the **Yom Kippur War** of 1973. A peace treaty was signed in 1979. It promoted decolonization and Arab unity under Colonel **Nasser**, and merged with Syria as the **United Arab Republic**, 1958–61. Under military rule, 1953–2012, the economic and political power of the armed forces was buttressed by American military aid after they brokered the 1979 peace treaty with Israel amid growing prosperity. President **Mubarak** led the government from 1982 until he was ousted in 2011, following the **Arab Spring**, when he was placed under arrest. The following free elections produced a narrow majority for the **Muslim Brotherhood**'s presidential candidate, Mohammed el-Morsi, but he was arrested and military control reasserted in 2013.

Egyptian Expedition (1798–1801)

Launched by the French under **Napoleon** and traditionally interpreted as the first step in the implementation of their ambition of replacing the British as the masters of **India**. Napoleon may, however, merely have wished to block Britain's access to India or, alternatively, to replace the Turkish **Ottoman Empire** with a new French one. He had once thought of enlisting in the Turkish Army, and he toyed with the idea of establishing a Jewish state in **Palestine**. The expedition proved a failure because, although Napoleon succeeded in capturing Malta, disembarking his troops in **Egypt**, defeating the **mamluks** there, and advancing into Palestine, the decisive British naval victory in the Battle of the Nile, 1 August 1798, made it impossible for him to receive supplies. His army remained locked up in Egypt through 1799. Invading Palestine in early 1799, he failed to take Acre, defended by British and Turkish forces, and was forced to retreat to Egypt with heavy losses. In July Napoleon returned to France, leaving his army to the command of subordinates. A British force landed and defeated the French at **Alexandria** in March 1801 and obtained the capitulation of all French forces in Egypt by September as peace preliminaries were being signed. The defeat left Britain as the dominant power in Egypt thereafter, but the French expedition with its complement of scholars and scientists did much to awaken Europe to Egypt's past and founded modern Egyptology.

Egyptian Revolution of 1919

The explosion of national sentiment triggered by the final collapse of the historic, though long nominal, power over **Egypt** of the **Ottoman Empire**, the promulgation of US President Wilson's Fourteen Points, and the success of many of the nationalist movements of central and eastern Europe in the wake of the defeat of the **Austrian, German** and **Russian Empires**. It also reflected the strong suspicion of most Egyptians that the British were minded to convert their 1914 protectorate over Egypt into formal colonial status. Immediately preceded by the foundation of the **Wafd** Party by **Sa'ad Zaghlul**, 13 November 1918, two days after the armistice, with the objectives of replacing the British protectorate with a directly negotiated treaty of alliance and of being heard at the forthcoming peace conference. The initial British refusal of those requests led to rioting and the arrest and deportation of the Wafd leaders, March 1919, although they were subsequently released and allowed to make their case. The revolution succeeded only in part. Egypt gained limited independence in 1922, but the British retained considerable influence until the **Egyptian Revolution of 1952**.

Egyptian Revolution of 1952

The revolution by the **Free Officers** movement which overthrew the Egyptian monarchy in the person of King Farouk (r. 1936–53), the descendant through his father of **Mehmet Ali**, the ethnic Albanian adventurer, khedive and virtually independent ruler of **Egypt** in the first half of the nineteenth century. Preceded by rioting and the burning of part of **Cairo**, January 1952, the revolution deposed the highly unpopular Farouk in favour of his baby son, Fuad II, 23 July 1952, prior to appointing Major General **Muhammed**

Naguib as head of state, 1953. Aimed to eliminate British as much as monarchical power in Egypt. In the context of the virtually independent rule of Muhammad 'Ali Pasha, the rebellion of **Ahmad Urabi Pasha**, 1882, and the revolution of 1919, the 1952 revolution must be deemed Egypt's first lastingly to achieve its aims.

Eisenhower Doctrine

The declaration by American President **Dwight D. Eisenhower** on 5 January 1957, and approved by Congress, that the **United States** would give economic aid and use its armed forces to maintain the independence of Middle Eastern states which faced 'overt armed aggression from any nation controlled by international communism'. The doctrine was an extension of the **Truman Doctrine** of 1947 which had promised similar aid to **Greece** and **Turkey** and had been interpreted as the American declaration of **Cold War**. The Eisenhower Doctrine was a continuation of the US policy of 'containment' and was prompted by the extension of Soviet influence in **Egypt** following the **Suez Crisis**, but could be criticized on the grounds that it dealt only with armed aggression which was the least likely vehicle for communist expansion and sidestepped the implications of the Arab–Israeli conflict. Most Arab states also resented the implication that they should take sides in the Cold War.

ejido

The Mexican Revolution's 1917 constitution, redeeming **Emiliano Zapata**'s goals, provided villages with *ejidos*, community-owned properties to be worked by individual families that could not be mortgaged, rented or sold. Presidents distributed millions of acres as *ejidos*. Over the decades, population increase and poor land made them impractical. A constitutional change under President **Carlos Salinas de Gortari** in 1991 allowed for their disposal or rental – regarded by many as the destruction of the revolution's heritage.

Ekwikwi (fl. 1876–1893)

King (*olusoma*) of the central Angolan state of **Mbailundu**, who ruled from 1876 to 1893. Ruling at a time when the long-distance trade in rubber was transforming central Africa, and seeking to modernize his country, Ekwikwi opened his lands to missionaries and freed trade. He was caught between a rising tide of independent local merchants that undermined his resistance and the demands of Portuguese imperialism which eventually overthrew them and integrated Mbailundu into **Angola**.

El Alamein, Battle of (1942)

A turning point in the struggle between the Allied and Axis powers in **World War II** over North Africa. A series of battles between 1 July and 4 November 1942 between the German–Italian Panzer Armee Afrika and the British Eighth Army were eventually won by Allied forces in a classic desert tank battle. The Germans suffered heavy losses and were forced to retire to **Tunisia** where eventually they were defeated.

El Niño

The normally cold waters of the Pacific off **Peru** (known as the Humboldt Current) are periodically warmed by deep currents, and this condition alters normal weather patterns around the world. In Peru, it produces severe rains and flooding in the north and prolonged drought in the south. Agricultural output declines and the government is forced into costly food imports and disaster relief. El Niño also causes the anchovy to disappear from the Pacific, causing fishmeal exports to plummet.

El Salvador

A small, densely populated nation on the Pacific coast of **Central America**. Rich volcanic soil enabled El Salvador to build its economy on agro-exports: indigo in the late 1700s and coffee by the mid 1800s. Its politics and society reflected a plantation model, with a tight-knit, wealthy elite dominating impoverished peasants. Leftist politicians in the 1920s focused on this social polarization and sparked the Salvadoran Army's 1932 massacre of tens of thousands of peasants. Military rule suppressed further unrest until the 1970s when civil war erupted in the wake of the **Sandinista** Revolution in **Nicaragua**. Significantly assisted by the US, the Salvadoran military prevented a victory by the leftist Faribundo Martí National Liberation Front (FMLN), and the warring sides joined the Central American peace process. After 1990, El Salvador witnessed a delicate return to democracy, though its social divisions remain an obstacle to national development.

elite culture (European)

Until quite recent decades, the term *culture* meant classical music, fine art, literature, opera and ballet, and the theatre. More recently, however, it has been extended to cover something closer to lifestyle, with concepts such as *working-class culture*. A term like *elite culture* or *high culture* has, therefore, become necessary to describe what was simply 'culture'. The new distinction is not completely helpful because 'high art' has always drawn vitality from 'low art' and vice versa, and what is 'elite' in one country or time may be 'popular' in another. Poetry reading in Britain, for example, has minimal public appeal but a Yevtushenko or an Akhmadulina could fill a stadium in **Russia**. Moreover, 'elite' can imply exclusive. Nevertheless, the production of high culture has always depended on the availability of wealth to reward its creators, whether in the hands of a church or an aristocracy or more recently a city or a business corporation. Elite culture is on the one hand the highest level of culture, but on the other the culture created for the elite in society, however defined. The opposite is folk art and dance, or vernacular architecture.

The culture of the eighteenth century tended to the elite in both senses, particularly in mainland Europe where the influence of the aristocracy remained dominant. The French comedies of Marivaux (1688–1763) have a highly sophisticated lightness of touch, reminiscent of the delicacy of Meissen porcelain, which is typical. Language remained similarly aristocratic – a common word such as *mouchoir* (handkerchief) being considered vulgar. The contrast with the much more robust English plays of the time written by Goldsmith (1728–74) and Sheridan (1751–1816) for much more middle-class (albeit upper-middle-class) audiences is striking. If anything, eighteenth-century architecture and music had an even more aristocratic bias than the theatre. The sheer number of princely courts in Germany and central Europe ensured a steady supply of patrons for composers and architects, and the fashionable baroque and rococo styles conveyed their sense of grandeur. The Zwinger in Dresden, commenced in 1709, and the Residenz in Würzburg of 1719 are leading German examples. The Roman Catholic Church in the Benedictine monastery of Melk, 1702–14, on the Austrian Danube was no less grand. Even in England, where the middle classes were ever more influential, their Georgian domesticity coexisted with the flamboyance of Castle Howard (1699–1712) and Blenheim Palace (1705–24).

The changes brought about by the **French Revolution**, the Romantic Revolution and, increasingly, the Industrial Revolution were profound. Eighteenth-century artists had been primarily craftsmen and their relationship to their patrons one of master and servant. The Romantic artist was a rebel believing in liberty, not least for himself. The concept of genius was born, and the artist saw himself as a guide. The great French novelist, Stendhal, declared that 'genius creates the taste by which it is appreciated', and the poet Théophile Gautier (1811–72) launched the concept of *l'art pour l'art* (art for art's sake).

However much artists were now seeing themselves as the new elite, they could not remain insulated from society, and that society was in profound flux, with the middle classes gaining cultural as well as political power. Balzac's *Comédie Humaine*, commenced in 1829, records the emergence of a new French society, and Dickens (1812–70) pioneered the depiction of working-class life for middle-class audiences. His exploitation of the cockney speech of the Wellers in *The Pickwick Papers* (1837) was as novel as it was comic. It must, however, always be remembered that Dickens subsequently, like Victor Hugo in *Les Misérables* (1862), was attempting to stir specifically middle-class consciences into social reform. Novels could not be written for the working classes because, until the later nineteenth century, few in those classes would have been literate enough to read them.

Nevertheless, the arts of the late nineteenth century were to become increasingly 'democratic'. The novels of Thomas Hardy (1840–1928) depicted rural life without sentimentality, as did those of Grazia Deledda (1871–1936) in Sardinia. Émile Zola (1840–1902) explored the grim conditions of the miners of north-eastern France in his masterpiece, *Germinal*, and the reality of prostitution in *Nana*. The same trend was reflected in painting where the French impressionists broached new subject matter, whether erotic, as in Manet's (1832–63) *Olympia* and *Déjeuner sur l'herbe*, or industrial, as in Monet's studies of the *Gare Saint-Lazare* in Paris. Toulouse-Lautrec (1864–1901) painted the seamier side of Parisian life as to some extent did Degas (1834–1917).

The part exceptions to this cultural democratization were opera and ballet. The staging of opera has always been expensive and its enjoyment exclusive in the absence of subsidy. Elite audiences, however, went to see and be seen and readily talked through performances. On the other hand, hired 'claques' booed and cheered Italian performances in the roughest manner. Verdi (1813–1901) and Puccini (1858–1924) nevertheless took Italian opera to new heights of achievement and popularity. The art of ballet has been elite since its modern origins in the French court of the seventeenth century and in the Imperial Ballet School founded in St Petersburg in 1775. Moreover, it is probably the most disciplined and sophisticated of all western art forms. Nevertheless Russian ballets with music

by Tchaikovsky have, like the Italian opera of Verdi, secured mass popularity.

The cultural history of the twentieth century was as fragmented as the political. Art forms became increasingly experimental and artists often self-absorbed. Much was conspicuously cerebral, and 'high-brow' became a meaningful classification. Elite meant 'intellectual'. Audiences claimed 'not to understand' modern art, literature and music. On the other hand, Berthold Brecht (1898–1956), in the febrile atmosphere of Weimar Germany, introduced both cinema newsreels and the street music of Kurt Weill into his plays, underlining their Communist message. The Bolshevik Revolution in Russia had led to an inversion there of the very meaning of the word *elite*. The elite were now the proletariat and the purpose of art was to serve the proletarian revolution. The Moscow Metro and Stalinist 'wedding cake' architecture were palaces for the people. Socialist realism prevailed in art, literature and even music. Prokofiev, Khachaturian and Shostakovich succeeded in producing accessible popular works, a number of which are twentieth-century classics, as well as their more introverted masterpieces.

Ellis Island

Ellis Island, in New York harbour, was the entrance point for over 12 million steerage-class immigrants to the **United States** from 1892 to 1954. First- and second-class immigrants entered without inspection. Prior to 1892 immigrants were processed at Castle Garden on Manhattan. After the 1920s Quota Acts, and in the Great Depression, Ellis Island became redundant. It was closed in 1954, and, after many years dereliction, became the National Museum of Immigration in 1990.

Emancipation Act (British)

Legislation to abolish the system of slavery in the British Empire was passed by Parliament in 1833. The 1833 Act of Emancipation freed all enslaved people in the British Empire as of 1 August 1834. The Act, however, did not free enslaved people unconditionally; for four years afterwards for skilled or domestic workers or six for field workers, the former slaves were considered apprentices. Slave owners were compensated for their lost property; the former slaves were not.

emancipation of the serfs (Russian)

A response to economic and military backwardness revealed in the Crimean War, the Emancipation Proclamation of Tsar **Alexander II** (1818–81) on 3 March 1861 (19 February, old style) released the third of Russia's population who were serfs of private landowners as part of reforms intended to encourage a market economy. Freed peasants remained liable to labour service to their former owners for nine years and to make redemption payments for land they were allocated.

Emancipation Proclamation (American)

Emancipation was promised by **Abraham Lincoln** in September 1862, and was put into effect through the final Emancipation Proclamation of 1 January 1863. This declared that all those enslaved in states 'in rebellion' against the **United States** were now free. Lincoln had initially harboured doubts about his authority to emancipate, but justified the measure by relating it to military necessity and the war powers of the president. He also believed that emancipation would end any chance that **Britain** or **France** would lend their support to the Confederacy. Word of emancipation spread, and while **African Americans** greeted the news with great joy, most waited for Union forces to arrive before claiming their freedom. Others enlisted in the Union Army. Since with very few exceptions the Emancipation Proclamation freed only those in Confederate states, and not slaves within Union lines, it was only with the passing of the 13th Amendment of 1865 that any doubts about the legality of emancipation were removed.

Embargo Act (1807) (American)

An act of Congress adopted on 22 December 1807 at the behest of President **Thomas Jefferson** which prohibited American exports until the trading rights of the **United States** were recognized. The embargo was intended to apply economic coercion to **France**, and particularly **Britain**, in order to prevent their interference with American trade during the prolonged war between those two countries. The embargo caused severe economic hardship within the United States while doing little to promote American rights abroad. It was repealed in March 1809.

Emecheta, Buchi (1944–)

Nigerian-born writer who immigrated to London and now lives and works in **Britain**. Emecheta was orphaned in her teens and had to work and attain her education on her own, eventually producing her first pubished work in newspaper columns. Although her early work was autobiographical, she took up African themes, best represented by her book *The Joys of Motherhood* (1979). She is often a harsh critic of traditional Africa, especially women's roles.

encomienda

A grant of Indian tribute and labour services initially given to individual Spanish conquistadors and early settlers in the Americas. The largest *encomiendas* appeared in Mexico and the Andes, where they underpinned an emerging commercial economy based on ranching, agriculture and mining. Declining indigenous population, royal restrictions and labour demands by non-*encomenderos* soon reduced their importance. In more peripheral regions, however, the *encomienda* remained a dominant socio-economic institution for most of the colonial era.

Encyclopédie

– *see also* **Enlightenment**.

Originated in the concept of the publisher, Le Breton, in 1745 to supply France with a modern dictionary by translating the *English Cyclopaedia* of Chambers including its technical plates. **Denis Diderot**, to whom the task was entrusted in 1746, transformed the *Encyclopédie* into a compendium of the latest knowledge in all fields, designed to promote progress and destroy prejudice. Aided by d'Alembert as scientific contributor and by other experts, Diderot as editor released the first two volumes in 1751, but hostility to the section on theology from Jesuits and Jansenists led to a ban on sales and the seizure of copies in 1752. The intervention of Mme de Pompadour and others, however, permitted publication of all seventeen volumes by 1765. The *Encyclopédie* sums up more than any other work the eighteenth-century faith in reason and its optimism that human happiness can be secured by the progress of civilization.

end of history

The philosopher Francis Fukuyama (1952–) borrowed this phrase from past writers and in 1992 used it in the title of a widely discussed book in which he argued that the end of the **Cold War** signalled the triumph of democracy and liberal capitalism over socialism, bringing to a conclusion an age-old struggle and ending history as hitherto conceived. Unlike other neoconservatives, Fukuyama was philosophically opposed to the continuation of militarism in American foreign policy.

energy

The eighteenth century opened with a pattern of energy use that had changed very little over the previous half a century. Industrial energy, in the sense of energy for such purposes as corn grinding and iron working, came predominantly from what would now be described as renewable sources. Water had been harnessed by creating a race which turned a mill wheel, or alternatively by damming to create a fall of water sufficient to power the iron-workers' hammers. Wind drove the windmills which provided another means of cereal grinding and, in lowland areas, most famously the **Netherlands**, powered the pumps integral to the vital tasks of land drainage and sea defence. It also provided much of the energy needed for transport not supplied by the horse, the donkey or the camel. The sailing ship was the most obvious, and was supplemented on inland waterways by the sailing barge, or wherry. For all their limitations, such forms of transport were frequently safer, faster and cheaper than overland transport, which suffered from bad or non-existent roads, the finite energy of horse or donkey, and often brigandage and punitive transit taxes.

Nevertheless, horse power had gained a new significance with the development of the horse-drawn canal barge. The eighteenth century saw a positive explosion of canal building in Britain, as the home of the Industrial Revolution, to meet the new demand for the mass transport of raw materials and manufactured goods. It was, however, **France** in the preceding century which had seen the first of the truly modern European canals, the Canal du Midi, constructed between 1661 and 1681, and finally commissioned in 1692. It linked Toulouse with the Mediterranean and, via the rivers Aude and Garonne, created a through waterway for the first time between the Atlantic and the Mediterranean.

Energy for heat in the home normally came from the best source locally available, which usually meant wood. Where wood was scarce, even dung could provide a poor substitute. **Ireland** long depended on peat, semi-carbonated, decomposed vegetable matter. Coal itself was a luxury in view of the difficulty of transporting it from the limited number of places where it could be mined from near the surface, although there had been an established trade in 'sea coal' between Tyneside and London by the fourteenth century. Much of the wood used, however, both in the home, particularly for cooking, and in industry for such purposes as smelting, was in the processed form of charcoal, which gave a much higher and much more consistent level of heat than was then possible from a traditional fire.

birth of the Steam Age

These traditional energy sources had real merits, notably in many cases their renewability and intrinsic economy. Nevertheless, given the technology of the time, they could not supply the much higher levels of energy required by many of the new inventions of the Industrial Revolution, most of which, therefore, depended on steam power generated from coal. Frenchman Denis Papin (1647–1714) is widely credited with first appreciating the potential of steam as a power source, but it was the British, Thomas Newcomen (1663–1729), James Watt (1736–1819) and Richard Trevithick (1771–1833) who developed and perfected the stationary steam engines on which the whole Industrial Revolution depended. Equally important, Trevithick developed the first working steam locomotive in 1804 – his 'Catch-me-who-can' ran round a demonstration track in London's Euston Square as early as 1808. The Stockton and Darlington Railway in the north-east of England followed as the world's first goods and passenger railway to be operated by steam in 1825, and with the appearance of George Stephenson's *Rocket* in 1829 the steam locomotive had acquired all its developed features. With the opening of the Liverpool and Manchester Railway the following year, steam was clearly the key to all future development in industry and transport, whether of goods or people. Canals across Britain rapidly fell into disuse and on occasion even provided the route for the substitute railway.

This new steam-powered economy, dependent as it was on coal and iron, not only generated wealth but also altered the whole balance of power within and between nations. The north of England and South Wales acquired an importance they had never known before and the Ruhr and Silesia were crucial to the power of the emerging new **Germany**. **China** and **India** are equally dependent today, with coal meeting the majority of their energy needs. European countries such as France and the new **Italy**, with limited resources of coal and/or iron, found themselves at a serious disadvantage. At a very basic level, coal and iron were the raw materials of an armaments industry, and **World War I** can be plausibly seen as the globe's first, and arguably last, war between economies as much as between armies.

Steam-powered railways were similarly strategic, contributing greatly to the development of **Canada**, **Russia** and the **United States** as modern nations. They were also a major factor in military calculations. It is well known that the German attack in the west in World War I was tied to the railway timetables but less well known that the Prussians in the 1850s had been opposed to a railway between Berlin and Görlitz because it might be used by an Austrian Army invading from **Bohemia**. The Russians were so conscious of this military dimension that their whole system was laid to a different gauge from that of their European neighbours as an integral part of defence planning.

coal gas

The developed world's dependence on coal was complemented by its wide use of coal gas for lighting, cooking and heating. Coal gas was produced by the destructive distillation of coal which turned it on the one hand into coke, a comparatively smokeless fuel which burned with less intensity than coal but with the greater consistency, which had previously been associated with charcoal, and on the other into coal gas. It was first used commercially for lighting in 1792, in Cornwall, England. By 1823, 213 London streets were lit by gas. It was only, though, with the invention of the gas mantle in 1887 by Carl Auer, a chemist in Bunsen's laboratory in Heidelberg, Germany, that gas lighting could become the genuine precursor of modern standards of lighting in the home.

Gas lighting of streets and other public places such as railway stations lasted in some places until the 1950s and even 1960s, when it was replaced by electricity, but coal gas, which could be used even in refrigerators, retained a highly competitive position for kitchen cookers and domestic fires, which it in practice still keeps, although coal gas was replaced by natural gas in the 1960s with beneficial effects for the industry's image. Coal gas was always disadvantaged by its pronounced smell, which gave its first major entrepreneur, William Murdoch, the sobriquet of 'stinker'. In practice, the main weakness of coal gas as an energy source was that to be economically viable it had to be produced comparatively near to the point of use, which largely confined it to urban areas although some remarkably small towns did in fact have their own local gas, light and coke company.

electricity

Compared with the harnessing of steam, the discovery of the principles of electricity and their subsequent application were a much more international endeavour. The Italian Alessandro Volta (1745–1827) invented, with his voltaic pile, the first instrument for generating an electric current, and the Frenchman André Marie Ampère (1775–1836) first propounded the theory that magnetism was caused by molecular electric currents. They were followed by the British scientist Michael Faraday (1791–1867), who produced comprehensive theories of electromagnetism as well as inventing the first electric motor in the 1820s and the first dynamo in 1832. Some decades later, American entrepreneur Thomas Edison (1847–1931) invented some of electricity's most familiar applications, with the phonograph in 1877 and, with Sir Joseph Swan, the electric light bulb in 1879. By 1881 the small English town of Godalming in Surrey had become the first town in the world to have electric street lighting.

It was only, though, at the very end of the nineteenth and the beginning of the twentieth centuries that electricity began to establish itself as the omnipresent energy source which we recognize today. Amongst its many revolutionary early applications was urban rail transport, and in particular underground rail transport. The world's first truly underground railway opened in London in 1890 and was soon followed by the other railway lines which comprise the nucleus of London's modern Tube network. Extensive new surface, sub-surface and elevated electrified metropolitan lines rapidly followed in Paris, Berlin, New York, Liverpool and elsewhere. Their humbler cousin, the electric tram, was to be found in towns and cities across the globe. It was, though, Berlin which claimed for itself the title of electropolis or electric city. Building on the genius of such household names as Siemens, it prided itself on the scale and variety of its applications of electricity. The world's first electric tram had run there in 1881, and the Potsdamer Platz was lit with arc lamps in 1882. It was increasingly, though, a worldwide phenomenon. Radio and then television, the telephone, the refrigerator, the washing machine, the dishwasher and a host of other applications, all powered by electricity, slowly became the norm in the developed world, although often some decades after their original invention. It is a phenomenon which is now spreading apace through most of the developing world.

There was, though, always a paradox at the heart of the development of electricity as an energy source. Although its applications could be as small and humble in scale as the light bulb or the clothes iron, and, with time, as intricate as the modern computer, electricity generation remained largely tied to the burning of coal. In **World War II** young British men were conscripted to work in the mines (the so-called 'Bevin boys', named after Ernest Bevin, the minister of labour) just as they were conscripted to the armed services. In post-war Germany and Britain alike, the coalminer was seen as one of the most vital of all workers.

The only major exception to this dominant role for coal was to be found in the developed world's mountainous regions, where rivers and torrents could be dammed and their energy harnessed in hydroelectric power stations. **Switzerland** and Scandinavia were amongst the pioneers, although their installations have since been dwarfed by those outside **Europe**, including Egypt's **Aswan Dam** built with Soviet aid in the politically charged 1950s.

political implications

In general, however, the world's constant thirst for energy ensured that coal, the mines and miners remained highly politicized. **Britain** nationalized its mines in 1947 although the United States blocked attempts to nationalize West Germany's mines likewise. On the other hand, the creation of the European Coal and Steel Community in 1952, which pooled the iron and steel resources of **Belgium**, France, Italy, Luxembourg, the Netherlands and West Germany and was the precursor of the European Economic Community founded in 1957, was a self-conscious attempt to make another western European war impossible by taking out of national control the raw materials of a future munitions industry. Relations between miners and governments, however, were often tense, particularly when left-wing miners faced right-wing governments. Britain's General Strike of 1926 was one such confrontation and the 1974 strike, which led to the fall of the Heath government, was another. That tension was finally resolved in Britain, however, at the miners' expense when a long and bitter strike in1984–5 was broken by the government's willingness to override traditional strategic considerations, close most of Britain's pits and import cheaper coal from abroad. That decision was facilitated by the British government's knowledge of the availability of new energy sources such as natural gas and oil, but some other national governments have been more conservative. Germany, for example, still heavily subsidises its domestic coal industry.

the rise of oil

Unlike coal, the first known reserves of oil were to be found mainly on the periphery of the developed world – in **Romania**, **Azerbaijan** in the **Caucasus** and the **Middle East**. Although oozing oil could be ignited by lightning, and bitumen, a semi-solid form of petroleum, had been exported from ancient Mesopotamia to **Egypt** for such purposes as the preservation of mummies, oil had been of little practical use as an energy source until the development of oil refining. The first well to be sunk specifically for oil was at Titusville, Pennsylvania, in 1859, but the importance of oil as an energy source really dates from the development of the petrol-fuelled internal combustion engine. Dutch physicist Christian Huygens (1629–95) appears to have been the first to conceive an internal combustion engine, but somewhat alarmingly it would have been fuelled by gunpowder. The first truly practical internal combustion engines were those of the Belgian John-Joseph Etienne Lenoir and the German Nikolaus August Otto (1832–91) in the 1860s, but their vehicles ran on coal gas, and the petrol-fuelled internal combustion engine as motive power dates from a three-wheeled vehicle produced by Karl Benz (1844–1929) in 1885–6, the precursor of the modern motor car. The diesel engine, invented by another German Rudolf Diesel (1858–1913) followed in 1892. Internal combustion engines powered the first aircraft and oil consumption increased rapidly to fuel the developed world's growing number of cars, lorries, aircraft, central heating and cooling systems, and industrial applications. It is a trend which has continued unabated, driven by, and itself driving, such social and economic developments as ever expanding car ownership, cheap holiday flights, the growth in out-of-town supermarkets and hypermarkets, specialization and globalization. No less has it been driven by the extension of western lifestyles to the developing world, most obviously to **China**, which by the early twenty-first century became the world's largest oil importer. The International Energy Agency estimates that the global demand for oil will almost double in the next twenty-five years.

The fact remains, however, that some of the world's richest oil reserves are still to be found in the developing world. Perhaps 40 per cent are in the Middle East, often in countries such as **Saudi Arabia** which are sparsely populated and culturally conservative. The main practical exceptions are **Russia**, together with **Venezuela** and the United States. Many of the most influential members of the Organization of Oil Exporting Countries (**OPEC**) are thus to be found in the Middle East, and some experts believe that the potential of **Iraq** is even greater than that of Saudi Arabia. Most Middle Easterners are convinced that the Anglo-American invasion of Iraq in 2003 was motivated primarily by the desire to control and exploit those reserves. Be that as it may, it is a reflection of the political tension which has accompanied the exploitation of oil since the first western oil companies moved into the Middle East in the early years of the twentieth century. The assumptions under which the companies worked were colonialist or neocolonialist in spirit and the royalties paid to the oil-producing countries themselves were meagre in the extreme. This led rather inevitably to growing internal pressures to take control of the industry for domestic benefit, and Dr **Mossadeq**, prime minister of **Iran**, 1950–3, led the way by nationalizing the Iranian oil industry in 1951. The times were not auspicious, however, for such a radical move. The developed world was now as dependent on oil as it was on coal, if not more so, and in the throes of the **Cold War** saw oil nationalization as an unacceptable threat to its vital interests. A coup organized by the American **CIA** with high British involvement led to the deposition of Dr Mossadeq in 1953 and the substitution of a regime more amenable to western interests. Despite this initial success, the West was faced throughout the 1950s with a rise of Arab nationalism and by pressures for decolonization which, despite some intense resistance, particularly by the French in Algeria, proved ultimately irresistible. By 1962 Algeria's large oil reserves were in nationalist hands. Equally significant was the overthrow by the military of pro-western neocolonialist regimes, first in Egypt (1952), but then in oil-rich Iraq and **Libya** (1958 and 1969 respectively). Iran did not finally depose the pro-western shah until 1979. The balance of power was changing. Iran, Iraq, **Kuwait**, Saudi Arabia and Venezuela established OPEC in 1960, and in September 1973 OPEC raised oil prices by 70 per cent, and a further 130 per cent increase was agreed at the Tehran conference in the December specifically to punish the West for its perceived support of **Israel** against the Arabs in October's **Yom Kippur War**. The cost of a barrel of crude oil rose from 3 US dollars in 1973 to 30 US dollars in 1980.

The oil shock to western economies was profound, provoking levels of inflation and depression at the same time, which economists had thought impossible and which earned the name 'stagflation'. Western governments everywhere struggled to contend with these new economic realities and with the accompanying social unrest. Many fell, notably the Labour administration of James Callaghan in Britain in 1979, following the 'winter of discontent'. The shock to some Communist regimes was, however, even greater. The originally plausible policy of the Gierek government in Poland to kickstart the economy on the basis of western loans totally collapsed under the burden of indebtedness, ending the regime's

hopes of acquiring political legitimacy. Romania and **Yugoslavia** laboured similarly under mountains of debt. Ironically, perhaps, the consequences of the oil price rises were economic and political rather than strictly practical. Governments fell and energy efficiency was taken more seriously, but the demand for oil soon resumed its upward rise, as new sources of oil were found in politically less sensitive areas, notably the United States and the marine shelf off north-western Europe. The benefits to the countries concerned have been mixed. Oil revenues boosted the balance of payments in the short term, but also introduced a new instability as petro-currencies became overvalued and more volatile, reducing competitiveness. Perhaps more seriously in the longer term, they encouraged unsustainable levels of consumption. Although Britain, for example, became self-sufficient in oil in 1981, production reached a peak in 1999 and Britain has become a net importer. Only **Norway** appears to still enjoy substantial reserves in the North Sea. Not surprisingly, perhaps, the oil industry remains in the political limelight. In **Nigeria**, the industry has been accused of bribery and corruption as well as gross environmental damage. In **Latin America** it is often seen as an exploiter. **Bolivia**'s populist president, Evo Morales, alarmed the global industry considerably in 2005 by nationalizing Bolivia's domestic industry, initially without payment of compensation.

natural gas

Many of the considerations concerning oil apply with equal force to natural gas. Although its comparatively late date of exploitation means that it has never been mired in the colonial and neocolonial struggles associated with oil, there is the same arbitrary distribution with regard to population, resources and style of government. The largest deposits are believed to lie in the Middle East, western Siberia, under the North Sea and in North America, with Russia enjoying the largest national endowment. The world's fifth largest reserves, however, are believed to lie under Turkmenistan. The strategic implications of dependence on gas reflect those of dependence on oil, although the endowments of the national suppliers obviously vary. President **Putin** (1952–) is clearly determined to reclaim control of Russia's energy resources and to use oil and gas supplies and prices as levers of political influence. He has himself, though, had to come to terms with Turkmenistan over prices and is likely to pass the increases on to consumers across the previous Soviet bloc, which remains highly dependent on cheap fuel imported from Russia. Russia currently supplies a quarter of Europe's needs, and 80 per cent of its exports to the **EU** pass through **Ukraine**. The EU was highly alarmed when Russia tried to impose a threefold price increase on Ukraine by temporarily cutting off its supplies on New Year's Day 2006, and Ukraine responded by diverting gas destined for the EU to its own national grid.

pipelines

Natural gas and oil have the further similarity that they are equally dependent on pipelines for large-scale distribution, and the routeing of those pipelines is every bit as politically sensitive as the choice of supplier. Indeed, strategic struggles over pipeline routes have been compared with the nineteenth century's Great Game when the British and Russian Empires vied for influence over central Asia and **Afghanistan** as the gateway to India. The war in Iraq, moreover, underlined the ease with which a hostile terrorist group can interrupt supplies. Russia favours pipelines over its own national terrritory but has also bought control of the pipeline being built between **Armenia** and Iran, which could have been an alternative source of gas for western Europe. Russia is also building a submarine pipeline under the Baltic jointly with Germany, partly to circumvent any possible interruption by **Poland** or Ukraine but also to link the EU and Russian economies to keep pace with China and India. The US is apprehensive of this growing European dependency, as it is of pipelines across Iran which it fears could be cut for political reasons. The EU also, however, wants to see a submarine oil pipeline across the Caspian Sea to link up with the 1,760-kilometre Baku, Azerbaijan–Tbilisi, Georgia–Ceyhan, Turkey pipeline opened in 2005 so as to link the oilfields of central Asia with Europe and reduce its dependency on Russian energy supplies. **Kazakhstan** alone holds potentially a quarter of the EU's needs.

The end of fossil fuels?

The demand for natural gas is growing as rapidly worldwide as the demand for oil, and some observers foresee a succession of global energy resource wars as the inevitable consequence, even seeing the **Gulf War** of 1991 as the first of such wars. The United States may have already consumed more than half its natural reserves. Other observers postulate, however, that the urgency of the need to control the accelerating problem of global warming, almost certainly caused by the emission of carbon dioxide into the atmosphere as a result of the burning of such fossil fuels as coal, oil and natural gas, will force an abrupt move away from all fossil fuels in favour of renewable sources and possibly nuclear power in the comparatively near future. In certain respects it would be a return in a much more sophisticated way to the energy generation practices of the pre-industrial age. The similarity would be heightened by the likelihood that much renewable generation would be small-scale and localized, avoiding the wastage associated with the present approach. It is estimated that up to 60 per cent of the electricity generated is lost during distribution through the grid. Although the US oil industry in particular has lobbied intensively against the existence of any connection between global warming and oil consumption, many others in the industry are preparing for the possibility of quite revolutionary change. BP symbolically changed the meaning of its initials from 'British Petroleum' to 'Beyond Petroleum' in 2000.

Denmark has set itself the target of being a carbon-free economy, and at 16 per cent generates more of its energy from wind than any other country. Most striking of all, perhaps, is the revolutionary change in California where state governor Arnold Schwarzenegger directly contradicted the whole thrust of federal government policy under President **George W. Bush** by introducing mandatory carbon emission limits, favouring carbon trading and suing the car industry, in a state which has hitherto been seen as the home of the car, for the damage it was causing to the state's environment. The governor feared in particular that global warming would melt the snow of the Sierra Nevada mountains and deny Los Angeles and other Californian cities their water supply.

steps to restrict emissions

Concern at the potential of global warming to devastate the globe's economies and societies led to the signature, at the United Nations Conference on Environment and Development (UNCED) held in Rio de Janeiro, **Brazil**, in 1992, of the UN Convention on Climate Change. The Kyoto Protocol of 1997, pursuant to that convention, commits the countries of the developed world to reducing their emissions of a basket of six greenhouse gases, notably carbon dioxide and methane, by an average of 5.2 per cent on 1990 levels by 2008–12. The administration of President **George W. Bush**, however, withdrew the United States from the Kyoto agreement in

Spring 2001, arguing that it would damage American competitiveness, particularly as it did not extend to such major carbon dioxide emitters in the developing world as China and India. There is nevertheless interest in some American states and in the developing world in extending the European Union's emissions trading scheme (ETS), which became operative in January 2005, to the world as a whole. Such a scheme, which was one of the so-called flexible mechanisms endorsed by the Kyoto Protocol, sets a maximum emissions level for the qualifying installations in each participating country, which is progressively reduced over time. Installations which emit more than their authorized maximum must buy credits accordingly from those which have emitted less, and in this way a market price for carbon emissions emerges. The ability of such a scheme to reduce emissions significantly remains unproven. Nonetheless, the United Nations Climate Change Conference in Paris in late 2015 saw 196 states pledge themselves to limit the rise of global temperatures to less than 2 °C by the latter half of the century and to make the target legally binding if fifty-five countries agreed to them. The mechanisms to achieve this target remained unspecified but they implied a huge reduction in fossil fuel emissions, particularly by the developed countries. For while alternative energy projects were being pursued energetically by newly developed countries such as China, they and other major emergent economies such as India remain heavily dependent on fossil fuels, particularly coal, China alone consuming over 3 billion tons of coal annually and India committed to coal-fired power stations for its energy requirement into the future.

renewable sources: potentials and problems

In addition to hydro-electricity, the main sources of renewable energy are the wind, the sun and biomass. Geothermal energy is harnessable in some areas of the world, including Iceland, Italy, **Japan** and **New Zealand**, but not generally elsewhere, at least with current technology. Current technology is also normally unable to tap the enormous power of the tides on a commercial basis. Such deficiencies could be seen as a direct result of inadequate investment by governments in the necessary research. Solar energy is growing in scope, both in the form of domestic installations and in industrial-style concentrations of solar cells, but remains essentially underdeveloped, particularly in the tropics

and sub-tropics where its potential is at its greatest. The use of wind power is expanding rapidly in western Europe with Denmark and Germany in the lead. The world's largest onshore wind farm to date, however, is planned for the Scottish Hebridean island of Lewis, with the capacity of two nuclear power stations. Nevertheless, inland sites are widely unpopular because of their impact on the landscape, particularly in upland areas. This unpopularity has encouraged the development of offshore sites, although these in turn can cause problems for shipping and migrating birds.

Biomass, an umbrella term for a range of energy crops ranging from rape seed to coppice wood as well as for forestry wastes, avoids such problems, although over-intensive cultivation can damage the soil. The biofuels distilled from energy crops, notably ethanol, can be used as direct substitutes for petrol but are more commonly mixed with it. Their development has the added attraction, for a Europe with more agricultural land than it needs to meet its food requirements, of providing a new source of rural prosperity. This attraction has been felt particularly in France where rural depopulation is perceived as a pressing problem. Others, however, envisage large-scale imports of cheaper biofuels derived from Brazilian sugar cane, thus switching dependence on the Middle East to dependence on Latin America. The argument is unresolved, but the European Union's bio-energy action plan of 2005 envisaged bio-energy meeting 8 per cent of EU energy requirements within a few years. This was just part of the European Union's wider target of generating 12 per cent of its overall electricity needs from renewable sources by 2010. Critics alleged that the technical resources necessary to meet such a demanding target were not available, and others doubted the overall ability of renewables to generate the volume of power needed by a modern industrial society. Such doubts, however, often ignore the extent to which energy is wasted. Effective energy conservation and efficiency measures, more demanding building regulation standards and more thought to solar capture in the design and location of buildings could do much to reduce the perceived gap in future energy supplies.

nuclear

Last, and most contentious of all, is the role of nuclear power, which the British government, controversially, now considers a renewable source. Unlike most renewable sources, its potential is fully proven and many countries across the globe, particularly those which formed part of the Soviet Union or its sphere of influence, depend on it extensively. In 2005 Lithuania generated more of its electricity from nuclear sources than any other country on earth. Nevertheless, the problem of what to do with radioactive nuclear waste remains unsolved. Current proposals to bury it deep underground sidestep rather than genuinely solve the problem. The possibility of generating power from nuclear fusion rather than nuclear fission, which would not give rise to long-term waste, remains essentially experimental. Nevertheless, in November 2006 the European Union, the United States, China, India, Japan, Russia and **South Korea** formally agreed a multinational programme to develop nuclear fusion, focused on a 10 billion euro reactor to be built at Cadarache in southern France. Most people, however, remain exercised by the problem of nuclear safety and, despite the generally admirable record of the global nuclear industry, regard another disaster of **Chernobyl** proportions as statistically inevitable. Public pressure has led a number of countries including Germany, **Spain** and **Sweden** to decide to phase out their existing capacity. Others including Austria overwhelmingly oppose it. Yet others, however, not least France and **Finland**, are fully committed to it. Japan, which shut down its nuclear facilities following the 2011 Fukushima disaster, started to operate them again in 2015, while the Chinese leadership in 2015 projected an ambitious programme of building eight to ten nuclear reactors each year to combat climate change and pollution. Britain seeks to build new nuclear plants and has extended the operating life of some of its existing stations to 2030.

Engels, Friedrich (1820–1895)

Propagator and funder of the ideas and status of **Karl Marx**. Engels was a child of privilege, having been born the son of a German industrialist, but was turned to social reform and **communism** through the experience of seeing poverty and working conditions in British and European factories and cities in the 1840s. An atheist who disbelieved in marriage and social convention, he was much influenced by **Hegel** as well as his life partner and fellow radical, Mary Burns. He began writing newspaper articles and pamphlets on social issues in 1843, moved on to a study of the English working class, and, in 1844 turned a hitherto cool relationship with **Marx** into friendship in Paris. This resulted in a number of works, the most significant of which was the *Communist Manifesto* of 1848.

Engels outlived Marx, who largely lived off Engels. As well as editing Marx's works, Engels became the driving force behind the organization and development of communism as a political and ideological force in Europe and a major theorist of communism in his own right.

enlightened despotism

– see also **Enlightenment**.
An eighteenth-century concept associated with **Catherine the Great**, **Charles III** of Spain and **Joseph II** of Austria, but also with the French philosopher, **Voltaire**, and the king of Prussia, **Frederick the Great**. It was born of Voltaire's enthusiastic response to the young Frederick's desire from 1736 to become his disciple, but was initially soured by Frederick's invasion of Silesia in 1741. Nevertheless, Voltaire was Frederick's guest in Potsdam, 1750–3, where they discussed literature, philosophy and politics in the spirit of the Enlightenment. Voltaire concluded there his *Le Siècle de Louis XIV* (*The Age of Louis XIV*) with the fanciful creation of a Chinese emperor, Young-Tching, who was an exemplar for all monarchs. The Chinese were to be admired for their deism, peacefulness and virtue, and the emperor for his achievement of material prosperity for his people and his exclusion of religious fanatics. Such ideas were consonant with Frederick's own sense of duty. Enlightened despotism has been seen as a justification for absolute rule through service to the state and reforming administration, including the provision of law codes, penal reform, rationalized administration and attitudes to serfdom. Style as much as substance, the principal rulers above all did embrace some enlightened policies, but rarely followed them in foreign policy and made few concessions to political rights for their subjects.

Enlightenment

A term popularized in the nineteenth century for the rationalist, positivist and secularist movement which swept across the social and intellectual elites of the Atlantic world from the late seventeenth to the late eighteenth century. As a belief system marked by **liberalism**, market economics and atheistic individualism, the Enlightenment also enjoyed a revival amongst middle-class intellectuals and globalists in the late twentieth century. The original movement was diverse, and marked by regional distinctions. For instance, in Scotland and **Northern Ireland**, Enlightened thinkers such as **Adam Smith**, David Hume, Francis Hutcheson and John Toland focused on economics, psychology and the removal of religious or moral precepts from public discourse. These thinkers tended to favour a strong but limited small state which functioned as a neutral regulator of society and the market without invading individual rights or property. They were proponents of republican or individual liberty. By contrast, in eastern Europe, 'Enlightened despots' such as **Catherine the Great** of Russia took Enlightenment to mean the generation from a rational centre of organized, systematized law codes based on classical or rational propositions. In **France**, an elite class of intellectuals and business people favoured a rational centre too, which would encourage innovation, remove superstition and tradition, and elevate reason. Some of them took their cue from the liberalism of **Voltaire** and **Montesquieu**; others from the incipient dirigisme of **Jean-Jacques Rousseau**. This led to a great split in French liberalism between those who supported the initial stages of the **French Revolution** for its abolition of feudalism and elevation of rationalist economic approaches, and those who supported the state-driven **Terror** and destruction after 1792. It was left to **Napoleon I** to attempt to reintegrate science, the development of a civil code, and ideas of the nation state equipped with an efficient rational and secular bureaucracy with a conception of individual liberty and rights.

In **Germany**, the Enlightenment gave rise in the Protestant north to the ideas of **Immanuel Kant** (one of the popularizers of the name). Kant focused on the idea of a transcendental consciousness integrating a faculty-based human intelligence, on the logical development of republics and international organizations based on the rule of law, and on the proposition that all individuals possessed of the desire to develop their reason would eventually come to the same intellectual and moral conclusions and behaviours. Like many of the enlightened, Kant doubted the material and traditional, preferring to argue that the world was really cognition and perception, albeit one which could be rationally mapped.

In North America, both before and after the creation of the **United States**, which in itself has been described convincingly as an Enlightenment project, the movement was characterized by attempts to apply science, innovation and mathematics to political, industrial and agricultural life as well as to architecture and the taxonomy of human beings. Individuals such as **James Madison** and **Alexander Hamilton**, for instance, argued from an Enlightenment perspective in the Federalist papers for the scheme of the American republic laid out in the **American Constitution** as well as for rational

economics; **Thomas Jefferson** asserted the primacy of rights to life, liberty, the pursuit of happiness and freedom of, from and for religion; and **Benjamin Franklin** and **George Washington** pursued practical inventions and innovations in their personal affairs.

The Enlightenment popularized the idea that society was based on a social contract, though the implications of the idea as explained by Thomas Hobbes, **John Locke** and Jean-Jacques Rousseau were radically different. It tended to value child-based learning, again thanks to Rousseau, and to be anti-Catholic, given the intellectual and traditional force of Catholic opposition to individualist freethinking and positivist conceptions of the law and philosophy. Not all the enlightened were atheists, but it is fair to say that those who were not were believers in a God 'outside the machine', known as Deists, or even simply Fideists (believers in faith as a social enterprise) rather than people with a theological view of the world. The representative products of the Enlightenment, after all, were calculus, classical architecture and the market.

All of these pursuits, as well as Enlightenment aesthetics, at some point or other were based around the assertion that some truths were self-evident from science and simply needed to be uncovered by reason. This resulted in the rather typical Enlightenment project of taxonomy, exemplified in the attempts by **Diderot** to compile an encyclopedia of knowledge, by Johnson to compile a dictionary of language, and by **Burke** to develop a theory of responses to art and the sublime. As the representative supranational and social institution of the West, the Roman Catholic Church found itself divided and attacked as no other church by the Enlightenment (not least in the papal lands themselves). One wing, associated with a papal and Jesuit party, asserted the primacy of Counter-Reformation sensualism and spiritual discipline as an antidote to freethinking and secularism, and associated the Enlightenment with Freemasonry and atheistic republicanism. This group, which indirectly contributed to the already evident anti-clericalism of enlightened thinkers, tended to value the economic and political influence of abbeys, local bishops and religious orders, and sought to strengthen concepts of monarchy, state and tradition in ways which led them into a conflict with French intellectuals and republicans that lasted into the twentieth century. Another group sought to accommodate church language and ideas to modern arguments, to counter rationalism via dialogue, and to question the capacity of unguided reason to ever function globally; it can be said that this group were ultimately successful, without fundamentally changing the church, in the twentieth century reforms which culminated in the second Vatican Council. The Enlightenment can be said to be the progenitor of both modern market **capitalism** and **socialism**, whereas fascism has been characterized as a reaction against its notions of rationality and human equality, and as such, the movement has been fantastically successful. In its own time, however, it gave way to romanticism and materialism, as first sentiment and emotion, and then the industrial elaboration of science replaced its somewhat elevated intellectual idealism. In that regard, the Emperor **Napoleon** is often seen as both an agent and then an undertaker for the European Enlightenment, although others in the Habsburg lands, **Portugal**, South America and the Atlantic public sphere of books and ideas carried it on. Its influence was probably best seen not in revolutions but in abolitionist and emancipationist movements, schemes of international law, and the development of public and higher education.

enosis

An idea which prevailed amongst Hellenic peoples between 1838 and 1960 that **Cyprus** and **Greece** should be part of a common political entity. The movement for union tended to antagonize both Turkish Cypriots and the British colonial authorities on **Cyprus**, though it frequently found backing amongst the authorities of the Greek Orthodox Church. An armed Cypriot resistance movement to the British, **EOKA**, upheld the idea between 1955 and 1960, but then accepted the emergence of the Republic of Cyprus. This republic was destabilized by a coup in Cyprus in 1974, sponsored by the Greek military regime, which resulted in a Turkish invasion, and the de facto division of the island. Cyprus was then partitioned, and populations remained divided until the gradual reintegration of the island in the early twenty-first century.

Entente Cordiale

The name given to a series of agreements between Britain and France symbolized by a declaration of 8 April 1904. The agreements sought to settle global differences between the two countries and to draw both into a network of amity, joint security and diplomatic coordination. The Entente led to the creation of a bloc involving **Britain**, **France** and **Russia** to counter **Germany**, **Austria** and **Italy** by 1907, and involved military discussions, especially on naval matters, with France by 1914. With the

Anglo-Japanese Alliance of 1902 it also formally ended Britain's tradition of 'splendid isolation' and neutrality in European affairs.

Enver, Ismail Pasha (1881–1922)

A prominent **Young Turk** who was a rival of **Mustafa Kemal**. A member of the pro-German faction in 1914, he was inspired by the pan-Turkism of **Ziya Gökalp** and led a reckless eastwards drive against the Russians, December 1914, but his army of nearly 100,000 men was destroyed. A fugitive, he was sentenced to death for his part in the Armenian genocide by an Allied war crimes tribunal, 1919. Chosen by Moscow to suppress anti-Bolshevik Basmachi rebels in Turkestan, instead he put himself at their head in November 1921. A year later he was killed by Bolshevik forces.

environment

– *see also* **climate change**; **Columbian Exchange**; **energy**.

One of the central historical processes of the past several centuries has been environmental transformation. Humans have always altered the environments in which they live, but their capacity to do so, and their sheer numbers, has intensified the process in recent times. The three most important world-historical processes bound up with environmental change – and related to one another – are the globe-girdling movements of people, plants, animals and microbes in the wake of Columbus, the modern rise of population after 1700, and the global impact of **industrialization** after about 1800.

global exchange

A famous pulse of ecological exchange followed upon Columbus' voyage from Spain to the Americas in 1492. After the original human invasion of the Americas towards the end of the last Ice Age, very little interaction took place between the Americas and the rest of the world. The history of the western and eastern hemispheres, although showing some parallels, remained separate. But after 1492, the flora and fauna of the two hemispheres mixed together with tumultuous results. Eurasian and African diseases ran rampant among Amerindian populations, reducing them by 50–90 per cent between 1500 and 1650. This paved the way for European peoples and powers to take over, politically and otherwise, the Americas. Eurasian livestock colonized the grasslands and some of the forests of the Americas. Wheat, barley, oats, African rice and a few other crops found niches.

Going the other way, maize and potatoes spread widely in Eurasia and (maize, anyway) in **Africa**. How different would Irish history be without the potato? **Argentina**'s without wheat and cattle? Or southern Africa's without maize and manioc?

The economic globalization that followed Columbus and other mariners of the fifteenth and sixteenth centuries brought effects beyond a flurry of ecological exchange. Commodity markets emerged with long-distance reach. The demand for silver in **China** drove a worldwide mining boom, most rewarding in **Japan**, **Mexico** and the Andes. Mining everywhere changed the face of the earth, spurred deforestation and, in the case of silver, which was most efficiently separated from its ores by use of mercury, brought lethal pollution to waterways near the mines. Fur and hide markets animated a global hunt for beaver, seals and deer, altering population dynamics and ecosystem balances in northern North America, for example, where beaver had before 1800 played a key role in shaping the landscape (and especially the waterscape). Markets for sugar inspired the creation of a plantation complex, first around Mediterranean shores, then on Atlantic islands, and on the largest scale in north-eastern **Brazil** and the Caribbean lowlands. Sugar meant deforestation, rapid soil nutrient depletion and biodiversity loss. The plantation complex of the Americas was as much an ecological revolution, especially at its core from Bahia to the Chesapeake, as it was a social revolution. The process of economic and ecological globalization that Columbus began is still in motion. Overlaid upon it, since about 1800, is the emergence of high-energy society, based on fossil fuels.

industrialization

The Industrial Revolution is often regarded as a turning point in world history as seen from an economic and social point of view. It is even more clearly a turning point environmentally, for many reasons. Central among them is the change in the human energy regime. For most of human history, our ancestors used, per capita, only 1–2 per cent of the energy we use today. Prior to the harnessing of fossil fuels, people had great difficulty deploying enough energy to get lots of work done. The main way to work was through human muscle power, supplemented with animal muscle and in a few select locations, wind or water power. Almost everything, from building pyramids to carrying freight, required muscle power. Human muscle power was limited to what people could ingest in the way of chemical energy in their food, which

their bodies converted to heat and mechanical or kinetic (muscular) energy. It was, in effect, a solar energy regime. Plants turn a tiny proportion of incoming solar energy (less than 1 per cent) into chemical energy via photosynthesis. People ate a tiny proportion of those plants, and ate an even tinier share of animals that also ate plants. This process captured an infinitesimal proportion of incoming solar energy. This inefficient energy regime was a great constraint on how much work could be done, and therefore how much wealth might be created. It also accounted for the widespread practice of slavery in the pre-industrial era, as there was no more effective way to get big things done than to amass human muscle.

Fossil fuels changed all that. They represent a subsidy from the geologic past, bestowed upon the last six or seven human generations (and probably the next several as well). Their ecological effects were, and remain, enormous. While fossil fuels have a prehistory that includes coal use in metallurgy in Song China and the Dutch reliance on peat, their true historical significance, especially for the environment, began in **Britain** just before 1800. Great Britain lay towards the north-western end of a carboniferous crescent, the landscape stretching from the Scottish lowlands to Silesia. In 1750 this region produced less than 5 million tons of coal annually (almost all of it in Britain). By 1900 it yielded more than 400 million tons a year, about 60 per cent of it mined in Britain. Coal was now king, supplying the majority of Europe's energy requirements and half of the world's needs. It shattered the grinding constraints of the solar energy regime, opening up new opportunities hitherto not only unimaginable but genuinely unattainable. Coal was king for the span of two human generations.

By 1900 primitive internal combustion engines existed; they eventually created a vast market for petroleum. Oil, liquid sunshine, another massive subsidy from the deep geological past, carries twice the energy per ton as does coal, and by virtue of its liquid form can be transported more cheaply, in pipelines and tankers. By 1960 oil accounted for more energy use around the world than did coal. Between 1800 and 2000 total worldwide energy use grew eighty- to ninety-fold, making it the most revolutionary process in human history since domestication. Fossil fuels accounted for almost all the growth, and today make up about 77 per cent of all energy use. The modern age is the age of fossil fuels. The power of cheap energy to enable sweeping ecological changes, to make things happen faster and more broadly than they otherwise could, reached every corner of the globe. Cheap oil made the fertilizers and pesticides of modern agriculture feasible, as well as the agricultural machinery and transport networks that helped bring food from fields to tables almost everywhere. Without oil, the yields of agriculture would be roughly half of what they now are, and the quadrupling of human population since 1910 could not have occurred. So fossil fuels, environmentally important in their own right, are also important because they helped make possible the modern rise of **population**.

The best estimates suggest global population was at, or about, 600 million by 1700 (a rise of around 50 million over the previous 100 years). By 1815 it had passed 1 billion, rising to 1.25 billion by 1870. When war broke out in 1914 it was around 1,800,000,000. Thereafter, world population exploded, reaching 2.5 billion by 1950, 4 billion by 1975 and passing 7.25 billion in 2016.

For reasons much debated, global population began to edge upwards in the second millennium, and to gather pace in the eighteenth century. Slightly lower death rates took hold, perhaps a result of ecological adjustment to some infectious diseases, perhaps a matter of improved nutrition and famine reduction. Then, in the course of the nineteenth century, population growth rates accelerated, despite difficult times in **China** and **India**. That acceleration nearly stalled in the years 1913–50, presumably a consequence of epidemics (the 1918 influenza pandemic may itself have killed up to 60 million), wars and economic depressions, which sharply curtailed birth rates. But after 1950, politics, public health and perhaps other factors combined to create a crescendo of demographic growth, briefly topping 2 per cent per annum in the 1960s and 1970s. Human numbers more than doubled between 1950 and 2000. In no other period of fifty years, in no other century, did human numbers ever double. (Nor will they again.) These modern growth rates are fifty to two hundred times as fast as those that prevailed for most of human history.

To feed, shelter, warm and clothe the burgeoning human population after 1700 required intensified mobilization of the earth's resources. New patterns emerged, mainly a consequence of industrialization, fossil-fuel-powered transport and population growth. Best known among these new patterns is the giant plough-up of the world's grasslands. Between 1800 and 1950 about 17 million square kilometres (equivalent to today's Russia) of the world's grasslands were converted to other uses,

mainly crops. Another 9 million square kilometres (equivalent to China) followed after 1950. The prairies of North America, the Argentine pampas, the Russian and Ukrainian steppe, big areas of northern China, south-eastern Australia, the West African Sahel and much grassland elsewhere was turned to cultivation, sometimes permanently, sometimes only briefly. The last big push in this global frontier process came in 1955–63 with the Soviet **Virgin Lands** scheme, in which wheat replaced steppe grasses over an area the size of Japan (or **Sweden**). The process from the outset was intimately linked with the trends in fossil fuels and demography. Growing populations required the grain that these former grasslands gave; railways and steamships allowed the grain to get to markets cheaply enough to allow (relatively) poor people to eat it; and, beginning in 1920 or so, oil-powered farm machinery such as tractors made it much more economical to plough up the densely rooted grasslands and harvest the resulting grains.

The second new pattern was an enormous expansion of the world's tropical and subtropical plantations. **Plantations** – large-scale agricultural enterprises geared towards the market and usually worked by coerced labour gangs if not outright slaves – had existed for millennia, and in the sixteenth to eighteenth centuries had become the standard means by which to produce sugar and sundry other crops. Steam-powered machinery could transform cotton into clothes very cheaply after 1840 (as water-powered mills had done somewhat less reliably in the decades prior to 1840). This ratcheted up the demand for raw cotton, inspiring a cotton frontier at the expense of forest in the American south, and new efforts to raise cotton in India, **Egypt**, the Anglo-Egyptian Sudan, French Polynesia and scattered locations in South East Asia and **Latin America**. But cotton was only part of a new industrial/plantation complex. Tea, coffee, tobacco, jute, palm oil, copra and various other stimulants, lubricants, foods and fibres made the Industrial Revolution hum as smoothly as it did. Most of these new plantations were carved out of former forest lands, often as a form of shifting cultivation because the crops and production methods wore out soils quickly. Tobacco, cotton and coffee, in particular, depleted soil nutrients rapidly, and, absent expensive conservation measures, required new soils, enriched by the ash of freshly burned forests, in order to be profitable. Keeping the growing populations of new industrial cities fed, clothed and caffeinated thus led armies of slaves in Virginia, **Cuba** and **Brazil**, and legions of labourers elsewhere, to burn off millions of hectares of old-growth forest. Chinese cities helped drive parallel changes in South East Asia; in **Thailand**, a traveller in 1822 noted plantations of cotton, indigo, sugar and tobacco, among other crops, all of which were built with Chinese labour, organized by Chinese entrepreneurs and geared to Chinese markets. This had nothing to do with fossil fuels, at least not until steamships took over long-distance trade in South East Asian waters. But it was an early example of a process much extended by steamships, railways and factories in East Asia. The rise of steam-powered textile mills in Japan after 1880 created a new source of demand for Asian cotton, and a new logic to hack out new plantations in places such as **Taiwan**, southern China and South East Asia.

Food and fibre frontiers formed only a part of the impact on the land in the age of fossil fuels. Cheap transport – railways and steamships –- made mining ores in remote locations more practical, and the industrial cities could buy all the copper, tin, iron, bauxite and other ores that **Chile**, **Malaysia**, **Australia**, Siberia and **Jamaica** could yield. Industrial methods, such as steam-powered hydraulic hoses, made mining worthwhile in alluvia that otherwise would have been left untouched in the nineteenth century. These methods debuted in the gold strikes around the Pacific Basin that began in the Californian Sierra in 1849 and shifted to Australia, **New Zealand** and the Klondike in **Canada**. Hard-rock mining, whether for South African gold and diamonds or Chilean copper, also required fossil-fuel powered machinery and transport. It inevitably pockmarked landscapes and occasionally, through surface collapses, altered topography. Late in the twentieth century huge oil-powered machines chewed their way through mountains and valleys, extracting coal in West Virginia or gold in Western Australia. These environmental changes could not have happened without cheap energy: no amount of slaves with pickaxes could have done the work economically. Furthermore, cheap energy created transportation networks that made feasible intercontinental migration for tens of millions. Between 1830 and 1913, some 60 million Europeans crossed oceans in search of better lives, and many of them ended up staffing the farms and mines of the Americas and the Antipodes (and a few million more in Siberia). Another 20 or 40 million Indians and Chinese migrated to the world's economic peripheries, to the mines and plantations of oceanic islands such as Fiji, **Trinidad** and Mauritius; and those of Malaya, Thailand, **Burma**, **Guiana**, Natal and Queensland.

Without these millions of strong backs and skilled hands, far less forest could have been cleared, far less slurry dumped, far less soil eroded and far less prairie ploughed. Fossil fuels, population growth and urbanization worked their transformative magic not only in the world's far-flung grain frontiers, plantation zones and mining camps, but also in and around the cities themselves.

First of all, in crucial ways fossil fuels made the big cities of the industrial era. As late as 1500 no city exceeded 700,000 in population (the seven largest were in Asia or Egypt). By 1800, Beijing alone had topped 1 million. Only about 3 per cent of humankind lived in cities. There were good reasons for this: supplying a concentrated population with enough food and fuel was a difficult technical and economic problem. Cities in temperate latitudes (northern Europe or China) needed to control forest areas fifty to two hundred times their size in order to meet their fuel-wood needs. This put a fairly firm limit on urbanization. So did stubborn constraints upon agricultural productivity. After 1800, however, the development of fossil fuels reduced the requirements for fuel-wood and, with technical improvements in engines and transport, allowed cities to extend their footprint, or catchment, over greater distances. By 1900 about 14 per cent of the world's people lived in cities, and by 2000 very close to 50 per cent. Thus the proportion of urban-dwellers among our species quadrupled in the nineteenth century and tripled in the twentieth. In raw numbers, the urban population in 1800 was about 30 million, in 1900 some 225 million, and in 2000 perhaps 3 billion. This equates to a hundredfold expansion in two hundred years, roughly the same as the expansion in energy use. Nothing like this ever happened in human history, nor can it again.

environmental consequences

Until a century ago, cities were lethal environments. Their infectious diseases killed people faster than others were born, so that cities survived only on the basis of continuing in-migration from rural regions. London around 1750, for example, killed off half of the population increase of the rest of England. Yet villages produced enough migrants that London survived, and even grew, if intermittently and slowly. But between 1850 and 1930 sanitation improvements revolutionized urban demography, so that after seven thousand years as black holes for humanity, cities by the early twentieth century actually contributed to population growth rather than pruning it. Rural landscapes continued to send their legions of young migrants to the world's cities, more of them than ever before survived and reproduced; hence the emergence of megalopoli (cities with more than 10 million) and the urbanization of our species. In short, improved sanitation allowed urban populations not to die young from water-borne disease while fossil fuels (and its associated transport) allowed them not to die from starvation or cold.

The new, bigger, healthier cities were nonetheless often hellholes. Early in the age of fossil fuels, the most conspicuous cases arose where industrial cities sprang up from former villages or small towns, as at Manchester, Berlin or Chicago. These were the 'shock cities' of the Industrial Revolution, the places where water power or coal came together with uprooted peasantries and raw cotton or iron ore in a particularly profitable mix. In parts of the carboniferous crescent, such as the Ruhr or Silesia, former farming landscapes almost overnight sprouted iron mills and coalmines, metallurgical plants and railway yards in, around and between cities. The same things happened even more quickly during the 1930s in the **Soviet Union** when state policy drove a particularly frenzied industrialization.

These cityscapes and industrial belts became the most polluted and unhealthy habitats of the nineteenth and early twentieth centuries. Their rivers and canals hosted all manner of industrial chemicals and biological wastes. A British royal commission found that one murky English river made a 'tolerably good ink', and demonstrated the point by writing part of its 1866 report in Calder River water. Rivers and lakes acquired a frothy foam cover and often became toxic to almost all aquatic life. Some rivers and canals frequently caught fire. Meanwhile chimneys spewed out ash, dust, smoke, soot, sulfur dioxide and all sorts of hydrocarbon compounds, blanketing homes, gardens, streets, pastures and fields – and filling lungs – with toxins. Environmental battles took shape within and around the cities, as victims of these 'nuisances' tried to stop, or win compensation for, the harm done them. For many decades they lost far more than they won.

As industrialization and urbanization spread, so did intense pollution of water and air. Cities dependent on high-sulphur coal and those situated so as to experience frequent temperature inversions (trapping the air of the lower atmosphere) developed especially dangerous local environments. Tens of millions of lives were shortened by urban air pollution in the two centuries after 1800, maybe more than a hundred million. Veteran newspaper editors in Britain knew to leave extra space for obituaries when winds died down or fog settled on their city. The air in cities of north China today gives some idea of likely conditions a hundred years ago in Glasgow or St Louis.

After 1950, urban air and water pollution got worse and then got better. With the arrival of the motor car (1920s in the US, 1950s in western Europe) as a routine middle-class possession, urban air acquired a new source of pollution. Exhaust pipes joined with smokestacks and chimneys in fouling the air, and introduced photochemical smog as a new ingredient in the toxic stew. Where strong sunshine and millions of cars combined, as in Los Angeles, smog occasionally fooled residents into thinking they were under attack with chemical weapons. Meanwhile, the rise of petrochemical industries added a new tang to the brew of polluted waters, and the rise of organic chemicals – often persistent in the environment for years or decades – further raised the risks to health and life in those landscapes within reach of industrial processes. But gradually effective political coalitions formed against pollution. Precursors go back to thirteenth-century London, but successful and comprehensive efforts to check pollution coalesced in **Europe**, North America and Japan in the 1960s. Regulations, lawsuits, adverse publicity – all helped to change the incentives governing the behaviour of major polluters. By and large, the technical problems involved in radical reduction of industrial pollution proved simple. Skies and waterways improved markedly from 1970 onwards. At the same time, however, industrialization and the spread of automobiles to other parts of the world created new pollution loads in Brazil, India, China and elsewhere. Indeed, the number of people affected adversely by pollution climbed, because intense pollution came to the more densely populated lands.

Towards the end of the twentieth century two additional environmental changes attracted widespread attention, even though they did not have much direct impact on human health. The first was biodiversity reduction. Although extinctions occur naturally, in recent centuries they have happened at accelerated rates due to human actions. Birds and amphibians have had the worst of it, especially those on small islands. The auk and the dodo led the way in the eighteenth century, hunted to oblivion mainly by sailors. Thousands of other species followed, more often due to habitat destruction than to predation. The pace of extinctions climbed after 1960 when large-scale deforestation in the tropics began. Tropical forests are the world's most diverse ecosystems, so when farmers and loggers in places such as Brazil, **Congo** and **Indonesia** rapidly eliminated huge swathes of forest, they inadvertently killed off many species too. Concerned scientists wondered whether the earth is in the early stages of another great spasm of extinctions, the last of which took place 63 million years ago. If so, it will be the first caused by the actions of a single species.

The second environmental change of note was global warming. Climate has always fluctuated on earth for natural reasons. Normally the warmings and coolings were gradual. For example, the earth's average temperatures warmed in the tenth to twelfth centuries, and then cooled in the fourteenth and fifteenth, but no one could tell. Only in retrospect, with the aid of the analysis of tree rings or oxygen isotopes trapped in glacial ice, can we detect the onset of medieval warming or of the so-called Little Ice Age. The Little Ice Age was a global event centred on 1550–1850, during which temperatures dipped by about half a degree Celsius. This was enough to cause great hardship to grain-dependent societies in northern Europe such as Scotland or Finland. Then a warming trend began in the late nineteenth century, which while checked during the decades 1950 to 1980, continues to this day. Global warming reached its apogee (to date) in the first decade of the twenty-first century, but further heating of the planet continues. That is because the chief source of the trend, increased concentrations of carbon dioxide in the atmosphere, cannot easily be reversed. Carbon dioxide lasts about a century in the atmosphere on average, so what has been added in recent decades has plenty of staying power. And more is added each day, because most of the carbon emissions come from the combustion of fossil fuels, also growing each day. The practical impacts of global warming to date pale beside what is forecast for the future. But if predictions widely endorsed by the world's most accomplished climatologists come to pass, with global average temperatures up by four to six degrees Celsius early in the twenty-second century, then everything we now think of as important about our own times will seem trivial.

Environmental Protection Agency (American)

A US agency created by President **Nixon** in response to public concern, to 'protect human health and safeguard the natural environment' via scientific research, monitoring and standard setting. Formed by consolidating several existing units of government, it began operating in December 1970. Despite arguments over enforcement powers, the EPA has overseen real advances in water purity, industrial pollution and vehicular exhaust emissions, and has become involved in global environmental issues such as climate change.

environmentalism

Environmentalism, in the modern sense of self-consciously seeking to live within the constraints imposed by the natural environment, dates essentially from the early 1960s and was engendered by the coalescence of three broad strands of concern. The first was a new awareness that the supply of many resources, including fossil fuels and other minerals, was finite and that the demand for many other resources, often including agricultural land and water, was outstripping their ability to renew themselves. The second was a new awareness that pollution could not be rendered harmless by dispersal to the wider environment, by means of high chimney stacks, long sea outfalls and the like, but that it could have a serious impact many hundreds of miles away from its source. The third was a much more nebulous, but arguably even more significant, evolution in outlook which was coming to see higher environmental standards as as much part of a higher standard of living as higher education, health and housing standards. It was paralleled by a return to an older sense – part moral, part religious, even mystical, part simply practical – that people were an integral part of nature and had to live with it rather than simply exploit it. It was a reminder that aspects of environmentalism were age-old.

The new environmentalism of the 1960s emerged unevenly, stimulated by impacts that were local even if the causes were global in their relevance. Amongst the more powerful stimuli were alarm at the incidence of tree death attributable to acid rain and fear of the risks associated with nuclear power. Acid rain, a dilute form of sulphuric acid, affected West Germany's forests in particular because they were contiguous to Soviet bloc industries dependent on highly sulphurous fuels. Moreover, all Germans were highly conscious that if nuclear war ever broke out between East and West, their own country would form the battleground, and hostility to nuclear warfare fuelled hostility to nuclear power even in civilian guise. It was therefore unsurprising that West Germany became not only one of the world's most environmentally conscious states but also effectively the founder of political environmentalism in the form of a Green Party. Environmental concerns were, however, increasing worldwide, and 1972 saw the first global conference, the **United Nations'** world conference on the environment in Stockholm. This was followed in 1987 by the publication of the Brundtland Report, which argued forcefully that the world could only address its environmental concerns and reduce the associated cleavage between rich and poor by pursuing the path of 'sustainable development', defined as 'development which meets the needs of the present without compromising the ability of future generations to meet their own needs'. Its influence was such that the ensuing UN Conference on Environment and Development at Rio de Janeiro, **Brazil**, in 1992 endorsed it as the way forward, establishing its own Sustainable Development Commission. Sustainable development became a formal responsibility of the **European Union** under the Treaty of Amsterdam in 1999.

EOKA

– see also **Cyprus**.

EOKA, the National Organization of Cypriot Fighters or, alternately, the National Organization of Cypriot Struggle, was a militant group under the leadership of **George Grivas**. With the support of the Greek government, EOKA organized Greek Cypriot paramilitary action against British control of **Cyprus** and envisioned eventual union with **Greece**. Ideologically, nationalist and anticolonialist, EOKA used attacks on British troops and assassination of Cypriots seen as sympathetic to the British to force London to withdraw. These efforts reached fruition in 1959, when the British agreed to relinquish control of the island, which they did in 1960. In 1971, Grivas founded EOKA-B, which used similar tactics to pressure the Cypriot government towards union with Greece. In 1974, with support from the military government in Greece, EOKA-B played a key role in the *coup d'état* which overthrew the government of Archbishop **Makarios III**.

epidemics

Epidemic refers to an outbreak of a contagious disease that occurs in excess of what is expected in a given time and region and spreads rapidly. The interactions of an agent causing the disease, susceptible hosts and a conductive environment prompts the disease to spread through physical contact, coughing or sneezing, contaminated water, food or intravenous fluids, inanimate objects such as bedding and clothing or biological vectors, including mosquitos or fleas. Although a toxic industrial process may produce outbreaks, bacteria and viruses cause most epidemics. Pandemics (global epidemics) include bubonic plague, smallpox, typhus, cholera, influenza, yellow fever, HIV/AID and avian flu. Endemic diseases, ailments at consistently high levels over long periods, become epidemic if the virus or bacteria is more virulent than usual and a greater number of the non-immune become infected. Cholera, endemic in parts of Asia, became a pandemic in the nineteenth century. Diseases, such as malaria, which are widespread in West Africa and which entered the Americas in the 1600s, are usually considered endemic. **Tuberculosis**, a major killer in Europe and the Americas in the nineteenth century, was never considered epidemic.

Epidemics have reduced the labour supply, encouraged migrations, fostered rebellions, reshaped economies, determined military defeats and shaped the rise and fall of empires. In the 1340s the bubonic plague, which originated in south-west China, spread along the Silk Road through **Asia** to **Europe** where it became known as the Black Death. It depopulated Asia causing labour shortages and weakening the Mongol regimes in **China** and Persia. In western Europe the plague killed 60–70 per cent of its victims and led to labour shortages, regional migrations and rebellions contributing to more deaths in the 1400s. Smallpox from 1518–30 in Hispaniola, **Mexico** and **Peru** and measles in 1530–1 killed most of the indigenous armies and 25–60 per cent of the population, assuring Spanish ascendancy. Cholera originated in nineteenth-century **India** and spread along trade routes to cause five pandemics. It was particularly deadly in North America, **Cuba**, Caribbean and Spanish America and **Brazil**. It was again deadly in Peru in the 1990s.

The Spanish influenza pandemic of 1918 killed over 50 million people worldwide. In India 5 per cent of the population died. While World War I did not cause the flu, the close quarters and mass movement of troops contributed to its spread. Since this epidemic, western governments have promoted annual flu shots. HIV/AIDS since 1959 has infected over 40 millon and killed 10 million to make it the most dangerous pandemic since the Black Death. Avian flu, a pandemic potentially as deadly as the Spanish flu because of the limited availability of a preventive vaccine, began in Asia and killed over 1 million people worldwide in 1957/8. Avian flu has reduced the income of farmers and provoked consumer concerns about poultry. The danger of a new pandemic can be seen in the 2002/3 SARS (severe acute respiratory syndrome) epidemic. Although representing only 8,096 cases with 9.6 per cent mortality rate, SARS, a previously unknown contagious disease, received massive media attention because it spread rapidly through air travel. **Globalization** makes government prevention efforts more difficult. Ebola was another case in point. The World Health Organization (WHO), a UN agency headquartered in Geneva, **Switzerland**, is responsible for coordinating international efforts to monitor and combat diseases by developing and distributing vaccines. The Epidemic Intelligence Service (EIS) of the US centres for Disease Control and Prevention assists in identifying and controlling epidemics.

Equatorial Guinea

A former Spanish colony which became independent in 1968 under Francisco Macias Nguema (1924–79), who repressed all opposition, declared himself president for life in 1972, and outlawed the Roman Catholic Church in 1978. A third of the population were believed to have fled the country during his rule. The following year he was ousted and executed by his nephew, Teodore Obiang Nguema Mbasogo (1942–). The country returned to civilian rule in 1982 and Nguema was, as sole candidate, elected president, an office he retained well into the twenty-first century. The opposition condemned this and subsequent elections as fraudulent (each time Nguema polled over 90 per cent of the vote). In 1996 oil and gas reserves were discovered and by the end of the century Equatorial Guinea had one of the world's fastest-growing economies, though wealth remained unequally distributed and there was international criticism of human rights abuses. The country is predominantly Christian, with a small Muslim minority. Subsistence agriculture still employs the majority of the population.

Equiano, Olaudah (c. 1745–1797)

Olaudah Equiano, aka Gustavus Vassa, an anti-slavery writer whose most famous book, *The Interesting Narrative* (1789), claims he was born in Igbo country, south-west **Nigeria**. He initially was held by a sea captain and much of his early life was spent travelling widely in **Europe** and the western hemisphere. He purchased his own freedom and was educated by a Quaker named Robert King, and eventually became an important spokesperson for anti-slavery causes.

Era of Good Feelings

The period after 1815 gained this name in the **United States** upon the decline of the intense partisanship of the previous two decades. After the election of the Republican **James Monroe** as president in 1816, the **Federalist Party** dropped its opposition to the national administration, which now advocated neo-Federalist policies. In 1820 Monroe was re-elected unopposed, though partisanship continued in some localities. The panic of 1819 and the **Missouri Compromise** brought new divisions and so ended the apparent harmony.

Era of Princes (Zemene Mesafint)

In **Ethiopia**, a period of political disunity occasioned by the death of Iyoas in 1769 in which a number of powerful noble king-makers upset the succession to the throne and eventually built strongholds where they supported pretenders. Their wars and intrigues forced the abandonment of the capital of Gondar and ruined the country. The era ended with the victory of Tedoworos II over all other pretenders in 1855.

Erfurt conference (1808)

The 27 September–14 October 1808 meeting between **Napoleon** and Tsar **Alexander I**, when Napoleon urged him to threaten **Austria** so as to discourage her from supporting the Spanish revolt. Napoleon's efforts were undermined by Talleyrand, who secretly advised the tsar not to comply. The resulting Franco-Russian treaty recognized Russia's acquisition of **Finland**, Moldavia and Wallachia, but did not include any formal military alliance against Austria, although Alexander informally promised help in the event of war.

Eritrea

East African state on the Red Sea ruled by the **Ottoman Empire** from the sixteenth century, an Italian colony from 1890 until occupied in 1941 by Britain. After being declared an Ethiopian federal region by the **United Nations** in 1952, Eritrea was annexed by the **Haile Selassie** regime in 1962. The Eritrean People's Liberation Front mounted guerrilla resistance, gaining independence following a UN-monitored referendum in 1993. President Isaias Afwerki (1946–) established the ruling People's Front for Democracy and Justice. National elections were arranged but postponed on various pretexts. Eritrea went to war with Ethiopia in 1995 over a border dispute, 100,000 dying before a fragile peace was negotiated in 2000. Sporadic clashes continued and there was additionally conflict with neighbouring Djibouti in 2010. Its repressive regime has earned Eritrea the title of 'Africa's North Korea'. In 2009 the UN imposed sanctions in response to Eritrea's support for Islamists in **Somalia**. The country's main economic activities are subsistence agriculture and mining and the population divides approximately between Christianity and Islam.

erosion
– *see* **deforestation**.

Estonia
– *see* **Baltic states**.

Ethiopia
An ancient kingdom in north-east Africa. During the sixteenth century Ethiopia was subject to attack by Muslim forces from Adal on the coast and later from Oromo from the south. **Portugal** assisted but tried to take control of the Ethiopian Church. Fasiladas (1632–67) restored both state and church but in the early eighteenth century rivalries among pretender kings during the Era of Princes broke the state. Restoration by Tedorowos II in 1855 led to political unity, renewed expansion, the repelling of a full-scale Italian invasion at the Battle of Adowa (1896) and a modernization drive under Menelek II (1889–1913). Modernization continued under **Haile Selasse** (r.1930–74), interrupted by Italian invasion and occupation in 1936–44. Selasse's increasingly autocratic rule led to a military coup and left-wing dictatorship of the Derg (Provisional Military Administrative Council) led by Mengistu Haile Mariam in 1974. Selassie was murdered in 1975 and the Derg instituted radical economic and social reform, including nationalization of land and all other economic activity and a large-scale literacy campaign. Famine and war with **Eritrea** crippled the regime in the 1980s and the withdrawal of aid from the **Soviet Union** after 1989 led to its collapse and the occupation of Addis Ababa by forces from Eritrea and Tigre. The Tigrean leader, Meles Zenawi, installed a new regime which inaugurated a limited process of democratization and provincial devolution. Zenawi was overwhelmingly elected president in 1995, confirmed in 2000 and 2005. War with Eritrea in 1998–2000 further damaged a war-and drought-ravaged economy. Popular unrest and ethnic divisions continue.

ethnic cleansing
– *see* **genocide**.

eugenics
The word eugenics (from the Greek *eu* meaning 'good + genes = birth') was coined in 1883 by Francis Galton (1822–1911) in his *Inquiries into the Human Faculties*. An Englishman and cousin of **Charles Darwin**, Galton applied Darwinian methods to develop theories about heredity. Eugenics developed into a social philosophy which advocated the improvement of human hereditary traits through various forms of intervention: selective breeding, prenatal testing and screening, genetic counselling, birth control, in vitro fertilization and genetic engineering. Eugenics as an academic discipline at universities lost its scientific reputation in the 1930s, when Ernst Rüdin applied its theories to support Nazi Germany's racial policies, which embraced experimentation on people, and the genocide of ethnic groups. After new developments in genetic, genomic and reproductive technologies at the end of the twentieth century (notably after the Human Genome Programme), debates over the effective modification of the human species have revived.

Eureka Stockade (Australia)
An armed rebellion by miners at the Eureka diggings in the Ballarat goldfields, Victoria, Australia, on 3 December 1854 provoked by dissatisfaction over the cost of licences, which they saw as taxation without political representation. Over twenty miners and five soldiers and police were killed in the rapidly suppressed rising, but a Goldfields Commission agreed to miners' demands, identifying Eureka Stockade as a milestone on the road to representative democracy in Australia.

euro
The Euro; a common European currency first mooted in the 1970s to draw together the states of the then European Community by reducing transaction costs and creating transparent prices across the common market. The idea was displaced by the economic troubles of the 1970s and did not re-emerge until the late 1980s, though an European monetary system with very broad bands of currency alignment had been created. In 1992 the states of the **European Union** with the exception of **Britain** and Denmark pledged to move towards a single currency in a renewed drive to integration in the **Maastricht Treaty**, with a single monetary policy under a European Central Bank. The euro was introduced between 1999 and 2002 and existing currencies in twelve countries including **France**, **Germany** and **Italy** were replaced by euros and cents. A common fiscal policy, the stability and growth pact, failed to stop European governments running up large debts and raising taxes, and the bank had a mandate only to lower inflation with a uniform interest rate; but by 2007 fifteen of the

twenty-seven EU states had adopted the euro and the currency began to seriously challenge the dollar as a reserve currency in the world, bringing with it major trading advantages for Europeans. However, the consequences of the 2008 financial crisis, which placed stresses upon sovereign debt, illustrated the weakness of the zone, which lacked a common fiscal union. Given German surpluses in trade, southern European government and private debt and trade deficits, and no mechanism to alter the imbalance other than pragmatic governmental agreements, the euro entered a period of crisis after 2009 which saw austerity imposed upon the southern members and **Ireland**, and pressure upon Germany and the northern members to lend vast sums through the European Central Bank and the IMF to their near bankrupt partners. This process resulted in huge instability, particularly from **Greece**, which came close to exiting the Euro in 2014–15 but did not do so. The belated adoption of 'quantitive easing' and firm statements of support for the Euro from the European Central Bank eased the crisis from 2014, though problems of low growth, unemployment and bank debt remain.

Eurocommunism

The name given to a movement in western Europe in the late 1960s and 1970s which sought to reconcile socialism, economic justice and democracy in the framework of multicultural rather than class-based policy. Eurocommunists, following the work of Antonio Gramsci and also the Frankfurt school, sought to establish 'hegemony' by changing the ways in which language was used and interpreted as well as gaining control of institutions which had previously been bastions of opposition. They were distinguished by their distance from the **USSR** and their appeal to anti-nuclear, middle-class voters as opposed to the traditional working class, which was often at odds with Eurocommunist views of feminism, homosexuality, student protest and immigration.

Europe

A continent roughly defined by the Ural mountains in the east, the Atlantic archipelago and **Iceland** in the west, Scandinavia in the north, and the Mediterranean coastline stretching from Iberia in the west to the Golden Horn and **Bosphorus** in the Balkans. At various times in its history, political and military authorities emerging from one or other of its regions have attempted to unite it, most notably the Roman Empire of antiquity, but generally Europe has been characterized by division. For instance, large parts of Europe were Christianized

after the split between Rome and Constantinople known as the Great Schism, so that a significant difference in civilizations has been discerned between western and eastern Europe on a line roughly defined by the Danube and the Vistula with an exception for **Greece** and the surrounding lands. A further religious division which has been seen as historically significant was established between a largely Protestant north-west and a Catholic south and centre during the Reformation. Europeans have also, largely in the nineteenth century, attempted to group their nation states (a European invention) into perceived racial and linguistic groups. In this analysis, a largely Germanic north, to which the English peoples are usually attached, can be contrasted with a Slavic east and 'Mediterranean' or Roman south, the Celtic, Greek and Turkish peoples identified as outlying. In truth, the Roman Empire was North African as much as European, and its successor was in many ways the **Ottoman Empire** rather than the European lands.

No conqueror since – the major ones being Charlemagne, **Napoleon** and **Hitler** – has ever managed to create a stable pan-European state, and in this Europe differs significantly from **China**. In fact, European intellectual life has often been marked by an attempt to create universal systems, but to associate them with confabulated states or groups, especially when justifying colonial missions or aristocratic networks of privilege and control. In the twentieth century Europe was subject to two devastating wars, which spread via the empires across the world, and which followed on from the Franco-German rivalry established by the unification of **Germany** in 1870–1. The Great War of 1914–18 and that of 1939–45 can lay claim to be the worst in history, and gave rise to totalitarian regimes, the **Holocaust**, multiple genocides, and the near suicide of the continent's culture. However, from 1905, Europe had been developing innovative structures of international law which, in 1919, meshed with the ideals of **Woodrow Wilson** to create the **League of Nations**, and thirty years later gave rise to the European Convention on Human Rights and the Council of Europe.

By 1956, western European nations which were outside the sphere of central and eastern Communist powers had arranged themselves into the **European Free Trade Area**, the European Economic Community, the European Atomic Community, the West European Union (a defence organization) and **NATO**. Three of these were joined in the EEC (Euratom and the WEU) and this body went on to largely displace EFTA, absorb the east and archipelago lands such as the **UK** and **Ireland**, and eventually become the **European Union**.

The EU, which does not cover all of Europe but which is associated with the European Economic Area (a wider grouping), has tended to claim the title of Europe for itself and to associate its own imperative for ever closer union with that of the whole continent. This led, in 1999, to the creation of the euro currency and to a significant decade-long attempt to constitutionalize and reify a pan-European state. In the meantime, the core states of the UK and **France**, whilst engaging in their own military cooperation, refused to give up their seats in the **IMF** and UN Security Council to the EU, and by 2010 worries about trade imbalances within Europe connected with the imbalance between Germany and everyone else had once again come to the fore. These worries, which threaten to break up the EU, are unresolved.

The twenty-first century thus sees Europe divided again, but with far less military and economic influence after a century marked by war and **decolonization**. 'Europe' as such, has considerable cultural or soft power and influence. This can be seen in the tendency of European languages, art forms and luxury products such as wine and clothing, to continue to be regarded as essential to the good life in a globalized world. The **Enlightenment**, and the subsequent cultural movements and reactions to it, were largely the product of European states, and therefore much of modern philosophy and academic life is in essence and context European. However, as with anything of the continent, a significant breach exists between the English-speaking areas and offshoots of Europe, and those influenced by the continental powers. This translates globally given the reach of the former British and continental empires into a clash of legal systems and business models. Europe also contains dynamic business and capital centres which form the matrix of a great deal of global investment, insurance and shipping, but this vitality is apt to conceal what appears to be a vulnerability to demographic decline and an unresolved, yet pressing, need to establish the real role of multiculturalism in the face of immigration. This latter point matters in that Europe has at various times been defined against **Islam** or **Turkey** (as the fifty-year postponement of Turkey's entry to the EU suggests) and the matter is considered potentially explosive, forming as it does a nexus for nationalist populism and resentment at the EU and globalization generally, as well as raising questions of identity which many Europeans once believed they had put behind them.

European Court of Human Rights (ECHR)

A judicial appeals body established at Strasbourg in 1949 which seeks to offer a remedy for any violations of the European Convention on Human Rights to those citizens of signatory states who cannot achieve domestic relief. The court as a whole contains judges drawn from every member state, none of whom are allowed to sit in judgement on a fellow national. Though non-binding, the decisions of the ECHR are usually respected, and often involve changes to domestic law and compensation agreements. They are also guiding influences for national laws. States which defy the rulings are often unable to participate in other European bodies or agreements.

European Free Trade Association (EFTA)

An organization established by the EFTA convention of 1960. Originally intended as a free-market alternative to the European community of the 'six', EFTA contained seven members (**Norway**, **Portugal**, **Switzerland**, the **UK**, Denmark, **Sweden** and **Austria**) but grew to include **Iceland**, **Finland** and Liechtenstein. EFTA was based on the idea of trade liberalization but suffered near collapse when the UK and Denmark left in 1973, then carried on as a neutral but efficient trading entity. Portugal left in 1986 and Austria, Finland and Sweden in 1995, leaving what many regarded as a 'rump'; however, common interests in forestry, fishing and oil, smaller populations, and more efficient institutions than the EU led to EFTA still accounting for a very lucrative 3 per cent of world trade and investment in 2003. The organization joined the European Economic Area in 1994 (excepting Switzerland) and thus enjoys a privileged status amongst the non-EU countries.

European Monetary System

A precursor to the **euro** established in 1972. The EMS sought to link currencies within the EC/EU to a central rate based on a notional 'european currency unit' or 'ecu'. The ecu was calculated with regard to the relative economic weights of member currencies. Members were allowed to fluctuate around the ecu within narrow and broad bands, in order to reduce uncertainty in transactions and to allow for transparent prices that allowed pan-European business decisions access to clear information. They maintained their positions by the use of interest rates and currency purchases. The system was very much associated with attempts to link other economies to the German economy, and was adopted as the formal 'path' to monetary union in the Maastricht

Treaty of 1992. This proved a problematic decision as the German economy slowed down after reunification and the British economy, which had joined the EMS in 1990, diverged from others. British membership was traumatic for the **UK**, leading to extremely high interest rates and deflationary policies and then to withdrawal from the system in September 1992 under market pressure which also forced out others. This crisis allowed a renewed system to function in a stable fashion and to move towards the monetary union of 1999–2002.

European Recovery Programme
– *see* **Marshall Plan**.

European Union (EU)
The European Union was by 2015 an organization of twenty-eight states which operates on the basis of a blend of supranational legislation and international cooperation. It emerged from the European Community via the Treaty of Maastricht in 1992, and can thus lay claim to a European tradition which dates back to the **League of Nations**. The union is based around seven institutions. The European Council is made up of heads of government and ministers from each state, and has an appointed president who acts as a secretary general. This council meets at least four times a year, and is not to be confused with the Council of Ministers, a shifting body of national ministers whose membership depends upon the particular law or issue to be discussed. The European Parliament, elected every five years, has powers of legislation and co-decision, and is based in Brussels and Strasbourg. A Court of Justice, with a subordinate General Court, issues binding rulings on the law of the Union (expressed in terms of directives, regulations, decisions and treaty articles) and a Court of Auditors monitors accounts. The European Commission acts as an executive body, with one commissioner drawn from each state and added to a president appointed by the Council for a fixed, renewable term. A seventh body, the European Central Bank, has what is termed 'quasi-privileged' status in that it can bring cases to the Court of Justice and is an EU responsibility, but it is most important for the seventeen members of the Union who have pooled monetary policy and currency behind the euro, an international currency. The EU operates on the basis of 'competences', and offers a model in which some key policies are within its exclusive jurisdiction, some are shared, and some are matters for the states, though the Union can offer help and money.

The EU is not officially a federal body, though citizens of states are citizens of the Union with Union rights which broadly correspond to the European Convention on Human Rights. Instead, it upholds – more often in the breach – the idea of pooled sovereignty and subsidiarity, with decisions being made and powers being exercised at the appropriate level. Nevertheless, many of those opposed to the Union – known as Eurosceptics – point out the tendency of the body either to expand its competences, deepen integration through new treaties every few years, or simply for the Court to make binding rulings. They also point to the lack of a state veto in Council decisions on directives about exclusive and shared competences to suggest that states within the EU are in fact limited jurisdiction facilitators of a federal body. The EU, through binding agreements, collects monies from each state, and possesses great budgets. It also has a flag, an anthem, a High Representative who acts as a coordinator of foreign policy and, nominally, an armed wing. A process for secession, involving the invocation of Article 50 of the Treaty of Lisbon plus a series of referenda in member states exists. It was formally invoked by the **United Kingdom** on 29 March 2017 following the UK referendum of June 2016. The level of integration in the EU, and its effective displacement of all other bodies within an European Economic Area in which only a small number of states are not EU members, has encouraged other regions and powers to pursue integration, and at present various schemes of Union based on aspects of the EU are to be found across the world.

evangelicalism (American)
From the Greek word for 'good news', evangelicalism is a strand of **Protestantism** that emphasizes Christ's redemptive death on the cross, the place of personal conversion (being 'born again'), biblicism and active propagation of the gospel. Like German pietism, it found its voice in opposition to rationalism, formalism and ritualism, stressing instead personal salvation and a true religion of the heart. It emerged in Britain and the American colonies during the first **Great Awakening** of the early eighteenth century. Whilst its focus on Christ as the means of deliverance, its scriptural literalism and transatlantic range recalled Puritanism, it was less inclined to respect formal learning, the elevated place of the clergy and the union of church and state. Evangelicalism made substantial headway in the American colonies, subsequently the **United States**, since its revivalist style and individualist doctrine more effectively reached

an increasingly mobile population than did the established churches.

The early and middle years of the nineteenth century witnessed a second Great Awakening of Baptist and Methodist gains over the colonial-era denominations, and evangelical involvement in reform movements such as **Abolitionism** and **Prohibition**. Evangelicalism declined from the late nineteenth century with the large-scale immigration of non-Protestants and the secularization of university learning. By the early twentieth century it appeared inseparable from Protestant **fundamentalism**, which combined a belief in biblical inerrancy with pre-**millennialism** and publicly challenged liberal trends in the mainstream churches. Evangelicals and fundamentalists built up an institutional base by founding their own colleges, but they kept a low public profile by offering no nationally cohesive message on the economics-oriented politics of the era. The formation of the National Association of Evangelicals (1942) hinted at differences with fundamentalism. After **World War II** prominent evangelicals such as **Billy Graham**, who founded Christianity Today in 1956, rejected fundamentalism's belligerent separatism from an increasingly **secular** world. They instead stressed **ecumenicism**, even with **Roman Catholics** from the late 1960s, and proactive societal outreach and conversion of new members as the more constructive method of engagement with the modern world. Evangelicalism thus represents a middling position between fundamentalism and liberal thought, though it draws more of its theology from the former. A similar post-war 'neo-evangelical' resurgence in Britain rekindled the Atlantic connection and bolstered the intellectual basis of the movement. Evangelicals from more than twenty countries formed the World Evangelical Alliance in 1951; it has since expanded into a hundred more.

Evangelicalism tends to be liturgically progressive and has enthusiastically exploited the mediums of radio and television in a manner that might seem to belie its emphasis on individual study of the written word of the Bible. In American political terms, however, the movement tends to be conservative. Support for creationism and prayer in schools, combined with opposition to **abortion** and **gay and lesbian rights**, has placed ever more evangelicals in the **Republican Party** since the late 1970s, although Graham himself has maintained a distance from the **Christian Right**. The end of the **Cold War** and the decline of the older Protestant churches has left evangelicals with an unclear counterpoint. Many now worry less about theological liberalism than they do about **secularism**, **postmodernism** and multiculturalism. The growth of Pentecostalism and the Charismatic movement has had an effect on evangelicals, who have become more interested in doctrines of sanctification than of justification, or of how one becomes holy oneself rather than the old debate about how God accepts a sinner. Any attempt at definition is inevitably problematic, but perhaps a quarter of the US population counts as evangelical. Along with Pentecostalism, it is the fastest-growing Christian movement in the world.

Exclusif

The *Exclusif*, a **mercantilist** policy, governed French colonial trade in the seventeenth and eighteenth centuries until it collapsed in 1789. Legislation began to be passed in 1670 that limited trade between French colonies and trading posts in New France, the Antilles, the Indian Ocean, **Africa** and **India** to French-chartered commercial companies or to metropolitan French merchants trading exclusively French goods. The policy was formally codified by two principal sets of letters patent in 1717 and in 1727. Both were pure expressions of mercantilist trade policy which laid out the conditions under which metropolitan interests dominated colonial interests in all matters of trade and manufacturing, including the prohibition on trade with non-French merchants. Modifications introduced in 1767 after France's defeat in the **Seven Years War** and in 1783 and 1784 (the *Exclusif mitigé*) reflected the growing commercial and political power of colonists, especially Caribbean planter elites, who argued vociferously against this metropolitan domination.

exploration

Exploration in the eighteenth century was essentially a continuation of that of the sixteenth and seventeenth centuries, which had been given irresistible stimulus by Columbus' discovery of the New World in 1492 and Ferdinand Magellan's circumnavigation of the globe in 1519. The prime goal was the pursuit of wealth, whether by outright plunder or by trade, usually on unequal terms. Closely associated with that was an assumption that the newly discovered lands would come under the sway of the discovering state and be evidence of its power. Exploration was to remain a key facet of imperialism until the twentieth century. Second was the search for land for settlement, then almost exclusively in the Americas, although **Australia**, first discovered by the Dutch, was designated a British penal colony in 1786–7. Little explored Siberia was to be used by Russian governments in a similar way. Third was the impulse to spread the Christian faith, which in the case of **Spain** and **Portugal** at one side of **Europe** and of **Russia** at the other was really a continuation of the struggle against the previously dominant **Islam**. Fourth, and a motive which remains powerful, was insatiable curiosity. The Spanish penetration of **Mexico** and **Peru** in the first half of the sixteenth century had revealed whole civilizations of which **Europe** had had no inkling.

The broad outlines of the continents, exclusive of Antartica and the polar north, were well known to Europeans by the beginning of the eighteenth century. The Portuguese, Bartolomeo Diaz, had rounded the Cape of Good Hope and reached the East African coast in 1488, even earlier than the discovery of the Americas by Columbus in 1492. Knowledge, however, was usually confined to the coastal strip and exploration was essential if the potential, real or imagined, of the new lands was to be exploited. The balance of activity was, however, changing. Pioneering Spain largely confined itself to the enormous space of South America, which then encompassed the Pacific littoral of the later United States, while Portugal, which had mounted the first expedition to India in 1497 under Vasco da Gama and had established the colony of Macau (Macao) on the Chinese coast in 1557, had lost its control of the oriental trade to the Dutch in the seventeenth century.

eighteenth century

It was now **Britain** and **France** who were to lead the exploration of North America and the Pacific. Englishman Captain **James Cook** (1728–79) explored **New Zealand** and Australia as well as the Newfoundland coast of **Canada**, and was the first both to sail south of the Antarctic Circle and to reach the edge of the icepack while circumnavigating **Antarctica** in 1773. No serious new attempt, however, was made to find a north-west passage above Canada, an endeavour which had resulted in the death of Henry Hudson in 1611. Exploration remained, and was to continue to remain, dangerous. Captain Cook himself was murdered by hostile islanders in Hawaii. Logically enough, exploration was the preserve of the maritime powers. Those of central Europe, **Austria** and **Prussia** did not participate and Russian exploration was as yet not across the seas but rather part of its peasant settler expansion into **Kazakhstan** and towards Siberia. Nevertheless, Russian sailors explored much of the northern shore of Siberia during the century.

The raw motive of curiosity was also becoming more sophisticated and more differentiated and, in particular, more scientific. Captain Cook gave Australia's Botany Bay its name because of the interesting plants he found there.

The eighteenth century, however, also witnessed the beginning of the reverse cultural phenomenon, with previously unknown or barely known lands having a marked impact on European taste. Chinoiserie was all the rage in crockery and furniture and even in construction, with such survivals as the Chinese bridge in Godmanchester, Cambridgeshire, and, supremely, Sir William Chambers' Pagoda of 1761 at Kew in south-west London. On a different level, the novelty of coffee had spawned London's famous eighteenth-century coffeehouses, which became the centre of its intellectual life, while the French *café* became almost a European word. Chocolate, from the Aztec *chocolatl*, had established itself similarly as a Spanish drink. On a different level again, the privations of exploratory seafaring caught the public imagination with the publication of Daniel Defoe's *Robinson Crusoe* (1719), based on the true story of a shipwrecked mariner, Andrew Selkirk. His Man Friday is probably the first of European literature's 'noble savages'. Such cultural impacts, which have multiplied and grown greatly in significance since, were, however, overshadowed at the time by the political impact of exploration. As noted, exploration, whatever the motive in any particular case, was almost always followed, usually sooner rather than later, by territorial claims or at the least by claims to exclusive rights and privileges. It was, in short, a facet of colonization and imperial rivalry that had become a major force in European politics by the 1770s. French defeats in Canada and **India**, and then in the **Napoleonic Wars**, gave the British a primacy which was not to be questioned until the 1860s and 1870s.

nineteenth century

Captain Cook's pioneering crossing of the Antarctic Circle was followed in 1820 by the first sighting of Antarctica itself, although the credit is divided between three men who made separate voyages in the same year: Russian Navy captain Fabian von Bellingshausen, British Royal Navy captain Edward Bransfield and an American sealer, Nathaniel Brown Palmer. A Frenchman, Jules-Sébastien-César Dumont d'Urville, then went on to become the first person to set foot on Antarctica, in 1840. In general, however, the style of most nineteenth-century exploration remained linked to colonization, although with some significant developments. Curiosity was becoming ever more scientific. Perhaps the best-known example is that of the British naturalist, **Charles Darwin**, whose *Origin of Species* (1859) followed his voyage round the world as naturalist on the *Beagle* in 1831–6. That scientific curiosity was, moreover, also becoming increasingly diversified to embrace such disciplines as archaeology and cultural history generally. This diversification made exploration a wider European enterprise rather than a preserve of the maritime powers. German scholars were prominent in this new field for exploration, with Heinrich Schliemann (1822–90) excavating Mycenae and Troy, both of which had been believed to be legendary. The most famous achievement, however, was probably the deciphering of Egyptian hieroglyphs initiated by French Egyptologist Jean François Champollion (1790–1832) following the discovery of the Rosetta Stone. These new forms of exploration also widened its geographical focus. Archaeologists such as the Briton, Sir Aurel Stein (1862–1943), were to explore the Silk Road linking Europe with **China** around the Gobi Desert, and to penetrate **Tibet**. Although this form of exploration did not have territorial implications, a disproportionate number of finds were transferred to Europe, as the collections of the British Museum in London, the Louvre in Paris, the Pergamon Museum in Berlin and the Hermitage in St Petersburg make all too clear.

The more traditional forms of exploration, however, were focused essentially on Africa and with the British in the lead, followed after the mid-century by the French, the Belgians, the Portuguese, and finally the Germans. The most famous of these explorers was probably **David Livingstone** (1813–73), who discovered the course of the Zambezi River, Victoria Falls and Lake Nyasa (Malawi). Believed lost, he was found by Sir Henry Stanley at Ujiji on 10 November 1871, the occasion of Stanley's almost legendary 'Dr Livingstone, I presume?' Both men subsequently explored Lake Tanganyika. This penetration of sub-Saharan Africa by European explorers, closely followed by traders and settlers, rapidly provoked the colonial rivalry dubbed the **'scramble for Africa'**, into which some sort of order was brought by the international Berlin Conference, 1884. The British were the prime beneficiaries and did not hesitate in 1890 to quash Portuguese aspirations to link their colonies of **Angola** and **Mozambique**, despite prior French and German acceptance.

Exploration was also resuming a sense which had somewhat receded into the background since the Spanish conquest of the Americas in the sixteenth century: exploration into mineral wealth – primarily gold and diamonds but also other precious metals and, increasingly, oil. The British were again prime movers, with gold and diamond prospectors flooding into the Cape Colony, South Africa, generating friction with the Dutch Boer settlers, and into western Australia.

Just as in the eighteenth century, exploration and discovery had a significant cultural impact at home, particularly on literature. They spelled adventure and spawned such boyhood classics as R. L. Stevenson's *Treasure Island* (1883) and R. M. Ballantyne's *Coral Island* (1857). The French novelist Jules Verne (1828–1905) had a more scientific, if equally imaginative, slant in his works *Journey to the Centre of the Earth* (1864) and *20,000 Leagues under the Sea* (1872). Even Switzerland was affected, with J. D. Wyss' *Swiss Family Robinson* published in German in 1812–13. Most remarkable of all, perhaps, was the English writer Sir Rider Haggard (1856–1925) – a respected agricultural expert, African administrator and settler but also an explorer and something of a mystic. His best-known work, *King Solomon's Mines* (1885), is a classic adventure book, but *She* (1887) and its sequel, *Ayesha* (1905) are a somewhat breathtaking fantasy taking the reader on a journey from Zanzibar to the monasteries and mountains of Tibet and central Asia.

Real-life exploration at the end of the nineteenth and beginning of the twentieth centuries, however, was the reverse of fantastical, but rather an increasingly scientific and technological investigation into those parts of the globe which had hitherto been the most inaccessible – the **Arctic and the Antarctic**. Scandinavians played a major role. The Norwegian explorer and scientist **Fridtjof Nansen** (1861–1930) crossed the Greenland icecap in 1888, before studying the movement of the polar ice in his north polar expedition, 1893–6, drifting in the ice north of Russia in his ship *Fram* for almost three years. A Swede, A. E. Nordenskjöld, successfully navigated the Northeast Passage for the first time in the *Vega*, 1879. Another Norwegian, Roald Amundsen (1872–1928), became the first man to sail the Northwest Passage and round the Canadian coast in his ship *Gjöa*, 1903–5, succeeding where Hudson and then Sir John Franklin's expedition in the *Erebus* and *Terror* (1845) had both failed with the loss of their own lives.

twentieth century

The end of the nineteenth and beginning of the twentieth centuries saw a continuing focus on the polar regions and a renewed interest in the Antarctic. An international research scheme was prepared, 1890, and the Norwegian C. E. Borchgrevink was the first man to winter in the Antarctic and to travel on the ice barrier, 1898–1900. The Frenchman Joseph de Gerlache de Goméry had brought back the first photographs of Antarctica in 1897. The British expedition of 1901–4 under Captain Robert Falcon Scott (1868–1912) sledged across the ice barrier and reached a then record latitude, 82° 17′ South. (Sir) Ernest Shackleton (1874–1922), a member of that expedition and leader of the British Antarctic (Nimrod) Expedition, 1907–9, then approached within 156 kilometres (97 miles) of the South Pole. Famously, however, it was Amundsen's meticulously planned expedition which was the first to reach the South Pole, 1911, and finally, in the company of the American explorer, Lincoln Ellsworth, and the Italian aeronautical engineer, Umberto Nobile, it was Amundsen who was the first to fly over the North Pole in a dirigible, 1926. Both Nansen and Captain Scott, the leader of the ill-fated British expedition which reached the South Pole after Amundsen, in 1912, were scientists as well as explorers. Indeed, the sponsoring Royal Geographical Society was clear that Scott's expedition would be 'scientific primarily, with exploration and the Pole as secondary objects'. It can never be proved but it has been speculated that his party might have reached safety if it had not been burdened with 35 pounds of valuable geological samples. Nevertheless, the public response to the death of Scott and his companions reflected the extent to which exploration was indelibly associated in the public mind with romantic adventure, heroism, sacrifice and national pride. The national element cannot be ignored – Shackleton had been typical in claiming Victoria Land Plateau for the British Crown in 1908, making the British Antarctic Territory the oldest territorial claim on the continent. The whole of Antarctica was subsequently to be divided into zones of influence much as Africa, Asia and the Americas had previously been. Britain, France, **Australia**, **New Zealand**, **Norway**, **Argentina** and **Chile** all made claims. Only the inhospitable nature of the terrain and the inherent difficulties discouraged exploitation prior to the conclusion of the Antarctic Treaty, 1959.

The technological advances which were making polar exploration practicable were even more in evidence in the whole new dimension of underwater exploration. The first major undersea survey had been undertaken by the multidisciplinary expedition of the British vessel, *Challenger*, in 1872–6, but it was the Swiss-born Belgian physicist, Auguste Piccard (1884–1962), and his son, Jacques Piccard (1922–2008), who jointly designed the bathyscaphe for deep-sea exploration. Their craft, *Trieste*, built by that city's local industry, successfully descended to a depth of 3,150 metres (10,330 feet) in 1953. In January 1960 Jacques Piccard descended in the *Trieste*, now owned by the US Navy, to a new submarine record depth of 10,912 metres (35,800 feet) in the Mariana Trench in the Pacific, accompanied by Lieutenant Don Walsh of the US Navy. Jacques Piccard also designed in collaboration with his father in the early 1960s the mesoscaphe for middle-depth exploration. Built with observation portholes and capable of carrying forty tourists, it was remarkably reminiscent of the submarine, *Nautilus*, imagined as science fiction by Jules Verne in *20,000 Leagues under the Sea* some eighty years earlier.

Meanwhile, terrestrial exploration had largely reached its limits. Colonel Fawcett, perhaps the last of the romantic explorers, disappeared in the Amazon basin in the search for a lost civilization in the early 1930s. On the other hand, scientific archaeological exploration made a series of spectacular discoveries, most famously the discovery of Tutankhamen's tomb in the Valley of the Kings near Luxor, Upper Egypt, by Howard Carter and Lord Carnarvon in 1922. Equally astonishing were the finds from the ancient city of Ur in southern Iraq excavated by Sir Leonard Woolley in the late 1920s and early 1930s, which revealed a quite unsuspected level of civilization and artistic achievement. Similarly spectacular finds were being made, primarily by American and national archaeologists, in the deserts and jungles of **Latin America**. Such exploration, however, did not need to be in remote areas for its finds to be spectacular. The excavation of the Anglo-Saxon ship burial at Sutton Hoo near Woodbridge, Suffolk, England, in 1939 prompted a drastic revision in appreciation of what historians had previously dismissed as the 'Dark Ages'.

cultural impact

It was, though, the recent exploration of Africa and Oceania which was to have the prime impact on European culture in the twentieth century. The great Benin bronzes, for example, had not been known to Europeans until 1897. Moreover, that impact was, perhaps for the first time, on mainstream art, rather than on adventure, literature or taste in decoration. The Spaniard Pablo Picasso's (1891–1973) revolutionary painting *Les*

Demoiselles d'Avignon of 1907 clearly shows the influence of African and Oceanic masks, as do celebrated paintings of the French artist Henri Matisse (1869–1954) such as *Madame Matisse* (1913). The English sculptor Henry Moore's (1898–1986) great stone figures meant for outdoor display clearly show the influence of those on Easter Island in the Pacific. 'Primitive' and 'modern' art went hand in hand. Even the stepped architecture of pre-Columbian central America was reflected in the wooden cabinets of twentieth-century wireless sets. One remarkable feat which combined aspects of archaeology, anthropology, the study of human migration and sheer exploratory adventure, and which attracted worldwide attention, was the Kon-Tiki expedition of the 1950s led by the Norwegian Thor Heyerdahl, which established that early man could have crossed the Pacific from the Americas using only the type of raft with sail still to be found on the Andean lakes.

The mid twentieth century also saw continuing significant advances in polar exploration, such as the first surface crossing of the Arctic Ocean by (Sir) Wally Herbert in 1969. The American nuclear submarine, *Nautilus*, had made the first voyage under the North Pole, 1958. The first crossing of the Antarctic continent via the South Pole was achieved by a UK party of the Commonwealth Trans-Antarctic Expedition led by Sir Vivian Fuchs, in ninety-nine days in 1957–8. Later, in 1994, Liv Arnesen of Norway became the first woman to reach the South Pole alone. Remarkable as these later exploits were, they were accompanied by political developments of arguably greater significance. In 1959 the twelve nations which then had scientists working in and around Antarctica signed the Antarctic Treaty, which came into effect in 1961. This was followed in 1991 by the signing by those twelve nations, together with thirty-four others, of the Protocol on Environmental Protection to that treaty. It did not assess the validity of any existing claims but defined Antarctica as 'a natural reserve devoted to peace and science'. The exploitation of natural resources for non-scientific purposes was unanimously banned until 2048. Unfortunately the signing of the protocol did not mean the end of national rivalries. Great Britain announced in 2007 that it planned effectively to extend its Antarctic territory by 50 per cent by claiming, through the United Nations, some 386,000 square miles of the Antarctic seabed, provoking Argentina and Chile to announce that they would contest any such claim. The deadline for lodging all such claims was 2009. Behind the claims is not only national prestige but also the hope that global warming will permit exploration for, and then the exploitation of, oil and other minerals.

Nevertheless, the main thrust of twentieth- and twenty-first century exploration has not been terrestrial; it has been of the upper atmosphere and then of space. It was again Auguste Piccard who led the way. Having designed a new type of balloon, with the sort of airtight pressurized cabin which has since become the norm in all high-flying aircraft, and attracted Belgian financing, he successfully ascended with Paul Kipfer to an altitude of 15,781 metres (51,762 feet) on 27 May 1931. He then bettered that with a new cabin, rising to 16,940 metres (55,563 feet) in 1932. Soviet and US balloonists rose even higher to 18,500 metres (60,700 feet) and 18,665 metres (61,221 feet) the following year. This was only a foretaste, however, of the drastic change to come. On 12 April 1961 Russian Yuri Gagarin (1934–68) became the first man in space, orbiting the earth for ninety minutes in *Vostok-1* at 274,000 kph (170,000 mph) and reaching a maximum height above the earth of 327 kilometres. The **Soviet Union** had already launched the first artificial satellite to orbit the earth, *Sputnik 1*, in 1957, and crashlanded its *Luna 2* rocket on the Moon the same year. In a pleasing touch, Gagarin's commemorative statue erected in London fifty years later faces that of Captain Cook. Reactions to the flight underlined the nationalistic and political dimensions of most exploration. In addition to the common pleasure at a great human achievement, of which many had dreamed but never expected to see, there was an awareness that it was a great triumph specifically of Soviet space engineering. The Soviet Union realized its propaganda value to the full, and was to build on it by inviting non-Soviet astronauts, drawn particularly but not exclusively from its Warsaw Pact partners, to join in future flights. The United States, on the other hand, was extremely alarmed to discover that its opponent in the **Cold War** had mastered a technology not only of the greatest propaganda value but also of enormous military potential. President **Kennedy** demanded that no resource be spared to put an American manned spacecraft on the Moon 'before this decade is out'. The propaganda reward for the United States was to make the American Neil Armstrong (1930–) the first man to set foot on the Moon, 12 July 1969. The largely unsung pioneers throughout were the German rocket scientists who had worked on the V1 and V2 weapons in the later years of **World War II** and who had been taken to the Soviet Union and the United States at its end, particularly Werner von Braun in the US.

Rather remarkably, space exploration, despite disasters to both American and Soviet spacecraft, seems to have proved safer than much earlier exploration. Gagarin's pioneering flight in *Vostok 1* was followed by sets of flights in 1962 and 1963, the latter including the first woman astronaut, Valentina Tereshkova. The Soviet Union then advanced to a three-man flight with *Vokshod 1* in October 1964 and to a two-man flight in March 1965 when the astronaut, Aleksey Leonov, became the first man to float free in space. The *Salyut* series of space stations launched between 1971 and 1982 permitted crews to live and work on board for an increasing length of time, reaching a record of 211 days. These protracted periods permitted rendezvous with astronauts from other Warsaw Pact states including Sigmund Jähn from East Germany in 1978, but also from France and India. Helen Sharman thus became Britain's first astronaut. Finally, in 1986, the Soviet Union launched its *Mir* space station with six docking ports for cargo transports and visiting manned spacecraft, together with expansion modules which made it practicable to accommodate a crew of up to six on board. The only cooperative US–Soviet manned space mission was the *Apollo–Soyuz* Test Project of 1975, when the three-man US *Apollo* and the two-man *Soyuz 19* docked in orbit for two days.

These manned journeys of exploration, which were, of course, paralleled by American projects, were complemented by extensive American and Russian programmes of unmanned flight which sought to explore first lunar and then interplanetary space. The American programme included limited collaboration with western European states including Britain and West Germany. The Soviet Union's *Luna* series succeeded with *Luna 3* in 1959 in photographing the far side of the Moon and *Luna 16* in 1970 returned a sample of soil to Earth. The first successful Soviet interplanetary launch was of *Venera 4* in 1967 which dropped an instrumental capsule into the Venusian atmosphere. *Venera 9* and *Venera 10* of 1975 provided the first photographs taken on the surface of another planet. Spacecraft sent to Mars in 1971 supplied limited scientific data. Russia has, as yet, found it difficult to recover the Soviet Union's prominence in space research. Its attempted return to planetary exploration in November 2011 for the first time since 1990, with its *Phobos-Grunt* probe to Mars, failed from an engine malfunction. It has been clear for several decades that future space exploration will involve such almost unimaginable distances and times that it will be unmanned. Unmanned probes have already provided information about Mars and Venus, while the American *Voyager* mission has examined other planets in the outer solar system. In July 2015 the NASA New Horizons mission, launched in 2006, flew by Pluto and on into the Kuiper Belt beyond. Orbiting space laboratories may be deemed research rather than exploration. Those distances and times suggest that radio astronomy, first discovered in the United States and pioneered in Europe by (Sir) Bernard Lovell at Jodrell Bank, Cheshire, England, in 1946–7, will remain a prime tool. It makes it possible to observe parts of the universe so far distant that the emitted radio waves have taken thousands of millions of years to reach Earth, and thus perhaps to explore the very beginning of the universe.

retrospect

For such reasons, the traditional human explorer – part adventurer, part scientist, part national hero – is probably passing into history. Mountaineering could never strictly have been described as exploration, but George Leigh Mallory's laconic response in 1923 to a question as to why he risked all to climb Everest of 'because it is there' summed up the spirit of much exploration as well. The surface of the globe is now too well known for that to continue. Nevertheless, scientific advances are facilitating anthropological and archaeological exploration and rich discoveries are to be anticipated in unlocking the stories of human evolution and the emergence of civilization. Archaeological exploration started with the 'gentleman amateur' in the late eighteenth century before becoming progressively professionalized, but the development of the metal detector has turned part of that wheel full circle. Weekend amateur explorers armed with detectors are routinely unearthing significant 'treasure troves' in the UK, of which the Staffordshire gold hoard discovered in 2009 has attracted the most attention.

However, most traditional forms of exploration always had a powerful strategic dimension, and this has returned to the fore in the Arctic, where global warming is turning a region which caused the deaths of explorers such as Hudson and Franklin into a new region of commercial, strategic and transport opportunity. Moreover, the strategic opportunities relate as much to resource exploitation as to military advantage. It has been estimated, for example, that perhaps a quarter of the world's oil reserves, equivalent to 375 billion barrels, and a third of its gas reserves are to be found under the Arctic Ocean. For reasons which are not fully understood, global warming appears to be running at double the speed in the Arctic than it is in the rest of the world. If it continues at its present rate, the Arctic will be free of ice in the summer of 2070–80, or even by as early as 2040 in the view of some scientists. The Russian vessel, *Akademik Fyodorov*, was the first to reach the North Pole without an ice-breaker in 2005, and in 2009 two German container ships navigated the North-East Passage through open water. All eight countries bordering the Arctic have their own claims and counterclaims on the continental shelf. Denmark claims the North Pole, arguing that it sits on Greenland's continental shelf, but Russia formally claimed the Pole on 2 August 2007. Russia's new national security strategy adopted in 2009 identifies the intensifying battle for ownership of vast untapped oil and gas reserves around its borders as a source of potential military conflict within a decade. Some later Russian diplomatic moves have, however, played down the risk of a new, very literal, Cold War.

Eyre, Edward (1815–1901)

A farmer who later became an explorer in south and west Australia. Eyre later held British colonial service positions in **Australia**, **New Zealand**, St Vincent and **Jamaica** during the nineteenth century. In 1865 he was governor of Jamaica when the Morant Bay rebellion broke out. Eyre declared martial law in the eastern part of Jamaica and had his most virulent political opponent, George William Gordon, transferred to Morant Bay to face a court martial. When Eyre returned to England, though he was popular with island planters, he faced many legal obstacles for his handling of the rebellion.

F

Fabians

British followers of a progressive, largely middle-class group, the Fabian Society. It was established in 1884 to promote socialist ideas in a non-revolutionary way, taking its name from the Roman general Fabius Cunctator, who used gradual attrition to wear down his opponents. Prominent early members included the social investigators Sidney and Beatrice Webb, the dramatist George Bernard Shaw, and the novelist H. G. Wells. The society played an important role in founding the Labour Party in Britain, adding an intellectual dimension to its trade union support, and to its character as a moderate 'gradualist' socialist party which rejected revolutionary **Marxism**. It continues to act as a research body attached to the Labour Party and a source of research and argument about a wide range of policy. The term is more generally applied to a supporter of gradual reform.

factories

– *see also* **industrialization**.

Generally any building or buildings carrying on manufacturing but increasingly with the emphasis upon production becoming centralized under one roof. In early industrialization the latter marked a key change from dispersed 'outwork', known as the 'putting out' system, to a concentration of production which permitted mechanization, the application of new sources of power and scaling up to unprecedented size, involving sometimes tens of thousands of workers. Places of concentrated manufacture existed from pre-industrial times for the production of Chinese ceramics, Middle Eastern carpets, in the large shipyards of Venice, Holland and **Britain**, the iron foundries of **Sweden** and **Russia**, the skilled metalworking centres of southern **Germany**, the large breweries and distilleries of eighteenth-century London and the luxury tapestry and porcelain centres of pre-Revolutionary **France**. Grouping of woollen workers into small factories was already common in the textile districts of eighteenth-century Britain, but it was the growing mechanization of textile production and the harnessing of first water power and later steam power which produced the first large factories for mechanized production of silk and cotton goods at places such as Cromford in Derbyshire and the Lancashire cotton towns. The scale of some of these enterprises and their ability to harness water and steam for virtually non-stop production made the multistorey 'factory', with its hundreds of workers, the symbol of the new industrial age, although the majority of factories until the middle of the nineteenth century were little more than large workshops employing less than fifty people. Some of the enterprises of the late nineteenth century operated on a much larger scale. Steelworks, railways workshops and chemical factories were soon employing thousands of workers on a single site and some early consumer goods such as sewing machines were produced by the Singer Company in Glasgow in a factory employing over 10,000 people in 1910. The development of assembly line production produced the giant automobile factories of Detroit, while the rapid industrialization of countries such as **Japan** and the **Soviet Union** produced factory complexes employing tens of thousands of workers. The use of electricity for power allowed greater dispersal of manufacturing into smaller units, while mechanization and robotization has reduced the numbers of workers required for assembly work. As a result, the size of factories has tended to be reduced.

Fahd ibn Abd al-Aziz (c. 1921–2005)

King of **Saudi Arabia**, 1982–2005. Fahd succeeded King **Khalid ibn Abd al-Aziz** in June 1982, although he had controlled Saudi affairs for many years as crown prince during Khalid's protracted illnesses. In 1986 Fahd adopted the title ' Protector of the Two Holy Places' (over His Majesty) to emphasize his religious role in **Islam**. Fahd's major political challenges included the decline in oil prices during the 1980s, which weakened the Saudi economy, and **Saddam Hussein**'s August 1990 invasion of **Kuwait**, following which Fahd invited American and other foreign forces to assist in the protection of the kingdom. Opponents challenged the legitimacy of the Saudi regime and demanded reforms.

Fahd ordered suppression of the opposition but also issued a series of decrees, including the constitution-like Basic Law of 1992. Crown Prince Abdullah ibn Abd al-Aziz assumed control of Saudi political affairs following Fahd's November 1995 stroke.

Faisal I (1885–1933)

King of Iraq, 1920–33; an experienced politician who despite the impossible pressures placed upon him, guided a nation through difficult and critical times. The son of Sharif Husayn ibn Ali, the emir of Mecca, Faisal was born in Taif, an ancient city in the Arabian peninsula, and grew up in Istanbul. During **World War I** he was the field commander of the **Arab revolt** against the **Ottoman Empire** and worked and fought alongside **T. E. Lawrence** (of Arabia). Faisal led the Arab delegation at the **Paris Peace Conference** of 1919, arguing for the establishment of a new nation in the Arab lands of Ottoman Empire in Asia. In 1920 the general Syrian congress proclaimed **Syria** an independent state with Faisal as its king. Though this action was greeted with enthusiasm in many quarters in the Arab Middle East, the French government was not as pleased, viewing the action as a usurpation of French claims to the region and a violation of various wartime agreements. Faisal had British support for his Syrian kingdom but the British backed off, wanting to preserve their alliance with **France**. The French Army invaded Syria and expelled Faisal. At the 1921 Cairo conference, perhaps guided by their sense of guilt over their abandonment of Faisal in Syria, the British decided that he would be the ideal ruler for **Iraq**, which the **League of Nations** had recently awarded to Britain. Even though Faisal had no local connections to the country, the British felt that because of his international reputation and the fact that he was a descendant of the Prophet Muhammad, the Iraqis would perceive him to be an attractive option to lead their country and to build up a new state and nation.

Faisal's coronation was held in August 1921, when he became the first king of the newly formed **Hashemite** Kingdom of Iraq. His position was precarious. He did not have a natural following in the country and he knew that his position was dependent on the British. His experience in Syria had taught him he was expendable if imperial interests demanded so. At the same time, he did not want to be perceived as being a British puppet. Initially there was little enthusiasm for Faisal, but there was little organized opposition and no obvious alternative. Furthermore, Iraq's governmental power was limited since the mandate of

the **League of Nations** put restrictions on the extent of Iraq's sovereignty. Despite these obstacles, in his twelve years as king Faisal used his considerable personal charm and political acumen to build a solid political base and to lay the groundwork for the development of many of the major institutions of the Iraqi state, such as the educational system and the military, and to inculcate a sense of Iraqi nationalism. The limitations of his power and of Iraqi independence were most visible in the 1925 agreement between Iraq and **Britain** that formed the Iraqi Petroleum Company. This 75-year concession provided Iraq with modest royalties but precluded their ownership in a company that controlled the the country's most important natural resource.

Faisal II (1936–1958)

King of Hashemite **Iraq**, 1939–58. Faisal II took the throne as a 3-year-old after his father King Ghazi was killed in an automobile accident in 1939. The infant king was placed under the regency of his uncle, Abd al-Ilah. He attended Harrow School in England with his cousin King **Hussein** of Jordan. When he came of age, in 1953, the young and inexperienced king continued to delegate much of his political work to his uncle. The 1950s were a turbulent time in Iraqi politics, coinciding with tremendous economic and cultural growth. In the 1958 military coup that overthrew the Hashemite monarchy in Iraq, the young and unmarried king was shot and killed by revolutionaries in the palace courtyard, leaving behind no descendants.

Faisal ibn Abd al-Aziz (1906–1975)

King of **Saudi Arabia**, 1964–75. Faisal was born in Riyadh and was educated by Abdullah ibn Abd al-Latif Al al-Shaykh, the grandson of Muhammad ibn Abd al-Wahhab, the founder of **Wahhabism**. From a very early age Faisal's father entrusted him with important duties such as leading the 1920 military campaign in Asir, representing his father at the 1921 Versailles conference and leading the 1925 campaign against the Hejaz. In 1930 he became the minister of foreign affairs and represented Saudi Arabia at the **United Nations** conference in San Francisco in 1945. He also commanded Saudi forces in the 1934 campaign against **Yemen**. When his brother Sa'ud succeeded **Abd al-Aziz** as king in 1953, Faisal became crown prince while continuing to serve as foreign minister. As crown prince, he and Sa'ud disagreed on the proper response to the threat of Arab nationalism and management of state funds. Faisal has often been characterized as being much more outward-looking, religiously conservative and pragmatic, and was supported by a group of his half-brothers known, after their mother's clan name, as the 'Sudairi Seven', whereas Sa'ud was more inward-focused, less religious and possessed a strong tribal base. A third faction within the royal family, the 'Free Princes' led by Prince Talal ibn Abd al-Aziz, favoured creation of a constitutional monarchy and economic reform.

These divisions first came to the fore in March 1958 when a group of princes forced Sa'ud to hand over power to Faisal, who immediately instituted political and economic reforms. However, family divisions allowed Sa'ud to retake power in December 1960. Sa'ud and Faisal continued to vie for power until 1964 when the crown prince consolidated his control of the royal family, including the Free Princes and the religious elite, and in November they forced Sa'ud out and Faisal became king. Faisal's reign focused to a ten-point programme committing state finances to the development of infrastructure, education, and health care for the first time, and to investing large sums in the military. Faisal also initiated the first five-year economic development plan in 1970, and reorganized the legal/religious institutions of the kingdom, replacing the office of Grand Mufti, who concentrated legal authority in a single person, with a Ministry of Justice, giving the government control over the judiciary, and a seventeen-member Council of Senior Ulema to serve as a kind of supreme court. In foreign affairs the king sought to counter Arab nationalism, first by supporting the Royalists against the Egyptian-backed Republicans in the **Yemen Civil War** and then backing the creation of the **Muslim League** as an Islamic counter to Nasserist secularism and socialism. Faisal also played an active role in the 1973 Arab oil embargo (*see* **oil shock**), attempting to link the kingdom's role as a leading petroleum producer to its goal of creating a Palestinian state and securing Muslim control over **Jerusalem**, **Islam**'s third holiest city. King Faisal died at the hands of a nephew, who shot him during his weekly *majlis*.

Faiz Ahmed Faiz (1911–1984)

Winner of the Lenin Prize (1962) and among the most acclaimed Urdu poets of the twentieth century. A Marxist whose poetry engaged social and political issues, Faiz began his literary career as a journalist, publishing his first collection of poetry in 1941. He was a member of the Progressive Writers movement, started in **India** in 1936 to promote more socially and politically conscious literature. He was also an avid opponent of **Zia-ul-Haq**'s military dictatorship in Pakistan.

Falkland Islands War (Malvinas War) (April–June 1982)

On 2 April 1982 Argentine forces seized the disputed Falkland Islands (the 'Malvinas' to Argentines) from the British, who had occupied the islands since 1833. Argentina's military dictatorship under General **Galtieri** hoped Britain would not retaliate, but Britain's Prime Minister **Margaret Thatcher** mounted a taskforce that defeated Argentine forces by 14 June. The humiliating defeat forced Argentina's military from power, while the victory bolstered Thatcher's flagging support at home, ensuring an overwhelming victory in the 1983 general election.

families/family systems

The structure, function, and even the definition of 'the family' have varied tremendously from culture to culture and for different social groups within each culture. Some groups practised polygamy and others monogamy; for some, the most important unit was the nuclear family of a man, a woman and their children, while for others the extended kin network was most important; in some groups, the family was primarily a unit of reproduction, while in others it was primarily a unit of production; in some groups, married couples lived with the husband's family (patrilocality), in others they lived with the wife's (matrilocality or uxorilocality), and in others still they set up their own household (neolocality); in some groups marital partners were chosen by parents or the family as a whole and in others by the individuals themselves; in some groups a woman brought goods or money to her husband or husband's family on marriage (a dowry) and in others a man gave goods or money to his wife's family (bride price); in some groups divorce was easy and in others impossible; in some groups the oldest son inherited everything (primogeniture) and in others all children or at least all sons shared in inheritance (partible inheritance); in some groups, people married within their group (endogamy) and in others outside of their group (exogamy); in some groups contraception, **abortion** and even infanticide were acceptable practices for limiting the number of children, while in others these were strictly prohibited. All of these variables often changed over time because of internal developments or contacts with other cultures. In the modern world, every major process had an effect on family forms, and conversely, family systems shaped the way economic and social processes developed.

European colonization

European colonization radically altered family forms in many parts of the world, as Europeans brought with them their own ideas of proper family life and the institutions designed to enforce those ideas. In Latin America, the Catholic Church and the Spanish and Portuguese crowns created a complex system of socio-racial categories that privileged white persons and defined as many as twenty different categories for persons of mixed background, termed *castas*. One's *casta* was in theory based on place of birth, assumed race and status of one's mother, but in practice was to a large extent determined by how one looked. This system had a direct effect on family formation. For members of the white European elite, concerns about bloodlines, colour and caste created a pattern of intermarriage within the extended family, for only among family members could one be sure about family background. For slaves, many persons of mixed race and poor people, family and property considerations did not enter into marital considerations, and in most cases people simply did not get married at all. The number of births out of wedlock in **Latin America** remained startlingly high by comparison with most of Europe. Thus, despite Christian norms, families in Latin America were extremely diverse.

As in Latin America, the family structures that developed in North America in the eighteenth and nineteenth centuries were class- and race-related. White families, especially in the North, tended to follow the north-western European model, with late marriage and a high proportion of people who never married. In the South, marriages between whites were earlier, and were accompanied by men fathering mixed-race children with non-white women outside of marriage. These children were defined as 'black', however, and were slaves like their mother. Unions between slaves were not recognized as marriages in most of the **United States**, so that black families were more fluid and often matrifocal.

European colonial rule in Africa and Asia generally did not disrupt existing family patterns to as great an extent as in the Americas; these continued to be shaped by Confucian, Hindu or Islamic ideals. Economic changes had a greater impact. The growth in mining and commercial agriculture

for export in colonial areas led many men to leave their families in search of wage labour, with women at home in the villages engaged in subsistence agriculture and caring for children; thus, like slavery, wage labour led to matrifocal family patterns. This occurred within legal structures that were often patrilineal, with formal rights to land held by men who were absent. Thus there could be a sharp contradiction between theory and practice regarding family structure and power relationships.

The growth of **industrialization** in the eighteenth and nineteenth centuries brought new forms of work organization that had a significant effect on family life. Young women were often the first to be hired as factories opened, which removed them from parental households and authority. Conservative commentators worried about this, and suggested that factory owners act as substitute fathers, and that young women give most of their wages to their families. Conversely, liberal social reformers and labour organizations increasingly advocated a 'family wage', that is, wages high enough to allow married male workers to support their families by themselves. This did not happen, and women and children continued to work in factories and mines in most parts of the world, for their labour was needed to allow working-class families to survive.

Governments intervened in family life in the twentieth century far more than they had earlier, with the most extreme examples in totalitarian regimes. In **Germany**, **Italy** and **Japan** in the 1930s large families were rewarded among groups judged to be desirable, while those judged undesirable were sterilized or executed. By the 1960s, as a result of explosive population growth, many governments were worried about overpopulation. Some condoned widespread sterilization, or penalized families that had more than one child. Coercive government measures provoked strong resistance from both religious and women's organizations, but by the end of the century worldwide fertility had been lowered, from 4.97 births per woman in 1950 to 2.59 in 2007. Curtailment of family size has been selective, with industrialized countries with strong systems of social support having the lowest birth rates because people did not have to rely on their children for support in old age. In 2007, Hong Kong had the lowest birth rate (0.98) and Mali the highest (7.38).

changing family patterns

Families in many parts of the world changed shape and became more varied from the twentieth century. Marital patterns in many parts of Africa remained polygymous, with over half the women in western Africa in the 1980s having at least one co-spouse, but urban marriages were increasingly likely to be monogamous. In Japan, **China** and the Arab world more than 95 per cent of people continued to marry, but in other parts of the world there was a dramatic decline in marriage rates. Male mobility and the lack of good jobs in developing areas meant that many people did not marry until quite late in life or never married at all. In both western Europe and the United States couples lived together but did not marry, and both divorce rates and remarriage after divorce rates increased significantly. Many families included the children from several different relationships, thus returning to an earlier pattern when spousal death and remarriage had created such 'blended' families. In some parts of the world, marriage between individuals of different races and religions became increasingly common, challenging centuries-old boundaries and definitions of who was family and who was kin. This diversity of family forms has been perceived by some observers as a social problem, but shows little sign of changing in the twenty-first century.

famine

– see also **agriculture**; **food**; **Green Revolution**.
Famine occurs when the food of a large and defined group of people becomes unavailable or falls below levels of availability required to sustain nutrition. It was for most of human history a recurring condition, but has become associated with four different sets of circumstances, as well as being a driver for various food policies in the developed world. Famine can be the consequence of a natural disaster when a population is dependent upon a particular staple or infrastructure which is damaged or depleted; it can arise as a deliberate consequence of governmental policy, to punish or remove a group from a certain area; it can arise as the consequence of a particular set of government policies; or it can interact with the dependence produced by a social system predicated upon a lack of access to economic, political or social resources by outsider groups. Hardly any part of the modern world was spared the impact of famine at some point in its history, but western Europe was one of the first to see an end to famine as a regular occurrence as agricultural development, improved communication and greater affluence allowed individual harvest failures to be overcome without major impacts upon death rates. The last 'killing

famine' of the traditional kind in England and Wales occurred in Cumbria in the 1620s and in France in the last years of Louis XIV's reign, though periods of shortage and high prices still caused hardship and gave rise to protest. Famine persisted longer in southern and eastern Europe, where agricultural productivity lagged and communications were less developed. Moreover, the introduction of the highly productive food crop, the potato, as a staple food of the poor, produced one of the greatest famines of modern times with the **Irish famine** of the 1840s, when blight destroyed the potato harvest on which the population depended, causing over a million deaths and large-scale emigration.

In the twentieth and early twenty-first centuries it is difficult to identify a famine that has had a purely natural cause, such as volcanic activity or flooding. Rather, where famines have arisen – such as in **Bengal** in 1943, **Bangladesh** in 1974 and **Ethiopia** in 1984–5 – they have been characterized by a combination of natural problems with the collapse of infrastructure, lack of political authority and economic systems that moved food away from affected areas. Famines have also followed directly upon government land reform policies, in which traditional farms were devastated as ownership was transferred or collectivized. The two greatest examples of such difficulty were the conditions which prevailed in China under **Mao Zedong**'s **Great Leap Forward**, which may have killed as many as 40 million people in the period 1958–61, and those in **Zimbabwe** as the government and its supporters sought to remove white landowners of large farms after 2000. **Joseph Stalin** is widely held to have either precipitated famine alongside natural causes, or to have deliberately restricted food supplies to the **Ukraine** in 1932–3 as a political action. This action resulted in the deaths of at least 6 million and possibly twice as many, and is given the title *holomodor* in history books. Famine has often been held to have been produced by the combination of **laissez-faire** and mass poverty, as in **Ireland** in the mid nineteenth century, or in the so-called third world during the **Cold War**. Proponents of such explanations usually point to the existence of urban surpluses of food or exports of staples, both for profit, alongside predominantly rural hunger, and blame the former in some way for the latter.

fear of famine

The fear of famine has been a driver of major social and economic programmes since **World War II**.

The European Common Agricultural Policy, for instance, has (alongside the **Green Revolution**), via a combination of subsidy and protectionism, managed to maintain European farm production at a level greater than that which is required for European needs. The United States has also used its grain surpluses and global capacity, in alliance with foreign governments, to reduce or prevent famine, such as in Bihar in 1966–7 and in **Haiti** in 2009. Similarly, the **United Nations** (UN) greatly expanded its operations to provide famine relief, agricultural advice through the **Food and Agriculture Organization** (FAO), pre-emptive policy advice and a global network of disaster response from the mid twentieth century.

Famine has been associated with the aftermath of war, particularly where 'scorched earth' policies were employed, but has also been a driver of war, through resource competition; it therefore makes pre-eminent sense for the UN to have behaved in the way that it does. Many scholars have followed the lead of **Amartya Sen** in drawing a link between famine and a lack of political representation. Famines have occurred on a large scale where governments have either felt no need to care for the bulk of their own people, or have followed the advice of international organizations to liberalize farming into dependence upon global markets (as in **Malawi** in the 1990s, for example). On the other hand, in **India** – a huge state geographically and historically prone to famine – democratic authorities have, since independence, largely managed to contain mass hunger. The emergence of viable mass property rights may also be a key to the reduction of famine, as states along the rim of the Pacific and Indian Oceans have found since the emergence of globalization. It is noticeable, however, that very few developed or newly developed states are prepared to abandon the security of food production, once achieved, for the lower prices of international markets, particularly when many rich and developed nations, such as those in the **EU**, the **USA**, **Russia** and Japan, maintain policies of agricultural protection and external food purchasing. It would be a mistake to think of famine as something from the past. Even with highly developed and sensitive political and economic systems, the emergence of very strong world population growth coupled with the depletion of stocks of fresh water and a long upward trend in the cost of goods essential both to fertilizer, livestock feed and farming, such as oil, famine (or at least the threat of it) is very likely to appear as a live danger in future history.

Faraday, Michael (1791–1867)

English chemist and physicist. His most significant contributions pertain to the field of electricity, where he established the foundations for electromagnetic induction, which are applied to devices such as electric generators, transformers, induction motors and rechargeable batteries. For chemistry, he established the oxidation numbers, formulated the laws of electrolysis, and more practically, invented the Bunsen burner and the halogen lamp. His works include *Experimental Researches in Electricity* (1832) and *Six Lectures on the Chemical History of a Candle* (1861).

Farouk (Faruq) I (1920–1965)

King of **Egypt**, 1936–52. Inheriting the throne from his father Fuad, Farouk had to contend both with the British, still influential in spite of granting Egypt formal independence in 1922, and growing nationalist sentiment, in particular the **Wafd** Party. Often alienating both sides and increasingly isolated, he was accused of corruption and incompetence. He was ousted by the Nasserist coup of 1952 and died in exile.

Fasci di Combattimento

A name bestowed upon a confederation of fighting gangs and paramilitaries by **Benito Mussolini** in 1919. Mussolini's core group was centred on Milan and drew together strands of the Italian radical right and streetfighters so as to form the core of the Italian Fascist Party, which he formally created in 1921. Fasci were named for the sticks which symbolized classical Roman strength, and were associated with an anti-modern taste for war, territorial aggrandisement and violence at all levels, rather than the rule of law, diplomacy or democracy.

fascism

Fascism is a more difficult political philosophy to summarize than most because, in many respects, it is not really a philosophy at all but rather an emotional response to a particular complex of European cultural, economic, political and social factors in the interwar years. It had no clear founders as communism did in **Marx** and **Engels**, although it certainly drew on many strands of eighteenth- and nineteenth-century thought, including **Rousseau**'s concept of the 'general will', **Nietzsche**'s of respect for strength and the man of destiny, and **Romanticism**'s cult of emotionalism, transcendence and transfiguration. Moreover, its practitioners, notably **Hitler** and **Mussolini**, were conspicuously pragmatic in their approach to government once in power.

It has often been said that it is easier to define fascism by what it was against, rather than what it was for, but certain characteristics were common to the great majority of fascist parties. Essentially they believed in the primacy of the holistic, usually ethnic, community at the expense of the individual, and saw such communities as living organisms, in which the individual could no more have significant independent meaning than could an individual human organ. The building bricks of the community were the family and a national tradition in which the dead could be as important as the living. This could easily acquire a mystical colouring and at its extreme veer towards a cult of death. Not least, the community had a natural leader or, pursuing the bodily imagery, a head, just as the human body had a head, who owed his position to his superhuman qualities. This doctrine of the superman owed much to the German nineteenth-century philosopher, Friedrich Nietzsche, and exercised great appeal across Europe, including amongst its disciples the great Irish writer, George Bernard Shaw. It was closely associated with a worship of violence as the means by which the will of the superman would be realized. The title of Leni Riefenstahl's famous film on the Nazi rallies, *The Triumph of the Will*, meant what it said. In practice, the worship of violence inevitably attracted the most brutal elements in society ranging from the thuggish to the psychopathic, as well as idealists who saw death in armed combat as the highest form of sacrifice for their country. The corollary of the primacy given to the national was a particular hostility to the cosmopolitan, the international and the universal, which always encompassed **Communism** and, in central and eastern Europe and in **Germany** but not in **Italy**, **Judaism**. In accordance with its stress on the primacy of the community organized as the nation state, the fascist approach to commerce and industry was **corporatist** and syndicalist. Cartels were encouraged and operated in close coordination with government. Independent trade unions were banned because they put the interests of their members before those of the state. Many other independent organizations were banned for similar reasons or because they competed with the state's own organizations, like the Boy Scouts in Germany with the Hitler Youth.

The public appeal of fascism in the interwar years was normally at its strongest where liberal democracy and liberal capitalism were perceived as having failed to provide strong government and to avert the economic depression and uncontrollable inflation which afflicted Germany, in particular, in the 1920s and early 1930s. The middle classes, who had lost their savings, were therefore amongst its strongest supporters. It was also a logical, albeit unforeseen, response to the acceptance of the ethnic nationality principle by the victors in the 1919–20 **Treaties of Versailles**, Saint-Germain and Trianon as the basis for redrawing the map of Europe. Both liberal democracy and liberal capitalism were at their most vulnerable in the countries which had been defeated in **World War I** – Germany and **Austria–Hungary** – because the psychological impact of defeat was so strong and the terms of the peace treaties were so harsh. Large sections of German society rejected the new order from the very beginning.

Fascism was also at its strongest in those countries where the national political, as distinct from cultural, identity was comparatively new and at its weakest where it was longest established – **France**, and particularly **Britain**. It reflected the Romantic artificiality of many of the political nationalisms east of the Rhine and the extent to which they relied on historical invention rather than on prosaic historical reality. It was a craving for an identity which had either never existed or only in the fairly remote past. Not surprisingly, it was a powerful force in many of the new ethnic states created by Versailles, Saint-Germain and Trianon. Partly for this reason, fascism was highly theatrical. Flags and banners, marches, uniforms, mass rallies and the like were exploited with genius, as were symbols like the swastika. The attraction verged on the irresistible, as was the intention. It also engendered responsiveness to the accompanying propaganda, to swell ever greater mass enthusiasm and indeed hysteria. Fascism also had a fluidity which was partly political cynicism but partly also an aspiration to be a genuine alternative to the extremes of capitalism and communism. It was to be a natural growth responding to the circumstances of the moment, and in Mussolini's Italy at least often meant what the leader that day thought it meant. Nevertheless, it was always essentially radical.

Within this broad tapestry of fascism, however, there were significant national differences of emphasis. Italian fascism, for example, never showed the German obsession with race or, until a fairly late stage, its **anti-Semitism**. It remained bullying rather than brutal. Its adulation of the leader never reached Hitlerian proportions, neither was there the same overwhelming role for the party. Romanian fascism was an unnervingly unstable mix, in Corneliu Codreanu's (1899–1938) paramilitary Legion of the Archangel Michael, renamed in 1932 the Iron Guard, of mystical Christianity, historicism and populism which terrorized and murdered Jews as well as political opponents. The Hungarian Arrow Cross, set up by Ferenc Szalasi (1897–1946) in 1939 as the successor to a number of right-wing, frequently anti-Semitic, anti-Communist groups, also pursued an agrarian agenda under the slogan 'Soil, Blood and Work'. Western European fascism showed different emphases. The Belgian Rexists, founded by Louis Degrelle (1906–94), though sharing the anti-Communism and anti-Semitism of other right-wing parties, drew heavily upon Belgian Catholicism and monarchism. The French Action Française capitalized upon the royalist, Catholic and conservative opposition to the **Third Republic** and later the **Popular Front** headed by **Leon Blum**. French fascism became deeply implicated in the **Vichy** regime which expressed many of its attitudes, including colluding in Nazi anti-Semitism. In Spain, the Falange, founded in 1933 by José Antonio Primo de Rivera (1903–36), the son of the Spanish dictator of the 1920s, idealized a Conservative, Catholic Spain shorn of socialist and cosmopolitan elements. It supported and was subsumed into **Franco**'s side in the **Spanish Civil War**, especially after the death of its leader at the hands of Spanish Republicans. Franco adopted its fascist trappings, installed Antonio as a martyr, and his sister formed a hugely successful women's section with 580,000 members by 1939. In **Great Britain**, Sir Oswald Mosley's British Union of Fascists formed in 1932. They borrowed the symbolism of Italian fascism, later of Nazi rallies, but added their own distinctive blend of imperial revival through protectionism and Keynesian economics. Mosley's party failed to develop significant electoral support and his adoption of anti-Semitism reduced him to fringe status and led to his arrest under emergency regulations following the outbreak of war. Outside Europe, minor fascist-style movements developed in the **United States** and there were overtones of European fascism in the military-dominated Japanese governments of the 1930s, where ultra-nationalism merged with the cultivation of a sense of national regeneraton and triumph over western interference.

Massively discredited by the behaviour and defeat of the fascist regimes in **World War II**, many pre-war fascist movements were consigned to oblivion in Soviet-controlled eastern Europe and actually outlawed in West Germany following programmes of de-Nazification. Fascist leaders in occupied countries such as **Norway**, Holland, **France** and **Belgium** were executed, imprisoned or forced into exile. Some fascist elements survived in the post-war Francoist and Salazar regimes, which lasted in Spain and Portugal until the 1970s, though increasingly without the revolutionary edge that had hitherto distinguished fascism from simple right-wing authoritarianism. However, immigration to Europe gave a fresh boost to the racial component of right-wing movements such as Mosley's Union Party after 1945 and to the much more successful French Front National formed by Jean Marie Le Pen (1928–) in 1972, which adopted an ultra-nationalist position courting anti-immigrant and anti-Semitic support. It was sufficiently popular in the presidential elections to achieve second place. His daughter Marie pushed the party to new heights in the presidential poll in 2017, adopting an anti-EU and anti-immigration platform.

Fascism has also been applied as a term for right-wing regimes such as those of **Perón** in **Argentina**, General **Pinochet** in **Chile** and the Colonels' regime in **Greece** during the 1960s, which were primarily conservative dictatorships.

Fashoda Incident

A near military encounter between French and British forces in southern Sudan, which grew out of imperial competition between **France** and **Great Britain** as both nations sought to expand their holdings in central Africa. A French expedition, under Captain Jean-Baptiste Marchand, sought a trans-African route that would anchor French influence across equatorial Africa. British forces under Major General **Horatio Kitchener** were engaged in securing control over the entire Nile river valley. The incident came to head when Kitchener moved to block further French movement after they raised a French flag at Fashoda in July 1898. Outnumbered, Marchand was in no position to resist militarily. Similarly, neither government was anxious for an armed confrontation. Marchand withdrew his troops in December. The incident led to the Anglo-French Treaty of 1899 that established boundaries of each empire in the region, with Britain gaining the Nile basin and France gaining the Congo basin.

Fatah

– *see also* **Palestine Liberation Organization (PLO)**.
The organization Fatah was officially founded by **Yasser Arafat** in the 1960s. Unofficially it had existed in **Kuwait** since 1957 at the impetus of

Palestinian refugees. Yasser Arafat, Khalil al-Wazir, Farouq Kadumi, Mahmoud Abbas and Khalid al-Hassan were the founding members. Fatah, or the Movement for the National Liberation of Palestine, was founded as a mouthpiece for Palestinian resistance and the reformation of an independent state. Its motto 'Revolution until Victory!' reiterates this position. Fatah was founded with the intention of being a popular movement giving a voice and power to the people. Although its stated purpose was revolutionary in nature, the movement did not have an armed organization until 1964 when it began attacks upon **Israel**, assuming the leadership of the **Palestinian Liberation Organization (PLO)** in 1968. It suffered a major setback when it was expelled from Jordan in 1970–1, but retained the leadership of the PLO under Arafat. Following the **Oslo Accords** it obtained the majority of seats in the Palestinian Council elections in 1996, on the one hand taking a lead role in negotiations with Israel but also playing a major role in the 2000 **Intifada**. **Hamas** defeated Fatah for control of the council in 2006 and a brief civil war saw Fatah lose control of **Gaza** while retaining its position in the **West Bank**.

Fath 'Ali Shah (1771–1834)

Shah of **Iran**, 1797–1834, having succeeded his uncle, **Agha Mohammad Khan**. He successfully subdued a rebellion in Khorasan, but was put on the defensive when Russia's General Tsitsianov provoked war by attacking Yerevan, 1804. He sought French help by signing a treaty of alliance with **Napoleon** in 1807. Napoleon then sent a strong military mission under General Gardanne to train the Iranian Army, but signed the Peace of Tilsit and lost interest in supporting the Iranians against the Russians before Gardanne had even arrived. Fath 'Ali Shah turned to the British for military advice on the recovery of **Azerbaijan** from the Russians, but to little benefit. Two serious Iranian military defeats by the Russians, 1812, resulted in the Treaty of Gulistan, 1813, which transferred northern Azerbaijan and the cities of Baku, Derbend and Gyanda to Russia. He was exposed to further Russian territorial claims, and to further military defeats, 1826–7. The resulting **Treaty of Turkmanchai**, 1828, transferred Iranian Armenia to Russia.

favela

The term *favela* is used most frequently in central and south **Brazil** since the first squatter shantytown in Brazil was established in Rio de Janeiro in 1897. Often built on hillsides or flood plains, some favelas have remained for decades and developed a sense of community. They consist of houses made of sheet metal, brick and cement blocks, and odd pieces of wood. Without official recognition, they lack city services and schools. Residents tap electricity illegally and carry water home from sources on the settlement's outer boundary. It is estimated that Rio de Janeiro has some 700 favelas with some 2 million largely black and mulatto inhabitants whose rate of increase is almost three times that of the city. Any services are often provided by non-governmental organizations. While the terms for them differ, these squatter settlements are common in the outskirts of cities throughout South America.

Federal Bureau of Investigation (FBI)

Named the FBI in 1935, this US law enforcement agency traces its bureaucratic antecedents to 1908 and its original inspiration to the establishment of the Department of Justice in 1870 and the use of federal detectives to crush the **Ku Klux Klan**. The bureau has fluctuated between fame (jailing mobsters) and notoriety (wire-tapping dissidents). Heavily criticized over 9/11, it has nevertheless expanded at home and abroad in the twenty-first century to combat terrorism.

Federalism (American)

The term usually applied both to the political philosophy of supporters of the ratification of the US Constitution in 1787 and 1788, and later, to the political programmes espoused by the **Federalist Party** of **George Washington**, **John Adams** and **Alexander Hamilton**. Whilst there is substantial overlap between the two groups, not every supporter of ratification would end up a supporter of the Federalist Party. In the 1790s, Federalism became closely associated with the centralizing and nationalizing philosophy of Alexander Hamilton. These policies, such as a national bank, a national debt and the cultivation of a mercantile and business elite, were modelled on the 'fiscal-military state' of **Great Britain**. Consequently, opponents labelled the Federalists 'Anglomaniacs'. Federalist belief in 'order' over 'liberty' caused them to support alliance with England over **France** in the 1790s, and the **Alien and Sedition Acts** in 1798, making it illegal to speak ill of the government. These policies contributed to Federalism's decline by the early 1800s.

Federalist Party (American)

As a partisan term, *Federalist* originally meant a supporter of the **American Constitution** in 1787–8. In the early 1790s, as supporters of

George Washington's presidency divided, it came to mean those who favoured the administration, Hamiltonian finance and cooperation with **Britain**. Faced by powerful opposition, the Federalists narrowly elected **John Adams** president in 1796 and enjoyed a surge of popularity in the 1798–9 war crisis with **France**. In 1801 they lost control of the federal government and suffered demoralization as **Jefferson** consolidated Republican hold on power. After 1807 the Federalists revived in the northern and middle states: they commanded state governments, regained congressional seats and in 1812 came within a state of defeating Madison's re-election. Severely critical of the war against Britain, they lost much support when the United States emerged unscathed in 1815. Dropping opposition to **Monroe**'s federalizing administration, they declined nationally but remained a force in some coastal states until the partisan realignment of the 1820s.

fellahin

A peasant or agricultural farmer in the Middle East and North Africa. Derived from an Arabic term for ploughman or tiller, the fellahin form 60 per cent of the Egyptian population. They traditionally provided **Egypt** with food and manpower. Fellahin farmers continue to live in mud-brick houses along the Nile, though many have moved into Egypt's expanding towns and cities.

feminism and post-feminism

There have always been women who have made their mark in male-dominated societies, such as Catherine the Great or Florence Nightingale, and many communities and societies have been strongly matriarchal in their arrangements, giving women considerable power in property rights, economic affairs and even political organization. Religious movements have also often provided an outlet for female spirituality in religious communities for women, as in Christianity and Buddhism, and female `saints' and holy women have a prominent place in many world religions. Women have also played a significant role in the animalist, magical and shamanistic practices of a wide variety of societies. The `wise' or `cunning' women of early modern **Europe** still have parallels in many societies where traditional beliefs remain well entrenched.

But whatever the role of women in society, feminism in the modern sense, with its insistence on equal economic, legal, political, sexual and social rights, is partly a legacy of the **Enlightenment** with its emphasis on the rights of all human beings and its quest to reform societies in a progressive manner. It also drew upon the Romantic movement with its emphasis on individualism and personal fulfilment. These movements found expression in the work of the English bluestockings, intellectual women who met to discuss a wide range of intellectual and cultural concerns. Out of this milieu sprang a flourishing group of female writers, especially in English and French, including women novelists such as Fanny Burney (1752–1840) and Maria Edgeworth (1768–1849). This activity found political expression in the writings of Mary Wollstonecraft (1759–97), the author of the *Vindication of the Rights of Women* (1792), advocating equal opportunities for men and women and demonstrating in her own lifestyle an `open' attitude to relationships with the opposite sex. Her daughter Mary Wollstonecraft Shelley (1797–1851) is remembered as the author of *Frankenstein* (1817) but demonstrated her sexual freedom by notoriously eloping with the poet, Shelley. In **France**, Olympe de Gouges (1748–93) was the author of the *Declaration of the Rights of Women and Citizens* (1791) and joined with other women in all-female radical clubs and in publications which flourished during the most radical phase of the French Revolution, only to fall foul of the Jacobins in the Terror and be guillotined in November 1793. In **Germany**, Madame de Staël (1766–1817) was one of the leading intellectuals of the day, hosting a literary salon in Paris which attracted opponents to the Napoleonic regime and whose novels *Delphine* (1802) and *Corinne* (1807) illustrate self-determining `modern' women as heroines. In North America, one outcome of the revolutionary period was a stimulus to women's rights with Abigail Adams (1744–1818) and Judith Sargent Murray (1751–1820) urging equal treatment for women. Murray's *On the Equality of the Sexes* (1790) signalled new thinking which resulted in a stimulus to women's education and some alteration by individual states of property rights and divorce laws in favour of women.

A flourishing cultural and literary climate in the West from the late eighteenth century reflected growing educational opportunities, especially for women from professional and middle-class families. While aristocratic and ruling-class women had commonly been educated at home by private tutors or at court both in Europe and elsewhere, the rise of a mercantile, urban society put an increasing premium on the education of daughters at least in the genteel accomplishments thought necessary to fit women for the marriage market. By 1800 most towns of any consequence in western Europe or North America had schools for women and teaching or running schools was one of the few respectable occupations available to women by the early nineteenth century. Early nineteenth-century feminism remained dominated by literary figures such as Jane Austen (1775–1817), the Brontë sisters and George Eliot (1819–80) in England, and George Sand (1804–76) in France. Significantly, these women often adopted men's names to facilitate the publication of their novels, but Sand was characterized by an ambiguity which has run through the history of feminism. Married with two children, she was notorious on the one hand for her wearing of men's clothing but on the other for a scandalous lifestyle, including amongst her many lovers the French poet, Alfred de Musset, and the composer, Chopin. A vastly more conventional figure than George Sand, George Eliot nevertheless lived with a married man for twenty-five years and her novel *Romola* is a powerful denunciation of the oppression of women.

However valid such concerns were, they nevertheless reflected a somewhat middle-class perspective. Working-class women had long been not only vital contributors to the peasant smallholding but also shopkeepers, market women, innkeepers and small traders. Feminism tended to overlook them. Moreover, economic and social developments throughout the nineteenth century muted the appeal of feminism for the majority of women, even if in sometimes contradictory ways. One such development was the growing popularity of the originally medieval romantic concept of woman as an idealized being, pure and spiritually superior – *das ewige Weibliche* (the eternal feminine) of Goethe's *Faust*. This fitted very easily into the ethos of the rapidly expanding middle class which, men and women alike, deemed it impossible for a woman both to work and be a lady. Not working was visible evidence to society that a family was not pauperized and the idealized woman was above worldly concerns. She was `the angel in the home'. This dissociation of middle-class women from the economy was further emphasized by the masculinization of business and the professions. Until the latter part of the nineteenth century women were excluded from higher education and places such as medical and art schools where professional training could be obtained.

At the other end of the social scale, the early Industrial Revolution brought women into factories and mines, often in areas where male labour was scarce. Early textile factories, in particular, used cheap and available female and child labour. Concern about the welfare of both led to the first factory legislation which banned women from working underground in the **United Kingdom** from 1842 and restricted hours of work. Well-meaning legislation to protect women and the fear of male workers and the early trade unions that women might be used to undercut male wages meant, however, that women were restricted to less well-paid areas of the labour force. In the West, the largest employment for women was in domestic service well into the twentieth century, and women tended to work outside the home or domestic sphere in poorly paid areas such as the clothing and garment industries and the so-called `sweated' trades such as match-making, millinery and later, assembly-style industries. A pattern emerged which spread across the world with **industrialization** that the majority of the female labour force were younger, unmarried women in relatively poorly paid occupations. As late as the outbreak of **World War II** in Europe and North America work outside the home was not the norm for married women of the middle or working classes in urban areas and only a small minority were involved in the professions, other than teaching. Outside the West, the progress of industrialization showed similar effects, with women drawn into early factories in **Japan**, **India** and, later, **China**, though excluded from the more highly skilled branches of the industrial workforce. While in many developing countries hard manual work by women has remained common in both industrial and agricultural contexts, the number of women engine drivers, engineers and managers has remained small.

Another feature that was exported from the West to the wider world was the desire on the part of Christian missionaries and colonial administrators to eliminate customs which they saw as immoral or uncivilized according to western values. A wide variety of traditional practices which affected women came under pressure from colonial elites, missionaries and the first generation of western-educated national leaders. They wrestled with the persistence of female slavery and concubinage, polygamy, suttee or wife-burning, child prostitution and dowry murder.

In the West, educational opportunities and the position of women were developing from the late nineteenth century. Secondary and higher **education** for girls advanced slowly but surely. Even by 1900, it had made scant progress in **Belgium**, **Italy**, the **Netherlands**, **Sweden** and **Switzerland**, but on the other hand a quarter of a million girls were receiving secondary education in **Russia** by 1900 and the same number in Germany by 1910. Progress in university education for women was less uneven. By 1914, France, Germany and Italy had some 5,000 students each and Austria 2,700, whereas Russia had more than 9,000. The class bias remained strong. Holloway College, now part of the University of London, was founded in 1883 'to afford the best education for women of the Upper and Upper Middle Class'. The award of the joint Nobel Prize in physics to the Pole, Madame Curie, in 1903 exploded any serious belief that women were innately inferior in intellect. Moreover, women were increasingly entering employment. Although only some 10 per cent of married women in Britain and Germany had a paid occupation in the period 1890–1910, some 50 per cent of unmarried ones had, and 40 per cent of widows. Young women were increasingly employed as clerks and primary school teachers as well as in the service industries generally. There were also some legislative advances in Europe and North America in women's property rights, divorce laws and child custody. The development of greater female assertiveness led to the phenomenon of the `new woman' by the end of the nineteenth century, cycling, smoking and also beginning to agitate for political rights.

In spite of the gradual extension of voting rights to men in nineteenth-century Europe and North America, women were excluded. Leading liberal intellectuals such as John Stuart Mill wrote in support of women's right to vote in 1867 and in 1848 American women in the Seneca Falls Declaration had called for the promise of the **American Constitution** to be fulfilled for women by giving them full citizenship, including voting rights. These demands remained unfilled before 1914, in spite of the vote being granted to women in **New Zealand** in 1893 and in **Australia** in 1902. In the face of the British parliament's refusal to accede to a female suffrage, the **Suffragettes** pursued a violent campaign of terror against property in the years before **World War I**. The war, however, proved a breakthrough as women's service in the war and the need to fully democratize votes for men saw the franchise extended to women in the United States in 1920, to women in Britain over 30 in 1918, and those over 21 in 1928. By the mid 1920s women had the vote in most European countries. The ascendency of the Bolsheviks in the **Soviet Union** following the 1917 Revolution led them to espouse the full equality of the sexes, through equal opportunities at work, the provision of nursery schools and access to birth control and abortion. Turkish women were given the vote under **Atatürk** in 1922 as part of a deliberate process of modernization.

But the achievements of 'first-wave' feminism were overtaken after World War II by a growing sense that the acquisition of voting rights had left women still in an inferior position even in western society, occupying few of the higher positions in society, suffering from unequal pay and still primarily seen as secondary to men in their traditional roles as homemakers and mothers. Works such as French philosopher Simone de Beauvoir's (1908–86) *The Second Sex* (1949) argued that womanhood was a social construct, while **Betty Friedan**'s *The Feminine Mystique* (1963) criticized the conventional role of women in American society. Second-wave feminism followed these lines of argument as it emerged alongside the radical civil rights and student movements of the 1960s. Groups such as the American National Organization for Women (NOW) and the Women's Equity Action League (WEAL) campaigned on a range of women's issues: equal pay, abortion law reform, maternity leave, domestic abuse, sexual violence against women and the gross under-representation of women in positions of power. As a result of political pressure an American Equal Pay Act governing federal employees was passed in 1963 while the British government passed an Equal Pay Act in 1970 and a Sex Discrimination Act in 1975. Second-wave feminism had a radical critique of the male oppression of women, dubbed in popular parlance `women's lib', that had far-reaching consequences in attempting a genuinely revolutionary shift in society's attitudes towards women and their position in society. Kate Millet's *Sexual Politics* (1970) treated sexual division as the binary divide in which women were an oppressed class. As a result, women's movements have shifted to wider issues, such as pornography, prostitution, gender stereotyping in advertising and language, violence against women in the home and in public, and the still wide gaps in pay and career profiles between men and women.

So-called 'third-wave' feminism has softened the anti-male language of oppression, while adopting the slogan `Different but Equal' to support causes specific to women's needs and to promote greater equality of opportunity. These issues have reached far beyond the West where they were born as part of the radical movements of the 1960s. Global feminism was spread by United Nations World Conferences on Women held in Mexico City in 1975, Copenhagen in 1980, Nairobi in 1985 and Beijing in 1995. Issues of sexual violence as an instrument of war, child marriage, female genital mutilation (FGM) and the education of women are currently major issues in the global feminist agenda.

Figueres Ferrer, José (1906–1990)

A towering figure in the political history of twentieth-century **Latin America**, Figueres served twice as president of **Costa Rica**, in 1953–8 and 1970–4. Following a civil war in 1948, he founded the National Liberation Party (PLN). He used this base to transform Costa Rica into a model of institutional stability, democracy and social welfare at a time when the wider Caribbean region faced intractable **Cold War** divisions, dictatorship and popular unrest.

filibuster, filibustering

Filibustering refers in one meaning to the unauthorized attempts of private individuals in nineteenth-century America to conquer sovereign states. The phrase most often pertains to the 1850s, when several Americans attempted to take over nations in the Caribbean and **Central America**, bringing slavery with them. However, filibustering can also refer to similar interventions in Florida, **Texas** and **Canada**. William Walker, who implanted himself as president of **Nicaragua** in the 1850s, is the most well-known filibuster. A second meaning refers to the parliamentary tactic of using up time in debate to 'talk out' a piece of legislation.

Fillmore, Millard (1800–1874)

Fillmore served in the **United States** House, 1833–5, 1837–43, and led its **Whig** members. Named **Zachary Taylor**'s running mate to secure the vote of New York State, Fillmore became thirteenth president, 1850–3, on Taylor's death. A conservative, he supported the **Compromise of 1850** and the **Fugitive Slave Law**, which, along with his purge of Taylor appointees, cost him renomination in 1852. The **American Party** named him its candidate in 1856; he finished a poor third.

Final Solution
– *see* **Holocaust**.

finance
– *see* **money**.

Finland
– *see also* **Finno-Russian Wars**.

A country in northern Europe which has been independent since 1919, having formerly been a duchy within the **Russian Empire** and a Swedish possession before that. Its autonomous presence within **Russia** was a cause of some concern before the **Russian Revolution**, and its secession a matter of annoyance to the Soviets afterwards. It fought a war with the **Soviet Union** in 1939–40 and was forced to cede territory after its defeat. Finland was the only democracy to side with Nazi Germany against the Soviet Union in Operation Barbarossa, though it did not participate in the associated genocides. It turned against the Nazis in 1944 and expelled German troops from its soil after an armistice with the **USSR**. Subsequently, Finland became a prosperous European state and a model of development from an agricultural to an industrial society with a highly egalitarian welfare system, appropriate for a small population and huge land mass. It was the site of the Helsinki Accords of 1975, as well as a 'bridge' between the Western bloc and the Eastern bloc. In 1995 the country (a parliamentary republic) joined the **European Union**, and followed into the eurozone in 2002. Finland is often featured in gun control debates, as its highly armed citizens enjoy a very high quality of life, and the state is often seen as one of the most stable in the world.

Finney, Charles Grandison (1792–1875)

Presbyterian, subsequently Congregationalist **evangelist** of the **second Great Awakening**. Trained as a lawyer, Finney experienced a religious crisis in 1821 and entered the ministry. He gained fame for his charismatic, extemporaneous and innovative revivalist preaching, which demanded an immediate acceptance of Christ. He found a home for his qualified Calvinism's social perfectionism and **abolitionism** at Oberlin College, Ohio, in 1835, assuming its presidency from 1851 to 1866, but kept up his itinerant revivalism.

Finno-Russian Wars

The 1939–40 'Winter War' resulted from the Finnish refusal of a Soviet demand to surrender territory better to defend Leningrad. The Finns were defeated, March 1940. The 1941–4 'Continuation War' followed the German invasion of Soviet Russia and saw the Finnish recapture, as Germany's ally under **Mannerheim**, of the territory ceded in 1940. Parts of Soviet Karelia were subsequently captured to create a 'Greater Finland'. The peace settlement with defeated Finland returned the territories to the **Soviet Union**.

Fire-eaters (American)

The radical shock troops of the **Secession** movement in the slaveholding states before the **American Civil War**. Strongest in the lower South, especially South Carolina, fire-eaters despised compromise, arguing that secession was the only way for Southerners to protect their liberty and honour in the struggle against free-state domination. Prominent among them were Robert Barnwell Rhett of South Carolina and William Lowndes Yancey of Alabama. With secession accomplished in 1861, the fire-eaters' political influence waned.

First International

The International Working Men's Association, formed in London in 1864 to unite a range of European anti-capitalist groups and trade unions on a class struggle basis. The International was riven by disputes between 'authoritarianism' and 'libertarianism'. **Marx** and his supporters favoured parliamentary activity and state socialism, while the followers of the Anarchist Bakunin argued for revolution against both capitalism and the state. The International moved to New York in 1872 but was dissolved in 1876.

First Nations

– see **indigenous peoples**.

First War of Independence

– see **Indian Mutiny**.

Fischer Thesis

An idea put forward in its full form by German historian Fritz Fischer in 1961. Fischer, who suppressed details of his membership of the Freikorps and Nazi Party in the 1920s, held that the unification of **Germany** in 1871 was achieved on such lines that Germany could only destabilize the peace of **Europe**. He further asserted that there was a clear line between Germany's responsibility (as he saw it) for **World War I** and the policies of **Adolf Hitler** in foreign affairs that led to **World War II**. Fischer believed that any German state since the Reformation would have challenged **Britain** and France for European and global leadership on military lines. His arguments allowed a debate to erupt about German identity and history which was intense and which led directly to the later 'historians quarrel' or *historikerstreit*.

Five-Year Plan (Soviet)

First implemented in Russia in 1928–32 by the Committee of Economic Planning (Gosplan) and backed by **Stalin**, the first Five-Year Plan aimed to break sharply with Russia's economic backwardness by promoting rapid industrialization. It set goals and priorities for virtually all sectors, and emphasized the need for large-scale investments in heavy industry. Under the plan, individual enterprises did not decide on inputs or production levels, but followed bureaucratic instructions. Considered an outright success in attaining remarkable growth in targeted sectors such as coal and iron production, which doubled, and electric generation, which tripled, the downside consisted of sharp falls in agricultural output that led to recurrent famines. Economic planning by means of Soviet-style Plans was copied by Communist regimes after the war. Western nations, developed and underdeveloped, also implemented forms of planning generally aimed at growth, regional balance, policy consistency or coordination among economic sectors in the context of market economies.

fleet system

Starting in 1564, armed convoys controlled by the Merchant Guild of Seville and the House of Trade theoretically departed annually from Seville and later Cadiz with goods for Spanish America. Uniting in **Havana**, they returned to the peninsula with silver from New Spain and **Peru** and gold from New Granada. Individual registered ships replaced the convoys in 1740 to reduce foreign competitors, but the fleet for New Spain resumed between 1757 and 1776.

Flexible Response

During the 1950s, President **Dwight Eisenhower** and Secretary of State **John Foster Dulles** made the threat posed by America's superiority in nuclear weaponry the cornerstone of their attempt to deter Communist expansion. Threatening **Cold War** adversaries with nuclear devastation was viewed as a way of achieving American foreign policy goals at a minimal cost. Flexible Response was in essence a critique by military pundits and liberal anti-Communists (such as **John Kennedy**) of this Eisenhower–Dulles approach. Proponents of Flexible Response argued that the **USA** should devise a wider range of approaches, including the development of conventional armed forces, so that it could react in a precise, calibrated way to challenges overseas. The intellectual justification for Flexible Response may have seemed clear, but it can be argued that it promoted a sort of tinkering and adventurism that resulted for the United States in the calamity of the **Vietnam War**.

Flying Tigers
– *see* **Burmese Campaign**.

FNLA (UPA)

The FNLA (National Front for the Liberation of Angola) was a military organization and later a political party, formed in 1954 in northern **Angola**. It was an armed movement that fought for independence from the Portuguese under leader **Holden Roberto**. During the conflict, the FNLA was variously supported by the **USA**, **China**, **Israel** and Zaire. At independence, it became involved in a drawn-out civil war with the **MPLA** and **UNITA**. In 1992 it became an official political party.

Foch, Ferdinand (1851–1929)

World War I French field marshal and overall commander of Allied forces in **France** and **Belgium** which finally defeated the German armies in 1918. He served as a military instructor, 1894–9, and wrote *Principles and Conduct of War* (1899), which extolled the values of the offensive and morale. Director of the École de Guerre, 1907–11, he served with distinction in early but costly battles in 1914–16, was appointed Chief of Staff in 1917 and from March 1918 acted as *generalissimo* in the succession of offensives which forced **Germany** to seek an armistice. At the **Treaty of Versailles** he argued that the settlement did not provide adequately for French security.

food

Among the most relevant aspects of contemporary food systems, **globalization** certainly looms large. The changes introduced by worldwide movements of ideas, information, goods, money and people are often indicated as a specifically modern phenomenon. Speed and intensity of change, heralded by massive industrialization and technological innovations in food production, processing, preservation, storage, transportation, distribution and retail, are often perceived in terms of loss of traditions, local identity and cultural heritage. Food as a commodity is the object of international trade negotiations, especially since the establishment of the World Trade Organization, which from 1995 has determined the principles and modalities of food-related global markets through specific agreements dealing with issues as diverse as tariffs, subsidies, safety and intellectual property.

globalization

On the consumption side, transnational industry and powerful marketing machines have meant the expansion of fast-food restaurant chains, the circulation of standardized, durable, cheap, mostly safe and mass-produced items, and the growing uniformity of global consumer cultures. The business decisions of transnational food corporations and retailers, which often invest directly in developing countries and dislocate manufacturing among distant localities, determine the availability and visibility of products. Some negative consequences of these epochal transformations, such as the shift of nutritional models from grain-based to meat- and dairy-intensive diets, the excessive consumption of sugar- and fat-rich foods, and the so-called obesity epidemic seem to affect the most remote corners of the planet.

However, it is necessary to adopt a nuanced approach when analyzing the complex and multi-layered phenomena connected with globalization. Many worldwide corporations operate in a mode that has been defined as 'glocal', adapting global priorities and strategies to different environments, while adopting and exploiting local products, often decontextualized and provided with new cultural meanings. Many fast-food chains rely on local products to assemble dishes that are the same across the planet and also create specialties that reflect or mimic local specialities. Globalization also manifests itself in the diffusion of ingredients, dishes and food-related traditions from one country to another, especially in urban environments where immigrant communities are more numerous. 'Ethnic' restaurants have become a fixture in urban landscapes across the world, with Italian, French, Japanese, Chinese, Indian and Mexican cuisines at the forefront, followed by Thai, Ethiopian, Moroccan and Lebanese, each of them occupying different segments of the local food scenes in terms of prestige and price point.

Looking at food systems from a historical point of view, however, we need not only to understand their origins and transformations over time, but also to ascertain if phenomena usually attributed to globalization are exclusive to our times. In fact, transfers of ingredients, materials, techniques, ideas, values and practices related to food and eating have been common since the origins of humanity. As a consequence, it is necessary to identify different aspects of food globalization across time and space and to analyze their specific dynamics, scope and duration.

crop transfer

Differences in geographical environment, culture and technology have always stimulated a wealth of diverse productions, which in turn encouraged exchanges and trade. Crop transfers have occurred since antiquity. Wheat, first domesticated in the Fertile Crescent, was adopted in far-away **China**, while citrus fruit slowly moved from East Asia to the Mediterranean. However, these movements often happened without any prearranged plan or political intervention and took centuries, if not millennia, to take place. Food also played a crucial role in local and regional trade. The Roman Empire was able to expand thanks to it capacity to organize production and distribution of grains, mainly wheat, and of cash commodities such as wine and olive oil. The Chinese Empire turned taxes on the production and trade of salt and alcohol into an important source of income, while developing a complex system of man-made canals to ensure the transportation of grains between the south and north. Only luxury goods – and in particular spices, which were relatively easy to transport and commanded impressive prices – travelled from one end to the other of the Old World along the land routes of the Silk Road and the maritime routes of the Indian Ocean, allowing the elites in different civilizations to enjoy forms of conspicuous consumption. However, in Oceania and the New World crop transfers and trade contacts were limited to the regional level.

This situation radically changed from the end of the fifteenth century, when the arrival of Spanish explorers in the Americas and the encroachment of Portuguese traders on the Indian Ocean routes marked the beginning of one of the largest movements of people, plants and animals in history, changing forever the way we grow, distribute, consume, and even think of food. In the following centuries, New World crops such as maize, sweet potatoes, potatoes, beans, tomato, chili peppers and peanuts were introduced in **Europe**, **Asia** and **Africa**, embraced by farmers who appreciated their high yields and adaptability to marginal lands. The modern period saw western European powers establish colonies – and later empires – whose profitability was mostly based on the production, control and trade of valuable commodities, including spices from Eastern Asia and a new category of stimulant substances that could be smoked, drunk or eaten. However, at least at the beginning of the colonial enterprises, many of these crops constituted natural monopolies. China was the sole producer of tea, while cacao originally grew only in **Mexico**, **Central America** and the Amazon basin.

To avoid the hurdles connected with these natural monopolies, the burgeoning European empires focused on transferring those cultivations to their own colonies. The new scientific approach to nature that was changing European mentalities proved to be the perfect partner of imperial expansion. In fact, great efforts were dedicated to studying tropical and exotic crops not only in their natural habitats but also in botanical gardens, where seeds and young plants were nurtured to be then redistributed across far-flung territories in the hope they would adapt and expand.

Some plants did not require much to prosper in the new environments. The Spaniards first introduced sugarcane in Caribbean islands, which was planted by the Dutch in the north-east of **Brazil** and then transferred to the French and English islands, in particular **Jamaica**, **Trinidad**, Martinique and Guadeloupe. While at first sugarcane was grown by European smallholders and indentured servants, over time the possibility of enormous revenues favoured the establishment of large plantations, modelled on Spanish and Portuguese cultivations in the Canary and Cape Verde Islands, manned by large numbers of African slaves in a production system that was highly organized, time-sensitive and requiring relevant investment of capital.

Traditional spices were introduced in the New World to break the East Asian monopolies. Over time, Grenada became a major producer of clove and nutmeg, and the French introduced pepper in Mauritius, Réunion and French Guiana. When cacao became a high-demand product the Spaniards, who had a monopoly on it, expanded its cultivation to **Venezuela**, Brazil and the **Philippines**. The Dutch transferred the plant to Curaçao in 1634, thus breaking the Spanish monopoly, the French introduced it in their Caribbean islands, and the Dutch brought it to **Ceylon** and **Indonesia**. Over time, cacao production spread also to West and Central Africa.

Arabica coffee, domesticated in **Ethiopia** and then transferred to Yemen, was sold at first under a tight monopoly controlled by the Indian and Arab traders in the Yemeni port of Mocha. Only later did it spread from there to many areas in the Islamic world. Across the **Ottoman Empire**, coffee drinking became associated with consumption in public places where men could gather and discuss current matters, to the point that coffeehouses were at times considered suspect as possible hotbeds of sedition. From the seventeenth century, the presence of Ottoman diplomats and merchants in Europe made the drink popular also among the western elites. Demand grew, and the Dutch managed to introduce some plants to Ceylon and Java and to bring specimens to the Amsterdam Botanical Gardens in 1706. From there, the

French transferred the crop to Martinique, Haiti and French Guiana, from where it spread to Brazil, thus eliminating the remnants of the Ottoman monopoly by the end of the eighteenth century.

Tea remained a Chinese monopoly until the eighteenth century, when European demand grew to the point where the exclusive production in China caused an enormous trade deficit and came to be perceived as a hurdle to free commerce. The British found the answer in a crop that grew in many areas of the Raj: poppy and its derivative, opium. The crop eventually lead to a series of devastating wars in the nineteenth century known as the **Opium Wars** (1839–42) and to the encroachment of western powers on Chinese territory. At the same time, the British found local varieties of tea in their Assam territories, which they later introduced in other parts of their empire, including the nearby Ceylon. Other crops were transferred not because of their commercial value but because of their potential as a source of nourishment. Breadfruit, rich in starch and consumed roasted or baked, was famously brought from Tahiti to the Caribbean by Captain William Bligh in 1789, in order to feed the local slaves, despite the fact that the native crops would have provided enough sustenance, if they had been taken into consideration by the plantation owners.

While New World crops expanded to the Old World, crops were transferred in the newly occupied territories in order to feed the colonists with foods they were acquainted with and that maintained cultural relevance as a connection to their lands of origin and as indicators of difference – and superiority – in the new environments. The French, Dutch and British colonies in the Americas saw the introduction of plants such as wheat, barley, oats, rice, onion, carrot and cabbage, as well as of domestic animals, above all cows, sheep, goat, pigs and poultry. In the Spanish and Portuguese territories in Central and South America, culinary customs connected with Christianity and its ceremonies were imposed as a way for the natives to reach salvation and as symbols of prestige and higher social status. As much as they wanted to distance themselves from the natives by displaying conspicuous consumption and by sticking to bread and wine, the colonial upper classes adopted a hybrid material culture that expressed itself in dishes such as the Mexican mole.

The African slaves working in the New World developed their own distinctive cuisines, with specialities that still survive, such as the Peruvian antichucos (beef heart skewers), the Caribbean callalloos (soups with taro leaves and other greens) and the Brazilian moquecas (coconut milk stews seasoned with palm oil). In the southern parts of the British American colonies, the increasing presence of slaves marked the introduction of crops such as okra, black-eye peas, collard greens and yams. At the same time, in Africa, the slave trade depleted local agriculture of labour, causing a decline of rural activities, especially around the European trading posts. When they could, farmers moved inland towards the forest, where the environment, however, limited production. In the long run, the slave trade contributed to the agricultural decline of the African continent, since little or no international interest was shown towards local crops, investments were non-existent and most of the crop production was geared towards subsistence.

The situation changed in the nineteenth century, when improvements in communication technologies and transportation boosted international trade and the expansion of colonial empires. The boom of palm and groundnut cultivation for oil production accompanied the establishment of European colonial control over Africa. Following the growth of consumer markets, urbanization and the industrialization of food production in most western European countries and later in the **United States** and **Japan**, the demand for commercial crops such as sugar, chocolate and coffee grew exponentially both in extension and in complexity of organization. However, the abolition of slavery dismantled the production model based on the plantation system, despite strong resistance from colonial landowners. The process – initiated by the **Haitian Revolution** in 1804 – ended only in the late 1880s with the elimination of slavery in **Cuba** and Brazil. Some Caribbean colonies shifted from sugar to other plantation crops such as bananas, pineapples, nutmeg and coffee, for which demand was growing in Europe. In others, for example Jamaica, plantations were divided among smallholders.

In order to maintain the plantations that the freed slaves often refused to cultivate, land-owners had to resort to forms of coercion such as contract labour or debt peonage, bringing workers from **India** to Jamaica, **Guiana**, Trinidad, Réunion and Natal, while Chinese peasants were shipped to Jamaica, **Cuba**, the valleys of the Peruvian coast, Java and Hawaii. These new mass movements heavily influenced the development of culinary traditions in many areas of the New World, especially the Caribbean. By the time the Indians arrived, some of their traditional ingredients, such as mangoes and tamarind, had already been introduced by the British colonial authorities, always eager to maximize the agricultural potential of their territories. While Chinese food traditions did not impact much on local cuisines (with the exception of pickled vegetables and the use of soy sauce for some meat marinades), Indian culinary habits and techniques have left a durable trace.

imperial effects

As western empires penetrated Asia and Africa in the nineteenth century, so European ingredients and culinary traditions acquired worldwide prestige, often proposed to or imposed on foreign populations as a tangible aspect of western cultural and moral superiority. Throughout the colonial world, from India to Mexico, specialties and ingredients of European origin were preferred to local ones by the ruling classes, to the point where at times products were exported to Europe, manufactured and then reimported as value-added and high-status delicacies. The French model of culinary excellence in terms of dishes, organization of the service and decor acquired particularly high status, also in other European countries. In **Indochina**, wheat baguettes, pastries, sausages and even asparagus became popular in urban centres, mixed by the locals with their traditional dishes and ingredients. French *haute cuisine* was also all the rage in Latin America, from Mexico to Argentina, where the Creole elites were trying to acquire global visibility and increase their distance from Indian and mestizo populations. Traditional foods such as Mexican tortillas were regarded with a certain suspicion, as a symbol of backwardness and at times even of racial inferiority.

These dynamics were visible also in Japan, where from the second half of the nineteenth century the local elites were engaged in a process of total renewal of the material aspects of society. Western food was embraced as modern, efficient and nutritious. The emperor made a point of showing that he consumed beef, against the widespread Buddhist vegetarian customs. In the twentieth century, when Japan itself became a colonial power by seizing large areas of East Asia, it promoted its own food traditions as superior to those of the occupied population all the while absorbing elements of Chinese and Korean cuisines.

However, despite the aspects of domination and exploitation that marked the relationships between western powers, their colonies and other independent but less developed areas of the world, elements of the subjugated cultures managed to affirm themselves and to be eventually adopted by the hegemonic culture, through processes of filtration, adaptation and appropriation. British colonists in India tended to adopt components from different local cuisines, integrating them in a unified gastronomic vocabulary. Curries, at first indicating only spices relishes that accompanied rice, came to denote all sorts of liquid or stewlike concoctions based on spice mixes, often accompanying meats. Only later was the name used for a specific Anglo-Indian dish, which became so popular that the British returning after their service in India made it also renowned at home. Over time, productions of curry powders for domestic use, Indian-inspired pickles and chutneys developed, catering first to Raj colonists and veterans, but soon embraced by the general population. Elements of the exotic culture of the colonized were often taken out of context and integrated in the productive processes that were shifting towards growing levels of industrialization. Nestle, for instance, discovered an Ottoman product, yogurt, that would later become an important component of its portfolio.

As the imperialist powers ensured cheap and reliable sources, goods that were previously limited to the upper classes became available to all walks of society. Towards the end of the nineteenth century commodity sales were organized in structured markets, with actual grading of products and the establishment of international standards. In the first decades of the twentieth century the economic exploitation of colonies became increasingly systematic. After the French made rice production a priority in their Indochina territories, and the British did the same in Lower Burma, it became more convenient for the neighbouring islands under Dutch control, such as Java, to buy rice from those areas to sell to farmers that could then switch from traditional cultivations, including rice, to export crops like sugar. Rice from Indochina was also imported into French West Africa, where peanut cultivation expanded, shifting labour away from staple production for subsistence and local trade. Colonial rule ensured that greater shares of peasants' production went to the foreign authorities, which were often more efficient and better organized in collecting taxes than their pre-colonial predecessors; as a consequence, life conditions worsened for farmers and unrest and riots increased, despite the fact that the occupants had recourse to modern weaponry to repress them, often negatively affecting production.

post-colonial world

After the global economic recession that followed the 1929 crisis, **World War II** was a period of food scarcity and hardship in many areas of the world. The years following the end of the war witnessed a widespread effort to jumpstart reconstruction and development, together with calls for political self-determination that eventually gave way to the dynamics of decolonization, as former territories that were part of global empires acquired independence, more or less peacefully. However, many new nations, especially in Africa, felt that the former colonial powers still controlled them through indirect political means and economic dependency, exploiting them under a new set of relationships that came to be known as 'neocolonialism'. Food security became one of the priorities for the leaderships of the young nation states, which considered it a fundamental source of political legitimacy. Debates about development and neocolonialism took place while the **Soviet Union** and China adopted radical politics of agricultural collectivization, which offered alternative models for growth and social change. Only in the late 1970s were a series of reforms introduced in China allowing farmers to grow crops to sell on the free market, albeit after meeting the quota assigned by the central planning authorities. In the 1980s agriculture turned into the engine of economic development in China, only to be later supplanted by the fast growth of industries, especially in coastal areas.

From the end of the 1960s, other Asian countries embraced what became known as the Green Revolution – a set of measures aimed at increasing agricultural yields to eliminate hunger that include the introduction of new crop varieties (at times genetically modified), the standardization of agricultural processes, intensive and mechanized techniques, the use of fertilizers and pesticides, and the intensification of irrigation. Attempts at introducing the **Green Revolution** in Africa were less successful, due to factors including corruption, lack of infrastructure and environmental features such as water scarcity and soil fragility.

In the 1980s, following the end of the **Cold War** and a global wave of neoliberal policies, many developing countries adopted various measures aimed at deregulating agricultural markets, such as the privatization of public enterprises, the dismantling of government agencies in charge of crop exports and international negotiations aimed at reducing, and eventually eliminating, subsidies, import quotas and tariffs. Production, distribution and consumption of food have been changing due to economic and social factors, such as rapid rates of urbanization, migrations – both domestic and international – the growing presence of women in the workforce, increasing inequalities and the overall transformation of food systems. In many areas of the world, both in rural and urban environments, large portions of the population still experience crises in food security and, at times, famine, due to problems requiring long-term interventions on issues such as climate change, political instability, structural socio-economic processes, lack of investment and environmental disasters.

nouvelle cuisine and fusion

The globalization of food is visible not only at the level of production, distribution and trade, but also in terms of terms of trends and fashions in restaurant cuisine, which over time tend to trickle down to domestic cooking thanks to the increasing relevance of food-related media. In the late 1960s a new generation of French chefs began to question the classical approach of French gastronomy. Among the main principles of their style, known as *nouvelle cuisine*, they included the refusal of excessively complicated dishes; decrease of cooking times to keep the flavours of the ingredients; attention to new technologies; use of fresh and seasonal ingredients; simplified menus with less dishes; abandonment of marinades, which were too long and strong; elimination of heavy sauces; attention to local cuisines, which could nonetheless be reinterpreted freely and creatively; and sensibility towards dietary issues. Similarly, in the early 1980s American chefs developed a cuisine knows as *fusion*, which reflected the multicultural nature of the USA by crossing cultural boundaries, collecting and experimenting with techniques and ingredients, especially from Asia, thereby creating something new and distinctly American. Fusion cuisine, which happened quickly and consciously as a deliberate act of creativity, quickly spread to the rest of the world. The changes in high-end cuisine and its influence on home cooking in post-industrial society continues, amplified by a media always looking for news. The last trend that has received worldwide attention is so-called *molecular gastronomy*, which creates new dishes and techniques by applying chemistry, physics and technology to cooking methods.

At the beginning of the twenty-first century, while traditional lifestyles and foodways are disappearing, the populations of post-colonial countries are showing a growing interest in food and cooking as constitutive elements of their national identities, often used to overcome class and regional tensions. National governments in developing countries, increasingly aware of the relevance of food for their tourist industry, are trying to create a marketable national cuisine almost by bureaucratic decree. Besides the growing interest of tourists in local food traditions, there is a growing interest for sustainable tourism, which intrinsically requires a larger involvement by local populations and the consumption of local food.

The interest in wine and food, and especially in culinary customs, local products and artisanal delicacies, is reaching new heights in western Europe, Japan and more recently in the US. In developing countries, still numerically limited but growing upper classes with disposable incomes have recently shown increased sensitivity to the cultural relevance of local and traditional ingredients and dishes, which in the past would have been considered embarrassing, uncouth and uncomfortably close to the rural realities and ethnic groups that had often been at the margin of national projects.

This global trend, which is quite visible in supermarkets and restaurants but also in green markets, is also promoted and exploited by the media, marketeers and politicians. These transformations in consumer perceptions are also having an impact on production and distribution. The sectors of trade dedicated to speciality products are acquiring increased relevance, with clear efforts to break down bulk commodities into smaller categories of value-added, more expensive foodstuffs. A central concept in the development and success of these products is *terroir*, according to which agricultural products are supposed to acquire their specific qualities from unique interactions between climate, geographic characteristics, earth composition and the presence of communities that have developed a particular connection with their environment. While *terroir* has become a central concept for understanding consumption in post-industrial cultures, different trends point to dynamics that highlight the modernity and creativity of culinary cultures in ways that would seem to transcend or even ignore the relevance of place.

Food and Agriculture Organization (FAO)

Following a preliminary meeting in Virginia, USA, in 1943, the Food and Agriculture Organization (FAO) was founded on 16 October 1945 in Quebec, **Canada**. It is currently based on Rome, **Italy**, as a specialized agency of the **United Nations**, and takes the lead in international efforts to defeat hunger. FAO aims to raise levels of nutrition, improve agricultural productivity, better the lives of rural populations and contribute to the growth of the world economy.

Ford, Gerald (1913–2006)

President of the United States from August 1974, following the resignation of **Richard Nixon**, to January 1977. He had acceded to the vice presidency in December 1973 after Spiro Agnew resigned over corruption charges; Ford was a popular choice after leading the Republicans in the US House of Representatives since 1965 and serving in the House since 1949. As president he presided over the withdrawal of the remaining US forces in **Vietnam** in 1975.

Ford, Henry (1863–1947)

Founder of the Ford Motor Company, pioneer of the moving assembly line (1913) and of relatively high wages (the five-dollar day) to promote worker retention, Henry Ford defined modern industrialism. His success rested on his robust and workable Model T car (1908). His assembly line enabled managers to regulate the pace of production and cut costs, and annual bonuses discouraged workers from leaving and gave them the means to buy consumer durables such as cars.

Formosa
– *see* **Taiwan**.

Four Modernizations (China)

These policies were proposed by the Chinese premier **Zhou Enlai** in the 1960s and reaffirmed in 1975, at the very end of the **Cultural Revolution**. The modernizations were of China's agriculture, industry, defence and science and technology, all of which Zhou felt had been seriously damaged by the chaos and xenophobia caused by the Cultural Revolution. However, Zhou died in 1976, and it was not until the ascendancy of the reformist leader **Deng Xiaoping** from 1978 that the policies were put into action, leading to significant changes in China's economy and society.

Fourth Republic (French)

The French constitutional system of 1946–58, the Fourth Republic covered both European **France**, modern **Algeria** and French colonial holdings.

The order which it created was a parliamentary one, with a President of the Council (Prime Minister) nominated by an otherwise weak President of the Republic to lead a cabinet which was nominally protected by obstacles to its removal by the Assembly. The system was designed to replicate but strengthen the order which had prevailed in the **Third Republic**, before the fall of France in 1940, but it failed to deliver stability, instead seeing twenty administrations in ten years. The life of the Republic was riven by movements for Algerian independence, Indochinese war, the deep splits in the body politic arising from resistance and collaboration with the Nazis and Vichy regime, the existence of multiple parties, a communist threat and the tensions produced by very strong but undirected economic growth. A final Algerian crisis, beginning in 1958, followed on from the **Suez Crisis** of 1956 and led to the collapse of the Republic and its replacement with a presidential system under **Charles de Gaulle**. The Fourth Republic is also notable for breaking with Anglo-American and Atlantic relationships in favour of the creation of an integrated European political system which began with the Coal and Steel Community.

fracking

– *see* **energy**.

France

The pivotal state and cultural heart of west European secular history, which emerged in the ninth and tenth centuries from Gallic, Germanic and Frankish origins. France was the epicentre of absolute monarchy and the **Enlightenment** after the civil wars of the seventeenth century, and experienced the first burst of modern nationalism as a direct consequence of the **French Revolution** of 1789–95. A culturally solid but politically unstable state, France has experienced three revolutions, five republics and two empires since 1789. Between 1214 and 1870 it was also the foremost military power of **Europe**, and had developed a tendency to view military leadership or qualifications as essential to governance. Defeat by **Prussia** in the 1870 war, devastation in the Great War of 1914–18 (which was largely fought on French soil) and occupation by **Germany** between 1940 and 1945 were thus searing experiences. These traumas gave rise to the **Third Republic**, which was instituted after the Paris Commune was crushed in 1871, a state of dangerous exhaustion leading to schemes such as the **Maginot Line**, appeasement and the Vichy regime between 1920 and 1943, and then to the **Fourth Republic** in 1946.

As a colonial power, France influenced or controlled regions from South East Asia through Africa to the **West Indies** after 1830, and eventually possessed the second most extensive global empire after that of the British. In contrast to **Britain**, it integrated territories into its government in a metropolitan and organized fashion. The mid-twentieth-century collapse of empire, in **Indochina** and **Algeria** especially, was thus particularly damaging, and caused the collapse of the parliamentary Fourth Republic and its replacement with a presidential fifth republic under General **Charles de Gaulle**.

Since 1956, France has been a driving force in the **European Union**, which has been characterized by many French statesmen as both a vehicle to retain global influence and to ensure the maintenance of a peaceful and democratic Germany, and has also possessed a permanent seat on the United Nations Security Council. It has also, however, experienced cultural pressure on both its language and its previous prominence in the arts and sciences, which has been magnified by the metropolitan tendency of French intellectuals to view things from Paris rather than the agricultural depths of the country. This pressure, associated with anglophone and especially American cultural, economic and military challenges, has sometimes resulted in attempts to introduce protectionism via control of language, television, the Internet and cinema, or through the promotion of subsidized industries or French-led military and monetary projects. These attempts have almost never seriously challenged the appeal of anglophone culture or foreign production, though from time to time, particular successes – such as the Airbus project – have registered. France retains extensive monetary and military interests in its former colonies in Africa, and is a major economy in terms of corporate wealth, GDP and global ownership.

Franco, Francisco (1892–1975)

– *see also* **Spanish Civil War**.

Dictator of **Spain**, 1936–75. Franco emerged from obscurity to become a commissioned officer in the often brutal Spanish Empire in Morocco, where he served from 1913. He developed an antipathy towards trades unions and working-class movements while breaking coalminers' strikes in Spain, and as deputy head, then head, of the Foreign Legion developed a particularly vicious reputation. By the mid 1920s he had begun a life of isolation as successive governments posted him overseas or to teaching posts. On the outbreak of the **Spanish Civil War**, in 1936, he was nominated *generalissimo* by his fellow generals – becoming commander-in-chief and head of the Nationalist state. He then formed strategic, if clandestine, alliances with Nazi and Fascist leaders outside Spain, and began to impose his forces on the country. Franco never joined the **Axis**, and, surviving the war, was seen as an anti-communist asset by the **USA** and allowed to join the **United Nations** in 1950. In 1969 he pledged to restore the Spanish monarchy and democracy under Juan Carlos, which followed his death in 1975. Primarily a right-wing authoritarian in a Spanish tradition which stressed national unity, Catholicism and conservatism, he initially balanced traditionalist and fascist elements but favoured the former. Regarded as a pariah in left-wing and democratic circles in the West because of the legacy of bitterness from the Spanish Civil War and his identification with fascism, he nonetheless allowed a new wave of foreign investment and tourism from the 1950s, which began the transformation of Spain from one of the poorest countries in Europe to a developing, increasingly urban society by the time of his death. The issue remains whether Spain could have modernized earlier under a more democratic regime without a renewal of civil war.

Franco-Prussian War
– *see* **German unification**.

Franklin, Benjamin (1706–1790)
A prominent printer, politician and diplomat during the colonial and revolutionary eras. Born in Boston, the youngest son of Josiah Franklin, Benjamin had trouble finding a trade until he was apprenticed to his brother James, a printer. In these years Franklin would frequently write using the pseudonym 'Silence Dogood'. In 1723, having served just five years of his nine-year indenture, Franklin ran away to Philadelphia following a dispute with his brother. After an unsuccessful attempt to procure a printing press on a trip to London (Franklin arrived in the city to find his supposed backer had no credit), he eventually established a successful printing business, most famously printing the *Pennsylvania Gazette* and *Poor Richard's Almanac*. He was prominently involved in the associational life of the city, including establishing the Library Company of Philadelphia in 1731. He retired from printing in the late 1740s, and from then on became far more prominent in political activities. In 1748 he helped form a colony-wide 'military association' in

response to the Quaker-dominated colonial assembly's unwillingness to raise a militia. In 1754 he (unsuccessfully) proposed a Plan of Union at the Albany Congress held to discuss strengthening ties between Britain's North American colonies. From 1766 to 1775 Franklin served as Pennsylvania's colonial agent in London. (For most of his years in London, Franklin was still voted to a seat in the Pennsylvania Assembly – a rare and notable sign of the esteem in which he was held.) While in London, Franklin continued his scientific endeavours and helped foster links between American scientists and Britain's Royal Society. He was in London during the early years of the Imperial crisis, where he famously defended colonial protests against the **Stamp Act** in front of a parliamentary committee, arguing that the colonists remained well disposed to the British Empire and that it was the unconstitutional actions of Parliament in taxing colonists without their consent that were to blame for the discord.

Franklin returned to Philadelphia in early 1775, having become a highly controversial figure in London as the dispute between Britain and its colonies intensified. Upon his return, he was prominently involved in national politics during and after the Revolutionary War. A delegate to the Second Continental Congress, he was part of the committee of five appointed to draft a Declaration of Independence (though most of that work was undertaken by **Jefferson**). He subsequently served as minister to **France** between December 1776 and 1785, and was instrumental in helping secure French aid for the war effort. He later played an important role in peace negotiations to end the war. Upon returning to America, Franklin served as president of Pennsylvania's Supreme Executive Council, and in 1787 as a delegate at the Constitutional Convention. Shortly before his death, his last political act was to sign an anti-slavery petition, submitted to Congress in February 1790.

Franz Joseph, Emperor (1830–1916)
Penultimate emperor of **Austria**, 1848–1916. An excellent civil administrator, but neither a strategist nor a statesman, he failed to reconcile the emergence of new nationalist loyalties with loyalty to the Habsburg dynasty. He lost **Italy**, and the leadership of **Germany** to **Prussia**, and the declaration of the Dual Monarchy of Austria and **Hungary**, 1867, satisfied Hungary but exacerbated relations with his Slav subjects. He authorized the ultimatum to **Serbia** which led to **World War I**.

Frederick the Great (1712–1786)

Frederick II (Friedrich der Grosse), king of **Prussia**, 1740–86. He built on the foundations laid by his father, **Frederick William I**, to make Prussia the greatest military power in Europe. The victim of a Spartan and bullied childhood, he sought unsuccessfully to escape to England, 1730, and was then placed on probation in the civil administration. On acceding to the throne, he proved to be a master of diplomacy and military strategy and tactics. He greatly enlarged the territory of Prussia, conquering the Austrian province of Silesia, 1741–45. His weakening of the hold on **Germany** of the Habsburg imperial monarchy in the Seven Years War, 1756–63, laid the foundations of the later Prussian leadership of the German states but also divided the Austrians from the other Germans. Although the Treaty of Hubertusberg which concluded the war in Germany, 1763, confirmed Prussia's hold on Silesia, and although the war further increased Prussia's military reputation, the cost in men and devastation made Frederick determined not to risk any further such struggle. His greatest diplomatic success was to persuade **Austria** and **Russia** to participate in the first partition of **Poland**, 1772, whereby Prussia gained the Polish province of West Prussia, minus Danzig, linking its previously isolated East Prussian territories with its core territories of Brandenburg and Pomerania. An autocrat who sincerely believed in the concept of '**enlightened despotism**' for the benefit of the individual citizen, Frederick liberalized the Prussian approach to such matters as censorship, religion and torture. On the other hand, his increasing reluctance to admit mistakes or change his mind, or to delegate decision-making, made both army and government increasingly inflexible and unable to adjust. Reflecting his appreciation of French language and culture, he built his palace of Sans Souci at Potsdam in the French **rococo** style and maintained the great French philosopher, **Voltaire**, there, 1750–3. In 1757 Voltaire persuaded Frederick in a letter not to commit suicide.

Time has mocked the man and his legacy. **Napoleon** took his sword to Paris and even his body was repeatedly moved and recoffined in and after 1945. All monarchs would then have agreed with **Clausewitz** that war was 'nothing but a continuation of political intercourse with the admixture of different means', but Frederick's emphasis on increasing the power of the state and on the primacy of the army gave Prussia a lasting reputation for militarism which overshadowed its other achievements, including its codification of civic values and constraint of corruption. Its very name was expunged by the Allies in 1947. His army and state collapsed before Napoleon in 1806, although it was soon restored and extended, but the independent Poland declared in 1918 recovered the territory lost in the 1772 partition. In 1945 the **Potsdam conference** swept away the rest of Frederick's military legacy by transferring Silesia, the whole of East Prussia, and the eastern parts of Pomerania and Brandenburg to Poland and the **Soviet Union**. In a final irony, it was the communist-dominated East German regime which was to rehabilitate Frederick in the 1980s.

Frederick William (Friedrich Wilhelm) I (1688–1740)

Second king of **Prussia**, 1713–40, who made Prussia financially and militarily strong. He completely freed the serfs on his own lands, which ultimately covered one third of Prussia, 1719, having replaced the aristocracy's feudal war service with a tax in 1717. He created the Prussian officer corps, introduced compulsory primary education, 1717, and a centralized administration, 1723; and promoted industry, particularly in wool, manufacturing and trade. He acquired Swedish Pomerania by the Treaties of Stockholm, 1719–20.

Fredericksburg Campaign (15 November–15 December 1862)

In the **American Civil War**, Ambrose E. Burnside proposed a winter offensive towards Richmond via Fredericksburg on the Rappahannock River. His troops arrived on 17 November but failed to cross the river until 11–12 December because of a delay in sending the pontoons forward. **Robert E. Lee** thus gained time to concentrate his army in the hills south-west of Fredericksburg. On 13 December Burnside assaulted this position in three disjointed waves, all of which were repulsed, costing him 13,000 casualties to Lee's 5,000.

Free French (FF)

The name given to the forces of resistance to Vichy France and the Nazi Occupation; led by **Charles de Gaulle** from London and aided by forces from the French colonies, North Africa, and the army that survived Dunkirk between 1940 and 1943. Thereafter, the FF merged into 'the Forces of Liberation' which included other leaders as well as de Gaulle. The symbol of the FF was the Cross of Lorraine.

Free Officers (Egypt)

A secret revolutionary organization forged by four officers in the Egyptian Army while serving in the **Sudan** in the early 1950s, with the objective of ousting from **Egypt** the British and the Egyptian royal family. Led by Colonel **Gamal Abdel Nasser**, Zakaria Mohieddine, later vice president of the United Arab Republic, Abdel Hakim Amer, later a field marshal in the Egyptian Army, and **Anwar as-Sadat**, Nasser's successor as president, with secrecy being maintained by the organization's membership being known to Nasser alone. Some ninety Free Officers carried out an almost bloodless *coup d'état* under Nasser's leadership, deposing King **Farouk**, 23 July 1952, and established a Revolutionary Command Council of eleven members led by Nasser but with Major-General **Muhammed Naguib** as head of state. Although the Free Officers organization had fulfilled its purpose, it arguably persisted in spirit in the military domination of Egypt which was not seriously contested until the deposition of President **Mubarak** in 2012.

Free Soil Party (American)

A short-lived third party in the **United States**. Founded in 1848 by disaffected New York **Democrats** who supported the **Wilmot Proviso**, it drew in **Whigs** and most of the **Liberty Party**. It avowedly embodied the lowest common denominator of northern anti-slavery, an opposition to the extension of black slavery into the western territories, and indeed to the presence of free **African Americans**, as something detrimental to the social, economic and political status of white settlers. Yet the party's **abolitionist** element and its actual legislative record rather qualified such claims. Its presidential candidate **Martin Van Buren** took 10 per cent of the vote in 1848 and arguably delivered the election to **Zachary Taylor**. The **Compromise of 1850** appeased many Democrats and thereby strengthened the abolitionist wing of the Free Soil Party. Its presidential vote dropped to 5 per cent in 1852 but its geographical concentration won it enough US representatives to hold the balance of power. The **Republican Party** absorbed it from 1854.

free trade

Free trade is an idealized model in which trade in goods and services between countries is unimpeded by barriers such as tariffs, quotas and subsidies. The concept dates back to **Adam Smith**'s *Wealth of Nations* (1776), which publicized arguments for free trade. Specialization in the production of certain goods in which a country possesses comparative advantages improves welfare for that country and its citizens achieve higher level of consumption. **David Ricardo** later refined Smith's argument into theory of relative comparative advantage. He insisted that trade, and specialization, could be beneficial even in cases when a country held an *absolute* cost advantage over another in all commodities. Despite its powerful influence as a theory, free trade is challenged by arguments for infant industries and late industrialization and lately by anti-globalization and also by political campaigners denouncing asymmetries of power in trade relations between countries.

Freedmen's Bureau

This was set up in 1865 following the ending of the **American Civil War** and the emancipation of those enslaved. False rumours had spread that freed people would receive 'forty acres and a mule', and the bureau has been criticized for offering moral advice but little practical help. It did, however, play an important role in providing humanitarian aid and in legitimizing the marriages of freed people under American law. It was allowed to decline in the 1870s as support for Radical Republicanism declined.

Freemasonry

Freemasonry developed from the seventeenth century from an organization for artisans into a social gathering and association of mainly middle-class members, accepting a vaguely charitable and moral outlook. A Grand Lodge was formed in London in 1717 and during the **Enlightenment** it spread to **Europe** and America as a secular promoter of learning, virtue and benevolence. The first lodge was formed in **France** in 1725 and in Boston, Massachusetts, in 1733. Acting as a mutual-aid society, it offered to its members an exclusive route to advancement and credit, proving a strong incentive to membership for urban elites and merchants. **Benjamin Franklin** and **George Washington** were masons, as later were **Danton, Garibaldi** and **Mazzini**, and the serious idealism expressed by the movement was encapsulated in Mozart's opera *The Magic Flute*. Surrounded by mystery and entry rituals, it earned the enmity of the Catholic Church in a Papal Bull of 1738, and of governments who identified it with secrecy, liberalism and secularism. The Anti-Masonic Party was formed in the United States in 1827, which won seats in

Congress and entered a candidate for the presidential elections in 1832. Although Freemasonry evolved into a primarily charitable organization, fears of its secret influence continued to surface and it was regarded as a direct threat to the state by authoritarian regimes such as the Nazis, who banned it in 1933, and by **Franco**, who bracketed it with Bolshevism as a threat.

Freeport Act of 1766 (British)

During the colonial era, each imperial power devised commercial laws to ensure that it had a competitive advantage in the international trade in the Atlantic World. The British adopted the economic philosophy of **mercantilism** and devised **Navigation Acts** to protect its trade. The French used *le exclusif*. But modifications were eventually implemented and some limited trade with 'foreign' nations allowed. It was the Freeport Act of 1766 that facilitated the importation and exportation of certain types of goods at certain ports in the British Caribbean by small vessels from neighbouring 'foreign' colonies. It was designed to allow only trade in goods which did not compete with the products of Britain and her colonies. The trade in African captives, North American supplies and the carrying trade between the Mother Country and her colonies remained firmly in British hands. Certain ports in **Jamaica** (Kingston, Savannah la Mar, Montego Bay and Santa Lucia) and Dominica (Prince Rupert's Bay and Rousseau) were made free to foreigners. The free ports at Dominica were intended to capture the French trade of the neighbouring islands of Martinique and Guadeloupe, while those at Jamaica should revive the Spanish trade. But no foreign tropical produce (except livestock and other colonial produce that the British islands did not have in sufficient quantity) or foreign manufactures were to be imported into Jamaica.

Frei Montalva, Eduardo (1911–1982)

Senator, 1949–64; president of **Chile**, 1964–70. Born in Santiago and trained as a lawyer, he was a founder of the Falange Nacional (1938), which eventually became the Christian Democratic Party (1957). As president, he proclaimed a 'Revolution in Liberty' which included agrarian reform and the gradual 'Chileanization' of the copper industry. An opponent of his successor's policies, he supported the military coup of 1973 but later opposed the military government of **Pinochet** (1973–90).

Freire, Paulo (1921–1997)

Born in Recife, **Brazil**, Freire abandoned law for a career in education, establishing himself in adult and worker education and especially literacy training. His best known of numerous books is *Pedagogy of the Oppressed* (1970). Educators around the world have drawn on a variety of his concepts of learning, although his reliance upon others' work has raised questions about his originality.

Frelimo

– *see also* **Mozambique**.

The Mozambique Liberation Front (also known by its Portuguese name Frente de Libertação Moçambique) was a guerrilla movement founded in 1962 by Eduardo Mondlane (1920–69) to liberate Mozambique from Portuguese colonial rule. **Mozambique** gained independence under **Samora Machel** (1933–86) in 1975 and in 1977 Frelimo adopted a Marxist–Leninist programme, though this was gradually abandoned. Frelimo was the country's ruling party after independence, first in a one-party state, going on to win successive majorities when multiparty elections were introduced in 1994.

French and Indian Wars

The North American dimension of the **Seven Years War**, which pitted the British, their colonists and their Native American allies against the French, their colonists and their Native American allies. The fighting, which was most intense in the Ohio River and St Lawrence valleys, but extended throughout eastern North America, occurred between 1754 and 1763. Although the French enjoyed early success, eventually the British prevailed, capturing Quebec and Montreal and driving the French from North America. Conquering eastern North America proved easier than governing it, as the British faced the challenge of administering two constituencies – Native Americans and European colonists – with different and competing needs. The former, concerned at the disruption to traditional trade and diplomatic relations caused by the defeat of **France**, immediately attacked the British in 1763 during **Pontiac's War**. Confronted by a substantial deficit as a result of the war, Parliament sought to impose direct taxes on the colonists in North America, setting in train a series of events which culminated in the **American Revolution**.

French Empire

The rise and fall of the French overseas empire, as distinct from the two Napoleonic Empires, paralleled in many respects that of the British. The first acquisitions were focused on the Americas with what is now Quebec becoming **Canada** or New France in 1534. Guyane (French Guiana) on the South American coast followed in 1604 and Martinique and **Guadeloupe**, both in the Caribbean, in 1635. A fort was however established at St Louis, **Senegal**, West Africa, in 1659. **Haiti** was ceded by **Spain** in 1697 and Louisiana was settled from 1699. Rivalry with the British, however, undermined French ambitions in **India** and only Pondicherry remained as a French enclave, although Réunion in the Indian Ocean, acquired in 1638, survived, as did Mauritius between 1715 and 1814. War with the British led, however, to the loss of Quebec in 1759, although not of the islands of St Pierre and Miquelon off Newfoundland, and Louisiana was sold to the **United States** in 1803. Conflict with the British also resulted in Haitian independence in 1804.

The foundation of what was effectively a second French Empire started with the acquisition of **Algeria** in 1830, stimulated by the need to suppress piracy, and the three northern departments of Algiers, Oran and Constantine were declared part of metropolitan France in 1881. With the exception of **Indochina**, of which the conquest commenced in 1858, and of the small Pacific territories of **New Caledonia**, French Polynesia and Wallis and Futuna, acquired 1842–53, the empire was to remain African until after **World War I**. Protectorates and colonies were progressively established across large tracts of sub-Saharan Africa from the mid nineteenth century, and were organized, other than Madagascar, as French West Africa and French Equatorial Africa from 1902 and 1910 respectively. **Tunisia** became a protectorate in 1883 and **Morocco** in 1912. The empire reached its greatest extent in 1919 when France acquired mandates under the **League of Nations** over **Syria** (including **Lebanon**), Cameroon and Togo, formerly Ottoman and German possessions respectively. The French was then the world's second largest overseas empire after the British.

Decolonization began with the declaration of an independent Lebanon in 1941, followed by Syria in 1946. In 1946 Guadeloupe, Guyane, Martinique and Réunion became overseas departments of metropolitan France. Pondicherry was ceded in 1954. The French, however, strongly resisted independence movements in **Vietnam**, **Tunisia** and **Algeria**, the latter an area of mass French settlement. France, however, had to recognize failure first in Vietnam after its defeat by the **Viet Cong** at **Dien Bien Phu**, 1954, then in Tunisia and finally in Algeria, after a war which earned France little moral credit. The battle against the communist Viet Cong in Vietnam, however, was continued by the Americans. Meaningful independence did not come to the three constituent parts of Indochina, Vietnam, **Laos** and **Cambodia** until the final American withdrawal of 1975. Tunisia gained its independence in 1956 and Algeria finally in 1962 after a struggle which had led to the fall of France's own **Fourth Republic** and the return to power of General **Charles de Gaulle** in semi-revolutionary circumstances. The decolonization of the rest of French Africa had proceeded swiftly, with autonomy being granted to the states of French Equatorial Africa and of French West Africa in 1958 and full independence in 1960. Only **Guinea** rejected the option of membership of the French Community in 1958 and became immediately independent. The Comoros, off Madagascar, became independent in 1975. Critics have since maintained that the French Community is a cloak for undue French financial and political influence.

French Guiana

An overseas department (*Département d'Outre-Mer*) of France located on the north-eastern coast of South America between **Surinam** and **Brazil**. The majority of the small, coastal population (approximately 200,000) is of African descent, though centuries of immigration from **Europe**, **Asia** and the **Middle East**, as well as contact with Caribbean and South-American neighbours, have produced great cultural diversity. Fitful French colonization of the teriritory secured a permanent settlement at Cayenne in 1664. Despite its potential as an exporter of natural resources, French Guiana stagnated until the mid nineteenth century, when a gold rush and a decision to establish penal colonies along its coast gave the territory some notoriety. After **World War II** it avoided the independence movements that largely dismantled the remaining European colonies in the Americas, choosing instead closer integration with its metropolis – and heavy economic subsidies – as a means to shed its colonial status.

French Revolution

The process of transition from the *ancien régime* feudal monarchy in **France** to a modern, secular and centralized entity, was one of the defining moments of the modern world. Whilst beginning in 1789, it is best seen as a series of changes rather than as a detonation. The ten years between 1789 and the rise to power of **Napoleon Bonaparte** saw six regimes in France. These were the monarchy and Estates General, the National Assembly (1789–91), the Legislative Assembly (1791–2), the Convention and Committee of Public Safety (1792–5), the revolutionary directorate (1795–9) and the consulate (1799–1804). They also comprised the execution of the king and queen, the First Republic, the French Revolutionary wars against a succession of European powers and the **Terror** associated with **Robespierre**. The Roman Catholic Church, which had hitherto been an estate of the realm whose canon law was French law, was deranged and traumatized by the events for some hundred years afterward, and the United Kingdom, including Ireland, was largely brought together as a power in competition for the world against France. In addition, the revolution became a model for subsequent change, and its association of targeted mass killing via scientific means with progress became embedded within a variety of radical political traditions. Feminism, nationalism, socialism, fascism and revolutionary internationalism can be traced to the revolution, and both modern metric systems of measurement as well as the widespread and systematized use of French are legacies of revolutionary innovation.

The crisis which produced the revolution originates in a combination of economic and agricultural crises with administrative failure. A punctuated century of European and global war, culminating in the default of France's American revolutionary allies on their debts, had left the French crown bankrupted. Poor harvests, some thirty-eight different tax jurisdictions, and the unwillingness of merchants, monasteries and aristocrats to pay tax rather than collect or avoid it undermined both the appeal and the capacity of the state. The over-centralized monarchy, which required that local leaders isolate themselves with the king at Versailles, was by 1760 reduced to demanding cooperation. When combined with a relentless series of criticisms of the constitution, criminal justice system, society and government of France during the **Enlightenment**, and contrasted with the growth and economic success of England and her institutions, it was obvious by 1787 that the French state was in drastic need of change. Following two failed attempts at tax reform, a conference of the Three Estates of the Realm – the clergy, nobility and people – was called for the

first time since 1614. Once called, the estates collapsed into the National Assembly, which in July was allied to the Parisien Mob in the 'Bastille Days'. The competing dynamic of a liberal parliament and a radical mob of various shades characterized the descent of the Revolution by 1792 into regicide and rapid alternations of governing regime. When added to foreign invasion, hyperinflation and civil strife (particularly in south-western France), this congealed into widespread revolutionary Terror, then stabilized in a counter-revolution of 1795 before being undermined by the military ambitions of Napoleon. Most of the symbols and political references of modern French history are today, unsurprisingly, traced to the Revolution, but the events of those years have also proved durable as inspiration for revolutionaries in France and elsewhere, and as a warning for conservatives of the dangers of resistance to timely reform.

Freud, Sigmund (1856–1939)

Founder of Freudianism and psychoanalysis. Freud was a member of the Austrian Jewish community in Vienna who developed ideas based around psychodynamics, the 'science of the unconscious'. He held that people never forgot anything, and especially not trauma, but instead confined painful memories and developmental experiences from the beginning of consciousness in the foetus onwards in an 'unconscious'. This unconscious could be understood in terms of three categories of active agent, the 'id' associated with desires and sensuality, the 'ego' associated with self-preservation and caution, and the 'superego' which mediated. That which was not consciously expressed was repressed, and could distort a personality unless brought forth by a 'talking cure' known as psychotherapy, which would cure neurosis and help control psychosis. Freud later refined his theory to include ideas of innate instincts such as 'eros' (a drive to propagation, eroticism and love) and 'thanatos' (a drive to the destruction of others and oneself). Many Freudian terms have passed into everyday language, such as 'oedipus complex', 'penis envy' 'phobia', 'projection' and 'fetish', and his insight that human sexuality is neither fixed nor uniform has become a cliché. Freud was initially close to Carl Jung before developing a strong disagreement over Jung's theories of a positive collective unconscious expressed by archetypes. Though forced out of Austria by the Nazi *Anschluss* of 1938 and exiled in London, where he died, Freud's greatest impact was on the psychiatric profession and popular culture of the **United States**, where his views became received wisdom in the twentieth century.

Friedan, Betty (1921–2006)

A powerful US women's movement leader, Friedan graduated from Smith College in 1942. She studied briefly at Berkeley, mixed with Marxists and for some years wrote for labour publications. In 1957 she conducted a survey of her fellow Smith alumnae and discovered a widespread dissatisfaction with their lives that were largely spent as housewives. She called this 'the problem with no name' and published *The Feminine Mystique* in 1963, analyzing the problems of American women and by implication those in other industrial societies. This became a best-seller and is often credited with sparking second-wave **feminism** in the United States and around the globe. She was one of the founders of the National Organization for Women in 1966 (becoming its first president) and later of the National Association for the Repeal of the Abortion Laws. She continued to write and speak widely for women's rights throughout her life.

Front de Libération Nationale (FLN)
– *see also* **Algerian Revolt**.

The Front de Libération Nationale (FLN) is a socialist party in **Algeria**, in power since independence from France in 1962. In 1954 several anti-colonial, paramilitary groups merged into the FLN under the leadership of **Ahmed Ben Bella**. A political organization with a military wing, it launched a harrowing but ineffective assault on French installations in late 1954. Its primary targets were Algerian collaborators. Internal strife within the group led to fractures, while rivalry with another nationalist group, Messali Hadj's Mouvement National Algérien, played out in France itself in a series of attacks aimed at the other's supporters. By 1959 FLN lacked the military capacity to resist the French, but their campaign to internationalize the struggle and the mounting costs of the war for France eventually helped bring Algerian independence in 1962. The FLN military wing came to power in a 1965 coup; officers have long continued to monopolize the highest levels in government.

frontier (American)

Outside the United States, the word *frontier* usually means 'international borderline'. More recently, it has acquired a metaphorical meaning (as in pushing back frontiers of science). Frontier is primarily

associated, however, with the conquest of North American lands. The concept was Americanized through application to the line between settled and unsettled (though rarely literally empty) lands and the unsettled area beyond. Federal census officials formalized prevailing usage in 1890 by defining unsettled territory as land with fewer than two colonists per square mile. Since 1893 the term has become irrevocably tied to historian Frederick Jackson Turner, whose influential `frontier thesis' situated the frontier at the heart of the American experience – a force responsible for democracy, individualism, opportunity and egalitarianism and that shaped the national character along non-European lines. Though the 1890 census pronounced the frontier closed, occupation of the public domain continued. Large western tracts (particularly Alaska) still qualify demographically as frontier.

Fuat Pasha, Mehmed (1815–1869)

Mehmed Fuat Pasha was one of the dominant figures of Ottoman politics during the mid nineteenth century period of reform known as the **Tanzimat** (1839–76), serving twice as grand vizier and five times as foreign minister of the **Ottoman Empire**. In domestic politics, he emphasized the need for reforms aimed at centralizing and modernizing the state, along with the development of an Ottoman patriotism, or **Ottomanism**, that would dampen the discontent of religious minorities. In international relations, Fuat Pasha aimed at developing sufficient European support for the Ottoman Empire to enable it to participate as an equal within European diplomacy. Of particular importance was the development of a de facto alliance between the Ottoman Empire and **Great Britain** as a check on Russian territorial ambitions. Fluent in French, he participated in the Treaty of Paris (1856) and accompanied Sultan **Abdülaziz** during the latter's official visits to Egypt and Europe.

Fuentes, Carlos (1928–2012)

Born in Panama City to Mexican parents, Carlos Fuentes is one of the world's best-known novelists and essayists, both in Spanish and in translation. His father's diplomatic career resulted in a childhood in **Latin America**, and Fuentes later had a diplomatic career until he became a writer. He wrote twenty-four novels, beginning with *La Región Más Transparente* (*Where the Air is Clear*) in 1958, and most recently, *La Voluntad y la Fortuna* (*Destiny and Desire*) in 2008. These have been widely translated, and *The Old*

Gringo (1985) was the first best-selling novel by a Mexican author in the **United States**, where it became a successful movie starring Jane Fonda, Gregory Peck and Jimmy Smits. In addition, Fuentes wrote numerous essays, short stories and opinion pieces for magazines and newspapers. He taught at major universities in the United States and received many international literary awards.

Fugitive Slave Laws (American)

The Fugitive Slave Act of 1793 required the return of all runaway slaves, although various Northern states passed 'personal liberty laws' in an attempt to impede its enforcement. The Southern states also passed various fugitive slave laws at the local level during the late eighteenth and nineteenth centuries. In 1850 the 1793 act was replaced with a more stringent act as a part of the **Compromise of 1850**. This granted Southern slave owners the right to bring back to the Southern states fugitive slaves living in the North, and also generated great fear of being kidnapped into slavery among **African Americans** in the free states. The ensuing outrage and protests did much to shape Northern sentiment in the decade preceding the American Civil War.

Fukuzawa, Yukichi (1835–1901)

Influential **Meiji** author and educator who founded Keio University, writing numerous books and articles that introduced western society to the Japanese public, most notably, *Seiyo Jijo* (*Conditions in the West*). Along with *Bunmeiron no Gairyaku* (*An Outline of a Theory of Civilization*), which enhanced the popular enthusiasm for education, Fukuzawa advocated *datsu-a-ron* (leaving Asia) through which Japan should subscribe to western knowledge and science rather than adopting Chinese and Korean anti-reformist directions.

fundamentalism (religious)

The response of many religions to modernization, industrialism, globalized and secularized societies, and the domination of culture by elites has been to return to 'fundamental values'. Particularly in religions which place a great emphasis on written texts, such as **Protestantism** and **Islam**, this desire has cohered into highly organized and intolerant movements which have sought to give meaning to the lives of those who feel alienated and humiliated. Hindu, Buddhist and Catholic fundamentalism, as well as that associated with other religions, has followed similar lines but drawn upon

opposition to social or sexual lifestyles or practices and the existence of priesthoods to crystallize ideologies. In the service of fundamentalism, many in the twentieth century saw themselves as having to reform or attack the modern world, and having to offer salvation or destruction either metaphorically or in reality to those seen as standing in the way of millennial faiths.

Protestant

Protestant fundamentalism (sometimes just dubbed 'Christian' or 'evangelical', wrongly) is particularly associated with the **USA**. North America from its European settlement has been home to both charismatic biblical fundamentalists and extremely strong Protestant and Calvinist social hierarchies. These two movements were located in the South and North of the USA respectively. A third distinctive American tradition was the creation on fundamentalist lines of new movements that demanded absolute fidelity and acquiescence to religious ideas that drew upon novel readings of texts and revelations, such as Mormonism and Islam within the African-American community. The interaction of all these groups with a dynamic, isolating and at times inhuman economy, great geographical mobility, immigration, and a highly secular society with institutionalized protection of speech tended to discourage moderation and humility. When added in the twentieth century to racial segregation, the perception of humiliation and defeat in the **American Civil War**, and a consumerized attitude to religious competition, organized political fundamentalism resulted. This involved campaigns against homosexuality, abortion, feminism, and moral relativism as perceived threats to decency, and even the support of the State of Israel in pursuit of biblical prophecies of the apocalypse. By the last third of the twentieth century, no American president and few political candidates could afford to demonstrate irreligiosity and expect to be elected easily or at all. In addition, vast numbers of people moved to support the teaching of biblical doctrines of creation in schools and at religious museums and theme parks which rejected scientific views of evolution and planetary chronology. Christian fundamentalists developed very sophisticated methods of communication, recruitment and organization and became very great business concerns, often pioneering methods of political organization through television or the internet, as well as ways of 'rating' candidates for voters. They also displaced a more liberal tradition of

Christianity on the left, partly because of increasing anti-religious sentiment and secularism after the sixties amongst self-styled progressives. The term 'moral majority' was coined in the 1970s after a decade of gestation and reflected movements associated with **Jimmy Carter**, **Ronald Reagan**, the Republican Party and ultimately **George W. Bush**.

Islamic

In the Islamic world, similar pressures developed by the end of the nineteenth century to offer a renewed and modern approach to Islamic spiritualism and society. Islamism was of course marked by the geographical and cultural distinctions of the Muslim world, but shared many features of Christian fundamentalism. Young and often well-educated men and women were drawn to an anti-secular and apparently purer way of living which put them at odds with domestic political institutions and what they saw as a corrupt western consensus. This way of life involved the organization of life according to a highly literal reading in Arabic of the Qur'an and radical proselytzing for a highly conservative and intolerant view of society, gender relationships and other religions. It also allowed them to associate on a quasi-democratic basis with peasants, traditionalists and poorly educated young men who felt disenfranchised, ignored, humiliated or manipulated by social groups and opponents who also opposed the Islamists. Very often, the response of governments within colonial regimes or post-Ottoman domestic administrations was to torture or threaten Islamic fundamentalists.

The process strengthened faith in many cases and also gave an air of holy suffering to proponents of a fundamentalist reading of the Qur'an and its associated bodies of law, the Hadith and shariah. Where court systems had become corrupt, tedious or cumbersome, ad hoc Islamic court systems thus proved a way of cementing fundamentalist social alliances in a similar way to the alliances created in opposition to elites, social reform based on civil rights and court decisions in Christian communities. Islamic movements in the modern period originated in three locations; Saudi Arabian **Wahhabism**, North African and particularly Egyptian Salafism and Iranian Shia fundamentalism. They were associated with intensely emotional networks of believers, distaste at western imperialism and policies, extreme hatred of the state of **Israel** and of Jews in general, and charismatic preaching. Reinforced by the oppression they encountered and boosted by the oil wealth of supporters and governments, young fundamentalists worked to remove non-Muslims from formerly Muslim territories, to block feminism and to reform society. After the humiliation of the Arab–Israeli War, they worked to oppose the state of Israel but also to remove secularizing military regimes. In **Afghanistan**, the Soviet invasion of 1980 led to generations of young men being trained in the arts of war and backed by the West, at the same time as the Iranian Revolution overthrew a pro-western and secular regime and replaced it with an Islamic republic.

Islamic fundamentalism then moved into a new phase, which became evident in the wars of the late 1980s and 1990s in **Lebanon**, Bosnia and the horn of Africa. Self-confident international networks of violence and conversion began to interact with civil wars and the emergence of relatively moderate Islamicizing movements and moved to attack the 'Great Satan' of the United States with highly sophisticated methods of suicide bombing and hijacking learned in Israel–Palestine. This resulted in attacks on the World Trade Centre in 1993; on the USS *Cole* in 1999; in **Sudan**; and, ultimately, in the vast and destructive September 11th operation of 2001. This latter attack, in which four large passenger airplanes were hijacked and driven into locations in New York and Washington DC, were a direct consequence of Islamic fundamentalism, and elevated spokesmen such as **Osama Bin Laden** to global leadership. Fundamentalist tactics such as violent protests against artists, writers and film producers who insulted Islam, comments by Pope Benedict XVI, and the **Iraq** and Afghanistan wars added to the internal determination of Islamic fundamentalists. The movement remains strong and developed further with the rise of the **Taliban** and, latterly, **ISIL**.

fur trade (American)

The fur trade loomed large in native settler relations and the economy of colonial North America. To secure guns, tools, clothing, alcohol and influence from French, British, Russian and (eventually) American traders, Indian hunters variously supplied beaver pelts from the northeast, deer hides from the south, buffalo hides from the Plains and sea otter pelts from the Pacific. Overhunting and a shift in fashion from beaver to silk hats killed off the trade by the 1840s. The modern fur trade has become of increasing concern to **animal rights** activists who have sought its restriction.

Futa Jallon

A highland region in modern-day Guinea, the source of the Niger, Senegal and Gambia rivers. It was the home of an important Islamic reform movement in 1726, which resulted in the foundation of a clerical republic. Its wars with its neighbours, and then between rival factions within the republic, resulted in the capture of thousands of people, who were sold as slaves. It was integrated into the colonies of **Portugal** and **France** in 1896.

G

Gabon

Under French influence since the 1830s, this area on the west coast of central Africa was incorporated into French Equatorial Africa in 1910. Gabon gained independence in 1960 under Léon M'ba (1902–67). French troops intervened to save M'ba from an army coup in 1964 and in 1967 he was succeeded as president by Albert Bernard Bongo (later known as Omar Bongo Ondimba on his conversion to **Islam** in 1973). Bongo (1935–2009) remained in power with French support until his death. Multiparty politics resumed in 1991 under a new constitution and in 1993 Bongo was again elected, with opposition complaints of fraud. In 2004 the government signed an agreement with **China** on iron ore extraction. Ali Bongo (1959–) succeeded his father as president in elections in 2009 that again aroused accusations of fraud, while relations with **France** soured. His victory in the 2016 elections was met with violence and protests. Gabon's population is 75 per cent Christian, with a 12 per cent Muslim minority. The economy, based at independence on timber and manganese, became reliant on oil production after the 1970s, the government depending on it for 70 per cent of its revenue.

Gaddafi, Colonel Muammar, al- (1941–2011)

Libyan leader. Entered the Libyan Army in 1965 and overthrew the monarchy in a coup in 1969 and headed the Libyan govenment. Sought to remould Libyan society in accordance with socialist Islamic beliefs and pursued abortive attempts to unite with neighbouring countries. Supported the Palestinian cause and funded terrorist movements abroad including the IRA. Clashes with US naval and air forces culminated in the US bombing of Gaddafi's headquarters in the capital in 1987.

Complicit in bombing of PanAm Flight 103 over Lockerbie in Scotland in 1988. A US trade embargo in 1986 was followed by UN sanctions in 1992. In 1999 Libya handed over for trial two of its intelligence officers allegedly responsible for the Lockerbie bombing. Secured resumption of diplomatic relations with all but the **USA** by 2002 and in aftermath of US 'war on terror' and capture of **Saddam Hussein**, Gaddafi opened his secret weapons' programmes up to international inspection and sought normalization of relations. Following the uprising of the **Arab Spring**, his regime was overthrown with British and French support and Gaddafi murdered by insurgents.

Gadsden Purchase (American)

In 1853 the US diplomat and railway tycoon James Gadsden negotiated the purchase from **Mexico** of a strip of disputed territory in what is now New Mexico and Arizona. The **Democratic Party** sought the territory to advance its plan to facilitate a southern transcontinental railway. The deal met with criticism in the Senate from anti-slavery politicians and contributed to rising sectional tensions. Though few thought so at the time, the Gadsden Purchase completed the continental borders of the **United States**.

Gallipoli Campaign (1915)

Considered one of the decisive battles of **World War I**, the Gallipoli Campaign saw Ottoman forces repel an Anglo-French invasion. In February 1915, England and France began their assault on the Gallipoli peninsula (the northern bank of the Dardanelles Straits) with the aim of defeating the **Ottoman Empire** and seizing its capital, Istanbul. By January 1916 the British and French governments acknowledged defeat and withdrew their troops. Ottoman troops had withstood a year of determined entente offensives launched from their beachhead on the peninsula.

Galtieri, General Leopoldo (1926–2003)

Briefly **Argentina**'s president, 1981–2. In the face of domestic economic and social crises, Galtieri ordered the invasion of the British-held **Falkland Islands** in April 1982. Despite his vain hope of US support, **Britain** won the war by April, and Galtieri was forced from power. Convicted of human rights abuses and mismanagement of the war, Galtieri received a presidential pardon in 1989, but was later convicted of additional abuses.

Gambia

Former British colony on the west African coast. Britain established a coastal settlement in 1843, moving inland in the 1880s and making Gambia a protectorate in 1894. In the 1960s **Britain** allowed political parties to form in the run up to independence, which came in 1965, with Dawda Jawara (1924–) as prime minister. The country became a republic in 1970, with Jawara taking the office of president. In 1980 and 1981 he faced military coups, surviving both with support from neighbouring **Senegal**. In 1982 Gambia entered into a Senegambia Confederation with Senegal, which broke down in 1989 because of Gambia's rejection of closer union. Jawara was overthrown by Yayah Jammeh (1965–) in 1994. Jammeh banned political opposition until 1998. In 2001, 2006 and 2011 he won widely criticized elections and the government provoked international condemnation for human rights abuses. The population is predominantly Muslim, with a small Christian minority. In 2015 Jammeh declared Gambia an Islamic republic and he also withdrew the country from the Commonwealth. He was eventually forced to quit after the 2016 elections were won by Adama Barrow.

Gandhi, Indira (1917–1984)

Indira Gandhi, the daughter of **Jawaharlal Nehru**, was **India**'s prime minister from 1966 to 1977 and 1980 to 1984. Following **Lal Bahadur Shastri**'s death in 1965, she was selected to succeed as prime minister by the Congress Party's powerful regional bosses who expected her to be a malleable figure. She soon outmanoeuvred them by successfully fielding her own candidate for the presidency of India in 1969, forcing a split in the party. In 1971, to consolidate her power, she separated parliamentary from state elections to minimize the impact of less easily controlled regional politics. Appealing to the electorate on national issues and from a populist platform, the strategy paid off as Congress and its allies won a solid majority at the centre. The military victory against **Pakistan** in 1971, leading to **Bangladesh**'s independence, further boosted her political profile and the Congress Party registered a landslide victory even at regional level in the states.

Indira Gandhi has been held responsible for deinstitutionalizing the Congress Party by centralizing and personalizing power, preferring to rely on hand-picked deputies and state leaders rather than basing the party on grassroots foundations. In 1975, amidst growing political and economic crises, pervasive protests involving politicians, students and labour, and in order to pre-empt an imminent fall from office following a judicial ruling holding her election invalid, she declared a national emergency. During the emergency, lasting until 1977, several organizations were banned, over 100,000 people including political opponents and Congress dissidents were arrested and detained without trial, a wide range of civil liberties were suspended, and programmes such as forced slum clearance and sterilization were pushed through. Gandhi finally announced parliamentary elections for March 1977, in the mistaken confidence of a Congress victory. However, the party was overthrown by the **Janata Party**, an unlikely coalition of various opposition groups, until factional struggles led to its own defeat and Gandhi's return through elections in 1980.

During this term, Gandhi demonstrated her old suspicion of state governments led by rival parties. In Andhra Pradesh, she engineered the removal of the popular chief minister N. T. Rama Rao of the Telugu Desam in August 1984, but widespread protest forced her to hand power back to him within a month. In Jammu and **Kashmir** she campaigned for the 1983 state elections by appealing to Hindu sentiments, especially in Jammu, implying a threat to national integrity from the Muslim majority of the state, which was then governed by the National Conference Party. Her deployment of the religious card and forcing out of chief minister Farooq Abdullah in 1984 was to have grave consequences, fuelling separatism in Kashmir. But her most catastrophic intervention was in the state of **Punjab**. During her years out of office, in 1977–80, she had worked to undermine the Akali Dal, traditional adversaries of the Congress in Punjab, by strengthening the Sikh revivalist Jarnail Singh Bhindranwale. Gandhi's strategy only fanned Sikh extremism, pushing the moderate Akalis also in that direction, and inaugurated years of terrorist violence. She quickly lost control over Bhindranwale, who turned the Golden Temple in Amritsar into an armoury and a shelter for his supporters, forcing her to order the Indian Army to storm the shrine in June 1984. Though successful in eliminating Bhindranwale and his supporters, this assault on one of their holiest sites alienated large numbers of Sikhs, and in October she was assassinated in New Delhi by two of her Sikh security guards.

Gandhi, Mohandas Karamchand (1869–1948)

The most influential figure of the Indian nationalist movement. Gandhi dominated the Indian National Congress from 1920 onwards and his leadership extended the Indian nationalist movement across the religious divide into the rural countryside. Popularly known as the *mahatma* ('great soul'), Gandhi's opposition to European colonialism, championing of civil rights and dedication to peace and non-violence has made him one of the twentieth century's most significant political influences.

Gandhi was born in the port town of Porbandar, Gujarat, in western British India. In 1888 he left for London to study law. Having been admitted to the Bar three years later, he returned to **India** in 1891. Failing to set up a law practice in Bombay in 1893, he took the offer of work for an Indian firm in South Africa. The racism he experienced in South Africa became a transformative experience and what was to be a year-long sojourn lasted for two decades. Reacting to an ordinance requiring Indians to carry identification passes, Gandhi organized a meeting in Johannesburg in September 1906, where *satyagraha* ('truth force') as a protest strategy was born. This non-violent fight involved disobeying unjust laws and suffering the hardships and penalties resulting from this defiance. The movement continued until 1914 when the repressive laws were repealed and Gandhi returned to India.

By 1919 Gandhi was at the forefront of the Indian National movement, having successfully used *satyagraha* in Champaran, Bihar (1917) and in Kheda and Ahmedabad, Gujarat (1918). Subsequently, he led three major political campaigns: the Non-Cooperation movement (1920–2), Salt Satyagraha (1930–4) and the **Quit India movement** (1942). British insensitivity to the Jallianwala tragedy (1919) coupled with Indian Muslims' concern over the dissolution of the Ottoman Empire after World War I mobilized Indians, both Hindus and Muslims, to boycott British manufacturers and institutions. These non-violent protestors defied the laws and courted arrest, but the burning down of a police station in Chauri Chaura and the killing of policemen by protestors in this remote eastern Indian village in February 1922 led Gandhi to call off the civil disobedience movement. On 10 March, Gandhi was arrested on charges of sedition and sentenced to six years, but was released two years later.

Challenging the imposition of tax on salt, which disproportionately affected the poor; in March 1930 Gandhi launched the salt *satyagraha* with more than 60,000 people courting arrest. In August 1942 the Congress leadership accepted Gandhi's resolution demanding an immediate withdrawal of the British from India, launching the Quit India movement. This led to the arrest of Gandhi and the entire Congress leadership. As a divided subcontinent gained its freedom in August 1947 with an independent India and **Pakistan**, Gandhi remained deeply affected by the communal riots between Hindus and Muslims and worked tirelessly to quell the violence. On the evening of 30 January 1948, on his way to his prayer meeting in Delhi, Gandhi was shot by Nathuram Godse, a Hindu fanatic who believed he was too lenient towards India's Muslims.

Gandhi, Rajiv (1944–1991)

Indian politician. Son of Prime Minister **Indira Gandhi** and originally a pilot, he entered politics after his brother Sanjay's assassination in 1980. Following Indira's assassination in 1984, Gandhi became prime minister, leading the Indian National Congress to electoral victory. The party lost office in 1989 in the wake of anger over **India**'s intervention in **Sri Lanka** and Gandhi's alleged corruption. He was assassinated by the Liberation Tigers of Tamil Eelam (**Tamil Tigers**).

Gang of Four

Four Chinese politicians became known collectively as the 'Gang of Four' after their downfall in 1976: Jiang Qing (1914–91), Zhang Chunqiao (1917–2005), Wang Hongwen (1932–92) and Yao Wenyuan (1931–2005). Jiang had status as **Mao Zedong**'s wife, and the other three were Shanghai-based radical politicians during the **Cultural Revolution**. They came to power as fanatical supporters of Mao's campaign against moderates in his own party, and became feared for their merciless launching of campaigns of persecution against their political enemies. They were arrested and put on trial by Mao's successor, Hua Guofeng.

García Márquez, Gabriel (José) (1928–2014)

Of Colombian birth, García Márquez is his country's best-known novelist and short story writer. He had authored more than fifteen books at the time he received the Nobel Prize in literature in 1982, and wrote several more subsequently. The English translation of *One Hundred Years of*

Solitude in 1970 expanded his audience and more than ten additional translated books are now available. Since its appearance in Spanish (1967), *One Hundred Years of Solitude* has sold over 30 million copies and been translated into more than thirty languages; some suggest it is the finest novel in Spanish since *Don Quixote*. García Márquez's literary success has made him one of Latin America's foremost representatives. Scholars have turned the study of his works into a large-scale industry.

Garfield, James Abram (1831–1881)

Born in Cuyahoga, Ohio, Garfield taught at Hiram College before enlisting in the Union Army in 1861. By the time he left the service to take up a seat in Congress, he had been promoted to the rank of major general. He served as a Republican in the House of Representatives from 1863 until his election as president in 1880. After only six months in office, his presidential term was abruptly curtailed by an assassin's bullet.

Garibaldi, Giuseppe (1807–1882)

A hero of the Italian **Risorgimento**, Garibaldi was largely responsible for first uniting southern Italy through military campaigns and then for linking it with the north to create an almost wholly unified peninsula under **Cavour** and Victor Emmanuel II in 1860. A native of Nice, Garibaldi travelled to South America as a young man, to **Uruguay**, where he settled and in whose wars he participated. He returned to **Italy** after revolutionary agitation in 1848 following the election of Pope **Pius IX**, hoping for national reunification, and led the defence of Rome before being evicted from Italian territory by French and Piedmontese forces after a great march. He then moved from Africa to New York, central America and **China** as a sailor and businessman, before returning to Italy to lead armies against the Austrian forces in the 1850s. By 1860 he was allied with Piedmont. He led a volunteer force of a thousand in the successful invasion of Sicily, and with British and Piedmontese support, defeated the forces of Naples in Italy proper to unify the south, which he then handed to Piedmont before retiring to his farm island near Sardinia. Subsequently, he offered himself to the US Army, fought the Pope in Rome, challenged the Austrians in the Alps, and encouraged Europe-wide nationalist revolution. He was extraordinarily popular. The incidental creator of the denim fashion in western Europe, he fathered multiple children by numerous wives.

Garrison, William Lloyd (1805–1879)

Born in Newburyport, Massachusetts, Garrison edited a strident **abolitionist** newspaper, *The Liberator*, from 1831. He founded the American Anti-Slavery Society in 1833, which admitted **African Americans** and women. From the late 1830s he rejected all political parties, organized religion and the **American Constitution** as thoroughly complicit in slavery, prompting abolitionist schism in 1840. The **American Civil War** dampened his pacifism, especially after the **Emancipation Proclamation**; rather conservatively, he considered his life's work complete by 1865.

Garvey, Marcus (1887–1940)

Jamaican-born Marcus Garvey established the United Negro Improvement Association (UNIA) in 1914, an organization dedicated to affirming race pride and solidarity among blacks. Two years later, Garvey travelled to the **United States**, where his movement flourished. He became a leading black nationalist and also established the Black Star Line, a shipping company that was part of a programme of return to Africa, known as **pan-Africanism**. Garvey was found guilty of mail fraud over shares in the Black Star Line and sent to jail in 1925. When his sentence was commuted two years later, he returned to **Jamaica**. By 1935 he had lost his family home and the UNIA headquarters' building in Kingston to creditors. He moved to London, where he died. In 1964, Garvey was declared a national hero in Jamaica, and his body was reinterred in a permanent memorial in Kingston.

gaucho

A much debated word used to describe both a type of person and a way of life and a culture in **Argentina** and surrounding regions. Gauchos were residents of the vast plains (pampas) of Argentina who spent much of their life on horseback, living independently off the land or on the estates of landowners. They influenced politics because they could serve as a private army for large landowners; gaucho cavalry facilitated the rise of strongmen such as Juan Manuel de Rosas in the nineteenth century. Modernized stock-raising led governments to use vagrancy and other laws to force gauchos into the labour market. Fences and immigrant labour also disrupted the traditional gaucho lifestyle, converting more gauchos into traditional ranch hands. In the face of massive European immigration in the late nineteenth century, many writers began using the gaucho as a symbol of Argentine identity, a symbol that has endured into the twenty-first century.

gay, lesbian, bisexual and transgender movement (GLBT)

It was not until the second half of the twentieth century that gay men had any legal rights of any kind. Sodomy had been a criminal offence in much of the common law world for centuries: American states inherited anti-sodomy statutes from their British colonial masters, for example. In the late nineteenth century Victorian Britain suffered a renewed outbreak of moral panic over sexual deviancy, exemplified by the trial and disgrace of the author Oscar Wilde. The term *homosexual* was coined in 1869 by Karl-Maria Kertbeny to describe same-sex love as a stable sexual orientation, and medical and psychiatric investigation into so-called 'sexual inversion' flourished in the very late nineteenth and early twentieth centuries in **Europe** and the **United States**. Although some of this work, notably that conducted by Magnus Hirschfeld's Scientific Humanitarian Committee in Germany between the 1890s and 1930s, was sympathetic to same-sex desire, much scientific enquiry considered homosexuality to be a mental illness. The American Psychiatric Association did not remove same-sex desire from its register of mental illnesses until the 1970s.

Male same-sex intimacy in the early twentieth-century western world was conducted in a secret demi-monde of bars, clubs and outdoor meeting places known to gay men as sites for gay sex. Lesbians also developed networks of bars and other public meeting places. Certain cities became renowned as cosmopolitan conduits of the exotic and urban landscapes where people of different backgrounds, ethnicities and sexualities could mingle freely, and gay men and women flocked to cities such as San Francisco, New York and London to develop queer communities and to indulge their sexual and social desires. In rural areas, and in many non-western countries, homosexuality remained taboo, though far from unknown, and in cities known as sites of same-sex networks regular police raids on gay bars and entrapment of those looking for public sex reinforced the fact that same-sex desire was far from being a 'right' in any locale.

World War II saw a major transformation in social relations as men and women in nations at war were uprooted from their social milieu to travel to far-off military bases and naval towns. Shortly after the war, the American sexologist Alfred Kinsey wrote his two volumes on sexual behaviour in men and women that defined same-sex desire as part of a broad scale of human sexual relations. These developments fuelled the emergence of a homophile activist movement, particularly but not exclusively in the United States and Britain, including the Mattachine Society and Daughters of Bilitis in the United States in the 1950s. In **Britain** a government-appointed commission headed by Lord Wolfenden in 1957 recommended the partial legalization of gay sex, which took place with the Sexual Offences Act of 1967. In 1962 the state of Illinois legalized gay sex and many American states followed in the 1970s. However, only the action of the US Supreme Court in 2003 finally mandated the decriminalization of sodomy in all states. Even at the present time, a number of countries, particularly in the **Middle East** and **Africa**, continue to prohibit sexual relations between same-sex couples. In many western countries since 2000, such as **Canada**, **South Africa** and **Spain**, same-sex marriage has been legalized.

Gaylani, Rashid Ali al- (1892–1965)

Iraqi politician and three-time prime minister during the Hashemite monarchy mostly known for leading the 1941 coup, often known as the Rashid Ali coup. Gaylani was a lawyer from a prominent Sunni Baghdadi family. As a member of the al-Ikha al-Watani (the Patriotic Brotherhood), he was often highly critical of **Iraq**'s close relations with the British. In 1940 he became prime minister and during this period of wartime tension the British felt that his loyalty to the Allied cause was ambivalent. In reality, Gaylani was attempting to follow a policy of neutrality which for the British meant a pro-Axis stance. In 1941 he orchestrated an operation that resulted in the expulsion of many pro-British Iraqi politicians. The British Army subsequently occupied Iraq, expelled Gaylani and brought back pro-British politicians. The military leaders who eventually toppled the pro-British Hashemite monarchy in 1958 claimed that they were carrying out the unfinished business of 1941.

Gaza

– *see also* **Occupied Territories**; **Palestine**.

Gaza can define either a strip of Palestinian-controlled land sandwiched between **Israel** and **Egypt**, or can be used to designate a city of the same name within the so-called 'strip'. This city, the largest in the disputed Palestinian Territories, lies along the Mediterranean Sea coast in the Gaza Strip. Gaza, or Gaza city as it is sometimes known, is populated by a majority of Arab Muslims. Though predominantly Muslim, there is a small minority of Arab Christians living in the Gaza Strip. As of 1993, and according to the **Oslo Accords**, the region came under the control of the Palestinian authority. **Hamas** won control of Gaza after 2006, after which it was periodically blockaded from both Israel and Egypt as a result of terrorist attacks by militants. Rocket attacks into Israel were met by devastating air and ground attacks on Gaza by Israeli forces causing several thousand casualties in 2010. In 2014 a further 51-day war erupted. The strip, which bears the same name as the city of Gaza, is one of the most densely populated regions in the world, with a little over 1.5 million people situated within roughly 360 square miles.

gender

– see also **feminism**.

Until the early 1970s the word *gender* was used primarily when discussing the classification of nouns in certain languages. At that point psychologists and sociologists first began to use it as a substitute for 'sex': 'sex roles' became 'gender roles', 'sex distinctions' became 'gender distinctions' and so on. The word was picked up by economists and educators, and then by historians and scholars in other fields. At the same time that 'gender' was emerging as a concept related to the sex of persons as well as words, women's history was developing as a research field. The first wave of the women's rights movement in the nineteenth century had been accompanied by great interest in **women's history**, and the second-wave feminist movement that began in the 1970s was as well. Students and scholars began investigating aspects of women's lives in the past, discovering and utilizing new sources and posing new questions to well-known sources. Initially these studies were often met with derision or scepticism, dismissed as a 'fad' that would quickly pass. This criticism did not quell interest in women's history, and may in fact have stimulated it, as many women who were active in radical or reformist political movements of this era were angered by claims that their own history was trivial, marginal or 'too political'. By the late 1970s hundreds of colleges and universities in the **United States**, **Canada** and **Australia** offered courses in women's history, and many had separate programmes in women's history or women's studies. Universities elsewhere in the world were somewhat slower to include lectures and seminars on women's history, though by 2000 these were a standard part of curricula in many places.

The very first women's histories often began with the premise that 'sisterhood is global' and that women of all places and ages shared many things. As historians delved into women's past, however, they quickly learned that statements about the 'status of women' in this or that society were far too general. Women's experiences differed according to race, class, religion, geographic location and a host of other factors, all of which came to be termed 'categories of difference'. Previous historical studies, which had generally focused on men (though only rarely stating this explicitly), had used some of these categories to differentiate the experiences of individuals or groups; they discussed, for example, 'the formation of the English working class' or 'the development of the Protestant ethic'. Women's historians added categories of difference that had rarely been noticed when focusing on men's lives, such as marital status and number (or lack) of children. They also emphasized that categories of difference were not discreet from one another, but 'intersected', that is, individuals' simultaneous location in many categories shaped their lives in complex ways. Thus the life of an urban, middle-class French Protestant was different from that of a village middle-class Protestant, urban working-class Protestant, urban middle-class German Protestant and urban middle-class French Catholic, to say nothing about how these lives differed from century to century or location to location.

Not surprisingly, women's historians noted that there was no such thing as 'a Protestant', for the experiences of a Protestant *woman* would have been strikingly different from those of a Protestant *man*. Picking up the word being used by social scientists, they increasingly began to use the word *gender* to discuss systems of sexual differentiation that affected both women and men, and to trace the ways in which societies fashioned their notions of what it means to be male or female. Gender was a category of analysis that complicated all the others. Take social class or nationality: if class was derived from one's relationship to the means of production, to what class did married women belong, as in many countries they could not own property. And if nationality is understood to imply certain political rights, then how is women's membership in a nation experienced or defined? Questions such as these made it clear that women could not simply be added to a story derived from the male experience, and that focusing on gender often necessitated a rethinking of other categories of analysis as well.

This disruption of well-known categories and paradigms ultimately included the topic that had long been considered the proper focus of all history – man. Viewing the male experience as universal had not only hidden women's history, it had also prevented the analysis of men's experiences as those of men. The very words used to describe individuals – *artist* and *woman artist*, for example, or *scientist* and *woman scientist* – made it difficult to think about how the experiences of Picasso or Einstein were shaped by the fact that they were male, while it forced one to think about how being female affected Georgia O'Keefe or Marie Curie. As they developed these ideas, historians – along with scholars in other fields – differentiated primarily between 'sex', by which they meant physical, morphological and anatomical differences (what are often called 'biological differences') and 'gender', by which they meant a culturally constructed, historically changing and often unstable system of differences. Most of the studies with 'gender' in the title still focused on women – and women's history continued as its own field – but a few looked equally at both sexes or concentrated on the male experience, calling their work 'men's history' or the 'new men's studies'. Several university presses started book series with 'gender' in their titles – 'gender and culture', 'gender and law' – and scholars in many fields switched from 'sex' to 'gender' as the acceptable terminology. Historians interested in this new perspective asserted that gender was an appropriate category of analysis when looking at *all* historical developments, not simply those involving women or the family. *Every* political, intellectual, religious, economic, social and even military change had an impact on the actions and roles of men and women, and, conversely, a culture's gender structures influenced every other structure or development.

sex and gender

Just at the point when historians and those in other fields were gradually beginning to see the distinction between sex and gender (and an increasing number were accepting the importance of gender as a category of analysis), that distinction became contested. Not only were there great debates about where the line should be drawn – were women 'biologically' more peaceful and men 'biologically' more skilful at mathematics, or were such tendencies the result solely of their upbringing? – but also, some scholars wondered whether social gender and biological sex are so interrelated that any distinction between the two is meaningless. Such doubts came from four principle directions. One

was from biological scientists attempting to draw an absolute line between male and female. Because the external body could be ambiguous, scientists began to stress the importance of internal indicators of sex difference, such as chromosomes or prenatal hormones. All these indicators still leave ambiguous intermediate categories, however, and some scientists began to question why the search for an infallible marker of sex difference was so intense. Might cultural norms that posited two genders be influencing science in this area, that is, might 'gender' actually determine 'sex' rather than the other way around?

A second source of doubts about the distinction between sex and gender came from anthropology. Though most of the world's cultures have a dichotomous view of gender, occasionally cultures develop a third or even a fourth gender. In a number of areas throughout the world, including Alaska, the Amazon region, North America, Australia, Siberia, central and south Asia, Oceania and the **Sudan**, individuals who were originally viewed as male or female assume (or assumed, for in many areas such practices have ended) the gender identity of the other sex or combine the tasks, behaviour and clothing of men and women. They are a distinct gender category, though outsiders often regarded them as homosexual men or unusually manly women. Among American Indians, such individuals are known as 'two-spirit' people, and often had special religious and ceremonial roles because they could mediate between the male and female world and the divine and human world. Comparative ethnography indicates that in many of the world's cultures, gender attribution is not based on genitals or other 'biological' factors, and may, in fact, change throughout a person's life.

The arbitrary nature of gender is also noted in a third source of doubts, psychology. Individuals whose external genitalia and even chromosomal patterns mark them as male or female may mentally regard themselves as the other, and choose to live and dress as the other. This condition is now labelled 'gender dysphoria' by the medical profession and is sometimes treated through sex-change operations. Not all people accept their situation as a medical condition in need of treatment, however; while some undergo surgery and become transsexuals, others understand themselves to be 'transgendered', that is, neither male nor female but another gender category entirely, and wish to remain such. They regard dichotomous gender and sexual categories as oppressive, and call for these to be 'queered' – that is, challenged and contested.

257

The fourth source of doubts came from within history itself. As historians of women put greater emphasis on differences among women and became increasingly self-critical, they began to wonder whether 'woman' was a valid analytical category. Some asserted that because gender structures varied so tremendously, and women's experiences differed so much depending on their race, class and other factors, there really is nothing that could be labelled 'woman' whose meaning is self-evident and unchanging over time. What is commonly called 'biology', from this perspective, is also a socially and historically variable construct – the word *biology* itself did not appear until 1802 – and those who argue for a biological or physiological basis for gender difference (or sexual orientation) are 'essentialists'. These historians noted that not only in the present is gender 'performative', that is, a role that can be taken on or changed at will, but it was so at many points in the past, as individuals 'did gender' and conformed to or challenged gender roles. Thus the only thing in the historical record is gender, so historians can never study women (or men, for that matter) as a sex.

All these doubts came together at a time when many historians were changing their basic understanding of the methods and function of history under the influence of literary and linguistic theory. This 'linguistic turn' emphasized the words and images of the past, generally described as 'discourse'. Historians should not be preoccupied with searching for 'reality', in this view, because to do so demonstrates a naive 'positivism'; instead, historians should simply analyze texts as texts, elucidating their possible meanings. The linguistic turn (which happened in other fields along with history) elicited harsh responses from many historians, including many who focused on women and gender. They asserted that it denied women the ability to shape their world – what is usually termed 'agency' – in both past and present by positing unchangeable linguistic structures. Wasn't it ironic, they noted, that just as women were learning they *had* a history and asserting they were *part* of history, 'history' became just a text and 'women' just a historical construct? For a period it looked as if this disagreement would lead proponents of discourse analysis to lay claim to 'gender' and those who opposed it to avoid 'gender' and stick with 'women'. Because women's history was clearly rooted in the feminist movement of the 1970s, it also seemed more political than gender history, and programmes and research projects sometimes opted to use 'gender' to downplay this connection with feminism.

In the first decades of the twenty-first century, however, it appears that the division is less sharp; gender history is increasingly recognized as an outgrowth of women's history rather than its replacement, and viewed as a related but separate approach. Historians using gender as a category of analysis no longer limit their work to textual analysis, but many instead treat their sources as referring to something beyond the sources themselves – an author, an event, a physical body – while recognizing that they do not present a perfect reflection. Scholars in many fields have accepted that 'social' gender and 'biological' sex are interrelated, but that the boundary between the two will remain contested and muddied.

recent theoretical trends

New theoretical perspectives are adding additional complexity and bringing new questions to the study of gender. One of these is queer theory, a field that began in the 1990s. The gay liberation movement of the 1970s encouraged both public discussion of sexual matters in general and the study of homosexuality in the past and present. Like women's history, it challenged the assumption that sexual attitudes and practices or gender roles were 'natural' and unchanging. Queer theory built on these challenges and on doubts about the essential nature of sex, sexuality and gender created by biology, psychology, anthropology and history to highlight the artificial and constructed nature of all oppositional categories: men/women, homosexual/heterosexual, black/white, public/private. Queer theorists argue that all dichotomies should be 'queered', that is, complicated so as to problematize the artificial and constructed nature of the oppositional pair. Some theorists celebrate all efforts at blurring or bending categories, viewing 'identity' – or what in literary and cultural studies is often termed 'subjectivity' – as both false and oppressive. Others have doubts about this (somewhat akin to doubts among many feminists about the merits of the linguistic turn), wondering whether one can work to end discrimination against homosexuals, women, **African Americans** or any other group, if one denies that the group has an essential identity, something that makes its members clearly homosexual or women or African American.

Related questions about identity, subjectivity and the cultural construction of difference have also emerged from post-colonial theory and

Critical Race Theory. Post-colonial history and theory has been particularly associated with South Asian scholars and the book series Subaltern Studies, and initially focused on people who have been subordinated by virtue of their race, class, culture or language. Critical Race Theory developed in the 1980s as an outgrowth (and critique) of the civil rights movement combined with ideas derived from Critical Legal Studies, a radical group of legal scholars who argued that supposedly neutral legal concepts such as the individual or meritocracy actually masked power relationships. Both theoretical schools point out that racial, ethnic and other hierarchies are deeply rooted social and cultural principles, not simply aberrations that can be remedied by legal or political change. They note that along with disenfranchising certain groups, such hierarchies privilege certain groups, a phenomenon that is beginning to be analyzed under the rubric of critical white studies. (This is a pattern similar to the growth of men's studies, and there is also a parallel within queer theory that is beginning to analyze heterosexuality rather than simply take it as an unquestioned given.)

Queer theory, post-colonial studies and Critical Race Theory have all been criticized from both inside and outside for falling into the pattern set by traditional history, that is, regarding the male experience as normative and paying insufficient attention to gender differences. Scholars who have pointed this out have also noted that much feminist scholarship suffered from the opposite problem, taking the experiences of heterosexual white women as normative and paying too little attention to differences of race, class, nationality, ethnicity or sexual orientation. They assert that the experiences of women of colour must be recognized as distinctive, and that no one axis of difference (men/women, black/white, rich/poor, gay/straight) should be viewed as sufficient. These criticisms led, in the 1990s, to theoretical perspectives that consistently attempted to recognize multiple lines of difference, such as Critical Race Feminism and post-colonial feminism. Such scholarship has begun to influence many areas of gender history, even those that do not deal explicitly with race or ethnicity. It appears this cross-fertilization will continue, as issues of difference and identity are clearly key topics for historians in the evermore connected twenty-first-century world.

gender in world history

World histories have taken many forms, beginning with the 'universal histories' of the ancient world such as those of Sima Qian and Herodotus. These early texts often included discussion of gender relations, generally as a symbol of the larger social order. Many medieval and early modern world histories took the form of biographical catalogues, in which the lives of great kings, writers, religious leaders or other types of people were described and compared, often as a way to demonstrate universal principles. These included catalogues of women, some produced to detail the prevalence of women's vices through the ages, and some, such as Giovanni Boccaccio's *De claris mulieribus*, to (at least ostensibly) discuss women's virtues. Reading a catalogue of women's vices inspired the Italian humanist Christine de Pizan to write her own universal history of women, *The City of Ladies*, in the early fifteenth century. Christine's work is part of the 'debate about women' (*querelle des femmes*) that involved many authors in Renaissance Europe. One part of this debate focused on women's capacity to rule, with historical examples of the disasters this had caused marshalled by John Knox in *The First Blast of the Trumpet Against the Monstrous Regiment of Women* (1558) and responses by many English courtiers hoping to win favour in the eyes of their monarch, Elizabeth I. The questions vigorously and at times viciously disputed directly concerned what would now be termed the social construction of gender: could a woman's being born into a royal family and educated to rule allow her to overcome the limitations of her sex? Should it? Or stated another way: which was (or should be) the stronger determinant of character and social role, gender or rank?

Universal histories continued into the nineteenth century, and in some of these gender relations are a key explanatory tool. The German scholar J. J. Bachofen, for example, asserted that human society had originally been a matriarchy in which mothers were all powerful; the mother–child bond was the original source of culture, religion and community, but gradually father–child links came to be regarded as more important, and superior (to Bachofen's eyes) patriarchal structures developed. Bachofen's ideas about primitive matriarchy were accepted by the socialist **Friedrich Engels**, who linked the transition from matriarchy to patriarchy with the development of private property. In matriarchal cultures, goods were owned in common, but with the expansion of agriculture and animal husbandry men began to claim ownership of crops, animals and land, thus developing the notion of private property. Once men had private property, they became very concerned about passing it on to their own heirs, and attempted to control women's sexual lives to assure that offspring were legitimate. This led to the development of the nuclear family and then the state, in which men's rights over women were legitimized through a variety of means, a process Engels describes as the 'world historical defeat of the female sex'.

More authors in Europe and America agreed with Bachofen's opinion of this transformation than with Engels'. They regarded the status of women as a way to judge societies: in 'primitive' societies, that is, those outside the West, women were sexual slaves, gathered into harems for oriental despots and polygamous marriages for savages, while in the West they were sheltered and cherished companions, providing havens in a heartless world for their husbands and sons. The female authors of biographical surveys of 'illustrious', 'celebrated' or 'distinguished' women – which remained a popular genre in the nineteenth century – generally agreed, though they often gave women an active role in enhancing progress and did not simply view them as victims. Echoes of this can be found in the twentieth century, in such works as Mary Ritter Beard's *Women as a Force in History* (1946) and even in the twenty-first, especially in series designed for the general public, such as those that focus on 'uppity women' in various historical eras.

Universal histories, generally based on earlier printed works and often designed with a pedagogic purpose, were popular reading in the nineteenth century, but increasingly disparaged as not really history by those who were transforming history into a profession. This process began in German universities, where young men debated one another in seminars and learned how to search archives for historical sources. Historical research carried out by those not trained in this system was increasingly regarded as amateurish antiquarianism, a judgement that spread to the rest of Europe and to present and former European colonies whose universities were modelled on those of **Europe**. The emphasis on archivally based research privileged those aspects of the past that produced the type of written records stored in archives, primarily political and institutional history.

The professionalization of history worked against both women historians and history that included considerations of gender. Women were excluded from studying at universities, and generally prohibited (along with children) from entering academic libraries and archives; whatever history they produced was therefore, by definition, amateur. The story of women's lives was less obvious in the archives created by various political bodies – cities, provinces, courts, dioceses, national governments – than were the more public lives of men. Perhaps not surprisingly, the world, national and local histories produced by the men trained through this system focused on the male experience, though they did not label it as such. They often described their research in highly gendered and sexualized terms, however. In an 1828 letter to his friend Bettina von Arnim (who had just given birth to her seventh child, and would later write several important novels), Leopold von Ranke, one of the creators of the seminar system, described documents in archives as, 'So many princesses, possibly beautiful, all under a curse and needing to be saved.'

World history in its most recent form, developed within the context of this understanding of what real 'history' is, was created in the nineteenth century: primarily a political story of public, institutional developments, in which intensive study of written sources is the primary key to understanding. This was the understanding of history within which women's history developed as well, and in many ways the paths of world history and women's and gender history have been parallel. Both have been, in part, revisionist interpretations arguing that the standard story needed to be made broader and much more complex; both have been viewed by those hostile or disinterested as 'having an agenda'.

The primary revisionary paths in world history and women's and gender history have been in opposite directions, however. World history has focused on the story of connections within the global human community, the linking of systems in the human past. As one founder of the field commented recently, world history has been the story of the 'great convergence'. In contrast, women's and gender history over the last decades have spent much more time on divergence, making categories of difference ever more complex. Both have also concentrated on their own lines of revision, and have not paid much attention to what has been going on in the other. Thus the use of gender as an analytical category has been slower in coming into world history than into some other historical fields.

This lack of intersection is changing, particularly in certain research areas, and especially in work on the modern era. Prime among these are studies of colonialism and imperialism. A few books on the gendered and sexualized nature of colonial encounters were published as early as the 1970s, and beginning in the 1990s many more have appeared. Most of this scholarship draws explicitly on feminist and post-colonial theory, exploring issues such as the construction of gendered national or ethnic identities during the colonial era. Work on the **British Empire**, particularly in south Asia, has predominated, with British masculinity in the colonial context particularly well studied.

gender and nationalism

Gender and nationalism has been another key area of scholarship, with edited collections and monographs. There are articles on gender and nationalism in many of the new collections on nationalism, and a special issue in 2000 of the journal *Nations and Nationalism* titled 'The Awkward Relationship: Gender and Nationalism'. Many of the major journals in women's and gender history have had special issues on nationalism, and there are chapters on nationalism in the new collections on global gender history. Thus the interpenetration is going both ways, as it must: gender is making it into considerations of nationalism, and nationalism into considerations of gender. The construction of nationalism and the imagined nature of national communities are important themes in this work, and women are viewed as important agents in that construction. Gender is also beginning to show up as a category of analysis in transnationalism.

The construction of gendered ethno-racial categories has been another strong area of research. Some of this work is about discourse and representation, but much of it is explicitly political, part of the burgeoning feminist work on gender and the state. Women's organizations are increasingly analyzed from a world-historical perspective, as so many of these organizations had (and continue to have) a global reach and mission. The ways in which the production, trade, purchase and use of consumer goods shape gendered identities is another area of growing interest. Certain areas continue to be under-studied, however. Gendered class analysis from a global perspective is very rare, as is gendered analysis of the technological changes that often structure the periodization of world history. On these and other issues, the insights gained from combining the strengths of both fields – the emphasis on interaction, exchange and connection from world history, and the stress on multiple categories of difference from women's and gender history – offer much promise.

general strikes

– *see also* **syndicalism**.

The general strike, meaning a cessation of work by all workers, originated in the British trade union movement of the early nineteenth century with the quasi-millennial idea of a `Grand National Holiday' or `Jubilee' that would signal the power of organized labour and bring about radical reform. British radicals, the Chartists, called a general strike in the industrial districts of Lancashire and Cheshire in the summer of 1842 in support of their petition for universal suffrage. The concept was adopted by European and other labour movements and left-wing thinkers as a means of mobilizing the entire workforce of an industry, area or country to bring about major change or the revolutionary overthrow of governments. The latter tactic was adopted by **syndicalists** and anarcho-syndicalists and general strikes were called in many countries in the late nineteenth and early twentieth centuries, though often only of partial or limited effect. One of the largest was called by the British trade union movement in May 1926 in support of a miners' strike, but was intended more to pressurize rather than overthrow the government and was deemed a failure. The general strike remained part of the left-wing agenda for political action; it was called on in **France** in 1968, and found a place in independence, anti-apartheid and post-colonial workers' movements.

genetics

– *see also* **eugenics**.

Genetics is the science associated with the discovery, study and application of knowledge about how characteristics are passed biologically from parent to child. It developed from the scientific work of the Catholic cleric and scientist Gregor Mendel (1822–84), who analyzed the way in which pea plants developed across generations. It was eventually associated with, but separate from, the theory of evolution which it tended to prove. In fact the science for many years was celebrated in a fog of ignorance, and was briefly associated with **eugenics** before being put on a serious basis by the discovery and mapping of the **DNA** molecule by various transatlantic teams between 1944 and 1953. The work of these teams culminated with Watson, Crick, Franklin and Williams at Cambridge in England, of whom only Watson and Crick became famous. Separately, between 1890 and 1965, research was conducted into the 'messenger' RNA of the DNA molecule. Identification of the processes involved in the copying and storage of genetic information via the DNA–RNA link proceeded through the twentieth century, and in 1990 a project was initiated called the Human Genome Project. The aim of this effort, which was initiated by the **USA** but ultimately comprised an international consortium, was the mapping of human DNA. With the aid of rapidly advancing computer and information technology, this aim was achieved between 2000 and 2003.

Sequencing, or mapping of DNA, allowed for the development of genetic therapies and genomic techniques which offered vast advances in medicine, but which also contained the risk of interventions to alter the nature, structure, appearance or behaviours of human beings in embryonic form. The consequent potential for a new birth of eugenics caused great debate and alarm. Nevertheless, the progress of genetic engineering in the late twentieth century had already led to the development of patented forms of crops, foods, animal therapies and insecticide combinations which together came to be known as 'genetically modified' food. Such foodstuff held out the hope of vast returns in terms of yields and a potential for therapies and other additions to become literally ingrained. GM food was seen as a threat to ecosystems and widely rejected in many jurisdictions across the world, partly because of the objections of ecologists and environmental campaigners. The public and political concern was partly that gene sequencing and manipulation had by the late twentieth century become an expensive preserve of corporations in the developed world, who were allowed to patent the technology they had developed or uncovered as their own property. Some governments, predominantly in Africa, were also concerned that once employed, GM food crops would tie a country or region to a corporation and undermine natural ecosystems, thus resulting in a new imperialism.

DNA techniques had also become associated in the public mind with police and criminal databases which had been accorded great predictive and preventative value, but which also raised concerns about privacy. Ironically, when DNA techniques were applied to past cases, police and prosecutors around the world found themselves facing a problem of credibility as the numbers of those convicted wrongly of crimes were publicized (even though more were eventually convicted safely because of DNA evidence).

A final source of cultural worry about genetics involved the popular belief, propagated in literature, films and speculative scientific grant applications, that DNA sequencing could somehow lead to the revival of extinct species (an almost impossible feat). In all of these matters, popular media tended to take a sensationalist line, with the ultimate result that popular perception of genetic research was disengaged from, and even hostile to, reality. This led to widespread calls that the technology be limited or controlled, which ultimately proved fruitless.

Geneva

Geneva, the second city of Switzerland is the most populous city of Romandy (the French-speaking part of **Switzerland**) and capital of the Geneva canton. It is situated next to Lake Geneva, where the lake flows into the Rhône. Initially settled by Celtic people, as the centre of Calvinism it was also known as the Protestant Rome during the sixteenth century, and is now headquarters base for numerous international organizations because of Switzerland's neutral status..

Geneva Accords (1988)

– *see also* **Afghanistan, Soviet invasion of**.

The Geneva Accords were a series of agreements intended to bring an end to the Soviet war in **Afghanistan** (1979–89). The product of multiple rounds of negotiations based in Geneva, **Switzerland**, beginning in June 1982 under the auspices of the **United Nations**, they were signed by representatives of Afghanistan, **Pakistan**, the **United States** and the **USSR** in April 1988. Afghanistan and Pakistan pledged non-interference in the other's affairs. The Soviet Union and the US agreed to act as guarantors of the settlement and to refrain from intervention in either state. **Mikhail Gorbachev** saw the accords as an opportunity to improve relations with Washington as well as a framework for Soviet withdrawal from Afghanistan. The last Soviet forces departed in February 1989. However, Pakistan, **Iran** and the US continued to back the anti-communist rebels, the **mujahideen**, and Moscow maintained its support for the Afghan communist Najibullah until late 1991. His government survived in power until April 1992, when it fell to mujahideen forces and defectors from among his former allies.

Geneva Convention

International agreement on the conduct of war initiated in 1864 and ratified in 1906. Chiefly concerned with the treatment of the wounded, the sanctity of the **Red Cross** and the treatment of prisoners of war, it was extended to the prohibition of certain weapons, such as 'dumdum' bullets, and in 1946 to the protection of civilians in time of war.

Latterly the rights of guerrilla fighters have been included in its provisions. In all, 100 treaties have been concluded under the aegis of the Red Cross with different states, and its four major conventions have been ratified by the great majority of states.

genocide

– see also **war crimes**; **Holocaust**.

Genocide is a legal term which arose in the twentieth century to describe the deliberate elimination of a people or culture. It was institutionalized in 1948 by the Paris Genocide Convention, and was subsequently incorporated into the statutes of the major international courts and by many members of the **United Nations**. As formulated by Rafael Lemkin (1900–59) in 1944, the term referred to the attempt by the Nazis and their associated governments to exterminate Jews and Roma in the Final Solution agreed after the 1942 Wannsee conference. However, it has come to also incorporate ideas of killing by the prevention of births, the creation of living conditions sufficient to destroy a people, the infliction of serious physical or mental harm via war crimes upon an ethnic group, ethnic cleansing and the forcible transfer of children. It is possible to commit, conspire to, incite or to instigate genocide. Signatory members of the Rome Convention are required to prosecute genocide, either within their own or the International Criminal Court (ICC), and in the absence of a charge from a state, the Prosecutor of the ICC, another government, or the Security Council of the United Nations can recommend proceeding. The charge has also been used in the international courts which were associated with the outcome of the wars in **Yugoslavia** and in **Rwanda**. This has not been true of the equivalent bodies in **Liberia** or **Sierra Leone**. At the **Nuremberg trials** no defendant was charged with genocide since the crime did not as yet exist, and in consequence convictions were secured for war crimes, or crimes against peace under a variety of customs and treaties. A similar condition applied in the Eichmann trial in **Israel**, when a key perpetrator of the Nazi genocide, Adolf Eichmann (1906–62), was tried by the state of Israel under its own laws, which ran parallel to the Paris Convention.

Genocide is also a term which is apt to be employed ahistorically and in debates in the social sciences and politics, to apply to the effects of European and settler policies in the Americas, as well as to the behaviour of the European (and especially German and Belgian) empires in Africa before **World War I**. Because it is a term with several meanings, it has also lent itself to debates over the British treatment of Maori and Aboriginal children in **Australia**, of the **Mau Mau revolt** in **Kenya**, and of the Irish people from the seventeenth to the nineteenth centuries. It has figured prominently and controversially in debates in the Middle East over the Armenian massacres, Israeli treatment of Palestinians, Islamist behaviour towards Christians in **Syria**, **Iraq** and **Egypt**, and to ethnic and religious violence in **Sudan**. The term has also been used of sundry other disputes. One reason for such varied usage has been the multiple iterations of genocide. The defining outrage, perpetrated by the National Socialist regime in Germany, was bureaucratized and industrialized. It was therefore comparatively easy to trace, but it was exceptional. No subsequent regime has ever behaved in the way in which Nazi Germany could between 1941 and 1944. However, it has been possible, as in the Rwandan and Yugoslav wars, to discern clear and intentional patterns of popular destruction inspired by racist and resource-driven attitudes. A consequence of this has been the creation of a debate over the requirement by outsider states to intervene in the affairs of another if they have evidence that genocide is taking place. Such a requirement has been characterized as a 'responsibility to protect'.

Lemkin (whose east European family were previously affected by pogroms) experimented with different words before settling on *genocide*, which he intended to convey a sense of modern mass killing aimed at non-national minorities. With the expansion of genocide studies in western universities, a debate has arisen as to whether genocide is specifically modern or simply built into human nature. This illustrates what has been termed an ontological problem in the fields of international relations and international law. These disciplines are at once both positivistic and prescriptive; they attempt to identify and universalize patterns in the fashion of scientists, but also to problematize processes and to suggest restraints or solutions based on the creation of norms and sanctions. This effort is obviously distinct from historical analysis. The tendency to see the prevention of genocide based on identified examples as offering an incentive to solve international problems led to United Nations-sponsored attempts in the 1980s to include the repression or elimination of sexual and political groups in genocide. This attempt failed, in part because of a coalition of disinterest from the developing world and diplomatic lawyers, who envisaged the diminution of genocide in a welter of tactical state-to-state lawsuits. It is a curiosity of the emergent awareness of states that they should prevent genocide if necessary by invasion that many major interventions, such as those in **Bangladesh** in 1971, **Cambodia** in 1978 and **Uganda** in 1979, did not mention the prevention of genocide, whereas occasions when states have failed to intervene, such as the Sudan or Rwanda in the late twentieth and early twenty-first century, did recognize it. It has also been the case that on occasions when states killed citizens of the same ethnic group as their rulers, such as the Holodomor, the **Great Leap Forward**, or the **Khmer Rouge** regime, there has been no legal basis on which to call the mass killing genocide. In recent years, examples of successful interventions have been few, such as the **NATO** involvement in **Kosovo** and Australia in **East Timor**.

George III (1738–1820)

George III (George William Frederick of Hanover, 1738–1820; King of Great Britain and Ireland, 1760–1820) was one of the longest-serving British monarchs. He presided over the rise of the **United Kingdom** to imperial power in the Atlantic and Indian Oceans, and is remembered for the defeat of **France** in the **Seven Years War** which ended in 1763, the 'loss' of the American colonies, and the defeat of France under the revolutionary and Napoleonic regimes by British-led coalitions. His personal descent into, and recovery from, madness has also been the subject of public interest and drama. George was the first of the Hanoverian Kings to be fully 'British' in the sense of being born in that country, and having English as a first language. George was closely associated with the rise of the British party system (being opposed to the Whig interest) and with **William Pitt the Younger**.

George, Henry (1839–1897)

An American journalist and radical political economist, George is best known for *Progress and Poverty* (1879), a best-seller that exposed the paradox of a deepening divide between rich and poor despite technological advances and nature's freely provided bounty. His solution to the concentration of land ownership was a single tax on land value to replace all others. Though more influential abroad (especially in Australia), his thinking inspired US foundations and think tanks dedicated to advancing his proposals.

Georgia

An historic state in the **Caucasus** straddling **Europe** and **Asia**, which emerged within the eastern Roman Empire. It spent three centuries as an important independent state until becoming subject to Persian, Mongol, Turkish and Russian domination, re-emerging as an independent state in 1991, having subsisted within the **USSR** for seventy years. Georgia has become a centre of liberal democracy and free market capitalism in the Caucasian region, and has developed wealth in the form of oil pipelines. In recent years, disputes over territory and Georgia's relationship with its ethnic Russian population (as in South Ossetia) have been the cause of military conflict with the Russian Federation, as well as an unreciprocated approach to the **European Union** and **NATO** on the part of the authorities in Tblisi.

German Democratic Republic

Declared in October 1949 in what had been the Soviet Zone of Occupation in response to the creation of the **Federal Republic of Germany** by the western Allies, September 1949, the German Democratic Republic was denied recognition by the West until 1973, when the Basic Treaty between East and West Germany normalized relations and **Britain** and **France** established diplomatic relations. Admitted to the **United Nations**, 1973, it defined itself by its anti-fascism and following of rigid communist orthodoxy. The link with the **Soviet Union** was recognized under the constitution. A member of **Comecon**, 1950–90, and of the **Warsaw Pact**, 1955–90, it enjoyed the highest standard of living in the Soviet bloc and achieved high cultural, educational and social standards which were missed by many after reunification. Nevertheless it remained unable to match the economic successes of its western neighbour, despite a high level of industrial output. All-party government was adopted in 1989, and East Germany adhered to the **German Federal Republic** in 1990 (*see* **German reunification**).

German Empire

Only unified in 1871, **Germany** was a latecomer to imperial ambitions beyond **Europe**. Initially hostile to colonial expansion, **Bismarck**, the German chancellor, yielded in the 1880s to business pressures to begin a process of `imperialism in a hurry', which also provided him with a useful diversion from domestic political difficulties. Beginning with territory in what became German South-West Africa, later **Namibia**, by 1914 Germany gathered a group of territories which covered 2.9 million square kilometres in **Africa** and the Pacific. The largest portion was in Africa where South-West Africa, German East Africa or **Tanganyika**, later **Tanzania**, Togo and **Cameroon** formed part of the late nineteenth-century `scramble for Africa'. Settlement was limited, but left a legacy in its two largest African colonies, South-West Africa and East Africa. Colonial rule was contested, in the former in the Herero and Nama rebellions in 1904–8 and in the latter in the **Maji Maji revolt** of 1905–7, which were brutally suppressed and followed by rigid separation between the races. The German colonies played an important part in imperial Germany's attempt to achieve great power status, its ruler Wilhelm II proclaiming in 1896 that Germany had become a `world empire'. Such statements, combined with German naval expansion, added a provocative air to its foreign policy in the years before 1914, as did quasi-imperial projects in the Near East, such as the unrealized **Berlin–Baghdad railway**. **World War I** saw serious fighting in Germany's African colonies, Germany's defeat leading to the loss of all its colonial empire. Article 119 of the **Treaty of Versailles** stipulated that Germany must surrender its territories because of `unworthiness in colonial matters'. Germany's colonies were distributed amongst the victorious powers, leaving another legacy of bitterness at the Versailles settlement in Weimar and Nazi Germany, though the latter increasingly looked to eastern Europe rather than the wider world to revive the expansionism of the Wilhelmine era.

German Federal Republic

Declared September 1949 in what had been the American, British and French Zones of Occupation (West Germany). Its federal form of government, enshrined in the Basic Law, respected tradition but was also designed to avoid both the instability of the Weimar years and any return to dictatorship. As West Germany, it joined the European Coal and Steel Community (ECSC) in 1951 and the European Economic Community (EEC – the common market) in 1958. It controversially rearmed under American pressure despite much internal opposition, and became a formal member of **NATO** in 1955. Admitted to the **United Nations** in 1973, despite criticism of the roles played by many former Nazis in its earlier years, West Germany was acclaimed for its lasting commitment to democracy. The reaction against nationalism, however, diluted its sense of identity, fuelling identification with the European ideal. The German 'economic miracle', based on the principles of the social market and co-determination, increasingly made West Germany Europe's most powerful and successful economy. It absorbed the

German Democratic Republic (East Germany) in 1990, under **German reunification**.

German historicism

Historicism was everywhere characteristic of the European Romantic reaction against the emerging bourgeois society of the earlier nineteenth century. The traditional craftsman was preferable to the machine; the Gothic to the classical; and the chivalrous, the emotional and the religious to the rational. This historicism went deeper in Germany than elsewhere, reflecting an ancient love of the forest and of legend. The Brothers Grimm collected folk tales from the Baltic, inspiring opera and literature to the present day. The academic study of Sanskrit unlocked Hindu mysticism, just as the German genius for lyricism and music was attuned to idealized visions of the past and the supreme Romantic ideal of transcendence, with Wagner as the greatest exemplar. At the domestic level, the *Heimat* movement created an enduring 'traditionalism'. Not least, historicism could redress the outcome of the Thirty Years War (1621–48), and embody a German Romantic nationalism which instinctively rejected the alien French concept of the rights of man.

German reunification

Consequent to the collapse of the Soviet bloc and more directly, the resignation of the ruling East German Politburo, November 1989 saw the opening of the inner-German border and the formation of a new all-party East German government. The rate of change took the international community, much of which was initially far from enthusiastic, by surprise, but reunification could not have happened without Soviet consent. Despite the desire of some intellectuals for a reformed East Germany and of many others for a confederal approach, the rejection by West Germany of military neutrality and of a requested financial 'solidarity contribution', and its counter-offer of immediate monetary union, made reunification on West German terms inevitable. The treaty introducing West Germany's currency and applying its economic, financial and social legislation to East Germany with effect from 1 July 1990 was signed on 18 May 1990, and the East German *Volkskammer* (Assembly) approved accession to the Federal Republic as of 3 October 1990 on 23 August 1990.

Much of the optimism surrounding reunification initially evaporated as the exchange of currencies effectively bankrupted the East German economy, generating mass unemployment and placing a heavy tax burden on the former West Germany. It also became clear that the outlooks of the two Germanys had diverged more profoundly than had been appreciated. The economic and social scars of reunification had largely healed, however, when the twenty-fifth anniversary of reunification was celebrated in 2015.

German Revolution (1918–1919)

Naval mutinies at Kiel on 29 October 1918 and at Wilhelmshaven triggered the creation of revolutionary workers' and soldiers' councils throughout **Germany** and on the Western Front. Kaiser Wilhelm II abdicated and fled on 9 November 1918. Social Democrat leader Friedrich Ebert became chancellor of a moderate socialist coalition, using the army and right-wing *Freikorps* to repress more radical ambitions, notably the January 1919 Spartacist rising. The fragile **Weimar Republic** was established in August 1919.

German unification

A process of consolidation in the German lands taking place in the nineteenth century which led to the creation of a 'Second Reich' or German Empire by **Otto von Bismarck** in 1871. **Germany** had originally been a geographical expression for dozens of states, in which **Austria**, **Prussia** and **Switzerland** were mixed with other entities roughly north of the Alps and between the Vistula and the Rhine, but also incorporating the eastern Baltic seaboard. Cross cut by the Reformation and Austro-Prussian rivalry, it would have remained so but for a conglomeration by the Congress of Vienna into the 39-member German Confederation. This loose grouping was replaced by a short-lived state in 1848, and then by a period of division which was resolved by the Prussian victory over Austria at the Battle of Königgrätz in 1866. Under the leadership of Bismarck, Prussia then proceeded to incorporate southern German lands into a new reich in 1871, following a war with **France** and initially via a customs and economic union. The creation of the empire, under a kaiser and a militarist, populist and quasi-democratic culture, destabilized Europe and led ultimately to the outbreak of **World War I**.

Germany

A cultural entity since the early Middle Ages but politically fragmented into numerous sovereign princedoms under the nominal suzerainty of the Habsburg Holy Roman Emperor after the Thirty Years War, 1618–48. The eighteenth century saw the rise of Brandenburg-Prussia, particularly under the rule of **Frederick II** (the Great), 1740–86, who made it the most powerful German kingdom after **Austria**. The **Congress of Vienna**, meeting after the fall of **Napoleon**, 1815, associated the thirty-nine surviving largely sovereign states in a loose German Confederation dominated by Austria, which opposed any move to German unification, seeing it as a threat to its imperial interests. Prussian Chancellor **Otto von Bismarck** promoted German unification by attacking and defeating first Denmark, 1864, and then Austria, 1866, permitting the annexation of most of the other north German states and the formation with seventeen further states of the North German Confederation. The declaration of the Franco-Prussian War, 1870, drew the southern states of Baden, Bavaria and Württemberg to the Prussian cause and victory allowed the annexation of the predominantly German-speaking French regions of Alsace and Lorraine. The German Empire, the Second (*Zweites*) Reich, with the king of Prussia as emperor (*kaiser*), was proclaimed in the **Palace of Versailles** in 1871.

The Second Reich ended with defeat in **World War I** and the abdication of the kaiser. The Weimar Republic survived the threat of revolution in the aftermath of the war, suppressing the communist revolutions of Kurt Eisner in Bavaria in 1918–19, and of **Karl Liebknecht** in Berlin in 1919. The **Treaty of Versailles** stripped Germany of her Polish territories, creating the **Polish Corridor** and the free city of **Danzig**, and of her colonies in Africa and elsewhere, and returned **Alsace-Lorraine** to France. Reparations of 33 billion dollars were imposed and severe restrictions placed on the German armed forces. Default on reparations led to the **occupation of the Ruhr** and was followed by hyperinflation in 1923. Gradual recovery was truncated by the return of economic depression, mass unemployment and political polarization in 1929–31. Having secured the status of the largest party, the Nazis under **Hitler** took power, exercising dictatorial control under the Enabling Law from 1933, making Germany a fascist state. Hitler began to unravel the Versailles Treaty, remilitarizing the Rhineland in 1936, and secured union with **Austria** (the *Anschluss*) in 1938. Germany annexed the **Sudetenland** following the Munich Agreement of 1938, absorbing **Bohemia** and Moravia into the Greater German Reich in 1939. The invasion of **Poland** in September 1939 provoked war with **Britain** and **France**, followed by invasion of the **Soviet Union** in 1941.

Defeat in 1945 was followed by occupation and division into American, British, French and Soviet zones and Berlin likewise, administered in accordance with decisions taken at the Potsdam conference. Surviving Nazi leaders were the subject of the **Nuremberg trials**, 1946, de-Nazification programmes were instituted, and the state of **Prussia** liquidated. Dissension over economic unification of the occupied zones led to the Soviet blockade of Berlin and the **Berlin airlift**, followed in 1949 by the establishment of the pro-western **German Federal Republic** (West Germany) and the **German Democratic Republic** (East Germany) under Soviet control. The former was involved in the founding institutions of the **European Union**, the European Coal and Steel Community, 1951, and the original 'Six' who formed the European Economic Community (EEC) by the Treaty of Rome, 1957. Normalization of West German relations with its eastern neighbours was achieved through **Ostpolitik** in 1969–73. **German reunification** and signature of the Treaty on the Final Settlement with respect to Germany (effectively the German Peace Treaty) in Moscow by East and West Germany and the four wartime Allies took place in 1990.

Gestapo

The German Secret State police (*Geheime Staatspolizei*), subordinate organization of the **SS** and charged with the security of the Third Reich. They emerged from the Prussian state secret police under Herman Goering and functioned as a domestic intelligence force that also executed the law, eliminated opponents of the Nazi regime and administered political punishments. Like the SS, they were bitter rivals of the **SA** and helped organize the destruction of the storm trooper organization in 1934. They were never fully staffed and ultimately depended upon the collaboration of ordinary Germans in the denunciation programme to function, which was forthcoming until 1945.

Gettysburg address (USA)

World-famous speech that **Abraham Lincoln** delivered on 19 November 1863 at the dedication of a military cemetery at a recent **American Civil War** battlefield. Not the main oration that day and less than 300 words long, it defined the purpose of the **United States'** war effort as that of preserving 'government of the people, by the people, for the people'. Contrary to popular legend, Lincoln did not write it on an envelope and it did receive contemporary praise.

Gettysburg, campaign and Battle of (10 June–14 July 1863)

In the **American Civil War** during the summer of 1863 **Robert E. Lee** sought a decision in the Confederacy's favour by invading Northern soil. By 28–29 June his troops were approaching Harrisburg, Pennsylvania, but Lee received inferior intelligence and underestimated the speed of the Union advance. On 1 July Union and Confederate forces collided at Gettysburg, and on succeeding days (2–3 July) Lee failed to organize concerted and concentrated blows, and was repulsed. Despite this defeat, a skilful retreat (5–14 July) permitted Lee to escape with his army intact. However, the battle was a turning point in marking the high-water mark of the Confederacy, after which it was forced on to the defensive and to eventual defeat. The bloodiest battle of the war with over 40,000 casualties, it became an emotive symbol of the heroism and sacrifice of both sides in the conflict.

Gezo (fl. 1818–1858)

Gezo, king of **Dahomey** (modern-day Benin), ruled from 1818 to 1858. He came to power in a coup against his brother Adandozan, and defied a hundred-year tributary relationship with **Oyo**, his interior neighbour. He was a skilled general, leading his forces in annual wars, and built up the army. He managed to redirect the economy of Dahomey from dependence on the slave trade as that commerce declined in the wake of British Abolition in 1807.

Ghalib, Mirza Asadullah Khan (1797–1869)

Pre-eminent Urdu poet in nineteenth-century India. Although his Persian works far outnumber his works in Urdu, he is revered in the subcontinent for the eloquence and imagery of his Urdu verse. While ridiculing religious orthodoxy, Ghalib explored the mystical and personal dimensions of **Islam** in his poetry. He emphasized the internal struggle of the believer and love for God as the true signs of faith. Serving as the court poet to the last Mughal emperor, Bahadur Shah Zafar, Ghalib wrote poignantly about the demise of the **Mughal Empire** and the rise of British colonialism, both in personal letters and in a diary he kept during the violent events of 1857. His poetry and prose continue to be among the most widely read and recited works in Urdu, and his life has been the basis for multiple plays, television serials and films.

Ghana

Once known as the Gold Coast, the present name was adopted after independence from the historic Ghana Empire, which existed *c.*750–*c.* 1240 to the north-west of the present state. Historically a rich source of gold and slaves, the Crown Colony of the Gold Coast became a British protectorate in 1874. The inland kingdom of **Ashanti** was annexed in 1901 following the overthrow of King Pempeh in 1896 and the suppression of a revolt in 1900, and parts of German Togoland were absorbed as mandated territory following World War I. Seen as the most prosperous and advanced of **Britain**'s West African colonies, in 1946 a new constitution gave Africans a majority in the colonial legislature. **Kwame Nkrumah** established the Convention Party in 1949 to campaign for independence, obtaining dominion status in 1957, followed by the declaration of Ghana as an independent republic within the **Commonwealth** in July 1960. Nkrumah introduced a one-party state and with Soviet aid built the Volta Dam project at Akosambo, completed in 1966, in an attempt to industrialize a country still dependent on agriculture and mineral exports. Blighted by economic mismanagement and corruption, Nkrumah was overthrown in that year in the first of five military coups in fifteen years. In 1979 Flight Lieutenant **Jerry Rawlings** seized control and attempted to end corruption, re-establish civilian government and seek western support to stabilize the economy. The first Ghanian leader to leave power peacefully in 2001, he was succeeded by President Kufour of the New Patriotic Party, who was re-elected in 2004. Ghana has since witnessed increased growth and debt relief, though it is still economically dependent on the price of its principal export, cocoa.

Ghatak, Ritwik (1925–1976)

Radical film director and author, hailed as a cinematic genius; he directed eight feature films. Haunted by the experience of the **Bengal** famine (1943) and the Partition of India (1947), his movies self-consciously range through individual melodrama and a universal political statement. Comparing himself to another filmmaker of epics, Misoguchi, he stands in contrast to Ray or Kurosawa. A director of the Film and Television Institute of India, he influenced future directors.

Ghazi, King of Iraq (1912–1939)

King of Hashemite **Iraq**, 1933–9. Born in Mecca, the son of **Faisal I**, he became king at the age of 21 upon his father's death. Though politically inexperienced, he was highly critical of British involvement in Iraq and in the region in general. His pan-Arab sympathies made him a vocal supporter of the Palestinian uprisings against the British and his Iraqi nationalism made him question British policies in the Persian Gulf. In particular, he claimed Iraqi sovereignty over **Kuwait** (the first time this was publicly voiced by an Iraqi politician). During his reign, the role of the military in Iraqi politics increased, especially after the 1936 Bakr Sidqi coup. King Ghazi died in a car crash which many claim to have been under suspicious circumstances. His 3-year-old son **Faisal II** succeeded him to the Hashemite throne.

Ghose, Aurobindo (1872–1950)

Philosopher and Indian nationalist leader. He forged transnational networks across continents, demanding absolute independence for **India**. He left for French Pondicherry (*c.* 1909), continuing writing and publishing. Hailed as the 'prophet and poet' of Indian nationalism, Sri Aurobindo, as he was later known, never emerged from the *ashram* that grew up around him into an international city, Auroville, which exists today; it also has a transnational network of support groups called Auroville International.

Giap, Vo Nguyen (c. 1912–2013)

Military commander of the **Viet Minh** and the People's Army of Vietnam (PAVN) responsible for leading major operations in the **Vietnam War**, such as **Dien Bien Phu** (1954), the **Tet Offensive** (1968) and the Ho Chi Minh campaign (1975). He served as Defence Minister (1946–80) and Deputy Prime Minister (1976–80) in the Vietnamese government and was a member of the Politburo until 1982. In 1992 he received the highest decorative honour of Vietnam, the Gold Star Order.

Gibbon, Edmund (1737–1794)

British historian and Member of Parliament most famous for his six-volume history of *The Decline and Fall of the Roman Empire*, conceived in 1764 and published between 1776 and 1784 to great sensation and lucrative reward. The book set the tone of interpretation of Rome for two centuries, partly because of Gibbon's innovative reliance on primary documentation and partly because of his powerful and seductive prose style. At various times, Gibbon's identification of the causes of the decline of the western empire, such as

Christianity, immigration and decadence, have been anachronistically applied to other states, and his relative disregard for the history of the Eastern Empire, which outlasted the West by 1,000 years, has been blamed for the comparatively smaller academic and popular focus on **Constantinople** which prevailed until the late twentieth century. Gibbon was an MP from 1774 to 1783, and a colonel in the Hampshire Militia. He wrote extensively in French and was self-consciously a man of the **Enlightenment**.

Gibraltar

A small British overseas territory at the southern tip of the Iberian peninsula, ceded perpetually by **Spain** to the **United Kingdom** in 1713, having been captured in 1704. 'The Rock' is a point of contention among the largely self-governing inhabitants, who are of diverse ethnicities and who have voted twice for autonomy as a dependent territory, in 1967 and 2002. Gibraltar is a significant British naval base and its defence and foreign affairs are the responsibility of Her Majesty's Government in London.

Girondins (France)

A loose grouping of moderate republicans, prominent in the Legislative Assembly and National Convention during the French Revolution, so described because a number of the most prominent members came from the south-western Gironde department. Predominantly lawyers and intellectuals and finding their support among middle-class businessmen, merchants and financiers, they feared the implications of the Jacobin appeal to the lower classes. The Jacobins secured the Girondins' arrest in June 1793 and their execution in October.

Gladstone, William (1801–1895)

Prime Minister of the United Kingdom, 1868–74, 1880–5, 1886, 1892–5; British Liberal leader. William Gladstone was the son of a Liverpool businessman who started his career in politics as a deeply conservative follower of Sir Robert Peel, rose to become Chancellor of the Exchequer and then moved, after the fall of Peel in 1850, to associate himself with Whigs, radicals and former Peelites in the grouping that would cohere into the Liberal Party in 1859. Gladstone was marked by intense Protestant religiosity and a combination of intellectual commitment to **laissez-faire** and individualist principles with highly successful electoral appeal. He pursued policies that sought to promote national self-determination abroad as far as his twin concerns of international law and the management of the **British Empire** would allow. He also sought to develop and uphold an accountable, efficient and transparent state within the boundaries of balanced budgets and low taxation. This latter policy did not conflict with his emphasis in office on individual self-improvement, and led to his supporting policies that clarified the court system, subordinated the armed forces, and which promoted education and international law whilst in office. Gladstone was, however, most associated with the attempt to 'pacify' Ireland, which, as an issue, was a major threat to Liberal electoral and parliamentary fortunes. Gladstone sought to reform Irish landholding, to disestablish the minority Anglican Church, to accommodate Irish leaders and, after 1885, to promote the establishment of a devolved Parliament in Ireland ('Home Rule'). He pursued these policies in the face of Fenian terrorism, and to the point of a split in the Liberal Party which caused Joseph Chamberlain to associate himself and his Liberal Unionist and Imperialist followers with the Conservative Party. His alliance with Charles Stuart Parnell and his attempt to pursue Home Rule was ultimately fruitless.

William Gladstone was hostile to foreign tyrannies, and is also remembered for campaigns in pamphlets and at the ballot box decrying the actions of the **Ottoman Empire** in **Bulgaria**. He shared an antagonism with Benjamin Disraeli, though he outlasted him, which defined both men, and was of such upright character that nocturnal efforts to save fallen prostitutes in the East End of London from their sad lives and for Christianity went unquestioned. Gladstone was phenomenally popular with ordinary Liberal voters, and many items associated with him or his image gained a great monetary value towards the end of the nineteenth century. He was heartily disliked by Queen Victoria, who thought him rude and a threat to her conservative ideas; he was also disliked by the military, particularly after what some perceived as his abandonment of **General Gordon** at Khartoum.

glasnost

A central policy of the **Gorbachev** administration in the **USSR**. Glasnost meant 'openness' and reflected Gorbachev's wish to engage in and sponsor debate, public discussion and open decisions within the Soviet lands. Gorbachev also used the policy to signal to others within the Soviet bloc that the USSR would not intervene to crush public debate, political reform or human rights protests, as in 1956 and 1968, and thus provided a powerful solvent for the communist hold on post-Yalta Europe.

Glele

Glele, King of **Dahomey** (modern **Benin**), ruled 1858–89. A modernizing king, he continued to expand Dahomey but failed to take Abeokuta, his cherished objective. Glele came under increasing pressure from **France** and **Britain**, but decided to cooperate with France. He signed customs agreements and allowed them a special treaty port at Cotonou. Disagreements with France marked the end of his reign, as France sought to expand its influence and commercial power further.

globalization

Globalization is a complex economic, political and cultural process that involves the interaction and interconnection of peoples, companies and governments of different nations. It is both an historic and an ongoing process by which regional economies, societies and cultures become integrated into a network of relationships, and where capital, goods, services, information, peoples, organizations, discourses, and ideas move across national borders, and help foster a growing interdependence among nations and their peoples.

Globalization can be conceptualized as a long-term process rather than as a political-economic condition that has only recently come into being. This has led to a focus on how it has occurred and is occurring in a dynamic process that is continually evolving. That ongoing process involves activities such as **migration**, transnational travel, Internet communication, international marketing, the transfer of employment from one place to another, transnational investment, and the development of a genuinely 'world' culture in areas such as sport and music. It can, however, also be seen as involving more than growing interconnections between nations but also within them, reshaping national territories and institutions. Local practices, institutions and cultures are reshaped by the process of globalization. For example, governments operating within the global economic system might make or be forced to make alterations to laws, regulations and practices to enable foreign merchants, firms and companies to operate in their territories or for their own to operate in ways advantageous to the nation concerned. The latter could range from legislative measures to encourage trade and overseas contact to the wholesale orientation of the state apparatus of war, empire and global influence.

Many states have orientated themselves to suit the needs of the global and are transformed in ways that blur the line between the global and the local or national. This blurring of lines raises serious theoretical questions about what constitutes the 'national'. For example, nation states which become more and more immersed in globalization can undergo a process that entails a degree of 'denationalization' where, to participate in the global economic system, state institutions are transformed and policies implemented which would not otherwise be adopted. Moreover, in addition to affecting the policies of nation states, globalization can affect individual lives in many diverse ways. One significant effect of exposure to globalization is to increase the diversity of cultural option available to individuals, often modifying the hold that customs and traditions play in shaping lives and identities.

a multidimensional process

Globalization is a multidimensional process. These dimensions include economic, political and cultural globalization. Economic globalization refers to the deep integration and rapid interaction of economies through production, **trade** and financial transactions by banks and multinational corporations with an increased role for global institutions like the **International Monetary Fund**, **World Bank** and the World Trade Organization. In the contemporary era, economic relationships are structured by a dominant ideology of **neoliberalism** that promotes the free market and free trade. This ideology shapes global economic policies that include trade liberalization (the reduction of tariffs and other barriers by governments in order to promote the free flow of goods and services between nations), privatization (the transfer of business ownership from governments to private sectors) and austerity (the reduction of government spending in order to shrink budget deficits).

Political globalization refers to an increased trend towards multilateralism in which the **United Nations** plays a key role, and national **non-governmental organizations** (NGOs) serve as watchdogs over governments, and international non-governmental organizations increase their activities and influence. Political activities transcend national borders through global movements and NGOs, and politics takes place above and beyond the confines of the state.

Cultural globalization refers to a worldwide cultural standardization – a trend towards cultural homogeneity as evidenced in the use of the terms *McDonaldization* and *Cocacolaization* by some scholars. Alongside this homogenizing trend, however, we find the formation of post-colonial culture, cultural pluralism and hybridization. This globalization has promoted growing contact between different cultures, leading partly to greater understanding and cooperation and partly to the emergence of transnational communities and hybrid identities. But globalization has also hardened the opposition of different identities. Indeed, there are various cultural movements across the world – some of them fundamentalist – that resist westernization in order to maintain their traditions. Within cultural globalization, then, there are degrees of cultural homogeneity (especially westernization) alongside a rich cultural diversity.

origins

Globalization is not a new phenomenon; it began well before the modern era if seen in terms of migration, trade and cultural contact. From the early modern period, globalization has been seen as integral to capitalist development because a key feature of capitalism is its tendency to be geographically expansionary in its search for new markets, resources and labour. Most scholars agree that for thousands of years people have crossed national borders trading goods, ideas and artifacts. An important period where we see the acceleration of globalization in the West is the sixteenth century, when European exploration and trade went beyond its borders and expanded into other parts of the globe including **Africa**, South Asia, the Caribbean and the Americas (referred to today as the 'global south'). During this period of colonization Europeans from **Britain**, **Spain**, the **Netherlands** and **France** resettled in these newly discovered regions and established economies that thrived on enslaved labour. The products of the enslaved labour force, and the slaves themselves, became part of a global triangular trade that linked the economies of the global south with those of the global north (especially Europe and North America). This early stage of the global economy thrived until the early to mid nineteenth century, when slave economies in the global south declined.

Thereafter, the nineteenth and early twentieth centuries witnessed huge waves of migration and the development of an increasingly sophisticated system of international trade and finance. The period after **World War II** was the precursor of contemporary globalization with the disintegration of the colonial empires and the creation of over eighty new nations. The collapse of the **Soviet Union** and of Soviet domination of eastern Europe

added another score of new states, followed by the break-up of **Yugoslavia**, which added several more. These 'new' countries were freed to sell their raw materials and products on the world market, to purchase goods and also to establish local industries that could compete with those elsewhere. In addition, the reconstruction of **Japan** following 1945 created a huge capitalist power in the Far East, joined from the 1980s by the emerging capitalist orientation of **China**.

contemporary era

Several factors have contributed to increasing globalization in the contemporary era. First, the ending of the **Cold War** and the collapse of Soviet-style economic doctrines in **Europe** and China have brought countries closer together in their economic relations. Second, the global flow of information and global marketing has been enormously enhanced by the **Internet** and information revolution, creating in effect a worldwide trading network even for individuals. Third, transnational corporations have grown in size and influence, building global networks of production, distribution and consumption, not only in traditional 'hard' goods but also in music, information and data. In addition to an increasing influence of transnational corporations, global financial institutions such as the World Bank and the International Monetary Fund (both created in 1944 in the United States) managed the global economy and helped foster economic cooperation among nations. Other global institutions such as the General Association of Trade and Tariffs (GATT) (succeeded by the World Trade Organization (WTO) from 1995), the Marrakesh Agreement of 1994 and the United Nations monitor economic (especially trade), political and social relationships between nations and seek transnational solutions to problems.

The process of globalization, especially in the contemporary period, has been accelerated by the development of information and communication technologies that have intensified the speed and scope of interaction among people worldwide. Because of technology, time and space is compressed: geographic distance and time no longer pose challenges, thus facilitating greater interconnection and interdependence among nations and peoples across the planet. The compression of time and space is also critical for capitalism. Modern technology has reduced the cost and time of moving commodities, labour and capital across the globe, and this has freed all sorts of activities from former spatial restraints. Major innovations in transport and communication technologies have facilitated and intensified the geographical expansion of the commercial economy that underpins the international capitalist economy.

the globalization debate

The literature on globalization is vast and has been intensely debated among scholars. These debates can be divided into three schools of thought: sceptics, hyperglobalists and transformalists. *Sceptics* view globalization as primarily an economic phenomenon that is not new. Nations have always interacted and traded with each other. What is new, is the intensity of that interaction among nations today. Sceptics argue that while there is more contact among nations today than before, the current world economy is not sufficiently integrated to constitute a truly globalized economy. From this perspective, globalization (i.e. the perfect integration of the world economy) is largely a myth. Current international processes are more fragmented and regionalized than globalized as the world economy is increasingly segmented into three major regional blocs (Europe, Asia–Pacific and North America) where the bulk of trade occurs, and where their national governments remain very powerful. Sceptics, then, focus on processes of regionalization as the primary characteristic of globalization as evidenced in the emergence of major financial and trading blocs. On this view, the growth of regionalization is evidence that the world economy is becoming less integrated and more fragmented than before. Sceptics reject the view that globalization is fundamentally undermining the role of nation states and national governments. From their perspective nation states are not passive victims; they are powerful actors governing and regulating economic activities. They argue, however, that deeply rooted patterns of inequality and hierarchy between nations in the north and south (the third world) remain largely intact, and the third world continues to be marginalized as trade and investment flows within the rich global north intensify to the exclusion of much of the rest of the globe.

Hyperglobalists view globalization as primarily an economic phenomenon. It is a process that is indifferent to national borders. From this perspective, globalization is a new era in human history in which peoples everywhere are increasingly subjected to the disciplines of the global marketplace. This new era is characterized by the declining relevance and authority of nation states brought about largely through the economic logic of the global market. Hyperglobalists argue that the most powerful economic actors are not bounded by

national boundaries; they are transnational (for example, transnational corporations). They argue that there exists a single global economy that transcends and integrates the world's major economic regions. In this 'borderless' economy traditional nation states are subordinated to the impersonal forces of the global market and demands of global institutions such as the International Monetary Fund, World Bank and World Trade Organization. At the same time, national governments decline in importance and influence, and have decreased control over their local economies. Hyperglobalists claim that economic globalization is generating a new pattern of winners and losers. A new global division of labour is replacing the traditional core–periphery (global north–global south) structure with a more complex architecture of economic power that creates uneven development and increasing inequalities within and between nations. However, while globalization may be linked with a growing polarization of winners and losers in the short term, many believe the whole world will eventually improve economically, politically and socially from this process.

Transformalists take a middle position between the hyperglobalists and sceptics. From their perspective, contemporary patterns of globalization are historically unprecedented, such that states and societies across the globe are experiencing processes of profound changes as they try to adapt to a more interconnected but highly uncertain world. Governments and societies across the globe are having to adjust to a world in which there is no longer a clear distinction between international and domestic, external and internal affairs. On this view, globalization is a multidimensional process not reducible to an economic logic. The global order is being transformed and these transformations are not restricted to economics but include transformations in politics, culture and personal lives. Globalization is having a differential impact across the world's regions and upon individual states. Transformalists view globalization as a dynamic, open process that is subject to influence and change. It is not a one-way process; rather, it is a two-way flow of images, information and influences. Globalization is complex, and at times contradictory where both integration and fragmentation exist.

As opposed to hyperglobalists who bemoan the weakened roles of states in the global economy, and sceptics who view the role of governments as strengthened, transformalists take a balanced approach. Many acknowledge that transnational corporations have increased their roles in the global field but insist that countries remain important actors. Indeed, while there has been some weakening of state power, transformalists believe governments are restructuring to fit into the current global landscape yet continue to retain a great deal of power in spite of global interdependence. Transformalists recognize that all countries in the world are linked in some way to a single global system, but all are not connected equally. Globalization is associated with new patterns of global stratification in which some states, societies and communities are becoming increasingly enmeshed in the global order while others are becoming increasingly marginalized.

contemporary trends

Scholars have identified several trends in the contemporary global era, two of which are (1) the formation and intensification of a *new international division of labour* and (2) the promotion of *economic neoliberalism* by international agencies. With globalization we see major shifts in labour patterns both locally and globally. One significant shift is the formation of what some term the new international division of labour, which refers to the division of production into different skills and tasks, and spreading them across regions and countries rather than confining them to a single company or country. This phenomenon reflects a spatial division of labour which occurs when the process of production is no longer confined to national economies. This new international division of labour has replaced an older form where the primary exports of countries in the global south to the north consisted of raw materials (minerals and agricultural commodities) and where exports from the north to the south consisted of manufactured goods. Under the new international division of labour, as underdeveloped economies in the global south merge into the global economy, more production takes place in these economies and they increasingly export more manufactured goods. In fact, economies of the global south have become more export-oriented over the last several decades and have developed substantial export flows of manufactured products to each other and especially to the north.

Labour is also divided among countries in the global north and the global south where multinational corporations based in the global north utilize labour in the global south because it is considered cheap and less skilled. Through processes of outsourcing and offshoring multinational corporations maximize their profits and minimize costs through the use of low cost, low-skilled labour located in the global south.

Multinational corporations take advantage of cheap labour pools all over the globe by either subcontracting with an overseas factory (usually located in the global south), relocating their own factories overseas (both are examples of offshoring) or subcontracting to another company within the same country in which they reside (outsourcing). Developing nations in the global south often compete with each other for these contracts by undercutting their citizens' wages and labour protections, and offering incentives to foreign corporations such as export processing (or tax-free) zones – a process often described as a 'race to the bottom'.

An important aspect of the international division of labour is its *gendered character*, in which men tend to be grouped in different jobs from women. In the global economy women are the majority of factory workers while men are the majority of managers. Women predominate in export-processing zones and other low-wage, low-skilled sectors of the global economy. One reason for this is that women are discursively constructed as cheap, docile, having nimble fingers and being 'easy' to exploit. It is also believed that young women are easy to discipline and are less likely to unionize, and as such they are a preferred source of labour for multinational corporations.

The impact of the new international division of labour has been uneven between nations, where some nations (especially those from the global north) have benefited more than others (especially those in the global south), and within nations where some groups (especially those from the elite classes and corporate owners) have benefited more than others (workers, especially poor women).

A second trend is the promotion of economic **neoliberalism**, a dominant ideology shaping global economic policies and production systems. Neoliberalism promotes the ideas of 'free market' and 'free trade'. It emphasizes the efficiency of private enterprise, liberalized trade and relatively open markets. It seeks to maximize the role of the private sector in determining the political and economic priorities of the state while minimizing the role of the state in the economy. In the global economy neoliberalism calls for free movement of goods, services, capital and money (but not necessarily people) across national boundaries. That is, corporations, banks and individual investors should be free to move their property across national boundaries and be free to acquire property across them, although free cross-border movement by individuals is not part of the neoliberal programme. Neoliberal policies are propagated through global institutions such as the International Monetary Fund, World Bank and World Trade Organization. This is achieved through the development and imposition by these global institutions of conditions which are attached to loans aimed at economic restructuring and debt repayment.

inequality and struggles in the global village

It is argued that while globalization is proceeding rapidly, its effects are uneven, marked by a growing divergence between the richest and poorest countries of the world. Wealth, income, resources and consumption are concentrated among the developed societies, whereas much of the developing world struggles with poverty, malnutrition, disease and foreign debt. This sense that growing inequality is linked to globalization made it a significant political issue in debates and protests from the latter part of the twentieth century. Left-wing critiques could argue it was the latest manifestation of international capitalism in which inequalities were the inevitable result while neoliberals saw it as an engine of growth and capable of raising the living standards of the poor. Attacks on globalization became prominent in the aftermath of the **Great Recession** with protest movements, mainly from the left of the political spectrum, blaming globalization as a contributor to inequality both worldwide and within nations. Often used as a synonym for the power of multinational corporations in producing a variety of ill effects – low pay, inadequate working conditions, pollution, climate change, tax avoidance – globalization moved from being an academic study to a political issue of current debate and analysis.

GM crops
– see **agriculture**.

Goa
Territory in western India conquered by the Muslims in 1310, then by the Portuguese in 1510. It became a centre of Catholic missionary activity and one of the major centres of the **Portuguese Empire** in the east for more than four centuries until its forcible occupation by the state of **India** in 1961.

Gökalp, Ziya (1876–1924)
– see also **Atatürk, Mustafa Kemal**.

An Anatolian Turk and the leading exponent of the pan-Turanian, or pan-Turkic, ideal, brought into being by Ismael bey Gaspraly under the stimulus of the **Russo-Turkish War** of 1877–8 and the absorption of the Turkic lands of central Asia into the **Russian Empire**. Gökalp argued, in his own translated words, that any group which existed had to have a prior potential for existence and that an ideal had to spring from the intensification of an existing group. It was the language group, which he equated with the nationality group, which had the greatest capacity for intensification. Likewise, just two things were sacred: the homeland of **Islam**, the *ummet* (*umma*), and the national home, which for Turks was 'Turan'. In practice, however, **Kemal Atatürk** in 1921 renounced any ambition of union between his new Turkey and the central Asian Turks, and the central Asian republics of **Kazakhstan**, Kyrgyzstan, Turkmenistan and Uzbekistan, established from 1924, have outlasted the Soviet Union. The 1991 initiative of Sultan **Demirel**, the then Turkish prime minister, to foster links appears to have borne only limited fruit.

Golan Heights
– see **Occupied Territories (Palestine)**.

Gold Coast
– see **Ghana**.

gold rush
Because gold is a scarce and precious metal, new discoveries have often attracted waves of prospectors and migrants eager to exploit the chance of sudden riches. As a result 'gold rushes' played a significant part in opening up new areas for European and white American settlement. The development of the telegraph, railways and oceanic shipping allowed news of fresh discoveries to attract large numbers of migrants to far-flung parts of the world. Notable gold rushes occurred in California (1848–9), **Australia** (1853), Colorado (1858–60), **South Africa** (1886) and the Canadian Yukon and Alaska (the 'Klondike') (1896–1901). From the outset they attracted romantic treatment in fiction, in books and later in film.

gold standard
A system of currency exchange based upon the convertibility of a currency to gold at a fixed rate. A gold standard is held by supporters to ensure that currency will not be issued recklessly and that trade imbalances will be a priority for government, and is

also a deflationary policy that necessarily imposes a fiscal discipline (though not immediately) upon its adherents. Gold, a limited and precious metal, was, at various times throughout western history and before, the basis of currency before becoming the British standard between 1689 and 1717. By the late eighteenth century British pounds had become a world currency accepted by most traders, and became pre-eminent until 1914. Other currencies found it convenient to base themselves on gold but were inevitably compared to the British currency and stability was therefore demonstrated by a link to the metal. During **World War I**, the gold standard collapsed alongside the pre-war economy. When the British tried to restore it in 1925 under chancellor of the exchequer **Winston Churchill**, they found that the high interest rates and fiscal restraint required proved an initial burden, though a housing boom in the late 1920s suggests that the British did gain some degree of economic confidence from gold-based pounds. However, the world economic crisis of 1929–31 saw the gold standard collapse and **Britain** and many other countries came off gold permanently. Under the **Bretton Woods** system between 1944 and 1973, the US dollar was linked to gold and all other currencies within the system to the dollar, which could be swapped for gold. Since most western countries owed the US money in dollars, and traded in that currency, the system worked so long as the dollar was neither inflated nor abundant; the **Vietnam War**, inflation and the US fiscal deficit after 1966 ended this system. Since 1980 there has been no formal basis for major world currencies except the confidence and needs of investors in their economies.

Golkar party

Also known as the Party of Functional Groups, Golkar was founded in **Indonesia** in 1964 as a federation of non-governmental organizations to counter the rising influence of the Indonesian Communist Party. In 1968, General **Suharto** joined Golkar and the federation was transformed into a political party. Consequently, Suharto was re-elected as president in 1971 and Golkar continued to win the majority in every election until 1999 when it was defeated by the Indonesian Democratic Party.

Golwalkar, Madhav Sadashiv (1906–1973)

Second head of the **Rashtriya Swayamsevak Sangh** (RSS) (1940–73), succeeding K. B. Hedgewar.

Having taught zoology at Banaras Hindu University, Golwalkar joined the RSS in 1931. His book *We, or Our Nationhood Defined*, published in 1939, nudged Hindutva towards ethnic nationalism. Although the RSS during Golwalkar's leadership focused on the cultural and psychological transformation of young people, the Jana Sangh began contesting elections in 1951. Golwalkar's emphasis on ideological discipline led to some tension with Jana Sangh members, who compromised for political ends.

Goncalves Dias, Antonio (1823–1864)

Born in the state of Maranhão, **Brazil**, but educated at the University of Coimbra in **Portugal**, Goncalves was the most popular of Brazil's Romantic poets as well as a playwright and linguist. He expressed strong nativist feelings in his glorification of Brazil's indigenous population. His poem *Song of Exile* (1843) is known to all Brazilian schoolchildren. Goncalves perished in a shipwreck.

Gorbachev, Mikhail (1931–)

Leader of **USSR**, 1985–91; General Secretary of the Communist Party of the **Soviet Union**, Executive President, 1988–91. Mikhail Gorbachev was, unusually for the Soviet leadership, trained in law and developed a Christian faith. Representing a new generation of Soviet leaders, he emerged from the Sevastopol agricultural region in the 1980s as the protégé of Yuri Andropov, and was promoted to the Politbureau just before Andropov's death. Following the interim rule of Konstantin Chernenko, he became leader of the USSR and began an intensive effort to inject new life and vigour into a regime in crisis. He first attempted to ease the military pressures on the USSR economy. To this end, he engaged in a successful effort to engage western public opinion and formed a strong bond with **Ronald Reagan** after an unsuccessful attempt to move to nuclear disarmament at the Reykjavik conference of 1986. Gorbachev concluded that the Soviet Union should pull out of **Afghanistan**, and work at all costs to prevent a costly and unwinnable round of competition with the US in space. In Eastern Europe he proclaimed the 'do it your way' 'Sinatra doctrine' which some associated with the end of communism, preferring not to attempt to hold back eastern **Europe** from liberal democracy by violent means.

Gorbachev's strategy was accelerated by the fall of communism in 1989 in eastern Europe, and achieved lasting arms reduction treaties in strategic, nuclear and conventional fields as well as a brief partnership with the USA under **George H. W. Bush** in global matters. Gorbachev, or 'Gorby', and his intelligent, attractive wife became wildly popular in western Europe and adopted western techniques of crowd greeting and campaigning. Gorbachev's second effort was to reform the USSR domestically. He engaged in policies of 'openness' (**glasnost**) and 'restructuring' (**perestroika**). The policies led to democratic criticism and debate, the emergence of civil society and disputed elections, ultimately bringing his former ally and bitter rival Boris Yeltsin to the presidency of the Russian republic by popular vote. Gorbachev also attempted to increase national productivity, and to ban the sale of highly alcoholic drinks, both of which policies failed. In 1991 he and his wife were held captive by elements of the Soviet state in their Crimean holiday home before Boris Yeltsin with mass popular support effectively broke the coup against Gorbachev and then moved to bring down the USSR, replacing it with a loose confederation of independent republics. Gorbachev retired to private life, ran unsuccessfully for the presidency, and became associated with western charity and advertising efforts. His wife Raisa predeceased him, and was accorded a Christian funeral.

Gordimer, Nadine (1923–2014)

South African writer and political activist. Born to Jewish immigrant parents, Gordimer began writing at an early age and was exposed to political activism through her participation in the Sophiatown cultural renaissance and membership in the **African National Congress**. Her novels reflect the moral and psychological consequences of racism under the **apartheid** regime, and many were banned by the South African government. In 1991 Gordimer was awarded the Nobel Prize in literature.

Gordon, Charles George (1833–1885)

British army officer. Commissioned into the Royal Engineers in 1852, Gordon served in the Crimean War, making his reputation as 'Chinese' Gordon suppressing the Taiping uprising in 1864. He acted for the Egyptian khedive as a provincial governor in **Sudan** and then as Governor General from 1873 to 1880. Dispatched by the British government in 1885 to evacuate Egyptian troops threatened by Mahdist forces, he disobeyed orders and was killed in the siege of Khartoum. In **Britain**, **Gladstone** was blamed for the failure to rescue him.

Gothic Revival

Renewed artistic interest in medieval ideals and motifs that spread throughout **Europe**, North America and the **British Empire** during the mid eighteenth and nineteenth centuries. The resurrection of this style coincided with the growth of **Romanticism, nationalism** and spiritualism. Gothic characteristics influenced the construction of universities, churches and public buildings. In Victorian Britain, the Palace of Westminster, designed A. W. N. Pugin and Charles Barry, epitomized the style and incorporated Gothic features in its design. In **France**, Eugène Viollet-le-Duc restored Gothic buildings destroyed during the French Revolution, including Sainte-Chapelle in Paris. Prussian architect Karl Friedrich Schinkel integrated pointed arches and vaulted ceilings in his buildings, including the Friedrichswerder Church. The Gothic Revival also influenced art and literature. Painters such as Caspar David Friedrich embraced the sublime and included Gothic motifs and designs in their work. The increasingly popular genre of Gothic novels rejected rationalism and merged medieval and modern ideas. Although **modernism** led to the decline of the Gothic Revival, it continued to influence art and architecture in the nineteenth and twentieth centuries.

Goulart, Joao (Belchior Marques) (c. 1918–1976)

Born in São Borja, Rio Grande do Sur, **Brazil**, Goulart, head of the Brazilian Labour Party, was elected vice president in 1955 and 1960. He replaced President **Jânio Quadros** following his resignation in August 1961. Political division and inflation pushed him towards the left and facilitated a military coup on 1 April 1964. Goulart died in exile in **Argentina** with his country still under military rule.

governance

The concept of governance has been developing since the late 1980s. Its birth can be traced back to the notion of 'governability', which represented the rule of law as the core of economic and political development. In the 1990s 'governability' gave way to the concept of 'governance', entailing a redesign or reinvention of public administration. *Governance* is, then, a new word in the English language and possesses many different definitions and the debate over its meaning is still open. For the **World Bank**, it means 'the traditions and institutions by which authority in a country is exercised for the common good. They include: (i) the process by which those in authority are selected, monitored and replaced, (ii) the capacity of the government to effectively manage its resources and implement sound policies and (iii) the respect of citizens and the state for the institutions that govern economic and social interactions among them.' In sum, governance is a society's or an organization's decision-making process that determines whom should be involved and how account should be provided. Even though the process of governance usually depends on the state, governance is not a synonym for government. The formal elements that shape decision taking and accountability (constitutions, by-laws, policies, conventions, etc.) define how the process is supposed to function in particular settings even though informal traditions, accepted practices or unwritten codes of conduct may also be significant. Governance should not be viewed as a synonym for politics, which involves processes by which decisions are taken according to rule (generally by majorities) and become binding to all. Governance, on the other hand, embodies the administrative and process-oriented elements of governing rather than the political processes of reaching decisions.

Governance also refers to corporate governance, understood as the manner in which an organization is managed, encompassing rules, laws and customs. Corporate governance means the relationships between a board of directors, managers, workers, shareholders or owners, regulators, customers and the community (people affected by the actions of the corporation).

Finally, 'global governance' denotes the regulation of interdependent relations among states in the absence of supranational political authority. In general, the term can be applied wherever a group forms and enters into regular economic and political relationships.

Government of India Act (1935)

The Government of India Act, 1935, passed by the colonial state in British India, abolished dyarchy and granted provincial autonomy with all government branches under the control of Indian ministers, although the central government reserved the right to dismiss these ministries. All power at the centre, including defence and finance portfolios, was kept in the hands of the British while the federal part of the act envisaged an Indian federation if one half of the princely states agreed to the plan.

Gowon, Yakubu (1934–)

Army general and president of **Nigeria**. A career soldier, Gowon took power after a succession of coups in 1966. When Lieutenant Colonel Ojukwu led eastern Nigeria, or **Biafra**, in a secession attempt, Gowon declared a state of emergency and launched a brutally repressive civil war that successfully prevented the secession by 1970. After the war, Gowon made his famous 'no victor, no vanquished' speech offering amnesty. The post-war years saw an economic boom fuelled by oil revenues but with massive corruption. Overthrown in a bloodless coup in 1975, Gowon is now regarded as an 'elder statesman' in Africa.

Graham, Billy (1918–)

US evangelist who first emerged to fame in the aftermath of **World War II**. Billy Graham's fiery preaching both in America and internationally won him not only a considerable following but invitations to the White House. His disappointment with **Richard Nixon** led to a distancing from politics and he was not among those evangelicals who later identified with the Christian Right. His son, Franklin Graham, however, became a leading figure among conservative evangelicals.

Gran Colombia

The name historians have given to the Republic of Colombia created by the Congress of Angostura in 1819 to replace, more or less, the earlier viceroyalty of New Granada. As constituted by the Congress of Cúcuta, it included three departments – **Colombia, Venezuela** and **Ecuador** – with **Simón Bolívar** as president and Francisco de Paula Santander as vice president. The dissolution of the republic in 1830 revealed separatism's triumph over unity among the former Spanish colonies.

Granger movement (USA)

The American National Grange of the Patrons of Husbandry ('Grange' for short – an English word for 'farm' derived from the Latin for 'granary') was one of the earliest of many late nineteenth-century agrarian protest movements. The Granger movement (founded in 1867, initially as a fraternal-style group) sought to regain economic and political power seized by the monopoly capitalism represented by railway and grain elevator companies that controlled the transportation and storage of their produce. Grangers organized into local `granges' nationwide, campaigned to regulate freight and grain elevator rates and set up cooperative elevators, stores and mills. Their political agitations yielded the most fruit. Establishing control over a number of Midwestern state legislatures, they secured laws governing railway and elevator rates (sustained as constitutional by Supreme Court ruling, 1876). Though the Grange's heyday was the mid 1870s (when it had over 800,000 members), the organization still exists, with a 300,000 membership promoting `Rural America'.

Grant, Ulysses S. (1822–1885)

American president and general. After a promising start in the Mexican War (1846–8), in 1854 Grant resigned from the army amid rumours of alcoholism. Reappointed in 1861 with a commission as brigadier general, in the **American Civil War** Grant proved a dynamic, offensive-minded commander with a consistent record of success at Forts Henry and Donelson, Shiloh, Iuka, Vicksburg and **Chattanooga**; his victory at Vicksburg was distinguished by persistence and ingenuity in overcoming the challenges of geography, and was rewarded by command of the Military Division of the Mississippi. In March 1864, promoted general-in-chief, he directed operations in Virginia against **Robert E. Lee**, culminating in Lee's surrender at Appomattox in April 1865. In 1869–77 he served two terms as eighteenth president of the **United States**. His Republican administration was tainted by a succession of scandals. Bankruptcy prompted him to write his *Personal Memoirs* (1885–6), a military literature classic.

Great Awakenings, first and second (c. 1720–1755 and c. 1800–1840)

Periods of evangelical revival, the first in Britain and its American colonies, the second more exclusively in the **United States**. On matters of free will, predestination and justification (atonement), the former was theologically Calvinist, although British **Methodism** bucked this trend; the latter was Arminian. The first Great Awakening challenged the prevalent ecclesiastical complacency, intellectual rationalism and liturgical formalism of the age. Charismatic preachers such as **Jonathan Edwards** would fierily demand conversion, then offer an electrifying sense of pardon. The revival divided the predominantly Calvinist denominations, the Congregationalists and Presbyterians, but bolstered the Baptists and Anglicans for their approval and disapproval of its methods, respectively. Its air of dissent was conducive to the **American Revolution**. The post-**millennialism** and Arminianized revivalism of the second Great Awakening stressed social sin as well as personal salvation, lending itself to **abolitionism**, **prohibition** and **women's rights**. It bolstered the

Methodists and Baptists over the old colonial churches, but they both split sectionally over slavery, as did the Presbyterians.

Great Britain

– *see* **United Kingdom**.

Great Depression (interwar)

The term given to the global economic collapse between 1929 and 1938 which witnessed an unprecedented deflation, unemployment, and a 25 per cent collapse in global production across all the industrialized economies. There had been 'great depressions' before; for example, in the 1840s and 1870s. However, the severity of the fall after 1929 is widely accredited with the rise of fascism and global conflict a decade later, and is therefore of supreme importance. The depression arose out of the conditions at the end of **World War I**. The world economic system had formerly been based on the maintenance of price stability and the transport of commodities by the British Empire, and financed by a few global banks. In addition, European dominance of capital flows and industry, an unregulated international money market and widespread price stability had characterized the period before 1914. After the Great War, the international economy was centred on the **USA**, which in turn maintained its vast international imports and investments from a stock market which was overindebted and based on speculation. The European economies had become dependent on American loans and exports to that country to maintain their balances of payments, and **Germany** in particular depended on the US to provide it with the cash to pay war debts to the British and French. In addition, resources and markets in **Russia**, **China** and **Asia**, usually open to imperial industries, had fallen to domestic disruption, civil war or communism. A vast global economic boom based on credit in the 1920s had overinflated the world economy. So, when countries raised protective tariffs against each other, starting with the US Smoot–Hawley Tariff of 1928, they damaged already precarious flows of cash; when the US stock market and then industrial production collapsed in the **Wall Street Crash**, it removed the source of global consumption and caused widespread bankruptcies in the USA; and when **Britain** and **France** on cue deflated, it plunged their economies into mass unemployment. European governments were forced off the gold standard since their governments could not pay for currency with gold; nor could they pay their debts to each other.

The effects of the depression were similar economically but varied politically. Most states, including Nazi Germany after 1933 and the USA under **Franklin Roosevelt**, adopted a form of Keynesian 'pump-priming' to get people back to work. The United Kingdom experienced mass unemployment on a similar scale, but established patterns of welfare provision, the devaluation of the pound, protection and continued economic activity saw it through the worst of the crisis. It then fell back upon the **British Empire** market to keep going. In France, a period of government crisis was inaugurated that was eventually to sap and then destroy the political will of the **Third Republic**, with disastrous results in the German war of 1940. Across **Europe**, radical political groups on the right and left prospered, and many lost faith in the democratic process in direct proportion to their inability to eat or to feed their families.

In Europe, the Great Depression led directly to the collapse of **Weimar Germany** and the rise of **Adolf Hitler**. In Britain, a National government was formed after the first Labour government collapsed; and, though Fascist Italy escaped the worst of the crisis because of its isolation and highly centralized economy, even there its markets diminished. In 1944 western governments met and resolved never to allow a depression to emerge again, resulting in the **Bretton Woods** agreement and widespread adoption of Keynesian policies until generational change and fading memories led to the abandonment of inflationary policies predicated upon the fear of depression and unemployment in the 1970s.

Great Divergence

A term used by Kenneth Pomeranz in *The Great Divergence* (2000) for the increasing disparity in **economic development** and wealth between the West, **Europe** and North America, and the rest of the world from the beginnings of **industrialization** in the eighteenth century to the twentieth. Growing wealth, industrialized weaponry and ruthlessly competitive nation states converted western superiority into political control over much of the rest of the world during that period, creating or expanding western empires and asserting western economic and cultural influences. Why this 'Triumph of the West' occurred has attracted many different interpretations, usually linked to the question of why industrial development occurred first in the West.

Max Weber's *The Protestant Ethic and the Spirit of Capitalism* (1904) traced the rise of entrepreneurial capitalism that drove mercantile expansion and the

Industrial Revolution to the culture of religious Puritanism and its emphasis on the relentless need to prove moral worth by economic striving. Others have sought explanations in the fortuitous coincidence of some European states, initially the United Kingdom, achieving agricultural self-sufficiency and prosperous trade with a high degree of technical inventiveness and access to raw materials, which generated unprecedented rates of economic growth and industrial development. This `divergence' underpinned the political and cultural dominance enjoyed by the West over the course of almost two centuries, but narrowed with the adoption of western models, first by **Japan** and increasingly in the latter part of the twentieth century with the industrialization of **China**, **India**, **Brazil** and several smaller Far Eastern states.

Great Exhibition (1851)

The Great Exhibition of the Works of Industry of All Nations (popularly known as the Great Exhibition) symbolized European progress and modernity and **Britain**'s industrial pre-eminence. Held at the Crystal Palace in Hyde Park, London, it began in May 1851 and lasted twenty-three weeks, playing host to over 6 million visitors. Displays included a range of goods, including machinery and manufactured items, decorative materials, household goods and weaponry. The 14,000 exhibits from Britain, **Europe** and colonies around the world exemplified the latest advancements in trade, science, industry and art.

Great Fear

The wave of mass panic that swept the French provinces in late July and early August 1789, following the outbreak of the French Revolution. It combined a realistic fear of hunger, because grain was not being traded, with an unrealistic fear of 'brigands' and an aristocratic 'plot' to starve the poor. Whole villages went into hiding and towns and cities formed defensive federations against these spectres of the imagination. The inspiration was the anarchy consequent upon the discrediting of the royal administration pending the advent of its revolutionary successor.

Great Game

– *see* **Afghan wars**.

Great Leap Forward (China)

The name given to a series of policies initiated by **Mao Zedong** in 1957 designed to promote agricultural production to balance an economy that privileged urban-based industry. Small farms were incorporated into People's Communes and peasants forced to engage in small-scale industry. By 1959 it became clear that there were serious problems, but the policies continued into 1960. Agricultural production dropped 25 per cent resulting in a famine in which an estimated 20 million people died.

Great Migration (USA)

The term applied in the **United States** to the large-scale migration of **African Americans** from the south to the north in the 1920s, though since the pattern continued it could usefully be applied to the whole period 1914–70. Americans, white and black, also streamed west. Consequently the proportion of blacks in the south fell from 90 per cent in 1910 to 53 per cent in 1970. The share of blacks in the whole US population remained at about 12 per cent, but their share in each region changed proportionately. Many northern and western cities hence developed dense black populations in impoverished ghettos such as Harlem or Watts. Significant numbers moved pre-1929, and the Great Depression checked but did not stop the migration, which accelerated to gain from war work and northern prosperity from 1940. The Great Migration exhibits the potential for economic efficiency, the gains in cultural diversity, the occasional severe social costs, and helped eventually to make possible greater black visibility in American politics.

Great Northern War

Provoked by the desire of **Peter the Great** to extend his territories at the expense of **Sweden**, **Poland** and **Turkey**. In 1700 Peter invaded Estland (now Estonia) in alliance with Denmark and Poland, but was defeated by **Charles XII** of Sweden at Narva. Peter rebuilt his army, occupied Livonia and Ingria (now Latvia) and in 1709 defeated Charles XII, who had invaded Poland with Cossack support, at the Battle of Poltava. The subsequent Russian invasion of Turkish Moldavia was repulsed by the Turks, but the whole of **Finland** was captured by the Russians, 1713–14. Peter's ally, **Frederick William I** of Prussia, acquired Swedish Pomerania, 1719–20. The war was concluded by the Treaty of Nystadt in 1721, which confirmed the possession by **Russia** of Estland, Livonia, Ingria and the city and district of Vyborg, but returned the rest of Finland to Sweden. It marked the end of Swedish domination of the Baltic. The war also reinforced Russia's control of **Ukraine**, extended its influence in Poland, and marked its emergence as the dominant power in the region.

Great Recession (2007–)

The financial crisis and economic downturn which began in the autumn of 2007 and whose effects are still being felt ten years later. It was the greatest economic crisis since the **Great Depression** following the **Wall Street Crash** of 1929, causing greater disruption than earlier cyclical downturns or that caused by the **oil shock** of the 1970s. As in 1929–33, the roots of the crisis lay in an unparalleled expansion of credit which overvalued many assets, principally in the housing market, which left banks, mortgage companies and even some countries exposed to financial collapse. Concern about the exposure of the financial system began with the collapse of the rapidly expanded fringe or `subprime' mortgage market in the **United States** in mid 2007. September 2007 saw the first run on a British bank for 150 years, the much expanded mortgage lender turned bank, Northern Rock, and in spring 2008 the United States federal government organized a bail-out for the investment bank Bear Stearns. But, intending to bring some discipline to the markets, their decision to allow the Lehman Brothers investment bank to fail in September 2008 instead sent shockwaves throughout the western financial system. The entire banking system teetered on the edge of breakdown, requiring unprecedented government support.

Huge sums were pledged by governments to support or even effectively nationalize their banks and measures put in train to purchase bank assets, so-called `quantitative easing', to reintroduce liquidity into their economies alongside a regime of record low interest rates. Small countries with large banking sectors, such as **Iceland** and **Ireland**, were threatened with national bankruptcy and had to seek international assistance and impose heavy cuts in state spending. The so-called `credit crunch' and financial instability plunged much of the industrial world into recession. Some European countries saw as much as a 6 per cent drop in output and very high levels of unemployment, especially amongst the young, but compared with the interwar depression, the fall in output and rise in unemployment was less severe in many countries. Unemployment in the United States was never higher than 10 per cent compared with three times that figure in the early 1930s. The worst effected were the southern European states where the austerity regime imposed on eurozone members of the **European Union** created high levels of unemployment and forced migration even after recovery began from 2011. For some countries, such as **Italy**, a return to pre-crisis levels of output was not achieved even a decade after it began. Other countries, however, were hardly affected; the Chinese economy continued to grow at a rapid rate, feeding a commodities boom in oil and raw materials which brought prosperity to the **Middle East**, **Australia** and emerging nations such as **Brazil** and **South Africa**.

Although recovery was widespread a decade after the financial crisis began, many countries were left with heavy government indebtedness, low or non-existent growth, and high rates of unemployment. Fears that the onset of recession would once again radicalize the political landscape were to some extent realized. Several established political parties across Europe lost support in favour of more popular parties both of the Right and the Left. The most successful, the Greek Syriza, actually took power in 2014. Elsewhere, the major effect has been to hollow out support from established parties, particularly social democratic parties of countries such as **Sweden** and Holland. On the whole right-centre coalitions fared better in the decade after the onset of the crisis, though in **Japan** the crisis encouraged a break with traditional politics and the election of Premier Abe in 2013 with a mandate to pursue non-traditional economic measures to free the country from endemic stagnation.

Great Society (USA)

A package of social reforms in the United States advocated by President **Lyndon Johnson**, largely enacted in law in the propitious political circumstances of the mid 1960s. Among its central elements were the 'war on poverty', federal aid to education, medical care for the aged, black civil rights, and environmental protection. After 1965 shifting political tides and implementation problems undermined the Great Society, which became a punchbag for generations of conservatives, although most of its programmes have endured.

Great Trek

A defining event in **Afrikaner** history, the movement of 12–14,000 **Boer** *Voortrekkers* north and north-east from Cape Colony across the Orange River into the southern African interior from 1835 and into the 1840s. The migrants, led by among others Hendrik Potgieter (1792–1852), Piet Retief (1780–1838) and Andries Pretorius (1798–1853), were impelled by resentment at growing British control, partly motivated by the abolition of slavery in 1834 and partly by different

conceptions of relations between blacks and whites. In Natal the *Voortrekkers* met with resistance from the **Zulus**, defeating them at the Battle of Blood River in December 1838, and going on to establish a short-lived Republic of Natalia (annexed by **Britain** in 1845). Others set up what became the Orange Free State and the Transvaal (the South African Republic), the former becoming an independent Boer republic in 1852 and the latter in 1854.

Greco-Turkish War (1919–1923)

Known variously as the Turkish War of Independence or the Greek Catastrophe, this conflict ended Greek territorial ambitions (the *Megale Idea* or 'Great Idea') in Anatolia. Apprehensive of Italian intentions, **Eleutherios Venizelos**, the Greek prime minister, ordered the occupation of Smyrna in May 1919. The **Treaty of Sèvres** (August 1920) recognized the Greek presence in Smyrna, but **Mustapha Kemal**'s resistance rejected the treaty. By this time the Greek military had commenced operations against the Turkish nationalist movement. Venizelos' electoral defeat and the return of King Constantine I to power resulted in a Greek invasion far into the Anatolian interior. At the Battle of Sakkaria River (August–September 1921) Kemal stemmed the Greek advance, resulting in a retreat culminating in the conflagration of Smyrna in September 1922, symbolically ending Greek ambitions. The **Treaty of Lausanne** (July 1923) restored Turkish Anatolia and Thrace and repatriated populations. The Turkish republic under Mustapha Kemal was subsequently officially proclaimed in October 1923.

Greece

– *see also* **Greek War of Independence**.

Part of the **Ottoman Empire** until it secured independence in the **Greek War of Independence**, the country of Greece was ratified by the great powers in 1830 with Otto I of Bavaria as monarch until he was deposed in 1863, in favour of George I of Denmark. The Ionian islands were ceded to it by **Britain** in 1864. As a result of the **Balkan Wars** of 1912–13 it gained Crete and western Thrace in Thessaloniki by the Peace of Bucharest, 1913. It entered **World War I**, gaining territory from Bulgaria by the Treaty of Neuilly, 1919. War with **Turkey** in 1919 to secure Anatolia proved disastrous for the Greek population, who were expelled following Greek defeat by **Mustafa Kemal**. Obliged to sign the **Treaty of Lausanne** with Turkey in 1923, Greek presence on the mainland of Anatolia was ended though Greece retained many of the Aegean islands off the coast. A republic was established 1923–35, but was superseded by the dictatorship of General Metaxas in 1936–41. Invaded by Italy in 1940, Greek resistance was broken by German intervention and resulting occupation in 1941–4. Rival resistance movements conducted the **Greek Civil War** from 1944 to 1949, with Royalist forces eventually taking control. Greece joined **NATO** in 1952, but persistent instability led to a military dictatorship in 1967–74. It was followed by a return to democracy and the abolition of the monarchy. Greece joined the **European Union** in 1981 ushering in a period of unparalleled prosperity, but was thrown into economic turmoil during the **Great Recession** of 2008, leading to the rise of a populist government which was forced to accept international intervention and austerity to stabilize its finances.

Greek Civil War

A struggle fought from 1944–5 and 1946–9 between Greek Communists and the British and American-backed government. When German occupation troops left Greece in October 1944 the resistance groupings – the Communist EAM–ELAS (National Liberation Front–National Popular Liberation Army) and the royalist EDES (Greek Democratic National Army) – formed a coalition government. The first phase of fighting began in December 1944 following attempts to disarm the Communist ELAS. A truce was agreed in February 1945. Following a right-wing royalist victory in the March 1946 elections and the restoration of the monarchy in September, the Communists proclaimed a 'Free Greek government' and began a guerrilla campaign. When British troops were unable to cope, the **United States** supplied Greek forces under the **Truman Doctrine**. The Communists declared a ceasefire in October 1949. Over 50,000 people were estimated to have died in a conflict that left a bitter legacy in Greek politics.

Greek Orthodox Church
– *see* **Orthodoxy**.

Greek War of Independence

In March 1821, Greeks revolted against Ottoman Turkish control. The massacre of the Turkish garrison in the Peloponnese (Morea) led to Turkish reprisals, notably on the island of Chios (April–June 1822). The Turks withdrew from their siege of Missolonghi in January 1823, but intra-Greek quarrels weakened their revolution.

Furthermore, Ibrahim Pasha arrived from **Egypt** (February 1825) with powerful forces and retook the Peloponnese and another Turkish army captured Missolonghi in April 1826. Nonetheless, the Greek Revolution inspired **philhellenism** (embodied by Lord Byron) and stirred European governments. By the Treaty of London (July 1827) the British, French and Russian governments insisted upon an armistice and the withdrawal of Egyptian forces. Ottoman refusal led to the allied destruction of the Turko-Egyptian fleet at **Navarino** (October 1827), which ensured Greek independence. Russia successfully waged war separately against the Ottomans (1828–9). The Treaty of London (1830) formally established a Greek monarchy.

Greeley, Horace (1811–1872)
American **Whig** then **Republican** journalist whose *New-York Tribune* newspaper stood for economic progress and all manner of reform movements, especially opposition to slavery from the 1850s. The **American Civil War** brought out an inconsistent streak that belied his radical inclinations on race and emancipation. Greeley lost respect with his calls for peace during 1863–4, his opposition to **Abraham Lincoln**'s renomination, his contribution to **Jefferson Davis**'s bail, and his position atop the **Liberal Republican** ticket (1872).

Green March
– *see* **Hassan II**.

Green Revolution
A term used in the **USA** from 1968 to describe the advances in food production which made it possible to massively increase food yields between 1943 and 1979. The advances are commonly associated with the work of Norman Borlaug (1914–2009), an American scientist, in **Mexico**, who led the team which developed varieties of wheat that were high in calories and which yielded much more than conventional fields when planted. However, they also encompass the development of mechanical technologies, fertilizers and irrigation techniques. The Ford and Rockefeller foundations, the **World Bank** and an International Secretariat propagated the processes and several governments, most notably that of **India**, not only averted **famine** but achieved spectacular success in food production by embracing them. As a consequence of the changes, **population** growth led to over 7 billion people sharing the planet by the early twenty-first century.

Greenback Party
– *see also* **Greenbacks**.

An American, predominantly Midwestern, agrarian party (1874–84) favourable to continued government issue of a paper currency – which increased produce prices and facilitated debt repayment – and hostile to the scheduled resumption (1879) of the **gold standard** (suspended since the **American Civil War**), which seemingly presaged banker control over prices and wages. Depression from 1873 polarized this debate, but Congress crucially conceded the limited monetization of silver in 1878 on the eve of the party's peak. The **Populist Party** would later support that policy.

Greenbacks

An American colloquialism for the paper money, printed with green ink, issued during the **American Civil War** under the Legal Tender Act of 1862. Their value greatly fluctuated in relation to gold. The controversial redemption of greenbacks into gold in 1879 fuelled the **Greenback Party** of the 1870s and the **Populist Party** of the 1890s. US currency notes are still referred to as 'greenbacks', though they now comprise other colours besides green.

greenhouse effect
– *see* **climate change**.

Greenpeace

One of the most militant of the environmental **non-governmental organizations** (NGOs). Founded by Robert Hunter in Vancouver, **Canada**, 1971, to lobby against nuclear power, it had become by 2015 the largest environmental organization in the world, operating in more than forty countries on behalf of over 3 million supporters. Greenpeace International has its headquarters in Amsterdam. It refuses money from both companies and governments. It achieved its greatest publicity with the sinking by the French Intelligence Service of its surveillance vessel *Rainbow Warrior* in harbour in New Zealand, 1985, and the reversal by Shell of its plan, endorsed by the British government, to sink the Brent Spar oil rig at sea, 1995. Its contribution to the conclusion of such international agreements as the London Dumping Convention, 1993, which officially banned the dumping of radioactive and industrial waste at sea, may, however, prove more significant in the longer term. The ultimate success of its core antinuclear campaigning remains uncertain.

Grenada invasion

The Grenada invasion (Operation Urgent Fury) occurred on 25 October 1983 and involved over 7,000 American soldiers and 350 Caribbean peacekeepers. It was triggered by the violent implosion of the Grenadian People's Revolutionary government; Prime Minister Maurice Bishop had been executed by government hardliners. Ostensibly concerned about the safety of American citizens in the region, President **Ronald Reagan** acceded to the Organization of Eastern Caribbean States' invitation to participate in a multinational operation to restore order to Grenada.

Griqua

The term used for the offspring of Dutch men and **Khoikhoi** women in the Cape of southern Africa. The Griqua spoke Afrikaans and led largely nomadic lives. Their leader Adam Kok I, a former slave, led the community north in the nineteenth century. Kok's successors founded two Griqua territories; both were annexed by the Cape Colony by 1877. The Griqua became part of the population known as 'coloured' in modern **South Africa**.

Grivas, George (1898–1974)
– *see also* **Eoka**.

Greek Cypriot guerrilla commander. Born in **Cyprus**, Grivas attended the Athens Military Academy and the Paris École Militaire, and was commissioned into the Greek Army in 1919, serving in the 1919–22 war with **Turkey**. He led the right-wing Organization X resistance movement during the 1940–4 Axis occupation of **Greece**, subsequently fighting against the Communists in the Greek Civil War. Retiring in 1946, he supported the campaign to unify Cyprus with Greece (*enosis*), establishing the **EOKA** (National Organization of Cypriot Fighters) guerrilla movement in Cyprus in 1954. He led Eoka's guerrilla campaign against British troops until independence in 1959. Following clashes between Greek and Turkish Cypriots in 1964, Grivas returned to Cyprus to lead Greek Cypriot forces but was removed at the Turkish government's insistence. In 1971 he formed EOKA-B in an effort to resume the struggle for *enosis*. He died in hiding in Cyprus.

Guadalajara

The regional capital of colonial Nueva Galicia, Guadalajara became the capital of the Mexican state of Jalisco. A railway hub after 1866, this infrastructural advantage elevated it to a regional distribution centre of goods from ranchos and small manufacturers. The 1960s Mexican miracle stimulated rapid demographic expansion, and industry and multinational corporations have spurred continued growth. The metropolitan area now has over 4 million inhabitants. The city is considered the country's cultural centre.

Guadalcanal, Battle of

First major offensive of the Allied Powers in the Pacific War during **World War II**. The Battle of Guadalcanal was a US-led naval campaign against Japanese possession of Guadalcanal Island. The conflict broke out on 7 August 1942 and ended on 9 February 1943. Although **Japan** still maintained naval superiority in the Pacific in 1942, their defeat at Guadalcanal provided the Allied Powers with a strong foundation that led to their ultimate victory in the Pacific campaign.

Guadalupe, Virgin of

Near Tepayac in **Mexico** where the Nahua had venerated the goddess Tonantzín, indigenous peasant Juan Diego experienced a mystical vision on 9 December 1531. Attracting clerical and lay Creoles as well as local people, the Virgin of Guadalupe became Mexico's nationalist symbol and **Latin America**'s most important female Catholic and spiritual icon.

Guadalupe Hidalgo, Treaty of (1848)

The treaty that ended the **Mexican–American War** (1846–8) was negotiated by Nicholas Trist and a special commission representing **Mexico**'s interim government, while American troops occupied Mexico City. Mexico ceded to the **United States** Upper California and New Mexico (parts of modern Utah, Nevada, Arizona, Colorado and Wyoming), relinquished claims to **Texas** (an independent republic after 1836, but still claimed by Mexico), and recognized the Rio Grande River as its northern border. The United States gave Mexico 15 million dollars, promised to protect property rights of Mexicans in the ceded territory, assumed debts of 3.25 million dollars owed by Mexico to American citizens, and agreed to control hostile Indian incursions from the US side of the border. Signed at the Villa de Guadalupe Hidalgo, the US Senate ratified the treaty (34–14) on 10 March 1848 despite objections from abolitionists and anti-war senators.

Guam Doctrine (Vietnamization)

First introduced by President **Richard Nixon**, this policy sought the gradual withdrawal of American troops in mainland Asia and stated that any future military operations would be carried out by indigenous forces. **Nixon** saw this as an attempt to reconcile conflicting political and military views over a complete communist takeover of **Vietnam**. The policy also signalled an effort to withdraw American troops from the prolonged **Vietnam War**.

Guaraní

An indigenous, semi-sedentary people of perhaps 300,000 that lived east of the Paraná and Paraguay rivers in the upper Platine region of South America. Those in central **Paraguay** initially allied with Spanish settlers, but later were assigned to labour for them. After 1610 many Guaraní entered Jesuit missions. Following the Jesuit Fathers' expulsion in 1767–8, their neophytes' descendants dispersed into northern **Argentina**, **Uruguay** and western **Brazil**. Most Paraguayans have some Guaraní ancestry.

Guatemala

A nation in northern **Central America** which has dominated the isthmus since the arrival of Spanish colonists early in the 1500s. Although the region's most populous and ethnically diverse society, with an indigenous majority and thirty distinct Mayan linguistic groups, westernized elites have monopolized political and economic power. In the 1800s Guatemala developed a viable agro-export economy – first coffee, then bananas – while under the traditional political and social order. A democratic revolution in 1944 inspired a decade of progressive reforms but collapsed following a US-sponsored coup in 1954. This intervention spawned a thirty-year civil war that pitted the restored oligarchy and its military allies against a leftist insurgency and much of the highland indigenous population. Despite the end of this conflict in the 1990s, Guatemala has failed to secure the political stability and economic growth that might serve as the foundations for national unity.

Guernica

The destruction in the Spanish Civil War of Guernica, the cultural capital of the **Basque** region, by German aircraft on 26 April 1937 opened the era of systematic bombing of civilians. In a daylight raid on market day, the German Condor Legion bombed the town for three hours, killing over 1,600 and wounding 900 of the 7,000 population. Though the Nationalist leader **Franco** denied prior knowledge, accusing Anarchists of burning the town, a telegram revealed he had requested the attack, while the German air force welcomed the opportunity to test its tactics. Nationalist forces entered the town three days later. The bombing outraged world opinion and fear of the effects of bombing civilians may have influenced Anglo-French appeasement of Nazi Germany in 1938. Picasso's painting *Guernica* remains a potent symbol of the callousness of the attack. In 1999 the German government offered a formal apology to Guernica's citizens.

guerrilla warfare

The word *guerrilla* has its origins in a Spanish diminutive for war, *guerra*. It may have originated during Wellington's Iberian campaigns against **Napoleon**, when Spanish and Portuguese *guerrilleros* or *irregulares* effectively disrupted French lines of supply and communications. After **World War II** with the rise of armed communist groups around the globe and their launch of people's wars and wars of national liberation, guerrillas became inextricably associated with left-wing insurgency. In general terms, guerrilla warfare is low in intensity, limited in range, and the scale of combat is small. Guerrilla operations tend to rely on skirmishes, ambushes, terrorism and sabotage. Another key feature is mobility of the cells to which guerrillas divide for flexibility in combat, and to avoid dependence on fixed bases of supplies that can lead to 'logistical tails'.

Theories of guerrilla warfare can be traced back as far as the Chinese general Sun Tzu in the fourth century BC who considered that military victory required deception and surprise and that a successful general 'avoids strengths and strikes weaknesses'. In antiquity these tactics were applied by the Roman general Fabius Maximus when Hannibal's armies invaded **Italy** during the Punic Wars, wearing down the enemy by ambushes and skirmishes after Roman defeats in full-scale battles. In the early modern era, guerrilla tactics were usually seen as auxiliary to formal military operations, as in the actions of the Spanish guerrillas against the Napoleonic armies alongside the battles and sieges carried on by the Spanish, British and French armies. Often, guerrilla operations took place in peripheral areas of conflict or in the aftermath of defeat, when guerrilla operations remained the only means of resistance. A significant example of the latter was the **Second Boer War** (1899–1902), which saw the Boers forced to use 'hit and run' tactics by 'commandos' of lightly armed horsemen when they could no longer contest British armies in the field, relying on the local population for supplies and support. But it also saw the development of anti-guerrilla

operations, the forerunner of counter-insurgency tactics, denying the Boer guerrillas support by burning their farms, putting their families in camps ('concentration' camps) and subdividing the open South African *veld* with barbed wire and blockhouses to restrict the mobile Boer forces.

Although the scene of intense industrialized warfare, **World War I** also saw one of the most highly publicized examples of successful guerrilla warfare with **T. E. Lawrence**'s campaign against Ottoman forces in Arabia and **Palestine**, described in his *The Evolution of a Revolt* (1920) and *Seven Pillars of Wisdom* (1926). In **Ireland**, **Michael Collins** also organized a highly effective guerrilla campaign in 1919–21 in support of Irish independence. Both suggested a greater role for guerrilla warfare and these ideas were developed into a full-blown doctrine of revolutionary warfare by **Mao Zedong** in organizing Chinese Communist forces against both the Japanese and, later, the Nationalists. Mao's victory established a pattern that was adopted by the **Vietminh** and **Vietcong**, the **FLN** in the **Algerian War of Independence** and anti-colonial movements elsewhere. The success of the **Cuban Revolution** produced **Che Guevara**'s *foco* theory (*Guerrilla Warfare*, 1961) that a small group could create revolutionary momentum, inspiring a wave of guerrilla insurgency in **Africa**, **Central America** and South America, some successful, some less so. It was in one such unsuccessful attempt, in **Bolivia** in 1967, that he was killed. But the 'war of the flea', as it was dubbed, became the default mode of operations for insurgent groups involved in long-running conflicts in places such as the **Sudan, Sri Lanka** and **Colombia**, as well as in anti-colonial wars in places such as **Angola**. Attempts to promote so-called 'urban guerrilla' warfare in **Brazil**, **Uruguay** and **Argentina** from the 1960s met with fierce and largely successful repression, but the defeat of American and South Vietnamese forces by the Vietcong and North Vietnamese regular forces in the **Vietnam War**, and of Russian forces following their invasion of **Afghanistan** by the largely guerrilla **mujahideen**, demonstrated the potency of guerrilla warfare, particularly when armed with modern explosives and hand-held automatic weapons, rocket launchers and missiles. There has been, too, an overlap between **terrorism** and guerrilla warfare, so that conflicts such as those pursued by **Hamas** or the **Tamil Tigers** utilize both as circumstances dictate.

Guevara, Ernesto ('Che') (1928–1967)

Born in Rosario, **Argentina**, Guevara graduated from the Colegio Nacional Dean Funes in Cordoba and received a medical degree in 1953 from the University of Buenos Aires. During his medical studies, he and a friend took the trip in the Andes that was subsequently memorialized in *Motorcycle Diaries*. Travelling with another friend, in July 1953 he went to **Bolivia** and in December reached Guatemala City where he acquired the nickname 'Che'. Soon after the US-sponsored coup against **Guatemala**'s President **Jacobo Arbenz**, in mid 1954 he left for Mexico City. A year later he met **Fidel Castro**, in exile there after his imprisonment in **Cuba** following the unsuccessful attack on the Moncada barracks in Santiago de Cuba on 26 July 1953. Che decided to join Castro as a result of both extensive reading and observations of exploitation of the poor throughout the Americas. He was among the group that reached Cuba from **Mexico** on the small ship *Granma* on 2 December 1956. Castro elevated Che to *Comandante* in mid 1957, at the time the only guerrilla aside from Fidel himself holding the rank. Following the flight of dictator Fulgencio Batista and the arrival of the Rebel Army in Havana in early January 1959, Che became a Cuban citizen, assuming important positions in the new regime and setting an example by his volunteer labour and almost puritan lifestyle. Che toured **Europe**, **Asia** and **Africa** in 1959 before his appointments as director of the newly created Industrialization Department of the National Institute of Agrarian Reform and president of the National Bank of Cuba.

In 1960 his manual on guerrilla warfare appeared and he visited the **Soviet Union**, East Germany, **Czechoslovakia**, **China** and **North Korea**. Che's antagonism toward the US as the embodiment of imperialism became ever more strident, as did his emphasis on armed struggle against imperialism originating with a *foco*, a small, armed guerrilla group in the countryside, and expanding into a populist uprising and lengthy 'people's war'. Although he drew upon Marxist–Leninist ideas, many Communist parties opposed an approach that placed him more on the side of China than the Soviet Union, a central political and economic supporter of Cuba during Castro's early rule. The most prominent Marxist among Castro's confidantes and ministers, in 1965 Che decided to personally lead an effort to apply his *foco* model in the **Congo**. After the African involvement failed, he tried again in **Bolivia** with a few mostly Cuban forces, arriving in November 1966. The result was his capture, execution and crude burial at a Bolivian airport in October 1967. Upon his death he became an icon of youthful

revolutionaries and a source of Marxist ideas. Both his early and posthumous publications continue to sell and an image of his face still appears on T-shirts, posters and other paraphernalia. In 1997 his body was disinterred and placed in a mausoleum in Cuba, where there is a large memorial in his honour.

Guianas

A 300,000 square kilometre area of dense tropical jungle in north-eastern South America. Colonized by the English, Dutch and French in the 1600s, the Guianas remain culturally, demographically and linguistically distinct from their neighbours on the continent. Politically, the region consists of the nations of **Guyana** and **Surinam**, as well as the French overseas department of **French Guiana**. These societies share a heterogeneous population consisting of indigenous groups, descendants of European colonists and African slaves, and more recent arrivals from southern Asia. Rich natural resources provide economic foundations, with timber, fishing and commercial agriculture the most common sources of wealth.

Guinea

Former French colony in west Africa, which became part of French West African Federation after resistance led by Samori (*c*. 1830–1900) was finally subdued. The first French African colony to gain independence in 1958 under President **Ahmed Sékou Touré** (1922–84), great grandson of Samori whose government proclaimed Marxism–Leninism. In 1960 he declared his Guinea Democratic Party the only legal political organization and stood as sole candidate for the presidency in 1961, 1968, 1974 and 1982. A Second Republic established after his death by Lansana Comté (1934–2008) abandoned socialism and instituted **International Monetary Fund**-approved market reforms. On Comté's death, a National Council for Democracy and Development led by Moussa Dadis Camara (1964–) took power, triggering a period of political instability that was ended only briefly by the election of Alpha Condé (1938–) in 2011. Guinea's population is 85 per cent Muslim and 10 per cent Christian. The country is rich in mineral resources, with reserves of bauxite and iron ore, gold and diamonds.

Guinea Bissau

Former Portuguese west African colony from the sixteenth century and a major slave-trading centre. The interior was not fully under Portuguese domination until the early twentieth century. In 1956

Amilcar Cabral (1924–73) formed the African Party for the Independence of Guinea and Cape Verde (PAIGC), launching an armed struggle in 1963. The country became independent under Luis Cabral (1931–2009) in 1974, with a socialist policy backed by **Cuba** and the **Soviet Union**. General João Bernardo Vieira (1939–2009) ousted Cabral in 1980, introducing **International Monetary Fund**-approved reforms to encourage foreign investment. Veira was elected president in the first free elections in 1994 but forced out by the army in 1999. The country was then riven by coups and army mutinies until PAIGC's José Mário Vaz (1957–) won the presidential election in 2014. The country's main economic activities are agriculture and fishing but there is a flourishing illegal drugs and logging trade. The population is predominantly Muslim, with a substantial Christian minority.

Gujarat and Gujaratis

A state in western India bordered by Pakistan and the Indian states of Rajasthan and Maharashtra. This historical region, as defined by the Gujarati language in the 1956 States Reorganization Act, was governed by rulers from a wide variety of ethnic and religious groups before its gradual incorporation into the Bombay Presidency of the **East India Company**'s government. Some rulers remained nominally independent as 'Princely States' under crown rule. Coastal towns in Gujarat had long been links between overseas trade to the Persian Gulf and western Indian Ocean littoral and central Indian textile production. In the nineteenth century the reach of the **British Empire** facilitated the movement of Gujarati merchants and indentured labour to British colonies, especially eastern and southern Africa. Despite **Gandhi**'s importance to Gujarat during his lifetime, its communal diversity and important pilgrimage sites have made the state a flashpoint for violence in the 1990s and 2000s.

Gulag

The Russian acronym for a prison camp administration in the **USSR** which officially operated from 1930 to 1960, though concentration camps were a feature of the regime from 1917 until the late 1980s. At their height, almost 500 camps saw between 14 and 20 million pass through their regime of hard labour, low-calorie nutrition, isolation and untreated disease. The camps catered for a variety of prisoners, including children, criminals, political dissidents, prisoners of war, economic offenders and those who had simply irritated some iteration of the Soviet regime, and contained at least 4 million people a year. In 1973 the name became synonymous with Soviet repression and internal exile because of the publication in the west of Alexander Solzhenitsyn's famous work, *The Gulag Archipelago*, detailing the existence of and conditions within the network. **Stalin** was given to using the inhabitants of the Gulag system as expendable workers in infrastructure projects, which perhaps explains the credible figure of over 4.5 million deaths within the system over the time of its existence.

Gulf War (1990–1991)

On 2 August 1990 Iraqi troops launched a surprise attack on **Kuwait** and invaded the country, which President **Saddam Hussain** then annexed and on 28 August declared it to be the nineteenth province of **Iraq**. The UN Security Council condemned the invasion and demanded the immediate withdrawal of the Iraqi troops. A similar declaration was made by the **Arab League** (only **Libya** and the **Palestine Liberation Organization** voted against the declaration). Owing to the failure of diplomatic means, the UN voted for economic sanctions against Iraq (6 August) and the **United States** – in alliance with other countries – started to build up their military forces in the area. On 28 November the UN Security Council authorized its member states to use force against the aggressor if Iraq did not withdraw its troops from Kuwait by 15 January 1991. After acquiring an absolute supremacy in the air within a matter of days, the US air force, together with its allies, bombed Iraqi positions and major cities for more than a month. In response, Saddam Hussain launched 'Scud' missiles on **Israel** and **Saudi Arabia**, had hundreds of thousands of tons of oil poured into the Persian Gulf, and set 500 Kuwaiti oil wells on fire. On 23 February a land offensive was also launched and by 26 February Kuwait was fully liberated. On 28 February – after Iraq's total defeat – US President **George Bush** ordered a ceasefire. A permanent ceasefire resolution was adopted by the UN Security Council on 3 April 1991 whereby the Security Council guaranteed the Iraqi–Kuwait border and Iraq accepted the destruction of all chemical and biological weapons and nuclear weapons-usable material under international supervision.

Gulf War, Second

– *see* **Iraq War**.

Guomindang
– *see* **Kuomintang (KMT)**

Guyana
Guyana is a large, sparsely populated and very poor country in north-eastern South America. It became Dutch in 1616 and was formally ceded to the British in 1814, though **Britain** controlled much of the territory from the late eighteenth century. Its coastal regions were ideal for the production of sugar and large numbers of Africans and, especially, Indians were imported as plantation labourers after slavery ended. Politics since independence in 1970 has often reflected a struggle between the Afro-Guyanese and the larger Indo-Guyanese population.

Guèye, Lamine (1891–1968)
Senegalese politician. Born in Médine in what is today **Mali**, Guèye trained as a lawyer in **France** before returning to **Senegal** where he founded one of Africa's first political parties and became mayor of Saint-Louis. In 1945 he was elected to the French National Assembly, where he lent his name to two laws: one in 1946 that declared all inhabitants of overseas territories to have the rights of French citizenship and the other in 1950 that stipulated the equality of French and African civil servants.

Gypsies
– *see* **Roma**.

H

Habsburg (Hapsburg) monarchy

The central European empire ruled by the Habsburg family from around 1273 which became **Austria–Hungary** in 1867. It was composed of lands which are today part of seventeen modern states, and was characterized by vast linguistic and ethnic diversity. Adherence to the monarchy, via local traditions or the rule of ethnic overlords such as the German and Magyar peoples, characterized its politics more than any centralized institution, although Chancellor **Clemens von Metternich** did show how reactionary central control could work in the early nineteenth century. The empire lost a devastating clash with **Prussia** for German leadership at Königgrätz in 1866, and was severely threatened by the rise of nationalism. The tensions thus produced caused a reversal in its economic prospects for several decades, despite its great resources, and made it ultimately dependent on **Germany** after 1869, and upon the intimidation of restive peoples in its southern and western borders. In turn, these factors led to the decision for war in 1914. The empire collapsed in 1918.

hacienda

Generally a largely self-sufficient agricultural estate with limited capital that produces for an internal market with resident labourers that initially were slaves or indigenous peoples. Although the word *hacienda* primarily refers to mixed farms in Spanish America, it can describe any large holdings, including cattle ranches (*estancias*) and export holdings, forerunners of the modern plantations, in Spanish America, West Africa, South East Asia or **Brazil**. By the eighteenth century the Spanish American hacienda, often owned by an absentee landowner and worked by **mestizos**, might include a main house, guest quarters, stables, corral, chapel, workers' quarters and granaries. After independence, patron–client links led workers to vote as instructed and assured owner control of political and economic power. The demand for equitable land distribution inspired the Mexican, Guatemalan, Bolivian, Cuban and Nicaraguan revolutions and peasant movements in **Peru**, **Chile** and **Brazil**, but large estates remain influential in Latin American rural society and economy.

hadj

– *see* **hajj**.

Haganah

Vladimir Jabotinsky helped establish this underground Jewish army (its name means 'defence' in Hebrew) in Palestine in 1920 to protect Jewish lives and property against Arab attack. It operated during the entire period of the British mandate, having some success repelling Arab attacks in Jaffa and the Old City of Jerusalem in 1921. During the **Arab Revolt of 1936–9** Haganah evolved into a nationwide, coordinated Jewish defence organization. It collaborated with the British during **World War II** but thereafter fought the British and clandestinely brought thousands of Jewish immigrants into **Palestine**. Between 1945 and 1947, and again with mixed success, Haganah defended the Jewish state-in-the-making against Arab attack. In April 1948 its leadership condemned the killings of Arab villagers in **Deir Yassin** by two irregular Jewish militias. Shortly after **Israel**'s establishment in May 1948, all Jewish fighting forces were combined into the Israel Defence Forces. At its height in 1944, Haganah had about 36,000 members.

Hague conferences

– *see also* **Geneva Convention**.

The conferences of 1899 and 1907 held at The Hague, in the **Netherlands**, were key steps towards the development of international criminal law and the laws of war, as well as precursors of the twentieth-century systems of conference and confederation which market European diplomacy in peacetime. They covered the issues of disarmament, arbitration and war crimes. The first conference was convened by Tsar **Nicholas II**, and saw the attendance of twenty-six nations, representing every inhabited continent and empire; the second attracted forty-four nations and produced thirteen conventions, mostly concerned with resticted weapons and rules of neutrality. The conferences did not produce a binding international court, but laid the groundwork for the Geneva protocols and the system of international conferences which prevailed after 1918. A third Hague conference was displaced by **World War I**, during which many of its rules were broken.

Haidar Ali (1722–1782)

Haidar Ali rose from the position of humble soldier to become the de facto ruler of the Indian state of Mysore. Employing European military experts, he built a modern army with which he successfully defended Mysore against encroachments by European and Indian powers. Forged by him into a compact and efficiently administered regional kingdom, Mysore allied with the French, posing a threat to British power in **India** until the British conquered the kingdom in 1799.

Haig, Douglas (1861–1928)

Principal British commander in **World War I**. The son of a Scottish distiller, he was commissioned in the British Army in 1885 and swiftly rose through the ranks in India. His experiences in the **Sudan** and **South Africa**, distinguishing himself in the **Boer War**, and an aristocratic marriage led him to the directorship of Military Training for the **British Empire** and the leadership of the Imperial General Staff by 1906. In this position he advised the reforming war minister, Haldane, creating the Territorial Army, a part-time reserve. He led the First Army Corps of the British Expeditionary Force in France in 1914, fighting at Mons and Ypres. In 1915 he succeeded French as British commander-in-chief on the Western Front. Haig has been fiercely criticized for the way in which he conducted the battles of attrition at the Somme in 1916 and Ypres in 1917, and his relations with **Lloyd George**, the British premier, were marked by mutual distrust. His determination and confidence overcame the shock of the German spring offensive in 1918 and he ably conducted the final battles which defeated the German armies during the summer and autumn. A subject of controversy in post-war writing about the conduct of the Great War, he devoted himself to charitable efforts for veterans through the Haig Fund.

Haile Selasse (1892–1975)

The last emperor of **Ethiopia**. Born Tafari Makonnen Woldemikael, the son of the governor of Harar, he became governor or Harar province in 1910. When his aunt Waizeru Zewditu became empress in 1916 he became regent and was effectively the country's ruler, attempting to build on the modernizing reforms of his uncle, **Menelik II**. He secured **Ethiopia**'s entry into the League of Nations in 1923, promising to abolish slavery, though the institution continued into the 1940s. Crowned king in 1928, he assumed the name Haile Selassie ('Might of the Trinity') on becoming emperor in 1930. In exile in London during the Italian occupation from 1936, he was restored to the throne by Allied forces in 1941. Aid from **Britain** and the **United States** financed a programme of modernization in education, health and the armed forces, and Haile Selassie became an international figure, notably in the Organization of African Unity (now **African Union**) and the **Non-Aligned movement**. In 1955 he introduced a nominally progressive constitution, though he retained complete power. But his authority was weakened by internal ethnic conflict, an independence struggle waged by Eritrea and growing army discontent. He survived a coup attempt in 1960, but mishandling of drought in 1973 exposed the state's inefficiency and, despite a belated attempt at liberalization, he was deposed by a radical military committee, the Derg, in 1974. He died under house arrest, believed murdered. Haile Selassie is regarded as the incarnation of God, the messiah, by Rastafarians, although he made no such claims himself.

Haiti

The western third of the island of Hispaniola discovered by Columbus in 1492. The native population was eliminated by the Spaniards by 1533 and progressively replaced by African slaves whose descendants comprise the modern population. Haiti was ceded to **France** by **Spain** in 1697, and the slaves were liberated by **Toussaint Louverture** following the **French Revolution**. Renewed French authority was terminated by the British. Independence was declared, 1804, under a self-styled emperor, and a separate regime was established in the north, 1806 – it was proclaimed a kingdom in 1811, while a republic was set up in the south. The island was reunited as a republic, 1820, and then united with what was later the **Dominican Republic**, 1822–44. A self-styled empire, 1847–59, it was occupied by the **United States**, 1915–34. It fell under the infamous dictatorships of François Duvalier ('Papa Doc'), 1957–71, and his son Jean-Claude Duvalier ('Baby Doc'), 1971–86, with democratic rule only being secured from 1994 following US and UN intervention against the military. Notoriously backward, voodoo continues to be widely practised by many nominal Christians and was recognized as an official religion in 2003.

Haitian Revolution (1791–1804)

The world's most successful slave revolt, the Haitian Revolution resulted in the creation of a black majority state, well before such states were contemplated elsewhere. It is both a component of the **French Revolution** – it would not have begun without the galvanizing effects of revolution being declared in **France** in 1789 – and directly connected to the **American Revolution** that preceded it. The revolt became the largest slave revolt in the Americas, going through a variety of stages and through a variety of participants (France, **Spain** and **Britain** were all involved) before the ex-slave general **Jean-Jacques Dessalines** declared the first black republic in the Americas, naming it **Haiti** (the original name of the region used by indigenous inhabitants) on 1 January 1804. It was also the most brutal war of the revolutionary era in the Americas, leaving at least 100,000 ex-slaves and nearly as many French and British soldiers dead.

Independence came at a heavy price besides the numbers of people killed. A decade of war left the economy in shambles and the plantation system, which before 1791 had been the most profitable in the world, in tatters. Moreover, Haiti was treated internationally as a pariah, mainly because its leaders were of African descent. Nevertheless, the Haitian Revolution reshaped the Atlantic world, showing in particular that slavery could be destroyed from within. In recent years, the Haitian Revolution has moved from the margins of history to occupy a central place in the understanding of the revolutionary era. It has been presented as a heroic example of successful self-liberation by an oppressed subaltern group. The reality is more complex.

The French colony of Saint-Domingue, was rich and prosperous for the small number of whites who dominated it in 1789. But it was a complex society, with a large population of free people of colour, who were as anxious as white colonists to use the outbreak of the French Revolution as a means to achieve political and economic independence. The initial stages of the Haitian Revolution involved fierce battles, mostly in the cities of Port-au-Prince and Cap-Français, between rich whites (*grand blancs*), poor whites (*petit blancs*) and free people of colour (*gens de couleur*). The latter were especially astute in using the rhetoric of human rights then current in France to ally themselves with a nascent abolitionist movement in order to get their voices included in the National Assembly of revolutionary France. They agitated for racial equality for themselves if not complete equality for people of all colours.

As the French Revolution became increasingly radical, previously unimaginable ideas of complete racial equality became feasible. Indeed, the two commissioners sent by revolutionary France to replace the colonial governor – Léger Félicité Sonthanax and Etienne Polverel – were so sympathetic to ideas of racial freedom that they abolished slavery in mid 1793. They chose to make such an unprecedented step partly from ideology but even more so from a desire to enlist aid from rebel slaves in an increasingly desperate struggle against both the Spanish and the British, as well as white colonists and enslaved people, all of whom wanted to maintain the status quo and keep slavery. The key event occurred on 20 June 1793 when a battle between French sailors, white colonists and free people of colour led to the complete breakdown of order in Cap-Français and the burning of the town. The destruction of Cap-Français provided the opportunity for the relatively small number of slave rebels who had launched an uprising against colonial rule in August 1791 to form themselves into an army determined to overturn French rule in the island.

The towering figure in the Haitian revolution was **Toussaint Louverture**, a first generation American-born, or Creole, slave who had been freed a decade before the French Revolution. Toussaint became the leader of an increasingly powerful army of ex-slaves in the plantation region of the north and exhibited both outstanding military skills against a range of opponents and superior diplomatic skills, negotiating independently of the French with the British and most importantly with the **United States**. His major problem was, however, economic: how to satisfy the aspirations of ex-slaves while retaining the productivity of the plantations. By the late 1790s, Toussaint was turning into a Caribbean dictator, causing dissension between his supporters, both elite and non-elite. In the south of Saint-Domingue, a different kind of war developed in which the interests of free people of colour were most important, as might be expected under the leadership of a free man of colour, André Rigaud. Throughout the long war, internal battles between various Haitians, including **Toussaint Louverture**'s successor, Dessalines, meant that independence, when it came in 1804, occurred in a deeply divided island.

Sonthanax wanted France to work with Toussaint Louverture and use the promise of emancipation as a weapon against the slave colonies of France's enemies. **Napoleon Bonaparte**, married to the daughter of a West Indian planter, had different ideas when he came to power in France. He wanted slavery – and its profits – reinstated and Saint-Domingue restored to the old order. In 1801 he sent a large expeditionary force to take advantage of the fissures in Saint-Domingue. Although the French managed to capture and deport Toussaint, they were unable to defeat a Haitian population determined not be re-enslaved. By late 1803 the French had been defeated. The few whites who remained were mostly killed in a series of massacres ordered by Dessalines in 1805. He became the first emperor of the northern half of Haiti while Rigaud became the leader of a republican south. Haiti did not become a united country until 1820, under the leadership of Alexandre Pétion, a free man of colour, educated in France. Although it gained a small measure of economic prosperity as its coffee economy grew during the nineteenth century, it continued to be isolated by other states and colonies, who feared the idea that blacks could rebel and live independently would spread to their territories.

hajj (hadj)

The annual pilgrimage to the holy city of Mecca during the Islamic lunar month of Dhu-ul-Hijja. The word in Arabic literally means `a setting out' and every Muslim whose health and wealth permit is expected to undertake it in their lifetime. Attracting no more than 20,000 pilgrims in the mid nineteenth century, it grew with the development of railways and steamships to attract as many as 50,000 by the 1920s, drawing believers from as far away as West Africa and South East Asia. After **World War II** the growing prosperity of **Saudi Arabia** and its assumed role as leader of the Islamic world, plus the development of air travel, have led the hajj to become one of the largest religious pilgrimage centres in the world, attracting hundreds of thousands of Muslims. It has also attracted terrorist and serious fatalities as a result of crowd stampedes.

Hajj Amin al-Husayni, Grand Mufti of Jerusalem

– *see* **Al-Husayni, Hajj Amin, Mufti of Jerusalem**.

Halabja

The Iraqi regime launched a chemical attack against Kurdish villagers in Halabja on 15 March 1988, killing approximately 5,000 civilians and committing the worst violation of international protocols against the use of chemical weapons since **Mussolini** in Abyssinia in 1935. In addition to the incident at Halabja, **Iraq** employed chemical weapons against their own civilians on several occasions during the *Anfal* campaign. In response to a united Kurdish military opposition supported by **Iran**, Iraq's government launched a brutal campaign to suppress the Kurdish parties in early 1987. Led by **Saddam Hussein**'s cousin 'Ali Hasan al-Majid, the Iraqi campaign relied on systematic ethnic cleansing to clear the Kurdish population from much of their traditional homeland. At the time, Iraq faced few objections to its policy as many western governments treated Kurdish claims of genocide as exaggerated. Later investigations vindicated that characterization of the Iraqi government's policy: more than a million Kurds were displaced, thousands of the villages razed and Kurdish civilians systematically arrested and executed by the Iraqi Army.

Hamas

Hamas is a conservative Islamic Nationalist organization that was founded in 1987 and is affiliated with the **Muslim Brotherhood**. The name *Hamas* is not the organization's full or official name. Hamas means 'zeal' in Arabic, but more fittingly, the name is an acronym of the organization's full name, which is Harakat al-Muqawama al-Islamiya. In English this translates as the Islamic Resistance movement, and is fitting because their purpose is to resist the Israeli occupation, maintain resistance and fight for the return of an independent Palestinian state. Founded by Sheikh Ahmed Yassin, the movement took up the cause of resistance against **Israel**, and in 1988 broke its ties with the non-violent Muslim Brotherhood, choosing to begin armed resistance and violent activities in their quest for independence and a Palestinian state. Although founded in **Egypt**, the organization is focused on Palestinian nationalism and resistance to Israel as an occupying force – its charter seeks the creation of a Palestinian state. The stated purpose of Hamas is not just to free **Palestine**, but to destroy the Israeli state and replace it with an independent Islamic state. Besides its political aspirations, Hamas also operates a substantial network of social services for Palestinians living within the Occupied Territories. providing infrastructure which includes, but is not limited to, education, aid and medical treatment, and in this way it seeks to support the Palestinian people while undermining the Israeli government. Also supporting a militant military wing, Hamas often deals in violent activities, such as rocket attacks and suicide bombings, to advance its cause. With two branches, the organization has a military faction known as the Izz ad-Dim al-Qassam Brigades, and also boasts a social services organization. Multiple organizations exist in the territories, and for many years the two prominent groups under the **Palestine Liberation Organization** (PLO) were Hamas and **Fatah**. Hamas remains deeply opposed to the decades of peace accords that have been attempted and the PLO's participation in peace talks with Israel. Following violent conflict within the PLO in 2005–6, Hamas became dominant in **Gaza** but ceded control of the West Bank to Fatah.

Hamilton, Alexander (1755 or 1757–1804)

Born out of wedlock on the island of Nevis in the West Indies, Hamilton early distinguished himself by his intellect and ambition. Securing a scholarship to study on the mainland, he entered King's College (now Columbia University) prior to the War of Independence. When the war commenced, he served as an aide and staff officer for **George Washington**. Hamilton served with distinction and was commended for his valour in combat during the siege of **Yorktown** in 1781. After the war he established himself as leading lawyer in New York. He was an early and strong supporter of political reform and supported replacing the **Articles of Confederation** with the federal constitution. He was one of three authors of the **Federalist Papers**, 1787–8, which were drafted in support of the proposed constitution. Hamilton served as Secretary of the Treasury in Washington's administration. In that role he helped to stabilize the finances of the new republic while establishing himself as the leader of the protean Federalist Party. He led the Federalists until his death in a duel; he was killed by a political and professional rival, Aaron Burr, who was then serving as vice president.

Harbin

Harbin is the capital city of Heilongjiang Province in north-east China. Originally a fishing village on the south bank of the Songhua River, the catalyst to Harbin's development was the construction of the China Eastern Railway by **Russia** at the start of the twentieth century. Although the city became a centre of heavy industry in the Maoist period, Russian influence has remained, and today Harbin is home to over 4 million people.

Harding, Warren G. (1865–1923)

Twenty-ninth president of the **United States**, 1921–3, and the first to be born after the civil war. An Ohio Republican, his 1920 campaign pledge to return the nation to 'normalcy' struck a chord with an electorate eager to repudiate **Woodrow Wilson**'s foreign policy. Harding's domestic accomplishments were modest; his foreign policy only marginally less so. His administration is chiefly remembered for a series of corruption scandals that came to light following his death.

Hariri, Rafiq al- (1944–2005)

In November 1944, Rafiq Baha al-din al-Hariri was born into a Lebanese Sunni family. Hariri attended Beirut University, earning a degree in business administration, eventually founding his business Oger Liban. In the 1980s, while **Lebanon** was being torn apart by internal and external forces, Hariri helped in mediation conferences including one in Geneva in 1984. In 1989 he played a key role in the agreement which ended the Lebanese Civil War, called the Taef Agreement. Three years later he was made president of the Council of Ministers, and helped to lead his country to the establishment of a more stable and cooperative form of government. While in his role as prime minister, Hariri was elected in 1996 to Parliament, and his party soon won a majority position under his leadership. He was assassinated a year after resigning as prime minister, in late 2004.

Harrison, Benjamin (1833–1901)

Twenty-third president of the United States, 1889–93. Harrison practised law in Indianapolis before enlisting in the Union Army in 1861, eventually rising to the rank of brevet brigadier general. An influential figure in the Indiana Republican Party, he was elected in 1881 to the US Senate and in 1888 to the presidency. As president, he championed orthodox Republican policies, including a commitment to the enforcement of African American voting rights in the South and a reinforcement of the protective **tariff** system. In 1892 he was nominated for a second term but defeated by **Grover Cleveland**, whom he had himself defeated four years earlier. The extravagance of the 'Billion Dollar Congress' (1889–91), elected along with Harrison in 1888, together with rising levels of industrial conflict and agrarian protest contributed to the outcome. After 1893 he returned to practising law.

Harrison, William Henry (1773–1840)

The shortest-serving US president, the Virginian Harrison saw active service in the US Army on the north-western frontier from 1791 to 1798, and served the Northwest Territory as secretary and then territorial delegate in Congress, where he fathered the Land Act of 1800. As governor of the huge Indiana Territory, 1801–12, he negotiated massive land concessions with the Native Americans. In 1812 he took command of the north-western armies, held off two British invasions, and won the decisive Battle of the Thames in 1813. He was elected to Congress in 1816 from the Cincinnati district, to the Ohio state senate in 1819, and in 1825 to the US Senate. In 1828 he was appointed minister to Colombia where he served until being recalled in 1831. In 1836, representing northern Whigs, he became the first presidential candidate to speak publicly on his own behalf. Winning the national Whig nomination in 1840, Harrison was triumphantly elected president – only to die of pneumonia and pleurisy after one month in power.

Hartford Convention (USA)

The Hartford Convention was long remembered – wrongly – as a **Federalist** attempt to bring about New England's secession from the **United States**. Commercial restrictions since 1806 and the disastrous War of 1812 alienated New England Federalists, and some talked of secession. Leaders of the party, however, recognized the continuing strength of the Republican Party locally and New England's commercial and political involvement with other states. The five states sent delegates to the convention called at Hartford, Connecticut, in December 1814 to protest against the war. In the end, the convention proposed a set of constitutional amendments requiring a two-thirds majority for a declaration of war or restriction on commerce, and removing the constitutional underpinnings of the Virginia dynasty. **Andrew Jackson**'s triumph at New Orleans and news of the Treaty of Ghent undercut their protests, the amendments were ignored in Washington, and the convention became a symbol of Federalist opposition to what was now seen as a triumphant war.

Hashemites

The Arab royal dynasty of **Iraq** (1921–58) and of **Jordan** (1921–) originating with **Husayn, Sharif of Mecca** and ally of the western powers during **World War I**. The designation 'Hashemite' denotes descent from the Prophet, and Hussein

vainly hoped to unify the whole Arab world under his rule. In practice he was only to see his sons **Faisal I** (1885–1933) and **Abdullah** (1882–1951) become client rulers for the British, as king of Iraq and emir of Transjordan respectively. Neither Faisal I nor his succcessors won the loyalty of the Iraqi people and **Faisal II** was assassinated in a military coup in 1958. Abdullah in Transjordan assumed the title of king in 1946, when a treaty with the British changed the name of the territory to **Jordan**. He was assassinated, 1951. Under his successors, Hussein and Abdullah II, the Jordanian Hashemites have retained the loyalty of the more traditionalist elements in the population but the limited nature of democratic reform has nevertheless engendered widespread unrest.

Hassan II, King of Morocco (1929–1999)

Hassan II was the second king of independent **Morocco** and a member of the Alawi dynasty. He ruled from 1961 until his death in 1999. After studying law at Bordeaux, as crown prince, Hassan was appointed chief of staff of the fledgling military, comprised of former anti-colonial guerrilla forces and officers from the colonial army. His father, King Mohammed V, died suddenly in 1961 and Hassan ascended. Perceived as unsuited to the throne, he quickly allied with the conservative Istiqlal Party and consolidated power. Close advisers penned Morocco's first constitution in 1962 that enshrined the monarch's political and spiritual authority by granting him total executive power and pronouncing him 'Commander of the Faithful'. The king maintained power through a system of patronage that started with him but filtered through every level of government. Military officers such as General Oufkir benefited the most, and most of the wealthiest Moroccans were members of the armed forces.

Turmoil described the 1970s, as Hassan survived two major coup attempts and launched an invasion of the Spanish Sahara territory long claimed by the monarchy as part of Morocco. In 1971, during the king's birthday party at the beach-side palace in Skhirat, soldiers under the command of General Medboh launched a coup. Legend has it, Hassan convinced a few rebels to give up the fight and help him retake the palace. A bloody purge of the army, led by Minister of Interior Oufkir, followed. The king's attempts at reconciliation with the opposition and reform did not sit well with entrenched elites, including his military allies. In 1972 the air force attacked Hassan's plane, but he miraculously escaped and rallied his trusted supporters. Hassan this time blamed Oufkir, who allegedly committed suicide the next day. His resilience boosted his popular reputation as a leader of destiny and good fortune. Hassan sought to stabilize and unify the country through irredentist expansion. He targeted the Sahara, still governed as a Spanish colony but claimed as part of a historical 'Greater Morocco'. After the International Court of Justice denied Morocco's claims, in 1975 Hassan led 500,000 Moroccan civilians in the 'Green March' into the Spanish Sahara. The Sahrawi independence forces saw a union with Morocco as a continuation of colonialism, and war soon broke out between the two sides. Hassan's army suffered setbacks, but western military aid helped tip the scales. By the early 1980s, Morocco controlled virtually the entire disputed territory. Food shortages and economic decline brought widespread unrest in the 1980s. Hassan responded with extreme repression at home while cultivating closer ties with **France** and the **USA**. During these so-called 'Years of Lead', Minister of the Interior Driss Basri crushed all opposition. In the 1990s Hassan opened the political field slightly: he granted more power to Parliament in a 1992 constitution, privatized state-held institutions and allowed the media to discuss human rights abuses by the regime. He died in 1999 and was succeeded by his eldest son, Mohammed VI.

Hastings, Warren (1732–1818)

Born in 1732 to a minor branch of an English land-owning family, Hastings took up a 'writership' in the English **East India Company** in 1750, learning the textile trade at up-country 'factories' in **Bengal**. The Company's conquest of Bengal after 1757 created new opportunities for talented administrators like Hastings, who was appointed governor of Bengal in 1772, and then Governor General of the Company's Indian territories (1774–85). Initially sceptical at the wisdom of new conquests, Hastings later tried to consolidate the company's power by devising more efficient modes of territorial taxation and judicial administration, and by prosecuting wars against other Indian powers. He also patronized British scholarship on Indian literature, history and law, hoping to found British power on indigenous forms of government. **Edmund Burke**, who regarded him as a corrupt tyrant, orchestrated Hastings' impeachment in the British parliament (1787–94). Finally acquitted, Hastings died in 1818, a controversial empire-builder who has continued to inspire debate about the morality of imperialism.

Hatt-ı Humayun (1856)

– *see also* **Tanzimat**.

Also known as the Reform Edict. In the second major decree of the **Tanzimat** period (after the Hatt-ı Serif of 1839), Ottoman Sultan Abdülmecid reaffirmed the equality, regardless of creed, of all Ottoman citizens. Conversion from **Islam** to **Christianity** was no longer punished amidst the expansion of state-mandated religious freedom. Legal equality produced new tensions between Muslims and non-Muslims for the remainder to the **Ottoman Empire**'s existence.

Hatt-ı Serif (1839) (Ottoman Empire)

A campaign of modernization preceded its promulgation – earlier reforms had focused on the Ottoman military – but the Hatt-ı Serif of Gulhane formally launched the **Tanzimat** reforms by declaring equality under the law for all Ottoman citizens. In addition, Sultan Abdülmecid's edict prescribed the abolition of tax farming as well as the inception of universal and impartial conscription. The Hatt-ı Serif enshrined protections for human rights into the Ottoman law books.

Hausa states

A group of independent city-states in modern-day Northern Nigeria. Although traditionally numbered as seven, Kano and Katsina were the most important. Converted to **Islam** in the sixteenth century, the states were nevertheless subjected to an Islamic Revival led by Usuman dan Fodio in 1804, which led to their consolidation under the caliphate of **Sokoto**, which in turn was taken over by **Great Britain** in 1903 and integrated into their colony of **Nigeria**.

Havana (La Habana)

Founded in its present location in 1519, Havana became **Cuba**'s colonial capital. Adjoining an excellent harbour, it protected the route to and from Vera Cruz, **Mexico**, and the exit from the Caribbean. The naval base for silver fleets returning to Spain, it was heavily fortified into the nineteenth century and regained strategic importance after Cuban independence. With over 2 million inhabitants, Havana remains **Cuba**'s capital, although with less glamour than in the pre-Castro years.

Hawaii

– *see also* **Pearl Harbor**.

A Pacific archipelago, the fiftieth American state since 1959. Named the Sandwich Islands by the British explorer **James Cook** in 1778, Hawaii was united under King Kamehameha I (*c.* 1736–1819) in 1810 and was briefly occupied by **Britain** in 1843. In 1893 sugar planters deposed Queen Liliuokalani (1838–1917), established a republic and called for American protection. In 1898, during the **Spanish–American War**, the **United States** annexed Hawaii for its value as a naval base, declaring the islands a territory in 1900. It housed the major American naval base at Oahu, as well as airfields attacked by the Japanese in December 1941.

Haya de la Torre, Victor Raùl (1895–1979)

Peruvian politican activist Haya de la Torre founded the Latin America-wide **APRA** (Alianza Popular Revolucionaria Americana) movement in 1923 and the first mass populist political party in **Peru**, the Partido Aprista Peruano (PAP) in 1931, which he led until his death. Elites and the armed forces blocked him from the presidency, but he presided over the Constituent Assembly that wrote a constitution which served as the transition from military to democratic rule in Peru in 1980.

Hayes, Rutherford Birchard (1822–1893)

Nineteenth president of the **United States**, 1877–81. Hayes practised law in Lower Sandusky, Ohio, before enlisting in the Union Army, rising to the rank of brevet major general. After serving one and a half terms as a Republican in the House of Representatives, he was elected governor of Ohio in 1867, in 1869 and again in 1875. The following year he was nominated for the presidency to resolve a deadlock between the supporters of James G. Blaine and Roscoe Conkling. The set of formal and informal agreements that resolved the contested election of 1876, commonly known as the **Compromise of 1877**, involved a commitment on his part to withdraw federal troops from the South in return for assurances from Southern political leaders that the rights of **African Americans** would receive adequate protection. This policy was hugely unpopular with elements of the **Republican Party**, and Hayes himself soon became disenchanted with its results. He also antagonized party leaders such as Conkling by his active support for civil service reform. Believing that the president should stand above

party politics, Hayes declined to run for the office again in 1880.

Hayford, Joseph Ephraim Casely (1866–1930)

Born in the Gold Coast (modern **Ghana**) to an elite family, he was educated at missionary schools in West Africa and became a journalist in his home region in 1886. After studying law in London, he served in politics in a variety of roles under the colonial government, always a spokesperson for the rights of indigenous people, and was an early advocate of **pan-Africanism**, forming the National Congress of British West Africa.

Haykal, Muhammad Husayn (1923–2016)

Influential Egyptian journalist, a close confidant of President **Nasser** and a member of the Central Committee of the Arab Socialist Union. Editor-in-chief of the leading Egyptian newspaper, *al-Ahram*, 1957–74, he was a regular weekly lecturer on the Arab television station Al-Jazeera in later life, giving him a major platform in the wider Arab world and a large following, not least among the young. The author of numerous books including *Nasser: The Cairo Documents* (published in English, 1972) and *The Sphinx and the Commissar: The Rise and Fall of Soviet Influence in the Arab World* (published in English, 1978), commenting in the latter: 'The Russians were unable to comprehend the dominating role of nationalism in the Arab world.' In his controversial *Khareef al-Ghadab* (*Autumn of Fury*), 1983, he sought to analyze reasons for the assassination of President **Sadat**, to whom he was never close, and for the rise of political **Islam**. Never afraid to generate further controversy, he strongly criticized President **Mubarak**, 2007, alleging that he lived in a 'world of fantasy'.

Haymarket Riot (USA)

In protest at police action against strikers at the McCormick Harvester plant, anarchists held a meeting at Haymarket Square, Chicago, on 4 May 1886. A bomb was thrown and police reacted by firing into the crowd, prompting widespread panic and the arrest of anarchists. The trial caused international controversy: although there was no evidence to link them to bomb throwing, seven were sentenced to death. Two were reprieved and later pardoned by Governor Altgeld (1893). The bomb thrower was never identified.

health and disease

– see also **epidemics**.

Health and disease have been key themes in modern history. Some of the most important developments of modernity are analyzed and assessed globally with respect to improving conditions of human health and the prevention of diseases. The rise of humanism and humanitarianism is associated with the growing concern for human health and well-being. The **Enlightenment** led to the rise of humanitarianism; a greater sense of sympathy for human beings combined with a faith in intellectual and social progress. These developed along with a view of seeing citizens as valuable resources of the state from the eighteenth century. Moreover, imperial warfare and losses to the eighteenth-century army from battle injuries and disease weighed heavily on the European powers. These gradually led European states to invest in better medical care for their civilian and military population from the eighteenth century. Yet, in other parts of the world, disease and epidemics remained a great, and sometimes became a greater, problem from the eighteenth century. There are limits to such an explanation of the rise of humanitarianism and modern medicine, however. Historians have questioned this general narrative of progress. They have highlighted some of the contradictions within the humanitarian Enlightenment project, which also led to the adoption of sophisticated modes of marginalization and ostracization of sick people in modern hospitals and asylums. Others have pointed out the gendered and racial predisposition of European humanitarianism. To understand the history of health and disease and the role of medicine in modern society, we need to focus on two main developments since the eighteenth century: changes in medicine and drugs, and the emergence and expansion of public health care facilities.

expansion of the European materia medica

European *materia medica* expanded and diversified rapidly from the eighteenth century. This started with the discovery of new trade routes and new continents by Europeans across the Atlantic and Indian oceans, which marked the global expansion of European trading and commercial networks. In Europe, the inflow of money and bullion and new items of trade led to the Commercial Revolution; the growth of markets, ports and towns, a rise in prices and of the merchant class. It also increased the import of exotic drugs into

European markets and transformed European pharmacopeia and medical theories. The supply of plant-based and exotic medicaments in Europe increased massively between the sixteenth and the nineteenth centuries. During the seventeenth century the import of drugs from **Asia** and America increased twenty-five-fold. Many exotic items, such as ipecacuanha, opium, cinchona, sarsaparilla, rhubarb, jalap, camphor and aloes, proved to be highly popular as medicine in Europe. Transformation in the philosophical reasoning and thinking within European natural history from the seventeenth century influenced the use of exotic plants in European medicine. Collecting became the hallmark of eighteenth-century natural history, started under the Royal Society in London and the Académie des Sciences in Paris. The new significance placed in this period on 'ocular demonstration' and observation of the 'phaenomena of nature' helped in the collection and study of exotic medicinal plants. At the same time, medical curricula in leading European universities laid stress on the study of botany and natural history. By the end of eighteenth century British pharmacopeia, particularly the *Edinburgh New Dispensatory*, became important depositories of various exotic drugs arriving from different parts of the world.

disease and environment

European theories of diseases changed as Europeans travelled to different parts of the world and encountered different climates. European physicians reworked their traditional medical theories to explain the diseases, particularly the various 'fevers', they experienced in hot climates. This led to the incorporation of climatic factors into the causation of fevers. French physicians such as Jean Fernel (1497–1558) shifted traditional attention from poisonous miasmas to the idea that different climates produced different types of fevers. The English physician Thomas Sydenham (1624–89) reinstated the significance of environment in Hippocratic medicine (airs, waters and places) in his treatise on fevers ('Method of curing fevers based on original observations') and thus made climate an essential element of understanding putrid fevers. These gave rise to the linking of disease with climate in the eighteenth century. Physicians such as James Lind (1736–1812) stressed the need for Europeans to acclimatize themselves in hot climates to gain immunity from the various illnesses that they experienced there.

The linking of disease with environment also led to a greater awareness of environmental hygiene in the eighteenth century. European physicians in this period viewed disease as the physical manifestation of lack of harmony between the body and the environment. The British physician John Pringle (1707–82) dwelt extensively on the so-called putrid or pestilential fevers that ravaged ships, jails and other confined spaces and argued that putrid diseases exhibited signs of physical and moral degeneration. In 1750 he published *Observations on the Nature and Cure of Hospital and Jayl Fevers* in which he attributed outbreaks of diseases in jails to air vitiated by filth, perspiration and excrement in which blood underwent putrid changes. Pringle suggested various means of 'purifying the air' by the use of antiseptics such as lime juice, vinegar and oil of vitriol, but also by maintaining cleanliness and hygiene. By the middle of the eighteenth century physicians and surgeons were stressing the importance of medical and sanitary intervention to ensure order and health in society. Empirical evidence had also proved the value of **inoculation** against smallpox, imported into Europe from the Near East, and then gradually replaced by the safer and more widely adopted **vaccination** pioneered by the British surgeon, Edward Jenner (1748–1823). These were the major pre-scientific developments in medicine and health. Meanwhile, sanitary reformers from the mid eighteenth century advocated the need for adopting hygienic practices including disposal of waste, maintain cleanliness and ensuring ventilation. Thus cleanliness and hygiene gradually became part of preventive medicine and state policy in the nineteenth century.

emergence of public health

Several outbreaks of cholera in the nineteenth century paved the way for the most important public health measures in **Europe** and America. Between 1817 and 1870 several cholera pandemics spread from Asia to Europe and America. By 1830 the disease had appeared in **Russia**, and then rapidly swept through Europe reaching **Britain** in 1831. A year later it appeared in Quebec, Montreal and New York and became a global contagion. Cholera caused huge mortalities wherever it visited. Between 1816 and 1832 millions of people died in Asia, during the 1832 outbreak 55,000 people died in Britain and 3,515 died in New York alone. During the second pandemic in 1849 over 33,000 people died in three months in Britain. In Europe, cholera prompted the emergence of modern public health and epidemiology. In 1842, Edwin

Chadwick (1800–90), the English social reformer and civil servant, published his *Report ... on an inquiry into the sanitary condition of the labouring population of Great Britain*, which demonstrated that poor living conditions, overcrowding and foul air predisposed urban populations to epidemic disease.

The main achievement of Chadwick's report was the mass of statistics it collected on the living and sanitary conditions of the poor in Britain. It connected cholera, and disease in general, with people's social and economic conditions. In **France**, Louis-René Villermé (1782–1863) provided a similar statistical record of the urban poor living in Paris even earlier, in the 1820s. The statistics and reports of Chadwick, Villermé and the German pathologist Rudolph Virchow (1821–1902), and the cholera maps of John Snow (1813–58) marked the birth of modern epidemiology. These evidences also prompted state intervention into the lives of the unhealthy urban poor. Cholera outbreaks proved critical in public health movements in Europe and in providing clean water for the public from the mid nineteenth century. These changes in public health were mostly confined to Europe and the **USA**, however. Public health care in the colonies in Asia and **Africa** remained very limited or non-existent.

laboratory medicine

Changes in medical research complemented developments in public health and epidemiology. By the late eighteenth century the introduction of laboratory research particularly in France started a new phase in medicine. This was part of a greater change in eighteenth-century science, known as the 'Chemical Revolution', initiated by the French scientist Antoine Lavoisier (1743–94). Lavoisier developed a new chemical taxonomy as well as a radically new understanding of all elements and compounds to define the active role and compositions of matter. This also led to the development of an important research tradition in medicine; the search for the 'active' ingredients of exotic medicinal plants. Laboratory research and the practice of chemical nomenclature led to the extraction of new medicinal elements in the 1820s, for example, quinine from cinchona, caffeine from coffee, emetine from ipecacuanha, morphine from opium and nicotine from tobacco. Modern chemistry and laboratory experiments transformed the observational and ocular traditions of medicine that developed from the late seventeenth century. In the nineteenth century laboratory experiments became important in producing medicines. This also contributed to the emergence of the modern pharmaceutical industry, particularly in France and **Germany**.

Laboratory research brought about important changes in other areas of medicine as well. By the 1830s, aided by new microscopes, laboratories and experiments, scientists discovered that yeast consisted of small and living organisms. By the 1860s the French scientist Louis Pasteur (1822–95) had established that fermentation depended on the vital and dynamic role played by living microorganisms, and in 1864 he proposed that subjecting milk and wine to an elevated temperature for a set period causes partial sterilization making it safe for consumption and preservation. This method, known as pasteurization, helped the food and agricultural industries and public health by improving diet. In medicine, this led to the emergence of the germ theory of disease, predominantly within French and German medical traditions from the 1880s. Germ theory suggested that specific germs or micro-organisms, not the miasma or humours, caused specific diseases. Robert Koch (1843–1910), the German physician, was the first scientist in 1875 to demonstrate that the bacterium *bacillus anthracis* caused anthrax. Pasteur extended his work on the sterilization of germs to develop bacteriological vaccines by partial attenuation of viruses. The most famous breakthrough came in 1885 when he developed the rabies vaccine. This led to the establishment of the Pasteur Institute in Paris in 1888. Soon, Pasteur institutes spread to different parts of the world, particularly the French colonies in Africa and South East Asia, and germ theory and vaccines became part of global and imperial medicine. In Europe, the Pasteur institutes carried out **vaccinations** in rabies, anthrax, tuberculosis and the plague and participated in public health undertakings of food preservation and diet. In the colonies, Pasteur institutes became part of the French imperial 'civilizing mission'. While carrying out vaccination and pasteurization, French scientists and imperial governors projected their science as a mission to spread the fruits of French civilization and progress to its colonies.

Germ theory brought new hope of eradicating diseases. It also marked a break from the traditional belief in humorology and miasmatic theories. However, ideas of miasma and environment continued to play an important part in medicine and public health. These gradually transformed

bacteriology, giving rise to a new idea of the human body with respect to the environment. Previously, physicians viewed the body in its natural state to be in harmony with the environment; now the human body no longer appeared to be in such harmony, but rather in need of protection from germs in the environment. This changing notion of the human constitution with respect to the environment had important implications in the tropics.

colonialism and tropical medicine

The introduction of germ theory in the tropics took place at a time when Europeans viewed tropical climate and environment as pathological. The combination of germ theory with concerns of tropical climate gave rise to the new medical tradition of tropical medicine by the end of the nineteenth century. Tropical medicine was based on the belief that certain diseases and pathogens were endemic to the tropics. It combined the cumulative European experiences of 'disease of hot climates' from the seventeenth century with the new science of bacteriology. Vectors and the climatic and environmental conditions of their life cycle, rather than the pathogens themselves, became the focus of tropical medical research. This started with Patrick Manson's (1844–1922) discovery in 1877 of the mosquito vector for the transmission of the parasite *filaria sanguinis hominis* (which caused the disease filariasis). In 1897, Ronald Ross (1857–1932) discovered that the *anopheles* mosquito was the vector that transmitted the malaria parasite. This started a tradition of medical research in the tropical colonies, which combined laboratory research with field surveys on vectors of diseases such as malaria, filariasis, trypanosomiasis, leishmaniasis and onchocerciasis in Asia, Africa and South America. The rise of tropical medicine also took place at a time of intense imperial expansion, particularly in Africa. Historians have shown how it played an important role in promoting late nineteenth-century ideas of 'constructive imperialism', which suggested that imperialism was ultimately for the benefit of colonized people and nations.

traditional medicine

Non-western countries and societies were not passive recipients of these various changes in modern medicine. Doctors and medical professionals in Asia and Africa engaged creatively with modern medicine, often defining their application in unique ways, but also by modernizing their own indigenous medicines. Traditional medicines in

Asia and Africa negotiated with modern medicine and emerged as alternative forms of medicine in the twentieth century. This took place through the marginalization and subsequent invention of indigenous traditions. Colonization and the expansion of European commercial and cultural dominance from the end of the eighteenth century led to the pre-eminence of European medicine often at the expense of indigenous medicine. The establishment of European hospitals and medical colleges legitimised western medical degrees and the introduction of European drugs, while the British medical acts in **India** restricted the use of the term *doctor* to only those who practised western medicine. Others were formally designated as 'quacks'. At the same time, Europeans took a keen interest in the drugs, exotic medical plants or substances local practitioners used and recorded them, thereby ensuring that they did not disappear.

Local practitioners in Asia and Africa responded to the dominance of western medicine by codifying and standardizing their own medicines, selecting certain drugs or practices which corresponded with modern ideas and requirements, introducing new medical substances and modern laboratory techniques and producing indigenous pharmacopoeias. They adopted some practices that they believed enhanced the 'scientificity' of their diagnosis, such as feeling the pulse of the patient, as well as a greater use of minor surgeries and the study of anatomy. In the process, indigenous medical practices were 'invented' as new forms of traditional medicine in the twentieth century.

In India, the most important developments in traditional medicine were in the professionalization of Unani (an Islamic medical system in India of Greek and Arabic lineage) and Ayurveda (a Hindu medical practice derived from Sanskrit texts). In Unani, this represented the translation of its texts from Arabic into Urdu, a more accessible language. Ayurveda reinvented itself and became associated with Hindu nationalism, which supported a 'revival' of Hindu scriptural knowledge. They also invented Sanskrit and Arabic names for modern ingredients. Several countrywide Ayurveda and Unani conferences were organized between 1904 and 1920 and the establishment of Ayurvedic and Unani College in Delhi helped to establish the two as mainstream 'Indian' traditions of medicine. The revival of traditional medicines from the ancient classics meant that the epistemological contribution and cultural accretions of several hundred intermediary years were

overlooked. (It is important to remember that modern Ayurveda or Unani do not include various marginal medical practices, which are not based on classical scriptures but are practised daily on roadsides in Asia and cater to a large section of the poor.)

In **China**, traditional Chinese medicine was reformulated in the twentieth century in response to western medicine. Western medicine had a dominant presence in parts of China in the nineteenth century, through the activities of the Jesuits from the eighteenth century and the modern vaccinations, hospitals and sanitarian policies introduced by the end of the nineteenth century. In the 1960s the Cultural Revolution invested heavily in reviving traditional medicine in an effort to develop affordable medical care and public health facilities. At the same time, the Chinese government revolutionized traditional medicine by establishing medical colleges, hospitals, standardizing treatment and drugs as well as medical training; a dynamic incorporation of modern medical concepts and methods with a revitalization of some selected aspects of traditional practices. Thus, a new tradition of Chinese medicine was invented known as traditional Chinese medicine (TCM), which adopted modern biomedicine in terms of its reliance on statistics and diagnostic tests, and standardization. TCM differs significantly from the different indigenous medicines practised in China by different communities for several centuries in the past in terms of medical orientation, physiological theories, aetiology, diagnostics, therapeutics and pharmacology. What is known as TCM today is a hybrid form of medicine that combines elements of folk medicine with that of western therapeutics and allopathic diagnosis and pharmaceutical production.

Traditional medicine in Africa emerged out of an interaction between African healing practices and Christianity. Colonization of Africa took place at a time of greater assertion of European superiority and of the 'civilizing mission', as well as at a time of growing influence of European biomedicine and vaccines. European colonial officials often misunderstood African medical practices as signs of African primitive culture and tended to lump them together with 'religion', witchcraft, 'magic' or 'superstition'. They instituted laws banning these practices. Christian missions were some of the places where a more hybrid medical tradition emerged from the late nineteenth century. While Africans adopted Christianity, they also imbued it with their everyday and traditional practices. African healing practices thus continued to survive, although they were increasingly infused with Christian ideas. At the same time, a selection took place whereby certain practices that European missionaries and mission doctors were more comfortable and familiar with and those, which appeared to be free from 'primitive' practices, were encouraged. There were also major demographic and economic changes in Africa in the first half of the twentieth century, with the establishment of mines, plantations, a market system, urbanization and labour migration. This led to new epidemics in AIDS, TB, influenza and typhoid, and to a breakdown of traditional institutions and belief systems. A new hybrid African medicine emerged in the twentieth century in this social and economic context, serving contemporary health and medical challenges, imitating modern biomedicine and reinventing African culture.

Thus, two major forms of medicine coexisted in the twentieth century; western medicine and alternative medicine. Both were relatively modern forms of medicine that developed from the late nineteenth century. It is also important to note that traditional and alternative medicine play a crucial role in global health care. In some Asian and African countries, 80 per cent of the population depend on traditional medicine for primary health care. The other important change in non-western health care has been the new modes of delivering medicine and health care to the poor, often a more challenging task than defining and discovering new medicines. A unique example of this was during the **Cultural Revolution** in China in 1968, when the Chinese Communist Party endorsed a radical new system of health care delivery for rural areas. A barefoot doctor (a medical person trained with the basic skills and knowledge of modern medicine) was allotted to every village to provide basic medical care. The main impact of this new programme was the introduction of modern western medicine and ideas of health care in remote villages.

the emergence of global health

The twentieth century was broadly speaking a period of international collaboration in health care. **World War I** caused huge mortalities. One of the most devastating global pandemics followed. The 1918/19 **influenza pandemics** (commonly known as the Spanish flu) killed around 50 million people worldwide. Outbreaks of typhoid in Russia and malaria in **Greece**, the **Balkans** and **Italy** soon followed. The war and subsequent epidemics led to the establishment of the first organization to ensure global preventive health care, the

League of Nations Health Organization, in 1921. This organization focused primarily on **Europe**, although major malaria eradication efforts were undertaken in India and Africa.

In the interwar period new visions emerged around medicine and global public health in the form of 'socialized medicine', a new ideology around health and development promoted by Henry E. Sigerist. Sigerist stressed the need for a national health service and a socially equitable distribution of health care with funding from the state. The model for his ideas was the **Soviet Union**, and in *Socialised Medicine* (1937) he promoted the Soviet structure of public health care for other countries. In Britain, a small group of radical socialist physicians formed the Socialist Medical Association (SMA), who were deeply influenced by Sigerst and the Soviet principles of 'socialist medicine'. The SMA played a critical role in instituting the post-war National Health Service in Britain.

World War II led to the formation of the World Health Organization (WHO) in 1948 in Geneva, Switzerland. The WHO marked a new era in global health and epidemic disease control. Its main activity was global vaccination campaigns, particularly for children, in measles, polio and smallpox, and it also sought to address questions of poverty and health and to ensure a basic medical infrastructure in different parts of the world. One of its major early successes was the smallpox eradication programme. In 1967 it intensified the programme and achieved its target by 1980. It achieved much less success with the eradication of infectious diseases such as malaria. The WHO adopted a formal policy on the control and eradication of malaria in 1955, mainly using DDT and distributing quinine, but despite the Global Malaria Eradication programmes and investments, malaria remains a global health problem, presenting a serious infection risk to several billion people. Consequently, the WHO has focused more on building health services and providing primary health care.

health and disease in the modern world

The study of mortality rates and the inequitable distribution of health care facilities worldwide have been important in addressing the main questions around health and disease in the modern world and in assessing the role of modern medicine in human welfare. In Europe and the US there was a noticeable decline in mortality from the end of the eighteenth century. In some countries such as Britain, the decline started early, and by between 1730 and 1815 Britain's population doubled from

5.3 million to 10 million. It doubled again in the next fifty-five years to reach 21 million in 1871. The rate of growth slowed only slightly from then on to reach 35.5 million by 1911. In **Switzerland**, on the other hand, death rates declined later, between 1890 and 1945. Historians have debated the role played by modern medicine in this decline. Thomas McKeown put forward the view that the growth in population in the industrialized world from the late 1700s was not due to advancements in the field of medicine or public health, but to improvements in overall standards of living, especially diet and nutrition, resulting from better economic conditions. These views were contested by historians such as Simon Szreter, who highlighted the importance of sanitary and public health measures such as clean water, milk supplies and vaccination campaigns and better medical facilities for declining mortality. Overall, the decline in mortality in the West has been ascribed to better primary health care, public health facilities and economic growth.

The link between public health, economic conditions and mortality rates has assumed even greater significance for understanding the role medicine played in the developing and poor countries. There has been a rapid decline in mortality rates in South America, south Asia and Africa, particularly in the post-colonial period, from the 1950s. Sometimes, mortality declines in underdeveloped countries have been more rapid than that in Europe, and less sustainable. One of the major mortality declines in the second half of the twentieth century came in sub-Saharan Africa. By the end of the century, mortality among children under 5 had decreased from about 500 per 1,000 to about 150. Similarly, the average life expectancy, which was less than 30 years about 100 years ago, increased to more than 50 years by the early 1990s. These too have been explained in terms of medical intervention through global and local measures in the control of epidemic diseases such as cholera, plague, malaria, vaccination campaigns, as well as in terms of economic growth.

However, mortality decline stalled and even reversed in many African nations from the 1990s. This is largely because of **AIDS**. By 2000, AIDS killed a million people every year, making it the world's biggest killer, and 95 per cent of these deaths took place in the developing countries, particularly sub-Saharan Africa. AIDS, more than any other disearse, has exposed the fact that global health, whether in inner-city New York or in Botswana, is a product of social and economic deprivation. HIV and tuberculosis spread particularly in those regions and among those communities which suffer from economic marginalization and lack of drugs and other medical facilities. Varying access to resources, political power, education, health care and legal services are examples of such structural problems. Similarly, the inequitable distribution of medical facilities in India – which suffers from a growing divergence in wealth and resources between poor and rich, where 30 per cent of the population is still under the poverty line and faces starvation and malnutrition, and where 71 per cent of the people do not have public or private health cover – has become critical.

Hebron massacre (1929)

According to the Hebrew Bible, Abraham was the first Jew to visit Hebron, stopping there to purchase the Cave of Machpelah as his family graveyard. King David chose Hebron as his royal capital. Hebron thereafter became a place of Jewish residence, study, prayer, retirement and pilgrimage. In 1929 Hebron had approximately 700 Jewish inhabitants out of a total population of 16,000. The city had a Jewish hospital and several rabbinical academies, notably the Slobodka Yeshiva. A well-planned Arab assault in that year resulted in sixty Jewish deaths, sixty wounded, and the main synagogue destroyed. The surviving Jews left. In 1931 thirty-five families returned, only to be evacuated by the British five years later during the **Arab revolt**. During the June 1967 **Six Day War**, **Israel** captured Hebron from **Jordan**. In 1968 Jews began to return.

Hebron massacre (1994)

The killing by Baruch Goldstein, a member of the far-right Israeli Kach movement, of twenty-nine unarmed Palestinian Muslim worshippers in the Ibrahim Mosque at the Cave of the Patriarchs at Hebron in the Israeli-occupied West Bank on 25 February 1994. A further 125 worshippers were wounded, and Goldstein was beaten to death by the survivors after he had run out of ammunition. Goldstein, who had emigrated from New York, 1983, and worked as a physician, had poured acid over the carpets inside the mosque, October 1993, and the Muslim authorities had written to the Israeli prime minister 'regarding the dangers'. The massacre provoked rioting across the West Bank and a further nineteen Palestinians were killed by the Israeli Defence Forces in the ensuing forty-eight hours. Although the great majority of Jews both inside and outside **Israel** condemned the massacre, a few rabbis and a number of settlers praised him as a martyr. A shrine was built at his burial site but demolished by the Israeli Army, 1999.

Hegel, Georg Wilhelm Friedrich (1770–1831)

A German philosopher who developed the ideas of historicism and idealism, dialectical synthesis, phenomenology and historical progress towards a moral end point. His ideas thus introduced concepts which would be of great value to **Karl Marx**, on the Left, and to British positivists. German philosophers in the twentieth century tended to define themselves against him, but words and phrases which he introduced – such as the concept of a *zeitgeist*, or an end of history, or the crepuscular influence of history on wisdom, have made their way into everyday language.

Hejaz railway

In 1908 the **Ottoman Empire** inaugurated a railway line connecting Damascus to Medina, ostensibly to ease the journey of those participating in the **hajj**. Unlike other railways in the empire, funded by European capital, the Ottoman government paid for and constructed the Hijaz railway with its own funds and donations from the global Muslim community. Sultan Abdul Hamid hoped to enhance his credibility among Muslims worldwide by coupling his modernization campaigns with the core symbols of the Islamic faith, the holy cities.

Helsinki Agreement

A term for the agreements reached between the American administration of **Gerald Ford** and the Soviet government in 1975 at Helsinki, in **Finland**. The agreements concluded with a declaration that both sides in the **Cold War** would accept and uphold the self-determination of peoples, **human rights**, sporting links and respect for freedom of conscience and faith. Though truisms in the West, there was some support for the idea that the effect of the agreements in the East was to expose the problems of communist states in dealing with **dissidents**. Many of the latter group associated themselves with human rights campaigns based around the agreements from 1976 onwards, and the self-confidence of Soviet ideologues suffered accordingly. The agreements, seen as one of the last acts of **détente**, may therefore also represent the slow but corrosive potential of human rights ideas on totalitarian states which adopt them, however cynically.

Henry, Patrick (1736–1799)

Patrick Henry was a Virginia legislator most famous for his speech 'Give me liberty, or give me death!', delivered in 1775 to convince the Virginia Convention to support military action against British forces in New England. Henry had risen to prominence as a legislator during the **Stamp Act** crisis of the 1760s. He would later serve as governor of Virginia, and was a notable opponent of ratification of the Federal Constitution.

Herero

– *see* **Namibia**.

Herzl, Theodor (1860–1904)

Herzl was the man who launched political **Zionism**, the movement to establish a Jewish homeland, amongst whom political mobilization as a nation had hitherto been an unknown and meaningless concept. A Jew of Austro-Hungarian origin, he was strongly influenced by encountering the same anti-Semitism in Paris, where he was a press correspondent, as he had in Vienna, which persuaded him that the answer to **anti-Semitism** was not the assimilation in which he had previously believed but emigration to a Jewish homeland. That perception was powerfully reinforced by the anti-Semitism which erupted in France during the **Dreyfus affair**, 1894–1906. Herzl claimed that it was the Dreyfus affair which had made him a Zionist. In Vienna, in February 1896, he published *Der Judenstaat* (*The Jewish State*), in which he claimed that the Jewish question was not a social or religious question but a national question, which was 'a political world question to be discussed and settled by the civilized nations of the world in council'. Failing to mobilize English Jews in support of his Zionist programme, he responded by organizing a world congress of Zionists, which was finally held in Basel in August 1897. The three-day world congress attracted some 200 delegates, mainly from central and eastern Europe including the **Russian Empire** but also a few from western Europe and the **United States**, of all social classes, together with some sympathetic Christians. The congress adopted the Basel Programme which declared that 'Zionism aspires to create a publicly guaranteed homeland for the Jewish people in the land of Israel', as well as establishing the Zionist Organization with Herzl as president.

Herzl then established a German-language Zionist weekly newspaper in Vienna, *Die Welt* (*The World*), and tried without success to negotiate with the Ottoman sultan a charter to permit the establishment of an autonomous large-scale Jewish settlement in **Palestine**. He had more success with the British, who might have been willing to see a Jewish settlement in British territory in the Sinai peninsula and, when that proved abortive, proposed 15,500 square kilometres of uninhabited **Uganda** as an alternative. Both Herzl and some other Zionists were willing to accept the Uganda proposal, but it was violently opposed at the 1903 Zionist congress, particularly by the delegates from the Russian Empire. It was a divide which Herzl could not bridge before his death. His remains were transferred from Vienna to Mount Herzl in **Jerusalem** in accordance with his hope, after the foundation of the Israeli state, in 1949. The Israeli city of Herzliyya is named after him.

Hezbollah

A militant **Shi'ite** organization established by Lebanese clergy after the Israeli invasion of 1982, and aimed at driving **Israel** out of **Lebanon** and establishing an Islamic state. It has played a political as well as a military role and, with its allies, largely comprised the October 2012 Lebanese government of Najib Makati. It enjoys considerable support from Shi'ite **Iran**. Responsible for numerous sophisticated attacks on US and Israeli targets, it was accused of involvement in the 2005 assassination of Rafiq al-Hariri, a former Lebanese prime minister. Hezbollah has been additionally motivated by the assassination, probably at Israeli behest, of Iranian nuclear physicists since 2011. It refutes as Israeli smears allegations that it has ties with international drug cartels and crime syndicates. All or parts of Hezbollah are classified as terrorist organizations by Israel, **Canada**, the **USA** and the **EU**. It intervened in the **Syrian Civil War** in 2013.

Hidalgo (y Costilla), Miguel (1753–1811)

Mexican priest and independence leader. Ordained in 1778, Hidalgo quickly rose to become rector of the Colegio de San Nicolás. Unorthodox theological opinions, radical political views and personal indiscretions derailed his academic career. While serving as parish priest in the town of Dolores, he joined other frustrated Creoles in organizing an anti-government conspiracy. Faced with arrest, he issued a call to arms, the *Grito de Dolores*, on 16 September 1810. He soon took the cities of Guanajuato, Celaya and Valladolid with a force that numbered nearly 80,000 rebels. But his call for the abolition of slavery and Indian tribute, and the violence of his peasant supporters, alienated colonial elites; moreover, his poorly armed and

inexperienced troops ultimately proved no match for the viceregal army. Bloody defeats near Mexico City forced Hidalgo to retreat north. Captured in March 1811, he was defrocked, excommunicated and executed.

high life

A music genre originating in **Ghana** in the early twentieth century. High life combines African, Caribbean and American musical influences and is characterized by jazz rhythms and a big band sound led by horns and multiple guitars. The heyday of high life came during the era of independence in the 1950s and 1960s, when the style spread across west African dance floors. More recently, highlife music has developed a more up-tempo, synthesized sound.

Himmler, Heinrich (1900–1945)

– *see also* **Holocaust**; **Nazism**.

German Nazi leader, chief of police and mass murderer. An early member of the Nazi Party, he was involved in the Munich putsch of 1923. Head of **Hitler's** bodyguard, the **SS**, from 1929, and of the **Gestapo** from 1934, subsequently of all police forces from 1936. Head of Reich administration from 1939, he became minister of the interior in 1943 and commander-in-chief of home forces, 1944. A major architect of the Nazi totalitarian state, he also bore central responsibility for carrying out the **Holocaust**. Loyal to Hitler almost to the end, he attempted to negotiate surrender in 1945. Arraigned at the **Nuremberg trials**, he committed suicide.

Hindenburg, Paul von (1847–1934)

The victor of Tannenberg and the Masaurian Lakes in **World War I**, chief of staff of the German Army (1916), a member of the Supreme Command (until 1918) and president of **Germany** from 1925. He was re-elected in 1932. He appointed **Hitler** as chancellor (a decision he regetted), allowed the new leader an election after the Reichstag fire, and signed the emergency decrees which suspended the Weimar Republic. Although he considered declaring martial law and governing personally in 1934, he was for most of his second term too ill and weak to do anything other than see his prestige and popularity gradually co-opted by the Nazis. On his death, Hitler called a referendum to merge the offices of leader and chancellor, taking supreme power in Germany for himself.

Hindu Mahasabha

Although a fringe Hindu communalist organization at its inception in 1915, it gained political prominence under the leadership of V. D. Savarkar in the 1930s. Its advocacy of a Hindu nation excluded other religious groups, especially Indian Muslims. The establishment of the Rashtriya Swayam Sevak Sangh in 1925 gave the Mahasabha a militant character. In 1947 it called for partition of **Bengal** and Punjab. It became a part of the Bharatiya Jan Sangh (a forerunner of the **Bharatiya Janata Party**) in 1951.

Hinduism

Hinduism is a mixture of beliefs and ideas subsisting in a religious system which can be traced back several millennia. It is intimately associated with the Indus valley (a source of the name) and therefore with **India** and the Indian diaspora. By number of adherents, it is the third largest religion on earth, but unlike **Christianity** and **Islam** it is not associated with any essential, ongoing or historic need to proselytyze and convert new believers. Given its longevity, it has also undergone several major revisions and regenerations. As a consequence, while it is possible to write that the tradition looks to no single scripture, hierarchy, eschatology or doctrine, there are significant numbers of believers who argue for commonality with western religions on the basis of the Vedic texts, the supremacy of the Brahman spirit which infuses the world, and the existence of holy men and interpreters who might correspond to a priesthood. In this analysis, gods, and other supernatural beings, are simply manifestations of the ineffable Supreme, which corresponds to St Anselm's ultimate imaginable being as much as to Tillich's Ground of Being. This allows for a plurality of forms of worship, but maintains the coherence of the whole. It also helps to explain the multiplicity of forms of Hinduism, which is replete with holy days, icons, statues and ritual.

A tendency towards integration can be observed in the transition from chants, rituals and texts known as the *veda* to a framework laid out around 3,000 years ago in the *Upanishads*, which culminated in the *Bhagavad Gita*. This compilation was in itself supplemented, however, by the development of epic poetry over the next thousand years, and by break-away movements such as Buddhism, which fed syncretistically back into Hindu thought and ritual. The first thousand years of the Christian era then saw a further elaboration, partly in the face of Islamic invasion, and more personal aspects of Brahma, such as Krishna and Rama, began to emerge as gods in the Indian canon. From the period of European invasion, the consolidation was filtered through both an incentive and a desire to counterbalance Christian monotheism

which resulted in further attempts to develop scriptures and beliefs that could be held in common, both on the part of western philosophers, the British administration, and Hindu thinkers. This is why, for some scholars, the idea of Hinduism as more than a broad ethical system overlying a theological plurality is an orientalist, modern and specifically Indo-British construct. Nevertheless, key ideas have been maintained in modern Hinduism, such as those of reincarnation, the consequentialist morality of karma, the indestructibility of the soul, the ethical necessity of a duty concept known as Dharma, and the viability of multiple routes to the union of mind and feeling which can be found through physical practices known as yoga. It is also possible to be Hindu while being atheist; indeed, the idea of Brahman as a ground of being, from some logical perspectives, requires this. This in no way eliminates the devas, or gods of the canon, since they simply reflect the recurrence of manifestation in the universe, but it does elevate the idea of individual contemplation, mantras and salvation through the divestment of the world's concerns in some Hindu schools. Hinduism tends to place an emphasis on karma as a form of right behaviour which ultimately reveals the transitoriness and meaninglessness of the sensual, and often leads to asceticism. However, the tradition is so rich that this isolation of some believers must be seen in the context of the emphasis on family and communal ritual which allows it to be sustained.

During the twentieth century Hinduism became prominent in four separate ways. Firstly, it functioned as an alternative system of thought and behaviour for those, such as **Mohandas Gandhi**, who wished to reject western domination in favour of the reassertion of Indian sovereignty. This in itself forced a re-evaluation of the religion, as at the beginning of the independence movement, more were inclined to follow the representative contempt demonstrated by **Winston Churchill** amongst others for the faith than to accredit it an equal status to established western beliefs. However, Gandhi's deep association with Hinduism led, in his view tragically, to an association of India with 'Hindustani' ideas of national religious identity, which in itself may have fed ethnic divisions and approaches to poverty and class within the new Indian state. Secondly, by the 1950s the interest of western minorities in aspects of Hindu practice and experience exploded into a desire to experience life lessons, to grow through vegetarianism and yogic practice, and to move beyond the West on the part of many westerners.

The Beatles, a phenomenally popular musical combination and in some ways the trendsetters of modern music, were, for instance, highly influenced by the beliefs of the Maharishi Mahesh Yogi from 1968 onwards. In this, they joined what became millions of American, European and Australian youth who wished to find an alternative perspective to that of industrial modernity. 'Yoga', in the form of a stylized combination of physical and spiritual exercise, became a mainstream occupation in middle-class communities across the West (though not, interestingly, in East Asia or the communist world). Some Christian divines even attempted to incorporate Brahmanic ideas into their thought, a process best seen perhaps in the works of Fathers Pierre Johanns or Pierre Teilhard de Chardin (1881–1955), both of the Society of Jesus. Whilst officially rejected, enough of the concepts of Catholic-Hindu coincidence, the idea of karma as conveying an everyday reward or punishment for actions in everyday life, and the possibility of reincarnation entered the popular and religious consciousness for western horizons to be permanently changed.

Thirdly, in the later twentieth century Hindu nationalism in India manifested in the form of the rise of a new party, the **Bharatiya Janata Party** (BJP) or Indian People's Party, which became a major party in the state and alternated in government. BJP leaders propounded the idea of Hindutva, which held that Indian culture and nationhood was based on Hinduism. This led to a political project involving the construction or defence of temples, an attempt to systematize scriptural beliefs and a sensitivity to the abuse or exploitation of cattle, as these were revered. Under Narendra Modi, the BJP has developed an appeal among those for whom status in the ancient Indian classification of people associated with the caste system has created a resentment of Indian elites and their perceived westernism. A final aspect of Hinduism in the twentieth and twenty-first centuries has been manifested in the attempt to create a usable version of Hindu law, political perspective and philosophy separate from BJP ideas.

Hirohito (1901–1989)

Emperor of **Japan** from 1926, as Crown Prince he was the first to travel abroad. Regent from 1921 when his father became incapable, he was largely aloof from politics, as emperor, during war with **China** in 1936 and the Japanese war on America and the West from 1941. He decisively intervened to support unconditional surrender in August 1945, breaking precedent to broadcast

to the nation. Controversially protected from war crimes charges as part of the process of rehabilitating Japan, he became a constitutional monarch under the new constitution imposed by the Americans in 1946. Abdicating his 'divine' status in January 1946, he remained the symbol of the Japanese nation and ensured continuity into the post-war era.

Hiroshima, bombing of

– *see also* **atomic bomb**.

On 6 August 1945 a United States B-29 bomber dropped an atomic bomb on the city of Hiroshima Prefecture in south-western **Japan**, causing an estimated 80,000 deaths and destroying 68 per cent of the city (an estimated 60,000 died subsequently from the effects of the bomb). This was followed three days later by the bombing of Nagasaki, unconditional surrender on 10 August, and public proclamation of the Imperial Rescript on Surrender on 15 August. Hiroshima was proclaimed the City of Peace in 1949 and became the centre of the post-war peace movement. With the famous slogan, 'No more Hiroshima', civil society networks organized anti-war and anti-nuclear movements, which gained worldwide attention. Hiroshima has been rebuilt as an industrial and business centre, and it holds an annual commemoration for the victims in the Hiroshima Peace Memorial Park and maintains the Atomic Bomb Dome as a reminder of Hiroshima's nuclear experience.

Hispanics (US)

In the **United States** this normally refers to people with ancestry in Hispanic America. There have long been Hispanics within the US, especially in California, **Texas**, Arizona and New Mexico, though from the mid twentieth century they were supplemented by new migrant streams. At least 400,000 Puerto Ricans migrated to New York City in 1945–60. Approximately a million migrants came from **Cuba** after **Castro** gained power in 1959. A major source of Hispanics has been the continuous arrivals from Mexico, 28 million identifying themselves as being of Mexican ancestry in 2006. There have been much smaller numbers from the Caribbean and South America. Most are white, though there are also black Hispanics and some of mixed race. Many are bilingual, though some speak only English or Spanish. From a diversity of national and cultural origins, together Hispanics now comprise the largest ethnic group in the United States with just under 14 per cent of the population, and are an increasingly important part of the political equation.

Histadrut

In 1920 **David Ben-Gurion** helped establish the Histadrut labour federation and, in 1930, the Histadrut-affiliated Labor Party (**Mapai**). Under Ben-Gurion's leadership, Histadrut steered a centrist political course 'without the Communists and without the Revisionists'. Histadrut considered settlement activity as the best way to achieve Zionist objectives. It trained young people in agriculture and industrial activities; founded the construction firm Solel Boneh and other industrial, agricultural and transportation cooperatives; established a full-service medical programme (Kupat Holim); merged its funds into Bank ha-Po'alim (1958); and sponsored a massive publication programme, including the newspaper *Davar* (1925) and the book publishing house Am Oved, in 1942. Histadrut's membership was 184,000 at the time of the rebirth of the state of Israel in 1948. It is now the largest organization in **Israel**, with about half of the population affiliated to it.

Hitler, Adolf (1889–1945)

– *see also* **Nazism; World War II**.

Leader of the National Socialist German Workers' Party (the Nazis), 1921–45; chancellor of **Germany**, 1933–45; president and leader (fuhrer) of Third Reich Germany, 1934–45. Hitler's name has become a byword for tyrannical madness, war, murder, demagogic speech and anti-Semitism and is often invoked as an example which can end debate. Hitler presided over and inspired (and probably ordered) the **Holocaust** of 1941–4, and was directly responsible for **World War II**, which cost some 100 million lives.

Hitler was born in Austria and grew up as the son of a customs officer, Alois, and a doting mother. He seems to have had a normal childhood, but developed an idea of himself as an artist in his teens. Rejected from leading art schools despite some talent, he became a vagrant until the outbreak of war in 1914. He refused to join the Austrian forces, which he saw as 'mongrel' because of their mix of different ethnic groups, and instead enrolled in the German Army, where he undertook dangerous missions as a bicycle messenger on the battlefield and rose to the rank of corporal, gaining the Iron Cross in the process. He suffered in an attack of poison gas and his recovery took place at the time of Germany's surrender whilst still on enemy soil in 1918. This experience, and the death of his mother before the war, seem to have combined to bring forth a deep hatred of Jews, democrats, socialists and others he held responsible for his condition.

The German Army, engaged in clandestine monitoring of and interference with politics, brought him into contact with the German Workers Party as an agent shortly afterward, and he swiftly displaced the leadership of that party. Renaming it the National Socialist Party, he attempted to use his considerable gift of stirring base emotions through speech to create a revolution in Bavaria in 1923. His attempted putsch failed in the face of strong local military resistance and he was sentenced to prison by a lenient judge for a short term. In prison, he developed ideas of *Lebensraum* and Aryanism which he proclaimed in **Mein Kampf** (My Struggle, 1925–6).

Hitler's primary ideas were twin. Firstly, he thought that Germany as a nation should be the expression of a racial group he identified as 'Aryans', characterized by blonde hair, blue eyes and a militaristic disposition, and that this group was threatened by an international conspiracy of Jews and 'Jewish Bolshevik communism' allied to Jewish capitalist interests in an attempt to subvert all other racial groups whilst keeping themselves pure. A strong collective government was therefore needed to purify, strengthen and advance the Aryan race at the same time as eliminating this Jewish threat. Secondly, he thought that Germany had been badly treated by the **Treaty of Versailles** and he wished to bring together all German-speaking peoples in a large new reich that would necessarily require 'living room' in the east of Europe. This living room of resources and farms would be acquired by displacing or enslaving the existing 'Slavic' races of 'subhumans' or *untermenschen* and replacing them with Germanic superior humans or 'supermen', and would have as a corollary the elimination of communist threats to the West.

Initially unsuccessful in politics, Hitler began to assume the leadership of the German extreme right, and was a serious candidate for president in 1928. He was beaten, though his Nazi Party acquired the backing of a great many financial interests, developed a strong if chaotic organization, and advanced its techniques of propaganda and intimidation through media manipulation and a large paramilitary party army of 'storm troopers'. As the world spiralled into the **Great Depression**, Hitler's message of blame and pride and the welfare programmes and uniforms provided by the Storm Troopers (**SA**), as well as his violent resistance to communism, attracted both voters, businessmen and the interest of the army. Hitler's party won around a third of the potential vote in the 1932 Reichstag elections and, to keep out the Left, other right-wing parties allied to the Catholic Centre Party to bring Hitler and his deputy Goering to power in 1933 at the head of a coalition government, as chancellor and police Minister of Prussia respectively. Hitler moved swiftly to promote the plans of the central bank to reflate the economy and end the depression with public works and government spending, and then took advantage of a fire at the German parliament to declare a state of emergency and lock up communists, socialists, liberals and other opponents. A period of consolidation with the connivance of the army followed, which resulted in Hitler's elimination of his internal party enemies and the suppression of the SA in the Night of the Long Knives of July 1934. Hitler then found himself unchallenged leader of Germany. He initially used this position to concentrate on economic reconstruction and rearmament, but by 1935 he had taken the first steps to undermine the **Versailles treaty** by reoccupying the Rhineland. He met with no resistance from western powers, which emboldened him; he intervened covertly in the **Spanish Civil War**, laid plans for a war-fighting air force, and began to progress to the absorption of **Austria** in the *Anschluss* of 1938; the partition and domination of Czechoslovakia followed later that year, which led ultimately to the Hitler–Stalin pact that led to the destruction of **Poland** and the beginning of World War II in September 1939.

Hitler's war began slowly, but by the summer of 1940 he had defeated the British in **Norway**, invaded the Low Countries and conquered **France**, and threatened to defeat **Britain**. Britain's successful resistance in the Battle of Britain and its determination to fight under **Winston Churchill** upset his plans, but in 1941 his plans to invade the east and to eliminate the Jews culminated in the Barbarossa attack on the **USSR**. Hitler was almost successful in his war on Russia, only being halted at the gates of Moscow and at Stalingrad a year later. Meanwhile, the Holocaust murdered over 6 million Jews, in addition to millions more political opponents, Slavs, Roma and homosexuals, coming close to wiping out European Jewry. However, the determined resistance of the USSR under **Joseph Stalin**, which lost some 20 million lives in the war to 1945, and the rash declaration of war against the **USA** in support of his Japanese Axis allies in 1941, ultimately sealed Hitler's fate. In spring 1945 the USSR and its western allies converged upon a defeated Germany, and on 30 April, Hitler, determined to leave nothing behind, committed suicide in his Berlin bunker with his new wife and dog. His body was burned and its few, unrecognizable remains captured but kept secret by Soviet forces until their ultimate destruction in 1972.

HIV
– see **AIDs**.

Hizbul Mujahideen
Founded in 1989 as the militant wing of the Kashmiri political organization Jamaat-i-Islami to provide an Islamic counter to the mostly secular Jammu and Kashmir Liberation Front, it is based in Pakistani-controlled Kashmir, and is active in the insurgency against the Indian government in the Indian state of **Jammu and Kashmir**. Headed by Syed Salahuddin, the group favours the integration of Jammu and Kashmir into Pakistan, and is considered a terrorist organization by the **EU** and **USA**.

Ho Chi Minh (1890–1969)
President of the Democratic Republic of Vietnam (**North Vietnam**) and chairman of the Vietnamese Workers' (Communist) Party. He was born Nguyen Tat Thanh, the son of a minor official in rural Vietnam, then part of French Indochina. An elementary school teacher, 1907, after being educated in a Franco-Annamite school, he worked as a steward on an ocean liner from 1912, gaining knowledge of European and other countries, before being employed as a kitchen hand in London's Carlton Hotel. He moved to Paris towards the end of **World War I**, earning a living by retouching photographs. He turned to politics, seemingly primarily motivated by a determination to secure justice for the non-white peoples of the world, not least black Americans, and to free them from the contempt displayed by the dominant whites. Vainly he tried to meet America's President Wilson during the post-war Versailles negotiations to seek his help in improving Vietnamese conditions. He joined the French Socialist Party and established the Inter-Colonial Union, a group of nationalists of colonial origin resident in Paris, editing its paper, *Le Paria*, as well as contributing articles to the Socialists' *Le Populaire*. He voted for the Third International at the Socialist Congress in 1920, and was a founder member of the French Communist Party. As such, he attended the **Comintern** Congress in Moscow, 1922, and remained there until 1925 as a student at the Toilers of the East University. He knew **Lenin** personally, accompanied the Borodin Mission to **China**, working as a translator in the Russian consulate in Canton and formed the Vietnamese

Revolutionary Youth League in which Soviet instructors trained young nationalists at Whampoa Military Academy.

In 1930 he founded the Vietnamese, later Indochinese, Communist Party in **Hong Kong**, but was arrested there the following year. Released, 1932, he was smuggled to Amoy despite a French application for his extradition. It is thought he visited Yenan, China, in the late 1930s, where he appears to have found **Mao Zedong** uncongenial. He joined Vietnamese exiles near the border, 1940, and formed the communist-dominated **Viet Minh**, which resisted the Japanese, at Chingsi, 1941. Imprisoned by Nationalist China, 1942–3, he then formally adopted, after many aliases, the name Ho Chi Minh (meaning 'Ho who seeks enlightenment'). He proclaimed the Communist-affiliated Democratic Republic of Vietnam under his own leadership in Hanoi immediately after the Japanese surrender and maintained it against the occupying Chinese, the returning French and his Vietnamese rivals until 1946. He went to war with the French after the breakdown of negotiations in November 1946, his forces, benefiting from Communist Chinese aid, finally defeating them at **Dien Bien Phu**, 1954. He became president of the north when the Geneva conference and the implementing **Indo-Chinese Treaty** partitioned Vietnam in 1954. He was obliged as the north's president to recognize China's war aid by initiating Chinese-style land reforms which proved totally unsuited to Vietnamese conditions and provoked peasant unrest. Spearhead of the Communist struggle in the civil war which broke out in the south and which increasingly became a nationalist war against the Americans, he did not live to see the final victory and reunification. Saigon was renamed Ho Chi Minh City in his honour. Personal charm, humour, linguistic ability and political intelligence gave this intensely secretive man a quite disproportionate influence, as recognized in the fact that 'Uncle Ho' is as publicly familiar as 'Uncle Joe' (Stalin) to the English-speaking world.

Ho Chi Minh Trail

– *see also* **Vietnam War**.

American term for the 16,000-kilometre (9,942-mile) network of roads and paths running from the Democratic Republic of (North) **Vietnam** through neighbouring Laos and Cambodia into the Republic of (South) Vietnam during the 1959–75 **Vietnam War**. The trail, named after the North Vietnamese president, facilitated movement of troops and supplies for the struggle waged by the northern People's Army of Vietnam and the

National Front for the Liberation of South Vietnam (the **Vietcong**).

Hollywood

– *see also* **cinema**.

This village became part of the City of Los Angeles in 1910, the year D. W. Griffith led the movie business from the east coast to this spot where the steadily sunny weather allowed for outdoor shooting for lengthy periods. By 1920 Hollywood was the film capital of the world. In the 1930s the studios Fox, MGM, Paramount, RKO, Warner Brothers, Columbia, Universal and United Artists controlled the business. **World War II** increased demand and Hollywood had its most profitable year in 1946. But in the 1950s competition from television and the loss of exhibition control undermined the dominance of the film companies. The television industry and major record firms were also based in Hollywood. Since the 1960s the studios have largely moved elsewhere in Los Angeles and the entertainment business has become far more international in its structure. However Hollywood is still widely seen as synonymous with the film and television business.

Holocaust

– *see also* **anti-Semitism; genocide; human rights; Jewish peoples**.

A collective term for a series of escalating actions taken by the Nazi regime between 1941 and 1945 which had as its aim the removal, exploitation and murder of the Jewish peoples of Europe by industrial means. It is known in Hebrew as the Shoah. The action gave rise to the definition of **genocide** after **World War II**. Called by the Nazis the 'Final Solution' (to a putative 'Jewish problem'), the idea represented the logical extension of the policies of **Adolf Hitler** and the National Socialist movement in **Germany**. Hitler viewed Jews as a racial threat, partly because Jewish communities maintained cultural distinctiveness across generations and partly because of a pseudo-scientific confusion of genes with culture which led him to an exaggerated fear of racial mixing and cultural decline. On coming to power, his initial plan was to exclude Jewish people from the civil service, and then from the economy, before driving people from Germany. This policy moved quickly to one of segregation, intimidation and potential exile to a national homeland elsewhere. Between 1933 and 1938 Jews were subject to increasing pressure, which broke into an orgy of violence on Kristallnacht in November 1938.

A policy of asset-stripping and ghettoization then followed.

Following Nazi successes in **Poland** and in the initial Barabarossa campaign, the occupation of areas containing huge Jewish populations changed the question. In 1941, Hitler and Goering tasked the **SS** under **Heinrich Himmler** and Reynard Heydrich with the production of an operation, which Himmler revealed in 1943, to require the physical elimination of Jews. Initially, the SS made efforts to build upon existing technology and the opportunistic destruction of particular areas, in pogrom fashion. However, after experimentation with carbon monoxide gassing, mass shootings and the use of special *einsatzgruppe* extermination forces, the Wannsee conference of 1942 settled on the idea of removing captured Jews by rail to extermination and slave labour camps, mainly in former Polish territory, alongside political opponents, Roma, homosexuals and Soviet and other prisoners of war. This operation was known as 'Reinhard' given the guiding influence of Heydrich. Though the camps built on lessons of construction and organization acquired from concentration camps, they were not, strictly speaking, the same thing. These were death or extermination camps, of which eventually there were six in Poland; Auschwitz, Sobibor, Treblinka, Majdenek, Belzec and Chelmno (of which Auschwitz-Birkenau was the most notorious). In 1942 a camp was added near Minsk, and the Jasenovac camp in Croatia which began operations in 1941 was also part of the system. In these extermination or death camps, human medical experimentation, slave labour and the deliberate destruction by gassing and cremation of large numbers of people took place. Cumulatively, these camps murdered almost 4 million, advancing in productivity as carbon monoxide was replaced with the cyanide chemical zyklon-B. Further deaths accompanied the Nazi retreat, via mobile facilities or 'death marches', leading to a total of over 6 million deaths.

The Nazis made great efforts to conceal the Holocaust and the associated murders of Roma and Slavic peoples which, by different methods, may have killed up to 5 million more. The **Nuremberg trials** in 1946, however, indicted the Nazi leadership of crimes against humanity and war crimes and began to formulate the legal concept of genocide for the wholesale destruction of European Jewry. But in spite of Nuremberg and trials of low-ranking figures in the Nazi hierarchy for their part in mass killing, in the years after 1945 the Holocaust tended to be subsumed in the larger horror and destruction of World War II. Denial affected not only many Germans but also large parts of eastern Europe where virulent anti-Semitism in the **Soviet Union** during the last years of **Stalin** also restricted acknowledgement of the full extent and nature of what the Nazis had perpetrated. Published accounts were relatively rare and many of the survivors, such as Primo Levi (1919–87), notable for his memoir of the camps, *If this is a Man* (1947), expressed the difficulty of articulating their experiences in a post-war world concentrated on reconstruction and the beginning of the **Cold War**. However, a major landmark in discussion of the Holocaust came with the trial and execution in 1961–2 in Israel of Adolf Eichmann, who played a principal part in implementing the exermination of the Jews. The publicity given to survivors' accounts lifted the veil of reticence surrounding the Holocaust, stimulating both academic research into Nazi policy and public recognition of it in memorials, museums and commemoration days. The designation of the former concentration camp at **Auschwitz** in Poland as a World Heritage site in 1979 and a museum to the Holocaust marked a significant point in recognition of its place in twentieth-century history. The fall of the Communist governments in the former Soviet bloc from 1989 also opened up the history and archives of areas subjugated by the Nazis to fresh investigation.

The historiography of the Holocaust is now considerable. Arguments about the specific role of Hitler's worldview and a direct continuum between his obsession with the Jews expressed in *Mein Kampf* and their physical destruction in the Holocaust have vied with explanations which relate more to an ad hoc process of dealing with the Jewish 'problem', which took a radical turn following the German conquest of Poland and large parts of the former Soviet Union, including the former **Baltic States**. That such a radical turn to a 'final solution' of mass extermination in 1941–2 is evident, but it could not have taken place without Hitler's clear support. His obsession with the Jews, in conjunction with the contingent events of the war, produced systematized mass murder not only in the areas of direct conquest but also of Jews throughout Nazi-occupied Europe. Hitler had ideological followers, particularly in the **SS**, and complicit anti-Semites assisted him in many parts of Europe, not only in the east, but it was his paranoid hatred which allowed the mass killing to take place.

The prevention of a new holocaust and of the conditions that might engender one, such as a return of mass unemployment and the polarizaton of democratic politics into extremes, particularly of the Right, has become the leitmotif of western, liberal societies since World War II. It has influenced a number of responses ranging from economic and humanitarian interventions such as the **Marshall Plan**, the creation of the **European Union** and support for the creation of the state of **Israel**. 'Holocaust denial' is a crime in some countries, as is incitement to racial violence.

Holy Roman Empire

Founded by Charlemagne, AD 800, but 'Holy' only from 1157 and a German rather than a universalist institution by the late fifteenth century (*Sacrum Romanum Imperium Nationis Germanicae*). Without permanent institutions, and theoretically elective but in practice hereditary, it had already become by the beginning of the eighteenth century little more than a loose federation of the autonomous German princes under Habsburg leadership. It came to its formal end when Emperor Francis II of **Austria** resigned the imperial Roman title to stop **Napoleon** becoming emperor himself in 1806. The medieval empire was deemed by unified Germany in 1871 to have been the First Reich, and the new empire to be the Second Reich. Nazi Germany, 1933–45, was thus the **Third Reich**. Despite its lack of political substance, the empire retained some symbolic resonance, and its remembrance of Charlemagne's rule over **France**, **Germany** and **Italy** from Aachen contributed to the thinking of the founding fathers of the future **European Union** (EU).

Homestead Strike (1892) (USA)

Strike and lock-out by Amalgamated Association of Iron and Steel Workers at Carnegie steel works in Pittsburgh. The strike was precipitated by new company president, Henry Frick, who attempted to reduce the workforce and smash the union. The strike saw violent clashes with Pinkerton guards, notably on 6 July 1892 when six workers and three Pinkertons died. State militia were called in, but the strike lasted until November when the union was forced to capitulate.

homesteads (USA)

The Homestead Act (1862) permitted any adult American, citizenship applicant or family head to claim 160 acres of vacant public domain. Title was bestowed after five years provided the homesteader had worked a portion and built a house of a certain size. The scale of the holding was subsequently quadrupled in recognition of the challenges farming faced in the semi-arid west. A total of 270 million acres were granted before repeal in 1976 (extended to 1986 in Alaska).

Honduras

A nation in northern **Central America** that became fully independent from **Spain** in 1821. During the 1800s, Honduras struggled to consolidate its historically fragmented and isolated settlements into a cohesive society. The banana industry brought some political and economic stability late in the century. Growing dependence on this export made Honduras the quintessential banana republic by the early 1900s, as the **United Fruit Company** and the Standard Fruit Company added unprecedented political and social influence to their vast economic power. A close ally of the **United States** during the **Cold War**, Honduras served as a strategic base in the struggle against leftist revolutionaries in neighbouring **El Salvador** and **Nicaragua** during the civil wars of the 1980s. Among the poorest countries in the hemisphere, it has witnessed uneven development in recent years. The country's political system has suffered a long series of military coups.

Hong Kong

Britain was ceded Hong Kong island in 1842, later adding neighbouring territories. Through much of the twentieth century, Hong Kong was a significant port providing access to southern **China**, but its status rose after other Chinese ports closed to the West in 1949. In the post-war period, Hong Kong became a centre for cheap manufacturing, and then from the 1970s, a major regional financial centre. In 1984, China and **Britain** agreed that it would revert to Chinese sovereignty on 1 July 1997 under the 'one country, two systems' formula. Transition passed peacefully, though there have been tensions over full democratic control of the Hong Kong Special Administrative Region, which covers the former colony. These erupted in the protests of 2014, known as the umbrella revolution.

Hoover, Herbert (1874–1964)

The thirty-first president of the **United States**, 1929–33. He was born into a **Quaker** family in West Branch, Iowa, graduated from Stanford University and forged a brilliant career as a mining engineer, travelling widely and amassing wealth. A gifted administrator, he earned worldwide acclaim for orchestrating the provision of food relief to the starving in German-occupied **France** and **Belgium** during **World War I**. In the 1920s he served as Secretary of Commerce in the Republican Harding and Coolidge administrations, impressively transforming his department. Despite these achievements, Hoover's reputation was defined by the **Great Depression**. He trounced Al Smith in the 1928 presidential election, but when the US economy collapsed in 1929 his limitations as a politician were exposed. Reluctant to show empathy for the poor lest it harm confidence, he struggled to adjust his inflexible economic principles to new realities and was defeated by **Roosevelt** in 1932. In later years he became a critic of the **New Deal**.

Hoover, J. Edgar (1895–1972)

A native of Washington DC and a lawyer, Hoover worked for the Federal Bureau of Investigation (FBI) and its precursors from 1919 until his death, from 1924 as director. An able administrator and publicist, he built the bureau into a formidable organization and became one of America's most popular public servants. His **FBI** defeated the Nazi threat in South America amongst other triumphs. But critics accused him of prejudice against blacks, homosexuals, women and political dissidents.

Horton, James Africanus Beale (1835–1882)

Doctor and political theorist. Born the son of a freed slave in **Sierra Leone**, Horton studied medicine in London and Edinburgh, taking the name 'Africanus' to symbolize his racial pride. He served as a military doctor in West Africa, retiring with the rank of Surgeon Major in 1880. Seen as a pioneer African nationalist, Horton's numerous writings include *West African Countries and Peoples* (1868), a criticism of white racial superiority.

Hossain, Rokeya Sakhawat (c. 1880–1932)

A Bengali Muslim writer best known for writing *Sultana's Dream* (1905), a utopian science fiction account of a society in which the roles of men and women were reversed, with the men kept secluded in *purdah*. In addition to advocating women's rights through writings in English and Bengali, Rokeya established Sakhawat Memorial Girls' High School, which is still in operation in **Calcutta**, and presided over the Indian Women's Conference in 1932.

Houphouët-Boigny, Félix

– *see* **Ivory Coast**.

Hountondji, Paulin (1942–2008)

Beninese philosopher and politician. Born in Abidjan, **Ivory Coast**, Hountondji studied philosophy at the École Normale Supérieure in Paris,

where he received his doctorate in 1970. After teaching in **France** and the **Congo**, he accepted a post at the National University of **Benin**. For a brief period he served as Minister of Education and Minister for Culture and Communities during Benin's return to democratic rule in 1992. Hountondji's philosophical work focused on a critique of ethno-philosophy and called for a genuine African philosophy that incorporates and transcends the theoretical heritage of western philosophy.

Hua Guofeng (1921–2008)

Briefly the successor to **Mao Zedong** as leader of **China**,1976–8. His major acts in power were officially to end the **Cultural Revolution**, arrest the **Gang of Four**, and allow a certain amount of political openness. Hua was nominated by Mao as party chairman, but he had little political support, and was outmanoeuvred by the lower-ranking but better connected **Deng Xiaoping**. At the Party Congress of 1978, Hua was stripped of his substantive power and, although he continued to hold official titles, lost any status as a power broker.

Huerta, Victoriano (1850–1916)

Born in rural Jalisco, this Mexican general, with a reputation for ruthless repression of indigenous peoples, usurped the presidency and held it from February 1913 to July 1914. He and General Félix Díaz, nephew of deposed **Porfirio Díaz**, contrived the overthrow of President **Francisco Madero** in Mexico City, an act known as the Tragic Ten Days, and Madero's murder shortly thereafter. The Constitutionalist Revolutionary forces of **Venustiano Carranza, Alvaro Obregón, Emiliano Zapata** and **Pancho Villa** almost immediately revolted against his dictatorship. US President **Woodrow Wilson** opposed his regime and arranged the **Veracruz incident** to prevent weapons from reaching him. With Constitutionalist victories mounting, Huerta fled to **Spain**, then El Paso, **Texas**, in the hope of retaking power (apparently with funds from the German military), but was gaoled on charges of violating US neutrality laws for a year and a half before dying during an operation at Fort Bliss, Texas.

Hugues, Victor (1762–1826)

A wealthy colonist from Saint-Domingue who played an important role in abolishing slavery in Guadeloupe on 4 February 1794. Returning to **France** from Saint-Domingue as the **Haitian Revolution** broke in 1791, he became a Jacobin and was sent to Guadeloupe where he led a revolutionary army of freed slaves who defeated royalist planters and their British allies. Victory allowed him to abolish slavery in Guadeloupe and encouraged him to export the French Revolution to neighbouring islands. Ex-slaves welcomed their emancipation but came to resent Hugues' reorganization of plantation labour in which most remained as peasant labourers. Their opposition, plus continuing planter resentment, led to Hugues' recall from Guadeloupe in 1797. He later returned to the French Caribbean as governor of **French Guiana** in 1799, and after a decade in France returned to the colony as governor in 1817, dying there as a private citizen.

Huk rebellion

The Hukbalahap insurgency occurred in the **Philippines** between 1942 and 1954. The name is a shortened form of Tagalog acronym, meaning anti-Japanese People's Army. After 1945 the Huk groups were connected to issues such as agrarian dissent, and shock at the anti-communist, anti-Huk ferocity of Philippine and US forces with whom they had previously been associated as guerrillas. Operating from the mountains of Luzon, they were highly successful in the face of the instability and political insecurity of the Third, or Independent, Philippine republic that emerged in 1946. In 1950 the tide turned because of their association with the Communists. This led to their ultimate defeat by President **Magsaysay** and the US forces.

human rights

Historically, many law codes have enshrined protections for life, against grievous assault, and dealing with some forms of sexual assault, but the explicit concept of human rights springs from the extension of common law in the Anglo-Saxon world and post-**Enlightenment** concepts of intrinsic human rights. Actions to reduce **capital punishment**, humanize the treatment of criminals, and anti-slavery and abolitionist movements implicitly recognized some principles about the treatment of human beings, and these ideas were extended during **industrialization** in **Factory Acts** and by colonial administrators and missionaries in curtailing inhumane aspects of indigenous cultures such as slavery, wife-burning and human sacrifice. There was also an impetus to humanize warfare through organizations such as the **Red Cross**, and the **Geneva Convention** implicitly recognized the rights of the wounded, prisoners of war and civilians, as well as deeming certain forms of weapons and their use as 'inhumane'.

But as a result of **World War II**, influenced by the **Holocaust** and the widespread ill-treatment of prisoners of war and civilians, exposed in the **Nuremberg trials** of Nazi leaders in 1945–6 and the Tokyo trials of Japanese military and political leaders in 1946–8, the newly formed **United Nations** formulated the view that international law and state behaviour should be based upon the protection of the defined and declared rights of any individual. On 5 December 1948 the United Nations General Assembly passed a Declaration of Human Rights, the first recognition that basic freedoms and rights, regardless of race, sex, nationality or religion, were a matter of international concern. Though passed unanimously, the **Soviet Union**, **South Africa**, **Saudi Arabia** and five east European countries abstained. The declaration did not have legal force but provided the basis for further developments in international law. A European Convention on Human Rights was drafted and agreed by the Council of Europe in 1949 and a European Commission on Human Rights and a European Court of Human Rights established at Strasbourg in 1959.

The European Court developed a body of case law as individual citizens brought cases against their states to uphold their rights, issuing non-binding but indicative decisions which governments were expected to agree to. The system was largely successful in restraining the behaviour of states and, for instance, abolishing the death penalty throughout **Europe** and providing a European-wide model of international law governing human rights cases. Under United Nations auspices several individual human rights agreements were signed on a voluntary basis, for example on **genocide** (1951), **apartheid** (1976) and discrimination against women (1981). In 1976 the original declaration was complemented by a covenant on social, economic and cultural rights (2004) and civil and political rights (2004), covering the right to domicile, freedom of expression, protection of minorities and prohibition of torture. A protocol of 1989 condemned capital punishment but did not command even a bare majority of UN members.

Human rights came to play a significant part in the **Cold War**. Democratic and liberal countries contrasted the positive rights of individual expression, movement, assembly and religion with the state tyranny, control of the media and restrictions on thought and expression found in totalitarian and communist regimes. The existence of the **Gulag** and the treatment of **dissidents** became major issues between the Soviet Union and the

West, leading to the **Helsinki Agreement** to ensure the human rights of dissidents. Similar arguments were laid at the door of Communist China, even following the rapid opening up of **China** from the 1990s, with condemnation of the abrogation of human rights in the suppression of the **Tiananmen Square** demonstration in June 1989 and its aftermath, as well as continuing persecution of individual Chinese dissidents well into the twenty-first century. Similarly, the rule of the Burmese Generals prior to 2015 and of the North Korean regime have been widely criticized for human rights abuses.

While some governments have remained beyond the reach of human rights law, under the authority of the Security Council of the UN, courts have been set up to deal with human rights abuses. In 1993 the International Criminal Tribunal for the former **Yugoslavia** was set up and has tried Serbian leaders for war crimes. An International Criminal Tribunal for **Rwanda** was set up in 1994 and in 2002 the International Criminal Court (ICC) was set up at The Hague to investigate human rights violations in cases of genocide war crimes and crimes against humanity. It acts when national law is inoperative and is accepted by 104 countries. Though the UN was instrumental in bringing it about, it is independent and has adjudicated on human rights abuses in **Darfur, Liberia, Congo** and **Uganda**. In addition to the ICC and UN activities, concern for human rights underlies the activities of a large number of NGOs, some of which are dedicated exclusively to its central place as a touchstone of respectability for states who wish to participate in international organizations and activities. **Amnesty International** and Human Rights Watch are dedicated to the defence of human rights across a wide range of issues, from torture and unlawful imprisonment to the exploitation of child, female and immigrant labour, human trafficking, and denial of asylum for refugees.

Hundred Days of Reform (China)

This was a series of political and social policies enacted by the Guangxu emperor from 11 June to 21 September 1898 in response to the perceived weakness of **China** after defeat in the **first Sino-Japanese War** in 1895. Over a hundred decrees were issued. They were designed to modernize the governmental bureaucracy, education, the economy and the military. The reform movement ended when Empress Dowager **Cixi** staged a coup and placed Guangxu under house arrest.

Hundred Flowers movement (China)

This is the name given to a movement begun by **Mao Zedong** in 1956 in which intellectuals were encouraged to criticize the Chinese Communist Party to push forward the modernization of the country. By the summer of 1957 initial debates on ideology had turned into criticisms of the party, and were being taken up by students and reported in the press. This led to a crackdown in the 'anti-rightist' campaign.

Hungarian Revolution (1956)

The eruption of nationalist, anti-Soviet sentiment, initially stimulated by the reburial, in October 1956, of László Rajk, a former communist foreign minister executed after a show trial, 1949. In the unpredictable climate following **Khrushchev**'s denunciation of **Stalin**, February 1956, Matyas Rakosi, the hardline communist leader, was deposed, and a new government installed, November 1956, under Imre Nagy, an independent communist seeking reform and international neutrality for **Hungary** (as agreed for **Austria**, May 1955). The Soviet Army responded to the appeal of a communist counter-government under Janos Kádár by attacking Budapest the next day, causing considerable loss of life and major damage to buildings. Many Hungarians fled to the West. The severity of the Soviet response, which contrasted with its more restrained approach to the parallel Polish unrest, may have reflected a lack of confidence in Nagy's ability to keep control and an awareness that Hungary had been one of **Hitler**'s loyalest allies.

Hungary

Central European country under Austrian Habsburg rule after 1699. It witnessed unsuccessful independence movements under Ferenc Rákóczi, 1703–11, and **Lajos Kossuth**, 1848–9, but secured equality in the **Austro-Hungarian Empire** with the compromise (*Ausgleich*) of 1867. Declared a republic, 1918, and briefly **communist**, 1919, it lost some two-thirds of its population and territory under the Treaty of Trianon, 1920. A monarchy with Admiral Horthy as regent, 1920–44, it turned increasingly **corporatist** and **fascist**, and entered **World War II** on the German side in 1941. A liberal democracy, 1945–7, it signed a peace treaty in 1947. A People's Republic, 1948–89. Member of **Comecon**, 1949–90, and of **Warsaw Pact**, 1955–91. The country sought neutrality and reform under the independent communist, Imre Nagy, but the **Hungarian Revolution** was defeated in 1956. The ensuing communist regime of Janos

Kádár won popularity on the basis that 'he who is not against us is with us' and the economic liberalism of 'goulash communism'. Alternative parties were legalized, 1988, and in 1989 the **Iron Curtain** began to be dismantled. Liberal democratic elections were held, 1990, the same year it became a member of NATO. It joined the European Union, 2004. Recent years have seen a marked nationalist policy pursued by Hungary.

Huq, Fazlul (1873–1962)

An important Muslim leader from **Bengal**, Huq was a lawyer from the Barisal district who was in the forefront of regional and national politics, first in undivided **India** and then in **Pakistan** for half a century. In 1935 he was elected mayor of **Calcutta**, and then as head of the Krishak Praja Party, he became chief minister of Bengal, 1937 to 1943, by allying first with the **Muslim League** and then with the Congress. In East Pakistan in 1954 he joined a coalition of parties which defeated the Muslim League and was home minister of Pakistan, 1955, and governor of East Pakistan from 1956 to 1958.

Husayn ibn Ali al-Hashimi, Sharif of Mecca (1854–1931)

Sharif of Mecca (1908–16), King of the Hejaz (1916–24) and Caliph (1924). Husayn ibn Ali al-Hashimi served at first as an Ottoman imperial official but on 5 June 1916 he declared an **Arab revolt** against the empire and allied himself with the British. While Husayn remained in Mecca, his sons Faisal (future king of Iraq) and Abdullah (future king of Jordan) provided leadership for the revolt. Meanwhile, Husayn found himself in conflict with the equally ambitious ruler of Najd, **Abd al-Aziz ibn Abd al-Rahman Al Saud**. Britain kept its two allies from fighting against each other throughout the war and the early 1920s, but in 1925 Saudi forces overran the Hejaz en route to the formation of the kingdom of **Saudi Arabia**. Husayn abdicated in favour of his son King Ali ibn Husayn, who ultimately lost to the Saudis. Husayn survived in exile in **Cyprus** and then in **Jordan**, where he died.

Hussein (al-Husayn), King of Jordan (1935–1999)

The son of Prince Talal bin Abdullah and Princess Zein al-Sharaf bint Jamil, Hussein bin Talal was born in Amman in what is now the nation of **Jordan**. Formally educated in both **Egypt** and at a British military academy, the future king remained close to his family. Surviving a successful assassination attempt on his grandfather, **King Abdullah**, at the al-Aqsa Mosque in 1951, Hussein bin Talal's father took over the crown. King Talal ruled for nearly a year before his son became King Hussein in August 1952. Not having reached his majority at the age of 18, a council was appointed to rule in his stead. On 2 May 1953 King Hussein was officially crowned, and began his reign. He is said to have been a direct descendant of the Prophet Muhammad. The young king worked to build the infrastructure of his country, developing a national system of roads and broadening and strengthening the economy. Great strides were gained in making sanitation and education widely available to Jordan's population. During over forty years of rule, the king became a renowned mediator in regional disputes and an advocate for pan-Arab issues. Involved in mediating an end to the **Arab–Israeli War**, he was also involved in mediations between **Kuwait** and **Iraq** during the Persian **Gulf War** and was an integral part of the United Nations' resolution that called for **Israel**'s withdraw from some disputed lands which were partially responsible for the Arab–Israeli War in the 1960s. The UN resolution, Resolution number 242, was an important stepping stone in the region's conflict-ridden politics.

An advocate for **human rights**, King Hussein made Jordan an example of human rights advocacy in the **Middle East**. He also provided a model for reconciliation and unification within the context of political nationalism. The creation of the Jordanian charter in the 1990s saw the coming together and representation of all political factions to create a highly representative government through its charter and constitution. Along with his political accomplishments, the king also wrote three books in the 1960s. *Uneasy Lies the Head, My War with Israel* and *Mon Métier de Roi* cover topics such as his early life, his political life and his struggles. Later in life he suffered from cancer. Treated in the **United States**, he returned from treatments to once again assume his duties as mediator in the region. In 1998, as one of his last political works, he mediated the Wye River Peace Accord, once again bringing a tentative peace to Israel and the Palestinians. King Hussein knew that his cancer was fatal, and thus appointed his son Abdullah to succeed him to the throne. King Hussein is credited with shaping the modern nation of Jordan, and with being a peacemaker in a volatile region.

Hussein (al-Husayn), Saddam (1937–2006)

President of **Iraq**, 1979–2003. Born in Tikrit, Saddam Hussein 'Abd al-Majid al-Tikriti became an authoritarian and repressive dictator. His twenty-four years in office proved to be disastrous on many fronts for the Iraqi nation. When Hussein took the helm, Iraq was one of the most prosperous nations in south-west Asia that had witnessed a great increase in the standard of living. During his reign of terror he took Iraq down a violent path of war and destruction. By the end of his rule, Iraq was an isolated country. A member of the **Ba'ath Party**, Hussein's status within the party rose significantly when his cousin Ahmad Hasan al-Bakr became Iraq's president in 1968. Hussein was in charge of the party's internal security apparatus, which became his personal power base. When al-Bakr resigned from the presidency in 1979, he appointed Hussein the next president.

Hussein immediately started to solidify his power. He conducted an extensive purge of Ba' ath Party members and governmental officials. He also started systematically attacking and killing Iraqi Kurds and Shi'ites whom he suspected would not be loyal to his regime. His rise to power was accompanied by an unparalleled personality cult. His image was omnipresent. In fact, his government, a republic of fear, was one of the most repressive police states in recent history. In 1980, Hussein invaded **Iran** and launched the disastrous eight-year **Iran–Iraq War**. Around 400,000 Iraqis lost their lives and the war cost the government an estimated 80 billion dollars. Towards the end of the war, with no clear winner in sight, the Iraqi regime saw an opportunity to settle scores with its internal enemies, particularly the **Kurds**. In the notorious Anfal campaign in late 1987, northern Kurdish villages were destroyed and subjected to chemical attacks.

In 1990 Iraq was facing an economic crisis. In order to solve it, Hussein decided in August 1990 to launch another disastrous war against a neighbour, this time **Kuwait**. As opposed to his invasion of Iran, the international community responded with alarm that a nation's sovereignty had been breached. An international coalition, spearheaded by the **United States**, launched Operation Desert Storm in January 1991 which involved massive air bombardments and an eventual ground invasion. The operation was successful in removing Iraqis

from **Kuwait** and also destroyed almost the entire infrastructure of the country. In order to punish Iraq for its actions and to prevent future attacks on its neighbours, the UN imposed extensive and comprehensive economic sanctions, which crippled Iraqi society even further. When the US invaded Iraq in 2003 as part of Operation Iraqi Freedom, the country offered little or no resistance. American troops entered Baghdad in April 2003, and the statues of Saddam Hussein were torn down. Hussein went missing but was found in December 2003 hiding at a small farm near Tikrit. The Iraqi Special Tribunal put him on trial for crimes against humanity, specifically his role in the 1982 massacre of Iraqi Shi'ites in Dujail. He was found guilty and sentenced to death by hanging.

Hussein (Al-Husayn), Taha (1889–1973)

Egyptian writer and intellectual. Blind from the age of 3, he studied religion and Arabic at **al-Azhar University** before attending the secular Cairo University; he also studied in **France**. Professor of Arabic literature and then of history at Cairo, 1919, he was a strong proponent of Egyptian nationalism, which he interpreted as Pharaohism or returning to **Egypt**'s pre-Islamic roots, arguing that Egyptian civilization was diametrically opposed to Arab civilization. He generated the anger of traditionalists and the *ulama* of al-Azhar with his book, *On Pre-Islamic Poetry*, 1926, which questioned the authenticity of some early Arabic poetry and implied that the Qur'an should not be read as an objective source of history. The book was banned but reissued with token amendments as *On Pre-Islamic Literature*, 1927. He lost his Cairo University post, 1930, however, but joined the American University in Cairo. Effectively minister of education, 1950, introducing free education. Dubbed the 'Dean of Arabic Literature', he was a convinced modernist and is particularly known for his autobiographical *Al-Ayyam* (*An Egyptian Childhood*), 1932.

Hutchinson, Thomas (1711–1780)

Hutchinson was the last civilian governor of Massachusetts prior to independence. He was educated at Harvard and was successful in business and public life. He held a variety of offices under the colonial government, eventually serving two stints as acting governor of Massachusetts before being appointed to that role between 1771 and 1774. Although a native of Massachusetts, he alienated many of his constituents by his outspoken support of British policies during the 1760s and 1770s. In 1765 his home was attacked and destroyed during the **Stamp Act** riots. Eventually he was forced from office and replaced by a military governor in the aftermath of the **Boston Tea Party**. Hutchinson died in exile in London. He was one of America's first historians, writing an unfinished history of Massachusetts, the first two volumes of which were published in 1764 and 1767.

Hyderabad

The regional successor state of the Mughal empire in south-eastern India, Hyderabad became a battleground for control of the region between the French and English **East India Companies** in the eighteenth century. Recognized as a princely state in the British Indian Empire in the nineteenth century, with a Muslim nizam ruling a majority Hindu population and a British Resident in the court to oversee state affairs. Today it is the capital of the Indian state of Andhra Pradesh.

I

Ibadan

A city in modern-day **Nigeria** founded in the early nineteenth century in the confused period following the fall of the **Oyo** Empire by refugees from various areas. It became the leading city of the region in 1840 when it defeated an invasion from **Sokoto**, and made an alliance, which it dominated, with New Oyo. As the most powerful of the Yoruba states in the region, it entered into major wars of expansion in the mid nineteenth century which saw it conquer most of the central part of modern Nigeria. A revolt against Ibadan's hegemony started a large-scale war that lasted from 1877 until 1886 and resulted in the formation of the Ekitiparapo Federation as its rival. Ibadan was integrated into the British colony of Nigeria in 1893, but continued to grow as a cultural and educational centre. Following independence it became one of the largest cities in Africa.

Ibáñez (del Campo), Carlos (1877–1960)

Military officer and president of **Chile**, 1927–31 and 1952–8. Born in Linares, he served as minister of war (1925) and minister of the interior (1927), vice president (1927) and president/dictator (1927–31). Ousted by widespread demonstrations in 1931, he went into exile in **Argentina**. After several attempts to regain power, he was elected senator (1949) and President (1952) in a campaign in which his symbol was a broom – to sweep the politicians and corruption from government.

Ibn Sa'ud

– see **Saudi Arabia; Abd al-Aziz ibn Abd al-Rahman Al Sa'ud.**

Ibrahim Sori (d. 1784)

A war leader and then ruler of **Futa Jallon** (modern-day **Guinea**), 1770–92. Cousin of Karamoko Alfa, the imam of Futa Jallon following the **jihad** of 1726, he was elected leader by a council. His reign was noted for the long and indecisive war against Wassulu and for his own attempts to wrest power from the council that directed affairs in Futa Jallon.

He won and executed many council members in 1788–9.

Iceland

An island situated between the Atlantic and Arctic Oceans, Iceland was ruled successively by **Norway** and Denmark, from 1918 as a monarchy in association with Denmark. Occupied by Allied troops during **World War II**, Iceland voted by plebiscite in 1944 to become an independent republic. It joined **NATO** in 1949, EFTA in 1970 and was involved in a 'Cod War' over fishing rights with **Britain** in 1958, 1972 and 1975. Iceland applied for **EU** membership in 2009 but withdrew the application in 2015.

Idi Amin

– see **Amin Dada, Idi.**

Idris, King of Libya

– see **Sanusiyah.**

immigration

– see also **migration.**

Immigration is a permanent movement of people from one nation to another for a variety of reasons: to find jobs, improve education, join family, flee wars and avoid persecution. Varying global interactions have changed the origin and destination of immigrations. From the sixteenth to the nineteenth centuries, 12 million slaves were shipped to the Americas. From 1492 to 1825, 2 million Europeans went to **Latin America**. With the age of **imperialism**, 1850–1914, colonial powers encouraged labourers to work on plantations, in mines and on railway constructions. Chinese migrated to **Vietnam, Peru, Cuba** and the **United States**; Indians moved to South East Asia and the Pacific islands. Industrialization encouraged European internal migrations, sending Poles to **Germany**, Italians to **France**, and western Europeans to **Russia**. The potato famine dispatched the Irish to England and the United States. Between 1870–1930, over 10 million, primarily Italians and Spaniards but also northern Europeans, Chinese, Japanese and

Syrio-Lebanese migrated to **Argentina**, **Uruguay** and **Brazil** to work in export economies. In the 1910s Botswanans travelled to the mines of **South Africa**. Between 1820 and 1920, over 38 million foreigners, the majority from north-western Europe, moved to the United States. From 1891 to 1921, 3.8 million immigrants went to **Canada**. Industrialization continues to effect migrations as Turks move to Germany and Scandinavian countries.

Since the 1930s many people have migrated because of war, political insecurity, religious and ethnic discrimination and for employment. **World War II** and the **Holocaust** resulted in Jews moving to **Palestine** and the United States; the independence of **India** and **Pakistan** forced the migration of Hindus and Muslims. The **Cold War** dispatched Soviet dissenters to western Europe and the United States. The revolutions in Vietnam, Cuba and El **Salvador** and the wars in the **Sudan**, **Afghanistan**, **Iraq**, the Horn of Africa, **Libya** and **Syria** forced groups to flee. The late twentieth century witnessed high immigration with nearly 9 million arriving in the US in the 1980s. Both the collapse of the USSR and the expansion of the European Union increased the migration of workers, illegal immigrants, asylum seekers and refugees. Ethnic cleansing, first noted in 883 BC in the Assyrian Empire, dispersed large populations in the 1990s from the former **Yugoslavia**, **Rwanda** and Darfur.

Immigrants often experience danger, high moving costs, loss of family support, exploitation, discrimination and difficult assimilation. Host country citizens frequently accuse them of lowering wages and living standards, undermining the culture with high birth rates, increasing tax-based services and disloyalty. Illegal immigrants lack legal rights in host countries and are often denied benefits. Trafficked female immigrants endure sexual abuse and confinement in domestic service. Leaving their children behind, they contribute to family fragmentation. With the exception of **Japan**, which has prohibited immigrants, few countries have consistent immigration policies. Developed countries control immigration for self-advancement and security and their policies often lead to a brain drain and global inequalities in third world countries. However, migrant monetary remittances support families and contribute to the economic development of countries of origin. Lebanese businessmen in West Africa, Indians in East Africa and Chinese in South East Asia have financed, provided jobs and acculturated later arrivals. Immigrants contributed to their host countries through cultural diversity, regional occupational specialities, labour and high birth rates.

Imperial Preference
– see also **protectionism**.

Imperial Preference was a highly controversial aspiration of protectionists who wished to knit the **British Empire** together via a system of tariffs and currency that promoted imperial goods. 'Tariff reform' split the Conservative Party and was a key element in electoral campaigns between 1900 and 1914. Subsequently, the loosening of the British Empire and the rise of the **United States** precluded any coherent agreement. A broadly protectionist system was eventually introduced by **Britain** in 1932, followed by the Ottawa conference, which favoured intra-imperial trade. This system was eliminated between 1937 and 1949 by a combination of the GATT agreements, the devaluation of the pound consequent upon debt and inflation, and gravitation of the dominions towards American markets.

imperialism

A form of political organization in which a central collective unit associated with a particular people, territory or idea of social organization imposes domination over others for the purposes of economic and cultural assimilation, the exploitation of resources for industrial purposes or the maintenance of security against domestic and foreign enemies, in the form of an empire. Empires have usually in history been monarchical bodies under an emperor or empress, but not always; the French Republic, for instance, laid claim for many years to large parts of the globe and some have seen in the later British Empire a decentralized and parliamentary strain. Imperialism was also associated explicitly by both **Marx** and **Lenin** with the struggle of capitalist states for resources as their economies expanded. During the **Cold War**, however, the term was directed back at the **Soviet Union**'s domination of the eastern bloc of European socialist states and the third world communist countries by anti-communists. Imperialism as a form of political and economic system should therefore be seen as a modern phenomenon and distinct from the simple, older concept of *empire*.

The term *imperialism* apparently dates to the mid nineteenth century and to analysis of the policies of the **United Kingdom** and the French Empire of **Napoleon III** by their critics and theorists. Imperialism upheld the idea of a 'special mission' for imperial countries arising out of racial supremacy, economic need or 'civilizing values'which involved imposing the latter upon the non-imperial world. Imperialists therefore developed a theory of history in which their actions would 'improve' those peoples they dominated by advancing their social or political evolution, or eliminating backward forms of knowledge, belief or organization. Unsurprisingly, such policies tended to produce reactions from nationalists and resistance movements both within and outside their borders, and to encourage each imperialist state to oppose others as being a less perfect entity competing for resources. Imperialists created new hierarchies based around titles, hereditary leaderships and subnational or regional associations, and associated themselves strongly with justifications based on faith (whether in reason, religion or some aspect of the identity of the leadership group) for their activities.

Imperialism encouraged both the development of markets within empires that spanned the globe and the competition for territory and resources that typified the **scramble for Africa**, the career of **Cecil Rhodes** or **World War I**. To do so, it tended to produce a characteristic combination of elite strata which assimilated talented young men through military or social structures early in their lives and gave them a coherent and highly powerful coda by which they could act and understand behaviour. Imperialists also encouraged values of aggrandizement, self-sacrifice and expansionism which increased their boundaries and resources, often at very little central cost to imperial exchequers. So powerful was the model of European imperialism that both the **United States of America** between 1896–1912 in the Caribbean and the **Philippines** and **Japan** between 1895 and 1945 in Asia adopted the model, with disastrous results. Imperialism was a model the proponents of which proclaimed colonization, peace and progress through the central model and its agencies as their aims, but which was almost completely associated with war and domination.

Imperialism did produce a very rich body of cultural products and changed the countries which adopted it significantly. Empires tended to bring food, commodities and production styles home to new industrial masses, for instance, and were the key bodies in the development of trade in tea, narcotics, metals, textiles and cotton, for instance. They also tended to rearrange domestic patterns of production, and to create huge economic corporations that associated their own aims with those of their empires, often in competition with foreign firms for innovation and growth rather than markets. They encouraged the movement of peoples around the world in unprecedented numbers, and in war spurred the development of transportation and communication technologies, as well as both the emergence and transmission of diseases and the creation and dissemination of their cures.

Imperialism was rejected as a model of political organization twice in the twentieth century, partly because of the rise of the **USSR** and USA as world powers, and partly because of the crippling costs of World War I. In place of imperialism, at the Congress of Versailles in 1919, and the **United Nations** after 1945, the primacy of international law and the nation state was proclaimed. The **Cold War** can be seen as a battle for the allegiance of the post-imperial nations, which grew from 38 in 1919 to 192 in number by 1999. By 1997, practically every major imperial colony had been replaced with functioning local states, though international legacy agencies such as the **Commonwealth**, the Hispanophone and the Francophone continued to exist. Moreover, the League of Nations Covenant held that imperialism was in part to blame for world catastrophe, and had to be replaced with a series of 'mandates' held by surviving empires who would pledge to move towards the creation of viable local nation states. The USSR explicitly denounced imperialism from its inception and added to this process. Thereafter, the term became polemical again, and was used by political critics to condemn (particularly western) policies of financial control, dissemination of the legally binding membership and authority of international bodies, and the activities of multinational corporations based in particular powerful countries. A short-lived attempt to revive the practical idea of empire in the 1976 Central African Empire under Jean-Bedel Bokassa ended in bloodshed and ignominy in 1979. Thereafter imperial terms, models and names have largely been consigned to popular culture and history with the exception of Japan, where the head of the democratic and constitutional state is still termed 'emperor'.

Inchon Landing

The Inchon Landing was a US assault in Inchon harbour on 15 September 1950 that shifted the tide of the **Korean War**. Led by General **Douglas MacArthur**, the assault split the North Korean Army that had occupied most of Korea. Defeating North Koreans in the south, the US went on to carry out a policy to roll back North Korean forces and unify the two countries.

indentured servants

Indentured servants (or *engagés*) consisted predominately of young men who, from the seventeenth century, voluntarily emigrated or were sent as a punishment to the North American mainland and Caribbean colonies for a period of between three and ten years. In return for their passage and upkeep, they agreed to work for a master and could expect to receive land or payment in kind at the end of their service period. Living conditions for indentured servants were often difficult and harsh; many sought to escape.

India

Constituting a major part of south Asia, India shares its border with **Pakistan, China, Nepal, Bhutan, Myanmar** and **Bangladesh** with much of the peninsula surrounded by the Bay of Bengal in the east and the Arabian Sea in the west. India is the second most populous country with approximately one-sixth of the world's population. With innumerable castes and tribes, and more than a dozen major and hundreds of minor linguistic groups belonging to distinct language families such as Indo-Aryan, Dravidian and Munda, India is one of the most ethnically diverse countries in the world. Hindus constitute a majority of the Indian population, while other religious minorities including Muslims, Christians, Sikhs, Buddhists and Jains make up slightly less than a quarter of the total population. In 1947 with the partitioning of British India, India along with Pakistan became independent countries.

It was in 1858 that Britain began the direct administration of India, but the foundations of British colonial rule were planted as early as 1757 following the Battle of Plassey, where **East India Company** forces under Robert Clive defeated the Bengal nawab, Siraj-ud-daula. The foundations of the Company were badly shaken in 1857 when northern India was caught up in a major rebellion. Reacting to these events, the British Parliament passed the Government of India Act transferring all the authority of the East India Company to the British Crown. In its aftermath the British affected a tighter control over India largely through administrative ordering of society.

During this period, a new group of Indians, educated in the new universities in the presidency cities of **Calcutta**, Madras and Bombay, took on leadership roles. They viewed themselves quite self-consciously as the leaders of a new conception of India, which eventually led to the formation of the Indian National Congress in 1885. The politically moderate and elitist Congress turned into an activist mass movement under the leadership of **Mohandas K. Gandhi** in the twentieth century. Several factors, for example the 1905

Partition of Bengal, the British government's decision to draw India into the **World War I**, and the 1919 Jallianwala Bagh massacre in **Amritsar**, added to growing Indian antagonism toward British rule. These sentiments when added to Gandhi's mass mobilization led to three major events: the Non-Cooperation movement of 1920–2, the Salt March of 1930 and the Quit India movement of 1942. During a period of shared rule from 1937 to 1939, the Congress, having won elections in many provinces, shared power with the British, only to resign in protest when **Britain** again drew India into **World War II**. Electoral victories and the **Quit India movement** deepened the rift between the Congress and the Muslim League under the leadership of **Muhammad Ali Jinnah**, ultimately leading to partition in 1947 and the formation of India and Pakistan. This affected some 15 million people mostly in **Punjab** and **Bengal**, and was accompanied by an unprecedented level of violence leading to the deaths of hundreds of thousands of people. The challenges of building and maintaining a modern representative democracy fell on the first prime minister of India, **Jawaharlal Nehru**.

India Act,1858

The India Act, 1858, or An Act for the Better Government of India, was passed after the Mutiny of 1857. It transferred responsibility for the government of **India** from the **East India Company** to the British Crown. It created the position of Secretary of State of India, assisted by a council of fifteen advisers, to oversee all Indian affairs. In India, the Governor General became a personal representative of the Crown under the title of Viceroy.

India Act, 1919
– *see also* **Montagu-Chelmsford Reforms**.
The British Act which recognized the principle of dyarchy. It created two parallel governments: one at the centre entirely under the control of the British, and the other in the provinces, less sensitive areas of which were to be run by Indian ministers answerable to provincial legislatures. Not only did the new franchise ensure the loyalty of Indians with property and education; the reforms provincialized Indian politics, thereby avoiding self-government.

Indian Councils Act, 1909
– *see also* **Morley–Minto Reforms**.
Passed by the colonial authorities in British India, this Act created religiously based concepts of majority and minority communities, and established

a political category of 'Indian Muslim' by granting separate electorates in which only Muslims could vote and reserving special seats for Muslims in legislative councils. It recognized the principle of elections at all levels so that wealthy and powerful Indians could hope to be elected to not only municipal but also provincial councils, and in some cases the Governor General's council.

Indian independence

After a long nationalist struggle starting in the nineteenth century, independence was achieved with the British withdrawal from **India** in 1947. The nationalist movement had become a mass movement under the leadership of **Mohandas K. Gandhi** from 1919 onwards. The pressure of the **Indian National Congress**, unrest generated by trials of members of the **Indian National Army** in 1945, along with the election of a Labour government in Great Britain, led to the decision by Prime Minister Clement Attlee that the British would leave no later than mid 1948. Under the last viceroy, Lord **Mountbatten**, the decision was made that the country would have to be divided into two new nations, India and **Pakistan**, the latter divided between two wings more than a thousand miles apart, as the British left. Indian nationalists had been demanding complete independence since 1929, but agreed, when the partition plan was agreed in June 1947, that India would remain a member, as a republic, of the **Commonwealth** of Nations.

Indian mutiny and revolt, 1857

Beginning in May 1857, an uprising swept through swathes of northern and central India, nearly ending a hundred years of **East India Company** rule. It began as a military mutiny sparked by various grievances including inadequate pay, forced service abroad, the annexation of Awadh in 1856 from where much of the Bengal Army was recruited, and, famously, the greasing of new Lee Enfield rifle cartridges with cow and pig fat, offending both Hindu and Muslim soldiers. The mutiny quickly became a civil rebellion drawing in dispossessed rulers and aristocrats, merchants, impoverished labourers and artisans, agrarian magnates, peasants and tribal communities hit by colonial taxation, as well as religious millenarian preachers. However, it remained confined to the Gangetic plain and pockets of central India. Though stimulated by several 'regional patriotisms', it lacked coordinated action and a single rallying ideology. Even religious rhetoric could not provide unity, sometimes pitting Sunni against Shia interests and

carrying the potential to divide Hindus from Muslims. The British were able to rely on the support or indifference of different groups of Indians as they played out old political, social and economic rivalries. With the revolt crushed by July 1858 and the abolition of the East India Company, authority over Indian territories passed to the British Crown on 2 August 1858.

Indian National Army

Designed by the Japanese, especially Colonel Iwaichi Fujiwara of their intelligence branch, the Indian National Army (INA), was formed from Indian Army prisoners taken at the surrender of **Singapore** in 1942. It was led at first by Colonel, later General, Mohan Singh. After a crisis in relations with the Japanese, Mohan Singh was relieved of his position and imprisoned. In 1943, under the leadership of **Subhas Chandra Bose**, the INA was reorganized and revivified and grew to approximately 40,000. This small force participated in the Japanese invasion of **India** in 1944. These forces advanced into India, but then were decisively beaten and retreated through **Burma**. In 1945 three leaders of the INA were tried for treason by the British in New Delhi. Although convicted, great nationalist demonstrations led to their release and contributed to the British decision to leave India in 1947.

Indian National Congress

The Indian National Congress was founded in December 1885 by seventy-two English-educated, urban, middle-class professionals. During the next twenty years its moderate leadership petitioned, rather than confronted, imperial authority for greater Indian participation in colonial governance and for economic policies that would develop India. By the early twentieth century a more militant strand emerged advocating full self-rule and assertive strategies of boycott to achieve it. These 'extremists' reached out to the masses but their rallying symbols – Hindu deities and historical figures – often alienated religious minorities. Indeed, most educated Muslims had eschewed the party even at its inception, concerned that its demands worked only to the political advantage of the Hindu majority. The Congress became a truly mass political party under **Mohandas K. Gandhi**. Capitalizing on already widespread political, economic, social and religious discontent, he drew to it wide segments of Indian society from educated professionals and capitalists to peasants and workers as well as large numbers of Muslims, at least for a while, when he launched a combined non-violent non-cooperation and pro-Khilafat movement in 1920. Until independence in 1947, and for some decades after, the Congress remained the dominant Indian political party, providing a standard for various anti-colonial nationalist movements elsewhere.

Indian Rising
– *see* **Indian mutiny and revolt**.

Indian Wars (American)
Between 1783 and 1890 the government of the **United States** pursued an aggressive policy of land acquisition at the expense of **Native Americans**. This was achieved through various means, including purchase, treaty and conquest. Force and the threat of force were integral to the process. Indians used a variety of methods to resist displacement and armed resistance was among these. As a result armed conflict between the United States and Indians was a regular feature of white–Indian relations in the century from the conflict between the United States and the Western Confederacy in Ohio, in the 1790s, to 1890 when the last major armed incident took place at **Wounded Knee**, South Dakota. Indians often achieved military success, as when Little Turtle of the Western Confederacy defeated Josiah Harmar and Arthur St Clair in Indiana in 1790 and 1791, and when the Sioux defeated **George A. Custer** at the **Battle of Little Bighorn** in 1876. Nonetheless, the superior numbers and technology of the whites meant that in the long-run the federal government prevailed.

Indies, Laws of the
Spanish legislation intended for the Americas, consisting of royal directives that often responded to specific colonial problems. This proliferating patchwork of regulations finally achieved codification in the *Recopilación de leyes de los reinos de las Indias* (1681), which included nearly 6,400 laws on a wide range of subjects. However, colonial officials, mindful of local conditions and power dynamics, exercised considerable discretion in how, or even if, they implemented its provisions.

Indigenismo
Born of early twentieth-century revolutionary movements in Latin American countries with large Indian populations, Indigenismo became an important campaign emerging from the **Mexican Revolution**, especially from 1920 to 1946, to recognize and incorporate the Indian population into national society. Major approaches came from

José Vasconcelos, Minister of Public Education, 1921–4, and leading anthropologist Manuel Gamio. Vasconcelos argued that the future of **Mexico** and **Latin America** belonged to the **mestizo** (the mixed population and culture of European and Indian peoples) that he called in his eponymous book, *The Cosmic Race* (1925). With *mestizaje* (the mixing of Indians with the European population) and acculturation of indigenous peoples especially replacing Indian languages, Vasconcelos sought to record the indigenous heritage and urged its incorporation into the nation's artistic traditions. In his most notable initiative, he sent educational missions to rural communities to teach Spanish and primary education and hired photographers and musicologists to document indigenous daily life and music. This music inspired classical and art song compositions by Manuel Ponce and **Carlos Chávez** and performances by Tata Nacho (Ignacio Fernández Esperón) of popular music. Photographs of indigenous peoples appeared in museums and world fairs' exhibits, tourism posters, postcards and calendars. Gamio's position changed over time, but generally he supported revitalizing indigenous communities and preserving their cultures. A student of Franz Boas at New York's Columbia University, he led efforts to investigate the needs of individual indigenous communities through intense fieldwork and development programmes. His early views appeared in *Forjando Patria* (1916), which called for Indian cultural assimilation. He also visited **Guatemala** and **Peru** to examine programmes to integrate indigenous peoples in those nations.

Mexico's revolutionaries attempted to complement education with administrative assimilation by making rural programmes such as the **ejido** available only to *campesinos* (rural workers), forcing communities to drop ethnic identification for land titles. The revolutionaries also created new agencies to assist Indians: in 1917, the Office of Anthropology within the Department of Agriculture, then in 1921, the office of indigenous culture in the Ministry of Public Education. These offices tried to record the extant indigenous groups. Carlos Basuri and Luis Mendieta y Núñez completed eleven studies on indigenous communities, finally published in 1940 as *La población indígena de México*. It provided information on all indigenous groups. Meanwhile, the lack of success of revolutionary programmes resulted in an effort by President **Lázaro Cárdenas** (1934–40) to discover what Indian communities believed they needed through a series of regional indigenous congresses. President Miguel Alemán created the

National Indigenous Institute (INI) that served as the major government agency until its abolition in 2003. President Luis Echeverría sponsored the First National Congress of Indigenous Peoples in 1975. Many see the failure of the indigenous programmes in the rebellion of the Zapatista Army of National Liberation (EZLN) in Chiapas in 1994; others point to success in the 1994 amendment to the constitution that defined the Mexican people as pluricultural on an indigenous base in recognition of more than 10 million indigenous peoples.

indirect rule

The theory of colonial governance whereby colonial officials ruled through local authorities and political structures. Most common in the British colonies of **Africa** and **Asia**, 'indirect rule' became a legitimizing discourse for the British Empire. Though precedents existed in both colonial **India** and **Uganda**, the ideology behind it was articulated by Lord **Frederick Lugard** in *Dual Mandate in British Tropical Africa* published in 1904 while he worked as high commissioner in Northern Nigeria. When conquering the **Sokoto Caliphate**, Lugard devised a system whereby each local emir would rule over their area on behalf of the colonial state, remitting part of their tax collection to the British administration. With fewer British administrators needed on the ground, the system reduced costs for the administration. Where recognized local structures of authority and political hierarchy did not exist, British officials invented and imposed institutions of chieftaincies.

Indochina

– *see also* **Cambodia, Laos and Vietnam**.
A former federation of states under French colonial rule in South East Asia. Indochina consisted of the French colony of Cochin China and French protectorates of **Tonkin**, Annam, **Laos** and **Cambodia**. The French gradually but systematically colonized parts of Indochina starting from 1862. In 1887 the Union of Indochina was established with the territories of Cochin China, Cambodia, Annam and Tonkin: Laos was the last to join, in 1893. Japanese forces gained control of Indochina during **World War II**. Parts of Laos and Cambodia, which had been tributary states of Siam prior to French annexation, were then given to the Thai government, which had entered into an official alliance with **Japan** at the beginning of the war. All territories of Indochina were returned to French colonial rule soon after the conclusion of World War II. In 1954 the Geneva Conference ended French control over Indochina.

Indochina War (1946–1954)

Also known as the First Indochina War, the Indochina War of 1946–54 was fought between the **Viet Minh** communist forces led by **Ho Chi Minh** and the French colonial forces. At the conclusion of **World War II**, the Viet Minh had already established a nationalist government in Hanoi. However, France insisted on re-establishing colonial rule in Indochina after the war. Viet Minh forces were initially driven to the countryside when the armed conflict broke out in 1946. In 1949 the French established a nominally independent government under former emperor Bao Dai. The violent conflict continued to escalate until the catastrophic defeat of French colonial forces in the Battle of **Dien Bien Phu** in 1954. The Geneva conference, which took place later in the same year, resulted in the end of French control over Indochina and the division of **Vietnam** into the Democratic Republic of Vietnam (North) and the Republic of Vietnam (South).

Indochinese Treaty (1954)

The treaty which enshrined the settlement reached by the American, British, French and Soviet foreign ministers with Asian representatives, including those of Communist China, in Geneva, 20–21 July 1954. Radically affected by the final French defeat at **Dien Bien Phu**, 7 May 1954, it allowed for a French withdrawal, created independent **Cambodia** (Kampuchea) and **Laos**, and also divided **Vietnam** at the 17th parallel between the Communist north of **Ho Chi Minh** and the south under the French-installed Emperor Bao Dai. They were to be reunited under free elections in 1956, but this never materialized. President **Eisenhower** did not consider the US bound by the Geneva decisions.

Indo-Chinese War ('Himalayan War')

A war in 1962 between **China** and **India** in the disputed Himalayan region over land on the Chinese border, which China claimed was mistakenly given to India by the McMahon Line decision in 1914. Clashes between Chinese and Indian forces occurred when Chinese forces crossed the McMahon Line into India. After Indian forces defended the territories it regarded as its own, Chinese forces continued to advance into Assam, until their withdrawal on 21 November.

Indonesia

– *see also* **Dutch Empire; Indonesian War of Independence**.

The Republic of Indonesia is located on a group of 17,508 islands in the South East Asian archipelago that stretches across the equator between the Indian Ocean and the Pacific Ocean. The capital city is Jakarta, and it is the fourth most populous country in the world, with a population of around 250 million. The majority of the population (88 per cent) is Muslim, making Indonesia the most populous among the world's Islamic states. The Indonesian islands are also rich in petroleum and natural gas. The country has played a significant role in the **Organization of Petroleum Exporting Countries** (OPEC) since 1962. The islands that make up today's Indonesia have been a vibrant centre of maritime trade since the earliest centuries of the Christian era. The Hindu-Buddhist kingdom of Srivijaya was established on the islands in the second century. Muslim invasion began in the thirteenth century and nearly the entire archipelago was converted to **Islam** by the fifteenth century. The Portuguese were to first Europeans to set up trading posts in the early sixteenth century. In 1595 the Dutch drove the Portuguese from the islands and established their first trading post in Java in an attempt to control the spice trade. The islands were included as a part of the **Dutch Empire** for the next three hundred years. During **World War II** Japanese troops seized Indonesia from the Dutch and used the islands' rich petroleum resource to fuel its war efforts in East and South East Asia. At the conclusion of the war, the Indonesian nationalist movement, under the leadership of **Sukarno** and Mohamed Hatta, declared independence for Indonesia on 17 August 1945. It was not until 1949 that the Dutch authorities fully recognized Indonesian independence. Sukarno became the first president and retained dictatorial power over the islands until 1966.

In the later years of Sukarno's rule serious conflicts arose between the **Communist Party of Indonesia** (PKI), which was rising in influence due to close ties with the president, and right-wing military leaders. In 1966 military forces loyal to General Suharto staged a massive purge of suspected communists in the government. Sukarno was eased out of office as Suharto assumed presidential powers in 1967. Under Suharto's rule, also known as the 'New Order', Indonesia assumed a firm pro-western standpoint and experienced dramatic economic improvements. Suharto's political party, the **Golkar**, won every election from 1971 onwards until Suharto finally stepped down in 1998.

Vice President B. J. Habibie succeeded Suharto during the last year of his presidency and ushered in an era of reform for Indonesia. During his short regime, Habibie agreed to hold a referendum in 2002 that would lead to the independence of **East Timor**, which had been invaded and occupied by Indonesian forces since 1975. In the 1999 elections the Indonesian Democratic Party-Struggle (PDI-P), under the leadership of Megawati Sukarnoputri, defeated the Golkar for the first time in nearly three decades. Despite massive economic setbacks from the Asian economic crisis in 1997 and the tsunami disaster of 2006, Indonesia in the post-Suharto era has made some progress in democratization of the political system. It has also witnessed the 2002 terrorist bombing on Bali.

Indonesian 'Confrontation' with Malaysia

Launched in 1963 against the new Federation of **Malaysia** by President **Sukarno** of **Indonesia**, who saw the Commonwealth state as a British ploy for protecting its interests in South East Asia. Indonesian soldiers posing as 'rebels' were infiltrated across the border of Indonesian Kalimantan in a policy of *Konfrontasi*, involving the British and the Malaysians in expensive guerrilla warfare until 1966 when a peace agreement was signed in Bangkok. The 'Confrontation' probably contributed to the British decision to withdraw from 'East of Suez' and indirectly terminated the concept of merging **Brunei** with **Malaysia**.

Indonesian Civil War

A violent conflict between forces loyal to President **Sukarno** and the right-wing military faction led by General Abdul Haris Nasution and Major General **Suharto** in 1965. President Sukarno had close ties with the **Communist Party of Indonesia** and was supported by the People's Republic of **China** and the Soviet bloc. Suharto's faction had the support of **Britain** and the **United States**. The war ended with the overthrow of Sukarno and led to Suharto's assumption of the Indonesian presidency in 1967.

Indonesian War of Independence

A war waged against the Dutch, 1945–9, over what had been the Dutch East Indies. The first action, however, the so-called 'Battle of Surabaya', was against the British, who had responsibility within the Allied Command for taking over **Indonesia** from the Japanese in 1945. Nevertheless, the new Dutch governor general, Hubertus van Mook, insisted, October 1945, that Dutch sovereignty be respected by all parties and envisaged a federal Indonesia within a union under the Queen of the Netherlands, making the 'Republic of Indonesia' proclaimed by **Sukarno** in August 1945 just one state among other Indonesian states. The first Dutch troops returned in February 1946, and skirmishes with Indonesian troops ensued, punctuated by negotiated ceasefires. The Dutch launched major military action, 26 July 1946, and had captured about half of Java by 4 August 1947, when the action was terminated. A round of unsuccessful negotiations followed, culminating in the Dutch seizure of Sukarno and other leaders and the occupation of strategic points. The resulting international protests and financial pressures finally forced a Dutch transfer of power to the United States of Indonesia on 27 December 1949.

Indo-Pakistan Wars (1947–1949, 1965, 1971)

These were three major armed conflicts involving the post-colonial states of **India** and **Pakistan**. The first and second wars involved disputes over Kashmir. During the colonial period the Hindu Dogras dynasty ruled over the princely state of **Jammu and Kashmir**, which had a majority Muslim population. On the eve of independence Maharaja Hari Singh remained ambivalent about whether he would choose to join India or Pakistan, leading to tensions in the region. Starting in 1947, Pathan tribesmen from the North-West Frontier Province began harassing the Maharaja's troops in the border regions, and although Pakistan remained officially neutral, Pakistani officers provided leadership and training to the tribesmen. Increasingly unable to resist internal and external pressures, Hari Singh signed an Instrument of Accession to India in October 1947. The government of India then sent in troops, pushing back the Azad Jammu–Kashmir forces, which were composed of local militia, tribal groups and Pakistani Army units. After clashes between the two forces reached a stalemate, the **UN** helped negotiate a ceasefire in January 1949, in which both groups agreed to respect what became known as the Line of Control, in which about one-third of the former princely state came under Pakistani control and the other two-thirds became part of India. The UN also passed Resolution 47 which promised that the fate of Kashmir would ultimately be determined by a plebiscite, although the conditions of the peace agreement have never been implemented.

The second war also involved Kashmir. Hostilities between the two countries began during skirmishes in April 1965 in the Rann of Kutch, a small region of Gujarat. In July 1965 Pakistan launched Operation Gibraltar, a clandestine plan in which militants crossed the border into Kashmir to promote an internal revolt. Although the operation did not result in the anticipated popular uprising, an alarmed Indian government responded by sending troops into Pakistan to cut off the operation. In September both countries escalated the conflict, with Pakistan launching major offensives in Indian Kashmir and India sending troops into Pakistan, including the regions around Lahore and Sialkot. When both sides decided that they had little to gain from further hostilities, the UN negotiated a ceasefire on 23 September. In January 1966 India and Pakistan agreed to return to their pre-war positions, signing the Tashkent Declaration, which was mediated by the **Soviet Union**.

The third war of 1971 involved East Pakistan, which would become the new nation of **Bangladesh**. The conflict began with a popular uprising against the Pakistani government after it instigated a massive crackdown on East Pakistan in March 1971. India opened its borders to a massive number of East Pakistanis fleeing the violence, and declared its support for an independent state of Bangladesh. War seemed imminent from November 1971, but Indian, Bangladeshi and international sources cite a Pakistani pre-emptive strike on Indian airbases on 3 December 1971 as the official start of the war. During the official thirteen days of conflict, India quickly advanced into East Pakistan, capturing Dhaka, and secured territory in West Pakistan. After suffering massive defeats, the Eastern Command of the Pakistani Armed Forces surrendered, following which the two countries negotiated the **Simla Agreement**, in which Pakistan agreed to recognize Bangladeshi independence in exchange for the return of tens of thousands of Pakistani prisoners of war, who had been left stranded after the official surrender.

Indus Waters Treaty

The Indus Waters Treaty was signed by **India** and **Pakistan** in 1960. It designates how the waters of the Indus basin are to be shared between the two countries. The Indus basin has six major rivers: the Indus, Jhelum, Chenab, Ravi, Beas and Sutlej. The treaty calls for the Indus, Jhelum and Chenab (barring a small portion used in Indian-administered Kashmir) to be used by Pakistan; and the Ravi, Beas and Sutlej by India.

Industrial Workers of the World (IWW) ('Wobblies')

The IWW was formed in 1905 as a radical American labour organization. Leaders including Big Bill Haywood promoted industrial unionism among the most exposed workers – miners in the far west, new immigrants in the east – willing if necessary to oppose employers with direct action. It was the antithesis of the exclusive craft unionism of the American Federation of Labour. At its peak it had about 100,000 members, but declined after the early 1920s though still survives in the **USA** and elsewhere.

industrialization

– *see also* **energy; factories; factory acts**.

1700–1815

The early eighteenth century continued to rely on water power to drive the comparatively simple machinery employed in iron foundries and textiles, whereas agriculture and cottage industries such as weaving relied on animal or manual labour. Jethro Tull had called, initially vainly, for the use of machinery in agriculture. The key changes which released the Industrial Revolution were first the development of coal and iron resources and second the substitution of steam power for water power, which was only possible once iron was available in quantity. The Industrial Revolution started essentially in **Britain** rather than elsewhere partly because, unlike, say, **France** and **Italy**, Britain was rich in both coal and iron, the resources often being conveniently contiguous, partly because manufacturing stimulated a rich new national vein of inventive genius, and partly because Britain had accumulated the reserves of investment capital needed to realize the potential of the new inventions to the full. As a result, Britain became the 'first industrial nation'.

Britain's production of coal doubled to 6 million tons between 1700 and 1770 and rose to 16 million tons by 1816. The increase in pig-iron production was even more startling, rising from 30,000 tons in 1760 to 250,000 tons by 1806. The increase was largely attributable to the discovery by Abraham Darby I, working in Coalbrookdale, Shropshire, from about 1708, that if coal were first turned into coke it could replace charcoal to produce the heat for iron smelting. Coal and iron were found conveniently close together in the English Midlands, which soon became known as the 'Black Country'. The uses of iron expanded widely from the traditional firebacks, nails, guns and cannon balls to the new machinery in equally new factories, to iron boats and even to an iron Methodist chapel. The world's first iron bridge was erected over the River Severn by Andrew Darby III at a cost of more than 6,000 pounds in 1779. Cast in the Coalbrookdale foundry using 378 tons of iron, the 30-metre-long single-span bridge remained in use for traffic until 1934, and it still survives, classified as a UNESCO World Heritage site. Meanwhile in the 1740s, Benjamin Huntsman of Sheffield had invented the crucible method to produce cast steel and some twenty Sheffield steel refiners were making cast steel by the late 1780s. In the same decade Henry Cort (1740–1800) introduced the rolling of iron to replace its being hammered into sheets.

The new machinery was employed in particular for cotton manufacturing, which became Britain's greatest machine industry, employing some 100,000 workers in factories and 250,000 weavers and other workers outside by 1815. John Kay had patented his Flying Shuttle, which enabled a weaver to do the work of two men and was soon adopted by cotton as well as wool weavers as early as 1733, but in 1764 James Hargreaves conceived the Spinning Jenny, which spun several threads instead of only one. (Sir) Richard Arkwright patented his Water Frame spinning machine in 1769 and by 1771 his mill at Cromford, Derbyshire, was being described as 'a palace of enormous size'. In 1775 Samuel Crompton combined the Jenny and the Water Frame in his Spinning Mule, which spun finer and stronger thread than its rivals and allowed England to make its own fine muslins rather than import them from the east. Edmund Cartwright followed with his power-driven weaving machine. Agriculture was potentially revolutionized by the invention of a threshing machine by a Scot, Andrew Meikle, in 1786. The significance of this series of inventions lay not so much in their intellectual originality, which was arguably modest by later standards, but in the huge boost to productivity which they permitted.

It was the application of the power of steam to driving machinery, however, which was to release the full force of the Industrial Revolution and carry it worldwide. The Frenchman, Denis Papin (1647–1714), the inventor of the condensing pump and the pressure cooker, had been the first to identify the potential power of steam, and the Englishman, Thomas Savery, had patented his steam pump at the beginning of the eighteenth century. It was Thomas Newcomen (1663–1729), however, who invented the first powerful engine, the atmospheric engine, for use in pumping water from the Cornish mines in 1705. The Scotsman, James Watt (1736–1819), then created the first truly efficient engine and is usually regarded as the 'father of steam'. Watt rectified the weaknesses in Newcomen's engine, patented his condenser, 1769, and built a rotative engine with connecting rod and crankshaft in partnership with Matthew Boulton (1728–1809) at his Soho works near Birmingham. Steam power was first introduced into a factory in 1789. Cartwright's machine, for example, had initially been driven by a bull but after that date by a steam engine. By 1800 Watt and Boulton engines were being widely used for pumping out mines and driving a variety of machines throughout the British Isles. Such stationary engines were followed from 1801 by increasingly successful steam locomotives, initially for colliery haulage but then for freight haulage generally. The steam railway locomotive prompted further growth in industrialized styles of production which had hitherto been inhibited by the absence of a comprehensive and efficient form of **transportation**.

By 1815, London had emerged as the most heavily industrialized part of Britain, but a number of other centres had established themselves for particular manufactures, many of which survived well into the twentieth century and even to the present day: Yorkshire and the West Country for weaving, Lancashire for cotton textiles, Sheffield for cutlery, Staffordshire for pottery, Leicestershire for shoes, south Wales for iron and steel, and Birmingham for metal goods of all kinds. Although the mass production associated with industrialization made Britain richer overall and made domestic products such as Wedgwood china affordable for a much wider range of people, it generated social problems and tensions. Many skilled craftsmen were displaced and some turned to violence, attacking machinery and factories in the Luddite riots of 1811–16. Even the employers made and lost fortunes from the very beginning. Crompton died penniless but Arkwright a millionaire. The Combination Acts of 1799 and 1800, passed in fear of a domestic repetition of the French Revolution, forbade workmen from combining to raise wages. Hardest to change in the longer term was the initial impact of **urbanization**: the unplanned new industrial towns and cities where thousands lived in extremely overcrowded conditions without sanitation, fresh water or fresh air. The economies of industrialization, however, were irresistible. It brought the cost of cotton yarn, for example, down from 38 shillings per pound in 1786 to 2 shillings and 11 pence in 1832. The price

of bar iron fell from 18 pounds per ton in 1750 to 3–4 pounds per ton by 1850.

Although the British unquestionably invented industrialization in the sense of factory-based mass production using specialized machinery, the French were perhaps the leaders in the eighteenth century in many of the sciences on which industrialization later came to depend. Antoine Lavoisier (1743–94) discovered oxygen and established that combustion is a form of chemical action. J. A. C. Charles designed the first hydrogen balloon in 1783, in which he made a two-hour flight covering 27 miles. André Marie Ampère (1775–1836) propounded the theory that magnetism was the result of molecular electric currents. They were not alone. The Italian, Alessandro Volta (1745–1827) invented the chemical battery and Swedish naturalist Linnaeus (Karl von Linné) (1707–78) made botany a science. Moreover, much of the technical knowledge which Britain so effectively applied came initially from other European countries which failed to capitalize on them. German mining engineers, Dutch canal builders and French civil engineers had all been the leaders in their fields in the seventeenth century but had faced popular conservatism and, in **Germany** and Italy, political division. On the other hand, the **Napoleonic Wars** had stimulated some branches of continental European industry, not least the metal and armaments industries of **Belgium**, Germany and **Switzerland**. Friedrich Krupp of Essen, Poncelet of Liège and Andreas Küller of Solingen were all producing cast steel by the beginning of the nineteenth century, and the cotton industry flourished in Saxony and in cities such as Ghent, Mulhouse and Paris.

Although industrialization had gained a momentum which excited many and was increasingly to inspire the nineteenth century across **Europe**, it also repelled many. The love of the medieval and of nature so characteristic of the Romantic movement in all the arts was in part a reaction against the scarring ugliness of industrialization, which became ever more widespread with the passing of time. Some, such as William Morris (1834–96), were to react by idealizing the medieval craftsman, and it has been argued that that disinclination to strive to create beauty in industrially manufactured products made industrialization more damaging than it need have been.

1815–1865

Britain was to retain its lead in manufacturing throughout the first half of the nineteenth century and to reinforce it with the invention of more advanced machine tools such as James Nasmyth's steam hammer in1832. Nevertheless, industrialization was spreading to the European mainland, initially to the Rhineland and Upper Silesia areas of **Prussia** and to Saxony. Britain's Great Exhibition of 1851 can perhaps be seen in retrospect not only as a celebration of Britain's industrial pre-eminence but also as a turning point after which the continuation of that pre-eminence could no longer be taken for granted. Britain herself had already exported industrial investment in textiles, coke smelting and metallurgy, but it was only with the adoption of Britain's pioneering steam railways that European industrialization could start in earnest. The European countries did not all start from the same position. Some suffered from a weak middle class, rigid class divisions and a peasantry whose conservatism was rooted in legal or virtual **serf-dom**, as in parts of Germany and in the Austrian and **Russian Empires**. The human resources for successful entrepreneurship and management, or to compose a mass labour force, were equally lacking. The French peasantry remained attached to the land and the family, and preferred to invest in land or government bonds than to buy industrial shares or trust to banks.

The general consequence was that continental European industrialization was always linked much more closely to government than was the case in Britain. Governments, whether directly or in the form of public corporations or local authorities, owned or controlled collieries, railways, ironworks and saltworks, arsenals and dockyards, and many other varieties of industrial installation in what they perceived to be the national interest, not in pursuit of any concept of socialism. Moreover, governments not only promoted industry directly in this way but also enacted, or if necessary repealed, legislation with the aim of encouraging their urban middle classes to engage in commerce and manufacturing. Such activities had the added advantage for authoritarian regimes of diverting any middle-class political aspirations. Continental industrialization was also more closely linked to the banks than it was in Britain, because Britain's pioneering machines of the eighteenth century had been rudimentary and comparatively cheap. The continental industrialization of the nineteenth century needed the services of credit banks, such as the French Crédit Mobilier or the Austrian Kreditanstalt, to mobilize the savings of small investors for investment in the planned new industrial enterprises.

Other wider developments accelerated the speed of European industrialization between 1840 and 1870. The rapid growth in population, particularly in Britain and Germany, enlarged the market for European manufactures, as did the growing number of colonies and the increased British, French and Russian authority over **India**, **Algeria** and Siberia and Central Asia, respectively. Extending railway networks, the substitution of iron steam-ships for wooden sailing ships and completion of the **Suez Canal** in 1869 all facilitated the transport of goods to these new and expanding markets. Not least, manufacturing growth was stimulated by a general steep reduction in tariffs, which had been particularly high in France. Moreover, the elimination of internal tariffs had been an essential dimension of the unification of both Italy and Germany and had been foreshadowed in the latter case by the conclusion of the *Zollverein* (customs union), 1834.

The spread of industrialization to continental Europe brought with it the same urban squalor as had mushroomed in Britain, with a general absence of clean water supply, sewerage and refuse disposal. Slum quarters such as St Giles in London, Little Ireland in Manchester, the Voigtland in Berlin and Saint-Georges and Croix-Rousse in Lyon became centres of crime and disease. It was the world of Fagin's den in Charles Dickens' *Oliver Twist* (1838). Minority groups such as the Irish in Liverpool and Manchester and the Poles in the Ruhr were crowded into the worst slums, accepting them much as African and Asian immigrants to Europe would in the following centuries on the basis that they were at least better than what was available at home.

Nevertheless, the period 1815–65 saw the first attempts in Britain to address some of the evils which industrialization had either created or, more often, intensified. Child labour, for example, was a traditional and often welcomed practice. Daniel Defoe had noted with approval at the very beginning of the eighteenth century that in the clothing dales of the West Riding of Yorkshire 'hardly anything above four years old but its hands were sufficient for its support'. The application of steam power to machinery, however, had led to the much wider employment of women and of children, who could be paid less and were found to be more amenable to the discipline of factory life. The manufacture of silks in the French city of Lyon in 1777 employed 9,657 people of whom 3,823 were children. A survey of the labour force in Scottish and Manchester textile mills at the end of the Napoleonic Wars found that half the workers were children. The children employed in the earlier domestic industries at least often had green fields to play in, but the child in the factory lived, worked and slept in unhealthy and overcrowded conditions. The British Parliament therefore passed, for both humanitarian and self-interested reasons, the Factory Act in 1833, the same year as it abolished slavery in the empire. The Act forbade for the first time the employment of children under the age of 9 in textile mills, limited the working hours of all those between 9 and 18 in them, and prohibited night-work in the mills for children and young people. Significantly, the Act appointed factory inspectors to ensure that the legislation was observed. The Ten Hours Act of 1847 limited the working week of women and young people in the textile factories to fifty-eight hours of which no more than ten might be worked in any one day. In practice it limited the work of adult men as well, as they could not work the machinery on their own. The principle of factory regulation was slowly extended in Britain to manufacturers other than textiles. The Mines Act of 1842 forbade the underground employment of women and children under 10, and an Act of 1850 brought adult men as well under the protection of the Mines Inspectorate.

Some other European countries acted similarly. Prussia in 1839 forbade the employment of children under the age of 9 in mines and factories and restricted the working day of those under 16 to ten hours. Young people were also prohibited from working at night, on Sundays or on public holidays. France in 1841 prohibited the employment of children under the age of 8 in factories and in 1851 extended some protection to other young people. The need was pressing. A parliamentary report of 1842 on child labour in England found 'the most frightful picture of avarice, selfishness and cruelty on the part of masters and parents, and of juvenile and infantile misery, degradation and destruction ever presented'. A report by Dr Villermé on the French textile mills shortly afterwards similarly found of the workforce 'many women, pale and thin, walking barefoot through the mud ... And there are also young children – still more in number than the women – not less pale, not less dirty, covered in rags, greasy with the oil of the looms, which has splashed on them while they worked'.

There was also an attempt by a small number of enlightened employers to improve the housing in which industrial workers lived. Robert Owen's New Lanark cotton mills in Scotland at the beginning of the nineteenth century had recognized that people were shaped by their environment and that that environment was under human control, but Titus Salt, a woollen manufacturer, probably exercised more long-term influence with his construction from 1851 of the model town of Saltaire near Leeds for his 3,000 workers. His provision of well-built houses with proper sanitation and other amenities was to inspire in due course a succession of new towns and urban estates aiming to end the squalor of overcrowded and unhealthy industrial slums. Similarly enlightened employers in Alsace inspired the construction of a 'workers' city' with modern amenities in Mulhouse in the same period, and the concept spread elsewhere in France, to Germany and to Switzerland. Also in France, Jean Baptiste André Godin (1817–88), a wealthy industrialist and philanthropist, inspired by the thinking of the early French 'utopian socialist', François-Marie-Charles Fourier (1772–1837), built his first *phalanstère* or phalanx – a self-sustainable community – near his iron foundry in the town of Guise (Aisne département) between 1859 and 1883. Nevertheless, such enlightened employers were very much the exception everywhere.

Just as Britain pioneered the Industrial Revolution it also pioneered some of the political reforms which had become necessary if industrialization were to be overall a positive rather than a negative European experience. In 1824–5, Parliament repealed the Combination Acts, and trade unions were henceforward legal. The year 1848 saw both the publication by **Marx** and **Engels** in London of *The Communist Manifesto*, with its famous conclusion 'Workers of the world unite, you have nothing to lose but your chains', and the revolutions in continental Europe, in which societies of skilled workers briefly played a political role. However their numbers were extremely limited and both trade unions and strikes remained illegal everywhere in Europe except Britain. Nevertheless, it was in Prussia that the first socialist mass labour movement emerged, Ferdinand Lassalle's (1825–65) Allgemeiner Deutscher Arbeiterverein (General German Workers Association) of 1863.

1865–1914

The fifty-odd years prior to the outbreak of **World War I** were characterized partly by the flood of new inventions from Britain, France, Germany and, increasingly, America – such as the phonograph, the internal combustion engine, the electric light bulb and the electric motor – which were later to revolutionize the products and styles of industrial manufacturing, but more immediately obviously by the spread of mass industrialization across Belgium and Germany and extending even to parts of **Russia**, together with some regions of the Austro-Hungarian Empire, notably **Bohemia** and Greater Vienna, of France, of northern Italy, of Sweden and of Switzerland. Newly unified Germany in particular was increasingly to rival Britain's position as Europe's prime manufacturing nation. This was partly an inevitable consequence of the spread of technological knowledge and of the more modern machinery available to newer entrants to the market, but also of weaknesses particular to Britain which remained conspicuous throughout the twentieth century. Product marketing remained attuned to the time when British manufactures enjoyed a monopoly and much labour training was old-fashioned. This itself probably reflected the extent to which Britain's pioneering industrial inventors had primarily been craftsmen advancing on the basis of trial and error, rather than research workers following scientific principles. They were, in the best sense, amateurs. Moreover, applied science rarely enjoyed the prestige in Britain which it gained in Germany as that country expanded into shipbuilding, chemicals and the electrical industry as well as into banking and insurance, generating sufficient wealth to satisfy her own domestic investment needs and to permit extensive foreign investment as well.

Nevertheless, industry everywhere now became more closely associated with the sciences, particularly chemistry, and inventiveness flourished in many countries leading to the establishment of companies which remain household names. Sir Henry Bessemer (1813–98) revolutionized steel making by inventing the process of converting cast–iron directly into steel. Also in Britain, W. H. Perkin in 1856 produced the first of the aniline dyes. It was the German firm of Friedrich Bayer & Co. of Elbersfeld, however, founded in the early 1860s to manufacture those dyes, which really pointed the way forward by investing heavily in research, under Carl Duisberg, into a wide range of new chemical products and establishing close links with the chemistry departments of the universities in Berlin and Würzburg. Also in the 1860s, Alfred Nobel in Sweden discovered the explosive potential of nitro-glycerine and earned the fortune from the manufacture of dynamite and blasting gelatine which funds the internationally famous Nobel Prizes. Efficient dynamos were first built in the same period by Werner Siemens

(1816–92), making it possible to use electricity for industrial power as well as for lighting and transportation. His Berlin electric tram of the 1880s then demonstrated the effectiveness of electric traction. Siemens, who had gone into partnership with J. G. Halske as early as 1847, then concluded an agreement with a newly founded rival, Emil Rathenau's German Edison Company, in 1883, and the two firms soon went on to establish the famous Allgemeine Elektrizitäts-Gesellschaft (AEG) electrical concern. The petrol-fuelled internal combustion engine appeared in France and Germany in the early 1870s, although its industrial applications lay in the future.

The story of industrialization from the 1860s onwards, however, was the story of economic and political change as much as it was of new inventions. Economic change took two broad directions. The first was the growing importance of the financier who was a banker or an accountant rather than a craftsman or an inventor, and who had to employ the managers and engineers needed to run the industrial enterprises they founded. The Pereire brothers in France in the 1830s and 1840s had perhaps been the first of this new breed of capitalist entrepreneurs, although their rivals, the Rothschilds, were to become more widely known. Such men were often Jewish with international interests, and their ability to survive the impact of the second broad direction of economic change, the emergence of the international trade cycle, was one factor in the growth of nineteenth-century **anti-Semitism**. Industrialization had started the movement towards a world economy which was to culminate in the globalization of the later twentieth and early twenty-first centuries, and the booms and slumps of the trade cycle had become international, not just national, in their impact. National slumps had occurred at roughly ten-yearly intervals, but the crisis of 1857 became the first world slump. It was followed in 1873 by the first 'Great Depression' which some consider lasted until 1896. German share values fell by some 60 per cent between the beginning of the 1870s and 1877, and almost half of the blast-furnaces in the world's principal iron-producing countries suspended operation. Nevertheless, it was not nearly as severe as that which was to follow between 1929 and 1934.

Economic change went hand in hand with political change. Organized labour became a powerful force, particularly in Germany, and its Social Democratic Party was formed in 1869. In 1875 it united with Lassalle's Workers Association to become today's Social Democratic

Party of Germany (SPD). The 1860s saw a general modification of the law across Europe to allow at least a measure of labour organization and strikes, although the legal position of unions remained unclear everywhere but in Britain. Again, except in Britain, organized labour was strongly influenced by Marxism.

1918 to the present

Industrialization since World War I has had five main aspects. The first is its spread across the **Soviet Union** after the 1917 **Russian Revolution** and then across the Soviet sphere of influence in central and eastern Europe after 1945. The Soviet concentration on heavy industry unquestionably permitted it to defeat Germany in **World War II** but it ignored the progressive substitution of light consumer industries for the traditional heavy industries, which had started in western Europe in the 1920s and formed the period's second main aspect. The **Great Depression** of 1929–34 caused mass unemployment in sectors such as shipbuilding, hence the Jarrow Crusade from a town where unemployment stood at over 80 per cent, but had little impact on the new consumer industries such as car and radio production. It was not until the 1950s, however, that the Soviet Union under **Khrushchev** belatedly put any emphasis on producing consumer goods.

The third aspect divides into successive phases of which the first was the introduction under American inspiration of production line mechanization, which dramatically increased productivity but rendered the operative a 'cog in the machine'. It was, however, to be widely subsumed in later decades by automation which dispensed with the operative altogether and then by computerization which could control the output of a whole factory.

The fourth aspect, which gathered pace from the latter part of the nineteenth century, was the development of industrial production in the wider world beyond Europe and North America. **Japan** took the lead in rapid industrialization, rivalling many European countries, the year 1920 producing more steel than Italy and more electricity than either **Spain** or **Sweden**. On the basis of virtually no indigenous raw materials, it had by the outbreak of war with America and Britain in 1941 a fully fledged industrial economy capable of producing warships, aircraft and other armaments, which permitted it to wage war for four years. Virtually the whole of India was connected by a major railway system by 1914 and thousands of workers were employed in the jute and cotton mills of Kolkata and Mumbai. Elsewhere, the elements of industrial development, railways and steam-powered factories for processing agricultural products, and large-scale mining were becoming commonplace, although few countries other than Japan had converted to primarily industrial economies by World War II. In 1951 the **United States** was on almost every measure the pre-eminent industrial power in the world, producing more coal, steel, motor vehicles and aircraft than any other country. Thereafter, industrialization spread much more rapidly. The southern European economies of Italy and Spain, which had hitherto lagged behind, saw rapid industrial growth in the post-war period, but the most striking developments came with the rise of Far Eastern manufacturers, initially in Japan but soon joined by **South Korea**, **Taiwan**, **Singapore** and **Malaysia**, who began to dominate older areas of manufacturing such as shipbuilding, textiles and motorcycles and motor vehicles while also becoming major producers of electronic goods such as radios, televisions, and latterly computers and mobile phones. Most dramatic of all was the industrialization of **China** following the death of **Mao Zedong**, becoming the second largest economy in the world by the early twenty-first century. By 2015 China produced over half the world's steel, consumed over 3 billion tons of coal and was a mass producer of manufactured goods of every type, accompanied by breakneck urbanization and many of the problems of pollution and environmental degradation which had affected the first industrial powers. India, too, was becoming an increasingly ambitious industrial power, rapidly developing high-tech computer industries, a space programme and extensive heavy and light industries. An intermediate category of emergent industrial powers, such as **Brazil**, **South Africa**, **Mexico** and **Turkey**, has also been recognized as having a leading part to play in the twenty-first century.

A fifth aspect has been the progressive liberalization and vast increase of trade in manufactured goods and a complication of trade flows from the nineteenth century pattern of primary products being brought to Europe for export as manufactured goods to a wider world. As late as 1914, the United Kingdom built three-quarters of the world's ships, produced half its cotton textiles and owned half the total merchant marine to carry its goods to every corner of the globe. By the twenty-first century Asian-manufactured goods flooded the world markets while China and Japan sucked in vast imports of raw materials and fuel and received counter-flows of services and luxury products from other parts of the world. To an extent, the countries of the first wave of industrialization have deindustrialized in favour of the new industrial powers in the East, though manufacturing still remains a significant part of their economies. After a period of protectionism between the two world wars during the Great Depression, there were deliberate attempts to liberalize world trade and establish worldwide agreement on tariffs. Following the **Bretton Woods conference** and the establishment of the **World Bank**, there were commitments to lower tariffs and regular meetings of GATT (the General Agreement on Trade and Tariffs), which covered 80 per cent of world trade by the late twentieth century. The World Trade Organization (WTO) provides a backdrop of liberal tariff arrangements, increasingly important since the opening of the former Soviet bloc and Communist China to world trade. Regular meetings of international groupings of leading economies such as the G7 and G20 are aimed at encouraging economic growth and dealing with incipient crises. As a result, world trade in manufactured goods and industrial development has grown considerably in the twenty-first century, in spite of a slowdown in growth produced by the **Great Recession** after 2008.

influenza epidemic

– see also **epidemics; health**.

Influenza epidemics remain a recurrent threat although in recent years those threats, notably that of avian or bird flu, have either failed to materialize or been successfully countered by the widespread vaccination of the most vulnerable. The threat, however, is likely to remain, because the influenza virus is subject to unpredictabe mutation. The most severe recorded epidemic was of Spanish flu in 1918–19 when 40–100 million people died worldwide, of which some 250,000 were in **Great Britain**, 400,000 in **France** and 500,000–675,000 in the **USA**. Fourteen European nations witnessed 1.98 million excess deaths, equivalent to 1.1 per cent of the population. Extrapolated to cover the 25 per cent of Europe not studied, the number of deaths rose to 2.64 million. The average rise of 86 per cent in the death rate in the fourteen nations included a maximum of 172 per cent in **Italy** and a minimum of 33 per cent in **Finland**. The rise in England and Wales was 55 per cent, in France 66 per cent and in **Germany** 73 per cent.

information revolution

– see also **information technology; Internet**.

The massive increase in the flow of electronic communication made possible from the late twentieth century, based upon the development of information technology (IT) in which computing power was increasingly miniaturized and global communication between computers was made possible by the worldwide web of telecommunication links. Computers for processing large amounts of data were pioneered during the 1940s but remained bulky machines, largely confined to government and large business institutions. By the 1980s the first personal computers (PCs) were made possible by the miniaturization of components and were soon followed by the first mobile or cell phones. Although early PCs were very limited in their computing power and early mobile phones weighed as much as half a kilogram and had a battery life of less than an hour, they set a trend for ever more powerful desk-top computers and hand-held devices. With further miniaturization and increasingly powerful silicon chips, processing power leapt by leaps and bounds.

A critical development came with the development of the World Wide Web, an invention of Sir Tim Berners-Lee, then a British employee of CERN in Geneva, which allowed computers to communicate worldwide through a `highway' of fibre-optic cables and ordinary telephone lines. The ability to use mobile phones using satellite and dedicated mobile phone networks provided a parallel line of development. Vodaphone made the first international mobile phone call in 1991. In 1995 a common operating system for personal computers, Windows 95, revolutionized the way in which people created and used information. Internet Explorer became almost ubiquitous as an operating system, permitting the transfer of data and personal communication by electronic mail (e-mail) and text messages. `Search engines' such as Google revolutionized access to information and also to a rapidly developing trend for all commercial outlets and government services to be accessible via a `website' on the **Internet**. Meanwhile, the digitization of archives, libraries, data banks and music made them readily available for the first time.

Similarly, Internet shopping had become well established by the early twenty-first century as most retailers moved online. What had been a parallel development in personal communication, mobile phones, developed rapidly. By 1999 more mobile phones were sold globally than cars or PCs combined, and by 2002 there were 1 billion subscribers worldwide to mobile phone networks. In 2007 the introduction of the Apple iPhone permitted mobile phones full access to the Internet, followed in 2015 by the first wearable IT devices with online capacity. From 2004 with the launch of Facebook a new wave of websites began to change expectations of how the Internet could be used for interpersonal use. By 2009 it was estimated that 1.67 billion people were using the Internet on a regular basis and 90 trillion e-mails were sent during the year.

Two years later, Facebook had 800 million users and Google, Amazon and mobile phone manufacturers Apple and Samsung were amongst the largest businesses in the world as e-commerce topped over 1 trillion dollars for the first time. In 2015 it was estimated that four-fifths of the world's population outside China had a Facebook account and mobile phone penetration was becoming almost universal. Full and speedy access to the Web remained strongest in the developed world and urban areas where fibre-optic connections were available but satellite-based systems promise connection for even the remotest areas.

information technology
– see also **Internet**.

The use of hardware and software artifacts for computing and telecommunication networks to convert, store, protect, process, transmit and retrieve information. Computing hardware devices, such as the abacus, have existed in many forms since the time of Babylon. The evolution of the modern computer was shaped by the development of electricity, advances in semi-conductor material and the invention of the transistor and the micro-chip, leading to the creation of the personal computer by IBM in 1978. Computing software devices have evolved along with the development of operating systems and programming languages, and of utility applications. The evolution of modern telecommunications technology may be represented by a sequence of innovations moving from the telegraph, on to telephony, radio, television, mobile telephony, the **Internet** and computer networks.

INGOs
– see **NGOs**.

Inkatha
A South African political party founded by **Gatsha Buthelezi** in 1975 primarily for **Zulus**. Initially Inkatha joined with the **African National Congress** to press for rights for black South Africans in the apartheid system, but by the 1990s it had emerged as its principal rival, leading to bloody clashes. After the end of **apartheid** and national elections in 1994

Inkatha was active in the government, especially for **KwaZulu** province.

inoculation
The practice of artificially inducing immunity against diseases such as smallpox through the controlled infection of a less severe form of the virus (*variola minor*), so as to make the recipient immune to reinfection. It is known to have been commonly performed in ancient **India**, **China** and the **Ottoman Empire**, by inhaling steam from smallpox crusts. The method used by eighteenth-century Europeans was to rub virus pustules into a scratch between the thumb and forefinger. Smallpox inoculation was replaced with the safer **vaccination** method derived from cowpox in the nineteenth century, pioneered by the British surgeon, Edward Jenner (1748–1823).

Inonu, Ismet (1884–1973)
On 11 November 1938, Ismet Inonu succeeded **Mustafa Kemal** (Atatürk) to become the second president of **Turkey**. He held that office until May 1950 when his ruling party met defeat at the ballot box. He adopted his surname in 1934, a reference to his leadership in the defence of the town of Inonu in January 1921 during a critical battle in the Turkish War of Independence. Inonu's legacy in power was to have carried the banner of Kemalist authoritarianism after Atatürk's death.

Institutional Revolutionary Party (PRI)
The official revolutionary party of **Mexico** in its third incarnation, first created in 1929 as the National Revolutionary Party (PRN), reorganized in 1936 as the Mexican Revolutionary Party (PRM), and in 1946 restructured as the PRI. It comprises three sectors: the National Confederations of Workers (CTM), of Campesinos (Agrarians) (CNC) and Public Workers (CNOP). From its creation, it controlled the national congress, and it held the presidency from 1930 until 2000. The PRI developed a reputation for election manipulation, corrupt practices with labourers and agrarians, and fiscal mismanagement. Efforts to reform the party led to the mysterious death of Carlos Madrazo and the departure of reform-minded members, called the Democratic Current, who founded the Democratic Revolution Party (PRD) in 1989, becoming a major party with the mayoralty of Mexico City. The PRI remains a powerful party especially successful in state and local elections and with strong presidential candidates.

Intermediate Nuclear Forces (INF) Treaty (1987)

This treaty was signed by US President **Ronald Reagan** and Soviet Premier **Mikhail Gorbachev** in Washington in December 1987, committing their countries to eliminating nuclear and conventional ground-launched ballistic and cruise missiles with ranges of between 300 and 3,400 miles. Each country had the right to inspect the military installations of the other. The treaty was the first agreement between the superpowers to reduce nuclear weapons and a major step towards ending the **Cold War**. By June 1991, 2,692 missiles had been destroyed.

International Bank for Reconstruction and Development
– *see* **World Bank**.

International Brigades
– *see* **Spanish Civil War**.

International Labour Organization (ILO)

This became a specialized agency of the United Nations in 1946 and is the only surviving institution created by the **Treaty of Versailles** of 1919. The ILO seeks to promote social justice and to recognize human and labour rights, by formulating international labour standards as Conventions and Recommendations. It promotes the development of independent employers' and workers' organizations and provides training and advisory services.

International Monetary Fund (IMF)

One of the three international organizations created during the United Nations Monetary and Financial Conference, commonly known as **Bretton Woods**, in 1944. Its purpose was to oversee the newly established system of fixed exchange rates, which collapsed in 1971–3, but the IMF continues to operate as an overseer of the global financial system. It monitors exchange rates and balance of payments, and offers technical and financial assistance when requested. Its headquarters are located in Washington DC.

Internet

An information system based around a network of computers that spans the globe and which are freely accessible (from 1992 onwards) to all those whose computer systems can accommodate HTML language. The Internet developed from several different technologies. As early as 1968,

researchers in the United States were creating ways to distribute their computer capacity between various 'hubs' so that a strike on one would not mean the end of the network. This technology, known as ARPnet, was soon supplemented by the rise of the microchip, which made computing power much more accessible. It was only in 1992, however, that a British scientist, Tim Berners-Lee, working at the European research centre at CERN, developed HTML language, which made the network easily accessible and capable of carrying large packets of information. Combined with improvements in telecommunications technology, these developments allowed computer engineers to develop systems that sent more and more complex 'packets' of information from computer to computer, and eventually made huge amounts of instantaneous information available to those users able to enter the network system, which was initially known as the 'Web' but which became the 'Internet'.

The Internet became the basis of new models of political organization, education, commerce and discussion and proved almost impossible to censor or control, leading, by the late twentieth century, to widespread worry amongst governments that it was subversive and open to criminal and pornographic abuse. Domestic and business use of the Internet was becoming commonplace by the early twenty-first century with personal banking and shopping being increasingly conducted online. Internet use, however, was transformed by the parallel development of the smartphone, introduced in 2007, which allowed people to access the Internet via their mobile phone. Whole industries, social media, music streaming and mobile gaming, as well as multi-billion-dollar companies developing apps (applications), have developed around the now almost ubiquitous personal access to the Internet, reaching billions of people worldwide. Concerns about hacking of personal data, sexual exploitation and international cyber-crime for political, financial or strategic purposes remain.

Intifada (First and Second)
– *see also* **Arab–Israeli Conflict**.

The word *intifada* is an Arabic word meaning 'shaking off'. From 1987 until 1993 Palestinians rose up against the Israeli occupation of the Palestinian Territories. This movement, both non-violent and violent, became known as the First Intifada – an attempt to shake off the Israeli occupiers. Originally the Intifada began as a protest turned riot by Palestinian refugees. However, soon organizations began to take advantage of the movement, orchestrated by the PLO. The Second Intifada occurred in 2000. Various causes are attributed to the actions, including Israeli incursions and the divisive border wall. The ongoing peace talks between **Israel** and **Palestine** at the time of the First Intifada caused the process to stall. Sometimes described as lasting until 2005, the Second Intifada has no real definitive ending date and the violence continues. Though neither intifada can be called a definitive success, the Second Intifada did succeed in causing the eventual Israeli evacuation of the **Gaza** Strip. Both are estimated to have cost over 6,000 Palestinian and 1,000 Jewish lives.

Iqbal, Muhammad (1877–1938)

Arguably the greatest Urdu poet of the twentieth century, he was born in Sialkot, near the Punjab–Kashmir border, and studied in Lahore, Cambridge and Munich. Trained as a lawyer, Iqbal found his calling as a poet, intertwining spiritual, political and philosophical themes in lyrical Persian and Urdu verse. He is known for his celebration of the spiritual development of the individual, his expressions of love for his homeland, and his calls for Muslim universalism as an alternative to narrow territorial nationalism. Iqbal also made significant contributions to the field of Islamic philosophy, most prominently in *The Reconstruction of Religious Thought in Islam*. He played an important role in anti-colonial politics, including a historic presidential address he made at the annual session of the All-India Muslim League in 1930 calling for the creation of a Muslim state in north-western **India**.

Iran

– see also **Iran–Iraq War; Pahlavi dynasty**.

In the longer perspective, an empire, the Persian, with a 2,500-year history and a powerful sense of cultural identity. The impact of its architecture, art, language and literature, all a source of great national pride, is felt far beyond the boundaries of modern Iran. The Persian Empire reached its greatest imperial extent of later centuries under **Nadir Shah**, who reigned 1736–47, to encompass modern **Iran**, Transcaucasia, central Asia, the Gulf emirates of **Bahrain** and **Oman**, **Afghanistan** and Mughal India. Weakened culturally and politically under the succeeding Zand and **Qajar dynasties** and the intervening civil wars, it was increasingly subject to pressure from the expanding **Russian Empire** and the British presence in **India**, and lastingly lost **Georgia** to **Russia**, 1801, and northern Azerbaijan and **Armenia** to Russia, 1828. It had to abandon

ambitions in Afghanistan under British pressure, 1856, thereby creating the nation state of today. Nevertheless, less than half the population speaks Persian (Farsi) and a fifth speaks a form of Turkish.

Persia failed to meet the challenge posed by the European great powers throughout the nineteenth century, either economically or socially. The Qajars did not nurture the social foundations on which a modern Iran might be built, perpetuating instead an administrative culture of suspicion and fear. Their personal corruption led to the granting of monopoly concessions to foreigners over significant sectors of the economy. Economic progress was slow, with Iran's first mainline railway not opening until 1938. The country's economic impotence was underlined by the Anglo-Russian agreement of 1907 dividing the country into economic zones. The impact of the 1905 Russian Revolution was, however, sufficient to generate the Iranian Revolution, 1905–11, whereby Iran haltingly, and often nominally, became a constitutional monarchy. In foreign affairs, it was to continue to try to play the British and Russians off against each other and to involve other countries such as America, **Belgium** and **Germany** as counterweights as best it could. The benefits were negligible.

The advent of the **Pahlavi dynasty**, 1925, marked an end to the stagnation of earlier decades and the introduction of reform and a new emphasis on material progress. The name of the country was also formally changed from 'Persia' to 'Iran'. Nevertheless, Iran remained dependent on the will of external powers. Britain and the Soviet Union forced Reza Shah into exile, 1941, fearing that he might cooperate with Germany, substituting his son, **Mohammed Reza Pahlavi**. He came under the sway of **Mohammed Mossadegh**, who nationalized the **oil** industry before being ousted in favour of the shah by the British and American secret services, 1953. Close relations with the **United States** thereafter contributed to the intense anti-Americanism of the **1978–9 Iranian Revolution** and the declaration of the Islamic Republic of Iran in which **Shi'ite** clergy exercise powerful influence. Attacked by **Iraq**, 1979, and at war until 1990, Iran has been at loggerheads with the United States since 1979 partly for historical reasons and partly because of US support of **Israel**. Iran is allied to Shi'ite groupings across the Middle East including **Hezbollah** in Lebanon. Recognized as a major regional player, especially after the fall of **Saddam Hussein** and the weakening power of Iraq, its rivalry with **Saudi Arabia** and antagonism towards Israel and the US have created tensions. These were heightened by its pursuit of nuclear facilities, leading to UN economic sanctions and the serious threat of military action to neutralize them. A major accord on Iran's nuclear programme in 2015 has led to the relaxation of sanctions and relations with the West.

Iran–Contra Scandal

The disclosure in November 1986 that the United States National Security Council (NSC) had been involved in armaments sales contrary to declared US policy and in consequent illegal financial transactions. Although the **USA** officially neither bargained with terrorists nor would aid Iran in its war with **Iraq**, arguing that **Iran** was a sponsor of international terrorism, the NSC in 1985–6 sold weapons to Iran in the unfulfilled hope that it would result in the release of Americans held in Lebanon by **Shi'ite** militants loyal to Iran. Part of the 48 million dollar payment was then diverted by the NSC to the **Contras** of **Nicaragua**, who were fighting its semi-Marxist **Sandinista** government. All military aid to Nicaragua, direct or indirect, had been legally prohibited by the Boland Amendment in Congress, 1984. The disclosure led to the sacking and prosecution of the NSC head, Rear Admiral John M. Poindexter, and the responsible officer, Lieutenant Colonel Oliver North, but the foreknowledge of President **Reagan** was never established.

Iran–Iraq War (1980–1988)

Following the 1979 revolution in Iran that toppled the pro-western government of **Muhammad Reza Shah Pahlavi** and brought to power Ayatollah **Ruhollah Khomeini** with the establishment of the Islamic Republic of Iran, Iraq's President **Saddam Hussein** sensed an opportunity. The country was in disarray. Hussein also believed it was necessary to strike Iran to prevent the Islamic revolution spreading to his own country and throughout the region, and also to gain full control of the Persian Gulf and Iranian oil fields. The war started on 22 September 1980, after a series of border skirmishes, and lasted for eight years with no clear winner. There was appalling destruction on both sides that included poisonous gas attacks on both civilians and soldiers, massive air strikes of infrastructure and oil fields and devastating loss of life.

At the start of the hostilities there were a number of issues that divided the two countries, ranging from cultural rivalries to specific disputes over navigation rights in the south and frontiers in the north. Ideologically, the war pitted a secular nationalist leader in Saddam Hussein against an Islamically motivated Khomeini. The war developed over several distinct stages. The first phase was characterized by Iraqi air and land attacks in south-western Iran, the site of the most lucrative oil fields. The Iraqis had expected that their invasion would turn Iranians against their own regime. But it had the opposite effect and the Iranians put up a vigorous defence. The second phase involved Iranian counter-attacks in the form of major campaigns in southern Iraq, especially near Basra. During this phase the Iranians utilized unarmed and untrained young men who were sent in waves to the battlefield with only a key around their neck, signifying their imminent entrance into heaven. This promise of martyrdom, a religious notion which the Iranian government extensively modified and secularized to great effect, demoralized the Iraqi troops.

The third phase, 1984–7, was essentially a trenched ground war of attrition. Both countries tried to internationalize the conflict by attacking tankers in the Persian Gulf. Though the **United States** remained neutral through most of the war, it aided Iraq in the last phases, selling it weapons. Towards the very end, as both sides became desperate, the Iraqi Army used poisonous gas against hundreds of Kurds in Halabja who they maintained were collaborating with the Iranians. Finally, with more than 1 million people dead (with most casualties on the Iranian side), the two countries agreed to abide by UN Resolution 598 on 20 August 1988, which brought a formal end to the war.

Ultimately, the war started a series of events in Iraq that subsequently resulted in its invasion of **Kuwait** in 1990, leading to comprehensive UN sanctions and the 2003 US invasion and occupation of the country. In Iran, the war served to solidify the revolutionary regime and enabled it to use the Iraqi threat to eliminate potential political opposition. Though the original intent of the invasion was to weaken the Islamic Republic, it effectively strengthened its relative position and militarized the society.

Iran Hostage Crisis

– *see* **Tehran Embassy Crisis**.

Iranian Revolution (1978–1979)

– *see also* **Iran**.

This revolution was the result of hostility to the autocratic rule and corrupt government of **Mohammed Reza Shah Pahlavi**, shared by students, merchants and traditionalist **Shi'ite** masses and inspired from abroad by **Ayatollah Khomeini**. It forced the departure of the Shah, on

16 January 1979. Unlike the great majority of twentieth-century Middle Eastern revolutions, it was a genuine popular uprising rather than a coup by the military. It was also successful at least in the medium term. It introduced theocratic fundamentalist rule under the Islamic Republic of Iran, and almost certainly was followed by the execution of many hundreds of members and servants of the previous regime and the suppression of all domestic opposition. The revolution's anti-Americanism soon generated the **Tehran Embassy hostage crisis**. Although the revolution was religiously and socially conservative and profoundly anti-western, it nevertheless embraced aspects of modernism, as evinced by Iran's development of nuclear power for civil and perhaps military purposes.

Iraq

– see also **Iran–Iraq War; Saddam Hussein**.

Iraq formed the Ottoman province of Mesopotamia from the sixteenth century until **World War I**. Occupied by British forces, 1916, and, following Turkey's defeat, created as a state by the **League of Nations mandate** to **Great Britain**, 1921, it was enlarged by the transfer from Syria of the district of Mosul in the early 1920s. It was designated a Class A mandate, indicating suitability for early independence. A kingdom under **Faisal I** of the Hashemite dynasty, who had first hoped to become King of Syria, its stability under him, his successor, **Ghazi** and the infant **Faisal II** was assured more by the political dexterity of the long-standing, pro-British prime minister, Nuri al-Said, than by any loyalty to the Hashemite dynasty. The country was formally independent, 3 October 1932. Arab nationalist Iraqi officers under Rashid al-Ghilani organized a military coup and tried to get German support for ousting both the British and their client Hashemite monarchy in 1941, but the coup was suppressed by the British. Nuri al-Said, who unbeknown to the British had also sought to contact **Hitler**, emerged as Iraq's strongman on whom the British could rely. He sought to counter the growing influence of **Gamal Abdel Nasser** throughout the Arab world in the 1950s by crafting the **Baghdad Pact** (CENTO) in 1955, which linked Iraq with **Turkey** and then Great Britain, **Iran** and **Pakistan**, but only succeeded in confirming the nationalist view that he was a western puppet. He was assassinated, together with King Faisal II and his family, in a military coup by General **Qassem** (Kassem) on 14 July 1958, which established a republic. The Arab Federation with **Jordan**, which was concluded 14 February 1958, lapsed

with the revolution. The country briefly claimed **Kuwait**, 1961.

Qassem was overthrown in 1963 and succeeded as president first by General **Abdul Salam Aref** (Arif) and then by his brother **Abdul Rahman Aref** (Arif), 1966. A successful coup by the Ba'ath Party in 1968 installed General Ahmed Hasan Al-Bakr as president. A peaceful transfer of power made **Saddam Hussein**, vice president since 1969, president in 1979. Fearing in part the intended export of the **Shi'ite** fundamentalism which had come to power in the **Iranian Revolution of 1978–9**, Iraq invaded **Iran** in September 1980, abrogating the 1975 Algiers Pact whereby it had been obliged to accept joint control of the Shatt al-Arab waterway. Despite an estimated cost of around 1 million lives, the war, in which Iraq sought to establish itself as the centre of power in the **Middle East**, proved inconclusive. It ended in a ceasefire under UN auspices on 20 August 1988, and peace terms offered by Iraq to Iran on 15 August 1990. Iraq invaded Kuwait on 2 August 1990, claiming it had once been part of Mesopotamia. Annexation was declared, 8 August 1990, unleashing the **Gulf War** of 1990–1, followed by Kurdish and **Shi'ite** insurrections in the north and south respectively, encouraged but not supported on the ground by the coalition The resulting air exclusion zones enforced by Britain, **France** and the US remained a source of tension as did international supervision of nuclear facilities, which was interpreted by Iraq as spying.

Tension was intensified by the 'war on terrorism' waged by US President **George W. Bush** following the **9/11** attacks by **al-Qaida**, his 29 January 2002 denunciation of an 'axis of evil' including **North Korea**, Iran and Iraq, and readiness to make a highly questionable connection between Saddam Hussein and fundamentalist Islamic terrorism. The US and Britain attacked Iraq without UN authority, 20 March 2003, claiming that Iraq was developing weapons of mass destruction, a claim later found to be totally false. The regime fell, 7 April 2003, ushering in several years of chaotic occupation and sectarian violence in which over 100,000 may have died. Since the parliamentary elections of 2005, power moved decisively from the traditional dominance by the **Sunni** minority to dominance by the Shi'ite majority in a context of continuing sectarian violence. The former Sunni vice president, Tariq al-Hashimi, was sentenced to death in absentia, September 2012, for allegedly running death squads. Sectarian violence was intensified by the emergence of the extremist **ISIL** movement, putting the future integrity of the state at considerable risk. A substantial tranch of northern Iraq, including Mosul, fell for a time under **ISIL** control in 2014–15.

Iraq War (2003)

Shortly after the terrorist attacks in the **United States** on 11 September 2001, the administration of **George W. Bush** launched their a global 'war on terrorism'. As part of that war, they focused their attention on Iraq and the presidency of Saddam Hussein. Although Iraq had not been involved in the terrorist attacks on 9/11, the Bush administration maintained Saddam Hussein had links to **al-Qaida** and in particular that his government had weapons of mass destruction that it could provide to various terrorist organizations to use against the United States. In autumn 2002 the UN Security Council passed Resolution 1441 calling on Iraq to disclose all its holdings of weapons of mass destructions and to allow unfettered access to all sites. In early 2003 the United States unilaterally proclaimed that Iraq was in violation of Resolution 1441. Subsequently, the Bush administration launched Operation Iraqi Freedom and on 20 March 2003 began a massive bombing campaign and land invasion of Iraq. Within three weeks American troops had entered Baghdad and statues of Saddam Hussein had been torn down. At this point, the US and its allies had encountered scant resistance from the Iraqis. On 1 May, President Bush announced the end of major combat operations in Iraq. However, the operation was far from over. The primary justification for the invasion, Iraq's weapon's arsenal, was misleading and illusory. The American ten-year occupation of Iraq proved to be disastrous with more than 4,000 American soldiers killed and hundreds of thousands of Iraqis either killed or displaced.

Ireland

– *see also* **Irish Civil War; Irish Famine; Irish Question; Irish Republican Army; Northern Ireland; Northern Ireland Crisis**.

An island in the British Isles located to the west of **Great Britain**. A Celtic land, never part of the Roman Empire and with a distinctive history and culture, it was claimed as part of an English 'empire' by Henry VIII in 1541, but there had been Norman, Anglo-Norman and Scottish incursions into Ireland before that time. Subdued by Oliver Cromwell (1599–1658) in 1649–50 and again by William III (1650–1702) after 1689, it retained its own parliament though subservient to any decisions made by the British Parliament at Westminster. Penal laws against the Roman Catholicism practised by the majority of the population in the south of Ireland and a legacy of expropriation of Catholic landowners produced an English Protestant 'Ascendency' over a largely landless Catholic population.

The northern part of the island, Ulster, was heavily planted as a result of the wars of the seventeenth century with English and Scottish settlers, many of them Protestants, giving it a distinctive character from the rest of the island. In the aftermath of the **American Revolution** the Volunteer movement obtained greater freedom for the Irish Parliament but moves towards religious toleration for Catholics were frustrated by the outbreak of the **French Revolution** in which fear of radical subversion by groups such as the United Irishmen led to repression and attempts by Irish radicals such as Theobald Wolfe Tone (1763–98) to solicit French assistance for a national uprising. A major rebellion in 1798 was crushed, at the cost of 40,000 lives. British Prime Minister **William Pitt** responded by passing an **Act of Union** in 1801 which ended the Irish Parliament and added 100 Irish MPs to the British House of Commons. He failed to pass an Act permitting Catholics to sit as MPs, but this was obtained in 1829 through the organized efforts of Catholics led by Daniel O'Connell. Absentee landlordism and heavy reliance upon the potato as a subsistence crop had created an unstable agricultural economy in which subdivision of plots, overpopulation, but a flourishing export trade in cash crops was vulnerable to crop failure. The **Irish Famine** brought disaster to millions, but eased land hunger and allowed a category of more prosperous tenant farmers to emerge. Extensions to the franchise allowed an organized Irish party to develop under Charles Stewart Parnell (1846–91) campaigning on land issues and for self-determination through 'Home Rule'. Attempts to obtain Home Rule failed in 1886 and 1892, and the issue was taken up again in in 1911–14, producing considerable animosity in Ulster.

Meanwhile substantial land reform had bought out many landlords producing a substantial Irish tenant class. Although Home Rule passed in 1914, suspended for the duration of **World War I**, a splinter group of Republicans mounted the **Easter Rising** in 1916. Its brutal suppression greatly inflamed Irish opinion, leading to the supplanting of the moderate Irish Nationalist Party by the nationalist Sinn Fein who triumphed in southern Irish seats in 1918 and set up a shadow government.

Attempts by the British government to impose devolved parliaments in Dublin and Belfast were a failure in the south and a guerrilla war with Irish nationalists ensued in 1919–21. A treaty in 1921 between the British government and Irish nationalists produced the Irish Free State as a dominion under the British Crown in the twenty-six counties of Southern Ireland, while the six counties of **Northern Ireland** remained excluded and part of the United Kingdom. Under their prime minister, Eamon De Valera, Southern Ireland was renamed Eire, in 1937, pursued an autarkic economic policy, and renounced its allegiance to the British Crown. Declaring neutrality in **World War II**, Ireland became a republic in 1949, but was one of the poorest countries of western Europe, almost totally dependent on agriculture and trade with the United Kingdom, plus persistent heavy emigration. Joining the **European Union** gave a great boost to Irish agriculture and attracted inward investment, for the first time in generations reversing the flow of emigration. By the early twenty-first century relations with the United Kingdom were much improved through joint efforts to resolve the **Northern Ireland crisis**, the Republic renouncing its claim to the North in 1999. Hailed for its economic boom as a 'Celtic Tiger', it suffered severely in the **Great Recession** which almost bankrupted the Irish State when it took over the debts of its banking sector, forcing it to seek EU assistance and pursue a major austerity programme, discrediting traditional political parties.

Irgun Zvai Leumi

The militant Zionist Revisionist movement of **Vladimir Jabotinsky** established this underground Jewish army in **Palestine** in 1930. Its symbol was a hand holding a rifle over a map showing both banks of the Jordan River. Irgun's motto, '*Rak kach*', specified that only by violence could its territorial objectives be achieved. Irgun's commanders included **Menachem Begin**. Until the middle of **World War II**, Irgun, like **Haganah**, emphasized Jewish self-defence against Arabs and illegal Jewish immigration into Palestine. In 1944, after collaborating with the British briefly in suppressing a pro-Nazi revolt in **Iraq**, Irgun declared war on the British. In this respect it differed significantly from Haganah, which still preached *havlagah*, or 'self-restraint', towards the British Mandatory authorities. On 22 July 1946 Irgun dynamited the British military headquarters in Jerusalem's King David Hotel, killing ninety-one Jews, Arabs and British. The British and Irgun engaged in floggings and counter-floggings and executions and counter-executions. On 4 May 1947 Irgun organized a spectacular prison break from the British fortress

in Akko, a feat dramatized in the movie *Exodus*. Almost simultaneously, and shortly before they were scheduled to be executed, Irgunist Meyer Feinstein and a fellow convict blew themselves up in Jerusalem's Central Prison. Begin is buried next to them on Jerusalem's Mount of Olives. On 9 April 1948 an Irgun force conquered the Arab village of **Deir Yassin**, which commanded the heights over the Tel Aviv–Jerusalem highway, in a controversial operation which resulted in 240 Arab and 5 Jewish fatalities. With the proclamation of the Jewish State on 15 May 1948, **Ben-Gurion** insisted on the incorporation of Irgun and all other militias into the Israel Defence Forces. The Irgun resisted, and on 28 June 1948 attempted to smuggle men and arms on to the Tel Aviv beachfront via the ship *Altalena* (Jabotinsky's pen name). A Haganah operation led by **Yitzhak Rabin** sank *Altalena* with loss of life on all sides, thereby eliminating Irgun as an independent military force thereafter.

Irish Civil War

A conflict waged from 28 June 1922 to 24 May 1923 between opponents (the **Irish Republican Army**) and supporters (the Irish National Army) of the 1921 Anglo-Irish Treaty, which had established the 26-county Irish Free State. The opponents, who were defeated, objected to the loss of the Northern Ireland six counties and the acceptance of an oath of allegiance to the British Crown. An estimated 4,000 were killed in fighting that left bitter long-term divisions in Irish politics.

Irish Famine

The name given to the devastating potato blight which struck **Ireland** between 1846 and 1852, removing through death or emigration around 3 million people (almost half the population of the island) and embittering the relationship between people of Irish descent and British authorities for a century. Though present in other European countries, the blight was particularly bad in Ireland because poor Irish rural communities, which were economically, culturally and linguistically isolated from the rest of the British Isles, had become dependent upon the potato as a crop and foodstuff for some 60 per cent of all requirements. The situation was aggravated by a combination of anti-Irish and economic opinion in the British press, which largely blamed Irish lack of productivity and unwillingness to export food to earn cash for the crisis, and inaction on the part of the British government, which held to **laissez-faire** doctrines of economic non-interference and anti-welfare moralism. One permanent effect was the creation of an Irish, largely Catholic diaspora in an arc which ran from London, through the industrial cities of England and Scotland, and then down the major cities of North America, before stretching to the Australian colonies. Another was the rise of the Land League and the Home Rule movement, leading to the **Irish Question** of the late nineteenth century.

Irish Question
– *see also* **Ireland; Northern Ireland; Northern Ireland Crisis**.
A term coined in the mid nineteenth century for a congeries of problems associated with the constitutional position and governance of the island of **Ireland**. At the centre, the problem was that a majority of Irish politicians and subjects, drawn largely from the Catholic and Anglo-Irish Protestant communities, wished for various degrees of self-government up to and including independence from the **United Kingdom**, whilst a majority of people from the Protestant communities of the north of Ireland did not. The question was also one that followed from the agrarian insecurity of tenant farmers dependent upon absentee landlords, the role of the Catholic Church in Ireland, the consequences of the Irish Famine of 1844–8, and the viability of devolution or secession in the context of a unitary constitution. It was exacerbated by the need of Liberal governments, and those of Mr **Gladstone** in particular, to win over the crucial bloc of Irish Members of Parliament in the 'Home Rule Party' in order to form an administration, as well as by the presence in the House of Lords of reactionary Irish landlords. The question was partly solved by the removal of most of Ireland from the United Kingdom in 1922.

Irish Republican Army (IRA)
– *see also* **Irish Civil War; Northern Ireland Crisis**.
First employed by Fenians in the US and Canada in 1866 to refer to the paramilitary and insurgent forces associated with Irish nationalism, this term gained greatest fame as the name for nationalist forces in Ireland after 1913, in the 1916 **Easter Rising** and in the Irish War of Independence from 1919 to 1921. Thereafter, IRA supporters and members split into a number of guerrilla, veteran and officially tolerated organizations until 1969, when the **Northern Ireland** troubles saw the re-emergence of the term for the largest nationalist paramilitary after a split between the Official and ultimately dominant Provisional IRA.

Iron Curtain
The term, coined by **Winston Churchill** in Fulton, Missouri, 1946, describing the line between communist and non-communist Europe. Initially a metaphor, it became a literal reality with the erection by East Germany along the length of its frontier of a barrier of barbed wire, minefields and watch towers in 1952. Similar barriers divided **Czechoslovakia** and **Hungary** from the West, but less obviously in the **Balkans** where **Yugoslavia** acted as a buffer. Completed by the **Berlin Wall**, 1961. Opened, 1989.

Ironclads
Steam-powered iron-clad warships, armed with explosive shells, were pioneered by **France** and **Britain** but first deployed in maritime combat during the **American Civil War**. Confederate ironclads operated on the Mississippi river in 1861, and on 8–9 March 1862 the CSS *Virginia* (a converted Union ship) clashed with the USS *Monitor* off Hampton Roads, Virginia in the first proper confrontation between the new armoured vessels. Ironclad technology and design soon spread throughout the world's navies.

Isandlwana, Battle of (22 January 1879)
An important opening battle of the Anglo-Zulu War of 1879 in which a British force of some 1,400 under the command of Frederic Thesiger, Lord Chelmsford, was surprised and annihilated by a **Zulu** force led by King Cetewayo, estimated at 22,000. Almost all the British soldiers were killed, while Zulu casualties were estimated at 6,000. Because of the defeat, Natal committed more forces to the campaign, eventually defeating the Zulu.

ISIS (Islamic State of Iraq and Syria), ISIL (Islamic State of Iraq and the Levant) and IS (Islamic State)
A self-styled administration and self-proclaimed caliphate of swathes of eastern **Syria** and northern **Iraq**, declared 29 June 2014. Ultimately inspired by the numerous reformers since **Muhammad ibn 'Abd al-Wahhab** in the early eighteenth century, who have argued that **Islam**'s ills would be cured by a return to the perceived purity of early Islam and the adoption in full of **sharia**, and also by the Salafism of Muhammad 'Abduh, with its goal of restoring the caliphate. Triggered by the perceived western attacks on Islam, notably in **Afghanistan** and **Iraq**, and by the Syrian Civil War, it has promoted a fundamentalist interpretation of **jihad**

with maximum publicity to acts of destruction, murder and terror, even blowing up the ruins of the ancient Assyrian capital of Nimrud as non-Islamic before turning its attention to Palmyra. Unremittingly **Sunni**, it has horrified many fellow Sunnis who first saw it as a saviour from **Shi'ite** oppression. A highly effective fighting force, it has resisted US drone attacks, holding the Iraqi city of Mosul and proving a magnet for radicalized Muslim youth in **Europe**. ISIL also spread to **Libya** in October 2014 and for a short time seized large swathes of the country in 2015, drawn both by its oil wealth and the absence of central authority.

Islam

The word in Arabic means 'submission' (to the will of God). The predominant, and often virtually universal, religion of the whole Arab world except **Lebanon**, and of **Albania**, **Azerbaijan**, **Kazakhstan** and the central Asian nations of the Commonwealth of Independent States, **Turkey**, **Iran**, **Afghanistan**, **Pakistan**, **Bangladesh**, **Brunei**, Malaysia and Indonesia, together with the Russian republic of **Chechnya** and the Chinese province of Xinjiang. **Bosnia–Hercegovina** is 40 per cent Muslim. There are also significant minority communities south of the Sahara, in India and in western **Europe**. Although divided into branches, of which the **Sunni** and the **Shia** are now by far the most important, all Muslims are strictly monotheistic and believe that the word of God (Allah) was revealed to Muhammad, the last and most perfect of a succession of prophets including Abraham and Jesus, in the seventh century and recorded by him in the Qur'an (the recital), which is also regarded as the peak of Arabic prose. Mecca (Makkah), his birthplace AD 570, and Medina, the destination of his migration (*Hijra*) AD 622, which marks the beginning of the Muslim era, are Islam's two holiest cities. Allah is omnipotent and every *sura* (chapter) but one of the Qur'an starts with the mesmeric '*bismi-lillaahi-ir-raahmaani-irrahiimi*' ('in the name of Allah, the compassionate, the merciful'). All Muslims are by definition members of the Muslim community (*umma*, cognate with *umm*, 'mother') which in orthodox Islam is a religious institution in its own right, making any sense of a 'Church' as an institution within society irrelevant.

Muslims have often regarded any attempt to achieve personal union with God through mysticism with suspicion, but Muslim mysticism, or Sufism, dates back to at least the eighth century and has sometimes been politically and socially influential, with the **Sanussi Brotherhood** as one

twentieth-century example. The polytheistic and magical tendencies of some Sufi cults, however, have led to the banning of Sufism in **Saudi Arabia** and the strict limitation of dervishes in Turkey. The popularity of Sufi cults and wider heretical tendencies led in the eighteenth century to the rise of the radical reformer **Muhammad ibn 'Abd al-Wahhab** (1703–92) in Arabia, who claimed that the then political eclipse of Islam was attributable to spiritual degeneration and could only be rectified by a return to the Qur'an and early tradition. The puritanical Wahhabi movement was to drive the rise to power in Arabia of the house of Sa'ud and the proclamation of the Kingdom of Saudi Arabia, 1932. The movement has ensured that the kingdom remains the most conservative and fundamentalist, and arguably the most reactionary, of the Muslim states.

That eighteenth- and nineteenth-century political eclipse was usually perceived by its European perpetrators as the natural fruit of human progress, and that progress also meant that more 'primitive' religions such as Islam would simply wither away in the face of Christianity. Muslims naturally felt differently and the conservative reaction, including the Wahhabi movement, was one response. The Salafis dreamed of a renewed caliphate and the reconquest of lands such as **Spain**, southern Russia and **Ukraine**, lost to Islam. The alternative reaction was to favour modernization and the absorption into Islam of progressive western ideas. The tension between the two responses remains unresolved and has to some extent been complicated by the growth of nationalism and of proud identification with the Islamic past. In fact, the most significant challenge to Islam from the late nineteenth century onwards was to come not from Christianity but from **secularism**. The impact on Islam of Christian missionary activity proved negligible in practice, while Muslim missionary activity proved highly effective south of the Sahara in areas such as Northern Nigeria. It was similarly effective amongst the nomads of Kazakhstan. Secularism, however, came in different guises. In the **Soviet Union** under **Stalin**, secularism meant revolutionary communism and from 1928 all religion was rigorously suppressed as 'the opium of the people'. Whereas the **Russian Empire**, exclusive of Bukhara and Khiva, had had 26,279 mosques in 1912 and probably much the same in 1927, that figure fell in the whole of the Soviet Union between 1928 and 1942 to just 1,312. It then rose to some 1,500 by 1953 only to fall even further under **Khrushchev** to about 400. Although there was no parallel drive against Islam as such under **Kemal Atatürk** after 1923, secular values were asserted over religious values in Turkey much as they were in Soviet central Asia. **Sharia** was abolished, Muslim brotherhoods such as the whirling dervishes suppressed, traditional dress outlawed and female equality promoted. Almost everywhere in the Muslim world the most important secular (and nationalist) force has been the army. Although obviously composed of Muslims, its officers have been imbued with western secular ideas and its leaders, ranging from **Nasser** to **Saddam Hussein**, presided over states whose legal systems and social institutions have shown strong modernizing and westernizing influence. As a corollary, the army has been the focus of resistance to the traditionalist interpretations of Islam associated with Islamist parties and the brotherhoods, and has been ready to thwart their democratic rise to power, notably in **Algeria** and **Egypt**. The relationship between the Turkish Army and the ruling Islamist Justice and Development Party can only be described as tense. The army, however, not least in Turkey has usually stood for modernism rather than liberalism. The prime secularist challenge, however, has come from the exposure to western lifestyles, which clearly exercise great attraction for many Muslims although they repel others. This sense of repulsion has proved strongest politically in Iran, but has been a powerful motivator of violence amongst a small minority of individuals and groups, such as **ISIL**, and amongst the offspring of immigrants in Europe and America.

The impact of Islam on international politics has been extremely variable, not least because of its uneasy philosophical relationship with the concept of nationalism and the nation state on which the present world order depends. Unified Muslim or even Arab action has always succumbed to opposing economic, national and political, or even purely personal, interests. The most consistent strand has perhaps been hostility to **Israel**, but this is compromised by numerous implicit and even explicit understandings, although **Hezbollah** in Lebanon has, with Iranian support, proved less accommodating. The most fundamentalist of all Muslim states, Saudi Arabia, is the close military ally of the United States, which itself is the close military ally of Israel. On the other hand, Islam helped to motivate national liberation movements in Bosnia, Chechnya and Kosovo, and numerous volunteer **jihadis** fought with the **mujahideen** against the Russians in Afghanistan and have since moved to conflicts including Chechnya, **Iraq** and **Syria**. Militant fundamentalist Muslim groups

are active in such countries as **Yemen**, **Nigeria** and other parts of West Africa as well as Afghanistan, tribal areas of Pakistan and Iraq. They have not always been welcomed by their fellow Muslims.

Ismail Pasha (1830–1895)

Ruler (khedive) of **Egypt**, 1863–79. During the reign of his father he successfully commanded troops, and upon his succession obtained the right to patrilineal succession of the Ottoman Sultan. He launched an ambitious modernizing plan for Egypt including building railways, modernizing Cairo and commencing the construction of the **Suez Canal**. These projects put Egypt heavily in debt, which required him to limit his sovereignty. Disaffected army members led by Colonel Urabi overthrew him in 1879.

Israel

– *see also* **Arab–Israeli Conflict**.

Rooted in the **Balfour Declaration** of 8 November 1917, when the British government responded to **Zionist** pressure by agreeing to grant a home to the Jews in **Palestine**, and the subsequent provision of the **League of Nations mandate** to **Britain** over Palestine that the immigration of Jews was to be permitted while respecting the rights of the Arabs. Israel was formally proclaimed by the Jews of Palestine on the day of the withdrawal, without a political settlement, of the last British troops on 14 May 1948. No corresponding Palestinian Arab state was established. The neighbouring Arab states invaded Israel unsuccessfully on 15 May, and by the time of the 3 April 1949 armistice Israel had increased its territory by a third and 800,000 Palestinian Arabs had become refugees. With the exception of the **Gaza** Strip, that part of Palestine still held by the Arabs, the West Bank, passed under Jordanian administration, December 1949, and was formally incorporated in **Jordan**, 24 April 1950.

Israel attacked Egyptian Sinai with British and French backing on 30 October 1956, unleashing the **Suez Crisis**. It attacked **Egypt**, **Jordan** and **Syria** in the **Six Day War** of 1967, when it captured Sinai and the Gaza Strip from Egypt, the Golan Heights from Syria, and the West Bank and East **Jerusalem** from Jordan. Despite United Nations Resolution 242 ordering it to withdraw from the occupied territories, Israel has effectively absorbed East Jerusalem and authorized numerous settlements, illegal under international law, in the West Bank: Egypt and Syria attacked Israel with some success in the **Yom Kippur War**, 1973. Peace was achieved with Egypt in 1978 under the **Camp**

David Accords between Egypt and Israel under US auspices and the subsequent 1979 treaty which in due course returned Sinai to Egypt. Nevertheless, Israel invaded Lebanon in 1982, in an attempt to expel fighters of the **Palestine Liberation Organization** (PLO), but with mixed results including the foundation of **Hezbollah**, which was to prove a highly effective opponent. The failure to resolve the Israeli–Palestinian problem resulted in the violent rioting known as the **Intifada** (shaking-off) by the Palestinians of Israel and the occupied territories from 1987. A series of interim agreements, the **Oslo Accords**, were agreed by **Yassir Arafat** for the PLO and **Yitzak Rabin** and **Shimon Peres** for Israel, 1993, whereby mutual recognition and a gradual transfer of authority to the Palestinians in the Occupied Territories were agreed, but the outstanding questions of the right of Palestinians to return, the status of East Jerusalem and the growing number of Jewish settlements on the West Bank have resulted in continuing conflict to which no end is in sight. The separation barrier built along the West Bank may have reduced the number of suicide attacks in Israel, but has increased Arab enmity. Many believe that the density of the settlements, with more than 500,000 settlers, has now become such that the two-state solution favoured by most negotiators has become impracticable. Israel proper has absorbed more than 3 million Jewish immigrants since its foundation. A peace treaty was, however, signed with Jordan, 1994. An unacknowledged nuclear power, benefiting from an exceptionally high level of US military aid and unlimited diplomatic support, Israel has still to achieve a lasting settlement with the Palestinians and several of its neighbours, including Syria and **Iran**.

Istiqlal Party (Morocco)

The Istiqlal, or Independence, Party was the primary organization of the nationalist movement in Morocco and remains an active political party. Officially founded in 1944, its roots stretch back to a scattered network of urban-based intellectuals. They organized their first successful demonstrations in 1930 when the French tried to establish a separate legal system for Moroccan Berbers. In its early stages, Istiqlal featured diverse ideological viewpoints, including Salafism, Arab nationalism and communism. In the 1950s it splintered, and Allal al-Fassi's more conservative wing took over. Unlike leading nationalist parties in other Arab states, Istiqlal was never revolutionary, but rather sought a capitalist, constitutional monarchy with an active parliamentary voice in lawmaking. Since

gaining nearly a third of the seats in Parliament in 1970, its popularity has steadily declined. It won only 11 per cent in 2011 but participated in the ensuing government coalition.

Italian Empire

A loose collection of areas under the control of the kingdom of **Italy**, established in piecemeal fashion around 1885–6 and finally relinquished in 1960. The **Risorgimento** and subsequent unification of Italy coincided with the expansion of European imperialism into Africa and the Near East. It was widely believed that viability as a great power required the territorial ownership of strategic points and economic resources, and Italian nationalists enthusiastically embraced this aim. By means of secret diplomacy, alliances and war the Italian state responded by establishing imperial territories. Holdings in the Horn of Africa centred on **Eritrea** and modern **Somalia** in the 1880s were supplemented with the acquisition of part of Tientsin in 1901, **Libya** in 1912, and **Albania**, the Dodecanese islands, Anatolia, Montenegro, **Croatia** and Trieste before or as a consequence of **World War I**. The Fascist government of **Benito Mussolini** sought to add to this collection a sphere of autarkic dominance in the Mediterranean and south-eastern Europe, as well as the kingdom of Abyssinia (modern **Ethiopia**) which Mussolini attacked and occupied in defiance of the **League of Nations** in 1935–6. The overall strategic design of these acquisitions, which had something of a post hoc rationalization about it, was to provide Italy with a dominance of trade and shipping in the eastern Mediterranean, at the entrance to the Suez Canal, and, eventually, on the east coast of Africa, thus making her a vital power in the considerations of others. However, the Italian Empire was more a matter of holdings which other imperial powers did not want than of intention.

The pursuit of empire, however, rather than the gain of it, is the key to understanding modern Italy's chequered diplomacy. A French snub to ambitions in Tunisia drove Italy into an alliance with **Austria–Hungary** and **Germany** in 1881, and then the prospect of gains in Libya drew Italy to war with Germany's ally, the **Ottoman Empire**, thirty years later. Faced with the prospect of more gains from the allies than the Central Powers in 1915, Italy again switched sides to support **Britain** and **France**; and disappointment with these powers, as well as a predatory eye towards **Spain** during the civil war then played its part in Italy's switch to support **Franco**, **Hitler** and the idea of a sphere of influence throughout the Mediterranean and the Balkans. Whilst the Axis agreement briefly extended Mussolini's power as an imperial ruler, **World War II** ultimately proved disastrous to Italian ambitions. By 1943 its empire was in ruins, and Mussolini himself a prisoner of Germany.

The empire was formally dissolved in 1947, though Italy carried out a UN trust in Somaliland until 1960. Italian imperialism ultimately proved to be a version of nationalism, as scholar-agitators such as Giovanni Pascoli argued at the time, aiming to win over working people, gain resources and resolve the national disunion of a state cleaved by class, geography, and the antagonism between a united Italy and the Catholic Church which went unresolved until the **Lateran Treaties**. This belied the grand claims of those who saw the empire as the nucleus of a restored or renewed Roman Empire, on the one hand, and romantic fascists who saw it as the territory for a new type of society to take wing, such as Enrico Corradini and Giovanni Gentile, on the other.

Italian unification

Between the sixth and nineteenth centuries the Italian peninsula was marked by the presence of a divided group of cities, regions, dukedoms, principalities and states, not least of which were the papal lands radiating across the centre of the country from Rome. By the thirteenth century the ideal of Italian self-government in the face of perceived foreign interference, and a revival of interest in classical forms and procedures, was upheld by many of those whose words and writings have survived, but a serious unification of the peninsula lands was simply not possible. However, with the emergence of modern nationalism after the **French Revolution**, the idea arose that a unified Italian state, speaking one language and governed in one way, was within reach, and that Italy was undergoing a *risorgimento* (resurgence) comparable in its cultural effect to the Renaissance. Those supporting or promoting the idea emerged from several strands, including Sicilian and southern revolutionaries, anti-papal agitators, liberals, revolutionaries and northern intellectuals, as well as those opposed to Austrian rule in northern areas. The movement was stirred by **Napoleon**'s recreation of the Frankish-era kingdom of (northern) Italy, and by the decline of the power of autonomous republics such as Venice.

After the Napoleonic Wars, which had a galvanizing effect, the first half of the nineteenth century was marked by revolts and uprisings against Austrian and local regimes which appealed to this nationalist spirit, in Sicily (1820), the Piedmont (1821), across the north (1830) and in 1848 (principally in Lombardy, Tuscany and Piedmont). In alliance with **Napoleon III**, who was motivated by the Orsini affair and anti-Austrianism, the kingdom of Piedmont, which incorporated Sardinia as well, began a serious push to unite the north and remove the Habsburgs in 1858. This push was led by **Camillo Cavour** and Napoleon III personally, and proved only partially successful since, appalled by the slaughter at the Battle of Solferino in 1859, Napoleon sued for an early peace. Piedmont continued alone, and united the remaining central and northern areas into the United Provinces of Italy, before merging them again with Piedmont–Sardinia. This, for Cavour, would have been satisfactory. However, the price of French intervention had been French occupation of Nice and Savoy, which had sufficiently antagonized **Giuseppe Garibaldi** that Cavour had to divert him from declaring war on France by pushing Garibaldi into a southern campaign. It was this campaign, which became famous, that united southern Italy, and then presented Cavour and King Victor Emmanuel (1820–78) with a practically united peninsula. Only Venetia, Rome, and the papal lands remained outside the new state. The antagonism between **Austria** and **Prussia**, which emerged in the 1866 war, and the removal of French troops from Rome, gave Victor Emmanuel and Garibaldi their chance and, allied against Austria and with Prussia, Venetia was under the control of the new Italian kingdom by 1867. That year, Garibaldi attempted vainly to overtake papal and renewed French forces. With the removal of the French in 1870, the way to Rome stood clear, and the Italian Army reoccupied the city, leaving the Papacy behind the Leonine Wall in the **Vatican City**, built on a hill outside the Tiber and therefore technically not a part of historic Rome. Italy had been reunified, and emerged as a liberal Nationalist parliamentary monarchy.

Italy

– *see also* **Italian unification**

A state which emerged during the **risorgimento**, 1861–71, and which was engaged in Italian imperialism, largely in the western Balkans, and North and East Africa between 1871 and 1942. Italy was a constitutional monarchy until 1924, then a fascist state until 1943, and has been a republic since 1947. Between 1947 and 1992 a combination of factors partly centred on the electoral system ensured that Italy underwent almost sixty administrations, though the politicians and parties involved were often the same. The corruption and instability which resulted was exposed at the end of the period, and a series of public and judicial protests led to a referendum which radically transformed Italian democracy in 1993. For this reason, many scholars date the rise of a second republic, which is often characterized as more stable, majoritarian, more secular and more legalistic than that which went before, from 1994. This latter republic is inescapably linked to the character and administrations of **Silvio Berlusconi**.

Italy is a major economic power within Europe, and a strong exporter. However, membership of the euro currency at too high an initial rate ensured a painful deflation after 2008, the effects of which are still ongoing. It is also the case that Italian unification yielded a state which was divided between a south, north, Austro-German Trentino and former papal lands. For a long time, the state was at odds with the Catholic Church, of which the overwhelming number of Italians were devoted members, until the **Lateran Accords** recognized the sovereignty of the Vatican State in a power and tax-sharing arrangement which persists. Italy has also been culturally divided, with dialects, regions, local family networks and urban communist centres forming horizontal divisions. In some ways, therefore, the 1947–92 republic was representative; deals were done behind the scenes, foreign and religious groups mixed with families and parties, laws were added to the constitution, and yet economic growth was intense, Italian standards of living rose and the **EU** and **NATO** functioned as external regulators.

Italy as a state has also enjoyed a great deal of cultural and 'soft power' influence because of its remarkable history from Roman times, its music, food, wine, and quality of life, and its global diaspora. The feelings of people of Italian descent have been effectively harnessed by the issue of second passports and the presence of regional senators elected by the diaspora in the Italian upper house, as much as by the vitality and beauty of Italy as a tourist destination. In recent years Italy has also experienced a serious challenge to criminal groups such as the **Mafia**, whose existence was rooted in the nationalism of the eighteenth century and the resistance movements of **World War II**, and a reconfiguration of its tax and banking regulation of the church, both of which have tended to strengthen the state.

Ito, Hirobumi (1841–1909)

A Japanese statesman who became prime minister four times, Ito Hirobumi played a central role in building the Imperial Diet and the **Meiji** constitution (1889). Influenced by Bismarck's **Germany**, he recruited Hermann Roesler from Germany as special advisor to the Cabinet. Under his guidance, the new political system gave supreme governing authority to the emperor by terminating the Council of State (*Dajokan*) system. Acting as the resident general of **Korea**, he was assassinated by a Korean nationalist.

Iturbide, Agustín de (1783–1824)

A Creole officer in the Spanish military, Iturbide secured Mexican independence in 1821 through a compromise with rebels led by Vicente Guerrero. Elected emperor of **Mexico** by a constituent congress, Iturbide's attempts to establish a strong fiscal base were inadequate. Government fiscal problems and political ideological tensions between federalists and centralists quickly ended this experiment with national monarchy. After a brief exile to Europe, he returned to Mexico and was executed.

Ivory Coast (Côte d'Ivoire)

Former French colony in west Africa. **France** imposed a protectorate on the coastal area in 1842, absorbing the country into French West Africa in 1910, though resistance to occupation continued for a number of years. The Ivory Coast gained independence in 1960 under Félix Houphouët-Boigny (1905–93). Anti-communist, he maintained close relations with France, and remained president until his death. The economy flourished in the 1970s, but falling world commodity prices provoked unrest and the government accepted democratization demands. Houphouët-Boigny's successor, Henri Konan Bédié (1934–) won an election criticized for irregularities in 1995 and the country suffered renewed economic recession. Laurent Gbagbo (1945–) became president in 2000. In 2002 civil war erupted between the Muslim north and Christian south and a ceasefire in 2005 left him weakened. Defeated in 2010 elections by Alassane Ouattara (1942–), he refused to relinquish office, was ousted by French forces and put before the International Criminal Court for crimes against humanity. Ouattara was re-elected in 2015. The country's population is 45 per cent Christian and 38 per cent Islam and the economy remains heavily dependent on coffee and cocoa cultivation.

Iwakura Mission (Japan)

A two-year-long visit of a Japanese embassy to twelve industrialized countries, departing 1871 from Yokohama to San Francisco, then on to **Europe**, returning via the **Middle East** and **Asia**. It was headed by Iwakura Tomomi and comprised forty-eight people including Okubo Toshimitsu, Kido Takayoshi and Ito Hirobumi, who intended to renegotiate earlier unequal treaties and to gather knowledge of western government administration, military and economic structures, trade and education. The ambassadors' failure to renegotiate the unequal treaties strengthened their conviction that modernization was essential to Japan's future.

Iwo Jima, Battle of

One of the Ogasawara Islands south of Tokyo was invaded by American forces in February 1945, at the end of **World War II**. The defenders had prepared 11 miles of tunnelled fortifications that were resistant to bombardment and tactically well sited. The severe fighting with US Marines lasted for over a month. The **USA** lost 6,800 soldiers and almost the entire Japanese garrison of 20,000 died. The Battle of Iwo Jima ended a few days before the start of the Battle of Okinawa, the final battle of the Pacific War.

Izmir (Smyrna)

Izmir is Turkey's third largest city and an important port. It was a renowned Ionian Greek centre and considered a possible birthplace of Homer. It retained its significance during the Byzantine and Ottoman eras. **Greece**, in pursuit of its expansionist 'Great Idea', seized Smyrna in 1919. The conflagration of the city in 1922 ended the Greek presence and symbolically the **Greco-Turkish War**.

J

Jabotinsky, Vladimir (1880–1940)
– *see also* **Zionism**.

Zionist leader raised in a secular family in Odessa, Jabotinsky's interest in Judaism was sparked by a 1903 **pogrom** during which he helped organize a Jewish self-defence organization – an activity which would be his passionate commitment thereafter. Hoping with **Chaim Weizmann** that Jewish support of **Britain** in **World War I** would help oust the Ottoman Turks from **Palestine**, Jabotinsky organized and commanded a 'Jewish Legion' within the British Army. David **Ben-Gurion** and many other early Zionist leaders were in that unit. Jabotinsky also participated in Jewish self-defence efforts during the Jerusalem riots of 1920. Opposing Weizmann's and Ben-Gurion's toleration of British Mandatory rule in Palestine, Jabotinsky withdrew from the World Zionist Organization in 1923. He founded the more militant Betar youth movement and the World Union of Zionist Revisionists, both antecedents of **Irgun Zvai Leumi**, the underground Jewish army commanded by **Menachem Begin** which pledged to expel the British from Palestine. Jabotinsky died in Hunter, New York, while on an inspection tour of one of his movement's training grounds. Because of their political differences, Ben-Gurion forbade Jabotinsky's reburial in an independent **Israel**, but in 1964 Prime Minister Levi Eshkol finally permitted it on Mount Herzl in **Jerusalem**. A Jabotinsky Institute in Tel Aviv, the Jerusalem neighbourhood of Pisgat Ze'ev, the West Bank settlement of Giv'at Ze'ev, the Nahalat Jabotinsky district of Binyamina, and many streets in Israel perpetuate his memory.

Jackson, Andrew (1767–1845)
This military hero and seventh US president was as a Tennessee lawyer and land speculator who served in Congress (1796–8), was a state judge and served in the militia from 1801. He led southwestern troops against the Creeks and Seminoles during the War of 1812 and successfully fought off a British invasion at New Orleans in January 1815. His Indian campaigns secured massive land acquisitions and opened the way for the 1819 annexation of Florida. Defeated for the presidency in 1824, Jackson triumphed in an innovative populist campaign in 1828. As president he conciliated the South, securing the removal of the Southern Native Americans and vetoing, on constitutional grounds, bills promoting national economic development. Winning re-election in 1832, Jackson's firm response helped defeat South Carolina in the **Nullification crisis**. His removal of government deposits from the Second Bank of the United States in 1833 brought on a financial crisis that divided his party, notably in the South, and led to the emergence of the American **Whig Party**.

Jacobins
The Society of the Friends of the Constitution, the radical party in the **French Revolution** formed in 1789. **Maximilien de Robespierre** and Louis de Saint-Just (1767–94) were leading figures. Initially a moderate grouping in the National Convention (where they were known as the Montagnards because they took the higher seats), the Jacobins – backed by the Parisian lower classes – became increasingly prominent in 1793, taking power in June on the fall of the Girondins as support grew in French cities for their advocacy of republicanism, universal suffrage, public education and separation of church and state. The Jacobins' violent suppression of counter-revolutionary enemies and of their former allies became known as the 'Terror'. When the Convention moved against what had become a dictatorship in July 1794, Robespierre attempted suicide but was executed on 28 July, ending Jacobin dominance. The last Jacobin club was closed in November 1794.

Jacobitism
Supporters of the Stuart descendants of James II following his expulsion in the Glorious Revolution of 1688. The movement's supporters generally included Catholics, Scottish clans and people opposed to parliamentary interference in monarchical affairs. It gained popularity throughout Scotland and England and received foreign

assistance, particularly from France. While Jacobites did pose a danger to Britain, attempts at uprisings, including the invasions in 1715 and 1745, ultimately ended in failure. The defeat at Culloden in 1746 effectively ended the Jacobite movement.

Jahn, Jahnheinz (1918–1973)

German journalist, historian and literary scholar. Born in Frankfurt and educated in Munich, where he studied Arabic, he became interested in understanding the new post-war African literature. He tried to develop, from the writings of African philosophers, an African model for criticism in his celebrated book *Muntu: An Outline of the New African Culture* (1961). This model was influential in many of the African and African American cultural movements of the 1960s

Jaja of Opobo (1821–1891)

Ruler of the city state of Opobo in modern-day **Nigeria**, 1867–87. Jaja was captured from the Igbo country of south-east Nigeria as a child and taken to the commercial port of Bonny where he served as a slave. Employed in business by his master, he came to lead the Anna Pebble House, an important commercial establishment dealing first in slaves and then in palm oil for the booming export market. Jaja absorbed most other Bonny trading houses into his own and hired ships to carry his oil directly to Liverpool. His attempts to block the access of foreign merchants to Opobo markets inland led to long disputes, especially with **Great Britain**. The British consul demanded that Jaja cease taxing British merchants and allow them unlimited access to the interior. In 1885 other European powers granted Britain permission to occupy Opobo and Jaja was captured by British consul Henry Johnston while under truce in negotiations and deported to St Vincent. He died on the way back to Africa.

Jamaica

The largest of the former British Caribbean colonial territories. The indigenous inhabitants of Jamaica are believed to have been the Tainos. There is still controversy over their origins but they appear to have come from South America 2,500 years ago and named the island Yamaye. On 5 May 1494, on his second voyage, Christopher Columbus landed in Jamaica. This opened the island to future European voyages of exploration, colonization and settlement. Under effective Spanish colonization, the indigenous

peoples and later enslaved Africans worked the land for the benefit of the colonizers. On 10 May 1655, Admiral William Penn and General Robert Venables led a successful attack on the island, wresting it from the Spaniards. The English remained in control of Jamaica until the island's independence in August 1962. Under the English, it was developed as a supplier of primary products to feed European industries, leaving the island underdeveloped. As a result of the slave trade, the island's population remains strongly African, although post-slavery and post-independence migration of other ethnic groups now makes the island multicultural, with Asians the largest minority. Jamaica has a 'first past the post' voting system and all adults age 18 and over may vote. Currently, there are two main parties, the People's National Party and the Jamaica Labour Party, the latter winning the 2016 election. Jamaica's economy is now more highly developed. It has an active stock market, many international banks, a large skilled labour force and a relatively broad-based economy. The economy, however, is dependent on imported consumer goods and raw materials that have exceeded earnings from tourism, bauxite, sugar and bananas, all of which are susceptible to erratic worldwide demand. The **United States** is Jamaica's major trading partner, accounting for around a third of the island's export and just over half of all its total imports. Tourism is the country's most important source of foreign currency while agriculture is by far the most important source of employment.

James, Jesse (1847–1882)

American outlaw. Born in Missouri, James and his brother Frank fought as Confederate guerrillas towards the end of the **American Civil War**, then turned to crime. From 1866 James led gangs robbing banks, trains and stagecoaches, killing an estimated fourteen people. He made spurious claims to be stealing from the rich to give to the poor. A fellow gang member, Robert Ford, killed James in pursuit of a 10,000-dollar reward.

Jameson Raid

An attempt in December 1895–January 1896 by British South Africa Company administrator Dr Leander Starr Jameson (1853–1917) to overthrow **Paul Kruger**, the **Boer** Transvaal Republic's governor, by leading a 600-strong force into the area and encouraging a rising of the non-Boer Uitlanders. The effort failed but a telegram supporting Kruger from German Kaiser Wilhelm II heightened Boer confidence on the eve of conflict with **Britain**. Jameson served a short prison sentence in England.

Jammu and Kashmir

– *see* **Kashmir**.

Jammu and Kashmir Liberation Front

Founded in the **United Kingdom** in 1977 by Maqbool Butt and Amanullah Khan, the Jammu and Kashmir Liberation Front demands independence for the state reunified along its borders as they existed before the 1949 partition into Indian- and Pakistani-controlled territories. It was led from Rawalpindi (Pakistan) by Amanullah Khan until splitting in 1995 into segments based in **India** and **Pakistan**. The Indian wing, led by chairman Yasin Malik, espouses a secular position and has renounced violence in its struggle to win independence.

Janata Party

Political party in **India** formed during the 'Emergency' of 1975–7. Leaders from the Bharatiya Lok Dal, Jana Sangh, Socialist Party and the wing of the Indian National Congress that had broken with **Indira Gandhi** in the 1960s met during their incarceration to devise an electoral strategy for the resumption of democracy. Janata won the 1977 election but quickly collapsed under the weight of its ideological contradictions. It reformed as the Janata Dal in 1989.

Janissaries

Ottoman professional military corps established in the fourteenth century and dissolved by Sultan Mahmud II in 1826. Initially one of the fiercest armies in Europe or Asia, the military significance of the Janissaries waned over time. Their numbers grew as recruitment expanded to include not only Christian slaves but also local Muslims (they had previously been prohibited from serving as Janissaries). By the seventeenth century the Janissary corps had lost its edge against European armies. A century later, most Janissaries were no longer full-time soldiers. They adopted trades outside of military service, settled in cities and benefited from a military salary and tax-exempt status. Meanwhile they became a critical political constituency and a force for corruption, opposing attempts at reform. A series of mutinies culminated in a murderous coup against Sultan Selim III in 1807. Selim had attempted military reforms unpopular among the corps. Sultan Mahmud II did not repeat Selim's mistake and when the Janissaries revolted against his reforms in 1826, his carefully planned military response killed thousands of Janissaries and Mahmud dissolved the corps in a key step towards modernization of the Ottoman military.

Japan

Japan was essentially closed to the outside world from 1600 onwards. Worried about the influence of western traders and Christian missionaries, the **shoguns** (regents on behalf of the emperor) of the ruling **Tokugawa** family forbade the Japanese from leaving the island and allowed only selected foreign traders to enter one port, at Deshima island in Nagasaki. Japan developed a highly stratified warrior culture in which firearms were banned, swordsmanship exalted and the shoguns maintained strict control over a class of *daimyo* (great feudal lords) who in turn supervised samurai (a warrior class). Nonetheless, the cities in particular developed a lively urban culture of spectacular art and drama, and knowledge of developments in the West was maintained by books brought in by Dutch traders for use at court.

In 1853 the American commodore Matthew C. Perry arrived with gunships in Tokyo Bay and demanded that the shogun open Japan to western traders. The shoguns reluctantly complied, but as a result lost their influence, and were eventually overthrown in a coup in 1868 led by aristocrats who had been marginalized under the old regime. They claimed to be seizing power in the name of the emperor by ending the regency of the Tokugawas. To mark the change, the emperor was given a new reign-title, **Meiji** ('brilliant rule'), which came to stand for the whole period until the emperor's death in 1912. Power now lay in the hands of an aristocratic oligarchy, who made a bold decision to reconstruct Japan as a modern nation state based heavily on the model of **Bismarck**'s **Prussia**. Among the changes were the establishment of a citizen army, an official religion (State Shintô), a constitution and a parliament, and the industrialization of Japan.

Among the modern reforms undertaken by the Meiji oligarchs was the establishment of Japan as a colonial power. Territorial acquisitions included **Taiwan** (1895), southern **Manchuria** (1905) and **Korea** (1910). During this period Japan also became a well-respected member of the international community, and developed a parliamentary democracy. However, its government was constantly under the influence of both military and civilian figures who argued that Japan needed to expand on the Asian mainland.

This encouraged army officers to occupy Manchuria (1931) and northern China (1935) and, finally, to launch an all-out war on **China** in 1937. This heightened confrontation between Japan and the West, leading to Japan's pre-emptive attack on **Pearl Harbor** in 1941. After four years of war, Japan was defeated by the Allied coalition, with the war ending abruptly after the atomic bombings of **Hiroshima** and Nagasaki in August 1945.

From 1945 to 1952 Japan was occupied by the **United States**, who established the country as a demilitarized, democratic and anti-communist **Cold War** ally. From the 1950s Japanese politicians stressed economic growth as a primary national goal, and politics was dominated by the Liberal Democratic Party, in power almost constantly from 1955. However, social issues such as opposition to industrial pollution and anti-nuclear protests helped to create a powerful civil society. The national mood altered in the 1990s, as the country fell into recession and China became more dominant in the region. There were attempts under Shino Abe (1954–), premier from 2006, to break free of a 'lost decade' of slow growth and increasing state debt. His 'Abeconomics' of quantitative easing, banking and labour market reform met with limited success but electoral opposition.

Java

– *see also* **Dutch Empire; Indonesia**.

Java is an island which forms the centre of the state of Indonesia. It is the world's most populated island, with around three times the population density of **Great Britain**. Over time, it has been of vital importance to the Hindu, Buddhist, Muslim, Dutch and **British Empires**. The island, which is volcanic, sits strategically at the east of the Indian Ocean between **Sumatra** and Borneo. It is also a `rice basket' that can provide for itself and elsewhere given its rich agriculture. This was supplemented by cassava and maize in the nineteenth century whilst Java was under Dutch administration, and was one reason why the population increased almost sixfold, from around 5 to 28 million, after 1850. The island was also the `ground zero' of Indonesian nationalism, and its combination of modernization, the effective secularization created by multiple religions under a colonial authority, and population growth led to the emergence of very powerful patriotic movements that later inspired **Indonesia** in general.

Java War

The Java War of 1825–30 was a war of rebellion and resistance to Dutch rule. The **Dutch East India Company** had ruled the island of Java with the cooperation, bordering on sufferance, of the native aristocracy. With the collapse of the Company, and the humiliation of **Java** being passed between the British and the Dutch states, both of which imported Chinese farm labour, the interests of common people and anti-Dutch-tax elites were the same. A key figure, Pangeran Diponegoro, arose to unite geographical and Muslim religious groups against the Dutch. After a four-year war which took the lives of some 22,000 Dutch and 200,000 Javanese, the conflict ended with the capture and exile of Diponegoro. Subsequently, the Dutch turned the island into a profit-making centre which produced enough cash to save an otherwise bankrupt **Netherlands** from ruin.

Jay's Treaty

Named after **United States** diplomat and chief justice John Jay, this 1795 agreement sought to relieve escalating Anglo-American tensions that resulted from **Britain**'s war with Revolutionary France. In the treaty Britain agreed to abandon forts located within the north-west territory of the United States and to refer various outstanding claims to arbitration (including those of Loyalists, British creditors and American shippers). Britain, however, made only a token gesture to open its markets in the West Indies to American shipping and refused to guarantee the neutral rights of American ships. Though the agreement avoided, for the time being, an Anglo-American war, it was unpopular in the United States. The Senate rejected the section pertaining to the West Indies on the grounds that the British concessions were too meagre. The controversy over the treaty contributed to the creation of 'the first party system', with **Federalists** supporting it and **Republicans** in opposition, as well as escalating US tensions with **France**, culminating in the 'quasi-war' of the late 1790s.

jazz

A distinctively American form of popular music that has its roots in American as well as African and European traditions. Typically polyphonal and syncopated and often using call-and-response either with the voice or between instruments, it is also heavily improvised and has spawned a large number of subgenres since it first received wide notice beyond the African American community around 1900. New Orleans was the first major centre for jazz, where it was improvised from a base of rural southern blues music and ragtime by King Oliver, Jelly Roll Morton and Louis Armstrong. Subsequently, Kansas City, Chicago and New York all became centres for development and jazz passed to white culture with composers such as George Gershwin blending it with classical forms, Duke Ellington blending it with a wide array of styles and Dave Brubeck making it 'cooler' and lighter. It remains a term used in reference to a diverse set of musical compositions that defies easy definition.

Jefferson, Thomas (1743–1826)

Over the course of a lengthy career Thomas Jefferson played a key role in the history of the **American Revolution** and the early **United States**. He was born in Albermarle County in central Virginia. His father, Peter Jefferson, was a land surveyor and his mother Jane Randolph was descended from a prominent family of planters from the Virginia Tidewater. At the age of 16 he entered the College of William and Mary. After leaving William and Mary (it is unclear whether he earned a degree), Jefferson read law under the tutelage of George Wythe, a prominent Virginia jurist. In 1767 he was admitted to the Virginia bar. In 1772 he married Martha Wayles Skelton, a wealthy widow. They returned to Albermarle where he established himself as a lawyer and planter and began to build his home at Monticello. Jefferson entered public life in 1774 when he was elected to represent the colony in the Continental Congress. He was unable to do so owing to illness yet prepared a set of instructions for Virginia's delegation that were published as a pamphlet, *A Summary View of the Rights of British America*, in 1774.

Jefferson eventually took his seat in Congress and was named to the committee which drafted the **Declaration of Independence** in June 1776. Although the final version of the declaration was substantially edited by Congress, most of the document, included its famous assertion that 'all men are created equal', was Jefferson's handiwork. After the adoption of the Declaration of Independence, Jefferson left Congress so that he could return to Virginia to assist in drafting a new code of laws made necessary by the state's newly independent status. Among his contributions was a bill adopted in 1786 which mandated the separation of church and state, the first of its kind in modern history. Between 1779 and 1781 Jefferson served two terms as governor of Virginia. The state was invaded by the British, who captured Richmond, forcing Jefferson and the legislature to flee. Although Jefferson was later exonerated by a special inquiry into his conduct as governor, this was the low point of his long public career.

In the mid 1780s he served as the American ambassador in Paris, where he witnessed the early stages of the **French Revolution**. He returned to the United States to join the cabinet of President **George Washington** as Secretary of State. He quickly came into conflict with Secretary of the Treasury **Alexander Hamilton** owing to personal and ideological differences. Jefferson and **James Madison** emerged as the leaders of the nascent opposition to the ruling Federalists. Frustrated by Federalist policies, Jefferson left the government at the end of 1793. He returned to run for president in 1796, losing to the Federalist **John Adams** and, as then mandated by the constitution, served as vice-president. In 1800 Jefferson defeated Adams in an election that marked the first peaceful transfer of power from one party to another in the history of the American republic. Jefferson served two terms as president. His greatest success was the **Louisiana Purchase** of 1803. Much of his second term was marred by international difficulties, particularly relations with **Britain** and **France** which he sought to resolve with the disastrous **Embargo Act** of 1807.

Jefferson began a long and productive retirement in 1809. He remained active in public affairs and his advice was sought widely by members of his party. He devoted his final years to helping to establish the University of Virginia. He died at Monticello on July 4, 1826, the fiftieth anniversary of his greatest achievement, the adoption of the Declaration of Independence. Jefferson was a polymath and autodidact with a wide range of interests and accomplishments, as reflected in his personal library, among the largest in the United States. He was a substantial slaveholder, which seemed to place him at odds with the sentiments he expressed in the Declaration of Independence. His apparent hypocrisy on the slavery question is underscored by the fact that he fathered at least one child and possibly as many as six children by his slave Sally Hemings.

Jehovah's Witnesses

An adventist, **millennialist** denomination that emerged from Charles Taze Russell's Bible Students Association (1872) and which adopted its current name in 1931. Witnesses believe that only they can survive imminent apocalypse and reject several 'unscriptural' doctrines central to mainstream **Christianity**, such as Trinitarianism. Popularly associated with door-to-door evangelization and a literalistic rejection of blood transfusion, their refusal to salute national flags or to fight incurred Nazi and **United States** government persecution during both world wars, the latter prompting major Supreme Court rulings on freedom of religion.

Jerusalem

One of the world's oldest continuously inhabited cities, dating back to the eighteenth century BC. Holy to Christians, Jews and Muslims alike. For Jews, it is the site of the capital of the Hebrews and their Jewish descendants until their ejection by the Romans in AD 70. The old city is dominated by Mount Zion, the site of the First and Second Temples where Jews believe David deposited the Ark, the portable wooden shrine in which God was thought to be present amongst the Israelites. All that is left of the Herodian Temple, however, is the West, or Wailing, Wall where Jews lament the destruction of the Temple and the dispersion of **Israel**. Jerusalem was God's chosen home, the focus of national loyalty, the geographical and spiritual centre of the world. Nevertheless, the suppression by the Romans of further Jewish revolts was so complete, extending to the ploughing up of the site and its total rebuilding as a Roman city, that Jerusalem ceased to exist as a Jewish city until the twentieth century and the advent of **Zionism**. For Christians, it is the site of the Crucifixion and the Resurrection, the cornerstones of the Faith, and the Church of the Holy Sepulchre, built over the traditional Rock of Calvary on which the body of Jesus is believed to have been laid, is one of Christianity's most sacred shrines. Although the present church was dedicated in 1149, during an interval of Crusader control, the crypt of Constantine's fourth-century Martyrion remains. Jerusalem was only a predominantly Christian city, however, between the fourth century and the Arab conquest of the seventh. For Muslims, Jerusalem is the most holy city after Mecca and Medina, the goal of Muhammad's mystic night journey and from where he is believed to have ascended to Heaven. Part of the original structure of the Dome of the Rock, or al-Aqsa mosque, founded in AD 687, remains under later rebuildings. Jerusalem was to remain an essentially Arab city for thirteen centuries.

The city came under the **Ottoman Empire** as part of **Syria** in the sixteenth century. Captured by the British under General **Allenby**, 1917, during World War I, it passed under formal British control when **Palestine** was detached from Syria to become a British **mandate** in 1920. It was the object of Zionist aspirations, strongly opposed by the city's Arab population. Recommendation by the British **Peel commission**, 1937, that it become part of a reduced British mandate for Jerusalem and Bethlehem only, with the remainder of Palestine partitioned, was never acted upon. The British headquarters in the city, the King David Hotel, was blown up by the Zionist **Irgun** in 1946. West Jerusalem was captured by Israel in the 1948 fighting but East Jerusalem, which included the old city, passed to Transjordan, later **Jordan**. East Jerusalem was then captured and occupied by Israel in the **Six Day War** in 1967, but Israel's claim that Jerusalem as its eternal and indivisible capital is not internationally recognized. Foreign embassies are therefore located in Tel Aviv. The Palestinians counter-claim East Jerusalem as the future capital of a Palestinian state. It remains a flashpoint for Israeli–Palestinian relations; riots in Jerusalem launched the second **intifada** in 2000.

Jesuits

The Society of Jesus (*Societas Iesu*; abbreviated to either SJ or SI) is a Christian religious order of the Roman Catholic Church in the service of the Pope. Initially Saint Ignatius of Loyola (1491–1556) and other students at the University of Paris met to bind themselves by a vow of poverty and chastity to engage in hospital and missionary work. The society was formally founded in 1540. Also known as the Company of Jesus, the Discipleship of Jesus or the Companions of Jesus, the Society is today one the largest religious orders in the Catholic Church. It was once regarded as the main promoter of the Counter-Reformation and then as a modernizer of the Church. It earned suspicion from several monarchies in the eighteenth century and was expelled from **Portugal** (1759), **France** (1764) and **Spain** (1767) and temporarily suppressed by the **Papacy**, but restored in 1814. Its modern work is focused on education and contributions to knowledge, providing high-quality university education and missionary work, human rights and social justice.

Jewish Agency
– *see also* **Zionism**.

In 1922 the **League of Nations** conferred a 'Mandate for Palestine' upon **Britain**, specifying that a 'Jewish Agency' be set up in **Palestine** to build a 'national home' for the Jewish people (*see* **Balfour Declaration**). The sixteenth Zionist Congress (1929) voted that the World Zionist Organization (WZO) work in close partnership with the Agency; thereafter, WZO's president served simultaneously as president of the Jewish Agency. In 1952 **Israel**'s parliament voted to make the functions of the agency and the WZO inseparable. These activities included Youth Aliya programmes, which brought young **Holocaust** survivors to Israel, and the establishment of *ulpanim*, or intensive language courses for all new immigrants. In 1948, after the **Deir Yassin** massacre, it sent **Jordan**'s King Abdullah a letter of apology, which he rebuffed. Prime Minister **Ben-Gurion** felt that the agency had outlived its usefulness after the establishment of the state, likening it to scaffolding which could be removed once a building was erected.

Jewish peoples
– *see also* **anti-Semitism; Holocaust; Israel; Zionism**.
At several points in history there was no extant Jewish state. As a consequence, the larger part of the Jewish national experience over the past five thousand years is one of exile and diaspora, and as a resulting consequence of this fact, the Jewish community of peoples is a diverse and global one. It comprises historic, geographic and ethnic groups. The most famous division is that between the Ashkenazi and the Sephardi, relating to the distinction drawn between those whose ancestry is associated with central Europe and the German lands, and those who descend from Jews settled in Spain in the late Roman and medieval period respectively. Jewish people are also represented in Chinese, African, Indian, Eurasian and Middle Eastern communities by families whose genetic lineage and cultural practices are as near to that of the original Jewish tribes as makes no difference. A famous elaboration of this point is the remarkable consistency of those belonging to the *Cohenim* priesthood line, whose families can be genetically traced back for at least 2,700 years on the basis of a single gene. There were also Jewish convert communities, of which the most famous was the Khanate of the Khazars, but in their case (as of that of the Russian subbotniks) there is little evidence of intermarriage or absorption with historic Middle Eastern communities. Given the persistence of anti-Semitic tropes in which Jews form a single group, it is important to note that the designation covers many social and cultural outlooks and linguistic groups, from the largely anglophone American community, through Yiddish-speaking people of German and Polish descent to the Beta Israel 'black' Jewish community of East Africa. Indeed, many Persian, Indian and Greek Jews could lay claim to very distinctive regional identities, and it would therefore be difficult to find agreement or commonality between any of them.

In modern **Israel**, which is built up of indigenous and settler groups under a law of return, and in large western cities with concentrations of Jewish people from all over the world, such diversity has led not only to a vibrant attachment to democracy but also to sensitivity to attempts to create a lumpen or monolithic group on the part of outsiders. Jews globally are no more likely to hold to any one religious interpretation of their ethnicity, or indeed any such interpretation, than to none; they are not marked by any consistent practice, profession or language, and they are not by any means outside the role of patriotic and cultural heroes within their given states. Jews have, however, frequently found themselves persecuted or marked out for their group status, and emotional or family ties to the wider group have sometimes been forced out of the public and into the private sphere.

Jhansi, Rani of
Rani Lakshmi Bai was the widow of the last Maratha ruler of Jhansi in central India. The state was annexed in 1853 under Lord **Dalhousie**'s 'Doctrine of Lapse' which allowed the British to seize states whose rulers failed to produce natural heirs. This ignored the right of sovereigns to adopt heirs, as Jhansi's raja had done before dying. In 1857 the dispossessed rani joined the **Indian mutiny** against the British, leading her troops in battle until she was killed in June 1858.

Jiang Qing (1914–1991)
Jiang Qing was the wife of **Mao Zedong** and a member of the radical group the **Gang of Four**. Born in Shandong, she became a film star in Shandong before marrying Mao in 1939. After 1949 she worked in the propaganda department and played a major part in the **Cultural Revolution**, launching attacks on moderate leaders such as Liu Shaoqi and **Zhou Enlai**. After Mao's death in 1976, Jiang was arrested and committed suicide in jail.

Jiang Zemin (1926–)
Secretary general of the Chinese Communist Party, 1989–2002, and president of **China**, 1993–2002. He was effectively nominated as successor to

Deng Xiaoping, although unlike Deng, he served fixed terms in clearly defined offices, thus making him the first leader in Communist China to take part in a defined handover of power. Jiang's period in office was marked by a desire to have China engage strongly with the outside world and a rush to domestic marketization which left many institutions, such as education and health care provision, out of reach for millions of poorer Chinese, although it did launch China on the road to becoming an economic superpower.

Jiaozhou (Kiaochow)

Jiaozhou was a German protectorate in **China**. In November 1897 German soldiers occupied Qingdao in response to the killing of two Catholic priests. Negotiations with the Chinese government gave **Germany** a ninety-nine year lease to the region. The Germans administered the territory, transforming Qingdao into a modern city. However, with the outbreak of **World War I**, the Chinese cancelled the lease, although the territory was not returned to China until 1922.

jihad

Arabic for 'fight' or 'battle', the word *jihad* refers to the duty of Muslims to spread **Islam** through battle. Contrary to much popular contemporary usage, however, this need not mean military conflict, because the duty of jihad can be discharged by the heart, the tongue and the hand, as well as by the sword. Discharge by the heart signifies spiritual self-purification by fighting against the inner devil. Discharge by the tongue or by the hand consists essentially of supporting right and opposing and rectifying wrong. Twentieth-century Islam particularly stressed the duty of battle with the inner devil, while armed war against other nations was only permissible to defend Islam. Even in earlier times, however, wars of Islamic conquest were not jihads when the opponents were Christians or Jews, if they either converted or paid poll and land taxes. Nevertheless, the description jihad has often been applied to conquests with mixed political and religious motives since at least the eighteenth century, initially perhaps in sub-Saharan Africa. The jihad of **Usman dan Fodio** which created the **Sokoto Caliphate**, 1804, in modern-day Northern Nigeria, is a significant example. The concept of armed jihad, however, was largely in eclipse throughout the nineteenth and early twentieth centuries, and the call of Ottoman Turkish sultan **Mahmud II** for a jihad against his enemies in the 1820s was as much a failure as Mahmud V's call in 1914. On the

other hand, the seizure of Mecca and Medina by **Wahhabi** reformers in the early nineteenth century created a base for the future propagation of their fundamentalist and intolerant interpretation of Islam in which armed jihad played a central role.

The exploitation of its enormous **oil** reserves made **Saudi Arabia** an extremely wealthy state in the second half of the twentieth century, with both the ability and the will to encourage and support militant jihadi movements outside its borders. This was of major importance first in **Afghanistan**, where holy warriors (**mujahideen**) fought the **Soviet Union** after the 1979 invasion with financial and military aid from Wahhabi Saudi Arabia as well as from western states. The West, again, supported the Islamic militants of the Kosovo Liberation Army (UCK) against the Serbian government from 1998, reasoning that western support for such liberation movements would reduce the influence of the fundamentalist jihadi element within them. The Russian Federation, where many jihadis joined the ultimately unsuccessful war for **Chechen** independence which broke out in 1994, had perceived more readily that the political and social agendas of that part of the mujahideen, which was to become the **Taliban**, and of some of the volunteer non-Afghan jihadis, were at best non-western and at worst anti-western. **Israel**, with many in America and western Europe, however, already feared **Hamas** and Islamic jihad in **Gaza**.

Western attitudes were to be profoundly affected, however, by the **September 11th** (9/11) attacks, deemed by the perpetrating **al-Qaida** group to be a jihad. **NATO** invasion of Afghanistan rapidly ensued on the grounds that it was a refuge for a concentration of al-Qaida fighters, including their leader, **Osama bin Laden**. The invasion of **Iraq** followed, in 2003. The invasions were interpreted by many Muslims, however, as an attack on Islam, particularly when President **George W. Bush** talked of a 'crusade', and the occupations proved bloody as jihadis, many affiliated to al-Qaida, flowed in to support the fight against the Americans and sectarian opponents. Their interpretation has since been reinforced by numerous civilian casualties from an increasing American reliance on unmanned drones in Afghanistan and **Pakistan**, and potentially in the Sahel and East Africa. The conflict zone spread to **Europe** when 191 people were killed on Madrid commuter trains in March 2004 and 56 on a London bus and on Tube trains by UK jihadi suicide bombers in July 2005. The **Syrian Civil War** became the most important global arena for jihadists, and its affiliated Islamic State of **Iraq** and ash-Sham (Damascus) (**ISIL**) fought for a new caliphate under **sharia** uniting **Sunni** areas of Iraq and Syria. Its 5,000–8,000 jihadis have proved equally as hostile to the anti-government Free Syrian Army as to westerners and the **Alawite** regime. Sunni clerics issued a call for jihad in Syria against the regime and its **Shi'ite** allies from **Iran** and Lebanon in June 2013.

Jim Crow laws
– *see* **segregation, racial**.

Jinnah, Mohammed Ali (1876–1948)
A leading Muslim politician in colonial **India** and Pakistan's first governor general. In **Pakistan**, Jinnah is known as the *Quaid-e-Azam*, or great leader. He was born in Karachi to a wealthy merchant family. At the age of 17 his family sent him to London to train with a business firm, but Jinnah instead joined Lincoln's Inn, becoming the youngest Indian to be called to the English bar. In 1896 he returned to India. In Bombay he gained prominence as a gifted lawyer, defending **B. G. Tilak** against charges of sedition in 1908. Jinnah joined the **Indian National Congress** in 1906. Although he at first avoided the **Muslim League**, eschewing their narrow focus on Muslim interests, in 1913 he joined. In 1916 he brokered the Lucknow Pact, in which Congress and the League presented joint demands to the British.

In 1920 Jinnah broke with Congress and **Gandhi** due to disputes over the **Non-Cooperation movement** and the **Khilafat movement**, which Jinnah viewed as a dangerous appeal to religious sentiments. During the 1920s he struggled to maintain the League's relevance in Indian politics, and in 1929 he drafted the Fourteen Points proposing constitutional reforms to safeguard the rights of Indian Muslims. After Congress rejected his plan, Jinnah spent from 1931–6 practising law in London. Returning to India, he embarked on the most influential period of his political life. The League did poorly in the 1937 elections. Faced with increasing political dominance by Congress, however, Muslim leaders of powerful regional political parties looked to Jinnah and the League to protect their interests at the all-India centre. During the late 1930s and 1940s, Jinnah struggled to balance the interests of Muslim majority and minority provinces in order to present a unified bargaining position that would give Muslims an equitable share of power in a post-colonial political arrangement. In 1940 the League passed the Lahore Resolution, which asserted that the Muslims of India were a separate nation. Some historians have labelled this controversial statement the 'Pakistan Resolution', while others have argued that Jinnah continued to envision a separate Muslim nation within a federated Indian state. Jinnah remained opposed to partitioning the provinces of Punjab and Bengal along religious lines. In 1946 he initially agreed to a three-tier federal structure for a united India, as outlined in the **Cabinet Mission Plan**. After negotiations between Congress and the League collapsed and the British announced their imminent withdrawal, Jinnah had little choice but to accept the proposal Lord Mountbatten presented in June 1947 for partition. Jinnah's role in the partitioning of India is hotly disputed; while he is popularly credited with single-handedly creating Pakistan, historical research has revealed his persistent attempts to broker power-sharing arrangements that would preserve some degree of Indian union. Despite ailing health, Jinnah became Pakistan's first governor general, struggling to steer the foundling nation through the rough waters of partition violence, fiscal crisis and war with India over **Kashmir**. His death came as a huge blow to the new nation.

Jobim, Antonio Carlos (1927–1994)
Born in Rio de Janeiro, Jobim was **Brazil**'s best-known songwriter. A pianist, singer, transcriber and arranger, his harmonic and melodic elements defined the bossa nova style. Inspired by Brazilian Heitor Villa-Lobos, considered **Latin America**'s foremost twentieth-century composer, Jobim worked with guitarist-singer João Gilberto and numerous other celebrated musicians. Internationally famous as a songwriter in the 1960s, he recorded numerous albums and influenced Brazilian musicians and jazz musicians worldwide.

Johannesburg
The largest city in **South Africa**. In the nineteenth century Voortrekkers migrating from the Cape established the **Transvaal Republic**. With the discovery of gold in 1886, the city of Johannesburg developed rapidly, dominated by goldmining prospectors and African male migrant labourers. After the union of South Africa in 1910, Johannesburg grew and spread into townships such as **Soweto** and Alexandra that became focal points of anti-**apartheid** activism in the twentieth century.

John Paul II, Pope (1920–2005)

John Paul II was one of the longest-reigning of modern popes (1978–2005) and had a decisive influence on the image, structure and attitudes of the Roman Catholic Church in the late twentieth century. His use of personal travel and association with political leaders and anti-communist trade unions introduced media techniques of the modern age to the Catholic Church. The first non-Italian pope in four centuries, John Paul II was born Karol Wojtyla in **Poland**, and lived through Nazi and Communist rule. A mystical thinker, his works of theology were highly respected before he became pope, and concentrated on the evils of objectification in relationships, sex and everyday life, and the value of the post-Wittgensteinian idea of personalism, which upheld the dignity of the human individual under God and natural law as central to existence. As pope, Wojtyla led the Catholic Church (the membership of which passed the 1 billion member mark, drawn from across the world, during his reign) in a conservative Catholic direction. His **papacy** was initially marked by anti-communism but, after the fall of the Communist regimes in 1989–91 in **Europe** and the **Soviet Union**, his thoughts turned to the materialism and secularism of the West. He suggested that the latter was creating, through soulless and relentless objectification and capitalization of life, a 'culture of death' which would inevitably devalue humanity.

John Paul II knew how to reach out to global audiences and exploit images and gestures, and this concern for the appearance as well as the integrity of Catholic structures led to an intense connection between him and the millions who converged upon Rome for his televised funeral in 2005, somewhat shocking the media. But it also led to a blindness in tackling the issue of child sex abuse by priests which became inordinately damaging for the Church in the late twentieth century. He had inherited a troubled papacy riven by tensions between reformers who wished to proceed beyond **Vatican II** and conservatives who wished to retreat from it, a banking scandal, and the need to balance anti-communism against communist regimes so fearful and antagonistic of him that an assassination attempt associated with the **KGB** and Bulgarian intelligence nearly took his life in 1981. He responded by giving support and inspiration to the **Solidarity** movement in Poland, which eventually broke the communist regime in that country, and upholding devotion to the Virgin Mary as a unifying force associated with the papacy. He ensured the election of a conservative successor by his appointments to the College of Cardinals, and his friend and colleague, Josef Ratzinger, when elevated to the papacy after John Paul's death, reciprocated by immediately beginning moves to set Wotijwa on the path to sainthood whilst referring to him as 'John Paul the Great'.

John XXIII, Pope (1881–1963)

Angelo Roncalli, Patriarch of Venice, was an unexpected selection as pope in October 1958, but used his time to call the Second Vatican Council, **Vatican II**, which made major reforms to the Roman Catholic Church after his death. As Apostolic Delegate to **Turkey** and **Greece** between 1934 and 1944, he was associated with the rescue of thousands of refugees and prisoners from Nazi Europe, including several thousand Jewish people. He was widely mourned upon his death in 1963.

Johnson, Andrew (1808–1875)

Seventeenth president of the **United States**, 1865–9. A tailor by trade, Johnson was political spokesman for the largely non-slaveholding population of eastern Tennessee in opposition to the slaveholding elite that dominated state politics in Nashville. He served as a Democrat in the US House of Representatives (1843–53), as governor of Tennessee (1853–7) and in the US Senate (1857–62). A devoted Unionist, he was the only senator from the seceding states to retain his seat when his state left the Union. In 1862 he was appointed military governor of Tennessee, and in 1864, to balance the Union Party's ticket, he was nominated for the vice presidency. On **Lincoln**'s assassination in April 1865, Johnson became president. The inflexible execution of his **Reconstruction** programme and his obstructive response to that of Congress soon led him into confrontation with Republicans in Congress. His efforts to win control of the War Department by dismissing Secretary Edwin M. Stanton, in contravention of the Tenure of Office Act of 1867, resulted in an attempted impeachment which only narrowly failed.

Johnson, Lyndon Baines (1908–1973)

Thirty-sixth president of the **United States**, 1963–9. Born in Texas, Johnson entered politics during the 1930s as a supporter of **Franklin Roosevelt**'s New Deal. As Democratic leader of the Senate in the 1950s, he displayed political pragmatism and a capacity for bending others to his will. Elected vice president in 1960, Johnson became president upon the assassination of **John F. Kennedy**, and earned plaudits for helping the US through that trauma and for using his legislative skills to steer through the most ambitious liberal reform programme since the 1930s. Re-elected by a landslide in 1964, his subsequent full term as president was soon consumed by his decision to send ground troops to **Vietnam** and by the eruption of serious ghetto riots. His damaged reputation helped make possible the election of **Richard Nixon** in 1968. Johnson's historical reputation is mixed, but he is often credited with having been an effective champion of black **civil rights**.

Jones, Sir William (1746–1794)

A scholar of Arabic and Persian who learned Sanskrit during his tenure as judge on the British Supreme Court in Calcutta (1783–94). He distrusted Indian legal experts, working to provide translated digests of Hindu and Muslim law for the British courts in **India**. As an orientalist scholar, he is most famous for demonstrating the affinities between Sanskrit and classical European languages, suggesting a common source on the ancient Iranian plateau, and thus pioneering the study of Indo-European linguistics.

Jordan, Hashemite Kingdom of

– *see also* **Hussein (Al-Husayn), King of Jordan**.
Middle Eastern nation formerly part of the **Ottoman Empire** but after the **Arab Revolt of 1916–17** under British control as part of a **League of Nations mandate** covering a wide area, including **Palestine** and **Iraq**. It became a separate mandate in 1921 under the **Hashemite** ruler, **Abdullah ibn Hussein**, becoming an independent state of Transjordan in 1946. Formed as a constitutional monarchy in 1952 under **King Hussein II**, the grandson of Abdullah, it absorbed East **Jerusalem** and the **West Bank** in the Arab–Israeli War of 1948–9, virtually trebling its population. A reluctant participant in pan-Arab militancy, it participated in the **Six Day War** of 1967, but lost both Jerusalem and the West Bank, which added another million refugees to the population, including highly radicalized elements of the **Palestine Liberation Organization** (PLO). The PLO used Jordan as a base for attacks on **Israel** but was expelled after a bloody civil war in 1970–1. In 1988 Jordan accepted PLO claims to the West Bank and Jerusalem as part of a Palestinian state. It held its first multiparty elections since the 1950s

in 1993, resulting in a moderate, pro-monarchy victory. Jordan followed **Egypt** in signing a peace treaty with Israel in 1994, following the latter's recognition of the PLO, King Abdullah II succeeding his father in 1999. With few economic resources beyond tourism, Jordan has followed a moderate course in Arab–Israeli relations, but has been buffeted by waves of refugees from the two **Gulf Wars** and the **Syrian Civil War** and been the subject of terrorist attacks itself from pro-Islamist groups.

Joseph II (1741–1790)

Holy Roman Emperor, 1765–90, co-ruler with his mother Maria Theresa, 1765–80, and then sole ruler of the Austrian **Habsburg** Empire, 1780–90. An enlightened despot, he issued the Universal Code of Civil Law, 1786, and developed the University of Vienna and the General Hospital in Vienna, as well as reorganizing the army. He abolished **serfdom** and established religious equality in law with an Edict of Toleration, with particular benefit to the Jews. He granted freedom of the press and reduced the power of the Roman Catholic bishops and dissolved more than 700 monasteries at the expense of conflict with the papacy, but encountered resistance in such traditional possessions as **Hungary** and the Austrian Netherlands (**Belgium**). He participated with **Frederick the Great** of **Prussia** and **Catherine the Great** of **Russia** in the first partition of **Poland** in 1772, gaining Galicia. Subsequently, he annexed Bukovina from **Turkey**. Other diplomatic successes, however, eluded him. A perceptive visionary, he could be too impatient to succeed in carrying his subjects with him.

Juárez or Ciudad Juárez

Mexican city located on the Rio Grande River, currently with over 1.5 million inhabitants and originally known as El Paso del Norte. Separated by the **Treaty of Guadalupe Hidalgo** from what became El Paso, **Texas**, it became a key border town. A supply centre for constitutionalists during the Mexican Revolution, it subsequently became an important manufacturing and commercial city. Since 2000 drug trafficking gangs have hurt business and caused population loss.

Juárez, Benito Pablo (1806–1872)

Mexican statesman and president, 1861–4 and 1867–72. Of Indian descent, he was governor of Oaxaca, 1847–52, but exiled under the conservative rule of **Santa Anna** (1853–5). He returned to join the Liberal government, proposing land reform, including the seizure of church lands, and established a liberal and anti-clerical constitution in 1857. During the ensuing civil war in 1857–60 he assumed the presidency. His refusal to pay foreign debts led to the occupation of **Mexico** by **Napoleon III's** forces under Ferdinand Maximilian (1832–67), who took the crown with the support of **France** and conservative groups in Mexico. Following resistance from the far north and the withdrawal of French forces and the execution of Maximilian, he resumed the presidency and restored the republic.

Judaism

– *see also* **anti-Semitism; Holocaust; Israel; Jewish peoples; Zionism.**

A term referring at times to a racial or ethnic group characterized by their fidelity to the principles, rituals, faith or line of descent identified as Jewish (a term derived from Latinization of the territorial noun *Judah*). Judaism can be traced back over nearly 6,000 years to the **Middle East**, and has at various times been sustained as an identity despite the immersion of Jewish people in other lands and cultures. Across the course of time, the association of Jews with a national territory in the Middle East has been physically, if not emotionally, broken on at least three significant occasions, the latest of which lasted from AD 70 to 1948. One consequence of this is that Judaism has evolved multiple ways of belonging, which can run together but which allow for a flexible interpretation of fundamental identity. Many Jewish people, for example, trace their identity to the European, African, Indian, Persian or Abyssinian diaspora, or to forms of food or Germanic dialects such as Yiddish which evolved during one or all of the long Jewish absences from **Palestine**.

Fundamentally, however, Judaism is defined by the character of Jewish religion, which is an ethics-based monotheism centred on a text (the Tanakh), a collection of scholarly writings (the Mishnah/Talmud) and religious law (the Torah). In the Tanakh, which broadly corresponds to the Christian Old Testament, God made various covenants with the Jewish people. These occurred at various times, such as those detailed in the Books of Genesis (four times), Job (twice), Exodus (twice) and Jeremiah. Within this multiplicity of promises and requisite duties, none are overriding, but the quality of Jewishness is broadly conveyed as one that upholds the idea of a promised land of **Israel**, ritual circumcision of males, matrilineal descent and scholarly priesthood associated with the status

of Rabbi, as well as dietary laws banning various combinations of foods, pork absolutely, and the consumption of any food not approved by a Rabbi. Jewish culture also allows for the celebration of meals related to historic events and narratives which remind group members of their cultural heritage, and a specific calendar which illustrates the longevity and history of Judaism. Symbols, such as a seven-pointed candlestick, the Star of David, and sundry works of religious art are incorporated by practice into the regular celebration of anniversaries as detailed by this calendar. The ability to read from the Tanakh in Hebrew at the age of 13 in a Bar Mitzvah ceremony is also often taken to define the entry of males into Jewish manhood.

There is therefore a multiple redundancy in Judaism, which allows for any number of means by which the culture might be maintained and sustained without it being substantially changed. Judaism is a remarkably plural religion, and can be iterated in orthodox, liberal, reformed or conservative forms as well as secularized identities. Some reform elements allow for female rabbinical scholarship, whilst some orthodox groups reject all but the most rigorous interpretation of clothing, social activity and lifestyle. It is therefore possible to be Jewish without following religious imperatives, so long as historic or cultural ideas are upheld and passed on. Jewish parents are expected, for example, having married within the faith as members of a community, to educate their children in the details of a history marked by persecution and oppression. At various times, multiple ancient and modern regimes have attempted to suppress or murder Jewish communities en masse, the latest of which were the **Russian Empire** and National Socialist Germany. This has led to a sensitivity to anti-Semitism on the part of many Jewish groups which often perceive darker purposes behind smaller slights, but the fact is that conspiracies, genocide and discrimination have been directed against all Jewish communities at almost every point in Jewish existence. Indeed, the twentieth and twenty-first centuries were historically unique in that various modern, non-religious narratives on the Left or within nationalist discourse incorporated a non-religious **anti-Semitism**, usually but not exclusively centred on denials of the legitimacy of the Jewish state, which were supplemented by a rise in Islamist condemnation of Jewry.

On the other hand, following the twentieth-century **Holocaust**, many Christian churches (some of which considered their traditional biblical narrative to be in some way to blame for anti-Semitism in the West) altered their teaching, so that accommodation with the Jewish faith has become typical. Translations of the Bible have generally been edited to remove an oppositional identification of the Jews as a people, the theology of the Crucifixion has been reinterpreted so that purported Jewish guilt as a people has been eliminated, and Christian leaders have generally ceased to question the legitimacy of the covenants detailed in the Tanakh. Pope **John Paul II**, for instance, referred to Jewish people as 'elder brothers in the faith' and de-emphasized super-cessionist ideas of Christian superiority. Many American evangelicals have also become **Zionist** supporters of the state of Israel for their own, Protestant reasons. In the twenty-first century a major fault line has developed within Judaism, which has incorporated members from all racial groups, over the issue of the Zionist project. Most Jews support the state of Israel, but many seek a global identity shorn of the socialist and nationalist sentiments involved in the support of the administration of a Jewish state in Israel with a titular capital in **Jerusalem**.

July Monarchy

A period of constitutional liberalism in **France** that began with the July Revolution in 1830 and the abdication of **Charles X**. **Louis Philippe**, the duke of Orleans, succeeded to the throne and adopted the title King of the French, instead of King of France, to denote his popular sovereignty and opposition to divine right and other principles of the *ancién regime*. 'The Citizen King' focused on creating a more bourgeois, progressive, populist and practical government following the absolutist rule of the previous regime. He upheld the revised Charter of 1815 and nearly doubled the electorate. However, fear of revolution and growing opposition, especially from the poor and working classes, caused the government to become increasingly corrupt and repressive. Following a series of economic crises, the July Monarchy ended with the abdication of **Louis Philippe** during the **Revolutions of 1848** and the succession of the Second Republic, led by Alphonse de Lamartine.

July Plot

A conspiracy to assassinate **Hitler**, take control of the German Army and mount a coup to oust the Nazi government, the culmination of long-standing military and civil resistance to the regime. On 20 July 1944, following a number of thwarted attempts, a leading participant, Colonel Claus von Stauffenberg, successfully exploded a bomb in the East Prussian military headquarters conference room, but Hitler escaped with minor injury. The majority of those involved were executed or committed suicide.

Junkers

The name given to the hereditary governing class of **Prussia**, who preserved the feudal nobility which Christianized Eastern Europe. Junkers, whose large estates covered most of Eastern Germany and a good part of modern **Poland**, formed the body of the Prussian officer class in the German Army. This was true even under **Hitler**, with whom they were frequently at odds. After 1945, Junker lands were expropriated and redistributed by the German Democratic Republic, although repurchases by surviving families were a feature of the late twentieth century.

Jutland, Battle of

– see **World War I**.

K

Kaarta

One of the two powerful Bambara states of modern-day **Mali** in the eighteenth century. The state was formed in 1753 by a branch of the ruling house of Segu who moved to the north and made their capital at Nioro. The later eighteenth century was marked by wars between Kaarta and Segu which nourished the external slave trade. In 1854 El Hajj Umar Tall conquered Kaarta and put the entire royal family to death.

Kabaka Yeke movement

The Kabaka Yeke or 'King Alone' movement, founded in 1961, employed a language of Ganda patriotism under the symbolic head of the Kabaka of **Buganda** (one of Uganda's four kingdoms). In April 1962, Kabaka Yeke formed a coalition with **Apollo Obote**'s **Uganda** People's Congress (UPC), and secured guarantees for the Kabaka and Buganda in Uganda's independence constitution. But this alliance proved short-lived. Kabaka Yeke was disbanded in 1965, the Kabaka were forced into exile, and in 1967 a new constitution abolished Uganda's four kingdoms.

Kabila, Laurent-Désiré (1939–2001)

President of the **Democratic Republic of Congo**. Born in what was then Belgian Congo, Kabila studied in France, returning on independence in 1960. Following the 1961 military coup, he waged an unsuccessful guerrilla struggle against the **Mobutu** government. In 1967 he formed the equally unsuccessful Marxist-orientated People's Revolutionary Party before setting up as a gold trader in **Tanzania**. As the Mobutu regime in the now renamed Zaire faltered, Kabila returned to lead the Alliance of Democratic Forces for the Liberation of Congo-Zaire in 1996, capturing the capital Kinshasa in 1997. He declared himself president and reinstated Democratic Republic of Congo as the country's name. Initially having apparent democratic intentions, Kabila's arrest of opposition politicians and human rights abuses provoked rebellion in the east of the country. Despite a ceasefire in 1999 fighting continued and Kabila was assassinated by a bodyguard in the presidential palace.

Kagwa, Sir Apolo (c. 1865–1927)

Kagwa fought on the Protestant side in the Bugandan Civil Wars, then served as chief minister or *katikiro* of Buganda from 1889 until 1926. He was a mediator between **Buganda** and the British, notably in the negotiations culminating in the 1900 Uganda Agreement. He embraced a vision of progressive modernity defined by **Christianity** and education, but sought to develop a Bugandan identity within this vision, publishing several books on Bugandan history and culture.

Kahlo (y Calderón de Rivera), (Magdalena Carmen) Frida (1907–1954)

Born in Coyoacán, Mexico City, Frida Kahlo married the celebrated Mexican painter **Diego Rivera**. A towering national artist herself, her style combined popular surrealism with expressions of the 'New Objectivity'. From the 1970s her memory and art were appropriated as a key icon of women's experience of life in general – a solitary, painful existence – as well as latterly by the LGBT movement.

Kamil, Mustafa (1874–1908)

Egyptian nationalist. He trained as a lawyer at the French law school in Cairo and at the University of Toulouse, **France**, and was a supporter of Khedive **Abbas II** in his opposition to the British occupation of **Egypt**. He initially proposed cooperation with France and the Ottoman Turkish Empire as a means to that end, but subsequently sought principally to activate Egyptians themselves. His nationalism is believed to have been primarily inspired by Egypt's Islamic past, and he unsuccessfully urged Khedive Abbas to introduce constitutional government. He displayed legal and journalistic talents with the launch of the newspaper *al-Liwa* (*The Standard*) in 1900, and garnered wide support following public anger at the **Dinshaway Incident**, 1906. Having gained the influential support of Mohammad Farid, a leading

Egyptian aristocrat, he launched the National Party, December 1907, which opposed the moderate nationalist Ummah Party, preferred by the British; Farid became its leader on Kamil's death. His funeral was an occasion of great public grief and his mausoleum, in Cairo, built 1949–53, is now a museum.

Kampuchea
– see also **Cambodia**.
Democratic Kampuchea was the name of Cambodia under the **Khmer Rouge** regime, which took control of the capital city of Phnom Penh in 1975. Kampuchea was governed as a socialist republic under the premiership of Khmer Rouge leader **Pol Pot**. In 1979 Vietnamese troops captured Phnom Penh and established a government, which renamed the country the People's Republic of Kampuchea. When the monarchy was restored in 1993, the country was renamed the Kingdom of Cambodia.

Kanagawa, Treaty of
The fifth **shogun**, Tokugawa Yoshinobu, signed a treaty with the **United States** at Kanagawa in 1854. This marked the end of **Japan**'s period of 'seclusion' (1639–1854) and was the country's first unequal treaty with a western state. In the face of the modern naval fleet of US Commodore Matthew Perry, the Tokugawa shogunate acquiesced to Perry's demand to open the ports of Shimoda and Hakodate, accepted US most favoured nation status, and received a US consul at Shimoda.

Kang Youwei (1858–1927)
Chinese reformer Kang Youwei was born in Guangdong, where he set up an academy to teach Confucianism and western learning. In 1895 he moved to Beijing and founded study societies and newspapers that pushed for reform. His proposals were implemented during the **Hundred Days of Reform** in 1898. The coup forced him to flee to **Japan**, where he founded the Protect Emperor Society, which advocated constitutionalism. After his return to **China** in 1913, Kang supported Yuan Shikai's bid to become emperor.

Kano
An important city of the Hausa states in modern-day Northern **Nigeria**. Founded in the eleventh century, it became an Islamic centre under Muhammadu Rumfa (1463–99) and was a major production and commercial centre. In the early nineteenth century it fell under the authority of **Sokoto**, founded by **Usuman dan Fodio**'s holy war. In 1903 it was integrated into the British colony of Nigeria, and is presently the capital of Kano State.

Kansas–Nebraska Act (1854)
A congressional act that produced **sectional conflict** in the **United States**. It came about through **Democratic** senator Stephen Douglas' attempts to organize territorial government on the plains in order to lay down a transcontinental railway. Such legislation inevitably brought up the place of slavery. As with the **Compromise of 1850**, Douglas offered 'popular sovereignty', but this clashed with the **Missouri Compromise**'s parallel 36°30′ north restriction on territorial slavery; southern ultras demanded and received the latter's explicit repeal. Horror swept the North, but Douglas argued that climate would effectively exclude slavery. He persuaded the Senate in March (37–14), then the House in May (113–100). The Act destroyed the **Whig Party** but brought about the **Republican Party**. Pro- and anti-slavery settlers clashed in 'Bleeding' Kansas and duly offered rival slave and free governments for Washington to choose from. The implications of the *Dred Scott* case and the thwarting of a clear anti-slavery majority in Kansas occasioned Douglas' break with **James Buchanan** in 1857.

Kant, Immanuel (1724–1804)
A philosopher who transformed western philosophy by developing transcendental idealism. Kant sought to respond to the challenge of Hume's scepticism by providing a transcendental argument for the necessary conditions of cognitive, moral and aesthetic experience. Combined with his arguments for an international democratic federation of states, Kant's theoretical, moral and political philosophy were major influences on the European **Enlightenment**. His critical philosophy continues to inspire contemporary liberalism, and is central to the developing discipline of international justice.

KANU
KANU is the acronym of the Kenya African National Union, formed in 1960 under the leadership of **Jomo Kenyatta** (c.1889–1978) by the merger of the Kenya African Union, the People's Congress Party and the Kenya Independent Movement. KANU ruled **Kenya** after independence from **Britain** in 1963, effectively becoming the sole political party in 1969. From 1982 to 1991 Kenya was officially a one-party state but KANU won

multiparty elections in 1992 and 1997. The party splintered following electoral defeat in 2002.

Karim Khan Zand (1705–1779)

Ruler of **Iran**, of tribal origin. A general under **Nadir Shah**, claiming power after the latter's assassination in 1747, he placed the infant grandson of the last recognized Safavid monarch on the throne as Ismail III to enhance his own legitimacy, exercising full personal power as regent (*vakil*), 1757. He controlled all Iran except Khorasan in 1760. An able and energetic ruler, he enabled Iran to recover from forty years of war, making Shiraz, which he embellished with many fine buildings and to which he attracted poets and scholars, his capital. He reorganized the fiscal system, easing the burden on the agricultural sector, promoted trade by permitting the British **East India Company** to establish a trading station at the port of Bushehr, 1763, and captured Basra, which had diverted the trade with **India** from Iranian ports, from the **Ottoman Empire**, 1775–6. The Iranian carpet industry was a major beneficiary. He never claimed the traditional royal title of *shahanshah* (king of kings).

Kasavubu, Joseph (1913–1969)

Born in 1913, Kasavubu qualified as a teacher in 1940 and taught for two years before joining the Belgian colonial administration. He came to politics through an interest in the rights of the Bakongo people and joined the Bakongo association Abako. As president of Abako from 1955, he was at the forefront of calls for political reform in the Belgian Congo. As independence approached, he argued for a federal constitutional structure against centralizers such as Patrice Lumumba. In July 1960 they found themselves in government together, Kasavubu as president and Lumumba as prime minister, but this arrangement did not last. An extended constitutional crisis saw Lumumba assassinated in September 1960 and power seized by Army Chief of Staff **Mobutu**. After the restoration of constitutional government in 1961, Kasavubu remained in power until he was overthrown by Mobutu in 1965. He died of a brain haemorrhage.

Kashmir

The valley of Kashmir is presently known as a region torn between the competing claims of **India** and **Pakistan**. During its early history, under the aegis of Hindu and Buddhist kings, it became renowned as a centre both of Shaivism and of Buddhism, the fourth great Buddhist council being held there in around AD 100. In the fourteenth century not only was Muslim rule first established there but **Islam** began to garner large numbers of converts mostly through the influence of Sufi orders. By the nineteenth century almost 93 per cent of its population was reported to be Muslim. In 1586, Kashmir came under Mughal hegemony following the defeat of Yusuf Shah Chak, the valley's last Kashmiri ruler for some time to come. Control over Kashmir would shift several times again, passing into Afghan hands in 1751, Sikh dominion in 1819, before being claimed by the British following the Anglo-Sikh War of 1845–6. The Sikhs transferred Kashmir along with several adjacent regions including Jammu and Ladakh to an ally, Gulab Singh, who was installed as maharaja of the new state. Given its Muslim majority population, many expected the state, especially its Kashmir valley, to join Pakistan following India's partition in 1947. However, a tribal invasion encouraged by Pakistan prompted the hitherto undecided last maharaja to accede to India in October 1947. Since a UN-brokered ceasefire in 1949, ending the first **Indo-Pakistan War** of 1947, about a third of the state has been under Pakistani control and the remaining part under Indian control. Kashmir remains a disputed territory, and since late 1989 the Indian wing has also witnessed an insurgency led by various groups, some calling for independence and others for a merger with Pakistan.

Kata'ib

– *see* **Phalanges Libanaises**.

Katanga

– *see* **Congo, Democratic Republic of**.

Kaunda, Kenneth David (1924–)

Zambian politician. President of **Zambia**, 1964–91. As leader of the Zambia National Congress, he was imprisoned for nine months, but was released in 1960 and became leader of the United National Independence Party. As president of **Zambia** he was the creator of the political philosophy of humanism and as one of the front-line presidents played an important part in independence negotiations in Rhodesia and **Mozambique**. He assumed autocratic powers in 1972 to prevent tribal break-up but, after a new constitution in 1973, his presidency was confirmed. Defeated in the multiparty 1991 elections following economic decline and years of one-party rule, he went into retirement.

Kazakhstan

A central Asian state, conquered by **Russia** in the mid eighteenth century. It experienced a series of anti-Russian risings, notably the 1916 anti-conscription revolt. Kazakhstan was part of the Russian Soviet Federative Socialist Republic from 1922 and in 1936 gained a measure of autonomy as the Kazakh Soviet Socialist Republic. In 1991 it declared independence from the collapsing **Soviet Union** under the presidency of former Communist leader Nursultan Nazarbayev (1940–). The country is rich in oil, gas and minerals and the population is predominantly Muslim.

Kazembe

A central African kingdom formed in the eighteenth century by migrants from the **Lunda Empire** on the border between modern-day **Congo** and **Zambia**. While it was probably originally a province of Lunda, by 1740 it had gained its independence. Kazembe emerged as a leading commercial centre in the late eighteenth and early nineteenth centuries, and attracted Portuguese visitors, first from **Mozambique** and then from **Angola**. However, the development of competitor states such as Msiri's kingdom caused both a military and commercial decline towards the end of the nineteenth century. In 1904 part of the state was incorporated into the Belgian Congo and the other part into the British colony of Northern Rhodesia, where its head of state became a chief in the indirect rule system. Under this system it was ruled by a number of modernizing chiefs, notably Mwata Kazembe XIV, who assembled its traditional history.

Kemal, Mustafa

– *see* **Atatürk, Mustafa Kemal**.

Kennan, George (1904–2005)

An American foreign policy intellectual, diplomat and historian, George Frost Kennan is best remembered for two documents that guided US strategy though the **Cold War**. The so-called '**Long Telegram**' was drafted while Kennan was at the US Embassy in Moscow in 1946, and its arguments were expanded in the anonymous 'X' article in *Foreign Affairs* in 1947. Kennan argued that the ideological fervour of Marxism–Leninism, and the territorial insecurity that had long driven the **Russian Empire**, had conspired to create a **Soviet Union** that was inherently expansionist in nature. He advised that America's role was to 'contain' this outward thrust through military and non-military means, for while the Kremlin was 'impervious' to

reason it was 'highly sensitive to the logic of force'. While Kennan later regretted the manner in which his advice was distorted to justify intervention in areas he deemed 'peripheral' – such as **Vietnam** – his containment doctrine, misinterpreted or not, was hugely influential through the Cold War.

Kennedy, John Fitzgerald (1917–1963)

Thirty-fifth president of the **United States**, serving from 1961 until his assassination in Dallas, Texas, on 22 November 1963. Previously a US senator, Kennedy narrowly defeated the Republican nominee **Richard Nixon** in the 1960 presidential election. His tenure in the White House was dominated by foreign affairs. In 1961, seeking to contest the **Cold War** with new vigour, Kennedy presided over the **Bay of Pigs** debacle, increased defence expenditures and an enlargement of the US commitment to South Vietnam. In 1963, strengthened politically by the successful resolution of the **Cuban Missile Crisis**, he negotiated the **Partial Nuclear Test Ban Treaty** with the USSR – the first major arms control agreement of the Cold War. At home, Kennedy committed the nation to the goal of a manned lunar landing before 1970 and sought to contain the confrontations between white Southerners and civil rights activists over racial segregation.

Kennedy, Robert (1925–1968)

US politician Robert Kennedy was appointed Attorney General by his brother, President **John F. Kennedy**, and engaged with the emerging **civil rights movement**. He also played an important role in counselling restraint during the **Cuban Missile Crisis** and led secret negotiations with Soviet Ambassador Anatoly Dobrynin. Elected to the Senate in 1965, he campaigned for the Democratic presidential nomination in 1968, on a progressive, anti-Vietnam War platform, during which he was assassinated by Palestinian extremist Sirhan Sirhan.

Kent State University, shootings at (USA)

On 4 May 1970 four students were killed and nine wounded when members of the Ohio National Guard opened fire during an angry campus protest against President **Nixon**'s decision to invade **Cambodia**. Two of those killed had not been involved in the protest. The shootings provoked further unrest on college campuses. Many were temporarily closed down. On 9 May a major demonstration against the shootings took place in Washington DC.

Kentucky and Virginia Resolutions (USA)

A series of resolutions adopted on 13 November and 24 December 1798 by the legislatures of Kentucky and Virginia respectively in response to the **Alien and Sedition Acts**. **Thomas Jefferson** was the author of the Kentucky resolves and James Madison those of Virginia. Taken together, they endorsed a strict construction of the constitution, asserting that the government had no authority to adopt such restrictive measures. The implication of the resolves was that individual states could nullify federal legislation. The resolutions were circulated among the other state legislatures. No other states endorsed them and ten explicitly rejected them. Although the resolutions were not legally binding, they were politically significant. They crystallized **Republican** opposition to **Federalist** policy and acted as a statement of the party's principles in advance of the 1800 presidential election.

Kenya

An east African nation whose name originates from German and British explorers' translations of the tribal names for Mount Kenya, it became a British protectorate in 1895. In 1920 it became a British crown colony and white exploitation of its best farmland, while transforming the economy, bred resentment among the Kenyan people who were excluded. The Kikuyu Central Association (KCA), formed in 1924 by **Jomo Kenyatta**, demanded compensation for expropriated land, education and opening up of commercial opportunities for Africans. Banned in 1940, the KCA was replaced in 1944 by the Kenya African Union, which developed a militant wing. Its attacks on white settlers and other Kenyans culminated in the **Mau Mau revolt**. Suppressed with considerable loss of life and thousands of arrests, including the deportation of Kenyatta, the 'Kenyan emergency' led to preparations for independence and the formation of two African parties, Kenyatta's **KANU** (Kenyan African National Union) and Daniel arap Moi's (1924–) KADU (Kenyan African Democratic Union). Released from exile, Kenyatta led KANU to victory in elections in 1961 and presided over independence in December 1963. KADU was dissolved and in effect Kenya became a one-party state. Moi succeeded Kenyatta as president in 1978, eventually retiring in 2002. A peaceful transfer to an opposition party, the National Rainbow Coalition, the first in Kenyan history, did not quell persistent criticism of corruption and scandal. Ethnic and inter-tribal tensions remain and violent incursions by Islamist al-Shabab terrorists from Somalia in the early twenty-first century threaten an economy and polity which has otherwise proved relatively stable and prosperous by the standards of its neighbours.

Kenyatta, Jomo (1894–1978)

Kenyan politician, anthropologist and first president of independent **Kenya**. Born Kamau wa Muigai among the Kikuyu, Kenyatta became involved in the Kikuyu Central Association in the 1920s, editing their newspaper and becoming the party's secretary general. He also launched the Gikuyu-language newspaper *Mwĩgwithania*, 'The Reconciler', with focus on Kikuyu culture, gender discipline, land conflicts and political activism. In 1935 he studied at the London School of Economics, publishing *Facing Mount Kenya*, a study of Kikuyu traditions and customs. Upon his return to Kenya, he took over the presidency of Kenya's first national political party, the **Kenya African Union**. In the 1950s he was accused of being the leader of the **Mau Mau revolt** and imprisoned until 1961. After his release he became the first president of independent Kenya in 1963, creating a strong one-party state, promoting pro-western, capitalist development and becoming increasingly authoritarian.

Kerala

State in southern **India**, bordered by Tamil Nadu to the east and Karnataka to the north. Kerala's tropical climate and abundant rain have long permitted the production of pepper, cinnamon and other spices desired by distant markets. Kerala's felicitous geographical position made it the ideal location to link trade routes of the western and eastern Indian Ocean from at least the first century BC. Commercial houses from the Arabian peninsula and elsewhere established expatriate enclaves, resulting in small but lively communities of Jews, Christians, Muslims and others by the fifteenth century. Portuguese and Dutch colonizers between the sixteenth and eighteenth centuries occupied some parts of Kerala, but Cochin and Travancore remained independent until incorporated as princely states under British rule. Communist parties or coalitions have led governments since the 1956 linguistic reorganization of states. Kerala has fared well in literacy and other quality-of-life indices.

Kerensky, Alexander (1881–1970)

Russian prime minister, July–October 1917. Kerensky was a moderate who served in the **Duma** before **World War I**. He then became, in sequence, a socialist opposition leader, minister of justice in the provisional government and war minister. After becoming prime minister (despite the failure of the Russian offensive named after him) he attempted to suppress both Bolsheviks and conservatives while proclaiming Russia a republic. On the occasion of the Bolshevik revolution, he escaped, attempted to organize resistance, and then adopted from exile a position of neutrality in the **Russian Civil War**. He lived variously in Paris, Brisbane and for the longest time in New York before his death, never again setting foot in **Russia** though he offered his (immediately rejected) services to Stalin in 1940.

Keynes, John Maynard (1883–1946)

Twentieth-century intellectual, financier and influential economist. Keynes was a Liberal who sought to develop a general theory of economics and to use economic insights to affect the policies of the **British Empire** and then the world. In 1926, having achieved some fame with his attack on the **Treaty of Versailles** (*The Economic Consequences of the Peace*, 1919) and the **gold standard** policies of **Winston Churchill** in the Baldwin government of 1925–9, Keynes produced his theory of economics. Using national income statistics, he held that the aggregation of demand in the economy powered consumption, which in turn led to investment, employment and further income. The chief aim of any government therefore, given that economies operated cyclically, was to stabilize aggregate demand by spending government money in recessions and removing money through taxation in periods of exuberance. Employment was, in such a Keynesian model, more important than the suppression of inflation, and only 'big government' operating through fiscal policy could achieve full employment. Keynes' ideas became extraordinarily important between 1945 and 1973, in part because the economic architecture of the post-war world was largely based on his designs from the 1944 **Bretton Woods conference** until his death two years later. Keynes died having secured a vast emergency loan for the bankrupt British Empire from the **USA** in 1946, but his goals of a neutral world currency and permanent world trading authority were rejected by the US in favour of a dollar-based gold standard and the pro-free market General Agreement on Tariffs and Trade, which favoured the USA. The **International Monetary Fund** (IMF) and the **World Bank** were also originally Keynesian in conception. Keynes' reputation beyond the academic world largely fell as Keynesianism became associated with inflation,

economic stagnation, deficits, high taxes and over-spending once politicians and industrial interest groups adopted his ideas without paying attention to investment, competition or supply-side economic issues, though his ideas are still very popular in **Japan** and continental Europe.

Keynesianism

The economic philosophy associated with **John Maynard Keynes**, **Britain**'s most influential twentieth-century economist, as set out primarily in *Treatise on Money* (1930) and *The General Theory of Employment, Interest and Money* (1936). Keynes argued that, in times of recession, national governments should use government spending and other active economic policies to stimulate demand and offset the cycle of boom and bust. He identified the 'multiplier' effect, by which putting one man to work not only benefits him but, by increasing his personal expenditure, puts six more men to work as well. He also noted that autonomous spending, defined as spending affected by such things as optimism about the future, government policy or anticipated exports, is the prime mover of income in an under-employed economy. The Keynesian model of the economy is driven by the aggregate demand resulting from the consumption and investment plans of households, governments and firms, and he, therefore, opposed the economic orthodoxy of retrenchment and wage-cutting widely favoured in the 1920s and early 1930s and particularly associated with Montagu Norman, the then governor of the Bank of England. Stanley Baldwin thus maintained as Conservative prime minister in 1925: 'All the workers of this country have got to take reductions in wages to help put industry on its feet.' Keynes himself first came to prominence as a British Treasury representative at the 1919 Versailles peace conference, publishing *The Economic Consequences of the Peace* that same year opposing reparations and arguing that Europe could prosper only when Germany was restored to her old economic strength. Opposed to Britain's return to the **gold standard**, 1925, he strongly believed that voluntary buyers and sellers both benefited from international trade, and was instrumental in the agreement of the July 1944 **Bretton Woods conference** of forty-four nations on the currency and financial-economic arrangements required to promote international trade after the war, to establish the **International Monetary Fund** and the **World Bank**. He led the British delegation to America, 1945, to negotiate the loan essential for economic recovery.

Although Keynesianism was always treated with a measure of reserve, even by the British Left, it set the tone for British economic policy until the 1970s and had wide international influence. The ideas fell from favour in the later 1970s when they appeared to offer no answer to the new problem of 'stagflation', the combination of inflation and stagnant economic growth – ultimately attributable to the more than doubling of the oil price by Middle Eastern oil producers, January 1974. Sidelined by **neoliberalism** and the **monetarist** theories of Austrian economist Friedrich von Hayek and American Milton Friedman, which strongly influenced **Margaret Thatcher**, Britain's prime minister, 1979–90, and **Ronald Reagan**, American president, 1981–9, Keynesianism has enjoyed renewed influence since the financial crash of 2008, which underlined the risks inherent in the concept of the self-regulating market, although some subsequent Keynesian economic stimuli such as quantitative easing appear to have had only limited success.

KGB

Komitet Gosudarstvennoi Bezopasnosti, the Committee of State Security (1954–91). The KGB was the security service of the **USSR** from 1954 (replacing the NKVD and MGB) until the demise of that state in 1991. It subsequently was the security service for the Russian federation until it was nominally disbanded and replaced by the FSB. The KGB evolved as an organization dedicated to the protection and advance of the Revolutionary communist state, and drew upon several Russian and Bolshevik traditions of secrecy, organization and the ruthless elimination of dissidence. It was organized into directorates and was an umbrella organization for other security and military intelligence services. In its time, the KGB was widely respected and feared by foes and allies. At the end of the **Cold War** many of the leaders and officers of the KGB, who had been recruited as able and idealistic young people, transferred to denationalized industries or new political groupings within the Russian federation. One of their number, **Vladimir Putin**, who had been an attaché in East Germany, succeeded Boris Yeltsin as president of Russia. These 'old hands' were widely suspected of rebuilding the organization and its base in the Lubyanka prison in Moscow. The name of the KGB became a euphemism in many languages, along with 'gestapo', for secret police, oppression and heavy-handed intelligence tactics.

Khalid ibn 'Abd al-Aziz, King of Saudi Arabia (1913–1982)

King of **Saudi Arabia**, 1975–82. Crown Prince Khalid became king upon King **Faisal**'s assassination in March 1975. Khalid was in ill health throughout his reign, and Crown Prince Fahd ibn 'Abd al-Aziz assumed day-to-day control of the kingdom during a turbulent era marked by the seizure of the Grand Mosque in Mecca in 1979 and a Shia uprising in the Eastern Province in 1980.

Khama, Seretse (1921–1980)

First president of Botswana, 1966–80, Khama was also the prime minister of (British) Bechuanaland in 1965–6. Educated in **South Africa** and **Britain** as a barrister, he became a symbol of multi-racialism after marrying a white Englishwoman against the wishes of his royal family in 1947. He presided over economic growth, the birth of a system of mass education, the development of a law-governed and honest regime, and a form of internationalism which brokered the end of the Rhodesian War. He died in office of pancreatic cancer.

Khan, Saiyid Ahmed (1817–1898)

A reformer, writer, educator and politician known for his role in leading the **Aligarh** movement in British **India**. Born into the Muslim nobility, he took employment with the **East India Company** and during the **Indian mutiny of 1857** remained staunchly loyal to the British. He wrote a short treatise on the causes of unrest which gained him a position of influence in official government circles. Convinced that Indian Muslims needed to embrace British rule and western education, he opened the Mohammadan Anglo-Oriental College in Aligarh in 1875. An opponent of the **Indian National Congress**, he urged Muslims to remain loyal to British rule and work for the protection of Muslim cultural and political influence. Despite his support for English-language education, he wrote prolifically in Urdu and published an influential literary journal and newspaper, contributing significantly to the development of modern Urdu prose.

Khan, Yahya (1917–1980)

Agha Mohammad Yahya Khan led **Pakistan**'s military regime in 1969–71 and presided over Pakistan's first national election held on the basis of universal adult franchise. In its aftermath, he prevented the **Awami League** from establishing a government although it had won a majority of the central legislature's seats. He then organized a military operation against the league, which resulted in Pakistan's civil war, war with **India**, and the creation of **Bangladesh**.

Khilafat movement

The Khilafat movement (1919–24) was a mass campaign waged by Indian Muslims in protest against the partitioning of the **Ottoman Empire** after its defeat at the end of **World War I**. Indian Muslims led by the charismatic brothers **Muhammad** and **Shaukat Ali** demanded that the Ottoman emperor be recognized as the *khalifa*, or leader of the Islamic community. The Ali brothers forged a partnership with **Gandhi**, linking the Khilafat movement and the **Non-Cooperation movement**. Widespread mass protests brought together **India**'s various religious communities and expanded the nationalist movement's reach into the ranks of lower-class and rural populations. At the height of the movement, thousands of Muslims left India for **Afghanistan**, an act of *hijrat*, or exodus, which ended tragically when many immigrants died due to lack of provisions. The movement declined significantly after 1922 when **Kemal Atatürk** declared **Turkey** a republic and abolished the office of the *khalifa*.

Khmer Rouge (Red Khmer)

– *see also* **Cambodia; Kampuchea; Pol Pot**.
A French term coined by the former Cambodian head of state, **Norodom Sihanouk**, to refer to the Communist Party which ruled **Cambodia** between 1975 and 1979. The movement originated as the Khmer People's Revolutionary Party in 1951, developing into the Communist Party of Cambodia from 1960, of which **Pol Pot** became general secretary in 1963. It organized peasant resistance to the Sihanouk regime, supported by North Vietnamese Communist forces. The latter's victory in 1975 brought the Khmer Rouge to power in Cambodia, presiding over an extreme Maoist, pro-Khmer regime in which cities were deliberately emptied and non-Khmer and other opponents ruthlessly slaughtered. As many as a million people may have died. The educated elite fled or were targeted for execution, torture and re-education, while the economy descended into chaos. North Vietnamese intervention in 1979 displaced the Khmer Rouge and Pol Pot, but they continued to wage guerrilla war against successive Cambodian governments. An amnesty in 1995 was followed by their surrender in 1999, a year after Pol Pot's death.

Khoikhoi

A pastoralist community living in south-western Africa since the fifth century. Translated as 'men of men', the Khoikhoi practised animal husbandry of goats, cattle and sheep and traded with their hunter-gatherer neighbours, the San. Cattle-raiding led to conflict between the Khoikhoi and the San. Bantu migrations into southern Africa brought Khoikhoi pastoralists into contact with Nguni agriculturalist chieftaincies to the east. Extended contact between the Khoikhoi and Nguni was clear in the characteristic Khoi 'click' sounds in the Nguni and Sotho languages. When Dutch traders arrived at Table Bay in 1652, the Khoikhoi provided their ships with meat and milk. Derogatorily termed the 'Hottentots', the Khoikhoi were forced into indentured labour. Saartjie 'Sarah' Baartman, the 'Hottentot Venus', was brought to **Europe** and displayed at exhibitions in the nineteenth century. From 1904 to 1907 the Namaqua, a Khoikhoi group in Namibia, revolted against German colonizers, during which 10,000 Nama died. Disease, displacement by European settlement and integration into other groups decimated the Khoikhoi lifestyle and population.

Khomeini, Ayatollah Ruhollah (1900–1989)

Iranian revolutionary leader. Born Ruhollah Musawi in the town of Khomeyn, the son and grandson of **Shi'ite** religious leaders or mullahs, he received an Islamic education, settling in the city of Qom in about 1922. He adopted the surname Khomeini from his home town in about 1930. The author of numerous works on Islamic philosophy, law and ethics and an advocate of a fundamentalist interpretation of **Islam**, he won support thereby and for his outspoken criticism of **Mohammed Reza Shah Pahlavi** and for his denunciation of western influences. Recognized as an **ayatollah** or senior religious leader in the 1950s and as a grand ayatollah in the early 1960s, which made him one of the supreme religious leaders of Shi'ite Islam in **Iran**, he denounced the shah's land reform programme, which reduced the extent of Iran's religiously held estates, and his policies of female emancipation, 1962–3. Anti-government riots were sparked by his resultant arrest. Imprisoned for a year and then exiled from Iran, 4 November 1964, he settled in the Shi'ite holy city of an-Najaf, **Iraq**, and made repeated calls for the ousting of the shah and the foundation of an Iranian Islamic republic. His influence within Iran rose dramatically from the mid 1970s as the shah's regime engendered growing public dissatisfaction. Obliged to leave Iraq by President Saddam Hussein, 6 October 1978, he settled in the Paris suburb of Neauphle-le-Château from where he sent tape-recorded revolutionary messages to Iran through his supporters – his messages received an enthusiastic reception from an increasingly angry population. He triumphantly returned to **Tehran**, 1 February 1979, following the shah's forced departure on 16 January, to be acclaimed as the religious leader of the revolution. He appointed the new government four days later, and settled again in Qom, 1 March. Named Spiritual Leader for life with supreme political and religious authority when a December 1979 referendum approved a new **constitution** establishing the Islamic Republic of Iran, he determinedly established theocratic rule, with Shi'ite clerics responsible for policy-making while he himself arbitrated between the different revolutionary groups and took the key final decisions. He relied on the deeply conservative forces which had brought him to power to forcibly implement a fundamentalist and intolerant interpretation of Islam whereby Iranian women were required to wear the veil, alcohol and western music were banned, and penalties were again determined by **sharia** law.

Khomeini reversed the shah's pro-western orientation in foreign affairs in favour of total hostility to both the **United States** and the **Soviet Union**, while endeavouring to export his variety of Islamic fundamentalism to Muslim neighbours. He endorsed the seizure of the US Embassy in Iran, provoking the **Tehran Embassy hostage crisis**. He long rejected the peaceful resolution of the **Iran–Iraq War**, launched by Iraq, 1980, hoping to overthrow Iraq's President **Saddam Hussein**, but ultimately had to accept failure and approved the 1988 ceasefire which heralded the end of the war. Despite the heavy losses of life throughout and the interrupted rate of economic development, his support amongst the masses remained unshaken and his position as Iran's supreme political and religious leader was impregnable until his death.

Like Dr **Mossadegh**, he strongly favoured policies of national economic autarky, rejecting foreign credits and loans, which were seen as instruments of foreign exploitation. As hostile to the liberal nationalism of the intellectuals as to the modernizing nationalism of the shah, he practised a form of what has been called Islamic state nationalism which did not threaten tribal and other traditional distinctions and the associated social practices and values. He is, therefore, more properly understood as a counter-revolutionary rather than as a revolutionary, and indeed acknowledged as probably the world's most successful counter-revolutionary of the twentieth

century. This may be attributable to the fact that, unlike most counter-revolutionaries, he was working with the majority rather than a privileged minority.

Khrushchev, Nikita (1894–1971)

Soviet premier, 1954–64. Originally a metalworker and electrician, Khrushchev rose through the Communist Party ranks to become a loyal servant of **Stalin** and member of the **USSR** leadership. Following the death of Stalin, he won out as a ruthless but underestimated member of the class of potential successors, and became known for his voluble, aggressive, yet open style of leadership. He travelled outside of the USSR, including to the **USA**, and attempted to invigorate Soviet agriculture through the Virgin Lands programme whilst boasting of Soviet space and missile technology. He also famously denounced Stalin in a leaked 'secret speech' to the Twentieth Party Congress in 1956. His 'thaw' of the **Cold War** gave way to new division between East and West after the invasion of **Hungary** in 1956, and Khrushchev developed a policy of 'rattling his rockets' to enforce compliance which almost came to grief during the **Cuban Missile Crisis** of 1962. Despite, or perhaps because of, the latter event, Khrushchev and President **Kennedy** grew in correspondence and closeness, and the Soviet leader associated Kennedy's end in 1963 with his own downfall in 1964. Subsequently, he was allowed to live out his life outside Moscow, where he wrote a memoir that was smuggled to the West. His son, also called Nikita, became an American citizen and respected authority in the USA on his father's regime which, though not bloodless, was more benign than many of those which had held sway in the USSR.

Kiaochow

– *see* **Jiaozhou**.

Kilwa

An important city-state on the coast of modern-day **Tanzania** founded in the ninth century. It was the location of an important coastal trading port and exerecised hegemony among many of the Kiswahili-speaking commercial towns along the east African coast, especially in its glory days in the thirteenth century. It boasted substantial mosques and the sultan had a large palace. When the Portuguese arrived in the early sixteenth century they temporarily decided to base themselves there, but local resistance and the political situation made it impossible. The city subsequently declined in importance, but underwent a renaissance in the eighteenth century as a centre for the ivory and slave trades between East Central Africa and the Indian Ocean. In 1886 it fell under the control of the German East Africa Company and was subsequently integrated into the British Colony of **Tanganyika**.

Kim Dae-jung (1925–2009)
– *see also* **Park Chung Hee; South Korea**.

Kim was the first opposition leader to serve as president of **South Korea** (1998–2003). During the 1970s and 1980s he was a leading political activist who protested and campaigned against authoritarian rule. He has been credited with successfully pulling South Korea through the 1997 Asian Financial Crisis and fostering closer and more peaceful relations with **North Korea** through his Sunshine Policy. His approach to North Korea helped him earn the 2000 Nobel Peace Prize.

Kim Il-sung (1912–1994)
– *see also* **North Korea**.

Kim served as the first leader of **North Korea** from 1948 to 1994. During the 1930s, in **Manchuria**, Kim waged guerrilla warfare against the Japanese in a quest to liberate Korea from colonial rule. His anti-colonial struggles influenced him to make self-reliance and sustaining independence the central goals of North Korea, which was articulated through ideologies such as Juche and carried out through movements including the Non-Aligned movement during the **Cold War**. Responsible for launching the **Korean War** in 1950 by invading **South Korea**, he used defeat to suppress opposition and develop an intense cult of personality.

Kim Jong-il (1941–2011)
– *see also* **Kim Il-sung** and **North Korea**.

Kim succeeded his father **Kim Il-sung** as leader of **North Korea** in 1994. Raised from an early age to be the future leader of the country, Kim assumed high-level positions in the government during the 1980s and early 1990s, including becoming a member of the Central Committee and head of Korean People's Army. After his father's death, he continued to promote Juche ideology through programmes for self-reliance, which were tested by a period of famine in the 1990s and the controversy over North Korea's nuclear programme. Following his death, Kim Jong-un, his son, became the new leader of North Korea and pursued an erratic, belligerent stance towards the **USA** and **South Korea**.

King, Martin Luther (1929–1968)
– *see also* **civil rights**.

Born into an affluent black Atlanta family, King became famous through his leadership of the Montgomery bus boycott (1955–6). A powerful preacher, he urged non-violence in contrast to the segregationists' use of terrorism and intimidation. In 1957 he established the Southern Christian Leadership Conference to coordinate protest efforts. By 1963, however, he was more highly regarded by liberal allies of the movement than by other activists. They complained he preached non-violence more than he practised it. But the political effectiveness of his Birmingham campaign and the public acclaim that followed his 'I Have a Dream' speech re-established King's pre-eminence. He won the 1963 Nobel Peace Prize and pressed President **Johnson** to pass the 1964 Civil Rights Act and 1965 Voting Rights Act. After 1965, King strove to apply non-violent tactics to issues of economic justice and to call for an end to the **Vietnam War**. A radical figure at the time of his death, he was assassinated in Memphis on 4 April 1968. Since 1983 he has been honoured by the creation of the Martin Luther King National Holiday when his 'I Have a Dream' speech is frequently rebroadcast.

Kinlaza and Kimpanzu

Two lineages which competed for power in the kingdom of Kongo following the disastrous battle of Mbwila in 1665. In the course of the Kongo Civil War each of these factions claimed their own kings and occupied parts of the country, fighting battles against each other leading to the export of slaves. In the eighteenth century a number of sub-branches developed as well, and a joint branch, the Agua Rosada, emerged after 1690.

Kissinger, Henry (1923–)

American national security adviser and secretary of state who played an important role in shifting US diplomacy towards a more 'realist' footing following the 'internationalist' activism of presidents **Kennedy** and **Johnson**. Kissinger was jointly awarded (with North Vietnamese counterpart Le Duc Tho) the Nobel Peace Prize in 1973 for his efforts in negotiating an end to the **Vietnam War** and was an important force behind the policy of détente towards the **Soviet Union**. He supported President **Nixon**'s plan to recognize the People's Republic of **China** and also recommended controversial actions such as the secret bombing of **Cambodia** (1969–70), the destabilization of the Chilean government of **Salvador Allende** (1973) and gave tacit approval for **Indonesia**'s invasion of **East Timor** (1975).

These policies – and his scepticism about 'morality' as a guide for diplomacy – made him enemies on both the right and the left of the political spectrum.

Kitchener, Lord Horatio Herbert (1850–1916)

British military commander. Born in **Ireland**, Kitchener was commissioned into the Royal Engineers in 1871, serving in **Palestine**, **Egypt** and the **Sudan** before appointment in 1890 as commander-in-chief of the army of British-dominated Egypt. He led the 1896–9 reconquest of Sudan, defeating Abdullah al-Taashi's forces at **Omdurman** in 1898. Kitchener was chief of staff and then commander-in-chief of British forces in the 1899–1902 **Boer War**, in which he introduced **concentration camps**. After commanding the army in **India** in 1902–9, he became British Agent and Consul General in Egypt, effectively the country's ruler. On the outbreak of war in August 1914, he entered the British Cabinet as Secretary of State for War, overseeing the recruitment of a mass volunteer army for what he foresaw would be a protracted conflict. Kitchener drowned when HMS *Hampshire* was sunk while conveying him to **Russia**.

Knights of Labor

An American trade union organization formed in 1869 in Philadelphia as the Noble and Holy Order of the Knights of Labor by a group of tailors led by Uriah Stephens (1821–82). It was aimed at those who produced goods of any kind, and expanded beyond the established craft unions to include Irish, Afro-American and women workers, but excluded Chinese and other Asians, supporting legislation to exclude Chinese immigration in 1882. By 1886 the Knights claimed almost 750,000 members, with 60,000 in New York alone. The Knights supported an eight-hour day, child labour legislation and equal pay for women, and was denounced as subversive by the authorities following the **Haymarket Riot** in 1886 for which one of its members was hanged. Membership declined rapidly thereafter as workers defected to the **American Federation of Labor**.

Kohima

– *see* **Burmese Campaign**.

Köprülü (Köprülüzade), Mehmed Fuat (1890–1966)

Turkish scholar and politician. A descendant of seventeenth-century Ottoman grand viziers, he was a professor of Turkish literature at Istanbul (initially **Constantinople**) University, 1913, and first director of the Institute of Turkology (Türkiyat Enstitüsü). Remembered particularly for his analysis of the fusion of central Asian and Islamic mysticism, *The First Mystics in Turkish Literature* (*Türk edebiyatinda ilk mutasavviflar*) (1919), and for his revision of earlier western theories about the rise of the **Ottoman Empire**. He entered parliament, 1936, and was foreign minister, 1950–4.

Korea

– *see also* **Chosŏn dynasty; Confucianism; Korean War; North Korea; South Korea; Tonghak Rebellion**. Before the seventh century, a number of small kingdoms ruled over portions of land throughout the Korean peninsula. In this period of decentralized rule, social, economic and cultural life centred on clans and village life. **Confucianism**, Shamanism and **Buddhism** served as guiding moral and religious principles for people. In the seventh century, Koguryo, Paekche and Silla emerged as the three largest kingdoms. After unifying the three kingdoms in AD 668, Silla inaugurated a period of centralized political rule (AD 668–935). During the early periods of Korean history, kingdoms on the peninsula had close political, cultural, economic and religious ties with **China**.

In 1231, Mongols from China invaded Korea and forced the Koryŏ government to submit to their rule. Foreign control of the peninsula ended with the downfall of the Mongol Empire and the birth of the Chosŏn dynasty (1392–1910). Founded by Yi Song-gye, the Chosŏn state adopted neo-Confucianism as the ruling ideology that informed the political, economic and social structures in society. This period featured a social hierarchy system with the royal court and the local gentry, who were known as Yangban, at the top. Because of the neo-Confucian ruling system, women experienced the loss of certain economic and social rights and customs from the Koryŏ period. Though the Chosŏn government formally closed Korea's border to the outside world, the country maintained robust relations with Asian countries.

In 1876, **Japan** forced the Chosŏn government to open the country's borders formally, thereby connecting Korea to the global world economy. From the late nineteenth century Korea became a pawn in international affairs. It ultimately lost its independence in 1910 when it officially became a Japanese colony. From 1910 to 1945 the Japanese colonial state ruled over Koreans while nationalist movements fought to create a new nation and achieve independence. In 1945 the country was entered by Russian forces from the north and American forces from the south. Korea briefly obtained its independence following Japan's defeat in **World War II**. The country, however, was quickly divided into two separate nation states because of **Cold War** politics between 1945 and 1948 that featured the **United States** seeking to establish an anti-communist regime that would be part of the capitalist global economy while a Communist regime was established in the north. Since 1948 the Korean nation has remained divided into the Republic of Korea (**South Korea**) and the Democratic People's Republic of Korea (**North Korea**).

Koreagate

This event in 1976 was considered a major political scandal that involved a Korean businessman, Tongsun Park, bribing members of the United States Congress in order to influence American policy in South Korea. Supported by the Korean Central Intelligence Agency (KCIA), Park gave money to a number of representatives from Congress for their support in reversing President **Nixon**'s decision to decrease the level of troops in South Korea. The scandal revealed the extent to which the South Korean government would act to preserve US military presence on the peninsula.

Korean War

On 25 June 1950, North Korean forces crossed the border established by treaty at the 38th parallel and broke the uneasy truce between the communist North and the US-supported South that had existed since the expulsion of the Japanese from the Korean peninsula at the end of **World War II**. The UN Security Council, which the **Soviet Union** was boycotting, authorized force to resist the invasion. Within two days the **United States** had sent air and naval forces to the area to help defend their South Korean allies, and on 30 June the **Truman** administration committed American ground troops to a war that would escalate and last until a truce was finally declared in July 1953. Other UN members also sent troops, though in much smaller numbers.

Though initially US General **Douglas MacArthur**'s forces quickly repelled the North Korean forces and continued to advance up into the northern part of the peninsula through the summer of 1950, the involvement of the Chinese after October, a development American military planners had not expected, turned the tide of

the war and inflicted heavy losses on the American-led forces. For the United States, the war was the first major military engagement of the **Cold War** and a major test of its evolving strategy of containment of communism around the world: US policymakers were convinced that the North Korean invasion was sponsored by the Soviet Union to gauge the willingness of the United States to defend its allies. American involvement in the war also reflected the growing importance of Asia more widely to American strategic concerns in the wake of the 'fall' of China to communism in 1949. For the new communist regime in Beijing the war represented the opportunity to flex its military muscles in the region and defend a client state. In October 1950 the Red Chinese Army mounted an attack on American and South Korean forces that had pushed the North Koreans back beyond the 38th parallel and now threatened to take the North Korean capital of Pyongyang. Emboldened by their ability to engage the Americans, the Chinese military authorized a massive deployment of troops the following month that pushed back MacArthur's forces towards the treaty border, and helped to create a military stalemate that would last until the eventual ceasefire agreement.

For ordinary Koreans the war did much to shape the social and political landscape of both North and South for the rest of the century. General MacArthur stated in 1951 at US congressional hearings that the 'war in Korea has almost destroyed that nation. I have never seen such devastation'. Millions died or became refugees, and the North was particularly badly affected as much of the fighting took place there: at least 12 per cent of the entire population died, a higher proportion than the Soviets suffered in World War II. Though a ceasefire was agreed in 1953, each of the two nations remained locked in a bitter dispute over the legitimacy of the other, and the demilitarized zone between the two countries became the most heavily militarized region on earth.

Kosciuszko, Tadeusz (1746–1817)

Polish nationalist, general and rebel leader. Kosciuszko is also honoured in Lithuania, the **United States of America** and **Belarus**. The son of a minor Polish noble, he rose through the Polish Corps of Cadets and received a military education in much the same fashion as **Napoleon Bonaparte** did in **France**. After emigrating rather than choose sides in Polish civil troubles which commenced in 1768, he studied in France for five years. Returning to **Poland**, he engaged in a doomed love affair with a student, having taken up teaching, which resulted in a beating from her father and emigration to America. There, he joined the Continental Army and became a celebrated Engineer, gained the rank of brigadier general, and was given citizenship and land. Despite this, he returned to Poland in 1784 (having vainly entrusted **Thomas Jefferson** with the manumission of his slaves). In 1791 Poland adopted a modern constitution and was invaded as a consequence by **Russia**, with the aid of conservative landowners. Kosciuszko assumed command of an army, won every battle he fought, and yet was undermined by the departure and surrender of the King of Poland. He then headed for France, of which he became a citizen in 1792, before organizing another uprising in Poland in 1793. This failed, and Kosciuszko was imprisoned, as indeed was Poland for 125 years. He was subsequently released, and spent his latter years between France, the United States and **Switzerland**, where he died.

Kosovo

Region of **Serbia** bordering **Albania**, considered by Serbs to be part of their traditional homeland, control over which they and the Albanian population dispute. Under Ottoman rule from 1389, Kosovo was retaken by **Serbia** in the 1912 Balkan War. Kosovo became a post-**World War II** **Yugoslav** Federal Republic province. Rising Albanian nationalism culminated in a declaration of independence in 1991, brutal war with Serbia, and the placing of Kosovo under **United Nations** transitional administration in 1999 pending agreement on the area's status between Serbia and the Kosovan Albanians. The population is 92 per cent Albanian.

Kossuth, Lajos (1802–1894)

Hungarian statesman and revolutionary. Kossuth was a lawyer based in Pest. Between 1825 and 1836 he served as an aide and deputy to Count Hunyady in the national Diet, whence his reports of activities became celebrated by liberal members and sympathizers. Kossuth rose so much in stature as a reporter of assemblies within the Habsburg lands that he was imprisoned in 1837–40. A career as a liberal journalist and agitator awaited on his release, until in 1847 he was elected in his own right to the Hungarian national Diet. From this position, he led the Treasury Department of the Hungarian revolutionary authority in 1848, rising to the presidency

of the Committee of National Defence shortly afterward. He issued the Hungarian Declaration of Independence, but was brought down by the combined forces of **Austria** and **Russia** in 1849. He then lived a life as a celebrated exile, travelling across the western world to much acclaim. He was feted by Lord **Palmerston**, and promoted the Hungarian cause as a refugee in England and **Italy**, before breaking with the bulk of Hungarian nationalists after the Austro-Hungarian compromise of 1867. He died in Turin and was repatriated with great national emotion to Budapest in 1894.

Kronstadt mutiny

Rising at the Kronstadt naval fortress in February–March 1921 by left-wing Russian sailors and workers following the Bolshevik repression of strikes in nearby Petrograd (later Leningrad, now St Petersburg). The rebels demanded a restoration of power to the Soviets (workers' councils), a lifting of the ban on socialists and anarchists, peasants' rights to land and the abandonment of 'War Communism'. **Red Army** troops under **Trotsky** captured the fortress on 18 March, executing many of the rebels.

Kruger, Stephanus Johannes Paulus (1825–1904)

Insurgent **Boer** leader in the 1881 (first) **Boer War**, who was also known as `Oom Paul' or `Uncle Paul'. Paulus was a Boer nationalist who became president of the Transvaal republic four times between 1883 and 1899. However, he was eventually forced to flee **South Africa** in 1900 because of British military pressure during the Second Boer War. He was unsuccessful in securing aid in **Europe**, and died in Clarens, **Switzerland**. Kruger remains a hero to many.

Ku Klux Klan (USA)

The Ku Klux Klan, a white supremacist terror organization, originally sought to overthrow the post-civil war **Reconstruction** governments in the American South. Initially organized at Pulaski, Tennessee, in May 1866, the Klan became a regional militia the following year under the leadership of Grand Wizard Nathan B. Forrest, the famous Confederate cavalry leader. Klan members often dressed in white sheets with white hoods, and the Klan's symbol was a burning cross. It targeted **African American** voters, landowners and militiamen. Klan violence played a major role in the collapse of Reconstruction governments and the reestablishment of white supremacy in the South. It has been revived at times during the twentieth century in response to immigration and threats to white supremacy. By this time it had become a national organization, appealing to anti-Catholicism and anti-Semitism in addition to its opposition to racial integration.

Kubitschek (de Oliveira), Juscelino (1902–1976)

President of **Brazil**. Born in Minas Gerais, Kubitschek became a doctor, participant in the formation of the Social Democratic Party, and governor of his home state. Elected president of Brazil in 1955 with only 36 per cent of the vote, he applied his energy to the construction of Brasilia, dedicated as the national capital in 1960. He promoted modernization and industrialization through public investment, but at the cost of rising inflation

Küçük Kaynarca (Kuchuk-Kainardji)
– *see* **Russo-Turkish War (1768–1774)**.

kulaks

The word was originally an abusive term for a class of peasant landowners who emerged in the wake of Pietr Stolypin's 1906 reforms in **Russia**. Kulaks were more productive than collective farmers, but associated with anti-Bolshevik forces in the **Russian Civil War** and were distrusted by **Lenin**. Nevertheless, Lenin made them the centre of his **New Economic Policy**. In the power struggle following Lenin's death, **Stalin** took advantage of a grain crisis to stir up popular resentment of the kulaks (whose holdings were larger than other farmers), and collectivized agriculture. He also oversaw the extermination of the kulaks as a class between 1928 and 1931, affecting an estimated 6 million farmers.

Kulturkampf

The name given to the political 'struggle for German culture' initiated by **Otto von Bismarck** between 1871 and 1878 within **Prussia**. The chief aim of the struggle was to demonstrate official and legal hostility to the Roman Catholic Church within the Prussian lands so as to win Protestant and liberal support for the new German Reich. The *kulturkampf* resulted in the exodus of many Germans to the **USA**, the persecution of priests and bishops, and the formation of German Catholic political movements such as the Centre Party. It also rebounded against Bismarck in the boost it gave to socialists and secularists.

Kun, Bela (1886–1939)

Hungarian revolutionary, born in Transylvania. He was a prisoner of war in **Russia** in 1916, where he joined the Bolsheviks. Founder of the Hungarian **Communist** Party, December 1918, and commissar for foreign affairs and effective leader of **Hungary**'s Communist–Social Democrat coalition government in March 1919. He created a successful national Red Army, but lost support and fled to Vienna and then Russia. A leader there of the Third International, he sought to promote revolution in **Germany** and **Austria**. He died in one of **Stalin**'s purges.

Kuomintang (KMT)

Also known as the Nationalist Party or Guomindang, and founded in 1912 by **Sun Yat-sen**, the Kuomintang (KMT) has been the ruling party in both **China** and **Taiwan**. In 1919 the KMT moved its base to Guangzhou, where Sun had established a revolutionary government, but after his death the party split. In 1927 the left wing under Wang Jingwei set up a brief government in Wuhan, while the right wing, led by **Chiang Kai-shek**, purged Communists from the party. The party was reunited in 1927 and established the capital in Nanjing under Chiang Kai-shek. During the second Sino-Japanese War the party was again divided between the Chiang's government in Chongqing and Wang Jingwei's collaborationist regime. After defeat by the Communists in the civil war, the Nationalists retreated to Taiwan, where the KMT was reorganized.

Kurds, Kurdish nationalism

A **Sunni** Muslim ethnic group of some 30 million people settled primarily across north-eastern Turkey, northern **Iraq** and north-western **Iran**, but also across Syria and the central Asian Turkic republics. Their origins go back to the ancient Medes and the earliest Indo-European migrations, but their most famous representative is Melik an-Nasir Salah ed-Din (1137–93), known to the West as Saladin, the great Muslim leader against the Crusaders. They have never forged a common political identity and the **Ottoman Empire** practised a deliberate policy of 'divide and rule'. There are still probably some 700 Kurdish tribes and clans in **Turkey** alone. They have been dubbed 'the largest nation without a state'.

The biggest concentration of Kurds is in modern Turkey, where they constitute a fifth of the population. They sided with the Turks against the Armenians during and after **World War I** and the **Treaty of Sèvres**, 1920, between the western Allies and the defeated Ottoman Empire, recognized the right of Kurdistan to independence, but the treaty was never to come into effect. The new **Republic of Turkey**, with its watchword of 'Turkey for the Turks', feared that the Allies still wanted its dismemberment, and in the same parliamentary sitting on 3 March 1924 as it abolished the caliphate it also closed down all Kurdish associations, newspapers and schools. Use of the language was effectively banned the same year. A consequent rebellion under Sheikh Said, with a force of 3,000–5,000 men, erupted on 13 February 1925 but was suppressed in a reign of terror, with several hundred people hanged, hundreds of villages destroyed and hundreds of thousands of Kurds deported. Kurdish revolts had been largely crushed by 1930, although the mountain province of Dersim, now Tunceli, held out until 1936–8.

Many Kurds have nevertheless intermarried and integrated, not least in Istanbul, and those who have established themselves in western Turkey have little desire to return to an independent 'Kurdistan' in the impoverished and mountainous east. On the other hand, attitudes have been hardened by violent governmental repression of the revolt by the Marxist Kurdistan Workers' Party (PKK), founded in 1978. Repression boosted Kurdish sympathy for an organization which few would probably have supported initially. This most sustained of Kurdish revolts commenced with a PKK attack in August 1984. Under the leadership of Abdullah Ocalan, the PKK proved both brutal and ruthless, and in the subsequent fighting perhaps 40,000 people were killed, more than 2,000 Kurdish villages destroyed and at least 300,000 people displaced. Hopeful initiatives on both sides, including the lifting of the official ban on the language in April 1991 and Ocalan's offer of a ceasefire in March 1993, repeatedly failed against entrenched interests and renewed violence. Ocalan himself was captured and jailed in 1999. The western nations have classified the PKK as a terrorist organization and the US has been supplying Turkey with intelligence on PKK movements since 2007. A ceasefire was called by Abdullah Ocalan in March 2013. It collapsed in July 2015 amidst renewed attacks and reprisals. The situation has been further confused by the reluctant acceptance by America and Turkey of the aid of Kurdish militants against the extremist **ISIL** movement from 2014 and the complications of the **Syrian Civil War**. The Kurds have proved to be the most potent force against ISIS/ISIL in **Syria**,

where, with Russian support, they have carved out a quasi-state, named Rejava.

The Kurds of Iraq again represent about a fifth of the total population but successfully negotiated an agreement on autonomy with the Ba'athist Iraqi government in 1970, the government constructing a parliament building in Arbil. Persecuted under President **Saddam Hussein**, particularly after US President **George Bush** called on them to rebel following the **Gulf War (1990–1)**, the now effectively autonomous Iraqi Kurds held free elections in May 1992, but parliamentary government collapsed into street fighting within two years, Turkey having encouraged factional divisions to stave off the precedent of a 'Kurdistan' on its borders. The Kurds are autonomous again in contemporary disordered Iraq and benefiting from access to Iraq's northern oilfields, but are embroiled in conflict with **ISIL**.

Some 9 per cent of Iran's multilingual population speaks Kurdish, but they rarely represent a political grouping. Turkey nevertheless suspects that Iran tolerates PKK rebels within its borders.

Kurile Islands

A string of Russian-controlled islands located north of Hokkaido, the Kurile Islands are at the centre of controversy between **Japan** and **Russia** because Japan claims ownership over four of them. A variety of ethnicities inhabit these islands, especially Koreans who were relocated there as forced labourers by the Japanese government during the 1930s. The disputed legal jurisdiction of the four islands has prevented the two countries from concluding a formal treaty to end **World War II**.

Kursk, Battle of (July–August 1943)

A decisive battle on the Eastern Front during **World War II**. **Hitler** hoped to pinch out a giant salient in the Soviet line in the **Ukraine**, which remained following the Soviet advance after **Stalingrad**, and seize the initiative in the conflict. He amassed huge forces including three-quarters of the armour on the whole front with many new types of tank used for the first time. Forewarned of the attack by intelligence, the Soviets under Marshal Zhukov (1896–1974) massed half of all their available infantry – over 1 million men with 500,000 in reserve, thousands of tanks and aircraft, protected by extensive minefields and thousands of anti-tank weapons. Eschewing **blitzkrieg** tactics, the German armies launched attacks on the northern and southern flanks of the salient and, although making inroads into the defences, became bogged down in very costly attritional warfare. On the southern front the largest tank battle in history took place with thousands of Soviet and German vehicles destroyed. The German forces were forced to call off the battle when news of Allied landings in the Mediterranean led Hitler to divert forces to that theatre. They had suffered over a million casualties and never recaptured the initiative on the Eastern Front. Soviet morale was bolstered and counter-offensives carried them beyond their original start line.

Kut-el-Amara

A city in eastern Iraq situated on the left bank of the Tigris River. The city was the site of a bloody battle during **World War I**. In an effort to protect its holdings and interests in **Asia**, the British attacked the **Ottoman Empire** from various fronts in the east. With relative ease, in November 1914 British Indian Expeditionary Force 'D' occupied Basra and secured access to the Abadan oilfields in south-west Iran. Lulled by futile Ottoman resistance, the British decided to continue upriver and proceed to the capital, Baghdad. Yet much to the British surprise, the Ottoman forces rallied. At Kut, under the command of German Baron von der Goltz, they surrounded and besieged the British troops led by Major General Charles Townshend for 140 days until the British surrendered unconditionally on 29 April 1916. This was a humiliating defeat for the British Army and a morale booster for the Ottomans and Germans. An estimated 23,000 British soldiers died at Kut, one of the highest numbers of casualties outside of Europe.

Kuti, Fela Anikulapo (1938–1997)

Nigerian muscian. Born into the distinguished clerical family of Ransome-Kuti, he was an accomplished entertainer and political activist. He studied music formally in London (1958–62) and began as a jazz musician. In 1969, following a US tour, he turned to popular music, creating the musical style Afro-beat. The music had radical and anti-government political messages and lyrics and he was often jailed and beaten by Nigerian officials.

Kuwait

Sheikhdom at the head of the Persian Gulf. Archaeological evidence suggests that Kuwait shared the Mesopotamian civilization of the third millennium BC, but subsequently declined until the foundation of Kuwait City, traditionally in 1710, and the autonomous sheikhdom by a member of the Al Sabah family in 1756. The Al Sabah family

has ruled ever since. Kuwait first became of interest to European powers in the late nineteenth century, when **Germany** sought to extend the **Berlin–Baghdad railway** it was sponsoring on to the port of Kuwait. Kuwait, however, resisted the encroachment of both German and Ottoman interests by concluding an agreement with **Great Britain**, 1899, whereby the British assumed control of the sheikhdom's foreign affairs. The establishment of a British protectorate followed with the outbreak of **World War I** against Turkey and the Central Powers, 1914. Relations with Nejd, a major constituent part of the later kingdom of **Saudi Arabia**, were resolved by the Treaty of Al Uqayr, 1922, which created a compromise neutral zone along part of the common frontier. The frontier with **Iraq**, then under British **mandate**, was determined the following year.

Kuwait became one of the wealthiest parts of the Arab world on a per capita basis following the exploitation of the sheikhdom's extensive oil reserves after **World War II**. The British recognition of full Kuwaiti independence in June 1961, stimulated Iraq to claim the sheikhdom as properly part of Iraq, but the claim was dropped following the dispatch there of British troops and the recognition of Kuwaiti independence by the **Arab League**, 20 July 1961. Kuwait sought to follow a neutral course in its relations with the rest of the Arab world thereafter. The neutral zone with Saudi Arabia, established in 1922, was partitioned between the two countries in May 1966. Kuwait tacitly supported Iraq during the **Iran–Iraq War** launched by Iraq in 1979, which endangered both Kuwait's security and its valuable oil exports. It extended large loans to Iraq throughout the war but was invaded by it, 2 August 1990, after talks about the repayment of those loans and other issues had broken down, provoking the **Gulf War, 1990–91**. Iraq announced the annexation of Kuwait on 8 August 1990, and the Kuwait government took refuge in Saudi Arabia throughout the war.

The defeated Iraqi troops caused significant economic damage to Kuwait on their retreat, most obviously by destroying almost half of the sheikhdom's 1,300 oil wells, many of which continued to burn for months afterwards. Kuwait sought after the war to ensure that Kuwaitis remained a majority of the population and many of the foreign workers who had fled the country were not permitted to return. Iraq recognized the independence and boundaries of Kuwait on 10 November 1994. In 2003 the country served as a base for the Iraq War which toppled **Saddam Hussein**. A modest measure of political reform was introduced in 1990, with the establishment of a National Council comprising fifty elected members and twenty-five appointed by the emir, as the ruling sheikh is formally known. The franchise was limited to men over 21 whose families had been of Kuwaiti nationality since before 1920 and the sons of persons naturalized after 1992, which gave an electorate by 1996 of just 107,169. In 2005 full political rights for women were introduced by Sheikh Jaber, who died in 2006.

Kuwait, Iraqi invasion and occupation of
– *see* **Gulf War (1990–1991)**.

Kwangju uprising
– *see also* **Roh Tae-woo**.

A mass uprising against authoritarian rule in **South Korea** in May 1980. Students and citizens in Kwangju, the capital of South Cholla province, protested against General Chun Doo-hwan's *coup d'état* of December 1979 and the declaration of martial law, but were violently suppressed by troops who reportedly massacred nearly 2,000 civilians. The Kwangju uprising and massacre became rallying points for democracy movements in South Korea.

Kwantung Army
A Japanese force established in **Manchuria** after Japan's victory in the **Russo-Japanese War** of 1905. Known for their aggressive stance, officers orchestrated the Manchurian incident in 1931. In 1937, they were involved in the **Marco Polo Bridge incident** that marked the beginning of all-out war with **China**. Although the Kwantung Army was successful against the Chinese, in 1939 it was defeated by Russian forces led by Marshal Zhukov (1896–1974) in the Battle of Nomohan (Khalkin-Gol). It later surrendered to the Russians in 1945.

Kwazulu
– *see* **Zululand**.

Kyoto
– *see* **environment**.

L

La Plata

The capital of the Argentine province of Buenos Aires since 1882. After decades of pressure, the Argentine government federalized the capital city of Buenos Aires in 1880 and provincial governor Dardo Rocha successfully proposed building a new city called La Plata to replace it as the provincial capital. La Plata is home to two top soccer teams as well as to the National University of La Plata, one of Argentina's most important universities.

Labor Party (Israel)

– *see* **Mapai**.

Ladino

An ethnic label designating non-indigenous people in Spanish America, most notably in **Guatemala**. The term emerged during the colonial era to describe Africans and Indians who spoke Spanish, then to label Indians who were alienated from their natal communities and became Hispanicized. This social category, long poised uncertainly between Indian and *mestizo*, gained greater significance and definition in Guatemala during the nineteenth and twentieth centuries. *Ladinos* moved into the western highlands as allies and agents of regional elites, expropriating indigenous land, taking control of local governments and recruiting plantation labourers. In the process, they increasingly defined themselves as modern, civilized proponents of progress and national development, in opposition to the supposedly atavistic Indians. The Maya cultural resurgence of recent years has made this identity problematic, but the *ladino*–Indian dichotomy remains the most important social division in contemporary Guatemala.

Lafayette, Marquis de (Marie-Joseph Paul Yves Roch Gilbert Motier) (1757–1834)

French aristocrat and military commander. A Continental army major general during the 1775–83 American Revolution, Lafayette commanded the National Guard in the **French Revolution** in 1789. Fleeing France in the face of rising Jacobin power, he was imprisoned by the Austrians until 1799. Following the French monarchy's restoration in 1815, he served as a liberal deputy until his death. The **United States** posthumously granted him honorary citizenship in 2002.

Lagos

Former capital and port city of **Nigeria**, with a population of over 8 million. Currently the second fastest-growing city in **Africa**, the region was originally inhabited by Awori hunters and fishermen of **Yoruba** descent. The area served as an important war camp for the Benin Empire before the arrival of Portuguese traders in the fifteenth century when it transformed into a major port in the **Atlantic slave trade**. Lagos was formally annexed as the British Lagos Colony in 1861, ending the slave trade and establishing British control over the palm oil trade and other resources. With the colonization of the interior, it became the capital of the Colony and Protectorate of Nigeria in 1914, which it remained until 1991 when the capital officially relocated to Abuja. Lagos experienced rapid growth throughout the 1960s and 1970s, is a major port for the export of crude oil and remains the industrial and financial hub of Nigeria.

La Guma, (Justin) Alexander (1925–1985)

South African novelist and activist. After working in a variety of jobs, La Guma became a journalist in 1955, going freelance in 1962. A Communist Party member from 1948 and **African National Congress** (ANC) member from 1955, he was placed under house arrest for his part in drafting the Freedom Charter. He lived in exile from 1966, acting as ANC representative in Cuba in the 1970s, but his writings encapsulated the anti-**apartheid** struggle.

Lahore

Lahore is the capital of **Pakistan**'s **Punjab** province. The city's history dates from the turn of the second millennium when it was incorporated into the Ghaznavid Empire (AD 977–1186). Subsequently, it was part of the Delhi Sultanate (1206–1526) and served for a time as the imperial capital of the Mughals (1526–1858). It was also the capital of the Sikh state of Ranjit Singh (1799–1949) and of the administrative province of British Punjab (1849–1947).

laissez-faire

Laissez faire, laissez aller et laissez passer, meaning 'let it do, let it go, let it pass', was first used by the Physiocrats against interference from **mercantilist** states with trade and as a synonym for free market economics by the early nineteenth century. In this strict view, laissez-faire assumes that markets are best left to their own devices, and that government interference simply creates inefficiencies. States should only do what is perceived as the minimum necessary to maintain peace security and property rights. Some extreme laissez-faire advocates even oppose taxation. The analogue of laissez-faire in international economics is freetrade, which opposes all use of protectionist measures designed to curtail trade between nations.

land warfare

European land warfare in the eighteenth century was limited in scale compared with later periods. Waged primarily for dynastic or territorial advantage, it was normally restricted in terms of the mobilization of manpower and resources. The largest of the **ancien régime** states, Bourbon France, could put as many as 300,000 men in the field, but battles rarely involved more than tens of thousands of combatants. Cumulatively, however, wars could prove costly in both men and materiel. The **Great Northern War** severely depleted **Sweden**'s relatively small population and the **Seven Years War** devastated **Prussia**, which lost 180,000 men out of a population of less than 3 million. Armies were professional organizations with service in the ranks, often of long duration, representing a separate cadre of society rather than the 'nation in arms'. Indeed, soldiering as a profession was often international, with soldiers from poorer parts of **Europe**, Scots, Irish, Swiss and Germans especially, ready to serve in the ranks of any who would pay them. The Prussian army of 1786, which numbered 190,000 men, included only 80,000 Prussian subjects. **Great Britain**, with a small standing army, called on regiments of Hanoverians and Hessians to campaign in its eighteenth-century wars in Europe and North America. On the fringe of Europe, the huge Ottoman armies which had struck terror into Christian Europe had diminished with the relative enfeeblement of the sultanate as a power from the early eighteenth century.

Armies, however, tended to grow in size in the late eighteenth century as competition between the major continental powers required them to maintain substantial standing armies, usually in excess of 150,000 men. But the French Revolutionary and Napoleonic Wars added a new dimension. The call *Aux armes, citoyens!* ('Citizens, to arms!') and the *levée en masse* announced a new kind of ideological revolutionary war in which the whole male population might be called on to fight. The French Revolutionary armies, which at their peak comprised more than 800,000 men, enjoyed high morale, meritocratic leadership and the benefit of less hidebound tactics. Systematized conscription organized by Lazare Carnot (1753–1823) provided Revolutionary and, later, Napoleonic France with hundreds of thousands of conscripts every year. Other powers were forced to reshape their military establishments to meet these new challenges, modernizing and rationalizing logistics, standardizing equipment, such as artillery and muskets, and improving officer training and recruitment. For example, Prussia's reaction to the crushing defeats by **Napoleon** in 1806 saw wholesale reform of the rigid structures inherited from **Frederick the Great** and the creation of a General Staff. The last years of the Napoleonic Wars saw the culmination of these developments with campaigns involving hundreds of thousands of men and battles on an unprecedented scale. Napoleon Bonaparte took an army of 600,000 men into **Russia** in 1812, lost most of it and then raised another of similar size the following year in order to campaign in **Germany**. Behind mobilizations on this scale lay unprecedented logistical and financial efforts. The victorious Russian armies which entered Paris in 1814 were supported by supply convoys which came all the way from eastern Europe, while the factories of industrial Britain supplied muskets and uniforms in their hundreds of thousands to friend and foe alike.

Tactically the Revolutionary and Napoleonic Wars not only used larger forces than was common in the eighteenth century, but also used them more flexibly. Napoleon's innovative use of independent army corps, operating free of supply trains and able to move rapidly, but concentrating when necessary, allowed more mobile and often devastating campaigns against traditionally organized armies. His use of massed artillery signposted the potential industrialization of the battlefield, which would grow apace as science and technology improved the firepower available to armies in the nineteenth century. In a contrary direction, the **American War of Independence** had demonstrated that irregular warfare could prove difficult for European armies to cope with and the use of **guerrilla warfare** by the Spanish in the Napoleonic Wars reinforced the point that conventional armies could be defeated by other means than conventional warfare.

Nonetheless, nineteenth-century land warfare reinforced the lessons of the Napoleonic era. Well-organized European states and the American Republic using the latest products of the early **Industrial Revolution** were able to defeat native powers on the battlefield, though geographical, medical and logistical problems might still hinder them. Americans were able to advance remorselessly westwards against native opposition, the French conquer **Algeria**, and the British defeat native rulers in the Indian subcontinent. Chinese armies armed with primitive gunpowder weapons proved no match for European forces carrying the latest weapons. When turned on each other even with muzzle-loading weapons, the scaling up of armies and the ability of states to mobilize for war over long periods meant huge casualties in the **Crimean War**, the **American Civil War** and the wars of Italian and German unification. Even where railways and steam shipping produced greater mobility, the greater concentration of forces they allowed produced pitched battles in which tens of thousands might be killed or wounded. Battlefield tactics of massed musketry and artillery fire produced over 600,000 dead in the American Civil War and over 200,000 in the Crimean War. By the second half of the nineteenth century colonial wars might still see reverses for western forces, as at **Islandwana**, Khartoum or Adowa, but the firepower of rifles, machine guns and breech-loading artillery could prove devastating on the battlefield against traditionally armed armies as demonstrated at **Omdurman** in 1898 when a small Anglo-Egyptian army inflicted almost 20,000 casualties on their Sudanese opponents in a matter of minutes. That battle also saw one of the last cavalry charges in modern land warfare.

The ability to project western armies thousands of miles by sail and later by steamship equipped with ever more effective weapons underpinned the imperial expansion of the late nineteenth and early twentieth centuries and the ability to crush native powers and challenges such as the **Zulu War** in **South Africa** and the **Boxer uprising** in **China**. The ability of modern weapons to turn the tables on imperial powers when in the hands of determined resistance was also demonstrated in the **Boer Wars** and the Rif rebellion in **Morocco**, especially when combined with guerrilla tactics. By 1914 land warfare in Europe, however, was predicated on a scaled-up version of the Napoleonic Wars or American Civil War with mass, conscript armies of millions rapidly concentrated by intricate mobilization timetables. War plans at the outbreak of **World War I** were predicated on speed of mobilization and, hopefully, a swift outcome by decisive manoeuvre as suggested by the German Schlieffen Plan to encircle Paris and achieve a swift victory, whilst the French hoped to launch a decisive attack in Lorraine. Once the impetus of these plans was spent, land warfare on the Western Front and in **Italy** became a static war of attrition, dominated by the firepower of artillery and machine guns and the ability of rail, road and horse transport to reinforce any threatened point. In the east, larger spaces allowed much more extensive manoeuvring with armies contesting hundreds of miles of territory. Casualties were massively increased; over 10 million Europeans died, though for the first time, battle casualties outstripped those caused by disease as medical advances increased survival rates for the wounded.

World War I had seen, in its final campaigns on the Western Front, the harnessing of the internal combustion engine to land warfare. Tanks plus ground supporting aircraft allied to more sophisticated infantry tactics had shown that mobile warfare could be achieved even against heavily defended positions. These developments found their expression at the outbreak of **World War II** in the **blitzkrieg** (lightning war) tactics which allowed Germany's armies to conquer **Poland** in 1939 and **France** in 1940 within a matter of weeks. Germany had learned, partly from the writings of British strategist Basil Liddell-Hart, how to use tanks, motorized infantry and air support effectively to achieve decisive results. Elsewhere, however, wars were fought with less sophistication; the **Russian Civil War**, the **Spanish Civil War** and the **Sino-Japanese War** proved lengthy and costly conflicts, the latter lasting from 1936 to 1945 before merging into a Chinese Civil War between Nationalists and Communists, not ended until 1949. Although blitzkrieg tactics brought Germany initial successes following the invasion of the **Soviet Union** in 1941, the war turned into an attritional conflict of mechanized armies waged over huge distances, from the outskirts of Moscow in late December 1941 to the heart of Berlin in May 1945. Tanks, artillery and ground support aircraft dominated the battlefield, leaving a legacy of weaponry and tactics which were utilized in the **Korean War** and prepared for during the **Cold War** for any future conflict in Europe between **NATO** and the **Warsaw Pact** forces. But World War II had demonstrated the increasing importance of an integration of land warfare with other forms. Air warfare, used to limit the productive capacity of opponents by bombing and air superiority, proved a crucial element in conducting land warfare. For example, the success of the Anglo-American **Normandy Landings** in 1944 was predicated upon almost total air superiority. Similarly, maritime control was what permitted the British **Dunkirk evacuation** in 1940 and the 'island-hopping' campaign with which American forces in the Pacific rolled back Japanese conquests from 1942.

The post-World War II era saw increasing sophistication in battlefield weapons such as tanks, with the addition of new developments, such as battlefield missiles, nuclear and conventional, new types of gas and helicopter gunships and unmanned drones for ground support. Nonetheless, the **Indo-Pakistan Wars**, **Arab–Israeli Wars** and **Iran–Iraq War** were fought in ways recognizable to veterans of World War II, while the **Gulf Wars** re-emphasized the integration of land warfare with the use of air power. The era also saw the extensive use of guerrilla war and insurgency, particularly in wars of colonial liberation, for example in **Vietnam**, Algeria and southern Africa, but also in resistance to the Soviet, and later **NATO**, invasions of **Afghanistan**. Both the United States and the Soviet Union, similar to the colonial powers before them, suffered humiliating reverses, respectively, in Vietnam and Afghanistan. Hostile populations armed with powerful hand-held automatic weapons and missiles, utilizing powerful modern explosives and infused with militant ideologies of different kinds even to the point of suicide bombing, have added an 'asymmetric' dimension to land warfare which continues into the twenty-first century.

landmines

Landmines are stationary explosives used against military troops or vehicles which came in to common use in **World War II**. They are usually placed just below the surface and are exploded by the weight of vehicles or troops passing over them. The name originates from the practice of sapping, where tunnels were dug under opposing forces or fortifications and filled with explosives. The clearance of landmines, which claim many civilian victims (especially children), is dangerous, slow and costly. As a result, there were moves to ban their use in the late twentieth century, though this has proved only partially effective. Charities have taken on the task of clearing mines from former war zones.

Laogai

Laogai, which is short for *laodong gaizao*, meaning 'reform through labour', was the system of prison labour camps instituted by the People's Republic of **China** in the early 1950s. It was formally abolished in 2013. Its ethos was supposed to be rehabilitative as well as punitive, but the system was in practice associated with lack of accountability and significant human rights abuses. Typically, prisoners held within the system would work a full day, followed by compulsory attendance at political 're-education' classes.

Laos

The Laos People's Democratic Republic was once the home of the fourteenth-century Lan Xang kingdom, but came under Siamese rule in the eighteenth century and in 1893 became part of the French protectorate of **Indochina**. The French ruled through the monarch, King Sisavang Vong, whose reign, 1904–59, saw the establishment of a French-educated elite and a basic administrative structure. Following **World War II** and Japanese occupation, attempts to resume French control by backing the monarchy gave way to a civil war between monarchists, neutralist nationalists and the communist **Pathet Lao** backed by the **Vietminh**. Formally independent in 1954, Laos remained divided with the Pathet Lao offering considerable assistance to the **Vietcong** in their struggle in **Vietnam** by allowing them to run the **Ho Chi Minh trail** through Laos. As a result, American bombing caused considerable damage to the Laotian infrastructure and economy. A coalition government was formed as the war in Vietnam ended, but was dominated by the Pathet Lao who collectivized agriculture in 1978. Liberalization began under the presidency of Phumi Vongvichit from 1986. Parliamentary elections in 1989 allowed a third of seats to opposition parties, collectivization was reversed in 1990 and foreign investment invited. Although the new constitution of 1991 confirmed a Communist monopoly of power, the country's fortunes were increasingly affected by the neighbouring capitalist economies, notably that of **Thailand**. The 1997 Asian banking crisis reduced the value of the Laotian currency drastically. A slow recovery under a succession of five-year plans left Laos still one of the poorest countries in the region and a major recipient of aid.

Laotian War

The civil war that followed **Laos**' independence from **France**. Armed conflicts, punctuated by brief ceasefires and failed coalitions, started in

1951. The two major factions involved in the Laotian War were General Phoumi Nosavan's pro-western revolutionary government in the south and the communist **Pathet Lao**, led by Prince Souphanouvong, in the north. The conflict ended in 1975 when Pathet Lao seized power. The Laos People's Democratic Republic was established with Souphanouvong as its first president.

Lateran Treaties

see also **Vatican City**.

A series of three agreements concluded in 1929 at the Lateran Palace in Rome between **Benito Mussolini** (for King Victor Immanuel III) and Pietro, Cardinal Gasparri (for Pope Pius XI). These agreements regularized the relationship between the Roman Catholic Church and the Italian state nearly fifty years after the rise of modern **Italy** had caused the loss of the Papal States in the centre of the country and the retreat of the Pope to Rome. The treaties settled questions of debt and established the **Vatican City** as a separate entity under the rule of the Pope. This ended the effective imprisonment of the popes, although the holders of the office were slow to leave the Vatican. In addition, Italy was dedicated to Catholicism, and social questions such as marriage and divorce were left to the church. This latter position, buttressed by the sponsorship after **World War II** of **Christian Democrat** parties by the church, only began to change in 1984. For its part, the church promised to be neutral in world affairs, which in the long term soured its reputation in the eyes of those who thought it should have done more to resist fascism. This position did not stop the church from an intense opposition to communism.

Latin America

Latin America refers to both a geographical and a cultural concept. The term originated in the nineteenth century as political leaders and intellectuals began considering the common heritage of nations where a Romance language is spoken – namely Spanish, Portuguese and French. Geographically, Latin America encompasses areas of the western hemisphere south of the **United States**, including all of **Mexico**, Central America, South America and the Caribbean.

The relatively isolated indigenous peoples of Latin America became part of the greater world system with Christopher Columbus' initial voyage across the Atlantic Ocean. Spaniards established permanent settlements throughout present-day Mexico, Central America and the northern and western regions of South America while the

Portuguese claimed **Brazil**. Violent confrontations erupted repeatedly between the European colonizers and the native populations. Armed with papal approval, the Spanish in particular sought to annihilate native religious practices and the Catholic Church emerged as a rich and powerful institution. By the end of the sixteenth century the indigenous population had declined precipitously as a result of epidemic disease, warfare and general mistreatment.

During three centuries of European rule a social hierarchy emerged based on race, ethnicity, wealth and occupation. The Spanish crown put in place a political structure that favoured the elite, white European population; a similar governing system developed in Portuguese-ruled Brazil. Economic activities centred on mineral wealth and the production of commodity goods and other raw materials, primarily through agriculture and raising livestock. Mining silver and other metals generated enormous wealth for the Spanish throughout the colonial period. Agricultural exports included sugar, tobacco, hides and various dyes; wheat, corn, cacao and other foodstuffs were grown for domestic consumption. Colonial elites owned large estates and mining operations where native peoples, African slaves and a racially mixed population provided the labour.

national formation

By the mid 1820s most of mainland Latin America had secured independence, while most Caribbean colonies and smaller mainland possessions controlled by the Dutch, French and British remained under European control. The new nations faced instability created by competing internal political factions and boundary disputes with neighbouring countries. In the midst of intense volatility, authoritarian yet charismatic *caudillo* leaders rose to power. Their autocratic rule brought much needed order to some regions, but in other areas infighting exacerbated the turmoil that followed independence. Wherever located, *caudillos* complicated efforts to establish constitutional processes. Besides internal conflict, many nations faced military invasions. The **United States** armed forces occupied much of Mexico during the **Mexican–American War** (1846–8); the conflict cost Mexico more than half of its national territory. The French Army invaded Mexico in the 1860s in an attempt to establish imperial rule in the Americas, while at the same time the Spanish attempted to recolonize the Dominican Republic. Private US citizens operating as soldiers of fortune – known as **filibusters** – led expeditions of conquest in Mexico and Central America throughout the 1850s and 1860s.

In the last half of the nineteenth century the disorder that had followed independence subsided. Elite oligarchies consolidated power in many nations and often imposed economic and political tenets that conformed to nineteenth-century liberal philosophy. Rejecting the closed economic model of colonial mercantilism, they actively pursued foreign investment to develop a commodity export sector. New constitutions outlined limited democratic processes that gradually evolved to allow more inclusive suffrage and representation. As a sense of order took hold, entrepreneurs from Europe and the US invested heavily in infrastructure and development projects. By 1900 railways and highways criss-crossed the region and electricity, telegraphs and modern sewage systems had arrived in major cities. These projects facilitated the development of foreign-owned capitalist agricultural ventures as well as an incipient industrial sector in countries that included Mexico, Argentina and Brazil.

twentieth century

By 1900 the United States had extended its influence throughout Latin America. It backed Cuban independence militarily in 1898 and forced **Spain** to surrender its remaining American empire. **Puerto Rico**, Guam and the **Philippines** became US protectorates and the 1901 **Platt Amendment** gave the United States the right to establish military bases in **Cuba**. In 1903 US leaders supported Panamanian independence and won the right to construct a trans-isthmian canal. As a result, US economic and military presence in Latin America expanded considerably, while western European and Asian nations also strengthened ties in the region through trade and migration.

Economic and political developments of the late nineteenth century fostered populist movements throughout Latin America in the twentieth century. A large working class and urban poor emerged in new industrial areas while political reforms aimed at expanding the electorate helped to create a sense of civil engagement. Populism manifested itself in the 1910 **Mexican Revolution** and in other nations through the labour unions, expanded suffrage and nationalist movements. After the onset of the **Great Depression** in 1929, populist leaders in Latin America changed their outlook on economic development and attempted to replace foreign investment with nationally owned enterprises. By the 1950s the preferred economic model was import substitution

industrialization, which stressed developing a national market for durable consumer goods, nationalizing major industries and expanding government spending. Those policies remained in place until debt problems and near financial collapse led Latin American leaders to embrace **neoliberalism** after 1980. Leftist policies often accompanied populist rhetoric, giving rise to concerns over the spread of communism during the **Cold War**. The success of the **Cuban Revolution** of 1959 seemed to validate such fears and for the next three decades US leaders worked with right-wing dictators to violently suppress leftist movements throughout the region. **Chile**, Argentina, Brazil and many other nations endured 'dirty wars', while Central American nations suffered decades of civil war. These violent tendencies eventually subsided with the end of the Cold War and the revival of democracy in Latin America in the 1990s, since which time a new wave of populism has swept the region, with the election of leftist leaders promising to combat poverty.

Latin America Free Trade Association (LAFTA)

A grouping formed by **Argentina, Brazil, Chile, Mexico, Paraguay, Peru** and **Uruguay** through the Treaty of Montevideo in 1960, coming into effect in January 1962 with the ambition of establishing a free trade area in goods (but not services) within twelve years. **Bolivia, Colombia, Ecuador** and **Venezuela** subsequently joined and in 1980 LAFTA became the Latin American Integration Association (LAIA or ALADI in Spanish). **Cuba** became a member in 1999.

Latin American independence

Latin Americans won independence from **France**, Spain and Portugal between 1804 and 1825. **Toussaint Louverture** ended slavery and made **Haiti** independent. Spanish American elites responded to the French invasion of Iberia and captivity of Ferdinand VII by seeking first autonomy within the empire and then independence. The military campaigns of **Simón Bolívar** and Antonio José de Sucre emancipated northern South America (**Venezuela, Peru, Colombia, Ecuador** and **Bolivia**); **José de San Martín** and **Bernardo O'Higgins** liberated **Chile**. Pedro I, heir to the Portuguese throne, declared **Brazil**'s independence. After the failures of **Miguel Hidalgo** and José María Morelos, Agustín de Iturbide negotiated **Mexico**'s independence, Central America split from Mexico, and Bolívar's dream of a united South America faded. With the exception of Brazil, where a monarch ruled, independence brought *caudillos*, internal conflict, political dissension, stagnant economies, inflated currencies and racial discrimination, but eventually new policies, expanded trade and democratic institutions.

Latvia
– *see* **Baltic states**.

Lausanne, Treaty of
An agreement signed on 24 July 1923 that established international recognition for the **Republic of Turkey**. It replaced the **Treaty of Sèvres** in the wake of the nationalist triumph in the Turkish War of Independence. Sèvres had envisioned the division of Anatolia between external powers. While Lausanne overturned Sèvres' attempted abrogation of Turkish sovereignty, it nevertheless forced the new government to renounce claims to all Aegean islands except two, as well as to the Iraqi city of Mosul. Another blight on Turkish sovereignty enshrined at Lausanne was the forced demilitarization of the Turkish Straits (*see* **Straits Question**). That condition restricted Turkey's control over the key waterways connecting the Mediterranean with the Black Sea until 1936. Despite those losses, Turkish negotiations under Ismet (Inonu) Pasha did glean important victories with recognition by European powers and retention of key territory in eastern Thrace chief among them.

Lawrence, Thomas Edward (of Arabia) (1888–1935)
Lawrence developed an early interest in the Middle East while an archaeology student at Oxford University. During **World War I** he became an intelligence officer in the British Arab Bureau in Cairo and was sent on an early mission to the Hejaz to establish an alliance with **Sharif Husayn of Mecca** in a revolt against the **Ottoman Empire**. Lawrence was subsequently dispatched to Husayn's army as a military adviser, assisting Husayn's son, **Faisal** (the future king of Iraq) in the **Arab Revolt**. Lawrence accompanied Faisal into Syria and advised the Arabs during the Versailles conference. But with the failure of the Syrian Arab kingdom, Lawrence returned to England in search of obscurity in the Royal Air Force under the name T. E. Shaw. He published his account of the war in the book *Seven Pillars of Wisdom*. Lawrence died in a motorcycle accident on 19 May 1935. A romantic hero for many, his campaign against the Turks became seen as a model of **guerrilla warfare**.

Laye, Camara (1928–1980)
A Guinean writer who was one of the founders of the Négritude literary movement. The son of a village goldsmith, he studied engineering in **France**. While in France, however, he began writing, especially about rural and traditional Africa and the loss of tradition in the colonial setting. Following Guinean independence he returned home, but became involved in political conflict and eventually died in exile.

Le Duc Tho (1911–1990)
Tho co-founded the Indochinese Communist Party in 1930. He joined the Lao Dong Politburo of the Vietnamese Workers' Party in 1955, and was the key negotiator of the ceasefire and American withdrawal from **Vietnam** in the Paris Peace Accords of 1973. Consequently, he was awarded the Nobel Peace Prize jointly with **Henry Kissinger** in 1973, but became the only person ever to turn down the prize, stating that there was still no peace in his country.

Le Pen, Jean-Marie (1928–)
A French right-wing Nationalist politician, former soldier, non-practising lawyer and intelligence officer who ran in five separate elections for the French presidency between 1974 and 2007. In 2002 he came second with nearly 17 per cent of the vote. Le Pen rose through the extremely violent world of monarchist and nationalist right-wing politics in Toulouse, via the Front National, which he founded in 1972. At various times, he was a member of the French National Assembly and European Parliament. Wealthy by inheritance, Le Pen was succeeded in the FN leadership by his daughter, Marine, in 2011. They subsequently had an open and bitter disagreement as the FN developed to become a major contender in French politics.

League of Nations
The League of Nations was an international body established after **World War I**. It was hoped that the League, the membership of which was intended to be made up of all sovereign states, would form a framework for a stable world in which secret treaties, military alliances and aggression did not exist and in which international law was brought into being. The organization, which was based in Geneva, was composed of an Executive Council, an Assembly and a Secretariat as well as sundry other bodies. The most important of this latter category were the International Court of Justice and the

International Labour Organization. The League was based around a constitution known as a Covenant that had emerged from the stated policy of the **United States of America**: it sought to guarantee international action and sanctions against acts of aggression, to promote disarmament and to sponsor the solution of international problems and disputes by diplomacy. It should not be wholly seen as an American enterprise, however (ironically, the USA did not join the League) but also as stemming from a strand of British and French thought which had envisaged the replacement of the global sway of empires with a internationally acceptable body grounded in a commitment to the rule of law and internationalism.

From the beginning, the League was beset by structural problems and the bad faith of particular members. It was, for instance, produced by the **Paris Peace Conference** and therefore associated with the **Treaty of Versailles**, which was seen by some potential members as a rebarbative and retributive punishment of the losers of the Great War. There was no global economic settlement, leading states resisted a commitment to racial justice, and **Britain** and **France** ensured that imperial control of particular key areas was maintained through a 'mandate' system. After the refusal of the American Senate to ratify Versailles, the United States sponsored alternative international agreements outside the League, such as the Washington Naval Treaty and the Kellogg–Briand Pact. By the early 1930s the combination of economic protectionism consequent upon the **Great Depression**, the aggression of the Japanese Empire in **Manchuria** and of **Italy** in **Africa**, and the attitude of the Nazi government in **Germany** – let alone the effective exclusion of the **USSR** and the appeasement policies of the UK and France – made the League a largely impotent organization.

Despite these difficulties, the League did subsist as a body that scored some early successes, attempted to sponsor diplomacy and disarmament, oversaw the development of international standards, and contained fifty-eight members at its height. However, its writ was effectively a dead letter by 1935. It was wound up in 1946, and its assets and buildings handed over to the **United Nations Organization**. The League is often seen as a comprehensive failure, but most historians would argue that it offered the first legitimate secular model of international organization in the modern period.

A republic situated along the Mediterranean Sea coast of the Middle East, Lebanon is also bordered by **Syria**, **Palestine** and **Israel**. The country covers an area of nearly 10,5000 square kilometres and has a population of almost 5 million. Lebanon formed a republic in 1943, when it shrugged of the yoke of the French **mandate**. Democratic republican in structure, the Lebanese government has a president, a prime minister and a cabinet, all of whom are elected. Parliamentary in form, the legislature is representative, with all religious and ethnic groups accounted for. The nation's guiding principles are set out in its constitution, which specifies a unique division of officials related to the nation's complex ethnic and religious factions. The elected president must be from within the Maronite Christian community, while the prime minister must be from the Sunni Muslim community and the speaker of the House from the Shia Muslim community in an attempt to balance power and create unity within the nation. This structure arises from the fact that the nation is among one of the most fragmented along religious and sectional lines, and has seen various civil wars and feuds which have had disastrous effects on the economy and quality of life in Lebanon. Beyond its borders Lebanon has had struggles with its larger neighbours as well. Israel has had a contentious history with Lebanon, who it accuses of harbouring Palestinian fugitives who use the nation as a base to attack Israel. Syria has also been accused of meddling in Lebanese affairs, and of committing high-profile political assassinations on Lebanese soil. Syrian troops had maintained their residence in Lebanon for many years, but in 2004 were recalled, having been accused of influencing Lebanese affairs for years. The **Syrian Civil War** has brought renewed tensions to Lebanon.

A member of both the **United Nations** and a founding member of the League of Arab States, the nation has sought a role in Middle Eastern and world affairs, and has attempted to retain ties to both western and eastern powers. Lebanon has few major economic activities beyond a generalized service industry, which makes up the bulk of its economy, with tourism a major source of revenue.

Lebanese Civil War (1859–1860)

The Lebanese Civil War began as a local class conflict, subsequently morphing into a regional sectarian conflagration. In the Kisrawan district of Lebanon, Maronite peasants revolted against their Maronite Catholic landlords in 1859. This show of power by peasants alarmed the **Druze** landholding class who responded by attacking the Maronite militias with their own irregular forces. The conflict quickly spread to other regions of Mount Lebanon and eventually to the Bekaa valley and Damascus. The Maronite militias lacked the coherence of their Druze adversaries, who looted Christian property and massacred civilians in the market towns of Zahlé, Dayr al-Qamar, Rashaya, Hasbaya and Damascus. Economic transformations of the preceding decades had privileged the Christian merchant classes of those towns disproportionately. The Ottoman Army intervened to stop the Druze militias, and **France** seized on the Christian loss of life to justify landing forces in Beirut in August 1860. In the ensuing peace agreement, France negotiated **Lebanon**'s autonomy from the **Ottoman Empire**.

Lebanese Civil War (1975–1989)

On 14 April 1975 four Christian political leaders in the Phalange Party were murdered in **Beirut** during an assassination attempt on Pierre Jumayyil, a Phalange Lebanese Party leader. In retaliation, Christian Phalange Lebanese Party members bombed a bus which was moving through a Christian neighbourhood carrying Palestinians. Twenty or so Palestinians who had been on the way to work were murdered in retaliation. The larger conflict which became the Lebanese Civil War may have been ignited by these events, but it had been a long time in the making. Politically based tensions between the various ethnic and religious groups, of which there were many, within **Lebanon** were based upon the 1946 decision called the National Pact, which made the ethnic minority Christians politically dominant. Religious tensions that had been so delicately balanced in Lebanon became a powder keg, and the fact that various factions, such as the **Druze**, tended to have their own militias for protection did not help the tense situation. Tens of thousands of people are still considered to be 'missing' from the disastrous war, and it has been estimated that as much as 7 per cent of the population was killed. The specific impetus of the war appears to have been related to the power of minority Maronite Christians in the political arena, where majority groups perceived themselves to be marginalized. As the fighting spread, the volatile situation descended even further into chaos, with other religious and ethnic factions choosing sides creating a deep rift within Lebanese politics and society.

Often seen as a Muslim versus Christian event, the civil war had deeper causes which were reflective of the complex political, social and religious make-up of the country. **Syria**, fearing the chaotic environment that was developing on its border, sought to mediate a compromise to restore order.

The **United States** also tried to intervene, but neither Syrian nor American attempts were completely successful in healing the divide that had torn Lebanon apart. The year 1989 witnessed the beginning of the end of the conflict with the signing of the Ta'if Agreement. The **Arab League** helped to get an agreement pushed through to begin to address the issues that underlay the conflict, such as confessional differences and perceived advantages and disadvantages due to religious and ethnic factors. Under the agreement the government was divided more equitably between Christians and Muslims, and a generalized disarmament was envisioned and attempted. In May 1991 factional militias were by and large dissolved and a non-partisan army of mixed religious backgrounds was built to attempt to calm confessional divides. Religiously based political disputes are still prominent in Lebanon, not having been totally healed by the end of the war and the various agreements, but the Ta'if Agreement has helped to mend the significant rifts. However, Lebanon's fragile balance remained threatened by the **Syrian Civil War** and the rise of **ISIL**.

Lebanon

– *see also* **Beirut**; **Lebanon Civil War**.

Lebensraum

An idea associated with **Adolf Hitler**, though only mentioned twice by him in his 1925 book *Mein Kampf*. *Lebensraum* was a concept of 'living space', which Hitler argued was vital for all great countries and which was constituted by large and fertile territories populated by a uniform national group. In pursuit of such 'living space', Hitler, **Himmler** and the **SS** sought to conquer territories in Europe and the **Soviet Union** after 1939; kill, enslave or displace their peoples in a way analogous to their image of the American Midwest; and settle them with 'Aryan' Germans who would then contribute to the new **Third Reich**. In that regard, the concept is best seen as a German domestic variant of racial Imperialism.

Lee Kuan Yew (1923–2015)

Lee Kuan Yew was a key figure in the negotiations for **Singapore**'s independence from **Britain** (1956–8) and became the first prime minister of Singapore in 1959. Under his management, Singapore became a major financial and industrial centre of the Asia Pacific region. He stepped down from power in 1990, receiving the honourary title of 'Minister Mentor'. The People's Action Party, which he founded in 1954, remains the sole political party with governing power in Singapore to this day.

Lee, Robert E. (1807–1870)

The outstanding Confederate general of the **American Civil War**. Lee's significance rests on his victories during the Seven Days of Battles and at the second **Bull Run** that prevented an early Confederate collapse. He also foiled two further Union offensives at **Fredericksburg** and **Chancellorsville**. Lee faltered while taking the war to the North at **Antietam** and **Gettysburg**. His entrenched campaign across northern Virginia shielded Richmond until in April 1865 Petersburg fell, and Lee's troops retreated westwards, surrounded and forced to capitulate at Appomattox. From 1865 to 1870 Lee served as president of Washington College.

Leeward Islands

The Leeward Islands is a collection of small islands (Nevis, **St Kitts**, **Antigua** and **Montserrat**) located in the north-eastern corner of the Caribbean Sea. Settled by French and English migrants after 1624, the Leewards became a centre for slave-produced sugar plantations. By the end of the eighteenth century, it was among the wealthiest places in the Americas. Antigua and St Kitts/Nevis gained independence from Britain in the 1980s. Montserrat remains a British Overseas Territory.

legal systems/rule of law

Most states have rules that they refer to as 'laws'. These are enforced generally in courts and by police forces, and bind all under the authority of the state. However, the term *legal system* is generally taken to refer to other ideas as well, including that of 'the rule of law' (as opposed to arbitrary tyranny) and the idea of justice. Most systems attempt to uphold consistent principles, often those in accord with human rights, and do so either by deriving principles from case law or by imposing a higher body of principles derived from philosophical or constitutional precepts.

The rule of law is in fact a set of ideas. The term covers the idea of equality of all citizens as are affected by a law before it in terms of their treatment; it seeks to restrict or prohibit retroactive laws; it upholds the idea that laws should be clear and comprehensible; and it restricts executive power by holding that citizens should be presented with evidence and given a chance to explain themselves before their guilt or innocence is ascertained and acted upon. At the heart of the idea is the notion that the state should itself agree to be bound by law and therefore should accept that sometimes its prosecutions may be wrong and that in any event they have to be founded on evidence and predictable clear rules.

Legal systems further break down into three strands; positive law, natural law and common law. Positive legal systems hold that all that is written by the state and legitimized by a constitution is the whole of the law, and that any other rules are partial, conditional or simply based on a relative ethical pretxt. In the **United States** in particular, liberal political philosophy cleaves to the idea that a body of principles exists which, if anonymous status-free observers were to create it, would correspond to all 'genuine' laws. Combined with the historic openness of American processes of compensation for injuries to the person, reputation, mental health or constitutional liberties of an individual, this has led to the idea of the 'rule of lawyers' through the American courts. Such a rule is held to be self-confident, total, and is enforced by damages claims added to punitive claims for money to punish bad behaviour.

Natural law systems look to the existence of higher or natural morals from which legal systems may derive principles to apply to particular situations, often with a minimum of explanation. Again, different interpretations of this type of law exist from Catholic natural law through Islamic sharia to traditional 'Roman' systems.

Common law systems are highly situational and adapt a usually restricted view of the sphere of law to the principles of fairness and natural justice; frequently they also hold to the idea that only that which is specifically prohibited is illegal. They are therefore an often unwritten combination of positive and natural systems as much as anything else, and typify the system in England and its former colonies. A legal system thus stands in contrast to a rule by dictators, parties or theocrats, and is also associated with courtroom argument and the prominence of lawyers in politics and political affairs. It allows for the peaceful transfer, purchase and maintenance of property, and is an essential adjunct of capitalism.

The idea of a legal system in the West has always been intimately associated with the process of secularization and the separation of church law and state action. A great many philosophers derive their inspiration from the **Enlightenment** attempt to codify law and to place it upon a logical basis of jurisprudence. A tradition therefore exists from Desiderius Erasmus (1469–1536) and Hugo Grotius (1583–1645), who wrote from the perspective of the early modern **Netherlands**, through William

Blackstone, J. Austin (1911–60), H. L. A. Hart (1907–92), Ronald Dworkin (1931–2013) and John Rawls (1921–), that law ought to be universal, explicable and reasonable. In recent years this idea, which in the nineteenth and twentieth centuries swept much before it, was challenged from Islamic sources. Though many institutions took a lead and example from Islamic law in the early years of that religion, modern Islamic law or sharia holds that its religious courts are competent to address, on the basis of the Islamic holy book, all matters of human activity and transgression. Sharia law holds, via the judgements of previous and existing religious scholars, that such a scholar armed with a holy book and set up as a local and itinerant judge, can supplement community and individual judgement and rule on the application of God's will to behaviour. Since Islamic law (like many religious systems) is concerned with harsh punishment, intolerance of non-normative sexuality, defined and usually subordinate female roles, and the prohibition of interest payments, the resurgence of Islamic law has posed a real challenge to the Enlightenment legal tradition. A subordinate challenge has been launched by Catholic scholars, who have claimed to derive law from God via several thousand years of Christian and Talmudic thought on proper process and principle. This has led to controversies over such issues as euthanasia, abortion and sexuality.

Legal systems ultimately seek to resolve problems in a predictable way that precludes violence and regulates expectations of the state and of property. Although it is possible to talk of early societies without one, it is impossible to find a state in the modern world that does not at least aspire to a legal system in Enlightenment form.

Lenin (1870–1924)

The name with which Vladimir Ulyanov, a Russian revolutionary, has become most closely associated. Lenin was the guiding genius of the Bolshevik, or Soviet Communist Party. A lawyer who based some of his theories on analogies drawn from the work of the physicist and philosopher Ernst Mach (1836–1916) and some from **Karl Marx** and **Friedrich Engels**, Lenin saw great violence done to his family in **Russia**. Escaping to **Switzerland**, he formulated the idea that the **Russian Empire** could be quickly advanced to the status of a modern power through ruthless industrialization, even at the cost of many lives. Lenin believed it was critical that a communist party which captured the state and then eliminated opponents by absorption, subterfuge or strategic violence, should direct this

effort. This became known as the core of Marxist–Leninism once Lenin was sent back to the Russian Empire in a sealed train by German officers eager to disrupt the liberal revolution associated with **Alexander Kerensky** in 1917. In alliance with Lev Bronstein (**Trotsky**) and Joseph Djugashvili (Koba, or **Stalin**), Lenin quickly established his new state of workers' councils, or Soviets, the Russian Soviet Federal Socialist Republic. He proved adaptable as well as ruthless, promoting a semi-capitalist scheme for small farmers when it became obvious that agriculture could not be easily collectivized after 1921, known as the **New Economic Policy**. He also guided Russia to a peace treaty with the western powers in 1917. During the **Russian Civil War**, Lenin, Trotsky and Stalin gradually picked off or isolated domestic and foreign armies. Lenin then offered to establish a voluntary Union of Soviet republics in the successor countries to the Tsarist Empire, but found that such a Union was unsustainable and decided to run it as a centralized communist tyranny instead. His health declined, and, though he found himself worrying about the capacities of his subordinate and mimic, Stalin, Lenin proved unable to execute his wish that Stalin not follow him in the Soviet leadership, despite the efforts of his formidable wife and partner, Krupskaya. Lenin died in 1923 and his embalmed body was subsequently placed in a tomb in Moscow's Central Square. From it, Soviet Leaders addressed the nation and watched military parades for the next sixty-seven years, and through it devoted worshippers of Lenin's secular religion passed. His cult became a keystone of Soviet and then international communist life.

As well as the idea of forced economic development, Lenin was also associated with a critique of **imperialism** that guided later Soviet leaders. In it, he asserted that the western liberal powers were degenerating into competing empires that would imminently consume each other. The policy of the **Soviet Union**, therefore, had to be to promote socialism in the West but also to understand that western states posed threats mainly to each other, and that future war could only benefit the USSR. This theory, when assimilated by Stalin, is perhaps one reason for the USSR's indifference to the Hitlerian regime of **Germany** and for the eventual Nazi–Soviet pact of 1939–41 which led directly to Nazi diplomatic and military success, and to the situation where **Hitler** could launch an attack which left 20 million Soviet citizens dead.

Lenshina, Alice (1920–1978)

Alice Lenshina (also known as Alice Mulenga Mubisha) was a religious leader in Northern Rhodesia (modern-day **Zambia**) during the colonial period. After an illness in 1953, she claimed to have met Jesus Christ and started a simplified Christian revival and anti-sorcery campaign which became the independent Lumpa Church in 1955. Lenshina was not interested in politics but the United National Independence Party considered the church a rival, and so arrested and detained Lenshina from 1964 until her death.

Lewanika (c. 1842–1916)

Lewanika II was king of the Lozi in modern-day **Zambia**. He came to power in the aftermath of the invasion and temporary rule of Lozi by the Kololo, a South African group that occupied the country until their expulsion in 1865. In 1877 Lewanika came to power and soon became involved in an attempt to modernize the country, working through Ovimbundu traders and European missionaries, especially François Colliard, to bring in modern techniques, western-style education and other modern cultural elements. In 1890 Lewanika arranged a treaty of protection with the **British South African Company**, which was seeking mining and agricultural rights in the country. Following the concession, Lozi moved into British control, losing considerable land to **Portugal** in 1905 and eventually being merged into the British colony of Northern Rhodesia. When Lewanika died his country lost its sovereignty.

Lewis and Clark expedition

The Corps of Discovery expedition (1804–6) led by Meriwether Lewis (1774–1809) and William Clark (1770–1838) was the first American overland expedition to the Pacific (Alexander MacKenzie had crossed **Canada** a decade earlier). The objective of the 8,000-mile, 28-month round trip, which reached the ocean at the mouth of the Columbia River, was to locate a transcontinental water route. It focused national attention on the recently purchased **Louisiana** territory, reinforced US claims to Oregon and provided information about resources and indigenous peoples.

Li Hongzhang (1823–1901)

Li Hongzhang was born in Anhui province, where he helped Zeng Guofan crush the **Taiping rebellion**. After this, he was appointed governor general of north-east **China**, where he supported the self-strengthening movement by founding the China Merchant Steamship Company and building arsenals near Tianjin. He negotiated the Treaty of Shimonoseki in 1895, which ended the first **Sino-Japanese War**, and then was recalled to Beijing to negotiate with the foreign powers after the **Boxer uprising**.

Liang Qichao (1873–1929)

Liang was born near Guangzhou in southern **China**, and studied with **Kang Youwei**. He accompanied Kang to Beijing and gained an official position during the Hundred Days of Reform, but was exiled to **Japan** after the movement's failure. Although he continued to work with Kang Youwei in Japan, he opposed the restoration of the dynasty under Yuan Shikai. After his retirement from politics, he became professor of history at Nankai University in Tianjin and wrote on synthesizing Confucianism with western liberalism.

Liaquat Ali Khan (1895–1951)

An influential leader of the **Muslim League** and the first prime minister of **Pakistan**. Educated at Aligarh, Oxford and the Middle Temple, he served as general secretary of the Muslim League from 1936 to 1947. One of **Mohammed Ali Jinnah**'s closest confidents, he played a key role in negotiations leading up to independence and the partition of India. As prime minister of Pakistan, he was initially overshadowed by Jinnah, Pakistan's first governor general. After Jinnah's death in 1948, Liaquat Ali Khan became the dominant force in Pakistani politics, negotiating a peace agreement with India to end hostilities in **Kashmir** and building diplomatic ties with the **United States**. He took steps towards drafting a constitution for the new state while struggling to balance the competing interests of different political factions and regional groups. In 1951 he was assassinated in Rawalpindi.

Liberal Democratic Party (LDP) (Japanese)

The largest and most influential party in post-war **Japan** that took control of the prime minister's office from 1955 to 1993. Japan became the second world economic power under the LDP. Influenced by prime ministers Kishi Nobusuke (1957–60), Ikeda Hayato (1960–4), and Sato Eisaku (1964–72), all of whom were former officials, LDP politics took a conformist approach of coordination and negotiation with business interests and bureaucrats. LDP politicians built strong give-and-take relationships with their personal support associations (*koenkai*) in their constituency. The prime minister was usually chosen from the largest faction of the party. LDP's national defence policy took shape under US–Japan security agreements, which originated in the US–Japan Security Treaty of 1951 signed by Prime Minister Yoshida Shigeru (1878–1967). Due to the monetary scandals that damaged the LDP's reputation, the party lost the election in 1993 and formed a coalition with its rivalling Social Democratic Party. It returned to power in 1996.

Liberal Republican Party (USA)

Break-away faction from the **Republican Party** (1870–2) that opposed the corruption of **Ulysses Grant**'s administration, demanded civil service reform and considered that **Reconstruction** had achieved its goals and that ex-**Confederates** should be allowed 'amnesty'. Its support for lower **protective** tariffs also helped win its candidate **Horace Greeley** the calculating support of a weak **Democratic Party**, despite the Liberal Republicans' contingent of former **abolitionists**. Grant won re-election easily but the mainstream party absorbed much of the Liberal reform agenda.

liberalism

Liberalism is the view that government is justified primarily to protect the freedom and property of individuals. Liberalism bases this belief on a commitment to the right of individuals to conduct their lives as they wish, free from interference by others. Liberalism is historically and intellectual diverse, and conflicting doctrines claim the title 'liberal'. However, common roots can be found in the early modern concern with the legitimacy of government in the light of increased political and religious pluralism. As traditional sources of political and moral authority dissolved under pressure from economic and religious transformation, writers such as Thomas Hobbes (1588–1679) and John Locke (1632–1704) sought to justify government on the basis of the rights, interests and reason of individuals. Hobbes' social contract theory expressed the view that legitimate political power was constituted by the consent of citizens to an undivided sovereign power. Their consent was derived from their interest in the protection government provided to their person and property. Locke's argument for legitimate government was also presented in terms of a social contract, but on his view, the role of political authority was to guarantee the natural rights of persons to property, freedom of speech, thought and religious observance. Thus at the origins of liberalism is a commitment to the moral importance of the rationality and interests of individuals.

The distinctive liberal turn was to define the legitimacy of government in terms of the reason and interests of individuals, and to charge political authority with the duty of protecting these interests with liberal rights, laws and institutions. This political project developed within the English Whig parliamentary faction, with which Locke was associated. The Whig political ascendancy during the eighteenth century coincided with the development of liberal economic theory. **Adam Smith**'s *Wealth of Nations* (1776) expressed a liberal concern with freedom in economic relationships, and argued that free economic interaction, on the basis of the interests and rationality of individuals would create prosperity and spontaneous coordination. The liberal concern with the moral, political and economic importance of individuals and their interests was taken up in the utilitarian thought of James Mill and **Jeremy Bentham**. Early utilitarianism condensed these liberal credos into a practical political programme of reform, generated by the utilitarian calculus of the greatest happiness of the greatest number. In the eyes of early utilitarians, political rights existed solely to protect the interests of individuals within a general utilitarian scheme, and were not derived from natural rights. In *On Liberty* (1859), James' son **John Stuart Mill** married utilitarianism and liberalism in his view that the state exists to protect individuals from harm caused by others. Mill developed many of the cardinal liberal doctrines in his political writings, advocating free speech as the best protection of truth and individuality, and supporting the extension of liberal political and economic freedoms to women. Later nineteenth-century liberal thinkers addressed the conditions for the exercise of political and economic freedoms, and argued that the state must not only protect individuals from harm by others, but also protect individuals from the harm of poverty, squalor and disease. Personal freedom requires minimum conditions of education, health and income, and New Liberal thinkers such as T. H. Green (1836–82) and L. T. Hobhouse (1864–1929) influenced the great welfare reforms of Lloyd George and William Beveridge (1879–1963).

The conditions for the development of liberalism varied widely. Whilst the French Revolution proclaimed the liberal values of freedom and equality, liberal constitutional reforms were only established in the **Third Republic** in 1871. The Italian **Risorgimento** was a liberal nationalist movement motivated by the goal of establishing a liberal republic within a united **Italy**. Post-colonial America embraced liberal political ideals. Key liberal freedoms, such as freedom of speech, association and worship, were embedded into the founding constitution. Liberal freedoms were also a motivating feature of **Simón Bolívar**'s revolutionary wars in Latin America.

In the twentieth century liberal political regimes have faced threats from extreme political ideologies such as communism and fascism. However, since fascism was vanquished 1945, and communism collapsed in 1989, liberalism has achieved increased global significance. Nations such as **Germany**, **Japan**, **Spain**, **Poland** and **Hungary** have developed strong liberal democratic institutions following varieties of totalitarian rule. International organizations such as the **World Bank** and **International Monetary Fund** promote both liberal political and economic reform. Developing nations across the globe are required to entrench laws protecting private property and democratic freedoms in order to benefit from financial assistance.

As the global political and economic influence of liberalism continues to grow, so liberal political theory has flourished. Since the publication of John Rawls' (1921–) *A Theory of Justice* in 1971, the established liberal devotion to political and economic freedoms has been augmented with a commitment to equality. Rawls' liberal egalitarianism returns to the social contract arguments of Hobbes and Locke, and continues the tradition of grounding political legitimacy in the consent of individuals. However, Rawls argues that such consent would only follow from a just distribution of political and economic resources. Consequently, distributive justice is now central to one strand of liberalism. An alternative liberal tradition has prospered in the writings of Friedrick Hayek (1899–1992) and Karl Popper (1902–94), where concern for equality is blamed for reductions in liberal political freedoms. Such neoliberal thinkers have been influential on governments from the late twentieth century.

Historically, liberalism was a political and economic project for nations: political rights and economic freedoms were established and protected through the institutions of the state. Liberal thinkers, politicians and politically motivated citizens are increasingly concerned with freedom and equality on a global scale. The human rights movement projects traditional liberal entitlements and freedoms beyond national borders. International organizations such as the International Criminal Court reflect the increased importance of the **human rights** movement. Opponents of liberalism complain about the emphasis on the rights of individuals, and claim that membership of communities and traditions ground moral and political relations. Others attack the moral licence that flows from liberal freedoms. Whilst liberalism remains contested, its significance remains as a theory and practice of the rights of individuals against the coercive powers of the state, and harmful interference by others.

liberation movements
– *see* **decolonization**.

Liberation Theology
A Latin American Catholic, intellectual movement recognized by **Vatican II** (1962–5), which explored the relationship between Roman Catholic theology and political activism through justice, social change and solidarity with the poor. Small groups, Basic Christian Communities (BCC), studied the Bible to apply it to everyday life. BCCs supported the overthrow of the Somozas in **Nicaragua** and challenged the state–church power structure in **Brazil** and **Chile**. Liberation theologians such as Gustavo Gutiérrez (1928–) of Peru, Leonardo Boff (1938–) of **Brazil** and Jon Sobrino (1938–), a Spanish Jesuit, supported roles for women in the Catholic Church and Asian/African approaches to economic development. In the 1980s Pope **John Paul II** attacked the movement by associating it with communism.

Liberia
A country in west Africa bordered by **Sierra Leone**, **Guinea** and **Ivory Coast**; composed of a coastline of mangrove forests and a less populous interior of forests and dry grasslands, the region was originally settled by a variety of groups moving westward. In 1820 the **American Colonization Society** sent freed blacks from the **United States** to establish a new settlement on the west African coast, founding the Republic of Liberia in 1847. From 1989 to 1996, after a *coup d'état* that brought **Charles Taylor** to power, Liberia underwent one of Africa's most bloody civil wars. In 2005 it elected Africa's first female president, Ellen Johnson Sirleaf (1938–). She instituted a truth and reconciliation commission and attempted to tackle corruption.

Liberty Bell (USA)
The Liberty Bell was cast in 1751 for use in calling legislators to session at the Pennsylvania State House (now Independence Hall) in Philadelphia. Inscribed with a quotation from Leviticus,

'Proclaim liberty throughout all the land unto all the inhabitants thereof', the bell began to crack in the 1830s. Its now distinctive crack was widened as part of a repair job. Though no longer in use, it has been used as a political symbol by abolitionists, womens' suffrage activists and civil rights movements.

Liberty Party (USA)

Minor American **abolitionist** party that agitated to separate the federal government from slavery with abolition in Washington DC, non-extension into the territories, and an end to the inter-state slave trade. It even came to regard an unamended **American Constitution** as adequate to abolish the institution in the states. It nominated James G. Birney for president in 1840, then again in 1844, arguably spoiling a potential **Henry Clay** victory. The **Free Soil Party** absorbed most of the Liberty Party in 1848.

Libya

Republic in north **Africa**. Established by the Italian occupation of 1911 out of two former Ottoman provinces, Tripolitania and Cyrenaica. In the eighteenth century Tripolitania had extensive self-rule under the Qaramanli dynasty, but Istanbul reintroduced direct control in 1835–1911. In Cyrenaica, Bedouins inspired by the **Sanusiyya** movement put up strong resistance to the Italians and were finally crushed only in 1931. A decade later, defeat in **World War II** ended Italian rule, and Libya was established as a kingdom under Sanusi leader Idris I in 1951. Oil was found in great abundance in the 1960s, but the monarchy was too weak to manage the new situation and was swept aside by the Arab nationalist coup of Colonel **Gaddafi** in 1969. Under his rule, Libya was prosperous but volatile; oil wealth was distributed while the political system was strictly authoritarian.

Internationally, Libya's position became fraught. Clashes with United States Air Force jets led to the **United States** bombing Gaddafi's headquarters in 1987, killing a member of his family; in turn, his regime was implicated in the bringing down in 1988 of PanAm flight 103 over Lockerbie in Scotland, killing all on board, mainly Americans. His support for terrorist movements, including the **Palestine Liberation Organization** and the **Irish Republican Army**, led to first the United States and then the **United Nations** imposing sanctions and almost 'pariah' status on the country. It secured resumption of diplomatic relations in the aftermath of the US 'war on terror' and the toppling of **Saddam Hussein**'s regime in 2003 by renouncing

its former role. However, Libya's rapprochement with the West was overtaken by the upheaval of the **Arab Spring** in which Gadaffi's threat of violence towards reformers based on Benghazi led to their backing with armed force by **Britain**, **France** and the US. In the ensuing civil war the regime was toppled and Gaddafi killed in 2011, but factional fighting prevented the emergence of a stable government and left one of the most prosperous countries in north Africa devastated, though some oil exports have resumed. In addition, Libya became a major jumping off point for migrants from Africa, the **Middle East** and further afield who sought to enter **Europe** by crossing the Mediterranean.

Liebknecht, Karl (1871–1919)

Co-founder with **Rosa Luxemburg** of the Spartacus League, later the German **Communist** Party. The first deputy in the Reichstag to vote against war credits, in November 1918 he declared the 'socialist republic' in Berlin at the same time as the German Republic was being proclaimed from the Reichstag. Like Rosa Luxemburg, he was arrested and shot by counter-revolutionaries in Berlin, and like her, is an icon of the later **German Democratic Republic**.

Likud

Israeli political party created by Ariel Sharon in 1973 with the merger of the old Revisionist party Herut, the Free Center Party and the La-Am party (consisting of former members of the Rafi party who had broken away from **Mapai** and did not wish to return to its fold). Likud ideology was rooted in **Vladimir Jabotinsky**'s notion not to repartition **Israel** after new territories were acquired in the June 1967 War. It feared that repartition was what the opposition Labor Party intended to do, hence the need for a strong nationalist coalition. Likud gained in strength in elections immediately after the October 1973 **Yom Kippur War**, winning thirty-nine seats in that year's election.

Likud paid special attention to, and gained popularity from, underprivileged Israelis of North African origin. Morocco-born David Levy was the energetic Likud city councilman from Beit Shean who led in the refurbishing of that impoverished development town. With the support of such Oriental Jews who constituted a plurality of the Israeli population, **Menachem Begin** was able, in 1977, to win forty-two parliamentary seats, oust Labour for the first time in Israel's history, and form a Likud government. He won forty-eight seats in the 1981 election and formed a second Likud government. After Begin's retirement from politics in 1983 and the elections of July 1984, in which Likud won only forty-one seats, **Yitzhak Shamir** formed a third Likud government in a chimera-like rotating national unity coalition with the Labor Party. In 1988 Shamir and Likud regained sole control of the government. In 1992 many Russian immigrants, unhappy with the manner in which the Shamir government absorbed them, spearheaded an opposition to Likud which elected **Yitzhak Rabin** as prime minister. In 2001 Sharon's Likud party regained national power. In 2005 Sharon created the Kadima party because a referendum among Likud members voted against his plan to unilaterally disengage from **Gaza**. Sharon was incapacitated by a stroke shortly thereafter and replaced by Kadima vice prime minister Ehud Olmert; Likud leader Benjamin Netanyahu then successfully challenged both Kadima and the Labor Party. From 2012 Netanyahu has been the Likud prime minister of Israel.

After 1977 Likud attempted to liberalize the vast socialist Israeli economy it inherited from Mapai. El Al, the national airline, was partially privatized. The national bus system, traditionally dominated by the Dan and Egged cooperatives, opened up to private competition. Likud's major foreign policy achievements since 1977 were **Camp David One**, the 1979 Israeli–Egyptian Peace Treaty, the destruction of the Iraqi and Syrian nuclear reactors, opening negotiations with the Palestinians at the 1991 Madrid conference, and the opening of substantial diplomatic, economic and military ties with **China** and **India**. Likud championed settlements but was also the first party to dismantle settlements, first in Sinai and then in Gaza. A crucial foreign policy crisis was **Israel**'s 2006 war with Iranian-backed proxies in **Lebanon**.

Lin Biao (1907–1971)

Lin Biao was born in Hubei province, central **China**, and enrolled in the Whampoa Military Academy in Guangzhou. He joined **Mao Zedong**'s forces after the purge of Communists from the **Kuomintang**, and took part in the **Long March**. Lin led Communist forces to victory in Manchuria during the civil war, and participated in the Korean War. He was designated Mao's successor in 1969, but died when his plane apparently crashed while fleeing a failed coup.

Lincoln, Abraham (1809–1865)

America's sixteenth president was born in Kentucky. The Lincolns were farmers who followed the moving frontier to Indiana and then to Illinois where they settled in 1830. Abraham received little formal education but he was a voracious reader with a passion for self-improvement. In 1834 he was elected to the Illinois legislature; two years later he obtained his law licence. A confirmed Whig, his hero was **Henry Clay** whose political principles he sought to emulate. In 1847–9 Lincoln served a single term in the US Congress during which he opposed the war against **Mexico**. Returning to Illinois, he spent the next few years building up a successful law practice. In 1842 he married Mary Todd from a prosperous Kentucky family. She bore him four sons, two of whom died in childhood.

The **Kansas–Nebraska Act** of 1854, which repealed the restriction on slavery's expansion, rekindled Lincoln's political ambition and led him to join the new **Republican Party**. Four years later he achieved national prominence in public debates with Stephen A. Douglas in the campaign for the US Senate. Lincoln's growing reputation combined with a moderate but firm position on the slavery expansion issue helped secure the 1860 Republican presidential nomination and, in November, the White House itself, albeit with less than 40 per cent of the popular vote. Within weeks seven lower South states had seceded from the Union after what they regarded as an abolitionist takeover of the federal government.

Lincoln was no abolitionist but he always regarded slavery as wrong and was determined that it would be contained. He was equally adamant that the Union would not be fractured, characterizing secession as undemocratic and illegal. The Confederate firing on Fort Sumter on 12 April 1861 ended political argument. Over the next four years Lincoln oversaw an unprecedented mobilization of the North's resources in order to save a republican experiment he described as the 'last best hope of earth'. Radicals in his party insisted from the outset on a war to destroy slavery, but, mindful of the conditional support of border state unionists and loyal Democrats, Lincoln resisted their call. In July 1862 after the failed Richmond campaign, however, his frustration at the lack of military success and at border state intransigence over slavery persuaded him that emancipation was now necessary to subdue the South. On 22 September he proclaimed that slaves in rebel-held areas would be free after 1 January 1863. Emancipation expanded the war's political and moral purpose, extinguishing any residual prospect of foreign intervention, and testified to Lincoln's capacity to 'think anew and act anew' in his struggle to save the Union. In generals **Ulysses S. Grant** and **William T. Sherman**, he also found commanders willing and able to fight his kind of war. After the president's re-election in November 1864, Confederate resistance crumbled. On 14 April 1865, only days after **Lee's** surrender, Abraham Lincoln was shot by the actor John Wilkes Booth, while attending Ford's Theater in Washington; he died the next morning.

Linlithgow, 2nd Marquess of (1887–1952)

Victor Alexander John Hope, 2nd Marquess of Linlithgow, was Viceroy of India between 1936 and 1943 and had been the chairman of the Royal Commission of Agriculture in **India** in 1926. His viceroyalty oversaw the election, formation of provincial ministries by the Congress and their resignation in protest due to his unilateral decision declaring India to be a participant in **World War II**. He suppressed the **Quit India movement** in 1942.

Lisbon earthquake (1755)

A massive geological event on 1 November (All Saints' Day) 1755 which resulted in the disastrous destruction of the Portugese capital and which is also frequently cited as reinforcing a crisis of religious faith in Europe which spurred the nascent **Enlightenment**. Lisbon had frequently suffered earthquakes before, including a seriously destructive event in 1531 and a lesser one in 1750; but when the 1755 earthquake struck just off the coast, the resulting tidal waves and seismic shocks destroyed tens of thousands of homes, killing possibly as many as 100,000 people and causing fires that lasted six days. European secular philosophers cited the disaster as evidence of a godless universe, and modern seismology began in an attempt to understand the secular causes of the earthquake under the **Marquis de Pombal**.

List, Friedrich (1789–1846)

A founder of the German Historical School, List was born at Reutlingen, Württemberg. His best-known book, *The National System of Political Economy* (1841), was written against free-trade doctrines that permeated classical economics. He was an advocate of the *Zollverein*, a commercial association of German states. He supported policies of protection for young industries and developing economies.

Lithuania

– *see* **Baltic states**.

Little Bighorn, Battle of (USA)

Battle of the **Native American** plains wars famous for **George Custer's** 'last stand' (25 June 1876).

Sioux and the northern Cheyenne had recently risen under **Sitting Bull** and **Crazy Horse** when the **United States** government ordered tribes to reservations. Custer opted for an unwise three-pronged attack; his outnumbered Seventh Cavalry unit was isolated and annihilated. News of the battle marred the centennial of the **American Declaration of Independence**, but a strong military response made it the fleeting zenith of Native American resistance.

Little Red Book

The Little Red Book is a collection of quotations of **Mao Zedong**. It contains thirty-three chapters with 427 quotations, and includes sections on class struggle, self-reliance, women and imperialism. It was originally compiled by **Lin Biao**, who wanted poorly educated soldiers to have access to Maoist thought. However, during the Cultural Revolution it was ubiquitous across **China** and carried by **Red Guards**. Now it is widely available across China as part of the commercialization of Maoist memorabilia.

Liu Shaoqi (1898–1969)

Born in Hunan and educated in Changsha along with **Mao Zedong**, Liu Shaoqi joined the **Chinese Communist Party** in Moscow. After his return to **China** in 1922 he spent time in Shanghai organizing workers, but fled north with Mao in 1934. He was a leader of the Communist Party in the countryside, and was eventually elected as state chairman in 1959. However, his moderate economic policies meant he was criticized in the **Cultural Revolution**, and he died in jail.

Livingstone, David (1813–1873)

Scottish missionary and explorer. Ordained in 1840, Livingstone went first to **South Africa** in 1841, subsequently exploring the Kalahari Desert in 1849 and 1851 and the territory from the Zambezi to the Indian Ocean in 1852–6, reaching and naming the Victoria Falls in 1855. In 1858–63 he explored central and east Africa on the British government's behalf, while continuing his missionary activity, and led an unsuccessful expedition to trace the source of the Nile.

Lloyd George, David (1863–1945)

British statesman and prime minister. Elected as a Liberal MP in 1890, he opposed the 1899–1902 South African War. Chancellor of the exchequer (1908–15) in the reforming Liberal government, he became prime minister of the **World War I** coalition government in 1916, continuing in coalition with the

Conservatives from 1918 to 1922. Influential in the 1919 **Versailles Treaty**, he lost power when the Conservatives withdrew following the Chanak crisis. Discredited by accusations of selling honours, Lloyd George led the declining Liberal Party in 1926–31, and was created Earl Lloyd-George of Dwyfor in 1945.

Lobengula (1845–1894)

Ruler of the Ndebele kingdom in modern-day **Zimbabwe** who came to the throne in 1869, in spite of resistance from supporters of other candidates. Lobengula made mining concessions to visitors from **South Africa** as early as 1870, but the 1889 concession allowed many settlers to come, leading to the Matabele War of 1893 during which Lobengula died and his country passed into the hands of the **British South Africa Company**.

Locke, John (1632–1704)

An English philosopher who argued that knowledge was created through experience and reasoning, and grounded in empirical observation. Locke's political works advocated a natural right to life, liberty, property and freedom of conscience. **Enlightenment** thinkers built upon his ideas to advocate contractual forms of government. Locke's ideas informed both the Atlantic Revolutions and the establishment of **liberalism** in the late eighteenth and early nineteenth centuries.

Lockerbie bombing

The bomb explosion on Pan Am flight 103 from Frankfurt to New York over Lockerbie, Scotland, on 21 December 1988, which killed all 259 people on board and 11 people on the ground. Abdul Baset Ali al-Megrahi, a former head of security for Libyan Arab Airlines, was indicted by the British and US authorities, 1991, following an alleged identification by a Maltese shop-owner, and was sentenced to twenty-seven years' imprisonment by a special Scottish court in the **Netherlands** in 2000. In 2007 the Scottish Criminal Cases Review Commission referred his case back to the Court of Appeal as a result of possibly unreliable evidence, saying that miscarriages of justice might have occurred. Al-Megrahi, who always protested his innocence and was by then suffering from terminal cancer, was controversially released by the Scottish Executive on allegedly compassionate grounds, August 2009. He returned to a hero's welcome in Libya, dying there on 20 May 2012. The full truth may never be known.

logging

– *see* **deforestation; environmentalism**.

Logwood

'Logwood' referred to a variety of dye-producing trees, but especially *Haematoxylon campechianum*, from whose wood a valuable black dye was generated. This wood was abundant on the Yucatan peninsula and could be found elsewhere in the West Indies. During the seventeenth century logwood cutters from **Jamaica** were particularly active on the eastern coast of the Yucatan, despite restrictions by the Spanish government. Their activities eventually led to a new British colony, British Honduras, now known as **Belize**, a sovereign nation within the British Commonwealth.

Lohia, Ram Manohar (1910–1967)

A member of the Congress Socialist Party, a subgroup within the **Indian National Congress**, he was jailed several times during **World War II** for his participation in the **Quit India movement** and public criticism of British war efforts. A strong opponent of Partition, he left the Congress in 1948 and joined the Praja Socialist Party in 1952. He advocated for Hindi as the medium of instruction, more effective birth control measures, abolition of the dowry system and the introduction of inter-caste marriages and dining.

Lomé Convention

An agreement on trade, investment and aid between the then European Community (later the **European Union**) and African, Caribbean and Pacific countries – predominantly the former colonies of **Britain**, **France** the **Netherlands** and **Belgium** – signed in Lomé, Togo, in February 1975 and coming into force in April 1976. The convention was subsequently renewed in January 1981, March 1985 and December 1989. The Cotonou Agreement, signed in Benin, succeeded it in June 2000.

Lon Nol, General (1913–1985)

Cambodian prime minister, 1966–7 and 1969–70. Lon Nol became head of state when the National Assembly voted unanimously to depose King **Sihanouk** in March 1970. His regime adopted a pro-western/anti-communist standpoint against Sihanouk's pro-Chinese/**Khmer Rouge** stance. Shortly before Khmer Rouge forces took control of Phnom Penh in the civil war, Lon Nol himself was exiled to **Hawaii** in April 1975. He later relocated to California where he remained until his death.

London, Treaty of (1839)

An international treaty signed by **Britain**, **France**, **Austria**, **Prussia**, **Russia** and the **Netherlands** that recognized **Belgium**'s independence from the Netherlands and also guaranteed its neutrality. The implications of the agreement would become significant in 1914 when **Germany** invaded Belgium. Britain subsequently entered the war on the pretense of protecting Belgium's neutrality as stipulated in the treaty, leading German Chancellor Theobald von Bethmann-Hollweg to remark that Britain and Germany would be going to war over a mere 'scrap of paper'.

London, Treaty of (1840)

The Convention for the Pacification of the Levant, signed on 15 July 1840 by **Austria**, **Britain**, **Prussia**, **Russia** and the **Ottoman Empire**. The treaty sought to end conflict between the Ottoman Empire and **Egypt** and secure the empire's integrity following a rebellion by Egyptian Pasha (governor) **Mehmet Ali**, in which he had occupied **Syria** and was threatening **Turkey**. The treaty proposed that the Ottoman Sultan Abdul Mejid I should name Mehmet hereditary Pasha of Egypt and lifetime governor of Syria. Mehmet rejected the offer but was forced into acceptance by European action. A second treaty signed in London on 13 July 1841 confirmed Mehmet as hereditary Egyptian Pasha under Ottoman sovereignty and restored Syria to the empire. The signatories, now including **France**, further agreed to bar foreign warships entry to the **Dardanelles** and the **Bosphorus** while the Ottoman Empire was at peace.

Long March

This was a year-long 6,000-mile trek to northwestern **China** by a large portion of the Communist People's Liberation Army to escape Nationalist forces. By 1934, attacks on Communist forces in Jiangxi forced them to flee west to Guizhou. The army then moved westwards through Sichuan, Gansu province, and the Long March ended in Yenan, Shaanxi province, near the Great Wall, where a base area was established. Of the 100,000 men who had started, only 7,000 survived.

Long Telegram

A key event in the **Cold War**, the Long Telegram written in Moscow by US diplomat George Kennan in February 1946 characterized the **Soviet Union**'s foreign policy as incorrigibly aggressive. Along with factors such as **Winston Churchill**'s 'iron curtain' speech and the crisis that spring over Soviet

influence in **Iran**, Kennan's Long Telegram convinced President **Harry Truman** that confrontation rather than cooperation with **Russia** was essential. This shift in US foreign policy was publicly revealed in March 1947 in the president's **Truman Doctrine** speech.

Lopez Portillo (y Pacheco), José (1920–2004)

Born in Mexico City, he served as president, 1976–82. He was a career bureaucrat whose administration suffered from a collapsing economy, especially declining oil prices, that resulted in a staggering foreign debt of 80 billion dollars. As his term ended, he nationalized the banking industry and devalued the national currency, the peso. He was accused of advising friends, before these actions, to move their money to the US, but was also responsible for guaranteeing an opposition bloc of seats in the Chamber of Deputies.

Lord's Resistance Army

Fundamentalist Christian movement formed in the 1990s, based in the **Congo** and active in northern **Uganda** under the leadership of Joseph Kony (1961–). The army waged a campaign of terror in Uganda, abducting children to train as fighters, with the aim of replacing Ugandan President Yoweri Museveni by a theocratic government committed to enforcing the Ten Commandments. The International Criminal Court issued arrest warrants for Kony and leading members in 2005.

Louis Philippe, King (1773–1850)

'King of the French', 1830–48, following the overthrow of **Charles X**. From a junior branch of the Bourbon dynasty, his 'middle-class' July monarchy sought a compromise with the Revolution, but his legitimacy was always contested. It could not survive the combination of the great European recession of 1846–8, the perception that the nation had been humiliated by the monarchy's common-sense policies, widespread corruption and lack of popular charisma. He died in exile in England.

Louis XV, King (1710–1774)

King of **France**, 1715–74. He failed to give firm direction to French policy, allowing his mistresses to exercise political influence. He also caused international confusion with his private system of secret diplomacy, and reduced the standing of the monarchy. He sacrificed French influence in central Europe and then in **India** and North America by involvement in the Wars of the Polish

Succession, 1733–8, and of the Austrian Succession, 1739–41, and the **Seven Years War**, 1756–63, against **Prussia** and **Britain**.

Louis XVI, King (1754–1793)

King of **France**, 1774–92. Well meaning, but lacking in political insight and strength of character, he failed to support the efforts of reforming ministers to reorganize France's finances, and by restoring the power of the judicial *parlements*, which supported aristocratic interests, 1774, he lost the opportunity to ally himself with the reforming middle classes. He successfully supported the **American War of Independence**, 1777, but at the cost of a national debt of one milliard livres. While recognizing that the outbreak of the Revolution, 1789, was the consequence of aristocratic intransigence, he continued to defend privilege. Unable to halt the outbreak of the **French Revolution** culminating in the capture of the Bastille, 14 July 1789, he was held in the Tuileries palace from October 1789, but fled with the queen towards the eastern frontier in June 1791. He was arrested at Varennes and returned to Paris a prisoner. A republic was declared on 21 September 1792. Following discovery of compromising royal correspondence with Austria, he was tried for treason and sentenced to death by the guillotine.

Louis XVIII, King (1755–1824)

King of **France**, 1815–24. Grandson of **Louis XVI**. He succeeded to the restored monarchy following the **Congress of Vienna**, and accepted the charter of constitutional rights as a matter of necessity in the France created by the Revolution. Personally, an eighteenth-century freethinker and a moderate, nonetheless he was unable to control the revengeful émigrés by whom he was surrounded. His desired policy of national reconciliation was undermined by their 'White Terror' of persecution and reaction, which enjoyed widespread clerical support.

Louisiana Purchase

The transaction agreed on 12 April 1803 under the terms of which **France** agreed to sell the Louisiana Territory to the **United States** for 80 million francs (approximately 16 million dollars). The territory in question included New Orleans and all French territory west of the Mississippi River, approximately 1,335,755 square kilometres. The United States sought to purchase New Orleans after France had acquired Louisiana from **Spain** in 1800. An economic and diplomatic crisis ensued when the Spanish (who had yet to vacate New

Orleans) closed the Mississippi to American trade in October 1802. Congress, at President **Jefferson**'s behest, appropriated 2 million dollars and authorized the American ambassador in Paris, Robert Livingston, to negotiate for the purchase of New Orleans. By the spring of 1803, with war in **Europe** looming, **Napoleon** authorized the sale not only of New Orleans but of all Louisiana. In the autumn of 1803 the Senate overwhelmingly ratified the Louisiana treaty.

Lourdes

A village in south-west France where in 1858 a young girl, Bernadette Soubirous, was believed to have received eighteen apparitions of the Virgin Mary, resulting in the emergence of healing waters in a grotto which subsequently became a major shrine and site of pilgrimage for Roman Catholics. The apparitions at Lourdes, which were associated by Bernadette with the doctrine of the Immaculate Conception (proclaimed in 1854 and purportedly spoken by the vision), were recognized by the papacy, which was closely associated with Marianism in the modern period. Bernadette was proclaimed a Saint of the Catholic Church in 1933, following on her death in 1879 at the age of 35 after a short lifetime as a nun.

Loyalists

Americans who sought to uphold British rule during the **American War of Independence**, Loyalists were a disparate group drawn from those segments of the population – particularly ethnic, racial, cultural and religious minorities – who felt threatened at the prospect of a rebel victory. During the war approximately 19,000 Americans enlisted in the British Army, serving in forty-two Loyalist units. Thousands more joined Loyalist **militias** during British campaigns such as the invasion of the southern colonies after 1780. Among the irregular Loyalists who took up arms in support of the crown were thousands of **Native Americans**. The largest single group of Loyalists, however, were African slaves in the southern colonies who fled to the British lines and sought to enlist in the royal forces. At the conclusion of the war the British transported approximately 100,000 Loyalists out of the **United States** (mainly to **Canada**). Among these, approximately 20,000 were **African Americans**.

Lu Xun (1881–1936)

Considered one of China's greatest twentieth-century writers. Born in Shandong, he studied medicine in Tokyo but changed to literature in 1906. In 1909 he returned to China and worked in the ministry of education. In 1918 he published the *Diary of a Madman*, which was the first ever story in the Chinese vernacular, and this made him famous. He continued publishing on a wide variety of topics until his death.

Luddites

A name given to a disparate movement of British skilled workers who attacked textile machinery between 1811 and 1817 in the hope of defending their jobs and raising wages. Luddites – followers of the fictitious outlaw hero of Sherwood Forest, 'General Ludd' – varied from midnight gangs intent upon criminal damage to large crowds of rioters and were especially active in areas of the English Midlands and north, which suffered from high food prices, unemployment and the exploitation of labour. In response to their activity, Parliament enacted the death penalty for machine-breakers, and transportation to **Australia**. Troops and special constables were deployed ruthlessly in the service of mill owners and manufacturers.

Luftwaffe

The air branch of the armed forces of the German Republic, and then the Nazi **Third Reich**. An armed air force for **Germany** was prohibited under the terms of the **Versailles Treaty**, but after the arrival of the Nazis to power in 1933, the treaty was gradually abrogated and subverted until a German capacity to use paratroop gliders, bombers and interceptors was developed. This capacity was integrated into military practice with fearsome effect in training schools, and in the **Spanish Civil War**, until the emergence of the highly armed and formidable German air force of **World War II**. This air force was innovative, and began steps to develop rocket, cruise missile, jet and helicopter technology before running out of resources and being degraded by 1944–5. It was associated in particular with infantry support and long-range mass bombing of urban areas in **Britain**, known as 'the Blitz'. After the defeat and occupation of Germany, both the Federal and Democratic German republics developed an air capacity, which was reintegrated in 1990, and again saw action from the Yugoslav and Afghanistan wars onwards.

Lugard, Frederick John Dealty, 1st Baron Lugard of Abinger (1858–1945)

British colonial administrator. Born in **India** and educated in England, Lugard was commissioned from Sandhurst in 1878 and served in the Afghan, **Sudan** and **Burma** campaigns. He joined the British East Africa Company in 1889 and, as military administrator of **Uganda**, secured British annexation in 1894. Moving to the Royal Niger Company, he established the Royal West African Frontier Force to counter French regional ambitions and local resistance to British rule. He served as high commissioner of Northern Nigeria in 1900–6, and as governor of **Hong Kong**, 1907–12, establishing a university in 1911. As governor general of **Nigeria**, 1914–19, he merged the northern and southern protectorates. Retiring in 1919, his book *The Dual Mandate in British Tropical Africa* (1922) was an influential exposition of 'indirect rule'. He was active in the League of Nations Permanent Mandates Commission, 1922–36, and the International Committees on Slavery and Forced Labour.

Lula

– *see* **Silva, Luis**.

Lunda Empire

Probably formed in what is now the **Democratic Republic of Congo** in the early to middle seventeenth century, it expanded both east to found **Kazembe** and west into modern **Angola** in the eighteenth century. It was a major source of slaves for the Americas, and during the nineteenth century was infiltrated by merchants, especially **Cokwe** merchants who sided with rival claimants to the throne, tearing the empire apart and allowing the Congo Free State to absorb it.

Luthuli, Albert Muvumbi (1898–1967)

South African politician, born in Southern Rhodesia (modern-day **Zimbabwe**). A teacher, Methodist lay preacher and union activist, Luthuli joined the **African National Congress** (ANC) in 1944, serving as president general in 1952–60. From 1952 he was a leading proponent of passive resistance to **apartheid** and was subject to banning orders. In 1960 he was the first African to be awarded the Nobel Peace Prize. His autobiography, *Let My People Go*, was published in 1962.

Luxemberg, Rosa (1871–1919)

Born in Russian Poland and a founder of both the Polish Social Democratic Party and the Spartacus League, later the Polish and German Communist Parties respectively. Her emphasis on democracy and spontaneous revolutionary mass action conflicted with **Lenin**'s emphasis on party discipline and democratic centralism, and continues to inspire reformed **communism**, particularly in

Germany. Arrested and shot as 'bloody Rosa' by counter-revolutionaries in Berlin, she subsequently became an icon, with **Karl Liebknecht**, of the later **German Democratic Republic**.

Lyautey, Louis Hubert (1854–1934)

The architect of the French protectorate over **Morocco**. Trained as a soldier at the Saint-Cyr Military Academy, 1873, he served in **Algeria**, 1880, and in **Indochina**, 1894, where he absorbed the doctrine of conquest as a path to civilization. He conquered Madagascar for **France**, 1895–6, and served under the French governor general of Algeria from 1904, encroaching on Moroccan territory to secure the frontier. Appointed resident general of the newly declared protectorate of Morocco, 1912, he replaced the then sultan with his brother after defeating insurgent tribes, and proceeded to conquer and pacify the whole country. He remained in Morocco until his resignation in 1925, apart from serving as French minister of war, 1916–17. He was a member of the Académie Française, 1912, and a marshal of France, 1921. In Morocco he pursued a policy of winning over its natural leaders, the sultan and the great *caïds*, while respecting the country's Islamic faith and way of life. He built modern European towns alongside the ancient cities of Fez, Marrakesh and Rabat but also rejuvenated Morocco's traditional arts and crafts.

M

Macao

A special administrative region in south-eastern **China** consisting of the Macao peninsula and two nearby islands. It was discovered by Vasco da Gama in 1497 and colonized by the Portuguese in 1557. In 1849, **Portugal** declared it a free port. Macao remained a Portuguese overseas province until 1999, when it reverted to Chinese sovereignty. It is connected to the Chinese province of Guangzhou.

MacArthur, Douglas (1880–1964)

A highly distinguished, outspoken and controversial American military officer, General MacArthur commanded Allied forces in the south-western Pacific during **World War II**, accepted the Japanese surrender in 1945 and led the Allied occupation there until 1951. He successfully commanded UN forces for the first months of the **Korean War** until his views regarding **China**'s entry into the war, suggesting possible use of the atomic bomb, and criticism of President **Truman**'s civilian command could no longer be ignored; he was recalled in April 1951.

Macartney Mission (1792–4)

In 1792 King **George III** sent Lord Macartney (1737–1806) and a British delegation to Qianlong's court to open northern Chinese port cities to British trade and establish diplomatic relations with **China**. The mission failed due to miscommunication between the two countries as a result of misunderstandings of customs and ritualistic practices.

Macaulay, Thomas Babington (1800–1859)

Author, Whig politician and member of Governor General Lord William Bentinck's Supreme Council of **India** (1834–8). Macaulay introduced the principle of education in English in India. This principle spread English as the language of instruction and exchange for the colonized world. He framed the Indian Penal Code, which was used as a model throughout the **British Empire**. His brief tenure of four years in India thus had subsequent global legal and linguistic consequences.

McCarthy, Joseph Raymond (1908–1957)

– *see also* **Cold War**; **McCarthyism**.

Born in Grand Chute, Wisconsin, McCarthy left school at age 14 before returning age 20 to complete three grades in one year. In 1939 he became Wisconsin's youngest elected circuit court judge, before enlisting in the Marine Corps, where he was nicknamed 'Tailgunner Joe' despite a predominately desk-bound role. Elected as US Senator for Wisconsin in 1946, he served two consecutive terms. He used the prevailing political climate to launch a crusade of rabid domestic anti-communism on 9 February 1950 in Wheeling, West Virginia, which he then pursued via the Committee on Government Operation's Permanent Subcommittee on Investigations. His targets ranged from former **New Deal** administrators to high-ranking federal employees, before a final televised assault on suspected subversives in the US Army in spring 1954. This gained him international notoriety and spawned the term **McCarthyism**. Censured by the Senate for 'unbecoming' behaviour in December 1954, McCarthy sank into alcoholism and oblivion.

McCarthyism

McCarthyism is usually used in reference to the excesses of American anti-communism, though the term is sometimes applied to other abusive campaigns in the US and elsewhere. It was first coined by Herbert Block in a political cartoon published in the *Washington Post* on 29 March 1950, which showed an elephant – the symbol of the **Republican Party** – being led unwillingly to stand on a shaky column of tar-filled buckets. The cartoon satirized the way in which Republicans had used domestic anti-communism to make political inroads against their **Democratic Party** rivals from the 1946 mid-term elections onwards. Republican Senator Joseph R. McCarthy of Wisconsin's high-profile campaign of domestic anti-communism was then only seven weeks old, leading Block to think of writing 'McCarthy's techniques' upon the buckets, before settling upon the snappier 'McCarthyism'.

In its most specific formulation, McCarthyism refers to the particular brand of domestic anti-communism practised by McCarthy: bold, brash and often unsubstantiated accusations of communist subversion delivered with great theatre and scant regard for accuracy, a reliance on guilt by association and the prioritization of the investigation of alleged subversives over the civil liberties of those being investigated. McCarthyism was not the historical aberration that some early chroniclers claimed, for there are rich traditions of anti-radicalism, anti-subversion and anti-communism in American life that both preceded and outlived McCarthy. As such, the fact that McCarthyism has fallen into general use as a synonym for anti-communism is not useful. Both the political and historical traditions of the **United States** have created a nation in which outbursts of public hysteria are common, examples of which include those nativists of the 1920s who railed against new waves of immigrants to the east coast and extreme conservatives who set up self-styled 'patriotic organizations' to purge positive references to un-American ideologies from all areas of US society.

Historians have begun to agree that McCarthyism was a 'multi-stranded', 'protean' or 'amorphous' beast, but continue to debate the impetuses that lay behind it. Early explanations sought to depict McCarthyism as a 'bottom up' phenomenon driven by 'status anxieties' at the grass roots of United States society, but these were countered by later analyses attributing McCarthyism's excesses to the 'top down' machinations of political elites, institutions and organizations including Attorney General A. Mitchell Palmer, **Richard Nixon**, the House Un-American Activities Committee, the Senate Internal Security Subcommittee, the Federal Bureau of Investigation and the Bureau's long-serving director, **J. Edgar Hoover**. Most recently, a series of detailed case studies has revealed a more complicated picture by showing that episodes of McCarthyism outside the federal bubble of Washington DC have been reliant on 'top down' forces at times, but equally reliant on populist surges at others. After McCarthy's death in 1954, the conservative and patriotic networks that sustained his particular brand of McCarthyism helped to feed the political campaigns of George C. Wallace, **Nixon** and **Ronald Reagan**.

McClellan, George B. (1826–1885)

American Civil War commander and politician. McClellan created the Army of the Potomac in a brilliant feat of organization. His Peninsular campaign was launched in March 1862, and he approached Richmond but was driven back during the Seven Days of Battles. He took command in Maryland, but on 17 September wasted his chance to crush **Robert E. Lee** at **Antietam**; inactivity – 'the slows' – provoked his final relief in November 1862. The unsuccessful Democratic presidential candidate in 1864, McClellan served as governor of New Jersey, 1879–81.

Machel, Samora (1933–1986)

Mozambican military commander, socialist thinker and first president of independent **Mozambique**. As a member of the Front for the Liberation of Mozambique (**Frelimo**), Machel became interested in Marxist ideology and **pan-Africanism**. In 1975 the fall of the government in **Portugal** led to the independence of Mozambique. Machel was president until his death in 1986. He instituted land reforms, nationalized key industries and invited rebel forces from **Rhodesia** and **South Africa** to train in Mozambique.

McKinley, William (1843–1901)

Twenty-fifth president of the **United States**, 1897–1901. Born in Niles, Ohio, McKinley joined a local regiment of volunteers at the beginning of the **American Civil War**. After a series of minor political appointments, he was elected in 1876 to Congress, where he served nearly continuously until 1891 and was particularly identified with the protective **tariff** legislation of 1890 that bears his name. During the early 1890s he served two terms as governor of Ohio. He won the Republican nomination for the presidency in 1896, basing his election campaign on a defence of the protective tariff and the gold standard against the agrarian policies of **William Jennings Bryan**. As president, he largely continued the Republican policies of the previous generation. The major exception was his association with the **Spanish–American War** of 1898 and subsequent annexation of the **Philippines** and **Puerto Rico**. He comfortably won re-election in 1900 but served only a few months of his second term. He was shot and fatally wounded by the bullet of an assassin while visiting the Pan-American Exposition in Buffalo, Ohio.

McNamara, Robert (1916–2009)

Best known for his tenure as US secretary of defence,1961–8, when he presided over the nation's escalating military commitment to South Vietnam. By 1967, McNamara was having second thoughts about the war, concerned that success was not achievable in a reasonable timeframe or at an acceptable moral cost. He resigned the following year, becoming president of the **World Bank**, where he dramatically increased funding for international development. He retired in 1981.

mad cow disease
– *see* **BSE**.

Madagascar
– *see* **Merina kingdom**.

Madero, Francisco I (1873–1913)
Born in Parras, Coahuila, Madero initiated the **Mexican Revolution** in 1910 after an aborted presidential campaign. He demanded democracy, no re-election of the president and major officials, and social reforms. His revolution overthrew the 35-year Porfirian regime at the Battle of Ciudad Juárez in April 1911. Elected president, he faced opposition, notably from Generals Félix Díaz and **Victoriano Huerta**, who contrived his overthrow in the Ten Tragic Days, and his murder in February 1913.

Madison, James (1751–1836)
Later renowned as 'father of the constitution' and fourth president of the **United States**, this legal colleague of **Thomas Jefferson** served in the Virginia legislature and Confederation Congress during the American Revolution. Elected to the constitutional convention of 1787, he drafted much of the **United States Constitution**, devising the federal system and establishing systems of indirect election for key institutions. He then worked for its ratification, writing (with **Alexander Hamilton** and John Jay) *The Federalist Papers*, the most important work of political philosophy produced in the United States. Elected to the House, he drafted the Bill of Rights, led opposition to Hamilton's financial programme and helped found the **Democratic Republican Party**. He became Jefferson's secretary of state (1801–9) and succeeded him as president (1809–17). After trying to protect neutral rights during the **Napoleonic Wars** through commercial pressure, he led the country into near disastrous war against **Britain** in 1812. Ineffective as a war leader, after 1815 Madison adopted more nationalist policies to overcome the internal weaknesses that had hampered the war effort.

Mafia
A name often used for a loose alliance of criminal gangs to suggest the coordination of racketeering, corruption and organized criminal activity. It derives from the existence of the Sicilian Mafia, an Italian network whose name became a byword for the activities of all regional crime groups from the mid nineteenth century. In the **United States**, *mafia* as a term came to be employed in the 1950s and 1960s by federal, state and city campaigners against crime, and suggested a syndicated entity against whom laws, executive agencies and suppressive action could be targeted. The word, unused by members, generally refers to secretive organizations run by families or close-knit groups who participate in a number of illegal and legal-front businesses with ruthless contempt for the sake of vicious ends. Members are subject to rules of non-disclosure, gang initiation and respect for established hierarchies within the group, but are typified by aggressive and often murderous actions outside it. Whilst undoubtedly a potent presence in public life at various times, the exact reach of various alleged Mafiosi in a number of states has never been adequately determined.

Maginot Line
A system of defensive fortifications, fortresses, hidden turrets and underground bases developed under the control of André Maginot (1877–1932), French minister of war in the socialist Poincaré government between 1928 and 1931. The line was designed to repel any attack and covered the French border with **Germany**, not with **Belgium**, and represented one of the largest civil engineering projects ever undertaken. It included huge hospitals, kitchens and train lines, and extended deep beneath French soil. In the German invasion of 1940, it was sidestepped and never frontally attacked, and in the allied invasion of 1944 it also proved of marginal importance. It was subsequently abandoned until sections were reopened as a museum. The construction and existence of the line was widely seen as contributing to the defensive-minded defeatism which led to **France**'s sudden collapse in 1940.

Mahan, Admiral Alfred Thayer (1840–1914)
American naval officer, geo-strategist and historian who stressed the importance of 'sea power'. His publications of the 1890s argued for the historical pre-eminence of navies in national supremacy and for the relationship between commercial and

military domination of the seas. Coming at a time of dramatic improvements in naval technology, his views influenced the Anglo-German **naval race** and the imperialists of the **Spanish–American War** era, though his direct involvement with them was limited. Seen as the father of American navalism.

Mahdi (Sudan) (1844–1885)

Muhammad Ahmad bin 'Abd Allah declared himself Mahdi, the messianic redeemer of **Islam**, in June 1882. Born in northern Sudan, he pursued a religious education. He gained prominence as a mystic and religious teacher in the Samaniyya, a Sufi order, before becoming leader of the order in 1880. Following his declaration as Mahdi, he declared **jihad** against the ruling Turco-Egyptian government of **Sudan** (the Turkiyya). Initially perceived by the government in Khartoum as a religious zealot, he continued to gain support from numerous tribes and sheikhs in northern and western Sudan. The Mahdi led his followers, known as *ansar*, in a military revolt against the Turkiyya, and by the end of 1885 his movement controlled most of Sudan – the Mahdi died unexpectedly of typhus in June the same year. Often characterized as the precursor to modern Sudanese nationalism, the Mahdi sought to restore the simplicity of Islam.

Mahdiyya (Sudan)

The term *Mahdiyya* refers to the uprising and rule of the **Mahdi**, or awaited messianic figure, in **Sudan** from 1881 to 1898. Muhammad Ahmad bin 'Abd Allah announced himself Mahdi in 1881 on Aba Island south of Khartoum, and called for his followers to rise up against the unjust Turco-Egyptian rule of Sudan. He fled to Kordofan with his *ansar*, or followers, calling it a *hijra* to draw on the Prophet's own *hijra* from Mecca to Medina. He continued launching attacks against the Egyptian forces and, after their 1883 occupation of **Egypt**, the British forces. The Mahdi's initial victories brought more *ansar* to the fold, and he gained support from Sudanese groups who were angry over colonial attempts to end the slave trade. In 1885 Mahdist forces surrounded Khartoum and crushed the Anglo-Egyptian forces of General **Gordon**.

The Mahdi died shortly after taking Khartoum, but his closest ally and confidante, 'Abdallahi al-Ta'ishi, took over and proclaimed himself Khalifa, the successor to the Mahdi. Although by no means a centralized state, the Mahdist government was headquartered in Omdurman on the west bank of the Nile, with 'Abdallahi holding full power. Omdurman grew

considerably and became a trading hub and spiritual centre for people from all over Sudan. The state's administration was staffed mainly by local veterans of the Turco-Egyptian regime. 'Abdallahi struggled to accommodate the wide-ranging interests of his followers, however, and had to put down challenges from the Mahdi's own kin. The most intense rivalries within the Mahdist-controlled territory were between cattle-grazing nomads of western Sudan ('Abdallahi's own background) and sedentary populations along the central Nile.

Under the Mahdist state slavery thrived. In 1896 British and Egyptian forces under **Kitchener** set out to halt the slave trade and re-establish control of Sudan, making gradual inroads with the help of a new supply railway to Wadi Halfa. The British had learned the lessons of the previous Sudanese campaign: this time a stronger, better provisioned colonial force overwhelmed the fragile Mahdist state. 'Abdallahi had to flee after a resounding defeat at **Omdurman** (Karari) in 1898; he was tracked down and killed a year later, marking the end of the Mahdiyya.

The historical memory of the Mahdi still looms large in Sudanese society and culture. Mahdism, too, survived as a powerful and popular concept. Omdurman, the Mahdist capital, still serves as a site of pilgrimage for many Sudanese. In the wake of the Mahdiyya's defeat, other self-proclaimed mahdis led uprisings against the British, but all were easily put down. Several descendants of the Mahdi played important roles in the formation of the Sudanese state. The Mahdi's son, born after his death, led the proto-nationalist Umma Party, while his great-grandson served two terms as prime minister of postcolonial Sudan.

Mahfouz, Naguib (1911–2006)

The father of the Egyptian novel and the first writer in Arabic to win the Nobel Prize in literature, 1988. On awarding him the prize, the Swedish Academy of Literature wrote: 'Through works rich in nuance, now clear-sightedly realistic, now evocatively ambiguous – Mahfouz has formed an Arabian narrative art that applies to all mankind.' Although celebrated for his three novels of ancient Egypt – *Khufu's Wisdom* (*Abath al-Aqdar*) (1939), *Thebes at War* (*Kifah Tiba*) (1944) and *Rhadopis of Nubia* (*Radubis*) (1945) – his masterpiece is the Cairo trilogy comprising *Palace Walk* (*Bayn-al Qasrayn*) (1956), *Palace of Desire* (*Qasr al-Shawq*) (1957) and *Sugar Street* (*al-Sukkariyya*) (1957). This work traces the lives of three generations of an Egyptian family in the years spanning the two world wars and has thus led to comparisons with Charles Dickens and Victor Hugo. His 1959 novel *Children of Gebelawi* (*Awlad haratina*) was temporarily banned in **Egypt** for its controversial religious content.

Mahmud II (1785–1839)

Ottoman Sultan, 1808–39. He acceded to the throne in 1808 following a coup plotted by the influential Mustafa Bayrakdar who, before Selim's murder, had wanted to restore Mahmud's reformist uncle, **Selim III**, and was himself killed by the conservative janissaries (the body of infantry forming the sultan's guard, most of whom were Christian-born) the same year. Mahmud suffered a long series of military reverses both within the Turkish Empire and in conflicts with the other powers. The Russo-Turkish War, 1806–12, concluded with the cession of Bessarabia (now Moldova) to the **Russian Empire** under the Treaty of Bucharest, 1812. He struggled against the movements for Serbian and Greek independence from 1804 and 1821 respectively, summoning the help of the khedive of **Egypt, Muhammad 'Ali Pasha**, in the latter case, but had to face British, French and Russian support for the Greek cause. The destruction of the Turkish-Egyptian fleet by the united navies of the three powers at the Battle of **Navarino** off southern Greece in 1827, presaged, despite Mahmud's declaration of **jihad**, defeat in the Russo-Turkish War of 1828–9. Serbian autonomy and Greek independence were both recognized by 1830.

The help sought from Muhammad 'Ali proved problematic. Mahmud had promised, 1830, to make him governor of **Syria** and of Tarsus in southern Turkey, but then reneged on his promise when Muhammad 'Ali claimed his due in 1831, as a reward for his assistance against the Greeks. Muhammad 'Ali responded by invading Syria and capturing Damascus and Aleppo before totally defeating the Ottoman-Turkish Army at Konya, Turkey, 1832, and advancing towards **Constantinople**. The frightened Mahmud sought help from the British, who, mindful of French interest in Egypt, refused, and then from the Russians. The result was the arrival of the Russian fleet in the Bosphorus and the conclusion of the **Treaty of Unkiar Skelessi**, 1833. Mahmud's final attempt at revenge, however, failed when his army was defeated by the Egyptians in Syria at the Battle of Nizip, 1839.

The quarter-century of defeats nevertheless brought some positive benefits to the **Ottoman Empire**. Administrative and military reforms were introduced in response, including the abolition and massacre of the archaic and conservative janissary corps in 1826. The military fiefs enjoyed by cavalrymen were abolished, 1831, and a new German-trained army created under the sultan's direct authority. A Turkish postal service was introduced in 1834, as well as a land survey and a census. Primary education became compulsory, as well as medical education and the practice of sending students to Europe. Not least, western dress was first adopted in a process culminating in **Kemal Atatürk**'s revolution of a century later.

Maji Maji revolt

A rising in 1905–7 in German East Africa (now **Tanzania**) involving twenty different ethnic groups against enforced cultivation of cotton and high taxes, inspired by Kinjiktile Nwagle, who told his supporters that Maji Maji ('magic water') would ward off German bullets. Over 25,000 rebels were killed in the fighting and a further 50,000 died in the German scorched-earth response. The revolt, though defeated, forced the German colonial administration to moderate the brutality of its regime.

Makarios III, Archbishop (1913–1977)

Archbishop Makarios III was a key figure of the Cypriot independence struggle against Britain and was the first president of the Republic of **Cyprus**. Born Michael Christodouros Mouskos, he took the name Makarios at age 13, when he became a monk. After study in Athens, Makarios returned to Cyprus, where he became a priest. In 1950 he was selected as the new archbishop of Cyprus. Over the course of the 1950s, Makarios' position made him a key figure in Cypriot politics and he worked to end British colonial control of Cyprus and towards union (*enosis*) with **Greece**. Exiled by the British, 1956–9, Makarios nonetheless remained a key figure in the Cypriot independence movement and helped to negotiate Britain's final withdrawal from the island. Returning to Cyprus, he was soon elected the country's first president. As president, however, he proved incapable of restraining intercommunal conflict between Turkish and Greek Cypriots. Although Makarios was able to win re-election in 1968 and 1973, his relations with the military regime that had taken control of Greece in 1967 quickly soured. In 1974 he demanded a withdrawal of Greek officers from the island. In July 1975 a Greek-sponsored *coup d'état* removed him from office and he fled to **Great Britain**. A Turkish invasion later that month precipitated the collapse of the military regime in

Greece as well as its client government in Cyprus. Makarios returned to Cyprus as president, but the island was now partitioned, with **Turkey** occupying the north.

Makeba, Miriam (1932–2008)

South African singer and anti-**apartheid** activist, nicknamed 'Mama Africa'. Her cameo in the 1959 film *Come Back Africa* set in Sophiatown on the eve of its destruction launched her to international recognition. After her South African passport was cancelled, in 1960, she remained in exile, recording several albums, performing and testifying against the **apartheid** regime before the **United Nations**. **Nelson Mandela** persuaded Makeba to return to South Africa in 1990.

malaria

Malaria (from medieval Italian *mala aria* meaning 'bad air') is a serious, recurrent infection characterized by periodic attacks of chills, fever, anaemia and, in severe cases, leading to coma or fatal complications. The infectious disease is widespread in tropical regions and is transmitted primarily by the Anopheles mosquito. Even in the twenty-first century malaria infects several hundred million people and kills at least a million every year. Most deaths are concentrated in sub-Saharan Africa.

Malawi

This former British colony in central Africa was a slave trading centre in the eighteenth and nineteenth centuries. British influence began in the 1870s and in 1893 a Central African Protectorate was established. The country was named Nyasaland in 1907. Hastings Banda (1898–1997) formed the Malawi Congress Party in 1959, becoming prime minister on independence in 1964. Two years later Malawi became a republic, with Hastings Banda as president. His regime became notorious for brutality and corruption. Unlike most African states, Malawi had diplomatic relations with apartheid **South Africa**. As the economy weakened in the 1990s, western aid donors pressed Banda to begin political liberalization. In 1994 the United Democratic Front leader Bakili Muluzi (1943–) became Malawi's first democratically elected president. Muluzi's protégé Bingu wa Mutharika (1935–2012) became president in 2004, to be succeeded on his death by Joyce Banda (1950–). Mutharika's brother Peter (1940–) was elected in 2014. The population is predominantly Christian, with a Muslim minority. Agriculture dominates economic activity, with tobacco a major export.

Malaya

–see **Malaysia**.

Malayan Emergency

The armed insurrection against British colonial rule in Malaya, now **Malaysia**, after **World War II**. Initiated by cooperation between the Malayan People's Anti-Japanese Army (MPAJA), comprising some 7,000 ethnic Chinese guerrillas who had fled into the forests to escape persecution by the Japanese after the 1942 invasion and who had been seen by the British as useful wartime allies, and Chinese trade unionists affiliated to the Communist Party. The scale of the insurrection led the British to proclaim a state of emergency in 1948, which was not formally ended until 1960. The British mounted a complex counter-insurgency campaign including the forcible resettlement of more than 1 million rural Chinese in about 500 'new villages' to prevent their assisting the guerrillas. The insurgents were defeated, however, only when the British under General Templar combined military action with a 'hearts and minds' campaign to win the confidence of villagers under Operation Service, 1952–4. A rare post-war example of the defeat of an anti-colonial movement.

Malaysia

The federation which succeeded the earlier Federation of Malaya, Sabah (formerly North Borneo), Sarawak and **Singapore** established in 1963, from which Singapore seceded, 1965. The strategic Malayan port of Malacca was captured by the Portuguese in the sixteenth century and the Dutch in the seventeenth. The British established an outpost on Penang, 1786, and a trading station in Singapore, the bridgehead of its future control of Malaya in 1819. Under British rule, many Chinese and Indians immigrated to work the mines and plantations, nearly making the Malays a minority in the country. Under Japanese occupation, 1942–5, when ethnically Chinese guerrillas, many communist, fought against the Japanese and then the returning British, provoking the **Malayan Emergency**, 1948–60.

An unpopular Malayan Union proposed by the British, recognizing the citizenship rights of Chinese and Indians but curtailing the privileges of the sultans, was dropped in favour of a Federation of Malaya in 1948, preserving special rights for Malays and their sultans, one of whom became head of state by rotation. Malaya became independent in 1957, and Malaysia in 1963. Immediately challenged by **Indonesian 'Confrontation'** and the secession of Singapore. Economic development in recent decades has put Malaysia amongst the so-called 'Asian tigers'. The United Malays National Organization (UMNO) has ruled the country since independence.

Malcolm X (1924–1964)

Born Malcolm Little, Malcolm X was the chief public spokesman for the Nation of Islam urging **African Americans** to separate themselves from white people and attacking integration as a goal and non-violence as a method. His indictment of whites was so spellbinding that he became a hugely sought-after public speaker by 1963. Visiting Mecca, converting to orthodox Islam and negotiating with African and Middle Eastern leaders suggest Malcolm was changing by 1964, but he was shot dead in Harlem in February 1965. His posthumously published *Autobiography* remains hugely popular and has ensured that he remains a powerful icon of black resistance.

Maldives

A nation made up of a chain of 1,200 coral and sandbank islands in the Indian Ocean. Commercial and intellectual links with **Sri Lanka** began in the fifth century BC and produced a Buddhist society until the islands' conversion to **Islam** in the twelfth century. The Maldivian sultanate became formally subordinate to Portuguese, Dutch and British colonial governors of Sri Lanka. Colonial rule ended in 1965, the sultanate was abolished in 1968, and a constitution aimed at guaranteeing multiparty democracy implemented in 2008.

Mali

A landlocked former French colony in West Africa, descendant of the once dominant Empire of Mali. **France** completed its conquest of what it named Soudan in 1898. In 1959 Soudan briefly united with neighbouring **Senegal**, but became independent as Mali in 1960. The country's first president, Modibo Keïta (1915–77), operated an authoritarian one-party state and was overthrown in 1968 by Moussa Traoré (1936–). Economically weak, Mali survived largely on foreign aid. Traoré was ousted in 1991 and the Transitional Committee for the Salvation of the People ruled pending elections. In 1992 Alpha Oumar Konaré (1946–) was elected president, and returned again in 1997 and 2002.

His economic liberalization won western approval and debt relief. Amadou Toumani Touré (1948–) became president in 2002 but was forced into exile in 2012 over mishandling of a Tuareg rising in the north. Mali's population is over 90 per cent Muslim, with a small Christian minority. Islamist groups allied to **al-Qaida** are active in the country. Farming and fishing are the major economic activities, with state revenue dependent on cotton and gold exports.

Malta

A strategically positioned Mediterranean island (along with Gozo) between North Africa and Sicily. **Britain** annexed Malta – formerly under Spanish and French control – in 1814 to operate as a pivotal naval base. Besieged and heavily bombed by **Germany** and **Italy** in **World War II**, the island was awarded the civilian gallantry medal, the George Cross, in 1942. Malta gained independence in 1964, retaining a British base until 1979, after which it continued as a **NATO** base. Malta joined the **European Union** in 2004.

Malthus, Thomas Robert (1766–1834)

English economist and early demographer whose most important work, *Essay on the Principles of Population*, argued, pessimistically, that population growth occurred in geometrical progression, whilst production growth tended to the arithmetical. Later on, he added evidence in order to validate his theory. Malthus also pointed out that populations would expand to reach subsistence limits and would be held there by famine, war and ill health. His work challenged the optimism of Godwin and Smith, by arguing that population growth would lead to the cultivation of less fertile lands to the point where agricultural output could not meet demand for food and raw materials. Thus, it would only be possible to avoid starvation if populations adopted moral conducts, such as late marriage, birth control and abstinence from sex.

Malvinas War

– *see* **Falkland Islands War**.

Mamluks

Egyptian ruling class until 1805. Originally slave soldiers, the name being derived from an Arabic word meaning 'slave', who had seized power in several Muslim states from the ninth century and established their own dynasties. Although the Mamluk sultanate over **Egypt** and **Syria** had been ended by the sixteenth-century Ottoman Turkish conquest, the mamluks remained intact as an influential class and successfully infiltrated and then dominated the Ottoman elite there. The mamluks themselves, however, divided into competing hereditary 'houses', such as the Qazdaglis, akin to those of medieval Italy. Nevertheless, the eighteenth-century Ottoman government had to recognize that the mamluks autonomously controlled the government, finances and army of Egypt subject to the payment of tribute. It was a mamluk state and army which resisted and then succumbed to **Napoleon** in 1798, but their power was finally destroyed in a massacre by the khedive (and virtually independent ruler) of Egypt, the ethnic Albanian **Muhammad 'Ali Pasha**, in 1811.

Manchukuo

– *see* **Manzhuguo**.

Manchuria

Manchuria, comprising the provinces of Jilin, Liaoning and Heilongjiang in north-east China, is home to the Manchus, an ethnic group that established the Qing dynasty in 1644. After 1900 Manchuria first came under Russian influence, and then after 1931 the Japanese gained complete control. During the Maoist period the area developed as a centre of heavy industry, although more recently commerce and finance have emerged, centred on the coastal city of Dalian.

mandates (League of Nations)

Commissions awarded by the **League of Nations** in 1919 to **Belgium**, **France** and **Great Britain**, and to **Australia** and **South Africa**, to administer the African and Oceanic territories of the former overseas **German Empire** and the Arab territories of the **Ottoman Empire**, following the defeat of **Germany** and **Turkey** in **World War I**. The mandates effectively brought the three European empires to their maximum geographical extent. In the distribution of Germany's African territories, Belgium was awarded **Burundi** and **Rwanda**; France, Togo and the greater part of **Cameroon**; and South Africa, South West Africa (now Namibia). Great Britain was awarded **Tanganyika** and the lesser part of Cameroon. The northern part of **New Guinea** was awarded to Australia.

The mandates awarded over the formerly Turkish Arab territories, which excluded the Arabian peninsula, were allocated by Britain and France between themselves with more regard to their own strategic interests than to internal coherence or historic ties. In accordance with a preliminary agreement between their negotiators, Mark Sykes and Georges Picot, (widely known as the **Sykes–Picot Agreement**), reached in January 1916, **Syria** went to France and **Mesopotamia** (later Iraq) to Great Britain, with the British having an outlet on the Mediterranean at Haifa. A pledge to satisfy **Italy** with a part of Asia Minor never bore fruit. **Palestine**, however, was taken away from Syria to become a British mandate in 1920 and the district of Mosul was similarly taken from Syria and transferred to British-mandated Mesopotamia. The British then created Transjordan in the 1920s by simply detaching the southern part of Palestine. However artificial, many of these changes remain on the modern map.

The mandates over the Arab world were something of a deception on two major counts. First, the British and the French had promoted Arab nationalism during the war as an ally against the Ottoman Turks only to deny it once the war was won. Their ally **Husayn**, Sharif of Mecca and head of Arabia's **Hashemite** dynasty which claimed descent from the Prophet, who had hoped to unify the whole Arab world under his rule, saw only his sons, **Faisal** (1885–1933) and **Abdullah** (1871–1951), become client rulers for the British, as king of Iraq and emir of Transjordan respectively. Second, and almost certainly with the greatest lasting impact, the mandate granted to Britain over Palestine included a provision that the immigration of Jews was to be permitted, although the rights of the Arabs were to be respected.

The mandates proved to be something of a thorn in the sides of British and French alike. The Hashemite dynasty imposed on **Iraq** by the British never won the allegiance of its people. The French found the numerous rebellious ethnic communities within Syria a permanent challenge to their authority and the **Syrian Revolt**, a rebellion by the **Druze**, a heretic Islamic group, was suppressed 1925–7. In Palestine, **Zionist**-inspired Jewish immigration made the country increasingly ungovernable. On the positive side, meaningful steps were made towards independence. Formal independence was granted by the British to Iraq, 1932, and to Transjordan, 1946. Formal independence was granted by France to Syria, 1943, and to **Lebanon**, which it had turned into a separate state in 1944. Palestinian independence, however, succumbed to the confusion surrounding the emergence of **Israel**. Independence was nevertheless highly conditional. Iraq's was circumscribed by a treaty which maintained Britain's right of access to the oil fields and guaranteed its military bases. It was only terminated with the military coup of

General Qassem (Kassem), 1958. Some would argue that the Anglo-American invasion of 2003 was an attempt to reassert those rights. Transjordanian independence was circumscribed by a parallel treaty. The French creation of a Lebanese state was inspired in part by a French hope of retaining influence there by promoting a special relationship with the Maronite Christian minority, and the French landed troops in Syria in 1945 to reassert their imperial status, not least against the British, even bombing Damascus in May. True independence only ensued with the withdrawal of British and French troops, 1946.

Mandela, Nelson Rolihlahla (1918–2013)

South African political activist and first president of **South Africa** elected by multiracial elections in 1994. Affectionately known as 'Madiba', the name of his father's Xhosa clan, Mandela was born in the Transkei region of South Africa. While attending Fort Hare University, he befriended lifelong ally **Oliver Tambo** and became involved in student politics. In 1944 he joined the **African National Congress** (ANC). Frustrated by the slow and moderate approach of older ANC leaders, Mandela, Tambo and Walter Sisulu formed the ANC Youth League in 1947 and the following year took over key positions on the executive council. With the victory of the **Afrikaner** National Party in 1948 and the installation of the **apartheid** government, the Youth League promoted a more radical and confrontational approach to activism enunciated in their 1949 'Programme of Action'. In 1952 Mandela organized volunteers and led the ANC's **Defiance Campaign** of civil disobedience and protest. Although initially wary of the participation of Indians, mixed race and communists in the anti-apartheid movement, the ANC joined with other groups to call for an end to racism and the redistribution of resources in the Freedom Charter of 1955, for which Mandela and 150 others were arrested and tried for treason. As the trial dragged on, a new generation of more militant African leaders emerged who promoted 'Africanism', the belief that **South Africa** was primarily an African nation. Despite his early commitment to **Gandhi's** theory of non-violence, the 1960 **Sharpeville Massacre** and the banning of the ANC convinced Mandela of the need for armed struggle. He co-founded Umkhonto we Sizwe, the 'Spear of the Nation', as the armed wing of the ANC and coordinated guerrilla training and sabotage campaigns against government, military and industrial targets. In 1962 Mandela was arrested and imprisoned on Robben Island, where he spent eighteen of his twenty-seven years in prison. During his time in prison he organized fellow prisoners, studied for his law degree by correspondence and his reputation as leader of the international anti-apartheid movement grew. By the late 1980s he was allowed visitors from international organizations and with pressure mounting, President F. W. de Klerk announced the unbanning of the ANC and the release of Mandela in 1990. Following his release, Mandela led negotiations with de Klerk to bring an end to the apartheid government and the institution of multiracial elections, for which Mandela and de Klerk jointly received the Nobel Peace Prize in 1993. In April 1994 Mandela was elected South Africa's first African president.

As president, Mandela promoted a policy of reconciliation, integrating the guerrilla forces and the apartheid military, supporting the hated 'Springboks' national rugby team to victory in 1995 and instituting the Truth and Reconciliation Commission. He furthered South Africa's economic development and its position as an important regional political force. In 1999 he retired and was succeeded by his deputy **Thabo Mbeki**. Despite early criticisms of inaction and ignorance, after the loss of his son to **AIDS**, Mandela publicly took on the issue and criticized Mbeki's AIDS policy. He remained an internationally respected activist and statesman until his death.

Manhattan Project

Variously regarded as a triumph and an instance of morally blinkered science, this joint British and American research and development programme was named after a unit in the Army Corps of Engineers and led to the building of the first atomic bombs. Costing 3 billion dollars and employing 120,000 people across America between 1942 and 1945, the project progressed from gun-type collisions of fissionable materials to implosion technology. After a trial detonation in Alamogordo, New Mexico, US bombers dropped the new weapon on **Hiroshima** and **Nagasaki** in Japan. Very few of the American actors realized that they had precipitated the world into a nuclear age. Amongst the scientists, Albert Einstein voiced serious concern. Klaus Fuchs, a German refugee physicist privy to Manhattan Project secrets, was later convicted in **Britain** of spying for the **Soviet Union**, having contributed to communist nuclear capability and the menace of proliferation

Manley, Michael (Norman) (1924–1997)

A three-time prime minister of **Jamaica**, 1972–80 and 1989–92, during his first two terms Manley promoted major economic reform, developed close ties with the socialist world and encouraged the non-aligned movement among developing nations. Among the achievements and significant legislation under his regimes are the minimum wage law, compulsory recognition of trade unions, maternity leave with pay, legal equality for children born out of wedlock, the Jamaica Movement for the advancement of Literacy and the National Housing Trust, Annual Labour Day and the Jamaica Nutrition Holdings and Jamaica Export Trading Corporation. As a member of the Third World and Non-Aligned movement, Michael Manley also gave Jamaica a more visible role on the world scene. He initiated several treaties, creating new links with **Mexico**, **Venezuela**, **Cuba** and other Latin American countries. He also opened Jamaica embassies in the **Soviet Union**, **Cuba** and **Nigeria** and negotiated joint economic projects with these countries. His democratic socialism was not widely supported at home and among some conservative international communities, some of whom equated it with communism, leading his party, the People's National Party, to later modify what was considered a too radical philosophy for Jamaica. Ill health caused him to pass on the leadership of the party to Percival J. Patterson in 1992. Manley is buried in Jamaica's National Heroes' Park in Kingston.

Mannerheim, Baron Karl (1867–1951)
– see also **Finno-Soviet Wars**.

Finnish soldier and statesman. Born at Villnaes of Finno-Swedish descent, he was commissioned in the Russian Imperial Army in 1889 and served in the Russo-Japanese War in 1904–5, rising to major general in World War I. Following the **Russian Revolution** and the Finnish declaration of independence in December 1917, he led 'White' forces, supported by a German expeditionary force, to victory over the Left, supported by the Soviets, in the Finnish Civil War of January to April 1918. He advocated Finnish intervention in support of 'White' Russian forces in the **Russian Civil War**, but was defeated in the presidential elections of July 1919. Following the **Soviet Union**'s recognition of Finnish independence on 14 October 1920, he retired from active service with the rank of Field Marshal. In retirement he maintained an active interest in the military readiness of Finland for any future war, including the fortification of the Karelian frontier with the Soviet Union. As chairman of the National Defence Council from 1931, he supervised the improvement of the line of defences across the Karelian isthmus, which became known as the **Mannerheim Line**. Recalled to active service in 1939, he commanded the Finnish forces in the war of 1939–40 and advised the government to seek peace in March 1940. He also commanded Finnish forces in the war of 1941–4 when the Finns joined the attack on the Soviet Union launched by **Hitler** in June 1941. Faced with certain defeat by the summer of 1944, the Finns elected Mannerheim president (4 August 1944); he secured an armistice with the Russians in September 1944, and retired from office on 9 March 1945.

Manto, Saadat Hasan (1912–1955)
Renowned Urdu short-story writer. A leading member of the Progressive Writer's movement, Manto explored controversial subjects in his stories, including sexuality and social injustice, and was repeatedly tried on charges of obscenity in British **India** and **Pakistan**. His stories about the partition of India are unrivalled in their ability to capture the physical and psychological violence of the period. Manto was also an accomplished script-writer and journalist.

Manzhuguo (Manchukuo)
The state established in Manchuria in 1932, after the Japanese Army initiated the 'Manchurian incident' in 1931. Manzhuguo was quickly incorporated into the Japanese Empire, providing raw materials for continued expansion as well as a base from which to invade the rest of **China** in 1937. Puyi (1906–67), the last emperor of China, was made puppet leader in 1934, although real power remained in the hands of the Japanese Kwangtung Army. In 1945 Manzhuguo returned to Chinese control.

Mao Tse-tung
– see **Mao Zedong**.

Mao Zedong (1893–1976)
– see also **Cultural Revolution**; **Great Leap Forward**; **guerrilla warfare**; **Maoism**.

Also known as Chairman Mao, he led the Chinese Communist Party (CCP) from 1935 to his death in 1976, and was the ruler of **China** after 1949. Mao was born in Hunan, and graduated from teacher training college in Changsha. He then worked as a librarian under Li Dazhao at Beijing University, and by 1920 defined himself as a Marxist. The following year he attended the first National Party Congress of the CCP in Shanghai as the delegate of the Communist Party in Hunan. He was elected to the Central Committee of the party in 1923. During this period, Mao worked with unions to organize strikes in Shanghai and then with peasants in Hunan. While there, he led the failed Autumn Harvest Uprising and formulated his ideas of rural revolution. Following the purge of Communists from the **Kuomintang** by **Chiang Kai-shek**, Mao fled to Jiangxi and built up an army of 200,000 troops. Nationalist attacks on the Communists forced him to embark on the **Long March**, 1934–5, which ended in Yenan in northern Shaanxi province. It was at the Zunyi conference, in Guizhou, in 1935 that Mao was appointed head of the party. While in Yenan, Mao began the policies of land reform and the alliance of peasants, workers and other classes known as New Democracy that were to be rolled out on a national basis after 1949. He also consolidated his position, and in 1945 Mao Zedong's thought was accepted as the official party line. With the victory of the Communists over the Nationalists in the civil war, Mao was elected chairman of the People's Republic of China (PRC) in 1949.

From 1949 to 1976 Mao was the leader of China, although he did not rule unopposed. The failure of the **Great Leap Forward** in 1959 forced his resignation as chairman of the PRC, although he remained in firm control of the party and the military. In 1966 he supported Jiang Qing and other radicals in a purge of moderates from the CCP that was known as the **Cultural Revolution**. This spread from the top levels of the CCP to local government and throughout society, and although its worst excesses were curbed with the disbandment of the **Red Guards** in 1968, turmoil continued until Mao's death in 1976. Mao was also active in foreign policy. He sent troops into **Korea** in 1950, and fought a border dispute with **India** in 1962. Meanwhile, he split with the **USSR**, which he believed had lost revolutionary impetus. In 1972 he signed the Shanghai Communique with **Nixon**, which agreed that **Taiwan** was part of China. After Mao's death, his body was embalmed and placed on display in Tiananmen Square, where it can still be seen today. In 1981 he was criticized by **Deng Xiaoping** for his part in the Cultural Revolution. Despite this and other failings, he remains an important icon for Chinese people and his ideas on **guerrilla warfare** have influenced revolutionaries throughout the world.

Maoism

The political and military doctrine inspired by Marxist–Leninism, but distinct from it, and formulated by Chinese Communist leader **Mao Zedong**.

At the core of Mao's thought is a view of antagonistic and non-antagonistic contradictions in society, which legitimize the need for revolution. Contradictions of the first type, as conceived by Mao, concentrated on 'us' or 'the people' against 'the enemy' or the Chinese bourgeoisie, and required revolutions that took form in the foundation of a Communist regime, the People's Republic of **China**, in 1949. Contradictions of the second order, such as ideological or policy-related differences arising within the Communist Party, called in theory for energetic debate and self-criticism, yet in practice materialized in more virulent campaigns for the rectification of thought of the 1940s and the 'Great Proletarian' **Cultural Revolution** launched in 1966.

The distinctness of Mao's doctrine was based on his agrarian focus and capacity to criticize the validity and appropriateness of Soviet-imported models and doctrines of revolution in a Chinese context. Unlike Marxist–Leninists, who assigned the task of revolution to the urban proletarians, Mao considered that in the tradition, culture and economic reality of a largely rural-based China the peasantry had the task and duty of promoting revolution. Mao believed peasants were the key to revolution, susceptible as they were to being mobilized both in political and military terms. The teachings and writings of Mao also integrated a rural-based military strategy to launch a People's War grounded on tactics and methods of **guerrilla warfare**. Mao's theory emphasized three points. First, widespread propaganda designed to broaden support and gain new recruits, accompanied by minor attacks on government personnel and their symbols. Second, a move forward into a protracted war through escalating attacks against military and other key state institutions through sabotage, terrorism and assassinations. Third, an extended insurgency against government forces in direct actions designed to seize cities, overthrow the government and take control of the country. Although the plan was never strictly followed by the Red Army itself, it became a blueprint for Maoist and non-Maoist insurgency around the world.

In economic and political terms, advocacy of Maoism in China after Mao's death in 1976 was more official and formal than real; and ironically, more flexible than in other countries. This evolution occurred for two reasons. First, failed industrial and agricultural modernization essayed with the **Great Leap Forward** (1958–63) is commonly viewed as a major economic disaster due to a combination of adverse weather conditions, technical mistakes and a bureaucracy that implemented the plan precipitously, which ended in millions of deaths from famine. Second, the excesses of the **Cultural Revolution** in purging Mao's enemies in the Communist Party led to hundreds of thousands of deaths and brought China close to civil war. Maoist doctrines are now regarded as counter-productive for both economic growth and social order.

Maori Wars

A term generally replaced with 'New Zealand Wars' which refers to the conflicts between British Crown forces, European settlers and the Maori tribes between 1845 and 1872. Following the Treaty of Waitangi, which British and settler groups insisted had transferred sovereignty and land to them, various Maori tribes reacted to missionary activity and land depredations by engaging in resistance to other Maori and to the British. This led to fierce, intermittent conflicts, latterly spawning a kind of Maori nationalism, which were eventually resolved by the destruction of the Maori economic base and land confiscations. Legal disputes over the loss of land have continued into the twenty-first century.

Maoris

– see also **Maori Wars; New Zealand**.
The term given for the Polynesian people of the islands of **New Zealand, Australia** and the Cook Islands. The Maori upheld a warrior culture which engaged with technologically superior Europeans in the seventeenth century, and which consequently suffered a great toll of disease and cultural crisis. Until the 1830s the Maori, who were organized in tribes, were powerful and integrated Europeans into their society. In 1840 the Treaty of Waitangi was signed between leading tribes and the British Crown, which purported to guarantee land in return for sovereignty. Thereafter, the internecine and British **Maori Wars** of 1845–72 broke out, and the Maori were subjugated. Their lands were in large part confiscated, and what seemed a successful attempt to assimilate Maoris into European politics and society began. In the 1960s a Maori cultural and political revival took place, leading to attempts to rebalance history and to settle land claims on the part of successive New Zealand administrations.

Mapai (Mifleget Po'alei Eretz Yisrael/ Israel Workers' Party)

A socialist Zionist political party founded by **Ben-Gurion** in 1930 and closely allied with Israel's **Histadrut** labour federation. Mapai was politically centrist, adhering to Ben-Gurion's notion that settlement work 'without the Communists and without the Revisionists' was the best way to achieve Zionist objectives. Mapai also represented **Israel**'s largest federations of collectivist settlements. From 1954 onwards Mapai's history was intertwined with the 'Lavon Affair', a botched attempt at officially authorized terrorism within **Egypt**. Responsibility for the operation's failure initially fell on Mapai Defence Minister Pinhas Lavon (1904–76), but his role in the affair has been debated ever since. As a consequence of the Lavon Affair, Ben-Gurion and **Moshe Dayan** led their Rafi faction out of Mapai in 1965. Rafi ran independently in the 1965 elections, and on 21 January 1968 it reunited with Mapai and other parties to form Israel's Labor Party.

Maquis

A term for dense thickets of bush in south-eastern Europe, which came to apply to rebel and resistance groups dedicated to the overthrow of Nazi Europe. The Maquis comprised a variety of groups, including people who wished to avoid forced employment in the Third Reich, which imported labour, those on the Left philosophically opposed to Nazism and Nationalists. Maquisards typically conducted raids and harassment of the German authorities and helped the Allies in the infiltration and extraction of agents. They were also of critical importance in the campaigns of sabotage and delay which aided the Allied invasion of Europe after the **Normandy landings**. Many Maquis adopted the beret as symbolic, but not exclusive, headgear, and later joined the French Army under **de Gaulle** or continued anti-fascist activities against the **Franco** regime.

March First movement (Korea)

Beginning on 1 March 1919, this mass, non-violent movement featured protests against Japanese colonial rule. Inspired by a formal declaration of independence by thirty-three intellectuals and religious leaders, half a million Koreans participated in numerous demonstrations throughout the country until the colonial police violently put an end to the protests in May 1919. As a result of the movement, the colonial government permitted limited forms of speech, print and organization under 'Cultural Rule', which led to a vibrant period of nationalist movements.

Marco Polo Bridge incident

On 9 July 1937 Japanese troops stationed at Yongding Bridge, also known as Marco Polo

Bridge, just west of Beijing, conducted a night manoeuvre firing blank cartridges. The Chinese fired back, but no casualties were recorded. However, at roll call the following morning a Japanese soldier was discovered missing, and it was assumed that he had been captured by the Chinese. This led to Japanese attacks which marked the outbreak of the second **Sino-Japanese War**.

Marconi, Guglielmo (1874–1937)

Born in Bologna, **Italy**, Marconi is best known for his development of a radio-telegraph system. Finding limited interest in his work in his native Italy, in early 1896 he went to London, where he was introduced to William Preece, engineer-in-chief of the Post Office. In 1897 he demonstrated that signals (Morse codes) could be transmitted over distances of 6 kilometres across Salisbury Plain. In December 1901, Marconi transmitted signals across the Atlantic between Poldhu, in Cornwall, and St John's, in Newfoundland, and proved that wireless waves were not affected by the curvature of the Earth. He received honorary doctorates from several universities and in 1909 shared the Nobel Prize in physics with Karl Ferdinand Braun, for contributions to wireless telegraphy.

Marcos, Ferdinand (1917–1989)

President of the **Philippines**, 1965–86. His regime enjoyed close ties and continuous support from the **USA** despite constant allegations of political repression, human rights violations and rampant corruption. Marcos was overthrown by the revolution that followed the murder of oppositional leader **Benigno Aquino**. He remained in exile in **Hawaii** until his death. **Corazón Aquino** (Benigno's widow) succeeded Marcos as president (1986–92).

Maria Theresa (1717–1780)

Archduchess of **Austria**, 1740–80. The only female ruler of the **Habsburg** Empire, she bore sixteen children, fought two wars (including the **Seven Years War**) against **Frederick II** of **Prussia**, transformed and stabilized the Austrian Empire and improved medicine, education and taxes in her realm. She was conservative in religion and stood at arms-length from the **Enlightenment**. She established Austrian rule in **Poland** following the first partition of that country in 1772, and is, unfortunately, remembered in part for a deep distrust of Protestant and Jewish people. She died of smallpox.

Mariátegui, José Carlos (1894–1930)

Born in Lima, **Peru**, Mariátegui founded the Socialist Party of Peru in 1928 which, after his death, became the Communist Party of Peru. An unorthodox Marxist, he combined **Indigenismo** (an ardent defence and advocacy of Indian culture and society) with **Marxism** and **nationalism** to create a unique blend of Andean Socialism. For such an innovative, autochthonous, if revisionist, Socialist perspective, he gained widespread fame in Latin American progressive circles, but eventual expulsion from the Communist International. A leading figure of the reform generation of 1919, along with his rival **V. R. Haya de la Torre**, Mariátegui was founder and editor of *Amauta*, a Peruvian journal of Socialist persuasion which published such international figures as Henri Barbusse, Miguel de Unamuno and **Diego Rivera**. His major work *Seven Interpretative Essays on Peruvian Reality* (1927) is considered a classic analysis of early twentieth-century Peruvian society.

Maritime Customs Service

This organization was established in 1854 by the British to collect taxes on maritime trade after the outbreak of the **Taiping** rebellion made it impossible for Chinese customs officials to carry out the task. Its functions expanded to include responsibility for domestic customs administration, the postal service, harbour and waterway management and anti-smuggling operations. It was disbanded in 1950.

market economy

– *see also* **liberalism**; **neoliberalism**.

An economy characterized by decentralized production and distribution of goods and services through free markets guided by prices. People decide how much they want to work and to consume simultaneously, given wage rates and prices. Producers decide what and how much to produce given input and output prices. The system is said to be decentralized because the coordination between consumption and work, on the one hand, and the production of goods and services, on the other, takes place through the equilibration forces of supply and demand. In practice, no economy has ever been a completely free market system. Some consider free markets to be features of modern societies that developed with the Industrial Revolution. Others see them as present for most of human history, spreading progressively to more and more social spaces. Moreover, even modern societies have experienced processes of increasing and decreasing intervention by states. The era of **mercantilism** was characterized by the intensifying interventions by states particularly in relation to shipping and international trade. Over the nineteenth century, states withdrew and allowed **laissez-faire**. The twentieth century saw increasing intervention in wartime to stabilize the economy. In Soviet-type economies, production decisions were taken by government bureaucracies and consumers and firms had little choice over what and how much to consume or produce.

The advantages of the free market systems of social coordination are embodied in three basic propositions: the invisible hand as elaborated by **Adam Smith**, efficiency as suggested by neoclassical economics and information processing as indicated by Friedrick von Hayek (1899–1992). Smith argued that in pursuit of profit, entrepreneurs are induced by prices to produce what people want to consume. The efficiency argument is based on the theory that entrepreneurs not only follow prices to produce what people want, but also produce commodities as cheaply as possible in order to sell and maximize profits under pressure of competition. Hayek's argument is based on his intuition that the market price of a good is a single number that is an indication of the overall social value of a good, and facilitates decision making by firms, as opposed to information on the costs of all direct and indirect inputs used in production. For these arguments to hold, markets must not be characterized by failures, in the form of monopolies and externalities. These are strong conditions. But the third advantage claimed for free markets implies that governments would have to generate and process huge amounts of information and develop sophisticated decision mechanisms to make decisions of comparable efficiency to those flowing from free markets, and the fall of Soviet command economies supports this idea.

Marlborough, Duke of (1650–1722)

John Churchill, Duke of Marlborough, served five monarchs, and as a commander of British and continental armies led ten campaigns which limited French power and raised British power in Europe. He was the leader of allied forces during the war of the **Spanish Succession** (1702–13) and is especially remembered for his great victory at Blenheim in 1704, the palace of that name subsequently built in England, and his elevation of the Churchill line in British politics. His dukedom was rare in that it could and subsequently did pass through the female as well as the male line.

Maroons

The name given to groups of run-away slaves in the Spanish, French and British Caribbean colonies; it derives from the Spanish *cimarrones*, referring to the inaccessible mountainous regions to which they fled (from the Spanish word *cima* meaning 'summit'). Substantial bodies of maroons existed in several islands, with some of the largest in **Jamaica**, against whom two wars were fought by British troops. Following the war of 1734–8 a peace treaty was concluded which guaranteed the Maroons two homelands of 2,500 acres in which their chief, Cudjo, had complete jurisdiction apart from the death penalty. In return the maroons were expected to help in the defence of the island and the return of run-away slaves. A similar treaty was signed with a second group in 1739. The Maroons helped suppress a major slave revolt in 1760–1, but a second Maroon War broke out in 1795, provoked by British fears of the spread of revolutionary ideas from French Saint-Dominigue, leading to the deportation of some of the Maroons to Nova Scotia and eventually to Sierra Leone. The remainer retained their privileges by continuing to assist in returning run-away slaves and as late as 1861 helped to suppress disorder on the island. On French Guadeloupe some Maroon bands survived until French slaves were freed in 1848. On Saint-Dominigue a Maroon leader, Mackandal, united the run-away groups but was caught and executed in 1758. Continued resistance, however, led to an accommodation with the governor similar to that in **Jamaica**.

Marshall, George (1880–1959)

Soldier, statesman and one of the most venerable servants of the **United States**. Marshall rose through the ranks of the US military before becoming in 1939 chief of staff with the rank of general. It was from this position that he played a central role in readying America's armies and coordinating its military campaigns during **World War II**. After the war he held a number of important positions: he was President **Harry Truman**'s special representative to **China**, secretary of state, and secretary of defence. As secretary of state, he delivered in 1947 the speech that unveiled the Marshall Plan, the initiative that not only helped to regenerate the war-torn western European economy but furthered Truman's policy of containing communist expansion. A reserved, taciturn man, Truman was not the only one to regard him as the greatest living American.

Marshall, John (1755–1835)

The great American jurist credited with establishing the authority of the United States **Supreme Court**. Marshall was a Virginian lawyer who, having fought in the Continental Army, defended the US Constitution in Virginia in 1788 and the Washington administration in the 1790s. After serving on the peace commission to **France** in 1798, he served in Congress, 1799–1800, and as secretary of state, 1800–1, and was appointed chief justice in the last days of **John Adams**. Initially concerned to defend the independence of the court against the **Jefferson** administration and to assert its right to invalidate congressional decisions, in 1810–24 Marshall's court made a series of famous decisions vetoing state laws and judicial opinions that broke the constitutional limitations of the federal constitution or diminished federal supremacy. After 1824 the decisions became friendlier to the states, but after disagreement with President **Andrew Jackson** over Indian rights in 1830–2, he recognized that the court could not effectively check settled political majorities.

Marshall Plan

The European Recovery Plan (ERP) drafted by the US State Department under the aegis of **George Marshall** and launched at Harvard in June 1947. It called for reconstruction of European economies and economic confidence on the basis of a share of some 13 billion pounds in aid monies and technical advice and assistance. The programme attracted the participation of sixteen European nations and lasted until 1952. The largest amounts were spent on the French, Dutch and British economies, but money also made its way towards states which had been neutral in **World War II**, such as **Ireland**, or hostile, such as **Germany** and **Italy**. Though offered, the **Soviet Union** and associated nations in the emergent Eastern bloc rejected the aid and its associated American coordination. Whilst small as a percentage of American GDP, the ERP is credited with creating the industrial conditions for high western European growth, political support for **NATO** in the nineteen fifties and containing the powerful communist movements in western Europe.

Martí (y Perez), José Julián (1853–1895)

Best known as a nationalist hero, he became the symbol of the Cuban struggle for independence against **Spain**. His literary work dealt with the idea of freedom and democracy. As head of the Partido Revolucionario de Cuba, he helped plan the invasion of **Cuba** in 1895, but died in military action on the plains of Dos Ríos on 19 May, becoming a martyr in the cause of Cuban nationalism.

Marwaris

A term referring to broad and disparate itinerant capitalist merchant groups originating in the princely states of western Rajasthan. By the mid nineteenth century they had settled in large numbers in Bombay, **Calcutta** and central India, as successful bankers, moneylenders, traders, small industrialists and brokers and commission agents to British firms. They continue to be a significant business group in contemporary **India** and the Indian diaspora.

Marx, Karl (1818–1883)

– see also **Marxism**.

Philosopher, journalist, polemicist and founder of **Marxism**. Marx was a Jewish thinker in **Germany**, forced to convert to **Protestantism** to get on in life. He was a lifelong critic of religion, especially after reading **Hegel** and Feurbach as a young man. His central concept of alienation – individual isolation from nature, progress and capacity because of exploitation and the control of property by others – perhaps speaks to this condition. Heavily influenced by the ideas of Georg Hegel, he developed as a journalist and polemicist in Paris in the 1840s, but then returned to Germany. Marx was driven out of **Prussia** in 1849 having been an enthusiastic supporter of the revolutions of 1848, during which he wrote *The Communist Manifesto*. He then moved to London, where he became an economist, philosopher, journalist and agitator, helping to organize socialist movements and international organizations as well as constantly skirting bankruptcy. His association with **Friedrich Engels**, a rigid thinker, industrialist and military man who helped craft his message and develop his theories, and with other socialist luminaries, was crucial in helping Marx avoid his creditors.

Marx held that all history was the history of class struggle, and that industrial society was moving towards an eventual communist state. He believed that the natural tendency of human beings is to accumulate property, either through the exploitation of others or in a way which necessitates such exploitation, but that as society developed so exploitation produced classes who caused a counter-movement and overturned the older order. Culture and language to Marx reflected this underlying economic order and were in an important sense caused by it, and religion represented a device of the ruling classes to hide this underlying unfairness and suppress the inevitable reaction against it. Marx identified the social order prevailing in the nineteenth century as 'capitalist' and 'bourgeois' and predicted that the exploited industrial working class would cohere around trade unions and communist parties and usher in a new age of industrial democracy leading to a state without money, waste or unemployment of any resource. He did not anticipate advances in technology and productivity, the flexibility of capitalist enterprises, or the possibility that large numbers of the working class might wish and work for a bourgeois lifestyle. Critically, his model depended upon rational and objective government-led plans informed by accurate information as replacements for the price mechanism employed by markets. Marx thought that revolution leading to communism would begin in industrial states, and particularly in Germany, but believed that it could be accelerated anywhere by a communist political party. He also believed that a communist order would be millennially different from everything that had gone before.

The secular, economic and rational-materialist arguments and complete explanations offered by **Marxism** attracted many in the nineteenth and twentieth centuries. Ironically, many of the middle classes who rejected religion while experiencing university or who wished to encourage social reform and the betterment of the poor, were the most enthusiastic supporters of Marxism. The collapse of traditional societies in **World War I** allowed the **Russian Revolution** of 1917, which eventually became a communist one and which encouraged revolutions with varying degrees of success across eastern Europe, **Asia** and **Africa** over the next sixty years. Under **Lenin**, the **USSR** which emerged from the Russian Revolution promoted Marxism, anti-imperialism and revolution across the world and inspired equally totalitarian movements to resist it, such as **fascism** and Marxism. Marxist states constituted the majority of humanity after the emergence of communist **China** in 1949, and the **Cold War** in which liberal and generally democratic states faced Marxist ones began, only ending in the collapse of communist states in 1989–90.

Marxism never proved able to win over large enough numbers in those countries where it was adopted that imprisonment, exile and execution for deviation were not necessary. It is reliably estimated that, within Marxist systems, political oppression of dissidents accompanied by economic mistakes and implicit difficulties with resource allocation were responsible for the deaths of at least 150 million outside of war in the twentieth century. Despite this, Marxism retains a great if diminished appeal as an intellectual system and as a vehicle of protest against both capitalism in its global twenty-first century form and the policies and culture of the hyper-powered **United States of America**.

Marxism

A strand of radical collectivist thought associated with **Karl Marx** and **Friedrich Engels** but which subsists in multiple iterations and forms. The key principles of Marxism are that all history is the history of class struggle, that production and technology give rise to culture and society, and that history progresses via the dialectical confrontation of social classes and ideas towards a communist state in which individuals should give and receive according to their needs and ability. Some Marxists have pursued the role of a 'vanguard' communist party in leading the workers towards the ultimate state, and others, such as **Lenin**, have attempted to force the creation of such a state via the mechanism of revolution and central state appropriation and redistribution of property. Still others have proposed the mechanism of permanent revolution within the institutions of the state via party bodies (**Trotsky**); a deliberate attempt to change language and ideas via campaigns of linguistic and institutional subversion (Gramsci); the physical elimination of all enemies of a national-communist state (**Stalin**); and peaceful evolution through example, international socialism, and democratic mandates. This latter iteration has not been generally symptomatic of the cause.

The term *Marxism* was popularized after Marx's death by Karl Kautsky, a Viennese Social Democrat who placed the idea in the context of Russian revolutionary conspiracism. Marxism itself is clearly a product of the industrial period. Its adherents generally accept, as in Marx's teleology (borrowed from **Hegel**), that private profit and property are a form of theft from the surplus value added to products by labour, which they assume to have been underpaid. Marxists also generally tend to see the working class as a 'proletariat' distinguished by its industrial activity and the bourgeois as appropriators who won over feudal aristocrats by the mechanisms of liberalism and rent. A further aspect of Marxism, which definitively places it within the nineteenth and early twentieth centuries, is the idea that as technology improves so workers are required to do more and more mundane tasks for less and less money in order to stay alive until they are in revolt and monopoly capitalism is exhausted. There is little role for technological step-changes, social mobility, individual or non-materialist outlooks or conservatism in the idea; indeed, Marxists would dismiss all of these as 'false consciousness'.

Marxism, of the Leninist or **Maoist** sort, was the basis of the **USSR** and is fundamental to the People's Republic of **China**. At one point, it threatened to spread to most of the world, and was found in various forms in **Cuba**, South America, **Africa** and **Asia**. It was viewed as so threatening by liberals, democrats and conservatives that, from one perspective, the **Cold War** was waged against it. Born in war and revolution, and deeply marked by anticlericalism, as well as dictatorship, it should not therefore be surprising that Marxist states are associated with more deaths and repression than any other form of government in history. No Marxist party in a free democracy has ever proven able to win the support of a democratic majority, and after the revolutions against East European Marxist states, the ideology has been very much in decline.

Masangano

Founded by the Portuguese governor Paulo Dias de Novais in 1586, Masangano was the principal Portuguese settlement in the interior of its colony of **Angola**. It became the refuge of **Portugal** when the Dutch invaded Angola in 1641 and was the headquarters for Portuguese campaigns into the interior. It was eclipsed by other towns in the nineteenth century and is today a tiny settlement surrounded by many ruins of earlier ages.

Masaryk, Tomáš Garrigue (1850–1937)

The 'father of **Czechoslovakia**'. Born in the Czech lands of **Austria–Hungary**, of a Slovak father and Germanized Czech mother, he was a university professor from 1882 and a member of the Austro-Hungarian *Reichsrat* from 1891, where he was a leader of the left-wing Slav opposition. He left **Austria**, 1914, to agitate for the Czechoslovak idea in western Europe and then in the **USA** during **World War I**. Sentenced to death 'in absentia' by the Austrians for nationalist agitation, he instead became president of the new Czechoslovak Republic in 1918. In office until 1935 under a constitutional provision personal to him, he was widely admired as a humanist and liberal democrat, but he did not succeed in the perhaps impossible task of winning the loyalty of the Sudeten Germans to the new state. Moreover, his failure to honour the 1918 Pittsburgh Agreement, whereby the Slovaks would enjoy autonomy in the new state, probably contributed to the ultimate failure of the Czechoslovak idea.

masculinity
– *see* **gender**.

Masekela, Hugh (1939–)

South African trumpeter, composer and singer. In 1959 Masekela joined the Jazz Epistles, the first African jazz group to record and perform to large audiences in Johannesburg and Cape Town. After the **Sharpeville Massacre**, he left **South Africa** and went on to perform and record with leading jazz musicians across the world. His 1987 hit 'Bring Him Back Home' became the anthem for **Nelson Mandela**'s world tour following his release from prison in 1990.

Masina (Hamduallah Caliphate)

A town on the Niger River in present-day Mali that was a centre for Fulbe and Islamic learning since the sixteenth century. In 1818, **Sekou Amadu**, a religious leader, led a reform movement against the Bambara Empire that controlled the region and overthrew it. This movement was part of a larger thrust towards Islamic reform in West Africa that had already resulted in the founding of the **Sokoto Caliphate** in 1804. In 1845 Masina expanded to include Timbuktu. He created a theocracy from his capital of Hamdullahi. Sekou Amadu was a strict reformer who banned alcohol, tobacco and music from this domains and built many mosques to intensify Islamic practice. The Masina theocracy also organized an extensive system of Islamic charity focusing on widows, orphans and the poor. In 1862 El Hadj Umar Tall, another Islamic reformer from the **Senegal** region, attacked and defeated Masina, razing its capital and killing its ruler.

mass production

Production of large amounts of standardized products on production lines. The system was introduced by Henry Ford in 1908–14 to produce his Ford Model T automobile. The evolution to mass production followed from the increased division of labour which began during **industrialization**, in the late seventeenth and eighteenth centuries, and from the development of standardized parts and production tools, during late nineteenth century – particularly in the production of arms, agricultural machinery, bicycles and other goods. Once standardized parts were available, it became possible to also standardize the process of assembly and to organize it along a production line. The resulting product is standardized and the process allows for very high productivity per worker and low unit costs. The system of mass production implies substantial set-up times and costs, making it really efficient for large and stable markets that allow for spreading initial set-up costs over large production runs.

Massive Retaliation

Massive Retaliation was an American **Cold War** strategy designed to minimize troop deployment through stressing the usability of nuclear weapons. Secretary of State **John Foster Dulles** explained in January 1954 that challenges to US interests would henceforth be met as the US determined and that 'local defence' would be strengthened by the threat of 'massive retaliatory power'. The premise was that the threat of nuclear annihilation would discourage aggressors from testing America's resolve at a fraction of the cost of conventional deterrence.

Matamba

A kingdom in modern-day **Angola** founded before the sixteenth century. In 1635 it was taken over by Queen Njinga of Ndongo, who was fleeing the Portuguese, and became her capital. The dynasty that was founded there controlled the central stretches of the Kwango river basin through the eighteenth century and was an important point in the slave trade. It lost its unity in the nineteenth century and was absorbed into Portuguese Angola in the 1890s.

Mau Mau revolt (Kenya Emergency)

Known by its members as the Kenya Land and Freedom Army, Mau Mau was the Kikuyu-based guerrilla resistance to British colonization which emerged from the Kenya African National Union's 1944 demand for access to land in the White Highlands. After sporadic Kikuyu attacks on white settlers and Kikuyu who refused to support the campaign, the British authorities declared a state of emergency in October 1952 and in 1953 imprisoned leading Mau Mau members, including **Jomo Kenyatta**. British tactics included 'villagization' and deportation to isolate the guerrillas. By late 1954 over 150,000 Africans had been detained in brutal conditions, culminating in the 1958 Hola Camp scandal in which eleven detainees died. Overall 11,000 Mau Mau were killed, 534 African and 63 white members of the security forces, and 1,817 African civilians, 32 whites and 26 Asians. Kenya

became independent in 1963, with Kenyatta as prime minister.

Mauritania

Mauritania is the eleventh largest country in **Africa** but its approximately 3.5 million inhabitants make it one of the least densely populated in the world. It borders **Senegal** to the south, **Mali** to the south and east, **Algeria** to the north-east, and the disputed **Western Sahara** territory to the north-west. Mauritania has long been a diverse place and a crossroads between empires. As part of the Sanhadja Confederation of Amazigh tribes, key Mauritanian towns were linked to other parts of north and west Africa. Important caravan routes between **Ghana** and the Songhay Empire and the Arab and Amazigh states north of the Sahara went through Mauritania. **Islam** arrived in the eighth century but initially blended with existing belief practices. The eleventh-century Almoravids unified the region under a more rigid and austere form of Sunni Islam that caused friction with the local population. The thirteenth-century invasion of the Beni Hassan, a devout warrior tribe from the Arabian peninsula, marked the most dramatic shift in cultural identity in the region. Quickly forming alliances with Amazigh tribes and militarily dominating other opposition, their arrival brought further Islamization and Arabization, and created a social hierarchy of tribes with the Beni Hassan at the top and black slaves at the bottom.

Prior to the late nineteenth century, **Spain**, **Portugal** and **Britain** erected temporary trading posts on the Atlantic coast without much lasting success. In the nineteenth century the French expanded into the Algerian Sahara and showed some interest in the 1860s in moving north from Senegal into Mauritania. In 1899, Xavier Coppolani (1866–1905) led an expedition north across the Senegal River into Mauritania, allying himself with Zawiya tribes against the Hassan. He was assassinated by the great sheikh and anti-colonial resister Ma al-Aynayn (1831–1910), but in 1909 Henri Gouraud (1867–1946) led a more concerted attack on Ma al-Aynayn's followers and took official control of the territory. **France** put very few resources into developing the Mauritanian economy or its state structures, compared to its other African possessions. Although administered as a distinct entity, all major decisions were made in French Senegal. Mokhtar Ould Daddah (1924–2003), allegedly Mauritania's only lawyer, led a conglomerate of political organizations in the push for independence and became Mauritania's first president. Ould Daddah's Parti du

Peuple Mauritanien quickly established one-party rule, interrupted only in the late 1970s. An ill-advised 1975 military foray into the Western Sahara failed miserably, with Sahrawi independence fighters routing Mauritanian troops and eventually invading Mauritania itself. The catastrophe ostracized army officers, who overthrew Ould Daddah in a 1978 coup.

Mauritania continues to struggle with deep and complex ethnic divisions. The Arab–Berber majority is itself divided into the dominant *bidan*, or white, Moors, and *haratine*, or black former slaves. Roughly 40 per cent of the country is black African (Peulh and Toucouleur, Soninké and Wolof), and slavery is illegal but still practised, especially in remote rural areas.

May Fourth movement

This was a series of demonstrations against the Chinese government for their secret agreement awarding Shandong to **Japan**, which became public knowledge during the **Paris Peace Conference** in 1919. On 4 May that year, students from thirteen Beijing universities and colleges drew up a resolution protesting against the agreement, proposing the formation of student unions and urging Chinese people to hold mass meetings in Beijing. Around 3,000 students gathered in Tiananmen Square and marched to the legation headquarters, where they beat the Chinese minister to Japan. The Beijing government imprisoned hundreds of students. In what is seen as the first mass public expression of nationalism in **China**, this sparked off a wave of popular protests and strikes in over 200 towns and cities. The cabinet was forced to resign, and the Chinese refused to sign the **Versailles Peace Treaty**. Japan later relinquished claims to Shandong at the Washington conference in 1921.

May Thirtieth movement

This was a general strike in Shanghai and other cities in 1925. On 15 May 1925 Japanese guards fired on workers protesting against the closure of a cotton mill in Shanghai, and killed a Communist sympathizer. This sparked off a series of demonstrations directed against foreign control of the city, and on 30 May protestors surrounded Lousa Police Station. The local commander panicked and opened fire, killing four people. The following day a general strike was declared. Within two weeks 160,000 workers were on strike and demonstrations had broken out in twenty-eight cities across **China**. The Chinese Communist Party had a leading role in organizing the strike, and this movement represents its most active period among Chinese workers before it was purged by **Chiang Kai-shek** in 1927. In Shanghai, the foreign-staffed volunteer corps was brought out to control the streets, and by November the strikes and protests began to decline.

Mayan languages

A family of thirty related languages spoken by more than 5 million people across Mesoamerica. The heaviest concentrations of contemporary Mayan speakers are found in southern **Mexico** and **Guatemala**, with smaller populations located in **Belize** and extreme western **Honduras** and **El Salvador**. Originating more than five thousand years ago in the Guatemalan Highlands as the Proto-Mayan language, linguistic unity quickly collapsed as communities split off and settled in different parts of the region. These languages survive today as powerful sources of ethnic and cultural pride in the face of increasing western pressures.

Mazzini, Giuseppe (1805–1872)

– *see also* **Risorgimento**.

A lawyer and journalist from Genoa at the time of the Ligurian Republic, whose writings on Italian nationalism and European federalism have proven inspirational. Beginning in the Piedmont, and then in Tuscany, Marseille and London, Mazzini was associated with movements such as the Carbonari, Young Italy, anti-Austrian republicanism and the **Risorgimento**. His works called for general European revolution so as to establish democratic republics on a national basis, and were closely read by the movements which contributed to the 1848 Revolutions in **Europe**. In that he was an exile, involved in various protests and disturbances, writing pamphlets, books and articles, and moving between national borders in pursuit of his cause whilst attaining almost legendary status amongst his followers, he helped to create the image of the modern revolutionary. In 1848 he became a Triumvir of the Roman Republic, but was then deposed, marking the beginning of a period of disappointment.

He was never reconciled to the monarchical **Italy** that emerged in 1861, and refused to accept its legitimacy. He turned down a seat in the Italian parliament in 1867, was briefly imprisoned in 1870, and died after a further period of exile in London and Pisa.

Mbailundu

One of several Ovimbundu states that formed in the central highlands of modern-day **Angola** in the eighteenth century. It grew to become one of the most powerful and a commercial centre for the slave trade and then for the long-distance trade in ivory, wax and rubber in the nineteenth century. The Portuguese attempted to take it over in 1896, which led to the Mbailundu War in 1903 and its final conquest by Portugal.

Mboya, Tom (Thomas Joseph) (1930–1969)

Kenyan politician. A sanitary inspector and trade union leader, Mboya studied at Ruskin College, Oxford. On his return to **Kenya** in 1956 he established the People's Congress Party, which became the Kenya African National Union (**KANU**) in 1960, and led the party's delegation at independence talks. Mboya was elected to Parliament in 1963, serving as justice minister in 1963–4 and as economic planning and development minister in 1964–9. He was assassinated in Nairobi.

Mecelle (Majalla) (Ottoman Code of Civil Law)

A massive reworking of the Ottoman Civil Code, the *Mecelle*, was a core Ottoman effort at reform in the nineteenth century. The aim of the new legal code, which was implemented in 1877, was to secularize and regularize most aspects of Ottoman law. However, it did not attempt to address the politically and culturally more sensitive question of family law. Unlike most of aspects of Ottoman legal reform during this period, the *Mecelle* was not simply the adaptation of European models, but an attempt to secularize long-standing Hanefi Islamic legal codes intended to be applied to both the secular (nizamiye) and Islamic courts. Elements of this legal code remained in effect through most former Ottoman territories in the Middle East well into the twentieth century.

Medellín cartel

Led by Pablo Escobar (1949–93), this violent criminal organization based in Medellín, **Colombia**, trafficked illegal drugs, mainly cocaine, between Colombia, Peru, Bolivia and Mexico, and the United States, Canada and Europe. From the early 1970s the Cartel brought several hundreds of billions of US dollars into the Colombian economy. In the process they changed socio-cultural patterns in Colombia, bought and killed presidential candidates and brought, through targeted assassinations and car bombs, Colombian society to its knees. The Cartel broke up into 'baby cartels' after Escobar's death and the drug trade mutated into

other criminal activities as the Colombian government was able to assert greater control.

Mehmet Ali (Muhammad 'Ali Pasha) (1789–1849)

Viceroy of Egypt, 1805–48. Khedive Mehmet Ali ruled **Egypt** for nearly half a century. While often characterized as the 'founder of modern Egypt', he never identified as an Egyptian and sought to extend his rule much further than the country's borders. Rather than as a peculiarly 'Egyptian' leader, he acted as an Ottoman statesman. Based on a series of successful military reforms, he became so powerful by the 1830s that he challenged the *Porte* itself for control of the **Ottoman Empire**. His gambit to unseat the Sultan militarily was thwarted with European help. In return for withdrawing his forces from **Syria**, the sultan agreed that Mehmet Ali's descendants would remains rulers of Egypt in perpetuity. His dynasty's rule over Egypt outlasted the Ottoman Empire, ending with the Free Officer's Revolt in 1952.

The life of Mehmet Ali remains shrouded in myth and mystery. He was born sometime between 1768 and 1771 (he himself gave more than one date). Hailing from the town of Kavala in modern-day **Greece**, it is generally accepted that he and his family were speakers of Albanian. Mehmet Ali distinguished himself as a commander of irregular forces and a competent collector of taxes as a young man. Those two professions were in fact one and the same: Mehmet Ali developed a strong track record of subduing peasants who revolted to avoid payment of taxes. Those talents foreshadowed his policies as ruler of Egypt wherein he subjected the peasant majority to new forms of financial and martial discipline. In 1801 he arrived in Egypt as an officer in an Ottoman Albanian brigade sent to quell an uprising of Mamluk officers that followed the withdrawal of **Napoleon**. Amidst the ensuing power vacuum in Egypt, Mehmet Ali proved a capable enforcer of law and order. Indigenous Egyptian allies became convinced of his abilities in this regard, particularly the religious establishment. Weary of unrest, powerful Egyptian constituencies appointed him khedive in 1805. The sultan subsequently confirmed his appointment.

The year 1811 was, in at least two ways, a watershed for Mehmet Ali's consolidation of power. A **Wahhabi** revolt on the Arabian peninsula threatened Ottoman control of **Islam**'s holy cities, and the sultan needed Mehmet Ali to intervene.

In March, Mehmet Ali invited Egypt's powerful Mamluks, descendants of a dynasty that had ruled Egypt for hundreds of years, to Cairo's citadel for a gathering purported to be the sending off for his son Tusun's military campaign in Arabia. Caught unawares, the Mamluks were massacred en masse by Mehmet Ali's guards. The khedive then had his forces track down and kill the remaining Mamluks, thus eliminating his main rival for power in the country. Meanwhile, Tusun's initial Arabian campaign met with failure in 1811. But, another campaign in 1812 subjugated the Saudi revolt, bringing the Hijaz back into the Ottoman fold. Mehmet Ali had proved his worth to the sultan and eliminated indigenous opposition to his rule.

In turn, he set about a series of modernizing reforms. To fund these, he nationalized Egyptian agricultural land, ending the tradition of tax farming and directly extracting surplus from the countryside. A census of agricultural land underpinned this new regime of taxation (1813–14). More ambitious projects were to follow. The construction of the Mahmudiyya canal linking **Alexandria** and the Nile has become synonymous with the forced mobilization of Egypt's peasant labour. Began in 1817, its construction employed as many as 300,000 labourers. Mortality rates, although not clearly quantified, were said to be appalling according to contemporary sources. Indeed, according to historian Khaled Fahmy (1965–) Mehmet Ali's consolidation of power was predicated on an unwelcome subjugation of the peasant class, which, rather than waiting for the nation he brought them, as nationalist histories charge, vigorously resisted the reforms. Perhaps the chief grievance of the peasant classes was the universal conscription inaugurated in 1820. Attempts at military reform had begun elsewhere in the Ottoman Empire previous to Mehmet Ali's creation of a properly national army, but in Egypt that modernization met with more success than in the imperial centre. Mehmet Ali's first large-scale campaign mobilized tens of thousands of soldiers to invade the **Sudan** in 1820 where his armies sought resources and slaves. That Mehmet Ali had developed a powerful army and navy was clear to Sultan **Mahmud II**, who called on him to help quell the Greek revolt, promising territory in return for aid. Mehmet Ali tasked his eldest son, Ibrahim Pasha, with leading an expedition of 16,000 troops to Greece in 1825. Eventually, the French and British navies intervened on the Greek side, destroying the Egyptian and Ottoman navies at the **Battle of Navarino** (1827). Incensed, this defeat led Mehmet Ali to demand that he become governor of all Syria as recompense for his destroyed fleet. Loathe to render him an even more powerful figure, the *Porte* demurred. Mehmet Ali then prepared a massive invasion of Syria that he launched in 1831, scoring lightning victories against inferior Ottoman forces. His armies would occupy Syria until 1840, threatening twice to march on **Constantinople**. British intervention on the side of the Ottoman Empire was critical to his army's defeat. Two decades of grandiose military campaigns required enormous sacrifices from Egyptians and resulted in protracted defeats.

Mehmet Ali's most debated legacy is his contribution to Egypt's economic development. Alongside military reform, as viceroy Mehmet Ali took measures to industrialize production in the country in the interest of import substitution. Without coal reserves, Egypt's industrial project was always going to be beholden to outside forces. Just as his military conquests faltered in the face of British and French antagonism, so those same powers undermined Egypt's economic projects. Britain forced all Ottoman territories, including Egypt, to cease protecting its markets – a necessary step for 'late' industrialization – with the **Balta Liman Convention** of 1838. Ultimately, the debt accrued to build manufacturing capacity eventually became prohibitive. Almost forty years after Mehmet Ali's death, Britain used Egypt's debts as a pretext to assert control over the country in 1882.

Meiji period

Headed by Emperor Meiji, **Japan** proceeded along a path of modernization and westernization from 1868 to 1912. To secure national independence and to revise the unequal treaties imposed by the Great Powers, Japan committed to political reforms under the slogan 'wealthy country and strong arms' (*fukoku-kyohei*). Whilst traditional systems were replaced with modern methods for rapid militarization and industrialization, the ancestor worship of Shintoism was re-emphasized in the modern schooling system. The first two decades witnessed an uprising of ex-*samurai*, Buddhist monks and peasants, who were discontented by the new oligarchic regime. Although this social unrest did not disrupt the central planning, it brought about the establishment of the National Diet and the promulgation of the Meiji Japanese Imperial Constitution (1889), which made clear the divinity of the emperor. Japan's victory in wars with **China** (1895) and **Russia** (1905) embodied Japanese success in developing strategic industries, railway, telegraph and banking systems.

Meiji restoration

The restoration of the Japanese imperial court in 1868 brought about momentous political change without bloodshed. Samurai leaders in the Satsuma, Choshu, Tosa and Hizen domains overthrew the **Tokugawa** shogunate that had responded badly to growing domestic problems and under pressure from US Commodore Matthew Perry opened **Japan** to foreign trade. With the cooperation of court nobles, the *daimyo* established a new central government, headed by Emperor Meiji, in Tokyo, formerly called Edo. The Charter Oath issued by the emperor in 1868 emphasized gradualism and equality, as well as cooperation between domains, in order to unify the Japanese nation under the legitimate authority of the imperial house. The Oath also officially terminated Tokugawa's policy of national isolation. The dismantling of the old feudal regime was largely accomplished by 1871, when the domains were officially abolished and replaced with a prefecture system; feudal class privileges were also abolished.

Mein Kampf

My Struggle, the autobiography and ideological programme dictated by **Adolf Hitler** during his imprisonment following the abortive 1923 Munich putsch. Hitler exaggerated the difficulties of his early life and set out his views on Aryan superiority, his virulent **anti-Semitism**, his conviction that there was a Jewish–Marxist conspiracy for world domination, and the need for **Germany** to conquer living space in **Russia**. Over 200,000 copies had been sold by the time Hitler took power in 1933.

Meir (Meyerson), Golda (1878–1978)

Israeli leader. Born in Kiev and taken to Milwaukee, Wisconsin, as an infant, Golda became a Labour Zionist and immigrated to **Palestine** with her husband Morris Meyerson in 1921. They joined Kibbutz Merhavya in the Jezreel Valley. Golda rose to become head of the Political Department of the **Jewish Agency**, representing it at the 1938 Evian conference on Jewish refugees. In 1948 she met secretly with Transjordanian Emir Abdullah in an attempt to forestall Arab–Israeli hostilities. She became **Israel**'s first ambassador to the **Soviet Union** and rose in the ranks of **Mapai** to serve as

foreign minister from 1956 to 1965. In that capacity she Hebraized her name to Meir and instructed other diplomats to follow suit, a practice that was abandoned in the late 1970s. After the death of Levi Eshkol in March 1969, Golda became Labour Party prime minister, serving until 1974. She was the third woman to head a modern state, having been elected shortly after **Sri Lanka**'s **Sirimavo Bandaranaike** and **India**'s **Indira Gandhi**. She was prime minister when eleven Israeli athletes were killed by the **Black September** organization during the 1972 Munich Olympic Games, following which she ordered Israel's Mossad secret service to assassinate those known to have been involved. Golda was prime minister when Israel was attacked in October 1973, the result of an intelligence failure for which she felt personally responsible. She was subsequently exonerated by the Agranat Commission. She considered the trade and political relations she developed with decolonialized **Africa** to be her greatest political achievement. She is buried alongside other leaders of Israel on Jerusalem's Mount Herzl.

Menderes, Adnan (1899–1961)

After membership in a short-lived opposition party in 1930, Adnan Menderes was elected to the Turkish parliament in 1931. In 1945 he became a founding member of the Democrat Party, which he led to victory in the free and fair general election in **Turkey**, 1950. Under his leadership, Turkey became a close ally to the **United States**, a member of **NATO**, and joined the UN forces in the **Korean War**. Relations with **Greece** became increasingly tense during his term in office over the question of **Cyprus**. One result of these tensions was a government-sponsored pogrom of Greeks and other non-Muslims in Istanbul in 1955. Domestically, aid from the United States, along with easy access to credit, led to the rapid industrialization of agriculture and the creation of a new capitalist class. Rural migration to the cities increased dramatically. Strictures on **Islam** were also relaxed. The increased role for religion, along with a progressively more authoritarian tendency to his governance, led to a *coup d'état* in 1960. Menderes was tried and executed the following year.

Menelik II (1844–1913)

Ethiopian ruler. Born Sahle Miriam, heir to the throne of the autonomous Shoah kingdom, he was proclaimed king in 1865, expanding the region's power and importing European technology. In 1889, after much manoeuvring, he was proclaimed Emperor of **Ethiopia** on the death of Yohannes IV. Menelik signed a treaty of friendship at Ucciali with **Italy**, which the latter interpreted as creating a protectorate over Ethiopia. Menelik decisively defeated an invading Italian Army at Adowa in 1896, gaining European recognition of the country's status as an independent state. As ruler he began Ethiopian modernization, creating a capital in Addis Ababa, constructing roads, a railway and telegraph, schools and hospitals, a national bank and state currency. From 1906 Menelik suffered strokes that diminished his power, which passed to his wife, to a regent Ras Tesemma, and eventually to his grandson, Lij Iyasu, who succeeded him as emperor.

Menem, Carlos Saúl (1935–)

Argentine politician. Elected governor of the province of La Rioja three times and **Argentina**'s president in 1989–99, Menem privatized state-owned industries, encouraged foreign capital and international trade, tied the peso to the US dollar, and supported Mercosur. Although these policies ended hyper-inflation and encouraged economic growth, corruption in privatizing, increased public debt and failed industries led to high unemployment, loss of middle-class purchasing power, currency devaluations and debt default.

mercantilism

– see also **market economy**; **protectionism**.

The economic doctrine, also known as the mercantile system, which estimated the wealth of a country by the amount of bullion it contained and viewed trade as a simple matter of gain or loss in which one country could only benefit at the expense of others. It is usually contrasted with **free trade** which in its theoretical formulations by economic theorists such as **Adam Smith** argued that trade could be mutually beneficial to the participants and would maximize outcomes in terms of output and wealth. Mercantilism has conventionally been seen as the dominant economic system of pre-modern economics. In spite of writings such as Thomas Mun's *England's Treasure by Forraign Trade, or the Ballance of our Forraign Trade Is the Rule of our Treasure* (1664), there is considerable debate whether mercantilism ever existed as a coherent economic theory, though it certainly reflected the practice of many governments who gave priority to accumulating resources for warfare and the amassing of bullion for its own sake and 'beggar my neighbour' policies of trade and warfare. In early modern Europe it was associated with the policies of the French minister Jean Baptiste Colbert

(1619–83), who sought to increase **France**'s manufacturing and restrict imports by protective tariffs. In **Britain** a long series of **Navigation Acts** beginning with a major Act under Cromwell in 1651 sought to restrict all trade between Britain and her colonies and with Britain herself to her own ships or that of the exporting country. These restrictions were only removed in the middle of the nineteenth century with the increasing adoption of free trade. By the nineteenth century European powers and the **United States** were increasingly involved in opening up restricted markets in less developed ports of the world, the **Mughal Empire**, **China** and **Japan**, sometimes involving wars, such as the **Opium War**, to enforce access to protected markets. Mercantilist ideas continued to have some purchase, particularly through the use of tariffs to protect newly industrializing countries such as **Germany** and the United States in the later nineteenth century (*see* **Protectionism**). Mercantilist views also informed the autocratic economic policies adopted by many totalitarian and post-colonial governments who wished to disassociate themselves from laissez-faire capitalism.

Debates on the advantages of mercantilism have persisted since Adam Smith's conceptual attacks. Classical economists focused on individual enterprise and saw clear benefits for free trade. The German Historical School saw mercantilist policies as means for a nation, and a social group within a nation, to achieve political power in a feudal world. Modern trade theory indicates that in a competitive economy the gains of trade are always superior to the benefits of protection, but this is not necessarily the case where strategic imperatives predominate.

Merina kingdom

The Merina kingdom developed in the central highlands of **Madagascar** in the early seventeenth century. Its founder, King Ralambo, led armies that conquered the other kingdoms of the island creating a unified state. During the eighteenth century the kingdom developed a central administration led by a council and became increasingly involved in European trade on the coast. A civil war in the mid eighteenth century disrupted the kingdom before it was reunited by Andrianampoinimerina around 1780. Nineteenth-century Merina abolished the **slave trade** in 1818 and began modernizing, experimenting with textile manufacture among other things, and entered into diplomatic relations with European countries and the **United States**. **France** and **Britain** competed over influence in Madagascar in the nineteenth century, leading to a French invasion in 1883 which took over parts of the island. In 1895 another French invasion captured the capital and integrated the Merina kingdom into their colony of Madagascar.

Merkel, Angela (1954–)

German chancellor from 2 November 2005. Born Hamburg, West Germany, the daughter of a Lutheran pastor in East Germany, she grew up in rural Brandenburg. A member of the Freie Deutsche Jugend (FDJ) (Free German Youth), she is a fluent Russian speaker, studied physics at the University of Leipzig, 1973–8, and worked and studied at the Central Institute for Physical Chemistry of the Academy of Sciences, Berlin-Adlershof, in 1978–90. She is a doctor in quantum chemistry. She joined 'Democratic Awakening', 1989, and became deputy spokesperson in the April 1990 East German coalition government under Lothar de Maizière. Elected for the constituency of Stralsund-Nordvorpommern-Rügen in the first Bundestag elections for unified **Germany**, 1990, she held the seat for the CDU in all subsequent elections. In September 1991 she succeeded de Maizière as deputy chair of the federal CDU.

Minister for women and youth (17 January 1991–16 November 1994) and then for the environment, nature conservation and reactor safety (17 November 1994–26 September 1998) she served in the cabinets of Chancellor Kohl. Chair of the CDU, March 2000, she was passed over as chancellor candidate for the German federal elections of September 2002 in favour of Edmund Stoiber, prime minister of Bavaria, who narrowly lost. Elected chancellor in November 2005, she led a 'grand coalition' with the Social Democratic Party (SPD), which had more cabinet seats than her own CDU. Re-elected 2009, leading a coalition with the liberal FDP, and again in 2013, leading a renewed 'grand coalition' with the SPD, she is the first woman and the first former East German to become German chancellor – a particularly noteworthy achievement in view of the traditional male dominance of the German political establishment. A loyal successor of Kohl and ultimately Adenauer in their insistence on the integration of Germany in **Europe**, as the EU's most powerful leader, she has insisted on German concepts of solid finance within it. Controversially, in 2015 she offered an 'open door' to refugees fleeing the **Syrian Civil War** and other migrants, precipitating an increased flow of over a million people into Europe, principally to Germany, **Austria** and **Sweden**. Widely criticized, it severely dented her

hitherto almost invulnerable position in German politics and fuelled populist opposition to immigration throughout Europe, especially in countries on the migration routes through the **Balkans**.

Mesopotamia campaign

– *see also* **World War I**.

In an effort to protect its holdings and interests in **Asia** and to weaken the **Ottoman Empire** that was allied with the Central Powers, the British attacked the empire from various fronts in south-west Asia. On 6 November 1914 the Mesopotamian Expeditionary Force landed at Fao and completed the first stage of the war against the Ottomans ten days later, after they had defeated the Turks and occupied Basra. This secured the access routes to the Abadan oilfields in south-western **Iran**, which were owned by the **Anglo-Iranian Oil Company**, and guaranteed the safe passage of all ships in the Persian Gulf. Initially the plan was confine themselves to the head of the Gulf. The relatively small force size and limited objective indicate that it was originally not the British objective to conquer all of Mesopotamia. But emboldened by the lacklustre Ottoman defence of Basra, the British India Office, Foreign Office and War Office gave conflicting advice to their field commander and put together ambitious plans to occupy all of Mesopotamia.

Although the British had taken Basra without much of a fight, their conquest of Mesopotamia would prove to be anything but easy. The British forces continued upriver in a quest to conquer Baghdad. At a loop in the Tigris River by the city of Kut al-Amara, the British, under the command of Major General Charles Townshend, found themselves surrounded by the Ottoman forces under the leadership of the German Baron von der Goltz. For the next 140 days Ottoman troops besieged the British Army, until the British, depleted of resources and on the brink of starvation, unconditionally surrendered on 29 April 1916, resulting in an estimated 23,000 lives lost in one of the biggest defeats outside Europe. After this significant setback, the British Army recalibrated and with a new commander at the helm, Lieutenant General Sir Frederick Maude, renewed their efforts to conquer Baghdad. After four months of fighting, the British captured it on 11 March 1917. General Maude issued a famous proclamation that the British Army were not there as occupiers but as 'liberators'. The victory in Baghdad rectified the humiliation at Kut. Yet the fighting continued and the British proceed northwards along the Tigris. Almost four years after they had first entered the country, the British finally occupied Kirkuk and effectively destroyed the Ottoman Sixth Army. At war's end, in November 1918, the British troops had reached just south of Mosul. The city was taken a few days after the signing of the Armistice of Mudros, which was supposed to guarantee an end to all hostilities between the Ottomans and the Allies. During the Mesopotamia campaign the British established civil administrations in the pacified area, which was largely based on the Indian administrative model but also included elements of indirect control. The British military and political presence in **Iraq** eventually led the **League of Nations** to award Iraq as a British **mandate** in 1921.

mestizo

A person of mixed European and indigenous ancestry. This social category first emerged as an unintended and disreputable by-product of Spanish colonization in the Americas. Springing largely from informal unions between Spanish men and Indian women, *mestizos* belong fully to neither group; they appeared anomalous, illegitimate and rootless, a threat to colonial stability. However, the boundaries and meaning of the word proved highly fluid. As their numbers grew they became an integral element of the Hispanic economy, ranked well above Indians and Africans in the racial hierarchy; indeed, many 'passed' as Spaniards. After independence, though scientific racism continued to cast grave doubts on the moral qualities of such 'hybrids', *mestizos* moved further into the social mainstream, and came to be favourably contrasted with the less assimilated indigenous populations. Especially in **Mexico**, the *mestizo* emerged as a symbol of nationalism, representing the fusion of diverse races into a single, unified people.

Methodism

A highly successful iteration of Protestantism that emerged in eighteenth-century England but which spread across the world. In England, the foundation of the faith was associated with the mission of **John Wesley (1703–91)** to criminal, working-class and lower middle-class communities, and his emphasis on personal salvation, intense faith and self-discipline. Wesley himself was an Anglican, but the faith he founded (which began as a form of Anglican renewal) became associated with synods, councils and committees, and lay-preaching, rather than bishops, priests or orthodoxy. It broke from conformity with Anglicanism

and by the late eighteenth century could claim to be a church in its own right, though it suffered numerous schisms and reunions. It was and is associated with missionary work, and has many adherents in **Africa**, **Asia** and the Americas. Methodism is particularly associated with charitable work, and it can also lay claim to a diverse hymnody deriving from the original songs of Wesley.

Metternich, Klemens von (1773–1859)

Austrian foreign minister, 1809–48, styled 'Prince' from 1813. Metternich was a German-born subject of the Habsburg Empire, remembered both as a reactionary and as a brilliant diplomat concerned with the maintenance of a balance of power in **Europe**. He blended the traditional Austrian policy of felicitous marriages with a new system of international congresses to create the lasting image of statesmanship as being the use of diplomacy to avoid war. His tenure coincided with the reawakening of Hungarian nationalism, the beginnings of Ottoman collapse, and the question of how to best contain and divert the power of **France**. He was exiled in the **Revolution of 1848** to England, before returning without great impact to **Austria** in 1851.

Mexican–American War (1846–1848)

The Mexican–American War marked the climax of American territorial expansion in the first half of the nineteenth century. The origins of the war principally lay in **Texas**, a territory claimed by both nations. Tensions along the disputed southern border of Texas (in the land south of the Nueces River and north of the Rio Grande) were exacerbated by the deployment of American troops to this sensitive region, eventually leading to hostilities in April 1846. The war was a decisive victory for the **United States**. In the **Treaty of Guadalupe-Hidalgo** (signed in February 1848), **Mexico** ceded nearly half of its territory (500,000 square miles) to the United States in exchange for $15 million and the US assumption of various claims against the Mexican government. From this territory would emerge the future states of California, New Mexico, Arizona, Utah and Nevada, as well as portions of Wyoming and Colorado. Though the war consolidated the continental empire of the United States, the question of whether or not to allow slavery in these new territories exacerbated sectional tensions and contributed to the coming Civil War.

Mexican Revolution

A major political and social revolution, 1910–46, begun by **Francisco Madero**, followed by

Venustiano Carranza, **Emiliano Zapata**, **Pancho Villa**
and **Alvaro Obregón**. Violence led to the death of
2 million people by 1920 and continued until
1940. The revolutionaries generally agreed on
the distribution of *ejido* lands, protection of workers, restrictions on the Catholic Church (including
nationalizing all properties), regulation of foreign
investors, promotion of public health and national
education, and incorporation of indigenous peoples into national life. These became fundamental
laws in the 1917 constitution, along with no re-
election of the president. Implementation of
the laws proved difficult and presidents chose
favourite campaigns: Obregón, land and labour
(1920–4); Plutarco Calles, the church and education (1924–8); and **Lázaro Cárdenas** (1934–40),
foreigners with the expropriation of their oil
properties in 1938. The last presidency of a revolutionary veteran ended in 1946, followed by
a younger, civilian generation without revolutionary zeal.

Mexico

– see also **Mexican Revolution**.
The former land of the Aztecs and the Mayas,
Mexico was the heart of the **Spanish Empire** until
1821 when it achieved independence. The name
comes from the word used by the Aztecs
themselves – *Mexica*. Today, smaller by half than
the nation created in 1821 because of the loss of
extensive northern territories, including **Texas**,
Arizona, New Mexico and California, to the
United States following the **Texas War of
Independence** and the **Mexican–American War**
(1846–8), its political history since independence
has been marked by foreign interventions: by the
French in 1838, the United States in 1846–8, the
French in 1861–7, and the United States in 1914
and 1916. Internally, there were numerous coups
from 1821 to 1854, revolts in 1854, 1872, 1876 and
1923; civil wars in 1858–61, 1923–6 and 1933.
There has been a pattern of authoritarian leaders
through the nineteenth and twentieth centuries.
The **Mexican Revolution** of 1911–17 led to a social
transformation with major land redistribution,
the curbing of the power of the Catholic Church,
and the eventual nationalization of the oil industry
in 1938. These developments were presided
over by the Institutional Revolutionary Party
(PRI) founded in 1929 and renamed the Mexican
Revolutionary Party (PRM) in 1938, incorporating
major interest groups under a one-party structure.
Criticized as increasingly institutionalized and corrupt, it controlled politics from 1946 to 2000, when
Vicente Fox (1942–) was democratically elected.

Fox was the first president who did not come from
the PRI. Although his tax reform and social agendas
were largely unproductive, he supported closer
relations with the United States and stabilized the
economy. His successor, Felipe Caldrón (1962–),
elected in 2006, stepped up campaigns against
drug-trafficking and drug cartels, which accounted
for thousands of deaths each year. Rapid economic
growth based on oil and low-cost manufacturing
for the United States market slowed in the aftermath of the **Great Recession**.

mfecane

Nguni term meaning 'the crushing of people' or
'annihiliation' used to describe a period of war,
devastation and displacement affecting southern
Africa in the early nineteenth century, arising
from a combination of aggressive **Zulu** expansionism under the rule of Shaka Zulu (*c.* 1787–1828) –
although the extent of this has been disputed – and
drought and soil depletion provoking conflict over
land and resources. By the mid 1820s an estimated
2 million people had been displaced as far as modern-day **Mozambique**, **Tanzania**, **Malawi** and
Zambia in the search for new land suitable for
cultivation and raising cattle. A further million
may have been killed, though this has been questioned. Depopulation made room for European
expansion into the Cape Colony in a period
described by **Boer** and English settlers as 'the wars
of calamity'. A series of new kingdoms arose from
migration, including the Ndebele, the Gaza, the
Sotho and the Swazi.

Miami Summit

– see also **NAFTA**.
The December 1994 meeting in Miami, Florida,
was the first of a series of summits held by the
leaders of the countries of North, Central and
South America. All countries of the Americas
were invited except for **Cuba**. The summit agreed
to work towards a Free Trade Area of the
Americas and to a series of principles in which
members affirmed their support for democratic
government. **NAFTA** (the North American Free
Trade Association) came into operation on
1 January 1994 and the Miami Summit sought
to further its work of extending free trade in
goods and services.

Michoacán

A central western Mexican state where the
Tarascans (Purépecha), a major rival of the Aztec
Empire, resided. Following a brutal Spanish
invasion, Bishop Vasco de Quiroga established

Christianity and promoted artisan crafts in new Michoacán communities comprised of previously dispersed inhabitants. The region was home to independence heroes **Miguel Hidalgo** and José María Morelos (1765–1815) (memorialized in Morelia, name of the state's capital) and the great twentieth-century president **Lázaro Cárdenas**.

Middle East

The Middle East is a commonly used term for the highly diverse countries between **India** and **Libya**, mostly former territories of the **Ottoman Empire**. The area has a Muslim majority but also includes Jewish-majority **Israel** and significant Christian minorities. It has many Arab majority countries but includes non-Arab countries such as **Iran** and **Turkey**. The growing usage of this term to refer to about twenty countries in scholarship and journalism after **World War II** illustrates the ambiguities of regional categories during the **Cold War**. Although there are many inconsistencies in the usage of the term, and multiple attempts to overcome it, it is still commonly used both in scholarly and non-scholarly writings.

American naval strategist **Alfred Thayer Mahan** was one of the first major figures to use the term 'Middle East' and offer its map to designate the area between Arabia and India. Mahan's map of the Middle East includes the Indian Ocean navigation zone connecting South Asia to Arabia, the **Suez Canal** and **Egypt**. His strategic vision of a region called the Middle East was mainly about the security of the **British Empire**'s vital sea routes in relation to its rivalry with the Ottoman and the Russian Empires. Mahan's usage of the term was popularized by British imperial strategists such as Valentine Chirol (1852–1929), yet, until the end of **World War II**, Near East and Far East were more frequently used to divide Muslim and non-Muslim areas of **Asia** after the fragmentation of post-Ottoman Arab populations. Only with the emergence of a Hindu nationalist-led Indian independence in 1948, and Indonesian independence, which separated the majority of the world's Muslims from the Arab lands of Asia, did the 'Middle East' begin to be used more commonly by British and US scholars and politicians. The popularization of the term also implied deep fragmentation in the pan-Islamic idea of the 'Muslim World' in the age of decolonization. What consolidated the usage was its adoption in the area studies of American universities during the Cold War, and its gradual appropriation by journalists and politicians during the 1960s. There are no intergovernmental organizations, such as the Arab League or Organization of Islamic Conference, that bring together all the countries in the Middle East in a world forum. However, many international aid agencies, multinational corporations and diplomatic branches use an area designation 'Middle East' to indicate a regional operation and interest, with the borders defined according to that purpose.

Boundaries of the Middle East have never been settled in either academic or non-academic usage of the term, and can extend from all of North Africa to **Pakistan** and from Caucasia to **Sudan**. In fact, annual meetings of the Middle Eastern Studies Association of North America host papers and panels that cover **Morocco** and **Algeria** as well as **Afghanistan**, **Armenia**, and also cover issues related to Muslims in the **Balkans**. In American and European colleges, the Middle East is one of the most common area designations for courses on world politics and history, with hundreds of textbooks and general audience books using the term in their titles. Despite discontent about its Eurocentrism and contradictions, as well as unsettled borders of this region, it has survived the debates on area studies and globalization in the aftermath of the Cold War. Nowadays, scholars and journalists use it with the awareness of its historicity and ambivalence, preferring it over the essentialism of civilizational categories such as the 'Islamic world' and focusing on the networks linking the region to other parts of the world.

The Middle East became an area of incomplete decolonization, a series of wars around the Palestinian question, Cold War conflicts and failed modernization projects. Added to the frequent devastating wars and military conflicts involving foreign military interventions and the confrontation between forces of political **Islam** and secular political projects, pro-democracy demands against authoritarian dictatorships also mark the region's modern history. Currently, many of the major countries of the region such as Iran, **Iraq**, **Syria**, **Egypt**, Libya and Algeria are either experiencing political struggles to establish a stable democratic order, or are embroiled in internal civil wars. Concurrent to a global image of the region as politically turbulent and undemocratic, is an image of growing oil wealth (**Saudi Arabia** and other Gulf countries) that has brought about developed Gulf cities such as **Qatar**, **Dubai**, **Abu Dhabi** and **Kuwait**.

Midhat Pasha (1822–1883)

One of the leading proponents of reform in the late **Ottoman Empire**, Midhat Pasha served in a dizzying array of administrative posts: as governor of the Danube province (1864–8), governor of Baghdad (1869–72), grand vizier (1872), minister of justice (1873–5), writer of the constitution (1876), grand vizier (1876–7) and governor of **Syria** (1878–81). Invariably, his attempts at progressive reform put him at odds with powerful interests. His second tenure as grand vizier ended only three months after it began. Sultan **Abdul Hamid** did not share his commitment to constitutional government. Politically, Midhat Pasha championed liberal ideas fashioned into an inclusive ideology of Ottomanism. After his tenure as governor of Syria, Midhat's political opponents accused him of organizing the assassination of Sultan **Abdülaziz**. Subsequently imprisoned in the Hijaz, Midhat was murdered while in his cell.

Midway, Battle of

A **World War II** naval battle (3–6 June 1942) over the Midway Atoll, in which the **United States** brought about **Japan**'s first setback in the Pacific. Admiral **Yamamoto**'s complex plan to destroy US naval power by capturing Midway Atoll and luring the US fleet to destruction failed when US cryptographers broke his coded battle plan. The result was a devastating ambush by the heavily outnumbered US Pacific fleet that sank four Japanese aircraft carriers. With his air power destroyed, Yamamoto withdrew.

migration

Alongside the themes of trade and empire, migration is a key concept in representing and accounting for cross-cultural interaction and encounter in the global past. Within the context of world history, migration is here defined as a permanent move across regional or national borders. It has always been an important part of human activity where mainly young adults have moved voluntarily or involuntarily, being pushed and/or pulled, to locations across cultural and social boundaries. In movement, migrants diffused knowledge and cultural practices, as well as contributed to regional and spatial shifts in economic production and consumption, and to changes in regional and global state power. In the early modern and modern periods of global history, these general processes and consequences of migration were relatively unchanged. However, what was distinctive about migration in these periods was the unprecedented demographic scale of human migration as well as the new means by which communication and transportation technologies, the globalization of consumption and production, and state policies

and regulations informed the size and pattern of human migration. In this sense, migration is not easily disentangled from other identified themes of global interaction and integration such as trade, empire and colonization.

The historiography of migration studies has generally mirrored the major shifts and trajectories within the historical profession. Until the late twentieth century, scholars of historical migration generally focused upon the 'macro setting' of large-scale migrations within the context of demographic shifts, economic patterns, push-and-pull motivational factors, and imperial and government policies. More recently, they have situated their research increasingly in the 'micro', and cultural and social, settings of migration with greater focus upon recovering the migrants' experience and sense of identity as well as personal decision making and inspiration. Both approaches remain central to the scholarship of migration and are associated with substantive disciplinary concepts such as networks and networking, and diaspora and diasporic communities. The term *diaspora*, which in ancient Greek meant 'sowed' or 'dispersed widely', has been an important concept in the historical study of migration. While the concept has assumed a variety of disciplinary meanings and contexts, within world history a diaspora is associated with those who have emigrated (freely or by force) from an original homeland to multiple distant locations while preserving an ancestral memory and identity shared with other members of the diasporic community and distinct from that of the host country. In world history, diasporic communities have served important roles in the long-distance transmission of knowledge, technology and cultural practice. They have also developed and sustained multiculturalism, hybrid cultural forms, transnational identities and in some cases cosmopolitanism – counter to nationalism and national identity formation associated with nation-building in the modern world.

early modern migration

When examined on a world historical scale, the early modern period takes on new significance as the intensity of trans-regional interaction and integration in Afro-Eurasia before 1500 became truly global by 1800. Migration, particularly in maritime basins, played a critical role in this process, and the scholarship addressing it is rich. The spread of advanced maritime technologies, and the transmission of knowledge pertaining to oceanic currents, established encounters and connections between peoples who had never before been in contact.

The expansion and intensification of long-distance maritime trade with the emergence of competitive maritime states and empires connected most of the world through largely seaborne networks by the end of the eighteenth century. These early modern global processes were both cause and consequence of significant shifts in the pattern and expanding scale of human migration. The early modern period was also distinctive in that the majority of large-scale migration was coerced, while voluntary human movement characterized the preceding and subsequent centuries.

As in the post-classical period, trade diaspora communities continued to develop and play significant roles in early modern long-distance trade and cross-cultural exchange. Settlements of resident foreign merchants learned local languages and customs, and familiarized themselves with local political practice to cultivate secure business relationships with host community merchants as well as with other settled foreign traders. Through such commercial relationships members of these trade diasporas also served as cultural mediators and promoters of not only commercial exchanges but cross-cultural exchanges as well. For example, Marwaris from Rajasthan in **India** established trading communities throughout the caravan routes of central Asia and established significant diasporic communities in **Russia**, **Afghanistan** and **Iran** where as many as 10,000 resided in the Safavid capital of Isfahan. Avoiding persecution and seeking commercial opportunity, Sephardic Jews left the Iberian peninsula and established trading communities in Amsterdam, Livorno (**Italy**) and London, as well as in the **Ottoman Empire** and in the port cities in southern India, where they served as important intermediaries between Christian and Muslim traders. Before being driven out by the persecution of colonial authorities in the seventeenth century, Sephardic Jews also established trade diaspora communities in the Americas. Another example was the Armenians who had been forcibly resettled from the Ottoman borderlands by Safavid Emperor Shah Abbas I in the early sixteenth century to New Julfa (a suburb of the capital Isfahan). Over two centuries, Julfan Armenians established an extensive and important trading network of diasporic communities throughout much of Europe, the Ottoman Empire and India, and extending as far as Manila on the Pacific Rim. Other significant early modern trade diasporas would include Bugis, Chinese, Gujarati and Portuguese migrants who established resident settlements and trade networks in the Indian Ocean and South China Sea.

In the early modern world, for the first time in human history, large-scale voluntary migrations took place by sea that were associated with the formation of western European maritime empires and settler colonies. Responding to demographic pressure and economic dislocation, as well as to the allure of wealth within colonial economies, roughly 700,000 Spaniards had emigrated to colonies in the Americas and the **Philippines** by the late eighteenth century. Similarly, approximately 500,000 Portuguese emigrated to the settler colony of Brazil or to trading-post colonies in **Africa** and **Asia**. Over the same time period, approximately 750,000 voluntary migrants travelled to the British Atlantic colonies in the Caribbean and North America. While the movement of persecuted religious groups such as Puritans and **Quakers** was notable, over three-quarters of the migrants settled in British America as indentured servants who signed contracts to offset the high cost of transportation that bound them to work on the land of others for a set number of years before they themselves became free farmers or wage labourers.

Throughout the late seventeenth century, given rapid population growth and declining economic opportunity at home, the majority of these indentured migrants were English peasants, cottage workers or urban labourers. Beginning in the late seventeenth century, English demographic pressure declined – partially as a consequence of previous colonial emigration. As English living conditions improved, so the majority of free migrants to the British Atlantic colonies were German, Irish and Scottish. Single young men dominated free migration to colonial settlements – especially amongst the earlier generations of settlers. Many married or cohabited with women from Amerindian communities and consequently populations of mixed race and cultural heritage grew, and racially hierarchical social structures developed in the colonies of the Americas. At the same time, the cohorts of biological descendants of European settlers grew generationally and established significant creole populations throughout the Americas. Creoles would play significant leadership roles in colonial governments and nationalist movements, wars and revolutions in both North and South America. Voluntary migration of the European poor was also an important component of the early development of plantation agriculture and extractive economic activities in colonial settings. The social mobility and economic advance of the descendants of migrants – many of whom were creole – also contributed to the importance of the American colonies by the late eighteenth century as a market for metropolitan manufacturers and merchants.

Of course the largest migration of the early modern period was not voluntary. The **Atlantic slave trade** was the biggest movement of people based on race and status in human history. From the early Portuguese movement of African slaves to sugar plantations on Atlantic islands such as Madeira in the late fifteenth century, through to the final abolition of slavery in **Brazil** and **Cuba** in the later nineteenth century, 12.5 million Africans were forcibly sent to the Americas, of which 10 million survived the passage. The numbers of Africans who died in the march to coastal slave-trading settlements is unknown. Driven in particular by the production of sugar in Brazil and the West Indies, the transatlantic slave trade peaked in volume in the last decades of the eighteenth century. Demonstrating the impact of sugar production, roughly 40 per cent of African slaves were sent to the West Indies and over 35 per cent to Brazil, while roughly 20 per cent were sold to mining and plantation owners in mainland Spanish America. Less than 5 per cent of the volume of the transatlantic African slave trade was associated with the plantation economies of mainland North America. African agency was critical in determining who entered the slave trade and how it was conducted. During the early modern period the African points of departure varied widely over time along the sub-Saharan Atlantic rim of Africa, and the ebb and flow was determined more by shifts in the location of war and the power of African polities than by the agency of European trading interests. The Portuguese were the dominant transatlantic slave traders in the sixteenth century, followed by the Dutch in the seventeenth century, and the British in the eighteenth.

Like voluntary Atlantic migrants, over two-thirds of Africans brought to the Americas were young men. In the Atlantic system of chattel slavery, plantation owners and mining operators valued physical strength while female slaves were more highly regarded in domestic systems of slavery that predominated in Africa. Given brutal working conditions on sugar plantations in particular, African rates of morbidity and mortality in the Americas were horrifically high. The relative absence of women meant that population replacement rates were almost entirely determined by continued forced migration. In the tobacco-producing plantations of the Chesapeake, African American populations became predominant in the early eighteenth century, but this was not the case for slave communities in the rest of the Americas

until after the end of the eighteenth century. In sub-Saharan Africa, forced emigration with a gender differential that was disproportionally male meant that African populations by the late eighteenth century were in decline while virtually all other parts of the world experienced significant demographic expansion.

Prior to the middle of the nineteenth century, forced African migrants far outnumbered voluntary European migrants in the Atlantic world. African migrants shaped the colonial societies of the Americas not simply in economic terms, but also in the formation of hybrid cultural practices that included new forms of religious observance and ritual, music and the arts, cuisine and the development of creolized language. Moreover, given the diversity of cultural groups brought from Africa, these hybrid forms were often developed within and across slave communities as well as with and between European and Amerindian populations. In early modern Brazil the most pronounced cultural syncretism was between different African cultures – 'African' culture was a product of American experience and a consequence of forced migration. Beginning in the 1970s, the recognition of African historical agency in the Atlantic world lead scholars to extend the concept of diaspora from a focus upon migrants involved in trade and colonization to labour diasporas where the term is often associated with collective trauma. This is most notable in the early modern period, where, inspired by Paul Gilroy's *The Black Atlantic* (1993), scholars increasingly conceptualize the African slave trade in diasporic terms.

Forced migration extended beyond the Atlantic world in the early modern period. The trans-Saharan and Indian Ocean African slave trades were still considerable throughout the early modern period, and the movement of Atlantic African slaves did not outnumber the forced migration of sub-Saharan Africans to North Africa and the Indian Ocean Rim until the seventeenth century. In the late eighteenth century demand for African slaves was increasing in the Muslim Mediterranean and the Indian Ocean Rim. Young women were sold as domestics and male slaves were purchased for construction, mining and agriculture in the Ottoman Empire. Beginning with the Portuguese in the sixteenth century, European traders also entered the Indian Ocean slave trade and supplied African slaves to markets in West and South Asia as well as to pepper plantations established in **Indonesia** by the Dutch in the seventeenth century, and to sugar plantations such as those established by the French in Mauritius in the eighteenth century.

Penal transportation was another means of forced migration in the early modern period. In North America, the British established a penal colony in Georgia in the early eighteenth century and later in Tasmania and **Australia** in the nineteenth century. The British **East India Company** began transporting convicts to a penal colony in the Andaman Islands in the late eighteenth century. Many early modern land-based empires also engaged in state-supported forced migration. Both the Ottoman and Safavid Empires forcefully moved ethnic groups such as the Armenians and Georgians to distant locations for purposes of security or frontier expansion. Conversely, the Russian and Ming Empires encouraged migrations of Slavs and Han Chinese to distant frontiers through enticements of land and economic opportunity.

modern migration

The involuntary migration of African slaves to the Americas and the Indian Ocean Rim continued into the nineteenth century. However, the transatlantic slave trade gradually declined after the 1807 abolition of the slave trade by the British and US governments until the 1850s when numbers began to decline rapidly with the spread of the abolition of slavery in **Columbia** (1851), the **USA** (1865), Cuba (1886) and finally Brazil (1888). However, over the same period the forced migration of East Africans to Muslim North Africa and West Asia, and to plantations in the Indian Ocean, continued to increase to over 50,000 per year by the mid nineteenth century. The long-distance forced internal migration of slaves was also a notable feature of this period as, for example, a million slaves were moved from the upper south of the United States to the cotton frontier in the south and west. Similar numbers moved from sugar- to coffee-producing regions in Brazil.

The nineteenth century witnessed a major shift in the character and pattern of mass migration. There was a significant expansion in free migration as the overall volume of the maritime slave trade declined. Also distinctive to the modern period were the relatively high numbers of migrants who eventually returned to their place of origin. In some cases, the numbers who returned were as high as 30 per cent. However, historians have much better data about the numbers of outbound migrants; figures for net migration are much more difficult to construct. The rapid expansion of free outbound migration was a consequence of a massive increase

in labour demand that was associated with the origins and spatial spread of industrialization in both the first and second Industrial Revolutions in western Europe and North America, as well as with population growth and rural labour surplus and dislocation in the societies of migrant origin. New communication technologies, such as the telegraph, steam-powered printing and eventually the telephone, all spread knowledge of opportunities abroad, and facilitated aggressive recruiting of labour from recipient societies. Steam-powered and steel-hulled shipping by the 1870s quickened and cheapened maritime migration, as did **canals** such as the **Suez** (1869) and **Panama** (1914). Railways moved immigrants transcontinentally across the United States (1869), **Canada** (1885), Siberia (1905) and Australia (1917). Also by the 1870s, railways and refrigerated cargo holds in ships created a global economy of food production that attracted European – and smaller numbers of Asian – migrants to the western United States, Australia and **New Zealand**, as well as to Argentina and Brazil, hoping for opportunities in farming and livestock production. The construction of railways and new transport facilities and conveyances also involved a significant migration of workers. For example, Irish workers built railways in **Britain**, the eastern United States and **South Africa**; Chinese workers constructed railways in the western United States, while Indians built those in East Africa, and Russian workers were used in eastern Siberia. Extractive activities such as coal and copper mining, and later petroleum drilling, also stimulated mass migrations of free migrants. Gold and silver strikes attracted migrants to California (1848), Australia (1851), Alaska (1880), South Africa (1886) and the Klondike (1896) in Canada.

Approximately 55 million voluntary European migrants crossed the Atlantic between the 1840s and **World War II**, roughly 35 million of which went to the United States. An additional 2 million Chinese, Japanese and Indians also crossed the Pacific to the Americas during this period with numbers peaking prior to the passage of the Chinese Exclusion Act in the United States in 1882. Initially, Germans and Irish in the wake of the Potato Famine (1846–8) made up the majority of Atlantic immigrants, but over time those from the Mediterranean and eastern Europe surpassed their numbers. In the same period, another 10 million Europeans migrated to other parts of the Americas – in particular to Canada, **Argentina** and Brazil; and to a lesser extent to **Chile**, Cuba and **Mexico**. By the later nineteenth century, in reverse of the early modern period, Atlantic migration had become characteristically 'white'. By the late nineteenth century, the majority of inhabitants in rapidly growing American cities were foreign born.

Imperial networks were important conduits for migration in the nineteenth and first half of the twentieth centuries. Free Irish and British migrants found administrative and military employment in India and other colonies throughout the **British Empire**. Metropolitan overseas investment within and without the British Empire stimulated economic activity that drew migrants from the British Isles and elsewhere. Through the British Empire and overseas capital investment, and migration associated with it, many British cultural practices became global, including for example the spread and use of the English language, and participation in the sport of football that had become a global game by the early twentieth century.

With the expansion of free mass migration of Europeans and the spread of slave emancipation, there was growing demand for other forms of cheap labour in the nineteenth century – the vast majority of which was supplied from India and **China**. Approximately 29 million Indians emigrated in the late nineteenth and early twentieth centuries. Most Indian migrants stayed within the confines of the British Empire, and more than half emigrated to **Burma** or **Malaysia**. Eight million Indians migrated to work mainly in the tea fields of Ceylon (**Sri Lanka**). Perhaps an additional million migrated to sugar-producing colonies such as **Trinidad and Tobago** in the Caribbean, Fiji in the Pacific and Mauritius in the Indian Ocean. About 10 per cent of Indian migrants were contracted indentured workers who were only partially free. However, Indian migrants who were not under indenture were often bound to assistance from colonial authorities or to other forms of debt obligation. The coercion and deception associated with indentures came under increasing public scrutiny and it was finally abolished in 1920. Notably, over 2 million Indians emigrated not as labourers but as merchants, shopkeepers, clerks or professionals to colonies such as **Kenya** and South Africa.

China was another major source of migrating labour in the late nineteenth and twentieth centuries. Mainly from the southern provinces of Guangdong and Fujian, around 18 million Chinese emigrated to South East Asia. Another million Chinese moved to islands such as Sumatra, the Philippines and Hawaii in the Indian and Pacific

Oceans. In total, less than 750,000 signed indentures with European colonial employers as most migrated under various forms of debt obligation and contract with Chinese employees. When combined with Indian emigration, migration to South East Asia and the islands in the Indian and Pacific Oceans was the second largest stream of mass migration (after European Atlantic migration) during the period. Indian and Chinese migrants were 'pushed' by overpopulation and severe El-Niño-inspired famines in the late nineteenth century, as well as by dislocation in China brought about by the Taiping and Boxer Rebellions. The mass migration of Indian and Chinese labour was 'pulled' by employment on island sugar plantations, and by expanding rice, palm oil and rubber production in South East Asia for global markets.

The third largest stream of mass migration in the period was for the most part land-based and involved the movement of approximately 30 million Chinese to **Manchuria** and Siberia. An additional 13 million Russians moved to Siberia and central Asia during the same period. In the 1860s Qing liberalization of movement regulations, in combination with the Russian abolition of serfdom, allowed labour to move to new agricultural, livestock and mining frontiers. In attempting to control these frontiers, both states encouraged settlement with homesteading incentives, and railway development further promoted migration.

The late nineteenth century witnessed a new role for the state in global migration. Initially some states began to implement restrictions on Asian immigration. Increasingly the creation and control of borders (and movements across them) became an important attribute of modern state sovereignty. By the early twentieth century, forced migration had been legally abolished. Free migration was determined increasingly by state regulation of entry and passport monitoring and control. Also as a harbinger of things to come, state violence and the expanding scale of war also became an important source of expanding numbers of refugee migrants. The Russian pogroms instigated the migration of almost 2 million Jews (mainly to the United States). The war and violence associated with the dissolution of the Ottoman Empire led to the migration of 5 million refugees, including a widely dispersed migration of 1 million Armenians expelled and fleeing genocide. The **Russian Revolution** and ensuing civil war led to the migration of 3 million people from the **Soviet Union**. World War II and its immediate aftermath would create a migration of refugees of unprecedented proportions.

contemporary migration

The growth of global migration slowed in the 1920s with the expansion of immigration restrictions by western nations, but it continued to expand as a consequence of forced and coerced migration in Siberia and Manchuria by Japan and the Soviet Union. The growth in global migration continued to outpace total population growth, and by the 1920s, 2 per cent of the world's population was foreign born – an unprecedented figure at that time. However, beginning in the 1930s, and continuing through the 1950s, migration declined as a consequence of the global impact of the **Great Depression**, World War II and the **Cold War**. Beginning in the 1960s, there was a resurgence of migration that has continued to expand unabated to the present. In 2000 close to 3 per cent of the world's population was foreign born. It would seem that the level of contemporary migration today is comparative with that of the early twentieth century.

The revival of migration in the second half of the twentieth century has multiple origins. With decolonization in the 1950s and 1960s, approximately 8 million white creoles returned to European colonizing states. Responding to post-war labour shortages, many colonial and postcolonial migrants took advantage of shared language and cultural practices to seek employment in western Europe. In some places, the process of decolonization was associated with violence and refugee migration. The partitioning of India and Pakistan in 1947 initiated a migration of up to 14 million displaced Hindus, Muslims and Sikhs – the largest mass migration in human history relative to time. Postcolonial nations faced immense economic challenges and the income gap between the developed and the developing world doubled in the late twentieth century. Highly differentiated economic development has drawn between 2 and 3 million migrants a year from the developing world to that of the developed in the late twentieth century. Movement across national boundaries was facilitated in some cases by the liberalization of immigration restrictions as demonstrated in the United States Immigration Act of 1965 and also by the creation of economic unions such as the **European Union**. The end of the Cold War facilitated the movement between East and West as well as initiating an emigration of Russians from former Soviet central Asian republics. The Cold War also initiated more open policies concerning the movement and status of political refugees. Currently about 500,000 applications for asylum are filed

each year. Since the 1980s, economic liberalization cheapened the cost of air travel, and the revolution in information and communication technologies has made it easier for potential migrants to learn about opportunities (real or imagined) in host societies.

Contemporary migration is marked by a number of distinctive shifts in pattern and trajectory. For the first time, global migration was oriented upon a north–south axis as opposed to east–west axis. By 2000 approximately 10 per cent of the population in developed nations of the northern hemisphere were – or were descended from – migrants from the developing world since 1945. Mexico became the largest single source of emigrants in the late twentieth century, most of whom went to the United States. The Caribbean and South East Asia, previously associated with immigration, are today regions of extensive emigration. Emigration from Africa ended in the later nineteenth century, but was very much revived in the later twentieth century. Temporary global mobility is clearly at an unprecedented level. However, given the relative ease of contemporary long-distance travel, it is more difficult to discern the level of permanent, even long-term, residence and settlement. Moreover, the increased motivation of the state to control and regulate migration has ensured that many long-distance migrants are 'illegal' and uncounted. Our data on contemporary trends is thus not very robust.

militias, American colonial

During the colonial period all able-bodied free men were expected to serve in local militia units committed to defending their communities in the event of attack. When the resistance movement to **Britain** developed during the 1760s, local militias helped to organize resistance and enforce boycotts. When the **American War of Independence** broke out – as the result of fighting between local militia in Massachusetts and the British Army – rebel militias served as crucial auxiliaries to the Continental Army. Pro-British **Loyalists** also organized militia to augment the British war effort.

Mill, John Stuart (1806–1873)

A key figure in the development of the European liberal tradition. *On Liberty* (1859) is an influential statement of the importance of freedom for individual and political well-being, presenting key arguments for freedom of speech. In *Utilitarianism* (1863), Mill distinguished between higher and lower pleasures, in opposition to **Bentham**'s view that all pleasures are of equal value. Mill was also a forceful advocate of female suffrage, most notably in his *The Subjugation of Women* (1869).

millennialism

A religious belief underpinning movements, such as the **Taiping Rebellion** and the characteristically anti-imperialist **Boxer uprising**, that seeks to establish an earthly paradise through apocalyptic struggle. In Christianity, the Book of Revelation obliquely prophesies that the Messiah will initiate a thousand-year reign of the Saints before the Last Judgement. Its sequential ambiguity produced a split in the American Protestant tradition. Pre-millennialists hold that the Second Coming *inaugurates* the millennium, and accordingly emphasize personal salvation; post-millennialists, that it *closes* a millennium of mortal perfection of society.

millet system

The term *millet*, in Ottoman Turkish, denoted religiously defined nations within the **Ottoman Empire**. By the mid nineteenth century the Ottoman government interacted with each *millet* via the head of their sect, the *millet başı*. For Christians, that figure was a patriarch resident in **Constantinople** and for Jews, the head rabbi. The head of each *millet* had an interest in presenting their authority as an original compromise with the Ottoman regime dating back centuries. However, the *millet* system was a modern arrangement. The Armenian patriarchate had no empire-wide ecclesiastical power, for instance, in the early modern centuries of the Ottoman Empire. Instead, the millet system emerged out of modernizing Ottoman reforms preceding and concurrent with the **Tanzimat** reforms. *Millets* represented an attempt at standardization of the status of minority populations. The term indicated some modicum of autonomy possessed by each 'national' religious community to organize its own affairs. This structure, according to some historians, increased the momentum towards cleavage amongst the empire's religious communities.

minorities (Ottoman)

– *see also* **Armenian genocide**.

In the Arab lands of the eastern Mediterranean, Christians remained the majority of the population for several centuries after the Islamic conquest. Slowly, Christians became a significant minority as conversion to **Islam** thinned their numbers. All the territories conquered by the **Ottoman Empire** contained Muslim majorities except Mount Lebanon and the European provinces. The Jewish population in the **Middle East**, meanwhile, increased significantly when **Spain** expelled its Sephardic population in 1492. Jews found safe haven in the cities of the Ottoman Empire, adding to the extant *Mizrahi* Jewish populations. Christians and Jews maintained their protected status in the Ottoman Empire, as they had in previous Islamic empires. Theirs was a sustained coexistence, never a situation of equality where minorities enjoyed the same rights as Muslims. Beginning in the eighteenth century, the economic and political pressures of the modern period slowly began to undermine the terms of that coexistence. In the twentieth century the ability of different religious groups to live in peaceful proximity with one another collapsed in most territories of the former Ottoman Empire.

Before the eighteenth century, the central authorities of the Ottoman Empire held little stake in the politics of Christian sects. Timely payment of taxes represented their primary concern with regards to minorities. In general, Christians could only garner the wrath of the authorities by proselytizing or publicly insulting Islam. However, with creeping European influence and diminishing central power as the eighteenth century wore on, the Ottoman state attempted to intervene more directly in the politics of Christian sects to reassert control. They adopted the *millet* system wherein the *Porte* appointed the head of each religious nation. Previously, different Christian sects had not been recognized as distinct national entities by the state.

Sectarian divisions between Christian sects, and between Christians and Muslims, hardened in the nineteenth century. Having achieved economic gain and more rights by developing relationships with Europeans in ecclesiastical, political and economic realms, local Christian populations became more prosperous. This perceived success made them a target, almost by proxy, for local anger at increasing European power. That anger exploded into sectarian massacres in Mount Lebanon and Damascus in 1860. In both places, groups who had suffered a concomitant relative decline in economic fortunes, the **Druze** and Bedouin Muslims respectively, became the primary perpetrators of the massacres. Nearly a century later, the Jewish populations of Arab lands faced a similar fate when they became targets by proxy for Muslim Arab anger at the creation of the State of **Israel**. Violence and fear obliged nearly all the Jewish populations of the Arab word to migrate to Israel or abroad. Meanwhile, inside **Palestine**, centuries of coexistence between Arabs, Muslims and

Christians collapsed as decades of Zionist immigration culminated in ethnic cleansing of the Palestinian population in 1948.

Before 1948, the Christian population of Palestine, **Syria** and **Lebanon** had already diminished amidst emigration to the West. Population growth and economic opportunities in the Americas convinced Arab Christians to leave their countries in large numbers. Twenty per cent Christian at the beginning of the twentieth century, Palestine's Christian population now stands at less than 2 per cent. The Christian population of Anatolia also stood at around 20 per cent in the first decade of the twentieth century; its decline came amidst less mundane circumstances than Christian Arabs. Armenians in Anatolia suffered the genocidal policies of Young Turk nationalism during **World War I**. Then, in 1923, the fledgling Turkish republic forced the Orthodox residents of Anatolia to leave their homes and relocate to **Greece**. **Gamal Abdel Nasser's** Arab nationalism afforded the Greek or Jewish populations of **Egypt** no room, and the populations were summarily deported during his nationalization campaigns of the 1950s. In broad outline, the rise of nationalism amidst the collapse of the Ottoman Empire spelled the end of more than a millennia of inter-religious coexistence in the Middle East.

Mirambo (*c.* 1840–1884)

Originally a Nyamwezi warlord who came to prominence in the 1860s in a period of commercial growth and political instability. Mirambo fixed his capital at Urambo in modern-day western **Tanzania** in 1870 and made a number of alliances with neighbouring people as well as engaging in warfare to increase his sphere of direct authority. His principal military force, known locally as the *ruga-ruga*, were mercenaries originally from **South Africa** who had spread north into East Africa. Mirambo manoeuvred the Swahili–Arab colony of Unyamyembe into his orbit. These connections, as well as his domination of the slave and ivory trade from the central African rain forest to the East Africa coast, led to an alliance with the sultan of **Zanzibar**, resulting in Mirambo becoming an important force in the whole of east central Africa. Mirambo's rule was never stable, and upon his death rival rulers and commercial brokers once again destabilized the region.

MIRV

An MIRV (multiple independently targetable re-entry vehicle) is a warhead containing a collection of nuclear devices carried on an intercontinental ballistic missile (or its submarine-launched equivalent), capable of hitting several separate targets. First developed by the **United States**, believing that it might enhance first-strike capability, both the United States and the **Soviet Union** came to possess many MIRVed missiles. In its Nuclear Posture Review of 2010 the United States proposed to de-MIRV its missiles to a single warhead each.

miscegenation

– *see also* **racism**.

The term used for the mixing of different socially or politically defined racial groups through sexual relations, cohabitation or marriage. The term makes little sense biologically, as it implies that 'races' are biologically distinct, even as scientific research suggests that the commonalties between 'races' vastly outweigh the differences. The term does have considerable historical importance, however, because it resulted in fundamental race-based legislation and policy in some of the least edifying regimes in modern history. *Miscegenation* is a word with a particularly American etymology, coined during the **American Civil War** as a term of abuse towards the Republican Party and its supposed policies of allowing blacks and whites to coexist. Concern over miscegenation, however, pre-dates the word's invention. The beginnings of its modern manifestation came about in the mid eighteenth century when scientific racism – the notion that biological differences between races were significant and measurable – began to emerge. Theorists such as the Comte de Buffon (1707–88) in **France**, Johann Blumenbach (1752–1840) in **Germany** and **Thomas Jefferson** in the **United States** suggested that mixed-race progeny between (mostly) white men and black or brown women would exhibit racial deficiencies inherited from their mothers and would be inferior intellectually and physically to white people. Although other societies besides western European and neo-western European societies were often concerned about racial mixing, it was in the former societies where laws and social practices intended to stop miscegenation were most pronounced.

Some early theorists, such as Jamaican historian Edward Long (1734–1813), posited that mixed-race people would be unable to reproduce, suggesting that humans originated by polygenesis rather than monogenesis. Such ideas went against biblical orthodoxy and also against reality – mixed-race people were growing rapidly in numbers in Long's Jamaica and in other racially diverse societies. Increasing numbers of mixed-race people were especially problematic in two kinds of society: slave societies (or ex-slave societies) in which most enslaved people were African and settler colonies in which politically dominant white populations were determined to deny political rights to people of other complexions. In these places, legislators attempted to limit both the spread of racial mixing and also it effects on white supremacy by passing laws that restricted the mixing of races. The first such laws were passed in the eighteenth and early nineteenth centuries but the greatest burst of activity in legislating against racial mixing, especially sexual connections, came in the late nineteenth and early twentieth centuries.

Notable examples of legislation placing restrictions on sexual mixing were in the segregation laws of the post-bellum American South from the 1890s to the 1960s, and in the anti-miscegenation laws of **apartheid South Africa** from 1948 to 1992. Probably the most notorious miscegenation legislation was that passed in **Nazi** Germany between 1933 and 1945 in which the state tried to legislate in favour of Aryan purity and against what was considered Jewish 'contamination'. Miscegenation laws have been steadily dismantled in recent decades, as more societies have embraced the ethnic diversity that has accompanied cultural diffusion.

missionary movement (Christian)

Although it existed previously, missionary activity accelerated and became more widespread in the early modern and modern eras, largely due to European imperialism. From the sixteenth to the twentieth centuries missionaries from across **Europe** established communities in **China**, the Americas, **Africa** and **India**. While various religious groups participated in overseas activities, Catholic and Protestant missionaries remained the most prominent. Although ostensibly focused on conversion and proselytization, missionaries' influence extended to global politics, economics, societies and culture.

The growth of Catholic religious orders during the sixteenth and seventeenth centuries led to a proliferation of missionary activity. Asia emerged as an early and important domain for missionaries, with **Jesuits** initiating missions to **Japan** and China in the late sixteenth century. While missionaries enjoyed some success in China, the destruction of traditional beliefs and ways of life generated hostility, which erupted in violent forms during the Tianjin Massacre (1870) and **Boxer rebellion** (1898–1901). Beginning in the seventeenth century, Catholic missionaries founded mission towns in America and established relations with native groups. While the dominance of Catholic missionaries declined in the eighteenth century, Catholic societies returned to missionary work and built communities in Africa and South America during the second half of the nineteenth century.

During the eighteenth century the British Protestant missionary movement expanded largely due to the growth of **evangelicalism**. Unlike Roman Catholic missions that were largely carried out by religious orders, the British Protestant movement relied upon lay societies. William Carey's influential *An Enquiry into the Obligations of Christians to Use Means for the Conversion of the Heathen* (1792) expressed the need to disseminate God's word abroad and acted as a handbook for missionaries. In the eighteenth century Protestants initiated work in the North American colonies. However, their work among slaves and free coloured populations generated hostility from colonial officials and white planters who feared Christianity's subversive influence. In Africa, British missionaries initially worked to provide a home for liberated slaves in **Sierra Leone**. They extended their focus to the **Cape Colony** in 1799, and later to eastern and central Africa.

In contrast to **Asia** and North America, missionary activity in India and the **Middle East** followed, rather than preceded, colonial institutions and remained intimately connected with imperial enterprise. The British **East India Company** expanded the British presence and provided missionaries with new opportunities for Christianization. However, they faced considerable challenges. Their conversion efforts were blamed for increasing sectarian tensions and contributing to animosity that led to rebellions against British rule, including the **India mutiny and revolt** in 1857. Consequently, missionaries shifted their focus from conversion to social and humanitarian services and sponsored medical and educational missions.

The missionary movement has a complex legacy. Despite its apparent good intentions, its interference in local cultures and connection to imperialism have generated much criticism. While some missionaries did denounce aspects of empire, religion provided an important rationale for imperialism. The continued subjugation of native peoples within missionary and church structures provoked resistance among colonised populations and anti-missionary movements. Despite these negative aspects, missionaries also had a positive influence. They facilitated cross-cultural exchange, established important educational and medical institutions, and led campaigns to end oppression.

Missouri Compromise

– see also **abolitionism**.

In December 1818 the Missouri Territory applied to Congress for statehood. In January, James Tallmadge, a New York Congressman, objected to slavery in the first newly settled state carved from the **Louisiana Purchase**, and moved an amendment requiring that no more slaves be admitted to Missouri and that the future children of existing slaves be freed at the age of 25. The amendment passed the House but failed in the Senate, in the face of Southern opposition. In the next Congress, meeting in December 1819, the argument intensified: the South blocked the intended admission of Maine, and some Southerners threatened secession if restrictions were placed on Missouri. Finally, in March 1820, Missouri was admitted as a slave state, the block on Maine was removed, and Congress voted to prohibit slavery in the Louisiana Purchase north of 36°30′. This compromise controlled westwards settlement until the South decided to insist on its repeal in the **Kansas–Nebraska Act** of 1854 in order to open up Kansas to slavery.

mita

Mita, from the Quechua *Mit'a*, was a system of forced labour used by Inca rulers. Under this mandatory public service, Inca subjects paid tribute, by working for a determined number of days every year. **Spain** adopted and used the system in its colonies in the Americas. Also called *repartimiento* or *cuatequil* in New Spain (**Mexico**), the mita remained largely unregulated through its existence. In the Spanish version, the viceroy would assign 5 to 10 per cent of the Indians living in a determined district to a colonist for work on plantations, ranches or, more commonly, in gold and silver mines. The system collapsed with the precipitous decline of the native population brought about by disease and harsh working conditions. The failure of the mita spurred the Spanish Crown to alleviate the terms and conditions under which Indians worked and to massively expand the importation of African slaves to the Americas after the sixteenth century.

MITI

A ministry which served as an architect of international trade and industrial policy in post-1945 **Japan**. MITI officials provided guidance and coordination with business enterprises as well as funding for research and development. With the growth of the Japanese economy in the 1980s, MITI's protectionist policy of the 1950s and 1960s was liberalized under diplomatic pressure from the **United States**. In 2001 it was replaced with the newly established Ministry of Economy, Trade and Industry (METI).

mixed courts (Tribunals) (Egypt)

Created in 1875 largely by the Egyptian foreign minister, Nubar Pasha, to administer Egyptian commercial life in a period of political uncertainty. Nubar Pasha sought both to restrict the arbitrary power of the sovereign through a system of legal procedures on the one hand, and to make foreign investment more secure while mitigating the effects on Egypt of the privileged status of Europeans on the other. The courts' legal codes, which applied a mixture of Napoleonic and Islamic legal procedures, were translated into Arabic by Muhammad Qadri Pasha (1821–86), a graduate of **Rafi Tahtawi**'s Cairo School of Languages. Judges were drawn from **Austria**, **Britain**, **France** and **Germany** as well as from Egypt. Western influences were perceived as being predominant and the courts were in regular competition with the religious courts. **Qasim Amin** was a mixed courts advocate from 1885. The Montreux Convention, April–May 1937, after the **Anglo-Egyption Treaty, 1936**, ordered the closure of the courts after a twelve-year transition period.

Mobutu Sese Seko (Joseph Désiré) (1930–1997)

Congolese dictator. Born Joseph-Désiré Mobutu, he spent seven years in the Force Publique, rising to the rank of sergeant major. In 1956 he left the army and turned to journalism, writing for the African weekly, *Actualités Africaines*. In 1958 he visited the World Exhibition in Brussels and remained in **Belgium** to work for the information agency Infocongo. He returned to **Congo** just before independence and joined Lumumba's government. After the mutiny of the Force Publique on 5 July, Mobutu was named army chief of staff. In September 1960, with Congo in political crisis following the breakdown of relations between **Joseph Kasavubu** and Patrice Lumumba and increasing American concern that the country was about to become the latest front in the **Cold War**, Mobutu seized power. President **John F. Kennedy** later praised him for saving Congo from communism, and an alliance between the Americans and Mobutu was established which would last until the early 1990s. Constitutional government was restored in February 1961, but Mobutu returned to power in November 1965 with his second *coup d'état*. He promised to restore peace after five years of turbulence, and moved quickly to recentralize power and reconstruct the state. His new party, the Mouvement Populaire de la Révolution, became the sole party under the 1967 constitution. He adopted a nationalist stance in economic policy, nationalizing the mining industry in 1967. He also began to develop his own personality cult.

In 1971 he changed the country's name to Zaire and called for 'authenticity'. He renamed himself Mobutu Sese Seko, meaning the 'all-conquering warrior who triumphs over all obstacles', and ordered his subjects to replace their Christian names with indigenous names. He developed a distinctive personal sartorial style, combining a form of 'Mao' suit with a leopard-skin hat and a carved cane, in the image of a traditional chief. From 1974 his personal style of rule reached a new level as he declared 'Mobutism' the country's new official ideology. From 1974, Zaire faced economic problems. The price of copper collapsed and petrol prices soared at the same time as Mobutu was undertaking a major programme to nationalize foreign business interests. The country became increasingly indebted and by 1976 it owed 3 billion dollars. In the decades that followed it became increasingly dependent on international support, particularly from America, **France** and **Belgium**. The debts were repeatedly rescheduled, and external forces supported the Mobutu regime when it was challenged by the invasions known as Shaba I and Shaba II in 1977 and 1978. Following the Cold War, Mobutu became less important to the West and pressure was put on him to follow other African countries in moving towards democratization. A national conference was held and political parties formed, with Mobutu doing his best to stay in control of the process and remain in power. He was finally toppled not through elections but by the advancing armies of Laurent Kabila. He was forced into exile in **Morocco**, where he died.

modernism

A cultural and artistic movement concerned with the development of new and more psychologically intimate and revealing forms of art, discourse and architecture which, while based on a command of previous techniques, deliberately rejected them. Modernism emerged in **France** in the closing decades of the nineteenth century and developed in the years before the Great War. The overarching aim of the modernists was to synthesize an aesthetic sensibility with the idea of progress and the use of modern technology. Paradoxically, however, they saw their society as one in which industrialism, institutionalism and social organization were geared to the alienation and destruction of the individual, and many saw the need for some great calamity to reset an hypocritical or inhuman imperialist civilization. Modernists sought to simplify and emphasize the subconscious and the relative. To that extent, the emergence in art of movements dedicated to the depiction of reality from the perspective of the artist and the elimination of ornament was typical, as was the deliberate narrative confusion of the works of James Joyce (1882–1941) in literature. Modernists wrote in the first person, rejected classical perspective for perception in art and, as in the works of Igor Stravinsky (1882–1971), deliberately sought to recreate music while rejecting traditional rules of composition.

They saw themselves as of a piece with the revolutionary effects of Einstein's relativity, socialism and the ideas of **Sigmund Freud** and **Friedrich Nietzsche**. For modernists, the self-directed artist, channelling emotional and world-transforming perspective and bringing on progress and destruction at the same time was the ideal, and often contrasted with what was portrayed as the staid and somewhat exhausted naturalism, ornamentalism and stuffiness of their chosen fields. In architecture, the movement inspired a blend of spare aesthetic with industrial process, reaching a pinnacle perhaps in the mid-century attempts of Mies Van der Rohe and Le Corbusier (1887–1965) to reform buildings as 'machines for living in'. Unlike many before or since, modernists viewed urban life and the growth of consumer and industrial machines, such as the internal combustion engine, with pleasure and anticipation. They associated them with emancipation of the individual, and with the possibilities of the car, the cinema, the radio, air travel and the telephone, to alter, compress or discard temporal limitation.

Modernism was greatly boosted after **World War I**, which weakened or destroyed traditional hierarchies and authority across a swathe of human endeavour. In their place, modernists elevated design, symbolism, the analysis of language and the creation of a new literary canon. This emphasis on novelty, and the rejection of traditional outlooks and techniques in which many of the modernists had been very well trained, led to a tendency to fetishize the irrational and primitive as things to be overcome, as much as it concentrated on the use of modern materials such as plastic and concrete. This had an inevitable impact on politics. The Atlantic Left, in the form of socialist parties, and communists, elevated a particular strain of modernism in which economic management, the provision of functional housing and schooling, and the development of a welfare state would create an industrial utopia for collective man. Fascists in Italy took some cue from the tradition-busting nationalism and plain-speaking of the Futurists, and the Nazi Party contained both modernist elements (associated more with its university youth and Strasserite wings) and people, such as **Hitler**, who were at some level motivated by a hatred and fear of the effect of modernist movements on art, society and the bourgeois domesticism of the nineteenth century.

In religion, the Catholic Church saw modernism as a continuation and enhancement of the errors which had exploded during the **French Revolution**. Pope St Pius X officially condemned the movement, which was characterized in his encyclical letter *Pascendi Dominici Gregis* as one of secularism, unaided rationality and philosophies which encouraged the idea of individual moral autonomy and republicanism. Between 1910 and 1967 Catholic religious officials across the world had to take an oath against modernism, and whilst other Christian churches never developed as coherent a philosophical opposition, it is safe to say that modernism and traditional or spiritualist Christianity were in many cases antagonistic despite the efforts of some 'evolutionist' reformers. Some Protestant and particularly Anglican traditions, however, came to appreciate the application of rationalistic exegesis to the study of the Bible, even though this tended to relativize and fragment their ecclesial communities.

Modernism reached a peak in the 1960s, but then declined for a variety of reasons (the 25-year period after **World War II** is sometimes referred to as 'high modernism'). Modernist architectural styles were viewed by many as alienating and anti-human when fully expressed in the form of the great post-war housing estates. Given that these were often associated with crime and constructed for the purposes of government-owned housing (which was then neglected and deprived of caretakers in the great British and American housing projects), modernist buildings came to symbolize the anti-human nature of statism. On top of that, the oil shocks of 1973 and 1978 undermined the cheap energy, plastic and petrol engines which had been so associated with modernity, and a political reaction towards individualism and the recovery of tradition began. Postmodernist architects felt a need to integrate their buildings both with ornament and human scale, but also with the wider environment, and tended to see buildings not as machines but as parts of quasi-organic constructs in which account had to be taken of ornament and human emotional needs. In literature, the introduction of parody, irony and magic realism ran against what many saw as the bleakness of modernism; and in philosophy, deconstructionists increasingly argued that modern discourse, rituals, institutions and offices were really ways of reifying a 'carceral' or prison-like system of social discipline. The most influential of these philosophers, Jacques Derrida (1930–) and Michel Foucault (1926–84), argued that modernist society and the Enlightenment quest for a universalized moral autonomy had in reality become a sort of intellectual cage, and that transgression, resistance and reaction were in themselves more interesting and more vital than this brutality. They were aided by the development of information technologies and globalization, which had the effect, ironically, of historicizing modernism within a particular western industrial moment, and of relativizing it in the face of other cultures and the democratization of information. By the 1990s this 'postmodernism' had become dominant in intellectual discourse and modernism had become an historical moment.

Mohammed Ali
– *see* **Mehmet Ali**.

monarchy
An ancient institution and form of government based around a crowned head of state in which formal power is held by a king, queen or emperor. Constitutional monarchy, in which a government under law exercised the powers of a monarch, leaving the actual person as a symbol of national continuity above politics, was the favoured form of government in Europe and the emerging world of the nineteenth century. Unitary states based around monarchs in northern Europe, **Britain**, **Japan**, **Spain** and **Italy** were seen as guaranteeing balanced government. In the twentieth century, particularly after the emergence of the **USA** and **USSR** to world power in 1917–18, monarchies fell out of favour as a constitutional model and were generally replaced by republics, particularly in decolonizing countries. Nevertheless, a number of monarchies persisted or re-emerged. Spain, **Saudi Arabia**, **Jordan**, Denmark, **Belgium**, **Canada** and

Australia retained kings or queens just as the Papacy, the British Crown, the **Commonwealth**, and post-1945 **Japan** demonstrated the continuing vitality of the model. It would be hard, however, to present the survivors of the twentieth-century breaking of crowns as the avatars of a viable model for new states, despite the stability and prosperity of most remaining kingdoms. Almost a hundred monarchs lost their thrones between 1900 and 2015. The reasons for these collapses can be divided into the effects of war and occupation; democratic, Islamic or socialist revolution; the break up of the states or empires on which some monarchies were dependent; and the peaceful transition of states to liberal republicanism.

Very few monarchies were or are either elective or temporary, although the Papacy, **Malaysia** and the **United Arab Emirates** maintain aspects of such a system. Most were based around a line of male succession through a royal family, and therefore monarchies tend to place the status and health of otherwise domestic institutions such as the family in the public sphere. They have also been closely aligned with religion and with the idea of an unbroken national narrative, and have consequently functioned as conservative institutions which have presented the public with a link to a past that is above politics. This was the appeal of the Spanish monarchy both to **Franco** and subsequently to Spanish democrats in the 1970s, and is an explanation for the otherwise paradoxical re-emergence of the Hispanic crown. An argument can be made that most monarchies allow for a public presentation and discussion of various stages of adult life, such as the dignity of age, the emergence of parental responsibility, or the exuberance of youth which would not be possible in a state where the principal figures were active politicians whose dominance rarely lasted a decade, and in this way they may allow for a public culture which is richer than one dominated by a cult of activity and change. Certainly, large majorities exist in the remaining monarchies in favour of their system of government, and in states which retain monarchical families as private individuals, titles are often deployed and individuals such as Habsburgs voted into office with some affection. It is therefore likely, barring war or disaster, that the age of abolition or abdication is, for now, over.

Mondlane, Eduardo (1920–1969)

Mozambican political leader. Born to a minor chief in northern Mozambique, he attended schools in **Mozambique**, **South Africa** and the **United States**, earning a doctorate in anthropology from Northwestern University. In 1962 he founded the Mozambican Liberation Front (**Frelimo**), but it was soon forced by Portuguese repression to adopt guerrilla war tactics, which were particularly successful in the north. The Portuguese managed to assassinate him in 1969 by sending him a bomb planted in a book.

monetarism

– *see also* **neoliberalism**.

Based on the theories of Milton Friedman (1912–2006), monetarism developed in opposition to post-1945 Keynesian demand management policies and had its heyday in the early 1980s. Monetarism argues that inflation has its roots in government deficits and is based on the quantity theory of money. The theory posits that if governments keep the supply of money steady, the economy would expand at a natural growth rate and market forces would efficiently solve the problems of inflation, unemployment and recession.

money

Money is believed by many to be the root of all evil, though it is acknowledged that it is not money itself that possesses this power but the actions of those who pursue its acquisition to the exclusion of all else. From that perspective money is seen as neutral, acting merely as a catalyst, and is thus not the cause of what has taken place. It is not money that generated wars and revolutions, propelled economic growth, or created class divisions but specific individuals, groups or governments. For them, money was either the end that they sought or the means used to reach another end. In treating money in this way there is no recognition of the different forms it has taken and the implications that stem from that. Money is what money does and this has varied both over time and in different countries. Money can range from being low-powered, as with the metallic coins and paper notes that circulate from hand to hand, to high-powered when it is in the hands of financial institutions such as banks or takes the form of bills and securities. As such, money is not neutral but can influence human behaviour whether that involves releasing destructive forces as with hyper-inflation and speculative bubbles or constructive ones such as providing credit and capital for short- and long-term investment.

The essence of money is that it is a unit of account. As such, it provides a way of measuring and comparing many different goods and services and thus facilitating their exchange. By providing an equivalent in money for all types of products and commodities, the needs of diverse producers and consumers wherever located can be matched. Without money civilization would continue to operate at the level of localized barter. Similarly, through converting payment for work into money all can participate and be remunerated according to the value society places on the contribution they make. As such, specialization and the division of labour are made possible with all the attendant productivity gains. Finally, money acts as a store of value permitting either resources to be accumulated for future use or future income to be used to support current expenditure. This can involve either delaying current consumption through not spending all available money or promising future payments in return for the immediate use of money. This means that money has the capacity to bridge space, time and type. It is thus impossible to imagine the existence of the modern world, with all it involves in terms of economic, political and social life, without the use of money.

the dynamics

Money has its own dynamic and interacts with both long-term trends and short-term events to help determine particular outcomes. Contributing to the dynamic effects of money is the fact that as a unit of account it has varied both over time and between countries. By 2010 the value of $100 (US) in 1774 had risen to $2,790. Even more dramatic was the changing value of the Japanese Yen, with 100 in 1879 being worth 417,000 by 2010. The explanation for the change is inflation, which, over time, has reduced the purchasing power of individual units of account. Inflation, especially that generated by governments when their finances were under strain, had major short- and long-term consequences as it unbalanced relative pricing and even destroyed trust in the unit of account. The hyper-inflation in **Germany** that followed **World War I** was one such example, leading to major political and social consequences for that country. The collapse in 1931 of the **gold standard**, under which the relative value of individual currencies was determined by the amount of gold each unit of account could purchase, had a devastating impact on international trade and finance leading to the climate of economic nationalism out of which came **World War II**. Since that war governments have accepted inflation as the price necessary to ensure social stability. However, that situation leads in turn to other crises as with the economic, political and social problems evident in many countries in the 1970s.

high-powered money

However, money is far more that the coins and notes in circulation, because financial innovation made it increasingly high-powered from the eighteenth century onwards. This power was a product of the invention and use of new financial products, the growing sophistication of financial markets, and the role and importance of financial organizations. Sometimes these developments in the form money took, and the way it was used, produced disastrous results ranging from the activities of John Law in early eighteenth-century **France** to the global financial crisis of 2007/8. In each case the result was attempts at greater regulation by governments of what could be done with money. The problem with regulating money is that it is like water. When blocked in one direction it will simply find another if the demand continues for what money can provide. Attempts by the US government to restrict the external use of the US dollar from the late 1950s, for example, led directly to the development of the Eurodollar market in London, and contributed to the failure of New York to emerge as the dominant international financial centre after World War II.

Over the centuries high-powered money has taken many different forms. Among the earliest was the commercial bill of exchange, which was a form of temporary money accepted among merchants and bankers. Bills were bought at a discount and then redeemed at face value, so generating a profit for the holder, unlike coins or notes. The huge expansion of international trade in the nineteenth century relied upon the use of these bills as they allowed producers to be paid before the products were sold to consumers. In turn, governments in the twentieth century increasingly relied upon treasury bills to bridge the gap between expenditure, that was often continuous throughout the year, and income, which varied depending on when taxes were paid. Bonds were another form of money that had a longer duration than bills. Bonds represented a loan on which interest was paid until redeemed. The issue of bonds made it possible for governments to finance expensive military campaigns as long as potential investors had faith in the ability and willingness of a government to pay the interest promised and redeem the debt when due. This is the position that **Britain** achieved in the eighteenth century but France did not, and that had consequences for both the political stability and military success of each country.

stocks and bonds

Allied to bonds were stocks, which represented a permanent stake in a business and on which dividends were paid if profits were generated. By issuing either bonds or stocks it was possible for a business to gain access to a sum of money far beyond that available to any individual or family group. It was in the nineteenth century that this ability became of major importance through the finance of railways, as their scale required a huge initial investment of capital before an entire system became viable. Throughout the Americas, for example, railway companies, financed through the issue of stocks and bonds, provided the transport system that opened up the interior of that vast continent and permitted its full participation in the global economy. Following on from railways, the issue of stocks and bonds was increasingly used by businesses of all kinds as a flexible means of raising finance, while such securities were favoured by investors searching for a remunerative asset that could be easily bought and sold in any amount and at any time.

What made bills, stocks and bonds high-powered money was the ability to repeatedly buy and sell them. When possessed of this facility bills and securities were also a means of exchange and a store of value. Money in all its forms benefited from a market in which it could be bought and sold if those holding them were to realize its full value. The variety of units of account, for example, required a mechanism in which different currencies could be traded. This was especially the case when the value of a currency was not underpinned by its actual metal content or the guarantee that it could be exchanged for a specific amount of gold or silver. The development of an active foreign exchange market, for example, provided a solution to the collapse of the fixed exchange rate era that had prevailed under the gold standard before 1914. It then came to the fore again from the 1970s onwards after the collapse of the post-World War II regime of fixed exchange rates. Similarly, the ability to buy and sell bills of exchange until redeemed provided a convenient means for both employing temporarily idle funds or accessing such funds. In the nineteenth century banks regularly bought and sold commercial bills between themselves when faced with either a temporary abundance or a shortage of funds. After World War I and then, especially after World War II, treasury bills became the main instrument used. Banks themselves also developed a market in which they could lend to and borrow from each other, with or without collateral such as bills, as a way of employing idle balances or covering temporary shortages on a daily basis. The effect was to simultaneously increase the use that could be made of the available money supply as less and less was left unemployed at any one time. In this way the low-powered money in the form of coins and notes was converted into high-powered money in the shape of bank deposits.

stock markets

To achieve the same result for stocks and bonds required the creation of much more formal markets such as stock exchanges. Due to the variety and complexity of stocks and bonds, and the number involved in buying and selling them, it was necessary to both introduce rules and regulations governing market behaviour and to cover counterparty risk, as when one side defaulted on a deal. These stock exchanges gave a visibility and certainty to the pricing and marketability of stocks and bonds that made them resemble money. Those stocks and bonds that could be easily, quickly and cheaply bought and sold, and whose prices were continuously updated through trading on public markets, could be used for both international exchange and as a temporary store of value. Instead of transferring currency or gold between countries, securities could be sold on one stock exchange and bought on another. When these stock exchanges were in different countries the result was a transfer of money as funds were received where the securities were sold and paid out where they were bought. Similarly, temporarily idle funds could be used to buy securities in the knowledge that they could be sold when necessary, while benefiting from any interest or dividends paid in the interim or appreciation of capital as the dates at which such payments were made came closer. Again, the effect was to convert low-powered money into high-powered money, and make it available to finance the long-term needs of governments and business.

However, the very visibility and marketability of particular stocks and bonds also generated speculative interest, with bubbles or manias occurring from time to time. The Mississippi/**South Sea Bubble** in France and Britain in 1720, the railway mania in Britain in the 1840s or the global dot-com boom at the end of the twentieth century are all such examples. The most famous was that in the **USA** in the late 1920s, which led to the **Wall Street Crash** of 1929. These bubbles left in their wake risk-averse investors, weakened banks, a rapid credit contraction and a depressed economy. For those reasons, in the aftermath of such bubbles governments often introduced controls such as restrictions on international financial flows or measures to reduce or eliminate speculation. This happened in the mid twentieth century and had the effect of creating a division between stocks and bonds and the other forms of money, and so reducing the role they had played. It was the ease of transferability possessed by stocks and bonds that made them into high-powered money.

banking

Important as stock exchanges were in transforming low-powered money into high-powered money, the most important development in this respect was banking. The essence of a bank as opposed to a moneylender is that the bank employs the savings of others when lending to borrowers. The bank obtained the savings of others in two ways. It could attract deposits by offering immediate access when requested and by promising to pay interest. The other way was to issue its own notes whose value was guaranteed by the assets the bank controlled. These notes did not pay interest but could be used as a convenient means of payment and redeemed against other forms of money. There were risks attached to the business of banking. Default was always possible on a loan, making the bank insolvent as its liabilities to depositors and note holders were now greater than the assets it possessed. Conversely, the demand by savers to withdraw their deposits or redeem their notes could exceed the funds currently available, making the bank illiquid. It was thus vital for a bank to maintain the trust of those who deposited money with it or used the notes it issued. Otherwise depositors would rush to withdraw their savings and those holding its notes would request that they be converted into another currency. For that reason a bank had to operate in such a way that it could meet withdrawals and conversions. That required it to have capital of its own which could be called on to meet losses, and so always remain solvent, and to balance its assets and liabilities in such a way as to be always able to meet withdrawals, and so remain liquid.

Though these principles applied to all banking, that did not mean that all banks were the same, even in those countries that were similar in terms of economic development. The degree to which earlier forms of banking survived, the intervention of governments, and the interaction with other components of the financial system, along with the nature of the demand for specialist services,

combined to ensure that a wide variety of banks existed. During the nineteenth century two main models of banking emerged. One was banks that spread risk through the use of extensive branch networks, and concentrated upon making short-term loans financed from the collection of deposits and the issue of notes. The other was the universal bank which offered the full range of financial services including making long-term investments and issuing and trading securities. Though two distinctive models of banking did develop in the century before 1914, the position was somewhat fluid. Universal banks were under pressure to open branches as a way of obtaining direct access to retail deposits while branch banks sought opportunities to expand into more profitable long-term lending. The difficult economic conditions experienced between the two world wars undermined the viability of the universal banking model because of its exposure to corporate failure, through long-term loans financed by short-term deposits and an inadequate level of capital. In contrast, the branch banking model proved resilient, because of its focus on short-term lending. In the more settled conditions that followed World War II universal banking re-emerged as a model that delivered benefits and could cope with risks. The result was growing convergence as universal banks expanded their branch network and branch banks expanded the variety of business they conducted.

The problem for every bank that operated on the deposits of savers, rather than on capital provided by investors, was the imbalance between supply of and demand for money. Depending on fluctuations in business, a bank could face either an excess of deposits but a deficit of demand for loans or a deficit in deposits but an excess in demand for deposits. The solution to this was the development of an inter-bank money market through which surpluses could be lent out and shortages made good. Such markets emerged in the major financial centres where banks clustered because of their need to make and receive payments from each other. By taking advantage of the low-cost money available in these markets, banks could finance highly profitable long-term lending. However, if the supply of short-term funds dried up temporarily, and a bank was unable to repay one loan through obtaining another, the result was a crisis that could spread throughout the banking system. In response to this situation a bank emerged that acted as a lender-of-last-resort to the inter-bank money market and thus to the banking system. Confidence that such a bank existed and would act in this way ensured that banks would continue to lend to each other even under the most extreme conditions, including war or a major financial crisis. This was the role increasingly undertaken by central banks, beginning with the Bank of England in the middle of the nineteenth century. Inevitably, however, the more extreme the conditions the more reluctant banks were to expose themselves to the risk of default among their peers.

When viewed from a perspective that recognizes the difference between low- and high-powered money, money itself can be seen to possess certain features that generate both risks and benefits. The benefits are self-evident because the functioning of all aspects of the modern world is dependent upon money in all its forms. In contrast, the degree of risk is related to whether money is low-powered or high-powered. Even at the level of low-powered money, there are risks attached to its fluctuating value which can have important economic, political and social consequences. However, when high-powered money is examined, whether in the form of bills and inter-bank transfers or bonds and stocks, the risks are greatly magnified. These range from the aftermath of speculative bubbles through the freezing of inter-bank markets to the collapse of large banks. It is for that reason that governments have a self-interest in ensuring the stability of the monetary system because its collapse has the potential to inflict serious and lasting damage. Both inflation and deflation create risks but even worse is the breakdown in the payments system or the collapse of trust in the banking system. For those reasons governments, through central banks, have greatly extended their oversight and supervision over time.

Mongolia

A nation in east central Asia situated in between **China** and **Russia**. Mongolia is mostly semi-desert, desert plains and grassy steppe, with mountains in the south-west. It is a landlocked country with a continental desert climate. In the thirteenth century Chinggis Khan (Genghis Khan) led the Mongols to establish a huge Eurasian empire, which was later divided into several powerful Mongol states. The Mongols came under Chinese rule during Qing dynasty in the late seventeenth century. Mongolia gained independence with Soviet support in 1921 when the Chinese were expelled. It was under Soviet control until the fall of the **USSR** in 1990–1. At present the country is governed under a mixed parliamentary/presidential system. The capital is Ulaanbaatar. The ethnic majority are Mongols (94.9 per cent). Roughly half of the population practises Lamaist Buddhism.

The official language is Khalkha Mongol, and the national currency is the Tughrik (MNT).

Monnet, Jean (1888–1979)

A French diplomat who, with Robert Schuman (1886–1963), is held to be the founder of the bodies which evolved into the **European Union**. Monnet was an economist for the allied forces in **World War I**, deputy secretary of the League of Nations, and then an international financier, all of which activities demonstrated his conviction for the international integration of Europe along liberal capitalist lines. He supported the Schuman Plan to pool economic resources that developed into the European Coal and Steel Community in 1951. This was the precursor of the European Economic Community, an idea driven in part by Monnet's Action Committee for the United States of Europe. After 1963 he retired and devoted himself to his memoirs. His ashes were committed to the Pantheon in Paris.

Monroe Doctrine (USA)

The Monroe Doctrine functioned as the conceptual and policy foundation of US foreign relations for most of the nineteenth century. Employed by presidents and secretaries of state with varying diplomatic views, its meaning and application were always contingent upon the circumstances in which it was invoked. What became known as the Monroe Doctrine was based loosely on **James Monroe**'s 1823 and 1824 messages to Congress, which proclaimed to European powers that the western hemisphere was no longer open to colonization and political intervention. Translating these negative principles into specific policies became a matter of great dispute. For instance, whereas **John Quincy Adams** read the doctrine as calling for participation in the multilateral Congress of Panama in 1826, **James K. Polk** interpreted it to justify pre-emptive territorial expansion in the 1840s. Others added 'corollaries', which transformed it from an instrument of transatlantic relations to one of hemispheric imperialism. Notably, the 'Roosevelt Corollary' (1904–5) sought to legitimize US intervention in the affairs of neighbouring states.

Monroe, James (1758–1831)

A diplomat and fifth US president, as a young Virginian James Monroe fought in the **American Revolution**, studied law under **Thomas Jefferson** and served in the **Continental Congress**. Elected to the Senate in 1790, he supported the opposition Republicans, but also served briefly as minister to

France (1794–6) and governor of Virginia, 1799–1802. President Jefferson appointed him special envoy to France in 1803, where he helped negotiate the **Louisiana Purchase**. As minister to **Britain**, 1803–7, he and William Pinckney attempted a new diplomatic settlement with Britain but Jefferson found the treaty unacceptable. In 1812 President **Madison** appointed Monroe secretary of state and in 1814 secretary of war as well. In 1816 Monroe was elected president and endeavoured to assuage partisan passions in the so-called **Era of Good Feelings**, but ill feeling triumphed in the Panic of 1819 and the **Missouri crisis**. Internationally, his administration gained Florida and the transcontinental boundary from **Spain** in 1819, recognized Latin American independence, and in 1823 issued the warning to Europe that became the Monroe Doctrine.

Montagu–Chelmsford Reforms

Officially known as the Government of India Act 1919, these reforms introduced the system of dyarchy into the provincial governments of British India. Under this arrangement, elected provincial legislatures controlled certain government portfolios, including education and agriculture, while executive councillors responsible to the governor general retained control over key portfolios, including defence, revenue and police. Disappointed with half-hearted concessions to the demand for self-government, Indian nationalists launched the **Non-Cooperation movement**.

Montesquieu, Charles-Louis de Secondat, Baron de La Brède et de (1689–1755)

French political philosopher, author of *The Spirit of the Laws* (1748). Montesquieu distinguished between despotic, republican and monarchical political regimes. He disputed the claims of Thomas Hobbes (1588–1679) and **John Locke** that the nature of a polity is characterized by a social contract, and instead argued that political cultures are constituted by a plurality of sources, including location, climate, moral characteristics and institutional formats. He rejected despotism as a corrupt form of government based on fear, and concentrated instead on the merits of republicanism, animated by virtue, and monarchy, characterized by honour. Republican virtue encourages shared values in the name of the common good, whilst monarchical honour promoted ordered hierarchy which allowed for expressions of individuality. Montesquieu admired both, but argued that each must also embody a separation of powers between executive, legislative and judicial authorities. This doctrine influenced the **American** and **French Revolutions**, and his wider approach to political analysis has informed contemporary discussions of global differences in political regimes.

Montreux Convention (1936)

– *see also* **Constantinople Agreements (1888)**.

The Montreux Convention was called at the request of the Turkish Republic to clarify Turkish control of the Bosphorus Straits and Dardanelles. The treaty was called in the context of concerns over Italian expansion in the Mediterranean; indeed, **Italy** was antagonistic to the convention and was the only participant in the **Lausanne Conference** that was not invited. The treaty allowed **Turkey** to remilitarize the straits, stipulated the free passage of civilian vessels in peacetime and placed restrictions on naval vessels of states not bordering the Black Sea.

Montserrat

A small volcanic island in the Lesser Antilles in the Caribbean Sea, Montserrat was first settled by the British in 1632. It is now a British Overseas Territory. Early in its history, it attracted a considerable Irish-indentured servant population. By the late seventeenth century it had become another plantation economy with a majority African population. Still volcanically active, a 1995 eruption led to half the island being abandoned and two-thirds of the population departing.

Moody, Dwight (1837–1899)

Prominent **evangelical** revivalist who operated in the cities of a rapidly industrializing **United States**. He divided his focus between his native Massachusetts and Chicago, and undertook extended tours of **Britain**. With the homespun authenticity of a layperson, Moody preached both a conservative, pre-millennial literalism and an Arminian, inclusive understanding of God. He reached the aspiring urban classes more than he did the poor, and attracted business sponsorship for his message of social regeneration by means of individual faith alone.

Moral Majority

An American pressure group formed in 1979, the Moral Majority was the leading organization of the Christian Right during its early years. Led by a Virginia pastor, Jerry Falwell, the organization vigorously campaigned against liberal Democrats, arguing that Christian values were under attack from abortion, homosexuality, feminism and the influence of secular values on America's elites. Highly visible during the **Reagan** years, by the 1990s it had become eclipsed by other right-wing Christian organizations and populist movements.

Morant Bay Rebellion

The Morant Bay Rebellion in **Jamaica** broke out in October 1865, when several hundred black people marched into the town, the capital of the sugar-growing parish of St Thomas in the East. Led by Paul Bogle, a native Baptist deacon, the crowd attacked the police station before confronting the militia and the parish authorities. In the subsequent melée, the crowd killed eighteen people. Over the next few days, local blacks killed two planters and attacked many plantations in the parish. The response of the Jamaican authorities was swift and brutal. The government forcefully put down the rebellion, and nearly 500 people were killed and hundreds more seriously wounded. A royal commission criticized the governor, **Edward Eyre**, for the severe repression used to quell the rebellion, and he was dismissed. More importantly, the political constitution of the colony was transformed and its 200-year-old Assembly abolished.

Morel, Edmund Dene (1873–1924)

Anglo-French radical writer and politician. Morel was born in Paris but taken by his mother to **Britain** in 1877. An active campaigner against slavery in **Congo** and a critic of Great Power secret diplomacy, Morel was a leading pacifist in **World War I** and a founding secretary of the Union of Democratic Control. A Liberal from 1912–14, he was elected an Independent Labour Party MP in 1922.

Morgenthau Plan

US Secretary of the Treasury Henry Morgenthau's plan for post-**World War II Germany** aimed not only to divide Germany but to make it pastoral by removing its heavy industry and war-making capability. Promoted by President **Roosevelt** and reluctantly accepted by **Winston Churchill** at the September 1944 Quebec conference, the plan encountered criticism for promoting a harsh economic peace that would destroy **Europe**'s industrial capability. The plan had some policy impact before being abandoned by the **Truman** administration.

Mori, Ogai (1862–1922)

Educated as an army medical officer in Germany, 1884–8, Ogai Mori was one of the leading **Meiji**

writers who was influenced by European, Chinese and Japanese literature. He established a modern literary tradition in **Japan**. His novel *Maihime* (*The Dancing Girl*) in 1890 was based on his affair with a German woman in Berlin. The news of General Nogi's *seppuku* after the death of the Meiji emperor led him to refocus his later work on the inner self in Japanese historical tales.

Morley–Minto reforms

Officially known as the Government of India Act of 1909, the Morley–Minto reforms were a response to nationalist agitation during the **Swadeshi movement** and the first time the British colonial government had permitted a limited number of elected members to join provincial legislative councils. The Act also introduced a system of separate electorates for Muslims. Minimal provisions for elected representation were counterbalanced by the predominance of non-elected members in the legislative councils.

Mormons

The Church of Jesus Christ of Latter-day Saints and its subsequent breakaway denominations trace their origins to Joseph Smith Jr's *Book of Mormon* (1830), which claimed to offer evidence of ancient Israelite immigration to the **United States**. The church claims to be a restored apostolic church with tenets merely supplementary to those of the Bible, but mainstream Christianity rejects that stance. The sect's **millennialism** and dreams of founding its own Zion produced a series of settlements in the Midwest in the mid nineteenth century. Repeated instances of local hostility eventually inspired an 1,100-mile leap to 'Deseret' (Utah). The Mormons' polygamy and an 1857 massacre of westbound pioneers incurred the hostile scrutiny of the federal government. The church outlawed polygamy in 1890, though not without splintering, and Utah achieved statehood in 1896.

The church rejects the distinction between laity and clergy, and has experienced worldwide growth through its adherents' compulsory mission tours. The Mormon work ethic, abstemiousness and conservative views on the family and marriage make Utah the most Republican state in the nation.

Moroccan Crisis, 1905

This crisis arose from agreements between Britain and **France** and between France and **Spain** in 1904 on making Morocco a French protectorate. In January 1905 France offered the Sultan of **Morocco** assistance in maintaining order. **Germany** had initially raised no objection to French ambitions but Chancellor Bernhard von Bülow (1849–1929) took the opportunity to test the recently agreed Anglo-French *entente cordiale*. In March 1905 Kaiser Wilhelm II landed at Tangier during a cruise and declared Germany's support for Morocco, subsequently demanding an international conference on the country's future and the protection of German commerce. Germany calculated that Britain would not risk conflict in support of France. Despite panic in France – the foreign minister was forced to resign – Britain fully backed the French at a conference at Algeçiras in January–April 1906, consolidating the *entente*'s effectiveness. Von Bülow was forced to explain the government's embarrassing miscalculation to the Reichstag.

Moroccan Crisis, 1911

Also known as the Agadir Crisis, this event was prompted by **Germany**'s deployment of a gunboat (the *Panther*) to the Moroccan port on 1 July 1911 in protest against French attempts to establish a protectorate. The British government, already antagonistic to German economic and naval rivalry, heightened its rhetoric and reinforced the *entente* with **France**. In ensuing negotiations, France's control of Morocco was accepted and Germany was compensated with parts of what are now **Congo** and **Chad**.

Morocco

An identifiable monarchical state since its foundation by Idris ibn Abdullah, a direct descendant of the Prophet Muhammad, in the eighth century, with a population and culture uniquely blending Arab and Berber traditions. The object of Great Power rivalry throughout the nineteenth and early twentieth centuries, led by the French who demanded Morocco's help in capturing the Algerian leader Abd-el-Kader, 1846. Favourable trading rights were then exacted by **Britain**, 1856, and a coastal region in the north-west declared a Spanish protectorate, 1859. Paradoxically, the internal weakness of the monarchy which made Morocco vulnerable to the Great Power predators made it harder for the Spaniards, and later the French, to control the Berber tribes within their respective protectorates. The scale of French ambition was in fact considerable, encompassing the foundation of a new 'Roman' empire, extending from Morocco to **Egypt**, which would compensate for the European empire lost with the defeat of **Napoleon**. **France**, therefore, opposed the British policy of reforming the North African states to

make them genuinely independent and the British-sponsored Madrid conference of the Great Powers, 1880, to reform Morocco collapsed under the weight of French opposition. Rivalry continued unabated. In 1902 a draft treaty prepared between France and **Spain** to hand all northern Morocco, including Fez, to Spain and the rest to France, succumbed only to the Spanish fear of antagonizing the British. It was not until 1904 that a durable Franco-British bargain was reached whereby the French would gain political control subject to British and Spanish commercial equality. The 'Moroccan question' was a threat to world peace in 1911. Germany had been encouraged to assert her claims in 1905, when France's ally, **Russia**, was distracted by the revolution, but had withdrawn them at the Algeciras conference, 1906, when Britain had supported France. **Germany** now sent a gunboat ready to seize the port of Agadir as some 'compensation' from the French for their impending protectorate over the country. A British threat to go to war on the French side terminated the crisis and the French protectorate was declared in 1912, with British interests safeguarded by the international zone of Tangier, established by Britain, France and Spain in 1923. The protectorate, with General **Lyautey** as resident general, operated through the country's natural leaders and respected the Moroccan way of life.

The independence movement was stimulated by **World War II**. France tolerated a coup by French settlers and the Pasha of Marrakesh, 1953, and then sought to replace the sultan by his uncle before negotiating independence, 1956, when the international zone of Tangier arrangement was also terminated. The northern strip of Spanish Sahara was ceded by Spain, 1958, and the former Spanish province of Ifni returned to Morocco, 1969. The coastal enclaves of Ceuta and Melilla, however, remained part of Spain. Morocco claimed and occupied the rest of Spanish Sahara, now Western Sahara, in 1976, fighting the guerrillas of the **Polisario movement** who enjoyed Algerian support. A UN-administered ceasefire has been in place since 2001.True parliamentary government was not introduced until 1977, when elections brought the king's supporters to power.

Moshoeshoe (1786–1870)

Nineteenth-century leader, diplomat and founder of the Basotho nation in southern Africa. As a chief, Moshoeshoe founded a kingdom in the Butha-Buthe mountains. During the '**Mfecane**/Difacane' upheaval, Moshoeshoe gained a reputation as a benevolent leader, integrating defeated enemies. As a diplomat, he welcomed French and British missionaries and traded with Europeans for guns. After wars with the **Afrikaner** states, he signed a treaty with the British in 1869, creating what would become **Lesotho**.

Mosquito Coast

The Caribbean Mosquito Coast is part of **Nicaragua** and **Honduras**. The indigenous inhabitants were described by British settlers as part of the `Misquito kingdom', although for the most part these Amerindians lived in small egalitarian groups. The Mosquito Shore was an object of competition between the Spanish and the British but in 1786 the British moved their settlers to British Honduras. **Spain**, **Britain** and the indigenous Misquito population continued to contest the territory into the nineteenth century.

Mossadegh, Mohammed (1876–1967)

Prominent Iranian politician of wealthy landowning stock close to the then ruling **Qajar dynasty**. He studied law in **Belgium** and **Switzerland**, gaining a doctorate in law from the University of Neuchâtel. The author of legal volumes in French and Persian, he was governor general of Fars province, 1917, and then of Azerbaijan province. Minister of justice and briefly minister of foreign affairs, 1922, he acquired the reputation of an honest reformer who passionately resisted 'foreign interference' in Iranian affairs. Opposed to the rise of **Reza Pahlavi** as, first, minister and, then, shah, he lost his parliamentary mandate and was banished to his estates in consequence, where he lived in obscurity until 1939 when he was imprisoned for two years, followed by forced residence in Ahmadabad, by the still vengeful shah. After the shah's obligatory resignation in favour of his son, **Mohammed Reza Pahlavi**, Mossadegh secured election to the *Majlis* (parliament) as deputy for **Tehran**, March 1943. Here he displayed the eccentric traits which were to become notorious, including tearful speeches and simulated fainting fits. As leader of the small National Front, he collaborated with the **Tudeh Party** and secured the passage of a law prohibiting **oil** negotiations with foreign interests until further notice, December 1944. Influential in achieving the rejection of a recently initiated Russo-Iranian oil agreement, October 1947, he attacked the revised agreement accepted by the Iranian cabinet and, as chairman of the Oil Committee, secured the agreement's rejection and the substitution of his committee's proposal to nationalize the whole Iranian oil industry, 1949.

He was appointed prime minister and enacted an Oil Nationalization Law, March 1951, establishing from 1 May a solely Iranian board of directors. He resisted British and American representations that the law was impracticable without modification, weeping and fainting when he spoke before the US Security Council. He presided over growing national economic and political disorder. A demand for increased personal power was rejected by the shah in July 1952, and he was dismissed by the shah with the support of the army, August 1953, but rejected the dismissal decree in a revolutionary atmosphere, causing the shah to leave the country. Following a brief period of anarchy, ended by a coup engineered by the British and American secret services supported by royalists in the armed forces and Mossadegh's many opponents in the population, he surrendered to the restored shah. Arraigned for treachery, *lèse-majesté* and illegal actions, he was sentenced to three years imprisonment, December 1953. Freed August 1956, he remained under house arrest until his death. Iran's oil production facilities, however, were to remain under Iranian government control. His personal probity and the sincerity of his patriotism were never in doubt, but the extent to which his wilder eccentricities, such as wearing pyjamas for public appearances and speaking to the *Majlis* from his bed, were the consequence of mental illness, as his supporters claimed, rather than the exercises in public relations alleged by his opponents, remains controversial.

Mountbatten, Lord Louis (1900–1975)

A member of the British royal family, Mountbatten had a distinguished career in the Royal Navy and became Supreme Commander of Allied Forces in mainland South East Asia in **World War II**. In 1947 he served as the last viceroy of India, presiding over the transfer of power from the British Raj to the new states of **India** and **Pakistan**. Although he was unhappy at the partition of the subcontinent, he felt blocked by **Jinnah**, the **Muslim League** leader, from any other course of action. He persuaded these new nations to remain members of the Commonwealth thereby achieving an important British goal. Remaining as governor general of India for a further year, he then returned home and resumed his naval career. He was helped throughout his career by his wealthy wife Edwina, who engaged in social service activities and died in 1960. Handsome, intelligent and decisive in action, Mountbatten was one of the most popular British leaders of the twentieth century. He was assassinated in 1975 by **IRA** terrorists while on holiday in Ireland.

Moyne Commission

The West India Royal Commission appointed by the British government on 5 August 1938 under the chairmanship of Walter Guinness, 1st Baron Moyne (1889–1944), to investigate the economic and social background to strikes and disturbances that had occurred in the Caribbean colonies since 1935 and to make recommendations on governing the region. The commission included the Trades Union Congress general secretary Sir Walter Citrine (1887–1983). The report exposed the desperate poverty of much of the population, poor health, deficiencies in the education system and the state of labour relations. Concluding that what lay behind the mid-1930s disturbances was a demand for improved living conditions, Moyne emphasized the need for widespread social welfare, health and labour reforms, together with a significant extension of the franchise. He completed his report in 1939 and although findings were not made public until 1945, the government introduced a Colonial Development Act in 1940.

Mozambique

Former Portuguese colony in southern Africa, a major eighteenth- and nineteenth-century slave-trading centre. The Front for the Liberation of Mozambique (**Frelimo**) was formed in 1964 and conducted an effective guerrilla war. Mozambique gained independence in 1974 under President **Samora Machel**, with Frelimo as the sole party, pursuing a socialist programme. The country was torn apart by civil war as the South African-backed Mozambique National Resistance (RENAMO) resisted the government. Joaquim Chissano (1924–), succeeding Machel as president in 1986, adopted an economic liberalization policy and negotiated a treaty with RENAMO in 1994. He was re-elected in 1994 and 1999, though RENAMO alleged irregularities. The Frelimo candidate, Armando Guebuza (1943–), was elected in 2005 and in 2006 the **World Bank** cancelled the country's debts. As clashes were renewed with RENAMO, Frelimo's Filipe Nyusi (1959–) was elected president in 2014. Mozambique's main economic activities are subsistence agriculture, mining and fishing and the population is mainly Christian, with a Muslim minority.

Mpungu a Ndongo

The seat of an important province in the kingdom of Ndongo in modern-day **Angola**. In the succession struggle in Ndongo in 1624–35, the rulers of Mpungu a Ndongo assisted the Portuguese in their war against Queen Njinga and provided major forces for other Portuguese operations, in exchange for being given the title of King of Ndongo. In 1670 Mpungu a Ndongo revolted and was defeated by Portuguese forces, becoming the *presidio* of Pungo Andongo.

Mubarak, Muhammad Hosni Said (1928–)

President of **Egypt**, 1981–2011. He attended the Egyptian Military Academy in **Cairo**, and the Air Academy in Bilbeis, graduating in 1949 and 1950 respectively. He received further flight and bomber training in the **Soviet Union**, and became director of the Air Academy, 1966–9. Appointed air force chief commander by President **Sadat**, 1972, he was responsible for its successes in the 1973 **Yom Kippur War**. Promoted to air marshal, 1974, he was appointed vice president by President Sadat, 1975. Involved in most subsequent Middle Eastern negotiations, he was chief mediator between **Algeria**, **Mauritania** and **Morocco** on the disputed future of Western, formerly Spanish, Sahara, achieving the tripartite agreement.

President of Egypt on Sadat's assassination, 1981, and also prime minister, 1981–2. Vice chairman of the National Democratic Party, 1976–81 and chairman, 1982–2011, he improved relations with the rest of the Arab world while cooling those with **Israel**, particularly after its 1982 invasion of **Lebanon**, but reaffirmed the 1979 peace treaty. Maintained warm relations with the **United States** which remained Egypt's largest aid donor. He was elected for further six-year terms in 1987, 1993, 1999 and 2005. The leading Arab supporter of the Saudi Arabian decision to respond to the Iraqi invasion of **Kuwait**, 1990, he invited the US to organize and lead a coalition force in the **Gulf War**, 1991. He mediated the bilateral Israeli-**Palestine Liberation Organization** (PLO) agreement, signed 1993, and was victim of an unsuccessful assassination attempt by al-Gama'a al-Islamiyya (an Islamic group) in June 1995.

He presided over a period of pervasive corruption, partly attributable to the lavishness of US military aid, which made the army a leading player in the civil economy, owning bakeries, banks, hotels, insurance companies, shipping lines, factories and publishing companies. It also runs many of the principal state organizations such as the lucrative Suez Canal. Officers shop in special malls, use exclusive hospitals and, subject to rank, live in the best neighbourhoods. He sustained himself domestically and internationally by claiming to be the only alternative to the **Muslim Brotherhood**, and oversaw the development of close relations between the Egyptian and Israeli secret services to check **Hamas** in **Gaza**, which caused many Egyptians to observe that the security interests cited by the US to justify its disregard for the human rights violations of the Mubarak regime were a euphemism for Israeli security.

Having failed to crush the mass demonstrations against him associated with the **Arab Spring**, he resigned in favour of the Supreme Council of the Armed Forces (SCAF), 11 February 2011. Effectively sacrificed by the military to preserve its own privileges, he was arrested and placed on trial with his sons and six former top police officials for corruption and failing to prevent the deaths of more than 900 protesters during the uprising in August 2011.

Mugabe, Robert (1924–)

Zimbabwean politician who was prime minister, 1980–7, and president from 1988. A graduate of Fort Hare University, Mugabe taught before his appointment in 1961 as publicity secretary for the National Democratic Party in Southern Rhodesia, then deputy secretary general of the Zimbabwe African People's Union (ZAPU) in 1962. When ZAPU was banned in 1963, he fled to **Tanzania** where he and Ndabaningi Sithole established the Zimbabwe African National Union (**ZANU**), Mugabe becoming secretary general. Mugabe was imprisoned on his return to Rhodesia in 1964. Escaping to **Mozambique** in 1975, he led a guerrilla campaign against the white Rhodesian government. Mugabe became prime minister of independent **Zimbabwe** in 1980 in coalition with ZAPU. ZANU merged with ZAPU in 1987 to form ZANU-PF and Mugabe became Zimbabwe's executive president. His return in subsequent elections aroused widespread claims of irregularities. Following flawed elections in 2008, Mugabe formed a unity government with Morgan Tsvangirai's Movement for Democratic Change. Despite increasing senility, Mugabe refused to relinquish power.

Mughal Empire

Established in 1526 by Zahiruddin Babur and lasting formally until 1858, the Mughal Empire was associated by contemporary observers with immense wealth, cultural magnificence and great power. Babur proudly traced his lineage from the Mongol conquerors Genghis Khan on his mother's side and Tamerlane on his father's. Following the loss of his central Asian patrimony in Farghana and Samarkand to invading Uzbeks, Babur turned to **India** where, after defeating the last Lodi sultan of Delhi, he ruled for merely four years until his death in 1530. In 1540 his son and successor, Humayun, was himself forced to seek refuge at the Safavid court of Persia, by Sher Shah, an enterprising Afghan warrior established in eastern India. Although Humayun returned in 1555 to reclaim his Indian kingdom, he died in the following year.

It was under his grandson Akbar (r. 1556–1605) that Babur's political legacy was transformed into an empire. Besides conquests extending the state's frontiers northwards to **Afghanistan** and **Kashmir**, west to Gujarat and Rajasthan, east to Bengal and Orissa, and south to parts of peninsular India (the Deccan), Akbar also created a vast, mostly loyal nobility inducted from a variety of ethnic and religious groups. This nobility was his instrument for military expansion, maintaining order, revenue collection and a records-based administration. Akbar's personal religious eclecticism found fruition in the *Din-e-Ilahi* (divine faith), the so-called new religion he established melding mystical strands from various faiths including **Islam** and **Hinduism**, which, however, remained a small cult involving only a few courtiers. His public religious policies, informed by the ideal of *Sulh-i-kul* (peace towards all), aimed at accommodating the predominantly non-Muslim subjects of the empire through measures such as the abolition of the pilgrim tax and the *jaziya* (a tax levied on non-Muslim 'protected' subjects).

Akbar's administrative and religious policies were largely continued by his son Jahangir (r. 1605–27) and grandson Shah Jahan (r. 1628–58). The latter added some of the best-known monuments, such as the Taj Mahal, to the dynasty's architectural achievements. Shah Jahan's son Aurangzeb's reign beginning in 1658 is often blamed for causing imperial disintegration by dismantling its cultural pluralism. Although Aurangzeb did push courtly culture in a more austere Islamic direction, the causes of central decline lay elsewhere. Whereas Aurangzeb realized the furthest extension of the Mughal frontier, the empire also outran its resources as it faced, in the last decades of the seventeenth century, a number of agrarian revolts in the north and powerful challenges from rival Muslim states and the Marathas in peninsular India. Aurangzeb managed to ward off these various threats, but his death in 1707 inaugurated an era of gradual imperial decentralization as his successors were weakened by Persian and Afghan invasions, factionalism at court, and the assertion of autonomy by former subordinates. The eighteenth-century context of the devolution of power to a number of successor states also provided the opportunities for the steady territorial expansion of the English **East India Company**. The British found it convenient to preserve the fiction of Mughal sovereignty and to extend their power under its aegis until the revolt of 1857, one strand of which enlisted the emperor as a rallying symbol, nearly ended their rule. Following the rebellion's suppression in 1858 the British exiled the last Mughal ruler to **Burma** and thus extinguished the dynasty founded by Babur.

Mugwumps

A group of American Republicans, mostly drawn from educated urban elites, who in 1884 declined to vote for the Republican nominee for the presidency, James G. Blaine, because his reputation was tarnished by allegations of corruption. It is doubtful that their votes were sufficient on their own to turn the election to the Democrat **Grover Cleveland**, but they represented a wider revulsion against the current practices of politics and a more extensive movement for political reform.

Muhajir Quami movement

A political party established in 1984 to represent the interests of Muhajirs, or Urdu-speaking migrants to **Pakistan**, who resided primarily in Pakistan's Sindh province. In 1997 the party changed its name to the Muttahida Quami movement (MQM) (Movement of the United). With this name change, the MQM attempted to launch itself as a national party advocating the interests of the lower classes.

Muhammad al-Kanemi (c. 1780–1837)

A military leader in the kingdom of Bornu in modern-day Northern Nigeria/**Chad**. A pious Muslim, al-Kanemi served the sultan Dunama and was rewarded by grants of land and slaves. He struggled to preserve Bornu's independence against the jihad led by Usuman dan Fodio in the early nineteenth century, writing letters protesting against its Islamic orthodoxy. He became effective ruler of Bornu in 1818, and continued defending Bornu until his death.

Muhammad Ali Shah Qajar (c. 1807–1848)

Third Qajar shah of **Iran**, 1834–48. The grandson of **Fath 'Ali Shah**, he asserted his claim to the throne against a rival with British and Russian approval and the help of British troops. Determined to restore the historic Iranian position in **Afghanistan** and specifically to reconquer Herat, he led an army against it in 1837, with Russian approval but in the face of strong British opposition. In 1838, therefore, the British occupied the island of Khar in the Persian Gulf and recalled their minister in **Tehran**. Muhammad 'Ali was forced to recognize that Russian support for Iran would not extend to hostilities with **Britain** and obliged to terminate the siege of Herat, December 1838. Like his chief minister, Hajji Mirza Aghasi, he was a man of strong Sufi beliefs, whose reign was marked by some shift in state patronage from the *ulama* and *madrassahs* to the Sufis and the *khaneqahs*. Nevertheless, his reign may be deemed an essentially static interregnum.

Muhammad 'Ali Pasha
– *see* **Mehmet Ali**.

Muhammad ibn Abd al-Wahhab
– *see* **Wahhabiyya, Wahhabism**.

Muhammad Zahir Shah (1914–2007)

Muhammad Zahir Shah was king of **Afghanistan** from 1933 to 1973. Educated in Kabul and **France**, he assumed the throne at the age of 19 following the assassination of his father. Relegating the daily conduct of government affairs to powerful relatives, his public role was largely ceremonial, but contemporaries credited him with a keen ability to manage domestic factions and to maintain Afghanistan's neutrality in the face of American and Soviet pressure. In 1964 he inaugurated a period of democratic experimentation with a new constitution that excluded royal family members from high office and established parliamentary elections and a free press. In 1973 his cousin Muhammad Dawud staged a coup against him and declared a republic. From his refuge in **Italy**, Muhammad Zahir remained the focus of various schemes to place him at the head of a government of national reconciliation, returning briefly to Afghanistan in March 2002 when he was awarded the honorific title 'Father of the Country'.

mujahideen
– *see also* **Afghanistan, Russian Invasion of**.

Afghans who fought against the communists and their Soviet backers between 1979 and 1989 under the banner of jihad, the legally sanctioned struggle in defence of **Islam**, became known as the mujahideen. Muslim clerics had warned of leftist penetration of **Afghanistan** from the 1960s and called for jihad after the communist coup in April 1978. Resistance groups formed spontaneously across the country and challenged the regime from early 1979. The Soviet invasion in December fuelled the resistance, which was increasingly dominated by political parties in exile in **Pakistan** and **Iran**. Seven **Sunni** parties based in Peshawar channelled resources provided by the **CIA** and Pakistani Inter-Services Intelligence, using their access to arms and cash to control the refugee camps in Pakistan and guerrilla commanders in Afghanistan. Nine **Shi'ite** parties similarly attemped to direct the jihad from Iran. Their patrons aided these parties in eliminating competing ideological groups in exile and in Afghanistan. In 1989 the Sunni groups formed an Afghan interim government, and in April 1992 the mujahideen captured Kabul, only to lose it, after years of infighting, to the **Taliban** in 1996.

Mukden Incident

This is also known as the Manchurian Incident. On 18 September 1931, Japanese troops set off bombs on the South Manchurian Railway outside the city of Mukden, the capital of Liaoning province, under the pretext of protecting it from Chinese attack. One hour after the explosion, troops from the Japanese Guangdong Army were mobilized, and within weeks the Japanese forces had overrun **Manchuria**. The following year, Manchuria was incorporated into the Japanese Empire and renamed **Manzhuguo**.

multiculturalism

Polices and systems, especially in education and public policy, which stress cultural pluralism and implicitly deny the superiority of one culture over another. The issue has proved a source of controversy mainly in European countries which in the mid twentieth century accepted considerable numbers of immigrants from other countries. **Germany** in the post-**World War II** period accepted hundreds of thousands of Turkish `guest-workers' and the **United Kingdom** millions of immigrants from the **Commonwealth** and latterly from the **European Union**. Broadly, the acceptance of the religious practices, culture and dress codes of non-European migrants was dubbed `multiculturalism' from the 1960s in anglophone countries. Seen

initially as a loose form of liberal toleration of difference, legislation was initiated in the United Kingdom in 1965 in the Race Relations Act to outlaw racial discrimination, strengthened in 1976. In the **United States**, multiculturalism merged into the **civil rights** and **Black Power** movements, but also found parallels in movements to respect the rights and culture of Hispanics and **Native Americans**. In **Australia**, multiculturalism elevated the rights of **aborigines** and offered greater recognition for their culture, as it did for the **Maori** peoples of **New Zealand**.

Claims by minority cultures that they are not given sufficient recognition continue to animate conflicts in many parts of the world and provide friction between majority cultures and minorities even where the latter's claims had been formally recognized. The `politics of difference' has also incurred a backlash from the end of the twentieth century, partly in reaction to Islamic fundamentalism but also as a reaction by majority cultures to the pressures brought about by immigration. Legislation in **France** in the first part of the twenty-first century against the wearing of religious symbols in state institutions and the wearing of the full female Muslim dress in public are examples of a retreat from multicultural ideals. More generally, **Europe** has seen attacks upon the ideology of multiculturalism with increasing stress upon the need for integration and acceptance by minorities of western values. Similarly, in **Japan**, Premier Abe in 2015 expressed the wish to avoid the `friction' caused in Europe by immigration from other cultures.

multinational corporations

Business organizations whose precursors were such sixteenth- and seventeenth-century foundations as the British Muscovy, Levant and East India Companies and the Dutch East India Company. Ever more profitable with the advent of novel commodities such as tea and coffee, international business was further boosted by the **Industrial Revolution** and improved communications. World trade increased by 260 per cent between 1850 and 1870 alone. **Great Britain** had invested 1 billion pounds abroad by 1875 and **France** ten times more by 1880 than in 1850. Liberalization was equated with economic progress and by the 1870s industrial capitalism had created a global economy.

The corollary was a concentration of economic power in a limited number of global companies. The logic was succinctly expressed by Carl Duisberg, the founder of Germany's I. G. Farben:

'The object of our amalgamation of capital and production units ... must always be the largest possible reduction in the costs of production, administration and sale, with a view to achieving the highest possible profits by eliminating ruinous competition.' That logic, now increasingly extended to services, proved to be a building block of the modern world, making manufacturers such as Ford, Hoover and Siemens household names. It can be found in oil giants such as Shell and Texaco and in other areas such as food and drink (Cocacolaization).

The distinctive contribution of the twentieth century was its reversal of economic geography with capital from newly developed countries such as **Japan** and **South Korea** and countries enriched by super-abundant natural resources such as **Saudi Arabia** penetrating the traditional developed economies, creating multinational corporations of immense wealth but with no national allegiance. The world's 100 biggest companies, almost all multinationals, were valued together in March 2015 at 16·24 trillion US dollars.

Munda, Birsa (1875–1900)

In 1899–1900, Birsa Munda led a **millennialist** revolt in eastern India provoked by the takeover of forests and the destruction of tribal ways by landlords, merchants, moneylenders and labour contractors from the plains. When redress through colonial courts or Christian missionaries failed, the Mundas turned to Birsa, a sharecropper's son who claimed prophethood, having had a vision of God. On 24 December 1899 they followed their 'saviour' into armed rebellion, burning churches and attacking the police until their defeat on 9 January 1900. Birsa was later captured and died in prison.

Munich Agreement

– *see* **Appeasement**.

Musharraf, Pervez (1943–)

Pakistani soldier and politician; chief of the Army Staff, 1998–2007; and president of **Pakistan**, 2001–8. He joined the Pakistan Military Academy in 1961, became an officer in 1964, rising to general in 1998, and in 1999, as army chief, executed a military coup which ousted Prime Minister Nawaz Sharif. Governing as chief executive, then as president, he attempted to reform the economy and improve relations with **India**. Allying himself to the Americans in the 'war on terror' following the 9/11 attack, he faced tensions within the country from supporters of the **Taliban** and increasing pressure from the international community to act

more effectively against them. Threatened with impeachment for his unconstitutional actions, he resigned in August 2008 and moved to London where he battled various charges brought against him, including involvement in the assassination of **Benazir Bhutto**. He was disqualified from taking part in future elections in 2013, and in 2014 charged with high treason.

Muslim Brothers (Brotherhood) (al-Ikhwan al-Musliman)

A religious and political organization that urges a return to the Qur'an and the Hadith (body of tradition) as the basis for a vibrant modern Islamic society, founded by **Hasan al-Banna** at Isma'iliyah, **Egypt**, in 1928. Rapidly spreading to the **Sudan**, **Syria**, **Lebanon**, **Palestine** and the rest of North Africa as well as throughout Egypt, it became increasingly politicized and fundamentalist from 1938, rejecting modernization, secularization and westernization, and demanding purity of religious practice within the Islamic world itself. It organized a terrorist wing directed against the monarchy of King Farouk and the governing **Wafd** Party. It assassinated Mahmoud el-Noqrashi Pasha, the prime minister, December 1948, then went underground with the **1952 Egyptian Revolution** and was forcibly suppressed after its failed attempt to assassinate President **Nasser** in **Alexandria**, 26 October 1954, six of its leaders being executed for treason. It remained generally underground throughout the 1960s and 1970s, and may have inspired, at least indirectly, the assassination of President **Sadat**, 1981. In Syria, the Brotherhood organized an uprising in the city of Hama against the **Alawite** government of President **Hafiz al-Assad**, 1982, which was suppressed at the cost of many thousands of lives. Although there was an unsuccessful attempt by al-Gama'a al-Islamiyya (the Islamic Group) to assassinate President **Mubarak** in 1995, the Egyptian Brotherhood had abjured violence from the late 1980s, as later the Islamic Group did to come into the political fold of the Brotherhood. Despite remaining banned, it fielded 'independent' candidates in the Egyptian parliamentary elections in 2005, winning 88 seats against the 14 of the legal opposition. This electoral success rested to no small degree on the popularity of its network of schools, hospitals and social services, deemed charities, which tended the millions of Egyptians largely neglected by the state, although the Brotherhood had also long built up a strong clandestine following among the professional classes.

The **Arab Spring** stimulated the Brotherhood across the Arab world, although in significantly different national forms. The Tunisian an-Nahda movement, inspired by the Brotherhood, is attempting to fuse Islamism and **democracy**, while the Syrian Brothers have been caught up in the **Syrian Civil War**. If it were to stand in **Jordan** it might win 30–50 per cent of the vote. **Hamas** in **Gaza** was founded by Brotherhood members, 1987, and is widely deemed by its opponents a terrorist organization. In **Bahrain**, however, the Brotherhood is a pillar of support for the ruling **Sunni** government against a rebellious **Shi'ite** population.

In its Egyptian homeland, its political wing was relaunched as the Freedom and Justice Party (FJP) following the overthrow of President Mubarak, February 2011. It won 41 per cent of the seats and 47·5 per cent in coalition with other parties in the parliamentary elections of winter 2011/12, its support being strongest in rural areas. The presidential contest of spring 2012 was then won by the Brotherhood's candidate, Dr Mohammed el-Morsi, over the army's candidate, Ahmed Shafiq, by 52 per cent to 48 per cent on a 51 per cent turnout, with some 8 million votes. The army was meanwhile pursuing its own agenda. The commander-in-chief of the armed forces and defence minister, General Abdel Fattah al-Sisi, warned on 29 January 2013 that the military would intervene if the country's stability was threatened, adding that the army would remain 'the solid and cohesive block' on which the state rested. National support for the government ebbed in the face of public disorder and a declining economy. By July 2013 armed robberies had increased twelvefold and the murder rate 300 per cent since the 2011 revolution. On 1 July, General al-Sisi issued the president with an ultimatum that within forty-eight hours he either meet the demands of the people or resign. The Muslim Brotherhood's headquarters in Cairo was ransacked by a crowd without police or army intervention, while the military made abundantly clear its support for the protesters gathered in Cairo's Tahrir Square.

On 3–4 July the army struck, executing a textbook *coup d'état*, arresting President Morsi and ultimately some 2,000 active members of the Brotherhood. **Saudi Arabia**, which had feared the Brotherhood might subvert its monarchy and could have had some involvement in the coup, approved a 5 billion dollar aid package within days followed by the **United Arab Emirates** with 3 billion dollars. America's President Obama initially declined to suspend military aid, although

US law prohibits martial assistance to a military regime. Saudi Arabia had already promised to make good any shortfall in aid to Egypt. On 23 September 2013 a court banned both the Brotherhood and its political wing in a ruling which could also both criminalize the Brotherhood's 1 million members and close its network of charitable organizations. Perhaps 1,000 Brotherhood supporters had been killed by the army by the end of the month, and its leaders awaited trial.

Muslim League

The league was founded in Dacca in 1906 to represent the interests of **India**'s Muslims. Until the 1940s it had limited influence. From the mid 1930s **Jinnah** worked to build the Muslim League into an all-India party with broad appeal. In 1940 the league announced the 'Lahore Resolution', stating that the Muslims of India were a nation, an ambiguous claim that some historians have subsequently labelled the 'Pakistan Resolution'. During the decade the league emerged as the vehicle for asserting Muslim's political demands at the national level. It won a sweeping victory in the 1945–6 elections, and the Muslim League and Congress were the key players in negotiations leading up to independence and partition. After independence the Muslim League split. In India it ceased to operate as a national party. In **Pakistan** it was sidelined by rising executive and military dominance, and after the late 1950s several parties adopted its name.

Mussolini, Benito Amilcare Andrea (1883–1945)

Leader of the Italian Fascist Party, prime minister of **Italy** 1922–43, first marshal of the Italian Empire 1938–43, and head of the Italian Social Republic ('Republic of Salo'), 1943–5. Known as 'Il Duce', Benito Mussolini rose from humble beginnings through journalism, teaching and the Socialist movement, as well as intermittent labouring jobs. He initially avoided Italian military service, despite his strong Italian nationalism, and spent time in **Switzerland** and **Austria–Hungary** before becoming a polemical novelist and prominent political writer. He broke with Socialism in **World War I**, when he first attempted to blend the ideas of **Friedrich Nietzsche** with those of **Karl Marx** and **Giuseppe Mazzini**, to create a sort of revolutionary socialist nationalism. This blend was a principal element in the creation of **Fascism**.

Mussolini was injured during nine months of military service in World War I, and was recruited by the British Intelligence Service MI5. Pay from his intelligence job allowed him to proseltyze for anti-Socialist fascism in Italy. He did so by rebuilding the movement as one of veterans who wore black shirts and who agreed with totalitarian fascism, and by becoming the editor of the *People* newspaper. From this editorial vantage point, he threw serious criticism at the Italian government for the outcome of the **Versailles** and Trianon **Treaties**, which he characterized as failures for Italy. He also played on middle-class fears of communism. By 1922 the National Fascist Party was strong enough to organize a March on Rome, which resulted in Mussolini being appointed prime minister as part of a coalition. Three years later he became, under the king, dictator and leader (*Duce*) of Italy. He pursued the creation of a one-party, corporatist (and anti-Mafia) state whilst attempting debt reduction, land reclamation, agricultural development and demographic growth, all of which were characterized as 'national battles', pursuing various tactics to suborn the industrial working class with after-work clubs, centralized working policies and jobs, laced with violence and the repression of dissent.

In the 1930s Mussolini applied his ideas of industrial intervention, the colonization of strategic resources within a *Lebensraum*-style '*spazio vitale*', and the promotion of totalitarian gender roles in policies geared to the growth of a new Italian Empire. This resulted in the Abyssinian campaign of 1935, Italian interference in the **Spanish Civil War**, the Axis agreement with Nazi **Germany**, and eventual intervention against Britain and **France** in **World War II**. Italy proved to be a complicated ally for Germany, requiring such support in the eastern Mediterranean theatre that Operation Barbarossa was fatally delayed in 1941. Italian forces also added little strategic or tactical value to the North African and Russian campaigns whilst suffering great casualties. Eventually, the alliance with **Hitler** also proved so unpopular to Italians that in 1943 Il Duce was deposed and imprisoned. He was rescued in a daring German operation, and set up as the head of a puppet government at Salo just after the Allied landings in Sicily. Italy was then occupied by Germany. The war became prolonged and bloody. Mussolini was forced to retreat with the Axis troops. His life ended in a bloody execution by Italian partisans and his body was displayed, upside down attached to a frame, alongside that of his mistress in April 1945.

Mustafa Kemal

– *see* **Atatürk, Mustafa Kemal**.

Mutesa I of Buganda (*c.* 1838–1884)

Ruled from 1856 to 1884. A modernizing ruler of a state in modern-day **Uganda** who opened up trade between the Great Lakes region of Africa and the East African coast initially through Swahili–Arab merchants. He was also very active in centralizing authority in his country and reorganizing it, making Buganda the pre-eminent state in the region. European merchants and missionaries began to arrive in his court in the 1860s and Mutesa witnessed the often factious competition between Muslims, Protestants and Catholics in his country. Many of his subordinates became adherents of these faiths and religious differences overlaid factional conflict in an increasingly centralized kingdom. Mutesa took a keen interest in developments in the outside world and often used Europeans as advisers to help him and his country become more modern. After 1879 Mutesa became ill and steadily lost control. His health never returned.

Mutsuhito, Emperor (1852–1912)

Known as Meiji Tenno, Mutsuhito was Japanese emperor from 1867 to 1912. He was a charismatic figure who symbolized both the maintenance of Japanese tradition and a new direction of modernization. His Charter Oath (1868) represented the end of **Japan**'s cultural and economic isolation and the beginning of the move towards modernization by the **Meiji** leaders, while the Imperial Rescript on Education (1890), promulgated under his name, became the moral code of the Japanese nation.

Muzaffar al-Din Shah Qajar (1853–1907)

Fifth Qajar shah of **Iran**, 1896–1907. Son of **Nasir od-Din Shah Qajar**, he proved both weak and incompetent in the face of ever-growing Great Power rivalry over his country and domestic revolutionary pressures. Essentially only an observer of the alarm felt by British and Russians alike at German economic expansion in **Iran** and, more significantly, of the ongoing negotiations between the British and the Russians over spheres of influence culminating in their 1907 agreement. Obliged to bend to the demands of a revolutionary movement inspired by nationalism, constitutionalism and the 1905 revolution in the **Russian Empire** and supported by both traditional Muslims and the new secular intelligentsia, he granted a new constitution limiting his power, 1906. The revolutionary movement had enjoyed some British but no Russian sympathy, and the constitution and parliamentary government were abolished by Muzaffar's son, Muhammad 'Ali Shah, who reigned 1907–9, with Russian support but at the cost of his own deposition in favour of his son, Ahmad Shah, then aged 11.

My Lai Massacre

The name commonly given to the killing of well over 300 unarmed and unresisting inhabitants of a hamlet in Son My village, **Vietnam**, on 16 March 1968, by a US infantry company. The killings were not exposed until November 1969; photographs of the victims then appeared throughout the world press. Only one soldier – Lieutenant William Calley – was successfully prosecuted for his role in the massacre. His trial attracted international attention.

Myanmar

The Union of Myanmar, formerly known as Burma, is located in South East Asia, bordering **China**, **Laos** and **Thailand** to the east and north-east, and **India**, **Bangladesh**, the Andaman Sea and the Bay of Bengal to the west and north-west. It has a total area of 678,500 square kilometres and a population of over 50 million. With the Burmans as the ethnic majority (68 per cent) occupying most of the central plains, Myanmar has a large variety of ethnic minorities residing in the rugged highlands and mountainous areas in the northern and western parts of the country. The majority of the population is Buddhist (89 per cent). The official language is Burmese. The capital city is now Naypyidaw.

Burma was first unified as a kingdom under King Anawrahta in the eleventh century. After Mongol invasion in the thirteenth century, the Burmese relocated their kingdom south to the ancient capital of Bago. The first agents of the British **East India Company** arrived for negotiations in 1612. However, Burmese political leaders resisted all efforts of British, Dutch and Portuguese traders to negotiate the establishment of ports along the Bay of Bengal. In 1824 the Anglo-Burmese War broke out, resulting in British victory in 1826. Burma was annexed as a part of British India in 1886, and in 1937 it once again became a separate colony within the **British Empire**.

During **World War II** Burma became a key battleground as it was the site of the 800-mile Burma Road, which was the Allies' major supply line to China. Japanese forces invaded Burma in December 1941 and managed to cut off most of the Burma Road during their four-year occupation. During the war the Burmese nationalist leader, Aung San, was persuaded to collaborate with **Japan** with the promise of post-war independence. However, Aung San switched allegiance to the Allies towards the end of the war when it became evident that Japan also had imperialist interests in Burma. Aung San remained the nationalist leader until his assassination in July 1947, only months before Burmese independence was finally achieved on 4 January 1948.

U Nu, a close colleague of Aung San, became the first Burmese prime minister in 1948. However, Aung San's assassination gave rise to another military leader, General **Ne Win**. U Nu relied heavily on Ne Win's forces to control frequent civil unrest arising from Burma's various ethnic minorities. When a rebellion broke out due to U Nu's refusal to grant semi-autonomy to the Shan and Kayins in 1962, Ne Win established himself as leader of the new military government. Ne Win ruled Burma according to the 'Burmese Way of Socialism', which essentially closed the country off from the outside world. In 1988, amidst escalating student demonstrations for democracy, Ne Win announced that he would step down from power. The military government agreed to democratic elections in 1989, but annulled the results when the oppositional National League of Democracy (NLD) won the majority. The NLD leader, **Aung San Suu Kyi** (daughter of the late nationalist leader, Aung San) was awarded the Nobel Peace Prize in 1991. She continued to lead the democracy movement despite being put under house arrest after the 1989 elections. After her release from house arrest in 2010 her party, the NLD, secured a majority in the 2015 elections, as part of a wider process of liberalization. A close friend of Suu Kyi then became a proxy president for her.

Mzilikazi (c. 1790–1868)

A Zulu who became king of the Ndebele kingdom (r. 1840–68). Originally a lieutenant of **Shaka** in the **Zulu** Empire, Mzilikazi fled northwards with his army into modern-day **Zimbabwe**. There he founded a kingdom among the Ndebele modelled on that of Shaka in Zululand. He successfully resisted **Afrikaner** invasions of his country in 1847–51, signing a treaty with **Great Britain** in 1852. He welcomed European settlers in his lands, especially following gold strikes in 1867.

N

Nadir Shah (1688–1747)

Iranian tribal ruler who created an empire. Born Nadr Qoli Beg of a Turkish tribe loyal to **Iran**, he became a bandit chieftain who supported Tamasp II, the Safavid claimant. He reformed the military to install Tamasp, defeated the **Ottoman** Turks of modern-day **Azerbaijan** and **Iraq**, and deposed Tamasp, proclaiming himself regent. He ejected the Turks from Iran and obliged the **Russian Empire** to surrender its Caspian provinces, and claimed the throne as Nadir Shah in 1736. He built an Iranian navy, capturing **Bahrain** and **Oman** from the Arabs, then invaded Mughal India, capturing Delhi and returning with the Peacock Throne and the Koh-i-Noor diamond. He attacked the Uzbeks of Bukhara and Khiva to expand his empire to its greatest extent, which compared with those of antiquity. Having sought unsuccessfully to change the Islamic practice of Iran from **Shi'ite** to **Sunni**, and intensely suspicious and tyrannical with solely military gifts, he grew increasingly unpopular and was assassinated by his own forces.

NAFTA

The North American Free Trade Agreement (NAFTA), in operation from 1 January 1994, was signed by **Canada, Mexico** and the **United States** creating a free trade zone among the three largest economies in North America. The United States and Canada had already signed a bilateral agreement in 1988, which under NAFTA was later extended to include Mexico. Canadian Prime Minister Brian Mulroney, US President **George Bush** and Mexican President Carlos Salinas de Gortari signed the trade agreement on 17 December 1992. After ratification by the national legislatures, it took effect on 1 January 1994. NAFTA is meant to reduce or eliminate trade barriers and tariffs between member states, similar to the common market of the **European Union**. Canadian and US companies gained better access to the Mexican markets in banking, insurance, advertising, telecommunications and trucking, though not without problems.

Nagasaki, bombing of

The second **atomic bomb** dropped by the **USA** on Nagasaki, Japan, on 9 August 1945. It killed more than 35,000 people outright and injured perhaps a further 25,000, as well as completely destroying or severely damaging about 40 per cent of the city's buildings. The city is now a spiritual centre for movements to ban nuclear weapons.

Nagorno-Karabakh

– *see* **Azerbaijan**.

Naguib, Major General Muhammed (Neguib, Mohammed) (1901–1984)

Popular Egyptian general, born in the Sudan, who first won prestige in the 1948 fighting between **Egypt** and **Israel**. Selected by the **Free Officers** led by Colonel **Nasser**, who were themselves too junior for the role, to be the figurehead for their planned new regime. Following their coup deposing King **Farouk**, July 1952, he became head of state of the new regime, then president of the republic, 18 June 1953. More traditionalist in outlook than Nasser and many other Free Officers, he sought the early introduction of parliamentary democracy and opposed summary justice for deposed politicians. Resigned February 1954, but persuaded to withdraw his resignation, he welcomed the revival of political parties and the summoning of a constituent constitutional assembly, opposed by Nasser. Remotely associated with the 1954 assassination attempt on Nasser, he was arrested 13 November 1954 and kept under house arrest until about 1970. Although it was eased in 1960, he thereafter ceased to play any political role.

Nahhas Pasha, Mustafa al- (1876–1965)

Leader of the Egyptian **Wafd** Party and a judge, 1904. He joined the Wafd on its foundation, but was dismissed from government service for taking part in politics, 1919. Elected to Parliament, 1923, he became minister of communications, 1924, and was then elected leader on the death of **Sa'ad Zaghlul**, in 1927. Prime minister, 1928, he was promptly dismissed by King Fu'ad after just three months. Again prime minister, he resigned over differences with the king in 1930. Reappointed to lead the Egyptian delegation, he negotiated the successful conclusion of the **Anglo-Egyptian Treaty** of Alliance, 1936, and obtained the abolition of the Capitulations at the Montreux conference, 1937. Increasingly authoritarian, he encouraged the paramilitary 'Blue Shirts' and demanded unqualified obedience, provoking widespread defections. Again dismissed, late 1937, he was reappointed February 1942, on British insistence, to ensure cooperation in the war effort, at the expense of maladministration and corruption. Ousted by King **Farouk** in October 1944, he became ultra-nationalist and helped to create the **Arab League**. Prime minister, January 1950, he was dismissed and dropped as Wafd Party leader in 1952, following violence in Cairo.

Naidu, Sarojini (1879–1949)

Indian nationalist leader and poet. Born Sarojini Chattopadhyay, she joined the independence movement after Curzon's partition of **Bengal**, and became famous across India as the *bharatiya kokila* ('nightingale of India') for her mellifluous voice. Brilliant, and deft in languages (Bengali, Urdu, Telegu, Persian, English), she was president of the **Indian National Congress** (1925) and the first secular biographer of Jinnah. She was goaled several times and died in office as governor of Uttar Pradesh.

Najibullah, Mohammad Ahmadzai (1947–1992)

Najibullah was head of the Soviet-backed communist government of **Afghanistan** from May 1986 to April 1992. Born in 1947 into a Ghilzai Pashtun family, he became politically active as a medical student. In 1965 he joined the People's Democratic Party of Afghanistan (PDPA) and was imprisoned several times. Following the PDPA coup of April 1978, Najibullah first played a major role as head of the dreaded Afghan security police (KHAD) under Babrak Karmal in late 1979. Backed by the Soviets, he replaced Karmal in 1986. Under pressure from Soviet leaders seeking an end to the war, he oversaw in 1987 a programme of 'national reconciliation' intended to stabilize the government by broadening its social base. In 1990 he further distanced himself from Marxist ideology. He was removed and executed after the opposition seized Kabul in 1992.

Namibia

Former German colony of South West Africa. Initially explored by **Portugal**, the area was occupied by **Germany** in 1884. In 1892–1905 German forces brutally suppressed Herero and Nama resistance. The territory came under South Africa as a **League of Nations mandate** in 1919. In 1946 the **United Nations** rejected a South African claim to annex it, but apartheid regulations were imposed. In 1960 Samuel Daniel Nujoma (1929–) was prominent in establishing the South West African People's Organization (SWAPO) to liberate Namibia. SWAPO opened guerrilla war in 1966, operating from neighbouring **Angola**, and the country gained independence under Nujoma in 1990, the last African state to do so. The government instituted a programme of land redistribution from whites to blacks. Hifikepunye Pohamba (1935–) became President in 2004 and was succeeded in 2014 by Hage Geingob (1941–). Namibia's population is overwhelmingly Christian. The economy is based on agriculture and fishing and is heavily dependent on diamond and uranium extraction for revenue.

Namik Kemal (1840–1888)

A leading **Ottoman** political and literary figure. He found initial employment in the empire's translation bureaux before joining a newly founded newspaper, *Tasvir-i Efkar*, in 1862. He soon expanded his literary repertoire to include expository political writing as well as poetry. As one of the founders of the Young Ottoman movement, Namik Kemal was a leading voice for political liberty and reform. In 1873 Sultan Abdülaziz had him exiled, objecting to his call for a new patriotism linked to the sovereignty of the people (instead of the sultan). Sultan **Abdul Hamid II** invited him to return from exile in **Cyprus**, and he went to Istanbul but was again forced out of the capital as Abdul Hamid turned against the **Young Ottomans**. He died while working as an administrator on the Aegean island of Mytilene.

Nana Sahib (1824–c.1859)

The adopted son of Maratha Peshwa Baji Rao, Dhondo Pant, better known as Nana Sahib, was a major leader of the 1857 Sepoy Mutiny against the British. Although his relationship with the English **East India Company** had been cordial even after the Company's refusal to recognize his right to the royal pension, he was forced by popular pressure to join the rebels in 1857. After the mutiny he fled to Nepal and little is known of his later life and death.

Nana Yaa Asantewa (c. 1840–1921)

Queen mother of the kingdom of Asante in modern-day **Ghana**. Wife of King Prempeh I, she was present when the British expeditionary force entered the capital of Kumasi and captured the king, demanding that the Golden Stool, an important symbol of Asante power, be turned over. After a stirring speech shaming male leaders, Nana Yaa led resistance against the British until her own capture and exile to the Seychelles in 1900.

Nanjing, Rape of

This is also known as the Nanjing Massacre. At the start of the second Sino-Japanese War, Japanese forces invaded Shanghai on 14 August 1937. After fierce fighting they pushed inland, reaching Nanjing in December. From then until March 1938, the Japanese troops murdered at least 200,000 civilians, although the Chinese claim the number is 300,000. They also raped and tortured countless women and children. The Nanjing Massacre remains a controversial issue in Sino-Japanese relations.

Nanjing, Treaty of (1842)

The Treaty of Nanjing concluded the first Anglo-Chinese **Opium War** (1839–42). The British imposed terms on the defeated government of the Qing dynasty, including the forced opening of five 'treaty ports' (Shanghai, Ningbo, Fuzhou, Xiamen and Guangzhou), the cession of **Hong Kong** island and the payment of reparations of 21 million silver dollars. The treaty is regarded in **China** as the first of the 'unequal treaties' that marred relations between the West and China for the next hundred years.

Nansen, Fridtjof (1861–1930)

Norwegian explorer, scientist and diplomat. He crossed the Greenland icecap, 1888, and studied the movement of the polar ice in his north polar expedition, 1893–6, drifting in the ice north of **Russia** in his ship *Fram* for almost three years. He personally negotiated the repatriation of 427,886 German and Austro-Hungarian prisoners of war with the Russian government on behalf of the **League of Nations**, 1920–2, and was active in Russian famine relief, 1921. He inspired the 'Nansen passport' for displaced persons, and was awarded the Nobel Peace Prize, 1922.

Naoroji, Dadabhai (1825–1917)

A mathematician and three-time president of the **Indian National Congress**, he argued for the rights of Indians as British subjects. In *Poverty and Un-British Rule in India* (1901), he provided an economic critique of British colonialism and articulated the theory of a 'drain' of **India**'s wealth to **Britain**. He was the first Indian elected to the British House of Commons in 1892 and was known by the sobriquet 'Grand Old Man of India'.

Napoleon (1769–1821)

French general and emperor. A Corsican by birth. He attended French military schools and became a general at the age of 24, his teachers at the École de Brienne recording perceptively: 'Wholly tending towards self-esteem, ambitious, aspiring to everything, liking solitude.' He married Josephine de Beauharnais, a Creole from Martinique, and was entrusted by the Directory with the French campaign against **Austria** in **Italy**, 1796 (see **Napoleonic Wars**). He helped the Directory reinstate the Jacobins as the war party, 1797, emphasizing the power of the military. Led an expedition to **Egypt**, 1797, revealing an ambition to take **India** from the British. Appointed consul in a *coup d'état*, appealing to both royalists and republicans. He entered office, December 1799, initiating an increasingly authoritarian regime, moving into the Tuileries palace to indicate both the continuity of power and the exclusion of the Bourbon monarchy. He believed the French preferred equality and glory to freedom, and sought to appeal to the centre while appeasing Left and Right and respecting the symbols of the Revolution. Granted a life consulate, 1801, by a majority of 3.5 million to 8,000 votes. He signed a **concordat** with the Roman Catholic Church, restoring religion, 1802, although he was a deist and a political, rather than a believing, Catholic. He personally supervised the creation of a new code of civil law (*code Napoléon*) unifying earlier laws, and lastingly reformed education along semi-military lines. He established the Grandes Écoles, which, rather than the universities, train the French elite of today, and created the *Légion d'honneur*, **France**'s highest honour.

He was invested with the foreign dignities of President of the Italian Republic and Protector of **Switzerland** and of the German Confederation. He forestalled an assassination plot, backed by the British, by kidnapping and executing the innocent Duke d'Enghien of the House of Bourbon, and crowned himself emperor of the French in the cathedral of Notre-Dame in Paris, in the presence of the Pope, 2 December 1804, swearing to defend equality, liberty, property rights and France within its natural frontiers. Always fearful of betrayal and a cynic as to human nature, he revealed his Corsican background by putting his relations on vacated thrones and marrying them into **Europe**'s royal families. He rejected Josephine to marry the 18-year-old Marie Louise, the daughter of the Austrian emperor and a niece of Marie Antoinette, to ingratiate himself with the European sovereigns and to secure an heir. Obliged to abdicate and exiled to Elba, 1814, he returned in March 1815 but was finally defeated at **Waterloo** on 18 June 1815. He gave himself up to the British and was exiled to St Helena, where he died. His remains were returned to France and placed in Les Invalides in Paris, 1840.

At one level, Napoleon changed little. The boundaries of France after 1815 were much as they had been before 1789. At another, he changed almost everything. Most of the medieval legacy of city-states and ecclesiastical states was swept away to be replaced by a more rational political geography. Similarly, feudalism was formally abolished everywhere under French control and nowhere re-established. Such Revolutionary innovations as the metric system became the norm in continental Europe, with even **Britain** slowly falling into line more than two centuries later, and continental European legal systems owe much to the Napoleonic code. It is France herself, however, which most clearly bears his enduring stamp.

Napoleon III (1808–1873)

Charles Louis Napoleon Bonaparte, last emperor of **France**. **Napoleon Bonaparte**'s nephew, Louis Napoleon lived in London following his abortive 'Bonapartist' coup attempts against King Louis Philippe in 1836 and 1840. In 1848 he was elected president of the Second Republic, becoming emperor of the Second Empire in 1852. Provoked into war with **Prussia** by **Bismarck** in 1870, Napoleon III was captured at Sedan, deposed following France's defeat and lived in exile in England.

Napoleonic Wars

The Napoleonic Wars follow the Revolutionary Wars declared in April 1792, which resulted by 1795 in the French occupation of the Low Countries, the Rhineland, parts of **Spain**, **Switzerland** and Savoy. The wars are significant not just militarily and politically but as the first expression of total war. They began with the entrustment to Napoleon (**Napoleon I Bonaparte**)

of the French campaign against **Austria** in **Italy**, 1796. With victories at Montenotte, Dego, Millesimo and Lodi, Napoleon conquered Italy within a month. He signed the Peace of Campo-Formio, 1797, led an expedition to **Egypt**, 1797, where he liberated it from the Mamluks, and entered the Levant, but had to return when Nelson destroyed the French fleet near Aboukir. Although he then wanted peace for home policy reasons, the Austrians resumed hostilities but were defeated at Marengo, 1800. He signed the Peace of Lunéville with Austria, 1801, securing the left bank of the Rhine and a zone of friendly states.

Fearing that the British would not accept a French Belgium except under duress, Napoleon conceived of a 'continental blockade', requiring the closure of all European ports to British merchants and the cooperation to that end of Denmark, **Sweden**, **Prussia** and **Russia**. Temporarily abandoning that plan, he signed the compromise Peace of Amiens with **Britain**, 1802, to which neither side was genuinely committed. Correctly he accused Britain of not evacuating **Malta** in accordance with the Peace, just as Britain correctly accused him of coercing Switzerland, annexing Piedmont and reorganizing **Germany**.

His declaration of the French Empire in 1804 provoked Britain, Austria, **Russia**, Sweden and Naples to form a new coalition, aiming openly to end his conquests and tacitly to reduce France to her former frontiers. Napoleon planned to invade England in 1805, but conscious of naval weakness first launched a campaign against Austria, winning a bloodless victory at Ulm only to learn of the great naval defeat at Trafalgar, 21 October 1805. He defeated the Austrians again, Austerlitz, December 1805, and then sought the tsar's friendship. He offered Prussia the British possession of Hanover but extracted the German Empire and Italy from Austria, then established the Confederation of the Rhine of sixteen rulers, including those of Baden, Bavaria and Württemberg, with himself as president, 1806. He drove the Bourbons from Naples, installing his male relations on the thrones of Naples and Holland, and marrying his female ones to other princes and kings.

He defeated Prussia at Jena and Auerstedt, and entered Potsdam, 1806; then defeated Russia at Eylau and at Friedland, 1807, but secured reconciliation with Tsar **Alexander I** at Tilsit and his agreement to closing Russia's ports to the British. Britain took the initiative by seizing the Danish fleet and bombarding Copenhagen. Napoleon extended the continental blockade to

Spain and **Portugal** and transferred his brother, Joseph, from Naples to Spain as king, having imprisoned the previous monarchs. Spanish insurgents backed by British, 1808, in **Peninsular War** but resurgent Austrians again defeated at Wagram, 1809.

Russia allowed the blockade to be broken, summer 1811, and Napoleon invaded, May 1812. Russia abandoned Moscow, forcing Napoleon to retreat in the depth of winter. Only 100,000 of his original 610,000 soldiers recrossed the Russian frontier. Prussia declared war, 1813, to be defeated at Lützen and Bautzen, but Napoleon was defeated by the allies at Leipzig and obliged to abdicate, 1814. Exiled as sovereign of Elba, he returned in March 1815, but was finally defeated at **Waterloo**, on 18 June 1815.

Narain, Jai Prakash (1902–1979)

Among the founders in 1934 of the Congress Socialist Party, a group within the **Indian National Congress** which attempted to radicalize its programme in a leftist direction. In 1954, Jai Prakash renounced party politics and devoted himself to the Gandhi-inspired Sarvodaya movement, which advocated service, non-violence and the equal rights of all to land and property. By 1974, amidst widespread corruption and economic and political crises, Jaiprakash suspended his political retirement to lead a popular movement against **Indira Gandhi**'s Congress party in power and, in 1977, was instrumental in uniting the opposition into the coalition Janata Party that won national elections. However, Janata's corruption and factionalism fell short of Jaiprakash's dream of 'total revolution'.

Nasir od-Din Shah Qajar (also ad-Din) (1831–1896)

Fourth Qajar shah of **Iran**, 1848–96. A younger son of **Muhammad 'Ali Shah Qajar**, he was nominated heir apparent through his mother's influence. Serious disturbances accompanied his accession in consequence, but were subdued by the efforts of his chief minister, **Amir-e Kabir**. Initially a reformer under Amir-e Kabir's influence until the Amir was forced from office by his enemies (and later disgraced, imprisoned and murdered), who included the shah's mother. Victim of an assassination attempt by two members of the Babi sect, 1852, he savagely persecuted the sect thereafter. Repeated his father's attempt to dominate **Afghanistan**, by capturing Herat, 1856, but similarly encountered British opposition, **Britain** declaring war on **Iran** and insisting on the return of Herat

and Iranian recognition of the sovereignty of the Afghan kingdom. The army was in any event in decline, whether in terms of men, equipment, discipline, or leadership, and its attempt to discipline the Yamut Turcomans was routed. The only comparatively disciplined and effective troops were to be the Russian-officered Persian Cossack Brigade presented by the tsar to the shah as his personal guards, 1878.

He was impressed by the technology he witnessed on his visits to **Europe**, 1873, 1878 and 1889, having already been persuaded (1872) by his chief minister to grant a concession to Baron Julius de Reuter, a naturalized British entrepreneur of German origin, to provide the investment necessary to exploit Iran's minerals and create a railway network, and thereby employ Iran's pool of underemployed labour. The size of the concession provoked such an angry public reaction, however, that it was withdrawn, 1877. Britain was, however, compensated for the cancellation by a new concession for the Imperial Bank of Persia to have the exclusive right to issue banknotes and to enjoy in addition extensive mineral exploitation rights, 1889. To keep a balance, the Russians obtained a concession to establish the Discount Bank of Russia. Even more inflammatory was the **Tobacco Regie** concession, 1890. All of these concessions were designed to be highly profitable in commissions and royalties to the shah and his ministers, but it has been persuasively argued that the grant and the withdrawal of the tobacco concession were the stimuli for the emergence of modern Iranian nationalism.

Genuinely responsible for a measure of modernization and reform, he introduced postal and telegraph services, remapping Tehran and providing it with street lighting and rubbish collections, and building roads, but refused to respond to the pressures for political reform which were growing in the later years of his reign, preferring the traditional arbitrary absolutism. Although there was no significant technical progress in either agriculture or industry, he is considered by some to be personally the best ruler Iran had had since **Karim Khan Zand**. Nevertheless, he was increasingly unpopular in many sectors of Iranian society, and was assassinated by a fanatic in 1896.

Nassau Agreement (1962)

Signed by US President **John F. Kennedy** and British Prime Minister Harold Macmillan in the Bahamas on 18 December 1962, the Nassau Agreement committed the **USA** to supplying the UK with nuclear-capable, submarine-launched Polaris missiles in exchange for the lease of a nuclear submarine base at Holy Loch, near Glasgow, Scotland. The agreement was a face-saving one for Macmillan, following the Kennedy administration's withdrawal of support for the jointly developed US–UK Skybolt air-launched nuclear deterrent.

Nasser, Colonel Gamal Abdel (Jamal 'Abd al-Nasir) (1918–1970)

President of **Egypt** and the Arab world's most charismatic twentieth-century leader. He graduated from Staff College, 1947, and was wounded in the war with **Israel**, 1948. Leader of the **Free Officers** organization which overthrew King Farouk, July 1952, he became prime minister on 17 April 1954, and, having ousted **Naguib**, president on 17 November the same year, until his death. A spellbinding orator in his native Arabic, whose espousal of colonial liberation and pan-Arab political unity was highly influential across the **Middle East**, he aroused western fears about the security of its **oil** supplies, and specifically French hostility because of his support for the **Algerian War of Independence**. **Ben Bella**, the future Algerian president, was a personal friend. Victim of an attempted assassination attempt by the then underground **Muslim Brothers**, in **Alexandria**, 26 October 1954.

He was a leading figure with **India**'s **Nehru** in the promotion of Afro-Asian solidarity and colonial liberation at the Bandung (**Indonesia**) conference, April 1955, and subsequently of the closely associated policy of non-alignment at the Belgrade conference, September 1961, where he, Nehru, and **Yugoslavia**'s **Tito** acted as a triumvirate. In accord with non-alignment he, like Nehru, cultivated good relations with the **Soviet Union** and its allies. He was greatly to annoy West Germany by inviting East Germany's Walter Ulbricht to pay a state visit to Egypt, 1965, which brought with it an economic and industrial aid agreement. Although he suppressed communism at home and Egypt was never a satellite, his relations with the Soviet Union had so alarmed the western powers that they cancelled their financial support for his Aswan Dam project, mid July 1956, to which he responded by nationalizing the **Suez Canal**, which was largely British and French owned, 26 July 1956, launching the **Suez Crisis**, 1956. The dam was then constructed by Soviet engineers with Soviet funding, its waters becoming Lake Nasser. He emerged from the crisis with his prestige greatly enhanced and was henceforth the unquestioned leader of the Arab world. President of the short-lived **United Arab Republic** of Egypt and **Syria**, 1958–61.

Domestically, Nasser, who considered himself an Arab socialist, sought to introduce a planned economy. He established a planning authority, 1957, and inaugurated an ambitious ten-year plan, 1960, which sought to increase gross national product (GNP) by 7.5 per cent annually. All industries, banks, insurance companies and the export trade were nationalized and from 1962 peasants and craftsmen were obliged to join cooperatives. The consequences included a flight of capital and mass migration from the countryside to the towns, but the planned economy was only revised after his death. His great setback was the defeat of Egypt by Israel in the Six Day War of 1967, a pre-emptive strike by Israel foreshadowed by his request for the withdrawal of the UN peacekeeping force from Sinai and his closure of the Gulf of Aqaba to Israeli shipping. He died suddenly of a heart attack in 1970.

Although many of his domestic policies were reversed by his successor, **Anwar as-Sadat**, Nasser may be credited with increasing the standard of living of Egyptian citizens and introducing long overdue social reforms.

Nasserism

Arab nationalist political ideology based on the thinking of the president of **Egypt Gamal Abdel Nasser**. It is a secular ideology, leading to conflict with the emerging Muslim fundamentalism, that argues for modernization, industrialization, opposition to colonialism, and views **Israel** as representing modern western colonialism. In world politics, Nasser's Egypt played a major part in the pan-Arab and Non-Aligned movements in the 1950s and 1960s.

Natal

– *see* **South Afica**.

nation state

– *see* **state formation**.

National Aeronautics and Space Agency (NASA)

The National Aeronautic Space Agency (NASA) was established by the **United States** in 1958 after the Soviets had launched *Sputnik*, the world's first orbital space satellite. It aimed to restore American technological prestige. Orbital satellites would yield information on Soviet military capabilities, but scientific exploration was an independent goal. In 1969, NASA's *Apollo II* landed a man on the Moon. The *Challenger* and *Columbia* disasters of 1986 and 2003 respectively, were setbacks to the attempt to create a reliable space shuttle service.

National Origins Quota System (USA)

Responding to massive European immigration, in 1921 and 1924 the American government put a ceiling on the number of immigrants from outside the western hemisphere and effectively excluded Asian immigration. The formula in the 1924 Act limited European immigration to numbers from each country not exceeding 2 per cent of the number of Americans living in the US in 1890 who had come from that country, thus assigning very small quotas to southern and eastern Europe. It remained law until 1965.

national parks (USA)

The United States established the world's first national park in 1872. Yellowstone (north-west Wyoming) was a new type of park: it was large, wild, publicly owned and with open access. The parks of the initial generation, enshrining examples of spectacular scenery in the mountainous west (eg. Yosemite, California), were set up to satisfy the needs of cultural nationalism and generate tourist revenue rather conserve flora and fauna. Their emphasis on a pristine wilderness led to the enforced removal of all indigenous peoples living in the areas. More recently, the preservation of wilderness and biodiversity have become more important priorities. The national parks theme has become a global phenomenon and now extends to marine reserves.

National Party

Former political party in South Africa. The National Party was founded in Bloemfontein in 1915 by **Afrikaner** nationalists in response to the **Union of South Africa** in 1910. Coming to power in 1948, the National Party promoted Afrikaner culture, established a republic and instituted the **apartheid** system. Under the leadership of F. W. de Klerk, it negotiated the establishment of the first full franchise, multi-party elections in 1994, which saw the victory of **Nelson Mandela** and the **ANC**.

nationalization

The term for public (rather than private) control of industry, finance or commerce. Nationalization was inspired in mainland Europe by the philosophy of **Karl Marx** and in **Britain** by Fabian socialists, notably Sidney Webb, whose clause IV(4) of the Labour Party constitution reads: 'To secure for the workers ... the full fruits of their industry and the most equitable distribution thereof that may be possible upon the basis of the common ownership of the means of production, distribution and exchange.'

Nationalization was pioneered in socialist Scandinavia and the communist **Soviet Union** whose command economy presupposed full state control. It was widely adopted for strategic industries across Europe after 1945 when capitalism was widely blamed for the rise of fascism, and extended to virtually the whole economy in Soviet-dominated eastern Europe.

Much was reversed in the process of privatization under right-wing influence from the 1970s and following the fall of communism, but the nationalized sector remains significant particularly in **France**. The financial crisis of 2008 resulted in emergency bank nationalizations in the UK and elsewhere.

nationalism

An ideology based around the idea of the nation. A nation is a collective unit made up of inhabitants of a particular area, or of a tribal group related by blood, or of the adherents of a civic culture associated with a particular defined territory. As such, nationalism is based on allegiance to such a unit as a basic feature of political life, and holds that members of other units are to be excluded from decisions as illegitimate. It is frequently contrasted with cosmopolitanism, imperialism, international religion, adherence to supra-national institutions and pluralism. Nationalists believe that different nations are possessed of different priorities, ethical systems and moral identities. Some go further and elevate their own associated nation above all others and seek to dominate or elevate themselves above others. One of the key features of nationalism is the identification of groups who do not belong to the nation within and without, and their use as elements against which a nation can be defined. Nationalists tend to want nations to conform to a nineteenth-century view of nationality as at least upholding a flag, anthem, language, particular ethnic group, passport, votes and citizenship for national citizens, and centralized government. They eschew regional differences, local dialects and diversity for a central monoculture to one degree or another. Paradoxically, nationalists tend to value membership, but deny the authority, of the **United Nations Organization**.

Nationalism has been one of the driving forces of western history since the **French Revolution** in

1789. During that event, ideas of the 'sovereignty of the people' people and 'French' institutions were defined against 'foreign' tyrants, a monarch with international connections, social hierarchies in which different groups used different languages, and foreign invasions. **Napoleon** went on, after his victories, to accept the reality of national difference and sought to reorganize states on ethnic lines, if subject to Napoleonic law. By the 1840s, liberal nationalists had associated the idea of democratic or liberal states with the idea of national resistance to overarching monarchies based around religious and traditional principles, and in combination with the romantic idea of a national 'soul' European nationalism emerged. Nationalism was initially therefore a radical force rather than a conservative one, but very much associated with firm views of social behaviour in which citizens would dress, eat and behave in particular ways and in which women would be expected to contribute by giving birth to and raising new citizens.

Such nationalism became an irritant to the great European monarchies, many of which presided over multiethnic or multinational states and sought to bring many peoples into vast multinational empires. It also created a violent form of intolerance based around national resistance movements and covertly organized armies. Some nationalist movements attracted a great deal of Romantic attention, such as that of **Garibaldi** in **Italy**, or Lajos Kossuth in **Hungary**. Irish nationalism became a key weakness in the British imperial scheme after the Act of Union of 1801.

The violent potential of European nationalism contrasted with that of 'Enlightenment' or 'civic' nationalism best exemplified by the ideas of the founders of the **United States** that nations did not have to be mono-ethnic and that people could join them if only they agreed with national ideas and political values. This still involved a corpus of national identity, and was also perhaps only possible in newer federal states in which Europeans of various descents mixed. It is instructive that American nationalists preferred the Roman term *patriot* to *nationalist* and that attempts to create a consensus on what an ethnic 'American' was failed in the mid nineteenth century. Instead, ideas of political allegiance, class or race filled the gap, a pattern repeated later in liberal democracies such as **Australia**, **Canada**, **South Africa** or **India**.

Nationalism attracted a great deal of attention from scholars in the nineteenth century, the most prominent of whom was Ernst Renan, who wrote *What is a Nation?* in 1882. Renan held that nationalists had to adhere to their idea of a nation every day, suggesting the imagined nature of their allegiance, and also that nationalists should encourage the public forgetting of past traumas and differences within a nation unless the memory strengthened collective feeling. By the time he wrote, nationalism was seen as a positive thing but one which had been appended to the highly militarized and conservative German Reich of **Otto von Bismarck**. Bismarck's Reich was therefore both a nationalist, modern and industrial state and yet a deeply anti-liberal and hierarchical monarchy.

A case can be made that nationalism was responsible for one of the greatest disasters of the twentieth century, the outbreak of **World War I**, in which empires either collapsed (the **Ottoman**, **Austro-Hungarian**, **Russian**, **German Empires**) or were placed under huge strain and forced to reorganize along national lines (**British** and **French Empires**). In addition, the new settlement in world affairs, the **League of Nations**, was imposed by the USA as an anti-imperialist power and explicitly elevated national identity as a key political requirement. In the interwar period, nationalism shifted definitively to the right as an anti-communist and often fascist creed, and was exemplified not by the 'small' and largely liberal nations which had emerged from Versailles in 1919 but by **Adolf Hitler** and **Mussolini**. They amongst others wished to build national empires as world powers, and their defeat with the rest of the Axis put paid to such models.

However, nationalism again became oppositional to the **Cold War** status quo following upon decolonization of the European empires and the rise of the modern international order. Some nationalists became associated with whichever ideological side opposed the allies of their rulers or past masters; Vietnamese nationalism was predominantly communist, for example, whereas Polish nationalism became pro-western. In this new order, international institutions developed ways of associating with nationalism; either, as in the case of the Roman Catholic Church, by translating into the vernacular languages and national parish system after Vatican II, or by upholding an essentially national version of identity under legally enforced common laws and human rights processes as in the **European Union**. Some existing units, such as those in **Britain**, **Belgium** and **Czechoslovakia**, as well as **Spain**, **Russia**, most of **Africa** and the **Middle East**, and **Asia**, had to cope with nationalist demands for separation or federalization of states which in some cases became very great strains indeed. Czechoslovakia, for instance, broke apart peacefully in 1992 whereas **Yugoslavia** did so violently and with much loss of life. By the twenty-first century, nationalism and nationalist political parties were however very strong or experiencing strong but not continuous growth in most parts of the world, especially in the face of globalization, and frequently became appended to racial, linguistic or political categories that disguised some of their more exclusionary and resentful aspects. Some noted the rise of English-speaking American nationalism in the United States of America as part of this process, whereas others called for an African Union to sponsor the redrawing of boundaries to better fit national lines in that continent.

Native Americans

Native Americans was a term used mostly in the **United States** to replace insensitive or inaccurate terms for the aboriginal or pre-Columbian indigenous peoples of North America, previously known as 'Indians' or 'Red Indians' as well as by tribal names. The term covers a huge number of groups, divided generally into eight to ten cultural groups, many of which can be traced back over 12,000 years. Native Americans were characterized by a mixture of nomadic hunting and pastoral activity, but were almost destroyed by a combination of European disease, forced displacement, war and, in some cases, genocidal elimination. Treated as sovereign nations, the remaining tribal groups are largely confined to reservations under treaty with the United States and the Bureau of Indian Affairs, though a revival of Native American culture and dignity began as part of the **civil rights movement** of the mid twentieth century. The US federal government and the states can each recognize tribes, and the actual status of some tribal governments is a significant issue in US legal debate.

nativism

Nativism (or anti-immigrationism) developed in response to the large number of immigrants to America, many of them Catholic, during the first half of the nineteenth century. Nativism played an especially important role in mid-century American politics, with the formation of the anti-immigrant Know-Nothing Party, which was then absorbed into the new **Republican Party**. Widespread nativist sentiment led to federal legislation restricting immigration during the late nineteenth and early twentieth centuries.

NATO

The North Atlantic Treaty Organization (NATO) is a body based upon a pact of mutual assistance and security signed in 1949, that grew out of the Brussels Treaty and the early **Cold War**. It cemented American and Canadian involvement in western Europe and is based in Brussels under an American Supreme Commander. NATO members coordinate their strategies, procurement and command systems to a very high degree, and operate in times of common military peril through a permanent command run by the Supreme Commander and Secretary General (traditionally a European). After the Cold War, NATO continued as a body which coordinated the deployment of forces and troops in **Yugoslavia** and **Afghanistan**, and a forum for defence discussions. It has a parliamentary assembly made up of delegations from member state parliaments. Its members officially engage in and therefore have an influence over the security policies of each other, from **Turkey** to the **USA**, and membership is incompatible with military conflict with a member state. NATO was the vehicle through which the occupation and rearmament of West Germany took place, and is still held in great suspicion by Russia, which viewed its expansion to the borders of the former **Soviet Union** in 1999 with alarm. NATO now faces a resurgent Russian nationalism (as in the **Ukraine**).

natural law

This doctrine posits that God has endowed all human beings with certain fundamental understandings which provide infallible guidance in every realm of behaviour. Franciscan and Jesuit neo-scholastics rigorously explored its theoretical and practical implications, developing detailed prescriptions for unified and moral polities, but their casuistical reasoning lost intellectual appeal after the seventeenth century. In recent decades, however, natural law has enjoyed a revival in conservative thought as an argument against secular statism.

natural resources

Natural resources are the basis for primary production associated with extraction and purification. Mining, petroleum extraction, fishing and forestry are generally considered natural resource-based industries, whereas agriculture is only partially based upon natural resources. Some natural resources can be treated as capital, since they are not renewable and thus subject to eventual biotic depletion. Renewable resources are generally living resources (fish and forests, for example) which can be restocked or renewed themselves if they are not over-harvested. Such resources can be used indefinitely if they are exploited in a sustainable way, which means that non-renewable resources can be used at the rate of their regeneration. For a non-renewable resource the sustainable rate of use can be no greater than the rate at which a renewable resource, used sustainably, can be substituted for it.

A nation's natural resources might determine its per capita income, wealth and status in the world economy as well as its political influence. The most striking example includes states that possess oil. However, some argue that there exists a paradox that countries with an abundance of natural resources tend to have less economic growth than countries without these natural resources. Various reasons may explain this fact, but they are usually embodied in the so-called Dutch disease explanations: the earnings from natural resource exports distorts the exchange rate and other domestic industries find it hard either to export or to compete against cheap imports. This tends to occur when a country over-specializes in only one resource but evidence suggests that the paradox does not hold when the country is abundant in several resources. Therefore, there is no necessary causality between natural resources and economic growth, with the latter being dependent upon how they are exploited and managed as well as the set of institutions that are created.

naval race (Anglo-German)

The naval race was a competitive arms race between **Germany** and the **United Kingdom** between 1898 and 1914 in which the participants competed to build and deploy large iron-clad big-gun warships. It was started by Germany's response to Britain's mooted capacity to blockade that state, and proceeded through the expensive creation of the Dreadnought class of ships by the Royal Navy between 1906 and 1910. By 1914, Germany had almost achieved a ratio of 2:3 in Britain's favour, but had turned towards expenditure on the army and submarine warfare. The race was extremely divisive, and spilled over into diplomatic alliances. However it was very popular amongst the press and as an economic stimulus in arms-producing areas. To some, the burdensome expenditures of the naval race were a spur for Britain and Germany to enter into agreements to restrain strategic weapons, but given the diplomatic and cultural

pressures of the period, attempts at agreements and 'naval holidays' failed.

naval warfare

Water covers around 71 per cent of the surface of the Earth. Naval power is therefore an essential feature of great power status, since control of the sea lanes, the capacity to launch attacks from the ocean, the maintenance of the key seaways for trade and transport, and most forms of invasion now require it. Naval warfare, however, has taken several different forms in the modern period. Before the 1890s, naval confrontation was modelled on the clashes of large wooden ships, firing cannon at close quarters and manoeuvring by sail, which had typified the exercise of naval power for some centuries previously. Tactics in such battles mirrored those in land warfare. Theorists such as Admiral Mahan and von Tirpitz essentially characterized the advantage as belonging to those countries capable of constructing enough ships. Though this model encouraged an arms race, it was already dated; the clash of the metal-clad ships USS *Monitor* and CSS *Virginia* during the **American Civil War** should have indicated how inconclusive naval clashes could become, and, if not, the efficient destruction by the forces of **Japan** of the Russian fleet at Tsushima should have shown the vulnerability of ships to massed assault in the home waters of a well-matched adversary. Nevertheless, this model persisted, with new life being blown into it by the British development of HMS *Dreadnought* and its iterative class from 1906 (*see* **naval race**). A Dreadnought was in effect an armoured, mobile, floating gun platform, and its development caused investment in extremely expensive heavy battleships around the world. Ironically, the great navies built up along these lines by the British and German commands spent most of **World War I** avoiding each other, until the Battle of **Jutland** in 1916 essentially resulted in a British victory with no real effect on the war. By the end of the war, two new forms of naval warfare had emerged; that based around the aircraft carrier, and that of the submarine. Both developments, when added to the over-the-horizon capacity of the heavy cruisers, changed naval doctrine and tactics. In **World War II** the capacity of the submarine to almost deal a decisive blow to supply lanes was demonstrated in the Battle of the Atlantic. Meanwhile, the Pacific war began with Japanese attempts to eliminate American aircraft carriers, proceeded through five great carrier battles, and ended at sea with the destruction of the imperial Japanese ship *Yamato* by air fighter and bomber assault.

This began a third era of naval tactics, centred around the dominance of carrier battle groups, in which a powerful central aircraft carrier (latterly nuclear powered) was surrounded by support ships and escort carriers. With the development of ballistic missile technology, such battle groups could arrive anywhere and fire deep into the territory of an adversary. In the context of the **Cold War**, only the **USA** and the **USSR** had enough economic strength to realistically deploy multiple numbers of such fleets, and after the Cold War, the USA was left with the advantage. However, there was some indication by the 1990s that new tactics were developing, which in the long run would be to the American disadvantage. Carrier groups are, for instance, very vulnerable to 'swarming' by large numbers of small, fast ships packed with explosives. They are also a standing temptation to launch a ballistic or nuclear device against the lead ship, and, further, they have struggled to deal with the re-emergence of piracy across the Horn of Africa, the Niger Delta and in the Malacca Straits. New developments in radar-cloaking stealth technology, unmanned aerial warfare, missile defence and rail gun technology, whilst at the moment benefiting the state with the money to develop them (the USA) could easily, if proliferated, undermine American advantages even more than the replacement of the idea of the high seas with an international law of the sea which would keep warships away from coastlines or transport hubs.

Navarino, Battle of (1827)

In response to powerful philhellenic sentiment domestically, the British, French and Russians signed the **Treaty of London** in July 1827, with Russia promising intervention in the **Greek War of Independence** if the belligerents did not accept arbitration. The Ottomans refused on the grounds that they considered the region sovereign territory and the suppression of the rebellion an internal matter. In response, a joint British–French–Russian fleet was sent to the region with orders to blockade supplies to the Ottoman forces. On 20 October 1827 the joint European fleet entered Navarino Bay, outside of modern Pylos, and destroyed the Ottoman–Egyptian fleet defending the harbour. The Ottoman defeat left their ground forces in **Greece** without reinforcements and ensured the eventual success of the Greeks in their war for independence. The battle also underlined the inability of the Ottomans to retain control of their territory without the political support of at

least one European Great Power and helped to define the empire's foreign policy for the following century.

Navigation Acts/Exclusif

In the early modern period the maritime empires of western Europe implemented a variety of policies to regulate overseas trade. Informed by mercantilist economic notions that characterized wealth as fixed, and that represented international trade as a zero-sum game, these economic policies aimed to protect and promote exports and to minimize imports. In **France**, such regulations were codified in the seventeenth century. Historians have referred to these policies – maintained throughout the eighteenth century – as the *Exclusif*. English parliaments passed a series of Navigation Acts beginning in the 1650s that restricted foreign shipping and mercantile activity within their colonial system. The *Exclusif* and the Navigation Acts were difficult to enforce, and smuggling and contraband trading proliferated throughout the eighteenth century. French physiocrats and British political economists such as **Adam Smith** offered a sustained critique of state regulation of colonial trade. Beginning in the 1730s, significant legislative exceptions to the Navigation Acts were made, and the remaining provisions completely repealed in 1849.

Naxalites

Indian peasant revolutionaries. An armed peasant uprising led by members of what was to later become the Communist Party of India (Marxist–Leninist) (CPI (ML)) ripped across Naxalbari, bordering **Bangladesh** (then East Pakistan), Sikkim, Nepal and Bhutan. The CPI (ML), also now called the Maoists or *Maobadis*, are embedded in the popular imagination as Naxalites, after Naxalbari. The first phase (1967–72) spread rapidly in rural areas ranging across **Bengal**, **Punjab** and Kerala. After its brutal suppression and the declaration of a state of emergency by **Indira Gandhi** (1975–7), it reappeared in various forms, both public and underground. It forged the 'Naxalite Corridor' from Andhra Pradesh to Nepal, where it joined forces with the pro-democracy movement in 2006. Ideologically multifaceted, its initial agenda had two basic aspects: it was anti-state, considering the state to be a neocolonial and neo-imperialist formation; and, given the agricultural mode of production, it was a struggle between feudal elements and the landless labourer in the countryside.

Nazism, the Nazis

The ideology of **Adolf Hitler**'s National Socialist German Workers Party. Hitler admired the successes of **Mussolini**'s Italian National Fascist Party, but developed a distinctively racial political creed. Hitler's Nazism was aggressively anti-Semitic, and advocated a voracious pursuit of *Lebensraum* – a massive expansion of German territory, particularly to the east, that could maintain a 'purified' racial state. Hitler's Nazis pursued their racial fascist ideology by invading **Poland**, **France**, **Belgium**, Denmark, Holland, **Yugoslavia**, **Greece** and **Russia**. The elite *Schutzstaffel* (**SS**) followed each military invasion with a political and racial purge of the newly conquered territory. Jews were collected into ghettos, and the Nazis built a system of concentration camps across Europe for racial and political prisoners. The Nazis used these camps to implement their racial ideology of 'purification', and systematically murdered at least 9 million Jews and members of other groups which included political opponents, Roma and Slav peoples, homosexuals, people with disabilities and prisoners of war. This murderous legacy is remembered as the **Holocaust**. German Nazism was finally defeated in war by the Allies in 1945.

Ndunduma (d. 1903)

Ruler of Viye, one of the Ovimbundu states of the central highlands of **Angola**. Ndunduma came to power in 1888 at a time when increased trade with the Portuguese and local social mobility was threatening political stability, and began a policy of raiding Portuguese interests, interfering with Ovimbundu merchants and threatening the North American Protestant missionaries. He was attacked and captured by the Portuguese in 1890, and died in exile.

Ne Win, General (1911–2002)

Military dictator of **Myanmar**, 1962–88. Ne Win was a key participant in the Burmese nationalist movement during **World War II**. He became commander in chief of the army and staged the coup that overthrew Prime Minister U Nu in 1962. During his reign of power, private enterprises were nationalized, foreign entrepreneurs were expelled and political parties and independent newspapers were banned. Ne Win announced his retirement in 1988, but remained an influential figure throughout the 1990s.

Negritude

A literary and ideological movement developed by black francophone intellectuals in the 1930s. Founded by Senegalese poet **Léopold Senghor**, Martinican writer Amié Césaire and Guianan Leon Damas, the Negritude movement promoted a common black identity as a rejection of French colonial racism and policies of assimilation. Negritude, translated as 'blackness', proclaimed the beauty of African culture and inserted African idioms and symbols into French literary forms. Inspired by the Harlem Renaissance and **Marxism**, Negritude writers founded important African journals and expressed their philosophy through poetry and cultural critiques.

While philosopher Jean-Paul Sartre exalted Negritude as the dialectical opposite to white racism, cultural theorist and psychiatrist Frantz Fanon felt it did not go far enough and criticized its promotion of a return to a pristine African past. **Wole Soyinka** and others criticized Negritude as a defensive ideology that reproduced the stereotype of Africans as 'noble savages'.

Nehru, Jawaharlal (1889–1964)

An Indian nationalist leader and statesman who was the first prime minister of independent **India** (1947–64), he was born in Allahabad, the son of **Motilal Nehru**, a wealthy Brahman lawyer whose family had originally come from Kashmir. The young Nehru was educated at Harrow, Trinity College, Cambridge, and Inner Temple, London. Returning to India in 1912, he practised law, married Kamala Kaul and in 1917 they had a daughter, Indira. In 1919 Nehru joined the **Indian National Congress** and became devoted to **Mohandas Gandhi**. Guided by Gandhi, he gradually learned about rural India and became an effective speaker to both western-educated sophisticates and Indian peasants. In time, Nehru's popularity was second only to Gandhi's. During this period he was imprisoned many times for civil disobedience, including from 1932 to 1935 and 1942 to 1945. In prison, he wrote *Toward Freedom* (1936), an autobiography; *The Discovery of India* (1946) and *Glimpses of World History* (1934). A talented and expressive writer in English, he and India's freedom struggle became more widely known through the circulation of his writings in the West.

Although he and Gandhi differed in terms of world view, they remained close. When the British formed an interim Indian government in 1946 preliminary to full independence, Nehru became prime minister. He participated in negotiations for a united and federated India between the British rulers, the Congress and the **Muslim League**. Nehru opposed the division of India on the basis of religion. He adhered to secularism and believed that all Indians regardless of religious affiliation should be equal citizens. The parties were unable to agree and the British government moved to turn over power to the Indian successors. The last viceroy, Lord **Mountbatten**, worked out a procedure for the transfer of power, with the division of British India between India and **Pakistan**. Nehru reluctantly agreed to the partition. At Mountbatten's urging, Nehru agreed to maintain India's membership in the **Commonwealth** of Nations.

Nehru became independent India's first prime minister on 15 August 1947, and remained its leader until his death in 1964. Upon taking office he moved to implement moderate socialist economic reforms by means of centralized planning. Successive five-year plans, beginning in 1951, sketched plans for the development of India's economy which stressed industrial development and national ownership of key areas of the economy. Nehru also backed plans for community development projects and the creation of many educational institutions. Throughout the Nehru years, India's economy achieved steady growth and its agricultural production increased, though not rapidly. Nehru also encouraged the development of India's nuclear energy programme. He served as foreign minister throughout his tenure as prime minister, and one of the first foreign policy challenges he faced was a conflict with Pakistan over the princely state of **Jammu and Kashmir** in October 1947. The **United Nations** negotiated a ceasefire agreement in January 1949, but no solution was reached.

As the **Cold War** developed in the 1950s, Nehru shaped a foreign policy of 'positive neutrality' for his nation, attempting to defuse international tensions without joining either of the international power blocs. He became a spokesmen for the non-aligned nations of **Asia** and **Africa**, championed the India–China friendship and backed the efforts of the People's Republic of **China** to gain membership in the United Nations. From the late 1950s, however, relations between the nations deteriorated over boundary disputes and over **Tibet**. In 1959 Chinese troops occupied territory claimed by both China and India. After diplomatic efforts failed to resolve the dispute, a border war broke out in 1962 between Indian and Chinese forces in the Himalayas. Indian troops were unprepared for the encounter and were decisively beaten. The Chinese took no additional territory, but continued to occupy the land they had annexed in 1959. India's crushing defeat prompted a re-evaluation of India's defence capabilities. The Chinese affair had a devastating personal impact on Nehru, whose health declined rapidly. He saw the border

war as a betrayal by a nation for whose place in the world he had fought. In January 1964 he suffered a stroke, and died in May. Throughout the period of Indian independence the Nehru family continued to play a vital role at the centre of power.

Nehru, Motilal (1861–1931)

An eminent lawyer and a moderate nationalist, he was a member of the Home Rule League. He became president of the Indian National Congress in 1919. At the end of the Non-cooperation movement, Nehru supported the proposal that Congress members should enter the Montagu–Chelmsford councils but was unable to persuade **Gandhi** and his followers. Consequently, in 1923, along with C. R. Das, he formed the Swaraj Party. In 1928 he authored the Nehru Report, which recommended that the Congress demand dominion status.

Nelson, Horatio (1758–1805)

A dominant British naval figure, seeing action in the French Revolutionary and **Napoleonic Wars** and against the American rebels. He entered the Royal Navy at the age of 12 and family connections helped his early career, but his subsequent advance owed much to his innovative tactics. Remembered for his role in the major battles of Trafalgar (1805), at which he was killed, Cape St Vincent (1797), the Nile (1798) and Copenhagen (1801).

Neoclassicism

An artistic style dominant during the late eighteenth and early nineteenth centuries that reflected renewed interest in antiquity and adherence to the ancient ideals of rationality and order. The formalism and serious subjects of Neoclassicism represented a reaction to the irrationality and ornamentalism of the **Roccoco** and **Baroque** styles. Neoclassical art borrowed themes from classical history and literature and interweaved ancient values with contemporary life. The works of the French painter Jacques-Louis David, most notably *The Oath of the Horatii* and *Death of Marat*, personified Neoclassical ideals by emphasizing self-sacrifice and loyalty to the state. Other significant artists include Benjamin West, John Singleton Copley and Bertel Thorvaldsen. This style also influenced sculpture and architecture. The works of Jean-Antoine Houdon and Antonio Canova evoked the refinement and elegance of Greek and Roman sculptures. Architects including John Soane and Karl Friedrich Schinkel incorporated the grandeur of ancient buildings in their designs. Neoclassicism declined in the nineteenth century with the growth of **Romanticism** and the **Gothic Revival**.

neocolonialism

A term attributed to **Kwame Nkrumah**, president of **Ghana**, 1960–6, that describes the ability of the western capitalist powers to retain economic and political control over their former colonies despite their formal independence. Examples included multinational companies, such as oil or mining companies, who could exercise enormous influence on the financial position of newly independent states. More widely the term has also been applied to the operation of `informal empire' by which more powerful states dominated and traded with less powerful ones without taking formal control. The division of **China** into spheres of economic influence by the West, the influence of the American **United Fruit Company** in **Central America**, the role of the major oil companies in the **Middle East**, and the position of major mining conglomerates in southern and central Africa were examples. Although often seen as fitting within a Marxist interpretation of imperialism as `the highest state of capitalism' in which capitalist companies impoverish the third world, economic activity by advanced states and their companies has been a significant factor in **economic development** and rising living standards in many parts of the world. Some major international organizations, such as the **World Bank**, the **International Monetary Fund** and United Nations agencies, have also been accused of neocolonialist attitudes in their distribution of economic aid and advice to third world countries.

neoconservatism (USA)

Emerging during the 1970s in the **United States**, neoconservatism grew out of opposition to what was seen as a leftward move on the part of the **Democratic Party**. Early neoconservatives, sometimes former leftists themselves, were strong supporters of the **Vietnam War**, believed the United States should continue to confront the **Soviet Union**, and were appalled at the rise of a permissive youth culture. Increasingly effective within the established conservative movement, neoconservatives were to become particularly influential in the aftermath of the **Cold War**. They called for a continued American global hegemony, and argued that the Gulf War should have been concluded with the overthrow of **Saddam Hussein**. When, following 9/11, the **Bush** administration decided to invade **Iraq**, critics accused the president of succumbing to the machinations of

a 'neoconservative cabal'. In turn, they compared their critics with those who had failed to stand up to **Hitler** in the 1930s. The term is now widely applied globally.

neoliberalism

A term used for the revival of pro-market and anti-statist policies associated with the policies of **Ronald Reagan** in America and **Margaret Thatcher** in the United Kingdom, opposed to the dominant **Keynesianism** of the post-World War II era. Hardened into what has been called the `Washington Consensus', it sought privatization, deregulation, trade and financial liberalization, a reduction in the role of the state and the application of these policies not only to the developed economies but also to the developing world. By emphasizing the role of the market, it explicitly rejected the primary role of the state in managing the economy and the socialist model adopted by communist states and some ex-colonial states such as India. The major theoretical opponents of the Keynesian consensus which had emerged from the interwar depression were the American economist Milton Friedman (1912–2006) and the Austrian economist Friedrich Hayek (1899–1992), both Nobel prize winners in the mid 1970s. The former was the foremost exponent of the belief that money supply was the key to the economy – `monetarism' as it became known – and served as an adviser to **Ronald Reagan** (1981–8). Hayek, who became a British citizen in 1938 but was later a professor in Chicago, believed government intervention in the economy led to inflation, unemployment, recession and, ultimately, dictatorship. Although rarely employed in the pure forms represented by the theorists, neoliberalism persuaded many western governments to adopt more market-orientated policies, seen particularly in areas such as privatization, and they were enthusiastically taken up by the states of eastern Europe freed from Soviet control after 1990 and even by the Russian state which succeeded the former Soviet Union. Similar policies were also promoted by the **International Monetary Fund** and the **World Bank** in the developing world. Critics of neoliberalism have included socialists, Keynesians and **anti-globalization** movements who characterize it as the economic ideology promoting capitalist globalization to the detriment of many of the world's poor.

Nepal

Himalayan country located between **India** and Chinese **Tibet**. Evidence from the first millennium BC suggests the population was restricted to the central Kathmandu valley and lower Tarai hill districts, which still generally obtains. Communications through several high passes fostered political fragmentation, intellectual growth and economic health. Gurkha ruler Prithvi Narayan Shah conquered several states in 1769 to form Nepal's modern territorial boundaries. Nepal concluded a treaty in 1860 that allowed the Indian Army to recruit Gurkhas and provided British security against the Nepali monarchy's foreign and domestic enemies. King Tribhuvan and the Nepali Congress replaced this system with a constitutional monarchy in 1950. Non-party politics resumed in 1962, and political pressure caused constitutional reforms in 1990. The murder/suicide of the royal family in 2001 led to a re-evaluation of the constitution, and persistent Maoist insurgency since 1996 led to the abolition of the monarchy in 2007. Maoist-led coalitions formed governments following the 2008 elections. A secular constitution was adopted in September 2015.

Neruda, Pablo (Neftalí Reyes Basoalto) (1904–1973)

Chilean poet, Nobel Laureate (1971) and diplomat. Born in Parral, **Chile**, he studied in the Liceo of Temuco and the Instituto Pedagógico in Santiago. He published poems in *Selva Austral* (1920) as 'Pablo Neruda', assuming the surname of Czech poet Jan Neruda. He adopted 'Pablo Neruda' as his legal name in 1946. In 1924 he published *Twenty Love Poems and a Song of Despair*, one of his most popular books. From 1927 until the 1940s he held consular posts in **Asia**, **Argentina**, **Spain** and **Mexico**, and in 1943 he joined the Communist Party and was elected senator in 1945. Forced into political exile, he published *Canto General* (1950) in Mexico, an epic poem relating to the struggle for social justice in **Latin America**. Neruda returned to Chile in 1952. Appointed ambassador to **France** (1970–2), he died in Santiago twelve days after the military coup that ousted Salvador Allende.

Netherlands

Independent of **Spain**, 1648, but its earlier maritime power declined during the eighteenth century. A member of the Frisian branch of the House of Orange-Nassau declared hereditary *stadhouder*, 1747. It became a French protectorate as the Batavian Republic, 1795–1806, following invasion by the French Revolutionary armies. The monarchy was restored under the House of

Orange in 1814, and a monarchical union established with Belgium and Luxembourg by the **Congress of Vienna**, 1815, lasting only until the Belgian independence revolt of 1830. Personal union with Luxembourg ended in 1890. A fully constitutional monarchy, modelled on the British, was established in 1848. Neutral in **World War I**, the Netherlands offered the kaiser asylum after his abdication, 1918. It sought neutrality again in **World War II**, but was occupied by the Germans, 1940–5. Reluctantly it accepted the independence of its former extensive empire in the East Indies as the Republic of **Indonesia**, 1949. A founder member of **NATO**, 1949, and of the European Economic Community, now **European Union**, 1957, and also of the **euro**.

New Caledonia

The Territory of New Caledonia and Dependencies has been a French territory since 1853. It is located in the South Pacific Ocean and has a total area of 19,060 square kilometres. The majority of the population is Roman Catholic (60 per cent). French is the official language. The capital city is Noumea. Referenda on independence were held in 1998 and 2014, but did not pass.

New Deal

The New Deal was the term for the response of the **United States** government to the crisis of the **Great Depression**. Though primarily associated with the array of domestic reforms introduced to restore the nation's economy between 1933 and 1941, its long-range significance lay more in its political effects. It was also important for its capacity to inspire subsequent generations of reformers (and their opponents), providing either a model to be emulated and exported around the world, or an archetype of excessive governmental intervention. The early New Deal was dominated by efforts to address the crises in agriculture and industry. The Agricultural Adjustment Administration (AAA) was created in 1933 to bring the purchasing power of American farmers back to pre-**World War I** levels. In 1936 its tax-raising provisions were struck down by the Supreme Court, but its basic principles were retained in the 1938 Farm Act, a mix of production controls, government payments and price-support loans. The industrial counterpart, the National Recovery Administration (NRA), was less successful. It established industrial codes to try to create a more orderly and cooperative relationship between government and industry; but the NRA never reconciled the interests of planners, who accepted large corporations as a natural part of economic life, and anti-monopolists, who did not. In the May 1935 *Schechter* decision, the Supreme Court ruled the NRA unconstitutional.

If these early experiments yielded mixed results, the New Deal's creation of a welfare state was one of its most enduring legacies. Previously, federal welfare provision was confined to benefits for veterans, pregnant women and widowed mothers. The New Deal's various work relief programmes, for example the Works Progress Administration, the Public Works Administration and the Civilian Conservation Corps, greatly raised Americans' expectations of government. These were heightened further with the passage in 1935 of the Social Security Act, which combined various forms of categorical assistance with the national provision of unemployment compensation and old-age pensions. Jerry-built in construction and conservative in its assumptions – it institutionalized racial and gender prejudices and eschewed a redistributive approach – the New Deal welfare state was nevertheless, in an American context, a major achievement.

The New Deal failed to bring about wholesale economic recovery, but it profoundly transformed the political landscape of the United States. It clearly made the **Democratic Party** the preferred party of liberals and leftists. Furthermore, its policies and programmes persuaded the overwhelming majority of **African Americans** (and most other racial minorities) to switch from the party of Lincoln to the party of **Roosevelt**. The New Deal also marked the emergence of organized labour as a major force in American political life. The rise during the New Deal of mass industrial unionism created an immensely powerful constituency which gave a tremendous boost in funding and support to the Democratic Party for more than half a century. These voting blocs may no longer be part of a winning national electoral coalition, but their continuing attachment to the Democratic Party speaks to the enduring power and long-range influence of the New Deal.

New Economic Policy

The term for **Lenin**'s attempt to preserve Bolshevik power by ending 'War Communism', compromising with the peasants and restoring elements of capitalism, announced at the tenth Communist Party Congress in March 1921. A fixed tax replaced requisitioning of grain, the right was restored to sell on the open market and employ labour, smaller factories were privatized and foreign investment

encouraged. Heavy industry and banking remained under state ownership. By 1928 most economic indices had returned to pre-1914 levels.

New Guinea

New Guinea is the world's second largest island, with a total area of 786,000 square kilometres. It is located at the eastern end of the Indonesian archipelago, north of **Australia**. Politically, the island of New Guinea is divided into roughly equal halves along the north–south line. The western portion is comprised of the West Irian Jaya and Papua provinces of **Indonesia**. The eastern portion is the independent state of **Papua New Guinea**.

New Left

A term given to intellectuals and political activists between the late 1950s and 1970s committed to a rethinking of leftist politics in response to a growing disillusionment with communism in the West and a parallel disappointment with mainstream left-of-centre democratic politics. The term became widely used in the late 1950s with the foundation of the *New Left Review* in **Britain** and *Studies on the Left* in the **United States**. Prominent new left intellectuals included Columbia University sociologist C. Wright Mills, author of works such as *The Power Elite* (1956) and the famous 'Letter to the New Left', which was published in the September/October 1960 issue of the *New Left Review*, and University of Wisconsin historian William Appleman Williams, author of *The Tragedy of American Diplomacy* (1959). Radical student groups sprang up in the early 1960s under the New Left umbrella, of which an important example was the US-based Students for a Democratic Society. An apogee of the movement was the 1968 student year of rebellion.

new religious movements

– *see* **Protestantism**.

New Right

A conservative American movement that emerged during the early 1970s. It criticized what it saw as compromises on the part of Republican politicians. It argued too that conservatives had failed to find effective issues to reach voters who were discontented with liberalism, and believed that anti-communism, defence of gun ownership and, above all, opposition to abortion and homosexuality would prove critical to disrupting the Democratic voting bloc. While tempted to break with the **Republican Party**, the New Right was drawn to

Ronald Reagan's presidential candidacy and was a highly visible force during his administration. Difficult to satisfy, it did not survive the Reagan years, and more recently its leading figures have been forceful critics of Republican policies. Many of the issues it championed, however, have become central to conservatism's appeal, and a movement which it played a central part in creating, the **Christian Right**, has remained a crucial force in the Republican Party.

Newfoundland

Newfoundland occupies a strategic position off the coast of **Canada** at the mouth of the Saint Lawrence River. Its earliest inhabitants were Inuit; after 1500, fishermen from many different European countries came to fish the cod on the banks off the east of the island. The British for many years contested fishery rights with the French. Newfoundland enjoyed a new importance as the easternmost site in the Americas during the early era of wireless telegraphy, and during the early years of transatlantic flight. Took Dominion status in 1917, but after economic problems in 1949 it joined Canada.

newspapers

A phenomenally popular and historically influential media of information and communication dating to the origin of the printing press, newspapers reached their greatest influence in the late nineteenth and twentieth centuries. This was because they exploited electric and steam technology to produce regular daily editions composed of news reports, advertisements and editorial opinion informed by the knowledge of staff and editors and up-to-date information. Newspapers also grew with the development of both leisure time and time spent on public transport, as much as with the standardized hours of the industrial working day and the growth of literacy. As a general rule, they were divided by the twentieth century into sensationalist tabloid-size papers, which carried information on sport, celebrity, public affairs and property, as well as items of human interest, to a wide audience, and broadsheets, which sought to reflect or to influence business and elite opinion. Major national newspapers were often based in key cities, and from time to time their support could make or break the careers of politicians and, occasionally, the reputation and operational freedom of whole administrations. Some proprietors, such as Lords Beaverbrook and Rothermere in the **United Kingdom**, actively attempted to sponsor or promote politicians or political movements, but for the most part papers focused on their audience and sales figures. Few politicians rose as 'newspaper products', though **Winston Churchill** – a journalist for almost as long as he was a politician – and Georges Clemenceau might be mentioned as exceptions. Many paid a great deal of attention to leading 'columnists' and editors, however, and actively sought their endorsement right up to the twenty-first century.

As a form, the division between the English-speaking and continental worlds mattered in that, on the European continent, political parties and companies tended to own newspapers and to run them in overtly partisan or class spirit, whereas in the English-speaking world, rich and powerful proprietors, editors and journalists were involved in a symbiotic and occasionally tense relationship with each other and the government. Some newspapers specialized in 'scandal' and the revelation of hypocrisy, corruption or contradiction on the part of public figures, which was seen by elites as deleterious and which contributed to the growth of cynicism about government and the emergence of privacy laws. However, others defended the medium as playing an essential role in democracy. This was particularly true in the **United States**, where the cosy relationship of correspondents with political figures was contrasted with editorial and corporate promotion of journalist-led investigations that often antagonized the powerful.

One solution, which political parties adopted from the 1940s, was to manipulate or 'spin' the press, but given competition, this strategy was often one which proved self-destructive in the end. The press, as newspapers were originally known exclusively, began to decline not with the rise of electronic news in the form of TV or radio (these played to different strengths) but with the Internet and the development of social media. These latter forms allowed individuals to reach beyond the newspapers for free, to editorialize through personal 'blogs', and to circumvent the perceived marketing *agendae* of the papers. In turn, the newspapers found that they suffered from decline as readers refused to pay for their product, and so they became dependent upon advertising, which tended to blunt their previous verve. Nevertheless, newspapers were still seen as vital to the political conversation, and by 2000 were still read globally by hundreds of millions, whilst being produced in over 6,000 different forms. The medium has also proven highly adaptive, and at the time of writing, there is nothing to suggest that the combination of networked tablet technology and subscription will not continue a model of the newspaper long into the century.

New Zealand (Aotorea)

Settled by the Maoris, a people of Polynesian stock, from at least the fourteenth century, but first found by Europeans in 1642, when Abel Janszoon Tasman, the Dutch navigator, discovered both it and the Australian island of Tasmania. The name is an anglicization of the Dutch 'Nieuw Zeeland' (New Sea Land). More than a century later, the coast was explored by British navigator **Captain Cook** in 1769, and it subsequently attracted whalers and traders principally from **Australia**. Annexation by **France** became a possibility in the 1830s but was forestalled by the foundation of the New Zealand Association in 1837 by Gibbon Wakefield, who argued that New Zealand could accommodate races other than the Maoris and whose association made the first British settlements there. Initially it was administered as part of the New South Wales (Australia) colony. Further settlement was facilitated by the conclusion of the Treaty of Waitangi in 1840, whereby the Maori chiefs ceded sovereignty to the British Crown rendering New Zealand a British colony.

White settlement soon provoked land disputes culminating in the **Maori Wars** of 1845–8 and 1860–70, before peace was finally established in 1871. The **Maoris** did, however, succeed in gaining parliamentary representation. Although New Zealand has probably had the most harmonious racial relations of all the British dominions, with a Maori, the opera singer Kiri Te Kanawa, achieving world renown, Maori grievances over loss of land and resources persisted and saw the establishment of the Waitangi Tribunal in 1975 to hear complaints against alleged breaches of the 1840 Treaty. The tribunal was empowered to hear claims against the Crown dating back to 1840 in 1984, and compensation was paid for losses of land throughout the 1990s.

Together with Australia, **Canada** and **South Africa**, New Zealand voluntarily participated in **World War I** and, like them, demanded full recognition of its nationhood subsequently, including individual representation in the League of Nations. Independence from **Britain** was formally conceded by the Statute of Westminster, 1931, but the British monarch remained, and remains, head of state. Its first decisive intervention in foreign affairs was perhaps in 1921–2 when, together with Australia and Canada, it opposed British Prime Minister Lloyd George's inclination to side with **Japan** against the **United States** in Far Eastern affairs, and persuaded Britain to abandon its wartime alliance with Japan. Continuing suspicion of Japanese intentions led New Zealand, together with Australia, to support appeasement of **Germany** in the late 1930s so that British military power could be built up against Japan instead. The New Zealand government nevertheless followed the 1939 British declaration of war on Germany immediately.

New Zealand has been a pioneer in home affairs, being the first country to adopt women's suffrage in 1893 and the first in the English-speaking world to lay the foundations of a welfare state with the introduction of non-contributory old-age pensions in 1898. Moreover farmers' cooperatives controlled the national dairy industry by 1900. The Cook Islands and Niue were annexed, 1901, and became self-governing territories in 'free association' with New Zealand, 1965 and 1974 respectively.

NGOs

A common acronym for non-governmental organizations of a national or independent kind which became increasingly important in the provision of aid and support, especially to poorer regions of the world, from the end of **World War II**. International organizations have the acronym INGOs. The earliest were primarily refugee agencies, formed under the auspices of the **League of Nations**, some of whose work was taken over by the different agencies of the **United Nations**. The United Nations Children's Fund (Unicef), formerly known as the United Nations International Children's Emergency Fund, established in 1946 to provide help for children in need after World War II, but given a permanent role in 1953, provides support programmes in over 160 countries relating to child health, nutrition and sanitation. Supported by voluntary contributions from the public and from governments, it also provides emergency aid. The World Health Organization (WHO) is a specialized agency of the United Nations formed in 1948 to seek international cooperation in the improvement of world health, concerned with the control of epidemic diseases, vaccination and clean water. It was able to announce the eradication of smallpox in 2010 and was heavily involved in controlling the outbreaks of Ebola in West Africa in 2014. Another branch of the United Nations, UNESCO (United Nations Educational, Scientific and Cultural Organization), provides educational and cultural work across nearly 200 states.

In addition to the UN agencies there are a large number of voluntary organizations providing long-term or emergency aid which have emerged from the mid twentieth century in addition to the nineteenth-century **Red Cross**. Oxfam was formed in 1942 as the Oxford Committee for Famine Relief but is now engaged in long-term development aid as Oxfam International. The Catholic Relief Organization (Cafod) is another NGO which is widely represented in aid and relief operations, alongside bodies such as Médecins Sans Frontières which specializes in medical assistance even in the most dangerous locations, Save the Children Fund, Water Aid and a myriad of other voluntary organizations. NGOs now make up a significant element in the direct provision of both long-term development aid and emergency relief in a very large number of countries.

Nicaragua, Republic of

A central American nation of over 6 million people. Nicaragua emerged from its colonial isolation in the early 1800s and entered the twentieth century as a minor exporter of coffee and bananas. Endemic political and economic turmoil led to a US invasion in 1912 that sparked a guerrilla uprising led by Augusto César Sandino. After US forces withdrew in 1933, the commander of its National Guard, Anastasio Somoza, established a family dictatorship that lasted until the revolution of 1979. In the 1980s the victorious **Sandinistas** (FSLN) tried to create a viable socialist state, but found themselves at war against the US and its proxy army, the **Contras**. Diplomatic intervention ended the war in 1989 and swept the opposition coalition (UNO) led by **Violeta Chamorro** into power. Political corruption and endemic poverty have plagued Nicaraguan society in recent years, a state of affairs which returned the Sandinistas to office in 2006.

Nicholas I, Tsar (1796–1855)

Russian monarch, 1825–55. Succeeding his brother Alexander I, Nicholas immediately faced the Decembrist Conspiracy, which encouraged his determination to strengthen tsarist authority with the maxim 'Autocracy, orthodoxy and nationalism'. He established a secret police in 1826 (the Third Section of the Imperial Chancellery), intensified censorship and discouraged higher education. Nicholas did, however, grant freedom to the serfs on state lands in 1838 and codify the laws. His eagerness to combat revolution in Europe – he

suppressed the Polish revolt in 1830–1 and aided **Austria** in crushing a Hungarian rising in 1849 – earned him the sobriquet 'the gendarme of Europe'. Nicholas coined the term 'Sick man of Europe' to describe the ailing **Ottoman Empire**. Having fought a successful war against the Ottoman Empire in 1828–9, his ambitions for **Constantinople** provoked the 1853–6 **Crimean War**, a conflict that revealed Russian weakness and inefficiency. Nicholas died while the war was in progress.

Nicholas II, Tsar (1868–1918)

Nicholas II, the last Tsar of **Russia**, succeeded his father Alexander III in 1894, in the same year marrying **Queen Victoria**'s grand-daughter Alexandra, who sustained his aversion to political reform. Nicholas' encouragement of Russian expansion into **Manchuria** provoked the disastrous 1904–5 war with **Japan**. Military defeat, mounting domestic discontent and the 'Bloody Sunday' massacre of protestors in St Petersburg triggered the 1905 revolution. Nicholas reluctantly agreed to limited constitutional government, establishing a largely ineffective Duma (parliament) in 1906 but at the same time coming under the reactionary influence of the monk Rasputin. The outbreak of war in 1914 temporarily boosted the monarchy's standing but Nicholas' decision to take supreme command of the army in 1915 ensured he was personally identified with Russian military failure. He was forced to abdicate following the February 1917 revolution and was executed with his family by Bolsheviks at Yekaterinburg on 16/17 July 1918.

Nietzsche, Friedrich Wilhelm (1844–1900)

A nineteenth-century German philosopher who became convinced that modern societies had no need for a concept of deity and that the idea of God, as such, was dead. In this context, his thought proceeded through his troubled life to contemplate how meaning which was other than relative could be found, and he came to the conclusion that it could not. Nietzsche has been often cited as a principal proponent of the idea that the strong should rise above the weak, and is sometimes portrayed as the originator of nihilism. His name was associated with the idea that those who free themselves of what he regarded as bankrupt Judeo-Christian morality could become 'supermen' aware of ultimate meaninglessness, the eternal recurrence of things and of their own capacity to remake the world through their will to power. Many of these views, which were actually those of his sister who obsessively popularized his works in **Germany**, and of **Adolf Hitler**, who misunderstood them, passed into the everyday understanding of Nietzsche. He was also depicted as the archetypical manic and humourless German philosopher in the works of cultural commentators and comedians. North Americans have tended to view Nietzsche more favourably than Europeans. Some of the former have seen him as a radical individualist with an overwhelming, honest and emotional appeal to the subjectivity of truth accompanied by an idea of the 'will to power' at the heart of human ambition. Others have attempted to claim him as an exemplar of the effects of repression on the homosexual community, given his mental breakdown, strong homoerotic writing and social isolation, though no one has ever proved he was in any way physically homosexual or that he acknowledged any such identity privately.

Niger

Former French West African colony, occupied in 1890 against major resistance. Niger gained independence in 1960 under President Hamani Diori (1916–87), who headed a one-party state riddled with corruption. The economy stagnated against a background of continuous drought from 1968. Diori was deposed in 1974 by Seyni Kountché (1931–87), who governed as head of an authoritarian Supreme Military Council. Surviving coups in 1975 and 1976, Kountché began moves to civilian government. He was succeeded in 1987 by Ali Saibou (1940–2011), and in 1993 Mahamane Ousmane (1950–) became president in the first free elections. Ousmane was deposed in a military coup led by Ibrahim Baré Mainassara (1949–99), who was assassinated in 1999. Coup and counter-coup followed until the election to the presidency of Mahamsdou Issoufou (1952–) in 2011. Niger's population is overwhelmingly Muslim and mostly engaged in subsistence agriculture, although the country holds significant uranium deposits. It has been affected by Boko Haram militants from neighbouring **Nigeria**.

Nigeria

Nigeria, a federal republic in West Africa, contains a territory that has been settled for over 2,500 years. Modern-day Nigeria holds the distinction of being both the biggest economy and the most populous state on the African continent. It is divided into thirty-six states and has one administrative capital, but is also split along confessional and ethnic lines. The north, for instance, is associated with the Islamic tradition, whereas the south is largely Christian, whilst the three largest ethnic groups – Igbo, Yoruba and **Hausa** – share the land with over 450 other groups, including some European and Asian groups. This is a legacy of the **British Empire**, which organized Northern, Southern and Lagos administrations from the nineteenth century through to 1960. Independent Nigeria, however, proved unstable, and has since 1960 been host to military rulers between 1966 and 1979, and again between 1983 and 1998, as well as suffering a civil war, an attempted **Biafran** secession between 1966 and 1970, and the more recent Boko Haram Islamist revolt. These periods of military rule have not been coterminous with stable regimes, and unfortunately *coups d'etat* both before and within the military periods were not uncommon. This instability and upheavals in leadership in part explains why Nigeria has been unable until the twenty-first century to exploit its vast oil and mineral wealth. It should also be noted, however, that, like **Congo**, Nigeria came to independence at a time of decolonization and the **Cold War**, and so was also subject to outside pressures from a number of regimes. In response, it has tended to take a leading role in the formation of international and supranational African organizations such as the Economic Community of West African States (ECOWAS), the African Union and the projected West African Currency Unit, the Eco. From independence, and throughout different regimes, Nigerian presidents have also been keen supporters of the Non-aligned movement.

Nigeria's anglophone inheritance has resulted in three specific similarities to other English-speaking states. Nigeria has an executive presidency similar to that of the **United States**, a National Assembly composed of a House of Representatives, and a Senate under the 1999 constitution, which owes a great deal to the US model. Functionally, however, it shares the Westminster parliamentary tradition of the **UK**, and political parties function within the Assembly, which is housed in the new federal capital of Abuja, in much the same way that they function in London and Westminster. Combined with the common law and statutory tradition, this was thought by some to ultimately guarantee the victory of democracy in Nigeria; yet engrained corruption, a systemic culture of human rights abuse, and the human cost of waste and executive domination have led to a situation where Nigerian freedom and justice are qualities that have to be defended and fought for daily. This is perhaps why the state has been so culturally productive in terms of literature, sport and music, forms of social capital which avoid central power and which also exist in defiance of it.

Nightingale, Florence (1820–1910)

Pioneering English nurse often associated, alongside Mary Seacole, with the foundation of the modern nursing profession, and alongside carbolic acid with the reduction of mortality in Victorian hospitals. Having first studied in Kaiserwerth, **Germany**, she began as a superintendent of nursing in Harley Street, London, in 1853. From there she went to the **Crimean War**, where she introduced new methods of hygiene and care. Nightingale returned to England and published her thoughts in 1860 in an acclaimed book. The same year she founded the Nightingale Training School for Nurses in London.

Nimeiri

– *see* **Sudan**.

Nixon, Richard Milhous (1913–1994)

Thirty-seventh president of the **United States**, 1969–74. Nixon's years in office were marked by intense partisan rancour and alienation arising out of the turbulent 1960s, culminating in the **Watergate** scandal that forced his resignation. From early in his career, Nixon attracted controversy, starting with his use of 'red scare' tactics to smear opponents. As president, policies such as affirmative action for blacks and welfare reform at first suggested a desire for a more unifying image, but this was undermined by his secret bombing of **Cambodia**, controversial judicial nominations and dirty tricks employed against political enemies. In 1972, Nixon won a landslide re-election, aided by two great achievements: the withdrawal of American forces from **Vietnam**, and détente with the **USSR** and **China**. Shortly thereafter details emerged of an array of illegal political activities during his first term, and Nixon's effort to cover up the scandal served only to make matters worse.

Nizam-1 Cedid

Nizam-ı Cedid, or the new system, refers to the Ottoman modernization campaign begun in 1792. The Russian Army had won two comprehensive military victories over the **Ottoman Empire** in the Russo-Ottoman Wars of 1768–74 and 1787–92. After the second defeat, during which the Ottoman Army failed to reconquer territory lost during the first war, Sultan **Selim III** launched sweeping military reforms. An independent

standing army was to be created with modern dress and discipline. The artillery corps was to be updated. Modern barracks were built and officers trained in new military schools. While aiming for broader impact, in the judiciary as well as the military, the energy of reform went into military affairs. The **Janissary** corps rebelled against Selim III's reforms (which threatened their interests) and helped depose him in 1807. Reform continued, however. The Ottoman military developed in the mould of western-style armies throughout the rest of the empire's existence.

Njoya, Ibrahim (1860–1933)

Ruler of the Bamoun kingdom in modern-day **Cameroon**, 1886–1930. Njoya sought to modernize his country by cooperating with merchants and missionaries from Europe, especially from **Germany**. He assisted the Germans in the conquest of Cameroon and was allowed considerable self-government. He developed a writing system for his language and established a network of schools in which to teach it. When the French took over Cameroon in 1918, his status changed and he was eventually deposed.

Nkomo, Joshua (1917–1999)

Zimbabwean nationalist leader who was president of the **Zimbabwe** African Peoples Union or ZAPU. In 1963 the nationalist movement split and soon afterwards Nkomo was detained. After the liberation war, Nkomo's party was soundly defeated in the independence elections of 1980 by its rival **ZANU**. The bitter and violent rivalry between the two parties ended in 1987 when Nkomo agreed to unite with ZANU and accepted the post of vice president.

Nkosi Sekelele Afrika

The traditional hymn and national anthem of **South Africa**. Composed in 1897 by Enoch Mankayi Sontonga, the original hymn translated as 'Lord, Bless Africa / Blot out all its wickedness /And its transgressions and sins / And bless us'. In 1925 the **African National Congress** adopted the song as its anthem. It spread across Africa as an anthem of resistance and anti-**apartheid** sentiment. A multilingual version became the national anthem of South Africa in 1994.

Nkrumah, Kwame (1909–1972)

Ghanaian politician. Born in Nkroful in the then British Gold Coast colony, he was educated in mission schools and originally became a teacher. Nkrumah went to the **United States** in 1935, attending Lincoln University and the University of Pennsylvania, going on to the London School of Economics in 1945. Active in England in the West African Students' Union, the **Pan-African** movement and with the veteran Trinidadian communist George Padmore (1902–59), in 1947 he was invited by nationalist leader Joseph Danquah (1895–1965) to become general secretary of the United Gold Coast Convention, the country's first political party. In 1949 he formed the Convention People's Party (CPP) to lead a civil disobedience struggle for independence. Imprisoned in 1950 for organizing a 'Positive Action' campaign that culminated in riots, Nkrumah was released to serve as prime minister when the CPP triumphed in the 1951 legislative assembly elections. In 1953 he presented a 'Motion of Destiny', demanding an end to British rule. **Ghana** became the first independent black African state in 1957.

In 1960 Nkrumah declared Ghana a republic and became president, establishing a one-party state in 1964 and making himself president for life. He followed a broadly socialist policy, attempting rapid industrialization and instituting initially successful education, health and welfare programmes, and was a beacon to African independence movements. He played a central role in establishing the Organization of African Unity (now the **African Union**) in 1963 and was awarded the Lenin Peace Prize. But mounting domestic debt and an increasingly unpopular personal cult led to his overthrow in a western-backed military coup in 1966. He fled to **Guinea**, dying in exile in **Romania**. Nkrumah was for a long time an influential theoretician whose writings include *Towards Colonial Freedom* (1946), *Africa Must Unite* (1963), *Neo-Colonialism, the Last Stage of Imperialism* (1965) and *African Socialism Revisited* (1967).

nomadism (Middle East)

A feature of Middle Eastern life since the earliest times, nomadism remains important in the more arid areas where it may be the only means of longer term survival. Nomads are best-known in the English-speaking world as the Bedouin, from the Arabic *badawii*, plural *badu*, meaning 'nomad', but the Tuareg of the Sahara are also familiar. The nomad may be defined as one of a group which moves from place to place to find pasture, but nomadism overlaps with tribalism and sometimes with trade. Measures to limit tribalism may therefore inhibit nomadism and vice versa. Moreover, the extent of nomadism at any one time reflects wider economic and social conditions. It will tend to grow if marginal farming becomes

unviable, because of, say, drought, and decrease in times of greater economic opportunity and political security.

Nomadism is characterized by loyalty to tribe and often recognizes only the authority of tribal chieftains. It readily rejects central government authority and disregards modern national frontiers, which are often unmarked. While having its own strict code of honour, it feels little bound by modern concepts of national law, whether civil or criminal. For such reasons, it has usually been suspect to government and been progressively curtailed as central authority has grown, particularly in the more sophisticated, urbanized states. **Mehmet Ali**, for example, deliberately neutralized the influence of the *badu* as part of his restructuring of Egyptian society in the early nineteenth century.

A not dissimilar approach has been seen in **Iran**, where throughout the nineteenth century the nomadic population remained stable at some 2.5 million while the population as a whole grew from some 6–7 million to some 8–9 million. In the 1920s Reza Shah succeeded for the first time in Iranian history in disarming the tribes, and sought to suppress tribal life and culture and to enforce settlement on the nomads with adverse effects on Iran's livestock production, basically because nomadism conflicted with his vision of a modern Iran. His campaigns in Loristan and Kurdistan were a success primarily because the nomads there were not organized in large tribal confederations. Nevertheless, the nomads remained resentful of central government and in particular of its national service law, implemented 1928, not least because the conscripts returned to the tribe with modern ideas, which was, of course, one of the government's intentions. The pressure on the nomads was increased in 1932 with the establishment of an office for the forced settlement of the tribes, which pursued its mission in a brutal manner. Although effective in the short term, the forcibly settled nomads virtually all returned to their familiar style of life as soon as the shah abdicated in 1941, while retaining a strong sense of grievance against central authority. The pressure on nomadism returned, however, under the White Revolution in the period 1962–77. The policy of forced settlement was renewed, with the government now commanding much more effective military and security resources to overcome resistance. The reasoning and the consequences remained the same. Nomadism was thought to be evidence of backwardness, but livestock production declined as sedentarization advanced.

All such policies of forced settlement, whether in Iran or elsewhere, tended to ignore the extent to which nomadism would diminish naturally as industrialization and other forms of economic development advanced. In the extreme case of **Saudi Arabia**, a traditional heartland of nomadism, the exploitation of oil after **World War II** had meant that only about 5 per cent of the population remained truly nomadic by as early as 1979. In **Egypt**, perhaps only a seventh or less of the *badu* of the Arabian and Libyan deserts remain true nomads, the remainder being semi-sedentary tent-dwellers.

Logically enough, it was to be in the nomad-friendly wastes of Arabia that nomadism played its largest military role in modern times. The first rejection of Ottoman rule by the Arabs was in 1913 when **Abdülaziz Ibn Sa'ud** captured the Ottoman province of al-Hasa, in what is now Saudi Arabia. This was followed in Mecca by the proclamation of Arab revolt against the **Ottoman Empire** by **Husayn, Sharif of Mecca** on 10 June 1916, during **World War I**. The size and composition of this initial Arab army cannot be known with any accuracy but it may have numbered some 30,000 tribesmen, many of them nomads but others marginal high-land farmers. What can be said with confidence is that the army included members of the Harith, Bani 'Ali, Bani 'Atiyah, Bani Salem, Juhaynah, Utaybah and Howeitat nomadic tribes and that the role of the nomad became more important as the campaign became more mobile. Such men were accustomed to a guerrilla style of warfare and excelled in raids on Ottoman positions but lacked discipline and were often reluctant to move outside their own tribal areas, posing a permanent problem of recruitment. They also had to be paid in gold coin. Furthermore, a distinction must be drawn between the regular Arab Army and the Arab irregulars, mainly nomads, associated with **T. E. Lawrence**, the almost legendary 'Lawrence of Arabia'. Their greatest joint achievement was probably to have pinned down some 20,000–30,000 Ottoman troops in Arabia for two years, but they also made a valuable contribution to the ultimate allied capture of the cities of Damascus and **Jerusalem**. Their political achievement was more limited, as the Arab lands passed under British and French control in the guise of **League of Nations mandates**, the seemingly value-less Hejaz alone being left to the Arabs under Abdülaziz Ibn Sa'ud to become the nucleus of the later Saudi Arabia.

The nomad has probably had the greatest politico-military impact since then much further

west in the Sahara. Droughts in the 1980s and 1990s destroyed the herds kept by the nomads, prompting many young Tuareg to join Colonel **Gaddafi**'s army in Libya as mercenaries. Displaced by his overthrow, they headed for **Mali** where they briefly sought to establish an independent state in the north called Azawad, 2011–12. The nomads also formed the backbone of the **Polisario**, originally founded in 1973, to fight Spanish colonial rule in what was then Rio de Oro and then fought **Mauritania** and **Morocco** for an independent **Saharawi Republic**, 1976–9, and Morocco alone, 1979–89. The future of what is now known as Western Sahara remains unresolved.

Nomonhan, Battle of (1939)

This was a battle between **Japan** and **Russia** fought over a border dispute in 1939. In May 1939 Japanese forces attacked the Mongolians who had crossed the northern border of **Manchuria**. The skirmish escalated, and on 20 August the Soviets attacked with 100,000 troops, driving the Japanese out of the disputed area and causing them heavy losses. This defeat caused Japanese leaders to abandon plans to fight the Soviets and concentrate instead on expanding their empire in South East Asia.

Non-Cooperation movement (India)

Launched in 1920 by **Mohandas K. Gandhi** at the helm of the **Indian National Congress**, the Non-Cooperation movement mobilized large numbers of Indians in non-violent resistance to the British. Beginning with a boycott of British goods and institutions, the movement escalated into the non-payment of revenue. Non-Cooperation was closely aligned with the concern of Indian Muslims over the post-**World War I** dismemberment of the **Ottoman Empire**, which also deprived its sultan, widely respected as the khalifa (caliph) of Sunni Muslims, of control over the holy cities of Jerusalem, Mecca and Medina. The joint anti-colonial programmes of Non-Cooperation and the pro-khilafat cause, however, ran into difficulties following rioting in 1921 in Malabar that pitted mostly Muslim cultivators against mostly Hindu landlords and moneylenders. In February 1922, following an incidence of violence in which peasant protestors were provoked into burning down a police station in Chauri Chaura, killing twenty-two policemen, Gandhi abruptly ended this first Non-Cooperation campaign.

NORAD (North American Defense Command)

The title of this organization changed in March 2007 to reflect the extension of its activities into space, but NORAD originally dates from 1958, when the **United States** and **Canada** combined their resources to establish a system that would give early warning of impending nuclear attack by Soviet bombers or intercontinental ballistic missiles. After the **Cold War**, NORAD diversified to help track drug-running aircraft and pre-empt 9/11-style attacks.

Noriega Morena, Manuel Antonio (1936–2017)

Gaining prominence under Panamanian dictator General Omar Torrijos (1968–81), Noriega controlled **Panama**'s National Guard and became de facto ruler during the 1980s. Long an intelligence asset for the **United States**, he lost American support following allegations of corruption, money laundering and drug smuggling. Deposed during the 1989 US invasion of Panama, he was convicted of drug charges and spent the subsequent period in US and French prisons.

Normandy landings

The accepted term for the 'D-Day' landings in north-western France beginning on 6 June 1944 that marked the invasion of Europe by the forces of the **United States**, the **British Empire** and the **Free French**. D-Day represented the biggest sea-borne invasion in history, and delivered over 100,000 men to five beaches – codenamed 'Omaha', 'Utah', 'Sword', 'Juno' and 'Gold'. Though casualties on some beaches, particularly Utah, were relatively high, the amphibious landings were ultimately successful in breaching the Atlantic Wall thrown up by the forces of the **Third Reich** and began the process by which **Nazi Germany** would be divided amongst western and Soviet forces. Soviet historians frequently point out that, though the western allies with sixty German divisions and accomplished a stunning military and intelligence coup with their invasion, the **USSR** during the contemporaneous operation 'Bagration' in the east of Europe destroyed 162 German divisions at the cost of almost a million casualties just before the Normandy landings began.

North, Lord Frederick (1732–1792)

The British prime minister, Lord North served in Parliament between 1754 and 1790. He was a junior minister in the Newcastle–Pitt government and became chancellor of the Exchequer from 1767 to 1770 during which period he was responsible for implementing the **Townshend Acts**. In 1770 he became prime minister, a post he held until 1782 when his government fell as a result of the failure of the **Yorktown campaign** in the **American War of Independence**.

North Borneo

– see **Malaysia**.

North Korea

– see also **Kim Il-sung, Kim Jong-il** and **Korea**.

Founded in September 1948 as the Democratic People's Republic of Korea, North Korea has its origins as an anti-colonial state. Through its leaders, **Kim Il-sung, Kim Jong-il** and Kim Jong-un, it has maintained a corporatist governing structure underpinned by Juche ideology and neo-Confucian principles. The country has faced numerous challenges since the 1990s, especially the struggle to balance the preservation of the ruling ideology and structure with economic reforms and confrontations with outside powers over its nuclear weapons programmes.

Northeast Passage

– see **exploration**.

Northwest Passage

– see **exploration**.

Northern Expedition (China)

This was a military campaign launched in 1926 by **Chiang Kai-shek** to unify China. In its initial phase, during which both Communist and Nationalist forces took part, it defeated or incorporated thirty-four warlord armies in south China. Following this, Hankou, Nanjing and Shanghai were all captured. A split in the Nationalist Party delayed further advance, but the expedition resumed in 1928, and on 8 June, Beijing was surrendered to Nationalist troops.

Northern Rhodesia

– see **Zambia**.

Northern Ireland

A formal political entity since December 1922 when the six north-eastern Irish Ulster counties refused to join the newly independent Irish Free State, now the Republic of **Ireland**. The partition reflected the cleavage between the predominantly Protestant north-east, which had been extensively settled by the British, particularly the Scots, since the seventeenth century, and the deeply Roman Catholic native, nationalist remainder. Partition was nevertheless flawed in that self-government within the **United Kingdom** established, in practice, a Protestant monopoly of power, although a third of the population was Roman Catholic, with major implications for employment, housing and policing. Communal relations remained antagonistic, particularly during the regular displays of Protestant triumphalism. The result from the 1960s was rioting, terrorist warfare by the Irish Republican Army (IRA), and counter-violence by the Ulster Defence Association (UDA) and Ulster Defence Force (UDF). A succession of negotiated approaches proved abortive before a power-sharing agreement of 10 April 1998 between the Protestant parties and the Irish nationalist **Sinn Féin** was finally reached, which has brought power-sharing and peace, or at least a cessation of violence.

Northern Ireland crisis

A term which can refer either to the civil disorder and sectarian state breakdown in Northern Ireland between 1969 and 1973, or to the entirety of the 'Troubles' between 1969 and 1998. Northern Ireland had emerged as a separate self-governing state within the **UK** in 1922, but by 1949 had become dominated by a Protestant majority who systematically segregated Roman Catholic Nationalists from civic life and amenities. This situation led to the emergence of a cross-community civil rights movement in the late 1960s. Unfortunately, it was met with violence on the part of the Northern Ireland government and sections of the Protestant, or 'Unionist' community. This encouraged the government of Harold Wilson to send in British troops, who were initially welcomed, but who were then isolated after attempts to suppress demonstrations and to eliminate the provisional IRA. Direct rule from Westminster, and the attempt to create power-sharing institutions, followed, but were brought down by a general strike in 1973. This ushered in an era of bombings and assassinations which claimed the lives of some 3,300 people. Eventually, a new power-sharing process, involving the Irish and British governments and representatives of all the traditions in Northern Ireland, gathered pace in the 1990s, leading to the Good Friday Agreement of 1998 and subsequent power-sharing.

Northwest Ordinance (USA)

An Act adopted by Congress on 13 July 1787 which established a system for the subdivision and sale of territory as well as the creation of local, territorial and, eventually, state governments in the Northwest Territory. The Territory was land in the public domain bordered by the Appalachian mountains in the east, the Ohio River in the south, the Mississippi River in the west and the Great Lakes in the north. The Northwest Ordinance established a process whereby five states could eventually be carved out of this territory and established a precedent for the creation of new states from western territory.

Norway

A Danish province, 1536–1814. Its surrender to **Sweden** in 1814 was immediately followed by a declaration of Norwegian independence, but then by a Swedish invasion and the recognition of the former French marshal, Bernadotte, as King Karl XIV Johan of a united kingdom of Norway and Sweden. Norway nevertheless retained its own parliament and constitution. The growing national consciousness evinced by the works of Henrik Ibsen (1828–1906), Edvard Grieg (1843–1907) and Edvard Münch (1863–1944) led to the dissolution of the union, 1905, and the election of Prince Carl of Denmark as King Haakon VII. Neutral in **World War I**, Norway again sought neutrality in **World War II** but was occupied by the Germans, 1940–5. It has been a member of **NATO** since 1949, a member of the Nordic Council since 1952, and a member of the **European Free Trade Association (EFTA)** since 1959, but **European Union** (EU) membership was rejected in public referenda, despite governmental support, in 1972 and 1994.

NSC-68 (USA)

The US National Security Council drafted the report commonly known as NSC-68 for President **Truman** in early 1950. The report detailed the Council's perception of Soviet intentions and capabilities in foreign policy. The authors asserted that the differences between 'free' and 'slave' states were irreconcilable, and that the **USSR** was determined to assume control over as much of the world as possible unless stopped by the threat of American military power.

Nu, U (1907–1995)

Burmese independence leader and prime minister of **Burma**, 1948–58 and 1960–2. A teacher and trained lawyer, he was prominent in the struggle for independence and was jailed by the British in 1940. By 1942 he had been freed by the Japanese and was serving as foreign minister. This ultimately led to a break with the Japanese, and upon liberation, Nu and Aung San continued as Nationalists.

With Aung San's assassination, Nu became leader of the Anti-Fascist People's Freedom League, and then prime minister. His various programmes of welfare reform, agrarian reform and nationalization were undermined by Communist and ethnic insurgencies. Despite this, he became prominent in the creation of the Non-aligned movement. His nemesis proved to be General **Ne Win**, who replaced him before the elections in 1958, before returning to power, and then permanently in 1962, after a coup. Nu subsequently endured prison until 1969, exile in **India**, life as a Buddhist monk, and rejection at the Myanmar polls in 1988 after an attempted comeback.

nuclear deterrence

The doctrine that possession of nuclear weaponry will deter enemy attack, and, in particular, that the corollary of mutually assured destruction (MAD) will deter nuclear powers from attacking each other. The doctrine presupposed that a nuclear exchange would be strategic and was severely compromised by any suggestion that it might be solely tactical. It was a fundamental feature of relations between the western powers and the **Soviet Union** throughout the **Cold War** and was widely credited with the avoidance of conflict.

nuclear energy

– see also **energy**; **nuclear weapons**.

The liberation of energy from an atomic nucleus is a phenomena reserved in nature only to the Sun and those stars that by undergoing nuclear reactions yield heat and light in truly huge proportions. For humankind, nuclear energy is a genuinely mid-twentieth-century achievement. However, the science of atomic radiation, atomic change and nuclear fission that made this development possible is older. Uranium, the heaviest occurring element in nature and also one of the favourite materials by which nuclear reactions are generated, was discovered in 1789 by German chemist Martin Klaproth. Ionizing radiation was discovered by another German, this time a physicist, Wilhelm Rontgen, who in 1895 by passing electric current through an evacuated glass tube produced unremitting X-rays. A year later a breakthrough took place. The French physicist Henri Becquerel found that an ore containing radium and uranium caused a photographic plate to darken due to beta radiation. Pierre and Marie Curie labelled such a phenomenon 'radioactivity' – the emission of α and β particles by unstable atomic nuclei of subatomic particles.

This accumulated stock of knowledge and experimentation of the late nineteenth century in the fields of nuclear physics and nuclear chemistry permitted the groundbreaking discoveries of the 1930s. In 1934 the Italian physicist Enrico Fermi bombarded uranium atoms with accelerated protons producing a lighter and diverse variety of artificial radionuclides. A few years later, Otto Hahn and Fritz Strassman showed that these new lighter elements were barium isotopes, thereby demonstrating that an atomic fission had taken place. This is the quintessential virtue of nuclear energy: nuclear fission. The nuclear fission of heavy elements such as uranium and plutonium are exothermic reactions that release substantial amounts of usable energy.

The most popular applications of nuclear energy since have been in two areas: nuclear power for electricity generation and nuclear weapons. Although fission had been discovered in Nazi **Germany**, the British acted promptly upon the 'uranium problem' and set up a scientific committee, the Maud Committee, to work on a report. On July 1941 Maud presented two final reports: 'Use of Uranium for a Bomb' and 'Use of Uranium as a Source of Power'. Efforts and resources focused on the use of uranium for the atomic bomb. When the **USA** entered **World War II**, leadership on nuclear development for the bomb passed from Britain to the US and from academic research with limited funds to a major US governmental concern directed for clear military purposes with 1,000 million dollars of funding under the Manhattan Project. In August 1945 the US dropped two atomic bombs on Japan causing over 150,000 deaths.

The use of nuclear energy for power generation only took off in the 1950s, but it was to do so on a massive scale generating cheap, clean and reliable energy, mostly in developed countries. Nevertheless, nuclear power generation is not problem-free and concerns have evolved around storage of nuclear waste and the threat of nuclear contamination by accident or sabotage (as, for example, at Chernobyl, Three Mile Island and Fukushima).

Nuclear Non-proliferation Treaty (NPT)

Signed by over sixty countries in 1968, and now by 190, the treaty came into effect in 1970 and was renewed in 1995. Its main objective is to prevent the spread of nuclear weapons, but it also upholds the eventual goal of nuclear disarmament and accepts the development of nuclear energy for peaceful uses. Five states with nuclear weapons are signatories (**United States**, **France**, **United Kingdom**, **China** and **Russia** replacing the **Soviet Union**), all of whom had signed by 1992.

nuclear weapons

Nuclear weapons are those weapons which utilize the energies released by the fission or fusion of heavy elements to create an explosion of very great power. Atomic bombs, based upon the fission of uranium, were the first to be developed, by the **United States**, and were deployed against the Japanese cities of **Hiroshima** and Nagasaki in August 1945. The use of these two bombs ended **World War II**. The explosive force of each was measured in megatonnes – a force equivalent to millions of tonnes of chemical high explosive. The United States went on to develop hydrogen bombs, which were much more powerful than the fission bombs as they depended upon the fusion of plutonium atoms and hydrogen. These weapons were also acquired, possibly by espionage, by the **Soviet Union (USSR)**.

An 'arms race' then began to develop as both sides sought to gain as many of the weapons as possible, so as to ensure the destruction of the other in the event of any attack. This capacity, which was soon exceeded by multiples of ten, would also have led incidentally to the destruction of civilization on Earth. Initially, the bombs were to be dropped from aircraft, but by the 1950s they were married with ballistic rocket technology to develop intercontinental forces. These were then supplemented by submarine-launched weapons. **Britain**, **France** and the People's Republic of **China** went on to acquire weapons of their own between 1953 and 1966. These were thought to guarantee their place on the Security Council of the United Nations Organization, and whilst the arsenals of the three powers were never as great as those of the US and the USSR, they were capable of being equally devastating. Eventually, a nuclear non-proliferation treaty was signed, but despite this **South Africa**, **India** and **Pakistan** went on to develop weapons; **Israel** was widely rumoured to have done so; and **Iraq**, **Iran** and **North Korea** at various times pursued weapons programmes, to great international disquiet and, in the case of Iraq, to the extent of provoking Israeli attacks in 1981 on development facilities.

The threat that Iraq was developing weapons again was used by the administration of **George W. Bush** to justify the **Iraq War** which began in 2003. The United States and the USSR at various times also developed 'tactical' weapons for use against opposing armies (sometimes called 'battlefield' nuclear weapons) and neutron weapons which depended upon releasing an intense and short-lived burst of radiation. The effect of this burst would be to destroy electronic and organic material. At the time of writing, no nuclear weapon has been used since 1945 in anger. Attempts were made, abortively, to use atomic bombs in civil engineering projects in the 1950s, and peace campaigners have pointed to the radioactive residue of uranium-tipped anti-tank bullets to designate such ordnance 'nuclear weapons'.

Nuclear weapons require frequent testing of stocks, which initially was conducted in the open air and the atmosphere, and then underground, until computer models evolved sufficiently not to require multiple tests. Such tests frequently caused controversy and anxiety during the **Cold War**, and amongst environmentalists

Nullification crisis (USA)

In December 1832 South Carolina declared Congress's tariff laws of 1828 and 1832 unconstitutional because they protected domestic industry. The state decided to obstruct the collection of import duties, but President **Jackson** and Congress determined to face down this challenge to federal authority, if necessary by military force. Congress also devised a compromise tariff that apparently gave up the protective principle in nine years' time, and South Carolina, finding itself isolated, accepted a concession that it could never enforce.

Nuremberg trials

The trials in 1946, after the end of **World War II**, of surviving Nazi leaders for war crimes including the newly defined concept of 'conspiracy to wage aggressive war'. Twelve defendants were sentenced to death, including one *in absentia*, three to life imprisonment, four to other long terms of imprisonment and three were acquitted. Scrupulously fair in their processes, they remained victors' justice in the sense that only the Germans and their allies were tried and only the victors determined the charges.

Nwapa, Flora (1931–1993)

Nigerian author. Born in eastern **Nigeria** to a wealthy family, Nwapa received degrees from University College, Ibadan and the University of Edinburgh. In 1966 her novel *Efuru* became the first written by an African woman to be published internationally. Her novels explore the condition of African women, **Igbo** traditions and motherhood. Following the **Biafra War**, Nwapa served as a government commissioner for health and social welfare before founding a publishing house dedicated to African literature.

Nyabingi cult

A religious movement in early twentieth-century East Africa, led initially by a woman named Muhumsa who claimed to be possessed by the spirit of a female warrior named Nyabingi. The cult resisted German occupation in **Rwanda**, **Burundi** and **Tanganyika**. Nyabingi was detained in Kampala by the British authorities from 1913 until her death in 1945, though the cult continued in a more quietistic mode after her arrest and continued for some time after her death.

Nyamwezi

An ethnic group in modern-day western **Tanzania**, famous especially in the nineteenth century for their commercial efforts. Nyamwezi did not possess a centralized state, but its merchants pioneered the trade route from Lake Victoria to the East African coast. Mirambo became an effective trading king of the Nyamwezi in 1860, though political unity was lost following his death in 1884. The region was eventually conquered by **Germany** in 1893.

Nyasaland

– *see* **Malawi**.

Nyerere, Julius (1922–1999)

Tanzanian teacher, politician and first president of independent Tanganyika, later **Tanzania**. Affectionately known as *Mwalimu*, or 'teacher' in Kiswahili, Nyerere was born to a chiefly family. He studied at **Uganda**'s Makerere University and at the University of Edinburgh where he was exposed to Fabian ideas and began to develop his own theory of African communal life. On his return to Tanganyika, Nyerere worked as a teacher and became president of the Tanganyika African Association (TAA) in 1953. He transformed the TAA into a more overt political party, the **Tanganyika African National Union** (TANU), with the explicit goal of independence from British rule. In Tanganyika's first elections, Nyerere was elected chief minister. Tanganyika achieved self-governance in 1961 with Nyerere as prime minister, then president the following year. After a coup in **Zanzibar** in 1964, Nyerere was instrumental in integrating Zanzibar into the new Republic of Tanzania. Nyerere He remained in power until his retirement in 1985.

An advocate for 'African socialism', he believed western models of capitalist development and industrialization were opposed to African forms of community and mutual aid. In 1967 he articulated his policy in the 'Arusha Declaration', which provided a model of African socialism that he called *Ujamaa*, translated as familyhood, community and cooperation. For Nyerere, *Ujamaa* was opposed to capitalism, which seeks to build a happy society on the basis of the exploitation of one another. 'We, in Africa, have no more need of being "converted" to socialism than we have of being "taught" democracy. Both are rooted in our past – in the traditional society that produced us', he said. His policy included the rejection of foreign aid and investment and the nationalization of banks and local resources. It also promoted 'villigization', a process through which the government established hundreds of *Vijiji vya ujamaa*, or solidarity villages. These villages were based on traditional African principles of communal labour that would increase productivity and produce a surplus to sell to towns or for export. Nyerere proposed that these villages would erase the class divisions created under colonial rule. While his policy focused on communal self-help, it was a top-down, highly regulated and state-imposed process. Peasant cultivators were reluctant to move. When persuasion failed, the government turned to compulsory villigization. A severe drought in 1973–4 prompted many to join the programme, and between 1973 and 1976 5 million people were moved into 8,000 *ujamaa* villages.

Villigization had devastating results. The new villages did not have the infrastructure to thrive, and peasant farmers felt their knowledge and skills were ignored by urban bureaucrats. Living standards in Tanzania fell between 40–50 per cent in 1975–83. Nyerere was however successful in creating impressive welfare services and extending local services of clean water, health and education throughout the country. A prominent **pan-Africanist**, he also allowed guerrilla forces from **South Africa**, **Zimbabwe** and **Mozambique** to train in Tanzania. Despite his socialist agenda, he maintained good relations with both the West and the Eastern bloc during the **Cold War**. He left power voluntarily in 1985.

Nyungu ya Mawe (d. 1884)

African ruler. Initially leader of a band of raiders in the Kimba region of modern-day **Tanzania**, his activities by 1871 had made him effective ruler over a large region in southern Tanzania. He moved gradually from raiding to trading, using the profits to increase his strength and create a centralized small state. His state was sufficiently durable to continue after his death, and only with German occupation was it defeated.

O

Obama, Barak (1961–)

Elected **US** president in 2008, the first African American to hold the office. Born in Hawaii to a white American mother and a Kenyan father (who returned to Kenya after divorce), Obama worked as a community organizer in Chicago before graduating from Harvard Law School and developing a career as a civil rights lawyer and law professor. Elected as a Democrat to the Illinois Senate in 1996 and to the US Senate in 2004, an opponent of the increasingly unpopular **Iraq War**, he defeated the former first lady, Hillary Clinton, for the Democratic presidential nomination in 2008, and won the presidency from the Republicans during a US financial crisis. As president he inherited wars in **Afghanistan** and **Iraq** and a collapsing economy. Within eighteen months he was also faced with one of the greatest environmental disasters in American history, when an offshore oil rig explosion in the Gulf of Mexico left huge quantities of oil gushing into the sea. Obama appointed Hillary Clinton (1947–) as his secretary of state and began to pivot US foreign policy towards the Pacific. Domestically, his first term was dominated by his successful extension of Medicare to almost every citizen, despite fierce opposition and dealing with the consequences of the **Great Recession**. An extensive policy of 'quantitive easing', low interest rates and federal infrastructure spending prevented a plunge into a deep recession and mass unemployment, at the cost of incurring higher debt. Obama won a second term in 2012 on the basis of a recovering economy and a boom in shale gas and petroleum production. He was unable, however, to act decisively against the Russian seizure of the Crimea from **Ukraine**, resolve the **Syrian Civil War** or further a settlement of the **Arab–Israeli conflict**. In 2015 he opened diplomatic contact with **Cuba**, breaking a long-standing embargo, making a successful visit early in 2016. He backed **Clinton** as Democratic candidate for the 2016 presidency. By then his election slogan of 2008, 'Yes we can', was widely cited by critics in relation to perceived impotence in foreign affairs.

Obasanjo, Olusegun (1937–)

Former army general and president of **Nigeria**. Of **Yoruba** descent, Obasanjo was a career soldier. He acted as a commander during the **Biafran War** and became **Murtala Mohammed**'s deputy after the military coup of 1975. After Mohammed's death in a failed coup in 1976, Obasanjo assumed the presidency. During his three-year tenure he banned student organizations, curtailed public political opposition, nationalized land and increased government control over the oil industry, leading to massive protests. Military rule ended when he handed over power to Shehu Shagari, a democratically elected civilian president. After being imprisoned for criticizing human rights violations by the government, Obasanjo was elected president in 1999 and served a further two terms.

Obote, (Apollo) Milton (1924–2005)

Ugandan politician. A teacher, Obote was elected to the Legislative Council in 1958 and formed the Uganda People's Congress in 1960. Prime minister on independence in 1962, he became executive president in 1966 after deposing the head of state, King Mutesa II. His unpopular government was ousted by **Idi Amin** in a military coup in 1980. On Amin's overthrow in 1980, Obote was elected president until being ousted once more in 1985.

Obregón, Álvaro (1889–1928)

Born in Alamos, Sonora, Obregón emerged as the best general in the **Mexican Revolution** and first of the Northern Presidents who implemented its social programme. He fought for **Francisco Madero**, led the troops that overthrew **Victoriano Huerta**'s dictatorship, defeated both **Pancho Villa** and **Emiliano Zapata**, and revolted against **Venustiano Carranza**. As president (1920–4), he initiated land and labour reforms and vigorously enforced anti-Catholic laws. He was assassinated by a Catholic fanatic.

Occupied Territories

– *see also* **Palestine**.

A disputed area, the Palestinian or Occupied Territories are currently 'occupied', or restricted by **Israel**. The **Gaza** Strip and West Bank make up the territories, with parts of the West Bank, such as portions of **Jerusalem**, being contested by both Palestinian and Israeli authorities. **Jordan** and **Egypt** have signed treaties with Israel giving up claims to lands which make up parts of the Occupied Territories; however Palestinian authorities were not a party to any agreements between these nations in reference to the lands. The territories which became known as the Occupied Territories to many Palestinians were gained by Israel in the wake of the **Six Day War**. The term 'Occupied Territories' is disputed by the Israeli government and scholars, but persists in use. Many of the areas called by this name, and which were occupied, and many of which continue to be occupied by Israel had been previously occupied by other Middle Eastern nations. The West Bank and Gaza Strip had been disputed and occupied territories for decades before the Israeli occupation, by nations such as Jordan and Egypt. Palestinians often refer to the areas of occupation as being a threat to Palestinian sovereignty as defined in the 1940 **Geneva Convention** because occupation denies the sovereignty of the whole. Some of the disputed 'occupied' territories were returned to Palestinian authority during the 1993 **Oslo Accords**, although settlements still exist illegally in some, and the legality of the occupations is challenged by both sides; Palestinian and Israeli.

The first and second **intifadas** which occurred in 1987 and 2000 respectively were sparked by popular uprisings over various aspects of occupation and its affect on the populace. The Occupied Palestinian Territories occupy a little over 6,000 square kilometres, and are home to millions of Palestinians and occupying Israelis. The Territories are predominantly Arab Muslim, with a small Arab Christian population. The country has a president and prime minister, as well as a legislative council. The capital of Palestine is Ramallah, but many of its governmental offices function out of the city of Gaza, as the nation is so divided by the Israeli occupation forces. The territory was split up in 1947 by a mandate creating a Palestinian state, an Israeli/Jewish state, and a separate entity for the shared holy city of Jerusalem. This plan was controversial, and is at the root of the current problems with land and settlement in Israel and the Palestinian Territories. A war commenced in 1948 when a Jewish section of the Palestinian mandate attempted to declare its independence thus depriving the Palestinian mandate of even more territory.

Sections of the Palestinian Territory were being controlled by the Israeli government and others by the Egyptian government. In 1967 Israel occupied the territories and cities of the West Bank and Gaza and continued to maintain their dominance of these areas until the 1993 Oslo Accords which forced Israel troops to withdraw.

O'Connell, Daniel
– *see* **Ireland**.

October War
– *see* **Yom Kippur War**.

Odinga, Oginga (1911–1994)
Kenyan politician, opposition figure and **Luo** chief. After serving on the Legislative Council under colonial rule and being recognized among the Luo as a *ker*, a spiritual leader, Odinga served as **Kenya**'s first vice president. By 1966 he had fallen out with President **Jomo Kenyatta** and the ruling party. He was jailed in 1969 but remained an oppositional figure in Kenya's one-party political landscape, mounting a failed presidential campaign in 1992.

Office of Strategic Services (OSS) (USA)
Established in 1942, the Office of Strategic Services (OSS) was supposed to coordinate the American intelligence effort and prevent another **Pearl Harbor**, to run covert missions behind enemy lines and supply the president with a comprehensive analytical intelligence service. Because of rivalries with the military and **FBI**, it never achieved an ascendant position and President **Truman** disbanded it in 1945, but OSS veterans would serve again after 1947 in the more durable **CIA**.

O'Higgins Riquelme, Bernardo (1778–1842)
– *see also* **Chile**.

Chilean independence leader. Of Basque and Irish origins, O'Higgins participated in a failed revolt against Spanish rule in 1810, returning to **Chile** in 1817 with Argentine General **José de San Martín** (1778–1850) and defeating the Spanish at Chacabuco. O'Higgins declared Chilean independence on 12 February 1818 and was proclaimed supreme director, but his proposed political and social reforms met with growing opposition and he was deposed in 1823 and exiled to **Peru**.

oil (Middle East)
– *see also* **Anglo-Iranian Oil Company (AIOC), Aramco** and **OPEC**.

Of limited significance as an **energy** source until the introduction of chemical processing in the mid nineteenth century, but important by 1900. The most familiar reserves then were in the **USA**, **Romania**, northern Azerbaijan (then part of the **Russian Empire**) and the **Middle East**. The potential economic and strategic value of these reserves was recognized by the British government's early purchase of a controlling share in the Iranian oil industry. Petro-diplomacy had emerged as a key factor in Middle Eastern affairs well before **World War I**, with the victors being the British, the French, European oil companies and the notorious 'Mr 5%', the Armenian Calouste Gulbenkian.

The allied victory over the Turks greatly strengthened the British position in the Middle East as a whole and over the areas then known to have rich oil reserves in particular. Britain felt free to establish a protectorate over **Iran**, although it was soon to be withdrawn under French and American pressure, but secured a more durable influence over **Iraq** and the Mosul oilfields under its **League of Nations mandate**. The British were similarly empowered by their military presence in **Egypt** to protect the Suez Canal, which had become more valuable as a route for Middle Eastern oil than as the route to India.

The benefits of oil exploitation to the Middle Eastern countries concerned were extremely limited, which generated considerable, but impotent, local resentment. Iraq remained under British influence even after its nominal independence and Iran was once more subject to the interests of **Britain** and **Russia**, now the **Soviet Union**. Nevertheless, **World War II** marked a watershed. The initial defeat of the European empires in the Far East by the Japanese boosted the confidence of national liberation movements, while the same European nations had been weakened by the war despite their final victory. Their imperial role was increasingly to be discharged by the United States, which was also trying to spearhead resistance to a perceived threat from the Soviet Union and international communism. At the same time, the dependence of the West on oil was growing ever greater. The politics of oil thus became embroiled in those of anti-colonialism, national liberation, economic prosperity and the **Cold War**.

The interplay of these factors was in due course to allow oil-producing countries to assert their own interests, but their first essay, in Iran, ultimately proved a failure. Dr **Mossadegh** succeeded in securing the passage of a law prohibiting oil negotiations with foreign interests until further notice,

December 1944, and in October 1947 secured the rejection of a recently initialled Russo-Iranian oil agreement. Then in 1949 he secured the adoption of his proposal to nationalize the whole Iranian oil industry. This was provocative when Ernest Bevin, Britain's Labour foreign secretary after 1945, had proclaimed Iran 'an intrinsic element in Britain's economic and strategic defence lifeline'. Iran was then also by far the largest Middle Eastern oil producer.

Despite its concern, the British Labour government had to recognize that it had itself nationalized 20 per cent of Britain's own industry and that America had emerged as a rival for control of Middle Eastern oil. Although military intervention had been deemed an option as early as April 1951, nationalization was in practice accepted by the Labour government, with Attlee himself warning against British association with the anti-Mossadegh elements around the shah, whose rule he described as the 'corrupt and undemocratic regime in Persia'. Concern was also felt at the standing of any such intervention under international law, and the Americans were strongly opposed. The option was finally ruled out by the Cabinet, 23 September 1951.

By 1953, however, there was a Conservative government in Britain and a Republican president in the US, and Iran was suffering economic and political disorder following a western blockade of Iranian oil. A successful coup was, therefore, masterminded by the American and British secret services to oust Dr Mossadegh. The 1954 consortium agreement then established a 50:50 division of proceeds between Iran and the consortium for twenty-five years, with American and British companies each receiving 40 per cent of the consortium shares. The Iranian oil industry was, however, to be fully renationalized under the 1979 revolution.

Despite the success of this blatant manipulation, the West was increasingly on the defensive in protecting its oil interests. The growth of Arab nationalism and of pressures for decolonization proved irresistible, and European-sponsored regimes succumbed in Egypt, Iraq, **Libya**, **Algeria** and ultimately Iran. Crises such as the **Suez Crisis**, 1956, were one consequence. On the other hand, the ceaseless increase in European demand was to some extent countered by the steady growth in the number of national producers. The discovery of ever wider reserves, however, had its own perverse implications. Although there were important exceptions, oil was often absent, or virtually so, in the more politically and socially advanced Middle

Eastern states such as Egypt, and abundant in the least advanced such as Libya and **Saudi Arabia**. Moreover, those same countries were those with the highest and lowest population densities respectively. Minor sheikhdoms such as **Kuwait** were suddenly endowed with quite disproportionate wealth. These discrepancies were further aggravated by the uneven social distribution of the new wealth. Social divisions in the shah's Iran widened as corruption was fuelled by growing oil income. In Saudi Arabia, little distinction was drawn between national wealth and royal wealth. Western powers were not slow to exploit these new class and national interests to their own benefit.

They were only partly successful. The oil-rich countries themselves proved increasingly willing to operate cohesively at least insofar as oil wealth was concerned. In 1960, Iran, Iraq, Kuwait and Saudi Arabia, together with Venezuela, established the Organization of Petroleum Exporting Countries (**OPEC**), to be joined by **Qatar**, Libya and **Abu Dhabi** from the Middle East during the decade that followed. Oil prices were raised by 70 per cent in September 1973 and then by a further 130 per cent in December 1973, specifically to punish the West for its perceived support of **Israel** against the Arabs in the October **Yom Kippur War**. The shock to western economies, both capitalist and communist, was profound, ushering in a phase of neoliberal economic thinking which was not to be seriously questioned until the banking crisis of 2008.

Such cohesion, however, never precluded national, strategic and, potentially, religious rivalries, in which oil wealth played a significant role. The precise motives for Iraq's annexation of Kuwait in August 1990 are open to debate, but it seems probable that Kuwait's immediate oil riches were one motive even though Iraq had enormous reserves of its own. It is even more probable that the American readiness to lead the coalition force in the ensuing **Gulf War (1990–1)** was predominantly motivated by its desire to guarantee the continued flow of oil from its Middle Eastern allies. Middle Easterners are convinced that the Anglo-American invasion of Iraq of 2003 was also motivated by oil.

The balance of forces, however, is permanently in flux. The discovery of North Sea oil temporarily reduced Europe's dependence on Middle Eastern oil, and the West's strategic concern to guarantee continued supply widened from the production of oil to its transit through pipelines from new sources adjacent to the Middle East, such as **Kazakhstan** and

Turkmenistan, and across Transcaucasia, which is an area of major Russian strategic interest. Nevertheless, 40 per cent of the world's oil is still shipped through the Persian Gulf via the Strait of Hormuz. The concern of Middle Eastern producers themselves was primarily focused on the European Union's drive to reduce its dependence on carbon fuels so as to combat climate change. Saudi Arabia has been a leader in opposing any binding international agreement to reduce carbon dioxide emissions, even arguing that it should be compensated for any future reduction in its oil income. The actual impact of new sources such as shale and of renewable energies is a further source of uncertainty, but Middle Eastern oil seems likely to remain a vital energy source for **Europe**, and increasingly **Asia**, for many years to come, even though over-supply caused prices to tumble in 2015 and they remain volatite.

Oil Shock (1973)

The Arab members of **OPEC** flexed their collective muscle by declaring an embargo on oil exports during the **Yom Kippur War** in October 1973. The embargo lasted until March 1974, quadrupling the price of oil in the **United States**. In 1967 a similar Arab embargo faltered; non-Arab production was then high enough to meet consumption. The intervening period saw a transformation of the balance of power between oil-producing states and western oil companies. Consumption of petroleum products was increasing rapidly and the United States was producing at full capacity. In this context of a tightening oil market, Arab nations took the opportunity to achieve goals on multiple fronts. The embargo furthered immediate military objectives meanwhile redefining the oil-producing states' position in the global political and economic order. The long-term economic effects of the oil shock, especially the end of 'cheap' oil and the ability of oil-producing states to demand higher revenues, were ultimately more salient than any impact the embargo had on the war.

Okinawa, Battle of

In **World War II**, this was the fiercest naval and land battle between **Japan** and the Allied forces lasting from late March to June 1945. It took place at Okinawa, an island in the Pacific, and resulted in the death of 12,000 US soldiers (and 38,000 wounded). The prolonged battle of eighty-two days was caused by the preparation of formidable tunnelled defences by an army that refused to surrender. A total of 130,000 Japanese were killed or missing and 11,000 captured. One estimate is 150,000 Okinawa civilians were killed or wounded (the lowest estimate is 42,000 killed).

Olmsted, Frederick Law (1822–1903)

The most renowned American landscape architect of the second half of the nineteenth century. His best-known creation was New York City's Central Park, but he designed public parks across the country as well as systems of interconnected green spaces (among them Buffalo's park network and Boston's 'initial generation of Emerald Necklace'). His contributions also include Stanford University campus, the environs of the US capitol in Washington DC, and early management plans for Yosemite National Park.

Olympic Games

A series of international sporting competitions first organized in the modern period in 1896 and intended to emulate the great meetings of ancient **Greece**. The Summer Olympics include athletes from most countries of the world, and are held every four years. Olympic games have therefore taken place quadrennially from 1896 with the exception of the war years of 1916, 1940 and 1944, beginning in London. Winter Olympics are also usually held two years after the summer games, and include tests of sporting skill in snow and on ice. The Olympics are strictly amateur games, with professionals barred from playing, and it is considered a great honour to win a gold, silver or bronze medal in one of the many competitions (an effect enhanced by the playing of national anthems and the raising of flags when the awards are given out). During the **Cold War**, and at Berlin in 1936, the Olympics were a stage for peaceful but serious competition between different countries and, implicitly, their different social and political systems. The Olympics were the scene of the 1972 Palestinian attacks on the Israeli team, and the subsequent German security catastrophe which resulted in the deaths of many of the Jewish participants. In 1980, at Moscow, and in 1984, at Los Angeles, the superpowers stayed away from each other's games. The games are staged in a different city across the world on each occasion, and are managed by an international committee which awards the prestigious and lucrative right to stage the games by a secret ballot of delegates. States have usually to accede to minimal human rights standards for the duration of the games and their preparation.

Oman

Also known as Muscat and Oman (until 1970), this is an Arab Muslim sultanate located in south eastern Arabia ruled, since 1749, by the Al Bu Sa'id dynasty with its capital in Muscat. Historically the economy was dominated by irrigated agriculture, fishing and extensive commercial activities throughout the Indian Ocean region. The beginnings of oil exports in 1967 transformed that economy. Politically, division has existed between those supporting the Ibadi Muslim principle of an elected imam and the sultanate form of government, and during the first half of the twentieth century an imam controlled the interior. Sultan Sa'id bin Taimur, with British support, unified the country in 1959, but his failure to modernize the country and defeat an insurgency in Dhufar resulted in overthrow by his son Qaboos ibn Sa'id in July 1970. Sultan Qaboos initiated wide-ranging social, economic and political reforms that successfully reunited the country.

Oman Civil War

Also known as the Dhufar War, this conflict began in 1962 over dissatisfaction in Dhufar province with the rule of Sultan Sa'id bin Taimur of Muscat and **Oman**. Arab and Dhufari nationalists joined the opposition to form the Dhufar Liberation Front. In 1968 the insurgency, backed by the People's Democratic Republic of **Yemen**, the Soviet bloc, **China**, and **Iraq**, adopted a Marxist ideology as the Popular Front for the Liberation of the Arabian Gulf (PFLOAG). By 1970 PFLOAG controlled nearly two-thirds of Dhufar. Sultan Sa'id obtained British military support but his failure to institute reforms resulted in replacement by his son Qaboos ibn Sa'id in July 1970. Qaboos initiated a more aggressive military campaign with support from **Great Britain**, **Iran** and **Jordan** and a civil development programme that brought roads, wells, schools and health services to the province. In December 1975 Qaboos announced victory in the war.

Omdurman, Battle of

The climax of the 1896–8 Anglo-Egyptian expedition to recapture the **Sudan**, fought across the River Nile from the capital Khartoum on 2 September 1898. The British commander, General Sir **Herbert Kitchener**, led 8,200 British and 17,600 Egyptian and Sudanese troops, together with a flotilla of twelve gunboats. His opponent, Abdullah al-Taashi, fielded a **Mahdi** force of 52,000. The one-sided battle was won by superior Anglo-Egyptian firepower, particularly from Maxim machine guns and gunboat-mounted artillery. Omdurman was also significant as the scene of the last British cavalry charge. Mahdist casualties were estimated at 9,700 dead and 13,000 wounded, with a further 5,000 taken prisoner. Anglo-Egyptian dead totalled 48, with 382 wounded. Kitchener was ennobled for the victory and the Sudan was restored to the nominal rule of the Khedive of Egypt. The remnants of the Mahdist forces were overcome at the Battle of Umm Diwaykarat in November 1899.

OPEC (Organization of Oil Exporting Countries)

International economic organization set up in 1960 with its headquarters in Vienna. Originally numbering thirteen oil producers, including the major Middle Eastern exporters and **Venezuela**, with the largest reserves. Its decision to embargo oil exports in response to the **Yom Kippur War** led to the **Oil Shock** of 1973–4 which quadrupled oil prices worldwide. Responses, including the development of non-OPEC sources of oil and alternative sources of energy, reduced OPEC's influence though its policies remained important. Latterly, the role of **Russia** as a major oil exporter and the revival of American domestic production through new drilling techniques have further restricted OPEC's ability to determine world prices, as witnessed in the fall in oil prices in 2015.

Open Skies Treaty (1992)

Originally suggested by American President **Dwight Eisenhower** in 1955, this was revived by President **George H. W. Bush** to encourage confidence between countries as the **Cold War** was ending by permitting the mutual observation of military activities. The treaty was signed in March 1992 by the **United States**, **Canada** and twenty-two European countries, ratified by the United States in 1993, and came into force in 2002. It permits unarmed aircraft to conduct observation flights over signatory countries.

Opium Wars

Two trading wars of the mid nineteenth century in **China**. The first (1839–42) was between China and **Britain**, and the second (1856–60) was between China and a British–French alliance. After the development of trade relations between China and western countries, the Chinese, accustomed to tributary relationships with others, required that westerners pay for Chinese goods with silver currency. To offset a growing negative flow of silver at home, the British created a market for opium in China and began illegally importing it to China. As demand for opium grew, China tried to stop the practice, and hostilities broke out. The outbreak of the second opium war led to the Treaty of Tianjin, which required further Chinese concessions and hostilities. The result of these conflicts was weakening of the Chinese imperial system and greatly expanded western influence in China.

Opus Dei

Roman Catholic organization, formally the Prelature of the Holy Cross and Opus Dei, founded in Spain in 1928 by Josemaría Escrivá de Balaguer y Albás (1902–75, canonized by Pope John Paul II in 2002). The organization is made up of priests and laity, the latter encouraged to demonstrate faith in their professional and everyday lives. Opus Dei (which is Latin for 'God's work') has been criticized for secretiveness, ultra-conservatism and for a past closeness to authoritarian regimes.

oral history

Oral history in the form of spoken or recited recollections of the past was commonly the only form of history available to societies before the invention of writing and the widespread availability of print. Even when these exist in societies of low levels of literacy, or where written records exist only in the forms compiled by an alien elite, whether dominant ethnically, politically or socially, oral history can be the only form of memory of past events. In the nineteenth century the literary figure Sir Walter Scott (1771–1832) drew heavily in his Waverley novels on the memories of his parents' and grandparents' generations of eighteenth-century Scotland. Similarly, the folklore collectors Jacob and Wilhelm Grimm (1785–1863 and 1786–1859 respectively) recorded traditional stories, published as *Grimm's Fairy Tales* (1812–22). Their example was followed by ethnographers and national historians who sought to recapture 'folk' traditions, tales and music, by the late nineteenth century using the first phonograph cylinders. Attempts to collect oral evidence about the past more systematically were organized in the **New Deal** by the Federal Writers' Project, collecting oral testimony from groups such as civil war veterans and ex-slaves, using both transcription and early tape recording. In 1948 an Oral History Record Office was established at Columbia University, New York. Oral testimony became an important component of 'history from below' with pioneers such as George Ewart Evans (1909–88) recording the memories of the last traditional English rural labourers, published as

Ask the Fellows that Cut the Hay (1958) and the American Stud Terkel's (1912–2008) *Hard Times: An Oral History of the Great Depression* (1970) and *The Good War: An Oral History of World War Two* (1985). Oral history developed its own journals in the early 1970s and the increasing ease of electronic recording and storage of material has made it a commonly available technique for recovering oral testimony of the past and establishing oral archives of contemporary events. Oral archives are now seen as a significant complement to written records for contemporary history with ongoing projects across the world to capture oral testimony of events within living memory, such as German Reunification or the 9/11 attack on New York.

Orange Free State
– *see* **South Africa**.

Oregon Boundary Dispute (USA)
Early attempts to resolve the protracted dispute between **Britain** and the **United States** over the Oregon territory failed, leading to an agreement in 1818 by which both would occupy the area jointly on a temporary basis. American migration and the ideology of 'Manifest Destiny' prompted US expansionists to claim the entire territory in the 1840s. The threat of war led both sides in 1846 to compromise on the present boundary of the 49th parallel.

Organisation Armée Secrète (OAS)
French right-wing underground movement formed by General Raoul Salan (1899–1984), Pierre Lagaillarde (1931–2014) and Jean-Jacques Susini (1933–) in 1961 to prevent **France** granting independence to **Algeria** at the end of the 1954–62 Algerian War. When an OAS coup in Algiers failed, the movement began a terrorist campaign, culminating in an assassination attempt on President **Charles de Gaulle** (1890–1970) in August 1962, five months after Algerian independence had been agreed.

Organization of African Unity (OAU)
– *see* **African Union**.

Organization of American States (OAS)
Established by charter in 1948 as a successor to the **Pan-American Union**, to promote solidarity and collaboration between states on the continent and to oppose the spread of Communism (Cuban membership was suspended following the 1959 revolution). The OAS was viewed as a vehicle for **United States** interests and shifted its emphasis as the **Cold War** ended towards encouragement of free trade, economic integration, sustainable development, democracy and human rights.

Organization of Petroleum Exporting Countries
– *see* **OPEC**.

orientalism
A term employed by the cultural historian Edward Said (1935–2003) from the 1970s to express European attitudes to the Orient, broadly defined as the non-European world of the **Middle East**, Far East and south Asia. Initially, it stressed the stereotypical views that were employed by romantic writers and artists to 'invent' a version of the Orient which derived primarily from their own preoccupations and fantasies. At the cultural level, there was a view of non-European civilizations, even some of the oldest, as exotic, backward and fundamentally static in comparison with a dynamic, progressive and culturally superior 'West'. But, at another, European 'orientalism' could be seen as justifying imperial expansion and the wholesale displacement of oriental culture with western models. As well as displaying often arrogant and ill-informed interpretations of other cultures, orientalism frequently meant a failure to perceive the subtleties and dynamic character of non-western societies. The orientalist cast of mind often proved inadequate to deal with anti-colonial movements and autonomous developments which it found incomprehensible or misunderstood as, for example, revivalist movements within **Islam** or the cultural sensitivities of Far Eastern societies. As an extremely fertile and multidisciplinary interpretation of many of the interactions between the West and other cultures over the past two centuries, the concept of orientalism has become an integral part and influence upon colonial and post-colonial studies.

Orozco, José Clemente (1883–1949)
Mexican artist. Born in Zapotlán el Grande, Orozco became, with **Diego Rivera** and **David Alfaro Siqueiros**, one of **Mexico**'s three greatest muralists. Less revolutionary in expression, he preferred to show caricatures of oppressors and to underscore human suffering. From 1926 to 1934 he created major works. Some observers consider his fresco at Pomona College among the finest murals ever painted. He subsequently worked in Guadalajara and painted walls of the Mexican Supreme Court.

Ortega, Daniel (1945–)

A long-time leader of the Sandinistas (FSLN), Ortega rose to prominence during the revolution that overthrew the Somoza regime in 1979. He became president of **Nicaragua** in 1985, a time when the leftist government faced both a severe economic crisis and an armed rebellion by the US-supported Contras. Defeated by **Violeta Chamorro** in the 1990 presidential elections, Ortega led the **Sandinista** movement into opposition until his re-election as president in 2006.

Orthodoxy

A division of the Christian faith encompassing around a third of a billion worshipers. The Orthodox Church is concentrated in the East of Europe, **Greece** and **Russia** and represents one of the 'big four' ancient traditions in apostolic **Christianity** (the others being Roman Catholic, Coptic and Armenian). Its faith is a Chalcedonian one, upholding the Nicene Creed except insofar as there is a dispute about the relationships within the Trinity of God the Father, Son and Holy Spirit. The Orthodox agree with Roman Catholics on the status of the Virgin Mary, the existence of angels, the communion of saints, and the continuity and integrity of the biblical tradition as affirmed by early Church Councils. They are administratively organized so that regional patriarchs work with autonomous synods of bishops, who are unmarried and usually drawn from monasteries, and who in turn preside over married priests who are adopted by a local church. These patriarchs arose with the Christian Church in **Constantinople**, and are the source of a main Orthodox dispute with Roman Catholics. The Catholic Church claims primacy for the Pope amongst all Church leaders because of his succession from the leader of the Apostles, whereas Orthodox bishops regard the Pope as the Patriarch of the West, and simply first amongst equals, and joint first with the Patriarch of Constantinople at that. The Roman Church contains a great many followers of orthodox rites and traditions, but its distinguishing characteristic is its requirement of fidelity to and communion with the **Papacy**, and in consequence it tends to view the non-Roman Catholic Orthodox as in schism (though not in heresy). The Orthodox, in turn, are wont to believe that the Romans are in schism, and that they have been since a famous, once repaired but often broken split which began in 1054.

The Orthodox Churches are possessors of a distinct aesthetic style, which is revealed in Byzantine church design, the use of chant and incense, the spatial organization of ritual, dress (including the requirement of beards on priests) and a distinctive style of iconography. Like Roman Catholics, the Orthodox use images to concentrate the mind on prayer to saints and God, and ornate two-dimensional icons, often of the Holy Virgin and Christ Child, have long been associated with the faith, though statues have not. Equally, the Church functions on an older calendar than that which prevails in the West, leading to the celebration of Christmas in January, and a date for Easter which is usually *sui generis* each year. These differences with the West have allowed the maintenance of a very distinctive tradition, which has often appealed to Anglican groups in inverse proportion to whatever is the current Anglican stance with regard to Rome or **Protestantism**.

Orthodoxy has been closely associated with the state in those areas where it was the majority religion. As a consequence, Churches have tended to add a national title to their rite (the Russian Orthodox Church, for example), but this should not convey any sense in which they are comparable to western establishments. Any orthodox church is in communion with any other unless it has deliberately disassociated itself, and so, for example, Russians, Bulgarians and members of autocephalous organizations in the **United States** and **Australia** may participate in each others' services. Nevertheless, there has arisen over the course of the past millennium a very close relationship between nationalists in Slavic lands, pan-Slavists and orthodox identity, and in other states, such as Greece, membership of the Church was for a long time an indicator of completed and full citizenship. This confluence of nationalist and mystical ideas, as well as an innate social conservatism, led the Orthodox Church into serious conflict with socialist regimes in the twentieth century, and to persecution thereby. By 1991, however, its restoration was in full swing, to the point where St Basil's Cathedral in Moscow, which had been destroyed by the Soviets, was rebuilt.

Because of its long history, the traditions of Orthodox Churches usually include a reference to two of the great disasters of Orthodox history; the sack by western forces of Constantinople in 1204, and the Muslim conquest of the same city in 1453. These were traumatic events for the Orthodox communion, and are often recalled in a perceived suspicion of the western and particularly Roman Church and its interests in eastern lands, as well as in a tendency towards intolerance of Islamic traditions. In the modern world, these features, plus social conservatism, have allowed for common ground to develop between Orthodox believers and American Protestant evangelicals, which has been buttressed by the growth of Orthodox numbers in the United States. Such ground is, however, by no means conducive to a majority movement or alliance. Instead, more effort has been placed on reconciliation with Rome, often at the initiative of popes such as **John Paul II** and Benedict XVI, who have re-emphasized patriarchal titles and engaged in dialogue and meetings with patriarchs of eastern regions.

Given its association with eastern Europe, the **Balkans** and **Russia**, Orthodoxy did not have a large presence as a missionary church in the past two centuries, although large numbers of Orthodox believers can be found in central Asia. Outside of its heartland, Orthodoxy is the religion of a diaspora of economic migrants and their descendants. It should not be confused with oriental Orthodoxy, western rite Orthodoxy, or the use of the term by various self-generated faith groups. The Orthodox Church suffered severely under **Communism**, but has revived strongly in such countries as Russia.

Oslo Accords (1993)

The Oslo Accords were an attempt to resolve major issues within the **Arab–Israeli conflict**. They were the first written agreement between **Israel** and the **Palestine Liberation Organization (PLO)** and established the framework wherein all 'final status' issues were to be resolved. Oslo was an outgrowth of the 1991 Madrid conference, where Israel for the first time openly negotiated with Palestinians who were part of a Jordanian delegation. Secret negotiations continued at the Fafo Institute in Oslo, **Norway**, and were completed on 20 August 1993. The Accords were signed at a public ceremony on the White House lawn on 13 September 1993 in the presence of PLO Chairman **Yasser Arafat**, Israeli Prime Minister **Yitzhak Rabin** and **United States** President **Bill Clinton**.

Oslo provided for the creation of a Palestinian National Authority which would administer territories under its control. It called for the withdrawal of the Israel Defense Forces from parts of the Gaza Strip and West Bank. Israel would grant interim Palestinian self-government in phases. Arafat, **Rabin** and **Peres** were awarded the Nobel Peace Prize for their efforts in reaching this historic step forward in the tortuous and still unresolved negotiation process between Israelis and Palestinians.

Ostpolitik

Chancellor Brandt's 'eastern policy' of 1969, of normalizing West Germany's relations with its communist neighbours – East Germany, **Poland, Czechoslovakia** and the **Soviet Union** – by renouncing force and by recognizing the integrity of all European states within their existing frontiers including the Oder–Neisse line as the frontier with Poland. Its main fruits were the Treaties of Moscow and Warsaw, 1970, and the 'Basic Treaty', 1972, on East–West German relations. It earned Brandt the Nobel Peace Prize in 1971.

Oswald, Lee Harvey (1939–1963)

Born in New Orleans, Louisiana, Oswald gained notoriety for assassinating **USA** President **John F. Kennedy** on 22 November 1963. Having been arrested, Oswald was himself shot dead on live television by Jack Ruby. In 1964 the Warren Commission identified Oswald as the lone rifleman in the assassination, but his contacts with Cuban officials, his Russian wife Marina Prusakova, and his sojourn in the **Soviet Union** continue to fuel portrayals of Oswald as a party in grand conspiracies.

Ottoman Empire

The Ottoman Empire originated in the thirteenth century, when it began to expand in Anatolia and **Europe** at the expense of other Turkic-speaking dynasties and the Byzantine Empire. In the centuries that followed, the Ottoman Empire conquered vast swathes of the European, Asian and African continents. **Constantinople**, conquered in 1453, became the empire's capital. Territorial expansion reached its apogee in the sixteenth century under Suleiman the Magnificent when Ottoman armies occupied a territory extending from the Danube to the Persian Gulf, and from Algiers to the Red Sea. The flexibility of its administrative arrangements accounted for its success. Ottoman policy was happy to accommodate Christian rulers in **Hungary**, for instance, as long as they obeyed the empire's edicts. The malleable reality of Ottoman administration stands in contrast to explanations of Ottoman expansion that have pointed to holy war as the driving force of the Ottoman *gazi* (or conqueror). Toleration, not religious zeal, was the main force behind Ottoman conquest.

Many have characterized the experience of the Ottoman Empire in the modern period as marked by inevitable decline. At the turn of the eighteenth century the empire lost its military edge over

European powers, and began to slowly lose its territory on the European continent, ceding Hungary back to the Habsburg Empire (1699). The depiction of total, inexorable decline should not be exaggerated, however. Despite a few temporary downward slips, real wages rose throughout the empire's history. The empire's prowess on the battlefield was sufficient to maintain its hold over an enormous territory for two more centuries after the Treaty of Karlowitz formalized the Ottoman withdraw from Hungary.

Rather than the objective decline of Ottoman fortunes, the relative military balance between European countries and the Ottoman Empire shifted in the eighteenth century. In particular, the Ottoman grip over its European provinces began to slip. By the latter part of the century, **Russia** had begun to defeat the Ottoman militarily on a regular basis. After one such defeat the Treaty of Küçük Kaynarca (1774; *see* **Russo-Turkish War**) enshrined the first Ottoman loss of territory with a Muslim majority (the Crimean peninsula). Military defeat sparked momentum for reform in the empire. **Selim III**, in the wake of another defeat to Russia in 1792, declared the inception of the **Nizam-ı Cedid** (New System) designed to be a comprehensive reform of Ottoman administration. The first object of reform was the Ottoman military. Despite objections of some established constituencies, especially the **Janissary** corps who opposed reform, Ottoman military reform had taken root by the end of the eighteenth century.

Sultan Mahmud II (1808–39) began the period of broader reforms that would characterize the Ottoman experience in the nineteenth century. He moved to crush the power of the Janissary corps in 1826 to facilitate further military reform. His son **Sultan Abdülmecid** formalized the inception of sweeping reforms, called **Tanzimat** (or reorganization). The Hatt-ı Sharif (1839), issued directly after Mahmud II's death, enshrined a series of financial reforms to standardize taxation and established basic human rights. The **Hatt-ı Humayan (1856)**, also issued by Abdülmecid, reiterated the equality of all Ottoman citizens regardless of sect. This period of reform coincided with accelerating change in Ottoman society. Hatt-ı Humayan aimed to reduce sectarian tension and, in particular, the momentum of separatist subnationalist movements driven by religious difference. In practice, Tanzimat corresponded with a heightening of ethnic tensions as foreign powers used the empire's minority populations as a conduit for their influence. Members of those same minority

populations manipulated foreign powers for their own economic and political benefit.

As well as interfering in the empire's internal affairs, European imperial powers increasingly sought to seize Ottoman territory in the final decades of the empire's existence. **France** struck at Ottoman North African territories, occupying **Algeria** (1832), **Tunisia** (1881) and **Morocco** (1912). **Great Britain** occupied **Cyprus** (1878) and **Egypt** (1882). Russia and the Ottoman Empire engaged in intermittent warfare throughout the modern period, culminating in a series of defeats in the Russo-Ottoman War of the late nineteenth century (1877–88) in which the Ottoman Empire had to abandon the bulk of its European provinces. Later, Russian-supported separatist movements in the **Balkans** would further imperil the empire's hold on its most productive territories. The first Balkan war (1912–13) saw the empire's military suffer defeats against the fledging armies of **Serbia**, **Greece**, **Montenegro** and **Bulgaria**.

Economic stress accompanied military defeat. The economy of the empire had always been agricultural. Global industrialization left the empire to export its own agricultural products and import manufactured goods. This economic disadvantage, despite increasing internal trade, left it deeply indebted to European powers. A sense of crisis, and the hope that reform could solve the empire's problems, inspired the revolt of the **Young Turks** in 1908. They restored the constitution and seized total power in 1913, briefly reinvigorating the inclusive ideology of **Ottomanism**, but the pressures of **World War I** led their administration to abandon inclusivity in favour of Islamist-tinged policies; deportations of Greek Orthodox subjects and the Armenian genocide (1915) represented the demise of the inclusive Ottomanist project.

In 1914 the looming Great Power conflict seemed to present an opportunity to the Young Turk leadership to escape economic and political subservience to Britain, France and Russia. The decision to enter World War I on the side of the Central Powers was, however, in retrospect, catastrophic. The Young Turks leadership reasoned that neutrality was not an option. Alliance with the Entente powers would have been difficult to swallow: Britain, France and Russia had actively abetted violations of Ottoman sovereignty and territory. Not unlike the rest of the Great Powers, the Ottoman leadership anticipated that the war would be quick and hoped to use delaying tactics to make the most of an alliance with the Central

Powers without risking too much in the war. Eventual defeat to the Entente spelled the end of the empire, along with the other large multi-ethnic territorial empires in **Europe**, Russia and **Austria–Hungary**, which also transformed into new political entities. The Ottoman sultanate was abolished on 1 November 1922, and the Turkish Republic was established a year later.

Ottomanism

– see also **Young Ottomans**.

An ideology pushed by reformers in the late Ottoman Empire to advocate for an inclusive political identity to bind together the empire's diverse populations, regardless of sect. During the **Tanzimat** reforms, officially inaugurated in 1839, contradictory forces pushed for more equality among Ottoman citizens while driving religious groups apart into sub-Ottoman nationalisms. Based on the introduction of new ideas of universal citizenship, Ottomanism became a moniker denoting an evolving series of rebuttals to particularist ideologies. In practice, Ottomanism gained traction among Ottoman elites of different sectarian orientations. After the **Young Turk** revolution and the reinstatement of the constitution in 1908, Ottomanism was resurgent. However, some of its earlier proponents among the Muslim intelligentsia turned increasingly pan-Islamic in orientation, which was at odds with Ottomanist inclusivity. During **World War I** the triumph of Islamist political currents over inclusive Ottomanism was complete.

Overland Trails (USA)

Before the first overland wagon trail was blazed (early 1840s), the way to the west coast was by boat around Cape Horn or via the Panamanian isthmus. The 2,170-mile (3,492-kilometre) Oregon Trail traversed the Rockies at South Pass, terminating in Oregon's fertile farmlands (the trek took four to seven months). Beyond South Pass, the Mormon Trail branched off to Utah and the California Trail led to the goldfields. The first transcontinental railway (1869) rendered them largely redundant.

Owen, Robert (1771–1858)

– see also **Cooperative movement**.

Born in Newton, Wales. At the age of 19 he became the manager of a cotton mill in Manchester and transformed it into one of the most successful firms in **Great Britain**. Owen moved to New Lanark in 1799 to manage a cotton mill, where he started developing his philanthropic activities supporting and improving the living conditions for his workers and providing education for their children. He published several works, became a utopian socialist and is the founder of cooperativism.

Oxfam

– see **non-government organization**.

Oyo

An important empire in West Africa (primarily located in modern-day **Nigeria**) founded in Yoruba-speaking country in the eleventh century. A smaller kingdom at first, it attained a large size in the mid to late seventeenth century, came to dominate the interior and played a major role in the coastal states as well. Famous for its cavalry armies, Oyo invaded **Dahomey** a number of times following 1728, eventually reducing it to tributary status. A series of civil wars beginning in the late eighteenth century weakened the empire, setting it up for subsequent invasion from the north by jihadists from the **Hausa** region. The empire broke up in 1835, following the sacking of the town of Oyo, dispersing refugees across Yoruba country. The town was refounded further south by refugees, and following the British occupation of the region in 1893, they attempted to create a new Oyo Empire as an instrument of indirect rule.

Özal, Turgut (1927–1993)

After an early career as a technocrat and minor political figure, Turgut Özal emerged as the dominant political figure in **Turkey** in the decade 1983–93. Under the military regime that followed the 1980 *coup d'état*, he was appointed deputy premier. In 1983 he founded the centre-right Motherland Party, which promised a return to civilian rule. Partially because the Motherland Party was not favoured by the military, it won in a landslide. Under Özal's rule, first as prime minister and then, after 1989, as president of the republic, Turkey moved towards a more liberal and political regime. In foreign policy, Özal's governance was marked by close cooperation with the **United States**, an aggressive effort to join the European Economic Community (EEC) and efforts at outreach to the emerging Turkic states of the former **Soviet Union** as well as Turkey's Middle Eastern neighbours.

P

PAC
– see **Pan-African Congress**.

Pacific Rim
A name applied to the political and economic space created between the fifty-six countries bordering or peripheral to the Pacific Ocean. The term is a largely American one, and has been used in three different ways by American geostrategists. In the nineteenth century variations were applied by believers in the 'manifest destiny' of the American republic to communicate liberal democracy to the world. In the **Cold War** the term was used to describe a nexus of defence and trading relationships, particularly by Californian politicians and those trained in universities on the American west coast. By 1991, it was being deployed as a cipher for the multiplicity of relationships which tied North America and **Australia** to the rising economies of **Japan** and continental Asia. There is no one Pacific organization, nor even a dominant one, as in the Atlantic world where **NATO** and the **EU** run alongside state-to-state relationships, but the term 'Pacific Rim' is often accompanied by references to the Asia–Pacific Economic Council (APEC), the Association of South East Asian Nations (ASEAN) or a putative Sino–US rivalry. Many scholars have noted that the term has waxed and waned in American discourse in direct proportion to the closeness of the **United States** and Japan, and in indirect proportion to the military engagement of the United States in Asia.

Though Pacific trade relationships certainly exist – Los Angeles, **Hong Kong, Singapore**, Shanghai, Shenzen, Pusan and Long Beach regularly number amongst the world's biggest ports – scholars of East Asia have questioned the existence of any real sort of 'Pacific community' comparable with the Atlantic world at all. Unlike the Atlantic rim, there is no necessary cultural linkage, history or political sympathy that links Pacific countries, and indeed many are arranged in vertical and cultural hierarchies and clusters against others in post-colonial relationships. In addition, the very long histories of **China, Indochina** and **Korea**, as well as Japan, have created cross-cutting barriers to community as strong as the legacy of the **Spanish, Dutch** and **British Empire**s in the region. Labour, social and political problems are broadly distinct in different zones, and it is difficult to identify any one cultural or ethnic relationship which unites the Pacific Rim beyond a complicated history of wars and exploitation. In such circumstances, and despite the very considerable money invested in universities that promote the idea of a community, the term remains a geographical expression sometimes appropriated by American geostrategists and elite graduates, rather than a living reality.

pacifism
The rejection of war on either rational or moral grounds, manifested in non-participation in wars, other than in non-combatant roles. Pacifists also seek to maintain peace and support disarmament. It has a long tradition in some world religions, notably **Buddhism**, and some Christian sects, notably the **Quakers**. The **Enlightenment** added the secular argument that war was 'the artifice of Princes' (Thomas Paine) and could be eliminated in a rational world where dynastic ambitions were set aside. Believers in **laissez-faire** also argued that free trade and the mutual interests of nations would encourage universal peace. Marxists argued that existing wars (other then proletarian uprising or revolutionary wars) simply pitted proletarians against each other for the benefit of the capitalist class.

Lenin refined the view to argue that war would be the outcome of capitalist competition for colonies while colonial wars and subsequent 'unequal treaties' with indigenous peoples were forms of capitalist exploitation. Later, pacifism like that of the Austrian Bertha von Suttner (1843–1914), who inspired the Nobel Peace Prize, which she won in 1905, was rooted in science and free thought. As an example, Norman Angell's (1872–1967) *The Grand Illusion* (1910), argued that war was impossible between great powers due to their mutual dependence on trade and would prove economically futile. Such ideas and faith in the international solidarity of the workers failed to prevent the outbreak of war in 1914. However, pacifism received an enormous boost from reaction to the slaughter of **World War I** and from the struggle of 'conscientious objectors' to escape military service, establishing parameters within which pacifists could object to conscription and military service of any kind.

Pacifist movements flourished after 1918 in a context where the **League of Nations** was promoted as an organization to prevent war by arbitration and to encourage disarmament. Anti-war works such as Erich Maria Remarque's novel *All Quiet on the Western Front*, published in **Germany** in 1929, quickly translated into English and turned into a film in 1931, caught the popular anti-war mood, symbolized in 1933 when the prestigious Oxford Union debating society voted against fighting for 'King and Country'. In 1934–5 the League of Nations Union organized a Peace Ballot of 11 million people which showed massive majorities in favour of the League and disarmament. A large majority were still in favour of the use of force against aggressors, but almost 2.4 million opposed it. In **Britain**, the Peace Pledge Union obtained a membership of 100,000 men pledged to renounce war and military service. Support for pacifism ebbed in the face of fascist aggression in the 1930s, the Left seeking to 'fight' fascism, particularly over the **Abyssinian crisis** and especially the **Spanish Civil War**.

Elsewhere, however, the cause of non-violent civil disobedience was proclaimed by **Gandhi** in his campaigns to remove the British from **India**, using boycotts and hunger strikes rather than violence to further his cause. Although pacifist movements survived in the maelstrom of **World War II** with conscientious objection given more sympathetic treatment in both Britain and the **United States**, pacifists were persecuted and killed in both Axis and other totalitarian states. However, post-war pacifism received a boost with the first use of atomic weapons in 1945. There was a strong pacifist component in anti-nuclear movements, such as the British Campaign for Nuclear Disarmament (CND), formed in 1958, which achieved considerable support across Europe from the 1960s, organizing marches, sit-ins and demonstrations. Similar non-violent tactics were adopted by the American **civil rights movement**, espoused by **Martin Luther King** and the Student Non-violent Coordinating Committee formed in 1960. Similarly, from the mid 1960s, anti-Vietnam War movements aimed, through sit-ins and marches, to

end American involvement in the conflict. Pacifists were heavily involved in anti-nuclear and anti-war movements across the world, for example against the siting of cruise missiles in **Europe** during the 1980s and in opposition to the **Iraq War** of 2003.

Pahlavi dynasty

– see also **Pahlavi, Mohammed Reza**.
The last Iranian imperial dynasty. Founded by Reza Khan (1878–1944), the commander after **World War I** of **Iran**'s Cossack brigade, who seized power in **Tehran**, 1921, soon becoming minister of war and, in 1923, prime minister. Elected shah by the *Majlis*, 1925, when the last **Qajar** monarch was deposed, he initiated the dynasty's policy of social modernization by disarming the tribes, emancipating women and requiring them to abandon the veil, and building schools, hospitals and Iran's first university; and of industrial modernization by building roads and railways. He abrogated all unequal agreements with foreign powers, 1928, but failed to break the traditional domination by **Britain** and **Russia**, now the **Soviet Union**, who occupied the country, 1941, and deposed him for suspected German sympathies, substituting his son, **Mohammed Reza Pahlavi**, who courted America and continued modernization until 1979. The revolution showed that the dynasty had failed to persuade enough Iranians that its social modernization was not an expression of western cultural imperialism.

Pahlavi, Mohammed Reza (1919–1980)

Second and last Iranian shah of the **Pahlavi dynasty**, 1941–79. Educated in **Switzerland**, he replaced his father, 1941, when **Great Britain** and the **Soviet Union** forced him into exile fearing that he might cooperate with **Germany** in **World War II**. He competed for power with Dr **Mohammed Mossadegh**, 1949–53, whose social origins were actually more distinguished than those of the 'arriviste' Pahlavi dynasty, but had little option in making him prime minister, following Mossadegh's hugely popular nationalization of the British-owned **Anglo-Iranian Oil Company** in 1951. The ensuing two years of growing economic and political tension culminated in the shah's being forced to leave the country, August 1953, after his unsuccessful attempt to dismiss Mossadegh as prime minister. Restored within days in a coup masterminded by the British and American secret services, he sought to execute a 'White Revolution' of development and modernization including transport infrastructure, irrigation, disease eradication, industrialization, land reform and education, but was increasingly fearful that the rate at which the fruits of his revolution would win him support would not match the rate at which Islamic traditionalism was winning adherents.

Ultimately, his foreign policy proved counterproductive. Although he developed a working relationship with the Soviet Union and its allies, his closeness to the United States, which led America openly to describe **Iran** as the West's 'policeman in the Middle East', offended other states and inflamed Islamic opinion. The perception of the shah as an American lackey contributed to the intense anti-Americanism of the succeeding Islamic Republic. It also countered the appeal to national pride inherent in the shah's highly theatrical (and arguably self-serving) celebration in Persepolis before the world's heads of state of the 2,500th anniversary of the foundation of the Persian Empire.

He faced renewed opposition from the 1960s, particularly after the 1973 increase in the value of Iran's **oil** exports, which exacerbated the existing inequality in the distribution of oil revenues. The autocratic nature of his rule, the corruption of his government, and the suppression of dissent by the secret police, **SAVAK**, all generated resentment and his policy of enforced westernization offended, in particular, both the lower classes and the clergy. Poorer farmers and traders perceived themselves as competing with western imports on unequal terms, while the clergy deemed westernization un-Islamic . Always supported primarily by the westernized upper and upper middle classes, opposition to him grew amongst the lower classes, the **Shi'ite** clergy, the merchants in the bazaars and the students, and following rioting in the major cities in favour of the Ayatollah **Ruhollah Khomeini**, the shah left Iran, January 1979. Although he did not abdicate, an April referendum led to the declaration of the Islamic Republic of Iran. He travelled to the US for cancer treatment in October 1979, provoking the **Tehran Embassy hostage crisis**. He was granted asylum in Cairo by **Egypt**'s President **Sadat**, where he soon died.

PAIGC (African Party for the Independence of Guinea and Cape Verde)

Founded in 1956, PAIGC led the struggle for independence from Portuguese rule in Cape Verde and **Guinea**. Under the leadership of Amicar Cabral until his assassination in 1972, the party combined armed struggle against the Portuguese with a programme of school-building, health care and legal reform in the areas under their control, while also seeking international recognition as the sole legitimate nationalist organization. PAIGC continued to rule Guinea and Cape Verde after independence.

Paine, Thomas (1737–1809)

Thomas Paine promoted revolutionary politics in England, America and **France** through his popular writings and political activism. In such works as *Common Sense* (1776), *The Crisis* (1776–83) and the *Rights of Man* (1791–2), he called for American independence, republican revolution in England and France, and social justice based on progressive taxation. Paine also attacked institutional religion whilst defending deism in *Age of Reason* (1794–5). Whilst his style and fervour were widely reviled or revered, he died poor and neglected.

Pakistan

Pakistan is a country in south Asia that is bordered by **India** in the east, **China** in the north-east, **Afghanistan** and **Iran** in the west, and the Arabian Sea in the south. It has a population of over 200 million, which although approximately 95 per cent Muslim encompasses several distinct regional cultural and linguistic groups. Formerly part of British India, Pakistan became an independent state in 1947. Introduced for the first time in 1930 by the poet **Muhammad Iqbal**, the concept of a separate Muslim state in north-west India gained popular currency during the Indian nationalist movement. In 1933 a Cambridge student, Chaudhri Rahmat Ali coined the term *Pakistan*, an acronym combining the first letters from Punjab, Afghan (North-West Frontier), Kashmir, Sind, and 'tan' for Baluchistan. While the demand for Pakistan gained increasing traction in the mid 1940s, different groups used the term to make diverse demands, including the possibility of a Muslim state within a federated India. The post-colonial nation state emerged as the result of complex negotiations between the British, the Indian National Congress and the **Muslim League** under the leadership of **Muhammad Ali Jinnah**, who later became the new nation's first governor general. On 14 August 1947 Pakistan gained independence, consisting of the north-west and north-east regions of the subcontinent, which were separated by roughly 1,600 kilometres of Indian territory. The result of the division of the provinces of **Bengal** and **Punjab**, the new nation was baptized in blood during large-scale violence accompanying **partition**.

It faced considerable challenges in its early years, including limited financial assets and industrial capacity and inadequate military resources to defend its extensive borders and key strategic location at the crossroads between south Asia, central Asia and the **Middle East**. Wars with India in 1947–8, 1965 and 1971 strained the country's resources. These financial and strategic liabilities led Pakistan to cultivate foreign allies to help bolster its position, eventually becoming a key ally of the **United States** during the **Cold War**. Early in its history, the unelected wings of the government, including the military and the bureaucracy, assumed an increasingly dominant position in comparison to elected political organs. In 1956 Pakistan ratified its first constitution and officially became an Islamic republic. A military coup in 1958 under the leadership of General **Ayub Khan** ushered in a period of military rule, lasting until 1971. In subsequent years, Pakistan has vacillated between elected civilian governments, including an extended period of civilian rule under **Zulfikar Ali Bhutto** in 1971–7, and unelected military rule, including the governments of General **Zia ul-Haq**, which lasted from 1977 to 1988, and General **Musharraf** after 1999.

Internally, Pakistan has struggled to integrate regions with diverse linguistic and cultural traditions. This trend was most pronounced in the increasing alienation of the eastern and western wings of the country. East Pakistan, where most of the population spoke Bengali, became increasingly dissatisfied with its position of political and financial subordination as west Pakistan and, particularly the Punjab, assumed a position of increasing hegemony. In 1971 Pakistan fought a civil war, eventually leading to the creation of the new state of **Bangladesh** in the former territory of east Pakistan. Pakistan now also faces major threats from Islamist militants and is in danger of becoming a failed state.

Pakistan People's Party (PPP)

Established in 1967 by **Zulfikar Ali Bhutto**, the Pakistan People's Party (PPP) called for the eradication of feudalism and the restoration of democracy by Pakistan's military regime. The PPP came to power in 1971 when democracy was restored, only to have its government dismissed in 1977 in a military coup. It returned to power in 1988–90 and again in 1993–6. In both terms its lifetime chairperson, **Benazir Bhutto**, served as prime minister.

Pal, Bipin Chandra (1858–1932)

Indian nationalist leader. Orator, author, editor of *Bande Mataram*, who along with Bal Gangadhar Tilak, Lajpat Rai and **Aurobindo Ghose** spearheaded the **Swadeshi** boycott movement after Curzon's partition of **Bengal** in 1905. The movement called for abandoning foreign commodities and replacing them with indigenous enterprise. Pal's vision involved facets beyond strictly defined territorial nationalism. He opposed Gandhian politics as narrow and 'papal', and retired from active politics in 1922, to die in poverty.

Palestine

Palestine is a self-proclaimed independent and self-governing nation, which is officially recognized by a number of countries, but not by some western nations. This self-proclaimed status, and the continued strife between **Israel** and Palestine, contribute to its instability and attempts to make a proper settlement and peace process between the occupying and governmental forces of Israel and the Palestinian authorities. The proper name for Palestine is As-Sulta Al-Wataniyya Al-Filastīniyya. Boasting a little over 4 million people, and a republican form of government, the nation is currently partly an occupied territory, with large swathes of the territories being occupied by Israeli forces and settlements. It is a very densely populated region, and tightly controlled by Israeli occupation forces. With only an estimated 1,000 kilometres in direct Palestinian control, and much of it disputed lands, the state is chaotic at best. The country has a president and prime minister, as well as a legislative council. The capital of Palestine is Ramallah, but many of its governmental offices function out of the city of **Gaza**, as the nation is divided by the Israeli occupation forces. Not only is the term used to delineate a 'country', but it is also used to name the same region in which the territory/nation exists that lies between the Mediterranean and the Jordan River. Its boundaries used to encompass parts of Israel, the Palestinian Territories, **Jordan**, **Lebanon** and **Syria**.

Originally a part of the **Ottoman Empire**, the Palestinian Territories were split up by the British mandate after **World War I**. The territory was again split up in 1947 by the creation of a Palestinian state, an Israeli/Jewish state and a separate entity for the shared holy city of **Jerusalem**. This plan was controversial, and is at the root of the current problems with land and settlement in Israel and the Palestinian Territories. A war commenced in 1948 when a Jewish section of the Palestinian mandate attempted to declare its independence thus depriving the Palestinian mandate of even more territory. Sections of the Palestinian Territory were being controlled by the Israeli government and others by the Egyptian government. In 1967 Israel occupied the territories and cities of the West Bank and Gaza and continued to maintain its dominance of these areas until the 1993 **Oslo Accords**, which forced Israeli troops to withdraw. In 1988 the Palestinian National Council, in Algiers, drew up a declaration of independence during a session, and installed **Yasser Arafat** as the president of Palestine within the ruling party/organizational influence of the **Palestinian Liberation Organization**.

Palestine is a territory that is largely economically dependent upon the larger occupying nation of Israel. The territory has natural gas resources and agricultural production, but lacks large industries. Its economic stability is at the mercy of political relations between Israel and the Palestinian authorities. Embargoes are frequent, and limit the available resources coming in to and out of the territory.

Palestine Liberation Organization (PLO)

The Palestine Liberation Organization, otherwise known as the PLO, was formed in 1964 during a Palestinian National Congress session in the city of **Jerusalem**. Though the organization's most internationally and nationally recognized leader was **Yasser Arafat**, its first leader was the Egyptian Ahmed Shukairy. Established by the Palestinian National Congress, the organization had been the brainchild of the Arab League, which met in January 1964 to discuss ways to help the Palestinian nationalist cause without hurting its own nations. Involved in the design of the organization were **Egypt**, **Jordan** and **Syria**, to name a few. The organization's goal is to establish a Palestinian state that exists independent of any other. To this aim, the first meeting of the PLO, a meeting of 422 individuals organized to represent the Palestinian masses, claimed that they would not allow Palestinian refugees to be exiled forever from their nation. Calling for an end to the state of **Israel**, they determined that one of their aims should be to bring the refugees home. The PLO began, in the late 1960s and early 1970s to reject Arab interference, and to proclaim Palestinian sovereignty above all.

The Palestinian National Covenant is the PLO's guiding charter, and in a bow to pressure from other Arab nations, it calls for a 'Palestinian entity', for a number of nations felt that the existence of an independent state would threaten their own sovereignty. The organization is a conglomeration of entities all seeking the same professed goal, and all governed by a parliament called the Palestinian National Council. This council and, indeed, the organization are helmed by an Executive Council made up of fifteen members. Though the greater Palestinian Territory is governed by the Palestinian Authority, the Authority, as it is commonly known, is dominated by members of the PLO.

The PLO became increasingly erratic in its behaviour in the decades prior to 2000. Violent activities such as hijackings, bombings, and even the murder of Israeli athletes attending the 1972 Olympic Games in **Germany**, were attributed to the PLO. The organization even extended its activities to Palestinian refugee camps in neighbouring nations such as **Lebanon**, which were used as training facilities and bases for attacks launched on Israel. In the 1980s concessions were made, and a seeming softening of ideology was witnessed. Israel was no longer to be totally done away with, but rather must respect and allow Palestinian independence. Such adjustments were in no way uniform, and at times it has been hard to see any softening in rhetoric or action. The PLO's importance and choke hold on the political and social life of Palestine declined with the death of Yasser Arafat in 2004, when what remained of the organization was incorporated into other Palestinian organizations, with the bulk of power being wielded by **Hamas**.

Palestinian refugees

The Palestinian refugee problem has its roots in the 1948 Israeli War for Independence. The division of the former Palestinian state, in 1947, into Jewish and Arab states displaced people and caused bitterness. Between 500,000 to 800,000 Palestinians were displaced according to estimates. Today the number is close to 4.6 million. Displacement continued in another war in 1967, and continues today in the displacement of Palestinians by Israeli settlement. Not all of the displaced reside in refugee camps; in fact only a little over a million reside in United Nations-run camps in **Gaza**, the West Bank, **Lebanon**, **Syria** and **Jordan**. Jordan is the only nation to have allowed refugees to settle permanently in their nation. According to UNRWA, the United Nations relief organization, Palestinian refugees are defined as 'persons whose normal place of residence was Palestine between June 1946 and May 1948, who lost both their homes and means of livelihood in the 1948 Arab–Israeli conflict'.

Palladianism

An architectural style based on Renaissance Venetian architect Andrea Palladio, that experienced renewed popularity in **Europe**, especially in England, during the eighteenth century. Inspired by Roman classicism, Palladio believed that the principles of classical antiquity should govern architecture. Inigo Jones, the architect to British monarchs James I and Charles I, exported the style to England. His designs for the Queen's House at Greenwich and the Banqueting House of the Palace of Whitehall embody the order, clarity and symmetry of Palladianism. Richard Boyle, Earl of Burlington, and Colen Campbell popularized the style through their designs of aristocratic homes and public buildings. Palladianism also spread to America and to other European countries. In **Prussia**, Georg Wenzeslaus von Knobelsdorff incorporated temple facades and Venetian windows into his works, most notably the Berlin Opera House. **Thomas Jefferson** designed his home, Monticello, in the style of a Palladian villa. The popularity of Palladian architecture declined in the nineteenth century with the **Gothic Revival**.

Palmerston, Lord (1784–1865)

Henry Temple, 3rd Viscount Palmerston, had a political career which spanned the rise of England to world power, from the period during the Regency when, at the age of 24 he became chancellor of the Exchequer, to the moment he resigned as prime minister in 1865. A Whig politician with firm views on public order and social discipline, Palmerston was also associated with populist 'gunboat diplomacy', the portrayal of British citizens as globally protected members of a new Roman Empire, and a loose sexual attitude towards women that won him the lasting enmity of **Queen Victoria**. Palmerston, also known as 'Lord Pumicestone' and 'Lord Cupid', led **Britain** through the end of the **Crimean War** in his first premiership, and, during his second from 1861, kept the United Kingdom out of the **American Civil War** despite pressure from members of his government such as **William Gladstone**. He sat in the House of Commons because he had an Irish hereditary title which allowed him to seek election as an MP in England, unlike English lords, but embraced a style of leadership which would have been well suited to the semi-democratic politics which followed him. Palmerston was, in theory, the first Liberal prime minister but is better thought of as a Whig who somehow survived and laid the groundwork for the later premiership of William Gladstone.

Pan-African congresses

Between 1919 and 1974 a series of six pan-African congresses were held which brought together African and African American intellectuals and politicians from North America, **Europe** and the African continent, and gave organizational content to the pan-African ideas which had been developing since the late eighteenth century. The first congress was held in Paris in 1919, organized by the African American intellectual **W. E. B. Du Bois**. It was timed to coincide with the Versailles peace conference, and a memorandum was presented to the peace conference which called for greater protection of African rights, though it did not call for independence. The fifth congress, held in Manchester in 1945, was the first to call for African independence and it was dominated by a new generation of young nationalist leaders from Africa, some of whom, such as **Kwame Nkrumah** and **Jomo Kenyatta**, would go on to lead their countries after independence.

Pan-Africanism

An historical movement with two main strands: an African strand seeking the liberation from European colonialism and the unity of the African continent; and an international strand looking to the unity and solidarity of black people throughout the world, the diaspora. Within the latter strand one element sought international black solidarity while a second envisaged the black diaspora's ultimate return to Africa. The Trinidadian American activist Henry Sylvester-Williams (1869–1911) organized the African Association in the late 1880s and he was a major figure in the establishment of the Pan-African Association in London in 1901. A leading proponent in the **United States** was **Marcus Garvey**, often described as the 'father of Pan-Africanism' and the leader of the United Negro Improvement Association. The movement appeared to gain momentum over six meetings of the Pan-African Congress between 1919 and 1974, but as the African nations gained independence it lost much of its radical impetus.

Pan-Africanist Congress

The Pan-Africanist Congress or PAC was founded at a meeting in Orlando, **South Africa**, in April 1959. Rejecting the multiracialism of the ANC and the concept of minority rights, its president, Robert Sobukwe, advocated African nationalism, pan-Africanism and government based on individual rights with equal citizenship open to all who accepted African majority rule. In 1960 PAC launched a campaign of non-violent protest which culminated in the Sharpeville Massacre of 21 March 1960.

Panama Canal

Built by the United States in 1906–14, the Panama Canal cuts through the isthmus of Panama allowing ships to cross between the Atlantic and Pacific Oceans. Years of negotiations involving the **United States**, **Great Britain** and **Colombia** (of which Panama was then part) ended in 1902 when the Colombian Senate refused to ratify a construction treaty that US President **Theodore Roosevelt** thought fair. When the Panamanians rose in rebellion, Roosevelt assisted their victory and a new treaty allowed the US to construct the canal and receive a 99-year renewable lease over a 16-kilometre wide strip of land that bisected the country. This caused increasing tensions including riots in 1964. In 1977 the US and Panama negotiated a treaty turning over the zone and the canal to Panama, full control of the canal being effected in 1999. As larger ships were developed, construction began on an enlarged canal, completed in 2016.

Panama, Republic of

A nation of just over 3 million people located in **Central America** between **Costa Rica** and **Colombia**. The narrowest point on the isthmus connecting North and South America, Panama has been a strategic commercial and transportation hub for the global economy since Spaniards first settled there. It achieved political independence from Colombia in 1903 when the **United States**, seeking exclusive rights to build a canal, encouraged a separatist movement. Completed in 1914, the canal cemented Panama's status as a US protectorate. For the next half-century the nation struggled to build a stable democracy in the face of anti-democratic elites, a politicized National Guard and an ongoing US presence. The 1989 US invasion to depose Panamanian strongman General **Manuel Noriega** underscored and amplified these challenges. In the years following this intervention, Panama has managed to preserve its fragile democracy and assume complete control of the Canal Zone.

Pan-American Union

Created in 1910 as a successor to the Commercial Bureau of the American Republics (1890) and the International Bureau of the American Republics (1902). In the first modern Pan-American conference (Washington DC, 1889–90), western hemisphere diplomats considered the possibility of a customs union, inter-American railway network, an isthmian canal, mandatory arbitration of disputes and commercial agreements. The conference responded to the policies of US Secretary of State James Blaine, who sought to expand his country's economic and political influence in the hemisphere. Between 1910 and 1948 the Pan-American Union held eight major conferences, while developing specialized agencies to deal with health, railways, copyright, civil aviation, a pan-American highway, postal affairs and communications, education, culture and science, and trade. It was succeeded by the **Organization of American States**, created in 1948. After 1970 the Conferences of American States were replaced by sessions of the OAS General Assembly.

pan-Arabism

– *see* **Arab nationalism**.

Pan-Asianism

Pan-Asianism was a racial, cultural and political ideology that grew popular during the 1920s and 1930s as a response to western imperialism. Pan-Asianism emphasized that Asians shared common racial characteristics, beliefs and history. Considering that many Korean, Taiwanese and Chinese people embraced pan-Asianism, this ideology served more than just the legitimizing of Japanese imperialism in east Asia; it expressed the frustration of Asians towards western racism and domination of the world and anxiety over the economic, social and cultural instability caused by capitalism. Pan-Asian ideology first grew in popularity as a discourse in the 1920s when **Japan** encountered discrimination from the western-controlled international system. A series of reforms and laws, such as western powers limiting the number of Japanese naval ships and policies in America prohibiting Japanese immigration, caused intellectuals and government officials in Japan to believe that westerners would never consider Japan and **Asia** as being equal to the West. They therefore called for Japan to move away from the West and instead 'return to Asia' (*Nyu-A*), which was believed to be the space where Japan shared common cultural and spiritual roots with other Asian nations. Believing that Japan to be the only Asian country to have successfully modernized, pan-Asianists envisioned it as the leading power to foster an independent Asian space that would be free from western imperialism.

In the 1930s a Japan-centred pan-Asianism served as a cornerstone for the expansionist policies of the Japanese state. It aimed to create a regional economy that would overcome the destabilizing effects of the **Great Depression** and enable Asia to be politically, economically and culturally independent from the West. Having already colonized **Taiwan** in 1895 and **Korea** in 1910, Japan sought to achieve its vision of an ideal pan-Asian nation state by creating the puppet state of **Manzhuguo** in 1932. Exhorting Korean, Chinese and Japanese people to live and work cooperatively, the Manchukuo authorities carried out political, social and economic experiments in order to cultivate and maintain a common Asian identity.

During the early stages of **World War II**, Japan sought to create a new pan-Asian order – the Asian Co-Prosperity Sphere – by connecting Japan and its colonies with the countries that had been previously controlled by western powers. Given the responsibility to forge this new autonomous space for Asians, the Ministry of Greater East Asia set up programmes to create a pan-Asian political, economic and cultural system. Though Japan promoted itself as a liberating power, Japanese forces carried out coercive practices and denied these former western colonies their independence. Japanese imperialism simply replaced western imperialism under the Asian Co-Prosperity Sphere. Yet, though many Asians saw pan-Asianism as an ideology that only legitimized Japanese imperialism, many Asian intellectuals supported Japanese-led pan-Asian projects as a way to resist western imperialism. Consequently, many collaborated with Japan to achieve its pan-Asian vision.

pandemics
– *see* **epidemics**.

pan-Islamism
Pan-Islamism has formulated multiple visions of global solidarity among Muslims in order to advance its causes in world affairs from the 1870s. Although there have been various other concepts describing a Muslim community since early **Islam**, such as the term *ummah*, pan-Islamism emerged as a modern concept during the 1870s with the assumption that there is a global 'Muslim world' that is in need of revival and empowerment through solidarity of its members. The rise of pan-Islamic ideas relied on the benefits of cheaper transport infrastructure with steamships and trains, and on the growth of Muslim publishing and journalism with more convenient forms of communication via telegraph and postal services as well as rising literacy levels. In its earlier forms, the term

was used to express the fear of Dutch, Russian, British and French colonial officers about a coordinated Muslim revolt and an imagination of educated Muslim leaders as a strategy to empower their communities. Pan-Islamists generally attributed to the Ottoman sultan, as the Caliph of Muslims, the role of leadership of a global Muslim community, and mobilized around various Ottoman Empire-related causes such as the **Red Crescent** society's aid campaign to victims of the **Balkan Wars** (1912–13), collecting donations for the construction of the **Hijaz** Railway, the boycott of the Italian Empire for its invasion of Ottoman Libya, and the Indian Khilafat movement to support the Turkish War of Independence. Early pan-Islamist intellectuals were critical of the ideologies of Christian and white supremacy within European empires, but were not necessarily against all empires. For example, some Indian Muslims could imagine a Muslim community in harmony with a revised **British Empire**.

Even though pan-Islamism is associated with the reign and unofficial international policies of Ottoman Sultan **Abdülhamid II** (r. 1876–1909), it originated during the reign of Sultan **Abdülaziz** (r. 1861–76) and peaked in its global appeal and influence from 1908 to 1924. In fact, pan-Islamism was utilized by the **Ottoman** and **German Empires** during **World War I** as part of war aims and propaganda, with the Ottoman Caliph issuing a jihad (holy war) proclamation. Upon the defeat of the Ottoman Empire, a pan-Islamic campaign was mobilized in south Asia to support a Wilsonian claim of self-determination of Muslims in **Turkey**, which greatly contributed to the success of the Turkish War of Independence under Mustafa **Kemal Atatürk**. When the National Parliament of the Republic of Turkey in Ankara decided to abolish the caliphate on 2 March 1924, pan-Islamic networks were still very active worldwide. Consequently, there were multiple failed attempts to revive the caliphate by organizing international congresses.

Pan-Islamist ideals survived the shock of the demise of the caliphate and the end of the Ottoman Empire. They were first transformed into a vision of international solidarity in support of decolonization of Muslim societies, often described as salvation and redemption of Muslims from the unjust rule of Christian and western colonizers. During **World War II**, the German, Japanese and Italian Empires all tried to appeal to pan-Islamic public opinion in their propaganda efforts. Pan-Islamism also expressed reasons for cooperation among post-colonial Muslim majority states to deal with shared political and religious issues. Thus, pan-Islamism persisted throughout the era of nationalism, westernization and **Cold War**, inspiring campaigns to support the causes of various dispossessed Muslim populations such as Palestinians, and to articulate discontent about the state of the post-World War II international order of nation states. New global non-governmental organizations emerged such as the Saudi Arabia-based Muslim World League, religio-political groups such as the **Muslim Brotherhood** and Hizbut Tahrir, and inter-governmental organizations such as the Organization of the Islamic Conference, all of which perpetuated references to a pan-Islamic cultural, political and social cause. From the aftermath of the Iranian Islamic Revolution of 1979 to the present, pan-Islamism has become part of the ideological repertoire of various national and international Muslim political and cultural trends, inspiring geopolitical debate about the role of religions and civilizations in the post-Cold War world order.

pan-Slavism

Pan-Slavism was a modern movement which sought to unify the Slavic peoples of eastern Europe. It reached its apogee in the nineteenth century, at the confluence of Romantic, Russian Slavophil and racialist thought. Pan-Slavism had two cultural centres, one in the Czech lands and the other in **Russia**, though its appeal went beyond both. It was, however, cross-cut by the divide between Roman Catholicism and **Orthodoxy** in the East, by western suspicion of Russian objectives, and by Polish nationalism, which, whilst Slavic, was distinctive and exclusivist. The desire of Slavic groups for equality within the **Austro-Hungarian Empire** was one of the causes of **World War I**, but with the end of the war, and the establishment of **Yugoslavia**, momentum for a union of all Slavs quickly faded. When, after **World War II**, the **Soviet Union**'s creation of a buffer bloc seemed to draw on such arguments, it in fact illustrated that the Slavic moment had passed; Soviet forces proved ultimately unable to construct or to draw upon a common identity with eastern Europe.

pan-Turanianism, pan-Turkism

Pan-Turkism is a vision of solidarity of Turkic-speaking Muslims of Euro-Asia for political, cultural and social empowerment. It emerged in late nineteenth century as an ideal to first create unity among Muslims of the **Russian Empire** and then to link them with the grand strategy of the **Ottoman**

Empire. Pan-Turkism was seen as a politically pragmatic and feasible version of pan-Islamism, with the assumption that it could receive the support of the **British Empire**, superpower of the early twentieth-century world order. This ideal was formulated mainly by reformist Muslim intellectuals of the Russian Empire such as Yusuf Akçura, in cooperation with some Ottoman Muslim intellectuals such as Ziya Gökalp. It relied on the late nineteenth-century scholarship on the linguistic and racial commonality of the Turkic peoples. During **World War I** and in the aftermath of the Bolshevik revolution, there were hopes of achieving some sort of pan-Turkic autonomy for Muslims of the Russian Empire. After the end of the Ottoman Empire and the consolidation of Turkic-speaking Muslim areas of the Russian Empire into the **Union of Soviet Socialist Republics**, pan-Turkism became a marginalized irredentist ideology, and at various times appropriated by the German Empire during **World War II** and the **USA** during the **Cold War** to weaken the Soviet Union. The emergence of independent Muslim republics in central Asia and **Caucasus** in the aftermath of the disintegration of the Soviet Union in 1991 revived hopes of a post-Cold War pan-Turkic unity. However, developments in international cooperation among these states in the following two decades failed to fulfil any pan-Turkic imagination. Pan-Turanianism takes the primary unit of solidarity as the Turanian race, defined by Ural-Altaic language use, and thus extends the political imagination of solidarity to non-Muslim societies of Hungarians, Finns, Koreans and Japanese. It gained adherents especially in **Hungary**.

Papacy

The name given to the government of the Bishop of Rome, generally known as the Pope, who is the incumbent of the Holy See (a sovereign state with observer status at the **United Nations**), monarch of Vatican City, Patriarch of the West and leader of the Catholic Church. Communion with and obedience to the Pope, rather than adherence to any particular rite, is a defining feature of Catholicism, which is the leading Christian religion with over a billion followers worldwide. The Papacy evolved from the Roman office of Pontifex Maximus during the Roman Empire, and was in many ways the defining institution of the West after the fall of Rome in the sixth century. In the modern period, popes have used communications technology and the resources of modern propaganda to communicate with and lead their flocks, and have in many ways become the 'face' of the Church, both in the eyes of supporters and critics. They are held to be infallible by their followers under very limited circumstances, when they are formally pronouncing on moral teaching, in such a way as to absolutely bind their successors. Otherwise, popes can be, and frequently are, contradicted. Popes are elected for life by a College of Cardinals, 'Princes of the Church' appointed by their predecessors, and have the power to call a general Council of the Church such as was seen at **Vatican I** and **II**, which can produce constitutions and change the structures through which Roman Catholicism operates. The Papacy has often taken a controversial role in politics, as the singular European and global institution, leading conservative social campaigns and spearheading efforts against Soviet communism, for instance.

However, it would be unwise to exaggerate the power of a body which is really the limited head of a mix of monastic, priestly, lay, academic and religious orders each of which are conscious of their privileges and rights. The Papacy's claim to primacy over all other Christian leaders (because of its unbroken apostolic succession from St Peter, the leader of Christ's apostles) is a particular source of contention with other faith communities, such as the Protestant denominations which originally broke from what they saw as a corrupt or illegitimate papal institution, or the Orthodox Church, which broadly agrees with Catholic doctrine but which does not recognize the primacy of the Pope. In addition, because it is so visible an institution, the Papacy tends to be blamed for its limitations. Pope Benedict XV, for instance, called in 1916 and 1917 for an end to **World War I** but was ignored by nominally Catholic politicians across Europe. In the run-up to and during **World War II**, Pope **Pius XII** condemned Nazism and **Adolf Hitler** in 1937, opposed the Nazi euthanasia programme, sheltered Jewish people in Rome, made strenuous efforts to stop Jewish deportations, and organized a worldwide network of humanitarian aid and shelter for displaced persons, prisoners of war and anti-Nazi elements. However, because statements were coded for fear of German escalation and aggression, and because some in the Church were sympathizers – and also because of its neutrality – the Church in general and the Pope in particular have been consistently attacked as not doing enough during the **Holocaust** or even as colluding by inaction. In the later twentieth and early twenty-first century, secularist and atheist groups also attacked the Papacy as being, as they saw it, enmeshed in extra-legal and illegal networks of money laundering and paedophilia cover-ups, none of which was ever proven. Despite this, the appeal of the Papacy in particular in the developing world and to young people was deepened by the pontificates of John Paul II and Benedict XVI, after a refoundation by **John XXIII**. The election of Pope Francis (the first non-European pope of modern times) saw stronger emphasis on tackling poverty, facing green issues and a greater compassionate attitude.

Papua New Guinea

Eastern part of the island of **New Guinea**, divided into north and south by **Germany** and **Britain** in 1885, the south being transferred to **Australia** in 1902. Australia occupied the German area in 1914 and held the combined territory under a post-war League of Nations **mandate**. Following Japanese occupation during **World War II**, Australia resumed control, granting independence to the renamed Papua New Guinea in 1975. Bougainville separatists waged an armed revolt in 1989–97, gaining autonomy in 2001.

Paraguay

A landlocked country independent since 1811, Paraguay is surrounded by **Brazil**, **Bolivia**, **Argentina** and **Uruguay**. The Paraguay River provides a north–south link that passes through the capital and deep-water river port of Asunción located about 1,530 kilometres from the Atlantic Ocean; the Paraná River marks the country's southernmost boundary. Its almost completely mestizo population of some 6.5 million speaks Spanish, **Guaraní**, or both of these official languages; almost 95 per cent of the population is literate. Since the end of Alfredo Stroessner's 35-year military dictatorship in 1989, several parties have contested elections for the presidency. The economy combines subsistence agriculture, imported consumer goods and exported commodities including soy and cannabis, and about 80 per cent of the hydroelectricity produced. The economy's informal sector is large and over half of the labour force is engaged in the provision of services. About half the country's roads are paved.

Paraguayan War (War of the Triple Alliance)

The Paraguayan War (1864–70) between Paraguay and **Argentina**, **Brazil** and **Uruguay** has been variously blamed on the leaders of Paraguay, Argentina, Brazil, Uruguayan internal disturbances, British intrigue and efforts to preserve a balance of power. The war increased territory and strengthened central governments for Argentina and Brazil and defined modern boundaries. Paraguay was defeated but remained independent, losing 8.7–18.5 per cent of its pre-war population and 38 per cent of its territory.

Paris Commune
– *see* **Commune (Paris)**

Paris Exhibitions
These were held in 1855, 1867, 1878, 1889, 1900 and 1937. They were celebrations of **free trade** and **industrialization**, but 1889 also specifically commemorated the centenary of the **French Revolution**. The further Paris Electrical Exhibition, 1881, displayed the novel Siemens tram and 1867 had featured one of the first large dynamos to be built, by Siemens and Halske. The 1900 exhibition drew 39 million visitors. The last, the World Exhibition of 1937, reflected the national and philosophical antagonisms of the period.

Paris Peace Conference (1919)
A conference held from 18 January to 28 June 1919 that settled the peace terms of **World War I**. Although thirty-two nations attended, the key players were French Premier **Georges Clemenceau**, British Prime Minister **David Lloyd George**, Italian Prime Minister Vittorio Emanuele Orlando and American President **Woodrow Wilson**. Competing national interests complicated negotiations. Wilson promoted a more idealistic and diplomatic agenda, embodied in his Fourteen Points. However, European powers sought harsher terms for **Germany** that would ensure it could not threaten European security again. The conference concluded with the negotiation of five treaties, including the **Treaty of Versailles**. These agreements established the **League of Nations** and created a new international order through the redistribution of European and colonial territories. However, the break-up of the Austrian Empire and the **Ottoman Empire** created instability and left many nationalist conflicts unresolved. Often considered a 'failed peace', the Paris Peace Conference created instability and resentment among the defeated powers that ultimately led to **World War II**.

Park Chung Hee (1917–1979)
– *see also* **South Korea**.
Park was the authoritarian leader of **South Korea** from 1963 to 1979. Trained as a military officer in the Japanese Army in **Manchuria** during the 1930s, he led a military coup against the democratic

government in May 1961. He initiated and oversaw South Korea's development into a powerful industrial capitalist economy as president while suppressing political and workers' rights. In 1979, at a time of growing social unrest, Park was assassinated by his chief of intelligence.

Park, Mungo (1771–1806)
Scottish explorer noted for his contribution to the history and geography of West Africa. In 1794 he entered the service of the African Association, an English geographical organization, and undertook an expedition to West Africa. In 1796 he reached the Niger River, the first European to do so. His books on his travels were very popular and provided a detailed description of West Africa at the close of the eighteenth century.

Parks, Rosa (1913–2005)
A key figure in the US civil rights movement. By refusing to give up her seat for a white passenger on a segregated Montgomery, Alabama, bus on 1 December 1955, Rosa Parks entered history. The subsequent bus boycott, under the leadership of **Martin Luther King**, lasted over a year and attracted international attention. A soft-spoken activist with the NAACP, Parks lost her job and was forced to leave the city, living much of her life in Detroit.

Partai Komunis Indonesia
– *see* **Communist Party of Indonesia**.

Partial Test Ban Treaty
Formally known as the Treaty Banning Nuclear Weapons in the Atmosphere, in Outer Space and Under Water, this treaty limited its signatories – the most notable of which being the **UK**, **USA** and **USSR** – to testing nuclear weapons underground. Designed primarily to curtail the release of nuclear fallout into the atmosphere, it was signed in August 1963, and signified a post-Cuban Missile Crisis thaw in US–Soviet relations. Notable non-signatory nuclear states include the People's Republic of **China** and **France**.

Pasteur, Louis (1822–1895)
A French scientist who developed vaccines, microbiology and a sterilization process for milk and wine in 1862 known as 'pasteurization', which greatly reduced early mortality in subsequent years. Pasteur was not a licensed physician when he tested his rabies vaccine in 1885, and could easily have become an example of scientific villainy had the vaccine not worked. Other great achievements lie in his propagation of medical sanitization, and his early work on the polarization of light. Pasteur was

a Catholic admirer of St Vincent de Paul, and modelled himself on both the saint and on Breton peasants.

Pathet Lao

A Communist organization in **Laos** broadly comprised of an army, the Lao People's Liberation Army, and a political movement, the Lao Patriotic Front, in which the principal organization was the Lao People's Revolutionary Party. It rose to power after allying with the **Viet Minh** against France in the **Indochina War** of 1946–54. It fought Royal Laotian forces during the 1953–75 civil war before ultimately triumphing and taking over the government of that country in alliance with Vietnamese forces. This led to attempts to ethnically cleanse Laos and **Vietnam** of the Hmong people, and an eventual breach between the two in 1989. Today, Laos is an independent people's democratic republic.

Paton, Alan (1903–1988)

South African writer and anti-apartheid activist. A teacher and reform school principal, Paton joined the South African Institute of Race Relations in 1930 and published his best-known work, *Cry, the Beloved Country* in 1948. He was a founder in 1953 of the multiracial anti-apartheid South African Liberal Party, acting as president until the government forced the party to disband in 1968. In 1964 he testified on **Nelson Mandela**'s behalf at the 'Treason Trial'.

Patton, George Smith (1885–1945)

Immortalized in the 1970 film that bore his name, Patton was an inspired and uncompromising if complex American military leader. A strong advocate of armoured tanks following his experiences in **World War I**, he was most famous for his command of the US Seventh Army during the invasion of Sicily in 1943 and the Third Army in **France** in 1944–5. Patton had a reputation for daring but was outspoken and nearly sacked for slapping a hospitalized soldier in 1943.

Paz Estenssoro, Victor (1907–2001)

Born in Tarija, **Bolivia**, he founded the National Revolutionary Party in 1941 and served as president of Bolivia in 1952–6, 1960–4 and 1985–9. In his first presidency he implemented an extensive agrarian reform, nationalized the tin mines and granted universal suffrage. Overthrown by the military in 1964, in his third presidency he introduced the New Economic Policy (NEP) that vastly diminished the state's role in the economy and encouraged the private sector.

Paz, Octavio (1914–1998)

Mexican writer and diplomat. Born into a radical intellectual family, Paz began writing early and in 1938 helped establish the journal *Taller* (*Workshop*). He entered the diplomatic service in 1945 and was posted to **France**, where he associated with Surrealist writers and produced *The Labyrinth of Solitude*, a study of Mexican consciousness. His appointment as Mexican ambassador to **India** in 1962 had a profound influence on his work, notably *East Slope* (1969) and *The Monkey Grammarian* (1974). Paz resigned from the diplomatic service in 1968 in protest against the government massacre of students during the Olympics Games protests. He subsequently worked as a publisher and editor, founding politico-cultural magazines (most notably *Vuelta*) and continuing to write poetry, essays and books of criticism, history and politics. Paz won the Cervantes Award in 1981 and the Nobel Prize in literature in 1990, the first Mexican to gain the award.

Peace Corps (USA)

A federal agency established by executive order by President **John F. Kennedy** in March 1961 to provide US government funds towards sending volunteer Americans to developing countries to undertake a variety of public works and other projects. The initiative was designed to help develop good relations between the **United States** and developing countries at a time when the **Cold War** was at its height, and when the break-up of many European empires had led to the creation of numerous new nations in need of economic development. Unlike many of Presidents Kennedy and **Johnson**'s domestic policies of the 1960s, the Peace Corps outlasted their terms of office and the agency remains in place today. The year 1966 saw the peak of the number of Americans, principally young people, working in the field: over 15,000.

Peace of Paris

This was the treaty ending the **Seven Years War** (including the French and Indian War) of 1756–63, signed by **Britain**, **France** and **Spain** on 10 February 1763. The terms of the treaty confirmed Britain's growing international prominence, with **Spain** ceding Florida and France abandoning any claim to North America east of the Mississippi and to **Canada**, her territories in **India**, four Caribbean islands and **Senegal** in Africa. Spain received Louisiana and New Orleans from France.

Pearl Harbor, attack on (1941)

The surprise Japanese attack on 7 December 1941 at the Hawaiian base of Pearl Harbor drew the **United States** into **World War II**. It left 2,390 Americans dead, 1,178 wounded, 21 ships sunk or damaged and 323 aircraft destroyed or damaged. The unannounced and unprovoked attack, an example of preventive warfare, was intended to destroy the US Pacific fleet so that **Japan** could expand freely into American, British and Dutch imperial territories in the south-western Pacific to secure access to raw materials including oil and rubber. However, despite the devastation, the attack was only a limited success: the harbour remained intact, fuel storage facilities were undamaged, and all aircraft carriers (at sea at the time of attack) remained operational. Significantly, the attack ended the bitter debate within the US regarding involvement in the war, and a declaration of war was passed against Japan the following day. **Germany** subsequently declared war on the US on 11 December 1941.

Pedro II (1825–1891)

Emperor of **Brazil**. Born in Rio de Janeiro, Pedro was the son of Brazil's Emperor Pedro I and Empress Leopoldina. His father abdicated in favour of him in 1831 and in 1840 Pedro II was declared of age and crowned as emperor. He grew into his position and, benefiting from rising revenues from coffee, by 1850 had established himself as an able ruler of the country and the embodiment of legitimate authority. His accomplishments included overseeing Brazil's participation in the defeat of **Paraguay** in 1870 and securing the Free Birth Law for children of slave mothers in 1871. Politicians increasingly favoured republicanism as Pedro's rule appeared ever more anachronistic. While in **Europe** seeking medical treatment, his daughter and heir Isabel secured the immediate abolition of slavery without compensation in 1888. The following year the army overthrew Pedro, who died an exile in Paris, and Brazil became a republic.

Pedro IV (r. 1696–1718)

Pedro IV Agua Rosada, King of Kongo, in west central Africa, one of three pretenders to the Kongo throne with a base at the mountain of Kibangu, Pedro sought to restore the country by reoccupying its capital. Beatriz Kimpa Vita's religious revival occurred during his reign with the same goal, and Pedro burned her as a witch. He refounded the capital in 1709 and established the principle that the crown in Kongo would rotate between various families.

Pedro V (r. 1856–1891)

Pedro V, King of Kongo, west central Africa. Originally the Marquis of Bemba, Pedro was established as king with the assistance of Portuguese troops from **Angola**. He became effectively independent when they were withdrawn in 1866 and gradually rebuilt his power through trading enterprises, though his real control was only over a fraction of the kingdom. He welcomed both Catholic and Protestant missionaries into the country and declared Kongo a vassal of **Portugal** in 1884.

Peel Commission, 1937

British royal commission chaired by former Conservative Cabinet minister Earl Peel, appointed in August 1936 to examine the causes of the **Arab revolt** which had broken out in **Palestine** earlier that year. The commission conducted investigations in Palestine from 11 November 1936 to 17 January 1937. Both **Chaim Weizmann** and Hajj Amin al-Husayni, the Mufti of Jerusalem, gave evidence. The commission's July 1937 report advised termination of the British **mandate** for Palestine (*see* **Balfour Declaration**). Instead, Palestine would be divided into Jewish-, Arab- and British-controlled zones. The report was rejected by the Arabs, with the exception of Transjordan's Emir Abdullah. Chaim Weizmann, **David Ben-Gurion** and the August 1937 Zionist Congress accepted, as it provided a much needed haven for Jewish refugees fleeing **Hitler**. **Vladmir Jabotinsky** and **Golda Meir** opposed so truncated a Jewish state. The British government, which initially accepted the proposal, abandoned it as unworkable in November 1938. In 1939 it was replaced as official Palestine policy by a white paper which limited Jewish immigration to a trickle and foresaw a future Arab majority state in Palestine.

Peninsular campaign (American Civil War)

The Peninsular campaign of 17 March–3 August 1862 was designed to end the civil war with a single blow. Its author, George B. McClellan, advanced cautiously, besieged Yorktown and fought indecisively at Williamsburg and Seven Pines, but got within 8 kilometres of Richmond. On 26 June **Robert E. Lee** launched the counter-offensive known as the Seven Days of Battles. McClellan withdrew across his front towards Harrison's Landing. His repulse of Lee at

Malvern Hill on 1 July could not disguise the full extent of his strategic failure.

Peninsular War (Napoleonic Wars)

Evolved out of the revolt, effectively a guerrilla uprising, by the Spaniards in 1808, against the imposition of **Napoleon**'s brother, Joseph, as king of **Spain**. It opened up a field of operations for the British, who landed armies in Spain and **Portugal**. **Sir John Wellesley** (soon to be Lord Wellington) with a small force of not more than 30,000 soldiers successfully pursued the guerrilla tactic of wearing out the enemy's forces while refusing to join battle. **Portugal**, however, was the base of the British expedition and Portuguese troops were drilled and commanded by British officers, while the Spaniards remained highly effective guerrilla irregulars. Wellington won increasingly decisive victories at Talavera, 1809, Salamanca, 1812, and Vitoria, 1813, against an ever more depleted number of French following the Russian campaign. The war was concluded with Wellington's entry into **France** across the Pyrenees, 1814.

Pentagon (USA)

A pentagon is a five-sided figure, but the Pentagon is the headquarters of the US Department of Defense (DoD) and is located outside Washington in Arlington County, Virginia. It was formally opened in January 1943, and was then the world's largest office building. The term is often used to apply to the US military or to the DoD, which was created by the consolidation of the separate military services in 1947 under the National Security Act, comprehending the army, navy, air force, and military intelligence agencies. It was thought that rivalry between the services had been a handicap during **World War II**. The DoD is headed by a cabinet secretary, providing unified and civilian control of the American armed forces. The Pentagon building itself was one of the **9/11** terrorist attack targets, when five **al-Qaida** members crashed a hijacked airliner into it, killing 125 people as well as those aboard the plane.

Pentagon Papers (USA)

The popular term for the *United States–Vietnam Relations, 1945–1967: A Study Prepared by the Department of Defense*, a 47-volume, 7,000-page, top-secret report of the United States Department of Defense that detailed the history of US involvement in **Indochina**. The report, which gave details of the ways in which the **United States** had deliberately expanded its involvement in the **Vietnam War** whilst telling the American people otherwise, was leaked to the *New York Times* in 1971.

Pentecostalism

– *see* **Protestantism**.

People's Liberation Army (China)

– *see* **Chinese Revolution**.

Peres, Shimon (1923–2016)

Peres was born in **Poland** and settled in **Palestine** in 1934. A protégé of **David Ben-Gurion**, he joined the **Haganah** and was deputy director of the Israeli Defence Ministry, 1953–9. In this capacity he built up the Israel Defense Forces in close cooperation with **France**. He was acting prime minister in April and May of 1977 and leader of the Labour Party (**Mapai**) opposition in 1977–84, during the invasion of **Lebanon**. He became prime minister again in 1984–6 in a rotating coalition with **Yitzhak Shamir**. As foreign minister in 1993 he shared the Nobel Peace Prize with **Yitzhak Rabin** and **Yassir Arafat** for negotiating the **Oslo Accords**. He went on to become president of **Israel**.

perestroika

Perestroika, meaning 'restructuring', was a key policy of **Mikhail Gorbachev** and became official **USSR** policy after 1987. It represented an attempt to democratize Soviet structures, make the economy productive and strengthen the Communist Party so that it could attempt to tackle Soviet economic decay. It also strengthened Gorbachev against more traditional foes within the Soviet State and Communist Party apparatus. Eventually, it resulted in inflation, contested elections, the toleration of public protest, legal rather than party institutions and the (almost) peaceful dissolution of the USSR.

Perez Jiménez, Marcos (1914–2001)

Army officer; minister of defence, 1946–52; president of **Venezuela**, 1952–8. Born in Michelena, he participated in the 1948 military coup and the military junta that followed. Ratified as president by a 'constituent assembly', he ruled as a virtual dictator. Faced with widespread protests against a second term, he fled to the **United States** in 1958. Extradited to Venezuela in 1963 and imprisoned during a lengthy trial, in 1968 he went to **Spain**, where he died in 2001.

Perón, Eva (Duarte de) ('Evita') (1919–1952)

One of the most polarizing figures of Argentine history, 'Evita' was the wife of President **Juan Domingo Perón**. An illegitimate child from a poor family, she had achieved some fame as a radio and movie actress when she married Perón in 1946. Her strong views about social justice helped fuel the government's anti-oligarchy rhetoric. Pro-child and other welfare policies of the regime, her foundation's charitable work and women's suffrage granted in 1947 demonstrated her influence and endeared her to the working classes. Although she considered running for vice president with her husband in 1952, she died of uterine cancer that same year. Her supporters called for her sainthood while her critics stole her body for seventeen years after Perón's overthrow in 1955. She remains an icon of hope for millions of Argentines, while others see her as a symbol of her husband's corrupt demagoguery.

Perón, Juan (Domingo) (1895–1974)

Argentine military officer, government minister and populist president,1946–55 and 1973–4. During the military dictatorships of the early 1940s, Perón served as minister of labour and intervened in labour disputes on behalf of workers. He founded the Justicialista Party, won the presidency in 1946, and with his wife 'Evita' continued pro-worker policies, although he used official government union structure to take control of the labour movement. Perón nationalized the British-owned railways in 1949 as part of his attempt to industrialize **Argentina**. Economic crises, along with conflicts with the Catholic Church, led to his overthrow and exile in 1955, but his popularity grew among leftists (as a workers' hero) and rightists (as a nationalist) despite attempts to stamp out his party. Faced with rising violence and revolutionary activity in the early 1970s, military leaders invited Perón to return in 1973. Elected president, he soon died in office, leaving his third wife, Isabelita, as his successor, only for her to be overthrown in the 1976 coup. Perón's legacy and the Justicialista Party remain politically important.

Perry, Commodore Matthew Calbraith (1794–1858)

Named commodore in the US Navy in 1841, Perry is best known for his missions to **Japan** in the 1850s. Seeking to 'open' Japan to international commerce, US President Millard Fillmore dispatched Perry's naval squadron to negotiate an agreement with the Japanese. The end result of Perry's visits was the Treaty of **Kanagawa** (1854), a basic commercial agreement that opened two ports to American ships and contained a 'most favoured nation' clause.

Persia

– *see* **Iran**.

Peru, Republic of

Comprising just under 1.3 million square kilometres on the west coast of South America, and, as a result of Spanish rule, a heterogeneous population of over 30 million people, Peru has a diverse climate and three major regions: the coast, the Andean sierra and the tropical Amazonian lowlands. Chronic political instability followed independence in 1825. New revenues derived from guano exports briefly stabilized the country during the mid nineteenth century, but a disastrous war with **Chile** (1879–83) ended the promise of guano-led development. By 1900 recovery began based on a diverse array of export commodities and elite rule. Peru was buffeted again by a failed radical, military-led reform effort in the late 1960s and 1970s and then by a lengthy guerrilla insurgency conducted by **Sendero Luminoso**. Political democracy and export-led growth, reaching 8 per cent annually, returned during the first decade of the twenty-first century. Peru now defines itself by its pre-Columbian past.

Peru, Viceroyalty of

The Spanish crown created the viceroyalty of Peru in 1542 with a viceroy in Lima to oversee all of Spanish South America. The viceroyalty of New Granada established in 1739 carved out modern **Colombia**, **Ecuador** and **Panama**. In 1776 Peru lost today's **Argentina**, **Paraguay**, **Uruguay** and **Bolivia** to the viceroyalty of Río de La Plata. **Chile** briefly reattached Bolivia, Peru was independent by 1825, and the viceroyalty of Peru disappeared.

Pétain, Henri Philippe (1856–1951)

French general and war leader. A career military officer and first commanding colonel of **Charles de Gaulle**, Pétain rose rapidly in **World War I**, partly as a result of his realization of the utility of defensive tactics; he ended the war as commander-in-chief and was then promoted to field marshal. In the interwar period he held ministerial and diplomatic offices. After the fall of France he moved from being ambassador to fascist Spain to leader of the **Vichy** regime, which resulted in his subsequent capital conviction for treason in 1944. Pétain's sentence was commuted by Charles de Gaulle, and he died in solitary confinement seven years later.

Peter the Great (1672–1725)

Acceded to the throne, 1689, as joint tsar with Ivan V until 1696, Peter the Great was the creator of the **Russian Empire**. He sought to win access to the Baltic, Black and Caspian Seas. A visionary with boundless practical energy, he studied shipbuilding at Saardam, in the **Netherlands**, and in Deptford, London, and founded the first significant Russian Navy. He sought to open **Russia** to western influences through major internal reforms and by founding St Petersburg on the Gulf of Finland. It was declared Russia's capital in 1712. As a result of the **Great Northern War** (1700–21), the empire made substantial gains in the Baltic, and Peter led the first Russian expedition into Transcaucasia. Larger than life in private as well as public, he was a towering figure at six and a half feet tall and subject to violent rages. He married a peasant but oversaw the murder of his own son. He remains almost a living presence in St Petersburg, where the humble hut from which he supervised the city's construction survives.

Petrobras (Petróleo Brasileiro)

Nationalists supported the creation of **Brazil**'s state petroleum monopoly known as Petrobras in 1953. The monopoly benefited during the military dictatorship (1964–85) and became the largest Latin American oil company by 1990. The government ended its monopoly in 1997, but in 2010 purchased enough stock to reverse the earlier privatization, a decision linked to the discovery of major offshore reserves since 2006, the year Brazil became self-sufficient in **oil**. Endemic corruption contributed to rising political anger by 2015.

Phalanges Libanaises (Kata'ib)

A paramilitary organization established by Pierre Jumayyil in 1936, Phalanges Libanaises was intended to protect Christian minorities within the Lebanese Maronite community. The organization actively pursued the Christianization of **Lebanon**, and sought Lebanese independence. In the 1930s and 1940s the organization focused almost exclusively on youth and paramilitary activities. Under Jumayyil during the 1958 Lebanese Civil War, it sought to protect and fight for Christian-led resistance to Muslim forces. The so-called 'bus massacre', perpetrated on a bus full of Christian Phalanges Libanaises members in 1975, is widely credited with setting off a new Lebanese Civil War. Pluralism in the Lebanese constitution is one of the main goals of the Phalanges Libanaises today, as it has been in the past. The organization is opposed to an Arab nationalism, although the group does acknowledge Arab ties. Despite its militaristic ties, Phalanges Libanaises has morphed itself into an almost exclusively political party since the early 1990s.

Phanomyong, Pridi (1900–1983)

A Thai politician and constitutional monarchist who served as regent, prime minister and as a sort of senior statesman without portfolio from 1941 onwards. Often called the 'father of Thai democracy', ironically for his role in the pro-democracy coup of 1932. He was exiled to **China** in 1949 after a second attempted coup failed, and died in Paris, where he had made his home from 1970. He was particularly associated with educational reform and South East Asian independence.

Phelps–Stokes Commission

A missionary-inspired commission set up to look into the state of education in the British colonies. In 1919 the Phelps–Stokes Fund, based in New York, sent a commission to West, South and Equatorial Africa. The commission's report provided the foundations for **Britain**'s interwar colonial education policy. Influenced by the American model of education for **African Americans**, the report promoted 'adaptation', a concept that called for the education of Africans to be simple, utilitarian and rooted in agricultural training.

Phibunsongkhram, Luang (Plaek Kittasangkha) (1897–1974)

Luang Phibunsongkhram operated under a variety of names and is most associated with the military regimes in **Thailand** between 1938–44 and 1948–57, which he led. Although associated with the 1932 pro-democracy coup, he was an army major who gravitated towards fascism as a governing ideology whilst minister of defence. He declared war on imperial **France**, allied himself to **Japan**, and declared himself field marshal. In these things, he was ultimately thwarted by the Free Thai movement and by his enemy, **Pridi Phanomyong**. However, he returned to power in 1948 after another coup, and was fiercely anti-Communist during the **Cold War**. He was ousted in 1957, and fled to Tokyo, where he died.

philhellenism

Pro-Greek sentiment. Politically significant at the time of the **Greek War of Independence** when it was widespread amongst the British and French educated classes, a fruit, no doubt, of their classical education, and extended to some of the high aristocracy, most famously the English poet, Lord Byron, who died of fever at Missolonghi, 1824. On the other hand it divided European governments who all feared rebellion against a sovereign monarch.

Austria supported the **Ottoman Empire**, as did the Duke of Wellington, British prime minister 1828–30, but Lord Canning, prime minister, 1827, favoured the Greeks. The calculation was the comparative benefit to British Mediterranean interests of a stable Ottoman Empire as against a small but friendly **Greece**. **Russia**, 1824, suggested the creation of three separate Greek principalities under Turkish suzerainty, but the diplomatic conference it convened in St Petersburg in spring 1825 broke up in disagreement. Greece gained independence, 1829.

Philip V (1683–1746)

First Bourbon king of **Spain** and Spanish America, 1700–46, but not of the Spanish Netherlands or part of Italy after the Treaty of **Utrecht**, 1713, ending the War of the Spanish Succession. Briefly abdicated January–August 1724. Instigated a number of economic and governmental reforms and reasserted Spain's international influence, securing the succession of Don Carlos, later **Charles III** of Spain, his oldest son by his second wife, to the duchy of Parma. Subject to bouts of insanity in his later years.

Philippine Rebellions

– *see also* **Platt Amendment**.

Philippine nationalist uprising against American colonial rule that took place at the end of the Spanish–American War in 1899. After the war, Filipino independence forces had taken control of the islands and declared independence. The US refused to grant full independence, and consequently there was a large-scale uprising in the islands. The insurgents were defeated by American troops in 1902. America did not grant independence to the **Philippines** until the end of **World War II**.

Philippines

– *see also* **Philippine Rebellions**.

The Republic of the Philippines consists of a group of 7,107 islands in the South East Asian archipelago, between the Philippine Sea and the South China Sea. It has a total area of 301,594 square kilometres and a population of around 100 million. The terrain is mostly mountainous with narrow coastal lowlands. The Philippines has a tropical marine climate and is influenced by the north-east and south-west monsoons. It became a colony of **Spain** in the sixteenth century. In 1898 the islands came under **USA** rule as a result of the Spanish–American War. The Philippines gained full independence from the US on 4 July 1946, having been occupied by **Japan** in **World War II**. At present, the republic is governed according to the presidential system. The capital, Manila, is located on Luzon, the largest island in the north. The majority of the population (82.9 per cent) is Roman Catholic. There has been a long-lasting Muslim autonomous movement on Moro. A ceasefire with Maoist-led rebels was signed in 2016. Filipino and English are the official languages, and the national currency is the Philippine peso (PHP).

Philippines, fall of the (World War II)

The Battle of the Philippines started on 8 December 1941 when Japanese forces invaded the islands and encountered resistance from American and Filipino forces. The battle ended on 8 May 1942 in Japanese victory. The Allies did not begin the campaign to recapture the **Philippines** until 1944. It was not until **World War II** had ended completely with Japanese surrender in 1945 that the Philippines returned briefly, in its entirety, to American rule.

Pied Noir

A French term meaning 'black foot', *Pied Noir* was used from the mid twentieth century to describe the colonists and their descendants in French-ruled North Africa, particularly in **Algeria** from the 1830 invasion until independence in 1962, predominantly French but including other Europeans. A million *Pieds Noir* migrated to **France** at the end of the Algerian War, bitter at the loss of their colonial home but with a sense of cultural alienation, and received with resentment by the mainland population.

Pierce, Franklin (1804–1869)

New Hampshire lawyer, **United States** Congressman (Democratic Party, House, 1833–7; Senate, 1837–42) and fourteenth president, 1853–7. Nominated for his obscurity, Pierce easily defeated a **Whig** candidate whose party was more divided than his own by the **Compromise of 1850**. He proclaimed an expansionist, domestically unifying foreign policy, but the Ostend Manifesto (1854) linked it to **filibustering** and **sectional conflict**, which Pierce inflamed by approving the **Kansas–Nebraska Act**. The only elected president ever to be denied renomination, Pierce's one achievement was the **Gadsden Purchase**.

Pill

The Pill was a key player in the birth control movement. The term refers to oral contraceptives pills – chemical compounds that physiologically affect the hormone levels in the female body so as to prevent ovulation, thus inhibiting normal fertility. As a birth control method, the Pill has outperformed all other practices, such as abstinence, coitus interruptus, induced abortion, male castration and contraceptives, in effectiveness, health risk or convenience. Since its invention in 1955 by Gregory Pincus, its use has been widespread in western developed societies.

Ping-Pong diplomacy

As part of its growing desire to normalize relations with the **United States**, Chinese Prime Minister **Zhou Enlai** invited the American table tennis team to **China** in April 1971. They were the first Americans to visit the People's Republic of China since the Communist takeover in 1949, and the move represented an unprecedented symbol of openness. The success of the trip contributed to a relaxing of tensions, making it easier for President **Nixon** to visit China in 1972.

Pinochet (Ugarte), Augusto (1915–2006)

Dictator who headed the Chilean military government, 1973–90. Born in Valparaíso, he was a military academy-trained career officer who became army commander in 1973. Pinochet's regime implemented neoliberal economic reforms, imposed a new constitution (1980), and harshly repressed political opposition. He claimed to have saved **Chile** from the threat of communist dictatorship, but is associated worldwide with massive human rights violations. At the time of his death, he faced indictments in hundreds of cases of kidnapping, torture and murder.

Pitt the Elder (William Pitt) (1708–1778)

Pitt the Elder (also known as Lord Chatham) led **Great Britain** in coalition with Lord Newcastle, who was widely credited with helping to win the **Seven Years War** with **France** and then **Spain** between 1754 and 1763, despite his own resignation in 1761. He became prime minister again between 1766 and 1768, during which time his policies radically alienated him from his colleagues and the American colonies, as much as his acceptance of a seat in the House of Lords alienated him from his natural constituency amongst commoners. A supporter of the American rebels insofar as they shared his Whig ideals, he died a disappointed man after intermittent ill health.

Pitt the Younger (William Pitt) (1759–1806)

The son of Pitt the Elder, William Pitt eclipsed his father as a war leader by virtue of his premiership during the wars following the **French Revolution**. Prime Minister at the age of 24 in 1783, Pitt won the 1784 general election, introduced income tax and excise taxes, attacked smugglers and attempted to assert government control over the largely private and commercial **British Empire** in **India**. Though he pushed through the Act of Union with Ireland in 1801, his attempt to lift anti-Catholic restrictions removed him from power until he was recalled in 1804. His final premiership, which broke his health, saw the formation of the Third Coalition against **Napoleon** and the Battle of **Trafalgar**. His health collapsed at the end of 1805.

Pius IX, Pope (1792–1878)

Born Giovanni Masti-Ferretti, he became Pope Pius IX in 1846. Pius IX was a railway enthusiast, an opponent of socialism, a centralizer and a modernizer who convened the first Vatican Council in 1868 to meet in 1869. He was elected as the candidate of liberals and moderates within the Catholic Church and presided over the end of the Papal States, the rise of the Italian state, the creation of a less dogmatic attitude towards Jewish people and the rise of the modern press. Pius IX began a tradition of centralizing the Catholic Church under the cover of the popular devotion to the Virgin Mary and the idea of papal infallability on matters of doctrine. These were very old ideas that had never been formally proclaimed before, but they characterized the Catholic Church for the entire twentieth century, culminating in the papacy of **John Paul II**. In some respects, therefore, Pius IX can be seen as the first modern pope.

Pius XII, Pope (1876–1958)

Born Eugenio Pacelli, he became Pope Pius XII in 1939. A diplomat-pope, he served as a papal ambassador in **Germany** from 1917, faced down communists, and negotiated concordats for the toleration of the Catholic Church by states throughout northern Europe. He travelled extensively before becoming pope, and was widely believed to have been elected because of his political skills in the midst of the crisis leading up to **World War II**. Early on, he had associated himself very strongly with criticism of Nazi ideas of nationalism, racism and national socialism, which he saw as 'idolatry'. Nevertheless, he tended to suppress public criticism of Nazis and fascists after he was elected, though not of communists. He was fully informed of the emerging **Holocaust** from a very early date, and took very few public stands against the murder of Jews specifically. He did attempt to arrange visas for Jewish Catholics to emigrate to **Brazil**, and appears to have ordered Roman convents and monasteries to hide Jewish refugees according to secondary evidence. After the war, he called for forgiveness for prisoners of war. He also accepted the idea of evolution as compatible with Catholicism. He is viewed by some elements on the extreme Catholic right as the last 'legitimate' pope given that he presided before **Vatican II** and also that he was succeeded by Pope **John XXIII** in an election which some suggested ought to have been disputed.

Plaatje, Solomon ('Sol') Tskekisho (1876–1932)

South African writer and activist. Born in the then Orange Free State, he was a court interpreter during the Siege of Mafeking and first general secretary in 1912 of the South African Native National Congress, forerunner of the **African National Congress (ANC)**. His book *Native Life in South Africa* denounced the discriminatory 1913 Natives' Land Act, while *Mhudi*, the first novel in English by a black South African writer, was written in 1919 and partially published in 1930.

planning

The term *planning* has long-acquired specific uses in the fields of urban development, as in planned cities and town planning, and in the military sphere, with war plans, strategic and battle plans. Then from the early twentieth century the idea of economic planning was developed, strategically identifying key economic objectives and attempting to implement them systematically by government-led direction and resource. Although not confined to socialist and communist theory, it gained its most prominent exponents as a reaction to capitalist **laisssez-faire** in which resources were allocated for private profit rather than for the good of society at large. Following the **Russian Revolution** the Soviet government set up a state planning commission, Gosplan, in 1921, 'to work out a single general state economic plan and means of implementing it'. With the drive to industrialization, Gosplan was given control of planning throughout the **Soviet Union** and charged with implementing the first **Five Year Plan** in 1928. The coincidence of this first grandiose example of state planning and its highly publicized prestige projects such as the Dnieper Dam (actually begun before 1928) with the **Wall Street Crash**, the **Great Depression** and unprecedented mass unemployment encouraged greater interest in economic planning than hitherto. In practice, many combatant states during

World War I had already exemplified the possibilities of greater state control and direction of resources, and these lessons were brought to bear in post-war projects such as state-subsidized housing in **Great Britain** and the reconstruction of war-devastated areas in **France**.

The Depression intensified demands for greater state involvement where laissez-faire appeared to have failed, even if below the level of full-blooded Soviet-style planning. **Keynesianism** suggested that even capitalist governments could manage the economy and determine, at least to a degree, where resources might best be allocated in the national interest, for example, in dealing with areas which had become 'depressed' due to long-term changes in economic conditions. Under the **New Deal**, a pioneer attempt was made from 1933 to regenerate a whole region through the Tennessee Valley Authority (TVA), combining flood control, hydro-electric schemes and agricultural improvement to raise living standards in one of the poorest regions of America. Also admired were the apparently successful public works schemes, such as the building of autobahns by the Nazis. Pressure groups such as Political and Economic Planning, founded in Britain in 1931, sought to promote the benefits of planning within a capitalist framework, though many on the Left sought to emulate the Soviet-style second and third Five Year Plans, which appeared to insulate the Soviet Union from the depression.

By **World War II**, planning was in vogue and the favourable experience of wartime control in countries such as Great Britain and the success of government-organized programmes in the **United States** such as the **Manhattan Project** to build the atom bomb seemed to indicate its effectiveness. With the coming of peace, communist and many ex-colonial states adopted planned economies, nationalized key areas of industry and resources, and sought to emulate the Soviet model of development. In the West greater state involvement in the economy was often a consequence of wartime experience, with state aid for regional development, nationalization of key infrastructure,and a variety of state-sponsored projects in defence and scientific research. In France, *dirigisme* was seen as a key component in turning the country into a first-rate industrial power. In Holland, massive state investment established huge flood defences and reclaimed thousands of acres following disastrous floods in 1953. In the United Kingdom, attempts to remedy a century or more of unrestrained urban growth resulted in state sponsorship of over twenty 'new towns' and restrictions on urban growth by 'green belts' around every major town and city.

In the last quarter of the twentieth century the rise of **neoliberalism** in economic thinking and the unheralded combination of inflation and high unemployment in the 1970s began to undermine faith in planning. Disastrous forays into planning by some developing countries and the sluggish performance of the Soviet and communist economies added to a sense that market reforms were necessary to optimize economic growth and avoid stagnation. In practice hybridization was usually the norm. Even under apparently neoliberal governments such as that of **Margaret Thatcher** in the UK or **Ronald Reagan** in the US, considerable state or federal sectors remained.

China, once the exemplar of a controlled, communist economy in which virtually all economic enterprise was state-controlled and governed by centralized planning norms had, by the early twentieth-first century, adopted a largely capitalist system of production while retaining overall state control of credit, currency and vital infrastructure, such as the railways. Some communist states, such as **Cambodia** and **North Korea** still adhere to a system of 'Five Year Plans' or their equivalents.

plantation/hacienda

The plantation and hacienda were large agricultural estates, common in the early modern Americas, though with persistence to the present day. The hacienda originated in Spanish land grants, mostly to conquistadores in **Mexico** and elsewhere. It was closely associated with the encomienda system, in which Spanish landowners were given power to control Native American labour and movement. The plantation, by contrast, tended to be based upon the labour of imported African slaves, who worked to produce tropical crops such as cotton or sugar. In **Brazil**, the owners of labour brought that labour to work on mills on plantations; in British and French America, all the operations of production were combined in a single operation. Oriented towards production for distant markets, mostly in **Europe**, the plantation proved to be a highly effective slave-based system in making American agriculture economically worthwhile. Planters, as plantation owners, formed significant ruling elites in places like antebellum America.

Platt Amendment (1901)

A rider by Senator Orville Platt to the Army Appropriations Act, the amendment specified conditions for **United States** troops leaving **Cuba** after the Spanish–American War (1898). It permitted US intervention in Cuban affairs when the United States deemed necessary and conceded rights to a naval base at Guantánamo Bay. Despite opposition from Cuban nationalists, the Cuban Constitution of 1901 incorporated the amendment as the price for US recognition of Cuba's independence.

pogroms

A term used by East European and Russian Jews to characterize the devastation and violence associated with groups involved in anti-Semitic attacks. Authorities in the **Russian Empire**, in particular, sponsored or encouraged official and mob violence against Jewish people, homes and businesses between 1821 and 1919. These tended to drive surviving Jews to emigration. The technique became a feature of Nazi German society after 1933, particularly during the **Kristallnacht** disturbances of 1938. Pogroms differed from mass lynchings such as the 1921 Tulsa race riots in the **USA**, in that they involved rapes, theft, arson and general violence as well as public murder, and were directed so as to destroy whole settlements rather than to intimidate. The last European pogrom was at Kielce in **Poland**, in 1946, but the term has also been used to describe subsequent violence against minority communities stopping short of genocide.

Pol Pot (1925–1998)

Pol Pot was the *nom de guerre* of Saloth Sar, leader of the **Khmer Rouge** and prime minister of **Cambodia**, 1976–9. His regime pursued drastic policies of population relocation and extermination of intellectuals and bourgeois enemies, which resulted in the deaths of approximately 1.5 million people. The regime was overthrown by Vietnamese troops in 1979. He was put under house arrest in 1987, and died under suspicious conditions while sleeping.

Poland

Entered the eighteenth century as a declining Polish–Lithuanian Commonwealth and partitioned, 1772–95, between **Austria**, **Prussia** and **Russia**. Unsuccessful national revolts, 1830, 1846 and 1863, provoked attempted Germanization and Russification, except in autonomous (Austrian) Galicia. Poland was re-established as an independent state by the **Treaty of Versailles**, 1919, and a year later the Curzon line was proposed as eastern frontier, but the Russian–Polish War gave Poland

land 150 miles further east and also part of Lithuania. A military dictatorship ruled from 1926 to 1939, when a German attack opened **World War II**. Partitioned by **Germany** and the **Soviet Union** along the Curzon line, 1939, a pro-Soviet government was in place after 1945. The Oder–Neisse line was set as the new western frontier and the German population expelled under **Potsdam conference** decisions, 1945. A member of **Comecon**, 1949–90, and of the **Warsaw Pact**, 1955–91, Poland became the People's Republic of Poland, 1952–89. Some independence was secured within the Soviet bloc in 1956. Solidarinosc (Solidarity) was formed under **Lech Wałęsa** in 1980. Martial law, 1981–3, was followed by a non-communist prime minister, 1989. A member of **NATO**, 1999, and of the **European Union**, 2004, Poland remains apprehensive of any renewed Russian expansion.

Polisario movement

The Popular Front for the Liberation of the Saguia el Hamra and the Rio de Oro, or the Polisario Front, was founded in 1971 as a national liberation movement in the Spanish Sahara. Polisario originally carried out guerrilla attacks against Spanish colonial installations. When **Morocco** and **Mauritania** claimed the territory in 1975 after **Spain**'s withdrawal, it turned its focus to expelling the two countries in order to establish an independent nation in the Western Sahara. A political party with no set platform, it claims to incorporate all viewpoints in the common struggle for independence. In 1976 it declared the establishment of the **Sahrawi Arab Democratic Republic**. Power remains concentrated in the hands of the Polisario leadership; Secretary General Mohammed Abdülaziz held the position after 1976, although an opposition group was established in 2004. In the 1980s a war of attrition featured the Moroccan building of a fortified sand barrier. Aspiring for a self-determination referendum, Polisario agreed to a UN-brokered ceasefire in 1991. In turn, Morocco offered an autonomy plan that Polisario rejected. Intermittent UN-sponsored talks between both sides continue.

Polish Corridor

The territory, formerly German, which became part of the new **Poland** recognized by the **Treaty of Versailles** in 1919, thereby separating East Prussia from the rest of **Germany**. The creation of such a corridor across Germany infuriated nationalist opinion and Poland's establishment there of the port of Gdynia disadvantaged the German-speaking free city of Danzig (Gdansk). **Hitler** demanded the corridor's return from Poland, March 1939. It disappeared with the incorporation of East Prussia in the **Soviet Union** and Poland, 1945.

Polish revolts

The 'November Uprising' of 1830–1 was an attempt by Polish radicals to restore Polish independence. The Battle of Grochów, February 1831, was claimed as a Polish victory, but the conflict at Ostreleka in May led to the fall of Warsaw. **Russification** was increased with a ban on the Polish language in administrative and judicial offices. The minor outbreak of rebellion at Siedlce in Russian Poland in 1846 was suppressed by the Polish peasants themselves, but the uprising in Austrian Galicia turned into a civil war between Polish gentry and peasants, and rival revolutionary factions fought in Kraków, annexed by **Austria**, November 1846. The ability of the Austrian and Russian authorities to exploit these internal conflicts curtailed the impact on **Poland** of the European revolutions of 1848. The revolt of 1863, triggered by the Russian decision to conscript Poles into the army, failed similarly from the division between the moderates who favoured cooperation to secure reform and the radicals who insisted on prior Russian recognition of Polish nationhood.

Polk, James Knox (1795–1849)

As eleventh American president, 'young Hickory' transformed the **United States** into a continental empire. A Tennessee slaveholding planter, Polk entered Congress in 1825 as a committed supporter of **Andrew Jackson**. His loyalty through the trials of the first administration and the bank war was rewarded by election as speaker of the house (1835–9) and governor of Tennessee (1839–43). Though defeated for re-election, he surprisingly won nomination as Democratic presidential candidate in 1844 because, unlike the favourite **Martin Van Buren**, he supported the expansionist demand for **Texas** and, unlike van Buren's opponents, was not associated with soft money and pro-bank policies. As president (1844–9), he backed the re-enactment of traditional Jacksonian domestic policies while pressing US territorial claims abroad. In 1846 he compromised with **Britain** over the Oregon country, but deliberately provoked war with **Mexico** over the **Texas** boundary. Military success brought huge territorial gains in 1848 and the intractable problem of slavery expansion that troubled his last months.

Pombal, Marques de (Sebastião José de Carvalho e Melo) (1699–1782)

Portuguese statesman. He was the dynamic chief minister of **Portugal** (1750–77) under King João I. Pombal imposed far-reaching economic and trade reforms, tightened tax collection, and legitimized mixed marriages with Indians and children born out of wedlock. He expelled the Jesuits from Portugal and the empire in 1759 and moved the viceregal capital in **Brazil** to Rio de Janeiro in 1763. Pombal fell from power with King João's death.

Popular Democratic Front for the Liberation of Palestine (PDFLP)

– *see also* **Palestine Liberation Organization (PLO)**.
Founded in 1967 by George Habash, the Popular Democratic Front for the Liberation of Palestine (PDFLP) is a radical group once under the umbrella of the **Palestinian Liberation Organization (PLO)**. The group professes Marxist–Leninist ideals and uses violence to promote its agenda. In the late 1960s to mid 1970s it famously carried out midair hijackings to highlight its demands and ideals. The militants who carried out these hijackings and other violent programmes were known as the Red Eagles. With the rise of other militant organizations, such as **Hamas**, the PDFLP has reorganized and formed coalitions with other groups to remain relevant on the national stage. Although their prominence has diminished, they gained national recognition, and seats in the Palestinian legislature in 2006, but under a different name; the Martyr Abu Ali List. This name change is reflective of the armed faction within the PDFLP organization, the Abu Ali Mustafa Brigades.

Popular Front

Policy adopted by Communist parties following the 1935 Treaty of Mutual Assistance between the **Soviet Union** and **France**, abandoning the ultra-radical 'class against class' line to secure the support of western European governments for alliances against Nazi Germany. Communists were ordered to work with Socialists, Liberals and even Conservatives prepared to oppose Fascism. Popular Front electoral coalitions won power in France and in **Spain** in 1936 but Communists were not given posts in either government.

Popular Front for the Liberation of Palestine (PFLP)

– *see also* **Palestine Liberation Organization (PLO)**.

The Popular Front for the Liberation of Palestine, or PFLP, was founded in December 1967. Born in the wake of the Six Day War, the group professed to maintain the Palestinian struggle for independence. The group's founding document professes profoundly Arab and Palestinian nationalist ideals. In 1968 The PFLP joined forces with the **Palestinian Liberation Organization**, or **PLO**. Through violence and resistance the PFLP sought to oust **Israel**, undermine Arab states who did not comply with a unified Arab world, and gain recognition for the struggles of occupied **Palestine**. Under the umbrella of the PLO the organization lost influence and was relegated to obscurity in the 1990s under the PLO leadership of **Yasser Arafat**. A major player in the resistance movements of the late 1960s and through the 1970s, the violent activities of the PFLP received international attention. Though still active in the 2000s, the group has attempted to perpetrate resistance operations.

population

Until the twentieth century, human population growth was set within relatively immutable limits. These parameters can largely be explained as war, famine, disease and climate change, which have all been responsible for checking what would otherwise have been geometric growth. For these reasons, most demographers have estimated the entire human population in 1800 at 1 billion people. This in itself represents an advance on projections of the previous period, but by 1927 had doubled, despite the Great War. Between 1927 and 2017, the figure rose to approximately 7.60 billion. This unprecedented rise – so great that by 1999, more people were alive than had ever lived – was largely caused by the Green Revolution in agriculture and the spread of medicine and medical techniques (and both were in part the consequence of the use of cheap oil, potash, nitrogen and petrochemicals).

The Green Revolution began in research conducted by Norman Borlaug in **Mexico** in the 1940s, and was proselytized by agencies of the **United States** government and the **United Nations**. It was directly applied to postcolonial India in the 1960s with the help of corporate concerns such as the Ford and Rockefeller Foundations, and of various third world governments. The concerns of the American government and foundations were not purely altruistic, but rather arose from a combination of progressivism and the understanding that lack of food and the decline of private farming and the landed class was associated with revolution and communist-inspired agrarian reform. Successful agricultural enhancement through technology was therefore a serious front in the **Cold War**, and the **Green Revolution** represented an approach which could potentially forestall support for socialism in states such as **India**.

The approach involved an integrated effort in which new strains of rice, wheat and maize were placed within artificially enhanced areas of irrigation and treated with oil-based fertilizers. Lessons from each successful effort were then filtered through an international network of research centres and foundations, which then formulated policies that were adopted by governments across the world. One problem of the approach was a tendency to shift supply to large agribusiness concerns and to particular forms of food, and another was the countervailing effort of governments in rich countries to protect or subsidize their own food production. The human diet across the planet largely changed as a result, with much more meat, refined carbohydrate and processed food being consumed than before, leading to concerns about obesity in most developed and rapidly developing states. Further concerns arose with the development of pesticides, which many critics associated with a worldwide rise in cancers (discounting longevity, lack of exercise or other environmental concerns) and with the 'next step' application of genetic and hormonal modification to flora and fauna beginning in the 1990s. Overall, however, these drawbacks were largely seen as being outweighed by the gains.

Medicine changed over a longer period than agriculture. Medical developments can be divided into public health and private progress, though a substantial overlap in the form of vaccination, antenatal and pregnancy care, and general hospital programmes exists. Public health involves the development of efficient sewage, clean water, waste disposal and the creation of clean food preparation and delivery systems. These require a complex urban architecture combining regulation and inspection with infrastructure and research. In European and American urban centres, cholera was largely eliminated by sanitary programmes by the late nineteenth century. This was followed by improvements in midwifery, antiseptic and gynaecological care, which meant that fewer women died in or as a consequence of childbirth. Major efforts to eliminate, suppress or manage disease followed in the period after 1945 when the spread of cheap antibiotic medicines, and medical technology (both

predicated upon the development of an oil-based pharmaceutical industry) meshed with international efforts to alleviate low living standards and to provide health care through national or international bodies.

By the late twentieth century the population rise caused serious concern to many policymakers and observers. Though this was relatively unrealized, the concern was rooted in resource depletion, fears about a global lack of sexual education and desires for population control. It is noticeable that criticism and fear of population growth was a first world or elite activity, whereas growth itself was evident in previously deprived regions. It is fair to say that it slowed or reversed only where female empowerment and the growth of living standards provided a countervailing incentive to fertility.

The subject of the extent, stratification and growth of populations has become important in modern history in at least four ways. Firstly, from the mid twentieth century in **Sweden**, **France** and then **Britain**, new techniques of measuring population based on church records, statistical back projection and family reconstitution have helped revolutionize the study of history and of population in general. Secondly, by the 1960s a consciousness of the rapidity of population growth resulted in a movement to utilize scientific techniques of prophylaxis, abortion and family control at the supposed cost of dire depletion of resources at the global and national level. Thirdly, techniques of statistical polling, social analysis and market targeting based upon demographic insights spread across business and politics from the 1970s. Fourthly, the growth and application of population studies is in itself a study of computing power, and of the interaction of scientific and medical explanations for growth with essentially cognitive preconceptions about the distribution of wealth and resources, and appropriate family size, which has had huge consequences for national populations. It is also related to the idea of human societies as systems within ecosystems, subject to the same rules of unsustainable growth and decline as other populations without intervention. As a consequence of such ideas, the population of **China**, in theory subject to a 'one child policy' by government decree, has become biased towards males; western and Japanese populations have begun to shrink partly because of the spread of contraceptive technologies and abortion; and African populations, for the first time in modern history, have boomed because of improvements in the capacity to sustain large populations and their food and energy needs.

population studies

The history of population studies in the modern period should be distinguished from a long tradition of concern with a perceived mismatch between geometric population growth across times of plenty and arithmetic resource growth best summarized in Thomas Malthus' 1798 *Essay on the Principle of Population*. Instead, modern studies can be traced to two influences. One was an international effort to promote both eugenics and birth control, which was intertwined with early feminism and the growth of international pressure groups. This influence can be seen in the international population conference held at Geneva in 1927, which gave rise to the International Union for the Scientific Study of Population. The IUSSP was (and is) a private corporation, organized by the eugenicist and sex education agitator Margaret Sanger but with a quasi-public charitable mission. Its effort (based on a model similar to that of the League of Nations Association) to propagate the causes of birth control, food depletion and population restriction by calling together international meetings of experts and then meshing them with national lobby groups became a modern trend, and was later applied by organizations such as the United Nations, the Club of Rome and the International Panel on Climate Change, to great effect. By these means, and in the wake of the Great War and its destruction of moral consensus about the exceptionalism of people and the absolute good of growth, the issue of population became a fashionable one. This was especially true for adherents of the emergent disciplines of social science, such as those associated with the foundation in 1936 of the Population Investigation Committee (PIC). The PIC was a direct creation of the British Eugenics Society, and given a perceived affinity was later housed at the London School of Economics.

A second influence was born of the overlap of social sciences and history, and emerged during and after **World War II** in France. It was particularly associated with the family reconstitution and demographic model of Louis Henry, who drew together amateur and piecemeal studies of parish registers, lineages and households across a long period of time and synthesized them with the ideas of the **Annales** school. This effort was parallel to that of Hannes Hyrenius in Sweden, but of wider appeal. Henry's principal concern was to explain the post-war 'baby boom' and to set it in context, since received opinion had for some decades been settled on the idea that Europe was in demographic decline but that any revival would place intolerable pressure on food resources. His work was therefore of interest to western governments and international bodies in general. Working through the 1950s with John Hajnal in Britain and a team in France, Henry linked fertility to nuptiality and placed stable marriage at the centre of European regeneration. This fed into a long-standing concern of the leading bureaucrats of France that welfare and legal systems might be constructed in such a way as to encourage the growth of the middle classes in particular through 'family planning'. However, Henry was forced to invent new resources to achieve breakdowns by age and live births, which ranged from statistical innovation to trawling international census and yearbook data. In this regard, his device of 'natural fertility' was a breakthrough as a reference point for researchers. By the time he propagated his technique, in the 1960s, the United Nations Organization had developed a population division which was eager to use it. Concurrently, the ability to reconstruct the *ancien régime* population of France which developed from Henry's work captured the imaginations of a generation of historians.

In the United Kingdom, E. A. 'Tony' Wrigley, Peter Laslett and Roger Schofield, amongst others, became fascinated by the French work. After founding the Cambridge Group for the History of Population and Social Structure in 1964, they went on to lead a generation of historians in the reconstruction of England's demographic past, particularly during the early modern and industrial eras. As in France, but without state help (they relied on John Rickman's collation of post-1538 parish registers and academic grants) they developed their arguments using church records to begin with. By the 1980s, however, improvements in information technology and the mining of publicly available state census data, which had been maintained since 1837, allowed them to devise new metrics. These included gross reproduction rates, expectation of life at birth rates and adjustments for bias. Amongst other things, these efforts yielded the production of Wrigley and Schofield's 'Population History of England 1541–1871', which provoked historiographical debates of international importance.

By the late 1960s the environmentalist movement which had been co-opted by the Nazi reaction against modernity had recovered its appeal to the democratic Left. Increasingly, debate around the societies of the North Atlantic rim and in **Japan** came to centre on the problems apparently posed by the combination of rising economic expectations based on resource depleting techniques, the extension of human longevity by medical science and the pollution of the environment. These debates were not simply left-wing ones, as they also concerned Italian industrialists such as Aurelio Peccei, management systems theorists such as Hasan Ozbekhan, and astrophysicists such as Eric Jantsch. The latter three were instrumental in creating the Club of Rome, an organization of scientists, civil servants and industrialists that promoted papers and commissioned studies on the deleterious effects of population growth and resource use. Their most famous publication, 'Limits to Growth' of 1972, was amongst their first. The Club of Rome, acting with the support of governments, and of the UN thus charged the issue of population control with dramatic importance. A debate began which was met by a reaction on the part of the Catholic Church and the Islamic revival, over the use of contraception and abortion. Initially, population control (which was embraced enthusiastically by communist countries) paid little attention to feminist concerns, and instead followed Paul Ehrlich's 1968 characterization of babies as a cancer the birth of whom required regulation. Concerned citizens began talking of a 'population bomb' and many pointed to the 1973 and 1978 oil price shocks, the emergence of media-driven awareness of famines and the iniquities of the global economy as the shape of things to come. This concern meshed with national security fears as to the future balance of the world population promoted by the **Nixon–Kissinger** administration which could be characterized as racist. Though agriculture, the financial sector and the energy sector proved resilient enough to deliver growth, which also empowered women and slowed, then halted population growth, these fears became embedded in international organizations. Amongst the most enthusiastic regulators, the People's Republic of China, the Republic of India and the Islamic Republic of **Iran** found themselves facing gender imbalances and a need for mass immigration based on policies as varied as the restriction of elective office to those with small families, forced sterilizations and hysterectomies, abortions and mandatory contraceptive education in return for marriage licences. They did not, however, produce smaller populations in absolute terms.

Marketing and opinion polling in the USA and UK are far older than modern demography. Perhaps because of its modern outlook, the UK Labour Party was the first of the Atlantic parties to attempt to identify segments of the electorate at whom a tailored message could be delivered.

The party formed a press and publicity department in October 1917, and by 1937 was running model public relations campaigns in the London County Council elections under Herbert Morrison. This followed on from Sidney Webb's 1922 advice to target particular sections of the population, which was enthusiastically embraced by party organizers. By the late 1940s and early 1950s the development of television, consumerism and de-alignment, which would later emerge in full force, was evident. In business, this meant a switch from reliance on loyalty to particular companies because of the quality of their product to an approach which elevated public relations and sales techniques which achieved sales in volume. This led to the growth of advertising companies, whose combination of modern methods, aesthetic modernism and charismatic consultancy spread throughout the business world. In 1969, Sidney Levy and Philip Kotler published an influential paper which pointed out how much the techniques associated with this business – based on an understanding of demographic 'segments' – could be applied to persons, organizations and ideas. In truth, this was something which political organizations had realized a generation before. For instance, the Truman 1948 campaign was aided by a comic book geared to young and less literate readers and the 1952 Eisenhower–Nixon presidential campaign was characterized by television advertising, positioning and the marketing of both Republican candidates. Avraham Sharma has identified the period between 1940 and 1960 as one in which political candidates on both sides of the Atlantic were marketed as products, but noted that by the 1960s demographic and market segmentation techniques based on the management of population information had become normal. These accelerated with the computerization of campaigns, to the point where, by the twenty-first century, highly sophisticated demographic, psychographic and population-based techniques were being employed at most political levels.

The application of techniques of political demography to practical politics has run parallel to the development of a subdiscipline of political demography in politics, international relations, and geography departments of universities. This discipline depended upon a mixture of government statistics, actuarial concepts and statistical methods. These in turn were based around measures of migration, nuptiality, fertility, mortality and morbidity as well as the back-projection methods developed by the likes of Louis Henry and the historical demographers. As with many social sciences, the origins of the subdiscipline are rooted in cognitive diversity. One strain, for instance, arose with the statistical study of crime in urban areas in the late nineteenth century, and is best represented in the work of Adolphe Quetelet. Another can be found in the concerns and techniques of Emile Durkheim, who studied religion, suicide and community cohesion as part of an effort to understand European modernity. For the first Parisian professor of demography, Louis-Adolphe Bertillon, demography was a branch of anthropology, while on the other hand, to William Lexis it was a branch of insurance. However, all these approaches have been synthesized into university programmes which are policed by national and international bodies of professionals.

The subdiscipline is still evolving, and in recent years has in itself given rise to an increasingly coherent body of political demographers, who attempt to apply population analysis to international relations and history in a new way, concentrating on the application of ethnicity, identity and demography to zones of cultural or military conflict, urbanization or migration. In recent years scholars such as Jack Goldstone, Jared Diamond, Neil Howe, Monica Duffy Toft and Eric Kaufmann have, amongst many others, sought to apply insights to topics as diverse as violence in the **Caucasus**, the rise of **Islam** or party formation in democracies. At the same time, graduates of political science schools have noted, for instance, how closely support for candidates can be aligned to a combination of marital status, religiosity, age and race in American elections. When added to computer databases gathered by the work of thousands of volunteers, the connection of social network technologies with a central computer program and public data, such insights have proved devastating. For instance, the 'Obama database', which built upon Democratic models and which has been maintained over the years, employed techniques to mine data which were widely accredited with providing 'demographic victory' for the **Obama** presidential campaigns of 2008 and 2012. In Britain, similar efforts were undertaken by the Labour and Conservative parties in the late 1990s and early twenty-first century through such systems as 'Excelsior' and 'Voter Vault', but given privacy laws and cost, were not pursued as diligently. They have not been evident in many elections in non-English speaking countries for similar reasons, though privately funded demographic marketing and consultancy have nevertheless proven lucrative for opinion research firms globally.

New trends. It is a paradox of population study that the years of its fastest global growth coincided not only with the greatest global economic growth in history but also with the most devastating wars in history, and with the unrealized threat of nuclear annihilation. In the early years of the Cold War, for instance, western populations experienced a 'baby boom' which lasted roughly for the two decades after 1945. This growth of 2 per cent or more per annum in childbirths followed from a similar rise in the period following the Great War of 1914–18, and has given rise in some quarters to an unsupported hypothesis that all wars result in population rebound. In fact, a more complicated picture has emerged from political demography, in which large wars may well result in growth, but small wars (which emerge over land, water or economic pressure associated with the interaction of economic maldistribution and population growth) result in migration, terrorism and stasis or decline. The field is in itself new, and therefore awaits confirmation.

One effect of twentieth-century population trends in the twenty-first is not in dispute, however, and that is the way in which the baby boom generation in the developed world did not replace itself after 1964. In societies such as those of western **Europe**, Japan and North America, this has resulted in a 'grey bomb' which has had an unprecedented economic effect only partly offset by immigration. Large numbers of older people, whose consumption and investment habits are very different from those of the young, are now alive and exist within schemes of medical and social insurance which are in large part funded by the taxation of younger groups and families. In addition, the accumulated wealth of the baby boomers is in many societies expressed in terms of the value of privately owned residential accommodation, or within pension funds which operate in a dominant way in stock markets. The combination of these factors has meant a decline in population, family formation, social mobility and disposable income for the young as well as low growth and budget deficits in many developed societies. The most acute example – perhaps the leading edge of the wave – has been the two-decade stagnation of Japan, which is also characterized by the lowest immigration rate of the group. One reaction at elite levels has been to embrace narratives in which human beings are described in terms of plagues or viruses, and to assert that population reduction, rather than control, should be at the heart of global policies. This has in turn resulted in political stances which promote abortion, euthanasia, sterilization and family limitation. Very briefly, in the fever of early space exploration in the mid twentieth century a potential solution in terms of the colonization of space, asteroids, the Moon and near planets or their satellites was mooted, but by the twenty-first century supporters of such ideas were either confined to largely honorary professional science positions or marginalized. This is not to say that the figures propounding such ideas, such as the internationally renowned physicists Stephen Hawking and Freeman Dyson, the former US Speaker of the House Newt Gingrich and Lord Rees, the then president of the Royal Society, were marginal, but simply that their ideas were. In addition, other scientists and futurists, such as Arthur C. Clarke and James Lovelock, were more concerned to emphasize the need to control or reduce earthbound population.

The increase in human population over the past two centuries has been unprecedented and has had unprecedented effects, such as the development of hundreds of cities – and slums, the growth of mass economies, the exponential depletion of resources and the creation of innovative and dynamic markets to meet problems. It has created multiple academic disciplines and resulted in medical and agricultural initiatives and networks which have provided a model of international action. However, the increase is ongoing and still inspiring dynamic change.

Populist Party (USA)

A third party of rural reformers in **United States** politics (1892–1908). Rooted in the **agrarian ideal** and **republicanism**, the Populist movement arose from the pincer effect of the deflationary reimposition of the **gold standard** combined with crop failures and low prices for southern cotton and the wheat of the western plains. The **Granger movement** and 'Farmers' Alliances' won some victories in the 1870s and 1880s, but learned that only a national organization could match the power of the **Democrats, Republicans** and the corporate interests that seemed to control both parties. The Populist Party platform of 1892 reached out to organized labour, promoting railway nationalization, direct senatorial elections and a progressive income tax. Its presidential candidate won a million votes and four states, and it made fruitful state-level alliances with whichever was the minority party. In 1896 it endorsed Democrat and ultimate loser **William Jennings Bryan** for his 'free silver' inflationism, but at the cost of its own identity. The **Progressive** movement adopted various Populist causes.

Port Royal earthquake

Port Royal was both the centre of commerce in seventeenth-century **Jamaica** and the leading haunt of Caribbean pirates. On 7 June 1692 a large earthquake, followed by flooding from the sea, struck and hundreds of people died. Some attributed the city's demise to divine intervention; Port Royal was thought 'the wickedest City in the West'. Local merchants moved to nearby Kingston, which replaced Port Royal as the leading centre of commerce and became a centre for Jamaica's slave trade.

Portugal

– *see also* **Portuguese Empire**.

In the eighteenth century Portugal enjoyed prosperity from the colonial wealth of **Brazil**, which was Portuguese from 1494 to 1822, and trade with **Britain**, particularly in port wine. It experienced semi-enlightened despotism under the **Marques de Pombal**, 1750–77, was invaded by **France**, 1807, in the **Napoleonic** and concurrent **Peninsular Wars**, and was subject to constitutional conflict thereafter until the 'Regeneration' of 1851–6. Failure to deal with economic and social problems stimulated republicanism after 1890, and King Carlos was assassinated, 1908. The First Republic spanned the years 1910–26, during which time the country was unstable, anti-clerical and punctuated by military coups. It suffered severely economically from British alliance in **World War I**. A military coup, 1926, resulted in the appointment of António de Oliveira Salazar, a professor of economics, as minister of finance with total power over expenditure. He secured collaboration from previously opposing groups. Authoritarian prime minister, 1932–68. Portugal declared a unitary, corporatist republic, 1933. Neutral in **World War II**, it joined **NATO**, 1949, and the **United Nations**, 1955. A democratic **Portuguese Revolution** took place in 1974, and its African colonies were declared independent, 1974–5. It joined the **European Union** in 1986.

Portuguese Empire

This global empire spanned the fifteenth century to the second half of the twentieth century and included territories in South America, **Asia** and

Africa. Along with **Spain**, **Portugal** dominated the first stage of European imperial expansion. While the desire to spread Christianity and interest in science and seamanship encouraged early discoveries, trade remained the primary objective for Portuguese expansion.

In Africa, the Portuguese established their first settlements in the mid fifteenth century. Their presence expanded on the continent with the development of trade in gold and slavery. Vasco da Gama's discovery of a sea route to **India** by travelling around the Cape of Good Hope allowed traders to circumvent middlemen along the Silk Road. This sea route led to Portugal's control of trade between Asia and **Europe** and established the country's dominance in the East. The Portuguese subsequently established outposts in India, **China**, **Japan** and **Indonesia**.

In the early sixteenth century Portugal founded colonies in **Brazil**, which would serve as its imperial centrepiece. Brazil differed from other areas of the empire in that the Portuguese did not simply establish trading posts but sought to colonize the area and establish a permanent presence. Settlement accelerated in the seventeenth century with the discovery of sugar and gold. These discoveries and their requisite intensive labour led to the beginning of slavery in the country. During the 'Golden Age of Brazil' in the early eighteenth century, the Portuguese amassed great wealth through the discovery of diamonds and the development of tobacco, mining and cotton industries.

The Iberian Union of Portugal with Spain in 1580 initiated rivalries with the British, French and Dutch, whose new imperial ambitions threatened Portugal's global holdings. While European rivalries helped precipitate Portugal's imperial decline, the country also faced internal problems. Imperial commerce brought wealth to Portugal, but little was invested into the country as a whole and instead remained concentrated in Lisbon. Consequently, imperial expansion ultimately led to the underdevelopment of Portugal's domestic economy. Moreover, Portugal's rapid imperial expansion over-extended the country's resources.

The achievement of independence by Brazil in 1822 led Portugal to focus its imperial ambitions on Africa, hoping that it would provide the same promise of wealth and prosperity as Brazil. The Portuguese established strongholds in modern-day **Angola** and **Mozambique** as well as Guinea-Bissau, Cape Verde and São Tomé and Príncipe. In the 1880s the **scramble for Africa** challenged Portuguese colonial holdings on the continent and initiated a rivalry with **Germany** which would re-emerge during **World War I**. Portugal entered the war after Germany threatened to conquer its African colonies to create German Central Africa.

During the interwar years Portugal's leader, **António de Oliveira Salazar**, viewed the African colonies as vital to the country's revival. However, the further exploitation of its colonies stimulated demands for independence. Following **World War II**, Salazar resisted demands for **decolonization**, despite the break-up of other European empires. From 1961 to 1974 Salazar fought against African independence movements in the Portuguese Colonial War. The overthrow of his fascist regime led to independence in Portugal's African colonies. Earlier, its enclave of Goa had been forcibly taken by India. The Portuguese Empire officially ended with the transfer of Macau to China in 1999.

Portuguese Revolution (1974)
– see also **Portugal**.
Initiated by a military coup on 25 April 1974 by the Movimento das Forças Armadas (MFA) led by Francisco da Costa Gomes against Marcelo Caetano, Salazar's successor, and known as the Revolution of the Carnations. Amongst political and social instability, the revolution moved to the far left, 1975, but a radical leftist coup in the army was suppressed by centrist officers, 25 November. Parliamentary elections on 25 April 1976 introduced a more moderate and stable phase.

post-feminism
– see **feminism**.

postmodernism
A comprehensive term for the large number of artistic reactions against the 'modern' movement which predominated throughout much of the twentieth century and remains a vital force, and which was characterized by its significant experimental, philosophical and theoretical elements. Modernism's leaders such as Le Corbusier in architecture, T. S. Eliot in literature or Schoenberg in music were self-consciously promoting new artistic doctrines, and some contemporary architects such as **Britain**'s Richard Rogers and **Italy**'s Renzo Piano worked in that same tradition.

Postmodernism, at least as yet, remains a series of reactions rather than a meaningful movement with its own manifesto. Insofar as it has a common thread it lies in its rejection of any artistic authority and its willingness to embrace parody, pastiche, quotation and self-reference in an eclectic manner. If it has a common quality, it lies in its frequent sense of humour – a quality in which modernism could be lacking. For its critics, it is the opposite of originality, the end of authenticity, laughing at history, self-conscious irony and even, for one, 'defecating on tradition'. The term was first used by Spanish writer Federico de Onis in 1938, and then by Arnold Toynbee in his *A Study of History*, 1938, who deemed it an irrational reaction to modernist rationalism. It came into wider use in connection with architecture in the 1970s and with painting and literature in the 1980s.

Postmodernism's leaders in architecture were Robert Venturi in America and Aldo Rossi in **Europe**, and Venturi's sardonic rejection in 1966 of Mies van der Rohe's famous formula that 'less is more' with 'less is a bore' was totemic. Venturi rejected what he saw as the 'puritanically moral language' of modernism in favour of 'elements which are hybrid rather than "pure" ... messy vitality ... richness ... rather than clarity of meaning'. Rossi argued in *L'Architettura della città*, the same year, that the city was an organic work of art, the rhythms, history and context of which had to be respected in any new architectural endeavour. This approach, with its echoes of Italian Fascist political thinking, was to be realized through a new formalism rooted in Renaissance values. Its few monuments include a controversial four-storey block of flats built at Gallaratese 2 within Milan's Monte Amiata housing development (1967–73) and the San Cataldo cemetery in Modena, designed in the 1970s. Hans Hollein's work in **Austria** and **Germany** owed much to Surrealism, but Les Espaces d'Abraxas in **France** by Ricardo Bofill of 1978–83 opted for formal, classical allusions.

The other arts were similarly wayward. Giulio Paolini's creation *L'Altra figura*, in which two faux-Grecian busts look down at their friend, a similar bust lying in pieces on the floor, typifies the postmodern approach to sculpture. The Italian, Alessandro Mendini was the king of redesign, so decorating an object that it became unrecognizable and perhaps intentionally ugly. Clothes were designed which were meant to disintegrate on the wearer within hours.

Postmodernism is perhaps too recent to evaluate but its genius for subversion may appear timely for the difficult second decade of the twenty-first century.

Potsdam Conference

The summit on the future of **Germany** held between President **Truman** of the **USA**, **Churchill** and then Attlee as prime minister of the **United Kingdom**, and **Stalin**, leader of the **Soviet Union**, at the Cecilienhof, Potsdam, outside Berlin, 17 July–2 August 1945. The conference agreed on the decartelization, demilitarization, de-Nazification and democratization of **Germany**. The arms industry and the monopolies were to be dismantled in favour of an economy devoted to peaceful purposes. The German people were to be supported in establishing a unitary, democratic state and a living standard at the level of Europe excluding Great Britain and the Soviet Union. The Oder–Neisse line was accepted, pending a peace settlement, as Germany's eastern frontier and the northern part of East Prussia including Königsberg (now Kaliningrad) transferred to the Soviet Union. Germans living in **Poland**, **Czechoslovakia** (*see* **Sudetenland**) and **Hungary** were to be transferred to Germany in an orderly manner. Germany was placed under an obligation to pay reparations, and to be treated as an economic whole. The French always resented their exclusion from the conference.

poverty, concept of
– *see* **economic development; social welfare; welfare state**.

Considerable debate has evolved over the best way to assess, define and measure poverty. Whether relative or absolute, poverty has been endemic throughout history. More interesting than measuring poverty is how different societies over time have perceived and reacted to it. Poverty existed in ancient **Greece**. Herodotus (*c.* fifth century BC) noted 'Greece has always had poverty as its companion' as it is situated in small plains surrounded by stony hills offering thin soil. Andrians bemoaned the 'poverty and helplessness' of their island home, whereas Menander's characters 'struggled with rocks that yield nothing but thyme and sage, getting nothing out of it but aches and pains'; while the Athenian tyrant Pisistratus wondered what taxes he could possibly extract from men working so thin a soil. Austere material conditions may well explain the incidence of petty crime and observations of Greeks sleeping rough on streets and in the entrances of temples, but could also account for some traits of Greek culture, specifically, their praise of frugality. Voluntary self-deprivation became a virtue in philosophy and delighted the gods. Ridicule and admiration, rather than stigma, encircled paupers.

During the Middle Ages two features can be said to characterize poverty and the poor. Firstly, the condition of poverty was one for which the poor themselves were not held individually responsible. As with wealth, poverty was seen as the result of God's grace and accepted with humility. Secondly, the poor were not equated with destitution; on the contrary they were regarded as an organic part of medieval societies, thought of as morally superior, often be welcomed to share local hospitality. Furthermore, the poor attracted the wealthy to cleanse sin from their souls through Christian charity and almsgiving.

The perception of poverty as a social pathology is modern. **Laissez-faire** and Malthusian views on rampant population growth perceived as harmful for economic progress conspired to stigmatize the poor and to ensure that relief was kept to a minimum. The advent of social Darwinism reinforced Malthusian views arguing that assisting the unfit could only delay their extinction and hinder social progress. The rise of modern welfare states has certainly alleviated poverty by means of labour legislation, unemployment insurance and housing subsidies, although stigmatization remains attached to the status of the poor.

As measured by life expectancy, infant mortality rates, health standards and general nutritional levels, it is undisputable that in modern times humanity suffers less from poverty and destitution than in previous centuries.

Prague Spring (1968)

The policy of liberalization within a **communist** framework launched by the new Czechoslovak communist leader, Alexander Dubček, as 'communism with a human face', in January 1968. Although enjoying overwhelming public support, it was suppressed by an invasion from five **Warsaw Pact** countries, involving the deaths of perhaps a hundred people, in August 1968. Led by the **Soviet Union**, the five had lacked confidence in Dubček's ability to control the situation and feared that the **Ukraine**, in particular, might follow suit.

prazos (Mozambique)

Portuguese landholdings in the Zambezi Valley originating from land grants made by the Mwenemutapa, the local ruler in the seventeenth and eighteenth centuries and subsequently regranted to the holders by the Portuguese Crown. Often held by females, they became more African in orientation over the following years and effectively independent of **Portugal**. When the Portuguese colonial government sought to reclaim the territory in the 1890s the *prazos* actively resisted until their final conquest in 1902.

Prebisch, Raul (1901–1986)

Prominent Argentine economist best known for his work with the United Nations' Economic Commission for Latin America (ECLA), where he worked in 1948–63. Prebisch argued that the structure of the free-trade world economy favoured developed countries (the 'centre') while developing countries (the 'periphery') lost ground. Thus, Latin American countries had to protect and develop their own industries from within. His ideas influenced structural economists as well as world system and dependency theorists.

Prempreh I

Nana Agymen Prempreh I, Asantehene (king) of **Ashanti** (r. 1888–1931). The last independent ruler of Ashanti whose succession was disputed and early reign was troubled by rebellion and secession movements. During his reign **Britain** attempted to extend the protectorate status they had proclaimed over the Gold Coast (coastal regions) to Ashanti. Britain supported coastal regions against his own attempts to extend his authority to the south, leading to war in 1896. As a result of the war, Prempreh was deposed and the British demanded that they be given the Golden Stool, a sacred royal symbol. Prempreh himself was arrested along with some members of the royal council and eventually exiled to the Seychelles in 1901, and Ashanti was annexed to the Gold Coast. He returned to Ashanti as a private citizen in 1924. He died the same year that Ashanti was restored as a subject kingdom under his nephew Prempreh II.

Prensa, La

Established in 1869, *La Prensa* became one of **Argentina**'s most popular national newspapers by 1900. Its conservative leanings led President **Juan Domingo Perón** to seize it in 1951. Although returned to its owners after Perón's overthrow, the paper never recovered its earlier prominence. Its conservative bent continued during and after the Dirty War (1976–83) when it published numerous articles defending the state's right to repress subversion, allegedly to save the nation from a communist takeover.

Prescott, William Hickling (1796–1859)

Of wealthy New England stock, Prescott wrote historical narratives in the romantic style. A scholarly historian, he insisted on 'impartial criticism' of sources despite never working in overseas archives. His publications on **Spain** and its empire include classic accounts of the conquests of **Mexico** and

Peru. His *History of the Conquest of Mexico* was widely read by US soldiers and citizens during the Mexican War (1846–8), although Prescott opposed the conflict.

Présence Africaine

Founded in Paris in 1947 by the Senegalese intellectual Alioune Diop, the mission of the journal *Présence Africaine* was to open a conversation between **Africa** and the West. In the first issue Diop called for contributors 'who might be able to define African originality and to hasten its introduction into the modern world'. Together with the publishing house of the same name, it provided a forum for the writers of **pan-Africanism** and the **Negritude** movement.

Presley, Elvis Aaron (1935–1977)

Singer and actor. Born Tupelo, Mississippi, Elvis's potent mix of traditional black and white musical forms, sensual movement on stage and heavily marketed commercialization led to over 1 billion record sales worldwide. The originality of his rock and roll sound atrophied while he appeared in thirty-one **Hollywood** musical films, until a revitalizing televised comeback in 1968. He became addicted to prescription drugs, eventually dying from their effects at his Graceland home. He married Priscilla Beaulieu in 1967; they were divorced in 1973. He remains an iconic figure.

Prestes, Luís Carlos (1898–1990)

Born in Rio Grande do Sul, Prestes followed a military career and led a three-year march of a rebellious force from São Paulo through the interior of southern and western **Brazil**, 1925–7. The 'Long March' of the 'Prestes Column' demonstrated the army's weaknesses and generational opposition to older politicians. Prestes returned to Brazil a Communist and was subsequently in and out of jail, hiding and exile.

Primo de Rivera, Miguel (1870–1930)

Spanish aristocrat from a military family who responded to the loss of empire and social disruption in **Spain**, and to a corruption probe against the Spanish Army, by leading a *coup d'état* in 1923 with the connivance of King Alfonso XIII, who named him prime minister shortly after. Rivera attempted to combine extreme repression through a miltary junta with the development of public infrastructure, social policies focused on the alleviation of poverty and inflationary monetary policies. Eventually, this unstable mix came apart and Rivera was forced to re-establish a parliamentary

state in 1925, though he retained the premiership. He resigned following loss of support from all sides in 1930, and died shortly afterward in Paris. His son's Falange movement was influential in the eventual dictatorship of **Francisco Franco**, though slightly distinct from it given its anti-monarchism after Alfonso turned against the de Rivera family in 1929–30.

privateers

Privateers and pirates were very similar in function, except that privateers had a patina of legality about them. A privateer was authorized by letters of marque and reprisal, issued by a European state, usually between the sixteenth and nineteenth centuries, to engage in the raiding of enemy vessels at sea. Famous privateers included Sir Francis Drake (1540–96) and Sir Henry Morgan (1635–88), both of whom were commissioned by the English to attack Spanish shipping. **Spain**, especially in the Caribbean, was the principal object of privateering attention from **Britain** or **France**, although **Bermuda** in the **American Revolutionary War** was also a place where privateers congregated, attacking American ships effectively. Privateers claimed to be acting legally because a state had licensed their activities, but if captured they were often treated as pirates. European powers often disowned privateers when it worked to their advantage, although also, as in the raids of Morgan and Drake, shared privateering profits.

privatization

A set of policies associated with the sale of public assets to, or the provision of public services by, the private sector. The phrase has some history but came to prominence in the early 1980s during the administrations of **Margaret Thatcher** in the **United Kingdom** and of David Lange in **New Zealand**. Early major privatizations began with the sale of British Telecom in 1983. This involved the sale of a public telecommunications company owned and run by the government to members of the public who were allowed to buy a limited number of shares. The company was to be regulated by an independent agency, and the idea was to transfer a liability from the state to the private sector where it could raise money whilst helping to create a share- and property-owning democracy. A second telecoms company was created and sold so that BT, as it became, would be subject to competition which would be legally allowed to share its networks. The policy became very popular and soon most of the British government's assets were broken up and sold in the same fashion. A second sort of privatization involved bringing in private companies to provide public services; a third involved the 'private finance initiative' where the government underwrote, rented and after a long time bought assets that were provided and maintained by the private sector. This kept debt off the national debt figures and borrowing down, which was seen as encouraging monetary stability. It extended to schools, prisons, hospitals and the armed forces. After the 1989 revolutions, privatization swept across the new liberal states of central and eastern Europe (though it was resisted in western Europe) and funds associated with privatized assets became a significant part of the global market.

Progressivism (USA)

A term most often applied to an American political movement of the early twentieth century, though it has had other applications in American political history. In general, Progressivism can be seen as part of the centre or left of the American political spectrum and most would agree that both major parties have had progressive wings. Progressives support the use of governmental power to limit the power of capital or businesses in order to protect the rights of individuals who are under at least a perceived threat by business (including banks). They often disagree on the amount of regulation that is appropriate, some support interference only to cure proven, long-term ills in society whilst others see a need for a structuring of American society as a European social democracy. The term has a positive connotation for most Americans, unlike 'socialism', which is widely opposed, and even 'liberalism' (which at times has been held in disrepute). For most of the twentieth century, however, significant parts of the political, journalistic, academic and legal classes identified themselves as adherents to progressivism, although they often disagreed as to what they meant by that appellation.

Progressivism was its most influential during the so-called Progressive Era, usually dated from 1901 when **Theodore Roosevelt** became president and lasting until at least 1917 when the **United States** focused on its entry into **World War I**. During this period, self-identified Progressives were a major force in federal, state and local government as well as in journalism. All three presidents of the period, Theodore Roosevelt, **William Howard Taft** and **Woodrow Wilson**, saw themselves as Progressive. Most historians would agree as to Roosevelt (who unsuccessfully ran as a third-party Progressive candidate for president in 1912)

and Wilson, but not Taft. At times those with Progressive beliefs held majorities in the House of Representatives and the Senate. They enacted progressive legislation that preserved land as national parks and forests; regulated the food, drugs and transport businesses such as railways; broke up monopolies in a wide range of businesses; limited hours of labour; introduced lower import tariffs; and established the Federal Trade Commission, the National Park Service and the Federal Reserve Board as well as passing constitutional amendments that allowed for the direct election of senators and a federal income tax. At the state and local level, Progressives passed health, safety, worker's protection, workmen's compensation and sanitation legislation.

After 1917 Progressives continued to assist in passing progressive legislation at all levels of government although they met with mixed success and some laws look unattractive today, such as immigration restrictions and miscegenation laws (that reflected the interest many Progressives had in white race 'purity'.) Senator Robert La Follette of Wisconsin ran for the presidency as another third party Progressive candidate in 1924, and former Vice President Henry A. Wallace also ran in 1948 as the presidential candidate of a Progressive Party. The Progressive Parties of 1912, 1924 and 1948 were different from each other but tapped into common themes of reform in the United States.

Prohibition era

The movement to prohibit the manufacture, sale and consumption of alcohol, wine and beer in the **United States** has its origins in the dissenting churches of colonial America. Many dissenters believed that alcohol interfered with one's ability to accept Jesus Christ as one's Saviour and encouraged the sin of idleness. In the 1830s the average personal consumption of alcohol was estimated at over 7 gallons a year. Fears of an 'alcoholic republic' led Maine to become the first state to ban alcohol in 1851 and twelve other states followed by 1855. After the civil war, the movement was led by women in the Women's Christian Temperance Union (founded 1874) and the Anti-Saloon League (founded 1893). They argued that alcohol was a threat to the family and American morality, and paraded and occasionally committed acts of violence against property in saloons to promote their cause. They were often supported by businessmen who wanted a reliable, sober workforce and opposed by immigrants who came from countries such as **Germany**, **Italy** and **Russia** where alcohol was a more integral part of the culture.

Twenty-one of the forty-eight states had banned saloons by 1916 and average alcohol consumption had fallen. With US involvement in **World War I**, Congress brought in prohibition as a war measure and also passed a constitutional amendment to ban it in peacetime too. The requisite three-quarters of the states ratified it and the amendment came into effect in January 1920. In many traditionally dry parts of the country, nothing changed. Advocates argued that with the widespread public support, enforcement costs would be low. Consumption did fall but by how much is unclear. Doctors reported fewer alcohol-related diseases. But it rapidly became clear that the lengthy American borders and coastline were porous as bootleggers imported alcohol, urban officials, police and government revenue agents were easily bribed, and the exceptions for medical uses and the sacraments were exploited heavily.

Still the majority of the country saw little of these problems first hand so that as late as 1928, the prohibitionist (or 'dry') candidate, the Republican **Herbert Hoover**, defeated the 'wet' candidate, the Democrat Al Smith, by a very wide margin in an election where prohibition was a central issue. After shocking events that showed the power of organized crime in the illegal alcohol trade, such as the St Valentine's Day massacre of 1929, and the beginning of the Great Depression that year, the public increasingly believed that the law was unenforceable, that the economic collapse was a more important issue, and that prohibition was an infringement on personal liberties. In 1931 the Wickersham Report admitted all the alleged problems but still supported prohibition. The Association Against the Prohibition Amendment demanded action and got it. The constitution was again amended in 1933, this time to repeal the previous amendment. Some states chose to remain 'dry' as late as 1966. Today thirty-three states allow local option and nineteen of those have over 500 municipalities that are dry.

proletariat

Derived from Latin word *proles*, meaning 'offspring', this is a term used to identify a lower social class, and a member of such a class is a proletarian. In Rome it identified those people who were poor landless freemen and small traders impoverished by the extension of slavery. The term was used in a derogatory way, until **Karl Marx** adopted it as a sociological concept to refer to the working class.

propaganda

Messages aimed at shaping the opinion, beliefs or behaviour of people, rather than simply providing information. Propaganda appeals to the emotions and is used in religion, politics and the marketing of products and services. Evidence that such techniques were used even in Roman times exists, but it was not until shortly after the Thirty Years War that Pope Gregory XV founded a committee to oversee the propagation of Christianity by missionaries sent to non-Catholic countries called the Roman Catholic Sacred Congregation for the Propagation of Faith, or Sacra Congregatio Christiano Nomini Propagando. **Industrialization** led to mass marketing, before studies of consumer behaviour explored consumers' reactions to alternative kinds of shops, packaging and publicity. Today, a substantial share of 'information' transmitted through the media is publicity for different commodities and services and the incessant process of advertising is monitored and regulated more or less effectively.

During **World War II** Nazi Germany used propaganda (especially associated with Goebbels) as a weapon against the Allies and earlier President **Woodrow Wilson** contracted Walter Lipmann and Edward Barneys to participate in the Creel Commission's campaign to gain support for the **USA** entry into the war against **Germany**. Propaganda campaigns, and the complementary activity, censorship, in the form of information control or news management, continued during the **Cold War** and still remains an important and specialized activity for states to pursue. Propaganda, misinformation and management of information on behalf of states, other organizations as well as private companies have developed rapidly and extensively during the past half-century, evolving industries of public relations and advertisement.

prostitution

The exchange of money for sex is both longstanding and almost universal, but it has been the target of social purity movements within the Christian tradition since the Reformation, citing injunctions against non-procreational sexual activity. Male intercourse and homosexual activity was a crime in English and American common law until the twentieth century, while female prostitution was hedged around with offences such as soliciting or living off immoral earnings which, while not making prostitution itself illegal, often criminalized prostitutes. Nonetheless, large capital cities such as London and Paris had tens of thousands of prostitutes in the eighteenth and nineteenth centuries, including poor women forced into casual prostitution, brothels which advertised their 'wares' in print, and high-class courtesans publicly acknowledged as such. Social purity movements in America and social reformers in **Europe** from the nineteenth century aimed to reform prostitutes and eliminate it as a 'social evil'. In Victorian England, Liberal Prime Minister **William Gladstone** took to the streets to 'reclaim' prostitutes, and child prostitution in 1880s London was exposed by the journalist W. T. Stead (1849–1912), leading to the rise in the age of consent. Prostitution remained commonplace in most parts of the world and was effectively legal in many European countries. The rise of women's movements in the late nineteenth and twentieth centuries ensured that the issue remained live, but was complicated with the rise of the feminist movement from the 1960s, which claimed that women who chose to had the right to sell sex. Hence, some countries such as **Germany** and **Sweden** have chosen to legalize brothels, while the sale of sexual favours has been made illegal in France and keeping a brothel is still technically illegal in the **United Kingdom** and some American states. Particular aspects of prostitution have attracted concern within the context of **human rights**. The forced prostitution of so-called 'comfort women', mainly from **Korea** and **Manchuria**, to serve the Japanese armed forces in **World War II** and the similar treatment of Bosnian Muslim women in the post-**Yugoslavia** civil war period 1991–5 have gained notoriety, as have concerns about human trafficking of women and children as sex workers, and the issue of 'sex tourism', particularly where associated with child prostitution in poor countries.

protectionism

An economic system under which imported products are taxed or prohibited in such a fashion that domestically produced goods become competitive or replace the imports. Protectionism tends to raise prices for consumers but is often held to guarantee the jobs of producers and the income streams from production. Developing economies have at various times used different devices, from import bans to currency manipulation, for protectionist ends. The policy runs the risk that other economies will reciprocate, that the efficient allocation of resources will be diminished, and that a lack of competition creates stagnation and a lower standard of living. Protectionism in the **United States**, in the form of the Smoot–Hawley tariff of 1930, is often held to have precipitated or deepened the **Great Depression**. In the early twenty-first century, it was mostly apparent in agriculture, being generally illegal under regional trade agreements and the rules of the World Trade Organization. Protectionist sentiment resurfaced in the second decade of the twenty-first century.

Protestantism

A generic term for forms of Christian belief that date themselves from the reformed religion that emerged from Martin Luther's protests against the Catholic Church of 1517. Protestant Churches typically elevate the Christian Bible to the level of revealed religion, accessible in the language of the reader and divinely inspired. Many not only reject the authority of the **Papacy** but of bishops (though some claim a reformed and renovated attachment to the apostolic tradition from which they believe Rome diverged in corruption during the Middle Ages). The Protestant churches also tend to reject the Catholic ideas of sacramentalism, celibate priesthood and supranational religious allegiance, but tend towards a great deal of diversity in their organization. Over time, Protestantism developed a distinctive moral calculus as a genre, which has been remarked on by many sociologists. Protestants, for instance, were associated with individual standards which did not brook the compromise of their faith or the idea of human frailty and sin. They were associated with a strong 'work ethic' (a term often synonymous with Protestant) and with standards of public openness, debate and political behaviour which contrasted with supposedly closed, hierarchical and sensual or corrupt Catholic models. Protestantism split soon after it emerged in different churches and organizations which contributed to this diversity. At the most extreme, Protestants who followed John Calvin (a great many of whom can be found in the **USA**) elevate both the literal idea of the Bible as containing absolute truth – a Qur'anic reading of a Christian text which has been through multiple revisions and that contains dozens of separate books – and the predestinarian idea that only some people were 'saved' to be righteous before their birth, the rest destined for damnation.

Part of the genius of this extreme form of Protestantism, however, was that nobody knew whether they were saved or damned, and God's favour was expressed by social respect, success in life and righteous behaviour – a combination of circumstances the attainment of which might drive an individual without rest or indulgence. Other forms of Protestantism retained bishops and held that salvation could be attained by good works, and also frequently assimilated to the nation state through the medium of national churches which were either established or nationally recognized in most countries where the plurality of the people, or at least the monied classes, were themselves Protestant. The greatest example of this latter 'Arminian' form of Protestantism is based around the Church of England, established in 1533 in defiance of the Church of Rome and possessed of the English monarch as its head. Members of the Church of England style themselves 'Anglicans' or 'Episcopalians' and, partly because they claim attachment to a catholic (but not Roman Catholic) tradition, maintain a worldwide 'Anglican Communion' and have close links with the Orthodox Churches. From the late 1990s, Anglicans became embroiled in a worldwide debate between Christians in the third world who were intolerant of the sexual and social practices of the West and those in **Europe** and America who supported the idea of openly homosexual priests and bishops and female clergy.

A third branch – Pentecostalism – is characterized by openness to the 'holy spirit' (not recognized as part of the godhead but still seen as an aspect of God), the charismatic influence of individual preachers, and itinerant revivalism associated with public displays of expression, conversion, immersion in cleansing water and public healing.

There is no characteristic liturgy upon which all Protestants agree, nor any clear attitude towards music, dance, women, indulgence, alcohol, sin, sexuality, nationalism, socialism, race, doctrine or any other point in relation to which a catholic or orthodox position can be discerned. In consequence, styles of Protestantism in the late twentieth and early twenty-first century became recognizable in terms of rituals, styles of preaching and social associations as well as evangelical and Bible-based approaches involving charismatic believers and practices rather than any one tradition.

Prussia

Early eighteenth-century Prussia was divided into two separate parts: East Prussia and Brandenburg. Frederick I (1688–1713) secured the title of king, 1701. His son, **Frederick William I**, acquired much of western Pomerania (1720) and his grandson, **Frederick the Great**, acquired first Silesia and then (Polish) West Prussia. Following the vicissitudes of the **Napoleonic Wars**, the **Congress of Vienna**, 1815, awarded Prussia substantial new territories. In addition to recovering Danzig, it gained what

became Prussian Saxony, the provinces of the Rhine and Westphalia, and more of Pomerania together with part of the Saar under the Peace of Paris, 1815. Prussia stretched continuously from the Neman (Niemen) to the Elbe and on, discontinuously, to the Rhine. Under **Bismarck**, it united **Germany** as an empire in 1871, with its king as emperor (*kaiser*). The province was, however, abolished by the Allies in 1947, as a symbol of militarism.

Pruth, Russian defeat at (1711)

Following the Turkish declaration of war on Russia, 1710, in the middle of the **Great Northern War**, **Peter the Great** marched into Ottoman Moldavia through Bessarabia, 1711, but found himself surrounded on the River Pruth (Prut) by numerically superior forces. He was obliged to make peace although on very light terms: he only had to surrender the coastal fortress of Azov, which he had captured in the war of 1695–6.

psychoanalysis

A form of therapy based on Freudian ideas. Psychoanalysis held that the troubles and tensions of individuals were a consequence of neurosis. This was a trauma associated with stages in the development of the individual as a child which were so unbearable that the later adult would be 'protected' from them by the existence of an unconscious, which, though motivating and inspiring their actions, would be hidden from their quotidien perceptions. By talking, playing word association games or communicating in states of hypnotic or chemical relaxation (during which pressure could at the discretion of a therapist be applied to the head of the analysand) an individual could be placed 'in touch' with their unconscious trauma. This trauma could then be identified, tied to early and arrested desires for bodily control, sexual fears or maternal feeding practices, and eliminated, leaving a well-balanced individual. Frequently, sociologists and commentators expanded what were perceived as insights from the psychoanalysis of individuals to social criticism and even to the description of policy.

Psychoanalysis was associated with rich and urban western areas, and in particular New York. It was frequently expensive, cures were not guaranteed and the process was often drawn out over years. Jungian therapists also denied that the unconscious was necessarily a source of trauma, and, as physiological and biological science improved in the later twentieth century, many began to see psychoanalysis as a coping strategy for the mind rather than a cure for agitation or cognitive difficulties best addressed by treating the brain or adapting behaviour to personality. Attachment theory, which very much influenced childcare, was associated with Freudian and psychoanalytic models, especially under the influence of trained psychoanalysts such as John Bowlby.

psychology

A social science which holds that it is possible by experiment and other scientific methods to develop rules about human cognition, behaviour, motivation and interaction which may be generally applied in a diagnostic or therapeutic sense. Psychology as a discipline is often closely associated with psychiatry, a medical offshoot. Both disciplines developed in the late nineteenth and twentieth centuries and were very influenced by **Freud** and Jung. Psychological establishments vary between states but the discipline is typically upheld by professional bodies and, in the case of psychiatry, requires medical training before an individual is allowed to practice. Some individuals, particularly some of those associated with religion but also those who point to the tenuousness, biological functionalism, faith in unproven forms of pharmacological sedation, or the sexual focus of many psychological theories, are very hostile to the psychological enterprise. Many social theorists and historians became interested in the way psychologists controlled the definition of the 'mad' in the twentieth century, and noted and employed the terminology of the profession. In particular, Freudian and Jungian terms had passed into everyday speech by the 1970s.

public lands (USA)

Public lands are those held in trust for the nation by the federal government. Located predominantly in the twelve farthest western states, they belong to various categories (including national forests and national parks) that serve the interests of resource extraction, conservation and recreation. Constituting 30 per cent of US territory, they represent what remains after much of the public domain was privatized. The most restrictive designation is 'wilderness' while Bureau of Land Management holdings are most permissive.

public sphere

The concept of the public sphere was first used by German philosopher Jürgen Habermas (1929–)

in *The Structural Transformation of the Public Sphere: An Inquiry into a Category of Bourgeois Society* (1962). Habermas appeared on the German intellectual scene in the 1950s thanks to an influential critique of Martin Heidegger. He had been working under the supervision of critical theorists Max Horkheimer and Theodor Adorno and in 1961 became a *privatdozent* in Marburg. In 1964 he returned to Frankfurt to take Horkheimer's chair in philosophy and sociology. He later moved to the Max Planck Institute as a director and during the twelve years he spent there he published his major work: *The Theory of Communicative Action*. In 1983 he returned to Frankfurt and finally retired in 1993. In 1986 he was awarded the highest honour in German research, the Gottfried Wilhelm Leibniz Prize of the Deutsche Forschungsgemeinschaft.

In *The Public Sphere: An Encyclopedia Article*, Habermas defines the public sphere as 'a realm of our social life in which something approaching public opinion can be formed. Access is guaranteed to all citizens. A portion of the public sphere comes into being in every conversation in which private individuals assemble to form a public body.' According to Habermas, 'public sphere' is a concept that contrasts with the private sphere, and is part of life in which one is interacting with others and with society at large. Basing his analysis on accounts of dialogues that took place in coffeehouses in eighteenth-century **France**, Habermas highlighted the fact that matters of political importance were being discussed in a public sphere. This became possible due to the development of bourgeois culture centred around coffeehouses and literary salons, and in print media. The outcome was parliamentary democracy. Eventually, structural forces, particularly the development of commercial mass media, undermined this bourgeois public sphere because even though media became much more widespread, it came under weaker scrutiny from the general public. According to Habermas, commercial mass media narrowed the channels through which a network for communicating information and points of view could be transformed into public opinion and influence states. In his view, the development of capitalist economies led to inequalities, limited access and eventually political control of the public sphere. Despite many criticisms that the idea of the public sphere is no longer relevant, the Internet has given it a provenance and some argue that it can emulate the political discussions that took place in early bourgeois societies. However, the Internet is sometimes viewed as too decentralized to play this role and unlikely to create identity, an essential element for the public sphere.

Puerto Rico

Puerto Rico is the smallest of the Greater Antilles with a population of around 4 million. Claimed by **Spain** after Columbus' second voyage in 1493, it remained one of Spain's last New World possessions until it was ceded to the **USA** following the Spanish–American War in 1898. Early gold mining, the death of almost all its native Taino population, African slavery (not abolished until 1873) and sugar production were major features of its Spanish period. Puerto Ricans became US citizens in 1917, have elected their own governor since 1948, and have had internal self-government under a constitution since 1952. They have rejected US statehood, but faced mounting financial problems, they are reconsidering this option.

Punjab

The Punjab is an area in the Indus basin of the Indian subcontinent comprised of the inter-riverine tracts of the Indus, Jhelum, Chenab, Ravi, Beas and Sutlej rivers. The area has historically served as a crossroads for east–west and north–south trade routes, which carried goods between **India** and the Near East and from Punjab south through Sind to access Indian Ocean trade. Much of the area came under the control of the Ghaznavid Empire at the beginning of the second millennium, and was subsequently incorporated into the Delhi sultanate (1206–1526) and then the **Mughal Empire** (1526–1858). The province was incorporated into the British colonial state in 1849, and was divided between India and **Pakistan** in 1947. Punjabis are the inhabitants of this area, and speak the Punjabi language. They are Hindu, Muslim, Christian and Sikh. Sikhs have a special relationship to the region as it is the birthplace of their religion and houses their holiest sites (such as Amritsar).

purges

An occasional activity of totalitarian governments in which officeholders and members of the security forces are removed from their jobs or party status because of a perceived or actual deviation from the government line. Purges have sometimes involved the reassignment of individuals to hard or isolated labour, and occasionally mass murder. They had a secondary function of creating a culture of fear and dependence on the leader or leadership which initiated them that tended to prevent the creation of alternate power centres or networks of resistance. In the Soviet purges of the 1930s, carried out under **Joseph Stalin**'s direction, over 1.5 million people were 'purged' from the governmental and military institutions, and often executed or removed from photographs, documents and memorials. Purges did not necessarily advance the state's purposes in general; Stalin's so-called 'great purge' of the late 1930s is often held to have dangerously weakened Soviet defences in the face of the German assault in 1941, for instance. **Hitler**, **Mao Zedong**, **Chiang Kai-shek** and a host of lesser individuals, such as **Pol Pot** in **Cambodia** and **Saddam Hussein** in **Iraq**, also engaged in the practice. Often, purges accompanied repressive economic or political measures, such as the Holodomor in the **Ukraine** or the **Cultural Revolution** in **China**, which had the added effect of killing millions more.

Putin, Vladimir (1952–)

Authoritarian Russian leader. The most powerful figure in post-Soviet **Russia**, alternating as prime minister (2008–12) and president (2000–8, 2012–). His nationalistic foreign policy supported pro-Russian rebels in the **Ukraine**, the annexation of Crimea and intervention in the **Syrian Civil War**. At home, political opposition was suppressed and state terror employed against dissidents. The ailing economy faced sanctions from the West, a collapsing oil price and long-term problems of population decline.

Q

Qadiriyya

A Sufi order. The first organized order in West Africa was the Qadiriyya-Mukhtariyya of Sidi Mukhtar al-Kunti (d. 1811). **Usuman dan Fodio** was also linked to the Qadiriyya. In East Africa, 'Uways al-Barawi spread the Qadiriyya to **Zanzibar** and beyond in the 1880s. The Qadiriyya is challenged by the Tijaniyya in the west and Shadhiliyya in the east, but remains a major order in sub-Saharan Africa, while it is smaller in the Maghreb.

Qaddafi, Colonel Muammar, al-

—see **Gaddafi, Colonel Muammar, al-**.

Qajar dynasty (Iran)

Iranian ruling dynasty, 1794–1925, succeeding the Safavid Empire, which had disintegrated in 1722, and the intervening rule of **Nadir Shah** and the Zand dynasty of **Karim Khan Zand**. Established by **Agha Muhammad Khan** of the Turkmen Qajar tribe, whose chieftains had become prominent in Iranian affairs following the disintegration of Safavid rule. Muhammad Khan dated his reign from 1779 but was not dominant in northern Iran until 1785 when **Tehran** was made the capital. He reconquered **Georgia** in 1795, running the risk of Russian intervention as it had been under Russian protection since the 1783 Treaty of Georgievsk, and finally reasserted central control over Khorasan, 1796. Although his period of rule saw the transformation of Tehran from a village to a town, his tight control of the exchequer and numerous wars were highly damaging to the Iranian economy. It was the misfortune of his successor, **Fath 'Ali Shah**, to reign during a period when the rivalry between **France**, **Great Britain** and **Russia**, focused on the **Eastern Question**, was at its height. Russia formally annexed Georgia in 1801. The French under **Napoleon** were primarily interested in using **Iran** and Russia as allies in Napoleon's projected invasion of British India. When Franco-Russian relations deteriorated, the British priority became reconciliation with Russia and their influence employed in favour of a Russo-Iranian settlement, which in practice meant subordinating Iranian to Russian interests. By 1828 and the treaties first of Gulistan and then of **Turkmanchai**, the Qajars had lastingly forfeited Iranian rule over northern **Azerbaijan** and **Armenia** as well as over Georgia.

Nevertheless, the Qajars continued to feel that the historically Iranian regions of Transcaucasia and **Afghanistan** were rightly theirs and sought to play the mutually suspicious British and Russians off against one another, but had to recognize that the British had no interest in helping them to recover Transcaucasia from the Russians. The British also opposed Iranian ambitions in Afghanistan, preferring the existing Afghan state which posed no threat to their position in India. **Nasir al Din**'s capture of Herat in 1856 was, therefore, as abortive as **Muhammad 'Ali Shah**'s expedition against the city had been in 1837 and for the same reason. Nasir al Din's domestic initiatives were, however, more positive if restricted in scope. Their limitations were underlined by the revolution of 1906 and the Anglo-Russian agreement of 31 August 1907. Under that agreement each power had a zone within which its own subjects might seek economic concessions to the exclusion of the subjects of any other power. The 'partition', which was not enforceable, gave the whole of northern Iran to Russia and the southeast to Britain, with the south and south-west being neutral.

The two last Qajar sovereigns, Mohammad 'Ali Shah (1907–9) and Ahmad Shah (1909–25), proved equally ineffective and Ahmad Shah was sidelined by Reza Khan in a *coup d'état* 1921. The Qajar dynasty was formally deposed, 1925, to be succeeded by Reza Khan's own **Pahlavi dynasty** until 1979. The Qajar sovereigns had proved essentially impotent as the viability of their regime and of Iranian institutions had crumbled under the impact of **Europe**, and had failed to embrace the constitutionalism introduced in 1906 which was to outlast them.

Qassem, Colonel Abdul Karim (1914–1963)

Iraqi military officer and leader of the 1958 revolution that overthrew the **Hashemite** monarchy.

He became the first president of the Republic of **Iraq** from 1958 until he was killed in the **Ba'ath Party** *coup d'état* in 1963. From a modest background, the son of a mixed Arab–Kurdish marriage, during his reign he established a personal military dictatorship not allowing elections to take place in the new republic. He withdrew Iraq from the **Baghdad Pact** and established closer ties with the **Soviet Union** and Eastern bloc states and his economic policies followed suit. Though he was an ardent Arab nationalist, Qassem was ambivalent about the Egyptian President **Nasser's** **pan-Arabism** and refused to join the newly formed Egyptian–Syrian **United Arab Republic**. He initially sought to bring about more Kurdish representation in the Iraqi government but eventually the 1961–3 Kurdish rebellion proved difficult to control and costly for his regime.

Qatar

Arab Muslim emirate in eastern Arabia ruled by the Al Thani family since the 1860s with its capital at Doha. The Al Khalifah family exercised nominal control over Qatar in the late eighteenth century, but that ended with a September 1868 treaty between **Great Britain** and the tribes of Qatar. The peninsula briefly fell under Ottoman influence but became independent under British protection with the November 1916 treaty between Great Britain and Sheikh Abdallah ibn Qasim Al Thani. Full independence came in September 1971. Historically, the peninsula's harsh environment limited economic activities to pearl fishing and camel husbandry, but oil exports in 1949 and subsequent natural gas discoveries greatly improved economic prospects. Despite massive oil revenues, the country lagged behind both economically and politically under Sheikh Khalifah ibn Hamad Al Thani, and his son Hamad ibn Khalifah deposed him in 1995. Sheikh Hamad initiated major economic and political reforms. Under the present ruler relations with Saudi Arabia reached new lows in 2017.

Qianlong Emperor (1711–1799)

The Qianlong Emperor was a **Qing** dynasty ruler who reigned 1736–95, during a period that is considered to be part of China's golden age. He expanded the Chinese Empire to include Xinjiang, and brought **Myanmar**, **Nepal** and **Vietnam** into the tribute system. He also sponsored scholarship and ordered the compilation of an encyclopedia. At the end of his reign, he received missions from **Britain's** Lord MacCartney, but refused to lift restrictions on trade.

Qing dynasty (1644–1911)

The Qing dynasty is the name given to the Manchu rulers of **China**, an ethnic group from the north in **Manchuria** who formed the last dynasty in the country. In 1644 an army from Manchu entered Peking (Beijing) and established the dynasty, although revolts from rebels loyal to the Ming continued until 1681. Under the three great Qing emperors Kangxi (1661–1722), Yongzheng (1723–36) and **Qianlong**, who reigned 1736–95, China enjoyed great prosperity. The emperors adopted a civil exam system, patronized scholarship, expanded the Chinese Empire to include **Tibet** and much of modern-day Xinjiang, and brought **Myanmar** and **Vietnam** into the Chinese tributary system. However, Han Chinese were forced to wear their hair long and Han–Manchu intermarriage was forbidden. In the nineteenth century later Qing emperors faced internal rebellions and foreign threats, which contributed to the fall of the dynasty during the Chinese revolution of 1911.

Quadros, Janio da Silva (1917–1992)

President of **Brazil**. Born in Mato Grosso, Quadros became São Paulo's mayor in 1953 and the state's governor in 1955. A populist running against corruption, he won the presidency of Brazil in 1960, but faced the economic crisis left by his free-spending predecessor, **Juscelino Kubitschek**. Thinking Congress would reject his stabilization plan, he abruptly resigned, apparently believing it would grant him extraordinary authority. Instead, Congress accepted his resignation and **João Goulart** became president.

Quakers

Otherwise known as the Society of Friends (from *c.*1800), Quakers are a religious group founded by George Fox (1624–91). Originating from the radical religious ferment which followed the English Civil Wars (1642–6 and 1648–9), they were organized as a distinctive Christian group in 1668. Extensively persecuted for their anti-hierarchical views, many sought emigration and in 1682 William Penn founded Pennsylvania on a Quaker basis. During the eighteenth century they came to regard themselves as a 'peculiar people', adopting distinctive dress and speech while actively pursuing trade and philanthropic activities such as prison reform. Gradually, the removal of their peculiarities of dress and speech made the Quakers less distinctive. Their theology stresses the 'Inner Light', which was deemed superior to the Scriptures and the Church and therefore rejected the Sacraments, the ministry and all set forms of worship. They have remained active reformers promoting philanthropy and pacifism. Many members refused military service in the wars of the twentieth century, for which some were killed in Nazi Germany, though elsewhere they were allowed to become conscientious objectors.

Quebec

Founded by Samuel de Champlain in 1608 to facilitate the French trade in furs with the Iroquois and Algonkin peoples, Quebec was the first French colony in the Americas and later became a permanent French settlement. Captured by the British during the **Seven Years War**, along with the Caribbean island of Guadeloupe, the French ceded Quebec to the British in exchange for having Guadeloupe restored to **France** in the Treaty of Paris that ended the war. In the twentieth century Quebec separatism became an important force.

Quemoy

–*see* **Mazu and Jinmen; Taiwan.**

Quezón, Manuel Luis (1878–1944)

The first president of the Philippine Commonwealth, who held office between 1935 and 1944. He promoted Tagalog as a Philippine national language, attempted agrarian reform and attacked corruption whilst standing close to the **USA.** This latter point is not surprising given his time as a non-voting representative in Washington DC between 1909 and 1916. Quezón pursued Christian Democratic ideas and policies when in office. He died in New York, of tuberculosis, and his remains were repatriated in 1979.

quilombo (mocambo)

Fugitive slaves who established communities in **Brazil** by the 1580s. Initially called *mocambos*, they were known as *quilombos* in the eighteenth century. They offered runaways sustenance and refuge, and in some cases tried to recreate the village life of **Africa**. All ten significant *quilombos* were destroyed, seven within two years of their founding. The largest, with as many as 30,000 residents, and longest lasting was Palmares, established by 1606 and destroyed in the mid 1690s.

Quit India movement

Set amidst the tensions of **World War II** and fears of a Japanese attack on **India, Mahatma Gandhi** drafted the resolution calling for the British to quit India in April 1942. Congress adopted the resolution on 8 August 1942. Gandhi believed that if the British were to leave India, the

Japanese would have no reason to invade thus saving the country from the devastating consequences of war. The top leadership of Congress were all imprisoned as soon as the Quit India resolution was passed, leaving lower-ranking Congress leaders to carry on the movement. Led by students and workers in the urban areas, it was repressed within a month but by late September 1942 it had spread across India, mainly to Bihar, the eastern United Provinces, western Bengal, Orissa and parts of Bombay province. Here large crowds of peasants attacked symbols of British authority such as revenue offices, railway lines, post offices and telegraph lines.

Qutb, Sayyid (1906–1966)

The most radical and controversial of the twentieth-century Islamic thinkers. Born in rural Upper **Egypt** and in his youth already a critic of specialist religious education, he received a British-style education, Cairo, 1929–33, becoming a teacher, author and literary critic, helping to promote the work of **Naguib Mahfouz**. He joined the Ministry of Education in 1939, but was appalled by a two-year visit to the **United States** in the late 1940s for further studies in educational administration, finding the US materialistic, racist, superficial and artistically primitive. Possibly a repressed homosexual, he was shocked by the relations between the sexes, which he considered depraved. He was later to claim that he never found a woman of sufficient 'moral purity and discretion' to marry. On his return to Egypt he joined the **Muslim Brotherhood**, becoming editor of its weekly journal, *al-Ikhwan al-Muslimin*, and then head of the Brothers' propaganda division. Welcomed the **Egyptian Revolution of 1952**, and consulted by **Nasser** until the hope of the Brotherhood that he would establish an Islamic government was disappointed. He then participated in the failed Brotherhood plot to assassinate Nasser, 1954, for which he was imprisoned for ten years. While in prison he wrote his two most important works, the thirty-volume Qur'anic commentary *Fi Zilal al-Qur'an* (*In the Shade of the Qur'an*) and the manifesto for political Islam, *Ma'alim fi-l-Tariq* (*Milestones*). Rearrested in August 1965, he was accused of plotting to overthrow the state, with many of the charges based on the text of *Milestones*, which he strongly defended in court. He was found guilty of participation in the assassination plot and hanged.

Qutb's mature philosophy marked a move away from his early more secularist inclinations. He found his early ideas incompatible with man's ability to accept knowledge from what he described as the imperceptible, an ability which distinguished man from animal. The secular mind, in his opinion, could never appreciate the power and danger of ignorance (*jahilliya*), and so-called 'progressive thought' was actually regressive. Like most Muslim reformers, he urged a return to the perceived purity of early Islam but went further in rejecting the schools of jurisprudence, all of which were later. Despite his dismissal of Marxism as contrary to human nature, there were nevertheless some parallels in his political philosophy, notably the concept of the withering away of the state, just as there were echoes of European anarchism and Leninist concepts of the revolutionary vanguard. The Qur'an should be approached as a means of changing society by substituting personal servitude to Allah for obedience to rulers, whether democratic, dictatorial or theocratic, for they and their agents were a violation of Allah's sovereignty (*Hakamiyya*) over his creation. All current Muslim governments were therefore heretical. The new freedom demanded the creation of a vanguard to defeat ignorance by preaching and practising offensive not defensive **jihad** throughout the Muslim and non-Muslim worlds alike.

There were also European echoes in his perception of a Jewish conspiracy to dominate the world through usury and deceit and the allegation that Jews were behind materialism, animal sexuality, the destruction of the family and the dissolution of society, two of the principal offenders being **Marx** and **Freud**. It was his conclusion in *Milestones*

that anything non-Islamic was evil and corrupt, and that total obedience to sharia would bring every benefit to humanity including appreciation of the beauty and harmony of creation. Indeed, the more people learned about nature, the more peaceful and harmonious their relationship with nature and the environment would be. Any notion of 'conquering nature' thus betrayed ignorance of the spirit and wisdom with which it had been created.

Qutb's works have since been much admired by some Muslims but also strongly criticized by others of both conservative and reformist views. They also appear to have influenced the ideology of **al-Qaida**, responsible for the **September 11th** attacks.

Quwalti, Shukri al- (1892–1967)

Shukri al-Quwalti, the first president of **Syria**, was elected in 1943. Born in Damascus, he rose to political importance during the period of the French mandate. Elected to lead the National Bloc in 1940, of which he had been a long-time party member, he went on to become the president before being ousted by a number of coups in 1949. Quwalti lived in exile for many years in **Egypt**. During his years of exile, Syria went through turbulent times, with one coup after another trying to take control of the government. In 1955, Quwalti returned from exile and was once again elected president. One of the instigators of the Union Pact with Egypt in 1958, he helped to initiate the establishment of the **United Arab Republic**. He died in Lebanon.

R

Rabat conference (1974)

Conference of the leaders of twenty **Arab League** states and representatives of the **Palestinian Liberation Organization (PLO)** in Rabat, Morocco, in October 1974. A final declaration affirmed the right of the Palestinian people to establish an independent national homeland under their own authority on land liberated from Israeli control. The Arab states unanimously acceded to the PLO's demand for recognition as the 'sole legitimate representative' of the Palestinian people and promised financial aid to states confronting Israel and to the PLO. The PLO representatives had threatened to boycott proceedings if their demands for recognition were not met. The decision represented a setback both for King **Hussein** of **Jordan**, who gave up his claim to represent the interests of the Palestinians, and for **Israel** and the **United States**, both of which preferred the prospect of dealing with Jordan rather than the PLO in future **Middle East** peace negotiations.

Rabin, Yitzhak (1922–1995)

Israeli chief of staff, 1964–8, and prime minister, 1974–7 and 1992–5. Rabin commanded a brigade of **Haganah** in 1943–8. In June 1948, on **Ben-Gurion**'s direct orders, he supervised the destruction of the ship *Altalena* on the Tel Aviv beach front. As army chief of staff during the **Six Day War**, he can be considered an architect of the Israeli victory in the June 1967 war. In 1968 he became ambassador to Washington. He succeeded **Golda Meir** as Labour prime minister, 1974–7. He left office under a cloud of financial impropriety involving his wife's breach of international currency regulations. In 1984 he returned to politics as defence minister in the Labour–**Likud** rotating coalition. As Labour prime minister from 1992 until his assassination by a right-wing Israeli in 1995, Rabin was responsible for the peace treaty with **Jordan** and for extended negotiations with **Palestine Liberation Organization**'s **Yassir Arafat**, which resulted in the September 1983 **Oslo Accords**. Many streets in Israel and the square in downtown Tel Aviv where he was assassinated perpetuate his memory.

race and ethnicity

The abuse of the concept of race, by Nazi Germany in particular on the one hand and by white imperialists and supremacists on the other, has brought the very term into such disrepute that 'ethnicity' is now often preferred. Some liberals even doubt whether race is a meaningful concept; others have called racism a disease. Any discussion of race must, therefore, ask first what it means from an objective, scientific perspective, and second what Europeans have thought it meant. Some six to ten historic geographic races are generally recognized by scientists, including the following:

1. African race of sub-Saharan Africa
2. European race of Europe, North Africa and the Middle East
3. Asiatic race of central, east and south-east Asia and western Alaska
4. American Indian race of the Americas, other than western Alaska
5. Indian race of that sub-continent
6. Australian race (the Australian aborigines)
7. Polynesian race of the Pacific islands including Easter Island, Hawaii and New Zealand
8. Micronesian race of Guam and other islands, which has continuities with the Polynesian
9. Melanesian race of New Guinea, which has continuities with the Australian

Such geographic races are, of course, essentially historic. Modern Australia is self-evidently populated essentially by settlers of European stock, not by aboriginal Australians, who number only around 250,000 of the 20 million population. Although *Homo sapiens* is almost certainly a single species, some experts have speculated controversially on whether some of the skeletal and biochemical differences between the geographic races might not even pre-date the emergence of *Homo sapiens* as a species some 150,000–100,000 years ago. Some of the differences between the geographic races are visible to the naked eye, but others, which are medically often more important, are not. Blood group B, for example, is common amongst sub-Saharan Africans, far less common amongst Europeans, and absent amongst American Indians.

Within these historic geographic races, scientists can identify local races. Modern Spaniards and Swedes, for example, share, as members of the European geographic race, characteristics such as 'white' skin, fairly narrow high-bridged noses, wavy to straight hair and a tendency towards the Rh-negative blood type. The Spaniard, however, as a member of the Mediterranean local race, will tend to have more in common with an Italian than either will have with the Swede, such as smaller stature and darker hair and complexion. Although **Europe**'s local races blend into each other, their centres remain distinct for social and political reasons. An even smaller classification is a micro-race, which can evolve when a population is isolated geographically or socially.

These biological differences between races are real, but they are also fluid because they are the result of ongoing evolution. However distinct a race may have become, its origins are always mixed and new races are in the process of formation as others die out. Although racial admixture has blurred many distinctions, studies into the native populations of European cities such as London and Rome have nevertheless identified genetic differences between districts, and similar differences have been identified in England as one moves from east to west.

The European, or Caucasian as it is often known, geographic race has often been subdivided by scientists in the past into long-headed (dolichocephalic) and broad-headed (brachycephalic) types (the head being viewed from above), the former being typical of both the northern and the southern regions of Europe and the latter being typical of the central region, hence its common description of 'Alpine'. These distinctively different skull shapes are of the greatest value, as they enable the archaeologist to trace from the skeletons in ancient burial places the migration across Europe of successive groups of peoples. The approach must, however, be used with caution because body measurements are affected by nutrition as well as by heredity, and genetic traits and blood type are therefore now viewed as being more reliable. Nevertheless, hereditary traits such as predominant hair colouring, physical build and physiognomy still sometimes reveal earlier population movements and relationships to the naked eye. The facial similarity between many modern Danes and many people from England's East Riding of Yorkshire is striking and may be attributed to the Viking settlements of the ninth and tenth centuries. The similarity in appearance of many from Iberia, Wales and Ireland likewise reflects the long movement of peoples along the Atlantic seaboard.

misunderstandings as to the meanings of race

It will be appreciated from this scientific introduction that race can rarely, if ever, be equated with nationality. Modern nations almost all comprise representatives of more than one local race and those local races themselves are an amalgam. The most that one can say is that there are a limited number of groups, of which the Basques and the Lapps would be good examples, where the gene pool has been significantly limited by geographic isolation.

Even less can race be equated with language than with nation. Throughout history, the latest wave of conquerors has tended to impose its language on the conquered. The conquered may well be willing to adopt it as representing a higher level of civilization or enhanced opportunity. This was true across much of the Roman Empire, where Latin was widely adopted, and to some extent of British India and French Africa in recent centuries. Nevertheless, although race or ethnicity can be equated with neither language nor nation, it is equally clear that over many centuries broad (albeit overlapping) categories of peoples have emerged, primarily held together by a common culture, including linguistic bonds, but also sharing a distinctive range of genetic characteristics. However mistakenly, such peoples have sometimes been described as races, as in 'the English race', 'the French race', 'the German race' or 'the Jewish race'. These peoples have developed their own distinctive cultural traditions in which successive generations could find inspiration. Sir Nikolaus Pevsner, the art and architecture historian, for example, christened his series of BBC Reith Lectures 'The Englishness of English Art'. What geneticists cannot tell us, at least as yet, is whether these cultural traditions have a genetic component. It is the same conundrum as is posed by families. The Brontë sisters had a common genetic inheritance, as to a lesser degree did the members of the Bach family. How much, if at all, was that the source of their genius for literature and music? It is a recurrently challenging conundrum. Is it genetics, the quality of North Sea light, or simple coincidence which links the genius in painting of the Dutch and Flemish masters and the fact that so many of the great English painters (Blake, Turner,

Gainsborough, Constable) have been born in London or the eastern counties? Are the violent swings in mood which we associate with the Slav peoples, particularly the Russians, genetic in origin or the product of living in an extreme and demanding environment? Is it even an evolutionary genetic adaptation in its own right, comparable with those engendered over time by nutrition? Such questions seem unanswerable and that is perhaps their true significance.

misunderstanding of race

The real significance of these facts for the historian is that they have so often been misunderstood in the Europe that has evolved since 1700. There is abundant evidence that human groups have always been wary of other groups and that a sense of difference has readily translated into either a sense of inferiority or a sense of superiority, or even sometimes both together. The duality of Russian attitudes to the West throughout the twentieth century and of contemporary Islamic responses to European lifestyles in the twenty-first could be cited as examples of that seeming contradiction. Both a sense of superiority and a sense of inferiority are reinforced by victory and defeat in battle, and the indigenous peoples of **Africa** and **Asia** could rarely resist the technologically more advanced West whose weaponry grew ever more sophisticated as western **industrialization** increased. Victorious Europeans in Africa, Asia and the Americas took their growing empires as proof of their inherent superiority and readily drew simplistic conclusions. The apparent absence of advanced civilization in sub-Saharan Africa was proof enough that black people were racially inferior. It may have been a jest that the Victorian Englishman believed that God was a white male who spoke English, but like many jests it contained a great deal of truthful observation. Such assumptions, or prejudices as we would now judge them, were the common currency of Europeans, not a preserve of the British. They would have been amazed to learn that, as we now know, *Homo sapiens* originated as a black human who lost the black colour after moving out of Africa into more temperate regions, and that 1–4 per cent of the modern human genome in Europeans and Asians, but not normally in Africans, comes from that allegedly most decadent of origins, the Neanderthal.

racial exploitation

Nevertheless, the initial response of Europeans to those of other races was unreservedly exploitative from the very beginning of significant contact in the sixteenth century. Asians suffered from increasingly unequal trading relations, and the Spanish hunger for gold meant forced labour in the mines for the native population of **Latin America**. The Native Americans of North America were progressively marginalized by growing European settlement, as the Australian aborigines would be in the nineteenth and twentieth centuries. The most savage European impact, however, was on Africa, where the slave trade was immensely profitable for the British in particular throughout the seventeenth and eighteenth centuries. The 1713 Treaty of Utrecht enshrined the domestically much applauded Spanish *Asiento*, giving Britain alone the right to send a ship to trade with Spanish America and to take there 4,800 black slaves. It was only the beginning of a much larger illicit trade.

Even in the eighteenth century, when human rights law was an unknown concept, there was clearly some feeling of moral guilt at such exploitation. The Spanish writers, Francisco de Quevedo and Juan Ginés de Sepúlveda, had acted as apologists for the Spanish depradations in Latin America by elaborating a theory that native peoples were not human in the sense that the Spaniards were and had a completely different origin from them. They did not therefore have to be treated like human beings. It was, perhaps, the first overtly racial literature.

In no way did the eighteenth century dent the European sense of racial superiority or dent European greed, but it did see stirrings of conscience over excess. The influence of **William Wilberforce** (1759–1833), drawing on the ideas of **Voltaire**, and of the founder of Methodism, **John Wesley** (1703–91), amongst others, led to the abolition of the slave trade by **Britain**, 1807, and the **abolition of slavery** in the **British Empire**, 1833. Viscount Castlereagh, the British foreign secretary, had been able at the Congress of Vienna, 1815, to persuade the other European powers, too, to subscribe to the suppression of the slave trade. None of this meant that Europeans felt any inhibition in acquiring the lands of other races for their own benefit or in subjecting their populations to their own purposes, however. This became particularly evident as the nineteenth century advanced and virtually the whole of Africa, other than Abyssinia which defeated the Italians at the Battle of Adowa, 1896, and much of Asia came under either direct European control or was divided into zones of influence. The **Ottoman Empire** and **China** retained weak control of their territories, but the real exception was **Japan**, which westernized determinedly to the extent of Japanese ladies undergoing cosmetic surgery to give themselves a more European racial appearance, but which defeated 'political' Europe in the **Russo-Japanese War**, 1905. This extension of European control was often a brutal process. Many massacres of resisting Africans or Asians were regarded with an official 'blind eye', or even authorized. Others never saw the light of day. Government documents which have recently become available in the **UK** confirm that torure and other forms of brutal treatment of Africans was similarly sanctioned in **Kenya** during the **Mau Mau** insurgency prior to independence in 1963.

racial perceptions

Despite the sense of superiority to those of other races, which was common to all Europeans, except perhaps in the **Balkans**, where the Turks had been the masters, European nations had distinctively different approaches to, and perceptions of, the races they had come to dominate. Many of these live on. The Chinese were perceived as 'clever', even 'fiendishly clever', although they could be seen as objects of fun. They were invariably inscrutable. Indians were always seen as civilized, however peculiar their beliefs and customs. Africans, however, were seen as being an inferior species and often dismissed as animals. The Australian aborigine enjoyed even less esteem.

These categorizations were never absolute. The British always respected wealth, and an Indian maharaja could stay in London's very best hotels. The French accepted those of any race who spoke, thought and wrote like Frenchmen. The gap between the general British acceptance of multiculturalism and the French banning of the Muslim burka in public places is the contemporary expression of this significant difference of approach. Perhaps because of their own warlike traditions, the British had a particular respect for warrior castes and peoples. Many also developed a real affection for things Indian, which is perhaps reflected in the fact that curry is one of the national dishes of modern-day Britain, but never achieved much rapport with the settled Arabs of the British Empire, notably in Egypt.

European explorers and traders of the eighteenth century and before appear to have interbred freely with local women, leaving a significant number of mixed-race descendants, as is evident in, for example, the former Portuguese territory in India of Goa, but only in Latin America did the Spanish and Portuguese influx lead to the creation of truly racially mixed societies on any scale. The earlier trend went into reverse in the nineteenth century when European administrators, traders and settlers increasingly took women out with them and created new white communities of their own. The colour bar became normal, the half-caste was shunned and 'going native' closed the doors of colonial society. The **Russian Empire** trod a somewhat different path. Perhaps because of the major role played by informal Russian peasant expansion into Siberia and **Kazakhstan**, and the absorption of much Turkic Tatar blood bequeathed by the thirteenth-century Mongol invasion, Russia never developed the racial consciousness of other European imperial nations. The colour bar was unknown. In areas such as central Asia the humblest jobs were often filled by those of European stock and supervisory jobs often filled by local Asians, and it was a pattern which persisted throughout the Soviet period. Indeed, the Soviet ideal was to create the 'Soviet Man' (*Sovetsky chelovek*) who would have risen above any sense of national or racial distinctions within the **Soviet Union**.

white man's burden

The European sense of superority was, however, a complex emotion, at least amongst the more sophisticated. However arrogant and prejudiced, superiority implied responsibility, and exploitation went hand in hand with a mission to introduce better administration, education, health care and, not least, religious enlightenment. Just as there were differences in approach between the European imperial powers, there were differences between approaches to the different colonial territories of the same power. British India attracted the highest administrative talents; British Guiana had a lower reputation. The dichotomy between mission and exploitation was often veiled in a generous measure of hypocrisy and self-deception. The French *'mission civilatrice'* and the British 'white man's burden' are cases in point. On the other hand, what we would now call 'racial discrimination' was a reflection of economic and political privilege rather than of racial theorizing. It was a justification of what existed rather than a policy blueprint for the future.

racial thinking: Gobineau and Chamberlain

Scientific, or more accurately pseudo-scientific, racial thinking can be traced back to the French senior diplomat and author, Arthur-Joseph, Comte de Gobineau (1816–82), who published his

L'Essai sur l'inégalité des races humaines (*Essay on the Inequality of Human Races*) in four volumes, 1853–5. Gobineau's childhood had been inspired by the knowledge of his Viking ancestors, and he maintained that the white race was superior to all others and that amongst them it was the Aryans who had reached the heights of civilization. He believed, quite wrongly as we now know, both that ethnic differences were permanent and that humans essentially differed from place to place.

Gobineau's adoption of the term 'Aryan' was to become the source of much confusion and misunderstanding. It really referred to those tribes comprising the easternmost end of the line of Indo-European-speaking peoples who migrated westwards and southwards out of the Eurasian steppe at least 4,500 years ago. Perhaps 4,000 years ago those easternmost tribes divided into two groups, one of which spread into **India** and the other into Persia to which they gave their own name which we recognize today as 'Iran'. Neither the Indo-European-speaking peoples as a whole nor any of the constituent European tribes were 'Aryans', and no Europeans are of Aryan descent. Despite this, European racial theorists appropriated the term to mean 'of Indo-European descent' and then found superior qualities in the Germanic representatives of the Indo-European world. This was to compound confusion with confusion. Indo-European was a language and it is from that tongue that almost all the languages of modern Europe (Basque, Estonian, Finnish, Hungarian and Turkish are virtually the only exceptions) together with many of modern western Asia and India, not least Persian, descend. The original Indo-European-speaking nomads may have comprised a 'local race', but they certainly intermingled with local populations wherever they settled to create new local races and the different populations we recognize today.

Gobineau's most important successor was an Englishman who spent most of his life in Germany, Houston Stewart Chamberlain, who published his *The Foundations of the Nineteenth Century* in German, proclaiming the mission of Germandom, in 1899. Like Gobineau, he insisted on the superiority of the Teutons, whom he identified physically as being of the Nordic type, tall, fair and dolichocephalic or long-headed. Chamberlain's theorizing was flattering to the Germans for whom he had 'scientifically' demonstrated the superiority of the Germanic spirit, and strongly appealed to Kaiser Wilhelm II (1859–1941) because it brought his own German and English heritage together. He wrote to the

Prince of Wales in 1901 that the two nations 'are of the same blood, and they have the same creed, and they belong to the great Teutonic Race, which Heaven has entrusted with the culture of the world'. For him, this meant that an Anglo-German alliance was a world-historical and racial inevitability. In 1913, barely a year before the outbreak of **World War I**, he was writing: 'In the long run it will be absolutely impossible for the Anglo-Saxons to ally with Slavs and Gauls against Germany (the Germanic people).' Time has shown just how wrong that deduction was.

Racial thinking was not a Franco-German preserve, but was shared by William Morris (1834–96), the English poet and textile designer, who, like Gobineau, despised modern society and idealized the medieval. It was a way of thinking which readily reinforced national sentiment and drew sustenance from tradition. Although Morris himself was an early socialist, racist thinking came more readily to the Right than the more cosmopolitan Left. It was actually a Turk, **Ziya Gökalp** (1876–1924), who brought out particularly clearly the assumptions underlying racial thinking and its bias towards exclusivity. He argued first, that those who speak the same language are usually descendants of the same stock, and thus a nation also means an ethnic unity. Second, that language is the carrier of ideas and sentiments, the transmitter of customs and tradition; hence those who speak the same language share the same aspirations, the same consciousness and the same mentality. Individuals thus sharing common and homogeneous sentiments are also naturally prone to profess the same faith. He went on to conclude that a state that is not based on a united spirit can only be a common source of subsistence – 'a public kitchen' – rather than the home of a nation.

racism as anti-Semitism

Such racial thinking was increasingly widespread across nineteenth-century Europe and its hostility to what we would now call multiculturalism targeted first and foremost the Jews, although many, particularly in **Germany**, were highly integrated and included such leading cultural figures as the composer Mendelssohn (1809–47) and the poet Heinrich Heine (1797–1856). Anti-Semitism was rife in **France** as was proved by the notorious **Dreyfus affair**, which ran from 1894 to 1906 and set the army, the Church and half of France against the other half which demanded justice for an innocent Jewish officer. **Anti-Semitism** in Europe, however, long pre-dated the racial theorizing of the nineteenth century. It was endemic in the Russian Empire, where Catherine II in 1791 had established the Pale of Settlement which confined Jews to the western and south-western provinces of the empire (basically modern **Belarus**, **Latvia**, Lithuania, **Poland** and **Ukraine**). Nineteenth-century anti-Semitism had therefore mushroomed in those areas rather than in **Russia** proper. **Pogroms** had resulted, in 1881 and 1882 in particular, and in 1887 upper limits (*numerus clausus*) had been set on the number of Jews to be admitted to secondary schools or universities. They were effectively prohibited from the Bar in 1889. Resentment at Jewish involvement in money-lending readily allied itself with a crude class hatred to create what the German socialist pioneer, August Bebel, derided as 'the socialism of the imbecile', but it was a powerful force when further reinforced by nationalism.

Anti-Semitism in Germany was always latent but long quiescent. It was rekindled by the financial crash of 1873 which occurred under a National Liberal government, and Jewish banks and liberals were equated by a public susceptible to conspiracy theories. Anti-Semitism was particularly strong in Berlin because of its large number of Jewish residents. By 1880 it had 45,000 when the whole of England had only 46,000 and the whole of France 51,000. This also contrasted with the 5 million in the Russian Empire. The 1892 Tivoli Programme of the German Conservative Party was uncompromisingly anti-Semitic, but on financial and political rather than racial grounds. Moreover, however widespread German anti-Semitism had become, its early strength should not be over-emphasized. In the 1907 Reichstag election, the Anti-Semite Party gained only sixteen seats.

The aftermath of **World War I** transformed racism within Europe. It became angrier, more pervasive, more violent, and above all more concentratedly anti-Semitic. No country was immune, but it was strongest in **Austria** and Germany with Poland, Latvia and Lithuania not always far behind. The German election of September 1930 pointed the way forward when the Nazis' celebrating their 107 seats in the new Reichstag' riotously shouted *Juda verrecke!*, a slang expression normally applied to animals and roughly meaning 'Perish the Yid!' or even 'Death to the Yid!' **Adolf Hitler** himself always acknowledged his indebtedness to Chamberlain for providing him with an allegedly scientific basis for his racist outlook, and the perceived mystical link between race and homeland was encapsulated in the concept of *Blut und Boden* (blood and soil). The *Reichsbürgergesetz* (German citizenship law) of 15 September 1935 made Aryan blood a requirement for citizenship, and the preamble to the Law for the Protection of German Blood and German Honour enacted by the Reichstag the same day proclaimed that 'the purity of German blood is the prerequisite for the continued existence of the German people'. Marriage between German citizens and Jews was prohibited and extramarital relations between citizens and Jews were punishable with imprisonment. By 1939, Hitler was assuring the Reichstag that if international Jewry once more plunged the world into war, 'then the consequence will not be the Bolshevization of the world and a resultant victory for the Jews but, on the contrary, the destruction of the Jewish race in Europe'. The decisions at the 1942 Wannsee conference to confirm and accelerate the extermination of the Jewish population in Europe, which claimed some 6 million lives, was the culmination of that way of thinking.

Nazi racism was not directed solely against the Jews. **Roma** were exterminated likewise, and the creation of *Lebensraum* (living space) for the German *Herrenvolk* (master race) to the east was to be at the expense of the resident Slavs. Himmler told a gathering of fellow **SS** officials in January 1941 that the destruction of 30 million Slavs was a prerequisite for German planning in the east, and in fact an even greater number were to die during **World War II**.

That particular form of racial hatred died in 1945 and racial discrimination has been progressively banned in European legislation since. Racism festered, however, in climates of dramatic change, insecurity and deracination, and those climates have now been renewed by globalization and economic liberalization. The immigrant is a target even in traditionally tolerant countries such as Denmark and the **Netherlands**. The Muslim is for many the new Jew. Anders Breivik, who massacred seventy-seven young Norwegian Labour Party supporters in 2011, declared it was a strike against traitors embracing immigration to promote the Islamic colonization of **Norway**.

racial discrimination

– see also **apartheid**; **segregation**.
Racial discrimination involves actions or behaviour that result in the unequal distribution of rewards and benefits among individuals based on their membership of a particular racial group. Racial discrimination provides members of privileged racial groups with disproportionate advantages and opportunities in social, economic and political spheres, while excluding or restricting members of other racial groups access to those same advantages and opportunities. One area where

racial discrimination is evident in the **United States** is in the criminal justice system where observers have found that racial minorities continue to be 'over-represented in delinquency, offending, victimization, and at all stages of the criminal justice process from arrest to pretrial detention, sentencing (including capital punishment), and confinement' (American Sociological Association, *Race, Ethnicity and the Criminal Justice System* (2007), p. 3). In New York City, for example, where people of colour make up about half of the population, 80 per cent of the New York Police Department stops were of blacks and Latinos.

Racial discrimination takes different forms: *individual racial discrimination* consists of overt acts carried out by one person against another person or his/her property because of that person's race. For instance, a racist landlord might discriminate against a South Asian couple by refusing to rent them an apartment, or a racist person may burn a cross at a home belonging to an African American. In contrast, *institutional racial discrimination* occurs when the social arrangements and accepted ways of doing things in society disadvantage a racial group. This can be done intentionally or not. The history of redlining – the practice of denying, or increasing the cost of services such as banking, insurance, access to jobs, health care and supermarkets to residents in racially determined areas – is one example. This practice has perpetuated racial residential segregation and has adversely affected **African Americans**. Institutional discrimination is more injurious to larger numbers of racial minorities than individual discrimination, but is often not recognized by majority groups as racial discrimination. Since patterns of racial discrimination are embedded in our social arrangements and every day practices, social inequality becomes normalized and invisible to majority groups.

Racial discrimination is often supported by racism: the 'attribution of characteristics of superiority or inferiority to a population sharing certain physically inherited characteristics'. Racism is a form of *prejudice*, which is an inflexible preconceived attitude about individuals or groups. These attitudes can be either positive or negative. These inflexible attitudes are often rooted in *stereotypes*, which are exaggerated generalizations about particular groups. Prejudice often, but not always, leads to racial discrimination since these attitudes can be used to justify the unequal treatment of racial minorities.

Today, racial discrimination operates in subtle forms in contrast to the past. Whereas in the Jim Crow era in the United States discrimination was openly enforced by 'whites only' signs, racial discriminatory practices in the present day operate under the false notion of 'colour-blindness'. Individual racial discrimination may be on the decline, but institutional racial discrimination continues to shape people's lives in subtle and not so subtle ways.

racial whitening

The overtly racist belief that **Brazil** would improve as its population became 'whiter' accompanied abolitionists' desire to free the country's slaves and was part of the rhetoric associated with immigration. Especially vocal after the end of the slave trade in 1850, advocates of racial whitening favoured the promotion of European immigration as a way to accelerate the 'whitening' process and opposed the immigration of Chinese workers because it would slow it down. Supporters of whitening assumed white superiority, as well as beliefs that whites had a higher birth rate, that miscegenation resulted in lighter-coloured descendants and that people selected lighter partners. This optimistic and positive view of miscegenation contrasted notably with the stereotype of degeneration resulting from racial mixing long prevalent in the **United States**. A multiracial society, Brazilians in recent decades have emphasized non-racial variables as the keys for individual success, despite the existence of informal rather than institutional discrimination.

racism

A form of social organization and ideology based upon the attribution to different racial groups of different moral, individual and political characteristics. Though recorded forms of prejudice and discrimination against others are as old as human civilization, the systematic oppression and enslavement of particular groups (especially black people and those of African descent, and Jews) is a relatively modern phenomenon. From the moment of the African slave trade's greatest extent in the eighteenth century to the 1850s, racist ideas were developing; but in 1850, Henri Gobineau became the most famous of the nineteenth-century systematizers of racial ideas. His divisions of humankind based upon skin colour and moral hierarchy, though not novel, refined various pseudo-scientific ideas that emerged with the combination of science and the age of European expansion. They gave aid, motive and comfort to imperialists and slave traders in the western hemisphere, and after the destruction of slavery in the **British Empire**, the **USA** and **Brazil** between 1833 and 1888, formed the basis for new social structures based upon the apartheid principle of human separation. To this was added the idea of a 'racial soul', outlined in the ideas of Houston Stuart Chamberlain, and a 'race consciousness', upheld by some proponents of the work of Carl Jung.

Racists believe that human groups are divided into three broad categories – white Caucasians, black 'negroids' and yellow 'Asiatics'. They further hold that human competition and hierarchy is expressed in the successful domination of 'lower' groups by racial superiors (typically whites, though Japanese and other Asian groups have sometimes sought to assert 'superior' status). Racists ignore genetic evidence that more difference exists within human groups than between them, and abjure racial mixing, interracial partnerships of most sorts, and pan-racial social movements and religions, in favour of the principle of institutionlized discrimination. Some racists have been accused of propagating unconscious discrimination through assumptions about individuals or groups which draw or uphold distinctions and race-based qualities. Anti-semitism in the twentieth century became a modernist offshoot of racism which held confused but ultimately violent, populist and genocidal views of Jewish difference.

In the modern period racism became allied to populism and propaganda in such a way that it was presented as a democratizing force. The thesis was propounded that all members of a superior group, regardless of class distinctions, were equally superior to the undergroups. This idea proved immensely valuable to racists in the European empires, Nazi Germany, the Southern states of the USA, and **South Africa** as they attempted to create structures that institutionalized and reflected white control and putative superiority. Racist scientists gave some spurious legitimacy to these claims, and magnified minor differences and varying susceptibilities to some diseases into foundational proofs of racism. This was also an enterprise of some religious groups, particularly but not solely Protestant, which argued that the Bible mentioned three 'sons of Noah' one of whom, Ham, was to expatiate sinfulness personally and through descendants by bearing a mark of slavery and submission.

Racism blighted the lives of millions before, during and after the decolonization of the European empires and the rise of the civil rights movement of the mid twentieth century, leading to reactions, stereotypes and self-defeating presumptions that have been held to have affected every single group on the planet. **Africa** has not proved immune from this process, having generated some groups within the decolonized countries who have sought to divide their human peers on lines describes as ethnic but actually no different from the racial categories that existed under foreign rule. Racism has typically proved limiting, murderous and only capable of being enforced by oppression and acts of violence.

Though public expressions of racist sentiment were suppressed and condemned by the twenty-first century almost everywhere in the West, economic conditions, perceived competition for welfare resources, resentment of upwardly mobile groups and a human tendency to fixate on difference meant that conscious and unconscious racism remained a feature of most modern societies in the twenty-first century.

Radama I (1793–1828)

King of Madagascar, 1810–28, often called the first king of Madagascar as he conquered much of the island by 1824 and annexed it to his original territory of Merina. He relied on British aid to equip his army, and to secure their aid, he abolished the slave trade in 1817. He sought to modernize the country by inviting missionaries to come and found schools, establish a printing press and develop an alphabet for his language.

Radcliffe Award

A decision which established the boundaries between **India** and **Pakistan** on the eve of partition. Headed by Sir Cyril Radcliffe, two commissions decided in just over five weeks which areas of **Bengal** and **Punjab** would go to each of the new nations, resulting in considerable controversy. The award was not announced until 17 August 1947, two days after formal independence, leading to confusion and anxiety about the physical boundary that resulted in mass migration and violence.

Raffles, Thomas Stamford (1781–1826)

Raffles was a historian, botanist, linguist and officer of the **East India Company** who is famed as the founder both of **Singapore** and of London Zoo. He was from the age of 24 proficient in the Malay language and culture, and in various positions in South East Asia he worked to deepen his knowledge. He was a principal influence in British policy to secure Malacca, launch the Java War and establish trading centres to take advantage of the markets of **Japan** and **China**. In 1819 he established Singapore as an 'Asian Malta', and subsequently laid out its laws, shape and style whilst serving as governor of Bencoolen. In 1824 he returned to London, where he was involved in petty disputes about staffing and deficits during his administration. After his death the Company took away his pension and earnings and the Anglican Church refused him burial as an **abolitionist**.

Rahman, Sheikh Mujibur (1920–1975)

A Bengali political leader who rose from student activist to became leader of the **Awami League** Party in **Pakistan**, which was victorious in the 1970 elections. Military leaders and politicians from West Pakistan prevented Mujibur and his party from forming a government, however. Instead, he and many other Awami League leaders were imprisoned during a military crackdown which led to a civil war between Bengali guerrillas and the Pakistan Army. In December 1971 **India** intervened on the side of the guerrillas and the Pakistanis surrendered. Upon his release Mujibur became prime minister of the new nation of **Bangladesh**. Although he had declared a programme of secularism, socialism and democracy, he had great difficulty in dealing with the severe problems of his country and declared himself president in 1975. Shortly thereafter, army officers carried out a coup, assassinating him and most of his family.

Rahman, Tunku Abdul (1903–1990)

Malaysian nationalist who was a key figure in negotiating independence from **Britain** in 1957. Also known as the 'father of independence' or the 'father of Malaysia', he was the first prime minister of **Malaysia** (1957–70) and president of the ruling United Malays National Organization (UMNO) for twenty years (1951–71).

railways

– *see* **transport**.

Rajagopalachari, Chakravarti (1879–1972)

A lawyer and Congress leader from Madras, he rose to national prominence during the Non-Cooperation movement and later the civil disobedience movement. In 1944 he most famously proposed that in return for the **Muslim League**'s endorsement of Congress's demand for independence, the issue of a separate nation for Muslims could be decided through a plebiscite within

Muslim majority areas after the war. This proposal did not find much support. He was the governor general of **India** after independence.

Rajputs

The Rajputs are a 'martial' caste prevalent in northern India whose name derives from the Sanskrit for 'son of a king'. Their origins are debated but most scholars agree on various ancestries with some clans descended from Scythians and Huns settled in **India** by the seventh century and others from indigenous tribal groups. The term *Rajput* was initially an open-ended category based on occupation which only gradually came to denote a hereditary, inbred group associated with royal lineage and the *kshatriya* (warrior) caste. This transformation began in the sixteenth century, as the more successful clans participating in the **Mughal** state began to 'close ranks' and legitimize their status in the language of aristocratic descent and kinship. The trend was strengthened in the nineteenth century by British colonial strategies of forging political alliances with Rajput kingdoms mainly in modern-day Rajasthan while, at the same time, refashioning Indian 'tradition' to enhance the prestige of their allies as high-caste martial groups.

Ramadan War

– *see* **Yom Kippur War**.

Ramakrishna Paramhansa (1836–1886)

Son of a temple priest, Ramakrishna became a foremost religious teacher in the **Calcutta** (Kolkata) area in the third quarter of the nineteenth century. He was devoted to Kali, a form of the mother goddess, and experienced rapturous religious experiences. But beyond these mystical experiences, he was able to guide many Bengalis in their religious quests through skilful teaching and a gift for pithy parables. Among his disciples was the young Narendranath Datta who became Swami Vivekananda, founder of the Ramakrishna Mission.

Ranade, Mahadev Govind (1842–1901)

A moderate nationalist and social reformer from Maharashtra, he became a judge in the Bombay High Court. He advocated reforms of social evils such as child marriage, seclusion of women and non-remarriage of widows and founded the Indian National Social Conference in 1887. He was also a founding member of the **Indian National Congress**. His economic critique of colonialism urged a dynamic policy of industrial and commercial development albeit under the auspices of the British.

Ranke, Leopold von (1795–1886)

German historian. Ranke taught at Berlin University from 1825–71, as a full professor from 1837, and pioneered the source-based study of history, seeking to discover 'how things actually occurred' through a close analysis of primary documents. He emphasized narrative political history (to the exclusion of economic and social issues) and was appointed Prussian historiographer by Frederick William IV in 1841. Ranke exerted a far-reaching influence on European and American historiography, although today his approach would be seen as too narrow.

Rao, P. V. Narasimha (1921–2004)

Congress (I) politician from Andhra Pradesh who served as prime minister, 1991–6, after **Rajiv Gandhi**'s assassination during the 1991 electoral campaign. Rao served for many years as a Congress activist, legislator and minister at state and federal levels. He presided over economic reforms usually credited to then financial minister Manmohan Singh, that dismantled Nehruvian socialism and eased the entry of multinational capital, which in turn promoted rapid economic growth.

Rashtriya Swayamsevak Sangh (RSS)

A cadre-based Hindu communalist organization founded in 1925 and composed largely of upper-caste Maharashtrians. Its leaders such as M. S. Golwalkar envisioned India as fundamentally Hindu in opposition to other minority citizens. Banned after one of its members assassinated **Gandhi** in 1948, the Rashtriya Swayamsevak Sangh (RSS) emerged on to the Indian political scene in the mid 1980s as a part of the **Bharatiya Janata Party**. In recent years it has incited and participated in communal violence against Muslims and Christians in **India**.

Rasputin, Gregori Yefimovich (1864–1916)

A peasant, faith healer and Orthodox monk who became close to the family of the last Russian tsar, Nicholas Romanov. Rasputin was hyper-sexual and reputed to be possessed of a brooding appeal and hypnotic skills, which, it was alleged, played upon the tsarina and her attendant women and gave the highly conservative Rasputin his cue. In fact, Rasputin also seems to have taken a hand in the treatment of the young heir to the throne, who was haemophiliac and prone to illness but badly treated by his doctors. This, and Rasputin's religious mysticism, is much more likely to explain his infiltration of the late tsarist court. Rasputin became both a trusted adviser and a cipher for discontent with the tsarist regime and was assassinated in 1915, after a career of sensual indulgence, prophesying that his death would guarantee the end of the tsar and a revolution in **Russia**. When the Soviet Union was established, the coincidental accuracy of Rasputin's observation elevated him in the superstitions of those raised in rural environments and disturbed by the Soviet Union's rush to modernity. Rasputin is also remembered for the manner of his death; hyper-suspicious, he had inured his body to poison and so was not only poisoned by his killers, but subjected to shooting and stabbing before he died.

Rathenau, Walther (1869–1922)

German minister of reconstruction, 1921, and foreign minister, 1922, Rathenau was a moderate conservative member of the German Reichstag following **World War I**. He supported worker participation in industry, the overall nature of the Versailles settlement of 1919, and stabilization under the Weimar constitution. As foreign minister, he recognized the **USSR** and helped solve the problem of Germany's eastern border in the Rapallo Treaty. This, and his Jewish background, was enough to prompt his assassination by two members of the army.

Rawlings, Jerry John (1947–)

Ghanaian military and political leader. An air force officer after 1969, Rawlings led a junior officers' coup in 1979. Briefly chairman of the Armed Forces Revolutionary Council, he purged corrupt politicians and military commanders before reinstating civilian rule in late 1979. He seized power again in 1981 but, as his popularity faltered, restored a democratic constitution in 1992. Elected president in 1993 and 1996, Rawlings relinquished power peacefully in 2001.

Raza Cósmica, La

José Vasconcelos's inverted racist theories espoused in the **United States** and **Europe** in *La Raza Cósmica* (1925). Instead of exclusionary, quasi-biological claims of superiority, he localized an amalgam of Iberian, Latin American and African 'races' in **Mexico**. His interpretation emphasized the aura of European romanticism and pronounced the existence of a 'fifth race' in Mexico. Only this futuristic race, born of an Iberian root, would bring about the desired 'era of humanity'.

Reagan, Ronald Wilson (1911–2004)
– *see also* **Reagonomics**.

Republican president of the **United States**, 1981–9. A former **Hollywood** film star, Reagan was California governor, 1967–75. As president, he articulated anti-communist rhetoric in opposition to the **Soviet Union** – 'the evil empire' – but pursued arms limitation negotiations, especially after the ascent of **Mikhail Gorbachev**. Easing **Cold War** tensions, the result was the Intermediate-Range Nuclear Forces Treaty of 1987. Domestically, a 'Reagan revolution' sought to attack the New Deal-era tradition of federal government activism and Keynesian economics by reducing taxes and spending (except military expenditure), by encouraging deregulation and by transferring government responsibilities from Washington to the state level. Insufficient spending cuts encouraged the growth of the federal deficit, but the 1980s was a period of economic growth. Supreme Court appointments of conservative justices supported the rightward impact of the Reagan presidency. A skilful politician whose optimistic persona buoyed national confidence, Reagan nevertheless experienced a second-term decline because of the **Iran–Contra scandal**.

Reaganomics

Reaganomics – or 'supply side' economics – was the popular expression for US President **Reagan**'s rejection of post-war Keynesian 'demand side' economic management. Reaganomics addressed 1970s 'stagflation' with sharp tax reduction and deregulation to encourage entrepreneurship, and tight money policy to control inflation. The result, after the sharp 'Reagan recession' in 1981–2, was rapid growth in the mid 1980s, but at the unintended cost of twin budget and trade deficits which later plagued the **United States**.

Reconstruction (USA)

The politics of Reconstruction after the **American Civil War** centred on two closely related questions. First, under what terms were the states that had so recently seceded from the Union to be readmitted? It was accepted, even by the most radical Republicans, that the final outcome would be their restoration to something like their former status as full and equal members of a reconstituted Union, and this expectation was an important constraint on what would be possible during

Reconstruction. Second, what status would be enjoyed by the 4 million or so men and women who had formerly been slaves but who were now free? What their freedom would entail and how it was to be enforced constituted the central issues of Reconstruction.

In fact, a process of Reconstruction had begun during the civil war, when President **Abraham Lincoln** had tried to establish loyal governments in the occupied South. His successor, **Andrew Johnson**, largely built on Lincoln's plan, which was founded on the assumption that, since **secession** was unlawful, the Southern states had never left the Union. Instead, certain individuals had been engaged in an insurrection against the authority of the **United States**, and the way to restore the seceded states to the Union was by an exercise of the pardon power. Those pardoned would then be free to create new state governments. All that Johnson required of them was that they should repudiate secession and acknowledge the end of slavery. State governments were established on this basis during the summer and autumn of 1865. However, while meeting Johnson's rather minimal requirements, the new state governments proceeded to pass a series of repressive laws, known as Black Codes, which defined the rights and liberties of freedpeople in a highly restrictive fashion.

Many Northerners were concerned that under this programme of 'self-reconstruction' the fruits of victory would be lost. It looked as if members of the old ruling class were taking advantage of Johnson's generous pardon policy to climb back into power and as if the freedpeople were in the process of being partially re-enslaved. Some Republicans, known as Radicals, many of them with a background in anti-slavery politics, worked to achieve equal civil and political rights for freedmen, and they were reluctant to allow the Southern states to be readmitted to the Union until they had undergone a substantial process of reconstruction. As Congressman Thaddeus Stevens put it, 'the foundations of their institutions . . . must be broken up and relaid, or all our blood and treasure have been spent in vain'. That would involve redistributing land from former masters to former slaves, creating public school systems open to all races, and promoting economic development along Northern lines, as well as giving blacks the vote. Other, more moderate, Republicans were happy to see an early restoration of the Union but were still troubled by the lack of protection given to freedpeople. They were afraid, as was Senator Lyman Trumbull, that the Negro would be 'tyrannized over, abused, and virtually reënslaved without some legislation by the nation for his protection'. And this, during the spring and summer of 1866, congressional Republicans such as Trumbull set out to provide: by extending the life of the Freedmen's Bureau, by passing a Civil Rights Act and by submitting to the states a 14th Amendment that wrote the principles of civil rights into the American Constitution.

Unfortunately, Johnson vetoed the civil rights legislation passed by the Republican Congress, arguing that it infringed on the independent sovereignty of the states, and ten Southern states refused to ratify the 14th Amendment, with the result that the first congressional plan of Reconstruction had stalled. When Congress reassembled during the winter of 1866/7, the Republican majority enacted a new programme which involved the reimposition of military government in the former Confederate states. However, the Reconstruction Act of March 1867 and its successors, rather than providing the framework for a protracted period of federal control, required military governors in the South to arrange for new elections, though this time on the basis of a bi-racial suffrage, the drafting of new state constitutions and the formation of new state governments. Once these new governments had been formed, with African American males enfranchised and discriminatory laws removed, once they had ratified the 14th and 15th Amendments (the 15th Amendment barred the states from denying citizens the right to vote on the grounds of race), the Southern states were fully restored to the Union.

With blacks voting and with many whites at least temporarily disfranchised, most of the former Confederate states enjoyed periods of Republican rule, ranging from a few months to several years. These Republican regimes brought major changes: democratizing state constitutions, expanding social welfare facilities, modernizing penal codes and, above all, establishing state publicly funded schools for black as well as white children. Although they did little to promote significant economic change, for example through the redistribution of land, the Republicans, particularly at a local level, provided political conditions under which **African Americans** received a fairer treatment in the courts and found it easier to enforce their economic rights than at any time before the late twentieth century. That enabled black labourers and tenant farmers to bargain for better terms from their landlords, even if they could not become independent farmers.

For all their achievements, Republican state governments that relied on the votes of former slaves and the leadership of northern 'carpetbaggers' lacked political legitimacy in the eyes of most white Southerners. Opposition sometimes took a violent form, as in the **Ku Klux Klan** outrages that flared up across the South between 1867 and 1872 and the more blatant campaigns of political intimidation in states such as Mississippi and South Carolina during 1875 and 1876. The federal government was at first quite effective in suppressing such outbreaks, but, as time went on, federal officials became more reluctant to intervene to defend Republican regimes in the South. This reflected a public opinion in the Northern states that was becoming increasingly distracted by other issues, especially after the economic crisis of 1873, increasingly disenchanted by the performance of Southern Republicans, and increasingly ready for reconciliation with their former adversaries. In 1877 the agreement made to resolve the contested presidential election of the previous year resulted in the overthrow of the last Republican governments in the South and the removal of federal troops. Although the federal disengagement was already well under way before 1877 and although Republicans held on to local power for many years after, the so-called **Compromise of 1877** is usually seen as marking the effective end of Reconstruction.

Red Army (Soviet Union)

The name given to the army of the Soviet Union which was organized by **Leon Trotsky** in 1918. The army fluctuated in size during its lifetime, but easily contained over 12 million men by the end of 1945. Soldiers and officers were consciously servants of the **USSR**, rather than **Russia**, and before 1939 had to swear an oath to socialism. The Red Army was noted for its fortitude in siege and its ferocity in victory during **World War II**, when as many as 20 million Soviet lives were lost, even though it had been subjected to merciless pre-war purges by **Stalin**. In 1946 the Red Army was formally transformed into the Soviet Army, although the title continued to be used unofficially.

Red Crescent

The generic name of national humanitarian organizations given the same principles as those of the **Red Cross** but organized in Islamic countries. The Turkish Red Crescent Society is the most venerable, having emerged in 1868, and is, as its sister organizations are, recognized in public international law as a body providing battlefield and war zone care for soldiers, prisoners of war and civilians. The Red Crescent was distinguished from the Red Cross, which had connotations of Christian and Crusader history, as a requirement of the Ottoman authorities during the 1876 war between the **Russian** and **Ottoman Empires**, and was then transmitted to Ottoman successor states and then copied, so that over thirty Islamic countries now use the emblem. An additional attempt on the part of **Egypt** and Persia to adopt a red lion and red sun emblem was accepted in the 1930s, but the expansion of emblems by national societies was then ended, so that the **Geneva Conventions** (which incorporated the symbols) was not to be subject to continuous addition. In 2015 the red crescent sat alongside the cross and a third, intentionally neutral crystal, as the only acceptable symbols of the humanitarian movements with which they were associated.

Red Cross
– *see also* **Red Crescent**.
An international Swiss-based humanitarian organization established in 1863 after lessons learned in the 1859 Battle of Solferino. It is run by an international committee based in Geneva, dedicated to the nursing and care of wounded and captured soldiers both on the battlefield and whilst under hostile internment. Semi-autonomous national societies complement the work of the International Committee in Geneva, and the symbol of the Red Cross on a white background has become associated with battlefield care. The Red Cross is a neutral organization which has won the Nobel Peace Prize three times, and was closely tied through one of its founders to the **Geneva Conventions**, which set out humanitarian limits to warfare. These conventions also provide the legal mandate for Red Cross inspections of prisoner of war camps, as well as its self-assumed responsibility to protect civilians who fall under the control of an occupying power.

Red Guards (China)
Young Chinese mobilized by radical elements of the Communist Party during the **Cultural Revolution**. Following rallies in Beijing in the summer of 1966, Red Guards began to attack the four 'olds' across the country. These were old customs, old habits, old culture and old thinking. During the campaign, buildings were vandalized and people beaten and humiliated. By 1968, fighting had broken out among different factions of the Red Guards, and **Mao Zedong** stepped in to disband them.

Red Scare (USA)
An intense period of anti-radicalism and perceived anti-subversion, particularly directed at communists or suspected communists, in the **United States**. The term was most commonly used in reference to the repression following **World War I**. Other American anti-radical scares have included the **Haymarket Affair** (1886) and the anti-communist crusades of Senator **Joseph R. McCarthy** (1950–4). The Red Scare of 1919–20 culminated in the raids on labour and leftist groups authorized by Attorney General A. Mitchell Palmer and the subsequent deportation of hundreds of those arrested. Similar hysteria has at times been whipped up by interested parties including ambitious individuals, patriotic networks, the news media and the agencies of federal and state governments. At other times, that hysteria has been fuelled by the pervasive fears of particular sections of the public. Federal government activity often legitimized smaller-scale local and regional red scares.

Reforma, La
After the **Mexican American War** a new generation of Mexican politician forged key political reforms. Promulgated in the constitution of 1857, these comprised La Reforma and became the basic planks of modern **Mexico**'s political system. Associated with President **Benito Juárez**, they emphasized nineteenth-century European political ideals centred around individualism and a society based on equality in law, against a societal vision that inspired the colonial corporatism of native Mexican villages, the Church and the army.

refugees
– *see also* **Afghanistan; migration; Palestine; Syrian Civil War**.
The political refugee is one of the enduring images of the twentieth century, but, historically, the refugee is not necessarily political or even the victim of circumstances beyond his or her control. If the asylum seeker fearing for his or her life is at one end of the spectrum and the economic migrant fleeing poverty is at the other, there are many in the middle whose political and economic motives overlap. The Pilgrim Fathers, for example, can be seen with equal validity as refugees from persecution and seekers of economic opportunity. This was particularly the case in the nineteenth century when the small but significant number of true political refugees, mainly either Italian or Polish nationalists fleeing from the **Austrian** and **Russian Empires** or Russian revolutionaries, were far outnumbered by the many

thousands of Irish who fled from hunger at best and starvation at worst during the Irish potato famine of the 1840s. Similarly the movement of large numbers of Jews into central and western Europe to escape the pogroms in the Russian Empire in the latter part of the nineteenth century was both economically and politically inspired.

A small number of refugees must also be categorized as voluntary refugees. The Belgian refugees of **World War I** were sometimes those who were wealthy enough to move to Britain away from the fighting rather than those whose lives were most threatened by it. Artistic emigrés such as composers Igor Stravinsky and Sergei Prokofiev, who left **Russia** during the **Russian Revolution**, the latter returning in 1934, are not dissimilar.

The European refugee can be a refugee from **Europe**, a refugee to Europe or a refugee within Europe. The number of refugees from Europe since 1700 has normally been limited, with the great exception of the Jewish exodus first to the **United States** and then to **Israel** before, during and after **World War II**. Many of the post-war emigrants, however, were not strictly refugees, as Nazi persecution had been ended. On the other hand, **Hungary** and **Poland** also had been violently anti-Semitic, and Jews had been killed in a pogrom in Kielce, Poland, in July 1946, more than a year after the end of the war, prompting a further 100,000 Jews to leave Poland. Refugees to Europe have almost all been attributable to decolonization since 1945. Dutch settlers in **Indonesia** and French settlers in North Africa, particularly **Algeria**, those of mixed blood, and all those who felt compromised by their links with the colonial regime, hurriedly came to Europe in significant numbers. The **Egypt** of **Colonel Nasser** expelled the Greeks, who had made **Alexandria** a Greek city ever since its foundation by Alexander the Great, as well as many French. Forty years earlier, the defeat of **Greece** by the Turks in the Turkish War for Independence in October 1922 had resulted in a reduction in the Greek population of what is now **Turkey** from 1.8 million to 120,000. There was a similar reduction in the Armenian population from 1.3 million to 100,000. Although many had been killed in the fighting, the majority had been expellees.

Until the 1930s the number of refugees within Europe had been limited and many, if not most, are more usually classified as the political exiles for whom **Britain** and **Switzerland** in particular offered safe asylum. Even in the eighteenth century **Voltaire** had thought it prudent to reside at Ferney close to the Swiss border. In the nineteenth

century **Marx** had worked in London and Victor Hugo lived in exile in Jersey, 1852–70, to be succeeded in England by his former foe, **Napoleon III**, after 1870. At the end of the century and the beginning of the twentieth, **Lenin** was the most prominent of such exiles in successive European cities, and Joseph Conrad's novel *Under Western Eyes* captures the conspiratorial atmosphere of the Russian exile communities. By far the greatest number of refugees in modern European history, however, is attributable to the rise, and even more the fall, of Nazi Germany. The intensifying persecution of Jews and all political opponents led to a steady exodus after 1933, including some of **Germany**'s most famous figures. Without emigration restrictions and the extermination policy adopted in 1942, the numbers would have been much greater.

The great flood of refugees, however, came after Germany's defeat in 1945. The **Potsdam conference** drastically redrew Germany's eastern boundaries and decreed that all the Germans outside those new boundaries, together with the Sudeten Germans of **Czechoslovakia** and the Germans of Hungary and pre-war Poland, were to be transferred to Germany 'in an orderly manner'. In what has been described as the greatest migration of peoples within Europe since the sixth century AD, some 13 million Germans were expelled, including 2 million from pre-war Poland, 3 million from the Sudetenland, 4.5 million from Silesia, now Poland, 2 million from East Prussia and 1 million from East Pomerania, now Poland. It was what has since become known as ethnic cleansing on the grand scale, and it was not always orderly.

The shifting boundaries during and after the war and the accompanying political changes also created far more of that particularly twentieth-century form of refugee: the stateless person, for whom the **Nansen** passport had been devised in 1922. The number of German refugees moving from east to west remained significant until the erection of the Berlin Wall in 1961, ranging from 125,245 in 1949 and 143,917 in 1959 to a high of 331,390 in 1953. Some were effectively in transit from eastern Europe – by January 1947, 4.3 million refugees had arrived in the Soviet Zone where they made up a quarter of the population; in Mecklenburg it was 43 per cent – others were economic and political refugees from communist East Germany. The economic cost to East Germany was high. Its leader, Walter Ulbricht, admitted to the Soviet newspaper *Pravda* in December 1961 that the movement of East German workers to West Germany since 1949 had cost East Germany some 40 per cent of its national income over that period. Later conflicts contributed further refugees. Thousands fled Hungary after the Soviet suppression of the 1956 uprising. The disintegration of **Yugoslavia** created many more. The capture of the Krajina and of Slavonia by **Croatia** in 1995 created perhaps 300,000 ethnic Serb refugees in total. The Bosnian conflict caused some 1,319,250 Bosnians to seek refuge abroad by 1996. By April 1999 there were some 300,000 ethnic Albanian refugees from Kosovo in **Albania** and 160,000 in Macedonia. Many ultimately returned there, provoking some 150,000 ethnic Serbs to flee in their turn.

Regency (France)

The period 1715–23, during the minority of **Louis XV**, when **France** was governed by Philippe II, Duc d'Orléans, as regent. With his having had more than a hundred mistresses, the Regency is remembered as a period of blatant sexual abandon, but the regent also led the reaction against the autocratic style of Louis XIV, establishing a number of advisory councils as well as dramatically reducing the scale of the court. He was also a free-thinking liberal and an anti-clerical who extended tolerance to Protestants. The Regency is particularly associated with John Law, a Scottish banker who argued that resources could be created by printing money but who did not recognize the necessity of adequate covering security. He established a General Bank, 1716, which became the Royal Bank, 1718, with the French state as sole shareholder. The fluctuating value of its security led to its crash, however, in 1720, bankrupting perhaps a million families.

reggae

– *see also* **pan-Africanism**.

Reggae and its earlier form, ska, are popular Jamaican music styles originating in the late 1960s. Ska is based on a four-beat rhythm and is performed by bass and electric guitar, drums and a 'scraper'. It expresses the problems of impoverished urban life in Kingston. The faster reggae music was pioneered with Toots and the Maytals, as well as the Wailers. Their lyrics address social and economic injustice. Reggae is strongly connected to the Rastafarian movement. In the 1970s reggae spread around the anglophone world, mainly through the songs of Bob Marley (1945–81).

Regulator movement (USA)

A rural protest movement that emerged in the western counties of North Carolina during the 1760s. The grievances of the Regulators included demand for more equitable representation in their colonial assemblies and fairer taxation. Anticipating more general American resistance to British rule, the Regulators took the law into their own hands and engaged in extralegal protests. The regulators were eventually suppressed by colonial **militias** representing the coastal counties of the colony at the Battle of Alamance in May 1771.

religion

Much of world history since 1700 has continued to be underwritten by religious beliefs, practices and conflicts. Moreover, modern world history has encouraged investigation into the nature of religion and its influence on both individual and social life. The spread in **Europe** of **Enlightenment** rationalism after 1700 led to the first efforts to define religion in an analytical sense. These efforts often involved scepticism concerning religious beliefs and traditions, though only rarely before the twentieth century did they entail outright atheism.

Since the history of religion in the world since 1700 has involved, on the one hand, scepticism concerning beliefs and traditions and, on the other, defence of them, analyses of religion still resonate in everyday life. In states where there was a volatile mix of strong inherited authority and vibrant intellectual inquiry – most notably **France** and **Great Britain**, including its American colonies – some men and women began to understand religion as a social institution, with perhaps little connection to the divine. This view could be atheistic, as with the French *encyclopédistes* Jean le Rond d'Alembert and **Denis Diderot**. But it could also be an effort to emend and rejuvenate a traditional religion, as with the British authors William Paley and Anthony Ashley-Cooper, 3rd Earl of Shaftesbury. So too could it be an effort to extirpate inherited and corrupt religion and replace it with a new and pure religion, as with the French *philosophe* **Jean-Jacques Rousseau** and the Anglo-American revolutionaries **Thomas Paine** and **Thomas Jefferson**. In these revisionist approaches, divine revelation and its transcriptions in religious texts, which together formed (and still form) one of the ancient sources of religion, were modified, even sometimes dismissed, by a modern, individual encounter with reality, whether construed as natural or supernatural.

Much of the modern world remains concerned with the difference between, on the one hand, religion as rooted in revelation, authoritative texts and traditions and, on the other hand, religion as a human creation – open to criticism, revision and even dissolution. In nineteenth-century **Germany**, both the idealist philosopher **G. W. F. Hegel** and the materialist philosopher **Karl Marx** emphasized the *human* sources of religion, whether as the evolution of a universal spirit partaken of by both humanity and God (Hegel) or as the 'sigh of the oppressed', 'the opiate of the people' (Marx). Hegel's contemporary, the Christian theologian Friedrich Schleiermacher, perceiving the danger to religion in such views, insisted on God's independence of any human activity and thought as well as on a human dependence on a divine power outside humanity, as did in the next hundred years the German theologians Rudolf Otto and Karl Barth. In this, Schleiermacher, Otto and Barth are part of a tradition that survives to the present day in the defence of traditional, supernatural religion against its deflation as a human creation.

In nineteenth-century Germany, the 'higher criticism' thrived in hermeneutics, questioning the authorship and chronology traditionally ascribed to the Bible and opening the door to a modern divergence between two types of believers – liberals who accepted some part but not all of traditional scriptures and fundamentalists who sought exactitude in adherence to ancient texts. (Fundamentalists can exist within any tradition, and **fundamentalism** thrives across the world in the early twenty-first century.) Charles Darwin infuriated traditionalists not only by discrediting age-old notions of creation, but also by implying that religious beliefs and practices could be part of natural selection in such a way that belief in an immortal soul was useful in evolution in the same way as was an eyeball or a hand with an opposable thumb. Those who sought to engage science and scholarship while retaining elements of a traditional faith, like the trailblazing French Roman Catholic theologian Alfred Firmin Loisy, were sometimes met with scorn (and, in Loisy's case, excommunication and a prohibition against Roman Catholics reading some of his works) within their own traditions.

In the twentieth and twenty-first centuries criticism of religion has become part of democratic culture (both where democracy has been achieved and where it remains an unrealized aspiration of part of the populace) even as the commitment to defend religious traditions and so-called fundamentals remains vigorous. Criticism and defence – distance and affiliation – sceptic and believer – all remain essential elements of religion in the modern world. Intellectuals, no matter what their individual beliefs, assume some distance in their analysis of religion.

The anthropological study of religion began in the 1870s with E. B. Tylor, who postulated animism as the original religion. Tylor defined the social scientist's stance as removed from that of ordinary believers, whose beliefs were irrational, or in other words the opposite of his own intellectualism. This stance allowed anthropology and psychology to thrive as scholarly approaches to religion, utilizing a language believers at first declined to adopt and still often resist. The psychologist **Sigmund Freud** argued that religious beliefs correspond closely with the phantasies of infantile life, mainly unconscious ones, concerning the sexual life of one's parents and the conflicts to which this gives rise. Somewhat less controversially, the sociologist Emile Durkheim (1858–1917) stressed the social role of religion as a unified system of beliefs and practices relative to sacred things, things set apart and forbidden, which unite into one single moral community called a Church all those who adhere to them. Freud's and Durkheim's are but two twentieth-century scholarly approaches to religion, yet their analytical style is now central to the lives of many believers. Alternatively, such distance and analysis seems inconceivable or even blasphemous or heretical to modern adherents of religious traditions. In some parts of the world, apostates (those who have forsaken an inherited religion) are subject to sanction. Today about 75 per cent of the world's population identifies with a religious tradition, either as liberals who accept the kernel of the faith and its institutions yet maintain a critical distance from some of its features, or as fundamentalists who seek to follow a faith in an original form untouched by the modern word, or as a believer who is situated somewhere between these two poles.

trends since 1700

Religion considered on a global scale and over several centuries will inevitably display great variety notwithstanding efforts to subsume all religions under one definition. However, a number of important – but inconsistent – trends are observable in the global history of religions since 1700. One trend, as noted, has been the capacity to regard inherited beliefs and practices with scepticism: as an atheist, an agnostic, a reformer or a scholar. Probably every society has had religious sceptics, but in the eighteenth century they gained a codified language and a clear self-identification that have survived to this day. Scepticism has been countered by an insistence on the validity of revelation and of tradition, sometimes with a fundamentalist tone.

A second trend in religious life has been nationalism, the identification of a church or a religion with a powerful interest group in a nation or would-be nation. This has been a common element of nation-building across the globe since 1700. The alternative, much rarer in history, has been a universal faith, sometimes called 'the religion of humanity', that denies that any polity is sacred or that any group of people is God's chosen one. Today, this is a radical view associated with the ideal that human rights should be respected in a global way, not only under the rule of sovereign states. Moreover, nationalistic religion has often been associated with militarism. Indeed, many parts of the globe at war in the early twenty-first century are border regions where different religious traditions, embodied in different societies, collide.

A third trend has been the growth of dissent and toleration. This has often meant the disestablishment of religion in the sense of a separation between church and state, although, in the words of the sociologist Robert Bellah, the alternative to establishment has sometimes been a 'civil religion', an ideology that sanctifies a national way of life. When there has been a reformist impulse there has usually been a proliferation of religious subsystems. Once a religious tradition begins to fragment, it is virtually impossible in the modern world to halt the process. Some splintered traditions have become strong and enduring, while others have disintegrated within a generation or two.

A fourth trend, accompanying colonialism and migration, has been an acceleration of syncretism. Colonialism and migration often forced people to confront new gods, new beliefs and new practices. Conquerors often sought to coerce indigenous people into accepting an alien religion, while migrants have been faced with the quandary of assimilating to new religious forms or maintaining old ones in a new environment. This process has itself led to the creation of beliefs and practices previously unknown in any of the syncretic traditions that arose as humans moved about the globe, whether in war or in peace.

Finally, among these major trends, all religious traditions have, to some degree, been faced with the choice of how much of the dominant part of the modern world – individualistic, capitalistic, acquisitive, yet also humane, democratic and, in the Internet age, interactive among the citizens of the

world in a way that has never been possible before – to accept or to reject. The impulse to accept much of the modern world and to square religious traditions with it can be called liberalism or modernism. The impulse to reject much of the modern world and to insist upon its subordination to religious traditions can be called conservatism, fundamentalism or primitivism. Much of the modern world still perceives a conflict between religion, on the one hand, and science and liberalization, on the other.

modern world religions

In modern world history, just as we see the defence and critique of traditional religion, we also see the continuity of religions and the creation of new ones.

Confucianism has underwritten a way of life for Chinese people since the fifth century BC. To his followers, Confucius imparted the notion of *ren* – excellence in morality and character as a corrective to the disorder and violence of his times. Gradually, various Confucians extended his teachings into politics, philosophy and literature. Although Confucianism functioned as way of life more than as a religion, it has had a spiritual dimension exemplified by Wang Yangming, who taught that heaven and earth are one and that people can come to share in a network of the sacred and the profane. By 1700 **Confucianism** had spread to **Korea** and, less fully, **Japan**. The **Qing** emperors (1644–1912) of **China** established themselves over scholars as interpreters of Confucianism. A marriage of politics and religion, with the virtually inevitable growth of social control, fostered scepticism and disillusionment, yet also defence and revival. Contact with western ideas and technology in the nineteenth century led intellectuals away from Confucianism, while the new People's Republic of China (1949) purported to replace it with Marxist–Leninist ideology. Some intellectuals came to regard Confucianism as an ideological backwater, and rapid economic development in East Asia in the late twentieth century made its moral and spiritual teachings, which emphasized harmony in family, society and, indeed, the universe, obsolete for many people. However, a revival has also been underway since the late twentieth century, as scholars and others throughout East Asia postulate that Confucianism possesses a humanistic tradition that can inform and improve modern political ideologies.

Buddhism was founded by Siddhartha Gotama in India in the fifth century BC and by 1700 had spread throughout **Asia**, then in the nineteenth and twentieth centuries to Europe and the Americas. The Buddha taught that the conditions of humanity – individuality, limitation, desire, suffering – can be overcome through the ethics of the Noble Eightfold Path: right views, right aspirations, right speech, right conduct, right livelihood, right effort, right mindfulness, and right meditational achievement. At the end of this path was Nirvana, which he did not define as nothingness (as many today believe), but rather as participation in the original, uncreated dimension of existence. Buddhist monks preserved the Buddha's teachings, and Buddhist monasteries often served as auxiliaries to government. By 1700, for example, Tibetan Buddhists had formed a government that would last until the Chinese occupation of their country in the 1950s. The cooperation between monasteries and political leaders was disrupted in the nineteenth and twentieth centuries by colonialism as well as by the **Meiji** rulers of Japan (1868–1912) who sought to establish Shinto (an indigenous faith pre-dating Japanese Buddhism) as the national religion. Bitter conflicts between Buddhists and non-Buddhist politicians (whether colonial or indigenous) occurred in **Sri Lanka**, **Myanmar** and Japan and do so still today in Tibet. During **World War II**, Buddhist leaders envisioned a vast Buddhaland in the East, dominated by Japan, but the post-war era saw new groups such as Soka-Gakkai and Rissho-Kosei-Kai that emphasized Buddhism as a religion of peace and fraternity. In the early twenty-first century Buddhism is thriving through adaptation in countries such as Japan, but it has been sorely pressed upon by political authorities in China, **North Korea**, **Vietnam** and **Tibet**. Moreover, Buddhist immigrants have created communities in countries such as **India** (where Buddhists had not been seen for centuries) and the **USA** (where some intellectuals and social critics have been attracted to Buddhism since the mid nineteenth century).

Hinduism originated in India's ancient oral traditions, which were later reduced to writing in the corpus of texts known as the Vedas (eternal truth), the insights of which were later elaborated in the *Upanishads*, *Manusmrti* and the *Bhagavad Gita*. Although Hinduism has a great tradition of philosophical reflection on scriptures and ritual, for most Hindus religion focuses on the proper ordering of life, one that will ensure a good rebirth (reincarnation) or even *moksa* (release from rebirth). To order life is to live according to *dharma*, one's cosmically ordained duties and occupation. An orderly life demands, thus, a social division of labour, which in India resulted in a caste system. Hinduism is in this sense an all-encompassing form of life and one that has taken many different forms, as seems inevitable in Indian society, which reached a population of 1.2 billion early in the twenty-first century (about 80 per cent of Indians identify as Hindus and about 30 million Hindus reside outside India). An orderly life leading to better rebirths brings one's *atman* (essence or soul) into union or correct relationship with Brahman (the origin of all) in such a way that the desires and disruptions of life as human beings first experience it are transcended. God appears in many entities in Hindu life, so there are many forms of devotion; God may be incarnated in a person, as some believe was the case with **Mahatma Gandhi**. Any occasion in Hindu life can involve devotion to one of a myriad of deities, yet three major devotional traditions, preserved by gurus and priests, have at any one time millions of adherents: to Siva, to Visnu and to Sakti. In the modern world a tension has developed in Hinduism between toleration of variety (long inherent in Hinduism and more recently in other religions) and assertion of Hindu particularity (even to efforts to re-establish Hinduism as the state religion of India). For an example of toleration, the Indian constitution created a secular state with protections for religious minorities and for the lowest caste among Hindus (untouchables, now called the scheduled castes). Yet, for an example of assertion of Hindu identity, around 1980 the **Bharatya Janata Party** emerged as a political force committed to the preservation of Hinduism in public life, and in 1992 Hindus whom secularists label as extremists destroyed a mosque built by Muslims in Ayodhya, a site traditionally considered sacred by Hindus. Toleration of untouchables has also been insecure. Although themselves Hindus, untouchables have long been considered a threat to Hinduism because of various forms of 'pollution' (unsanitary occupations or a mixed caste or foreign background).

Judaism began among a network of families calling itself *b'nai* Jacob (the descendants of Jacob), who transitioned from a nomadic to a sedentary way of life shortly after 2000 BC in the part of western Asia often called the Fertile Crescent. A sedentary life required defence of territory, later conquest of new lands. The social foundation of such security was the covenant, an agreement of common defence that came to be sacralized in a covenant, later a series of them, with Yhwh (the one god above all other deities, later the only God). The Jewish Bible (Torah, Nevi'im and Ketuvim) recounts God's creation of a harmonious world, its disturbance by disobedience, the covenants (always challenging for human beings to keep) God offered to allow Jews to return to harmony, and prophecies of restoration of divine order. Military conflict with Roman occupiers of Jewish land pushed the Jews into diaspora by AD 135 as well as into a codification of faith and ritual by rabbis. The two major groups in diaspora were the Sephardim (who settled in the Iberian peninsula but were expelled in 1492) and the Ashkenazim (who settled in northern France, Germany, **Poland** and **Russia**, were subject to pogroms during most of modern European history and targeted in the Holocaust in the 1930s and 1940s). Like all major European religions, Judaism underwent liberalization as a response to Enlightenment ideas and values, resulting in Reform Judaism in the nineteenth century and Reconstructionist Judaism in the twentieth century. The **Holocaust**, in which 6 million Jews were slaughtered, and a way of life, *shtetl* culture, destroyed, was the most extreme example of an anti-Semitism that dates at least to medieval Europe and that in some places continues today. Responses to the Holocaust have included meditations on the nature of evil, the role of God in the world, the possibility of a new covenant, and the power of ideas such as **anti-Semitism**, which had so long been promulgated by Christians.

Christianity emerged in the first century AD among the followers of Jesus, a Jew who some viewed as a messiah (Hebrew, *ha-Mashiach*; Greek, *ho Christos*) but who most Jews did not accept. Judaism and Christianity thus separated and by 1700 Christianity was the dominant religion in Europe and in European colonies in the western Atlantic. Many elements of Jewish scriptures (the Old Testament to Christians) survived, most notably the covenants between God and humanity, although they were usually reinterpreted. The covenant, for example, became potentially universal, not offered only to a particular chosen people: it was Jesus' crucifixion and his miraculous resurrection and ascension that opened the possibility of reconciliation with God to all humanity. In its early centuries, Christianity came to have two conflicting faces that have continued in the modern world. One was Christians as those inspired by the Holy Spirit (the third person of the triune God comprising the Father, the Son and the Spirit) and having equal status before God. The other was Christians as those organized in a hierarchical church modelled on the Roman Army (Rome occupied the land of Jesus' birth), with ordinary believers subject to the authority of deacons, priests, bishops and, ultimately, the pope, Pontifex Maximus.

The Orthodox (often called Eastern) Church split from the Roman Church after disputes over the authority of the pope; this division remains in the modern world and the Orthodox Church has spread across the globe. Challenges to the Roman Church, whether real or imagined, were suppressed by means such as the Inquisition. A momentous split occurred in the sixteenth century as Protestant (Reformed, Lutheran and Anabaptist) churches left the Roman Church. Although in the eighteenth century Christianity was harshly attacked by some adherents of the Enlightenment, the individualistic, capitalist and democratic tendencies of Europeans and Americans invigorated the religion and fostered movements that thrive in the twenty-first century. Individualism, capitalism and democracy all legitimized the inner spiritual experience and the religious insights of believers in ways that were inconceivable in a traditional authoritarian religion. The eighteenth century brought into better focus the first face of Christianity – believers inspired by the Holy Spirit – and it encouraged revivalistic religion (continuing today), a voluntaristic model of religious affiliation and a splintering process in which new theologies, new types of ministers and new groups are continually created. In American history, this process is often called 'the democratization of Christianity', but in fact it has occurred worldwide, albeit not at the same pace in all places. Inherent in the early church, just visible in the Reformation and in full swing by 1800, the legitimization of the spiritual experience of ordinary believers has allowed Christianity to divide and subdivide into a vast array of religious bodies.

Although in theology, practice and social views, Christianity in the early twenty-first century seems kaleidoscopic, much of the religion in its modern forms can be traced back to the post-Reformation unleashing of the spirituality of ordinary men and women and the possibility of choosing one's religious affiliation. The success of Christianity as an evangelical religion lies in its adaptability to the lives of ordinary people the world over. Even the Roman Church possesses only a shred of the authority it once had. Still, popular Christian faith remains prone to the criticisms of those such as Karl Barth who resist the deflation of the supernatural into the ordinary ways of life and thought. A religion based in miracles and transcendence of the world, as in the Christian Bible, will always seem to some believers not totally adaptable to social circumstances.

Islam began with Muhammad, who believed that the competing claims made in his time about god or the gods could not all be true and who felt the lack among of his own people, the Arabs, of a written revelation such as had been given to the Jews and the Christians. Prayer and meditation, accompanied at times by anxiety, led him, in a cave on Mount Hira, to a revelation from an angel of one god, Allah, as all powerful in the creation and rule of the universe. Islam as a faith is submission to the will of Allah. As prophet, Muhammad began speaking of his convictions, which were recorded by his followers and later collected in the Qur'an, which itself came to be supplemented by the Hadith, the earliest interpretations (now accepted as traditional) of Muhammad's words and deeds.

Sharia was the legal code of Muslim life, though open to interpretation on points, as indeed are all laws. Islam from its beginnings was both spiritual and social. Not until the twentieth century were there efforts, as in **Turkey**, to disengage the religious and secular spheres, while in 2011 the leaders of a successful resistance movement in **Libya**, having deposed the former head of state, announced that sharia would guide new Libyan legislation and that laws that contradict Islam would be nullified. After Muhammad's death in AD 632, controversy over his successor led to a split in Islam between the **Sunnis** and the **Shias** that continues today. By means of both conquest and conversion, Islam spread rapidly from the **Middle East** and in the modern world both interacted and collided with European colonialism: Muslims controlled some of the routes of the slave trade that provided sub-Saharan Africans for European and American slave ships, yet Muslims were leaders of resistance against European colonialism in some parts of **Africa** in the twentieth century. Moreover, European achievements in science, including geography, rested on borrowings from the Islamic world.

In the early twenty-first century Muslims number more than 1 billion and are successfully carrying Islam to new believers. Indeed, about half of the 2 million pilgrims who make the annual hajj, the visit to Mecca enjoined upon each believer at least once in his or her life, are citizens of non-Arab countries. Islam has spread so far from its place of origin that it, like Christianity, has engaged with the indigenous traditions of its converts. Insofar as this syncretism is disdained by the more orthodox, it is often unacknowledged, as in Christianity. Among West African Muslims, home shrines to various deities are common, although Islam is strictly monotheistic. Artistic representations of

Allah are easily found, particularly in *souweres*, paintings on panes of glass, although such images are forbidden as idolatrous in Islam. In both central Asia and **Indonesia** a mix of indigenous and Muslim beliefs and practices still survives, including religious notions, codes of law and social hierarchies that depart from normative Islam. The Nation of Islam, formed in the USA in the 1930s, followed the opposite path in that it originated outside the Muslim world but joined it in the 1970s.

In the second half of the twentieth century a fundamentalist movement gained strength in Islam. As with other fundamentalist impulses, the impetus has been a clash between the ancient texts and laws, on the one hand, and modern practices, on the other. Islamic fundamentalists have defended the literal truth of the Qur'an and traditional prohibitions against, for instance, divorce, consumption of alcohol and interest on loans – all parts of an inherited faith that are under pressure in modern society. Moreover, modern events often lead enquiry into the foundations of a faith. Honour is widely thought in the early twenty-first century to be a Muslim trait, particularly a masculine trait. Conflicts between Islamic societies and the non-Muslim world are often interpreted as affronts to Muslim honour, while the enforcement of sharia within Muslim societies is often described as a matter of honour. Yet an open question remains: does the Qur'an itself mandate honour, or was it rather a feature of the tribal societies among which Muhammad first spread his message and therefore a compromise of the moment but not essential to Islam?

Religious Right
– *see* **Christian Right**.

religious toleration

Religious toleration is the phenomenon whereby adherents of a sect other than the official religion of a polity are permitted certain rights, whether civil in nature or pertaining to the practice of their faith, or attain at least a modus vivendi with the followers of an established religion. The latter group normally, but not invariably, represent the majority or plurality of the population or profess the same faith as members of the ruling regime. In theory, religious toleration represents one of rather a wide range of positions between the systematic persecution of dissenters and a separation of church and state that is more associated with modern **secularism**; 'toleration' necessarily presupposes deviation from an official faith. Older accounts in the Whig tradition tended to posit a somewhat linear history in which medieval intolerance and the bloodshed of Europe's wars of religion of the sixteenth and seventeenth centuries inspired an **Enlightenment** reaction from figures such as **John Locke** and **Voltaire** against the notion that temporal status should depend on individual conviction, thus laying the foundations of nineteenth- and twentieth-century laicity and of a **liberalism** that grew to encompass secular rights as well.

Recently, historians have moved away from treating toleration as an abstract concept and have explored the multivalency of the word to stress its uneasy yet inherent coexistence with currents of persecution throughout the medieval and early modern periods as well, and the frequently contingent, localized and transient nature of its manifestation. 'Toleration' might describe anything from a polity's strategic concession of religious and/or civil rights to attract or retain a skilled stratum of the population, or an established church's grudging emphasis on religious concord – short of **ecumenicism** – and avoidance of further conflict, or the practical acceptance of dissent that keeps a low profile and does not seek to proselytize followers of the official faith. As to the ideological equation of toleration with the Enlightenment, *philosophes* could themselves be ambivalent about an idea that premised religious plurality on the grace and favour of the authorities rather than on the rights of the individual. Some of their number were also less celebratory of the human conscience where it strayed into religious 'enthusiasm' and 'ignorance'. Indeed, the question of how one tolerates the (potentially) intolerant has continued to prove intellectually problematic.

There was little change in the official religious arrangements of Europe for almost all of the eighteenth century: **Roman Catholicism** was established in **Spain**, **Portugal**, **France**, **Poland**, most of the **Habsburg** dominions, and the Italian and some German-speaking territories; **Protestantism**, in northern central and western Europe and most of the British American colonies, though it had various denominations; and **Islam** in the **Balkans**. Whatever the intellectual developments of the Enlightenment, dissenters still had good reason to fear both state and popular persecution during this era; **anti-Semitism** was especially persistent. Edicts of toleration (**Russia**, 1773; Holy Roman Empire, 1781–2; **France**, 1787) were generally limited by denomination or in their scope. Probably more so than conviction, they reflected the calculation of **enlightened despotism** which sought to bolster internal cohesion in the face of recurrent international wars, and whose burgeoning frameworks of state were beginning to assert themselves over those of the Church. More thoroughgoing and principled emancipation would have to await the effect of the **French Revolution** throughout Europe.

In England, political circumstances occasioned the Toleration Act (1689), which covered only religious rights, and those just for non-conformists; it completely excluded **Unitarians** and Catholics, on the latter of whom penal restrictions were lifted over a period of decades culminating in the Catholic Relief Act (1829). In the new **United States**, the **First Amendment** to the **American Constitution** prevented federal establishment of religion. In the individual states, the **American Revolution** witnessed accelerated liberalization and disestablishment, processes to which the existing religious diversity had rendered them prone. In more recent times, the **Universal Declaration of Human Rights** (1948) of the **United Nations**, and the **Vatican**'s decree *Dignitatis Humanae* (1965), have reaffirmed the individual's right to religious freedom.

reparations

The term for payments demanded of a defeated nation by a victor to compensate for war losses. It gained its most prominent airing in the **Treaty of Versailles**, in which **Germany** was required to pay monies to the victorious allies which would have resulted in the extraction of billions from the German economy until the 1980s. Reparations were once seen as a principal cause of German grievance and revanchism, and as an essentially unfair burden. Recent historical work has suggested, however, that the United Germany of 1919 would have had to pay less over sixty years than West Germany paid to other members of the European Community between 1957 and 1989, and that the burden of reparations was therefore exaggerated, though the method chosen to pay (inflated Reichsmarks) may well have contributed to the great inflation of 1921–3. The uncertainty of reparation bond repayment was also a key distortion leading to the world economic crash of 1929–31.

Republican Guard (Iraq)

– *see* **Hussein (al-Husayn), Saddam**.

Republican Party (US)

Supportive of isolationism and unilateralism, **laissez-faire** capitalism (albeit with **protectionist** tariffs), fiscal orthodoxy and conservative social policies, the 'Grand Old Party' is the historic main rival of the **Democratic Party**. Its birth in opposition to the **Kansas–Nebraska Act** (1854) heralded the third American party system, though its economic programme and evangelical social reformist impulse recalled the **Whigs**. The **American Civil War** vindicated its anti-slavery stance and confirmed it as the party of business and sound money. Although the end of **Reconstruction** lost it the South, the Republican Party was marginally preponderant in national elections up to 1896, then hegemonic till 1932. That very domination incurred occasional splintering, such as with the **Mugwumps** and **Progressives**.

The **Great Depression** destroyed the party's electoral standing and it accepted the tenets of the Democratic **New Deal** by the 1950s. Disaffection over the **Great Society**, the **Vietnam War** and African American **civil rights** won it working-class and Southern voters from the 1960s and bolstered its conservative wing. It dominated presidential elections from 1968 and won control of Congress in 1994. In the ascendant during the **Bush** era, it became divided by vocal right-wing activists. In 2016 it won power with the surprise victory of **Donald Trump**.

republicanism

Commonly, the ideology of governance without hereditary rule, although earlier definitions allowed for constitutional monarchies too. More specifically, republicanism refers to an **Enlightenment** tradition that saw people as being inclined to political participation but also liable to undermine the common good with corruption unless they were 'virtuous' or economically disinterested. It accordingly celebrated the **agrarian ideal** whilst mistrusting elites, merchants, bankers and people without property, for their dependence on dealings with others. Its emphasis on communitarian needs and positive law distinguished it from the **liberalism** of **John Locke**, in which a government of negative liberties protects the individual's property. It regarded actual republican government as liable to instability, factionalism and the passions of pure **democracy** unrestrained by law, which ultimately invited dictatorship. **Montesquieu** and **Rousseau** doubted that the model was viable for entities larger than city-states of homogeneous interests. Whilst republicanism was fundamental to the new

United States, **James Madison** had to address and contest these points in his case for the **American Constitution**.

resistance (World War II)

The occupation of **Europe** by the Germans and the Italians (and by the Bulgarians) provoked resistance movements almost everywhere, as did the Japanese occupation of the Far East. These resistance movements, however, were constrained by a political background which in many countries was highly ambiguous. Many Europeans were persuaded that the Nazi New Order in Europe was the face of the future and that it was pointless and counterproductive to struggle against it. Many French agreed with **Marshal Pétain** that collaboration was the only rational course. Many again saw the Germans and the Italians as actual or potential supporters of their own particular subordinate nationalism. The creation of a Slovak state under German auspices in 1939 was an attack on the integrity of the Czechoslovak state, as was that of a Croat state in 1941 on the Yugoslav state. Many Flemings, Ukrainians and others had parallel aspirations, as did many in South East Asia who hoped that the defeat of the Americans, British, French and Dutch by the Japanese would further their own ambitions for independence. Not least, most European countries had their own significant political movements of the far-right which found the Nazi creed sympathetic. These ambiguities were accentuated by the German attack on the **Soviet Union** of 1941 and the progression towards total war. The Germans promoted the war as a crusade against Bolshevism and many across Europe preferred fascism to communism and would have preferred to fight with **Germany** against the Soviet Union rather than fight with the Soviet Union against Germany.

The consequences for resistance movements were significant. On the one hand, they were bolstered by large numbers of communist recruits who proved to be amongst the best organized and the most highly motivated, contributing to the important role played by communists in post-war governments in **France**, **Italy** and elsewhere. On the other, they led to deep fissures, most obviously in **Yugoslavia**, where the failure to agree of communist Partisans under **Tito** and Royalist Cetniks under Mihajlović led to a civil war running in parallel with the war against the occupiers. The Cetniks ultimately collaborated with the occupiers.

The Germans in particular forfeited any acceptance of their overrule by the brutality of their occupation, which was at its most marked in the east where the Slavs were to be displaced. Oradour in France and Lidice in **Czechoslovakia** became symbolic of the savagery of reprisals for resistance although they helped to cement the movements together. Nevertheless, despite the heroism of individuals, the military value of the resistance movements was usually limited. Only in the **Balkans** where the rugged terrain lent itself to guerrilla warfare did they have a major impact. Tito's Partisans succeeded in containing a score of enemy divisions, but the Albanians alone liberated their country without outside assistance. The significance of the resistance movements was sometimes greater after the war than during it. In France, the very existence of the resistance and the accession to power of its leader, **General de Gaulle**, helped to restore national confidence and pride after the collapse of 1940. In both **Albania** and Yugoslavia, meanwhile, the communist resistance became the national government for more than fifty years after the end of the war.

revolution, counter-revolution

Human history, and indeed prehistory, has been punctuated by revolutions – in agriculture, in technology and in social organization as well as in culture, ethics and philosophy. It could even be argued that human history is the history of revolutions. Amongst all these revolutions, however, the political revolution stands apart. It is incomparably more violent and seemingly sudden, often exploding on a single day. Its nearest parallel is perhaps the religious revolution. The Reformation, for example, can be dated from Martin Luther's nailing of his theses on the church door at Wittenberg on 31 October 1517. Furthermore, political and religious revolution are equally likely to be bloody. The political revolution can also be distinctly 'catching'. The **revolutions of 1848** spread across much of Europe with remarkable speed just as did the **Arab Spring** of 2011–12 across the **Middle East**. Such revolutions, however, are usually the least likely to achieve their aims. Nevertheless, political revolution is often the fruit of earlier revolutionary economic and social change to which the pre-existent structure of power cannot, or will not, adjust. The French *ancien régime* prior to 1789 and tsarist **Russia** prior to 1917 are both excellent examples. Moreover, political revolutions do not exist in isolation. There are close links, for example, between the **French Revolution** and the Romantic movement in the arts across Europe. Most political

revolutions, however, are primarily associated with economic and social revolution. **Lenin**'s pronouncement that 'Communism is the electrification of the whole country' clearly underlines that particular duality. It is this lack of association which prevents many of the military coups, which have been such a feature of Latin American and Middle Eastern history since the mid nineteenth century, from being usefully classified as political revolutions. The replacement of one military officer by another of similar background may bring about a change of government but probably not a change of regime.

Political revolutions are inherently untidy explosions of public feeling. Nevertheless, they are normally driven by one or more of three basic aims: securing more democracy, however that may be defined; securing national liberation; securing modernization. Those aims are, however, always likely to be modified or even thwarted by the incidence of counter-revolution, either as a phase in the longer-term revolutionary process or as a pre-emptive political act to forestall revolution. The Unilateral Declaration of Independence (UDI) by Rhodesia (now **Zimbabwe**) under **Ian Smith** in November 1965 is a particularly clear example of the latter.

Just as it is possible to see distinctly different, albeit overlapping, common aims in the untidiness of all political revolutions, so it is similarly possible to identify a common underlying pattern in their course of development, although there will be major differences in the duration of individual phases. Moreover, some political revolutions, such as the German after 1918, will not run their full course and others may seemingly omit a particular phase. The underlying pattern is, however somewhat different in the case of democratic, liberation and modernizing revolutions, although there are significant parallels. Despite these common patterns, some revolutions appear to be appreciably more significant than others, not so much because of the power or size of the country concerned, although that is clearly a factor, but because of the applicability of their ideas and spirit to the much wider world. The French Revolution was so significant because its espousal of the concept of the 'rights of man' and its ideals of equality, liberty and fraternity were of universal application. It was as an acknowledgement of the enduring power of those ideas that the French **Vichy** regime in occupied France during **World War II** substituted for them its own trio of *famille, travail, patrie* (family, work, fatherland). That power to inspire can give revolutions and revolutionary ideas a sudden unexpected potency centuries later. English parliamentarians prior to the English Civil War (1642–6) drew on the ideas of Magna Carta (1215) giving them an interpretation remote from the concepts of the barons for whom Magna Carta had been drafted. Similarly, the ideas behind the **American Declaration of Independence** (1776) were widely adopted by colonial peoples of **Asia** as arguments for their own independence following the defeat of the Japanese, primarily by the Americans, in World War II. The response of Chinese prime minister **Zhou Enlai** to the question what he thought of the French Revolution, 'It is too early to say', may have been meant as a joke but may yet prove profoundly true.

democratic revolutions

The most notable democratic revolutions of the modern period might be considered to be the English revolutions of 1642–9 and 1688–9; the French revolutions of 1789, 1830, 1848 and 1870–1; the liberal revolutions across the **Austrian, German** and **Russian Empires** of 1848–9; the Spanish revolutions of 1873 and 1931; the Ottoman and Iranian constitutional revolutions of 1876 and 1905–11, respectively; the Portuguese Revolution of 1910; the Mexican social revolution of 1910–21; the **Chinese revolutions** of 1911–12 and 1949; the **Russian revolutions** of 1905 and March and November 1917; the Hungarian communist revolution of 1918; the German revolutions of 1919; the communist revolutions in central and eastern Europe following World War II; the **Cuban Revolution** of 1959; the **Prague Spring** of 1968; the Ethiopian Revolution of 1974; the **Portuguese Revolution** of the Carnations of 1974–5; the Sandinista revolution in **Nicaragua** of 1979; the 'People Power' revolution in the **Philippines** in 1986; and the **Arab Spring** of 2011–12. Some of these, notably those of 1848, had a strong national liberation element, but their mutual connection was primarily liberal. The 'Rose Revolution' in **Georgia** of 2003 and the 'Orange Revolution' in **Ukraine** of 2004 shared a complex mix of democratic, nationalist and counter-revolutionary characteristics. Just as democratic revolutions may have a national liberation element, so national liberation revolutions have usually had an important democratic dimension.

For all their national differences, the foregoing democratic revolutions share a common pattern of development. In their first phase there is an uprising against an autocracy, usually monarchical, which has lost its moral authority through defeat in war, extravagance and corruption, remoteness from reality or simple incompetence. The targeted autocrat is typically a comparatively ineffectual leader whose claims ring hollow – Charles I of England's belief in his divine right to rule or **Louis XVI** of France's continuation of the absolutism crafted by Louis XIV, *le roi soleil* (the sun king), for his much more commanding personality. The autocrat is challenged by an influential group which demands a share in power, or at least the right to be consulted. The English parliamentarians of the 1640s insisted on 'no taxation without representation'. The French in 1789 demanded the summoning of the States General, which had not met since 1614, and the Russians in 1905, the establishment of a state Duma which would, in effect, be a successor of the consultative Boyars' Duma of the period before **Peter the Great**. The Turks in 1876 and the Iranians in 1905 demanded their first ever constitution. In some cases, such as **Russia** in 1917 and **Germany** in 1918, defeat in war may lead to mutiny in the armed forces and the evaporation of traditional autocratic power. In other, particularly more recent cases, such as **Cuba** in 1959, **Nicaragua** in 1979 and **Egypt** in 2012, the power of the autocrat – **Fulgencia Batista**, Anastasio Somoza and **Hosni Mubarak**, respectively – is significantly undermined by the perception of corruption. The uprising may take the form of little more than widespread public disorder, but is often much more dramatic, with the capture and destruction of the Bastille castle prison in Paris which launched the French Revolution on 14 July 1789, commemorated annually as the French national holiday, being perhaps the most famous example. The phase ends with the dissolution, or at least temporary dilution, of the established power structure. The more violently the regime is overthrown, the more likely the revolution is to succeed in securing its aims.

The second phase, which is occasionally omitted, is marked by growing disorder verging on anarchy as the old structure of power has been destroyed and a new one is yet to take its place. The infant Chinese republic declined into warlordism (1912–27). One common response is for the revolution to become ever more radical. The climate of anarchy may well be exacerbated by civil war between supporters of the previous power structure and the revolutionaries, as in the English Civil War (1642–6) and in the **Russian Civil War** (1917–22), or by war with outside powers opposed to, and probably fearful of, the revolution's aims, as in the French Revolutionary Wars, or even by both side by side, as in Russia where the western allies intervened, with **Churchill** famously wanting to strangle Bolshevism in its cradle. In yet other examples, for example Nicaragua, the foreign intervention, in this case by the US, may remain significant but be much less overt, as was revealed in 1986 by the **Iran–Contra scandal**. There is also the possibility of invasion by an outside power motivated by the belief that the ability of the disordered state to defend itself has been seriously compromised, as was the case with the Japanese invasion of **China** in 1931. Much more common, though, is conflict between the moderate revolutionaries, who are usually those who have instigated the revolution, and the more radical revolutionaries who seek to transform society. This conflict occurred virtually spontaneously in Berlin on 9 November 1918 when the social democrat Philip Scheidemann improvised the declaration of the German Republic from a Reichstag balcony and the communist **Karl Liebknecht** proclaimed the German Socialist Republic from a balcony of the Royal Palace at the other end of the city centre. The conflict, however, more usually develops over months rather than hours or days, and usually flows to the advantage of the more radical faction. In France, the Jacobins supplanted the Girondists, in Russia the Bolsheviks supplanted the Mensheviks. In the **Middle East** the **Muslim Brotherhood** emerged as initially the strongest force from inchoate discontent. It is a personally dangerous phase for revolutionary leaders and deposed monarchs alike. Danton and Ropespierre, Louis XVI and Marie Antoinette in France, Charles I in England, Karl Liebknecht and **Rosa Luxemburg** in Germany, and **Tsar Nicholas II** and his family in Russia all met the same fate. The communist victims of the 'show trials' in the **Soviet Union** in the 1930s, together with **Trotsky**, murdered in 1940, and Rajkin in **Hungary**, and Kostov in **Bulgaria** in 1949, and Slansky in **Czechoslovakia** in 1952, are in many respects comparable.

The third phase is probably the most confused and most subject to national variation, but is broadly a phase of reaction or at least retrenchment. In the case of the least effective revolutions, most obviously the liberal revolutions of 1848–9, the autocratic power then in the shape of the Austrian, German and Russian imperial governments, succeeds in reasserting its control. Only in France did the liberal impulse succeed in establishing a republic which, however short-lived, marked the final end of royal government in that country. The slightly greater degree of success of the national liberation face of the 1848 revolution is further discussed shortly. In the **Ottoman Empire**

after 1876 and **Iran** after 1905, the sultan and shah respectively, progressively rescinded their constitutional concessions and resumed their former autocratic rule. In Hungary in 1919 the forces of Admiral Horthy quickly overthrew the communist regime of **Bela Kun**. In the rather unusual case of Germany, social democrat chancellor Friedrich Ebert allied himself with the former imperial army in 1919 to defeat the communist Spartacists, which weakened the **Weimar Republic** throughout its fourteen-year existence. The rather similar savage repression of the Paris Commune by the infant French Third Republic in 1871, in which more Frenchmen died than had in the Franco-Prussian War, left equally deep scars. Circumstances may require even the most determined revolutionaries to compromise, at least temporarily, as with Lenin's New Economic Policy of 1921. In other cases again, as in England in the 1640s, the phase of reaction may either simply not occur or be postponed to a subsequent counter-revolutionary phase. More recently, the killing of **Che Guevara** in 1967 by US-trained Bolivian troops ended hopes of extending the Cuban revolution across **Latin America**.

In the fourth phase an authoritarian leader, often drawn from either the revolutionary army, such as Cromwell in England and **Napoleon I** in France, or from the dominant revolutionary party, such as Lenin and more obviously Stalin in Russia and then the Soviet Union, and Mao Zedong in China, or from both, such as Tito in Yugoslavia and Hoxha in Albania, acquires total authority. The seizure of personal power by elected President Louis Napoleon, later Emperor **Napoleon III**, in France in 1852, which was facilitated by the public memory of his uncle, the great Napoleon, was atypical. In any event, the leader imposes order in a manner which may be remote from the ideals of the first revolutionaries. Lenin's dictum that the challenge is not to destroy autocracy but to capture it underscores that point.

The fifth phase is as confused and subject to national variation as the third. Domestic fatigue and reaction, or defeat in war, may lead to a counter-revolution and reversion to the previous status quo; the restoration of the monarchy in England in 1660 and in France in 1815. Such reversions, however, are conditional. Any attempt by the monarch to revert to the previous absolutism sparks renewed revolution; the English 'Glorious Revolution' of 1688–9 and the French 'Three Glorious Days' of 1830. Alternatively, the authoritarian leader may die of natural causes and be replaced by appreciably more moderate but still authoritarian successors, particularly if power flows from control of a revolutionary party. The Soviet leadership after Stalin's death in 1953 followed this pattern, as has China's since the death of **Mao Zedong** in 1976. Policy is likely to become less 'revolutionary' in tempo. Indeed, the period of **Brezhnev**'s rule in the Soviet Union (1964–82) has been dubbed 'the age of stagnation'. At the other extreme, China has largely substituted state capitalism for state communism with economic effects the reverse of stagnant.

In the sixth and final phase, the experience of the revolution has been absorbed and equilibrium achieved. Its benefits have been consolidated, its excesses acknowledged and remedied, and a basic consensus secured. The length of this phase will vary considerably between different facets of national life. French social life absorbed the economic impact of the Revolution comparatively quickly, as the novels comprising Balzac's *Comédie Humaine*, written in the 1830s and 1840s, testify, but political life saw a long search by its institutions for legitimacy, with two monarchies, two empires and five republics exercising power between 1789 and 1958. Britain has been unusual in its ability to secure general acceptance of the principle of constitutional monarchy in 1688–9, only thirty-nine years after the execution of Charles I in 1649. Whether Russia or China has yet reached that level of equilibrium is a matter for future historians.

This overview is an analysis, not an evaluation, of the revolutionary process. One may conclude that the overall impact of a revolution was negative rather than positive. Some historians have opined that the Revolution set France back, and it is no secret that the commemoration of its bicentenary in 1989 would have been appreciably less celebratory if a right-wing president rather than the Socialist François Mitterrand had been in office. Moreover, the very definition of *democracy* has historically been contentious with proponents of, for example, 'liberal' and 'socialist' democracy denying the validity of the alternative interpretation. All that can be said is that a revolution has become inevitable by the time it erupts, and that England is unusually fortunate in being able, with so little dissent, to summarize its civil war in the comic formula of *1066 and All That* that the Cavaliers were 'Wrong but wromantic and the Roundheads right and repulsive'.

national liberation revolutions

Revolutions to achieve national liberation have been numerous, largely because the world since 1700 has moved away from a dominant imperial pattern of organization to an almost exclusive pattern of nation state organization. On the other hand, national liberation has often been achieved without the need for an armed struggle which can remotely be described as revolutionary. In a further complication, a revolution of national liberation may exclude or even frustrate the call for a democratic revolution which is an integral part of the wider independence movement. This is simply because the creation of a nation state may be seen as a means of securing the privileges of an elite or a majority rather than of enfranchising the population as a whole.

As with democratic revolutions, revolutions to achieve national liberation may be broadly grouped and there are similarly common underlying patterns. The first group includes the most celebrated of them all – the **American War of Independence** (1775–81) – but also comprises those it inspired, directly or indirectly, first in **Haiti** where the French precedent was the stronger influence in 1804, and then across the whole of Latin America under the leadership of **Simón Bolívar** and José de San Martín (1778–1850). By 1830 the Spanish and Portuguese Empires in the New World were at an end. The second group comprises the Balkan nation states which first secured autonomy and then independence from the Ottoman Empire from 1829 onwards, finishing with **Albania** in 1912. Only **Egypt** amongst the Ottoman Empire's Afro-Asian domains secured somewhat comparable autonomy but as a result of the adventurousness of Mohammed 'Ali rather than of an independence movement.

The third group is represented by the European liberal revolutions of 1848 which, France and Germany proper aside, all had a strong nationalist component. Only in Italy where **Austria** had to surrender Milan did they have any immediate impact, although the 1867 *Ausgleich* converting the Austrian into the **Austro-Hungarian Empire** was arguably a belated concession. The revolution in Brussels in 1830 against the decision of the **Congress of Vienna** in 1815 to unite the former Austrian Netherlands with the Kingdom of the **Netherlands** may perhaps be associated with this group. It led to the international recognition of modern **Belgium** in 1839. The fourth group comprises the numerous nation states of central and eastern Europe which emerged following the collapse of the Austrian, German, Russian and Turkish Empires at the end of **World War I**. It could be argued that they all emerged in a power vacuum and cannot be validly classified as revolutions. On the other hand, the Polish independence movement in particular had a history of violence behind it, and it was a south Slav nationalist who had triggered the outbreak of World War I by assassinating Archduke Franz-Ferdinand in Sarajevo in 1914. The true nationalist revolutions of the period were actually against the victorious western allies: in **Ireland** which secured independence from **Britain** after violent unrest starting with the 1916 **Easter Uprising** in Dublin, and in Turkey, where **Kemal Atatürk** repudiated the allies' intention of dismembering the national territory and established the present Turkish nation state, reluctantly recognized by the allies under the Treaty of Lausanne (1923).

The fifth group is the largest, comprising all those where there was a violent reaction to the attempt by the European powers or the US to re-establish their colonial authority after World War II or to deny the call for liberation from colonial status more generally. They include French North Africa (now **Morocco**, **Algeria** and **Tunisia**) and French Indochina (now **Vietnam**, **Laos** and **Cambodia**), the Dutch East Indies (now **Indonesia**), and certain British territories where either strategic interests prevailed (Aden, **Cyprus**) or there was a strong white settler interest (**Kenya**, Southern Rhodesia). The unique case of **South Africa**, where the imperial power was effectively the white settler government, can be included with this latter group for the present purpose. A subgroup, including Egypt in 1952 and **Iraq** in 1958, and perhaps **Cuba** in 1959, comprises states where there was a revolution against a client regime and a determination to assert untrammelled independence. A small seventh group arguably comprises the states arising from the dissolution of the Soviet Union and Yugoslavia after 1990. Within the former Soviet Union, however, the process of dissolution saw limited violence only in Lithuania, and in Yugoslavia the conflicts between the Serbs, Croats and Bosnian Muslims were ethnic rather than revolutionary.

A comparatively small final eighth group comprises those regions which have sought separation by violent means from a state, normally African or Asian, which has either reasserted or acquired its full independence comparatively recently: Iranian **Azerbaijan** from **Iran** (1946), **Tibet** from China (1959), **Biafra** from **Nigeria** (1967–70), **East Timor** from **Indonesia** (1976–2002), Chechnya from the **Russian Federation** (1994–6), Kosovo from **Serbia** (1998–2008) and South Sudan from **Sudan** (1962–2009). Several more sporadic or less focused movements could perhaps be added – the **Kurds** of Iran, **Iraq** and particularly Turkey, and the Naga

from India. The rather exceptional European cases of the revolutionary Basque ETA movement, which officially abandoned its armed struggle for independence in 2011, and of the **Irish Republican Army (IRA)**, which abandoned its armed struggle for Irish unification in return for power-sharing in **Northern Ireland** in 2007, share some of the characteristics of this group, which may well grow over time.

Although worldwide in their incidence, these revolutions for national independence do share certain characteristics. The first is their almost total success. Even South Africa abandoned apartheid and accepted black majority rule in 1990. Only those of the eighth group have sometimes failed, at least to date. This is particularly remarkable when the imperial powers, notably the French in Algeria and **Vietnam**, replaced by the Americans in the latter case (1954–73), put very substantial military resources into their attempt to retain control. A second common characteristic is their almost universal rejection of liberal democracy for at least a substantial period after independence. Apart from a few minor cases, including Ireland and perhaps **Malaysia** and Turkey, the only real exception to date is South Africa. Democratic India is precluded by the fact that its independence was willingly granted by Britain in non-revolutionary circumstances.

modernizing revolutions

Although perhaps only one revolution can be classified as solely a modernizing revolution – the 'White Revolution' of the **Pahlavi dynasty** in Iran, particularly under Shah **Reza Pahlavi** – some other revolutions, both democratic and national liberation, have had a powerful modernizing dimension. It featured in the French Revolution of 1789 from the beginning under the influence of such eighteenth-century philosophers as **Diderot** and **Voltaire** who had attacked obscurantism, prejudice and blind traditionalism, but has its greatest impact under Napoleon, who swept away feudalism, clerical jurisdictions and archaic forms of law and social organization virtually wherever the revolutionary armies went.

It was an even more overt feature of the communist revolutions of the twentieth century, starting with the Russian Bolshevik Revolution of 1917. Lenin's concept of progress as encapsulated in his dictum 'Communism is the electrification of the whole country' was virtually deified in the Soviet Union under Stalin and across Communist-dominated central and eastern Europe after the Word War II. Party banners read 'Forwards' and publishing houses were 'Progress Publishers'. Religion was persecuted as a non-progressive force which indeed it often had been. Socialist realism demanded positivism, and negativism was an unforgivable sin. The headlong progress of China's contemporary state capitalism under communist auspices may perhaps be construed as just a continuation of that same revolutionary dynamic, only in different dress.

It was also a crucial component of Kemal Atatürk's primarily nationalist revolution in Turkey. It was his specific intention to mould a new Turkey as a nation state on western lines. Latin script replaced the Arabic, the new legal system was based on the Swiss civil and Italian penal codes, traditional dress was discouraged or banned, and the *ulama* abolished as a class. Indeed, there was little difference between his own social reforms and those concurrently being imposed on the Turkic lands by the Soviet Union.

counter-revolutions

As has already been implied, the aforementioned three broad groupings of revolution are complemented by, and may well include a phase of, counter-revolution. It is perhaps important to repeat that the present description is analytical, not qualitative. Counter-revolution may be described as a move to undo the achievements of a preceding revolution or, less commonly, to forestall a revolution which is anticipated will happen. The Rhodesian Unilateral Declaration of Independence of 1965 has already been mentioned as a particularly clear example of the latter. Other examples include the *coup d'état* of General Pinochet in **Chile** (1973) to forestall a radical popular revolution under President **Allende**, and slightly less clearly that by the military in **Argentina** in 1976. General **Franco**'s ultimately successful invasion of **Spain** in 1936, which launched the **Spanish Civil War** against a democratic, albeit weak, republican government which was moving to the left, may be included, as may the *coup d'état* by the Colonels in **Greece** (1967).

Counter-revolutions, as part of the longer-term revolutionary process, include the monarchical restorations in England in 1660, and in France in 1815, and arguably the collapse of Communism in the Soviet Union and central and eastern Europe (1989–91). The uprising in Hungary in 1956 had combined national liberation with counter-revolutionary characteristics, as did the renewed independence of the **Baltic States**. The most interesting example of counter-revolution, however, is probably the Islamic Republic of Iran with its rejection of the shah's 'White Revolution' of western-style modernization. Usually described as a revolution rather than a counter-revolution, its future evolution remains unclear.

Revolution of 1830 (French)

The Paris insurrection of 27–29 July (the 'July Days') that forced the abdication on 2 August of the reactionary Bourbon King Charles X (1757–1836) and his replacement on 9 August by his Orléanist cousin **Louis Philippe** (1773–1850). It was provoked by Charles' rejection of an opposition election victory and his suspension of the 1814 constitution. The new regime, the 'July Monarchy' of the 'Citizen King', represented the triumph of the bourgeoisie and survived until 1848.

Revolutionary Calendar (French)

Adopted in October 1793 but applied retrospectively from September 1792, those months being year one of the Republic, deemed the dawn of a new age in human history. The months, each comprising three weeks of ten days, were: Pluviôse, Ventôse, Germinal, Floréal, Prairial, Messidor, Thermidor or Fervidor, Fructidor, Vendémiaire, Brumaire, Frimaire and Nivôse. Abolished by **Napoleon** on 1 January 1806, but briefly resuscitated by the Commune, May 1871, it was used by some French historians when referring to the Revolution.

Revolutions of 1848

Series of revolutions and attempted revolutions that occurred throughout Europe in 1848. The spread of nationalism, the growth of liberalism and economic crises challenged the conservative establishment and acted as catalysts for revolutionary activity. The first revolution occurred in France, where radical socialists forced the abdication of **Louis Philippe**. This uprising produced a domino effect. In Germany, protests led by university radicals, liberals and nationalists achieved limited reforms, including the establishment of the Frankfurt Assembly and creation of the Declaration of the Basic Rights of the German People. Revolutionary activity in **Italy** strengthened the nationalist cause and provided the foundation for unification. Inspired by nationalist movements, minority groups – including Czechs, Poles, Hungarians and Croats – demanded freedom from Austrian rule. Despite the ultimate failure of the revolutions, the events of 1848 succeeded in expanding the public sphere and brought a new consciousness of republican, democratic and nationalist ideologies that would continue to shape European politics and diplomacy in the nineteenth and twentieth centuries.

Rhee, Syngman (1875–1965)
– *see also* **South Korea**.
Rhee served as the first president of **South Korea** from 1948 to 1960. He participated in various anti-Japanese colonial efforts through organizations such as the Independence Club in 1896 and the Korean provisional government. Rhee became president of South Korea through the support of conservative Korean leaders and the **United States** government. Pushing an anti-communist agenda, his presidency was marked by corruption, violence and authoritarianism. In April 1960 mass protests that resulted in the police shooting and killing scores of students and older citizens forced Rhee to resign from office.

Rhineland, reoccupation of the
Under the terms of the Armistice of 1918 and the **Versailles Treaty** which ended **World War I**, allied troops occupied the Rhineland area of **Germany**. The area was administered by an Inter-Allied Commission. The occupation forces consisted of American, French, British and Belgian forces. The occupation, which lasted until 1920, was highly controversial for three main reasons. Firstly, a large part of the French forces consisted of colonial African troops, against whom racial objections were raised. Secondly, **Belgium** incorporated several Rhineland territories into itself. Thirdly, the Rhenisch independence movement, which would become important in the 1920s and which wished to break away from Germany, was inadvertently encouraged.

By 1925, the Locarno Treaties provided that, though a part of Germany, the Rhineland was never to be remilitarized, as this would pose an obvious threat to **France** and Belgium. In March 1936, **Adolf Hitler** sent troops, airplanes and light infantry into the Rhineland, at the risk of a backlash and coup should there have been French or **League of Nations** resistance. Given that there was none, his aggressive act was seen as a great success for Germany and is often viewed as the beginning of the road to **World War II**.

Rhodes, Cecil (1853–1902)
A British businessman noted for his major role in the colonization of **South Africa**. When in his teens, Rhodes went to South Africa as a treatment for his poor health, and for a time worked as a farm owner. In 1871 he joined a number of other British settlers in prospecting for diamonds in Kimberley. He formed the De Beers Mining Company (subsequently chartered as the British South Africa Company) in 1880 and consolidated large holdings in the mine fields. He organized a private police force initially to patrol the lawless diamond district, but later as a private army which helped him extend control over neighbouring areas, taking over Mashonaland, the nucleus of later Rhodesia (modern **Zimbabwe** and **Zambia**) in 1893. His company was instrumental in arranging for the development of the migrant labour system of South Africa. He and his followers were active in the South African War (1899–1902).

Ricardo, David (1772–1823)
Born in London, England. He articulated and rigorously formulated the Classical system of political economy. In his most famous work *Principles of Political Economy and Taxation* (1817) Ricardo advances a labour theory of value and introduces the theory of comparative advantage. He was also a businessman, financier and speculator, and amassed a considerable fortune.

Rida, Rashid (1865–1935)
Islamic thinker, born in what became Lebanon. Influenced early by Muslim reformers and nationalists, notably Muhammad 'Abduh, the founder of the Salafi movement, with whom he launched in Cairo in 1898 the widely influential journal of Qur'anic commentary, *al-Manar* (*The Lighthouse*). Rida attributed the vulnerability to colonialism of Muslim societies to blind traditionalism, intellectual stagnation amongst the *ulama*, and Sufi excesses resulting in a lack of scientific and technological progress. His answer was a return to the purity of early **Islam**, interpreted (*ijtihad*) to address the modern world, thereby incorporating both the traditional and the radical. The unification of the Muslim community (*umma*) should be achieved through a true caliph who would guide Muslim governments as the supreme interpreter of Islam. Rulers should respect and consult the *ulama* in the formulation of policy, and the implementation of **sharia** law and its punishments was mandatory. On the other hand he supported Darwinian evolution and the need sometimes to interpret the Qur'an allegorically. Moreover, usury (*riba*) could be permissible and social relations should reflect differing generations and societies.

Risorgimento
The name given by Italian nationalists and historians to the re-emergence over the course of the nineteenth century of a united **Italy**.

The beginning of the Risorgimento is usually placed at around the time of the **Napoleonic Wars**, when Italian cultural affiliation began to become more than an expression. A sense of Italian identity pervaded the press before and during the failed 1848 revolutions, and had been evident in the activities of the Carbonari revolutionary movement since 1820, but a full drive to unity did not begin until mid-century. Under the leadership of **Camillo di Cavour** in Piedmont from 1852, and **Giuseppe Garibaldi** from 1860, and in the face of opposition from the papal lands and Rome, Italy was gradually united – a process that was completed by the withdrawal of French troops from Rome in 1870. By 1871, Austrian, Sicilian, Neapolitan, papal and aristocratic regimes had been displaced by a unitary parliamentary monarchy. This process, which had proceeded via insurgency, war, diplomacy and annexation, failed to fulfil Republican dreams but largely completed the Risorgimento.

Rivera, Diego (1886–1957)

One of **Mexico**'s greatest muralists, Rivera was born in Guanajuato, underwent traditional art training at Mexico City's Academy of San Carlos, and travelled to Europe to study Italian fresco wall painting. He was inspired by the tumultuous innovations of Cubism and Expressionism. After the Mexican Revolution, Secretary of Education **José Vasconcelos** chose him to express revolutionary ideals visually as frescos on public buildings. He fused the European fresco style with Mexican colours and popular images of native Mexican cultures. He refused the cheap utilitarianism of socialist realism and non-individualistic state-ordered paintings of communist parties. While he developed a unique Latin American revolutionary ideal, he lived as a communist painter, a Stalinist, a Trotskyite, an occasional **FBI** informer and a skilled provocateur. Out of favour with Mexico's revolutionary elite after 1929, his technical and visual innovations inspired US painters of the **New Deal**. His wife and partner was the famous painter **Frida Kahlo**.

Rizal, José (1861–1896)

Philippine nationalist, polymath, doctor, opthamologist, writer and poet whose life was defined and ended by the struggle for independence from Spain. He came from a wealthy family, but through dissent and common feeling sympathized more with Filipinos than the West, which nevertheless fascinated him. He travelled widely, and was married to an Irish woman in **Hong Kong**.

However, he was arrested in Spain during the anti-Spanish revolution of 1896 as a Cuban sympathizer, and, once returned to the **Philippines**, was executed for treason. Rizal is simultaneously one of the great political and cultural heroes of his homeland.

roads

– *see* **transportation**.

Robespierre, Maximilien (1758–1794)

French lawyer, revolutionary, leader of the Committee of Public Safety and instigator of the Terror of 1793–4. Robespierre began as a provincial lawyer and devotee of the works of **Jean-Jacques Rousseau**, rising from comparative obscurity through academic merit to the rank of criminal judge, which he abjured out of distaste for the way in which the death penalty was applied against the poor. He was elected to the Estates General in 1789 as a deputy from Arras, arguing for the 'Rights of Man'. He gravitated towards the Jacobin left, and was a powerful voice in the decision to execute **France**'s dethroned king in 1793. From then on, Robespierre became the leading force of the revolution, encouraging the guillotining of enemies of the revolution in a campaign of purges and terror, and also the promoting of a new civil religion based around a cult of a Supreme Being. When his threat of revolutionary violence based on suspicion was directed towards the National Convention, it turned on him, and he was himself executed, along with fellow Jacobins. He remains the icon of the **French Revolution** in its most bloody phase.

Rococo

The term for an art movement which developed from the Baroque tradition in the eighteenth century in the aristocratic capitals of Catholic Europe. *Rococo* is a compound wordplay on the French word for 'stones', the Spanish *barocco*, meaning 'pearls', and is a near homophone for 'seashells'. It referred to sensuous, asymmetric elaborated designs of furniture, jewellery, costume, landscapes and art which played on free-flowing naturalism (unlike the more stylized Baroque). Variations on seashells and foliage were particularly characteristic. Rococo was associated with the 'totalization' of interior design, indulgent theatrical wordplay (especially in pre-Revolutionary **France**) and with the artistic visions of Roman and French architects and painters in the early and mid eighteenth century. It was a term of derision used alongside 'old-fashioned' in the early to mid nineteenth century (though it has enjoyed periodic returns to favour) and the style itself was supplanted by the much more formalized, austere Neoclassicism of the later 1700s.

rock 'n roll

Musical form drawn from twelve-bar blues, rhythm and blues and boogie-woogie piano, with a strong rhythm section and accentuated 4/4 back beat. Developed from what was termed 'race music' in the 1940s **United States**, the term 'rock and roll' had been in use – particularly in song lyrics – before the genre itself fully crystallized. Its precise starting date remains disputed: a 'rhythm and blues' event organized by radio personality and DJ Alan Freed in Cleveland, Ohio, on 21 March 1952; **Elvis Presley**'s first recording, 18 July 1953; Presley's first commercial recording, 'That's All Right, Mama', 5 July 1954; or the opening sequence of *Blackboard Jungle*, over which Bill Haley's 'Rock Around the Clock' played, released 20 March 1955. The genre's energetic sound, charismatic performers, racial ambiguity and sexually charged lyrics both appealed to a new generation of teenagers and aggravated a conservative society. Rock 'n roll spawned numerous subgenres and laid the groundwork for future musical styles including rock music. It rapidly became a global phenomenon, generating many iconic rock groups.

Rockefeller, John Davison (1839–1937)

American **oil** magnate who pursued a number of business interests in Cleveland, Ohio, before entering the newly established oil-refining business in 1863. Rockefeller expanded his operations continuously until by 1879 his Standard Oil Company controlled 90 per cent of the country's refining capacity. Although Standard Oil lost ground to its competitors as new oilfields were opened, it retained a position of power and was regarded as one of the most dangerous of the so-called 'trusts' that dominated American industry.

Roe v. *Wade* (USA)

Decision of the **United States Supreme Court** (22 January 1973), authored by Justice Harry Blackmun, that found a fundamental, constitutionally protected right to an abortion, based on a woman's privacy right implicit within the US Constitution. Politically controversial, the decision spurred a 'pro-life' movement that successfully raised abortion's electoral importance, as well as a 'pro-choice' movement in *Roe*'s defence. Anti-*Roe* litigation has limited access to abortion but has left the right itself intact.

Roh Tae-woo (1932–)

– *see also* **Kwangju Uprising** and **South Korea**.

Roh served as president of **South Korea** from 1988 to 1993. His most notable role in Korean politics before 1988 was his participation in the December 1979 *coup d'état* led by Chun Doo-hwan – a military general who preceded Roh as president. Considered the first openly held democratic election in South Korea, Roh's election as president ended authoritarian rule and inaugurated a new period of democracy. His conviction for corruption and conspiracy in the **Kwangju Uprising** in August 1996, however, tarnished his presidential legacy.

Roma (Gypsies)

A generic and sometimes pejorative term for nomadic peoples of Romany and Calo extraction who emerged from **India** in the 1100s and whose culture generally mandates that they travel as a community in caravans. The word *gypsy* suggests an Egyptian origin for the group which is misconceived, but which took root early in its encounter with European natives. Some Romanies in southern Europe have settled but retain linguistic or cultural links with their past. In the English-speaking world, the term has been extended to cover Irish travellers and nomads of choice. There are over 10 million subsisting Roma peoples, many of whom are subject to frequent racial discrimination, and persecutions of gypsies – including in the **Holocaust** – have been historically common in Europe. Romany and Calo or Kale peoples can now be found, often upholding inter-group dialectical and regional differences, across the world.

Roman Catholicism

A global church belonging to no one country which forms the largest single Christian denomination of over 1 billion people. The Roman Catholic Church is distinguished by the existence of a **papacy** based in the Vatican city-state, its worldwide network of priests, orders, non-ecclesiastical or 'lay' groups and its role in western history since the time of the Roman Empire in which it took initial institutional existence. The Church claims an apostolic succession of its leader from Saint Peter, whom Jesus Christ designated controller of the keys of Heaven and a rock for his church according to Catholic tradition, and of its archbishops and bishops from the apostles in general. It has senior members known as cardinals who draw their authority from an tradition dating from the Middle Ages; is generally but not absolutely associated with unmarried, celibate priests; and has a sacramental approach to religion in which only recognized priests and bishops can administer forgiveness after confession of sin, sanctify marriage and conduct the transubstantiation of bread and wine into the body and blood of Christ. Three further sacraments of baptism, the last rites before death and confirmation in the faith are usually but not theoretically exclusively administered by priests or bishops.

The Church employs Latin in its official dealings, though since **Vatican II** has not required it for its distinctive ritual of Mass (during which worshippers are asked every week to restate their creed as a group and occasionally to repeat baptismal vows), and is less dependent upon the Bible than other Christian groups for its authority. Indeed, the remarkable discipline and rigidity of authority within the Church, stretching from a pope, who on some matters is viewed as infallible, down to ordinary members, who are generally inducted from just after birth, contrasts with other Christian denominations. Catholicism employs an agreed catechism, or system of religious logic, which is highly coherent and therefore rigid in the face of dissent, and is associated with networks of schools, welfare institutions, social and political teachings such as Christian Democracy, and functional orders of monks and nuns which further buttress its organization. It considers itself the only true church, and sees other churches as having worth only insofar as they approach Catholic doctrine.

Though highly complex and developed over nearly 2,000 years, Catholic doctrine broadly holds that God is actually a trinity of Father, Son and Holy Spirit; that Jesus Christ was the son of God, was born of a virgin, crucified, died and resurrected; and that he charged the apostles with spreading his message after he ascended into Heaven bodily, to be followed a little later by his immaculately conceived mother. The status of Jesus' mother, Mary, is a point of disagreement between Catholics and other Christians. Catholics have been closely associated with Marianism, the devotion to and elevation of Mary, which has gone hand in hand with the strengthening of the central papacy against local bishops and archbishops. Catholicism has also been associated with other distinctive doctrines, such as the idea of original sin. This holds that all people are flawed and imperfect, and so is any human institution, even the Church may be; it has often been attacked as therefore forgiving crimes and sins too easily, and as internalizing guilt. Protestantism began as

a protest against the Church's manifest corruption, its sale of 'indulgences' and its proclaimed monopoly over the creation of saints and the gates of Heaven, as well as its promotion of belief and duty over individuality and the work ethic of individual success.

Because of the Church's past and its intense anti-communism (which led it in some cases to either support or indulge fascist movements which almost exclusively arose in Catholic countries), anti-Catholicism has been a key feature of western history. Anti-Catholics associate the Church with sinfulness, sensuality, hypocrisy and arrogance. They question its Christian commitment, point to its perceived anti-Semitic past, and note the bitterness of Catholic disputes with Orthodox and Protestant churches. They point to the Church's record of inspiring wars, dominating central **Italy** as a ruler, its opposition to republics, and the fact that **Hitler**, **Mussolini** and all other fascist leaders were raised as Catholics. Such commentators also note the superstition implicit in Catholic recognition of miracles, exorcism and apparitions such as that of the Mother of God at **Lourdes**. Critics further point out the enormous impact of the Church's modern hostility to artificial contraception in the struggle with **AIDS** in the third world, its blanket opposition to **abortion**, its tendency to repression in matters of sexuality, and its highly conservative system of natural law. Such critics also point to the way in which a global wave of sexual scandal principally involving paedophilia was covered up in the Church until it was exposed in the 1980s and 1990s, with the Church hierarchy often allowing perpetrators to escape justice.

The Church has in recent years attempted to reform, and has undergone a process of internal debate about whether a conservative or progressive tradition should be emphasized. Its social teaching is anti-capitalist as well as anti-communist, and some groups within the Church, particularly the Society of Jesus or **Jesuits**, have become closely associated with campaigns for land reform, social democracy and human rights in the face of authoritarian regimes. During the **Cold War** the Church worked closely with western intelligence groups and was feared by communist leaders, who saw it as a resolute global opponent. This may have influenced the selection of some popes, as in 1958, when the cardinals who select the pope sidestepped hard-line anti-communists in favour of **John XXIII** in case of reprisals in eastern Europe.

Nevertheless, the role of **John Paul II** in particular in the destruction of communism in **Poland** and then elsewhere in 1989 should not be underestimated. World leaders of all denominations have made a point in recent years of attending papal funerals (that of John Paul II attracted global media attention and 4 million visitors) and of conferring with, listening to and occasionally reacting against such popes as Benedict XVI and Francis I. Both Muslim and Christian fundamentalists have attacked the Papacy as the symbol of a corrupt West and, in western history, have looked for its destruction as the sign of the end of the world and the emergence of a new religious order. To that end, some have sought to physically attack the Church. This is reflected in the Church's maintenance of the martial tradition that gives the pope three orders of protection, principally in the (fully armed) Swiss Guard, and which allows him to maintain orders of knighthood such as the papal Knights of Malta who have diplomatic status at the **UN**. Despite this, John Paul II did suffer an assassination attempt at the hands of a Turkish gunman involved with a Bulgarian offshoot of the **KGB** in 1981. The pope's protection is much enhanced by his status as head of a state, the Vatican, recognized as an observer state at the UN, by Italy since the **Lateran Treaties**, and by over a hundred other states by ambassadorial accreditation.

Romania

An integral part of the **Ottoman Empire** from the fourteenth and fifteenth centuries and the only 'Latin' state in the **Balkans**. Its core of Wallachia and Moldavia became autonomous in 1856, and independent under the Treaty of Berlin of 1878. It gained Bukovina from **Austria**, and **Transylvania** and most of the Banat from **Hungary**, under the treaties of Saint-Germain, 1919, and Trianon, 1920. Its gain of Bessarabia under Saint-Germain was not recognized by Bolshevik Russia, which reclaimed it, 1940. Deeply unstable throughout the 1930s as the crown, the government and different fascist groups, notably the Iron Guard, struggled for power, it signed the Axis Pact, 1940. Armistice, 1944, was followed by a peace treaty, 1947. It became a republic, 1947, and a people's republic, 1948–65. A member of **Comecon**, 1949–90, and of the **Warsaw Pact**, 1955–91, it remained highly independent and nationalistic in its policies. Following the overthrow of **Nicolae Ceauşescu** in 1989, his associates introduced liberal democratic economic and political policies. Romania became a member of the **European Union** in 2007.

Romanticism

The intellectual and cultural movement that spread throughout **Europe** during the early nineteenth century. The defining principles of Romanticism reflected the tumultuous events of the period. The chaotic changes of the **French Revolution** and the **Napoleonic Wars** led Romantics to question the objectivity and rationality of the **Enlightenment** and instead embrace emotion, the spiritual and the irrational. The destruction of traditional rural life due to **urbanization** and **industrialization** fostered a new reverence for the natural world. While the preceding Neoclassical movement emphasized self-sacrifice for greater causes, Romantics focused on individualism and personal experience. The emphasis on human individuality and self-determination led to a renewed interest in expressing national uniqueness and sovereignty. Writers, artists and musicians helped construct national narratives through their celebration and preservation of culture, traditions and language. Despite common characteristics, the complex and multifaceted movement varied greatly, especially depending on location and generation.

Romantic painting, music and literature represented artists' quests to understand the rapidly transforming world. Painting challenged traditional artistic conventions and expressed greater emotionality. For instance, Eugene Delacroix's painting *Liberty Leading the People* experimented with different forms to convey the authenticity and spontaneity of life. Francisco de Goya used painting to support radical political causes. His works, particularly the series *The Disasters of War*, epitomized the Romantic appreciation for the irrational and supernatural. John Constable, J. M. W. Turner, Theodore Géricault and Caspar David Friedrich created landscape paintings that emphasized humanity's subservience to nature and focused on vastness, beauty and the mysteriousness of the natural world. In America, the Hudson River school idealized peasant life and expressed nostalgia for pre-modern society.

Like painting, architecture shifted from the formalism of Neoclassicism to a more ornamental style. Renewed interest in medieval architectural principles stimulated the **Gothic Revival**. Music also conveyed greater emotionality and innovation. Johann Bach, Ludwig van Beethoven, Richard Wagner and Franz Liszt utilized new instruments and orchestration to intensify expression and sentimentality. Influenced by the growth of **nationalism**, Romantic musicians, most notably Frederic Chopin, incorporated traditional ballads in their compositions and used music to express national aspirations.

The Romantic emphasis on freedom, sensibility and imagination encouraged new innovations in literary subjects and forms. In England, poets Lord Byron, John Keats, William Wordsworth, Samuel Coleridge and William Blake celebrated nature, intuition and the supernatural. French writer Victor Hugo challenged literary traditions in his works, most notably *Notre Dame de Paris* and *Les Misérables*. Hugo and other French novelists – including Theophile Gautier and Stendhal – earned the description of social Romantics for their social commentaries and criticism. German author Johann Wolfgang von Goethe explored the complexity and uniqueness of human experience in his masterpiece, *Faust*. Fyodor Dostoevsky and Alexander Pushkin helped create the modern Russian language and facilitated a golden age for Russian literature. The Gothic novel became a popular genre and reflected the Romantic interest in the supernatural and sublime. Mary Shelley's *Frankenstein*, which critiques the corruption of reason, remains the quintessential Gothic novel.

The Romantic movement declined in the mid nineteenth century, particularly after the failure of the **Revolutions of 1848**. Despite its decline, Romanticism marked an important epoch that redefined European culture, politics and social life.

Roosevelt, Eleanor (1884–1962)

A leading American humanitarian, she was born into an elite political family and married her fifth cousin **Franklin D. Roosevelt**, president from 1933 to 1945. Crippled with polio, President Roosevelt trusted her to move amongst the people and be his eyes and ears, but at the same time she spoke with an independent voice. As a **USA** delegate to the **UN**, she later helped push through the 1948 Declaration of Human Rights.

Roosevelt, Franklin Delano (1882–1945)

Thirty-second president of the **United States**, 1933–45, and the only president to serve more than two terms. A man of few fixed principles, he was a supremely gifted communicator whose nature was fundamentally political. His instinct for action and willingness to experiment made him a particularly effective leader in an era of global depression and war.

Born into a wealthy Episcopalian family of Dutch descent in the Hudson Valley, Roosevelt attended Harvard University before entering New York State politics, serving as a Democratic state senator (1911–12). President Woodrow Wilson appointed him assistant secretary of the Navy (1913–20). After contracting polio in 1921 his career was thought to be over (the effects of

the disease made him dependent on a wheelchair for the rest of his life), but he was twice elected governor of New York (1928 and 1930), won the Democratic presidential nomination in 1932, and then defeated Herbert Hoover in the presidential election, pledging a **New Deal** for the American people.

Roosevelt's New Deal began with a frenzy of legislative action in the first hundred days of his presidency. He backed the creation of new public works schemes, the regulation of the stock market, agricultural price control and subsidies, labour legislation and ambitious public power and regional development projects. He was criticized from the right by those who said his reforms were tantamount to socialism, and from the left by those for whom the New Deal was not radical enough. He used a series of 'fireside chats' – radio addresses on major topics – to appeal to the American people over the heads of an often hostile press. He was re-elected by a huge margin in 1936, but the pace of domestic reform slowed during his second term, in part due to a botched attempt to reform the Supreme Court, which had struck down some major New Deal legislation. Throughout this period, Roosevelt's wife, Eleanor, established herself as a remarkable First Lady, who proved a powerful campaigner for social reform, civil rights and international justice.

In the late 1930s, as the international climate deteriorated, Roosevelt was faced with the complex task of negotiating between his basic internationalist inclinations in foreign policy, and a Congress and people markedly reluctant to go to war. He was prepared to support **Britain** through material aid, most notably in the form of lend-lease, but the United States remained officially neutral until the Japanese attack on **Pearl Harbor** on 7 December 1941, which Roosevelt termed 'a date which will live in infamy'. Roosevelt, who became increasingly frail over the course of the war, went on to play a key role in shaping the post-war world. He attended the wartime conferences, most controversially at **Yalta** (February 1945), where East–West spheres of geopolitical influence were delineated; and led the effort to establish a new post-war international organization – the **United Nations** – to maintain peace and ensure global stability after the war. He died just thirteen days before the San Francisco conference at which the United Nations was established.

Roosevelt, Theodore (1858–1919)

Twenty-sixth president of the **United States**, 1901–9. He served as assistant secretary of the Navy

(1897–8), resigning to become a colonel of the volunteer regiment, the 'Rough Riders', that fought in the Spanish–American War. He was elected governor of New York in 1898 and vice president in 1900. He became president in 1901 when President William McKinley was assassinated, and was elected to a full term in 1904. An active president, he oversaw Progressive reforms, including attempts to regulate big business and promote conservation. He was responsible for securing the **Panama Canal**, and issued the 'Roosevelt corollary' to the **Monroe Doctrine**, justifying US intervention in **Latin America** to avert European interference. His mediation in the **Russo-Japanese War** of 1904–5 earned him the Nobel Peace Prize. He retired in 1909 but ran again as a third party (**Progressive**) presidential candidate in 1912, thus dividing the Republicans and allowing the election of Democrat **Woodrow Wilson**.

Rosas, Juan Manuel de (1793–1877)

An Argentine *caudillo* who rose from rancher and regional militia commander to govern the province of Buenos Aires. Supporter of the gauchos, urban poor and Afro-Argentines and vilified by Buenos Aires elites despite policies favourable to merchants and landowners, he forcefully centralized and ruled **Argentina** from 1829 to 1852. Fighting various wars with the Littoral provinces of **Brazil** and **Uruguay**, and with **Great Britain**, he was defeated and exiled to Great Britain.

Rostow, W. W. (1916–2003)

An economic historian by training, Rostow served as deputy assistant for national security affairs and as national security adviser during the **Kennedy** and **Johnson** administrations. He played an important role in expanding America's foreign aid programmes and believed that the **US** had to accord more attention to the developing world. Rostow advised strongly in favour of the Americanization and escalation of the **Vietnam War** and played an important role in shaping US military strategy.

Rousseau, Jean-Jacques (1712–1778)

French composer, writer and political philosopher. Rousseau's early fame followed the success of his opera *Le Devin du village* (1752). He befriended Diderot and contributed entries to the *Encyclopédie*. In 1750 he wrote *Discours sur les sciences et les arts*, arguing that humanity is by nature good, but defiled by society. This theme was developed in *Discours sur l'origine de l'inegalité* (1755), where he argued that natural physical inequalities are compounded by artificial inequalities derived from private property. Later in *Du Contrat social* (1762), Rousseau claimed that government should not merely protect property, but rather promote liberty. Rousseau's notion of liberty remains controversial. He argued that freedom consists in self-legislation by the general will. The general will is different from the aggregation of individuals' wills, and is akin to the common good. But Rousseau famously suggested that citizens may be coerced to obey the general will: to be forced to be free. Consequently, Rousseau's legacy is contested.

Roxas, Manuel Acuna (1892–1948)

The third and final president of the Philippine Commonwealth and first president of the independent **Philippines**. He held office in 1946–8 during the transition from one regime to another, and died during his term of a heart attack. He had emerged from Capiz City and was distinguished as a law student; he became a representative, speaker of the House, secretary of finance, economist, brigadier and senator. During **World War II**, in which he was captured by the Japanese, he operated as a facilitator and protector of guerrillas within the occupied administration. During the conflict he won and maintained the support of General **MacArthur**, who was critical to his later election. After the war he broke with the official National Party to help found the Liberal Party, of which he was the successful presidential nominee. In office, he maintained strong ties with the **USA** but failed to control peasant unrest, the Huk (formerly anti-Japanese) insurgents or organized crime and corruption. However, he did help the new Philippine state avoid bankruptcy and collapse by engineering a massive sugar harvest, thus acquiring capital and foreign currency. He was succeeded by his vice president, Elpido Quirino.

Roy, Manabendra Nath (1887–1954)

Indian nationalist. Born Narendranath Bhattacharya, he joined the underground Indian revolutionary movement and left **India** on a mission to bring German arms to India in 1915. The mission failed. He took the name M. N. Roy and joined the third Communist International after visiting the **Soviet Union**. He tried to organize an Indian Communist Party from outside India, was purged by **Stalin** in the late 1920s, and returned to India in 1930. Gaoled until 1937, upon his release he formed the Radical Democratic Party and later converted it into the Radical Humanist movement.

Roy, Rammohun (1774–1833)

Known as the 'father of modern India', Roy was highly educated in Sanskrit and Persian traditions and became wealthy working with the British in the late eighteenth century. From 1815 he turned to educational and religious reform, advocating English education, the purification of Hindu traditions and constitutional rights for Indians. In 1817 he helped to found the Hindu College, later Presidency College, **Calcutta** (Kolkata). His religious teaching stressed the monotheism he found in Hinduism. He opposed image worship and *sati*, or the self-immolation of widows. He engaged in many controversies with orthodox Hindus and Christians, coming close to Unitarian friends in **India**, **Great Britain** and America. In 1828 he founded the Brahmo Samaj. He went to Britain in 1830 to testify before Parliament in support of the Reform Bill of 1832 and for the extension of constitutional rights to Indians, dying in Bristol in 1833.

Royal African Company (English)

Founded in 1672, the Royal African Company (RAC) was the last, and most important, of a number of English joint stock corporations established to promote trade with **Africa** and to supply overseas plantations with slaves. The RAC charter provided its London investors with a trading monopoly as well as the authority to build forts and factories in West Africa. Colonial planters and merchants outside London increasingly opposed this monopoly. In 1698, Parliament ended it, which expanded the number of merchants and the significance of ports such as Bristol and Liverpool, in the Atlantic slave trade.

Royal Navy

– see **naval warfare**.

royalty

– see **monarchy**.

Ruhr occupation

The Ruhr was a major industrial area of **Germany**. Under the terms of the **Treaty of Versailles**, Germany was required to pay reparations to the allies until 1980. When in 1922–3 it failed to do so, **France** and **Belgium** invaded the Ruhr and began to appropriate materials to the value of the reparations in arrears. The behaviour of French troops caused outrage both in Germany and internationally. Germany passed into economic and monetary collapse before stabilizing on the basis of repayments for withdrawal in 1924–5, after a rescue package known as the Dawes Plan proposed by the **USA** in 1924 was implemented.

Rusk, Dean (1909–1994)

As US secretary of state to Presidents **Kennedy** and **Johnson**, Dean Rusk participated in key flashpoints of the **Cold War**: the Berlin and **Cuban missile crises** and the Americanization of the **Vietnam War**. Committed to the logic of domino theory, Rusk supported military intervention to protect South Vietnam's pro-western independence. He was a loyal member of Johnson's administration, although he was not as vocal or influential in his post as some of his predecessors.

Russia (Russian Federation)

– see also **Putin, Vladimir**.

The world's largest country by area. Politically it consists of a Russian federation of twenty-one republics and the forty-nine provinces of Russia proper. Just over 80 per cent of the Federation's population is ethnically Russian. Moulded by its severe climate and absence of natural frontiers, which have repeatedly left it open to invasion, most notably by the Mongols, the French under **Napoleon** and the Germans in two world wars, the resulting sense of exposure has long led to an acceptance of autocratic styles of government which will guarantee security. The prime title of the tsar was 'autocrat of all the Russias', and **Lenin** famously declared that the challenge was 'not to destroy autocracy, but to capture it'. Effective change has always come from the top. Russian distinctiveness has also been bolstered by the influence of the Russian Orthodox Church, which, as the heir of Byzantium and ultimately of Persia rather than of classical **Greece** and Rome, draws no clear distinction between church and state.

The rejection of Mongol rule, the assertion of Muscovy as the heir to the initial Russian state of Kiev Rus and the consolidation of its power in the west were accompanied by the eastwards movement of Russian peasants and hunters who had reached Siberia by the second half of the sixteenth century. In 1689 the Treaty of Nerchinsk fixed the border between **Russia** and **China**. Russia was also extending its power southwards at the expense of the Muslim Tatar khanates, absorbing much Turkic blood in the process. The last, Crimea, was conquered in 1783. The motive was primarily political but the struggle against **Islam** in the name of the Russian Orthodox Church helped to shape Russia's sense of identity. Russia was also seeking from the

1820s onwards to secure the western Caucasus, but it met determined opposition, in Dagestan and **Chechnya** in particular, which meant that the **Caucasus** as a whole was not under Russian control until 1864. Under **Peter the Great**, Russia had become the **Russian Empire**, and it did not fully reappear as a constitutional entity until the proclamation of the Russian Soviet Federal Socialist Republic (RSFSR) as part of the **USSR** in 1924. Its capital, renamed Petrograd, had been the focus of the **Russian Revolution**, 1917, and Russia had been torn by the **Russian Civil War**. Communist victory led to the mass programmes of education, industrialization, collectivization and **urbanization**, and to the command economy of the Soviet period, as well as to victory in the Great Patriotic War, 1941–5.

Although the other Soviet republics became separate states on the demise of the USSR in 1991, the RSFSR remained intact as the present Russian Federation and the only serious threat to its internal security appears to come from the northern Caucasus, particularly Chechnya. The enclave of Kaliningrad, formerly Königsberg in German East Prussia annexed by the **Soviet Union** in 1945, is an integral part of Russia itself. The Russian-speaking Moldovan area of Transdniestria has expressed the wish to become a second detached part of Russia. Vladimir Putin, believes that 'the gravest problem facing Russia' is demographic. The declining population could drop to as little as 100 million by the middle of the twenty-first century unless current trends are reversed.

Russian Civil War

The Russian Civil War broke out in 1918 following the German-imposed Treaty of Brest-Litovsk, between the Bolshevik 'Reds', who controlled Moscow, Petrograd (St Petersburg) and most of the industrial belt, and the 'Whites', anti-communists under former imperial officers, with other groups such as the 'Greens' in the **Ukraine**, the Mensheviks in the **Caucasus** and dissident Socialist Revolutionaries on the sidelines. The Whites were also to enjoy much financial and material support from **Russia**'s former **World War I** allies. Victory went to the Reds by mid 1920, primarily because of **Trotsky**'s military gifts in creating and leading the new **Red Army** but also because their lines of communication were much shorter and they were ruthlessly determined. The Bolsheviks, however, lost control of the **Baltic States** and **Finland**. The Reds pursued the civil war by instigating War Communism, a harsh economic policy of

expropriation of private commerce and industry and of food requisitioning, backed up by the power of the new Cheka – the political police – and by a lasting militarization of approach.

Russian Empire

The only European empire, other than the Austrian, to be a continuous geographical entity, apart from Alaska settled by traders in the eighteenth century but sold to the **United States**, in 1867. Muscovy formally became the Russian Empire under **Peter the Great** (r. 1689–1725), but the nature of much Russian expansion and the comparative absence of natural barriers have often made it difficult to draw a meaningful distinction between Russia and its empire. The Slav peoples of what are now Belarus and **Ukraine** have more in common in many respects with the Russians than have many of the Asiatic citizens of the Russian Federation itself. One consequence was that the Russian Empire never developed a colour bar.

It was Peter who, in 1722, strengthened Russian control over the then Ukraine, a loosely defined border region covering some of contemporary Belarus as well as Ukraine, which had been under Russian overlordship since the Pereyaslavl agreement of 1654. Under the Treaty of Nystadt of 1721 Peter had already acquired modern **Estonia** and **Latvia**. Much of **Azerbaijan** followed in 1723–4, but Bessarabia finally only in 1808. Further European expansion followed with successive partitions of **Poland**, and by 1797 the Russian Empire included eastern Poland including Warsaw, Lithuania and the remainder of Belarus. Following the defeat of Sweden in the **Napoleonic Wars**, **Finland** was united with Russia in 1809 through the person of the monarch, but kept its own laws and institutions. In the **Caucasus**, **Georgia** became a voluntary protectorate in 1783 following occupation by both Persia and Turkey, but was annexed in 1801, and **Armenia** was ceded by Persia under the Treaty of Turkmanchay, 1828. The expansion into the southern steppes, however, like that into Siberia, was led initially by fugitive serfs, and facilitated by subsequent requests for protection by the nomad Kazakhs. Nevertheless, Russian settlement provoked revolts in the 1830s and by 1850 the Russians had established a line of forts along the course of the Syr Darya river, broadly marking the southern boundary of **Kazakhstan**. Expansion into Central Asia soon followed, raising British fears of Russian designs on **India**. The Tashkent region was annexed, 1865, and a Turkestan governor generalship established, 1867. The khanates of Bukhara and Khiva became Russian protectorates in 1873. The penultimate act was played out in Turkmenia where the Russians suffered a major defeat in 1879 at Dengil-Tepe, but by 1881 Turkmenia was Russian, as were the Pamirs (modern Tadzhikistan), 1890–5.

The Russian Revolutions and defeat in **World War I** marked the end of the traditional empire. **Finland** declared its independence, 1917, and under the Treaty of Brest-Litovsk, 1918, Russia ceded Latvia and Estonia. The **Treaty of Versailles**, 1919, recognized the independence of Lithuania and Poland. Russia did not, however, recognize the Romanian acquisition of Bessarabia. The remainder of the Russian Empire was reorganized as the **Union of Soviet Socialist Republics (USSR)** in 1924. The USSR reabsorbed the Baltic states and Bessarabia in 1940, but all the constituent republics became independent in 1991. The newly independent states, other than the three Baltic nations, created the rather insubstantial Commonwealth of Independent States (CIS) in 1991, but later agreements between Russia, Belarus and Kazakhstan may prove genuinely significant.

Russian Orthodox Church
– *see* **Orthodoxy**.

Russian Revolutions (1917)

The name commonly ascribed to events of the year 1917 inside the **Russian Empire**, which experienced three changes of regime and the beginning of a civil war in a very short space of time. The main changes were the 'February' and 'October' revolutions, which, given calendrical differences from the standard calendar, actually happened in March and October. February saw the end of tsarist rule and its replacement with a provisional government, driven by exhaustion and disgust at the conduct of **World War I**. However, the provisional government, which was based in Petrograd (St Petersburg), whilst made up of popular parliamentary figures, effectively shared power with councils of workers, soldiers and sailors known as Soviets, which were under socialist control (known as Bolshevik or Communist given political divisions within the Left). A third element in the governance of the revolutionary empire were those elements of the army who were still loyal to the tsar, or at least not to the provisional government, and the units under their command. By April, after a series of convulsions, the leadership of the provisional government had passed to Alexander

Kerensky, who proposed to reform **Russia** whilst continuing the war. This led to a failed offensive, a near collapse of governmental legitimacy, and an attempted socialist coup in July 1917. The coup failed, and led **Lenin** (freed from Swiss exile by Germans wanting to destabilize Russia) to flee to Finland. Fearing radical influence, hypersensitive army commanders then attempted their own coup in August, leading to the provisional government in Petrograd becoming dependent on the Soviets and Socialist leaders.

From that point on, Lenin and **Trotsky** gained an ascendancy which allowed them to launch their own, successful revolutionary strike in October. The result was a Communist government based on revolutionary Soviets, which in turn were opposed by liberals and monarchists, and heralded the beginning of the **Russian Civil War**. During the early days of this war, the tsar and his entire family were murdered by Communist forces. The ultimate result of 1917, via Trotsky and Lenin's creation of a revolutionary state based on the **Red Army**, powerful and invasive intelligence forces and emergency economics, was the creation of a Marxist–Leninist state. This state sought, with some success and much bloodshed, to rapidly modernize the territories of the former Russian Empire and to inspire world revolution. Communist success did indeed inspire a wave of revolutions and attempted revolutions conducted in the name of Workers but often led by intellectuals in subsequent years, leading to short-lived Soviets in such places as Bavaria, **Hungary**, Alsace, Slovakia and Finland in 1918–20, as well as the creation of the USSR. It also inspired ferocious anti-Communist actions, ranging from 'White terrors' in which all socialists of whatever stripe were imprisoned or stripped of rights, through 'red scares' in which democratic states deployed police and propaganda power against Communists. During the twentieth century, 'Red October' would become a model, example, or inspiration for a socialist movement which at one point seemed poised to sweep the world.

Russification

The popular majority of the **Russian Empire** was at no time Russian. As a consequence, various tsars, but particularly those who ruled from the mid nineteenth century, promoted Russification by the use of the Russian language, alphabet and administrative structures, as well as Orthodox Christianity. Occasionally, in the face of local nationalism or culture, this process was moderated or delimited. Under the **Soviet Union**, the process was continued without the Christian elements, and was expressed in terms of language, Soviet ideology, technological integration and education. It never extended successfully, however, into the destruction of traditional borders, dialects and nationalities.

Russo-Japanese War (1904–1905)

A conflict which dealt a severe blow to the **Russian Empire**. In essence a naval battle for a warm-water port at Port Arthur, the war also represented an attempt by the tsarist state to put down growing Japanese power and create a wave of popular legitimacy based on military success. It failed in all three aims, with land defeats at Mukden and a naval disaster at Tsushima. The resulting peace agreement (the Treaty of Portsmouth), brokered by the **USA**, inflamed the **Russian Revolution** of 1905, ensconced **Japan** in **Korea** and encouraged European powers to underestimate Russian military strength.

Russo-Polish War (1918–1921)

A war fought between Bolshevik **Russia** and **Ukraine** against the Polish Republic and supporters from the Ukrainian People's Republic. The war is associated in some minds with the aggrandizing and federalizing ambitions of the Polish leader, Piłsudski, and by some is viewed as a final theatre of the **Russian Civil War**. Facing an apparently stronger and better organized Soviet force, **Poland** was expected to lose, until a stunning series of victories by Marshals Sikorski and Piłsudski turned the tide. The decisive Battle of Warsaw in August 1920 was extremely important in European history, as it precluded a Soviet move into Europe in the 1920s; the subsequent Treaty of Riga saw Poland gain large areas of land in Ukraine and Lithuania.

Russo-Turkish War (1768–1774)

Instigated by Sultan Mustafa III to demonstrate that the **Ottoman Empire** remained mistress of the Black Sea, in response to the probing by Catherine the Great's **Russian Empire** of the northern Caucasus, which was theoretically part of the Turkish Empire, and more specifically of Crimea, which was a vassal state. The Black Sea mattered to the Ottomans for prestige and for the taxes payable by merchants shipping goods down the River Danube from central Europe or down the Rivers Dnestr and Dnepr from Russia. The **Battle of Cesme**, 1770, however, proved disastrous and the Treaty of Kücük Kainardji, 1774, concluding the war, obliged **Turkey** to recognize the loss of its monopoly over the Black Sea and the surrender of its northern coasts, the preponderance of Russian power in the northern Caucasus and increasingly in **Georgia**, and the theoretical independence of Crimea, which had been a valuable source of troops. The war announced the end of the military and political strength of the Ottoman Empire, with the sultan having the sole compensation of being recognized as protector of the Muslims. The parallel recognition of the tsar(ina) as protector of the Ottoman Empire's Christians was to bedevil the **Eastern Question**.

Russo-Turkish War (1877–1878)

– *see also* **Berlin, Congress of**.

The Russo-Turkish War of 1877–8 was one of a series of wars resulting from the disintegration of Ottoman control in the **Balkans** and the rise of new, national states in former Ottoman territory. **Russia**, anxious to support these new national states, was soon joined by **Serbia**, **Romania** and Montenegro in its efforts to push the Ottomans out of the Balkans. Ottoman defences quickly collapsed and, by January 1878, Russian troops were nearing **Constantinople**. Fearful that its ally might collapse entirely, a British fleet was sent to the area and the Russians ceased their advance. The Treaty of San Stefano resulted in Ottoman recognition of the independence of Romania, Serbia and Montenegro, as well as the autonomy of **Bulgaria**. These results were modified somewhat by the **Congress of Berlin** in 1878. The Russo-Turkish War was accompanied by significant sectarian conflict and ethnic cleansing. Ottoman atrocities against Christians in Bulgaria received widespread condemnation, while Christian violence against Muslims resulted in hundreds of thousands fleeing to Ottoman territory after the war.

Rwanda

A country in Central Africa bordered by **Burundi**, the Democratic Republic of **Congo**, **Tanzania** and **Uganda** with a population of over 10 million. The country has a temperate climate and fertile terrain composed of lakes, mountains and rolling hills. Migrations of agriculturalists and pastoralists into the region led to interaction and the development of one common language, Kinyarwanda. The Kingdom of Rwanda emerged in the mid fifteenth century as a loose confederation with a central monarchy. It grew in importance and extended beyond the current borders of Rwanda. The German colonizers who arrived in 1897 viewed the **Tutsi** monarchy as a superior race and imposed Tutsi chiefs over the **Hutu** majority population. After **World War I** control of the colony shifted to **Belgium**. Rwanda gained independence from Belgium in 1961 and has experienced a series of political crises and periodic violence culminating in the civil war of 1990–3 and the genocide of 1994.

Rwandan Civil War (1990–1993)

This war began when the Rwanda Patriotic Front (RPF), composed of Tutsi refugees based in **Uganda**, invaded **Rwanda** to fight the Hutu-dominated government forces. The war was characterized by guerrilla tactics, massacres on both sides and numerous attempts at a ceasefire. For the RPF, it was an armed repatriation and an attempt to redress perceived inequalities after the **Hutu** majority reversed colonial power relations at independence. For the Rwandan government and many within the Hutu community, the RPF invasion represented a 'recolonization'. The Arusha Peace Accord of 1993 called for the integration of the RPF into the national assembly and army, the establishment of a transitional government and the institution of multiparty elections. The violence, language of invasion and assassination of President Juvénal Habyarimana in April 1994 can be seen as crucial precursors to the Rwandan genocide the same year.

S

SA (Sturmabteilung)

Sturmabteilung, or Storm Troopers, was the name given to the paramilitary wing of the Nazi Party after 1921 in **Germany**. The Storm Troops, who copied the name of the shock batallions of the German Army in 1915, started as thugs and party enforcers in the Bavarian Beerhalls, but grew to contain over 4 million members by 1934, and were as such bigger than the German Army. Their distinctive uniform, bought wholesale from the former (brutal) colonial forces in German South West Africa, gave rise to the name 'brownshirt', and their membership tended to be working-class rather than bourgeois, unlike the rest of the Nazi Party. The Storm Troopers were subordinated to **Adolf Hitler** and lost autonomy after a bloody purge in 1934 known as the 'Night of the Long Knives' during which their leaders were killed with the connivance of the German armed forces.

Saad Zaghul

– *see* **Zaghlul, Sa'ad**.

Sabah, Al

The ruling dynasty of **Kuwait** since 1752. Al Sabah were originally a clan of the Anaizah tribe from Najd who migrated to the Kuwait region and associated themselves with the Bani Utub tribe. In 1899 Sheikh Mubarak ibn Sabah al-Sabah placed himself under virtual British protection, although the 1913 Anglo-Ottoman Convention recognized Ottoman sovereignty. With the collapse of the **Ottoman Empire**, the British proclaimed nominal Kuwaiti independence under Al Sabah, who remained under British control until 19 June 1961. Al Sabah rule is not strictly hereditary as a family council chooses the ruler. Article 3 of the constitution also grants the parliament some authority in the selection of the emir, power they exercised in the January 2006 succession crisis when they deposed Sheikh Sa'ad Al Abdallah al-Sabah for health reasons, thereby paving the way for Sabah Al Ahmad al-Sabah to assume power.

Sadat, (Muhammad) Anwar as- (1918–1981)

President of **Egypt**, 1970–81. Sadat graduated from the Cairo Military Academy in 1938 and was imprisoned by the British in 1942, for planning to expel them from **Egypt** with German assistance, but he escaped. He joined the **Free Officers**, 1950, and was active in the 1952 coup against the monarchy. He wanted King Farouk's immediate public execution, but was overruled by **Nasser**. A supporter of Nasser's election as president, 1956, he duly became vice president, 1964–6 and 1969–70. Elected president after Nasser's death, 1970, he revised Nasser's planned economy and political controls, and concluded a friendship treaty with the **Soviet Union**, May 1971, following the increase in the number of Soviet military advisers in Egypt under Nasser, March 1970, but then expelled some 15,000 Soviet military advisers as well as technicians, July 1972, in response to allegedly inadequate support from the Soviet Union against **Israel**. Threatened without any outcome to make 1972 a 'year of decision' with Israel, which may have been merely an attempt to demonstrate Egyptian independence, he launched with Syria a surprise attack on Israel on 6 October 1973, the Jewish holiday of Yom Kippur, and succeeded in his objective of gaining US respect when Secretary of State Dr **Henry Kissinger**, who was anxious to restore US influence there, came to Cairo to discuss the post-ceasefire arrangements between Israel and Egypt, and the US–Egyptian diplomatic relations broken off in 1967 were restored, 2 November 1973. Subsequent conciliation efforts by Kissinger resulted in Israeli–Egyptian agreement on disengagement, 18 January 1974. Although the benefits to Egypt and the Arab world from the **Yom Kippur War** were largely intangible and would not be fully realized until 1979, the much better performance of the Arab forces greatly boosted Sadat's domestic prestige, and his prime objective of securing American respect recognized by US President **Nixon**'s visit to Egypt, **Syria** and other Arab states, 10–19 June 1974. Egypt's 1971 treaty with the Soviet Union was abrogated, 15 March 1976.

Despite his perceptible and often criticized weakness for somewhat grandiose and militaristic uniforms, Sadat emerged as a potential peace negotiator, declaring his readiness to talk to the Israeli Knesset, 9 November 1977. Invited to **Israel** by its hard-line prime minister, **Menachem Begin**, 14 November 1977, he accepted and addressed the Knesset, 19–21 November 1977. He attempted to organize a conference between the Arab states, Israel, the Soviet Union and the **USA** in Cairo for 14 December, but was thwarted by willingness of only the US, Israel and the **UN** to attend. He met Begin again, in Egypt, on 25–26 December 1977, and then with America's President **Carter**, 6–17 September 1978, when the **Camp David Accords** were reached whereby Israel would evacuate the occupied Sinai peninsula in return for formal recognition – Sadat shared the Nobel Peace Prize with Menachem Begin the same year. The Egyptian–Israeli peace treaty which implemented the accords, was signed by him on 26 March 1979, against much popular opposition as it sidestepped the Palestinian problem, which was to remain a source of Arab–Israeli conflict. Domestically unpopular also because of worsening economic conditions, Sadat was assassinated on 6 October 1981 by members of his guard belonging to Egyptian Islamic Jihad (Ayman-al-Zawahir).

Saddam Hussein
– *see* **Hussein (al-Husayn), Saddam**.

Saghlul, Sa'd
– *see* **Zaghlul, Sa'ad**.

Sahrawi Arab Democratic Republic (SADR)
This is the sovereign political entity formed in 1976 by the Polisario independence movement. It claims the disputed Western Sahara territory almost completely occupied by **Morocco**, but functions as a state in exile, operating in the Sahrawi refugee camps across the border in Tindouf, **Algeria**. Its structure is closely tied to that of the **Polisario movement**, with the party's secretary general Mohammed Abdelaziz serving as president of SADR from 1976 to 2016. Its 1999 constitution called for multiparty democracy and a free-market economy but postponed their establishment until formal territorial control of the Western Sahara is established. The constitution defines the Sahrawi people as Muslim, Arab and African. Algeria provides SADR with most of its diplomatic, political and financial support. SADR is not a member of the UN, but it gained full membership of the **African Union** in 1984. The conflict remains unresolved.

Said, Nuri al-
– *see* **Nuri al-Said**.

Sa'id Pasha (1822–1863)
Khedive (viceroy) of **Egypt**, 1854–63. Fourth son of Muhammad 'Ali Pasha and successor to **Abbas I**. He was granted the concession to build the **Suez Canal**, 1856, but failed to terminate the slave trade. Remembered for his introduction, under pressure from western financiers, of western forms of land ownership and taxation at the expense of the traditional system whereby the village headman (*sheikh*) had had the right, either on the death of a peasant or at set intervals, to distribute land amongst the village peasantry.

Said bin Sultan, Sayyid (fl. 1804–1856)
Sayyid Said bin Sultan, Sultan of Muscat and **Oman** (r. 1804–56), was originally ruler of a trading empire in the Arabian peninsula. He transferred his capital to the island of **Zanzibar** in 1820 and used it as a base to expand his commerce into East Africa. Thanks to slaves from East Africa, he developed thriving plantations, growing primarily cloves on Zanzibar, and held an informal empire over much of the adjacent coast and into the interior.

Saigo Takamori (1827–1877)
As a leader of the **Meiji restoration**, Saigo promoted the idea of an expedition to **Korea** (1873), which gained widespread support from disenfranchised former samurai that posed a threat to the government, but the return of the Iwakura Mission abruptly terminated the plan. He resigned and on returning to Kagoshima, created a military academy for his samurai followers. Government forces attempted to disarm the academy, which resulted in the Satsuma Rebellion (1877), reluctantly led by Saigo, that was quickly crushed by imperial forces.

St Christopher's/St Kitts
St Christopher's, also known as St Kitts, is an island located in the English-speaking Caribbean. Its capital city is Basseterre. In 1623 English forces captured the island from Spanish colonists. In 1625 French colonists invaded St Christopher's, controlling the island until 1783. Before 1640, the island's inhabitants produced tobacco for the international market. In the eighteenth century colonists turned

their efforts to producing sugar, using enslaved Africans as labourers. In 1783 British forces regained control of the island.

St Eustatius

St Eustatius or Sint Eustatius is an island located in the Dutch-speaking Caribbean. Its capital is Oranjestad. It is one of five islands that form the Netherland Antilles. Christopher Columbus visited in 1493, and in 1636 Dutch colonists captured the island and used it for several centuries to carry on a smuggling trade with neighbouring Caribbean colonies and also the thirteen North American colonies (later the **United States**). The island is now known mainly for its tourism.

Sakarya, Battle of the

During the Turkish War of Independence, the Greek Army's advance into Anatolia threatened the Turkish nationalist capital at Ankara. On 13 September 1921 fighting from positions along the Sakarya river, forces under the command of **Mustafa Kemal** (Atatürk), forced the Greek Army to retreat. With the front thus stabilized, the nationalists were able to amass supplies and eventually reconquer all of Anatolia. The battle marked the end of the Greek advance and gave Atatürk a crucial victory that confirmed his supremacy in the nationalist movement.

Sakoku system (Japan)

Foreign relations of **Tokugawa** Japan were under the strict control of the Tokugawa government. The 'Seclusion' policy towards the West banned Christianity and limited trading posts to the Dutch, the only approved western traders, at Dejima in Nagasaki. The Japanese were forbidden to leave and return to the country. Trade with East Asia was conducted through Dejima, Tsushima and the Ryukyu Kingdom. The system was ended by the visit of US Commodore **Matthew Perry** in 1853.

Salazar, António de Oliveira (1889–1970)

Salazar was prime minister of **Portugal** between 1932 and 1968, and ran a repressive conservative nationalist regime on extreme Catholic lines. A dictator, he was neutral in **World War II**, and his anti-communism made his regime extremely useful to **NATO** thereafter. Salazar attempted not only to quarantine **Portugal** from modernity, emphasizing traditional conservative values in an *Estado Novo*, but also to hold on to its empire via

a policy called *lusotropicalism*. Despite setbacks in **Goa** in **India** in the 1960s, when Goa was forcibly retaken by India, this aim was achieved in **Mozambique** and **Angola** until the mid 1970s at the cost of escalating civil war in the colonies. Salazar himself suffered a stroke in 1968, and died two years later.

Samori (1831–1900)

Political and military leader and founder of an Islamic state in modern-day **Guinea** that controlled a broad swathe of West Africa from Guinea to modern-day **Ivory Coast** and **Mali**. His early life was spent as a soldier in various armies, and he was named general of the army of Kamara in 1861. Samori engaged in fighting against El Hadj Umar Tall's Islamic army and had gained enough strength to found the Wassulu Empire in 1878. Much of his success lay in purchasing and manufacturing modern weapons for his army, and in establishing diplomatic relations with European countries. In 1884 he took the title 'alimany' and declared Wassulu an Islamic state. In 1886 French forces, advancing from **Senegal**, began to engage his army and after a long struggle, which included a ruthless scorched earth campaign, he was forced to surrender in 1898. He died in exile.

San Francisco, Treaty of

A peace treaty signed by **Japan** and forty-nine nations of the Allied Powers on 8 September 1951 and coming into effect on 28 April 1952. It attempted to normalize the position of Japan following **World War II**. Japan lost virtually all of the territories it had occupied between 1895 and 1945, but regained national independence. Okinawa and other Ryukyu islands were put under US trusteeship. The treaty was considered a 'separate peace', because representatives of **China** and **Korea** were not invited; the **Soviet Union** did not recognize the treaty.

San Martín, José de (1778–1850)

A hero of the independence era, San Martín was born in present-day **Argentina** but spent twenty years as a Spanish officer in **Europe**. Returning in 1812, he joined the patriots, recruited an army that included numerous Afro-American slaves, and in early 1817 crossed the Andes into **Chile**. Victories at Chacabuco (1817) and Maipú (1818) allowed Chile to declare its independence. On 10 September 1820, San Martín disembarked his army in **Peru**, where he proposed independence under a monarch. When royalists rejected this, he occupied Lima. Yielding to his pressure, on 28 July 1821 the irresolute town council declared independence. The new government began deporting peninsular Spaniards while ending the slave trade and Indian tribute. In July 1822 San Martín met **Simón Bolívar** in Guayaquil (**Ecuador**). Convinced that Peru lacked 'enough space' for both of them, he went into exile, dying in **France**.

San Remo Agreement (1920)

Signed by **Britain** and **France** on 25 April 1920, the agreement sought to resolve the fate of the former Ottoman territories conquered in 1918. Both powers sought international recognition for their **mandates** to rule **Lebanon**, **Syria**, **Palestine** and Mesopotamia (**Iraq**). While the agreement granted provisional independence to the **Hashemite** governments in Syria and Mesopotamia, it laid the legal groundwork for the formal assertion of French and British control over those territories less than a year later. France had already colonized Lebanon and Britain had asserted its control in Palestine. Unlike previous colonial arrangements, the mandate system promised the eventual independence of the colonized territories. The **League of Nations** formally ratified the mandates in July 1922, giving them international legal backing two years after Britain, France, **Italy**, **Japan** and **Belgium** had formalized them at San Remo, Italy.

San Stefano, Treaty of

– *see also* **Berlin, Congress of**; **Russo-Turkish War (1877–1878)**.

The treaty of San Stefano (3 March 1878) ended the Russo-Ottoman War of 1877–8, enshrining devastating territorial losses for the **Ottoman Empire**. Ottoman surrender came as Russian forces threatened Constantinople and the treaty was to deprive the defeated empire of nearly all of its European provinces. **Britain**, **France** and **Austria** considered the extent of Russian gains to be an unacceptable affront to the balance of power in **Europe**. Subsequently, the **Congress of Berlin** significantly revised the treaty in favour of the Ottoman Empire.

sanctions

A response by an individual, group, country or international organization to provocation by another and designed to discourage that behaviour. Sanctions between individuals include punishments, avoidance and physical violence. Sanctions can be informal and come from other individuals, or formal and institutional, as forms of social control. International sanctions include diplomatic actions to reduce activities by embassies, economic sanctions such as tariffs, quantitative restrictions or bans to reduce trade, and military sanctions which may take the form of wars. Countries that have been subjected to sanctions include **Iran**, **Russia** and **North Korea**.

Sandinistas

Adherents of Augusto César Sandino, a hero of nationalist Nicaraguans, who fought against US Marines in **Nicaragua** from 1927 to 1933. The Frente Sandinista de Liberación Nacional (FSLN, founded in 1962) took Sandino's name in their successful military struggle against dictator Anastasio ('Tachito') Somoza Debayle. Despite the US government's support of armed opposition, the Sandinistas governed Nicaragua from 1979 to 1990. In 2006, **Daniel Ortega**, Sandinista president in 1990, was again elected Nicaraguan president.

Sanhuri, Abd al-Razzaq al- (1895–1971)

Abd al-Razzaq al-Sanhuri was one of the foremost legal scholars of the postcolonial period in the Arab world. He authored the civil codes of several countries, including his native **Egypt**, **Iraq**, **Syria** and **Jordan**. After studying law at the University of Lyon in **France** in 1925, he began an academic career teaching law in Cairo and Baghdad. He is best known for composing the Egyptian Civil Code of 1948, although his insistence that civilian rule be restored following the **Free Officers**' coup of 1952 pushed him into exile. Sanhuri spent the rest of his career working to modernize legal frameworks across the Arab world, with his stated goal being to synthesize the western civil codes with classical Islamic legal thought. He was also a prolific scholar throughout his life, publishing a twelve-volume analysis of the Egyptian civil code just before his death.

Santa Anna, Antonio (López de) (1794–1876)

Mexican *caudillo*, political opportunist and general who served as president of **Mexico** eleven times during 1833–55. Victories over invading Spanish troops in 1829 and French troops in 1838 made him a national hero. Recognition of **Texas** independence in 1836 and loss of half of Mexico's territory (over 1.5 million square kilometres) to the **United States**, in 1846–8, contributed to his downfall and subsequent erratic Mexican–United States diplomatic relations.

Sanusiyah

Islamic Sufi brotherhood founded by Muhammad ibn 'Ali al-Sanusi (1787–1859). Born in **Algeria**, Sanusi was influenced by the Sufi reformism of Ahmad ibn Idris and established the first lodge of his brotherhood in al-Bayda, eastern Libya, in 1841. The order rapidly gained support among the Bedouins of Cyrenaica with a message of piety and practice of Islamic ritual. It was well organized with a centre in Jaghbub (on the **Libya–Egypt** border) and provided education and social and economic services, favouring trans-Saharan trade. At the end of the century the centre was transferred to Qiru (present-day **Chad**), later to Kufra in south-eastern Libya. Attacked by French colonialists, it became the focus of Bedouin resistance to the Italians in Libya, 1911–31. Most lodges were destroyed in this war, and attempts at reviving the order during the kingdom (1951–69) proved largely ephemeral.

Sanussi Brotherhood

– see **Sanusiyah**.

Saratoga Campaign (USA)

During the summer of 1777 British General John Burgoyne undertook a campaign down the Hudson River valley from Montreal to New York. Burgoyne led a combined force of British regular soldiers, Hessian mercenaries, Native Americans and Canadian militia with the intention of isolating New England from the other rebellious colonies. After a series of defeats by rebel **militia** and Continental Army forces at Bennington and Freeman's Farm, Burgoyne was compelled to surrender his army to General Horatio Gates at Saratoga, New York, on 17 October 1777. His defeat led **France** to enter into a formal alliance with the **United States** in 1778.

Sarekat Islam

Sarekat Islam was an Islamic Union in the Dutch East Indies (now **Indonesia**) in the early twentieth century. It emerged as a mass nationalist Islamic movement in 1911, though precursors had evolved by 1905. In the beginning, the Sarekat was primarily a trade union (and named as such) geared to the protection of east and central Javanese native workers in the face of Chinese immigrant enterprise. Though similar groups existed in west Java, Sarekat Islam quickly developed an anti-colonial and anti-Christian aspect. The organization grew rapidly, and though its own claim of 2 million members is disputed, half to a third of that figure is not unrealistic. Sarekat Islam became a party in

1921, but had in effect sponsored different movements within its congress from 1915 onwards. This led to a dependence upon charismatic leaders, such as Tjokroaminoto and Agus Salim, amongst others. When the pressures of communist infiltration, an ill-fated attempt to link Muhammad and **Marx**, the contradictions of Islamic modernization, and the Dutch use of an Advisory *Volksraad* or people's council from 1917 came together in the 1920s, the movement became impossibly strained. It proved unable to survive the imprisonment of its leaders and the rise of the Community Party of Indonesia, and it declined into irrelevance in subsequent decades.

Sarmiento, Domingo Faustino (1811–1888)

Argentine statesman, educator and president, 1868–74. Coming from the interior province of San Juan, Sarmiento took advantage of every educational opportunity offered him. He joined the liberal literary group known as the 'Generation of 1837' and went into exile during the long rule of dictator **Juan Manuel de Rosas**. From exile Sarmiento produced volumes of anti-Rosas writings. His classic work *Facundo* (1845) spelled out his views that Argentina's environment and political culture were backward and the country needed to import enlightened foreign ideas and immigrants to reshape them. He travelled to the **USA** where he became enamoured with many aspects of American society and especially its educational system. Elected president of Argentina in 1868, he pursued a number of modernizing projects, including importing dozens of female teachers from the United States to help expand Argentina's growing public school system – perhaps his greatest legacy.

Saro-Wiwa, Ken (1941–1995)

Nigerian author, television producer and environmental activist. Saro-Wiwa led a non-violent campaign against the environmental destruction and political corruption caused by oil extraction. In 1995, Saro-Wiwa and eight others were hanged by the military government. The execution sparked international criticism and prompted Nigeria's suspension from the **Commonwealth** of Nations. In 2009, Royal Dutch Shell agreed to settle out of court and awarded the Saro-Wiwa family 15.5 million US dollars.

Saudi Arabia

– see also **Abd al-Aziz ibn Abd al-Rahman Al-Sa'ud**; **Wahhabism, Wahhabiyya**.

Arab, Muslim kingdom in the Arabian peninsula ruled by the Al Sa'ud family with its capital at Riyadh. The origins of the kingdom date to the mid eighteenth century when Muhammad ibn Sa'ud, the emir of the town of Diriyya in Najd, allied with the religious reformer Muhammad ibn 'Abd al-Wahhab to form an ideal Islamic state. Over the next four decades Al Sa'ud consolidated control over much of Arabia, including the holy cities of Mecca and Medina. However, **Mehmet Ali**, the Ottoman governor of Egypt, overran the Saudis in 1818. A second Saudi state arose during the late nineteenth century in central and eastern Arabia, reaching its peak under Faisal ibn Turki Al Sa'ud. Al Rashid of Jabal Shammar overthrew the second Saudi state in 1888. The modern state began in January 1902 when **Abd al-Aziz ibn Abd al-Rahman Al Sa'ud**, popularly known as ibn Sa'ud, captured Riyadh from Al Rashid. Ibn Sa'ud then conquered central Arabia and with his Bedouin army, the Ikhwan, inspired by the teachings of ibn Abd al-Wahab, overran al-Hasa, Jabal Shammar, Asir and the Hejaz and proclaimed the Kingdom of Saudi Arabia in September 1932.

From its earlist years, Saudi Arabia has struggled with issues relating to economic development and security while adhering to the strict principles of Wahhabi Islam. Even before proclaiming the kingdom, Ibn Sa'ud had to remove his Ikhwan army when it revolted against the introduction of 'innovations' such as the telegraph and automobiles. Economic stability became assured when Ibn Sa'ud awarded an oil concession to what became the Arabian American Oil Company, which discovered and began exporting oil in 1938. Ibn Sa'ud died in 1953, leaving more than thirty sons, with state wealth in the hands of the royal family and only rudimentary governmental institutions. King Sa'ud (r. 1953–64) did little to change his father's policies, and the kingdom found itself under the external threat of progressive Arab nationalism. Faisal (r. 1964–75) replaced Sa'ud and began to direct oil revenues to infrastructure projects, education, health care programmes and military development, while seeking to counter Arab nationalism with the creation of the **Muslim League**. He also used Saudi oil policy to promote the Palestinian cause by leading the 1973 oil embargo. However, modernization promoted religious opposition, which peaked with the capture of the Grand Mosque in Mecca by religious extremists in 1979. Decreased oil revenues and massive defence spending in the 1980s increased social and political tensions. King Fahd's (r. 1982–2005) invitation to American and other foreign forces into the kingdom to assist in its protection against a threatened Iraqi invasion in August 1991 raised questions about the legitimacy of the Saudi regime from both religious groups, who opposed the entry of foreign troops, and the more liberal opposition, who questioned the failure of heavy military expenditure at the expense of social development. Fahd introduced some reforms, such as the constitution-like basic law of 1992, while suppressing all criticism, but opposition from groups such as **al-Qaida** continue to threaten the kingdom under King Abdullah and his successor after 2015, King Salman..

Savak

The Shah of **Iran**'s internal security organization established 1957–61, with the aid of advisers from the American **CIA**, and aimed at identifying, controlling and suppressing all political opposition. This expanded during the 1960s and 1970s to the suppression of any dissident views. Its ruthless suppression of all criticism, even in private, was, however, ultimately counter-productive because the fear and humiliation it engendered politicized much of the population. Around 70,000 people may have been imprisoned for months without trial by the late 1970s. Widely held to be responsible, probably wrongly, for the deaths of intellectuals **Jalal Al-e Ahmad**, 1968, and **Ali Shari'ati**, 1977, but much more plausibly behind the death in one of its prisons of the militant Tehran preacher Seyyed Mohammad Reza Sa'idi, which it maintained was suicide, in 1970. Its use of torture was notorious. One leading Marxist theoretician of the 1970s, Mostafa Shoa'iyan, was killed in a street battle with SAVAK, 1976. Its chief, General Nasiri, was executed by the new Islamic Republic.

Savignoran de Brazza, Pierre (1852–1905)

Italian traveller and explorer who played a significant role in establishing French claims in Equatorial Africa. De Brazza first visited **Africa** as a French naval officer in 1875, travelling in the Congo and Ogooué river basins. He signed treaties with local authorities, which were presented in Africa as commercial agreements but in **Europe** as treaties of protection. His actions and international reaction to it provoked the first steps in the 'scramble for Africa'.

Schlieffen Plan

The plan of 1905 for German victory in a war on two fronts formulated by Field Marshal Alfred von

Schlieffen (1833–1913), chief of General Staff, 1891–1905. Schlieffen's strategy envisaged a rapid enveloping attack on **France** through **Belgium** and the **Netherlands** while holding superior Russian forces at bay. He had doubts about its success because of the numbers and mobility of troops required. Modified in 1911 by Schlieffen's successor, the strategy failed in 1914.

Schoelcher, Victor (1804–1893)

The leading French voice for the abolition of slavery in the **French Empire**. Initially inspired by a commercial visit to **Mexico**, **Cuba** and the southern United States, 1829–31, which led him to analyze the positive consequences of emancipation in the British colonies. Effective as a journalist and writer, 1829–48, in his condemnation of the barbarism of slavery. He was under-secretary of state for the colonies following the 1848 Revolution, and chair of the commission responsible for the decree abolishing slavery in all French colonies, adopted by the provisional government, 27 April 1848: it emancipated more than 260,000 slaves. Elected to the National Assembly as deputy for Martinique, 1848, and Guadeloupe, 1849, he went into exile in England during the Second Empire, 1851–70. Regaining his seat, 1871, as a left-wing deputy urging social and political reform, he was elected senator for life, 1875. His ashes transferred to the Panthéon in Paris, 1949.

science and technology

The Industrial Revolution began in England in the eighteenth century, unleashing a social and economic transformation that has proved even more explosive in its effects than the comparable Neolithic and urban Bronze Age revolutions of so many millennia earlier. It opened a new era in world history and gave birth to a new mode of human existence, industrial civilization. In 1700, while the technologies of humankind were much more sophisticated than they had been at the dawn of civilization, the world was still overwhelmingly rural, agrarian, craft-based and traditional, and not categorically different in nature from the first civilizations of 5,000 years earlier. In eighteenth-century Europe, as elsewhere, science and technology were still largely separate enterprises. Sociologically and intellectually, the world of artisans, the crafts and everyday technologies unfolded at considerable remove from the parallel world of science and natural philosophy. Contemporary science was a literate culture, required schooling, was decidedly urban and was well institutionalized

in universities and specialized schools, learned societies, observatories, botanical gardens and hospitals. Governments supported science and medicine for their perceived utility, and to that extent we can speak of contemporary 'applied science'. But the vastly larger world of contemporary technology, on the other hand, was not institutionalized and not part of a literate tradition for which one went to school, but was craft-based and required hands-on training or apprenticeship. Manufactured goods were for the most part the products of either cottage industries in farming communities or of skilled urban craftsmen. Technology affected everyone every day and was, notably, present in the countryside as well as the city.

industrial revolution: England and beyond

Several factors help explain why early industrialization began in England. One is the dramatic population increase in England and Wales, that jumped from 5.5 to 9 million across the century, putting pressures on all kinds of resources. Another is what is known as the 'timber famine'. Shipbuilding, for example, consumed vast quantities of timber. The smelting of iron ore, another major industry, which depleted whole forests and added to pressures on sylvan resources, created something of an energy crisis, and induced consideration of alternatives. New farming techniques known as the 'Norfolk system' provided the necessary agricultural surplus to support the rise of industrialization in England. Finally, one can speculate that profits from British colonial trade and the sugar and slave trades provided some of the extra capital necessary for industrial development.

Technological responses to this set of pressures and shortages, to critical bottlenecks, and to surprising synergies by the nineteenth century stepwise created a new world and new way of life no one had anticipated. As with the Neolithic and urban Bronze Age revolutions previously, once this change was under way, there was no going back to earlier modes of social or economic life. In the iron industry, for example, plentiful coal presented itself as a natural substitute for scarce wood and charcoal. In 1709, Abraham Darby, a Quaker ironmaster, succeeded in using coke (charred coal) instead of charcoal in the blast furnace. In 1784 English inventor Henry Cort developed the 'puddling' process for converting pig (or cast) iron to wrought iron using coal directly, a technique that involved stirring the melt. These changes rendered English iron production geographically and materially independent of the forest and launched a new iron age. As for coal and other mining, mine shafts were sunk deeper and filled with more groundwater as superficial deposits became depleted. Traditional methods employed pumps of various designs driven by animal power, but in 1712 an obscure English ironmonger, Thomas Newcomen, invented the first practical steam engine to pump water from the mines. Newcomen engines proved sufficiently economical and were widely adopted because they operated primarily at coalmines where coal was cheap. Around the mid eighteenth century two English craftsmen, John Smeaton and **James Watt**, using entirely different approaches, improved the Newcomen engine, with Watt in 1765 introducing a fundamental technological novelty that resulted in a radical improvement in efficiency, the idea of condensing the steam in a separate vessel kept cold apart from the hot cylinder. The Watt engine could be set up and used to drive mills virtually anywhere, thereby promoting the expansion of manufacturing in urban centres. Another Englishman, Richard Trevithick, designed a high-pressure steam engine in 1800, and this development made the railway possible. In 1814 British engineer **George Stephenson** unveiled his first steam locomotive. The age of the railways truly dawned with the first public line opened between Liverpool and Manchester in 1830. As rail transportation developed, it interacted synergistically with the iron and coal industries: railways were made possible by the availability of increasingly cheap iron, and, in turn, rail transportation spurred – indeed demanded – increased iron and coal production.

Mechanized textile production is the paradigmatic industry of the early Industrial Revolution. Textile production, even as a 'cottage' industry, was already highly developed in Europe and elsewhere, but alternating technical innovations in spinning and weaving machinery propelled development in England. In 1733, John Kay, initially a clockmaker, invented the 'flying shuttle', which improved weaving but thereby created a production bottleneck in spinning. A combination of technical developments elaborated by a series of artisans and engineers in the 1760s and 1770s resulted in fully mechanized spinning; these improvements left weaving as the constriction point in the production process, an imbalance intensified by the invention of cylinder carding in 1775 which made spinning even more efficient. After 1785, with the

mechanically powered loom, to which the steam engine would ultimately be applied as an independent power source, weaving became mechanized. In 1813 some 2,400 power looms operated in **Britain**; by 1833 the number had skyrocketed to 100,000. Worker productivity in the cotton industry shot up two hundredfold. The mechanization and industrialization of textile production marked the arrival of industrial civilization.

The new factory system that arose with the Industrial Revolution came to involve centralized and standardized production using machines, wage labour and an organization of the production process that involved hierarchies of supervisors and managers. For workers, the factory imposed an unprecedented alienation of work from home and family life. The clock, the medieval device to tell time, became the industrial master that governed time and the workplace. Especially in its early phases in England, the factory system entailed a severe exploitation of labour. An industrial, urban-based labour force formed a new working class that rivalled the traditional rural peasantry, and new forms of class conflict arose. The so-called American system of manufacturing with interchangeable parts – developed in Britain, but widely applied in the **United States** – represents a key innovation that emerged in the mid nineteenth century. With machine tools and experts migrating across industries, the formal assembly line, perfected by Henry Ford in the automobile industry in the second decade of the twentieth century, culminated in the evolution of the modern factory.

The Industrial Revolution only coincidentally followed the Scientific Revolution of the sixteenth and seventeenth centuries. Effected for the most part by unlettered mechanics in the countryside, the early Industrial Revolution in England had nothing to do with science in the city or any effort to apply science in industry. The ideology of Francis Bacon that science could or should be tapped for its useful application was without direct effect. Science, rationality and experiment had a large cultural impact at the time, but science and contemporary industry had little to do with one another, again sociologically or intellectually.

Industrialization brought fundamental social and cultural changes. Urbanization is a telling indicator. The urban population of England topped 50 per cent in 1850; it achieved the same figure in Germany in 1900, and in **France** and the United States by 1920. Urbanization on a world level was only 15 per cent in 1900, but that figure rose rapidly, and humanity crossed the watershed of 50 per cent urban dwellers in 2004. New coercive institutions such as public schools and well-regulated prisons came into being as agents of social control. The family ceased to be a centre of production, and a new division of labour took hold – typically men secured employment in factories while women were mainly restricted to domestic duties. The advent of industrial civilization brought about significant changes in available energy resources and patterns of energy consumption. The production of coal and then oil rose exponentially from the eighteenth century to the point where per capita energy consumption in industrialized societies today is two orders of magnitude greater than in traditional pre-industrial societies. A money economy replaced traditional exchanges of goods and services. Like labour, capital and new means of financing were essential for industrialization, for which the London Stock Exchange, opening in 1773 and offering its first list of stocks in 1803, can stand as the exemplar. The ideological effects of industrialization proved no less powerful. Not coincidentally, new ideas about markets and free enterprise or **'laissez-faire'** capitalism emerged with the Industrial Revolution. **Adam Smith**'s *The Wealth of Nations* (1776) signalled the new ideology of the marketplace. As the Industrial Revolution gained momentum, however, other voices began to speak in opposition to free-market capitalism, in particular, **Karl Marx** (1818–83), whose *Das Kapital* (three volumes from 1867), provided an analytical critique of the new economic circumstances.

The processes of industrialization gained momentum in England in the nineteenth century, and industrialization and industrial civilization soon spread to the Low Countries, **Belgium**, **Germany**, France and North America in places such as Lowell, Massachusetts and Patterson, New Jersey.

wedding of science and industry

The important story behind science and technology in the nineteenth century concerns the union of science and industry. The connection between science and government did not go away, but expanded as industrialization proceeded. A potent novelty in this new era was the emergence of modern applied science in industry. It is not too crude to say that science moved from the superstructure of natural philosophy to unite with technology to become part of the base and the means of production of contemporary industrial

civilization. Over the course of the nineteenth century the intellectual accomplishments of science, particularly the physical sciences, were tremendous, and it was this body of knowledge that leaked into practical and world-transforming new technologies. The creation of the battery by Alessandro Volta in 1800 marks a turning point. Current electricity was virtually a new phenomenon of nature created by science, and it had wide scientific and technological impact. For science, the ramifications passed through Humphry Davy (1778–1829) and electrochemistry, John Daton (1766–1844) and chemical atomism, and the mathematization of electricity and magnetism by way of André-Marie Ampère and the calculus. Compliments of Hans Christian Oersted and **Michael Faraday**, by 1831 scientific understanding had led to the technological development of motors, generators and electromagnets. A technological result was the telegraph in 1837 and in 1882 with **Thomas Alva Edison**, the first electric lighting systems. The telephone, invented by Alexander Graham Bell in 1876, is a related and likewise consequential technological outcome stemming from science. Another branch of this river flows out of James Clerk Maxwell's science and the mathematization of Faraday's electromagnetic field, notably in Heinrich Hertz's discovery of radio waves in 1887 and their almost immediate application by **Guglielmo Marconi**, as 'wireless telegraphy', which ultimately turned into radio and then television.

The dye industry in Germany proved another influential locus of applied science in the nineteenth century. This confluence depended on the formidable maturation of analytical and organic chemistry in the context of German universities revived as research institutions, as well as peculiarities of German patent law and the state of German unification. Beginning with the first synthetic aniline dye by William Perkin in 1856 and moving on to the whole spectrum of coal tar dyes and their widespread application in dying, cosmetics, pharmaceuticals and explosives, companies like Bayer embraced science and forged tight links with university chemistry departments. The novelty in this case was the creation of the first industrial research labs, where industrial research and development (R&D) began to be formally practised. The research division created by Bayer in 1874 was taken up by other industries. The invention of invention and technology as applied science had finally arrived.

As much as we need to highlight new connections between science and industry in the nineteenth century, the continuing connections between science and governments and the industrialization of war that took place on a vast scale cannot be overlooked. Governments thereby supported and added to the momentum of industrialization and the integration of science into government as well as industry. Chemical warfare used in **World War I** is a telling example. It should be noted that applied science in the military increased the ability of the West to impose itself on the rest of the world. In this way science and technology became tools of empire.

By 1900 the world had become a very different place from what it had been in 1800, as industrialization worked its transforming effects. But this deep-rooted technological and social metamorphosis occurred unevenly and in stages, with scientific and technological haves and have-nots to be found both within and among the nations of the world. We need to distinguish between and among the Industrial Revolution that unfolded in Britain, the larger process of industrialization that spread around the world, and industrial civilization as the practical and social/cultural outcome and modus vivendi. Historians of technology debate whether there has been one or multiple 'industrial revolutions': the age of steam followed by the electo-chemical age or perhaps now the digital age. The categories themselves seem problematic, even if distinctions do need to be drawn. But looked at in broader perspective, one overarching, snowballing process seems to have been at play, transforming the world as we know it. Especially after **World War II**, industrialization has proceeded on a truly multinational and global basis. Furthermore, unlike the Neolithic and urban Bronze Age revolutions of prehistory, industrialization has unfolded with amazing rapidity.

science and technology

Historians of technology introduced the concept of a technological system, or the idea of an entire set of things and ways of doing things required for any working technology, distinguishing, for example, between the artifact of a light bulb from all that's required to make it glow. The concept has proved useful in conceptualizing technologies in general, but especially so in unpacking the technologies that sustain today's world. The major technological systems that weave together in industrial civilization today are not hard to identify. The motor car is a wonder of technology and an icon of industrial civilization. Motor vehicles powered by internal combustion engines, a potent new prime mover,

first developed in the 1880s. Their manufacture powers whole economies and their social effects have been dramatic. What can be said about cars can be said forcefully about trucks and the place of trucking in the world economy today, including links between trucking and railways. This global transportation revolution is thrown into higher relief when one considers the technology of containerization and shipping across the world's oceans.

In this connection the industrialization of agriculture stands out. The mechanization of agricultural production began in the nineteenth century, but horses and humans then supplied the power. The tractor-driven plough, an offshoot of the automobile industry, changed matters significantly and, with other motorized farm equipment, accounted for a substantial increase in food production. The industrialization of agriculture has produced unprecedented reductions in the numbers of people directly involved in farming and food production. That figure stands at less than 5 per cent in many industrialized countries today, compared to the historical norm of greater than 90 per cent.

Electricity is an especially versatile energy source that also can stand as a surrogate for industrial civilization as a whole. The development of the electric power industry and near universal electrification in the twentieth century introduced novel and complex technological systems involving generators, power lines and meters, to name but a few of its elements, and changed social behaviours that came with it. The production and consumption of electricity have grown spectacularly in tandem with the rest of industrial civilization.

With the Wright brothers' first powered flight at Kitty Hawk in 1903, aviation, too, has taken off as an emblematic and essential technology of today's world. In World War I, less than fifteen years after the Wrights' primitive flyer, aeroplanes mounted with machine guns and carrying bombs flew in war over **Europe**, and military aviation has developed substantially since. Civilian aviation got off the ground in the early 1930s, with commercial airliners combining hundreds of techniques and materials, many of them newly invented. Passenger air travel expanded after World War II, eventually developing into the complex global air transportation system that exists today, where we and our baggage are processed (in factory-like fashion) through Security and on to stupendous flying machines of extraordinary technological scale and complexity that are maintained by other elaborate components of the system. It seems almost miraculous that today's traveller can get from virtually anywhere in the world to any of a thousand destinations in a single day.

A profound change has taken place regarding domestic technologies that has affected billions of people in their everyday lives, particularly women. A host of powerful and power-hungry machines replaced the simple appliances and techniques traditional for running the home, including, for example, vacuum cleaners (1901) and washing machines (1910). And let us not forget frozen and prepared food and the differences these technologies have made. Even a small-scale modern home embodies wonders that were rare or unimaginable in mansions prior to industrialization. The lift made possible skyscrapers and high-rise office and apartment buildings. The suburban house comes with its own range of ancillary equipment. The system of the home plugs into the world of the motor car, for in so many cases getting into a car is the first thing a person does when leaving their home. In less-developed parts of the world and among the world's poor everywhere, however, shelter remains primitive, if not precarious. Most women are still restricted to the kitchen, and it is a kitchen with few amenities.

An extraordinary constellation of sociologically and economically significant new technologies developed in the twentieth century centred on personal and mass entertainment. Radio broadcasting reshaped everyone's lives. The invention of the phonograph and recorded music represent another powerful technology. Synergy arose between the radio and recording industries, as radio stations played music that listeners purchased to enjoy at home on their own record players. To this list we need to add moving pictures or 'movies', a powerful new medium of art and entertainment that has remained popular. In 1930 the first commercial television was already broadcasting. The impact of television cannot be overemphasized, even as it is becoming overshadowed by other great technologies of the modern age: computers and the Internet.

In the meantime, modern science itself underwent its own revolutions, including conceptual ones, that further integrated it with technology and society. This story can only be suggested here by waving at Einstein and general and special relativity, the discovery of radioactivity and subatomic particle physics, the quantum theory of light and then quantum mechanics and uncertainty as articulated by Werner Heisenburg and Erwin Schrödinger and later Niels Bohr. Edwin Hubble and Big Bang cosmology represents another area where theorists forged profound conceptual novelties in the twentieth century, confirmed in Arno Penzias' and Robert Wilson's discovery of the $3°$ kelvin background radiation in 1965. A notable theoretical and practical development in twentieth-century science was the revival and success of Darwinian evolution along with Mendel's genes and their confirmation in the discovery of the double helical structure of DNA by James Watson and Francis Crick in 1953. Subsequent developments in genetics, consequential for natural philosophy and for practical application (DNA forensics, for example), have been spectacular over the last half of the century, and evolutionary thinking has refracted into huge areas of scientific thought, not least in sociobiology and evolutionary psychology. With the full panoply of scientific knowledge today, we are well equipped to tell unprecedentedly sophisticated stories about ourselves and the natural world around us.

The exponential growth of science in the modern era is exceptional. The scale of the scientific enterprise has increased dramatically since the seventeenth century, until recently outpacing the growth of industrial civilization itself. One result has been scientific research fractionating into hyper-specialized areas of enquiry. Another has been the professionalization of science and engineering and the elaboration of technical careers and gainful career paths in academe, university and industry. Science, engineering and medicine have generally not been inclusive in terms of gender or race, although those circumstances are changing. Another feature of science and technology in the modern world concerns the industrialization of scientific research itself in what is known as Big Science or Technoscience. In Big Science, teams pursue pure and applied science research in huge facilities on an industrial scale. The **Manhattan Project** to build the atomic bomb in the 1940s is a paradigmatic example; the best currently is the Large Hadron Collider (LHC), the world's largest and highest-energy particle accelerator. The expenses involved in this kind of research are enormous, with funding coming mostly from governments, but also from industry and in the case of the LHC from national, inter-agency and regional sources. Industrial and military research may be less multinational and cosmopolitan, but it is no less industrial and managerial in this regard. The industrialization of scientific research is such a marker of modernity on a global scale that it has been given the name *Technoscience*. The term is a loose one, with shades of meaning suggesting a seamless merger of what might be thought of separately as science and technology.

Science and science-based technologies have self-evidently contributed to the making of industrial civilization. How exactly has science been tapped and applied in the technologies of contemporary civilization? Applied science in industrial contexts is mostly empirical and trial and error. It involves what historian Derek Price labelled 'boiled-down science' or the mundane (but hardly trivial) exploitation of knowledge by engineers or R&D specialists using what is available in textbooks, say, or online. The invention of xerography and photocopying is exemplary here. Chester Carlson, a chemist and lawyer, developed the process by himself in his kitchen in 1938 using what he knew of optics and photochemistry. That photocopying machines did not come into general use until the 1960s says that much else is always involved when 'science' gets transmuted into 'technology'. A particular, atypical kind of applied science involves the transformation of theoretical work from the forefront of scientific research directly into practical, useful technologies. The atomic bomb represents an iconic case and a powerful exemplar. 'The Bomb' was a clear-cut and direct application of scientific theory to a practical use, with theoretical novelty in 1938 being turned into practical technology and the obliteration of Japanese cities in 1945.

Business and industry have now eclipsed government as the main underwriters of research in science and technology. Industry is almost entirely oriented towards immediately useful and profitable applications of knowledge. Government remains the major player supporting basic research. Through a complex system of grants, the basic research takes place in universities and federal research centres. These days, scientific discoveries are regularly patented as intellectual property. The melding of science and technology at the forefront of research has produced today's high-tech industries and high-tech world. Computers in particular have transformed technology and society. A key step was the creation of the first solid-state transistor in 1947 and teams at IBM to carry projects forward. A computer and digital revolution followed. Mainframes, followed by personal computers, then the Internet, and today's myriad of chip-enhanced devices successively changed everyone's lives. Industrial civilization and our networked society are now inconceivable without the computer, and an untold story is how standards have evolved in these high-tech industries to allow industrial civilization to function.

Computers and computing transformed the music industry and created video games. With the maturation of cellphone and satellite communication technology along with computers and the Internet, a further global communication revolution unfolded. Computers and the Internet provide instantaneous communications through a variety of platforms. Unique in history, people around the globe now have instant access to one another via phones, live television, email and social network media. And, we should not overlook scientific medicine and the modern miracles that have resulted from the applications of scientific research in biology, chemistry and a host of related fields. Highly sophisticated, science-based medical technologies have emerged that have transformed medicine and improved the health and welfare of humankind. The gamut of modern medicine is its own example. The modern science-based and high-tech pharmaceutical industry is likewise remarkable, and materials science and biomedical engineering have contributed much, not least with dental technologies. Nuclear power is another example of a non-trivial high-tech industry, as are genetically engineered crops and genetically modified foods that have effected a further historic agricultural revolution. Any number of examples of continuing connections between science and the military tell the same story of science and cutting-edge technologies as key elements of industrial civilization.

In the period following World War II science enjoyed an unquestioned moral, intellectual and technical authority. Through the operations of its apparently unique 'scientific method', theoretical science seemed to offer an infallible path to knowledge, while applied science promised to better human existence. As the effects of a fused science–technology culture began to refashion advanced societies, so, too, beginning in the 1960s did a wave of reactions lead to the questioning of science and technology as the triumphant bearers of human progress. Technological failures such as the implosion of the Fukushima nuclear reactor in 2011 and the spread of new diseases make many people suspicious of the benefits of science and technology. The dark side of industrial civilization, with its weapons of mass destruction, industrial pollution, climate change, depletion of resources, deforestation, the loss of biodiversity, and so forth, is inextricably interwoven with the miracles, benefits and comforts of the same. How humanity lives today is astounding, and modern science and technology are in no small measure responsible. Yet because of them also, the future of industrial civilization is in doubt. The destructive and constructive powers inherent in science and technology will play key roles in the unfolding of that future.

'scramble for Africa'
– see also **imperialism**.

The carving out of new African colonies by European states following the 1884–5 Berlin conference, which increased European holdings from 10 per cent to 90 per cent of the continent. Those gaining from the scramble for land were **Britain** (acquiring 7.7 million square kilometres of territory and 88 million people), **France** (5.8 million square kilometres and 37 million people) and **Germany** (1.6 million square kilometres and 17 million people). Within twenty-five years only **Ethiopia** and **Liberia** remained independent.

SEATO
– see **South East Asia Treaty Organization**.

Secession (USA)
– see also **Sectional conflict**.

In 1860–1, after more than a decade of sectional agitation, eleven slaveholding states seceded from the Federal Union to form the **Confederate States of America**. Southern politicians claimed secession as a legal right; the denial of that claim by President Abraham Lincoln led to the **American Civil War**. State secession proceeded in two distinct stages: 20 December 1860–1 February 1861 and 17 April–20 May 1861. The first group of seven lower Southern states seceded in response to the victory in the 1860 presidential election of a **Republican Party** committed to opposing Southern demands for the further expansion of slavery. South Carolina acted first, followed by Mississippi, Florida, Alabama, Georgia, Louisiana and **Texas**. The Confederate firing on Fort Sumter and Lincoln's decision to force the rebellious states back into Union precipitated a second secession, this time from the upper South, beginning with Virginia and quickly followed by Arkansas, Tennessee and North Carolina.

Second Empire
– see **Napoleon III**.

Second Republic (Spanish)
Established after the electoral defeat and flight of King Alfonso XIII in April 1931, the Second Republic survived until the Nationalist victory in the civil war in 1939. A centre-left administration instituted modest reforms but the right won the 1933 elections, provoking anti-government strikes and an uprising in 1934. The narrow electoral victory of a left-wing Popular Front coalition in February 1936 was followed by military revolt in July, opening a bloody three-year civil war.

Sectional conflict
A conflict between the Northern and Southern **United States** lasting from the **American Revolution** to the **American Civil War**, notably but not exclusively over slavery. Its analytical counterpoint would be partisan conflict, though friction could entail both; party alignment might itself be rather sectional. In the first **American party system**, a slave South that exported primary products challenged an essentially free North that had diversified into banking, shipping and nascent industry over matters of **tariff policy** and **protectionism**. **Federalist** decline mitigated such sectionalism, although the **American War of 1812** inspired its New England stronghold to murmurs of **Secession** at the **Hartford Convention**. The **Era of Good Feelings** and **Missouri Compromise** revealed growing differences over slavery's expansion, whilst the **Nullification crisis** betrayed somewhat sectional economic divisions, but the nationwide scope of the second party system counteracted such tendencies. The **Mexican–American War**, the **Compromise of 1850** and the **Kansas–Nebraska Act** divided the two sections over slavery's extension into a third, the west, and made of the North's long-held majority an actual political bloc.

secularism
It could be plausibly argued that the history of Europe over the last five hundred years has been about the assertion of the primacy of secular over religious institutions and ultimately of secular over religious values. It can be traced back to the struggles for primacy between the emerging monarchies of medieval Europe and the **Papacy**, which culminated in the decision of Henry VIII of England to make the king, rather than the pope, the supreme governor of the Church of England. Religious authority in England and much of northern Europe was further tempered by the continuing impact of the Protestant reformation. It was a common feature of the new Protestant churches that there was a balance of power between the clergy and the laity, and the 'lower' the church, the lower the inherent authority of the clergy. They ceased to be priests administering the sacraments and became ministers or elders. In the

extreme case of the **Quakers**, founded in the late seventeenth century, the concept of clergy disappeared altogether. Only the English, however, then asserted the primacy of the secular power by establishing a national church under the authority of the crown. It was their settlers in the **United States** who were to take the opposite course, which has been much more widely influential, of completely separating church and state as a guarantee of religious toleration.

It was only in the eighteenth century, however, that secularism started to emerge as a coherent force in its own right. The French philosophers, notably **Denis Diderot** (1713–84) of the *Encyclopédie*, wrote in a notably rationalist spirit which prompted religious hostility. **Voltaire** ridiculed religious superstition and was drawn to a non-doctrinal deism. Other intellectuals and members of the upper classes were attracted by free thought. The licentious, notably the Marquis de Sade (1740–1814) in **France** and Sir Francis Dashwood's Hell Fire Club at Medmenham Abbey in England (1750–74), perverted religious ritual for sexual ends. Much more widespread in Roman Catholic countries, however, was anti-clericalism and contempt for the religious orders.

The advance of secularism, though, was in general much more subtle. Scientific discovery slowly explained the previously inexplicable. The progress of science accelerated in the nineteenth century and in 1859 **Charles Darwin** (1809–82) published *The Origin of Species* which not only rendered the biblical account of the creation untenable but explained how all living creatures, including humans, could have evolved without divine intervention. Religious hostility to what was perceived to be an attack on the fundamental pillars of Christian belief was intense. The *Syllabus* promulgated by Pope **Pius IX** reverted to medieval absolutism by condemning the nineteenth century's basic philosophies as 'monstrous', declaring the Church superior to the state, requiring for it a monopoly in education and opposing both freedom of the press and freedom of worship for non-Catholics. Papal infallibility in doctrine was proclaimed at the Vatican Council of 1870. With time, however, most Christians absorbed evolution into their understanding of the world and it is probably only in the modern United States that there remains significant resistance to it. What has happened, however, is that, rather than being all encompassing, religion has been confined to more specifically spiritual fields.

Notwithstanding religious hostility, secularism in the modern sense had become an important force by the middle of the nineteenth century. Overt atheism could be expressed, at least in western Europe, and materialism was on the ascendant as a philosophy. Anti-clericalism grew stronger and in Roman Catholic countries usually implied the rejection of all religion, which it always sought to deprive of any status in society. It was in collision with the Roman Catholic Church in particular but also with any church which upheld orthodoxy and tradition, and not least with the temporal power if it defined itself in religious terms. The Habsburg monarchy of **Austria** and then **Austria–Hungary** was an avowed defender of Catholicism.

Secularism, therefore, became associated with left-wing thought and its faith in progress almost by default, but the link between left-wing thought and science was confirmed by the foundation in **Germany** of 'scientific socialism', which maintained that the correctness of socialism could be proved scientifically. Secularism remained, therefore, somewhat suspect to the middle classes, who valued the sense of stability and order conferred by religion. Consequently, a certain cleavage opened up in all the developed countries between continued church-going and people's lifestyles and attitudes, which grew ever more secular.

The twentieth century was to see the increasing separation of church and state. In France, the *loi laïque* of 1905 imposed a complete severance, with the church losing the legal power to conclude marriages and a ban on religious education in state schools. The concordat concluded in 1929 between the Papacy and the Italian government restricted the pope's temporal claim to all but the Vatican City and recognized state supremacy in the rest of Italy. By the end of the century the secular authority had established the primacy over the religious pioneered by Henry VIII in England everywhere in **Europe**, with the possible exception of **Poland**. The trend was strenuously resisted by the Roman Catholic Church in many countries. It actively backed the nationalist side in the **Spanish Civil War**, 1936–9, and the Catholic Clericals were in conflict with the Austrian Socialists during the 1930s. In the Nazi puppet state of **Croatia** during **World War II**, the Orthodox were threatened with death if they did not convert to Catholicism.

The greatest triumph of political secularism, or more properly, state secularism, however, was not against Roman Catholicism but by the Communist Revolution of 1917 against the Russian Orthodox Church. Churches (and mosques where relevant) were closed wholesale and social organizations reorganized on strictly secular lines. Major cities had museums of atheism. It was only under the pressures of the German invasion of 1941 that some churches and mosques were reopened to harness traditional national sentiment. The same secular revolution was imposed in all the central and eastern European countries which came under Communist control after 1945 until the collapse of Communism in 1989.

Nonetheless modern Europe is an essentially secular continent despite the continuing influence of the churches on education, most notably in **Ireland**, and much religious belief is residual. Homosexuality and the use of condoms are accepted despite religious prohibitions. It is only in general in its immigrant communities that faith is stronger, often in Islamic guise. The Vatican has even considered working with **Islam** to promote spirituality in a Europe which no longer appears to feel great need for it.

segregation, racial (USA)

The Jim Crow racial segregation laws were passed by Southern states during the late nineteenth and early twentieth centuries. They covered many aspects of Southern life, from public amenities to transport. The Supreme Court endorsed Jim Crow in *Plessy vs. Ferguson* (1896), which ruled in favour of 'separate but equal' rail travel. The imposition of segregation ran alongside the disenfranchisement of African American voters and a rapid rise in racial lynchings. The segregation era was also one of intellectual support for **social Darwinism** and the rise of demeaning black images in popular culture. There was widespread support for Jim Crow from white Americans living beyond the South – indeed, segregation was practised in many Northern schools. African American resistance often delayed the imposition of Jim Crow. During the twentieth century civil rights organizations challenged Jim Crow through the courts, and famously in the direct action protests associated with **Martin Luther King Jr.**

segregation (South Africa)

– *see* **apartheid**.

Segu

The capital of the **Bambara Empire** in the eighteenth and nineteenth centuries and current capital of **Mali's** fourth largest administrative region. While its origins remain contested, Soninke settlers arrived in the region by the eleventh century, followed by Mandinka settlers. Located on the Niger River, Segu provided the capital of the Bambara Empire that ruled over parts of central and southern Mali from 1712 to 1861. The capture of Segu by

El Hadj Umar Tall's mujahideen in 1861 signalled the end of the empire. Umar Tall handed control of Segu over to his son Ahmadu, who ruled until 1890 when the French colonial army invaded. Guadeloupean writer Maryse Condé chronicled the life of Segu in the late eighteenth century in her novel *Segu*. Currently, it is the fifth largest city in Mali.

Self-strengthening movement (China)

This was a movement in the 1870s and 1880s in **China** to strengthen the country in the face of a threat from foreign imperialism. Led by Feng Guifen, it was also supported by officials such as Li Hongzhan and Zheng Guofen. In 1861 the *zongli yamen* was established in Beijing as a foreign office. Railway, steamship companies and military arsenals were set up, while the study of western science and technology was also promoted.

Selim III (1761–1808)

Enlightened Ottoman sultan who responded to the forces released by the **French Revolution** and the chaos in his own empire by introducing a range of reforms after his accession in 1789. His 'new order' (*nizam-i cedid*) incorporated reformed provincial governorships, taxation and land tenure, together with embassies in **Europe**'s major capitals. A new body of European-style infantry was introduced and army and naval colleges set up. Selim accepted the treaties terminating the 1787–92 war with **Austria** and **Russia**, and allied himself with **Britain** and Russia in response to **Napoleon**'s invasion of **Egypt**, 1798. He declared war on them in 1806, however, having recognized Napoleon as emperor in 1804. He lacked the determination to defend his reforms and French concepts against conservative reaction led by the janissaries and the *ulama*. Abandoning troop reorganization in the **Balkans** following the Edirne mutiny, 1805, he abolished the 'new order', 1807, after a further mutiny. He was murdered on the order of his immediate successor.

Sembène, Ousmane (1923–2007)

Senegalese author, filmmaker and cultural theorist. After working as a docker and in the Senegalese Tirailleurs during World War II, Sembène began writing short stories and novels. In 1966 he directed *La Noire de . . .*, considered the first feature film by a sub-Saharan African director. Known as the 'father of African cinema', his films and novels question themes of colonialism, modernity and tradition, gender, religion and are a critique of the postcolonial African bourgeoisie.

Sen, Amartya (1933–)

Indian economist and philosopher. An undergraduate of Presidency College, Kolkata, he completed a PhD in economics at Trinity College, Cambridge, in 1959. He was awarded the 1998 Nobel Prize in economics for his work on welfare economics, economic inequality, poverty and famines, and social choice theory. He was appointed master of Trinity College, Cambridge (1998–2004) and then became Thomas W. Lamont University Professor at Harvard University.

Sendero Luminoso (Shining Path) (Peru)

A fundamentalist version of Maoism that sought to capture the Peruvian state, the Shining Path revolutionary movement was organized and led by a charismatic university professor, Abimael Guzmán Reynoso. In the 1980s and early 1990s it plunged **Peru** into a catastrophic civil war that cost upwards of 70,000 lives, nearly wrecking the economy and almost toppling the government. Guzmán's capture in 1992 punctured his almost mythical invincibility and led to the movement's quick demise.

Senegal

Senegal became the first French colony in **Africa** in 1854. The coastal area had a history of slave trading involving the **Netherlands** and pre-Revolution **France**. A member in 1959 of a brief **Mali** Federation with French Soudan, Senegal gained independence in 1960 under **Léopold-Sédar Senghor** (1906–2001), founder of the Senegalese Democratic Bloc (subsequently renamed the Socialist Party). Senghor instituted a one-party state and initially aimed at constructing a socialist society. He was succeeded in 1980 by Abdou Diouf (1935–), who moved towards a market-oriented economy. A confederation, **Senegambia**, established with neighbouring **Gambia** in 1982 foundered as Gambians complained about Senegalese attempts at dominance. With political parties legalized, an opposition candidate, Abdoulaye Wade (1926–), won presidential elections in 2000 and 2007. Senegal is one of the few African nations never to have experienced a military coup. Macky Sali (1961–) was elected president in 2012. The population is predominantly Muslim, with a small Christian minority.

Senegambia

– *see* **Gambia**.

Senghor, Léopold Sédar (1906–2001)

Senegalese poet, cultural theorist and first president of independent **Senegal**. In 1928, Senghor left for **France**, studying first at La Sorbonne and graduating from the University of Paris. While teaching outside Paris, he and other intellectuals from the African diaspora began the movement called **Négritude**, a response to French racism that proclaimed the pride and beauty of African culture. His writing reflected debates over race and the place of Africa in world history. After serving in the French military and being interned by the Germans during **World War II**, Senghor became a member of the French National Assembly representing Senegal–Mauritania. He drew his support from among workers and trade unions and in 1948 founded the Senegalese Democratic Bloc. In 1960 he became the first president of Senegal and penned its national anthem. He resigned in 1980 and in 1983 became the first African member of the Académie Française.

Senusi

– *see* **Sanusiyya**.

September 11th (9/11)

The airborne attacks on the Twin Towers housing the World Trade Center in New York and the Pentagon in Washington on 11 September 2001, executed by three pilots of Palestinian origin under the auspices of the **al-Qaida** (the 'base') Islamist terrorist group headed by Saudi Arabian **Osama bin Laden**. In Islamic eyes, the World Trade Center epitomized the capitalist sin of usury. Brilliantly planned and executed to attain the maximum physical and psychological impact and with total disregard for the cost in lives (nearly 3,000) and human suffering, 9/11 must be deemed one of the greatest terror attacks on record. It was followed by a call from US President **George Bush**, echoed by UK Prime Minister Tony Blair, for international support for a 'war on terror' and the invocation for the first time of Article 5 of the NATO charter, declaring that September 11th was an attack on all nineteen member states. The inconclusive war in **Afghanistan**, where al-Qaida had many training camps, soon followed.

Serbia

Balkan country. Its historic heartland was what is now **Kosovo** and southern Serbia, but under the Ottoman Turks many Serbs emigrated northwards as far as modern-day Vojvodina and **Croatia**. Serbs north of the Danube were under Austrian rule after 1699, those south had formed part of the **Ottoman Empire** since the fourteenth century. Serbia gained autonomy within the empire, 1829, and independence, 1878, when it also gained more territory. A victor in the **Balkan Wars**, 1912–13, it acquired much of Macedonia. Attacked by **Austria–Hungary**, 1914, following the assassination of Crown Prince Franz-Ferdinand in Sarajevo by a Bosnian Serb, it was defeated, 1915, but the end of **World War I** saw the proclamation of the Triune Kingdom of Serbs, Croats and Slovenes, later **Yugoslavia**, with the Serb monarch as king. Independent again after 1990, it sought to gather all the Serbs in a Greater Serbia and sought to retain Kosovo, which brought it into conflict with **NATO** and the **European Union**. It has applied to join the EU.

serfdom (European)

A key feature of medieval European feudalism outside **Russia**, whereby, in return for a measure of protection, a serf delivered much of what he produced to his lord, to whom he was totally subservient. The main difference between a serf and a slave was that a serf was bound to a designated plot of a lord's land, and that if that land were transferred to a new lord, he was transferred with it.

A clear distinction had emerged in the fourteenth and fifteenth centuries in the amount of personal liberty enjoyed by the serfs of western Europe, on the one hand, and of central and eastern Europe, on the other. Louis XIII of France (d. 1515) had revised compulsory feudal obligations and feudal tenures had been abolished in England by statute in 1660, although they had been largely inoperative since the Hundred Years War (1337–1453). In the east, however, the great wars of the period, notably against the Turks, had enhanced the power of the aristocracy and depressed that of the serf. The status of the peasant remained depressed from eastern Germany to Moscow until the eighteenth century when **Frederick William I** of Prussia completely freed the serfs on his personal domains in 1719. Nevertheless, more than two-thirds of Prussians remained serfs, and general emancipation was not begun until 1807. Serfdom was not abolished in the **Austrian Empire** until 1848, although its abolition had been ordered by **Joseph II** (r. 1765–90). Nevertheless, much of the central and eastern European peasantry retained a semi-feudal status until the Communist revolutions after **World War II**. The great Romanian peasant revolt of 1907 was suppressed at the cost of some 10,000 lives.

Even in parts of the West, however, significant vestiges of feudalism, if not legal serfdom,

remained a source of resentment until the *coup de grâce* delivered by the **French Revolution**. Feudalism was formally abolished in France in 1793, and the Convention had ordered its generals in 1792 to abolish the tithe and feudal rights everywhere they went – 'War on castles, peace to cottages'.

The origins of serfdom in the **Russian Empire** were different from those elsewhere in Europe. It had evolved here out of the growing financial dependence of the peasantry on the nobility as tenants in the fifteenth century and their agreement to remain on the same land until they could repay their debts. Serfdom had become widespread by the end of the sixteenth century but only legally established in 1649, the law decreeing that noblemen alone might own estates tilled by serfs. There were 3,400,000 serfs in 1743–6 and 5,700,000, excluding the Baltic provinces and Russian Poland, by 1794–6. Their position actually deteriorated during the eighteenth century because **Catherine II** bound them to their landowners but not to the land. They could thus be bought and sold in a marketplace, although not in **Ukraine** after 1798. Landless serfs were emancipated in the Baltic provinces, 1811–19, in what might have been envisaged as a pilot project for Russia as a whole. **Nicholas I** saw serfdom as an evil, 1842, but concluded that 'to attack it *now* would be something still more harmful'. Defeat in the **Crimean War**, serf restlessness and moral considerations, however, changed opinion and Tsar **Alexander II** issued the Edict of Emancipation, 1861.

settler colonialism

Settler colonialism is a process whereby foreign migrants, also known as settlers, permanently reside in a country or nation with the intent to displace the indigenous population. With the assistance of their home country, settlers seek to colonize the indigenous population by imposing their culture, politics, economy, religion and social institutions. In many instances, settlers seize the land of the indigenous population while creating 'native' reserves on undesirable land. The indigenous population is forced to migrate to the reserves, while the settlers occupy and transform the landscape of the country. For example, some settlers are in search of agricultural land, or natural and mineral resources such as gold and diamonds. The settlers are able to extract from or utilize the land with the removal of the indigenous population. In recent times, indigenous populations in **Australia**, **Canada**, **Kenya**, and **South Africa** as well as South and North America, argue that they have been affected by settler colonialism.

Seven Years War (1756–1763)

The first global conflict, fought between an coalition of **Austria, France, Russia**, Saxony and Sweden and against the **Prussia** of **Frederick the Great** and his allies **Britain** and Hanover, arising from Austria's attempt to regain Silesia from Prussia, lost during the War of the Austrian Succession. Prussia met with early successes in **Bohemia** and Saxony in 1756–8 but suffered a setback at the hands of Austria and Russia in 1759. After concluding peace with Russia in 1762, Prussia drove Austria from Silesia. Britain, meanwhile, engaged in a colonial and maritime contest with France and **Spain**, driving France from **Canada**, ending French influence in **India** and winning two sea battles in 1759. The result of the war in Europe confirmed Prussia as a major power on the continent and within **Germany**, while Britain's victories in North America and **India** established the foundations of the **British Empire**.

Sèvres, Treaty of

– see also **Lausanne, Treaty of**.

Paris Peace Conference agreement signed on 10 August 1920. This treaty dealt with the fate of the **Ottoman Empire**. Under its stipulations, the sultanate lost its non-Anatolian possessions, the Hijaz to the Arabs, **Palestine** (and what would be Transjordan) to the British, and **Syria** to the French. **Greece** received Smyrna for five years and gained Thrace and islands in the Aegean. **Italy** acquired Rhodes and the Dodecanese Islands. **Armenia** attained independence. The Straits (the Dardanelles and the **Bosphorus**) and **Constantinople** were demilitarized and placed under international control. **Mustapha Kemal**, who had mounted a national resistance, denounced the agreement, and subsequently defeated invading Greek forces. The Treaty of Lausanne (24 July 1923) nullified the Treaty of Sèvres. **Turkey** accepted the loss of non-Turkish territories but regained territory in Thrace. Turkish populations were also repatriated. The Treaty of Lausanne led to the official declaration of the Turkish republic in October 1923.

sexual equality

Two hierarchies have been universal in human cultures: age and gender. Patriarchy, the gender hierarchy in which men are understood to be superior and women inferior, has varied in its intensity, but has been remarkably resilient to change, surviving political and economic revolutions as well as intellectual and technological transformations. Some women were able to ignore or overcome patriarchal restrictions because of their position in other social hierarchies, and others decried them, but only in the mid nineteenth century did an organized movement supporting greater gender egalitarianism develop.

Reformers advocating for women's rights in the nineteenth century – what has since been termed the 'first stage' of the women's movement – called for women's suffrage, greater access to education and property rights, more equitable marriage and divorce laws, and protection for women workers, though with different emphases in different parts of the world. Reformers in **India** urged an end to *sati*, female infanticide and the prohibition of widow remarriage; those in **Europe** worked for women's rights to own property and control their own wages; those in the **United States** worked for temperance and dress reform; those in **Latin America** sought improvements in working conditions and a restructuring of civil law codes.

Groups specifically devoted to women's suffrage and political rights communicated with each other in what became an international feminist movement. They were initially ridiculed and attacked physically, and in many countries anti-suffrage groups were formed. The efforts of suffragists, combined with international events such as **World War I**, were ultimately successful, however, and suffrage rights were gradually extended to women around the world. This movement was especially slow in the conservative, religious societies of the **Middle East**. After gaining suffrage, many women's groups turned their attention to other types of issues, such as educational, health and legal reforms, or to world peace.

By the 1960s women in many parts of the world were dissatisfied with the pace at which they were achieving political and legal equality, and a second-wave women's movement began, often termed the 'women's liberation movement'. Women's groups pressured for an end to sex discrimination in hiring practices, pay rates, inheritance rights and the granting of credit; they opened battered-women's shelters, day care and rape crisis centres, and pushed for laws against dowries and sexual harassment. By the early 1970s advocates of rights for homosexuals had also mobilized in many countries, sponsoring demonstrations, political action campaigns and various types of self-help organization.

The United Nations declared 1975–85 to be the International Decade for Women, and held a series of meetings discussing the status of women around the world. These meetings were sometimes divisive, highlighting the great differences in women's concerns. Because of these differences, international measures promoting greater gender equality are always worded very carefully. The 1979 United Nations Convention on the Elimination of All Forms of Discrimination Against Women (CEDAW) did describe discrimination against women as a violation of 'the principles of equality of rights and respect for human dignity', but it was also careful to stress the effects of such discrimination on families, society and women's countries, and not simply on women as individuals. CEDAW has been ratified by nearly all countries, with the United States the only industrialized country not to do so; some ratifications have exempted customary, family and religious law, however, which lessens its impact considerably.

sexuality

The word *sexuality* is quite new, coming into English and most other western languages in about 1800. Ancient Greek, medieval Latin and many other early languages did not even have words for 'sex' or 'sexual', so that they did not define or classify ideas or behaviours in this way. Every human culture, however, has developed norms of sexual behaviour and provided positive consequences for following those norms, along with negative consequences for deviating from them. World history is often told as a story of interactions between cultures, along with the creation of traditions within cultures. Sexual issues have been central in both of these processes.

Encounters between cultures may have taken the form of military campaigns or voyages of trade, but permanent contact often brought laws regulating sexual relationships between groups. Laws and norms regarding marriage and other sexual contacts work to keep groups distinct from one another, and also to preserve hierarchies within cultures, which depend on those in power marrying people which that society defines as 'like themselves'. Thus socially defined categories of difference such as race, nation, ethnicity, caste, noble status and social class are maintained by sexual restrictions, for if they are not, those distinctions literally disappear. These restrictions are gendered, for almost everywhere women's sexual activities are more constrained than are those of men of the same social group.

Sexual categories and norms within a culture are often so deeply ingrained that they appear 'natural', the result not of human decisions but of divine mandate or the 'laws of nature'. 'Unnatural' sexual practices became a standard feature of groups other than one's own, a sign that they were radically 'other'. During the era of European colonialism and imperialism, indigenous peoples were often feminized, described or portrayed visually as weak and passive in contrast to the virile and masculine conquerors, or they were hyper-sexualized, regarded as animalistic and voracious. (Or sometimes both.)

Many scholars see several developments from the late eighteenth century to the early twentieth century as creating a distinctively 'modern' sexuality, though most of this research has focused on the West. The most important of these was a change in the basic paradigm of sexuality from religion to science. Church courts in **Europe** and the European colonies heard fewer morals cases, as aberrant sexual desires and actions were no longer viewed as sin, but as 'degeneracy' or 'perversion'. They were still 'unnatural', but any correction or prevention was to be done by scientifically trained professionals such as doctors, not by pastors or priests. Western governments sought to promote a healthy society as a way of building up national strength, and anything that detracted from this became a matter of official and often public concern. Masturbation, prostitution, pornography and venereal disease all came to be viewed as sexual issues and health problems.

Attitudes towards same-sex sexual activities and the social context of those activities also shifted in the West. In the sixteenth and seventeenth centuries 'sodomy' was a capital crime tried by secular or church courts, although the actual number of sodomy cases was small. The early eighteenth century saw several waves of sodomy trials and executions, but by the end of the century punishment was more likely imprisonment or banishment than the death penalty of earlier years. In the nineteenth century same-sex desire was medicalized, first labelled 'inversion' and then with a term devised in 1869 by the Hungarian jurist K. M. Benkert: 'homosexuality'. During the same period, homosexual subcultures and communities – with special styles of dress, behaviour, slang terms and meeting places – became more common, developing among men in some European cities as early as the seventeenth century, and in many more places by the twentieth century, when they more often involved women as well as men.

Heterosexuality also became a matter of identity in the early twentieth century, of a permanent 'sexual orientation' that eventually became a legal as well as medical term and a central part of modern western notions of the self. The word *heterosexual* was originally used by sexologists to describe individuals of different sexes who regularly engaged in non-procreative sex simply for fun; it was thus a type of perversion, though a mild one. Increasingly the term came to be used for those who were sexually attracted to the 'opposite' sex, with the proper development of this attraction a matter of health.

These scientific and medical studies of sexual attitudes and behaviour led to two somewhat contradictory ideas about sexuality in the West. On the one hand, one's choice of sexual partners or sexual behaviour was increasingly regarded as a reflection of a permanent orientation, a 'sexual identity' as a homosexual or heterosexual. On the other hand, homosexuality and other types of 'deviant' sexuality were at first defined as illnesses, curable through drugs, surgery or psychoanalysis.

Whether expressed through religion or medicine, western ideas about gender and sexuality were largely dichotomous – there were two genders, and one was attracted to either one's own or the opposite gender – but in a number of areas throughout the world, certain individuals combined the tasks, behaviour and clothing of men and women. Though outsiders often regarded such individuals within the framework of *sexuality*, that is, as homosexuals, they are better understood as a third *gender* category. Sexual activities or relationships between such individuals and either men or women thus cannot be categorized as homosexual or heterosexual.

Third-gender individuals highlight what became a prominent theme in the study of sexuality in the late twentieth century, and in political activism surrounding issues of sexuality. At the same time that discrimination on the basis of sexual orientation was prohibited in many areas – largely as a result of the gay rights movement that began in the 1970s – many people (including some gay rights' activists) argued that sexual orientation, sexual identity and even gender identity were completely socially constructed and could or should be changed, adapted and blended at will. They asserted that 'sexual orientation' and 'gender identity' had indeed been part of 'modern' ideas about sexuality, but in a postmodern world such concepts were outmoded.

Both 'modern' and what might be called 'postmodern' sexuality are often seen as western

developments, with groups in other parts of the world regarding these as yet another example of cultural imperialism. In some areas, however, individuals and groups have blended traditional indigenous third-gender categories and more recent forms of homosexual or transsexual identity, asserting that toleration or even celebration of those with distinctive sexuality has roots in their own cultures and is not simply a western import. At the same time, fundamentalists in many religious traditions, including **Christianity**, **Judaism**, **Hinduism** and **Islam**, oppose alternatives to heterosexual marriage, and support the expansion of existing laws regulating sexual relationships. It is clear that sexual issues have not lost their power as points of conflict both within and among cultures.

Sha'rawi, Huda (1879–1947)

Egyptian feminist pioneer. Daughter of the first president of the Egyptian Representative Council, she received an elite education at home, studying French, her first language, as well as Arabic, Farsi, Turkish and the Qur'an, which she had memorized by the age of 9. Betrothed to her much older cousin as a second wife at age 13, but, following her protests, the marriage was suspended until she was 21. She started organizing public lectures for women in Cairo and established a women's welfare society, 1908, and a school for girls, 1910. A participant in the **Egyptian Revolution of 1919**, she helped to organize the largest women's anti-British demonstration, and became president elect of the Wafdist Women's Central Committee (WWCC). She attended the ninth session of the International Feminist Conference, May 1923, the first session at which **Egypt** was represented, and then founded the Egyptian Feminist Union to fight for a feminist agenda and full national independence. Its lifelong president, she resigned from the WWCC, 1924, after the government ignored women's suffrage. She founded the All Arab Federation of Women in 1944.

Shaka Zulu (c. 1787–1828)

One of the most famous **Zulu** kings, creator of an empire. Born in present-day KwaZulu Natal, the illegitimate son of Zulu chief Senzangakhona, and Nandi, princess of the Langeni clan, among whom he was first brought up. Shaka subsequently became first a soldier for and then a protégé of the Mthethwa leader **Dingiswayo**, rising to command a regiment. On the death of his father in 1816, Shaka seized control of the Zulu clan, and in 1817 succeeded Dingiswayo following his assassination.

He expanded Zulu power through a combination of alliances with smaller neighbours and efficiently organized military prowess. An autocratic and reputedly brutal ruler, at the height of his powers, of around 250,000 people (a fifth of whom were warriors), Shaka's sanity faltered after his mother's death in 1827 and, as he grew increasingly unpredictable, he was assassinated by his half-brothers Dingane and Mhlangana.

Shamir, Yitzhak (1915–2012)

Underground leader in **Palestine**; leader of **Likud**; prime minister of **Israel**, 1983–4 and 1986–92. Shamir was born in Poland, educated at Warsaw University, and immigrated to Palestine in 1935. A protégé of **Vladimir Jabotinsky** and **Menachem Begin**, in 1937 he joined the *Irgun Zvai Leumi*. In 1941 he was a founding member of the militant breakaway militia known as the Stern Gang. He was arrested by the British in 1941, escaped, and became one of the three heads of Stern in 1942–6. The British exiled him to **Eritrea** in 1946, He escaped a second time and returned to Israel in 1948 by way of **Ethiopia** and **France**. From 1955 to 1965 he served in Israel's foreign intelligence service, Mossad. He was Likud speaker of the Knesset in 1977–80, where he initially opposed **Camp David One**. Upon the resignation of **Moshe Dayan** in 1980, Shamir became foreign minister, serving until 1986, even while serving as prime minister in 1983–4. Following the 1984 general elections he shared the rotating leadership of a government of national unity with **Shimon Peres**. Shamir was again prime minister in 1986–92, during the **Intifada** period and Israel's deepening military involvement in **Lebanon**. Under him, Israel participated in its first open negotiations with the Palestinians, who formed part of the Jordanian delegation to the 1991 Madrid Peace Conference. It was also under Shamir that Israel established full diplomatic relations with **China** and **India** and reopened diplomatic offices in Warsaw (1986) and Budapest (1988). In 1992 Likud was defeated in the general election, after which Shamir resigned the party leadership.

Shanghai

Shanghai is located on the east coast of **China**. In 1843 it was designated a treaty port, and grew from a trading town to a major centre of commerce, industry and culture often known as the Paris of the East. It was occupied by the Japanese after 1937, and then formed a centre for **Mao Zedong** during the **Cultural Revolution**. It is now a major international commercial and financial centre, as well as having the largest port in the world.

sharia law
– see also **Wahhabism**.

Arabic for the 'Highway', *sharia* describes the Holy Law which lays down the perfect standard for earthly society and embodies the unity and ideology of **Islam**. Codified in the eighth and ninth centuries, it is derived not only from the Qur'an and the *sunna* (the way of the Prophet) but also from universal agreement (*ijma*) and analogical reasoning (*qiyas*). *Ijma* is an elusive concept, although of prime importance in determining doctrine and practice, which has evolved from relating to past agreement to being a democratic force opposed to tradition and as such a source of toleration of differing Islamic traditions. *Ijma* and *qiyas* together provide a flexibility which might otherwise be lacking. Sharia is communicated with authority through the systems of jurisprudence elaborated by the four orthodox schools of law, namely the Hanafi, the Maliki, the Shafi'i and the Hanbali.

The concept of the Law plays an important role in Islam as it is, in theory, rooted in divine revelation rather than in human reason, with the *ulama* being responsible for the interpretation of the Hadith (tradition) in which the *sunna* is recorded, and because it, rather than theology, as is the case in Christianity, is the decisive expression of the Islamic faith. Moreover, Islam has produced, much more than Christianity, an inclusive system of morality and ethics pervading both the private and the public dimensions of society. The *umma* constitutes the whole community of believers and is not therefore either amenable to the separation of church and state of western Christianity or satisfied with the fusion of secular and spiritual authority characteristic of Eastern Orthodoxy. It aims, rather, at the fusion of the secular and spiritual worlds themselves, and many Muslims would argue that it is not possible to derive the principles of social and political life from a secular morality.

Such an understanding has proved a major source of tension in modern conditions, with a cleavage having opened up between the limited number of adherents who might be willing in private to question orthodoxy and the large number who endorse tradition in its entirety. **Saudi Arabia**, where sharia is the common law of the land, is the voice of the latter: **Turkey**, where sharia was abolished by **Kemal Atatürk**, is the voice of the former. Indeed some Turks will voice highly cynical opinions about the true profundity of the faith espoused by the more orthodox. In practice, however, most Muslim countries have legal systems which have been strongly influenced by, although not normally replaced by, western norms. Many of the punishments laid down by sharia, such as the cutting off of limbs, have long been abandoned by most, though not all, Muslim states. Saudi Arabia still frequently applies the death penalty for murder, rape, sodomy, armed robbery, sabotage, drug trafficking, adultery and apostasy, with executions sometimes being in public.

The cleavage appears to have widened rather than narrowed since the 1970s with the westernizing 'White Revolution' of the shah being reversed by the **Iranian Revolution of 1979**. A legal system based on sharia was introduced by the **Constitution of 1979, Islamic Republic of Iran**, and a new criminal code on similar principles introduced, November 1995. The president of the Supreme Court and the Public Prosecutor General are both appointed by the Spiritual Leader. A total of 109 criminal offences, together with economic crimes, carry the death penalty. **Mauritania** adopted Islamic jurisprudence, 1980. **Sudan** announced in 1990 that the Islamic law courts, which had always administered justice for the Muslim population, would henceforth apply sharia to the non-Muslim south of the country as well. **Yemen** introduced a civil code based on sharia, 1992, and sharia courts decide all issues relating to Muslims' personal affairs in **Qatar**. In **Pakistan**, a presidential ordinance of August 1990 decreed that the criminal code must conform to sharia and it was incorporated in the legal system by parliament in May 1991. Saddam Hussein's **Iraq** also introduced the amputation of a hand for theft in 1994. It was enforced by **jihadi** groups in **Egypt**'s Sinai peninsula when it slipped out of government control with the overthrow of President Morsi, 2013, and by radical rebel groups in **Syria** in areas under their control during the ongoing civil war. Not fasting during Ramadan incurred a year's imprisonment.

Islamic traditionalism including sharia also appears to be increasing its appeal amongst the immigrant communities of western Europe, particularly amongst descendants of original immigrants who often seem readier to adopt fundamentalist positions than the communities from which their forebears sprang. Although a sense of deracination may be the prime cause, extremist preaching and teaching in mosques and religious colleges, both in Europe and countries such as Pakistan, benefiting from Saudi Arabian

finance, are widely considered to be a contributory factor. In any event, sharia could even be recognized as a basis for settling civil legal disputes between Muslims in **Britain** provided both parties were in agreement and the judgement was compatible with English law.

The spread of sharia has caused considerable alarm amongst the more westernized sectors of the population, particularly in countries such as **Egypt, Tunisia** and Turkey, whose legal systems show strong European influence, not least with regard to the rights of women. A Gallup Poll conducted in Egypt in 2011 found, reliably or otherwise, that fewer than 1 per cent of its respondents wanted sharia implemented. Tunisia promulgated a Personal Status Code on independence in 1956, making divorce subject to a court decision and abolishing polygamy. Alarm has been shared by the military which seized power in **Algeria** in 1991 to keep the fundamentalist Islamic Salvation Front out of office, and by the armed forces that reclaimed power in Egypt in 2013 ousting the **Muslim Brotherhood**, whose December 2012 draft constitution had raised fears that it would usher in a theocracy governed by sharia. The Turkish Army has been similarly restive, reflecting the concern of many Turks that the Islamist government is progressively re-Islamicizing the nation. Parallel concerns have been expressed in Tunisia.

Shari'ati, 'Ali (1937–1977)

Iranian intellectual. Shari'ati contributed articles to newspapers as a trainee teacher, aimed at solving the challenges faced by Muslim societies in reconciling Islamic traditions with contemporary philosophy and sociology. As a teacher, 1952, he founded the Islamic Students' Association. He joined the National Front, 1953, graduated, 1955, and was repeatedly arrested. He studied in **France**, obtaining a doctorate from the Sorbonne, 1964. He collaborated with the Algerian **Front de Libération Nationale (FLN)** from 1959. Translator of the revolutionary philosopher, Frantz Fanon, into Persian, and a founder of the Freedom Movement of Iran, 1961, but briefly imprisoned for subversive political activity abroad on his return to **Iran**, 1964. He taught at the Ershad Institute, Tehran, where he expounded a highly influential and revolutionary interpretation of **Shi'ite** Islam which he described as 'red Shi'ism' as distinct from clerical 'black Shi'ism', calling on Shi'ites to accept change and fight for social justice so as to hasten the return of the twelfth Imam. Denounced by **Ayatollah Khomeini** and held in solitary confinement by the government for eighteen months, he was released in 1975. He died in England.

Sharpeville Massacre

South African police fired on and killed sixty-nine unarmed protestors against the **apartheid** Pass Laws in the black township of Sharpeville, near Johannesburg, on 21 March 1960. With the country close to civil war, the government declared a state of emergency, banning and driving underground the main anti-apartheid organizations, the **African National Congress** and the **Pan-African Congress**. The massacre demonstrated the extent of government oppression of the black majority, prompting an international outcry.

Shastri, Lal Bahadur (1904–1966)

Indian politician. Active in the movement against the British, Shastri was imprisoned a number of times. A minister in Uttar Pradesh in 1947, he was Congress Party general secretary during the first post-independence elections. In 1952 he was appointed minister of railways and transport, subsequently becoming minister of commerce and industry, home minister in 1961 and prime minister in 1964. Successful in the 1965 **Indo-Pakistan War**, he died the day peace was signed.

Shays' Rebellion (USA)

Shays' Rebellion was an uprising in western Massachusetts in 1786 led by militia captain Daniel Shays. Farmers and other middling and lower-class citizens protested against taxes they viewed as favouring commercial and mercantile elites in the east. The inability of the national government to send troops to put down the uprising, which attacked a federal armoury at Springfield, Massachusetts, spurred many to support the Philadelphia Convention, which ultimately resulted in the writing of the US Constitution.

Sherman, William Tecumseh (1820–1891)

American military commander. Sherman did well at Shiloh, and his reputation survived disappointment at Chickasaw Bluffs. He played an important part in the fall of **Vicksburg**, and in November 1863 commanded the Army of the Tennessee at **Chattanooga**. In March 1864 he commanded the western theatre and in September seized Atlanta before completing his marches through Georgia and the Carolinas, a herald of twentieth-century

psychological warfare against civilians. His initial lenient surrender agreement with Joseph E. Johnston at Durham Station was repudiated. In 1869–83 he served as commanding general of the US Army.

Shi'ites

– see also **Islam**.

Members of the lesser of the two main branches of **Islam**, comprising some 10 per cent of all Muslims and predominant in **Iran**, **Iraq**, **Bahrain** and **Azerbaijan** and approaching parity in **Yemen**, with significant communities in **Syria**, **Lebanon**, **India**, **Pakistan** and East Africa. Although Shi'ites share with **Sunnis** the same core Islamic beliefs, they differ in regarding 'Ali, the Prophet's son-in-law, as Muhammad's true successor as spiritual and temporal leader rather than the Umayyad and subsequent caliphs recognized by the **Sunni**. The beheading of 'Ali's son, Husain, in the civil war between the two factions is commemorated annually as his martyrdom, and the concept of martyrdom pervades Shi'ite Islam. Shi'ites are in general more hostile to non-Muslims than the Sunni, but on the other hand they have absorbed many Zoroastrian, Christian and gnostic ideas. It is partly for this reason that there are many ultimately Shi'ite sects whose practices and tenets are remote from orthodoxy, including the **Alawis**, the **Druze** and the Ismailis. Most remote of all is **Baha'ism**, founded by Mirza 'Ali Muhammad, who claimed in 1844 that he had superseded the prophet Muhammad as the forerunner of a coming messiah. It has become a separate religion and is savagely persecuted in its Iranian homeland. The more esoteric Shi'ite splinter sects tend to have their own secret doctrines and secret interpretations of the Qur'an, and the armed members of one such group sought to seize the Holy Mosque at Mecca in 1979. The largest Shi'ite sect, the Ithna Ashariyah, or 'Twelvers', believes in a series of twelve infallible *imams*, or leaders, the first being 'Ali and the last, Muhammad al-Mahdi, known either as the 'Hidden Imam' or the 'Expected One', who allegedly retreated to the mountains in around AD 880 to return at some future date to effect the victory of Islam and introduce the rule of righteousness, prosperity and peace. The most recent claimint to the title of *mahdi* or 'Rightly Guided One' was Muhammad Ahmad al-Sayyid, who in 1882 led the capture of the Sudanese capital Khartoum in which British general **Charles Gordon** was killed.

Shi'ite Islam is visibly different from Sunni Islam in its acceptence of images of the Prophet, which are widely seen in Lebanon and Syria, and in the existence of a highly influential body of clergy with its own hierarchy, although not of a priesthood. The political importance of Shi'ite Islam rests essentially in its role in Iran, where it has effectively been the state religion since the sixteenth century. Iran has been under theocratic rule since the 1979 **Iranian Revolution**. Its spiritual leader (*wali faqih*) was proclaimed the 'Source of Knowledge' (*Marja e Taghlid*) as the head of all Shi'ite Muslims, December 1994, and the country has been fundamentalist and intolerant in domestic policy, demanding the exclusion of western influences and the implementation of **sharia** punishments including the execution of homosexuals. Westernized opponents have either had to conform or leave. A fatwa was passed on the British author Salman Rushdie, which remained in place until 1996. Uncompromisingly independent in foreign policy, Iran has determinedly opposed the United States and is the sworn foe of **Israel**; it is closely linked to the Shi'ite **Hezbollah** and is a supporter of the Alawite government of Syria.

Shi'ites are influential in Iraq, where they presently form the majority and exercise secular power incurring Sunni hostility and suspicion, but not in Bahrain, where demands by the Shi'ite majority for democratic rights were forcibly suppressed in 2013 following the **Arab Spring**.

Shiloh, Battle of (6–7 April 1862) (American Civil War)

The Confederate general P. G. T. Beauregard resolved to attack **Ulysses S. Grant**'s Army of the Tennessee at Pittsburg Landing on the Tennessee River before it could be joined by Don Carlos Buell's Army of the Ohio. Almost 45,000 Confederates caught Grant unawares, but a faulty deployment that sacrificed any concentration on key objectives, prevented exploitation of their advantage. Buell arrived in the late afternoon, and thus reinforced, on 7 April Grant launched a counter-offensive that regained the battlefield, but only after the bloodiest American battle to that date.

Shimonoseki, Treaty of (1895)

This was the treaty that marked the end of the first **Sino-Japanese War**, during which **China** was defeated. It was signed on 17 April 1895, and named after the city where it was negotiated on the Japanese island of Honshu. The terms of the treaty included cessation of the Liaodong peninsula to **Japan**, a large indemnity, granting Japan most favoured nation status, which allowed it full access to treaty ports and recognition of the independence of **Korea**.

Shining Path

– *see* **Sendero Luminoso**.

shipping

– *see* **transportation**.

Shiv Sena

A Maharashtrian political party founded by Bal Thackeray in 1966 in Bombay, the Shiv Sena had a clear 'sons of the soil' ideology that championed the economic interests of Marathis. In addition, it had a clear anti-communist and anti-Muslim stance. From its inception it acquired a reputation for violence and combined extreme methods of political action with a populist programme of providing services to local neighbourhoods and slums. It later became a close ally of the **Bharatiya Janata Party**.

shogun

The shogun was the regent who ruled on behalf of the Japanese emperor. In the early modern period the shogunate was for a long period in the hands of the **Tokugawa** family (1603–1868), who built up a complex and highly stratified social system under their rule, with the emperor himself being confined to the royal palace. The shogunate was abolished during the **Meiji restoration** of 1868, when **Japan** moved instead to an aristocratic oligarchy.

shuttle diplomacy

Shuttle diplomacy consists of negotiation between two sides carried out by a third party who moves between them. It is particularly useful when the two sides in question refuse to recognize each other. The first and most famous example was US Secretary of State **Henry Kissinger**'s Middle Eastern diplomacy in the aftermath of the **Yom Kippur War** of 1973, which saw him fly frequently between **Egypt**, **Israel** and **Syria**.

Siam

– *see* **Thailand**.

Sierra Leone

A west African country bordered by **Guinea** and **Liberia**. The diverse environments of the region are rich in mineral resources. While dense rainforests insulated it from expanding west African kingdoms, its coastline received some of the earliest European explorers and traders. In 1772 the Sierra Leone Company founded Freetown for the settlement of freed slaves. It was taken over as a British colony in 1808. It became independent in 1961. In 1991–2002 civil war devastated the country.

Sihanouk, Norodom (1922–)

Former Cambodian head of state. Sihanouk was first selected to be king by the Crown Council in 1941. He was deposed of as head of state by Prime Minister Lon Nol and the National Assembly in 1970 and exiled to **China**. Sihanouk returned to **Cambodia** in 1991 and was restored as king in 1993. He abdicated in 2004 and his son, Norodom Sihamoni, was appointed as his successor.

Sikhism

Sikhism is today the fifth largest religion in the world. It originated in north-west India in the early sixteenth century with the teachings of Nanak (1469–1539), the first of Sikhism's ten gurus (or spiritual teachers). Nanak's religious philosophy emphasized the oneness of a formless god, Vahiguru, and the equality of all. The former tenet was in broad agreement with **Judaism**, **Christianity** and **Islam**, and the latter a critique of the Hindu caste system into which Nanak had been born. Nanak institutionalized the equality of his followers through the *langar*, or communal kitchen, in which people cooked and ate together irrespective of their caste backgrounds. Subsequent gurus elaborated Guru Nanak's religious message, while adding rites and rituals for their followers, and codifying a sacred text, *The Adi Granth*, in 1604, which includes the poems of the first five gurus as well as other religious sages, both Hindu and Muslim. Many of its adherents are in the Punjab and its holy city is Amritsar.

Silva, Luis (Ignacio da) ('Lula') (1945–)

Labour leader, politician and president of **Brazil**. Born in Caetés, Pernambuco, but brought up primarily in São Paulo, Lula was a factory worker who helped to found the leftist Workers' Party in 1980. Elected president in 2002, he served two four-year terms and left office highly popular with Brazil's poor. He expanded social programmes and successfully promoted economic growth, building on the anti-inflationary programme of his predecessor **Fernando Henrique Cardoso**.

Simla Peace Agreement (1972)

The presidents of **India** and **Pakistan** signed the Simla Peace Agreement in the aftermath of the 1971 war between their countries. The agreement, signed in 1972 in the Indian city of Simla, laid down principles for a future and sustained peace between its signatories. Among these principles were that in future India and Pakistan would respect one another's territorial integrity, and seek to settle their differences through peaceful means and bilateral relations. Simla (Shimla) had earlier been famous as the summer capital of the British Raj.

Singapore

The Republic of Singapore is located in South East Asia, between **Malaysia** and **Indonesia**. It has a total area of around 690 square kilometres and a population of over 5 million, the majority of whom are of Chinese descent. Singapore was established as a British trading colony in 1819. It joined the Malaysia Federation in 1963, but was forced to separate in 1965. Since then it has become one of the most important financial and commercial cities and trading ports of South East Asia.

Singh, Ranjit (1780–1839)

Sikh ruler of an independent state in the **Punjab**, established through marriage alliances and the capture of Lahore in 1799 from Sikh competitors. When the **East India Company** checked his expansion to the south-east by treaty in 1809, he acquired territory in other directions, including Multan (1818), **Kashmir** (1820) and the trans-Indus (1823). Though he facilitated British adventures in **Afghanistan**, including the first Anglo-Afghan War, the Company annexed his state in 1849.

Sinn Fein

Sinn Fein ('Our own selves' or, popularly, 'Ourselves alone' in Irish Gaelic) is the name for a number of Irish Republican parties associated with nationalism and the revolutionary cause in **Ireland** beginning in 1905. Sinn Fein was established as a nationalist political party which agitated for Irish self-rule and then, after a period of militarism, for an Irish republic in 1917. The original party broke with Fianna Fail and a successor after 1923, and was then marginalized. A new, provisional version emerged during the Northern Ireland crisis in 1970, leading to further splits and spin-offs, but the present-day Sinn Fein (closely connected with the IRA) was eventually to enter government in **Northern**

Ireland after the Good Friday Agreement and is also a serious party in the Republic. It is generally viewed as being of the Left, though it is also associated with Catholics of conservative personal views on social matters.

Sino-Japanese War, first (1894–1895)

A conflict between **China** and **Japan** for control of the Korean peninsula in the late nineteenth century. In 1895 the **Treaty of Shimonoseki** declared Korea independent and provided for Chinese cession of Taiwan, the Pescadores and the Liaodong peninsula to Japan. Within a week of the treaty being signed the diplomatic intervention of **Russia**, **France** and **Germany** forced Japan to return the Liaodong peninsula to China. Under a subsidiary commercial treaty in 1896, China allowed Japanese nationals the right to open factories and engage in manufacturing in China's trade ports. This right was also extended to the western maritime powers.

Sino-Japanese War, second (1937–1945)

A conflict that took place on the Chinese mainland between combined nationalist and communist Chinese forces and Japanese troops. The 'Manchurian incident' of 1931 reflected early signs of Japanese expansionist desires, and a full-scale war broke out after Chinese and Japanese troops clashed near the **Marco Polo Bridge** in July 1937. The Japanese overran northern **China**, penetrating up the Yangtze River and along railway lines, capturing Shanghai, Nanjing (the scene of horrific brutalities by the Japanese), Guangzhou and Hankou by the end of 1938. By 1941 the conflict had been absorbed into **World War II**, and the second Sino-Japanese War had reached a state of near stalemate as the Japanese military and its aerial superiority were unable to overcome Chinese resistance and the problems posed by distance and poor communications. The war concluded in 1945, with **Japan**'s surrender to the **United States**.

Sino-Soviet conflict

This refers to a period from the late 1950s to the 1970s when hostility developed between **China** and the **USSR**. The split was precipitated by several factors, including **Khrushchev**'s denunciation of **Stalin**, which was seen as an attack on the cult of **Mao Zedong** in China, and the **Great Leap Forward**, which diverged from the Soviet model of centrally planned industrialization. In 1960 the Soviets supported **India** in a skirmish with China and by 1962 Mao had denounced the Soviet leaders for their

revisionism. Relations continued to deteriorate during and after the **Cultural Revolution**, as the Chinese believed that Soviet aid to the Vietnamese invasion of **Cambodia** and the invasion of **Afghanistan** were an attempt to encircle China. It was the failure of this invasion and the change of leadership in China that led to a thawing of relations, and in 1989 a summit was held in Beijing to normalize the relationship.

Siqueiros, David Alfaro (1896–1974)

Mexican Marxist and artist. Born in Camargo Chihuahua, **Mexico**, Siqueiros engaged in anarcho-syndicalist politics before going to **France** to witness the Cubist and Impressionist revolution in painting. After returning to Mexico, in 1923 he fused Marxist politics with art that attacked bourgois individualists and led to his exile to the **United States**. He participated in a failed attack against **Leon Trotsky** in 1940. After **World War II** he employed social realism in his art.

Sitting Bull (1831?–1890) (USA)

Indigenous North American leader. Sitting Bull was a Lakota Sioux chief and holy man who had a vision of Sioux victory prior to the Battle of **Little Bighorn** in June 1876. Eventually he was compelled to move to the Standing Rock Reservation on the Cheyenne River. Because of his stature as a holy man and warrior, Sitting Bull retained a great deal of influence over the Sioux. With the advent of the Ghost Dance movement, which stressed native cultural renewal, the federal government feared renewed native resistance. In an attempt to suppress the Ghost Dance, tribal police killed Sitting Bull while seeking to arrest him.

Six Day War (1967)

The **Middle East** conflict from 5–10 June 1967 between **Israel** and an alliance of **Egypt**, **Jordan** and **Syria**. Israel argued that events in May 1967, against a background of years of tension over Israel's existence, suggested the country faced imminent attack. On 15–16 May Egypt moved troops to the border with Israel after ordering the withdrawal of a United Nations Emergency Force deployed in the Sinai peninsula since the 1956 **Suez Crisis**. Two days later Syria began military preparation on the **Golan Heights** overlooking Israel. Israel mobilized reservists on 19 May and by 20 May Egyptian and Israeli forces stood face to face. The crucial move came on 22 May when Egypt blockaded the Straits of Tiran in the Gulf of Aqaba, intent on preventing Israeli shipping from leaving the port of Eilat and denying access to oil imports. This was in effect an act of war. On 30 May, Jordan signed a five-year mutual defence treaty with Egypt and on 4 June Iraq entered into a military alliance with Egypt, Jordan and Syria.

The blockade of the Straits was a major factor in Israel's decision to mount a pre-emptive attack on 5 June. Israeli aircraft destroyed the bulk of Egypt's air force on the ground while troops advanced into **Gaza**, Sinai and – following Jordanian cross-border artillery shelling – east Jerusalem. In the afternoon of the first day Israeli aircraft struck Jordan and Syria and by evening the Egyptian, Jordanian and Syrian air forces posed no further threat to Israeli ground troops. As the Israeli Army advanced deeper into Sinai on 6 June, Jordanian troops were meanwhile withdrawing from the West Bank, leaving the Old City of **Jerusalem** in Israel's hands. Jordan agreed to a ceasefire on 7 June. The Israeli push into Sinai reached the Suez Canal on 8 June. Egypt accepted a ceasefire on the same day. On 9 June, Israeli troops moved against Syrian forces on the Golan Heights, capturing the area and negotiating a ceasefire with Syria on 10 June. In the course of the fighting, an estimated 11,000 Egyptian, 6,000 Jordanian, 1,000 Syrian and 760 Israeli troops were killed. By the conclusion of the lightning campaign, Israel occupied the Sinai Peninsula, the Gaza Strip, the West Bank of the Jordan and the Golan Heights, henceforth known as the **Occupied Territories**. The land Israel controlled tripled from 8,000 to 26,000 square miles, with new responsibility for almost a million Arabs. The decisive military defeat was a shattering blow to morale in the Arab world and more specifically to the standing of the Egyptian president, **Gamal Abdel Nasser**. In November 1967 the **United Nations** passed Resolution 242 calling on Israel to withdraw 'from territories' (not 'the territories') occupied in June but recognizing Israel's right to secure its borders. The resolution formed the basis for all subsequent attempts to achieve a Middle East peace settlement. In 1978 Israel returned Sinai to Egypt under the **Camp David Accords** and in 2005 Israeli forces evacuated the Gaza Strip.

sixties

A term relating to the decade of the 1960s, though one which sometimes also includes the late fifties and early seventies. The sixties was a period of social change and experimentation during which the assumptions and protocols of western society fundamentally changed. Popular culture became characterized by new, youth-oriented electric music and the use of illegal drugs, politics came to be driven by the destruction in appearance or reality of established hierarchies, and civil rights, individualism and consumerism came to dominate public behaviour. Tradition was rejected in the key institutions of the western world, and feminism, radical social attitudes and sexual diversity were celebrated. In reaction, many white, male and traditional communities adopted a pessimistic 'backlash' approach and associated the decade with the subsequent inflation, rise in crime and loss of social authority. Many of the political leaders of the sixties were assassinated, discredited or removed from office by the 1970s. In the Islamic world, the worldwide rise in youth-oriented politics helped give rise both to **Ba'athism** and fundamentalism, and in **China** to the Maoist **Cultural Revolution**. In the West, by contrast, most of those affected by the sixties embraced 'flower power', 'hippy' pacifism and a sometimes overtolerant approach to social disorder and associated behaviours, though some became involved in spiritualized cults which styled themselves as 'new religions'.

slave revolts (USA)

Comparatively speaking, there appear to have been fewer attempted slave insurrections in North America than there were in South America and the Caribbean, with most of those enslaved practising 'day to day' resistance to the regime instead of outright revolt. The propensity to rebel also declined over time as slaveholders increasingly consolidated their degree of control over the enslaved in the antebellum period. In 1739 the Stono rebellion in South Carolina resulted in the deaths of more than sixty people, and there was also an attempted insurrection in 1811 in St John the Baptist Parish, Louisiana. Neither the 1800 Gabriel Prosser plot in Richmond, nor the 1822 Denmark Vesey plot in Charleston got beyond the planning stage, but Nat Turner's revolt of 1831, in which fifty-seven whites of Southampton County, Virginia, were killed, resulted in more stringent laws and restrictions being imposed upon all those enslaved in the Southern states.

slave trade (Atlantic)

A term given to the transatlantic transport of captives, 'purchased' in exchange for manufactured goods from West Africa to be sold as slaves in the Caribbean and Americas, so as to produce the rum, molasses, tobacco and cotton which would then be sold back to European markets. Occasionally, an extensive older Arab practice focused on east and north Africa is also subsumed under the term, as are indigenous African practices emerging from the treatment of prisoners of war and defeated enemies. However, the trade generally referred to emerged as a specific and racialized process conducted by European traders in the 1500s. It is sometimes styled the 'African holocaust' or 'the disaster' by African historians. This is not least because it removed over 25 million people from **Africa**, leading to a cultural and economic collapse which in some ways was unrecoverable. The slave trade tended to generate huge profits, and was associated with cruelty, inhumane practices and the murder, neglect or vicious physical coercion of millions of people. Recent estimates, for example, suggest that over a million died on the so-called 'Middle Passage' taken from Africa to the New World, sometimes because slaves were thrown overboard, but usually because of the packed, unsanitary and starved condition of those transported. Unlike previous examples of slavery in history, the status of slaves and their descendants tended to be fixed in host societies, and associated with theories of racial and natural dominance and subservience which served the purposes of the slaveholders. This fed a culture of plantation life and cheap food in the Americas, as well as one of pseudoscience and engineered religiosity bought at the expense of black mortality.

Those who escaped slavery, such as Olaudah Equiano, in alliance with British parliamentarians, began a campaign of agitation against the trade in the **British Empire** in the late eighteenth century. Others, from the foundation of the **USA** onwards, aimed for the **abolition of slavery** itself, often citing the cruelty of the trade in evidence. Inspired by the agitation, **William Wilberforce** conducted a long campaign that eventually ended in the British abolition of the trade and the enforcement of that rule by the Royal Navy in 1807. By this time, however, colonial and postcolonial slave states in the western hemisphere had developed self-sustaining slave cultures themselves, and were in fact averse to the continuation of a trade which undermined their own marginal revenues. Virtually every city and state on the Atlantic rim by that time had been materially enriched by the trade in humans, with Liverpool, Manchester, Charleston, Amsterdam and **Portugal** being obvious examples. In the twentieth century some groups argued that reparations to those of slave descent, accompanied by the cancellation of African debts, could form the beginning of an acknowledgement of the importance of slavery's profits to the developed world's accumulation

of capital, but no action was taken on this prompting.

slavery

Slavery is both an institution and a condition. Formally, it is a type of exploitation in which one human was owned by another person and in which the slave hovered uncertainly between the contradictory positions of being both a piece or property and a person. Slavery has existed for millennia and was only outlawed officially in the aftermath of **World War II**. While it has been illegal by UN decree since 1956 everywhere in the world, forms of slavery still exist in many parts of the world, notably sub-Saharan Africa and South Asia. It is estimated that as many as 40 million people were living in conditions resembling slavery in 2017. These people are not formally slaves as they cannot legally be sold; in the past millions of people were enslaved property that could be bought or sold.

While forms of slavery are varied, and range from quasi-familial arrangements to people being chattels, the principal differences between forms of slavery depend on the degree to which slavery was essential to the workings of society. Moses Finley, a historian of ancient Greece, usefully divided societies into slave societies where slavery suffused every aspect of life, and societies with slaves, where slavery was significant but not vital. Only a few societies – ancient Greece and Rome and the tropical societies of the early modern and nineteenth-century Americas and West Indies – became slave societies in this definition. In these places, slaves made up between a third and 90 per cent of the population. They were essential, in these societies, to how the economy operated, being both expensive items of property themselves and, as importantly, integral to how wealth was produced through their hard work in extracting wealth on behalf of their owners.

In the early modern slave societies of tropical America most slaves were not natives, but were imported Africans, racially distinct from the dominant racial and political groups in society. What was true about slaves across the world was that they were always political and social outsiders, and often ethnically distinct from those who enslaved them. Slaves were, as the French anthropologist and Africanist Claude Meillasoux postulated, alienated individuals who become subordinated people within social structures with a status normally below that of any other people in those social structures. In some cases, slaves became considered perilously similar to beasts, as can be seen in listings of slaves in colonial America where they were combined with listings of livestock. There were profoundly dehumanizing effects. It is for this reason that sociologist Orlando Patterson described slavery as a form of 'social death', where the social existence of slaves was extinguished by owners in order that a slave might be considered a physical and ideological extension of the owner. Patterson considers this 'natal alienation' and believes that it served to create huge psychological crises of selfhood for slaves expected to have no independent existence separate from that of the master but who, of course, maintained a considerable measure of their own selfhood.

This crisis of identity was exacerbated in societies such as those in the Americas where scientific racism accompanied the development of slavery, suggesting to owners and slaves that slaves were 'naturally' preordained to be slaves by virtue of racial characteristics, such as a presumed ability to work well in hot climates and a presumption of mental inferiority. The purpose of slavery, however, was to extract work from slaves and this purpose always gave slaves a measure of power, albeit lesser than that exercised by their masters. Masters used a variety of means to get slaves to work; slaves had well-developed moral economies about what they would do and what they would not do. Moreover, contrary to Patterson's argument that slaves were just extensions of their owners' wills (an argument often advanced by masters who suggested that their primary relationship with slaves was paternal rather than as exploiters of their labour), they had other relationships that were important to them. Enslaved people formed their own communities, established families, practised religion in ways that were significantly different from religious practices of free people and in many ways showed that they had value systems and forms of behaviour that differed from the social norms of non-slaves. While much of slaves' lives were taken up with labour, especially if working in agriculture in ancient Rome or on sugar or cotton plantations of early modern tropical America, they participated in a range of cultural activities that had long-lasting influences. Take music, for example. Africans brought musical traditions with them in their transit to the Americas and developed those traditions in combination with European musical norms that they saw around them into distinctive, syncretic forms of music-making. These forms of music-making were later adopted by other people and formed the bedrock for the dynamic and innovative musical patterns of the contemporary Americas.

Nevertheless, slaves' lives were hard, especially before the beginnings of abolitionist movements in the late eighteenth century. Owners constructed legal systems designed to control the movements of slaves and to punish them for any indiscretion. In some systems, such as the **French Empire**, the state, under the *Code Noir*, exercised great control. In other systems, such as in Portuguese America and the **British Empire**, masters were given close to unlimited power to discipline their slaves. Resistance from slaves was violently put down. The ferocity of planter control helps to explain the relative paucity of slave rebellions in the Americas in the eighteenth century. The only broadly successful slave revolt came in Saint-Domingue, later **Haiti**, where slaves overthrew French colonial rule in a thirteen-year war, ending in 1804. Elsewhere, slavery ended either by government fiat or, as in the **United States**, by a bloody civil war between 1861 and 1865. Slaves contributed to their own emancipation in numerous ways such as running away. Forms of slavery persisted far longer in parts of the **Middle East** and in African countries such as **Mauritania**.

Slovakia

A central European state, absorbed into the Great Moravian Empire in the ninth century, then part of the Hungarian Kingdom and subsequently the **Austro-Hungarian Empire** until 1918. Nineteenth-century Hungarian attempts at imposing linguistic and cultural hegemony encouraged Slovak nationalism and sympathy with neighbouring Czech nationalism. At the end of **World War I** the Slovaks and Czechs united in the state of **Czechoslovakia**, but a strong Slovak autonomy movement remained. During **World War II** Slovakia allied with Nazi Germany as an independent state, with Vojtech Tuka (1880–1946) as prime minister. Czechoslovakia was restored at the war's end, coming under Communist rule and Soviet dominance in 1948, with a thwarted attempt at liberalization in the 1968 **Prague Spring** under Slovak Alexander Dubček (1921–92). The 1989 'Velvet Revolution' ended Communist control. On 1 January 1993 Slovakia again divided from what became the Czech Republic under the 'Velvet Divorce'. It joined the **European Union** and **NATO** in 2004.

Slovenia

Part of the **Austro-Hungarian Empire** until 1918, when the area joined the Kingdom of the Serbs, Croats and Slovenes, known as **Yugoslavia** from

1929. Occupied by **Germany** and **Italy** during **World War II**, Slovenia became a constituent republic of the new socialist Yugoslavia in 1945. In 1990 the population voted for independence in a referendum, fighting a successful ten-day war against Yugoslav federal forces. Slovenia joined **NATO** and the **EU** in 2004, adopting the euro as its currency in 2007 – the first former Eastern bloc country to do so.

Smith, Adam (1723–1790)

Scottish political economist and moral philosopher. His book *Inquiry into the Nature and Causes of the Wealth of the Nations* (1776) was one of the earliest attempts to study the historical development of industry and commerce in **Europe**. He developed the idea of the invisible hand and became the founding father of political economy. Smith argued for free trade and against **mercantilism**. He died in Edinburgh.

Smith, Ian (1919–2007)

Southern Rhodesian (later Zimbabwean) politician. After wartime RAF service, Smith was elected to the Southern Rhodesian Parliament as a Liberal in 1948. A founder of the Rhodesian Front in 1962, he became party leader and prime minister in 1964. In 1965 he declared illegal unilateral independence from **Britain** (UDI), serving as prime minister of white minority who ruled Rhodesia until 1979. Following independence under majority rule in 1980, Smith remained an MP until 1987.

smuggling

Smuggling, in its broadest sense, refers to the trade or sale of goods carried out in deliberate contravention of existing legal frameworks governing the commerce in question. The laws relating to trade that were broken by smugglers most commonly concerned tariffs or taxes on the exchange of particular goods across state boundaries, tariffs that smugglers wished to avoid paying. Smuggling has existed in many places for as long as trade has been a human activity regulated by states. After 1700 it took on particular importance in the increasingly globalized world that was taking shape, of which it was both a constitutive component and a powerful emblem. States attempted more and more to tie together transatlantic and transpacific empires – largely built on trade – through the creation of legal regimes that set out colonies' economic dependence on metropoles and protected metropolitan trading rights. For instance, the British Parliament passed the Molasses and Sugar Acts (1733 and 1765) to put tariffs in place to discourage extra-imperial trade in a valuable commodity (molasses) between the British New England colonies and the non-British Caribbean islands. Smugglers largely bypassed these regulations, and molasses remained a heavily smuggled good until the laws themselves were relaxed after the **Seven Years War**, principally because of the colonists' ongoing intense pressure to liberalize trade.

Because smuggling by definition constitutes the contravention of law, legal and other primary sources can only reveal instances of unsuccessful smuggling. Amounts of successfully smuggled goods must thus remain unquantified, and both their proportion to legally traded goods and their overall role in expanding economies remain unknown. A corollary of this unknowability is that, because of the prevalence of smuggling, accounts of state economies in the post-1700 periods must necessarily admit a certain degree of inaccuracy.

The study of smuggling, although it cannot reveal even approximate values and volumes of goods smuggled, can however uncover deep economic, social and cultural patterns in the nature of state, imperial and metropole–colony relations. One example is the clear links between widespread smuggling and the evolution of free trade regulation in the eighteenth-century Atlantic world. Another example is the smugglers themselves, who, although operating outside the law, often did not exist apart from the formal political and social worlds of trade and trade regulation, but were rather embedded deeply within them. Smugglers were often the very merchants who lobbied for and benefited from legal regimes put in place to protect trade, or were, for instance, the customs officials charged with enforcing these laws. The lines of legality that surrounded trade were most easily breached by those who knew them well and were in a position to do so. Indeed, the **Opium Wars** represents a case in which one state (**Britain**) actively promoted the contravention of the trade regulation of another state (**China**) in order to establish a set of exchanges from which it derived profit. Overall, smuggling represented a challenge by individuals or collectivities to the regulation of trade by states, and charting the reaction of governments to these challenges permits a deeper understanding of modern ideas and institutions surrounding political economy.

Smuts, Jan Christiaan (1870–1950)

South African soldier and politician. Smuts fought the British during the 1899–1902 **Boer War** and was a government minister before leading the campaign against German forces in South West Africa. In 1917 he joined the Imperial War Cabinet and in 1919 attended the **Paris Peace Conference**. He was involved in the formation of the **League of Nations** and the **United Nations** and was **South Africa**'s prime minister in 1919–24 and 1939–48.

Smyrna

– *see* **Izmir**.

Sobhuza I (also known as Ngwane IV) (fl. 1815–1839)

Ruler of Kangwane, a kingdom in modern-day Swaziland, from 1815 to 1839, and a member of the Dlamini, a royal group that had controlled the kingdom for many years. When Sobhuza took to the throne southern Africa was in the throes of the **Mfecane**, a time of troubles created by the rise of the **Zulu** kingdom, the arrival of **Afrikaners** in the region and an emerging slave trade. Sobhuza was able to stave off conquest by the kingdom of Ndwandwe and then the Zulu kingdom, both of which had powerful armies, during the first decades of the nineteenth century. However, for strategic reasons he decided to abandon much of the south of his country and conquered the regions to the north, integrating them into what was in effect a new kingdom which would eventually be known as Swaziland.

social capital

A relatively modern term used to describe attributes of economic value an individual may possess due to his or her location and relationship with certain social groups, or the valuable attributes of certain social groups to society. Elements frequently adduced as components of social capital include the organization and structure of communal life in clubs or societies, engagement in legally defined public acts such as elections or protests, engagement in not-for-profit activities such as voluntary or community projects, and informal activities such as friendships. While various aspects of the concept have been developed by several social sciences, its modern usage has been attributed to Jane Jacobs in the 1960s. During the late 1980s and 1990s, James Coleman and Robert Putman diffused her ideas to wider audiences.

Social Darwinism

Charles Darwin's scientific theory concerned with explaining the evolution of species inspired a number of writers and philosophers to theorize about the evolution of human societies by way of analogies between human societies and other biological organisms. Notions of stages of evolution, belief in social progress by means of competition among individuals and cultures, and the notion of the 'survival of the fittest' in human evolution are among the key ideas. They found fertile ground in the geopolitics of late nineteenth-century European history characterized by increasing militarization, strong imperialist ambitions and economic laissez-faire. Social Darwinism legitimized further governmental actions and shaped citizens' attitudes in line with these phenomena. Key exponents of these ideas were Herbert Spencer, Francis Galton, Benjamin Kidd and Lewis Morgan.

social history

Social History is the practice of studying the ordinary lives, affiliations and behaviours of people within the historical discipline. It is usually contrasted with history based on war, prominent individuals or major institutions, and with the sociological swing in the historical profession during the 1960s, though in truth it is as old as the proper study of history itself. For example, the works of J. R. Green in the late nineteenth century, and of Eileen Power in the 1930s, pre-date the working-class focus of E. P. Thompson, or the demographic study of Wrigley and Schofield. Nevertheless, the 'New Social History' refers to a definite, post-**Annales** school phase of study in the English-speaking world, which explored urban, industrial and agricultural experiences, population trends and economic and gender histories which departed from the traditional schools. By its nature, the study attracted a mix of leftists, liberals and materialists, though unlike most of the work of the academic left it also proved capable of redefining popular opinions and elite prejudices outside of the Academy in ways that more conservative histories did not. The social history of divorce, for instance, and of crime, revealed how many marriages had ended early through death in childbirth, or had subsisted with the barest of social validation under the common law, as much as the historicity of illegitimacy and homosexuality. Labour historians such as Eugene Genovese, and those interested in the history of ideas such as Christopher Lasch, found themselves moving from left to right whilst avoiding liberalism as they deepened their studies of slavery, wage labour and the historic idea of progress in American society.

In popular history, social historians were a spur to the development of amateur genealogy, television dramas, the historical recreation movement and the rediscovery or reinvention of folklore. Indeed, whilst many academic social historians took their cue from the intellectual implications of Keith Thomas' work about the disenchantment of the world through modernity, *Religion and the Decline of Magic*, ordinary people were in fact more willing to study or be entertained by the past as long as it could be seen as a more spiritually elaborated time. The New Social History encouraged new ways of using documents, expanded and rescued the study of the hitherto discarded, and made almost anything capable of supporting a thesis if it was studied properly.

Combined with the use of the workshop rather than the seminar, it ultimately functioned to popularize and democratize the teaching of history, at the expense of forcing many of those who wished to be academically distinguished to either embrace a highly conservative view of the profession or take an antagonistic and *soi-disant* radical stance towards it. As social history has expanded into the classical past and united with the continental influences which helped to shape it, so debate has begun over the legacy of social history. In particular, historians are now inclined to argue that it has become necessary to rise above the fragmented specialization. Other historians have begun to posit the view that their discourse needs to move away from the promotion of comfortable heritage into a more disturbing but full version of the human past in which most lives were characterized by frustration and struggle.

social media
– see **information revolution**.

social welfare
This can be defined as state activities designed to protect and promote the well-being of citizens, based on principles of equality of opportunity, equitable distribution of wealth and public responsibility for those falling below a poverty line or those highly exposed as they go through certain stages during the life cycle, including childhood and old age. A welfare state also provides benefits during periods of unemployment as well as health, education and other social services. The legal system is defined as being outside the welfare activities of states. Justice is a necessary activity provided by any democratic state and an inalienable right of any individual, while welfare is subject to discussion and varies from country to country. There are close links between the social welfare and justice systems, because they often encounter the same people. The distinction hinges on personal responsibility. People involved in the social welfare system are generally unable to control or influence their own circumstances, while those in the justice system are generally responsible for the situation in which they find themselves. Assistance to the latter is more about allowing an individual to receive fair treatment rather than social welfare. In some countries, access to social welfare services is considered to be a basic and inalienable right, as in the UN Convention on Social and Economic Rights.

Industrialization and urbanization transformed and transferred activities within the households into social and political responsibilities. Secularization has also undermined traditional relationships such as marriage, while social mobility and the alienation of city life have also loosened the ties between people. Initially poverty and incapacity were seen as personal failure by Malthusians, social Darwinists and others. Poverty, economic crises and high unemployment led to the development of special programmes to insure against unemployment, poor health and old age, initially in **Bismarck**'s **Germany** and England and then in **Austria**, the Scandinavian countries, the Low Countries, **France** and **Italy**. By 1930 only the **USA** remained outside comprehensive programmes of social security as developed by the richest nations in the world. During the 1980s welfare states experienced substantial reform and privatization of functions previously executed by states. The introduction of different institutional arrangements establishing the incentives and disciplining forces of competition has reshaped the organization of welfare states.

Social welfare works in different ways in different countries. In the US, unemployment and health cover is less extensive than in many European countries, and a bitter debate rages over welfare. The Nordic countries have developed a system that takes care of most of their population during most of the stages of life. In some countries, investment in social welfare services have been justified by savings made in the justice system, in personal health care and in the private costs of legal services.

Social Realism
An art movement dominated by the leadership of the **USSR** in the 1930s which emphasized Marxist–Leninist theory and depicted the heroic struggles of working people towards a communist society. It was conceived as a revolutionary attempt

to appropriate painting and the arts from the bourgeois, and was formally adopted at a Congress of Soviet Writers in 1934. The influence of state-directed art policy chilled the creative atmosphere inside the USSR, and then the Soviet bloc for some thirty years before declining in the 1960s.

Society of Friends
– *see* **Quakers**.

sojourners
Sojourners is a somewhat archaic term for people who temporarily migrate to another country. Some sojourners migrate for an extended period of time, but they generally plan to return to their native country at some point in the future. Because they choose to leave and are not necessarily forced to migrate due to religious or political persecution, they behave differently from other migrants in the society to which they move. It is therefore important to distinguish sojourners from other types of migrants. A more modern term is *economic migrants*.

Sokoto Caliphate
An Islamic state in Northern **Nigeria**, *c.* 1808–1903. Founded by the Fulani-led **jihad** of **Usuman dan Fodio**, the caliphate unified the seven previously separate Hausa kingdoms. Each of these continued as an emirate, ruled by a merged Hausa–Fulani aristocracy. The caliphate (led at times by **Muhammad Bello**) dominated West Africa politically in the nineteenth century, and prospered economically. After the British conquest, the emirate structure was retained under British overlordship.

Solidarity movement
An independent trade union movement in **Poland** which began during the industrial disturbances at the Gdánsk shipyards in 1980, which by 1981 contained nearly 10 million members. Solidarity became a rallying call and a centre of civil resistance in the run up to and during the Polish Revolution of 1989, and then a political coalition led by the most famous of the Gdánsk strikers (and later Polish president) **Lech Wałesa**. Solidarity was trade unionist, Catholic, nationalist and democratic, but found that its influence over Poland's parties had collapsed by 1991. It is now primarily a trade union again.

Somalia
East African state on the Red Sea, parts of which were British and Italian colonies. In 1960 the colonies gained independence as the United Republic of Somali under President Aden Abdullah Osman Daar (1908–2007), succeeded in 1967 by Abdirashid Ali Shermarke (1919–69), the first democratically elected African president. His assassination in a coup led by Mohamed Siad Barre (1919–85) in 1969 opened a long-running phase of political fragmentation, intensified by defeat in the 1977–8 war with **Ethiopia**. Barre was ousted in 1991 by a militia coalition and power was disputed between rival clan overlords. A UN peacekeeping force failed to deliver stability as successive individuals and organizations claimed authority. In 2006 the Union of Islamic Courts proclaimed Somalia an Islamic state before their defeat by Ethiopian troops the following year. In 2012 the first legislature for twenty years met and Hassan Sheikh Mohamud (1955–) was named president. Political instability and an Islamic insurgency have effectively made Somalia a failed state. Agriculture is the main economic activity and the population in overwhelmingly Muslim.

Sons of Liberty (USA)
This semi-secret organization emerged during the **Stamp Act** crisis to coordinate resistance to British taxation in North America during the 1760s. The Sons of Liberty began as informal protest organizations in various American cities and towns. They drew their membership from among small shopkeepers, tradesmen, sailors and apprentices, and their leadership from local elites. Opposed to British taxation, they coordinated boycotts and other protests. Owing to the extralegal nature of these activities, the Sons of Liberty often acted in secret.

Soong family
A prominent Chinese family during the Republican period. Soong Qingling was the wife of **Sun Yat-sen**, and after his death became a member of the Chinese Communist Party and was elected to high office after 1949. Her sister, Soong Meiling, married **Chiang Kai-shek** and worked as his interpreter and secretary. Their brother, T. V. Soong, held various posts in the Nationalist government in the 1930s and 1940s, and then retired to America after 1947.

Soshangane (d. 1856)
Soshangane was a military leader originally associated with the rivals of **Shaka Zulu** in modern-day **South Africa**. In 1819, following a defeat, Soshangane took his army northwards into modern-day **Mozambique**, attacking Portuguese posts at

Imbanhane, Delgoa Bay and Sena, demanding tribute and repelling an attack by Shaka in 1828. He continued building a kingdom for himself in the region known as Gaza, establishing a civilian administration and government.

Soukous

Soukous (formerly called 'African rumba' and also known as 'Lingala') is a musical genre with stylistic roots in Afro-Caribbean and African traditional music. It typically features finger-style guitar, acoustic bass, brass, drums and vocals. Soukous emerged in the late 1930s in French and Belgian Congo. It spread throughout the francophone Caribbean as well as central and east Africa in the 1960s before becoming popular in European metropoles such as Paris and London in the 1980s.

Souphanouvong, Prince (1909–1995)

First president of the People's Democratic Republic of **Laos** after 1975. A royal renegade, Souphanouvong threw in his lot with the communist **Pathet Lao** because of an admiration for **Ho Chi Minh** garnered during his education in **Vietnam** and Paris. He was primarily anti-French when he joined the first cabinet of free Laos in 1958, but was driven from office by anti-communist forces a year later. In 1960 he acted on the side of the Pathet Lao whilst in hiding on the **Ho Chi Minh Trail**, and then as a delegate to the Genevan Peace Conference. Despite a further return to government at the prompting of his half-brother, Souvanna Phouma (Souphanouvong's mother was a commoner), he became fully associated with the Pathet Lao from 1963. He was viewed with suspicion by his colleagues, and ceased to be acting president in 1986.

South Africa

European interest in South Africa began with the establishment of the Cape Colony in 1652 by the Dutch East India Company. The possibility of conflict between predominantly Dutch settlers, the **Boers**, and the British began when **Britain** took the Cape of Good Hope in 1806. In the 1830s the Boers began moving from Cape Colony in the 'Great Trek', clashing with the **Zulu** population of Natal and going on to establish the republics of **Transvaal** and **Orange Free State**. The discovery of diamonds in 1867 (and of gold in 1886) encouraged greater European immigration into the republics and heightened British ambitions to assert control. Britain annexed Transvaal and, after defeating the Zulus in 1879, met with stronger Boer resistance. The 1880–1 **Anglo-Boer** war ended in

a negotiated peace, with Transvaal restored to independence. The Boers were defeated again in the war of 1899–1902, which was ended by the Treaty of Vereeniging by which Transvaal and Orange Free State became self-governing colonies within the **British Empire**. In 1910 the British colonies of Cape and Natal amalgamated with Transvaal and Orange Free State to form the Union of South Africa, a state marked by growing subjugation and exploitation of the majority black population. The 1913 Land Act, for example, denied the black population the right to purchase land outside designated reserves. The South African parliament asserted the country's independence from British authority in 1934 by passing the Status of the Union Act. There was reluctance among many **Afrikaners** (as the Boers had come to be described) to join Britain in the war against **Germany** in 1939, as there had been in 1914. The 1948 electoral victory of the National Party, the voice of the Afrikaners, presaged an intensification of discrimination against the non-white population through the system of **apartheid**, described by the Afrikaners as 'separate development', aimed at forcing the black population into 'homelands'.

The main opposition to apartheid came from the **African National Congress** (ANC), established in 1912. In 1950 the ANC responded to the Group Areas Act, intended to segregate blacks and whites, with a civil disobedience campaign. The ANC was banned and its leaders, including **Nelson Mandela**, imprisoned following the 1960 **Sharpeville massacre** of black demonstrators, leading to international boycotts and sanctions against South Africa. In 1961 the country became a republic and left the British Commonwealth after a whites-only referendum. What proved to be the final phase of apartheid began with clashes at the Johannesburg township of **Soweto** in 1976, leading ultimately to widespread black revolt and a state of emergency. In 1989 F. W. de Klerk became president and instituted a rapid unravelling of apartheid, releasing Mandela from prison, legalizing the ANC and other anti-apartheid parties, setting the scene for the first multiracial elections in 1994. The ANC secured a majority and Mandela became state president. There was an ANC–National Party coalition government until the National Party withdrew 1996. The ANC went on to win successive elections with overwhelming majorities, but it has become increasingly criticised amidst corruption scandals and economic malaise, particularly under President Zuma.

South African Wars

– see **Boer Wars**.

South Arabian Federation

Short-lived British-sponsored union of the fifteen sultanates and sheikhdoms of the Federation of Arab Emirates of the South and the Aden Crown Colony in January 1963. The Federation expanded to seventeen territories when the sultanate of Upper Aulaqi joined in June 1964. The weak federal government faced major challenges from the conflicting interests of the member states, the refusal of the states of the Protectorate of South Arabia to join the federation, and the rejection of the National Liberation Front (NLF) and Front for the Liberation of South Yemen nationalist movements. The nationalists, dominated by the NLF, launched a guerrilla war in 1963 against both the British and the traditional states and during the summer of 1967 succeeded in overthrowing the conservative sultanates. The British–NLF negotiated settlement abolished the Federation and established the People's Republic of South **Yemen** on 29 November 1967.

South East Asia Collective Defence Treaty (1954)

Signed in Manila on 8 September 1954, the South East Asia Collective Defence Treaty founded a regional defence organization whose members included representatives from **Australia**, **France**, **New Zealand**, **Pakistan**, the **Philippines**, **Thailand**, the **United Kingdom** and the **United States**. It led to the establishment of the South East Asia Treaty Organization (SEATO) in 1977. SEATO, which shared the same founder members as the Collective Defence Treaty of 1954, was established to block further Communist developments in South East Asia.

South East Asia Treaty Organization (SEATO)

Created in September 1954 as a South East Asian counterpart to **NATO**, SEATO was an international organization for collective defence whose signatories were **Australia**, **France**, **New Zealand**, **Pakistan**, the **Philippines**, **Thailand**, the **United Kingdom**, the **United States** and **South Korea**. This alliance of European, American and Asian nations required unanimity among its members to launch military intervention. But unity of purpose was rare throughout its existence, particularly with respect to the **Vietnam War**. SEATO was formally dissolved in 1977.

South Korea

– *see also* **Kim Dae-jung; Korea; Kwangju uprising; Park Chung Hee; Roh Tae-woo; Syngman Rhee**.

Established in August 1948 as the Republic of Korea, South Korea was founded as a direct result of **Cold War** politics dividing the peninsula. It survived its greatest challenge in the **Korean War** and authoritarian rule backed by military force prevailed mostly from its inception to 1988. South Korea today is a leading democratic country that has one of the largest industrial capitalist economies in the world.

South Ossetia

– *see* **Georgia**.

South Sea Bubble

The name given to events surrounding the emergence of a share-based scheme which financed a boom in London between 1719 and 1720. Shares were sold in a company which purported to have a monopoly of a fabled and lucrative trade in the South Seas; the directors of this South Sea Company then reinvested their monies in other companies and inflated their values, causing more credit and profit to be generated. The scheme was touted with the assurance of inevitable growth and success. When the South Sea Company suffered a withdrawal of funds, the companies with which it was associated crashed, and then the London markets. The effect was accelerated by the sale of shares by those who had over-invested in the market to pay debts which they had pre-allocated to profits that no longer existed. At one point, a third of the British Parliament was brought to bankruptcy or near default by the scheme, and its progress and crash stand as one of the first examples of the booms and crashes to which share-based markets are prone.

South Sudan

– *see* **Sudan**.

South Tyrol

A province of northern Italy based around Bolzano, also known as Alto Adige, characterized by the presence of a German-speaking majority who were incorporated into **Italy** by the Treaty of St Germain when the area was annexed from **Austria–Hungary** in 1919. Under **Mussolini**, the Italian state made aggressive efforts to Italianize the region, and to prevent any Nazi claims on the territory, ultimately unsuccessfully. After 1945 the region became an autonomous province of Italy, with occasional secessionist violence before 1967 disguising a largely amicable example of a 'euro region' linked to the Austrian Tyrol as well.

South-West Africa
– see **Namibia**.

Soviet Union
The Union of Soviet Socialist Republics (USSR), which existed as the leader of the Communist bloc centred on Moscow between 1922 and 1991, though many date its emergence to the Bolshevik seizure of power in 1917. The USSR existed nominally under three constitutions in 1924, 1936 and 1977, but in reality was constantly governed by the Communist Party and mostly by the acknowledged leader of that party via personal dictatorship (although there were periods of collective leadership). It transformed the backward but growing economy of the old **Russian Empire** into that of a global superpower at the cost of the destruction or impoverishment of tens of millions of lives. Its attempted destruction was the object of **Adolf Hitler**, whose war in **Russia** between 1941 and 1945 cost at least 20 million lives. Though recognized by the **British Empire** in 1924, and a western ally between 1941 and 1945, the USSR was isolated and confronted in the pre-war and **Cold War** periods through a variety of strategies which, in common with its deep internal flaws, brought it to the point of collapse by 1991. At its height, allied to **China** and in control of eastern Europe, the Soviet Union was a nuclear-armed alternative to liberal democracy which convinced many that the future of world would be at least in part socialist for some time to come.

Soweto Uprising
One of the key episodes in the struggle against **apartheid** in **South Africa**. In 1976 schoolchildren in the black township of Johannesburg demonstrated against the imposition of Afrikaans in education; by the end of the year over 500 had been killed as anti-apartheid protests intensified. The violence of the reaction further hardened world opinion against the apartheid regime, though the South African government refused immediate concessions. School boycotts were repeated by coloured schoolchildren in Cape Town in 1980 and there was widespread violence and school boycotts in black townships again in 1985, resulting in the declaration of an indefinite state of emergency and hundreds of arrests. For outside commentators, Soweto became the symbol of resistance to the apartheid regime.

Soyinka, Wole (1934–)
Nigerian activist, playwright and poet. Born among the **Yoruba** community, Soyinka studied literature in **Nigeria** and England. An outspoken political activist, often using satire as a mode of expression, he protested against political corruption and was imprisoned several times in the 1960s. His literary works are influenced by Yoruba and Greek mythology, traditional beliefs and Christianity, Yoruba idioms and Shakespearean dramas. In 1986 he became the first African to be awarded the Nobel Prize in literature.

Soyo
The coastal province of the Kingdom of Kongo, founded in the fourteenth century. Its ruler was baptized in 1491. In the early seventeenth century it became independent of Kongo, and its interference in Kongo's civil wars both prolonged and intensified them. Soyo was an important commercial centre, and many slaves were exported through its port of Mpinda. Soyo was brought under Portuguese rule in 1905, and became the site of major oilfields.

space exploration
– see **exploration**.

Space Treaty (1967)
This established the principles that were to govern the exploration and use of outer space by nation states. In particular, it outlawed claims of ownership over celestial bodies and the creation of military bases thereon. It also outlawed the deployment of nuclear weapons in space. Signatories were obliged to assist any astronauts landing in their territory and return them to their country of origin. The treaty entered into force on 10 October 1967.

Spain
Spain is a constitutional monarchy which has continuously existed in one form or another since the Roman Empire. After the fall of Rome in the west, Spain fell to a number of Germanic and Byzantine conquerors until it came under the sway of the Muslim Abbasid regime. By the late fourteenth and early fifteenth centuries it was removed from Islamic control by the Christian *reconquista*. It is located on the Iberian peninsula, and was at one time after its resurgence the possessor of the first European empire in the Americas as well as colonies and holdings in the Indian and Pacific Oceans of which the **Philippines** (named after a former king of Spain) was the prime example. Spain entered a period of decline in the eighteenth century, when it became embroiled in the **Napoleonic Wars**, and subsequently was subject to the rapid loss of its South American colonies, guerrilla wars conducted between royal families and the loss of

Cuba and the Philippines in the **Spanish–American War** of 1896–8. This created a crisis in Spain's African holdings as well as on the Iberian peninsula proper, which in turn led to the rise of the armed forces and in particular of **General Franco**. Though Spain escaped both world wars, it did suffer the **Spanish Civil War** and the control of a fascist regime until 1975, when the monarchy was restored under King Juan Carlos. Democracy was consolidated after a failed coup attempt in 1981, and Spain joined the European Community (subsequently the **EU**) in 1986.

Spain flourished under the initial expansion of the EU, and redeveloped its trade and cultural ties with the wider hispanophone in the 1990s, but became subject to a capital and property boom which worsened when it joined the **euro** as a founder member. When the global economy collapsed in 2008, Spain's bubble – created in part by overly low interest rates and by joining the euro at too high an exchange rate – turned into a deflation which was rare in its severity. Unemployment reached 26 per cent in 2012 and political instability and turmoil ensued. Spain also participated in **NATO** from 1982 onward (its membership was confirmed by referendum four years later), and was a participant in the coalition of the willing assembled to fight the 'war on terror'. However, a series of bombings in Madrid in 2004 helped cause a change of government and a withdrawal from allied military activities.

Spain is, like many European monarchies, a compound state in which power has been devolved to different ethnic and regional groups and cities on an inconsistent basis. In consequence, island holdings such as the Balearics and and the Canary Islands are self-governing, some regions which consider themselves nations are politically and fiscally autonomous (such as the Basque Country and Navarre) and some are functionally independent, such as Galicia and Catalonia (Catalonia has a thriving nationalist movement). Spain also maintains two cities in North Africa, Ceuta and Melilla, and in recent years has asserted a claim over the British holding of **Gibraltar** (which was transferred by treaty to Britain in 1713). Spain is renowned for its dance, art, history, cuisine and literature, and is split culturally between an historic and conservative Catholicism and a powerful history of urban socialism.

Spanish Civil War

The conflict between the Republican government and Nationalist rebels lasted from July 1936 to April 1939 and began with an attempted military coup in response to the narrow election victory of the centre-left Popular Front in February 1936. General **Francisco Franco** took command of the Nationalist forces. Anarchist and Socialist trade unions and left-wing parties thwarted the rising in the cities of Madrid and Barcelona, but the Nationalists rapidly gained control of a third of Spain. While **Britain** and **France** refused aid to the Republic under the terms of a non-intervention agreement, **Germany** and **Italy** assisted the Nationalists and the **Soviet Union** supported the Republic, including raising the volunteer International Brigade. Barcelona fell to the Nationalists on 26 January 1939 and Madrid on 27 March. Half a million people are estimated to have died during the war and a further 100,000 executed following the Nationalist victory.

Spanish Constitution of 1812

The elected *Cortes* (parliament) gathered in Cadiz on 24 September 1810 after **Napoleon** had invaded Spain in 1808 and detained King Ferdinand VII. The Cortes drafted a constitution that sought to create a unitary state with a tripartite division of authority. It defined the Spanish nation as all Spaniards in Iberia and America and affirmed its sovereignty, created a hereditary, constitutional and limited monarchy, established a unicameral legislature and guaranteed civil rights. By excluding persons of African descent from citizenship it ensured that peninsular deputies would be a majority and thus confirmed South America's second-class status despite protestations of equality. Ferdinand VII returned in 1814 and abrogated the constitution. Colonel Rafael de Riego's liberal *coup d'état* in 1820 reinstated it, but it was abolished again with the restoration of **absolutism** in 1823. The constitution served as a model for many independent American countries.

Spanish Empire

One of the first and most extensive of the European empires, which lasted from 1493 until 1975. Spanish conquerors colonized most of South America, the West Indies and the **Philippines** as well as large sections of North America. The devastating effect on the indigenous peoples and native empires, such as that of the Inca, is still referred to today. **Spain**'s American Empire largely unravelled due to a series of uprisings in 1811–20 associated with **Simón Bolívar**, **Bernardo O'Higgins** and **José de San Martín**, as well as the separate revolt of Mexico. This left various holdings in the Atlantic and Pacific, including **Cuba**, **Puerto Rico** and the **Philippines**, and new acquisitions in western and northern Africa. The martime colonies were lost during the **Spanish–American War** of 1898, though Spanish Morocco remained and provided enough troops and opportunities to suppress colonial troubles to effectively train and equip the likes of **Francisco Franco**, who ruthlessly used his African army and experiences to aid in his rise to *generalissimo*. Many scholars have drawn a link between the attitudes and practices of Spanish military elites and conservatives with regard to the Caribbean and African Empires and the rise of Spanish fascism. However, Spanish liberals were also marked by Iberocentric nationalist and populist taste for empire in the period, given the way in which Spain dispensed citizenship to all who were not slaves anywhere in the empire after 1812. Within Spain, contemporary regional nationalists who wish to be removed from the rule of Madrid draw attention to the way in which empire strengthened an absolute monarchy and therefore the administrative centre both within the Iberian peninsula and without at the expense of regional autonomy, and argue that this legacy explains their grievances. Outside, ongoing problems in the **Western Sahara** (*see* **Sahrawi**) as well as the social inequality which has marked much of the existence of **Equatorial Guinea** have often been traced to Spanish rule. The Spanish Empire was unusually predatory and did not encourage the development of stable institutions or democracy; its on–off association with the Catholic Church also tended to encourage French-style revolutionary anti-clericalism in the American colonies. Such anti-clericalism on the part of radical and urban groups, as in Spain, has tended to encourage reaction in the countryside and an ongoing bitter cleavage over religion which undermined the creation of cooperative political networks and unifying government coalitions.

The legacy of empire is also evident in the worldwide reach of the Spanish language, which has been reckoned to comprise some 500 million native speakers. Spain itself endured a long descent into fascism in the twentieth century, but since the 1970s the re-emergence of the Spanish monarchy and universities, as well as Spanish investment in the Americas, has allowed the creation of an annual Ibero-American summit, bringing together Spanish-speaking heads of state. Alongside the efforts of linguistic and cultural groups dedicated to the development of a plural, global hispanicity, the summit has proven perhaps more useful to Spain's diplomacy and economy than the equivalent **Commonwealth** of Nations has to **Britain**, not least because of the greater political enthusiasm of Spanish business and elites for the initiative.

Spanish Succession, War of ('Queen Anne's War')

The conflict between the forces of Louis XIV's Bourbon **France**, **Spain** and Bavaria on the one hand, and the United Provinces ('Holland'), England (later the **UK** or Great Britain), **Prussia** and **Austria** on the other between 1700 and 1714. To these twin cores, other states such as Savoy and **Portugal** were sometimes attached. The war began after the death of **Habsburg** Spanish King Charles II, and his designation of Louis' grandson as his heir. This caused the European powers to worry about the eventual unification of France and Spain under one family and ultimately one monarch. Such a unification would not only have guaranteed the creation of a huge and destablizing empire in Europe, stretching from Naples and Milan through France and down into Spain, but would have linked the foreign possessions of an hitherto declining Spain with the French state and placed great pressure on the Asian and Atlantic colonies of Britain and Holland. These complications were deepened by the antagonism of the Houses of Bourbon and Habsburg, and by the French patronage of the pretender to the British throne, James Stuart.

The war is widely divided into three periods. There was an initial stage of diplomacy, alliance-forming and encounter-stretching from just before the beginning of formal hostilities until the rise of the Franco-Bavarian Army in 1703. This was followed by a 'middle period' of very serious warfare during which the forces of Savoy and England under John Churchill, Duke of Marlborough, won great battles at Blenheim, Ramillies, Orleans and Turin. This period also saw the acquisition of **Gibraltar** by England, a backward and forward invasion of Spain, and English victories at Oudenaarde and Lille. Pressure of the war and war finance, as well as English worries about the stability of the throne at home, contributed to the Union of England and Wales with Scotland in 1707, and thus to the creation of Great Britain. The war approximated to a global conflict with confrontations in North America allowing for the cession of some Canadian territories to England from France, and battles over South America and the Caribbean ships of Portugal and Spain featuring in the conflict.

The second part of the war ended with multiple attempted invasions of France. The combination of devastating losses in the technical British and allied victory at Malplaquet in 1709, and the bloodiness of the subsequent allied victory at Mons resulted in a sea change in attitudes and a resolution by British Tories to remove the UK from the war at the earliest opportunity when they came to power in 1710.

The third episode spans the period between 1710 and the staggered treaties that closed the conflict. In part the drive to peace was powered by the recognition by Britain and Holland that a victory in which the new Austrian emperor gained the Spanish throne would be as dangerous as one in which a French king did. Gradually, the alliance which had begun at the Hague fell apart. Marlborough was dismissed, the **Peace of Utrecht** in 1713 removed the UK and Holland from the fighting (and the pretender to the British throne from France). It left the conflict to the French and the Austrians. Eventually, Philip V of Spain was secured in his throne on the understanding that he had renounced succession to the throne of France. This secured the European balance of power. The cost of doing so, however, had been the depletion of the financial and administrative architecture of France, the exhaustion of Spain, and the cession of the New World to a commercial Britain. Much more than Holland, Britain's separate peace elevated the standing of, but undermined continental trust in, the United Kingdom.

Spanish–American War

Also referred to as the War of 1898, the Spanish–American War resulted in the **United States'** acquisition of a formal, overseas empire in both the Caribbean and the Pacific. Though the causes of the war were manifold, chronic rebellion in **Cuba** was its immediate pretext. With **Spain** unwilling to grant independence to Cuba and the unrest on the island threatening US interests and ideals, the US Congress, at the request of Republican President **William McKinley**, declared war in April 1898. Following a decisive US victory, the Treaty of Paris (December 1898) transferred the Spanish colonies of the **Philippines**, Guam and **Puerto Rico** to the United States. Cuba was granted independence, though the US quickly established a protectorate there that effectively placed the island under its control. These territorial acquisitions provoked great political controversy in the United States, fuelling a protracted debate over the nature and aims of American foreign policy.

Speer, Albert (1905–1981)

Albert Speer was head of German armaments production, 1943–5, and chief architect to **Adolf Hitler**. In the latter capacity, he planned a new Berlin which would have arisen had Hitler won **World War II**, renamed 'Germania'. At Nuremberg, he pleaded guilty to crimes against peace and humanity, and was sentenced to twenty years in prison. Upon his release, he became the 'good Nazi', who was presented as an urbane intellectual product of **Germany** who had repented of his folly and who wished to explain his association with the Third Reich. Speer was also one of the few men to defy Hitler's orders to his face and live in 1945, when he refused to set a 'scorched earth' programme of physical destruction in motion. By these means his reputation was distinguished from some of the more obvious criminals of the Hitler regime. His grandiose and bombastic architectural plans became well known with the post-war rise of interest in **Nazism** as a movement, and computer simulations and movies added to this process.

Speke, John Hanning (1827–1864)

Born in Devon, England, Speke joined the Indian Army and in 1855 travelled to Somaliland with the explorer British Richard Burton. Although that expedition ended badly, in 1857 he and Burton returned to **Africa**, this time in search of the true source of the Nile. Speke reached Lake Victoria and claimed to have discovered the source of the Nile, but this claim was disputed by Burton. In 1860 Speke returned to prove his claims.

'splendid isolation'

A foreign policy associated with the British Conservative Party (though the phrase was coined by a Canadian Member of Parliament, George Eustace Euler, about New Brunswick, and popularized by the Liberal Lord Goschen after 1895). It was associated particularly with **Benjamin Disraeli** and Lord Salisbury in the latter third of the nineteenth century. 'Splendid isolation' held that **Britain** would hold itself distant from European alliances and concentrate on global and imperial matters, involving itself only to the extent of influencing major treaties and minimizing threats to British interests in the eastern Mediterranean. It was a form of isolationism which ended with the declaration of an Anglo-French entente in 1905.

Spoils System (USA)

Whenever a new party took over the US government, it dismissed many existing office-holders and appointed its own supporters. Initiated by Thomas Jefferson in 1801 and repeated on a similar scale by Andrew Jackson in 1829, this politicization of the administrative system did not become common practice until the 1840s and 1850s, when it was blamed for growing corruption. The demand for a professional civil service, recruited through public examinations, resulted in the Pendleton Civil Service Act of 1883.

sport

– *see* **Olympic Games**.

Sri Lanka

Island nation located across the Palk Strait from south-eastern India. Millennia of communication with the Indian subcontinent produced a pre-modern culture grounded in both Brahmanical and Buddhist ideas. Its central position along the lucrative Indian Ocean trade routes made it a sure target for colonial control. Portuguese, Dutch and finally British rule made colonial Ceylon (as Sri Lanka was called before independence) highly cosmopolitan, though dominated demographically by two ethnic groups, Sinhalese and Tamils. British tea planters imported Tamil labour to central upland districts. The British governed Ceylon through the Colonial Office rather than the India Office, and Sri Lankans won their independence in 1948. Postcolonial politics increasingly defined nationality in terms of Sinhalese language and Buddhism. By the 1980s this resulted in demands for an independent Tamil state in the northern districts and guerrilla violence executed in pursuit of Tamil Eelam. The Sri Lankan government declared victory in the civil war in 2009, but there were widespread claims of massive human rights abuses.

SS (Schutzstaffel)

The black-clad 'special protection staff' of the German **Nazi** Party, the SS emerged as a squad of bodyguards for **Adolf Hitler** in 1925, typified by fanatical devotion to the Nazi cause. Under leader Heinrich Himmler they became an elite nucleus of the future Nazi state, and were viewed as the seeds and advance guard of a new racial and moral order based around Nazi ideology after 1933. They functioned as a state within the German state, and developed an armed force, the Waffen-SS, which fought alongside the regular army. The SS deliberately associated themselves with fear, torture, the death's-head symbol and the subordination of modern technology to an upturned moral universe in which they would breed a new master race outside of all conventional morality. They were the principal agents of the **Holocaust**, but in carrying it out they were following Nazi policy and supported by the rest of the German state.

Stalin, Joseph (1879–1953)

The pseudonym of Joseph Djugasvili, a renegade Georgian Orthodox priest who became unchallenged leader of the **Soviet Union** and one of the most homicidal dictators of the twentieth century. Stalin, the 'Man of Steel', was attracted to Communism as its Russian iteration and his disillusion with Orthodox Christianity rose. He robbed banks for the movement during its time of struggle in the **Russian Empire**, and after the October Revolution became a critical member of its party apparatus. Quietly, he gathered the levers of bureaucratic power to himself, acting as an apparently subservient general secretary to **Lenin**'s Bolshevik Communist Party, until the illness of the latter allowed him to adopt a position of primacy in 1923. Once in the ascendant, Stalin worked to gain the support of conservative elements opposed to Lenin's quasi-capitalist New Economic Policy, and specifically to the kulak class of farmers. He also attempted to isolate elements within the Soviet establishment who favoured the claims of Serge Kirov and Nikolai Sverdlov to leadership. Stalin made his move for total domination in 1928, having Kirov murdered and himself placed in pole position as Soviet leader. The displacement of Sverdlov followed, and was itself succeeded by show trials and semi-permanent purges that eliminated or cowed not only actual opponents but any potential opponents. Stalin set the Soviet Union on a pattern of forced development aided and abetted by the secret police structures created by Lenin that resulted in apparently great economic gains. These were achieved at the expense of any truthful approach to production quotas, and at the cost of vast amounts of prison labour and broken lives.

Stalin also organized the international Communist organization (Comintern) controlled ruthlessly from Moscow to promote his cause, but believed with Lenin that all opponents of Communism were in the process of destroying themselves in competitive capitalism and military tension. As a consequence, he held democratic countries in greater contempt than totalitarian fascist regimes, even signing a pact with Nazi Germany in 1939 to guarantee mutual defence and to divide any conquered **Poland**. Stalin promulgated a doctrine of minimal direct intervention in western theatres, preferring to give aid and support to communist forces in the **Spanish Civil War** and to promote spies and occasional assassinations abroad. This was called 'socialism in one country'.

The full folly of Stalin's relationship with the Third Reich and his constant purging of the army leadership became apparent when his ally **Hitler** launched Operation Barbarossa on 20 June 1941. A massive invasion of the **USSR**, greater than any previous blitzkrieg and involving some 200 German divisions, left Stalin reeling and unbelieving; and though the Germans were stopped at the gates of Moscow, Hitler's gamble almost succeeded. That it did not is in part thanks to Stalin, who refused to leave Moscow and who directed a murderous fightback that left 20 million Soviet soldiers dead but which eventually stopped the Germans and their allies at **Stalingrad** in 1943, and then, in Operation Bagration, destroyed their armies and moved on Berlin. **World War II** and the **Yalta** agreements left Stalin in control of most of eastern Europe, eastern Germany and a vast militarized state which nominally represented a workers' republic. His death camps and forced starvations of millions were kept secret.

Between 1945 and 1953, Stalin tightened the grip of the Soviet centre on conquered countries, using international spy networks to acquire atomic weapons. He ruled the Soviet Union with a combination of personal worship and terror. At the time of his death – which if not caused may have been ensured by his terrified and exasperated colleagues – he was preparing a new terror against Jews and medical staff.

Stalin was a failure in his personal life. His first wife killed herself; his daughter fled the country he established, and his son surrendered to the Germans in World War II; and though his body was embalmed and virtually worshipped in the USSR in Moscow, his reputation was more or less destroyed by his sometime lieutenant **Khrushchev** in 1954, when he revealed to the Soviet Congress the full details of Stalin's crimes in a 'secret speech' which was in time completely leaked.

Stalingrad, Battle of (1942–1943)
A battle fought between German forces and the **Soviet Union** which was centred on the city of Stalingrad (now Volgograd) between August 1942 and February 1943. Costing almost 2 million lives, the battle hung upon the failure of the German forces to seize the city, and the consequent demonstration of their logistic and strategic isolation once the initial phase of Operation Barbarossa (the battle plan to defeat Russia) failed to result in a quick Soviet defeat. The battle saw the defeat of German, Romanian, Croatian, Hungarian and Italian armies and marked the moment when Nazi Germany was pushed on to the defensive in **World War II**. It demonstrated the salience of German Army concerns that **Adolf Hitler** and the

Wehrmacht leadership had led **Germany** to the point of destruction in the East, which eventually resulted in an attempted army coup against Hitler in July 1944.

Stalinism
A form of political organization associated principally with **Joseph Stalin**. Stalinism is a by-word for repression, totalitarian control of political and administrative bureaucracies, and the functional but violent deployment of ideology by leaders to suit their immediate political purposes. Stalinists were devoted to their leader and his interpretation of ideology, enforced whatever line however contradictory the centre wished in the name of the people, and perpetrated or ignored whatever atrocity the leadership wished to be executed. Stalin himself upheld or ordered the nationalist idea of 'socialism in one country', the destruction of capitalist elements and the suppression of their supporters as working-class rule was established, the elimination of the **kulaks**, and the slow, deliberate construction of socialism, but avoided using the word *Stalinist*, preferring others to do so. Abroad, Communist parties which took their politics and direction from Moscow were known as 'Stalinist'. The ideology was responsible for millions of deaths and blighted lives, but reached an apotheosis in **World War II** as **Stalin** and the **USSR** engaged in a mortal struggle with **Hitler** and the Third Reich (with whom they had been allied from 1939) in 1941–5.

Stamp Act (1765)
The Stamp Act of 1765 was the first major crisis point of the American Revolution. The British Parliament demanded that colonists pay a tax to use stamped paper for a variety of legal and recreational purposes, to help defray expenses incurred during the **Seven Years War**. Colonists protested that British subjects could not be taxed without representation in Parliament. Protests, both by petition and by riot, aimed to force the resignation of the hated stamp collectors, and thus the repeal of the Act. The Stamp Act was never collected in the colonies, and was repealed in 1766.

Stanley, Henry Morton (1841–1904)
Welsh American journalist and explorer, born John Rowlands in Denbigh, Wales. In 1871, while working for the *New York Herald Tribune*, Stanley found the missing explorer and missionary David Livingstone in present-day **Tanzania**, going on to further explore central Africa. Stanley was criticized for his ruthlessness in his role in helping

King Leopold II of **Belgium** establish the Congo Free State. A Liberal Unionist Member of Parliament in 1895–1900, he was knighted in 1899.

Stanton, Elizabeth Cady (1815–1902)

American women's rights advocate. She organized the women's rights convention at Seneca Falls, July 1848, drafting its manifesto, the Declaration of Sentiments. After the **American Civil War** she founded the National Woman Suffrage Association with Susan B. Anthony. She toured the country speaking for woman's suffrage and wrote widely on women's education, property rights and women's role in society, religion and the economy. She caused great controversy with the publication of *The Woman's Bible* (1895) and her uncompromising radical feminist ideology.

Star Wars
– *see* **Strategic Defense Initiative**.

state formation (European)

It is often assumed that the nation state is a natural phenomenon. Such familiar expressions as 'fatherland' and 'motherland' reflect that sense of a natural bond between state and people. It is a perception, however, for which there is very little historical evidence. There is even less evidence that there has been anything inevitable in the evolution of the European nation states we know today. The number of examples of earlier quite different allegiances is endless. England in the early eleventh century was part of King (Knut) Canute's Scandinavian Empire. Less than 150 years later Henry II of England (r. 1154–89) was ruling more of what is now France than was the king of France.

In fact, almost all modern European states are deliberate constructs, and most in western Europe are the constructs of their monarchs, not their peoples. Over significant periods of time the monarchs and their courts sponsored the cultures and the standardized languages which then supported them. The 'king's English' was literally that. Loyalty was owed to 'the Crown', not to the nation, the people or the state. British citizens remain to this day 'subjects of the Crown' and British civil servants are in law responsible to the Crown through the monarch's ministers in Parliament, and not to Parliament itself. The Académie Française was founded by Cardinal Richelieu in 1635 specifically to promote national unity under royal authority by determining the correct usage of the French language – a function it performs to

this day, although the monarchy is long gone. The national sentiment which had emerged in England and France by at least the sixteenth century was the consequence, rather than the cause, of this monarchical state formation, and self-definition had been further prompted by the Reformation and the ensuing religious wars.

The pattern of development in central and eastern **Europe** including **Germany** and **Italy**, prior to 1700, had been significantly different. Natural frontiers were comparatively absent in central and eastern Europe. Germany had been divided into 350 states at French behest by the Peace of Westphalia in 1648, which ended the Thirty Years War, and the states' theoretical loyalty to the **Holy Roman Empire** had little practical meaning. In **Italy**, the vigour of medieval city-states had discouraged the emergence of a single centralizing monarchy, as had the temporal ambitions of the **Papacy** and, later, Franco-Spanish rivalry to dominate the peninsula. In central and eastern Europe, stretching into **Russia** in one direction and into the **Balkans** in the other, state formation had been profoundly affected by the invasions of the Mongols and of the Turks respectively. Muscovy had emerged as the state most able to resist and eventually absorb the Mongol invader and by the time of **Peter the Great** (1672–1725), Russia had become an empire stretching to the Baltic, the **Caucasus** and Siberia. The earlier Balkan states, with the one exception of Montenegro, had succumbed in turn to the Turks, whose empire had incorporated **Hungary** in 1526. By 1649 the Turks were at the gates of Vienna. Modern central and eastern European history could be said to start with the defeat of this siege, which was followed by the progressive expansion of the domains of the House of Habsburg, which was not to come to an end until 1908 with the annexation of **Bosnia–Hercegovina**.

It could thus be said that the map of Europe in 1700 was dominated by the expanding **Russian Empire** in the east, the similarly expanding Austrian Empire in the centre, and the equally expansive nation states of England, **France**, **Spain** and **Sweden** in the west. The major 'gaps' in that map were northern Germany and **Poland**, where **Prussia** was yet to assert itself, and Poland, yet to fall apart. Government was everywhere monarchical with the part exception of the **Netherlands**. Other than in the Papal States and states ruled by an (arch)bishop, such as Salzburg, loyalty was due to the Crown.

None of these states was yet a unified nation state in the modern sense. **Britain**, France, the

Netherlands, **Portugal** and Spain all had overseas empires geographically larger than themselves. Many Welsh could still not speak English, and **Ireland**, held by the Crown since the Middle Ages, was so split between Protestant Anglo-Scottish settlers in the north and the disaffected majority Roman Catholic Celtic population in the rest of the island that the latter had supported a Jacobite restoration and the French interest prior to the decisive English victory at the Battle of the Boyne in 1690. France itself permanently feared Breton separatism.

Moreover successive French kings had sought to extend the national territory to the north-east, not least to reduce the power of Spain there, acquiring lands in the process which were traditionally Flemish or German in culture, history and language. Most of Alsace had been acquired in 1648 by the Treaty of Westphalia. Louis XIV had secured part of Flanders by the Treaty of Nijmegcn, 1678, and had annexed the Alsatian capital of Strasbourg by a judicial decree of 1681. All of modern French Flanders, including Lille, was confirmed as French under the Treaty of Utrecht, 1713. Opposition led by Britain had, however, thwarted his ambition of extending France to its 'natural frontier' on the Rhine, which would have meant the absorption of what is now Belgium.

The Scandinavian monarchies of Denmark and **Sweden** were similarly by no means the nation states of today. Sweden owned **Finland** as well as what are now Estonia and Latvia, together with part of Pomerania including what are now the German town of Stralsund and the Polish town of Szczecin. **Norway** had been a Danish province since 1536.

It was only with the end of the monarchical union with Portugal in 1640, the loss of the Netherlands in 1648 and the death of the last Spanish Habsburg monarch, Charles II, in 1700 that Spain could begin to evolve into a nation state on modern lines under the Spanish Bourbon dynasty.

1700–1815

However erratically, the trend towards state consolidation continued throughout the eighteenth century as **Austria**, Britain, France and Spain in particular, but later Prussia as well, jockeyed for dynastic and strategic advantage in a series of wars, notably but not exclusively those of the **Spanish Succession**, 1701–13, the Polish Succession, 1733–8, the Austrian Succession, 1740–8, and the **Seven Years War**, 1756–63. The main exception to the trend was Italy, which was to remain profoundly divided and a political football between the great powers. A sequence of treaties marked Europe's evolving political geography. The first was the Second Partition Treaty of 1700, whereby the first Spanish Bourbon monarch, Philip V of Anjou (r. 1700–46), a grandson of Louis XIV of France, was to rule over Spain, the Spanish Netherlands (now **Belgium**) and Spanish South America, but not the Kingdom of Naples. The Treaties of Utrecht, 1713, and of Rastatt, 1714, which concluded the War of the Spanish Succession, allocated the Kingdom of Naples together with Sardinia and the Duchy of Milan and Mantua to the Austrian Habsburgs. Sicily then gravitated to Austria by the Treaty of The Hague, 1720, with the Piedmontese House of Savoy gaining Sardinia in compensation.

Italy was to remain deeply divided throughout the eighteenth century. Renewed French and Spanish influence was expelled from Lombardy and Sardinia by the Austrians and the Piedmontese at the Battle of Piacenza, 1746, but the Treaty of Aachen, 1748, confirmed Don Carlos, the Bourbon Infante of Spain, as King Charles VII of Naples and Sicily. Tuscany was Austrian but central Italy remained subject to the pope as a secular monarch and Venice retained its independent identity.

Britain provided probably the greatest contrast. In 1707, the Act of Union united the parliaments, although neither the churches nor the legal systems of England and Scotland, which had enjoyed a monarchical union since 1603. Although the enactment itself was peaceful, its consequences were less so. Scotland was more Jacobite and Catholic than England and the accession of the German Elector of Hanover as King George I in 1714 rekindled resentment at the loss of independence and led the following year to a significant rebellion in Scotland and an attempt to claim the throne by James, the son of James II, dubbed the 'Old Pretender'. It failed through lack of any significant English support. The second Jacobite rebellion, led by the 'Young Pretender', Prince Charles Edward (Bonnie Prince Charlie), in 1745 was a much more serious affair, but it never had any real chance of success and its true significance lay in the severity of the English response. The Duke of Cumberland, dubbed both 'Butcher Cumberland' and 'Sweet William', broke the Highlanders at Culloden in April 1746 and Highland traditions and customs were ruthlessly swept away at great human cost. Britain was made more uniform to make it less rebellious.

France continued its expansion with the cession to it of Lorraine in 1738, but the province was granted by **Louis XV** to his father-in-law, the former Polish king, Stanislas Leczinski, and only returned to France on his death in 1766. The island of Corsica was purchased from the Genoese in 1768 over the heads of Corsican patriots.

The greatest change, until the end of the century, was the emergence of Prussia as a great power. **Frederick William (Friedrich Wilhelm) I** made Prussia financially and militarily strong and started the enlargement of Prussia, which was to make it the most important element in the ultimate united German state formed by **Bismarck** in the following century, by acquiring Swedish Pomerania, 1719–20. It was his son, **Frederick the Great** (Friedrich der Grosse) (1712–86), who took that process much further by conquering the Austrian province of Silesia, 1741–6, and weakening the grip of the Habsburg imperial monarchy on the German states through the Seven Years War, 1756–63. As was always likely to be the case, the developing formation of one state was at the expense of a weaker neighbour. Prussia inspired the first partition of Poland in 1772, whereby it gained the Polish province of West Prussia, less Danzig, and was able to link its previously isolated East Prussian territories with its core territories of Brandenburg and Pomerania. The further second and third partitions of Poland under Frederick William II (r. 1786–97) increased Prussia's holdings in the east even further, with Poland ceasing to exist as a state.

This eighteenth-century trend towards the consolidation of a limited number of states was accompanied on the European continent, but not in Britain, by the emergence of the concept of 'the state' as something beyond the will of any particular monarch or politician. Louis XIV of France had maintained '*L'état, c'est moi*' ('I am the state'), but Frederick the Great had seen himself as the servant of the state and subject to its laws. The state was continuous and capable of surviving military defeat, change of regime and even the loss of independence. It called for a new form of loyalty quite different from the ultimately feudal personal loyalty to an individual monarch. It was French thinkers, though, particularly **Rousseau** (1712–78), technically Swiss, who were producing the ideas which were most to influence subsequent approaches to state formation. Rousseau argued in his *Du Contrat Social* of 1762 that a state was a community of citizens who freely chose to live together under laws of their own making, who, in short, had entered into a social contract. It was no longer the creation of a monarch sustained by divine right or even simply the grace of God. Such

thinking had contributed to the **American Declaration of Independence** in 1776, but bore more direct fruit in the **French Revolution** of 1789. The ensuing Revolutionary and **Napoleonic Wars** repeatedly turned the map of Europe on its head, sweeping away the remains of feudalism in areas under French control, the **Holy Roman Empire** and many ecclesiastical and local jurisdictions, and shaking the great powers to their foundations. The final defeat of **Napoleon** in 1815 led to the restoration of a monarchical Europe, except for republican **Switzerland** whose territorial inviolability and perpetual neutrality were guaranteed, but one subject to forces which the signatories to the Congress of Vienna settlement in all probability barely appreciated.

Romantic nationalism

The Napoleonic Wars had everywhere created a nationalist reaction and that reaction coincided with the flowering of the Romantic movement, which sought to glorify nature and saw the medieval as a source of inspiration. The emotional and the individual were prized more than the rational. Romantic nationalism looked back to what it perceived to be its roots in a distinctive language, a distinctive culture, a distinctive homeland, and not least a distinctive national character. Above all, romantic nationalism was about national liberty. It was a flawed concept in that much of what it perceived as decisively distinctive was exaggerated or even imagined. More seriously, romantic nationalism was deeply divisive – a consequence to be felt most strongly in areas such as Alsace-Lorraine and **Transylvania** where peoples had intermingled for centuries. Such flaws became even more serious when they were reinforced by the increasingly popular concept of **race**. Nevertheless, romantic nationalism was one of the most potent, perhaps the most potent, of all European nineteenth-century ideas, and it retains all its vigour two hundred years later. It could be absorbed in most of western Europe where the nation states had genuine medieval roots and state and culture were mutually supportive. It was only in Ireland that it was potentially explosive.

It was a very different matter in the rest of Europe. The cultures of the **Austrian**, **Russian** and **Ottoman Empires** were cosmopolitan, and tolerant of diversity provided it was not consciously disloyal, but essentially German, Russian and Ottoman in character, particularly in the cities. Culture, however, was not linked to a specific state. German culture was common to Austria and Prussia, and had reached its peak in the politically insignificant state of Weimar. Italian culture was similarly flourishing, but common to Austrian Milan, papal Rome and the Bourbon kingdom of the Two Sicilies. The Habsburg emperor in Vienna, on the other hand, counted on the personal loyalty of his subjects regardless of their language, religion or ethnic affiliation. The seemingly irresistible force of romantic nationalism meant that he was ever less likely to receive it as the nineteenth century advanced.

1815–1914: The Balkans

There was the same contrast in the Balkans, where there was a rich cultural heritage of Byzantine art and architecture associated with the Orthodox Church but the commissioning monarchies such as those of **Bulgaria** and Serbia had long succumbed, although they remained discernible in the autocephalous structure of Orthodoxy. The earlier monarchical boundaries of those states had in any event been extremely fluid, with the first Bulgarian Empire, for example, encompassing much of what is now **Albania**, Macedonia and Serbia as well as Bulgaria itself. Stimulated by western nationalist thinking, a new Balkan nationalism now percolated downwards from artists, intellectuals, the military and even the Church. It was a nationalism that was taught, and sometimes taught without sophistication. In the West, the nation state had given birth to national sentiment; elsewhere, national sentiment called for the creation of a nation state to express it. That call was heard more clearly as the political power of the Ottoman Empire weakened. **Greece** and Serbia led and others followed. In Greece, the call for a state was echoed by western **philhellines**. Serbia, exceptionally, had an aristocratic dynasty of its own, the Karadjordje family, to lead its struggle. It rebelled from 1804 onwards and gained autonomy in 1829, but had to wait until 1878 for full independence. Greece, however, gained full independence in 1829. Recognition of the autonomy of Moldavia and Wallachia, the core of modern **Romania**, followed in 1856. The full independence of Romania ensued in 1878, when Bulgaria gained its autonomy, although it had to wait until 1908 for full independence. Albania won independence of a sort in 1912. The resulting states were not, however, quite those familiar from the modern map. **Turkey** still held Thrace, Macedonia and Crete, and Transylvania remained part of the Austro-Hungarian Empire.

The progress of independence of the Balkan states from Turkish imperial rule underlined, however, one of the key flaws in the romantic nationalist ideal. Cultural allegiances had long been extremely fluid and peoples had so intermingled that in a number of regions they had no clear potential national identity. Virtually every one of the new national boundaries could therefore be contested. The consequences were the First and Second **Balkan Wars** and opposing allegiances in **World War I**. The ultimate consequence was that the predominantly Greek-speaking southern part of Macedonia, focused on Thessaloniki, together with western Thrace and Crete, became part of an enlarged Greece and almost all the predominantly Slavonic-speaking north, focused on Skopje, went to Serbia, with a small portion to Bulgaria.

The unrest in the Turkish Empire was mirrored in the Austrian Empire but Austria remained strong enough to retain control until 1918. Indeed, it had been strong enough to acquire Bosnia–Herzegovina from the Turks in 1878 in its first expansion since the loss of Italy in the 1850 and 1860s and of any role in Germany with the Austro-Prussian War of 1866. Its big concession had been the *Ausgleich* (compromise) of 1867, which had created a dual monarchy of **Austria–Hungary**. Although it remained under Habsburg rule, Hungary had thereby reasserted its national identity for the first time since 1699. Hungary also returned to its previous frontiers, which meant that Croats, Slovaks, Transylvanian Romanians and Ruthenian Ukrainians of the Habsburg Empire now passed under Hungarian imperial rule.

1815–1914: Italy, Germany and the West

The **Congress of Vienna** settlement was first challenged in the west by the rebellion in Brussels in 1830 against the union of what had once been the Spanish, and then the Austrian, Netherlands with Holland, in a united kingdom of the Netherlands. Modern Belgium had emerged. The great European change, however, came after mid-century in first Italy and then Germany, and it operated in reverse to what was happening further east. There, the pressure was to dismember empires and create small successor nation states. In Italy and Germany, the pressure was to amalgamate jurisdictions, some very small and backward, into new unions of all Italian-speaking and all German-speaking peoples, led by their most dynamic constituent parts, Piedmont and Prussia respectively.

The stimulus in Italy had been the Napoleonic Wars, which, however temporarily, had united the whole of Italy other than Sicily and Sardinia, directly or indirectly, in a Napoleonic framework. The successful route to unification was plotted by the Piedmontese minister, Count Camillo di Cavour, who relied on international diplomacy rather than the revolution favoured by **Giuseppe Mazzini**. Having first concluded an alliance with France, January 1859, he provoked the Austrians to declare war in the April. The allies were victorious, notably at Solferino in June 1859, acquiring Lombardy and leading Parma and Modena to call for unification with Piedmont. Despite the alarm of **Napoleon III**, who had gained Nice and Savoy for France as the price of his support, but no more wanted a united Italy than had his predecessors, British support led to plebiscites in favour of unification across Tuscany, Emilia, the Marches (*Marche*) and Umbria, 1860. The Expedition of the Thousand under **Garibaldi** undermined the Kingdom of the Two Sicilies, 1860, and the Kingdom of Italy was formally proclaimed in Turin, 17 March 1861. The Italy of today came closer with the cession of Venezia (Venetia) by Austria, 1866, and the surrender of Lazio (Latium) and the city of Rome, except the Vatican, by the pope, 1870. Trentino-Alto Adige (south Tirol) and Istria (including Trieste) remained Austrian.

German unification started similarly, with the final destruction of any Austrian hegemony over the German states in the Austro-Prussian War of 1866, a war preceded by the forcible acquisition of Schleswig-Holstein from Denmark, 1864. The unification of the German-speaking peoples (outside Austria and Switzerland) was then completed by the defeat of the French in the **Franco-Prussian War**, 1870, and with the cession of Alsace and part of Lorraine to the new **German Empire** proclaimed 1871. The map of Europe outside the Balkans was then only to be altered prior to World War I by the Swedish recognition of the independence of **Norway** in 1905.

impact of World War I

This state of comparative equilibrium was completely disrupted by the defeat of the Austrian, German, **Russian** and **Turkish Empires** in World War I. The resulting peace treaties saw Poland reappear as a sovereign state. Austria and **Hungary** appeared as nation states confined to their German-speaking and Hungarian-speaking cores respectively. Estonia, Latvia and **Finland** became states for the first time, and Lithuania was as independent of Poland as of Russia. The greatest innovations, however, were the creation of a unified **Czechoslovak** state, which

combined the Czechs of Austrian Bohemia with the Slovaks of Hungarian Slovakia, and a new Kingdom of the Serbs, Croats and Slovenes (later **Yugoslavia**), which united the former independent **Serbia** and Montenegro with formerly Austro-Hungarian **Bosnia–Hercegovina**, **Croatia** and Slovenia. These radical changes were accompanied by others a little less important. Linguistically divided Alsace-Lorraine returned to France, and Bukovina and Transylvania became part of a much enlarged Romania. Italy secured Trentino, the south Tirol, Trieste and Istria. **Danzig** became a free city. In the far west, the conflicting goals of Catholic Irish nationalists and Protestant Ulstermen led to the 1921 division of the island into an Irish Free State and a semi-autonomous **Northern Ireland** linked to Britain in the **United Kingdom** of Great Britain and Northern Ireland of the present day.

The new dispensation did not bring peace. Poland seized the Lithuanian capital of Vilnius, 1920, amongst aspirations for a new empire embracing **Ukraine**, and having been in conflict with **Soviet Russia** over their joint border since early 1919. The Treaty of Riga of March 1921 set the border 150 miles east of the Curzon Line recommended by the allies in July 1920 and included territory whose population was probably less than a quarter Polish. In 1923, Italy seized Fiume (Rijeka). The new Irish Free State suffered civil war over acceptance or otherwise of the island's division. The most serious problems, however, were to be in the German-speaking areas. The **Treaty of Versailles** had preached the principle of national self-determination but had declined to respect it for the defeated Germans. Austria had been forbidden from uniting with Germany under the Treaty of Saint-Germain and solidly German Danzig had been declared a free city. The new Czechoslovakia included more than 3 million reluctant (Sudeten) Germans. The creation of Poland had split Germany in two with an isolated East Prussia. The resulting rise of extreme German nationalism dominated the history of the 1930s and culminated in **World War II**.

impact of World War II

For all its savage destructiveness, World War II finished with remarkably little change to most of the map of Europe. The German and Italian redrawings of 1938–41 had sometimes been radical but none survived 1945. The Soviet Union had reclaimed the three Baltic states and Bessarabia in 1940, the latter becoming with the northern part of Bukovina the new Moldavian

SSR. In 1947, Yugoslavia gained Istria and Rijeka (Fiume) from Italy. The great exceptions were Germany and Poland. By the Potsdam Agreement, Poland was moved bodily westwards, relinquishing its territory east of the Curzon Line to the Soviet Union and being given in compensation eastern Pomerania and Silesia. East Prussia was split between Poland and the Soviet Union and Danzig became Polish Gdánsk. The other big change was the progressive division of Germany between the western Allies and the Soviet Union which resulted in the declaration of the German Federal Republic (West Germany) and the German Democratic Republic (East Germany), 1949.

Iceland gained independence from Denmark in 1944. France grew technically larger with the inclusion in metropolitan France of its former colonies of Guadeloupe, Guyane, Martinique and La Réunion, but shrank with its recognition of Algerian independence, in 1962. Similarly the Netherlands' Antilles was granted internal self-government as an integral part of the Kingdom of the Netherlands, 1954. The British granted **Malta** independence, 1964, and created an independent **Cyprus**, 1959.

fall of Communism

The years 1990 and 1991 saw much more sweeping changes. The Soviet Union dissolved into its constituent soviet republics and the Baltic states returned as sovereign states. The two German states were united. Ukraine, **Georgia** and **Armenia** recovered a long-lost independence and **Belarus**, **Kazakhstan** (western strip) and Moldova appeared on the map of European states for the first time, almost by default. Significantly, however, the Russian Federation itself remained intact. The Yugoslav Federation disintegrated into its constituent states of Bosnia–Herzegovina, Croatia, Macedonia, Serbia and **Slovenia**. The disintegration was often violent for familiar reasons. The boundaries between the Yugoslav republics were historic and did not allow for the more recent movement of people. The resulting wars evicted the Serbs from Croatia and created a barely functioning federation of two constituent entities in Bosnia–Herzegovina, which the so-called Bosnian Serb Republic (Republika Srpska) is threatening to leave. It was forbidden under the 1995 Peace Agreement from joining Serbia.

The converse situation applied in the Serb province of Kosovo, which was its historic heart but which had become 90 per cent ethnically Albanian

from immigration. The Albanian Kosovar cause attracted western military support and Kosovo declared its independence in 2008. It was not, however, recognized by Russia and some EU member states. The former Yugoslav Federation came to a formal end with the separation of Montenegro from Serbia, also in 2008. Czechoslovakia had dissolved itself by agreement into the Czech Republic and Slovakia in 1993.

The dissolution of the Soviet Union in general proved much less violent than that of the Yugoslav Federation, but there were exceptions for reasons parallel to those in the Balkans. Armenia was at war with Azerbaijan over the disputed enclave of Nagorno-Karabakh until 1994. Georgia suffered civil war focused on its Russian-leaning regions of South Ossetia and Abkhazia until 1993. The Georgian attempt to assert direct control over them resulted in a Russian invasion in 2008. Moldova saw fighting in 1992 with separatists in the largely Russian-speaking areas east of the River Dniestr, which had been declared the Republic of Transnistria in 1991. It sought independence and probable future inclusion in the Russian Federation. The most important conflict was in Ukraine.

The trend towards the formation of ever more European states seems likely to continue. The secession of Flanders from Belgium, of Catalonia from Spain, of Scotland from the United Kingdom, of the Faroes and Greenland from Denmark, and of the north of Italy from the rest of the country all enjoy significant political support. The number of European sovereign states has already doubled in a century. The countervailing trend towards some sharing of sovereignty is represented by the European Union and the Commonwealth of Nations.

states' rights (USA)

This tradition saw the United States as a confederation of independent states that created a federal government only to satisfy a few shared needs. Though the Constitution of 1787 had deliberately replaced the confederation by a more centralized system, the balance thereafter shifted back with the 10th Amendment; then **Jefferson**'s doctrine of strict construction limited the federal government to the powers specifically authorized, while the Virginia and Kentucky resolutions of 1798–99 argued that states could determine the limits of federal power. After 1801 the Jeffersonians themselves increasingly leant towards broad construction, thereby aggrieving some states-rights ideologues who subsequently found redress when

Andrew Jackson's vetoes of 1830–2 committed his party to a more strictly constructionist view favouring inactive federal government. After 1848 Democrats denied that federal power could decide the issue of slavery expansion, though pro-slavery Southerners also asserted federal power whenever it suited them. Southern secession in 1860–61 utilized the ultimate (but disputed) right of a state; inevitably the Union conquest put state's rights to sleep for a generation after 1865.

Statue of Liberty (USA)

A gift from the French Republic erected in New York harbour in 1886, it was one of the first features of the New World to be seen by millions of European immigrants. Its pedestal carries an inscription by the author Emma Lazarus celebrating the welcome that the **United States** offered to 'your huddled masses yearning to breathe free'. Ironically, at that very moment, pressure was mounting for at least a partial closing of the 'golden door' that was celebrated in Lazarus' poem.

Stephenson, George (1781–1848)

A British inventor and engineer who developed a safety lamp for miners and the first commercial use of steam locomotive technology in railways. He began as a colliery worker who repaired watches and stripped engines in his spare time, before becoming a colliery engineer. This allowed him to build his own locomotive to pull coal. He was then hired by railway companies to build their engines and tracks, for which purpose he formed his own company. He served as chief engineer and the provider of rails and engines for major British rail companies, and thus became known as the 'father of the railways'. His most famous invention was the *Rocket*, a steam locomotive produced for the Liverpool and Manchester Railway in 1829.

Stevens, Siaka (1905–1988)

An important political leader in **Sierra Leone**. He began his career in the colonial service in 1923, and became a trade unionist while working for a mining company. He was an advocate for the people of the interior against the otherwise dominant Creoles as head of the All People's Congress. He became president in 1967 and eventually developed a one-party state in 1978, turning the reins of power over to Joseph Momoh in 1985.

Stock Market Crash

– *see* **Wall Street Crash**.

stock markets

Stock markets may have originated in Cairo in the eleventh century as a trade in paper assets among Islamic and Jewish merchants, but became first institutionalized in late thirteenth-century Bruges when commodity traders associated in the house of a man called van der Beurse, giving birth to the 'Beurse'. The idea quickly spread and 'Beurzen' opened in Ghent and then for continuous trade in Amsterdam. Nowadays, the term 'stock market' stands for an institution that enables and facilitates the trade in stocks, bonds securities and derivatives. Stock exchanges can operate as a corporation or mutual organization, specialized in bringing buyers and sellers of stocks and securities together.

Stowe, Harriet Beecher (1811–1896)

American writer and **abolitionist**. In 1832 she followed her father, the Congregationalist minister Lyman Beecher, from Connecticut to Lane Seminary, Cincinnati, Ohio. Her proximity to a slave state and the passage of the Fugitive Slave Law (1850) inspired *Uncle Tom's Cabin* (1852). The book's potent depiction of the human impact of slavery won it a wide audience; it was adapted for the stage and drew heated southern rejoinders about the 'wage slavery' of the free north.

Straits Question

The right of passage for warships through the Straits of the Dardanelles and the **Bosphorus** was always a highly sensitive diplomatic issue between the **Ottoman Empire** and the European powers because **Russia** needed naval forces strong enough to defend its southern coast against attack by **Turkey** and any other power, but not so strong that Turkey felt the need to ally itself with a power hostile to Russia. The bilateral treaty of Unkiar Skelessi, 1833, which committed Turkey to closing the Straits to all foreign warships if so requested by Russia, concerned the British and was succeeded in 1841 by the Straits Convention, between the five then European powers and Turkey, which forbade warships of foreign powers from entering the Straits while the empire was at peace. The situation when Turkey was at war, as in the **Crimean War**, 1853–5, was not covered. That war's concluding Treaty of Paris, 1856, neutralized the Black Sea until the provision's cancellation, 1871. It was a Russian aim in **World War I** to have permanent control of the Straits.

Strategic Arms Limitation Talks (SALT I and SALT II)

The Strategic Arms Limitation Talks (SALT) between the **United States** and the **Soviet Union** placed numerical limits on long-range nuclear weapons systems. SALT I (1972) consisted of an interim agreement limiting the number of intercontinental and submarine-based ballistic missiles, and an anti-ballistic missile (ABM) treaty restricting the number of ABM systems to two per nation. SALT II (1979) agreed to limit the number of strategic missile launchers, but was not ratified by the US following the Soviet invasion of **Afghanistan**.

Strategic Arms Reduction Talks (START I and START II)

The Strategic Arms Reduction Talks between the **United States** and the **Soviet Union** built upon the earlier SALT talks, aiming to reduce the total number of nuclear weapons. START I (eventually signed 1991) aimed to halve the total number of nuclear warheads. START II (1993) promised to cut warheads by almost half again, and banned the use of multiple independently targetable re-entry vehicles (MIRVs) from 2003. **Russia** withdrew from START II in 2002 when the United States withdrew from the ABM treaty.

Strategic Defense Initiative (Star Wars)

Announced by President **Ronald Reagan** in March 1983, the Strategic Defense Initiative, or 'Star Wars', as it was popularly known, aimed to build a defensive shield around the **United States** through the creation of a space-based anti-ballistic missile system which would destroy incoming nuclear missiles with lasers or particle beams. Critics argued that it was reckless, scientifically flawed and would lead to an escalated arms race; supporters claimed it forced the Soviets to the negotiating table.

Stratford de Redcliffe, Viscount

– see **Canning, Stratford**.

Stroessner, Alfredo (1912–2006)

Dictator of **Paraguay**, 1954–89. A military officer, Stroessner deposed Federico Chávez to become president. Utilizing the Colorado Party and military, he stabilized the currency and improved roads, schools and health facilities. With Brazilian cooperation, he constructed the Itaipu Dam. He also encouraged contraband, harboured international criminals, forcibly assimilated the indigenous population, controlled the media and ruthlessly and brutally eliminated his opponents until overthrown by the military.

Stuart, James Ewell Brown (1833–1864)

American Confederate cavalryman. Stuart's skill as a cavalryman made him an important contributor to the Army of Northern Virginia's record of success. He discovered exposed Union flanks before the Seven Days of Battles and at **Chancellorsville**. He screened the army offensively, denied intelligence to Union cavalry while gaining it for his chief, **Robert E. Lee**. He failed at these tasks at **Gettysburg**, but retained Lee's confidence. In May 1864 he fell mortally wounded at Yellow Tavern while preventing Union cavalry from entering Richmond.

Sublime Porte

– see also **Ottoman Empire**.

The French term to denote the Ottoman government, coined in the sixteenth century and adopted by other European languages including English. Also used in Ottoman Turkish, *Bab-ı Ali*, or the 'High Gate', referred to the literal gate that acted as the entrance to the office of the grand vizier and as a symbol for the seat of the Ottoman administration. The gate still stands in the Sultanahmet district of Istanbul where it now protects the offices of Istanbul's municipal administration.

Sudan

– see also **Sudanese Civil War**.

The Republic of Sudan is located in north-eastern Africa along the Red Sea between **Egypt**, **Eritrea** and **Ethiopia**. Ruled by Ottoman and later Anglo-Egyptian forces in the nineteenth century culminating in the **Battle of Omdurman**, .continued resistance marked Sudan's colonial period. Since gaining independence in 1956, Sudan has experienced significant political and ethnic turmoil, with governance alternating between military regimes and civilian parliamentary systems. After 1989 the government was a coalition between the three leading political parties headed by Umar al-Bashir. Ethnic and religious conflict has shaped Sudan's political, economic and social development. It suffered two civil wars: from 1956 to 1972 and from 1983 to 2005. The Comprehensive Peace Accord in 2005 initiated a ceasefire between northern and southern forces, set up the current coalition government and called for a referendum regarding southern autonomy. Southern Sudan voted overwhelmingly for independence in January 2011, but since independence has itself been plagued by internal warfare.

Sudanese Campaign (1883–1885)

In 1881 a Muslim messianic figure known as the **Mahdi** successfully organized tribes and Sudanese notables in a revolt against the Ottoman–Egyptian khedival authority. Angered by **Britain**'s termination of the slave trade in the region, the *ansar*, or the Mahdi's followers, joined the cause. Britain, which occupied **Egypt** in 1881, sought a withdrawal from **Sudan** and, in late 1883, sent General **Charles Gordon** to organize the evacuation. A previous expeditionary force tasked with putting down the Mahdist rebellion had been defeated a few months previously. Once he arrived in Khartoum in February 1884, Gordon ignored orders and set out to establish a civil administration of the city and prepare to crush the Mahdi. In March the Mahdi's forces had closed in on Khartoum, eventually cutting supply lines north towards Egypt. After nearly ten months of siege, the Mahdi launched a full assault in January 1885 that destroyed British–Egyptian forces and killed Gordon, ending colonial rule in the region until a second **Sudanese campaign** of 1898.

Sudanese Campaign (1898)

With Italian and French interests threatening **Sudan** from the south and east, the British sought to re-establish control after being pushed out by the **Mahdi**'s forces in 1885. In 1896, Anglo-Egyptian forces under Lord **Kitchener** began a steady advance south into the country. Learning the lessons of their defeat a decade earlier, they constructed railways and posts to ensure good communication and supply for the invasion. By 1898 they had won several important victories in northern Sudan and threatened Khartoum. Although Mahdist forces – now led by the Mahdi's successor, Abdallahi ibn Mohammed – greatly outnumbered the British and Egyptians, the chief Mahdist commander, Mahmud Ahmed, was indecisive and allowed British technology and firepower to overwhelm his ranks at the **Battle of Omdurman**. Abdallahi himself fled but died a year later. The British set up an Anglo-Egyptian administration of Sudan that lasted until Sudanese independence in 1956.

Sudanese Civil War (1956–2009)

This conflict was rooted in Sudan's ethnic fragmentation and the cultural divide between the 20 million Muslims in the Arabic-speaking north and the 5 million traditionalist animists and 2–3 million Christians in the black African south. Under the Anglo-Egyptian condominium prior to independence in 1956, the British had first sought from 1902 to produce a modern educated Sudanese Arab elite, but that policy had not influenced the south. Moreover, the approach had been changed with the introduction of the British 'Southern Policy' in 1930, which deliberately divided the south from the north because the British believed at the time that southern Sudan was a better fit with the adjacent British East African colonies than it was with the Arab north. The 'Southern Policy' was, however, reversed in 1946 with the British now maintaining that the north and south belonged together and should have a common legislature. In practice, the position of the south worsened as independence approached. In the 1953 parliamentary elections, only 22 of the 142 seats were reserved for the south, although about a third of the population were southerners. The position in the civil service was even worse. Sudanization of the posts vacated by the British was so executed that southerners received just 4 of the total of 800. The victorious National Unionist Party (NUP) under **Ismail al-Azhari**, which then favoured union with **Egypt** and was to lead the country on independence, dismissed the plea of the newly formed Southern Party, which had won 16 of the south's 22 seats, for the establishment of a federal state with a degree of autonomy for the south. One early consequence was a mutiny of southern army officers in 1955, which heralded the civil war which broke out in 1962. The rebellion in the south, now organized as the **Sudanese People's Liberation Army (SPLA)**, saw conflict peaking in 1963–71 and from the 1980s, and was further exacerbated by the seizure of power in 1989 of the Islamic fundamentalist Revolutionary Command Council under **Omar al-Bashir**, which declared its intention of turning the Sudan into an Islamic state. It announced in 1990 that the Islamic law courts which had always administered justice for the Muslim population would henceforth apply sharia to the non-Muslim south of the country as well.

The continuing conflict had serious consequences for Sudan's ability to feed its rapidly growing population, and parts of the south suffered severely from famine in the late 1980s and 1990s. Both Egypt and **Libya** acted as mediators in 2001, and the SPLA opened negotiations with the government, 2002. The SPLA leader, John Garang, met President Bashir, 2003, and a power-sharing agreement was signed, 2005. A peace agreement followed in 2006, but killing continued. In 2008 the

United Nations assumed control of the Darfur peace force established by the **African Union**, and in 2009 it declared the end of the war in Darfur. The Sudanese legislature passed a law authorizing a referendum on independence for south Sudan, 2009, and following such a referendum in the south, in which 99 per cent voted for independence, January 2011, the south finally seceded, 9 July 2011. The two countries have, however, since teetered on the brink of war. Civil war broke out in the new South Sudan in 2013, causing a massive refugee crisis. The International Criminal Court called in 2008 and 2009 for President Bashir's arrest for war crimes in Darfur, including genocide.

Sudanese People's Liberation Army (SPLA)

– see also **Sudanese Civil War (1956–2009)**.
Established as a guerrilla force in 1983 by southern-based mutineers from the Sudanese Army led by John Garang de Mabior (1945–2005), and aided by neighbouring **Ethiopia**, the SPLA fought initially for a secular **Sudan**, condemning the imposition of Islamic law. The SPLA launched its first major attack on government forces in 1985 and provided the basis of South Sudan's regular army when the area gained independence from Sudan in 2011.

Sudetenland

The largely German-speaking border regions of pre-war **Czechoslovakia** incorporated in the new state by the **Treaty of Versailles** to give it allegedly defensible frontiers. Highly responsive to the Nazis, the 3 million Sudeten Germans supported the region's transfer to **Germany** under the 1938 Munich Agreement. They were dispossessed and expelled under the **Potsdam conference** decisions and Czechoslovakia's Beneš decrees, 1945. Any hopes of return were lost with the Treaty on the Final Settlement with Respect to Germany in 1990 and Czechoslovak legislation in 1991.

Suez Canal

Attempts to construct a canal linking the Mediterranean to the Red Sea culminated in 1858 when the French diplomat and engineer Ferdinand de Lesseps (1805–94) secured the agreement of Egyptian Viceroy Mohamed Said to the project. The joint Franco-Egyptian Universal Suez Canal Ship Canal Company was established in 1858 and construction work began in April 1859. The canal was 163 kilometres (101 miles) long and was completed in November 1869. The company was authorized to operate the canal for ninety-nine years, after which the right reverted to **Egypt**. In 1875 Egypt sold her shares in the company to **Britain**. An 1888 international convention allowed all shipping to use the canal but in 1948 the Egyptian government barred access to Israeli shipping. From 1936 Britain deployed troops in the Suez Canal Zone controlling entry, finally withdrawing its forces in 1954. Egyptian nationalization of the canal in 1956 triggered the **Suez Crisis**.

Suez Crisis (1956)

Unleashed by the conspiracy in 1956 between the leaders of **France**, **Great Britain** and **Israel** militarily to seize the nationalized **Suez Canal**. The British had resented **Nasser**'s assertion of Egyptian interests prior to the crisis, which had included the nationalization of the canal in July 1956 and a readiness to be equidistant from the western powers and the **Soviet Union**. Such non-alignment challenged Britain's traditional pre-eminence in **Egypt**. The British prime minister, Sir Anthony Eden, also appears to have been almost obsessed by his memories of fighting the European dictators in the 1930s and of the 1938 Munich crisis, and mistakenly to have believed that Nasser personally was another **Hitler** who should on no account be appeased. Eden was also conscious that pressure from Nasser had led to the disbandment in 1956 of Transjordan's Arab Legion under General John Glubb, a final remnant of imperial glory. The French, who had first planned the action with Israel, were smarting from their defeat by the **Viet Minh** at **Dien Bien Phu** in **Indochina**, May 1954, and resented Nasser's support for **Algeria**'s Arab nationalists. Both feared the impact of Nasser's pan-Arab nationalism, both on their wider strategic interests and on their Middle Eastern oil supplies in particular. Israel feared Nasser as the first Arab leader who appeared to be strong enough to unite Arab forces against them.

The British and the French, therefore, encouraged Israel to attack Egypt so that they could intervene on the pretext that they were seeking to restore peace, 30 October–5 November 1956. In strictly military terms, the attack was a success, but politically it was a complete failure, most of all perhaps for the British. It was denounced by the opposition Labour Party under Hugh Gaitskell, but more crucially, it infuriated US President **Eisenhower**, who had not been advised of the conspiracy in advance. Sir Anthony Eden was obliged to resign under **USA** pressure and

President Nasser scored a major diplomatic victory, becoming the Arab world's undisputed leader thereafter. The nationalized canal remained closed to Israeli shipping but otherwise, contrary to much expert western prediction, remained open with the assistance of Russian pilots.

The Suez Crisis was the last occasion in British foreign affairs when the UK would try to act independently contrary to US wishes, although the French, particularly under **de Gaulle**, were to remain obdurate in defending perceived national interests. It was also counter-productive, at least for Britain and France, in a wider context. It needlessly exacerbated tension with a strongly felt but essentially moderate form of secular Arab nationalism with which constructive engagement would have been more rewarding. It effectively enhanced Soviet influence and cancelled out the opprobrium which the Soviet Union had incurred with its suppression of the Hungarian uprising at exactly the same time. Lastly, it immeasurably boosted President Nasser's standing not only in the **Middle East** but across the whole developing world, while humiliating not just one but two western European prime ministers at a time when many of their peoples still regarded Arabs in a poor light. It presaged the end of the age of empire.

suffragettes

– *see also* **democracy**; **feminism**; **women's rights (American)**.

Generically, women who campaigned for the vote from the late nineteenth century, but more specifically, supporters of the British Women's Social and Political Union (WSPU), founded in 1903 by Emmeline Pankhurst (1858–1926) to campaign for votes for women. The movement distinguished itself from other groups (such as the 'suffragist' National Union of Women's Suffrage Societies) by its adoption of militant tactics, including violence against property when parliamentary leaders refused to include women's suffrage in their legislative programmes. Faced with imprisonment, suffragettes resorted to hunger strikes and were met by forced feeding, 'cat and mouse' release and rearrest legislation. Though attracting great publicity, there was no legislative advance prior to 1914. On the outbreak of **World War I**, Pankhurst committed the movement to winning the war. Women over the age of 30 obtained the vote in the fourth Reform Act of 1918; women over 21, in 1928. The WSPU's contribution is still controversial alongside that of other pressure groups and the general democratizing effect of World War I.

sugar

Although the production of sugar, derived from a giant grass called sugarcane that thrives in tropical areas, has occurred throughout world history, large-scale cultivation is mostly a consequence of the **Columbian exchange**. The production of sugar – a luxury crop until the nineteenth century – took off in the Americas, beginning in **Brazil**, and spreading to the Caribbean and Louisiana. Brazil, the first major region of sugarcane production, dominated production in the first half of the seventeenth century. Brazilian planters pioneered both the distinctive form of labour used to cultivate it – African chattel slavery – and also the use of specialized machinery – sugar mills – to increase sugar production and make it economically feasible. A major advance was made in the mid seventeenth century, when sugar cultivation spread to the Caribbean island of **Barbados**. Sugar planters developed the integrated plantation, in which both the growing and the processing of sugarcane occurred on a single plantation. Planters employed a gang-labour system of production. They also developed, through the commission system, an effective way to market their crop in Europe. These innovations made sugar the premium tropical crop of the eighteenth century.

Sugar is closely associated with slavery; labour in sugarcane fields was especially arduous and notably similar to the harsh factory discipline later adopted in the Industrial Revolution. Over time, planters learned how to use African labour effectively, employing men as disciplinarians, tradesmen and boilers while reserving much of the hard labour for women. The employment of women in back-breaking field labour had strongly negative consequences on reproduction. The demographic consequences were dire: no sugar-producing area maintained a self-reproducing slave population. Thus, sugarcane production was heavily reliant on fresh importations of Africans through the Atlantic **slave trade** in which declining populations of slave labourers were regularly supplemented by new arrivals. In the eighteenth century the leading areas of sugar production were **Jamaica** and (until the **Haitian Revolution** of 1791–1804) Saint-Domingue. **Cuba** benefited most from the end of sugar production in Saint-Domingue and, adopting industrial techniques, became the leading producer of sugar in the nineteenth century. Both Cuba and Louisiana benefited from active slave trades long after the ending of the Atlantic slave trade in the **British Empire**. By the nineteenth century sugarcane production in the Caribbean had been supplemented by sugar beet production in **Europe**. Sugar beet production and the development of increasingly sophisticated forms of mechanization made sugar cheaper to produce and easier to consume from the mid nineteenth century; it also allowed sugar production to survive the abolition of slavery in the Americas between 1834 and 1888. Sugar, given its addictive properties, is now consumed in vast quantities and forms an essential part of modern diet in many places. Even so, despite the abolition of slavery, the production of sugarcane remains associated with poverty in the developing world and with poor working conditions and adversarial labour relations.

Sugar Act (UK)

The Sugar Act of 1764 was a British imperial law; the first to explicitly raise revenue from North American colonies (as opposed to trade regulation). Though the Act halved the duty payable on sugar imported from non-British colonies, it was accompanied with a move towards rigorous enforcement and a crackdown on smuggling. Protest against it was strongest in New England, where most rum distilleries in the colonies were based. Further south, there was little concern over the new legislation.

Suharto (Soeharto), General (1921–2008)

Authoritarian president of **Indonesia**, 1967–98. Born, Java, in the then Dutch East Indies. He joined the Dutch colonial army and after the Japanese invasion, 1942, a Japanese-sponsored home defence corps, where he received training as an officer. After **Japan**'s surrender, he joined the guerrillas in the **Indonesian War of Independence**. He rose steadily in the Indonesian Army after 1950, becoming a major general in 1962. He suppressed the coup against President **Sukarno**, 1965, and instigated an anti-communist, anti-left-wing purge in which perhaps 500,000 people died. As army chief of staff, he effectively took power on 12 March 1966, although Sukarno formally remained president until Suharto was appointed acting president, March 1967. Elected president, March 1968 and at five-yearly intervals thereafter until 1998, his 'New Order' reinvigorated the chaotic economy, curbed inflation and substantially improved living standards at the cost of engineered elections and military penetration of both the economy and government. His personal rule also tolerated the inequitable distribution of wealth and blatant corruption and family favouritism. Opposition intensified with the 1997 economic crisis and, having lost the support of the military, he resigned in May 1998. Corruption charges against him failed in 2000.

Suhrawardy, Husain Shahid (1892–1963)

Son a prominent Muslim family from Midnapore, **Bengal**, Suhrawardy was called to the Bar from Gray's Inn, and shortly after entered politics in Bengal. He was a minister in several provincial cabinets, and then chief minister of Bengal under the British Raj, 1946–7. He formed the Awami Muslim League Party in 1949, which became the **Awami League** in 1953. Joining a coalition of opposition parties, he helped defeat the **Muslim League** in 1954. Suhrawardy was law minister of **Pakistan** and then prime minister of Pakistan, 1956–7. He attempted to decrease the disparity between the two wings of the country.

Sukarno (Soekarno), Ahmed (1901–1970)

The founding father of **Indonesia**. A civil engineer educated at Bandung Technical College, he founded the Partai Nasional Indonesia (PNI), 1927. Imprisoned by the Dutch, 1929–31 and 1933–42, when he was released by the Japanese. He led a nationalist mass movement with M. Hatta during the occupation and proclaimed the independence of the Republic of Indonesia, 17 August 1945. The new republic was opposed by the Dutch in the **Indonesian War of Independence**. Power was, however, transferred to a federalist United States of Indonesia, 27 December 1949, but it was dissolved by Sukarno within months and absorbed by a unitary Republic of Indonesia under his presidency. He abandoned parliamentary democracy in favour of 'guided democracy' when the 1955 elections emphasized regional differences, threatening the integrity of the country, and proclaimed the restoration of his August 1945 presidential constitution, July 1959. In August 1960 he banned several leading political parties, and in 1963 instigated the **Indonesian 'confrontation' with Malaysia**. Narrowly surviving a coup allegedly by communists in 1965, he was deposed by **General Suharto** amidst economic and political chaos in 1967.

Sumatra

Sumatra is the largest island completely within the Indonesian jurisdiction, coming under Dutch control from the seventeenth century. It became part of an independent **Indonesia** in 1949. Unlike neighbouring **Java** which retained Hinduism, it is primarily Islamic and Buddhist in faith. The former independent Sultanate of **Aceh** occupies the northern portion of the island and was only fully reincorporated into the Republic of **Indonesia** in 1959 after a serious rebellion. Like Aceh, the coastal regions of Sumatra were devastated by the 2004 tsunami which caused tens of thousands of deaths. The exploitation of its rich timber resources in recent years has excited concern from environmentalists.

Sun Yat-sen (1866–1925)

Sun Yat-sen was leader of the revolutionary movement that overthrew the **Qing** dynasty and is regarded as the founder of modern **China**. Born in Guangzhou, he went to **Hawaii** in 1895 to study medicine. In 1899 he settled in **Japan**, where he founded the Tongmenghui (Revolutionary Alliance), and travelled around the world raising money. He also drew up his three people's principles of Chinese nationalism, democracy and people's livelihood. He helped instigate eight failed uprisings in China, but was able to return to the country after the revolution in 1911. Sun was elected provisional president of the Republic of China on 24 December 1911, although he gave up this position to Yuan Shikai, who secured the abdication of the emperor. He established the Nationalist Party in 1912, and became leader of a military government in Guangzhou in 1920. He died in Beijing, after being invited to reorganize the national government there.

Sunnis

– see also **Islam**.

The estimated 90 per cent of Muslims who follow the Sunna (habitual practice) and may be described as mainstream or orthodox Muslims. The Sunna itself, or way of the Prophet, is derived from the six canonical books of the Tradition (Hadith), which records the spoken tradition attributed to Muhammad, and authority is enshrined in sharia law, on the interpretation of which **Al-Azhar University** is supreme. Orthodox **Islam** is a religion of observance, and Muslims are expected to practise its five 'Pillars', or key duties, namely: to make the profession of faith with complete conviction at least once in one's lifetime; to observe the five daily prayers; to give alms, generously including provision for the poor; to fast during the month of Ramadan; and, if possible, to make the pilgrimage (**hajj**) to the holy city of Mecca (Makkah). Other duties include the avoidance of drinking alcohol or eating pork, and practising **jihad**. The avoidance of usury, defined as living off interest, is taken much

more seriously than in Christian countries, where there is a parallel biblical prohibition, and the concept of Islamic banking, which endeavours to pursue western banking practice without relying on interest, has been significantly developed in recent years with **Malaysia** emerging as a major centre. Islamic mortgages, which likewise seek to circumvent usury, have become common amongst Muslim immigrant communities in western Europe.

Such creative reconciliations of western and Islamic ideas are both conceptually and technically complex and the same observations apply to the concepts of democracy and nationalism. The Muslim tradition relates much more readily to achieving consensus within the *umma* (community) than it does to the competitive individualism which underpins liberal democracy, particularly in the Anglo-Saxon world, but it remains much easier to identify what Islamic political thought is against than what it is for. There has been a similar Islamic reserve, sometimes amounting to hostility, over the concept of nationalism, which can be seen as a threat to Islam as an agent of social bonding. One such critic was Sadeq al-Mahdi, a former prime minister of the Sudan, who maintained: 'The concepts of secularism, humanism, nationalism, materialism and rationalism, which are all based on partial truths, became deities in their own right; one-eyed superbeings. They are responsible for the present Euro-American spiritual crisis.' Sincerely held as such reservations may have been, the contemporary Muslim world is divided into nation states, not least because an outgrown tribalism and an as yet unrealizable unity appear to be the only alternatives. As nation states, they are being drawn into the struggle between **Shi'ite** Islam, focused on **Iran**, and Sunni Islam, funded by **Saudi Arabia** and the Gulf states, for dominance in **Syria** and **Iraq**, in which **Israel**, **Russia** and the **United States** all have a powerful interest, but which has developed a possibly uncontrollable momentum of its own. The position is further complicated by the emergence of the self-proclaimed Islamic State of Iraq and the Levant (**ISIL**). The Sunni–Shia split is the great fault line of the **Middle East**.

Surinam

The Republic of Surinam lies on the northern coast of the South American continent bordered by **Guyana**, **French Guiana**, **Brazil** and the Atlantic Ocean. Its capital, and largest city, is Paramaribo. After various attempts at settlement by the

Spanish, British, Dutch and French, Surinam became a Dutch colony in 1667 and gained its independence from the **Netherlands** in 1975. Today, Surinam is a constitutional democracy whose population is racially, ethnically, religiously and linguistically diverse.

Suu Kyi, Aung San (1945–)

Aung San Suu Kyi is the daughter of Burmese nationalist leader General Aung San. She became leader of the National League for Democracy in 1988. Despite being put under house arrest by the military dictatorship from 1989 to 2010, her party won the general election in 1990, but the result was annulled by the military junta amidst widespread international outcry. A symbol of democratic resistance, she was awarded the Nobel Peace Prize in 1991 and her National League for Democracy emerged as the largest party when the first free elections were held for a generation in 2015. A government was subsequently formed with her as deputy leader.

Swadeshi movement

The Swadeshi, or 'own country' movement was formed in **Bengal, India**, in 1905 in response to the division of the province by the viceroy, Lord Curzon, ostensibly for administrative reasons but in fact to curtail the nationalist activities of Bengalis, mainly Hindus. The movement involved protests in the form of marches and the mobilization of the population to boycott British goods. It was supported by the **Indian National Congress** and lasted, in one form or another, for three years. The British reorganized the provinces in 1912, reuniting the two parts of Bengal and moving the capital of India from **Calcutta** (Kolkata) to Delhi.

Sweden

Officially neutral parliamentary monarchy in Scandinavia which is a member of the **EU** but outside the eurozone. Sweden was in the seventeenth and eighteenth centuries a major European power though it suffered little from its decline, and in the nineteenth century it experienced strong population growth but little economic development. This in turn led to large-scale emigration to the **USA**, on the one hand, and to the emergence of a state based around agrarian attitudes to social solidarity and provision, and government intervention, on the other. The solidaristic mentality of a poor country, dependent upon support for agricultural enterprises from the centre, transferred into the urban trade unions and parliamentarians of the twentieth century, and Sweden became very much associated with Social Democracy and a practical gender

equality based on shared work. In the 1990s Sweden's oligopolistic economy faced a major challenge from the collapse of a land and credit bubble, which began a process of reorganization and modernization leading to a move towards neoliberalism, lower taxes and more individual autonomy in health and education.

Switzerland

An Alpine federal republic in the heart of Europe famed for its wealth, longevity and neutrality. Switzerland is a confederation of several major linguistic groups and is organized on the basis of twenty-six highly autonomous cantons, which are subject to varying degrees of direct democracy at cantonal and communal level. These cantons are federated under a rotating presidency and a bicameral federal parliament, and are defended by a militia and a small, specialized army. The state is a centre of international banking, and was seen for a long time as a safe haven in which any assets could be stored anonymously, and without question, though this status has recently changed, with the rise of tax treaties and agreements which allow for the disclosure of holdings. From 1815, Switzerland took no side in external conflicts, and was thus viewed as an appropriate centre for diplomacy. This was why the **League of Nations** was based there, and why many international bodies, including the **UN** and the **Red Cross**, maintain a presence there. Neutrality has, however, allowed for serious criticism and punitive law cases to be launched on behalf of those, principally in the **USA** and **Israel**, who believe that Swiss banks aided in the dispropriation of European Jews by the Nazis at the same time as facilitating Nazi transactions.

Sykes–Picot agreement

Finalized in May 1916 with the approval of the tsarist regime, the agreement concluded between **France** and **Britain** established zones of influence to be asserted after the Ottoman Empire's anticipated collapse. This secret agreement informed the principle of the eventual settlement by dividing territories seized from the **Ottoman Empire** between France and Britain. However, the map they produced differed greatly from the ultimate borders adopted in 1920. According to the agreement, **Palestine** was to become an international zone, Mosul was to be French and broad swathes of interior **Syria** were to be under indirect French influence, not the direct control that France asserted under the **mandate** system. In the lead up to negotiations with the French, British diplomats had promised **Sharif Hussein** that they would support Arab independence in what

became known as the Hussein–McMahon correspondence. The Sharif, and the rest of the world,
would be apprised of the content of the secret treaty,
and Britain's conflicting promises, when the
Bolshevik regime published the treaty in the aftermath of the October Revolution.

syndicalism

From the French *syndicalisme*, meaning 'trade unionism', the most historically significant manifestation
was anarcho-syndicalism, which advocated organization to defend workers' interests in the short term
as a preliminary to establishing non-state socialism
under workers' self-management in the longer term.
Anarcho-syndicalists argued for direct action by
workers rather than participation in party politics,
seeing the revolutionary general strike as the
means of overthrowing capitalism. Notable examples
of revolutionary syndicalism were the Confédération
Générale du Travail in France, which set out a radical
programme in its 1895 constitution, the Industrial
Workers of the World, established in the **United
States** in 1905, and the Confederación Nacional del
Trabajo (CNT) formed in **Spain** in 1910. Prominent in
the pre-1914 labour movement in **Europe** and the
Americas, anarcho-syndicalism lost ground following
the 1917 Bolshevik Revolution in **Russia**. The CNT
resisted the 1936 Spanish military rising and
instituted examples of workers' industrial self-
management and agricultural collectivization.

Syria, Republic of

The Republic of Syria is a secular parliamentary
republic which boasts a president and a secondary
ruling body, the People's Council, or Parliament.
Syria, as it is more commonly known, was formed
after the end of the **World War I**-era French mandate
in 1946, with its most current incarnation of its constitution being ratified in 1973. After 2000 the president of Syria was Bashar al-Assad, who after
inheriting the presidency upon his father's death,
was re-elected in 2007. Before Assad, his father,
Hafez al-Assad, was the nation's leader from 1971
to 2000. The 2011 uprising against Assad led to the
bloody conflict of the **Syrian Civil War**. The nation is
bordered by **Turkey**, **Iraq**, the Israeli controlled Golan
Heights, **Jordan**, **Palestine**, **Lebanon** and the
Mediterranean Sea. Occupying over 114,000 square
kilometres, Syria has a diverse geography that
includes mountains and coastal regions with fertile
lands in between. The dominant ethnic majority in
the nation is Arab, and **Islam** is the predominant
religion.

Syrian Civil War (2011–)

An ongoing conflict between the **Alawite** government of President Bashar al-Assad and its diverse
and frequently mutually hostile opponents.
It started with protests in Spring 2011, which the
government sought brutally to repress, but disorder
spread and by 2015 the government had lost control of large swathes of the country, albeit often
areas of sparse population. The revolt must be
seen in the context of the **Arab Spring**, but the
government has always maintained that it was
prompted from abroad – a position regularly denied
but given some credence by the acknowledged later
flow of funds to the rebels from the Gulf states. **Iran**
and increasingly **Russia** have given consistent
military and political support to the government,
as an ally against Salafism, and America, military
training to the rebels; but western support for them
has been compromised by its lack of coherence and
an awareness of the growing power of extremist
Islamic groups, notably **al-Qaida** and **ISIS**. The war,
which had created over 4 million refugees and
killed over 400,000 people by summer 2017, has
been increasingly subsumed in the wider **Sunni–
Shi'ite** religio-political struggle and the parallel
struggle for political influence between the West
and **Russia**.

Syrian Revolt (1925–1927)

The uprising of the **Druze** tribes of **Syria** and part
of **Lebanon** against the French administrators of
the **League of Nations mandate**. It was inspired by
the introduction by the French, but Druze-
elected, governor, Captain Carbillet, of modernizing administrative and social reforms which
went against Druze traditions and tribal hierarchy, and aggravated by the arrogant handling of
their complaints by the high commissioner,
General Maurice Sarrail. Triggered by Sarrail's
arrest and detention of Druze leaders
in July 1925, mass rebellion ensued resulting in
a victory over the French by the Druze under
Sultan al-Atrash in August 1925. They were
joined by Syrian nationalists of the People's
Party the next month. Rebellion extended to
Damascus causing the French to bomb the
city but failing to contain the rebellion's spread
into southern Lebanon. There was continued
fighting throughout 1926 with further bombing
of Damascus, but French control was largely re-
established by mid 1927. Druze isolationism
encouraged by the French thereafter to reduce
the attraction of **Arab nationalism**.

T

Taft, William Howard (1857–1930)

Twenty-seventh president of the **United States**, 1909–13. From a noted Republican family, Taft pursued a legal career until he became the first civil governor of the **Philippines**, 1901–4. After serving as secretary of war, he succeeded **Theodore Roosevelt** to the presidency but failed to continue Roosevelt's reform programmes because of his belief in a more passive presidency. He lost the 1912 race for re-election but became Chief Justice of the United States in 1921.

Tagore, Rabindranath (1861–1941)

A towering figure in Bengali literature whose poems, songs, short stories, novels and essays have immensely enriched Bengali culture. Tagore occupies a prominent place among the cultural icons of the Indian subcontinent and his poems are the national anthems of **India** and **Bangladesh**. In 1913 he was awarded the Nobel Prize in literature for his collection of poems entitled *Gitanjali* (*Song Offerings*). The news of this award startled many worldwide, and for Indians, it was a vindication of Indian culture vis-à-vis the West.

Rabindranath was born into the very prominent Tagore family and was the fourteenth child of Maharshi Debendranath Tagore. Much like Rabindranath himself, many of his siblings were artistically inclined with interests in music, theatre, literature and art. Rabindranath was not too keen on formal education and in the 1870s he returned to India without having completed his studies in England. Moving away from formalized education, he tried to make schools appealing to both boys and girls, principles that were prominent in the co-educational school he founded in rural West Bengal at Santiniketan ('Abode of Peace') in 1901. Santiniketan became Rabindranath's permanent home where he focused on promoting creative and performing arts leading to his opening of Visva Bharati University in 1921, which further fostered global cultural interchange with many programmes devoted to **China**, **Japan** and the **Middle East**.

Rabindranath was an avid traveller and soon after receiving the Nobel Prize became an international celebrity who rarely refused invitations from all parts of the world and was seen as the spokesperson for the East. While he travelled extensively in India, he also lectured in the **United States**, across **Europe**, in Japan, China, South America, **Soviet Russia** and South East Asia. This allowed him to address audiences particularly in the West at a time when very few views from **Asia** were available. Rabindranath addressed western audiences by saying that modern civilization with its attachment to power and money had to be mitigated by the spiritual wisdom of the East, and particularly after **World War I** he pointed out the evils of **nationalism** and materialism. In his worldview, it was Asia's obligation to lead the way forward toward a spiritual reawakening. Yet, his was not a wholesale repudiation of the West; instead, he tried hard to maintain the distinction between opposing western imperialism and rejecting western civilization.

Rabindranath was a strong critic of British colonial government of India. He strongly opposed the 1905 British proposal to partition Bengal into two provinces along religious lines. Following the **Amritsar Massacre** of 1919, where 379 unarmed people were gunned down, he denounced the brutality of British rule and a month later wrote to the viceroy asking to be relieved of the knighthood he had accepted four years earlier. Rabindranath's sympathy for the impoverished in rural Bengal, the source of much of his early writings, and masterly style, which revolutionized Bengali language when viewed alongside his commitment to championing human freedom, made him one of the foremost thinkers of the period.

Tahtawi, Rafi Rifa'a (1801–1873)

One of the first Egyptian scholars to attempt the reconciliation of Islamic and western concepts and values. He experienced the West as a religious teacher to Egyptian students in Paris, 1826–31. He became head of Cairo's School of Languages, 1836, then headed a bureau translating western books on geography, history and warfare, 1841, until the accession as khedive of **Abbas I**, 1848, which heralded a new distrust of western influences. Tahtawi taught that the social order with the ruler at its head was God-given. The ruler had a duty to be just and care for the well-being of the people, the only constraint being his own conscience. Such an approach reflected a significant strand of European conservative thinking including benevolent despotism and, later, **fascism**, but totally ignored the inheritance of the **Enlightenment**, particularly the rights of man.

Tai'erzhuang, Battle of (1938)

This was a conflict between Chinese and Japanese forces in 1938. In April 1938, Japanese troops began an assault on Tai'erzhuang as a prelude to attacking Xuzhou, a major railway junction. They were encircled by Chinese forces with superior numbers, and driven back. Although Xuzhou was lost later that year, this marked the first victory of the Chinese in the second **Sino-Japanese War** and was a major boost for morale.

Taino

The Tainos were Amerindians who migrated from South America to the Caribbean region. They were the first native peoples that the Spanish encountered in the New World and, in 1492, and were predominant in the Greater Antilles. Although the Tainos did not possess writing, they impressed the Spanish with their sophistication in agricultural techniques. They were unable to withstand the impact of European diseases and harsh labour regimes and had largely died out by the early seventeenth century.

Taisho (Japan)

From 1912 to 1926, under the reign of the Taisho Emperor, who had virtually no political capability, a liberal, democratic society began to take shape in Japan. The Taisho democratic movement was characterized by both economic development and social problems. The promulgation of the General Election Law and the Peace Preservation Law in 1925 signified positive changes in parliamentary politics on the one hand, but severe penalties for subversive acts on the other.

Taiwan (Formosa)

A Pacific island comprised of the main island of Taiwan, several islets and the Pescadores group. The island was originally named Formosa by the Portuguese in 1590 until the Dutch assumed full control in 1641. It relinquished its control to **China**

until 1895, when it was ceded to **Japan** after its victory in the first **Sino-Japanese War**. In 1949, the Kuomintang government fled there after the Chinese Communist Party's victory of mainland China. An independent nation, it is dominated by its relationship with mainland China.

Tal, Wasif al- (1920–1971)

Three times Jordanian prime minister, 1962–3, 1965–7 and 1970–1. A captain in the British Army during **World War II**, he fought with the Arab forces in the war against **Israel**, 1948, becoming a major in the Jordanian Army. He graduated from the American University of Beirut, entered the Jordanian civil service, rising to become chief press officer and then ambassador successively to West Germany, **Iran** and **Iraq**. He acted as defence minister during his third term as prime minister. In 1970 he forcefully repressed the Palestinian uprising in **Jordan** led by the Black September organization, a radical offshoot of the **Palestine Liberation Organization**'s **Fatah** movement. Accused by **Black September** of personally torturing and killing one of Fatah's leading field commanders, Abu Ali Lyad, he was assassinated by four Black September gunmen in the lobby of the Sheraton Hotel, Cairo, while attending an **Arab League** summit, 28 November 1971. **Yasser Arafat**, as leader of Fatah, accepted political responsibility.

Taliban

The Taliban are a militant movement that since 1994 have contended for power in **Afghanistan**. Promising a pure Islamic order and social justice, they drew their name from the Persian word for students (*taliban*) and their ranks from religious schools on the Afghanistan–**Pakistan** frontier. This collection of ethnically Pashtun students and clerics became, with Pakistani backing, a military force. They were led by a charismatic cleric, Mullah Muhammad Umar, who in April 1996 assumed the title Commander of the Faithful. His troops took Kabul in September of that year and eventually controlled 80–90 per cent of the country. They proclaimed the Islamic Emirate of Afghanistan, but only **Pakistan**, **Saudi Arabia** and the **United Arab Emirates** recognized it. Their record of human rights abuses and refusal to extradite **Osama bin Laden** led to confrontation with the **United States**, which following the **al-Qaida** attacks of 11 September 2001, invaded Afghanistan and dispersed the movement. Their leadership regrouped in Pakistan and waged a guerrilla war against the Afghan government and international forces to restore the emirate. In 2014 there was a resurgence of activity following the withdrawal of most foreign forces and parts of the country came again under Taliban control.

Tamil Nadu and Tamils

State in south-eastern **India**. Extensive agricultural production in the interior connected coastal Tamil Nadu to trading partners along the Indian Ocean littoral and beyond, at least since the first millennium BC. Chola rulers by the eleventh century unified Tamil-speaking territories, but later periods experienced political fragmentation. British, French, Dutch and Danish companies established trading houses beginning in the seventeenth century, and intervention in local wars resulted in British political supremacy by the end of the eighteenth century. In the nineteenth century Tamil labourers migrated to other British colonies, especially to Ceylon (**Sri Lanka**), South East Asia and the Caribbean. Brahmin domination of the colonial administration of the Madras Presidency engendered a non-Brahmin political backlash in the early twentieth century. Non-Brahmin identity and Tamil language has shaped politics in independent Tamil Nadu. Flows of Sri Lankan Tamil refugees and of funding from Tamils abroad have affected politics since the 1980s.

Tamil Tigers

The Liberation Tigers of Tamil Eelam, a Tamil (mainly Hindu) separatist organization established in 1976 by Velupillai Prabhakaran (1954–2009) to campaign for an independent state in north-eastern **Sri Lanka**. The majority population is Sinhalese and predominantly Buddhist. The Tigers waged a protracted and bloody armed struggle against government forces from 1983 until their eventual defeat in 2009, assassinating Sri Lankan President Ranasinghe Premadasa in 1993 and former Indian Prime Minister **Rajiv Gandhi** in 1991. Both sides were accused of human rights abuses.

Tammany Hall (USA)

Founded in 1786 as a fraternal organization, Tammany Hall became identified in the nineteenth century with New York City's Democratic Party machine. Fernando Wood's mayoral election in 1854 consolidated Tammany's control, which was sustained by its vigorous courting of the immigrant vote. Tammany's most notorious figurehead was

'Boss' William Tweed, who defrauded the city of millions of dollars between 1865 and 1871; its authority declined after Mayor James Walker was forced from office in 1932. The name is synonymous with corrupt machine politics.

Tanganyika

– see **Tanzania**.

TANU (Tanganyika African National Union)

Leading national political party in late colonial Tanganyika and independent **Tanzania**. In 1954 the Tanganyika African Association transformed into the more political TANU led by **Julius Nyerere** to advocate for independence. TANU spread across the country on a multi-ethnic and strongly nationalist platform. After campaigning for elections, TANU won 70 out of 71 seats in 1960 and in 1961 Tanganyika became independent. TANU remained the ruling party until 1977.

Tanzania

Former German and British colony in east Africa. **Germany** occupied the area, with British agreement, in the 1880s, putting down the Maji Maji revolt in 1905–7. Britain took Tanganyika as a **League of Nations** mandate in 1919. In 1952 **Julius Nyerere** founded the Tanganyika African National Union to press for British withdrawal. The country gained independence in 1961, with Nyerere as prime minister (subsequently president) of the republic. Tanganyika united with **Zanzibar** in 1964 to form Tanzania. Nyerere's 1967 **Arusha Declaration** set out his 'African Socialism' programme. War with **Uganda** in 1979 achieved **Idi Amin**'s overthrow. Nyerere's successor in 1985, Ali Hassan Mwinyi (1925–), instituted multiparty democracy and a market-oriented economy. The shift continued under Presidents Benjamin Mkapa (1938–), Jakaya Kikwete (1950–) and John Magufuli (1959–). Tanzania is largely Christian, with a significant Muslim minority. The bulk of the population is engaged in agriculture but the country has major natural resources and is an important tourist destination.

Tanzimat

– see also **Ottoman Empire**; **Midhat Pasha**.

Tanzimat, meaning 'reorganization', refers to the period of reform in the **Ottoman Empire** lasting from 1839 to 1876. The **Hatt-ı Şerif** of Gulhane, an imperial edict (*ferman*) issued by the Sultan Abdülmecid, inaugurated Tanzimat in November 1839. Reform efforts pre-date the Hatt-ı Sherif, but none attempted the systematic refurbishment of the relationship between the Ottoman state and its citizenry attempted by Tanzimat. Financial reforms were the focus of the first edict. In particular, a standardization of the tax system aimed to strengthen the state's financial and political position by replacing the tax farming system with direct taxation. The second Tanzimat declaration, **Hatt-ı Humayun** of 1856, signed in the wake of the **Crimean War**, began the second round of reforms. As with the first edict, Hatt-ı Humayun emphasized the equality of all citizens, regardless of sect. Tanzimat reforms were implemented unevenly. They were at once a progressive but destabilizing force.

Taoism
– *see* **Daoism**.

Tariff Policy (American)
Essential as sources of federal revenue in the early American republic, tariffs had been employed to protect sectors of the domestic economy from foreign competition. They often prompted great political discord, as in the **Nullification crisis** of the 1830s and the party conflict of the late 1800s. During the twentieth century the American attempt to liberalize the international economy has not prevented Congress from periodically increasing tariffs, most notably in the Smoot–Hawley Tariff (1930).

Tawfiq, Muhammad, Khedive of Egypt (Tawfik Pasha) (1852–1892)
Appointed khedive (viceroy), 1879, when **Khedive Ismail** was perceived as thwarting the interests of the Great Powers. His lack of support in **Egypt** made him dependent on political rivals, notably the army officers under **Ahmad Urabi Pasha**. The British, alarmed by the growth of anti-European sentiment in **Egypt**, tried to suppress it by bombarding **Alexandria** in July 1882, but that further increased Urabi's popularity. Tawfiq, proclaimed a traitor, was reduced to seeking British protection and the British occupied Egypt in August 1882, reinstating Tawfiq as their puppet.

Taylor, Charles McArthur Ghankay (1948–)
Liberian politician. Initially working for the post-1980 Samuel Doe government, Taylor underwent military training in **Libya**, returning to lead the National Patriotic Front in the 1989–96 Liberian

Civil War. Elected president in 1997, he was accused of war crimes and crimes against humanity during **Liberia**'s involvement in the Sierra Leone Civil War. He ceased to be president in 2003 and in 2012 was sentenced to fifty years by the Special Court for Sierra Leone.

Taylor, Zachary (1784–1850)
Twelfth president of the **United States** and a veteran of the **American War of 1812** and the **Mexican–American War**. In 1848 he won the nomination of a **Whig Party** keen to run a war hero and political unknown. A slaveholding Virginian, Taylor subsequently shocked Southerners by declaring that he would not veto the **Wilmot Proviso** and encouraging the admission of a free New Mexico and California. He died in the early stages of the **Compromise of 1850**, likely from gastroenteritis.

Tehran
Declared the capital of **Iran** by **Agha Muhammad Khan**, 1788. Although then a village, it was the site of the ancient capital of Rayy, which had been sacked by the Mongols, 1220. A township of some 15,000 by the time of Agha Khan's death, in 1797, it grew significantly under the **Pahlavi dynasty** to approaching 6 million. It was the venue for the wartime conference of 28 November–1 December 1943 – sandwiched between the two **Cairo conferences** – attended by America's President **Roosevelt**, **Britain**'s Prime Minister **Winston Churchill** and the Soviet leader **Joseph Stalin**.

Tehran conference (1943)
The Tehran conference (28 November–1 December 1943) was the first wartime meeting of **Franklin Roosevelt**, **Winston Churchill** and **Joseph Stalin**. It was agreed that the **United Nations** would be created, that a second front in **France** would be opened in 1944, and Stalin agreed to join the war against **Japan** following the defeat of **Germany**. However, few concrete decisions were made regarding post-war eastern Europe, and plans for Germany and **Poland** remained uncertain.

Tehran Embassy hostage crisis (1979–1981)
This event ensued from the seizure of the US embassy in Tehran and the capture of more than fifty Americans there by Iranian revolutionary activists, 4 November 1979, following Shah **Mohammad Reza Pahlavi**'s admission to the

United States for cancer treatment. The shah's extradition was demanded as a precondition of the release of the Americans held as hostages, but the demand was refused. A subsequent failed US helicopter rescue attempt seriously diminished President **Carter**'s domestic standing. The hostages' release was eventually negotiated in 1981.

Terror (France)

The Terror was a period of state-driven political persecution from September 1793 to July 1794. It took place during the **French Revolution**, and was in part a product of tension between **Girondin** and **Jacobin** groups, which resulted in the execution by guillotine or otherwise of more than 40,000 people. It was driven by a Committee of Public Safety, which in turn was dominated by **Maximilien Robespierre**, who fed on the conspiracism and psychological crisis of a revolutionary regime beset by powerful internal and external enemies to deliver 'justice' to anti-revolutionaries. He was aided in this by an atmosphere of mob rule, revolutionary tribunals which were strangers to due process, assassination, high bread prices and war fever. Eventually, elite fears for their own safety (the majority of Terror victims were working people) led Robespierre himself to the guillotine via a failed suicide attempt. His death inaugurated a period of relative political stability.

terrorism

A form of political action in which targeted violence is used against military or civilian populations and political leaders for a political reason by non-state groups. Terrorism rose to prominence in the latter half of the twentieth century. In its modern usage, the term is distinguished from state and criminal terror campaigns, but can be linked to the nationalist and ideological use of violence by anarchist and other groups in the nineteenth century. Terrorist techniques and strategies can be likewise distinguished. Some groups who employed bombings, assassinations and coercion to meet their ends, such as the Provisional IRA or the **Palestine Liberation Organization**, have found themselves negotiating for governmental roles with those whom they initially opposed. Others, often associated with religious causes, such as Islamism or anti-abortion protests, have drawn attention to their unwillingness to compromise and their undefeated nature, as well as to that against which they are protesting, with shootings, bombings or campaigns of intimidation. A third class, which has been associated with planned acts of mass killing, political assassination or civil

disruption but which has been characterized by the individual action of disturbed individuals, is usually not called terrorism at all.

Terrorism as an act of war in which suicide bombings against military targets are particularly used, has become something of a trope, having been employed in the **Tamil Tiger** campaign against **India** and **Sri Lanka**, as well as in Israel and the **Middle East**. One major cause of terrorism was the **Cold War**, which promoted the manufacture of large numbers of small arms and explosives in client states of the great powers. As the arms race intensified between 1960 and 1980, more and more serviceable weapons entered black markets and were exchanged for dollars acquired from global resource revenues or migration streams, leaving stockpiles available at low or falling marginal cost for those who had been affected by the totalitarian mindsets produced by Cold War ideologies, or fundamentalist reactions against them. In addition, in over a hundred global trouble spots both the **USA** and the **USSR** sponsored groups which effectively trained global mercenaries and fundamentalists in their craft without providing permanent employment. These factors, added to the anomie and alienation common to western and Japanese society, tended to produce either terrorists or terrorist movements. However, they also produced a response in states which, allied to new technologies, created in many countries a structure of surveillance in which closed-circuit TV cameras, microwave eavesdropping, extended police powers, restricted public and individual liberty and forensic financial demands became the norm. This process reached its apotheosis in the USA with the **'war on terror'** launched after eight years which began with the Oklahoma bombing of 1995 and ended with the events of 9/11. This commitment on the part of Presidents **Bush** and **Obama**, to attack organizations coordinating or employing terrorists, such as **al-Qaida** and later **ISIL**, plus any states which might have been harbouring them, was open-ended. It employed extralegal methods which verged on torture, Internment, drone aircraft and a generalized right of pre-emptive self-defence within international coalitions of the willing that skirted UN law. In that regard, terrorism in the twenty-first century could be seen as facilitating international anarchy and the globalization of fear.

Tet Offensive (Vietnam)

A military campaign launched by the People's Army of Vietnam (PAVN) and the forces of the National Front for the Liberation of South

Vietnam (NLF) on 30 January 1968. The aim was to seize strategic sites, including towns and cities, and to disable and disrupt the control systems of the government of South Vietnam (GVN), the South Vietnamese Army (ARVN) and their US military ally. A general uprising against the GVN was expected to follow. It did not; most strategic targets were quickly retaken by ARVN and US forces, and the PAVN and NLF suffered heavy losses in the fighting, which lasted into September. Nevertheless, the offensive called into question US military accounts of progress in the war. President **Lyndon Johnson** turned down requests from his commanders for substantial increases in troop numbers, and announced a partial halt in bombing as evidence of his interest in peace negotiations.

Tewodoros II (c. 1818–1868)

Emperor of **Ethiopia**, born Kassa Hailu. Taking the throne in 1855 after a struggle with feudal chiefs, Tewodoros attempted to construct a modern, non-feudal state, with an effective administration and army and a weakened church. His imprisonment of missionaries and officials provoked the despatch by **Britain** in 1867 of a punitive expedition led by General Robert Napier. Tewodoros committed suicide in the wake of his army's decisive defeat at Magdala in April 1868.

Texan War of Independence

In 1835, Mexican President **Antonio López de Santa Anna** imposed a centralist constitution that triggered revolt by the peripheral states of Coahuila and Tejas. Ethnic separatism by white, US pro-slavery settlers led to the Battle of González on 2 October 1835. Despite a Mexican victory at the **Alamo**, the war ended in 1836 with Sam Houston's forces defeating Santa Anna's army at the Battle of San Jacinto and securing Texan independence.

Texas

In the settlement with **Spain** in 1819 the **United States** gave up its claim to Texas, the north-western province of Spanish Mexico. On winning independence in 1821, **Mexico** invited Americans to settle the largely unpopulated province. When Mexico abolished slavery and adopted a centralizing constitution, the 30,000 settlers rebelled and won de facto independence at the Battle of San Jacinto in 1836. But Mexico would not recognize it, **Native American** tribes warred on the new state, and the United States refused annexation. After a decade of independence, strained by war and large debts, Texas

again requested annexation, stressing that the alternative was British protection. The issue divided American opinion, many Northerners objecting to the annexation of a slave state, but the narrow victory of James K. Polk in 1844 sealed the issue. Texas joined the Union in May 1845, but ever since has taken pride in its status as the only US state to have once enjoyed independent power.

Thailand

The Kingdom of Thailand is located in South East Asia, bordering Myanmar (**Burma**) to the west, **Laos** and **Cambodia** to the east and **Malaysia** to the south. It has a total area of 514,000 square kilometres and a population nearing 70 million. Thailand's geography includes mountainous areas in the north and south, river delta plains in the centre and a plateau in the north-east. The country has a tropical climate and is influenced by both north-east and south-west monsoons. Thailand is the only country in South East Asia to remain independent from European imperialism throughout its history. It was traditionally an absolute monarchy, but a bloodless revolution in 1932 transformed it to a constitutional monarchy that remained a major unifying force during the long reign of King Bhumipol from 1946 to 2016. However, political instability resulted in nineteen coups or attempted coups between 1932 and 2016. The majority of the population is Buddhist, with a minority of Muslims concentrated mostly in the far south, where there is an insurgency movement, and also near Bangladesh.

Thant, U (1909–1974)

The third secretary general of the **United Nations**, 1961–71. U Thant, from **Burma** (Myanmar), was also the first Asian to hold this key position. While serving, he played an important role in diplomatic negotiations over the **Cuban Missile Crisis** and the conclusion of the Congolese Civil War, and deployed peace-keeping troops to **Cyprus**.

Thatcher, Margaret (1926–2013)

A chemist, barrister and politician. Margaret Thatcher became the first female leader of the British Conservative Party in 1975 and the first woman prime minister of the **United Kingdom** in May 1979. She was associated with the philosophy of 'Thatcherism', though in fact many conservative and libertarian thinkers had been involved in that body of ideas, which combined a low tax philosophy of relative economic liberalism or libertarianism with conservative social moralism. Thatcher also defined herself as a fierce opponent of socialism and Keynesianism, which she saw as agents of national decline, and sought during her ten and a half years and three election victories to challenge the power of trade unionists, progressive social theorists and those who believed in compromise and conciliation over confrontation and argument in diplomacy.

Though she began as a supporter of the European Economic Community (the Common Market), and campaigned for British membership of the organization in the 1975 national referendum (and also pushed through supranational powers for the European Commission in the 1986 Single European Act), she became a fierce critic of the European Community, which she saw as embodying the economic lassitude and corporatism that she rejected domestically, as well as undermining the nation state. Previously, she had seen it as a free-market antidote to British trade unionism and inefficiency and a spur to the liberalization of continental markets.

Thatcher became Britain's first successful war leader since **Churchill** after the **Falklands War** of 1982 transformed her from the most unpopular prime minister since records began to the herald of national rebirth (a role she came to believe in with disastrous personal results for her leadership and relations with colleagues) and weathered a world recession in 1980–1, the year-long 1984 miners' strike of the sort that brought down her predecessor Edward Heath, the 1987 stock market crash and unemployment of 4 million to win a record three election victories (1979, 1983 and 1987). She also sold off most of Britain's nationalized industries under her 'privatization' policy, ended exchange controls to boost the City of London's financial markets in 1979, sold state-provided rental housing controlled by local councils to residents, and encouraged a culture of mortgage-driven credit, car driving and small business as a way of reinvigorating the country.

Despite these achievements, or possibly because of them, she became increasingly out of touch with her party and neglected her political colleagues in Cabinet and the House of Commons, often only acknowledging them to antagonize them with argument. In her first and second administrations she relied heavily on the emollient skills of her deputy, William Whitelaw, but even he could not prevent the resignation of her defence secretary, Michael Heseltine, in 1986, whose challenge to

her leadership over the subsequent four years eventually brought about her downfall. She also lost her chancellor, Nigel Lawson, and eventually her deputy, Geoffrey Howe. This final loss, combined with losses in critical by-elections, an economic collapse which affected the housing market, and the rise of the opposition Labour Party to political contention, forced her resignation in 1990, though the actual cue was a victory by less than the required majority in a leadership election caused by the Heseltine challenge.

Margaret Thatcher continued in politics as a not necessarily benign influence on her successor, John Major, whom she promoted to stop Heseltine. Major found his administration assailed by Thatcherites who accused him of being too 'pro-European', not Atlanticist enough, weak in the Bosnian crisis, too conciliatory and incapable of firm, Thatcher-style leadership. Thatcher was closely associated with these views. She withdrew to a lucrative career of lecturing in the **United States**, but was severely weakened by two strokes. Deeply unpopular in the north of England's former industrial communities, Scotland and Wales but equally as popular in the south of England and amongst aspirational voters, the shadow of which profile helps to explain the geography of Conservative Party performance in the 1990s and early twenty-first century.

Thiers, Louis Adolphe (1797–1877)

French politician who wrote a ten-volume *History of the Revolution* and established the newspaper, *Le National*, opposing the rule of **Charles X**. Premier under **Louis Philippe**. A patriot loyal only to himself, he was the model for Balzac's Rastignac and was described by Lamartine as a 'weathercock'. He argued for early negotiations with the Germans, 1870–1, and was elected 'head of the provisional government of the French Republic'. He maintained he was 'a monarchist who practises the Republic', ruthlessly suppressing the **Paris Commune** in 1871. He lost the presidential election of 1873.

Thieu, Nguyen Van (1923–2001)

President of South **Vietnam**, 1967–75. Thieu helped lead the military coup that overthrew President **Ngo Dinh Diem** in 1963, after which he served as the ceremonial head of state for Prime Minister Nguyen Cao Ky's government. He became executive president of South Vietnam, but fled to **Taiwan** when Saigon was captured by northern troops in

1975. He later relocated to Boston, **USA**, where he remained until his death.

Third Reich

An alternative name for Nazi Germany from 1933 to 1945, the Third Reich first emerged in German nationalist circles in the 1920s. The 'First Reich' was the medieval German empire of Frederick Barbarossa; the Second, the **German Empire** brought into being by **Otto von Bismarck** in 1871, which perished in 1918. **Hitler** used the term infrequently, preferring '**Germany**', but with greater consistency during **World War II**. The Third Reich was also a term favoured by the Allies as a description of their principal enemy in the world war, and has survived in popular speech, especially in English-speaking countries.

Adolf Hitler's *reich* or empire was never based on any consistent legal principle, nor was it ever formally established. The Nazis themselves were brought to power under the **Weimar Republic**, which was suspended after the Reichstag fire in favour of a permanent state of emergency. Nevertheless, a sort of structure can be discerned, especially after the Nuremberg laws of 1936 attempted to set out the rules under which Hitler's racist state pretended to operate. The first and most striking feature of the Reich was the absolute primacy as president, chancellor, party leader, commander in chief and ultimately simply 'fuhrer' or leader, of Adolf Hitler. The German armed forces swore personal allegiance to him; the Nazi state ultimately reflected in large part his approaches and wishes. Though the historians' quarrel has established a degree of disagreement over the extent of his primacy and the functionality of German culture for the purposes of dictatorship, there is no disagreement about Hitler's public primacy.

Beneath Hitler, administrative chaos reigned. Various quasi-independent groups such as the **SS** were in effect a state within a state, plotting racial empires far beyond the borders of Germany. Semi-legal bodies and institutional husks such as the German Central Bank and the Foreign Office were in effect in competition with personal offices of the deputy fuhrer, the **Nazi** party, most ministries and coordinating agencies. The army leadership and its associated intelligence and security departments were also quasi-autonomous, as was the navy (the Luftwaffe having emerged fully under the Nazis was the most thoroughly Nazi force). The army in particular also contained the bulk of the aristocratic leadership of **Prussia**, the old Junker groups, and after 1934 exerted control over the **SA** storm troopers as well.

Despite this administrative confusion, however, certain consistent and developing policies were evident. One was the fierce and constantly escalating **anti-Semitism** of the Nazi regime. On coming into power in 1933, and with great emphasis after 1934, the Nazis systematically excluded Jews from professional life, educational and welfare establishments and German cultural organizations. The Nazis initially perpetrated low-level physical oppression of Jewish groups, and public rhetoric was bitterly anti-Jewish. From Kristallnacht, November 1938 onwards, Nazi violence towards those Jews who had not been able to emigrate massively increased. Jewish shops, stores and services were attacked, and Jewish people publicly humiliated; they were sent in greater numbers to ghettoes and prison camps; and some Nazis began contemplating a 'final solution' to the 'Jewish problem'. On the outbreak of war, for which Hitler particularly and publicly blamed Jews and communists, anti-Jewish policies increased, leading ultimately (especially given the German invasion of areas with large numbers of eastern European Jews) to the 'death camps' of the **Holocaust**.

A second theme was the extreme blend of state-sponsored monopoly capitalism and controlled labour with which the Nazis engineered an economic boom and rearmament and oppression of communists, homosexuals and dissidents. The Nazi state was under-manned in this regard, and depended upon ordinary Germans to 'denounce' enemies of the state, which they did in great numbers. This fidelity in part was achieved by appeals to German nationalism and racist sensibilities, by oppressive policing and by appeals to a traditional culture of order and hierarchy. For this reason Nazis were, paradoxically, under the most pressure in urban Berlin and to a lesser extent in other cities, where the semblance of a free press and economic mobility were maintained by behind-the-scenes coordination of resources and intimidation of editors.

The Nazi state was also perhaps the culmination (or the depth) of nineteenth-century attempts to meld scientific methods and insights with unsupported ideas of race, perversions of **Darwinism** and contrarian science. Never quite intruding into 'flat earth' ideas, these attempts sometimes proved productive (as in rocket and jet science, and the discovery of a link between cancer and smoking tobacco) but at other times utterly wasteful (as in research into 'field theory' rather than 'Jewish' particle physics, SS expeditions to Tibet to find the 'Aryan' birthplace, or cataloguing of supposed racial physiognomies). The Third Reich was a paradox in another sense as well; a highly conservative state which wished to see women with 'children, church and cooking', was also one in which professional women were more evident than they were in many other western states and which upheld the idea of fast cars and motorways as much as *Lebensraum* and Germanic philosophy. It was a state which could 'scientifically' murder thousands of 'defective' less able children until public outrage stopped it from doing so in 1938, and at the same time organize an increasingly pagan and 'Germanic' Reich church harking back to pre-medieval forest religions.

In wartime the Third Reich accelerated to an institutional apotheosis. It became a state of ghettoes and death camps, oppressive security, lunatic racial schemes and militarism, which was unprecedented and remains unparalleled. By 1945 it had been reduced to the bunker in Berlin wherein Adolf Hitler committed suicide to escape advancing Allied armies. Though the German state passed to Admiral Doenitz before accepting its defeat, surrender and de-Nazification, the Reich as such died with him.

Third Republic (French)

The Third Republic, which was to be to date the longest lasting of **France**'s five republican regimes, began in 1871. Its birth took place in the rubble of twin defeats, both of France at the hands of **Prussia** and of the **Paris Commune**, the shadow from which the conservative, rural and somewhat anti-Parisian imperial and parliamentary republic which emerged never quite shook off. The state only rejected monarchy in a referendum in 1877, for example, and experimented with highly conservative systems of election between 1885 and 1889. The Assembly of the regime, too, maintained seats for the lost provinces of Alsace and Lorraine until its fall at the hands of the Nazi invasion in 1940. The republic, dominated by rural and extrametropolitan figures, kept Parisien radicalism at bay, and, though it encouraged a dizzying number of governments, gave weight to the conservative figures who typically staffed them through their different iterations and not to aspirant national saviours or radical parties. The regime was culturally split, between urban and non-urban, Catholic and Republican, and imperial and domestic concerns. These splits broke into the open in matters as diverse as the **Dreyfus Affair**, the **Panama scandal**

and the revanchism which led to **World War I**, before a sense of national exhaustion, division and collapse fell upon France's political class. Though by 1940 the Republic had survived one great war and proved able to lose more casualties in six months against the German Army than America had lost in the whole **Vietnam War**, the state collapsed into three. One segment fled to England to nurture its vision of an independent and liberated France under **de Gaulle**; one operated a collaborationist regime at Vichy; and one eventually and uneasily located itself in French North Africa, under Admiral Darlan. After Darlan's death, and the later victory in which de Gaulle participated, the Republic was restored and swiftly replaced by a short-lived **Fourth Republic**, its splits apparently replaced by new ones which brought it down in the Algerian crisis of 1958.

The period of the Third Republic spanned some of the greatest events in French history, and is associated with ministerial figures such as **Clemenceau**, Gambetta, **Blum, Laval, Pétain** and **de Gaulle**, as well as a cultural efflorescence that has rarely been matched, though oddly, its figurehead presidents have largely been forgotten or are remembered only in scandals. It was in this period that Paris was briefly (in 1919) acknowledged as 'the Capital of the World', during the Versailles conference, and the cultural centre of **Europe** between 1890 and 1930.

third world

The 'third world' was identified by Alfred Sauvy in 1952 as the area comprising those states which were decolonizing or independent but which were not associated with the western or communist blocs during the Cold War. It is generally taken to have applied to Africa and Asia outside the Middle East. The term initially conveyed a sense of suppressed potential, but came to refer to areas that were economically underdeveloped. Some academic theories, such as the Harrod–Domar model, were adapted, and some, such as the Prebisch–Singer hypothesis, the Rostow Model and the Lewis Model, were adapted to explain how the third world could either develop or become stuck as a resource provider for the rich, but by 1980 the term was increasingly falling out of use. Instead, terms referring to specific regions, the pace of industrialization, or the geographical nature of dependency came into vogue, before themselves being displaced by the effects of **globalization**.

Threshold Test Ban Treaty (1974)

The Threshold Test Ban Treaty – formally the Treaty on the Limitation of Underground Nuclear Weapon Tests – was signed by the **USA** and the **USSR** on July 1974 but was not ratified by either party until December 1990. The treaty prohibits the underground testing of nuclear weapons with a yield in excess of 150 kilotons. This mutual restraint limits signatories' ability to increase the explosive potential of nuclear weapons beyond that range.

Tiananmen Square

This square is a public space of approximately a single square kilometre, located at the centre of the Chinese capital Beijing. 'Tiananmen' means 'Gate of Heavenly Peace' and refers to the front entrance to the Forbidden City complex. The square was built in its present form in 1958 on the orders of the Chinese **Communist Party**, which wished to create an open space in clear contrast with the close-knit buildings that marked the pre-modern Chinese city. In 1989 it became the scene of large popular demonstrations by workers and students, about a million strong at their height, which were eventually put down by troops, resulting in many deaths.

Tianjin, Treaties of

The Tianjin Treaties were signed between **China** and **Great Britain**, **Russia**, **USA** and **France** in 1858 and 1859 after the defeat of China by the British in the second **Opium War**. The terms included the most favoured nation clause, which guaranteed all powers equal rights in treaty ports. Four new treaty ports were opened along the Yangtze River, while Christian teaching was protected and foreigners were granted the right to travel in China.

Tibbu Tip (*c.* 1840–1905)

A central figure in the economic and political life of late nineteenth-century East Africa. Born to a trading family in **Zanzibar** around 1840, he made his first journey to Ujiji with his father when still a teenager. He conducted a lucrative trade in ivory and slaves in the region to the west of Lake Tanganyika in what is now the Democratic Republic of **Congo**, using the wealth he accumulated and also firearms to impose himself politically – the name 'Tibbu Tip' is commonly said to refer to the sound of gunfire. As European power and ambition in the region increased, he found himself competing with Europeans to ensure the continued supply of ivory to Zanzibar. With the

establishment of Congo Free State, he first accepted a governorship, then in 1890 retired to Zanzibar where he died, leaving behind an autobiographical account of his life.

Tibet

An autonomous region of **Asia** to the north of the Himalayas surrounded entirely by mountains and the source of some of Asia's largest rivers. Ruled by Buddhist lamas since the seventh century, Tibet was conquered by the Mongols in the thirteenth century and the Manchus in the eighteenth century. **China** reasserted its authority over Tibet in 1951 but only gained full control after suppressing a revolt in 1959, during which the **Dalai Lama** sought refuge in **India**. Recent decades have seen a massive influ of native Chinese into Tibet. The principal religion is Tibetan Buddhism. Many of Tibet's monasteries and shrines were destroyed in multiple unsuccessful attempts to change its national culture and consciousness.

Tibet, Chinese Invasion of

China invaded **Tibet** after the establishment of the People's Republic of China in 1949. Its failure to adhere to or uphold the Seventeen Point Agreement, which guaranteed that China would not alter Tibet's political, cultural and religious institutions, led to the March 1959 uprising in Lhasa. The people of Lhasa called for the Chinese to leave, marking the beginning of the uprising and leading to a harsh crackdown by the Chinese government.

Tientsin, Treaties of

– *see* **Tianjin, Treaties of**.

Tierra del Fuego

Archipelago separated from the South American mainland by the Strait of Magellan. A Boundary Treaty in 1881 divided the territory between **Argentina** and **Chile**. Its indigenous peoples were decimated by disease and slaughtered by settlers and gold-seekers in the 1880s. Tierra del Fuego's main economic activities include oil and natural gas, sheep ranching, tourism and light industry. Ushuaia (Argentina) and Puerto Williams (Chile) both claim to be the world's southernmost city.

Tijaniyya

Founded by Ahmad al-Tijani (d. 1815, **Morocco**), this 'reformist' Islamic Sufi order was introduced into West Africa by the *jihad* state of Al-Hajj Umar Tall (d. 1864). In the twentieth century its piety (*fayda*) spread rapidly particularly through the teachings of Ibrahim Niasse of **Senegal** (d. 1975). It is also widespread in North Africa and is now found in many other Muslim regions. Uniquely, its members cannot join other Sufi orders.

Timor Este
– *see* **East Timor**.

Tipu Sultan (1750–1799)
The ruler from 1783 until his death of the southern Indian state of Mysore, founded in 1761 by his father Haidar Ali. He and his father distinguished themselves among eighteenth-century Indian rulers for their decisive steps to stem British expansion: the defeat of Mysore came only after four wars. Internally, Tipu sought to eliminate the privileges of various scribal, commercial and agrarian intermediary groups. He asserted firm control over mercantile groups while also providing opportunities for them to prosper, and established efficient revenue collection directly from the peasantry. With well-organized infantry and artillery forces added to the traditional cavalry, in the 1780s Mysore nearly expelled the **East India Company** from Madras. Tipu Sultan shrewdly, though ultimately fruitlessly, sought diplomatic alliances with the great powers of peninsular **India**, the Marathas and the Nizam of Hyderabad, and with the French. His determined resistance to the Company earned him British denunciation as the archetypal 'oriental despot'. In the end, the fall of Mysore was wrought not only by greater British economic resources but also by help to the Company from intermediary groups within Mysore that Tipu's policies had alienated. Tipu Sultan died defending his capital, Seringapatam, during the fourth and final Anglo-Mysore War.

Tirailleurs Sénégalais
A corps of colonial infantry in the French Army recruited from French West Africa. Translated as 'skirmishers', the all-African regiment was first formed in 1857 in **Senegal**. The forces provided hundreds of thousands of troops in both **World War I** and **World War II** and in numerous colonial wars and counter-insurgencies. During World War II thousands were killed and interned in German camps, and after the war protests erupted over unfair pay, discrimination and mistreatment and many joined nationalist movements.

Tito (Josip Broz) (1892–1980)
Born Josip Broz. Secretary general of the Yugoslav Communist Party, 1939–80. Famous Partisan guerrilla leader, 1941–5, he served as prime minister, 1945–53, when he determinedly put national interests before those of the **Soviet Union**, leading to the break with **Stalin** in 1948. A pioneer, with **Nasser** and **Nehru**, of active non-alignment internationally and of direct worker management at home, he tragically failed, however, to bequeath a **Yugoslavia** strong enough to resist internal nationalisms once his own authority and charisma had been removed.

tobacco
Tobacco rivals cotton as the world's most important non-food crop. Native to the Americas and long cultivated by Amerindians, the commercial production and global distribution of tobacco was an important component of Atlantic colonialism. In the seventeenth century tobacco plantations were successfully established in the Caribbean and Chesapeake area to meet growing European demand for pipe smoking and snuff. Commercial tobacco production spread to much of **Latin America**. Nineteenth-century tobacco consumption and production was supported by the expansion of hand-rolled cigars and the commercial production of chew. Most important was the mechanized production of cheap cigarettes. Industrial companies such as the American Tobacco Company (1890) mass-produced cigarettes and used modern methods of advertising to promote smoking. By 1950 half of all tobacco was consumed in the form of a cigarette, and the **USA** was the largest grower and producer. Research in the 1960s linked smoking to cancer, and western demand for tobacco began to drop precipitously in the 1970s. It has, however, increased in the developing world.

Tobacco Regie (Iran)
The fifty-year monopoly concession granted in 1890 to the British firm, Talbot, by **Nasir od-Din Shah Qajar** on the purchase, sale and processing of all tobacco in **Iran**, 1890. The imperial grant, facilitated by the shah's personal corruption, provoked rioting, an uprising and an unusually effective nationwide boycott of the sale and use of tobacco, backed up by a fatwa in which even the shah's own wives participated. The tripartite organizers of the protests – a small number of radical westernized intellectuals, merchants in the bazaars (*bazaris*) exposed to foreign economic competition and the

Shi'ite *ulama* with their links to the traditionalist majority – represented the same popular alliance as was to generate the revolutions first of 1905–11 and then of 1978–9. Merchants feared in particular that the tobacco concession might act as a precedent for other profitable areas of trade, and the unrest caused the concession to be withdrawn by the shah, 1892.

Tocqueville, Alexis de (1805–1859)

French politician and writer, whose *Democracy in America* (published in two volumes, 1835–40) testified to the new egalitarian political society developing in the former colony. Tocqueville argued that American democracy was characterized by an equality of condition that would become the model for European polities. Whilst Tocqueville admired America's democratic egalitarianism, he feared for the atomizing individualism that might proceed from the demise of traditional hierarchies that mediate between individuals and the state. Tocqueville's writings remain influential in the disciplines of sociology and political science.

Tokugawa era (Japan)

The last feudal era in Japan (1603–1867), in which the Tokugawa family established indirect control of domains and an inflexible caste system comprising four classes (samurai warriors, farmers, artisans and merchants). Whilst the Tokugawa shogunate provided the rules of society and the court of appeal, *daimio* (feudal lords) with regional administrative power paid homage to the shogun and left hostages in the capital, Edo. Tokugawa Japan adopted the policy of national seclusion which restricted foreign trade and contact: Christianity was totally banned as a subversive religion. Tokugawa's success in maintaining peace led to growth of the national economy and of urban cities such as Edo, Osaka and Kyoto, but the heavy taxation imposed by *daimio* and financial difficulties caused social unrest and uprisings of peasants in the eighteenth century. The late Tokugawa period witnessed the dissolution of Tokugawa governance, which failed to resist insurgent forces in southern Japan and a foreign threat.

Tonghak Rebellion (1893–1894) (Korea)

This rebellion was one of the largest peasant rebellions in Korean history that lasted from early 1893 to December 1894. Inspired by Tonghak (Eastern Learning), which was a nativist religion founded by Ch'oe Cheu in the early 1860s, peasants sought to achieve economic security and to expel foreigners, especially the Japanese, who threatened Korea's independence. Though peasants had successfully battled government troops, a combined fighting force of Japanese and Korean troops finally put an end to the rebellion.

Tonkin

The northernmost part of **Vietnam**. Tonkin is located in the fertile delta of the Red River, west of the Gulf of Tonkin. It is also the former name of Hanoi, which had been the capital of Vietnam since the seventh century. Tonkin became a protectorate of **France** in 1884 and part of French **Indochina** in 1887. It later became an important base for **Viet Minh** forces during the **Vietnam War**.

Tonkin Gulf Resolution

Passed by US Congress on 7 August 1964 in response to two reported attacks on US vessels by North Vietnamese torpedo boats in the Gulf of Tonkin. The second attack is now thought not to have occurred. The resolution approved 'all necessary measures' to repel and prevent attacks on **USA** forces in South East Asia. It was subsequently cited as a legal authority for the **Vietnam War**. The resolution was repealed in 1971.

Tortuga (Île de la Tortue, Isla de la Tortuga)

Located off the north-west coast of **Haiti**, opposite Port-de-Paix. The island covers an area of 180 square kilometres. The name in both French and Spanish means 'Turtle Island' or 'Tortoise Island' because its shape resembles a sea-tortoise. This island was a major centre for Caribbean piracy in the seventeenth century.

torture

– see also **abolition**.

Any act causing pain, whether physical or psychological, which is intentionally inflicted on a person as a means of intimidation, coercion, punishment, information gathering, or as a tool to control groups, particularly religious and political groups, seen as threats by governments. Torture is almost universally considered to be an extreme violation of **human rights**, and most countries have signed up to the treaties expressly forbidding the practice (**Geneva Convention** and UN Convention Against Torture). Many countries do not abide by these treaties.

totalitarianism

A political system which seeks to explain, control and reform every aspect of existence and which recognizes no distinction between the private, the personal and the public but which rather views all things through a founding idea. The term developed in the Hegelian idealism of Italian fascist thinkers such as Giovanni Gentile in the 1920s, and was then promoted as the operating principle of fascist doctrine in 1932. It was adopted by Hannah Arendt in 1951 in her study of the Nazi and Communist regimes, and was used throughout the subsequent **Cold War** to describe both forms of government. It is a curiosity of the term that, after **Mussolini**, it was more used by its liberal and democratic opponents than by those who were held to practise it.

Totalitarian regimes hold that it is not enough for citizens to agree or comply with the state; rather, they must demonstrate that they have internalized and identified with the truth which totalitarians claim their ideology embodies. Often, this truth is presented as a simple or brutal one which can be adapted to explain any event in life – class or race struggle, or war, or the immutability and liberating quality of violence, or hierarchy, or cupidity and self-interest, for example. Once dedicated to the central insight, the state then proceeds to force all potential counterbalances in civil society, such as churches, academies, guilds, vocations or indeed any autonomous organization, to either assimilate or disappear. Occasionally, as in **North Korea**'s putative tolerance for religion, the outer form of the assimilated organization was left intact to serve state purposes so long as absolute loyalty is demonstrated. More often, as in Communist Budapest, churches were closed or destroyed and society 'regeared' through technology, ritual, parades, the destruction of the family and universal surveillance. No institution can be left untouched, and in particular popular forms of entertainment or diversion are often diverted into demonstrations of the principles of, and superiority implicit in, the system. Despite this, there have been different manifestations of totalitarian regimes, which have been characterized either by the personal rule of a dictator, a junta or a party.

The term is intimately connected with modernist and futurist ideas in art, in that it merges a convention-shattering, radical approach with what is often the expert use of propaganda, social manipulation and mass communication. Unsurprisingly, it has proved difficult to establish and maintain, and in the twentieth century only really caught hold where previous institutions (including the armed forces and the nation) had been deeply weakened by war, inflation, famine, disease or any combination thereof. Equally, liberals in the twentieth century took to lauding

'dissidents', who were people who were certain enough in their own beliefs that they remained distant from the immanence of totalitarian ones. Such people were often imprisoned and tortured whilst attempts were made to re-educate them, often to no avail. It was this determination to try to force agreement, above all, which distinguishes authoritarians from totalitarians.

tourism

Tourism is the name given to the practice of visiting different places for the purposes of rest, relaxation and edification. It is intimately associated with the development of the idea of the holiday, or leisure time, during the Industrial Revolution, and with the emergence of mass forms of transport which could move people to, and return them from, new destinations quite quickly. Tourism has evolved with the spread of incomes. For instance, the first tourists, in the early modern period, were European aristocrats who, as a part of their education, would undertake a Grand Tour around **Europe** as young men, travelling with a minimum of servants and moving through the great cities and sights of the Continent. As a middle class emerged in the early nineteenth century, trips to the seaside or to spa towns to bathe in the waters during the summer season created an attendant network of industries and infrastructure, such as hotels, piers, railway stations and entertainments which provided employment and income for coastal towns. Concurrently, a few cities and places in the south of **France** or New England, such as Biarritz, attracted celebrities and the richer middle classes to a more sophisticated type of holiday. Finally, the integration of railways, hotels and even steamships by the likes of Isambard Kingdom Brunel allowed the extension of tourism to the working class.

In the twentieth century this pattern of travel, visiting a foreign location and returning within a period mandated by statute or offered by employers as holiday time was extended by **globalization**, but not overtly changed. However, the control of tourism, and the earnings from it, did become areas of political and cultural contention. The **USSR** tourist organization, which provided guides, itineraries and facilities for foreign tourists, became one of the most extensive in history between 1929 and 1991, spreading its bureaux and representatives across the world and earning huge amounts of foreign capital for the Soviets. In Fascist Italy, the Dopolavoro, an after-work recreational club, sought to win over workers from the Socialist and

Christian clubs which had emerged, and later, the Nazi Party established the Strength Through Joy Organization (KdF) on the Dopolavoro model. The KdF became one of the biggest domestic tourist agencies ever, moving workers and the middle classes around **Germany** and on cruises with the aim of legitimizing the regime's dominance of the work place and civil society with the reward of relaxing, regime-organized recreation. Tourism thus meshed with propaganda, much in the same way that movements of people for work or immigration had meshed with Christian urban reform influences to provide the network of Young Mens' Christian Associations which sprang up globally, offering hostels for travellers, in the nineteenth and twentieth centuries.

By the later twentieth century tourism had become a very valuable source of foreign capital and investment for developing countries. However, it also became a worry, as it tended to encourage the development of air travel, motor infrastructure and hotels which in turn brought pollution, despoliation and liberal moral values to areas of already great social inequality, orienting economies towards the pleasure of foreigners and the pickings from their spending. Sex tourism became of major concern in such countries as **Thailand**. At the turn of the twenty-first century this process had in some cases become associated with the growth of unsustainable debt in some countries, and was a check on the industrial or urban development of tourist areas, as well as a cause of dependency and the distortion of terms of trade.

Touré, Ahmed Sékou (1922–1984)

Trade union leader and first president of independent **Guinea**. Born into the Mandinka community, Touré worked in the postal service and quickly became involved in labour unions. In 1952 he became the leader of the Guinean Democratic Party and advocated for the decolonization of **Africa**. In 1956 he organized a regional trade union across French West Africa and was elected to represent Guinea in the French National Assembly. His most famous saying, 'We prefer poverty in liberty to riches in slavery', referred to his decision to demand immediate independence and leave the French community in 1958. As president, he adopted a Marxist policy of nationalization and instituted a one-party state in Guinea. He often invoked his lineage to **Samori**, who mounted a great military resistance against French colonialism in the nineteenth century. Touré remained in power until his death.

Toussaint Louverture, François Dominique (1743–1803)

Born a slave in French Saint-Domingue, Toussaint Louverture acquired a limited education and free status before a massive slave revolution engulfed this plantation society in 1791. He joined the uprising and quickly became one of its leading military commanders. A passionate advocate for independence and opponent of slavery, he became the de facto dictator of the colony, a position he held in the face of political turmoil in **France**, foreign invasions from **Great Britain** and **Spain**, and intractable divisions within the colony's racial castes. In the end, Toussaint's deliberate steps towards independence, his efforts to consolidate and perpetuate his hold on power, and the rise of **Napoleon** in France proved to be his undoing. In 1802 he surrendered to a French expeditionary army. He was taken to France where he died in prison, months before the new nation of **Haiti** achieved independence.

Townshend Acts (UK)

The Townshend Acts, adopted by Parliament on 29 June 1767, introduced a series of customs duties for the American colonies including taxes on wine, porcelain, lead, glass and tea. The duties would be collected by an American Board of Customs Commissioners, which would be paid for with the revenue generated by the duties. Americans, who drew on the experience acquired during the **Stamp Act** crisis, revived the Sons of Liberty and immediately protested against the duties. A series of prolonged boycotts eventually led to their repeal in March 1770.

trade (Atlantic)

The term 'Atlantic world' was coined by scholars to refer to the four continents bordering the Atlantic Ocean: **Europe**, **Africa**, **North America** and **South America**. Historians of the Atlantic world focus mainly on the regions nearest the Atlantic Ocean, namely western Europe, West Africa, the eastern coast of North America (from Newfoundland south to Florida), the Caribbean islands, **Central America** and the eastern coast of South America, particularly **Brazil**. There was little contact between western Europe and West Africa until the mid fifteenth century, and there was almost no contact between the Old World, Europe and Africa, and the Americas, or New World, before Christopher Columbus and his crew invaded the Caribbean in 1492. Trade within the Atlantic world can be said to have started on a large scale with the colonization of the New World by the Europeans, and in particular after they created commercial agricultural enterprises and started the transatlantic trade in Africans. But it is important to remember that the indigenous peoples on all sides of the Atlantic had their own intra-regional trade; and while not on a large and regular scale, contact between Africa, **Asia** and the Americas had been established long before the fifteenth-century European voyages of discovery. Before the establishment of an international commercial system that connected the Americas to Europe, there were trading links among the territories of the South Atlantic system, such as indigenous long-distance trade and communication throughout the region. For example, the Incas of **Peru** traded in products such as cacao with the Aztecs of **Mexico**. Trade links to South America and, to a much lesser extent, Central America, were set up from time to time. Conquest destabilized some of these indigenous lines of trade and exchange and replaced them with new ones.

The enslavement of Africans on American plantations allowed Europeans to extract profit, which in turn was central to the development and continuation of trade in the Atlantic world. It transformed the Atlantic into a complex trading area, turning it into the centre of the international economy especially during the eighteenth and nineteenth centuries, with Caribbean products destined more for external than for local and regional markets. As Europeans explored and conquered the Caribbean and American mainland, they created new economic and social systems so as to subdue the indigenous peoples to produce commercial crops that could be sold in Europe, and to mine the mineral wealth of the North American and South American continents. These enterprises required a system of organized labour. Europeans tried three labour systems: indigenous labour under the *encomienda* system, white indentured servitude, and the large-scale enslavement of Africans. The dramatic indigenous population loss that resulted from colonization, the eventual racism that deemed it inappropriate to exploit white, but not black, labourers in colonial societies, as well as the ready supply of forced African labour caused a shift towards the system of black chattel slavery by the end of the seventeenth century. Indeed, over the entire period of the transatlantic slave trade, perhaps as many as 15 million Africans were forced to migrate to the Americas, the majority from West Africa.

The Iberians (first the Portuguese and then the Spanish) pioneered the large-scale trade in Africans via the Atlantic Ocean. The Spanish in Hispaniola (present-day **Haiti** and **Dominican Republic**) imported enslaved Africans for their properties as early as 1510 and later used them on the mainland. The Portuguese exported African captives to work plantations in Brazil. Other European colonists followed their example, especially as coffee and sugar cultivation spread across the region. Once formalized, European commerce in enslaved Africans rapidly expanded. The volume of the trade at the various import points in the Atlantic islands and the Americas increased from less than 300,000 between 1451 and 1600 to nearly 1.5 million between 1601 and 1700. The Spanish American colonies received about 27 per cent of the total transatlantic trade before 1600, with Brazil getting 18 per cent. For the entire seventeenth century, Spanish America received nearly 22 per cent of the volume, with Brazil getting nearly 42 per cent, reflecting the growing importance of the sugar revolution there. But the volume of the trade had expanded so much that the 22 per cent that the Spanish Americas received during the seventeenth century almost equalled the number of the previous half-century.

Without African enslaved peoples and the transatlantic trade, Europeans would never have been able to realize such large profits from Africa, the Atlantic islands, the Caribbean and the Americas. They purchased large numbers of Africans, shipped them via the Middle Passage, mobilized them into gangs to work plantations and exported the fruits of their labour to Europe. Indeed, firm and enduring trade links between Europe and America were not forged until the introduction of slavery. Trade, especially transnational trade, was central to the development and sustenance of the Atlantic world during slavery. 'The continuous and varied activity in international trade, the sophisticated markets in foreign exchange, and the wide assortment of business done by international bankers were all symptomatic of an economic life which transcended national boundaries as a matter of routine,' says the economic historian William Ashworth in confirming the existence of an international economy (discernible in the Atlantic world) before 1850. Through trading links, the constituent parts of the geographic zone that made up the Atlantic world introduced hitherto unfamiliar products into each other's social space.

Several sectors of the economy reflected the enormously increased trade. Shipping expanded, with thousands of ships crossing the Atlantic, even after European nations, starting with Denmark in 1792, made the slave trade illegal. To supply these ships, a wide range of goods had to be provided. No other type of trade could equal the broad-based economic stimulus of the

European trade in Africans; and to ensure that the status quo continued, economic laws were devised and implemented to prevent imperial competition and discourage any other line of trade. Indeed, from the seventeenth century, Europeans tried to control the volume and direction of trade, creating virtually exclusionary economic zones in the Atlantic world and directing the bulk of what was produced towards the export market. To ensure the efficient transfer of wealth from colonies to their metropoles, European powers attempted to partition the Caribbean into exclusive economic zones and established bilateral trading arrangements with their colonies. To effect such a bilateral trade, **Britain**, like the French through the *exclusif*, worked out a strategy. They embraced and attempted to enforce the tenets of **mercantilism**. The underlying ideology of mercantilism was that colonies were primarily sources of supply for the metropole; that foreign trade could be made to serve the interests of government, who would in turn ensure that it facilitated this process, usually through imperialism and imperial ideologies.

In turn, colonies were expected to import their necessities from the `mother country'. Imperial self-sufficiency was the goal desired by this 'mutual' commerce and thus such valuable possessions required strict commercial control; one which would effectively exclude foreign trade. Between 1651 and 1660 the English, for example, devised **Navigation Acts** to impose such control. By these Acts, staple produce from the Caribbean colonies – sugar, rum, molasses, indigo, pimento, ginger and coffee – were to be carried in English ships. Some degree of peacetime trade was allowed between the English and foreign colonies in several commodities, but these did not qualify as 'staple produce'. Ships were to be manned by a majority of British crewmen and goods consigned solely to English ports. The French and Spanish had similar commercial restrictions.

Despite these mercantile laws, international (as opposed to intra-imperial) trade within the Atlantic was not eliminated entirely; and not all commodities produced in the colonies were destined for the extra-regional markets in Europe. Slavery and the plantation system also had a catalytic function in the emergence of internal marketing systems in different territories and in the linking of the disparate Caribbean and wider American territories through the intra-regional trade. The making of an integrated market culture in the Atlantic has particularly overshadowed the study of intra-Caribbean trading links before and after the conquest. Any understanding of trade in the larger Atlantic world must take greater cognizance of intra-American labour mobilization and resource exchange that operated within the panoramic context of what the historian Immanuel Wallerstein has described as the world system. For example, by the mid to late sixteenth century a recognizable trade had developed, as indigenes were traded for food to sustain emerging Spanish colonial settlements. The quantitative dimensions of this 'Indian slave trade' have not been measured accurately, but estimates for the period 1527–49 for **Nicaragua** alone range from 100,000 to 500,000. Inter-regional trade from an early period took place in other commodities, and the large numbers of ships that transported goods from one part of the region to the other led Ruggiero Romano to describe the region as an 'American Mediterranean'. Cocoa from **Venezuela** to Mexico, livestock between Cuba and Santo Domingo, and grain from Mexico to **Cuba** established at an early date a busy network of trading links which continued throughout the entire period of Spanish domination. In the British and Spanish Caribbean, those who produced the commodities to supply the needs of this intra-regional trade were primarily non-elite whites and free people of colour who were not wealthy enough to invest in the export production of commodities.

Internal markets and local industries also emerged. Most colonies produced 'clay' sugar and distilled rum; and while most of these products were exported, the islands consumed about 15 per cent of their output of rum, sugar and molasses. **Jamaica** provides a good example of the ways in which internal markets functioned and intra-regional trading links were maintained. The island's colonial economy was diversified and led not only to the availability of a wider range of export crops, but also to the emergence of non-staple producers who traded their goods on the domestic market. Anthropologists Sidney Mintz and Douglas Hall have shown that enslaved people maximized the surplus from their provision grounds and through huckstering, helped to sustain the markets in the island and enlarge the sphere of domestic economic activities. But white settlers and free coloured property holders also traded with each other (using cash or kind as payment), sustaining a domestic trade in sugar, coffee, food provisions, meat, livestock and other products. The livestock farms, which were known as pens (mostly dominated by whites), played a large role in the internal commodity trade in Jamaica. They were thus engaged in three levels of exchange: export of commodities, primarily `minor staples', and various woods; domestic trade in provisions and livestock in which money was used as a medium of exchange; and a type of informal, non-monetary exchange of commodities with other properties.

Plantation inputs that were not produced and traded internally were outsourced not only to the metropole, but to North and South Atlantic sections of the Americas. As many historians have argued, the development of capitalist export agriculture severely limited the production of food crops for internal consumption. Further, the export-led nature of Caribbean economies, that is, the production of staples (primary, resource-intensive products) stifled the domestic sector and limited the successful production of plantation inputs locally. Had most of the Caribbean colonies been able (or willing) to produce a suitable supply of food and livestock – bulky items (relative to value) that are not only expensive to transport but are perishable, and thus maintain a strong comparative advantage in the production of its own supplies, the import of these items might not have been necessary.

As it happened, such inputs had to be outsourced. Many were therefore dependent on regional suppliers such as the North American colonies, especially the English colonies in what later became the **United States of America**, both before and after the War of Independence. Trade between the West Indies and North America was vital, for without a steady flow of food and lumber the prosperity of the plantations with their thousands of slaves would have been impossible. In the seventeenth century England and **Ireland** at first furnished the greater part of the corn, salt, meat, cheese and butter they consumed. It took English mercantilists a long time to see that the sugar colonies and Pennsylvania, New York and New England were as dependent on each other as 'belly and members', that without the Caribbean trade North Americans would be unable to accumulate capital for economic expansion or for settling their adverse trade balance with the mother country. The Caribbean, in fact, dominated New England's exports. This is not surprising: New England had well-developed trading links with most parts of the **British Empire** by the mid eighteenth century, importing manufactures from Britain and tropical foodstuffs from the Caribbean and exporting in turn a variety of goods including whale products, livestock, fish and building and packaging materials. This international trade was a solution to the chronic trade deficits New Englanders faced with Britain.

The development and maintenance of intra-Caribbean trading links, for example between Jamaica and the Spanish Caribbean, also emerged. The trade between Jamaica (English after 1655) and the Spanish Caribbean may seem surprising in an age of mercantilism and during the existence of the English Navigation Acts. But the restrictive mercantilist policies under the Restoration so contrasted with the virtual free trade of Cromwell's day during which the Spanish trade to Jamaica had developed, that such laws were virtually ignored. In spite of Britain's efforts to implement the Navigation Acts, the importance of the Spanish trade to Jamaica had been long recognized and moves had been made to legalize it. **Spain** had consistently refused to sanction any such freedom of trade. Nevertheless, successive governors from the time of Modyford encouraged a contraband Anglo-Spanish trade, granting licences to traders to sell enslaved Africans and commodities to Spanish America and to import livestock. Spain did not reciprocate by granting similar licences. On the contrary, the illegal nature of the trade was emphasized in the Anglo-Spanish Treaty of Madrid in 1670, article 8 of which stated: 'Subjects of the King of Great Britain shall on no account direct their commerce or undertake navigation to the ports or places which the Catholic King holds in the said Indies, nor trade with them. Reciprocally, the subjects of the King of Spain shall not sail to or trade in the places that are possessed there by the King of Great Britain.' However, articles 9, 10 and 11 opened up certain loopholes, which were fully exploited and facilitated the continuation of the smuggling trade. These provided that if for any reasons – whether pirate attacks, storm or revictualling – ships of either nation found it necessary to enter the other's ports, such ships should be allowed. Furthermore, it was stated that if in the future 'either king shall deem it convenient to grant any general or special license or any privileges to the subjects of the other for navigating and trading ... the said navigation and commerce shall be practiced and maintained'.

The passing of the Free Port Act of 1766, however, further opened up Spanish trading to Jamaica. It sanctioned a branch of colonial trade that had hitherto been conducted in a clandestine manner, facilitating the importation and exportation of certain types of goods at certain ports in the British West Indies by small vessels from neighbouring 'foreign' colonies. This did not, however, represent a departure from the Navigation Acts, which still attempted to control the trade of staple commodities and English manufactures. The Free

Port Act was designed to allow only trade in goods which did not compete with the products of Britain and her colonies. The trade in African captives, North American supplies and the carrying trade between the mother country and her colonies remained firmly in British hands. In Jamaica, Lucea, Savanna-la-mar, Kingston and Montego Bay were declared free ports in 1776 and with the passing of the Act and the opening up of ports other than Kingston, the Spanish trade with Jamaica was revived. Moreover, the trade remained illegal from the Spanish perspective.

It should, perhaps, be noted that the South Atlantic system was able to maintain trading links with the Caribbean in products such as labour, cattle, **cotton**, animal hides and tortoise shells because, while certain sections (Brazil and coastal Venezuela, as well as the US South) produced staple crops for export to Europe, for the most part they successfully developed independent subsistence agriculture and a livestock industry and were less dependent on the two-way trade with Europe. Part of this was because, as economic historians have shown, the Iberian powers were never able to absorb fully Latin American products in the same way that England was unable to absorb fully the exports of the Mainland Colonies, especially New England. Regional markets (and trade with 'foreign' powers) played a more crucial role in **Latin America**'s economic development. They were forced to view their economic relationships in even more regional terms than did the plantation colonies of the Caribbean.

Trade continued even where the Spanish recaptured some of the territories that had passed to Britain, as the case of links between Jamaica and coastal settlements in Central America, San Andrés and Providencia, demonstrates. Jamaica and the Colombian islands of San Andrés and Providencia (originally Santa Catalina) developed trading relations from the eighteenth century. Indeed, well into the twentieth century there was limited economic and cultural interaction between the islands and **Colombia**. Their inhabitants have largely been descended from planters and enslaved people from Jamaica and other western Caribbean territories. In 1835 an English visitor to Providencia reported that 30,000 pounds of cotton and 170 pounds of shell were traded annually to Jamaica for English goods such as calicoes and cloths. Trade with Jamaica (even though these islands only became free ports in the twentieth century) and Latin America facilitated the development of the maritime industry in Providencia. Providencia fishermen traded along the coastal areas of **Honduras**,

Nicaragua, **Costa Rica**, **Panama**, the Cayman Islands and the Colombian port city of Cartagena. Costa Ricans tended to be better connected to the commercial networks of the Atlantic coast of Central America and the Caribbean rather than to the international capitalist markets of Europe. Trade led to marital ties, emigration and permanent settlement of men from Providencia in places such as Corn Island, Bluefields, Puerto Limón, Bocas del Toro, Colón, Grand Cayman, Cayman Brack islands and Jamaica.

The links between San Andrés and Jamaica developed along a similar trajectory as Providencia. Cotton was the mainstay of the economy from the 1620s to 1853, after which coconut exports took over (1853–1953). But trade was mainly with the USA. Early settlers, mainly from Jamaica, were involved in the extraction of wood, the planting of cotton using enslaved labour, and the export of turtles.

The impact of long-distance voyages on livestock vital to the productive aspects of the sugar industry and the inability of plantation colonies to maintain significant herds, also opened up a market for working stock with Spanish American suppliers. Within the British Caribbean export-led economies, only Jamaica developed what could be categorized as a 'domestic sector', shaped by the demands of the major staple, sugar. But, as in **Barbados**, Nevis, **St Kitts** and **Antigua**, the commitment to sugar prevented lands eminently suitable for livestock to be put into this product, making import vital, giving rise to internal controversies between the livestock and sugar sectors (where they were distinct). The island attempted to supply its own livestock needs by maintaining a significant number of pens; despite their efforts, pen keepers and planter/pen owners were never able to supply the total livestock needs of the island during slavery. The Spanish, who could undersell local producers, picked up the slack. Spanish cattle, horses and mules were generally about a third to a half the price of local breeds. From 1794 to 1845 the principal suppliers of livestock from Spanish America to Jamaica were Chagres, Rio de la Hacha, Coro and Santo Domingo. Modern authors also indicate that Puerto Rico participated in this trade along with the Spanish Main.

trade cycles

The idea that the economy manifests cyclical behaviour which can be identified and predicted has a long provenance, having been suggested by the astronomer Herschel in 1800, and by Sismondi in 1819. Over subsequent years, **Robert Owen**,

Clement Jugler, William Jevons, **Karl Marx**, Joseph Schumpeter, the Rothschild family, Kuznets, Kondratiev, Raymond Wheeler, Alexander Chizvesky, Hyman Minsky, Robert Elliot and **Milton Friedman**, amongst others, have assumed or put forward specific forms of cycle. Cycles – beginning with growth, then boom, then recession, then recovery – have been a specific feature of the modern world since the **French Revolution**. The nineteenth century in particular was characterized by a very great number of financial panics (for instance in 1825, 1837, 1857, 1873 and 1893), which marked the end of economic booms. In the twentieth century the **Great Depression** and post-war business markets in the West all demonstrated elements of cyclical behaviour. As a consequence, Keynesian economic theorists in particular developed ideas of counter-cyclical spending and saving to smooth out fluctuations in gross domestic product. A division exists within the economic and political community between those who believe that the cause of cycles is exogenous, and those who believe that cyclical change is an inbuilt feature of markets. Secondary differences arise over the length of cycles, with variations having been established in a range between Kondratiev's fifty-four years, Kuznet's eighteen years, the Rothschilds' fourteen-year consol cycle, a twelve-year solar cycle and the seven to eleven years for the business cycle established by Jugler.

The mechanism that gives rise to cycles has been disputed. Early astronomers and economists saw a link between solar cycles, wheat harvests and the behaviour of populations, with political change and crashes following on poor food supply. Others have identified loose fiscal and monetary policy causing interest rates to decouple from prudence, leading to over-production and over-consumption, whilst Keynesians have tended to think of excess savings as causing depressions and aggregate demand increases as giving rise to reflation and recovery. In financial markets a variety of cycles, including Elliot's intersecting temporal functions of the Fibonacci sequence (the Elliot wave), have been mooted but never properly explained. Longer-term waves and cycles have been associated with the development, spread and exhaustion of particular technologies such as the Kuznet's and Kondratiev waves, and the inability to expand the supply of land to meet demand for it (a feature of Henry George's models).

The significance of the distinction of mechanisms lies in the consequences for public policy. If markets are implicitly stable, for instance, but prone to outside shock, then policy should be geared to controlling outside influences such as interest rates, money supply and supply-side flexibility. On the other hand, if markets are implicitly unstable, then counter-cyclical policy, government control and economic management are appropriate. Some schools blend elements; in the 2008 crisis, for instance, many formerly monetarist, exogenous-shock economists called for bailouts and bank rescues to preserve the clearing system. Austrian economists also tend to welcome periodic collapses as ways of purging the system, returning interest rates to 'proper' levels, whilst encouraging 'creative destruction' and the growth of new business.

trade unionism

The practice of workers banding together in labour organizations to negotiate with employers and provide mutual support. Initially developed by skilled workers in **Europe** and later North America, **industrialization** led to larger-scale organizations for semi-skilled and unskilled workers, leading ultimately to national confederations to represent and defend their interests in national politics. The earliest trade unions developed in eighteenth-century England and the word *strike* dates from the 1760s when trade disputes rippled through London. Distinct from medieval guilds, early craft unions sought to regulate apprenticeships and maintain wage rates amongst skilled groups such as printers, tailors and shipwrights. The British government's attempt to outlaw trade unions through the **Combination Laws** failed to prevent their growth and they were substantially legalized after 1825 though still subject to legal action over taking oaths or in conducting strikes. Trade unions spread amongst both traditional and newer textile workers facing the onset of new machinery and trade liberalization; organizations of workmen lay behind the Luddite attacks and mounted strikes in Regency England. By the early 1830s the Grand National Consolidated Trade Union claimed a million members and the first **general strike** was called in northern England in 1842 in support of a Chartist petition for democratic rights by a wide range of early industrial workers.

Although Napoleonic France outlawed trade unions, they soon sprang up, playing a significant part in the revolutionary outbreaks in Paris in 1830 and 1848 and mounting a large-scale revolt of silk workers in Lyons in 1834. In the **United States** in 1869, the **Knights of Labor** were formed to represent different groups of workers and in Britain the Trades Union Congress (TUC) was formed in 1868, initially to represent workers' organizations seeking clarification of the legal position of unions but eventually providing a significant coordinating body for organized labour. The first nationwide Dutch organization of workers dates from 1871 and in 1898 Belgian workers formed a socialist Syndical Committee. The American Federation of Labour (AFL) was founded by thirteen craft unions in 1886 and had expanded to over 1.5 million workers by 1904, while the growth in union membership among dockers, miners and other unskilled and semi-skilled workers in Britain increased TUC membership to over 4 million by 1914, mirrored in **Germany** by rapid union growth to the largest membership in Europe.

Union growth and effectiveness were characterized, however, by religious, ideological, gender and skill differences, which often restricted their effectiveness. Spanish trade unionism was split between the anarcho-syndicalist National Confederation of Labour (CNT), formed in 1911 and the largest group until 1939 when it was suppressed by **Franco**, and the socialist General Union of Workers (UGT), dating from 1882. The Dutch set up rival Protestant, Catholic and 'neutral' labour organizations to combat socialist labour organizations. In **France**, the General Confederation of Labour (CGT), formed in 1895, split in 1921 with the setting up of a rival communist organization (the CGTU). In Great Britain, the TUC was instrumental in setting up the gradualist Labour Party in 1901 along with moderate socialist intellectuals from the **Fabians**, giving it direct access to parliamentary politics, a moderate character and over 8 million members by 1920. The similarly moderate American AFL rose to 3.25 million members in the same year, outstripping militant socialist groups such as the **Industrial Workers of the World (Wobblies)**. In 1935, however, it was challenged by the formation of the more militant and politicized Congress of Industrial Organizations (CIO), reaching 5 million members by 1943 especially through the unionization of mass assembly workers, though the two movements merged in 1955.

Broadly speaking, the moderate trade union movements of **Europe**, North America and **Australia** learned to live within a capitalist framework, negotiating the best deals they could for their members and eschewing more militant positions. The British TUC was forced into a humiliating retreat after the general strike of 1926 and turned increasingly to improving workers' positions through the Labour Party and traditional wage bargaining. In America, union support for the

Democratic Party and opposition to both **communism** and organized crime made them an accepted feature of American industry, though unionization remained lower than in many European countries. In totalitarian states such as Fascist Italy and Nazi **Germany**, independent trade unions were forcibly dissolved and workers organized within state-sponsored organizations. Similarly, the **Soviet Union** subsumed within the organs of the Communist Party the former role of the trade unions in tsarist **Russia**.

In the post-**World War II** era moderate trade unionism coexisted with liberal democracies, often flourishing as service and white collar workers were unionized. Attempts were made to recreate western-style trade unions in **Japan**, though they largely failed to displace employer loyalty to their own industrial enterprise. Anti-imperial movements often had their origins in trade union organization, seen for example in the Caribbean, which saw its first unions formed early in **Trinidad** (1897) and **Jamaica** (1898) and witnessed a series of labour revolts in the 1930s. Similarly, in Poland, **Solidarity**'s call for 'free' trade unions was one of the rallying cries of the democratic movements which led eastern Europe out of Soviet control. In contrast, neoliberal criticism of 'union power' for creating rigidities in the market, inhibiting growth, combined with new technology such as robotics and information technology, deindustrialization and the effects of **globalization**, have tended to reduce union numbers and influence in both Europe and America. Elsewhere, emerging industrial superpowers such as **India** and **China** represent distinctive traditions. China relies on the Communist Party for the needs of workers and has no 'free' unions in the western sense. India, on the other hand, has a long history of trade unionism stretching back to the nineteenth century, with strong union representation in some states and some sectors of industry, such as textiles.

Trafalgar campaign (1803–1805)

A naval engagement between British and allied French and Spanish forces that began in May 1803 following the collapse of the Peace of Amiens. In the most famous battle, British forces under the command of Admiral **Horatio Nelson** met the Franco-Spanish fleet near Cape Trafalgar on 21 October 1805. The Battle of Trafalgar marked a decisive victory for the British and ended **Napoleon**'s plans for an invasion of southern England. The French defeat secured British maritime supremacy.

Transcendentalism

American **Romantic** philosophy of the 1830s–1850s that drew on an eclectic mixture of European and Asian writings to hold that personal intuition could 'transcend' received wisdom, logic and experience to discover universal truths in the human conscience. Originating in Concord, Massachusetts, through Ralph Waldo Emerson's dissatisfaction with **Unitarianism**, the movement attracted such luminaries as Henry David Thoreau, Margaret Fuller and Orestes Brownson. Its criticism of the established social order lent itself to a range of reform impulses.

transhumance

– *see* **nomadism (Middle East)**.

Transjordan

– *see* **Jordan, Hashemite Kingdom of**.

transnational history

Traditional focus upon national history or alternatively global trends leaves an important gap in the history of regions or themes which cross national boundaries but do not fit a truly global context. Early examples include studies of whole regions such as those by **Braudel** of the Mediterranean world, aiming to convey the experience of a geographically defined area rather than one bounded by state boundaries or a particular ideology. Analogies can be found in studies of the Eurasian Steppe, the Irish Sea `world', the Indian Ocean, the Caribbean and the Pacific Rim. Similarly, many issues have been studied across national boundaries, such as slavery, migration, gender relations, childhood and religious and cultural movements and beliefs. For the modern period the latter has included studies such as those of the **Enlightenment** by Jonathan Israel, R. R. Palmer's studies of the `age of the democratic revolution' and Jane Randall's studies of the rise of feminism in North America and Europe. Transnational non-governmental organizations (NGOs) such as Médicins Sans Frontières, War Resisters International and Global Vision play an increasingly important role.

transportation

In the early eighteenth century personal transport on land meant, as it long had, either walking, riding a horse, donkey or mule, or being carried, normally in a cart or carriage but for the rich possibly in a sedan chair. Personal transport by sea meant, again as it long had, travel by sailing ship. Goods transport was similarly traditional:

the donkey panier, the packhorse, or the horse or ox-drawn cart, and the cargo ship for sea-borne goods. River transport was sometimes an option but much circumscribed by the many natural obstacles. The sledge or sleigh was another possibility for the cold winters of northern, central and eastern Europe. Transport was remarkably expensive, extremely slow and often dangerous, whether from a bolting horse, a storm at sea or from brigands. It was also extremely uncomfortable. For all these reasons, personal transport for the great majority meant walking to the next village or market town and back in a day. Nevertheless, sea-borne transport had long been highly developed.

1750–1820

Change came with the work of two Scotsmen, Thomas Telford (1757–1834) and John Loudon Macadam (1756–1836). Telford constructed Britain's first roads since Roman times to have solid foundations, good drainage and a firm slightly curved surface. The Shrewsbury–Holyhead road along north Wales with the Menai Suspension Bridge at its end is his masterpiece. Macadam invented the system of road surfacing with 'tar macadam', which is still in use today and which made road building cheaper because it only needed a 12-inch (30-centimetre) layer of small stones to provide an adequate base. The work of the two men meant that a wheeled vehicle could henceforth travel as fast as a horse could pull it and foreigners were agreed that **Britain** had the best system of roads in **Europe**. However limited by later standards, this was a vast advance on the previous situation when, for example, the Flying Coach had advertised in 1754 that 'however incredible it may appear, this coach will actually (barring accidents) arrive in London in four days and a half after leaving Manchester'. The journey was some 183 miles (295 kilometres).

The invention of the macademized road was rapidly exploited by private companies, which levied tolls for the use of the improved road, or turnpike, introducing the golden age of the stagecoach. Coach services ran from London to Scotland and to Holyhead for **Ireland**. However much the road had been improved, though, the speed of the coach was limited to that of the horse, some 12 miles an hour. Nevertheless that was fast enough to permit the birth of longer-distance London commuting. Gentlemen began to travel the 50 miles (80 kilometres) from fashionable

Brighton to London by the morning coach to do business before returning by the evening coach. It was also fast enough to permit the introduction of Britain's first efficient national postal service. Mail coaches left the General Post Office in London for all parts of the country and travelled to strict timetables with the accuracy later attributed to the Swiss Railways clock. Innkeepers who failed to meet the tight schedules for changing horses were subjected to financial penalties. Nevertheless, despite the romance it was later to enjoy, coach travel remained slow, expensive and extremely uncomfortable. Large leather overboots stuffed with straw were employed in an attempt to keep out the piercing cold of an unheated coach in winter, but the thickest of travelling cloaks worn by 'outside' travellers, who were in the majority, became waterlogged in wet weather.

Goods or freight transport was similarly revolutionized, at least in western Europe, over the same period. The French had actually built the first of the great modern canals, the 150-mile (240 kilometre) Canal du Midi, between Toulouse and the Étang de Thau on the Mediterranean, in the second half of the seventeenth century, but the first stirrings of the Industrial Revolution provoked a wave of canal building in Britain, primarily to transport coal. It is the Duke of Bridgewater who was called the 'father of inland navigation' but it was the uneducated James Brindley (1716–72) who actually built the Duke of Bridgewater's canal of 1759–61, its extension to the Mersey and the Grand Trunk Canal. In Scotland, the Firth and Clyde Canal opened in 1790 and work started on the Caledonian Canal in 1803. The Grand Junction Canal, built 1793–1805, linked London with Oxford and the English Midlands. These canals were remarkable feats of engineering with their own aqueducts and tunnels, but most of them had serious limitations. The barge had to be pulled by a horse on a towpath and most canals were, therefore, small. In some tunnels, including Brindley's own 2,800-yard (2,560-metre) tunnel at Harecastle, there was no towpath and 'leggers' were employed to propel the barges by pushing with their feet against the wall. In some other cases, such as the Wey and Arun Canal designed to link Portsmouth with London, annual rainfall proved too low to keep the canal reliably full of water.

For such reasons, most canals could no more compete with the future railways than could the stagecoach, but they played an invaluable role in facilitating Britain's Industrial Revolution. Perhaps their most significant indirect impact was the stimulus they gave to the expansion of Britain's

ports. The programme of modern dock construction which was to make London the biggest port in the world, started with the construction of the West India Dock in 1802. Shipping remained, as yet, traditional, although there were attempts to apply the new technology of the atmospheric steam engine developed by Thomas Newcomen. Jonathan Hull designed a steamboat with a paddle-wheel, 1737, but experimental steamships were actually built in France on the River Saône, in Scotland, and in the **United States** in the 1780s. An atmospheric steam engine powered the *Charlotte Dundas* which sailed on the Forth–Clyde Canal, 1801–3, Henry Bell inaugurated a daily steamship service on the Clyde in 1812 and William Denny's *Rob Roy* began a regular steam service between Glasgow and Belfast in 1818. All were paddle-ships built of wood.

1820–1870

Shipping remained a pioneer. The first iron steamship, the *Aaron Manby*, sailed from London across the Channel and up the River Seine to Paris, 1822. The first efficient screw propellers were invented by the Briton, Sir Francis Pettit-Smith, and a Swedish engineer, Captain John Ericsson, 1836. The revolutionary change, however, was on land, and it was the emergence of the steam railway locomotive as an efficient form of traction. The concept of the railway was not in itself new. Small handcarts running on parallel planks had been used in mining districts since the sixteenth century and wooden rails had been laid at some English collieries at the beginning of the seventeenth century. Such colliery tramways, using horse haulage, were common by 1700. It was not until 1768–1771, however, that Richard Reynolds of the Coalbrookdale ironworks introduced the cast-iron rail to replace wood. Although such horse-drawn industrial railways had become common in Britain by 1800, they remained rare elsewhere in Europe. The steam locomotive appeared in 1801 when Richard Trevithick invented the first steam-powered vehicle to carry a passenger, and 1804 saw the first application of steam power to rail transport when a Trevithick locomotive ran on an industrial line at Penydarren in south Wales, hauling 10 tons of iron and seventy men along 9 miles (14.5 kilometres) of track. He caused something of a sensation in London in 1808 by demonstrating his *Catch-Me-Who-Can* locomotive on a circular track in Euston Square at a shilling a ride.

Increasingly successful locomotives for colliery haulage were built, including William Headley's

Puffing Billy of 1813. Although Trevithick (1771–1833) must be considered the inventor of the steam locomotive, it is **George Stephenson** (1781–1848) who was the father of the railway age. Together with his son, Robert (1803–59), he built *Locomotion* for the Stockton and Darlington Railway, opened in 1825 as Britain and the world's first steam-hauled passenger railway, although some horses were still used. His greatest achievement was the *Rocket*, which won the Rainhill Trials for the new Liverpool and Manchester Railway in 1829 with the unparalleled speed of 30 miles (48 kilometres) an hour. The Liverpool and Manchester Railway opened in 1830 as the world's first line to use steam alone, and the Great Western, from London to Bristol, and the London to Birmingham soon followed. Two thousand miles (3,218 kilometres) of railway were brought into operation in Britain by the first railway boom of 1836–7 alone. Turner's famous painting, *Rain, Steam and Speed, The Great Western Railway*, of 1844 captures the sheer physical excitement of the early Railway Age. Continental Europe quickly followed with the first line in **France** (Lyon–St Etienne) opening in 1832, in Bavaria (Nuremberg–Fürth) in 1835 and in **Belgium** (Brussels–Antwerp) in 1835–6. The emerging Belgian network radiated from Brussels, and in **Prussia**, Cologne and Berlin became long-distance railway centres. **Russia**'s first line, linking St Petersburg with the royal resort of Tsarskoe Selo (15 miles/24 kilometres) distant, opened in 1837. Political uncertainty retarded the construction of a French network, however, before 1842.

The impact of the railways on transportation can hardly be exaggerated. The speed of the railway put the stagecoaches out of business within a decade and the inns that had served them fell into neglect. The new railways were, however, as socially conservative as the world into which they had been born. They had little interest in transporting the poor, and third-class coaches were open trucks with benches and were often omitted from trains altogether. This contrasted with the plush and spacious accommodation in first class, but even in second class the coaches, although covered, had open sides and wooden bench seats. This situation was ameliorated in Britain by an Act of Parliament of 1844 which required all British railways (which then included the Irish) to operate at least one train a day in which the 'lower orders' could travel for one penny (1d) per mile in covered accommodation at an average speed of not less than 12 miles (19 kilometres) an hour. 'Covered accommodation', however, often still meant only enclosed goods vans with bench seats.

Speeds were meanwhile increasing at a remarkable rate. By 1845 express trains were running from London Paddington to Exeter in four and a half hours at an average speed of 46¾ miles (75 kilometres) per hour. By 1847, the 53 miles (85 kilometres) from London Paddington to Didcot were being covered at an average speed of 58 miles (93 kilometres) per hour – five times the speed of the fastest stagecoach. This potential led to an explosion in railway building in Britain and across Europe. Britain's 'railway mania' of 1844–8 expanded the network to 5,000 miles (8,046 kilometres) in 1848. There were nevertheless significant differences in approach between Britain and many continental European states. Britain's railways were built by a large number of private companies, who only had to seek parliamentary powers. The consequence was an unusually dense but poorly coordinated network. In Belgium and Prussia, however, railways were state enterprises from the beginning. Belgium welcomed them as instruments of national unification after independence in 1830. France struck a middle course of laying down the routes of future trunk lines by law and of providing that railways should be built by private enterprise in association with the state. The government defrayed the cost of the infrastructure while the private sector provided the track, signalling, stations and rolling stock. The capital expenditure on railways in 1848 was 955 million francs of which 331 million had been contributed by the state. By 1857, 9,320 miles (15,000 kilometres) of track had been laid, and the number of companies reduced under government pressure to six, each serving a major geographical region. This logical and efficient structure remains clearly visible today. A further railway law of 1859 guaranteed investors their interest payable on new lines, and by 1870 the network reached nearly 11,184 miles (18,000 kilometres). European-wide, railways expanded both rapidly and steadily: 1,700 miles (2735 kilometres) by 1840, 14,500 miles (23,335 kilometres) by 1850, 31,900 miles (51,338 kilometres) by 1860, 63,300 miles (101,871 kilometres) by 1870 and 101,700 (163,670 kilometres) by 1880. Everywhere the impact on the transportation of freight was as significant as on passenger transport. Ports such as Antwerp, Hamburg and Le Havre expanded rapidly. Many rural lines were built primarily to move fresh agricultural produce to market, with passengers a very minor consideration. The stimulus to engineering was no less remarkable. **Austria**'s Südbahn (Southern Railway) crossed the Semmering Pass at almost 3,000 feet to link Vienna with Trieste as early as 1854. The 7½-mile (12-kilometre) Mont Cenis Tunnel piercing the Alps to link Lyon and Turin opened in 1871, having been begun in 1857.

The USA's first passenger-carrying railway (railroad) company, the Baltimore and Ohio, was incorporated in 1827 and began operation in 1830. By 1849, 3,328 miles (5,355 kilometres) of railway track had been laid, 9,000 miles (14,484 kilometres) by 1850, and over 35,000 (56,327 kilometres) by 1865. Owned by different private companies with different gauges, the railways had dramatic effects in opening up the American frontier to settlement and establishing the United States as a truly 'continental' power 'from sea to sea'. The first transcontinental line was completed when the Union Pacific and Central Pacific lines were connected in Utah in 1869. The network reached its maximum of 254,000 miles (408,773 kilometres) in 1916, but began to retreat thereafter as motor cars and road freight began to eat into profits. A similar process of unification was achieved in **Canada** by the completion of the Canadian Pacific Railway (CPR), constructed in 1881–5 and overcoming even greater engineering obstacles than in the United States, followed by the Canadian National Railway (CNR) in 1922, running from Halifax Nova Scotia on the North Atlantic in the east to Vancouver on the Pacific in the west. One of the other great railway systems largely completed during the nineteenth century was in **India**, where over 37,000 miles (59,545 kilometres) of track had been constructed by 1924, linking most of its major cities and ports and reaching into the frontier district of the North-West Frontier.

The substitution of steam for sail and of iron for wood in shipping advanced much more slowly. As late as 1847 British steamships had a total tonnage of 116,000 out of the 3 million tons of the merchant navy as a whole. In 1871, 51 per cent of the world's shipping capacity was still under sail. The fastest sailing ships, the tea clippers, were, at the peak of their fame in around 1870, taking an average of 110 days for the journey to Canton. The great achievement of the steamship before 1870 was accomplished by the then largest steamship in the world, Brunel's *Great Eastern*, the laying of the first successful North Atlantic cable in 1865. Within a further five to six years cables circled the globe inaugurating the virtually immediate transportation of

facts and news, if not of people. A new world was on the horizon.

1870–1920

The following fifty years were characterized by the contrast between the railways, which in almost every European country reached their greatest extent as the almost exclusive carriers of both passengers and freight, except at the strictly local level, and the new modes of transport which were increasingly to compete with them. By 1880, Belgium had the highest density of railways in Europe with more than 1,000 kilometres of railway per 10,000 square kilometres, followed by Great Britain with more than 750 kilometres and by **Switzerland**, **Germany** and the **Netherlands** with more than 500 kilometres each. France, Denmark, **Austria–Hungary** and **Italy** had 250–499 kilometres, **Sweden**, **Spain**, **Portugal** and **Romania** had 100–249 kilometres and **Norway**, **Finland** and Russia just 10–49 kilometres.

The self-confidence of the later Railway Age was mirrored in commercial shipping where the sailing ship finally succumbed to steam. The world tonnage of steamships increased from 803,003 to 1,939,089 in the ten years between 1861 and 1871 alone. The combination of railway and steamship was directly instrumental in the development of the new concept of tourism, and the opening up of the Mediterranean, the Alps and the continental spas to the wealthy. Railway dining cars, Pullman cars and sleeping cars now became familiar although the London and Birmingham Railway had actually provided a 'bed coach' as early as 1838. The famous Wagon-Lits Company was founded in 1876. The almost legendary Orient Express began running in 1883 between Paris and Bucharest, extended to **Constantinople** (now Istanbul) in 1889. This luxury train market contrasted with the slowly expanding mass market, which was, ultimately, to be the more important. First in Britain and then elsewhere, the railway facilitated the lower middle-class and working-class seaside holiday and seaside day trip, but it was not until 1872 that Britain's railways earned half of their receipts from third-class traffic.

The mass market, however was increasingly making itself felt, not least in the new industrial conurbations, so was the growing significance of **Germany** as a transportation pioneer. The first electric tram, built by Siemans and Halske, ran in Berlin in 1881, and the electric tram soon became a popular urban feature. Inner suburban railways were similarly electrified, but somewhat later and only sporadically. Much more immediate was the impact of electricity on underground rail transport. The electrification of London's Metropolitan Railway began in 1890, the same year as the opening of the capital's first electric deep-level 'Tube' line, the City and South London. Most of Europe's underground systems, such as the Paris Metro and Berlin's U-Bahn, were, however, to be sub-surface. Mainline rail electrification was pioneered by Switzerland's Bern–Lötschberg–Simplon which opened in 1913 as the world's first purpose-built long-distance electric railway.

Transportation, however was no longer the story of rail, horse and shipping alone. The German firms of Gottlieb Daimler and Wilhelm Maybach and of Karl Benz both demonstrated motorcars to the public for the first time in 1885 and Daimler produced the first motorcycle the same year. Benz produced a 'popular' car, the Velo, in 1894, which cost £100 and had a speed of 12 miles (19.3 kilometres) a hour. Even more startling was the success of the Wright brothers in America in 1903 in making the first controlled sustained flight in a powered heavier-than-air machine. Development of both the car and the aeroplane was rapid. By 1909 Frenchman Louis Blériot (1872–1936) had flown across the English Channel from Calais to Dover. The motor car was an increasingly common sight, but remained prohibitively expensive for the great majority. It was the motor bus, rather than the motor car, which mattered. As so often, war stimulated technical development, to the benefit of the aeroplane and the motor vehicle.

Significant as these technical advances were to prove, the lives of most people were much more affected by a much simpler transportation development – the introduction of the modern bicycle. The primitive 'hobby-horse' and the somewhat hazardous 'penny-farthing' gave way in the 1890s to the cheap and convenient bicycle, which introduced a quite new level of personal mobility, not least for increasingly emancipated young women.

1920–1939

The interwar years saw intense competition between the railways, the motor bus or coach and, increasingly, the private motor car. Although Captain (Sir) John Alcock and Lieutenant (Sir) Arthur Whitten Brown successfully made the first transatlantic flight in 1919, large-scale air travel was still in the future. The crash of Britain's R101 in 1930 and the destruction of Germany's *Hindenburg*, however, terminated the airship's rivalry with the aeroplane. The railways suffered

from the changed economic climate, and those in Britain grouped for economy in 1923. Only Southern Railway competed by extensively electrifying its short-haul routes. The LNER took steam traction to its limit with the unbroken speed record of 126 miles (202 kilometres) per hour by *Mallard* in 1938. Some other European countries, however were more forward-looking. Mainline electrification was vigorously promoted in **Italy** after 1928 and was accompanied by major infrastructure improvements including the Great Appenine Tunnel, the second longest mountain railway tunnel in the world. **Hungary** introduced mainline high-voltage alternating-current electrification, now the European standard, between Budapest and the Austrian frontier at Hegyeshalom in 1933. Underground railways expanded and the grandest, Moscow's Metro, was built under **Stalin** as a prestige project.

Rail was on the defensive particularly in North America and Europe with growing competition. In the United States, domestic airlines were already beginning to compete with rail for lengthy journeys and the development of an inter-state highway network opened up the bus and motor vehicle traffic. By 1930 the United States was producing over 3 million motor cars and the great giants of the industry, Ford and General Motors, were each producing 2 million motor vehicles of every kind. Mass motoring had arrived, not only as a means of transport but also as a desirable consumer product, with Ford's basic Model 'T', produced from 1912 to 1928, replaced by a Model 'A' in 1928, followed by new models from Ford and other manufacturers, aiming to compete on styling and performance. The United Kingdom was the leading European producer, with both satellite manufacturing from the United States (Ford) and domestic producers such as Lord Nuffield's Morris motors. By 1939 there were over 2 million motor cars in Britain and traffic 'jams' on holiday weekends and congestion were already leading to plans for new road layouts and town plans by 1939. Buses and coaches were replacing trams in Britain and North America, but with fewer motor cars many European cities retained large tram networks as the basis for urban travel.

International trade and travel remained dominated by shipping. Sail had virtually disappeared apart from coastal traffic and relatively small motor ships and 'tankers' for oil and petrol carried virtually all the seaborne trade of the world. The interwar years were the heyday of the ocean liners, and the largest liners, such as the *Queen Mary* and the *Queen Elizabeth*, both completed in the

1930s, enjoyed unique prestige from their sheer size. Less prestigious were a vast range of smaller passenger vessels which were vital to the maintenance of the European empires, the conduct of international business and the continuing migration of millions of people from one part of the world to another.

International air travel was a minor component but growing by the outbreak of **World War II**. Britain's Imperial Airways was specifically set up to carry mail and key personnel throughout the empire. Its early Handley Page biplanes carried up to forty passengers to the **Middle East**. An 8,000-mile (12,874-kilometre) service from London to **South Africa** in 1932 and to Australia in 1934, was carried out in the late 1930s by Short Brothers Flying Boats completing the journey in several hops, using rivers and lakes.

post-war world

By the late 1940s rail was suffering from ever greater competition from road and within North America and Europe, by air travel for more affluent travellers. Mass motoring came to western Europe with popular models from Fiat, Volkswagen and Citroen aimed at average families. **Japan**, too, saw a rapid renaissance of its motor industry, which had started before World War II with foundations laid by Toyota, Nissan and Honda, becoming a post-war giant in the automobile industry and breaking into European and North American markets from the 1960s and 1970s. By the early twenty-first century, Japan's Toyota and American General Motors vied as the world's largest producers of motor vehicles. Mass motoring was complemented by expansion in air travel, which was becoming safer, more comfortable and more affordable. Incorporated into the 'package holiday', it offered millions of north Europeans the opportunity to holiday in the Mediterranean and further afield, transforming parts of the coastlines of Spain, Majorca, Italy, **Greece** and its islands into mass holiday resorts. Similarly in North America, Florida and the desert resorts of Las Vegas and Reno flourished with sun-seekers from northern states. The range and speed of airliners also transformed long-distance travel. The last age of the great liners was in the 1950s, as air travel became the overwhelming means of moving between the continents or any long distance travel within them. The future of the liners lay in cruise liners offering holidays afloat. By the early twenty-first century, these had become immense floating hotels producing some of the largest ships ever seen, with accommodation for thousands of passengers. While the Soviet Union maintained the **Trans-Siberian Railway** as a vital link over its immense length, the transcontinental systems of North America came under pressure. In 1970 Amtrak took over the much reduced passenger network in the United States, and Canada's transcontinental lines were effectively nationalized in 1978.

Railway networks were reduced in many European countries to cut expenditure on little used lines; France lost about 40 per cent of its network and Britain about a third under the Beeching Report of 1963. Passenger numbers dropped on both sides of the Atlantic, other than on dedicated commuter networks where some renewal took place. The San Francisco Bay area developed a new transit system from the 1960s and in Cologne/Bonn the tramway network became a light railway system with underground lengths in the denser urban areas and penetration into the surrounding countryside.

Similar schemes were widely implemented in many European cities as mass transit systems were seen as a means to avoid road congestion where underground systems were too expensive or difficult. The development of more high-speed roads in Britain and Europe, large schemes such as the Peripheral motorway around Paris and the M25 around London, and urban renewal with road traffic provided for, increased competition for freight traffic to the point where road was overwhelmingly dominant apart from particularly bulky commodities.

A revival in rail transport came through modernization and high-speed passenger lines. France began rail electrification in earnest after World War II and in 1955 achieved a rail world record speed of 205 miles (330 kilometres) per hour. Such speeds, however, called for dedicated lines and France started its first high-speed line between Paris and Lyons in the early 1970s. It was pre-empted, however, by Japan whose 'Bullet train' of 1964 offered high-speed travel between Tokyo and Osaka. The French TGV (Train de Grande Vitesse) system is planned to total over 4,000 kilometres by 2025 with speeds of 300–320 kilometres per hour and has been copied in Spain and elsewhere in Europe. Britain has been slower, though a dedicated high-speed link through the Channel was completed in 1994, linking London with Paris and the Continent. By 2015, **China** had completed thousands of miles of high-speed line and drew up plans in 2014 for a network of new rail 'silk roads' linking Beijing to Moscow, Tashkent and Karachi by high-speed rail.

In many parts of the world, the most modern modes of transport available in the early twentieth century remained buses or river craft. Neither **Africa** nor **Latin America** saw the transcontinental railway lines built in North America and across Eurasia and railway development has lagged. On land, motor lorries, usually diesel-powered, carry the vast majority of all freight, as they still do in Europe, Asia and North America. At sea, however, the great transformation after 1945 came with 'containerization', the placing of many commodities, especially consumer goods and vehicles, into standardized containers which could then be placed on lorries for distribution, while bulky commodities such as oil, ore and timber used ever larger tankers or bulk carriers, some up to 300,000 tons. Most freight was handled by specialized ports with the equipment to store and sort containers, leading to the decay of many traditional dock areas in London, New York and Liverpool, where general cargoes had once been unloaded by thousands of dockers. New container ports, such as Felixstowe and Rotterdam, can handle the latest container giants such as the Chinese-registered *Globe*, launched in 2015, displacing 186,000 tons and capable of carrying over 19,000 standard 20-foot shipping containers.

While larger container ships are possible, limits have been reached with the capacity of restricted waterways such as the Straits of Malacca and the Straits of Dover to accommodate them safely. A growing alternative for specialized high-value produce and perishable goods is air freight, estimated in 2014 to be carrying approximately a quarter of international trade by value. Recent transport developments have been affected by international concern at the environmental impact of transport, focused on the effect on human health of vehicular emissions and on the phenomenon of climate change, generally attributed to carbon emissions. This concern has led not only to the favouring of high-speed rail over short-haul air transport and to the expansion in urban light-rail systems already noted, but also to sustained and successful **European Union** pressure on motor manufacturers to make radical improvements in vehicular emission standards. Some predict that the motor vehicle itself will soon have been rendered obsolescent by the electric car. Environmental concern is particularly strong in the sensitive Alpine regions and major infrastructure improvements are being made to transfer freight from road to rail. The largest is the 8 billion euro Brenner Base Tunnel between Austria and Italy on which work started in 2011 and was completed in 2016. At 64 kilometres it became the longest rail tunnel in the world. The European Commission's 2011 white paper on the future of transport envisaged a 50 per cent reduction in the use of conventional cars for urban transport by 2030 and a 100 per cent reduction by 2050. A European high-speed rail network would be complete by 2050 and the length of the existing network tripled by 2030 permitting the greater part of medium-distance passenger journeys to be by rail by 2050. Not least, 50 per cent of road freight would be transferred to other modes, such as rail or inland waterway freight, for distances of more than 3,000 kilometres by 2050, with an interim target of 30 per cent by 2030. The extent to which this vision will be realized is conjectural.

Trans-Siberian Railway

Authorized in 1891 to promote Russian penetration of the Far East, the 5,900-mile (9,495-kilometre) line from Moscow to Vladivostok was completed, 1903, except for the loop around Lake Baikal, where there was a ferry service. The loop was completed in 1905. The 800-mile (1,287-kilometre) section first laid across Chinese territory was supplemented by an alternative Russian section to create a continuous railway on Russian soil in 1915. Doubled throughout and largely electrified in the Soviet period.

Transvaal

– *see* **South Africa**.

Transylvania

The large region forming modern northern **Romania**, with its capital in Cluj inhabited, historically equally, by ethnic Hungarians and Romanians. A Hungarian territory of the Austrian and then **Austro-Hungarian Empires** until December 1918, when representatives of the Transylvanian Romanians proclaimed the Union of Transylvania and Romania, and the union of all Romanians in one state. Formally transferred to Romania under the Treaty of Trianon in 1920. Most of the region returned to **Hungary** under the second 'Vienna Award' imposed by **Germany** and **Italy** in August 1940, only to be restored to Romania under the Hungarian armistice agreement of January 1945. The Transylvanian town of Tirgu Mures was the scene of ethnic rioting in which three people died in 1990, and Romanian sensitivity to any expression of interest by Hungary in the ethnic Hungarians beyond its borders remains live. The Hungarian revolutionary, **Béla Kun**, was Transylvanian-born.

Treaty of Utrecht
– see **Utrecht, Peace of (1713)**.

Trent Affair
In November 1861, US Navy Captain Charles Wilkes boarded the *Trent*, a British steamer, and illegally captured James Mason and John Slidell, two Southern emissaries en route to Europe to lobby for the recognition of the Confederacy. The ensuing diplomatic crisis threatened British intervention in the **American Civil War**. Under pressure from the British, and acknowledging their breach of international law, the Lincoln administration disavowed Wilkes' action, released the captives, and drafted the apology London demanded.

Trinidad and Tobago
Located at the southernmost tip of the Lesser Antilles in the Caribbean archipelago, the Republic of Trinidad and Tobago is a geological extension of the South American continent located north-east of **Venezuela** and south of Grenada. First colonized by **Spain**, the islands came under British control in the early nineteenth century and remained so until 1962 when they achieved independence. In 1976 the islands became a republic and subsequently followed a parliamentary system of government. Trinidad's economy is largely dependent on oil, making it among the wealthiest of the Caribbean countries.

Trotsky, Leon (Lev Bronstein) (1879–1940)
Along with **Lenin** and **Stalin**, Trotsky was one of the key leaders of the **Russian Revolution** and the **USSR**. He was an intellectual who became the organizer and leader of the Red Army in the **Russian Civil War** of 1917–21. He established the doctrine of revolution from the bottom, and developed ideas of permanent revolutionary change which sat ill with the desire of Lenin and especially Stalin for central control. Stalin moved against him in 1925, and he became an exile in **Mexico**, where he wrote and influenced the national cultural scene. His murder – with an icepick in the back of the head, probably on Stalin's orders – whilst in Mexico became one of the most celebrated examples of political assassination and passed into ordinary language in the twentieth century. In the 1960s Euro-communists and 'entryists' who wished to radically change the Left in democratic **Europe** whilst in the guise of other parties adopted 'Trotskyite' ideas of infiltration and personal involvement in contrast to **Maoism** and **Stalinism**.

Trujillo (Molina), Rafael (Leonidas) (1891–1961)
Dominican dictator. After rapidly rising in the National Guard, Trujillo seized control of the **Dominican Republic** in 1930 and established a dictatorship marked by the brutal persecution of all dissenters, the massacre of thousands of Dominicans of Haitian descent, and the appropriation of vast personal wealth. An anti-communist alliance with the **United States** kept him in power until his unrelenting attacks on political opponents led to his assassination.

Truman Doctrine (USA)
The term used to describe President Harry Truman's message to Congress on 12 March 1947 asking for authorization for 400 million dollars in US military aid to **Greece** and **Turkey**. Greece was in the midst of a bloody civil war at the end of **World War II**, and American policymakers feared that a victory for the communist guerrilla forces there would allow the **Soviet Union** to dominate south-eastern Europe. The British government had informed Washington it lacked the financial muscle after six years of war to defend the region on its own, and Truman's advisors feared that failure to maintain Greece and Turkey as allies of the **United States** would not only destabilize the whole Mediterranean basin but would also cause concern amongst its allies in western Europe. The speech was the first major example of the policy of containment that dominated US policy towards the **USSR** for the next two decades.

Truman, Harry S. (1884–1972)
President of the **United States**, April 1945 to January 1953. Born in Independence, Missouri, Truman served as an army officer in **France** during **World War I**. In 1934 he was elected US senator from his home state. He became vice president at the party's convention in 1944, becoming president following the sudden death of **Franklin Roosevelt**. In domestic policy he tried to maintain the reformist impulse of the New Deal in a difficult political climate of rising prosperity and a resurgence of political conservatism. His foreign policy placed the United States firmly on the world stage, involving his country in the defence of non-communist Europe (**Truman Doctrine** and **Marshall Plan**) and in a war to defend **South Korea** from communist invasion in 1950–3. He presided over a growing national obsession with communism that did much to shape the **Cold War**.

Trump, Donald (1946–)

Billionaire property developer and television presenter, elected as forty-fifth president of the **United States** in November 2016 as the **Republican Party** candidate. He won the Republican nomination as a rank outsider on a controversial populist platform, attacking immigration, the effects of **globalization**, and American weakness abroad. His slogan that he would 'Make America great again' and pledge to revive the economy earned him a victory that confounded pundits and the media, winning a clear majority in the electoral college though behind in the popular vote.

tsarism

Russian tsars inherited the Orthodox Church's interpretation of the Byzantine concept of the emperor (*autokrator*), and their prime title, *samoderzhets vsekh Russ* ('autocrat of all the Russias'). The church was identified with the state and the aristocracy was the instrument of the autocracy and never an autonomous force. The law was the will of the autocrat and he and his instruments were free to break it. All power came from the top. The notorious arbitrariness and capriciousness of Russian imperial administration flowed directly from this distinctively Russian background. As in Byzantium, the role of the emperor as regent of God on Earth did not sanctify his person. Conspiracies to dethrone the tsar were common in eighteenth-century Russia and Tsar Paul I was strangled by a group of army officers in 1801. **Stalin**'s rule, with its bending of religious ritual to Communist purposes, can be interpreted as a form of neo-tsarism.

Tshibumba Kanda Matulu (1947–*c*. 1980)

Zairean painter. Born in Lumbumbashi in what was then the Belgian Congo, Tshibumba was a genre painter and historian whose historical paintings, produced in the early 1970s, tell of Zaire's pre-colonial, colonial and post-colonial history. His paintings, together with writings and interviews with western scholars including Johannes Fabian and Bogumil Jewsiewicki, constitute a striking historical account of colonial and post-colonial rule. Tshibumba disappeared in 1978 and his fate thereafter is uncertain.

Tshombe, Moise Kapenda (1919–1969)

Born in the province of Katanga in the Belgian Congo, Tshombe was educated by American Methodist missionaries and in 1951 became a member of the Katanga Provincial Council. In 1959 he was one of the founders of Conakat (Confédération des Associations Tribales de Katanga) and as Conakat's president argued for a federal system for the independent Congo. On 11 July 1960 Conakat declared Katanga independent and Tshombe became head of state. While external support was crucially important in financing and defending the secession and Tshombe's regime, he also sought to build internal legitimacy. In 1963 the secession ended and Tshombe went into exile, but was recalled to Congo as prime minister in 1964 in the hope that he could restore order. He was dismissed in October 1965 and again went into exile. He died in prison in **Algeria**.

Tsushima (1905)

An archipelago in the Korean Strait located between southern **Japan** and **Korea**. From the twelfth century to 1868 Tsushima served as an important Japanese gateway for trading and diplomatic contact with Korea despite the Tokugawa policy of national seclusion. It was the site of a decisive sea battle: in 1905 the Russian Baltic Sea Fleet commanded by Admiral Rozhestvensky was intercepted and defeated by a Japanese Fleet under the command of Admiral Togo Heihachiro. After this defeat, **Russia** negotiated peace.

Tuareg

– *see* **nomadism**.

tuberculosis

An infectious disease which affects the respiratory system; its symptoms include chest pain, fever, chills and coughing up blood. It was prevalent in ancient **Egypt** and was a major cause for concern in ancient **Greece**. Its bacillus was first identified in 1882 by Robert Koch. Successful immunization came in 1906, and widespread **vaccination** in the 1950s. Around a third of the world's population has the infection in a latent form.

Tubman, Harriet (*c*. 1820–1913)

Probably the most famous 'conductor' on the Underground Railroad. She escaped from bondage in Maryland in 1849 and then reputedly ventured into the Southern states around nineteen times to help the enslaved who wished to flee to the Northern states or to **Canada**. She later served the Union Army as a nurse in the low country sea-islands.

Tubman, William (1895–1971)

Nineteenth president of **Liberia**, 1944–71. Tubman was a proponent of cautious and gradual African liberation, and aligned his country both with the **United States** in **World War II** and with non-aligned and African unity movements in the

1950s and 1960s. He attempted to encourage economic development, and built up the Liberian merchant marine, mineral industries and foreign investment. However, his authoritarian tendencies created divisions and reactions which saw his successor overthrown by Samuel Doe in 1980, prompting the descent of Liberia into civil war until the second decade of the twenty-first century.

Tudeh Party

The Iranian Communist Party. Founded as an anti-fascist popular front in 1941, led primarily by Marxist intellectuals known as the Fifty Three, who had been in prison under Reza Shah. It sought far-reaching social reform within the context of constitutional monarchy and parliamentary government, and was sympathetic to the **Soviet Union**. Mostly supported in the northern, central and north-western regions of **Iran**, where it stood out as the only political party then to be well organized, possessed of a clear political outlook and enjoying popular support. The principal voice of intellectuals and the secular elite, it also enjoyed the sympathy of the small Iran Party, established by leading technocrats of liberal and social democratic outlook. It returned eight deputies to the *Majlis* after the 1943 parliamentary elections.

Under Soviet pressure, it uncritically supported the autonomist revolt in Iranian Azerbaijan, which was then under Soviet military occupation, December 1945. Briefly in governing coalition with the Democrat Party under Ahmad Qavam, 1946, whereafter Soviet troops withdrew and the Azerbaijan revolt collapsed. It boycotted the 1946 *Majlis* elections following the savage reprisals by government forces against the autonomists in **Azerbaijan**. Increasingly pro-Soviet, it unsuccessfully supported the grant of a concession for north Iranian **oil** to the Soviet Union, 1947, which lost it the support of many members.

Banned by the shah following the failed assassination attempt of 4 February 1949, in which one of the Tudeh leaders, Nureddin Kiyanuri, but not the membership, was involved, it went underground, becoming one of the monolithic communist parties typical of the time. Nevertheless, it maintained secret relations with the government prior to Dr **Mossadegh**'s oil nationalization bill, 1951, which it was the only domestic political force to oppose because it considered it a plot to deliver Iranian oil to America. Suppressed by the shah, 1953–5, when many of its activists were jailed and

more than twenty members of its military network of more than 450 army officers were executed, it largely lost credibility by the mid 1960s when Soviet–Iranian relations became warmer, and suffered a split in 1965 when its Chinese-inspired Maoists defected to form the Revolutionary Organization of the Tudeh Party of Iran (Sazman-e Enqelabi-ye Hezb-e Tudeh-ye Iran).

Tudeh resurfaced with the **Iranian Revolution**, 1979, when its exiled leaders pledged their loyalty to **Ayatollah Khomeini**, but did not recover its one-time popularity partly because it was seen as too pro-Soviet and partly because it was seen as having behaved poorly in 1953. It was, however, very well organized and had established itself effectively in intellectual circles, in women's and youth movements, and in due course the armed forces, establishing a military wing. It also had influence over the Fada'i Marxist–Leninist guerrilla organization. It supported the 1979 occupation of the American Embassy in **Tehran** which provoked the **Tehran Embassy Hostage Crisis**.

The party came to an end in 1983 when the exposure of its military network led to the arrest and trial for treason of many of its leaders and activists and their execution or imprisonment. Following torture, its leader, Nureddin Kianuri, admitted to espionage on behalf of the Soviet Union over forty years. Others fled to **Afghanistan** and the Soviet Union.

Tunis

Capital and largest city of a Tunisia which, under its bey, was a dependency of the **Ottoman Empire** until the establishment of a French protectorate by the Treaty of Bardo with the bey on 12 May 1881, which greatly angered the Italians, who regarded Tunisia as an area of settlement. Second only to Algiers as a centre for the **Barbary pirates** in the eighteenth and early nineteenth centuries. A focus of German resistance to the Allies during the North African campaign of **World War II**, its fall, May 1943, led to the capture of more than 250,000 prisoners. Tunis became the headquarters of the **Arab League**, 1979–90, and of the **Palestine Liberation Organization (PLO)**, 1982–94. The scene of the first change of government achieved by the **Arab Spring** when President Zine el-Abidine Ben Ali was ousted in January 2011, but subsequently of the assassination of two prominent critics of the successor Islamist government: Chokri Belaid, 6 February 2013, and Mohamed Brahmi, 25 July 2013.

Tunisia

Republic in North Africa. Formally a part of the **Ottoman Empire**, Tunisia achieved de facto independence under the Husaynid dynasty of beys from 1705. After a period of grave financial problems, Prime Minister Khayr al-Din Pasha (1873–7) introduced one of the most comprehensive reform programmes of the Arab world. This was in part continued by the French, who made Tunisia a protectorate from 1881. Nationalist movements, like the Destour and Neo-Destour, grew after **World War I**, demanding self-rule and later independence, which was achieved when **France** withdrew in 1956. Tunisia since then has had two important presidents: **Habib Bourguiba** until 1987, and Zine el Abidine Ben Ali. Tunisia is a West-oriented and secular society, but with a strong presidentialist rule, where the Neo-Destour (now RCD) has for long been the single political party. The radical uprising of 2010 gave its name to the **Arab Spring**. However, continuing unemployment and soaring inflation threaten its political stability.

Tupac Amaru (1738–1781)

Wealthy Andean nobleman José Gabriel Condorcanqui took the name Tupac Amaru after the Inca executed by the Spaniards in 1572 and led the great Andean Indian Rebellion of 1780–2 in **Spain**'s viceroyalty of **Peru**. He attempted to tap into popular currents of millenarianism and peasant discontent as a way to mobilize the Indian population against the colonial system and to support reform and a possible restoration of the Inca Empire.

Tupamaros (Movimiento de Liberación Naciónal Tupamaro)

Named after **Tupac Amaru**, leader of a major insurrection in **Peru** in 1780–2, the Tupamaros, founded in 1963, engaged in urban guerrilla warfare to create socialism in **Uruguay**. The military government that seized power in 1973 killed hundreds and tortured several thousand captured Tupamaros. When democratic rule returned in 1985, the Tupamaros reorganized successfully as a political party. In 2009 a former Tupamaro, José Alberto Mujica, who spent fourteen years in prison, was elected Uruguay's president.

Turabi, Hasan al- (1932–)

A Sudanese political and religious leader, Hasan al-Turabi was a supporter of the establishment of an Islamic state. Educated in Khartoum, London and Paris, his political activity began with the Islamic Charter Front, the political arm of the Sudan Muslim Brotherhood, which promoted an Islamic constitution. He has continued to advocate for an Islamic state, holding leadership positions in a succession of political parties including the National Islamic Front, the National Congress and most recently the Popular National Congress Party. Additionally, he held a number of key positions in various governments ranging from attorney general to minister of justice and minister of foreign affairs. Active in Umar al-Bashir's rise to power in 1989, al-Turabi fell out with al-Bashir in 1999 over attempts to limit presidential powers. Al-Turabi's political career has alternated with periods of arrest and imprisonment, most recently due to conflicts with al-Bashir's government regarding the **Darfur** region.

Turkey, Republic of

Established in 1923, the Republic of Turkey emerged from the ruins of the **Ottoman Empire**. Its establishment did not represent a clean break with the Ottoman past as Turkish nationalist propaganda suggested, but rather a radical reformulation of the imperial state. **Mustafa Kemal**'s practices and ideology grew from his experience as a prominent member of the Committee of Union and Progress (see **Young Turks**). Despite the continuity between the two states, the demographic circumstances of the new polity were transformed. In a decisive break with the Ottoman past, the Turkish-speaking population formed an outright majority in the new state. The **Armenian genocide** and the population transfer of 1923 had largely removed the Christian population of Anatolia that had represented 20 per cent of the inhabitants before **World War I**. Gone, too, were the Arab and Balkan provinces. Now, with a population 98 per cent Muslim, the state set out to construct a secular, Turkish nationalist identity by undermining institutional and popular forms of religious expression.

Mustafa Kemal (Atatürk) oversaw the liberation of Anatolia from the invading Greek, Italian, French and British forces during the Turkish War of Independence. Turkey benefited greatly from inheriting the Ottoman Army. Other regions of the former umpire were unable to resist the reassertion of colonialism After the war, Atatürk consolidated his power after an initial period of pluralism, tolerating no political dissent after 1925. Instead of relying on a systematic ideology to create its legitimacy, the primacy of the state itself became the bedrock of the Turkish republic. Atatürk's policies represented a conscious response to many of the perceived failures of the Ottoman Empire. The acceptance of Turkey as a 'modern' nation, so coveted by the late Ottomans, was finally won by the state's uncompromising reformist stance. Atatürk's reforms aimed to revolutionize the daily lives of Turks; language reform brought the introduction of the Roman alphabet and cultural reforms – such as banning the wearing of the Ottoman fez – aimed to symbolically bury the past.

Never forgetting the disaster an alliance brought them during World War I, Atatürk's successor, his long time deputy, Ismet İnönü, resisted significant pressure from the Allies and remained neutral during **World War II**. Having only tolerated token political opposition before the war, the increasingly unpopular ruling party, led by İnönü, allowed free and fair elections in 1950. The Democratic Party (DP) under Adnan Menderes defeated the nationalist party and adopted liberal economic policies and eventually a kind of Islamic populism that would prefigure the politics of Recep Tayyip Erdogan's Justice and Development Party of the early twenty-first century. The DP ruled for ten years before a military coup displaced it in 1960. A troubled democracy, the country always moved back towards elections after the military coups of 1960, 1971, 1980 and 1997. The army, once in power, attempted to devolve power back to the politicians, and in each instance, evinced scant interest in establishing a permanent military dictatorship. Democracy had its limits and the military intervened when the political process broke down intractably (as in 1980) or when Islamists were perceived to threaten the state's core ethos of secularism (as in 1997). More recently, President Erdogan has stamped his authority on the country, particularly after the failed coup of 2016. In the economic sphere, Turkey was similarly Janusfaced in late twentieth century. Periods of prosperity and growth punctuated economic downturns and crises, with successive governments changing their stance toward state intervention in the economy. In the long run, Turkey's nationalist project succeeded in creating a robust national identity and relatively vibrant economic life. Prosperity was not spread evenly however, and 'Turkification' had its discontents among the country's Kurdish population, where a renewed conflict is taking place.

Turkish Empire
– see **Ottoman Empire**.

Turkish Invasion of Cyprus
– see **Cyprus**.

Turkmanchai, Treaty of (1828)
Signed 22 February 1828 between **Iran** and **Russia**, bringing their war of 1826–7 to a close. The militarily defeated Iranians surrendered to the Russians the territory in **Armenia**, including Yerevan and Nakhichevan, which they had acquired from **Turkey** in the seventeenth century, the border with Russia being fixed on the River Aras (Araxes) with a small deviation south of its mouth to include the Lenkoran district. Tabriz, occupied by the Russians in 1827, was, however, returned to Iran. The treaty gave the Armenians a Christian ruler in the person of the tsar, to whom they would prove extremely loyal, hoping that he would ultimately wrest the western part of Armenia from the **Ottoman Empire**. It no more united the Azeris than it did the Armenians. Although the greater number were in the **Russian Empire**, a minority remained in Iran, which shared their **Shi'ite** interpretation of **Islam**.

Turks and Caicos
Located south-east of the **Bahamas**, the Turks and Caicos is a British overseas territory consisting of eight major islands and numerous uninhabited cays. The islands are named after the indigenous Turk's head 'fez' cactus, and the Lucayan term *caya hico*, meaning 'string of islands', and were formerly smuggling entrepôts. Presently the islands are under direct rule by the UK's Foreign and Commonwealth Office and run by an appointed governor. The economy is based on tourism, offshore financial services and fishing.

Turner, Nat (c. 1800–1831)
Nat Turner was an enslaved preacher who led an insurrection in Southampton County, Virginia, **USA**, in August 1831. The revolt resulted in the deaths of fifty-seven whites in the local area before it was quashed by the white authorities. At the subsequent trial seventeen participants were hanged, including Turner, and seven deported. The revolt led to much more stringent restrictions on the enslaved throughout the 1830s and thereafter.

Tutola, Amos (1920–97)
Nigerian writer. Born in western **Nigeria** to **Yoruba** Christian cocoa farmers, Tutuola received only six years of formal education. His first and most famous novel, *The Palm-Wine Drinkard*, was lauded internationally for its ability to capture oral

tradition in the written form but criticized in Nigeria for its crude style and use of broken English. His writings use Yoruba traditions and folktales to explore themes of greed, betrayal, morality, death and spirituality.

Tutu, Desmond Mpilo (1931–)

South African cleric. Ordained an Anglican priest in 1961, Tutu was appointed dean of Johannesburg in 1975 but was removed following white protests, becoming bishop of Lesotho in 1976. He used his role as South African Council of Churches secretary general, 1978–84, to denounce **apartheid**. Awarded the Nobel Peace Prize in 1984, he was the first black archbishop of Cape Town, 1986–96. He was also chairman of the post-apartheid Truth and Reconciliation Commission.

Tutu, Osei (c. 1660–1717)

First leader of the **Ashanti** kingdom, who began his career about 1675 in Kumasi. His important victory over the rival state of Denkyira in 1701 marked the start of the confederacy that would become Ashanti. He and a religious leader Okomfo Anokye, created the Great Oath of the Ashanti and the Golden Stool, a symbol of the new state, which expanded dramatically during his reign. He was killed fighting against Akyem.

Tweed Ring (USA)

The circle of men centred on **Democratic** 'Boss' William M. Tweed (1823–78) who systematically defrauded New York City of tens of millions of dollars. Tweed consolidated his hold on the party through control of **Tammany Hall**, exploiting its power of nominating candidates. A new city charter (1870) allowed him to grossly overpay contractors who diverted their gains to Tweed personally. Widespread bribery and generous provision for the poor could not save him from internal party opposition that assisted in his 1873 conviction.

Twenty-One Demands

This was a set of demands made to Chinese President Yuan Shikai in 1915 by the Japanese. They included ceding Shandong to the Japanese, an extension of **Japan**'s lease of Port Arthur, commercial rights in **Manchuria**, and making **China** a protectorate of Japan. The final demand was rejected, but the others were accepted, although when they became public during the Paris Peace Conference in 1919, Chinese protestors took to the streets during the **May Fourth movement**.

Tyler, John (1790–1862)

The tenth president of the **USA** began as a Virginia lawyer, and served in Congress (1816–21) and as governor of Virginia (1825–7). As a strict constructionist Democratic Republican, he opposed nationalist legislation and the **Missouri Compromise** and became a Jacksonian in the late 1820s. Serving in the US Senate (1827–36), he turned against Jackson during the **Nullification crisis**. Elected vice president on the Whig ticket in 1840, he became the first 'accidental' president on Harrison's sudden death. In 1841–2 Tyler vetoed the nationalist legislation passed by the congressional Whigs, leading to their alienation. Looking for support elsewhere, in 1843 he turned to an expansionist programme. His administration negotiated the acquisition of **Texas** but its apparent pro-slavery purposes prevented it from acquiring the necessary two-thirds support in the US Senate; however, Congress passed a resolution recognizing the annexation of Texas at the end of his presidency. Tyler emerged from retirement to chair the Virginia peace convention of February 1861, and then spent his last days in the Confederate Congress.

Tzu Hsi

– see **Cixi**.

U

U-2 Incident

In May 1960, during the **Cold War** era, an American U-2 reconaissance aircraft flown by Gary Powers was shot down over Soviet airspace. Powers survived, but the episode triggered a diplomatic crisis in which Soviet leader **Nikita Khrushchev** demanded but did not receive an apology from President **Dwight Eisenhower**, resulting in the aborting of the Paris summit meeting. With Soviet–American relations damaged, it was not until 1963 with the signing of the **Nuclear Test Ban Treaty** that clear signs of superpower cooperation became evident.

Uganda

– see also **Buganda**.

Former British colony in east Africa. The agreement in 1875 between Bugandan King Mutesa I (1827–84) and Christian missionaries entering his territory culminated in Uganda becoming a British protectorate in 1894. There was significant early twentieth-century Indian settlement. Uganda gained independence in 1962 under Mutesa II (1924–69), though **Milton Obote** (1925–2005) exercised actual authority as prime minister. Obote ousted Mutesa, declared a republic and became president. In 1971 army commander **Idi Amin** (*c.* 1923–2003) deposed Obote. Ruthlessly authoritarian, Amin expelled the large Asian community. Obote returned to power on Amin's overthrow in 1979 but was again ejected in 1985, Yoweri Museveni (1944–) taking power and introducing market-oriented economic reforms. He won successive presidential elections from 1996, bringing political stability to the country, though his human rights record aroused criticism and the opposition was stifled and persecuted. The Ugandan population is predominantly Christian with a Muslim minority. Agriculture provides most employment – coffee is a major export – and there are copper, gold and other mineral deposits, together with oil.

ujamaa

– see also **Tanzania**.

From the Swahili word for 'brotherhood' or 'togetherness', ujamaa is the Tanzanian form of socialism based on decentralized communal village units outlined by President **Julius Nyerere** (1922–99) in his 1967 **Arusha Declaration**. The scheme – based partly on an idealistic vision of pre-colonial Africa – emphasized rural development and economic self-sufficiency through popular ownership of the means of production rather than the centralized Soviet model, though Nyerere's Tanganyika Africa National Union (TANU) remained the country's sole legal political party. Participation – initially voluntary but subsequently imposed through forced collectivization in 1973 – rose from 58,000 farmers and workers in 1968 to over 12 million by the late 1970s. While there were definite successes in terms of education and health, widespread resentment at the scheme's growing bureaucracy and tendency to corruption provoked growing disillusionment and a fall in agricultural productivity. **Tanzania**'s attempt at a new socialist model was diluted in 1977 and abandoned completely in 1987, with a return to individual ownership.

Ukraine

The name means 'borderland' and broadly referred to the area between Galicia and the River Don and between the Pripyat Marshes and the Black Sea, bisected by the River Dnepr on which Kiev stands. The site of the first Russian state, Kievan Rus, founded in AD 862, and hence of emotional significance to modern Russians and Ukrainians alike. In the seventeenth century **Ukraine** was a 'no-man's land' between **Russia**, **Poland** and the Muslim Tatar khanate in the Crimea, the final political vestige of the Mongol invasions. West of the Dnepr was nominally Polish with a religiously Orthodox peasantry, speaking a range of Ukrainian (or 'Little Russian') dialects similar to but distinct from Russian, together with **Cossacks** supposedly defending Poland from Tatar raids. East of the Dnepr was inhabited largely by fugitive Russian serfs and autonomous Cossack bands, and the Cossacks controlled the area around the Dnepr rapids. The Slav population used the same name for itself as for the Russians (*Rus* and *ruskii*), but its legal and cultural traditions were more western and it lacked the collectivist traditions of **Russia** proper.

Eastern Ukraine came into the Russian orbit under the Pereyaslavl agreement of 1654, concluded after a major rebellion against Poland, and Russian control was strengthened by **Peter the Great** following the **Great Northern War**. Kiev had become Russian in 1667. Much of western Ukraine followed with the second partition of Poland in 1793, but Ukrainian-speaking Galicia went to the Austrian Empire under the first and third partitions of 1772 and 1797. Modern Ukrainian nationalism was born in largely Uniate (Orthodox but in communion with Rome) eastern Galicia and was directed as much against the Poles as against the Russians. The literary language was created by the poet Taras Shevchenko in the 1840s. Ukrainian national sentiment spread in both Austrian and Russian Ukraine in the second half of the nineteenth century but was largely confined to the intelligentsia and the peasantry, and was probably still quite weak in 1900. The concentration of Jews made Ukraine one of the parts of the **Russian Empire** subject to mass anti-Semitism.

Ukraine first appeared as a political unit with the declaration of an 'autonomous Ukrainian republic' in June 1917. The establishment of the Ukrainian Soviet Socialist Republic followed in December 1919 and it joined the future **Soviet Union** in December 1920. This new Ukraine, however, did not include a strip some 240 kilometres (150 miles) wide on its western boundary, including Lviv (Lvov, Lwow), and east Galicia, which was acquired by Poland under the Treaty of Riga, 1921. It was united with Soviet Ukraine under the **Yalta** agreement of February 1945, and Ukraine was given its own seat in the **United Nations** that year. Some Ukrainian nationalists hoping for independence, notably Stepan Bandera, had sided with the Germans in 1941, but their hopes were usually disabused by the brutal German drive for *Lebensraum*. Soviet Ukraine was enlarged finally in 1954 when the adjoining Crimea, Russian since 1783, was transferred to it. Amongst the most dramatic events of the Soviet period was the **Chernobyl** nuclear disaster, 1986.

Independence came on 5 December 1991 with the dissolution of the Soviet Union, but Ukraine joined the **Commonwealth of Independent States** (CIS) the same month. The former establishment was deposed in the 2004 Orange Revolution and its populist leaders, Yuliya Tymoshenko and Viktor Yushchenko, pursued a more pro-western course but brought neither competence nor stability. The more pro-Russian Viktor Yanukovych, elected 2010, fled in January 2014, following a revolt by those enraged by his cancellation of a proposed association agreement with the EU and substitution of a trade agreement with Russia. The traditional divide between the more Russianized and the more westernized halves of the country deepened and conflict broke out between the Ukrainian military and armed separatists in the east in April 2014. Crimea was annexed by Russia in March 2014, with the nearly unanimous support of its Russian-speaking majority.

ulama

Literally 'those who possess *'ilm* (learning)', in practice the religious leaders of Islamic society with expertise in the Muslim sciences, notably philosophy and jurisprudence. They include theologians (*mutakallimun*), canon lawyers (*mufti*), judges (*qudaa'a*), professors and high state religious officials. Historically, it was the consensus of the *ulama* which established the key **sharia** legal principle of *ijma* (universal agreement). Although never the equivalent of the Christian priesthood, they may be equated with the clergy of Christianity in **Shi'ite** regions, notably **Iran**, but in the mainstream **Sunni** Islamic world they are closest to the Jewish rabbis or teachers. Their influence over Islamic societies has been pervasive since early times, leading governments including those of the most powerful Muslim empires, such as the Ottoman Turkish Empire, habitually to seek their support. The corollary was an ability to shape policies.

Like most religious establishments, the *ulama* have normally been a conservative, and sometimes reactionary, force. The Turkish *ulama*, for example, in cooperation with the janissaries, led conservative reaction against the reforms and French concepts of Sultan **Selim III**, represented by his 'new order'. Some Muslim thinkers, including **Rashid Rida**, have gone further, accusing the *ulama* of intellectual stagnation. The Iranian chief minister 1848–51, **Amir-e Kabir**, was convinced by his time on the Ottoman Iranian frontier commission that the elimination of clerical influence on affairs of state under **Mahmud II** had been the key to Ottoman recovery. The conservatism of the *ulama* is, however, for better or worse, a bulwark against all radicalism whether backward- or forward-looking. Following **Sayyid Qutb**'s execution in 1966, for example, the *ulama* of **Al-Azhar University** put him on their index of heresy, declaring him a 'deviant' (*munharif*) for his propagation of armed **jihad** to overthrow the established governments, institutions, societies and traditions of the Muslim world. The conservatism of the *ulama* has sometimes provoked a reaction akin to the anti-clericalism of Roman Catholic societies, notably the abolition of the *ulama*, as a class, in **Turkey** by **Kemal Atatürk**.

Their clerical status has given them particular influence in Shi'ite lands, notably Iran, where by ancient tradition state power has been widely seen as illegitimate. Their autonomous power there grew during the nineteenth century, particularly under **Fath 'Ali Shah**, for a complex of arguably contradictory reasons including state patronage, with the *ulama* even marrying into the **Qajar** nobility, on the one hand, and the Islamic concept that the state was usurping the kingdom of Allah, and was, therefore, illegitimate, on the other. Fath 'Ali Shah did not appreciate that his deference to the *ulama* and need for their support would result in the ineradicable entrenchment of their power under his successors. **Amir-e Kabir**, chief minister, 1848–51, sought with only limited success to reduce their influence in the legal sphere through the sharia courts and ability to offer refuge (*bast*) to criminals. Their power rose yet further with their successful leadership of the revolt against the **Tobacco Regie** in 1890.

Initially the *ulama* preferred the rule of Reza Khan to a republican regime which might have introduced secularization on the new Turkish model, but resented the official imposition of western dress codes, including the unveiling of women, from 1928. They supported the 1953 coup which returned **Shah Mohammed Reza Pahlevi** to power, but were increasingly dissatisfied after 1955. They supported the critical stance of **Ayatollah Khomeini** to the concentration of power in the person of the shah and the resulting public demonstrations, 1963. They formed the backbone of the **Iranian Revolution, 1978–9**, and were directly involved in government thereafter, contrary to traditional Shi'ite thinking that they should refrain from any such involvement. Indeed, 1979 constitution of the Islamic Republic of Iran, drafted by Ayatollah Khomeini, enshrines the supreme authority of the Spiritual Leader and the duty of the Council of Guardians to ensure that legislation is compatible with the Islamic code.

underground railroad (USA)

This term refers to the systems of support given to fugitive slaves attempting to escape bondage and flee to the Northern states or **Canada**. The extent of support and methods employed remain uncertain, with most help seemingly being given on an ad hoc or individual basis. Nevertheless, obtaining food, shelter, clothing and advice about safe areas was essential to fugitives. Those who provided help were known as 'conductors', the most famous example being **Harriet Tubman**.

Unilateral Declaration of Independence

The declaration made by British settlers in Southern Rhodesia, later **Zimbabwe**, of independence from the **United Kingdom**. Under the leadership of Ian Smith, white settlers in Rhodesia voted in 1965 to declare independence. Britain, the **Commonwealth** and the **United Nations** declared the move illegal and imposed economic and political sanctions. Guerrilla forces led by **Robert Mugabe** and Joshua Nkomo eventually succeeded in toppling the white settler government in 1980.

Union, Act of (1707) (Scotland)

The Act of Union 1707 united the two kingdoms of Scotland, on the one hand, and England and Wales, on the other, under a common set of institutions in the Kingdom of Great Britain. It was instituted on the English side as a hedge against growing Scots sentiment for a separate Stuart monarch after it became clear that Queen Anne would be childless, and because of fears of Scottish insurgency, and on the Scots side because of financial instability mixed with protestant sympathy on the part of the elite. The Act provided that Scotland maintain a separate system of laws, but that the political authority of both countries would be the Parliament in Westminster, composed of a House of Commons and a House of Lords under a common monarch. There are now persistent demands for Scottish independence.

Union, Act of (1801) (Ireland)

The Acts of Union 1801 (in **Great Britain** and **Ireland**) united the Kingdom of Ireland with that of Great Britain under a common set of institutions. It followed on British concerns that a Catholic or autonomous Ireland would become a base for French Revolutionary and Napoleonic forces, after the 1798 rebellion in that country, and also upon the failure of the Irish elite to secure the Constitution of 1782 granted after the **American Revolutionary War**. As in Scotland in 1707, the Act was unpopular, but unlike Scotland, serious religious and social differences prevented cultural union with Britain, to the point of continuous Irish attempts to break with the Union and the iteration of different nationalisms across the island, resulting in regular attempts at constitutional change for the next two centuries.

Union Minière de Haut Katanga (UMHK)

The Union Minière du Haut Katanga was founded in 1906 by the Société Général de Belgique and operated in the rich mineral province of Katanga in the Belgian Congo. The UMHK's mining activities began slowly, but the company soon became one of the world's largest suppliers of copper as its output increased from 19,000 tons in 1920 to 137,000 in 1929 and 280,000 in 1957. By the time of **World War II**, the UMHK was not only a major copper producer, but was also the world's largest supplier of cobalt and uranium. It was also the largest employer in the Belgian Congo. State finances were heavily reliant on the UMHK, and the company attracted international attention at independence in 1960, when Katanga was declared independent and survived until 1963 with UMHK backing. The company was nationalized in 1967 by Mobutu, and subsequently replaced by the state corporation GECAMINES.

Union of Soviet Socialist Republics (USSR)

– *see* **Soviet Union**.

Unitarianism

A liberal **Christian** movement that rejects trinitarianism, human depravity and biblical infallibility. The **Enlightenment** witnessed its rationalism and Arminianism assume the shape of a formal denomination in Britain and America from the late eighteenth century. It provided a label for the American founders' deism and took particular hold in New England, where adherents founded the American Unitarian Association in 1825. With no creed or hierarchy, conventional Christian elements dropped out from the late nineteenth century, confirming this small denomination's universalism, liberalism and humanism.

United Arab Emirates (UAE)

Arab, Muslim federation of seven emirates located in eastern Arabia with its capital at **Abu Dhabi**. The UAE formed on 2 December 1971 when six of the former Trucial States (Abu Dhabi, Ajman, Dubai, Fujairah, Sharjah and Umm al-Qiwain) became independent of British protection. Ras al-Khaimah joined the federation in February 1972. A president, who was Sheikh Zayed ibn Sultan Al Nahayyan of Abu Dhabi from 1971 to his death in 2004, serves as head of state of the federation while the Supreme Council of Rulers ensures participation of the sheikhs of the seven member states. Border disputes, most notably with Iran over Abu Musa and the Tunb Islands as well as with **Saudi Arabia** and Oman, remain unresolved and dominate the UAE's international affairs.

United Arab Republic (al-Jumhuriyah al-Arabiyah al-Muttahida) (UAR)

– *see also* **Egypt**; **Nasser, Gamal Abdel**.

The political union of **Egypt** and **Syria** proclaimed on 1 February 1958 and ratified in national parliamentary plebiscites, 21 February 1958. It lasted until 28 September 1961 when Syria declared independence following a military coup. Egypt retained the title of United Arab Republic (UAR) until 2 September 1971. The union required the creation of a new governmental structure, and the 1956 Egyptian Constitution was, therefore, abolished. The provisional constitution of the new union was promulgated by decree, March 1958, and featured four vice presidents, two Egyptian and two Syrian, a central union cabinet and two regional councils of ministers, one for each constituent country. Syria's political parties were officially dissolved and replaced by the National Union on Egyptian lines. The UAR was the only tangible result of **Nasser**'s promotion of pan-Arabism although the concept generated wide public enthusiasm. The only other example of Arab union, the Arab Federation of **Iraq** with **Jordan**, had lasted only five months in 1958.

United Fruit Company (UFCO)

Formed by multiple mergers of US banana importers, United Fruit emerged after 1900 as, perhaps, the most powerful multinational corporation ever to operate in **Latin America**. Across the Caribbean, Central America and northern South America, UFCO was the guarantor of economic stability and largest landowner, employer and exporter in many countries where it did business. The company earned the sobriquet the 'Octopus' for its pervasive presence and willingness to leverage influence to maximize commercial and economic positions. This power was best exemplified in UFCO's concerted efforts to undermine the government of Guatemalan president **Jacobo Arbenz** by branding his reform agenda a communist conspiracy, a strategy which contributed to his overthrow in a US-sponsored coup in 1954. The influence of UFCO waned in the 1960s and 1970s as its monopoly collapsed. The company survives today under the name Chiquita Brands.

United Kingdom (UK)

– *see also* **British Empire**; **Commonwealth**; **industrialization**; **Ireland**; **Northern Ireland**; **transportation**.

The United Kingdom comprises England, Scotland, Wales and **Northern Ireland**. Wales became part of the United Kingdom as early as the fourteenth century, the crowns of Scotland and England were joined in 1603 followed by an Act of Union in 1707, and **Ireland** became formally part of the United Kingdom in 1801. The creation of the Irish Free State in 1922 led to the current name of the state. The English monarchy has a long history from Anglo-Saxon times and its governing institutions, such as Parliament, also date from the Middle Ages. Parliamentary government was established from the eighteenth century and its bicameral character remains in the House of Lords and the House of Commons. The powers of the former were decisively limited in the twentieth century. Initially comprised of hereditary aristocrats, it was joined by appointed life peers after 1945, and the number of hereditary peers was much reduced by the early twentieth-first century. The House of Commons has been democratically elected since 1928, following a long process of reform over previous centuries.

The parliamentary, legal and constitutional legacy of the United Kingdom has been exported worldwide, and aspects of fundamental documents such as Magna Carta (1215) have been incorporated into the constitutions in other states states and into the **United Nations** Universal Declaration of Human Rights of 1948. Internally, the rise of nationalist sentiment since the 1960s and a bloody conflict in **Northern Ireland** have seen devolution of powers in recent years to a Scottish parliament and to Welsh and Northern Ireland assemblies. A referendum for Scottish independence in 2014 failed to obtain a majority but did not settle the issue.

The expansion of the United Kingdom from the late sixteenth century with the acquisition of colonies led to the creation of the **British Empire**, which, reaching its largest extent in the period after **World War I**, became the largest empire the world has ever seen, both geographically and in size of population. Over the course of the twentieth century the empire was dismantled and converted into the **Commonwealth**, numbering in the early twenty-first century over fifty states, comprising approximately 30 per cent of the world's population. The effects of that expansion have been immense, including the early colonization of what would become the **United States** and creating English-speaking or part English-speaking nations such as **Canada**, **South Africa**, **Australia** and **New Zealand**, heavily populated with migrants from the United Kingdom. Many non-European states are

substantially the creation of the British colonial experience in their frontiers' experience and cultures, with outposts as far flung as **Hong Kong**, **Singapore**, **Fiji** and the Falkland Islands. Cultural influence includes the use of English as the world's most widely spoken language and the widespread adoption of a common sporting culture with games such as football, cricket and rugby. The monarch remains the nominal head of several Commonwealth countries and also Supreme Governor of the Anglican (Episcopalian) Church, the largest Protestant communion, with adherents in many parts of the world, notably **Africa**.

Militarily, colonial and imperial expansion was dependent on maritime power. British involvement was worldwide as early as the **Seven Years War** (1756–63), with British forces involved in **India**, the Caribbean, North America and the Mediterranean, as well as **Europe**. Over twenty years of war with Revolutionary and Napoleonic **France** (1793–1815) not only defeated Napoleonic hegemony in Europe but also gave the United Kingdom almost complete maritime supremacy. This underlay imperial expansion in the nineteenth century and involvement in numerous colonial conflicts. In the twentieth century the United Kingdom was a major participant, and victor, in both world wars, again seeing worldwide involvement of its armed forces. It became a nuclear power in 1951 and remains so. It has fought alongside the **United Nations** in the **Korean War**, but saw conflict during the retreat from empire in Malaya, **Kenya** and **Cyprus**. The United Kingdom became a member of **NATO** at its inception and maintained substantial armed forces in Germany until the end of the **Cold War**. It participated in the two wars against **Saddam Hussein** and in the overthrow of the Libyan regime of Colonel **Gaddafi** in 2011. It has been a member of the UN Security Council since its formation. It joined what became the **European Union** in 1973, subjecting membership to referenda in 1975 and again in 2016. The June 2016 referendum produced a political sensation, with a majority of people opting to leave the EU, although both Scotland and Northern Ireland voted to remain.

The first industrial nation, Britain achieved a dominance in manufacturing in the early and mid nineteenth century when it was the 'workshop of the world', pioneering factory, mining and transport developments in many parts of the world as well as supplying the majority of the world's manufactured goods. This lead was already being eroded by1914 when it was overtaken in production of leading commodities such as steel by the

United States and **Germany**, but with extensive trade and the largest merchant marine in the world it also retained its position as the financial capital of the world, based on the City of London. Latterly, an overwhelmingly service-based economy, the United Kingdom, after a period of concern about economic decline in the 1970s, had retained a position in the twenty-first century as the fifth largest economy in the world. The City of London remains one of the world's major finance centres.

United National Independence Party (UNIP)

A political party in **Zambia** that governed from independence in 1964 until 1991. Founded in 1959, the party served as a vehicle for political protest under the leadership of **Kenneth Kaunda**. At independence, it won the country's first elections and Kaunda established a one-party state. After riots and an attempted coup in 1990, Zambia introduced multiparty democratic elections and UNIP was defeated by opposition party Movement for Multiparty Democracy led by Frederick Chiluba.

United Nations Organization (UN)

An international parliamentary and security body established after **World War II** as successor to the **League of Nations**. The United Nations (UN) was a style adopted by the Allies after the Atlantic Charter, and in its early form was a military alliance. By 1944 extensive planning for the post-war world had begun, and the UN was projected, principally by the **United States**, as a body which could develop and enforce international obligations, offer a forum for the resolution of disputes, preclude war and promote global welfare. The San Francisco conference of 1945 formally established the organization, and the first meeting of its General Assembly was held later that year in London.

The UN was distinguished from the League in that its executive body, the Security Council, contained five permanent members – **Britain**, **USA**, **France**, **China** and **USSR** – that had the power to veto its actions. This, it was thought, would safeguard the sovereignty and interests of the Great Powers whilst other seats on the Security Council would allow for a rotation of world states. Other states – whose numbers would expand rapidly after 1945 – would be represented in the General Assembly, which would be able to pass non-binding motions and offer a global audience for state grievances. There

would therefore be no incentive for states to leave in order to protect their interests, as had been the case with the League. In addition, the removal of the seat of the international body from Geneva to New York, it was thought, would 'lock in' the USA and prevent a repeat of America's failure to ratify the **Versailles Treaty**, as well as acknowledging the new position of the US as essential to world peace and prosperity.

Though it was not the only international body, the UN from the beginning was projected as a nexus for international action, and its principal organs – the international Court of Justice, Security Council, Economic and Social Council, General Assembly, Trusteeship Council and Secretariat – were designed to reflect that. The UN was also capable of creating agencies and commissions, such as the **World Health Organization** and the High Commission on Refugees, which were geared to the management or solution of real world problems. There are currently almost a hundred specialized funds, conventions, agencies, organizations and executive bodies within the UN System, appointed by the Secretary General, the Security Council, or particular national governments, which seek to coordinate world affairs or to solve world problems. Some, such as the International Criminal Court, the **World Bank** and the **International Monetary Fund**, are autonomous but share facilities and some processes, and others are wholly at the disposal of relevant UN administrators. The UN System has been credited with the effective elimination of major diseases such as polio, as much as with the emergence of international private and public law.

The UN Charter specifically tasked the UN with the elimination of the 'scourge of war'. This has manifested itself in various ways. Peace-keeping and peace-making operations have from time to time formed a large part of UN work. Since the UN lacks its own armed forces, the organization has been reliant upon member states and regional security organizations to carry out the resolutions of the Security Council. In the case of peacekeeping operations, this has meant the maintenance by 'blue beret' forces of negotiated peace agreements within or between states or in disputed territories. Many states have deployed armed forces almost purely for UN service. Peace-making has been more controversial, and has involved the imposition by military force of solutions to regional or national problems where sovereignty has broken down or been abused and where the international community via the Security Council has resolved to uphold a responsibility to protect local peoples and general peace.

In UN history, peace-making has also been complicated by the tendency of Great Powers to take action in the name of their own interpretation of international law and UN Security Council Resolutions. This was evident, for instance, in the **Korean War**, the **Suez Crisis** and the second US–Iraq War. During the **Cold War**, problems arose because of occasional boycotts by the USSR and the dispute between the People's Republic of China and **Taiwan** over the 'ownership' of the Chinese seat. These, and the basic dynamic of the Cold War, precluded the development of any coherent 'UN military system'. High hopes were raised in 1991 after the end of the Cold War; but the Yugoslav, Bosnian, Iraqi, Syrian and Rwandan crises demonstrated that international order was better expressed in post-conflict tribunals rather than in any international ability to end war.

The UN has been particularly notable as a sponsor and negotiator of talks and peace agreements between potential belligerents. The US–USSR confrontation of 1962 during the **Cuban Missile Crisis** was allowed a 'safety valve' via formal and informal connections of the two in the Security Council, for instance, and the **East Timor** problems, as well as resolution of many East Asian and African border disputes, have been particularly notable successes. Where problems have been ongoing, the example of international conventions, ministerial meetings and the potential for meetings at the UN can be identified as mollifying.

The United Nations now contains within its membership some 193 states, as well as offering status to the Holy See, indigenous and stateless peoples and disputed territories. It has sponsored the occasional break-up of states such as **Sudan**, and has also acted to provide a common system for the international seabed and outer space. It has also survived **Indonesia**'s temporary attempt at withdrawal in the mid 1960s and sundry Soviet attempts to move its seat to **Australia** or to sponsor rival organizations. It has nevertheless attracted criticism from those who suspect it or its leaders, supporters or particular bodies of seeking to establish world government and to replace absolute national sovereignty with a limited and regulated version thereof. This criticism has from time to time been particularly virulent in the USA, and has resulted in the US Congress witholding funds from the whole body or organs such as the attached cultural organization. However, the UN in its eighth decade is still sponsoring conventions, the rule of law and diplomacy, and the absence of a major direct confrontation between the Great Powers owes more than a little to its existence.

United Nations Education Scientific and Culture Organization (UNESCO)

A specialized agency of the United Nations established in 1946. Its original purpose was to rebuild schools and museums destroyed in **Europe** during **World War II**. Since then it has focused on contributions to peace and security by promoting international collaboration through education, science and culture in order to achieve universal respect for justice, the rule of law, human rights and other fundamental freedoms proclaimed by the UN Charter.

United Negro Improvement Association
– *see* **Garvey, Marcus**.

United Provinces
– *see* **Netherlands**.

United States of America

The Declaration of Independence of 1776 pronounced the independence of thirteen of Britain's North American colonies and articulated the 'self-evident' individual rights that provided the political and ideological foundation of what would become the United States. Having earned their independence from Britain in the 1783 **Treaty of Paris** that ended the **American War of Independence**, representatives from the newly independent states composed the Constitution in 1787 that still governs the nation today. Though early American elites were suspicious of democracy, American states gradually adopted universal, white male suffrage in the early nineteenth century. However, on the issue of emancipation, only the Northern states acted, leaving slavery to become central to the economies and identities of the Southern states. **Slavery**, as evinced in the Missouri crisis and disputes regarding territorial expansion, would dominate politics of the mid nineteenth century. Ultimately, the issue could only be resolved through force during the **American Civil War** (1861–5). Though the Northern states emerged triumphant and amended the Constitution to provide, in theory, basic protection to **African Americans**, the Southern states soon constructed a rigid system of segregation called Jim Crow that would remain in force until the mid twentieth century.

The late nineteenth and early twentieth centuries saw the United States develop its vast territory and emerge as the world's leading economic power. However, ethnic tensions, labour unrest and agrarian decline made this a period of social and political conflict. So-called progressive reformers attempted to tackle these issues with a series of piecemeal reforms in the early twentieth century. More fundamental changes in the nation's political system and economy would occur during the **New Deal** of the 1930s, which strengthened the federal government's regulatory powers and increased social programmes and spending. The **Cold War** had a paradoxical effect on the growth of the state: it encouraged high defence spending, but generally undermined attempts to enlarge the welfare state. There were exceptions to the latter trend, most notably **Lyndon Johnson**'s 'Great Society' programmes of the 1960s, which increased social spending on health care, and the 'war on poverty'. Though conservatism emerged as a dominant political force in the late twentieth century, as embodied in the electoral success of **Ronald Reagan** in 1980, this impulse failed to fundamentally reduce the powers and scope of the federal government.

Central to the history of the United States is racial, ethnic and cultural diversity. Populated by successive waves of immigrants (both voluntary and involuntary), the diversity of its inhabitants has been central to the nation's history. A powerful theme in American history is the process in which ethnic and racial groups, as well as women, have struggled (and continue to struggle) to secure equality – in political, constitutional, social and economic terms. These struggles, most notably the **feminist** and **civil rights movements** of the mid twentieth century, have made pluralism and diversity a central component of national identity. The history of the United States has also been marked by religious diversity. In the 1st Amendment, the architects of the Constitution rejected the notion of an established church, thus enshrining religious pluralism – though usually understood to be Christian pluralism – into the constitutional structure of the new nation. This separation of church and state – though periodically challenged by some evangelical Christians – has helped contribute to the religiosity of Americans by introducing a competitive free market in religion.

Another notable feature of the history of the United States is the transition it has made from former colony to global empire (albeit one that usually has eschewed formal control of peoples outside of its own borders). Early American foreign policy sought to confine **Native Americans** to isolated reservations and to limit European involvement in the western hemisphere, as evinced in the **Monroe Doctrine** of 1823. The United States also sought to protect its commercial interests and promote freedom of the seas – issues which led to a second conflict with Britain in 1812. Later in the nineteenth century, it became more aggressively expansionist, establishing a 'continental empire' during the **Mexican War** and annexing overseas territory in the aftermath of the War of 1898 with **Spain**. In the twentieth century it emerged as the world's pre-eminent power in the aftermath of two world wars. The position of the United States was strengthened further with the collapse of the Soviet Union at the end of the Cold War. Twentieth-century American statecraft has vacillated from internationalism, particularly in economic policy, to unilateral diplomatic and military interventions. Though the United States became the world's strongest military power by the end of the century, its influence and power was more often projected through the means of economics and culture.

The rise of the United States has been directly linked to the development and success of its economy. The classic developing economy in the nineteenth century, the nation benefited from foreign investment, high tariffs that protected nascent industries, bountiful natural resources, a near monopoly on the world's production of cotton, technological innovation, slavery and immigration that provided much needed labour, and a transportation revolution that linked its internal markets. By the late nineteenth century the US economy began to surpass its European competitors. The **Great Depression** of the 1930s demonstrated that American prosperity was contingent upon an open, international economy and compelled the nation's leaders to promote 'globalization' in the second half of the century. In recent years the American economy has begun to resemble itself in the late nineteenth century in being the world's greatest debtor nation as well as the world's greatest recipient of immigrants.

United States Supreme Court

The US Constitution defined the jurisdiction of the Supreme Court, and provided that judges would be named by the president, approved by the Senate and hold office 'during good behaviour'. Congress filled in the details, including the court's size and its relationship to lower federal courts, in the Judiciary Act of 1789. In the first decade the court's standing was uncertain, though most people assumed that it could decide the meaning of the Constitution. Its position was firmly established under **John Marshall**, who defended the court's independence of the **Jefferson** administration, notably in the trial of Aaron Burr (1807), and incidentally established that the court could overrule acts of Congress (*Marbury* v. *Madison*, 1803). Between 1810 and 1824 the Marshall court asserted its authority by overriding state laws and state judicial opinions that exceeded constitutional rights (*Fletcher* v. *Peck*, 1810) or entrenched on federal jurisdiction (*M'Culloch* v. *Maryland*, 1819). These nationalist decisions provoked a **states' rights** reaction in the South and among western debtors which demanded the repeal of the 1789 clause authorizing the review of state judicial decisions. This proposal had little effect, and controversy between the Jackson administration and the court arose over the court's decisions protecting the treaty rights of Southern Indians. Though these decisions proved unenforceable, Jackson in his farewell address (1837) acknowledged that disputes over the meaning of the Constitution could be determined only by the Supreme Court.

Jacksonians were fully reconciled to the Supreme Court when Jackson appointed Roger B. Taney chief justice in 1835. Under Taney, the court displayed more respect for state authority while continuing to make the legal context friendly to commercial development (*Charles River Bridge*, 1837). The 1837 Judiciary Act increased the size of the court in a way that ensured a Southern majority, ensuring that decisions relating to slavery would favour slave-owners. In 1857 the court tried to settle the sectional dispute by ruling, in the *Dred Scott* case, that Congress lacked the power to prohibit slavery from the territories, an opinion that roused a storm of protest in Northern states and undermined the court's standing. In the civil war the Taney court endeavoured to limit the power of the executive, notably over the suspension of *habeas corpus*, but the national emergency made the court largely irrelevant as the federal government asserted its authority over the states during and after the war.

In the 1870s the court began to limit the impact of the 14th Amendment, ruling in the 1883 civil rights cases that its prohibition on discrimination applied to states, not individuals, and in *Plessey* v. *Ferguson* (1896) that the protection of equal rights did not forbid segregation. In the same period the court approved some state regulation of economic activity, but only if it did not encroach on federal jurisdiction or violate property and contract rights other than by due process. Involvement in cases affecting corporations, labour and government hugely increased the court's caseload until the justices were relieved, in 1891, of the duty to serve also on circuit courts of appeal.

Universal Declaration of Human Rights

Adopted by the General Assembly of the **United Nations**, Paris, 1948, and inspired in part by US President **Franklin D. Roosevelt**'s 'four freedoms', declared 1941: freedom of speech and expression, freedom of religion, freedom from want, and freedom from fear. The declaration proclaims that 'All human beings are born free and equal in dignity and rights' (Article 1), that 'Everyone has the right to life, liberty and security of person' (Article 3) and that 'No one shall be subjected to torture or to cruel, inhuman or degrading treatment or punishment' (Article 5). Article 7 provides that 'All are equal before the law and are entitled without any discrimination to equal protection of the law', Article 9 that 'No one shall be subjected to arbitrary arrest, detention or exile', Article 10 that 'Everyone is entitled in full equality to a fair and public hearing by an independent and impartial tribunal', and Article 11 that 'Everyone charged ... has the right to be presumed innocent until proved guilty.' The declaration is mirrored in the Council of Europe's Convention on Human Rights, but many UN members had no serious intention of respecting it in its entirety.

Unkiar Skelessi (Hūnkâr Iskelesi), Treaty of
– *see also* **Straits Question**.

The bilateral eight-year treaty of defensive alliance between **Ottoman Turkey** and **Russia** (8 July 1833), which committed Russia to giving armed assistance to the **Ottoman Empire** if so requested. It was prompted by Sultan **Mahmud II**'s fear that he would be defeated by **Muhammed 'Ali Pasha**, the governor of **Egypt**. A secret article committed the Turks to return to closing the Straits of the Dardanelles to any foreign vessels of war except those of Russia. This provision caused the British great concern and it lapsed under the 1841 London Straits Convention.

Untouchables
– *see* **Caste**.

Upper Volta
– *see* **Benin**.

Urabi (Arabi), Pasha al-Misri, Ahmad (1839–1911)

Leader of the first Egyptian nationalist movement. Of Egyptian peasant stock, he attended **Al-Azhar University**, Cairo, before conscription into the army, rising to the rank of colonel. He shared the widespread resentment of all classes of Egyptians at foreign control, and joined the officers' revolt against Khedive (viceroy) **Ismail Pasha**, 1879. A member of the secret society within the military aiming to displace the Turkish and Circassian officers who exclusively filled the senior ranks, he led the army revolt against them in 1881. Minister of war in the nationalist government of Mahmud Sami al-Barudi in 1882, he coined the slogan 'Egypt for Egyptians' (*Misr li'l Misriyin*). Following the British bombardment of **Alexandria**, he organized resistance as commander-in-chief of the Egyptian Army, proclaiming Khedive **Muhammad Tawfiq** a traitor, but was defeated by the British at Tel-el-Kebir on, 13 September 1882. Captured, court-martialled and sentenced to death, his sentence was commuted to exile in Ceylon (**Sri Lanka**) following British intervention. He was allowed to return to **Egypt** in 1901.

urbanization (Europe)

– see also **economic development; population**.

Urban living can be traced back at least 8,000 years to the Neolithic township of Catal Hüyük in Anatolia and the subsequent classical world contained a number of major cities. The European medieval world similarly included many great cities, particularly in the south, a number of which, including **Constantinople** (Istanbul), Florence, Seville and Venice, still retain their historic fabric. Such cities were essentially centres of administration, finance and trade, and sometimes of defence, and trade, primarily agricultural, was the lifeblood of the smaller market towns which mushroomed across **Europe**. Virtually all survive, although their market function is much diminished.

Urbanization, however, conveys more than the slow migration of people from the countryside to the town which had supported traditional urban living. It conveys the much more dynamic process which started in **Great Britain** as early as the late seventeenth century, when capital accumulation combined with scientific and technological advance to launch the Industrial Revolution. Increasing economic specialization and industrial styles of manufacturing moved wealth generation away from agriculture and the land and into the factory and the industrial city. In so doing, it progressively undermined the economic structure of the village and throughout the later eighteenth century, and even more the whole nineteenth century, people migrated in ever increasing numbers to the new industrial centres, depopulating large tracts of the English countryside. It is a transition which has almost always created poverty and squalor as well as wealth and brought major political and social problems in its wake. The writings of **Marx** and **Engels** were strongly influenced by their personal experience of conditions in industrial Manchester. Socialism itself was an early fruit of the new urbanization and the concentration of large numbers of workers in factories and the slum housing which surrounded them. Despite the noise, dirt and disease, industrial cities remained magnets because they offered work, a wage, however low, and a measure of freedom from the constraints of village life. **Lenin** maintained that it was the urban proletariat which was the most politically advanced of all social classes. Much more widely, the city had come to be seen by the late nineteenth century as the focus of progress.

The transition from rural to urban in Britain was soon reflected in Europe, starting in those regions where local coal and iron facilitated a similar industrial revolution, notably **Germany**'s Ruhr and Silesia. First the canals and then the railways abetted the process by greatly reducing transport costs and making mass production yet more profitable. Advances in health and wealth prompted rapid population growth in both Britain and Germany, although not in **France**, and the growing populations were concentrated overwhelmingly in the cities. Berlin grew from some 120,000 in 1760 to 547,000 in 1861 to almost 2 million in 1919. Vienna grew from over 400,000 in 1846 to 700,000 in 1880; and Paris from 1 to 1.9 million and London from 2.5 to 3.9 million in the years between 1851 and 1881. All were characterized by slums and overcrowding. As the nineteenth century advanced, banking and other service industries joined manufacturing as a stimulus to urban growth, particularly in such capital cities as Berlin, London, Paris and Vienna, and their proportionate importance has increased with time, particularly in London and Paris. Political change has also sometimes played a role. The declaration of Athens as the capital of an independent **Greece** and of Rome as the capital of a unified **Italy** progressively transformed them into the cities of more than a million people of today. Working in reverse, the immigration of Czech-speaking peasants turned Prague from a German-speaking city into a Czech-speaking one and **Czechoslovakia**'s unquestioned future capital.

The transition from rural to urban, however, which **United Nations** statistics show has now made the whole world predominantly urban, has always been uneven in Europe. Although the urban population was well established in Britain by the eighteenth century, in Russia it was just 328,000 in 1724 and still only 1.3 million in 1796. Together with much of central and eastern Europe, Russia remained overwhelmingly rural until the Communists took power in 1917 and after 1945 introduced the industrial transformations with which much of western Europe was long familiar. Contemporary Russia has thirty-two cities of 500,000 people or more. France has followed a slightly different path, perhaps because its rate of population growth has been so much lower. Although people have left the land in very large numbers since 1945, they have migrated less to big cities on the British or German model and more to big towns. Paris and Marseilles remain the sole towns of more than 500,000 people.

A rather different but still significant stimulus to urbanization has been provided by tourism, in which the British again were leaders.The health benefits claimed for sea air took the Prince Regent to Brighton, on the Sussex coast, then little more than a village, and the fashionable aristocracy rapidly copied him. The middle classes and then the working classes followed in large numbers, facilitated by the opening of the railway from London in 1841. The city of Brighton and Hove now has a population of more than a quarter of a million. The British seaside resort had been born, and villages and towns around the coast including Blackpool and Bournemouth were similarly transformed. The process was more modestly repeated on the French Atlantic and Channel coasts, but it was the Mediterranean which was most changed. The French Riviera became the playground of Europe's rich and urbanization spread apace. Nice became the fifth largest town in France. Coastal development, however, was at its most extreme on the Mediterranean shores of **Spain** in the years after **World War II**, when the 'package holiday' and increasingly cheap air travel brought millions, from Britain and Germany in particular, in search of sea and sunshine. Much of the natural coastline disappeared under hotels and leisure complexes and boards announcing future *urbanización* became almost monotonous in their ubiquity.

Current urban developments are somewhat contradictory. Deindustrialization has provided many of the traditional great manufacturing cities of Europe with a major challenge to reinvent themselves which some have achieved more convincingly than others. The more service-oriented cities, particularly the capitals, have generally prospered, although at the expense sometimes of generating potentially destabilizing extremes of wealth. They remain magnets for immigration, although some observers suspect that the ultimate impact of information technology will be to so individualize work and leisure that the traditional urban environment will have lost much of its point.

Urquiza, Justo José de (1801–1870)

Argentine president. Governor of Entre Ríos province during the rule of **Juan Manuel de Rosas**. In 1851 Urquiza rebelled, eventually defeating Rosas in 1852. Urquiza called a constitutional convention that soon produced the constitution of 1853, the first of the unified country. He served as president of the Argentine Confederation (1854–60), but Buenos Aires province's refusal to join the Confederation provoked further conflict until Buenos Aires finally yielded in 1859.

Uruguay

A pastoral colony populated by indigenous peoples, Spaniards and people of mixed ancestry, Uruguay emerged as an independent state in 1828 as a result of British mediation in the conflict between **Brazil** and **Argentina**. It was then known as the Oriental Republic of Uruguay. Characterized by three distinct plains, this small country subsequently attracted numerous European immigrants. Beef, wool, wheat, flax and their processed products anchored its export economy. Two parties, Colorado and Blanco, emerged from civil wars in the nineteenth century. Political stability in the early twentieth century accompanied redistribution of wealth to end social conflict. Uruguay reached its apogee in terms of prosperity and political consensus at mid-century. Urban guerrillas (**Tupamaros**) challenged the government by 1970 as inflation rocked the economy. The military assumed power in 1973 and ignored civil liberties. Open elections were reinstituted in 1985.

US–Japan Security Agreement

A series of security pacts between the United States and Japan from 1951 onwards. The first bilateral security treaty was signed on the same day as the San Francisco Peace Treaty, 8 September 1951. Whilst the United States was obliged to defend

Japan, Japan did not have the same obligation due to the 'renunciation of war' contained in Clause 9 of the Japanese Constitution. Despite the massive public protests against the security revision in 1960, US–Japan alliance has been maintained.

Usuman dan Fodio (1754–1817)

Islamic preacher and leader. Born in Maratta in the **Hausa** state of Gobir (now northern **Nigeria**), Usuman dan Fodio had an Islamist religious education before becoming a travelling preacher in 1774, spreading **Islam** through the Hausa region. His mounting criticism of local rulers provoked an assassination attempt and in 1802 he led his followers into the countryside, developing a reform programme and an increasingly influential politico-religious movement. Attacked by a Gobir Army in 1804, he pronounced **jihad**, appointing military commanders to conduct a campaign. A prolific writer, he set out the structure of a theocratic caliphate in 1806. The capture in 1808 of Gobir and other Hausa city-states enabled the establishment of the **Fulani** Empire, the largest west African empire with a population of 20 million. His success encouraged the spread of Islam throughout the Hausa states and neighbouring regions, from modern-day **Chad** to **Senegal**.

Utilitarianism

– *see* **Mill, John Stuart**.

Utrecht, Peace of (1713)

A sequence of treaties involving **Britain**, the Dutch Republic, **France**, **Portugal**, **Spain** and Savoy in March and April 1713 concluding the **War of Spanish Succession**. The treaties marked Britain's rise as a significant European and global power, put a brake on French expansion, weakened Spain and consolidated the European balance of power. Britain gained territories in **Canada** from France, while Spain ceded **Gibraltar** to Britain together with a monopoly in the slave trade to Spanish America.

V

vaccination

The introduction of antibodies that stimulate immune responses in the human body is one of the most formidable public health advances in history. Vaccination has prevented illness and death for millions. Early credit goes to Edward Jenner, an English doctor, who in around 1795 observed that milkmaids did not suffer much from smallpox, a virulent killer of the time. Jenner hypothesized that the pus in the blisters milkmaids received from cowpox protected them from smallpox. By introducing cowpox (from Latin *vacca*, hence, 'vaccination') virus into humans Jenner immunized them against smallpox. His vaccine spread quickly throughout **Europe** and North America, where laws requiring vaccination appeared as early as 1805. Development of other first generation vaccines included rabies in 1885, plague in 1897, diphtheria in 1923, pertussis (whooping cough) in 1926, tuberculosis and tetanus in 1927, and yellow fever in 1935, along with national programmes of immunization through regular maternal and child health services.

Vajpayee, Atal Behari (1924–)

An author, editor and award-winning Hindi poet who served as prime minister of **India** briefly in 1996 and a second time in 1998–2004 as head of a coalition of political parties known as the National Democratic Alliance. He was a member of the **Bharatiya Janata Party** (BJP), although he retired from active politics in December 2005.

Van Buren, Martin (1782–1862)

Eighth US president, Van Buren combined reverence for Jeffersonian principles with sharp political astuteness. When the New York Republicans divided after 1815, this Albany lawyer became leader of the regular (Bucktail) faction and sought fruitlessly, as US senator (1821–8), to hold the national party together. After 1825 he worked to reconstruct it behind **Andrew Jackson**, reconciling the North to a Southern candidate and appealing to old-party loyalties. Serving as governor of New York, 1829, secretary of state, 1829–31, and minister to **Britain**, 1831–2, he became Jackson's vice president and heir apparent in 1833. As president, he responded to the Panic of 1837 by separating government from banking, and to the Canadian rebellions of 1837 by preserving US neutrality and good relations with Britain. He lost the Democratic nomination in 1844 because he opposed the annexation of **Texas**, and when proslavery opponents again won control of the party in 1848, ran as candidate of the new Free-Soil Party.

Vargas, Getulio (Dorneles) (1883–1954)

Brazilian president. Vargas took power in 1930 after a military rebellion. With military support he created in 1937 the New State (Estado Nôvo), which he ruled without Congress, political parties or elections until he was deposed in 1945. Elected president in 1950, he could control neither high inflation nor ultra-nationalism. After revelations of corruption among his close followers, military pressure forced his resignation on 24 August 1954. He committed suicide the same day.

Vasconcelos, José (1882–1959)

Born in Oaxaca, **Mexico**, he espoused political liberalism, supported **Francisco I Madero**, and fought against dictator **Victoriano Huerta**. As secretary of education in the early 1920s he emphasized *Indigenismo*, integrated Mexican traditions into a national curriculum and further weakened folk and Catholic cultural legacies in education. His most famous publication was *La Raza Cósmica* (1925).

Vatican City

The name given to the sovereign state within the City of Rome (an observer member of the UN) formed in February 1929 following the Lateran Pacts. The Vatican functions as the effective headquarters of the Roman Catholic Church and is an absolute monarchy ruled by the Pope. Technically, it is distinct from the Holy See, which is the name for the episcopal entity which actually forms the basis of the Pope's authority and which travels with him. The Holy See is accredited with diplomatic relations by nearly all states and territories, and is governed through the Roman Curia, which can legitimately trace itself back to the Roman Empire and therefore represents the oldest governing institution in the West. Since being granted by the Emperor Constantine to the popes, the Holy See has at various times been supplemented by other centres as the power and authority of the popes has waxed and waned, both within Rome and without. The Vatican's status as a self-governing entity with its own army and police allows the Roman Catholic Church access to most international meetings and maintains its role as the chief and most influential religious institution of Christendom.

Vatican I

A major Council of the Catholic Church proclaimed changes to official Roman Catholic institutional and doctrinal positions in 1870. The Conference, convened by Pope **Pius IX** in 1869 and attended by the better part of a thousand bishops, cardinals, priests and observers, set out Catholic reactions to modernity. It condemned materialism, atheism and communism, set the Church formally against the revolutionary tendencies of freemasonry, and re-emphasized Catholic self-definition as the Universal Church. The Congress is particularly remembered however, for two decisions. One was the elevation of the Holy Virgin and mother of God, Mary, above all other saints, and the other was the full emergence of the doctrine of papal infallibility. This latter doctrine holds that, when the Pope comments on the 'deposit of the faith' (the body of church teaching) on a matter of morality, and when he says he is doing so, his comments are infallible and irreversible because they are directly inspired by God. This has often been misinterpreted to suggest that the Pope is held infallible on all or even most things. This misinterpretation of the doctrine is a notion which the Papacy has never popularized but which is undeniably incorrect. The misreading has been a major obstacle to Catholic efforts to develop dialogue and meaningful cooperation with Protestants and members of the Orthodox Church.

Vatican II

The second Council of the Roman Catholic Church to be held in the grounds of the Vatican, in 1962–5. Vatican II represented the attempt of the largest Christian Church to adapt to global change in the twentieth century. It abolished the mandatory use of Latin for church services, allowing more engaging and quasi-democratic masses to be conducted in the vernacular language of worshippers, created

a new church constitution called *lumen gentium* (the light of the ages) and attempted to isolate and eliminate **anti-Semitism** and organizational sclerosis in the global church. In associated gestures, Pope John **XXIII** and Pole Paul VI, who dealt with the immediate consequences of the Council, abandoned practices such as the papal triple crown, complex styles of dress and excommunication in favour of attempts to engage with the modern world. These were not wholly successful as the Church did not compromise its views on sexuality, abortion, divorce or other features of late twentieth-century life, and renewed its anti-communism and opposition to artificial contraception. A strong movement emerged within the Church which opposed Vatican II, though only a small part broke away from the new church, and a restoration of some more traditional practices (adapted and elective) such as Latin masses where congregations wished it and the elevation of Catholic fundamentals over ecumenical engagements with other faiths began under Polish-born Pope **John Paul II** in 1978 and continued under Bavarian-born Pope Benedict XVI, elected in 2005.

Velasco Ibarra, José Maria (1893–1979)

A spellbinding orator and charismatic, if opportunistic, political figure, he served as **Ecuador**'s president five times between 1934 and 1972, building a formidable political machine to win power, but the military overthrew him four times. Velasco was a poor administrator with authoritarian tendencies and little understanding of economic issues. A conservative populist, he shifted to the left after 1960 under the influence of the **Cuban Revolution**.

Vendée, revolt in

The revolt against the 1789 Revolution in the deeply Catholic and economically backward Vendée region of western **France**, sparked by the February 1793 conscription acts. Under joint peasant and aristocratic leadership, its 'Catholic and Royal Army' captured Saumur and then Angers in June, but the main insurgent army of some 65,000 was heavily defeated at Cholet in October 1793. Further defeats at Le Mans, where perhaps 15,000 rebels died, and then at Savenay, both in December 1793, ended general warfare.

Venetian Republic

The City of Venice was the centre of a major post-Roman Mediterranean empire in the eastern Mediterranean, north-west **Italy**, and the Dalmatian coast between the end of the seventh century and 1797. It was independent of both the **Papacy** and **Constantinople**, and based on trade. It is widely held to have developed double-entry bookkeeping, the art of accounting, shipbuilding, navigation, banking and glassblowing. Known as *La Serenissima*, or 'most Serene', Venice was intimately involved in the Crusades and the sacking of Constantinople in 1204. Its energies and dominance were sapped by struggles with the **Ottoman Empire** and the Papacy in the seventeenth century, and decline became headlong in the eighteenth. A much denuded republic was conquered and divided by **France** and **Austria** in 1797, occasioning poetic regret and nostalgia from across **Europe** and Italian nationalist grievances closer to home.

Venezuela, Republic of

Marked by the Andes, Maracaibo lowlands, central plains and Guiana highlands, Venezuela was the first department to exit **Gran Colombia**, becoming an independent republic in 1830. Its diverse population numbers around 30 million, with over 3 million living in the capital, Caracas. Cacao and coffee were important exports in the nineteenth century. During the rule of strongman Juan Vicente Gómez (1908–35), Venezuela became a major exporter of petroleum products. The country ranks behind only **Saudi Arabia** in proved reserves of crude oil and may have the largest reserves in the world. Domination by *caudillos* continued from independence to the mid twentieth century. The 1998 election of Hugo Chávez, a former military officer enamoured with **Simón Bolívar**, inaugurated the 'Bolivarian Revolution' with a new constitution in 1999 that renamed the country the Bolivarian Republic of Venezuela. Under Chávez and his chosen successor Maduro, the country faced increasing economic and political chaos, exacerbated by the oil price collapse of 2015.

Venizélos, Eleuthérios (1864–1936)

Eleuthérios Venizélos began his career as a leading politician and a central figure in the independence movement of his native Crete, then still Ottoman territory. Venizélos represented the Cretan rebels in their negotiations with the Great Powers and became minister of justice after Crete became an autonomous Ottoman territory in 1899. By 1905, however, he was leading a movement to unite Crete with **Greece**, and in 1909 was recruited into the electoral politics of the Greek mainland. By 1910 he was the head of a new party, the Liberals, and prime minister of Greece. Venizélos' policies as prime minister tended to promote the

interests and sensibilities of an urban bourgeoisie domestically, while aggressively pursuing a policy of national aggrandizement internationally: Greece expanded territorially during the **Balkan Wars** and **World War I**. Attempts to expand into western Anatolia after World War I, however, resulted in a costly war and the defeat of the Greek Army in 1922 by a resurgent **Turkey**. This defeat marked the end of a period of irredentism in Greek foreign policy. Venizélos left office in 1924, only to return in 1928. In 1932 he was defeated and left office once again. He fled a deteriorating political climate for Paris in 1936, dying of a stroke the same year.

Veracruz Incident (1914) (Mexico)

US President **Woodrow Wilson** wanted to assist **Venustiano Carranza**'s revolutionaries in their bid to prevent an arms and ammunition delivery to Mexican usurper president **Victoriano Huerta**, which it was hoped would lead to the ousting of the president. Fabricating a cause, Wilson ordered US Marines to occupy Veracruz. The occupation lasted seven months and prevented the weapons' delivery. Upon their departure, the US left their military supplies to assist **Álvaro Obregón**'s revolutionary army. The US awarded its troops fifty-five medals of honour.

Verdun, Battle of (1916)

Verdun, a small city in the north-east **France**, has at various times been a great national symbol. It held an important place in the Gaulish, Carolingian and Holy Roman Empires before becoming a fortress city in the 1620s. It was nationally critical in the French Revolutionary Wars, being regained from the Prussians, and was the last non-metropolitan fortress to surrender in the **Franco-Prussian War** in 1870. For most of 1916 Verdun (which was reinforced under the **Third Republic**) was the site of one of the most bitter battles of **World War I**, in which almost a million casualties fell in Allied and German lines. Verdun was proclaimed a redoubt of France in romantic terms by Generals **Pétain** and Nivelle, who both had a hand in the battle, and is now the site of a French national cemetery and an American cemetery.

Versailles, palace of

Versailles began as a small hunting base before being repeatedly expanded to the status of *château* by Louis XIII, beginning in 1624. It was then converted to a monumental palace by Louis XIV, who moved the French court there between 1678 and 1682. Except for a brief interlude between 1715 and 1722, the kings of **France** were not to leave it – and thus, neither were the nobility allowed to avoid it – until 1789. For over a century the gardens, rooms and layout of the palace centred on the royal bedchamber, the effective capital and base of France's absolutist, and non-Parisien, state. In 1871 the Second Reich was proclaimed by victorious German invaders at Versailles, in the Hall of Mirrors, and in revenge, Clemenceau forced the Germans to acknowledge defeat in **World War I** at the same location in 1919. Versailles thus gave its name to the treaty which marked the attempt at post-war peace.

Versailles, Treaty of (1919)

Significant peace treaty signed between **Germany** and the allied powers, with the exception of the **United States**, during the **Paris Peace Conference** on 28 June 1919 at the conclusion of **World War I**. The treaty's complicated negotiations revealed the differing ideologies and security concerns of allied leaders. While the United States sought a more amicable and considerate solution, European powers advocated harsher terms to ensure that Germany would not threaten European security again. One of the more controversial parts of the treaty, the war guilt clause, focused responsibility for the war on Germany. Germany was forced to reduce its armed forces, demilitarize the Rhineland, pay significant reparations and cede colonial possessions as well as territories in **Europe**. The treaty also established the **League of Nations**, inspired by **Woodrow Wilson**'s Fourteen Points. The treaty's conditions cultivated resentment among German people and weakened the economy, which **Adolf Hitler** and the Nazis would exploit in their rise to power, ultimately leading to **World War II**.

Verwoerd, Hendrik Freusch (1901–1966)

South African politician known as the 'architect of **apartheid**'. Born in the **Netherlands**, Verwoerd was an academic in **South Africa** before editing the National Party newspaper in 1937. He opposed his country's involvement in war with Nazi Germany. Elected to the Senate in 1948, he became minister of native affairs in 1950 and prime minister in 1958, playing a central part in formulating, instituting and enforcing the policy of apartheid. He was assassinated.

Vichy France

The name given to the administrative authority of the French state between 1940 and 1944. Vichy was the capital of a southern zone (unoccupied by the Germans) from which the French

civil service and secret police sought to govern, though its nominal authority extended alongside that of the German forces in the northern part of **France**. From 1942, all of France was occupied and Vichy formed an administrative scaffolding for what was in effect a German satellite. Vichy was faced with several varieties of resistance movement, both internal and external, including the **Free French** under **Charles de Gaulle**, and contrasted them with the leadership of **World War I** hero **Phillipe Pétain** and individuals such as Pierre Laval and Joesph Darnand. After 1942 it became associated with the **Holocaust** and extreme reaction; by 1944, though recognized by some of the Allies, it fell, and its leaders were eventually executed or imprisoned on war crimes and treason charges, and tens of thousands of other collaborationists were purged or condemned.

Vicksburg, Campaign and siege of (1862–1863) (US Civil War)

Following the failure of his first campaign, **Ulysses S. Grant** spent the early months of 1863 astride the Mississippi River but failed to create a water route. He moved south of Vicksburg and by 1 May had crossed the Mississippi at Hard Times. The seizure of Jackson permitted Grant to shift westwards unchecked and he won victories at Champion's Hill and on the Big Black. Vicksburg surrendered on 4 July, followed by Port Hudson on 9 July, cutting the Confederacy in two.

Victoria, Queen (1819–1901)

Queen of **Great Britain** and **Ireland**, 1837–1901; Empress of **India** 1876–1901. Victoria was the niece of King William IV and the last of Britain's Hanoverian monarchs. Her name is associated with the era of British ascendancy to global empire, through which she lived, though often her younger period, which she shared light-heartedly with her consort, Prince Albert, is displaced in the public mind by her later serious-faced widowhood after 1861. Victoria was the longest-reigning English monarch and the longest-reigning female monarch in history until overtaken by Elizabeth II in 2015. Her long reign was punctuated by periods of unpopularity which were often reversed by assassination attempts, rallying public support. Her progeny, by blood, descent or marriage, expanded her influence across the capitals of **Europe**. Though she regularly exerted her prerogative behind the scenes, Victoria helped create the idea of the modern, constitutional monarchy which still prevails in Britain today.

Viet Cong

Short for Viet Nam Cong San, also known as the People's Liberation Armed Forces in South Vietnam. The Viet Cong were guerrilla forces working against the South Vietnam government during the **Vietnam War**. They were supported by the government of North Vietnam and integrated into the People's Army of Vietnam after the war. American forces typically referred to the Viet Cong as 'Charlie', which comes from the NATO phonetic alphabet pronunciation of VC, 'Victor Charlie'.

Viet Minh

Shortened form of the Vietnamese for 'League for the Independence of Vietnam'. A Communist-led national front organization founded by **Ho Ch Minh** in **China**, May 1941. The Viet Minh initiated guerrilla warfare under General Vo Nguyen Giap against the occupying Japanese, late 1943, and had liberated large areas of northern **Vietnam** when the Japanese surrendered at the end of **World War II**. They seized Hanoi and established the independent Democratic Republic of Vietnam, which the French, as former colonial rulers, initially recognized. The breakdown of negotiations, however, led to conflict and a French naval bombardment of Haiphong with the deaths of at least 6,000 Vietnamese civilians on 23 November 1946. In the ensuing first **Indochina War**, the Viet Minh benefited from popular support and could, therefore, dominate the countryside. The majority of the leadership was absorbed, 1951, into the Lao Dong (Vietnamese Workers' Party, later Vietnamese Communist Party), which was to remain dominant in North Vietnam. Viet Minh elements joined the Viet Cong in the second Indochina War in South Vietnam, and its leaders remained important after reunification, in 1976.

Vietnam

The Socialist Republic of Vietnam is situated in South East Asia, bordering **Laos** and **Cambodia** to the west and the Gulf of Tonkin and the South China Sea to the east. It has a total area of 329,560 square kilometres and a population of around 90 million. The country includes low and flat delta areas in the north and south and mountainous highlands in the centre. It has a tropical climate in the south, a monsoonal climate in the north, and often suffers serious damage from typhoons originating in the South China Sea. Vietnam became part of the French protectorate of Indochina in 1887. After **World War II** it became one of the most well-known battlefields of the **Cold War**. It was divided in 1954. Communist forces of North Vietnam eventually took over and reunified the country in 1975. The country then became a socialist republic.

Vietnam War (second Indochina War)

The Vietnam War was the longest conflict in US history: America's declared military participation lasted from 1965 to 1973. In **Vietnam**, the conflict is known as the American War and is remembered as a necessary formative struggle in which a small, impoverished nation fought the world's strongest nation to a standstill, and successfully reunified the nation. It is estimated that up to 2 million Vietnamese and 58,000 Americans died.

The conflict's immediate origins can be traced to 1954, when colonial **France** was defeated on the battlefield by the **Viet Minh**, a combination of Vietnamese communists and nationalists. The **Geneva Accords** split Vietnam at the 17th parallel between a communist north, led by **Ho Chi Minh**, and a western-inclined south, where Ngo Dinh Diem eventually assumed the presidency. The Geneva Accords stipulated that nationwide elections should be held in 1956 to reunify the nation but Diem, fearing defeat to Ho Chi Minh at the ballot box, declined to participate, a decision supported by the **United States**.

In December 1960 North Vietnam sanctioned the creation of the National Liberation Front (NLF) in the South, with the purpose of overthrowing Diem's government and securing reunification with Hanoi. President **John F. Kennedy** responded to the NLF threat – and to the weaknesses of Diem's administration – by strengthening US military support, increasing America's 'advisory' commitment from 800 to 16,000 personnel and sanctioning the use of chemical defoliants to strip away the protective jungle foliage which hid NLF insurgents. With America's tacit blessing, the ineffective and polarizing Diem was toppled and subsequently assassinated in a military coup in November 1963. Chaos in South Vietnam followed his removal, as one military government after another came to power. Following the assassination of President Kennedy, his successor **Lyndon Baines Johnson** faced some painful choices.

Fearful of Republican attacks on his anti-communist credentials, Johnson escalated America's commitment to South Vietnam through his presidency, although never to the degree counselled by more hawkish advisers such as General William Westmoreland and National Security

Adviser Walt Rostow. Johnson's decisions were influenced by the fear that US actions might provoke Chinese military intervention, as had been the case during the **Korean War**. Johnson made it clear that he was not going to 'be the President who saw South East Asia go the same way China went' and instructed his advisers to 'tell those generals in Saigon that Lyndon Johnson intends to stand by his word'.

On 4 August 1964 two American ships appeared to come under attack from North Vietnamese torpedo boats in the Gulf of Tonkin. North Vietnamese responsibility was murky – Johnson later remarked that the US ships might have been 'shooting at whales out there' – but it was enough for Johnson to seek open-ended Congressional authorization to respond militarily to North Vietnamese aggression. Johnson's request was passed by Congress on 10 August in the form of Joint Resolution 1145. There were just two dissenters during the vote in the Senate. With Congressional support in hand, Johnson decided to Americanize the war – itself a testimony to South Vietnam's weakness – with the dispatch of ground troops and the launching of a US bombing campaign against North Vietnam to compel it to cease infiltration and its support for the NLF. In March 1965, 2,500 US Marines landed at Danang, South Vietnam. By the beginning of 1968 there were half a million American troops in South Vietnam, the largest deployment since **World War II**.

The Rolling Thunder bombing campaign against North Vietnam lasted from 2 March 1965 to 1 November 1968. In its early stages, heavy restrictions were placed on what North Vietnamese targets were destroyed, but these fell away as it became apparent that the campaign was failing to curb north–south infiltration or affect North Vietnamese morale. US military strategy was two pronged, focusing on aerial bombardment and search-and-destroy missions against NLF battalions. Statistical measures such as 'body count' were deployed to measure progress. Yet, North Vietnam refused to halt its support for its southern communist comrades and sent North Vietnamese Army (NVA) regulars down the so-called **Ho Chi Minh trail** – the main north–south infiltration route – in ever-increasing numbers as the conflict progressed. On 30 January 1968 the NLF launched a nationwide assault on every major town and city in South Vietnam to coincide with the passing of the lunar new year. This Tet offensive was a clear military defeat for North Vietnam and the NLF – 40,000 communist soldiers were killed by a highly effective US counter-attack. Yet, it was also

hugely damaging to President Johnson's credibility; whatever the immediate battlefield situation, it was clear that 'light at the end of the tunnel' was an illusion. The president concluded that the war was unwinnable in its present form and announced his withdrawal from the presidential race.

The 1968 US election was won by **Richard Nixon**, who pursued a two-pronged strategy to secure peace. He extended the US bombing campaign to **Laos** and **Cambodia** in 1969, and dispatched combat troops to both countries in what were termed 'incursions'. Commensurately, he pursued a policy of 'Vietnamization', withdrawing US combat troops steadily while shifting the burden of the fighting to the South Vietnamese Army (ARVN). Following a particularly heavy US bombing campaign against Hanoi and Haiphong in December 1972, National Security Adviser **Henry Kissinger** and North Vietnamese lead negotiator Le Duc Tho signed a peace treaty in Paris in January 1973 which ended hostilities between the two nations, but allowed the NLF to remain in place in the South as a legitimate political party. Both Kissinger and Tho were subsequently awarded the Nobel Peace Prize for this achievement, although Tho declined the award, a sign that North Vietnam did not view the war as over.

In 1975 the North Vietnamese Army launched a conventional invasion of the South and routed the ARVN, whose regulars fled southwards in disarray. Saigon was taken on 30 April 1975 and Vietnam was reunified under communist rule. The Vietnam War was a clear victory for South East Asian communism and represented the worst military defeat in American history. While most orthodox historians deem the conflict a tragic geostrategic blunder, many others continue to agree with William Westmoreland's retrospective judgement that the United States fought with 'its arm tied behind its back'; that with stronger political leadership, fewer restrictions and clearer war aims the outcome might have been different.

Villa, Francisco 'Pancho' (1878–1923)

Mexican revolutionary. Born a peasant as José Doroteo Arango Arámbula, Villa (one of many aliases) was a bandit before allying with Francisco Madero in the 1910 removal of dictator Porfirio Diaz. Following Madero's overthrow in 1913, Villa resumed fighting, emerging as a leader in a ruling alliance but subsequently returned to banditry. Retiring with a government land grant in 1920, he was assassinated when he appeared about to resume political activity.

Virgin Lands Campaign (1956)

A campaign associated with **Nikita Khrushchev** to develop the grain-producing areas of **Kazakhstan** and Altai with displaced labour and prisoners beginning in 1956. The campaign was initially successful and eventually resulted in the greatest production of grain in Soviet history (some 125 million tones). However, reliance on peoples displaced before and during **World War II** (including Volga Germans), who inevitably became both tired and resentful of their work, and overproduction meant that the programme resulted in declining yields and land exhaustion quite quickly, and by 1960 it was a diminishing part of the Soviet food production effort.

Vivekananda, Swami (1863–1902)

Indian Hindu mystic and religious leader. Born Narendranath Datta and western-educated, in his twenties he turned to a mystical temple priest, Ramakrishna, as his guide. Devoted to him, but able to speak and write English with facility, Vivekananda formulated his own version of his guru's teaching, which stressed its Vedantic monistic underpinning with less stress on image worship. After the death of Ramakrishna, Vivekananda took his teachings to the West, particularly to the World Parliament of Religions in Chicago, 1893. He taught **Hinduism** and yoga in the **United States** and **Great Britain** for several years and returned to India to found the Ramakrishna Mission, an order of *sannyasi*, or 'monks', who continued to spread his message of Vedantic Hinduism and social service to **India** in succeeding generations. His skill at recruiting disciples and powerful defence of Hindu customs earned him enduring fame as a religious teacher in his native land.

Vladivostok Accord (1974)

The Vladivostok Accord was part of the arms control process between the **United States** and the **Soviet Union**. It was an informal agreement reached in late 1974 by US President Gerald Ford and Soviet Premier **Leonid Brezhnev** during the **SALT II** negotiations, limiting the number of strategic launchers (some of which could carry **MIRV**s) and heavy bombers for each superpower. It helped lay the groundwork for the SALT II treaty of 1979.

Voltaire (François-Marie Arouet) (1694–1778)

French dramatist, novelist and philosopher. Voltaire's life and work were characterized by a passionate and often irascible opposition to intolerance, traditional religious authority and oppression. Through works such as *Zaïre*, *Candide* and *Lettres philosophiques* he found popular success in **France** and across **Europe** for his witty satires and humane rationalism. Such qualities often resulted in official opprobrium, and Voltaire also experienced imprisonment and exile. He lived in England in 1726–8, and was influenced greatly by performances of Shakespeare's plays, practices of religious tolerance and developments in philosophy and science. Whilst Voltaire praised England's liberal freedoms, he also admired enlightened absolute monarchs who valued rational progress, such as **Frederick II** of **Prussia**. Voltaire was associated with Diderot's *Encyclopédie*, contributing both money and entries. His rationalism extended to aspects of religion, where he opposed revelation and church dogma and favoured rational deism. Voltaire's popularity and influence extended to the courts of Prussia, **Russia**, and the cantons of **Switzerland**, cementing his importance in the European Enlightenment.

Voortrekkers

Boer migrant farmers who left Cape Colony in the two decades after 1834 on the 'Great Trek', seeking independence from British control and moving into the interior of present-day **South Africa**. Moving into new territory, they clashed with the Matabele and Zulus, notably at the battle of **Blood River** in December 1838. The Voortrekkers established Natal and the independent Boer territories of the Orange Free State and the **Transvaal**.

W

Wadai (Ouadaï)

Pre-colonial state in eastern Chad (capital Abéché).
Traditionally founded by sultan 'Abd al-Karim in
the early seventeenth century, Wadai conquered
neighbouring states to dominate the area between
Darfur and Lake Chad, across what is now central
Chad. It reached the height of its power during the
reign of Sultan Muhammad al-Sharif (1834–58), its
economy flourishing with the rise of the east
Saharan trade route from Wadai to Benghazi in
the last half of the century. A Muslim country, its
leaders were influenced by the **Sanusiyah** to the
north. After French occupation in 1912, Wadai
became a prefecture, later region, of **Chad**. It has
suffered from continual unrest from the 1970s, and
in particular from the conflict in neighbouring
Darfur in the Sudan at the turn of the millennium,
since the populations of Wadai and Darfur are
closely related.

Wafd (al-Wafd al-Misri)

– see also **Zaghlul, Sa'ad**.

Egyptian nationalist party. Founded by **Sa'ad
Zaghlul**, 13 November 1918, two days after
the Armistice, as a permanent delegation of the
Egyptian people, seeking the abolition of the
British protectorate over the country and its
replacement by a treaty of alliance. The Wafd also
sought permission to go to London to negotiate
such a treaty with the British government direct
and to be heard at the forthcoming peace conference. The refusal of these requests prompted
rioting organized indirectly by the Wafd, and its
leaders were arrested and deported to **Malta**,
March 1919. Their subsequent release eased public
unrest and Zaghlul made the Egyptian case at the
peace conference. It organized itself as a political
party in September 1923, with a programme of
internal autonomy, constitutional government,
civil rights and Egyptian control of the **Suez Canal**
and of the **Sudan**, winning 90 per cent of the seats
in the 1924 parliamentary elections and forming
the government. It dissolved in 1953 but reconstituted in February 1978, prior to dissolving again
in June 1978.

Wahhabism, Wahhabiyya

More properly Muwahidun (Unitarian). A conservative Sunni religious movement associated with
the eighteenth-century central Arabian reformer
Muhammad ibn Abd al-Wahhab (c. 1703–91), who
preached an austere form of **Islam** that based all
practice on the Qur'an and the traditions (Sunna)
of the Prophet Muhammad. Ibn Abd al-Wahhab
rejected the interpretations of all four schools
of Islamic jurisprudence that were not consistent
with the Qur'an and tradition, although in practice
Wahhabism follows the Hanbali school and
the teachings of medieval scholar Ibn Taimiya
(d. 1328). Although rejecting all 'innovation'
(bida'), ibn Abd al-Wahhab did recognize reason
(ijtihad) as a source of law. In determining doctrinal
and legal issues, Wahhabis rely on the Qur'an, the
Sunna, the consensus (ijma') of the Salafiyah (the
companions of the Prophet and their immediate
descendants) and the consensus of legal scholars
who have drawn reasoned analogy with the
Qur'an and Sunna.

Wahhabi teaching emphasizes oneness or unity
of God (tawhid) and that all acts of worship should
be directed solely to God. Hence, Sufi practices such
as the veneration of saints and even the visiting of
tombs and graves is forbidden as these behaviours
might indicate some mediation between an individual and God. Secondly, Wahhabi teachings
emphasize absolute application of religious practices and sharia law, a teaching that again attacked
Sufi mystical practices, music in general, and added
tobacco and coffee (along with alcohol) to the stimulants forbidden to Muslims. Ibn Abd al-Wahhab
also forbade all forms of ostentation such as the
decoration of mosques and even personal finery.
Finally, he took an uncompromising attitude
against those who did not follow his particular
teachings on tawhid, charging them with apostasy
and subjecting them to death.

Although originally rejected by the people of his
region of Najd, ibn Abd al-Wahhab found a strong
supporter in Muhammad ibn Sa'ud of Diriyya.
The Wahhabi–Saudi alliance lead to the formation
of two Saudi states before the religion became

firmly established with the creation of the modern state **of Saudi Arabia** by **Abd al-Aziz ibn Abd al-Rahman Al Sa'ud**. Wahhabism is the official dogma of Saudi Arabia, as evidenced by the central political role of the Council of Senior Ulama, often including members of the Al Shaykh family, descendents of ibn Abd al-Wahhab, and the *Mutawi'* or 'religious police' who enforce strict compliance with Islamic law. Although still the official dogma, recent 'liberalizing' tendencies in Saudi Arabia have resulted in tensions between legal scholars and the state.

Wahhabism has also begun to assert greater influence throughout the world. It is the major form of Islam practised in **Qatar**, and inspired other reformist movements, such as a Wahhabi movement in nineteenth-century India. In the twentieth century the Saudi government has actively promoted Wahhabi thought through major financial support for religious activities throughout the world. Wahhabi teaching influenced the political philosophers Rashid Rida and Sayyid Qutb and has provided inspiration and the ideological basis for radical Islamic movements such as **al-Qaida**, the **Taliban** and **ISIL**.

Wakefield, Edward Gibbon (1796–1862)

London-born Edward Wakefield believed that many of the problems of England were caused by over-population and overcrowding. Inspired the Durham Report on Canadian colonial policy, he became the advocate for colonization of South Australia and **New Zealand**. He died in Wellington, New Zealand.

Wałęsa, Lech (1943–)

Polish trade union leader and politician. Initially an activist in the Lenin Shipyard, Gdansk, he led the Interfactory Strike Committee which won workers' right to free and independent organization, 1980. Chairman and leading negotiator of the succeeding Solidarinosc (Solidarity). Imprisoned for nearly a year, 1981–2, and leader of the union's underground movement while Solidarinosc was banned, 1981–9, he became president of **Poland**, 1990–5, but withdrew from politics, 2000, following two successive defeats. He was awarded the Nobel Peace Prize in 1983.

Waliullah, Shah (1703–1762)

A religious scholar from Delhi who is sometimes called the founder of Muslim modernism in South Asia. He advocated religious reform and wrote on subjects ranging from Islamic jurisprudence to political and economic topics. While Shah Waliullah's writings are most influential in South Asia, where he inspired many of the reform and revival movements of the nineteenth century, his works in Persian and Arabic are read throughout the Muslim world.

Wall Street Crash

– see also **Great Depression**.

The Wall Street Crash heralded the **Great Depression** of the 1930s. The exact origins of the late 1920s boom, the mechanisms of the consequent stock market euphoria, the failure to control it and the relationship between the ensuing crash and the depression are still debated. Low bank rates in 1927, lax regulation and mishandling by the authorities encouraged the boom. The crash and consequent destruction of wealth then exploited many pre-existing weaknesses in the banking system and institutional and social structure. Income and wealth were especially maldistributed in the 1920s, and the crash coincided with the end of a long construction boom. Unlike in 1987 when a severe crash had few long-term effects, the 1929 collapse was not offset by competent fiscal and monetary policy. The initial shock and its escalating reciprocation aborted the necessary transfer of resources from old declining industries and agriculture to new rising industries, until the whole economy revived in **World War II**.

Wallachia

– see **Romania**.

Walpole, Robert (1676–1745)

Generally regarded as the first prime minister of **Great Britain**, 1715–17 and 1720–42. Walpole created the idea of a senior minister, trusted by the Crown, who could dominate the Houses of Parliament, organize a party behind him, chair the Cabinet and conduct the affairs of state as though he was the Executive. Thus Walpole could hold a variety of offices, but attract the initially abusive term 'prime minister'. His ascendancy depended upon his being in favour with, and of use to, George I, and later George II, to the avoidance of odium and scandal, the bribery of allies and opponents, and the good favour of the electors aided by the occasional war.

Wang Jingwei (1883–1944)

A Chinese Nationalist leader, Wang Jingwei became a member of the Revolutionary Alliance in **Japan** and worked with **Sun Yat-sen**. After Sun's death, he was leader of the left-wing faction of the Nationalist Party. He formed a rival government to **Chiang Kai-shek** in Wuhan in 1927, and led the reunified Nationalist government in 1932–4. After the outbreak of the second **Sino-Japanese War**, he became president of the collaborationist reorganized Nationalist government in Nanjing.

war

War is an activity characterized by assaults on the persons or resources of a collectively defined opponent, who may or may not reciprocate the action. It has been found in every human society at all times, and has therefore been classified in different ways and elaborated according to available technologies. War has also been a source of economic and technological development as well as demand destruction. In the modern period, the industrialization of war and the development of different technologies of coercion and elimination has complicated the categories of warfare. For example, nuclear, chemical and biological warfare have generally been viewed as atrocious or illegal activities, and an attempt has been made to make the latter two forms illegal under the law of nations, at the sanction of war crimes charges and invasions by the international community. There is also a widely held belief amongst scholars of international relations and history that the mere threat of general nuclear war creates a deterrent which allows for the imposition of a 'cold' peace in which states refrain from direct attacks upon possessors of atomic weapons. This concept of deterrence has been a principal explanation of the restraint which the superpowers showed towards each other in the **Cold War**, but has also been proffered as an explanator of the acquisition of atomic weapons by the North Korean, Indian and Pakistani governments. On the other hand, the generally escalated development of light arms and explosive production during the same Cold War, as both blocs built up stocks, and the release of these stocks in the post-Cold War period has been held to explain the development of asymmetric warfare and terrorism. These are situations in which one side begins with a very great disadvantage in terms of the amount of power and destructive capacity available, but then through the acquisition on global markets of small weapons and their calculated deployment can concentrate actions so as to damage opponent morale, populations, societies, economies or leaders.

In the modern period war has changed substantially and has also demonstrated a capacity to change social values. The historian of war Robert

O'Donnell, for instance, has demonstrated how an emphasis on ferocity and aggression as an expression of manliness transmuted with the development of the rifle into a weakness, to be contrasted with the concept of calm and courage under fire. Absolute obedience as a virtue in turn changed in the modern age into an obligation that soldiers recognize and disobey unethical orders, in western armies marked by the lessons of the **Holocaust**, air bombing capacities or nuclear potential. Because war is in part a function of society, the more organized the society, the more armed conflict moves from the clash of individuals in duels or of armed gangs in internecine and intermittent civil conflict to organized violence on a large scale. The rise of the modern army, composed of citizens or sympathizers seeking citizenship and often augmented by territorial or militia groups and enlisted people, is a function of the rise of the state. As the state industrialized, so battles became campaigns and successful states developed a capacity to lose the former whilst winning the latter, as was evident in the **American Civil War**.

The industrialization of warfare should be seen as an holistic process. It is often the case, for instance, that technologies which were developed for business – such as the code-creating cypher machine which was designed to protect the confidentiality of commercial transactions which became the Enigma device – were accelerated by war. Propaganda, supply and an industrial war effort would likewise have been very difficult without typewriters, telephones and telegraphs, paper and paper-copying technology, and uniforms, let alone canned and concentrated foods and drink. In the atomic age, this synchronicity often led to the interaction of commercial and military supply in remarkable ways. For instance, in planning a 'nuclear howitzer' and bomb-based space transport in the 1950s and 1960s as part of 'Project Orion', serious consideration was given by the US Department of Defense to adopting the technology employed by the Coca-Cola company to bottle their beverage in order to deploy atomic weapons. Indeed, across the twentieth century, administrative correlation spread from borrowed methods to borrowed forms of organization. By the mid twentieth century almost all states had integrated previously separate departments of war, army, air forces and navy into a single department or ministry of defence or defence force. Often, these were subject to the control of integrated management boards drawn from joint chiefs of the various military arms and national security figures from the worlds of politics, academia or intelligence organizations. These departments in turn worked with the media to persuade civilians to volunteer for armies or to support the war efforts of professionalized forces. Such collaboration followed from lessons learnt from the Crimean, American, Franco-Prussian, world and East Asian wars about communication, the 'home front' and the need for popular support. In a parallel academic development, the education and training of warriors as professional employees developed apace. This took place at the levels of strategy, operations and tactics, and involved the development of sophisticated military colleges and vocational training programmes. This process has made strategic leadership a key medium through which political and military elites connect. It has resulted in a satellite development of civilian 'national security studies' through which political leaders have sought academic and professional non-military advice as well as recommendations from the leaders of their armed forces. In many jurisdictions, this has led to the development of a national security council, which functions at times like a consultative body for the executive, and at others as a sort of war cabinet.

Modern warfare has also allowed the progressive development of force-multiplying technologies, such as radar and automatic electronic targeting, which have allowed for the destruction of any and every target on the battlefield without close engagement. Such force multiplication has run alongside the development of 'area denial' weapons such as anti-ship and anti-aircraft ballistic missiles, landmines and nuclear technology. These have reversed the historic advantage of states and armies which had more men and a greater population to draw upon, and replaced it with an emphasis on the capacity to construct or to buy high-technology weapons systems and to integrate them with highly trained forces. War has therefore been linked to purchasing power and GDP in new ways. A corollary of this is that there is now no 'front' and that the battlefield is only one area of war. Armed forces must now plan for assaults at home, via ballistic or fast-moving air and seaborne assaults, and for attacks on opponent logistics and resources. Another curious modern development can be found in the fact that weapons have been deliberately limited in use or made smaller, or certain weapons have been anathematized. Treaties, and international and domestic law, have largely contained the development of very large atomic bombs, such as the Tsar Bomba of 1961, and have precluded the exploration and utilization of particular pathways, such as those of

chemical, biological or radioactive weapons, weather and sea-wave alteration, and fragmentation projectiles. This, and the development of asymmetric weaponry, has added something of an advantage to terrorist, guerrilla and insurgent nationalist groups since **World War II**, and has led from time to time to the victory of groups employing such tactics over stronger opponents.

The laws of war have also changed to reflect technology, in such a way that the absolute destruction of opponent forces or targeting of civilians has in effect become illegal under sanction of the International Criminal Court and the Security Council of the **United Nations**. In the context of 'setpiece' state-to-state conflicts, this has not proven controversial; indeed, the notion of crimes against humanity or war atrocities has a very long provenance and was prosecutable in all legal systems once a commander or army had been declared *hostis humani generis*, or 'enemies of all mankind'. The term can be dated to the Roman view of piracy and linked to the Holy Roman Empire's view of chivalry (as evidenced in Peter von Hagenbach's 1474 trial for atrocities). However, in more typical colonial and insurgent conflicts, which have arisen with the confluence of a market in captured or internationally sold arms and the rise of sub-state rebel, ideological or regional nationalist groups, things have become more complicated. Such wars have been set about with many more stringent and legal restrictions on traditional powers than have been applied to insurgents, leading to asymmetry and bureaucratic military hostility to police operations.

Unsurprisingly, multiple explanations have been developed for the existence of war. The greatest theoretician of the practice, Carl von Clausewitz, famously viewed war as an extension of politics, but this was in the context of military clashes between forces which could largely be separated from their populations. The nineteenth and twentieth centuries saw the industrialization of war and the development of 'total warfare' in which a home front was expected to demonstrate support, provide labour, resources and logistical support, and to emotionally identify with the national war effort. This ran alongside the rather curious separation of 'military' and 'civilian' targets, which was often honoured more in the breach than as a rule.

Other theoreticians have viewed war as essentially explicable in economic terms. The greatest exponents of this view were, as befitted materialists, the Marxists. Following **Marx**, **Vladimir Lenin** and **Rosa Luxembourg** argued that warfare was a consequence of **imperialism**, as industrial societies came to be dominated by rapacious monopolies and networks of interest which would ultimately seek new resources and consumers in the territory or population of others. This was similar in itself to the ideas of Thomas Malthus, who held that demographics (though he did not use the term) could explain war, although Malthus himself would have been among the first to note that his explanation was not original.

War has frequently been linked to economics, and not just by Marxist or Leninist thinkers. In the **USA**, for instance, historians and political scientists from Charles and Mary Beard to Eugene Genovese have seen war as intimately related to **capitalism**, in for instance the destruction of the old South during the **American Civil War**. For supporters of **John Maynard Keynes** (and some critics), the real end to the **Great Depression** came with the price-controlled expansion of wartime demand after 1939. In addition, war has been held responsible for the inflation during and after **World War I** which undermined aristocratic and psuedo-aristocratic rents and incomes around the Atlantic and within western Europe while boosting those of public employees and those paid in fiat currency, thereby effecting a social revolution which ultimately elevated the working and middle class. The idea that war actually boosts demand, and that preparatory spending (in the form of a military-industrial complex) is a kind of disguised industrial programme is really quite new. For most of the history of economics, war was seen as a form of demand destruction. However, it has also proven a way of efficiently destroying debt and competition while securing resources.

Psychological and psychoanalytic theories of war have been propounded by Franco Fornari, Konrad Lorenz and John Bowlby, among others. For these thinkers, war in some sense is a consequence of the identification of a repressed or damaged community of individuals with the group to the point of self-sacrifice. One logical consequence of this idea is that past wars sow the seed of future war among the next ones, as children and youths view the progress and development of war in their own community. Closely allied to this view is the idea that war results from the combination of an over-identification of the nation with one or both parents in the minds of war's supporters, and a degree of socialized repression and psychological damage resulting from trauma or bad parenting in repressed or violent societies. Biological and behavioural theorists such as Steinmetz and Lorenz tend

to agree on this latter point, but see mood and ideas as an outgrowth of natural pressures on group resources, membership and territory, which characterize many animals in complex social organizations.

War has, somewhat lazily, been linked with religion. It is certainly the case that people at all military levels have embraced monotheistic or culturally evocative spiritual poses in the prelude to, passage of, or subsequent explanation for war. In theory, for example, the Conquistadores, proponents of the various Islamic military expansions from the beginning onwards, Buddhist anti-Catholics in East Asia and Hindu nationalists in India have all enjoyed religious justification. During the Cold War, 'godless' communism was often contrasted with the supposed non-material aspirations of Catholics, the Orthodox, Baptists, Jews, the mujahideen and other western groups or allies. In World War II the spirit of the Crusades was frequently evoked against Nazi 'paganism' or 'perversion', and chaplains were encouraged to serve and practise religion in combat units.

At home, preachers and politicians frequently interpreted and invoked religious texts to justify their actions, and both nursing and field medicine (as seen in the work of **Florence Nightingale**, the **Red Cross** and the **Red Crescent**) were very much affected by religion. However, religious figures were also very important in the 'depopularization' and moral condemnation of war. This not only included Mennonite and **Quaker** communities, who rejected war outright, but also thinkers and activists such as Reinhold Niebuhr, Pope Benedict XV, Dorothy Day, the entire Society of Jesus, the Berrigan brothers and **Martin Luther King**.

One historian of war, John Keegan, has argued that the embrace, practice and consequence of war needs to be assessed in cultural and political terms. This observation meshes with that of some scholars (and practitioners such as Hermann Goering) that it is hard to argue that most ordinary people ever want war. Instead, views of law, leadership, morality and obligation, particularly among elites, have from time to time overlapped with specific unstable flashpoints and either through accident or design an opportunity has been afforded to leaders and factions to launch war. This was the approach towards World War I which was propagated by Barbara Tuchman in *The Guns of August*, a best-selling work which argued that the combination of an unstable European alliance system and complications arising from the assassination of Franz Ferdinand at

Sarajevo in 1914 'explained' World War I. Regardless of the veracity or not of this explanation, it was cited by **John** and Robert **Kennedy** as a key influence on their restraint of war during the **Cuban Missile Crisis**, and has become a political trope in the United States.

Significant tension has developed between popular and political explanations of the causes of war, academic analysis and the views propounded in war colleges. For instance, for a large body of western opinion in the earlier twentieth century, war was a matter of failed general disarmament and failed collective security. The proposed solution therefore was coordinated and binding global treaties, arbitration and open diplomacy based upon nation states bound together by finance and trade. This was the basis upon which President **Woodrow Wilson**, Secretary of State Frank Kellogg, French Foreign Minister Aristide Briand and the **League of Nations** operated at various times in the interwar period.

It proved impossible to maintain a system based upon these principles but without institutional elaboration and the determined support of the rising great powers. The system which arose after World War II, in which the United Nations, the **Bretton Woods** system and **NATO** managed the decolonization of the European empires and the passage of the USA through the Cold War via world leadership, was an enhanced version of the earlier system. Critically, it largely excluded states opposed to a liberal world order such as **China**, **USSR** and the Republic of **South Africa** from stopping trade and alliance cooperation while providing a forum for leaders and elites to communicate and develop relationships. 'Cold warriors' and later the neoconservatives tended to oppose this process and instead to promulgate the idea of clandestine and open rollback of communism and fascism employing war, intelligence operations, local representatives and strategic military campaigns at particular focus points.

After the Cold War this realist view-point, in which international anarchy outside of alliances was tamed by security guarantees and economic agreements, took on a stronger ideological tinge. For western nations, led by the **Clinton** and **Bush** administrations, regime changes so that governments became law-governed and friendly to trade and democracy became orthodox policy. This led to the idea that the rapid development of overwhelming and highly technological (usually American or Anglo-American) force, followed by popular engagement and the creation of democracy,

would end wars and security threats quickly. The high point of this notion of war as a reintegrated part of politics was the period between the Yugoslav campaigns of the 1990s and the Afghan and Iraq campaigns following the terrorist attacks of September 11th. The subsequent progress and academic analysis of that period has somewhat blunted its appeal.

War, and not simply in the form it took during the two world conflicts, has had a very significant role as a creator, mirror and propagator of culture. This was in part because of the institution of a draft, or national service, in the **United Kingdom** and the United States between 1916 and 1972 (the US never formally abolished the draft, but has not used it en masse since 1972). This mechanism inducted civilians into armies on the basis that the men involved were required by their country to present themselves for potential sacrifice. It therefore involved a great deal of persuasive advertising (initially known as propaganda) and a media strategy directed at men, families, the construction of gender roles and the creation of an anti-pacifist ethic. It broke down in the US after severe opposition to the **Vietnam War**, and a pattern of 'draft-dodging' and resistance to conscription arose. In the UK, national service was riven with class antagonism and tainted by the memory of the Great War, in which (because of recruitment from regions) whole villages and towns had found their young men removed, traumatized, killed or wounded. It ended between 1957 and 1963 as the **British Empire** unravelled.

Subsequently, Anglo-American militaries returned to a professional status, and for a time struggled with a mismatch between military views of hierarchy, nationalism, gender separation, sexuality, intoxication and personal discipline, on the one hand, and social mores, on the other. By the late twentieth century, however, the militaries of the English-speaking world, which were experiencing regular use, had been elevated again in popular culture and invested with levels of public trust which other institutions had lost. This was partly because of media management, and did nothing to reconnect political and governing elites, who had largely avoided or not been required to engage in service, with armed forces. In other countries, the situation was different, as drafts were maintained in the form of service to the state in countries such as **South Korea**, and up to the 1990s in **France**, **Italy** and **Germany**. In these countries, service in the military and preparation for war was seen as an essential element of citizenship. This attitude could be dated to ideas which emerged from the **French Revolution** about citizen republicans, or **Bismarck**'s partnership of welfare benefits with time in the military, though of course it only applied to men.

The **Crimean War** is generally acknowledged as the first in which the propagation of photography and reports from the scene in newspapers affected public opinion and the course of the war. However, in that and subsequent nineteenth-century conflicts, an aesthetic distaste for war, which was new in European history, began to emerge. Poets such as Tennyson, for instance, were encouraged to turn to criticism in verse of commanders, and to call for world government and peace. In World War I rejection of the values of industrial war became a flood, and a generation of war poets, artists and filmmakers, some of whom died on the battlefields of France, emerged. They typically employed modernist methods, para-rhyme and blank verse, and powerful imagery to condemn war as a waste, and to meditate upon the destructiveness of weapons and the fleeting nature of life. In the interwar period, this sensibility, enhanced by the global outbreak of influenza at the end of World War I, has been held to have created a fascination with death, uniforms and violence which bled through into political expressions of fascism, communism and political rhetoric in general. It is noticeable, for instance, how the works of Siegfried Sassoon, Wilfred Owen, ee cummings or John Dos Passos, extending through Ernest Hemingway, all revealed a concern with war and violence which was the obverse of the Nazi and Fascist celebration of the practice. The **Spanish Civil War**, and Picasso's meditation on air bombing, has been held to be revealing of the confluence of modernism and fear of technological war not only because of the emotions which arose from Spain's internecine conflict, but because of the way in which it spoke to fears of apocalypse shared and propagated, for example, by H. G. Wells. World War II produced a slightly more celebratory view of heroism and war, both in the 1950s and 1990s, but the Vietnam and Algerian conflicts, which came in between, were important referents for a sense of rebellion, rejection and social revolution which characterized the 1960s generation.

In the decades after 1990, war had a somewhat unexpected revival as ethnic conflicts, resource disputes and internecine fighting spilled over into the post-Cold War world. Wars of choice, ostensibly to remove bases for terrorism, effect regime change or discipline rogue states were launched by NATO forces in **Yugoslavia**, **Kosovo**, **Afghanistan**, **Iraq**,

Libya and **Mali**. Russian forces intervened in **Georgia** after aggressively prosecuting the war in Chechnya and more clandestinely in eastern Ukraine, and China at various times threatened war over disputed islands with **Japan**, and also its neighbours whilst confronting India, itself in a state of tension with **Pakistan**, in the Himalayas. **Israel**, **Syria**, **Lebanon** and **Iran** became involved in direct or proxy wars, and **Sudan**, **Somalia**, **Burma**, **Mexico** and **Colombia** all experienced serious substate level violence. The most devastating and regionally destabilizing war of the late twentieth century, in **Zaire-Congo**, also threatened continually to flare, as did the possibility of a renewed conflict in the Korean peninsula. Despite this development, one curious feature in popular culture, in the consensus of international business and political opinion, and among most world governments was the lack of a fear of general war. The most devastating armies in history, trained to the height of military doctrine, armed with the greatest technology and embedded in an unprecedented web of human and capital mobility, treaties, organizations and markets, seemed set only to be used in internationally sanctioned, humanitarian or strictly limited operations. This in itself suggested a fundamental change in the postmodern condition to something relatively unseen since the 1648 Peace of Westphalia.

war crimes

A tenet based on the assumption that a common moral framework governed the laws of sovereigns and states, and that consequent duties were owed to fellow Christians, medieval Europe developed the idea that some activities were contrary to God, justice or the peace of the continent. In such a manner, the idea that a particularly brutal or unlimited form of warfare could be made infamous, on the basis that it was *hostilis humanis generis*, or an enemy of all mankind, was transformed into the idea that some commanders could be arraigned for their decisions in war. Similarly, the growth of organizations such as the **Red Cross** was accompanied by the idea that a moral duty existed to provide and care for those soldiers who were too wounded to fight, or who had been taken prisoner and who were therefore no longer belligerent. As a consequence, conventions were agreed at Geneva in 1864, 1906, 1924 and 1949 which were accompanied by later protocols which created a mandate in international law for such care. At around the same time, in The Hague an attempt was made to create binding limits, including some blanket prohibitions, to particular types of weapon and behaviour which resulted in the Hague Conventions of 1899 and 1907 and the Geneva protocol of 1925. These treaties were soon accompanied by the Kellogg–Briand Treaty, which sought to outlaw aggression and war as a tool of policy.

Although the treaties were universally impressive to contemporaries, they proved too weak to prevent the **Holocaust**, or indeed the proliferation of destruction targeted at civilians as well as technology based on firebombing or terror during World War II. Indeed, such was the enormity of the Holocaust that a new war crime – that of **genocide** – had to be invented to describe it. At **Nuremberg** and Tokyo, various individuals were tried for their participation in crimes of aggression and war, and many sentenced to death. The UN System then proceeded to build on earlier treaties and, along with the International Court of Justice, to uphold an idea of international law.

The **Cold War** placed something of a freeze on the development of public criminal law, and disputes arose as to whether any of the three categories of crime – crimes against peace, crimes against humanity, or crimes of war – were to be tried under a general duty by all UN states (the Israeli argument in the Eichmann case) or by international bodies. The surge of ethnic cleansing and genocide at the end of the Cold War in **Rwanda** and the **Balkans** brought the issue to the fore again, and, after a series of experiments with ad hoc international bodies which could try crimes, a permanent International Criminal Court was set up to run alongside sovereign states and the UN Security Council and to prosecute war crimes. Under the 1999 ICC protocol, several dozen people, including heads of state, have been indicted or tried, and though conviction rates have been very low, signatory members agreed to proceed with an expansion of the definition of crimes of aggression in 2017. It is still the case, however, that several states, including the US, are outside the International Criminal Court and possessed of the view that, while the identification and definition of war crimes may be an international matter of customary or public law, their prosecution is a matter for national domestic courts.

War of the Pacific (1879–1884)

Fought by **Chile** against **Peru** and **Bolivia**, primarily over the control and commercial exploitation of nitrate deposits. After Chile's victory, the Treaty of Ancon (1883) gave it the Peruvian province of Tarapacá and temporary control of Tacna.

By a truce in 1884, Bolivia relinquished Antofagasta and its Pacific coast. Diplomatic conflicts and resentment over the war persist; Bolivia still continues to demand access to the Pacific from Chile.

War of the Triple Alliance

– *see* **Paraguayan War**.

War on Poverty (USA)

The label attached by US President **Lyndon Johnson** to a package of anti-poverty programmes whose central element was the Economic Opportunity Act of 1964. Johnson pledged to eliminate poverty not by redistributing income but by equalizing opportunity. This was to be achieved by educational reform, job training and 'community action', but controversy erupted when radicals construed the last as an invitation to challenge established power structures, alienating Johnson and stimulating a conservative assault on the **Great Society** more generally.

Warsaw Pact

Military alliance formed by the **Soviet Union** and the eastern European communist states of **Albania**, **Czechoslovakia**, the German Democratic Republic (East Germany), **Hungary**, **Poland** and **Romania** under the Treaty of Friendship, Cooperation and Mutual Assistance signed in Warsaw on 14 May 1955 in response to the entry of the Federal German Republic (West Germany) into the **North Atlantic Treaty Organization**. Pact forces invaded Czechoslovakia in 1968 to curb liberalization. The Warsaw Pact was dissolved in 1991 after the fall of communism.

Warsaw Uprising (1944)

A 63-day rebellion in Warsaw's Jewish ghetto against Nazi forces from August to October 1944. The uprising represented an attempt by the Polish government in exile in London to encourage the self-liberation of Warsaw in order to avoid Soviet domination after the by then inevitable defeat of Nazi Germany. During the course of the rising, some 188,000 Jews, soldiers and civilians were killed by the ferocious forces of the **SS**, while Red Army troops waited, apparently on **Stalin**'s orders, before moving into the city. As the Germans retreated, Warsaw was razed to the ground, and the Soviets were able to take the area with no resistance.

Wasif al-Tal

– *see* **Tal, Wasif al-**.

Washington Naval Conference (1920–1921)

The Washington Naval Conference was an important exercise in naval disarmament. It was sponsored by the **USA** partly to demonstrate that, although the country had rejected the **Treaty of Versailles** and **League of Nations**, it had not abandoned the hope of international law, and partly to provide a way of containing the growing power of **Japan**. The talks resulted in three major treaties that significantly reduced the number and size of ships placed on the seas by great powers, and which sought to maintain 'open door access' to **China** as well as the avoidance of military confrontation in east Asia, together with a number of bilateral agreements.

Washington, Booker T. (1856–1915)

Booker T. Washington was by far the most powerful **African American** leader in the **United States** at the end of the nineteenth century. In 1895 he gave a famous speech in Atlanta in which he urged African Americans to accept segregation and in turn called on white Americans to fund industrial training schools. By this time Washington was principal of Tuskegee Institute in Alabama. In private, Washington funded some court cases challenging segregation.

Washington, George (1732–1799)

First president of the **United States**. Born into a wealthy family of Virginia planters in 1732, George Washington's early ambition was to be a soldier. He realized that desire in 1754 when, commanding a detachment of Virginia militia asserting a claim to disputed lands in the Ohio River Valley, he came into conflict with a detachment of French soldiers, igniting the **French and Indian War**. He served in that conflict acquiring valuable combat experience before returning to civilian life in 1759. He married a wealthy widow, Martha Dandridge Custis, and settled down to life as a Virginia planter at Mount Vernon. In 1775 he was elected to the Second **Continental Congress** and was present when the **American War of Independence** broke out in Massachusetts. In June 1775 he was appointed to command the Continental Army, a post he held throughout the war. Although he won several notable battles, such as Trenton, Princeton and Yorktown, he recognized early in the war that the struggle was as much political as military. Under his leadership the Continental Army assumed an enormous symbolic importance as the embodiment of the revolutionary cause. As such, Washington

appreciated that keeping the army intact was a greater strategic priority than defeating the British on the battlefield. As a result he pursued a Fabian strategy of avoiding large set-piece engagements which might risk the existence of his army. Rather he drew out the British supply lines hoping to sap the British will and ability to carry on the struggle. He only fought when absolutely necessary and drew on the combined resources of the Continental Army, local **militias** and the French (after 1778) to do so. The strategy succeeded when, in the aftermath of the siege at Yorktown, war weariness caused the fall of Lord North's government and the British agreed to recognize American independence.

After the war Washington resigned his commission (he had served without pay) and returned to civilian life. When he did so he was probably the best-known and most popular man in the United States. When the Constitution was ratified in 1789 he was a near unanimous choice to serve as the first president of the United States. Inaugurated on 30 April 1789, he served two terms as president. His tenure was marred by increasing partisan bickering between his Federalist supporters and the Republican opposition. The partisan division was reflected in his own cabinet, where **Alexander Hamilton**, the treasury secretary, emerged as a forceful advocate for Washington's Federalists, while Secretary of State **Thomas Jefferson** helped to orchestrate the Republican opposition.

The major foreign policy question facing Washington concerned the wars of the **French Revolution**. Hamilton advocated a policy which was sympathetic towards the British while Jefferson favoured France. In the end Washington opted for strict neutrality. Closer to home, Washington's administration was confronted by armed resistance by the **Native Americans** of the Western Confederacy in the Ohio River Valley. After several embarrassing defeats, the United States managed to defeat them in 1794. In domestic affairs, Washington's major task was to establish the national government on a sound financial footing in the aftermath of the war (which he achieved largely thanks to Hamilton) and to maintain the authority and dignity of the government in the face of domestic opposition from the Republicans and occasional violent resistance such as a **Whiskey Rebellion**. Washington retired in 1796 and died at Mount Vernon three years later.

Watergate (USA)

A political scandal in the **United States** that caused the resignation from the presidency of **Richard**

Nixon (9 August 1974), to be replaced as president by Gerald R. Ford. It involved attempts to cover up White House connections with a break-in on 21 June 1972 at the headquarters of the Democratic National Committee, then housed in the Watergate complex in Washington, DC. Although investigations did not uncover evidence that Nixon had prior knowledge of the break-in plans, tape recordings that he maintained of his White House conversations showed that within a week the president was involved in cover-up efforts and the obstruction of justice. The scandal helped foster public scepticism about government, reinforcing a trend connected with the **Vietnam War** and becoming a key element of the US 1970s political landscape. Nixon's assertion of executive privilege to fend off scrutiny of the White House role in Watergate exacerbated the episode's status as a constitutional crisis concerning the limits of presidential power.

Despite the early revelation of a connection between the break-in and the Nixon campaign committee, the crime had little impact on Nixon's November 1972 victory by a landslide over Democrat George McGovern, demonstrating the success of White House denials of involvement. Investigations of the scandal soon overshadowed Nixon's second term as president, however, implicating his closest aides and undermining the pursuit of his political agenda. In handling the court case against the burglars, Judge John J. Sirica's uncompromising approach persuaded them to break their silence and began the process of exposure. The Senate Watergate Committee gathered evidence on the scandal that led to the indictment and prosecution of administration officials, as well as House of Representatives impeachment proceedings. Meanwhile a Watergate special prosecutor – first Archibald Cox and later Leon Jaworski – conducted investigations within the Department of Justice. Television broadcasts of Senate hearings boosted public concern, as did journalistic coverage, most famously by the *Washington Post*'s Bob Woodward and Carl Bernstein. Investigations uncovered a larger disregard within the administration for legalities in such areas as fund-raising.

The July 1973 revelation in the Senate Watergate Committee by aide Alexander Butterfield of a White House taping system led to significant and protracted conflict between the investigators, who sought access to the tapes, and Nixon, who attempted to deny access. The Supreme Court's July 1974 decision in *United States* v. *Nixon* found against the claims of executive privilege. In the same month, House of Representatives impeachment hearings led the House Judiciary Committee to recommend three articles of impeachment against Nixon: obstruction of justice, abuse of power and contempt of Congress. The release of a 'smoking gun' tape, which documented a plan by Nixon to mislead the Federal Bureau of Investigation's break-in inquiries through the claim that national security was at stake, deprived Nixon of most remaining support in Congress, leading to his decision to resign, the first US president to do so. Nixon received a pardon from his successor, Gerald R. Ford, on 8 September 1974 for any involvement in Watergate crimes.

Waterloo, Battle of (1815)

Decisive defeat of **Napoleon Bonaparte** on 18 June 1815 by British, Dutch and Prussian forces which ended the **Napoleonic Wars**. Following his return from exile in Elba and resumption of the imperial crown, Napoleon sought to inflict swift defeats on the British and Prussian forces in **Belgium**, aiming thereby to open the road to Brussels where allied leaders were beginning to deliberate on the future shape of **Europe** and force a settlement that would restore his position as ruler of **France**. Initial French successes at Ligny forced the Prussians under **Blucher** to withdraw, pursued by a substantial portion of Napoleon's forces who remained unavailable for the major battle which followed two days later. **Wellington** took up a defensive position with 68,000 British and Dutch troops, opposed by 72,000 under Napoleon. Sustained attacks by the French failed to break Wellington's lines. The approach of Prussian forces in late afternoon forced Napoleon to commit his Imperial Guard, who were also repulsed, throwing the French Army into wholesale flight. One of the bloodiest battles of the era with over 45,000 killed or wounded, it destroyed Napoleon's ambitions to regain power. He abdicated on 7 July and was sent eventually into final exile on St Helena.

Watt, James (1736–1819)

A Scottish inventor who changed steam-engine design by introducing a condenser to steam engines in 1763, and in 1784 by developing the rotary steam engine. The condenser radically reduced heat loss and improved performance; the rotary engine allowed for great versatility. In alliance with his business partner Matthew Boulton, Watt thus revolutionized mining, the textile business and the commercial use of steam power, and opened the way for a vast expansion of industry. He also developed the concept of horsepower when licensing his systems. His other contributions to industry include the development of a document copier and chemical bleaching.

Weber, Max (1864–1920)

A German political economist who developed the discipline of sociology. In his most popular work, *The Protestant Ethic and the Spirit of Capitalism* (1904–5), he argued religion had profound implications for the work ethic, and was behind the ways cultures of the Occident and Orient had evolved, which, in turn, also had implications for the development of western capitalism and bureaucracies.

Webster, Daniel (1782–1852)

American politician. Webster is remembered as the eloquent spokesman for conservative nationalism and Boston business. Initially, the young New Hampshire lawyer and Federalist Congressman (1813–7) opposed the War of 1812 and spoke for a sectionalist New England. In 1816 he moved to Boston, extended his legal reputation, and, as Massachusetts Congressman (1823–7), helped bring about the Adams–Clay coalition, which associated New England with nationalist Republicans. In the Senate (1827–41), he spoke powerfully for national unity and resisted concessions in the **Nullification crisis**. In the bank war Webster defended the national bank and became a leader of the **Whig Party**, but never its presidential nominee. He served as secretary of state, 1841–3, securing the 1842 settlement of the north-eastern boundary with Britain. Returning to the Senate in 1845, he advocated the Compromise of 1850, in a notorious speech that marked his separation from the Conscience Whigs of Massachusetts, and served as Fillmore's secretary of state, 1850–2.

Webster–Ashburton Treaty (1842)

This diplomatic agreement (also known as the Treaty of Washington) settled a border dispute between **Britain** and the **United States** in the area between **Canada** and Maine. Lord Ashburton and Daniel Webster, the British and American negotiators respectively, were intimately involved in the Atlantic economy and greatly desired a settlement. The treaty resolved the north-east border issue but was otherwise more symbolic than substantive. It sidestepped several controversial issues, most notably impressment and the Oregon Territory.

Weimar Republic

The name given to the German Reich under the constitution agreed at Weimar in 1919, which lasted until it was suspended in 1933. Weimar represented an attempt to turn the former German Empire into a federal republic, with a relatively strong presidency and parliament under a system of proportional representation. Though from the beginning it was faced with border issues, the near secession and then occupation of the Rhineland, agitation from the Left and the Right, and hyperinflation, by 1924 it stabilized and enjoyed five 'good years' before plunging into the **Great Depression**. Faced with turmoil on the streets, economic collapse, isolation and mass unemployment, the state fell into the hands of a Hitler-led coalition and then of a full Nazi government, which contrived to use a 'war on terror' after the Reichstag fire of 1933 to suspend the constitution and replace it with their own structures of 'emergency' rule until 1945.

Weizmann, Chaim (1874–1952)

The first president of **Israel**. Son of a timber merchant who had imbibed the Russian *haskalah*, or Jewish Enlightenment, Weizmann graduated from high school in Pinsk, **Russia**, and received a doctorate in chemistry from the University of Freiberg, **Germany**. In 1904 he began a career as a chemist at the University of Manchester, where he met Conservative Party leader and future foreign secretary Arthur James Balfour. Weizmann had engaged in Zionist activities in Russia and attended the second Zionist Congress in Basel in 1898, where he met leader **Theodore Herzl**. He opposed the scheme to settle Jews in **Uganda** rather than **Palestine** and was an early advocate (1901) of a Hebrew University in **Jerusalem** to serve as a refuge for ostracized Jewish intellectuals.

Weizmann felt that the interests of **Zionism** and of Britain converged on a worldwide level. During World War I, when Britain opposed the **Ottoman Empire**, Weizmann directed Britain's Admiralty laboratory, where he developed methods to produce large quantities of acetone, a key ingredient in the manufacture of the explosive cordite. His contribution to the war effort was recognized by British Minister of Munitions, **Lloyd George**. Weizmann also worked with **Vladimir Jabotinsky** for the recruitment of a Jewish Legion within the British armed forces. In November 1916, Lloyd George became prime minister. He, Weizmann and Balfour were all inclined to support some sort of joint British pledge in favour of both the war effort against the Ottomans and the Zionist cause. The fullest expression of this convergence of views was Britain's 1917 **Balfour Declaration**, calling for a Jewish national home in the then Ottoman province of Palestine. After British General **Allenby**'s conquest of Palestine, the British government asked Weizmann to go there and make recommendations for the future status of the province. In 1918 Weizmann participated in the founding of the Hebrew University of Jerusalem. Realizing the importance of Arab cooperation for any future Jewish endeavour in Palestine, he signed a formal agreement to that effect with Emir Feisal.

Weizmann was repeatedly elected World Zionist Organization (WZO) president. He was always a general Zionist, rejecting the socialism of **Ben-Gurion** and the revisionism of Jabotinsky. In 1935 he presented the Zionist case before Britain's **Peel Commission**, and during **World War II** once again urged Jewish participation on Britain's side, this time in the formation of a Jewish Brigade. After the war he was disappointed with the anti-Zionism of British Prime Minister Clement Attlee. He nevertheless continued to hope for some sort of independent Jewish state affiliated with the British **Commonwealth**, but his approach turned out to be a minority position within the WZO. Weizmann was defeated as WZO president in 1946 in favour of Ben-Gurion's more confrontational, activist approach. Weizmann continued his unofficial efforts on behalf of Zionism, meeting US President **Harry Truman** twice in 1948 to secure American support for Israel. He was rewarded for his efforts when, despite his differences with Ben-Gurion, he was elected Israel's first president in 1948. Today, many streets in Israel and a research institute in Rehovoth perpetuate his memory.

welfare state

A term introduced in 1941 by William Temple, Archbishop of Canterbury, to refer to a state which provided for the welfare of its citizens as well as the protection of their property and security. Welfare itself had from the early twentieth century onwards acquired the meaning of health, education and social security payments, insurance or provision. This meaning distinguishes the idea of the modern welfare state from that derived from the 'one nation' organic Tory paternalism of **Benjamin Disraeli**, the Christianity of the Catholic social tradition, or the more common 'social state' seen in **Germany** and **Italy** after 1870. This is because the welfare state was associated with the creation of individual opportunity and the removal

of barriers to individual success, rather than with the strengthening of communal solidarity under God or the authorities.

The idea caught the imagination of the modern liberal establishment directing the war effort in the Atlantic community, and in 1942 Sir William Beveridge produced a blueprint designed to employ state benefits and insurance against the 'evils of want, ignorance, disease, squalor and idleness'. This implied a vast post-war programme of home-building, health care, state education and benefits to maintain social security and prevent poverty in unemployment which went beyond any insurance principle. The idea found welcome support in the ideas elaborated by supporters of T. H. Green and **John Maynard Keynes**, which held that people were altruistic, wanted to live in an egalitarian community, and that the centralized management of aggregate demand by the state could deliver strong economic growth.

Following victory in 1945, the idea of a welfare state was put into practice in the **UK** by the Labour government of Clement Attlee, which was aided by the relative impotence of any economic opposition given the devastating costs of the war and the way in which it had encouraged a centralized, nationalizing economy. By 1951 a national health service (the NHS) and a system of payments 'from the cradle to the grave' (in the form of funeral grants and benefits for dependants) was in place. Given its socialist flavour, the Attlee administration rejected the option of making these benefits conditional upon pre-payment or financial contribution, though it employed the language of 'national insurance', which was a legacy tax system held over from the reforming financial policies of **David Lloyd George** and Herbert Asquith before **World War I**. The Conservative Party between 1951 and 1964 largely maintained and expanded the welfare state, and in subsequent years most administrations proved unwilling to engage in reform; the Wilson administration, in fact, expanded the implications of educational welfare to lay the foundations of a nationwide, open access college system called the Open University, and for the introduction of comprehensive schools in place of a diverse historic system of selection-based schooling. By 1979 the **Thatcher** administration had committed itself to 'rolling back the state' and therefore to attempting to restrict welfare benefits, introduce an element of market discipline to the NHS and to sell off housing stock, but the elaborated form of a benefit system was maintained. An attempt was made to replace benefits with tax credits by the Blair administration, and carried through by the Conservative–Liberal Democrat coalition of 2010–15 with the planned creation of a consolidated, computer-based 'universal benefit payment' system.

In the rest of the English-speaking world, insurance principles rather than benefits and the government provision of health care prevailed, though a lively debate began in the **USA** in the Truman administration on how far the 'Economic Bill of Rights' proposed by President **Roosevelt** should translate into the 'Fair Deal' policies of President Truman. By 1949, Truman had achieved or was arguing for an extension of the GI bill principles of subsidized education and health care for veterans, improvements in unemployment compensation, education and civil rights reforms, and comprehensive health insurance as well as federal minimum wage legislation, housing policies and farm aid. Truman was unsuccessful in most of his efforts, and his successors did not push the issue until **Lyndon Johnson**. Johnson declared 'war on poverty', introduced the **'Great Society'** welfare programme and generally promoted the vast expansion of welfare. This then resulted in a backlash coinciding with a budget deficit, the **Vietnam War**, and a fracturing of American politics and society to the point where successive Democrat and Republican administrations sought reform of welfare (ironically in a fashion which made it more generous under **Richard Nixon**) before comprehensive reform and withdrawal from welfarist principles in 1996. Nevertheless, the tradition of welfarism in the USA, which was bound up both with federal power, the rise and decline of modern liberalism, and the role of lobbyists for insurance providers and anti-statists in both parties, is often held to have resulted in the **Obama** health care reforms of 2010–14.

From the beginning, welfare attracted a collection of critics, who were not necessarily in agreement and who often were not concerned with strictly empirical facts. These ranged from those who argued that welfarism institutionalized dependency and gave the state a permanent reason to displace traditional and more effective forms of welfare delivery, such as charities and churches, as well as the family. Some believed – as **Winston Churchill** discovered, to initial ridicule – that welfare states could only be functional if attached to an expansive and intrusive state bureaucracy which would eventually function as a drain on the private sector and tax payers in general. The ethical effects and moral hazard associated with the abandonment of the principle of insurance, coming at roughly the same time as the post-war boom in

services, deindustrialization in the West and the rise of what was perceived as a therapeutic, narcissistic culture of the 'baby boom', 'permanent teenage' generation were also much debated. Civil rights, multiculturalism and race relations were often (wrongly) filtered through the application of such criticisms to the perceived decline of the ethnic and racial minority family structure, though these may have had more to do with capitalism, consumerism and the revolution in sexual mores and divorce of the 1960s. Finally, some critics on the Left associated welfarism with the German tradition of a militarized state, and saw in welfare a sedative or anaesthetizing correspondent of crony capitalism and the wars prompted by the development of a military–industrial complex. Many pointed to perceived Asian examples of economic success without welfare as indicators of the correctness of their ideas. These indicators, however, somewhat paled in the face of the reality of north-east Asian adoption of welfare principles as developmental states matured. In the twenty-first century, the debate is still raging.

Wellesley, Arthur, 1st Duke of Wellington (1769–1852)

Anglo-Irish leader who was a dominant military and political figure in **Britain** during the first half of the nineteenth century. Born Arthur Wellesley, he earned the title Duke of Wellington after leading forces in the **Peninsular War**. In 1815 he defeated **Napoleon** at the Battle of Waterloo. Wellington occupied several important governmental offices, including Chief Secretary for **Ireland** and Foreign Secretary, and served as prime minister from 1828 to 1830. His Tory government passed Catholic emancipation but suppressed other changes, including parliamentary reform.

Wellesley, Richard Colley, 1st Marquess (1760–1842)

An Anglo-Irish aristocrat, Richard Wellesley (who changed his name from the plainer Wesley), succeeded his father as second Earl Mornington (1781). A well-connected politician in England, in 1798 he was appointed governor general of **India**, where he joined his younger brother, Arthur (later Duke of Wellington), an up-and-coming army officer. Wellesley responded to the perceived threats from rival Indian powers, from French expansion in Asia, and from the global spread of republicanism by championing an aggressive form of military imperialism. Created marquess, after the conquest of Tipu Sultan's Mysore in 1799 he ran up a massive debt for the **East India Company** by further annexations and an inconclusive war with the Marathas. He was recalled in 1805, but his assertion of British supremacy in India helped to set the later tone of the Raj. An ineffectual but grandiose lord lieutenant of **Ireland** (1822–8 and 1832–4), Wellesley supported Catholic emancipation (in opposition to his more conservative brother).

Wesley, John (1703–1791)
– see also **Methodism**.

Wesley was an ordained Anglican minister, a major figure in the religious **Great Awakening**, and founder and organizer of the Methodist movement. While a Fellow at Oxford, he and other Oxonians formed a group to study and live as devout Christians, including visiting prisoners and caring for the sick. After unsuccessful missionary efforts in Oglethorpe's new Georgia colony, Wesley returned to England and soon began a lifetime of preaching outdoors to the working-class poor, working outside of established churches in homes and local 'societies'. He differed from most other revivalists by rejecting the doctrine of predestination, and teaching that loving God and others, meekness, abstaining from evil and repentance could result in salvation in this life. A separate Methodist Church only developed later.

West Bank
– see **Occupied Territories (Palestine)**.

Western Sahara
– see **Sahrawi Arab Democratic Republic**.

western thought in East Asia
Mostly starting in the sixteenth century, western ideas and practices circulated around East Asia as the countries of **Europe** established religious and economic ties. Originally, through merchants and Christian missionaries, western knowledge of science and technology was the most popular form of knowledge that spread throughout East Asia. In **China**, Matteo Ricci introduced scientific instruments and mathematical concepts. Japanese businessmen and intellectuals after 1720 studied medicine, physics and other forms of western science with Dutch merchants. Protestant missionaries in **Korea** during the late 1800s established schools where Koreans learned about western knowledge and technological innovations. These different forms of knowledge produced new political, economic, social, cultural and religious categories through which many people interpreted

and gave meaning to the natural world and society. In the late 1800s political and economic concepts such as democracy, **Marxism**, **capitalism** and **industrialization** captured the East Asian imagination as people confronted western imperialism and the impact of the global capitalist economy on society.

West Indies Federation
Established by the British government in 1958, the West Indies Federation aimed to facilitate independence in many of the British Caribbean colonies. The British believed that independence for small island colonies could only be viable on a wider regional basis. The Federation foundered when **Jamaica**, fearing that it would have to subsidize smaller islands within the Federation, voted to withdraw in 1961. **Trinidad** soon followed suit, and the Federation was dissolved in 1962.

Whig Party (American)
Supportive of **Henry Clay**'s 'American system' of protectionism and federal infrastructural improvements, Whigs opposed the **Democratic Party** during the second American party system. Emerging from the Era of Good Feelings, the Whigs coalesced awkwardly around opposition to President **Andrew Jackson**, encompassing both National Republicans and Southern supporters of states' rights and **Nullification**. Jackson's 'war' against the Second Bank of the United States and an economic depression (1837–43) vindicated Whigs' claims of executive tyranny and brought them cohesion and much needed electoral viability in the South. William **Henry Harrison** and **Zachary Taylor** won the presidency in 1840 and 1848 but died in office; their successors John Tyler and Millard Fillmore proved internally divisive.

Claiming to stand above partisanship, the Whigs nevertheless offered the Democrats close competition outside the western states. Sectional conflict arising from the **Mexican–American War** and Compromise of 1850 wounded a party that straddled Southern slaveholders and Northern evangelicals imbued with the social reformism of the second **Great Awakening**, and in 1854 the Kansas–Nebraska Act killed it.

Whig Party (British)
Major party that dominated British politics along with the rival Tory Party from the late seventeenth century until the mid nineteenth century. The party's central principles included opposition to absolute monarchical power and support of a parliamentary monarchy as well as toleration

and equality for all Protestants. Members supported the Hanoverian, and more broadly Protestant, succession. The party enjoyed an era of dominance during the early eighteenth century, when its support largely came from merchants and aristocratic landowners. Towards the end of the eighteenth century, the Whigs faced ideological divisions that led to the creation of factions within the party. In the nineteenth century Whig governments enacted significant reforms, including the emancipation of slaves in the **British Empire**, poor law reform and, most significantly, the Reform Act of 1832. Following the decade of reform in the 1830s, the popularity of the Whigs began to decline, and the party essentially disappeared with the rise of the Liberal Party in the mid nineteenth century.

Whiskey Rebellion (1794) (USA)

During the summer of 1794 a series of violent altercations took place in western Pennsylvania in response to a federal excise tax on whiskey. The protestors, mainly small farmers hard hit by the tax, sought to prevent its collection by attacking tax collectors. In response to the unrest, in the autumn President **George Washington** dispatched an army under the command of treasury secretary **Alexander Hamilton** to suppress the rebellion. The rebels fled without offering resistance.

'white man's burden'

– *see* **racism**.

White Russians

The name given to those subjects of the **Russian Empire** who fought against the Bolsheviks in the **Russian Civil War** and who, to one degree or another, supported the former tsarist constitutional settlement. The origins of the term are ambiguous, and may refer to uniforms or commitment to absolute monarchy in a Russian context, but should not be confused with the same term used of Belarussians. White Russians were organized in different and uncoordinated armies between 1917 and 1921, and were split on foreign policy and war aims beyond the defeat of communism; in this lies the main explanation for their destruction by the Red forces of the Bolsheviks. The defeated Whites, who were often of wealthy or aristocratic background, formed a very significant if small diaspora in **Asia**, **Europe** and the **United States** for the rest of the twentieth century. Many members of the cultural, business and intelligence communities in the modern West can trace their families to White émigrés.

Wilberforce, William (1759–1833)

The abolition of slavery in the **British Empire** was the life obsession of William Wilberforce, who was central to this humanitarian reform. The son of a wealthy Yorkshire merchant, he became close friends with **William Pitt** (the younger) (1759–1806), whom he greatly influenced to oppose slavery. In 1784 he became a committed evangelical Christian and this religious enthusiasm, combined with a paternalistic moral conservatism, shaped his campaigns against slavery and in favour of other moral reforms in early nineteenth-century **Britain**.

Wilderness Campaign (4–6 May 1864) (American Civil War)

This military operation arose from a collision in a congested forest. **Robert E. Lee**'s army remained scattered and victory would be achieved by the first concentrated thrust. On 6 May **Ulysses S. Grant** attacked, but was foiled by James Longstreet's counter-stroke, which drove in his left. A draw resulted, for Lee could not exploit his advantage and Grant would not give up the campaign. The following day, Union troops headed for Spotsylvania Court House.

Willard, Frances (1839–1898)

American temperance advocate and woman's suffragist. After an early career as an educator in Evanston, Illinois, she joined the Chicago Women's Christian Temperance Union (WCTU) in 1874. She was elected president of the national WCTU, 1879 and of the world WCTU, 1891 – positions she held until her death. She lectured widely in the **USA** and **Europe**, wrote extensively in cause of temperance and prohibition, and edited the *Union Signal*. She associated the WCTU demand for women's suffrage – 'home-protection ballot' (1876) – and other reform causes with a 'do everything' policy.

Wilmot Proviso (1846) (USA)

In August 1846 David Wilmot, a Democratic Congressman from Pennsylvania, moved an amendment to a bill appropriating money for the **United States**' war against **Mexico**. Requiring that 'neither slavery nor involuntary servitude shall ever exist' in any territory acquired from Mexico, it produced a major sectional confrontation, passing the Northern-dominated House but failing in the Senate. After the South secured new prospects of slavery expansion in 1850 and 1854, the nascent Republican Party made Wilmot's proviso the key article of its programme.

Wilson, Woodrow (1856–1924)

The twenty-eighth president of the **United States**, 1913–21. Wilson initially developed a career as an academic, becoming president of Princeton University, 1902–10. He was elected as Democratic governor of New Jersey in 1910. He won the Democratic presidential nomination in 1912, campaigning successfully with a progressive domestic reform programme, and during his presidency, to which he was re-elected in 1916, oversaw a number of reform measures. With the outbreak of **World War I** he tried to keep the United States neutral, but continued trade and finance meant in effect that the US supported the Allies. The US finally declared war in April 1917 following German attacks on American shipping. Wilson participated in the Paris negotiations on the post-war settlement but failed to persuade his country to join the newly created **League of Nations**. Semi-paralytic strokes in autumn 1919 left him an invalid for the rest of his presidency and his life.

Windward Islands

The Windward Islands lie in the eastern Caribbean and consist of both the French island of Martinique and former British islands. The British Windward Islands comprise Dominica, Saint Lucia, Saint Vincent and the Grenadines, Grenada and **Barbados**. These islands were governed as a single colony between 1833 and 1960 and now comprise several independent states. British occupation led to massive investment in plantations, though before the British permanently occupied these islands they switched between British and French control quite regularly.

Wobblies

– *see* **Industrial Workers of the World**.

World Council of Churches

– *see* **ecumenicism**.

women's history

Women's history has a long history. In 1405 the Italian humanist Christine de Pisan wrote *The Book of the City of Ladies*, providing examples of just queens, loyal wives and pious virgins from the near and distant past. The nineteenth-century women's rights movement occasioned intense interest in women's history, resulting in books such as Lydia Maria Childs' *The History of the Condition of Women, in Various Ages and Nations* (1835). When history became a professional academic field in the late nineteenth century, however, its primary focus was the public realm of politics and war; women were viewed as part of the 'private' realm, and their past was not understood as history by university-trained historians, who were all male.

As universities began to admit women to graduate study in the twentieth century, a few pioneers examined women's history, but such work remained rare. This changed with the feminist movement of the 1960s and 1970s, when advocates of women's rights in the present looked at what they had been taught about the past and realized they were only hearing half the story. They began to investigate the lives of women in the past, first fitting them into standard historical categories – nations, historical periods, social classes, religious groups – and then realizing that this approach, sarcastically labelled 'add women and stir', was unsatisfying. Focusing on women often disrupted familiar categories, forcing a rethinking of the way in which history was organized and structured. The European Renaissance and **Enlightenment** lost some of their lustre once women were included, as did the democracy of ancient Athens or Jacksonian America. Newer historical approaches, such as an emphasis on class analysis or world systems theory, were similarly found to be wanting in their consideration of differences between women's and men's experiences.

When it initially developed, this newest version of women's history was often regarded as a subfield of social history, but over the last forty years it has widened to include investigations of intellectual, political, economic and even military and diplomatic history. Historians of women have demonstrated that there is really no historical change that does not affect the lives of women in some way, though often very differently from the way it affects the lives of men of the same social group. This scholarship has called into question many basic historical paradigms, including capitalism, modernity and even how historical periods are divided and designated. It has also become increasingly self-critical, putting greater emphasis on differences among women.

Building on studies of women, some historians during the 1980s shifted their focus somewhat to ask questions about **gender**, by which they meant a culturally constructed, historically changing and often unstable system of sexual differentiation. Gender history has developed in tandem with women's history, and has led to a self-conscious 'men's history' that examines men's experiences in history *as men*, rather than simply as 'the history of man' without noticing that their subjects were men. Both women's and gender history have been factors in the development of the history of sexuality, though this is also rooted in the gay rights and now LGBTQ movement. Though resistance to all of these approaches remains among some historians, increasing numbers integrate gender as a category of analysis in all of their work.

women's rights (American)

Initially influenced by revolutionary ideals of 'all men are created equal', though the **American Revolution** brought women few rights of citizenship. Women's demands were first fully articulated at the Seneca Falls Convention of July 1848, claiming equal rights for women. Before the civil war there was no independent movement, but in the later nineteenth century two rival national organizations concentrated on the fight for women's suffrage, merging to form the National American Woman Suffrage Association in 1890. Federal suffrage was achieved in 1920 after a long struggle. During the 1920s the movement splintered as the National Women's Party fought for the Equal Rights Amendment while social feminists sought to ensure women's protection based on their difference from men. Alongside political demands, attempts were made to legalize birth control and improve women's place in the economy. Until the 1960s there were few gains, but prompted by the civil rights movement and publication of **Betty Friedan**'s *Feminine Mystique*, second-wave feminism sought to gain women's equality in society, the economy and politics. Some progress was achieved, but backlash caused the defeat of the amendment in 1982.

World Bank (International Bank for Reconstruction and Development)

The International Bank for Reconstruction and Development was conceived at **Bretton Woods** in 1944 to replace the international investment machinery destroyed by the **Great Depression**, although initially the **Marshall Plan** helped reconstruct post-war Europe. In the 1950s and 1960s the bank supplemented faltering international aid to the third world. Recent Chinese and Indian industrialization has been achieved with private multinational company assistance, but the bank and the International Development Agency

(created 1960) have assisted many substantial developments in poorer countries.

World Council of Churches

– *see* **ecumenicism**.

World Economic Forum (Davos)

Title adopted in 1987 by the informal meeting of European business leaders and key figures in the worlds of academia, arts and politics which met annually from 1971 at the Swiss ski resort of Davos, the name by which it is more usually known. Founded by German academic Klaus Schwab in 1976, it offered membership to the '1,000 leading companies of the world', plus notable invitees. Increasingly not just a forum for economic discussion, it witnessed some important diplomatic initiatives, including the so-called 'Davos declaration' between **Greece** and **Turkey** in 1988 to avoid war between the two countries, and a draft agreement in 1994 between **Shimon Peres** of Israel and **Yasser Arafat** of the **PLO** on **Gaza**. In 2007 it expanded to establish a summer Davos in **China** for `global growth companies' from emerging economies. The winter Davos meeting has increasingly attracted world leaders and opinion formers and growing attention from journalists and news media, though its discussions have no formal status.

World Trade Centre bombing (1993)

The explosion in the underground car park of one of the two towers comprising the World Trade Centre in the south-western tip of Manhattan, near Wall Street, New York, on 26 February 1993. Planted by Ramzi Yousef, a Pakistani, the bomb killed six people and injured about a thousand, as well as damaging the base of the tower, which was later repaired. The Centre had been built by the Port Authority of New York and New Jersey as a focus for businesses and government agencies promoting international trade, and the 110-storey towers at 417 metres (1,368 feet) and 415 metres (1,362 feet) were the world's tallest buildings when built, in 1972. Ramzi Yousef was the nephew of Khalid Sheikh Mohammed, the alleged mastermind behind the **September 11th** bombing of the Centre some eight years later.

World War I (1914–1918)

The Great War, as World War I became known, was a general European military struggle which began with the Balkan crisis of July 1914 and ended in the armistice between the Allied and Associated

Powers (**Britain, France, Italy** and the **USA**) and the Central Powers (**Germany** and **Austria–Hungary**) on 11 November 1918. The conflict devastated western and central Europe, helped cause the collapse of the **Ottoman, Russian** and **Austrian Empires**, and created social and economic revolution through mass mobilization, inflation and political change in eastern and central Europe, Germany, France and Britain. It saw the transition of Great Britain from a creditor to a debtor nation, began the process of breaking up the **British Empire**, and gave rise to the **Russian Civil War** (and therefore indirectly to the **Soviet Union**). The war cost over 8.5 million lives lost in combat, plus around 25 million wounded or unaccounted for out of a general mobilization of some 65 million soldiers, and the United States emerged from it as a central economic and cultural world power.

The peace settlement which followed the war required German representatives to accept responsibility for the start of the war, but the real causes of the conflict have been controversial since 1914. The immediate cause was the effect on **Europe**'s alliance system of an ultimatum by Austria to **Serbia** following the assassination of Serbian heir apparent Archduke Franz Ferdinand and his wife in Sarajevo by Serbian nationalists. Russia, in support of Serbia, then mobilized against Austria and its ally, Germany, and this caused France to mobilize in support of its ally, Russia. Given that the British were also allies of France and Russia, the commitment of His Majesty's Government to war on 4 August 1914 set Europe up for conflict. The Italian state refrained from joining its allies in Germany and Austria, and in 1915 switched allegiance and began a campaign against Austria which lasted until 1918. Similarly, **Romania, Japan, Greece** and in 1917 the USA associated with the Allies, while **Bulgaria** and the Ottomans supported the German-led coalition.

The fatal instability of the alliance system in Europe, which had largely arisen from the late 1890s, sits alongside other reasons which are usually preferred for the start of the war. For example, historical works have focused on the rivalry between England and Germany in naval production, the inability of states to rescind battle plans once launched, the personality of the German kaiser, the effects of European imperialism, the economic rivalry of Germany and Russia, and the instability of Austria–Hungary as proximate explanations for the start of the war. Other explanations have been offered for the continuation of the conflict, such as the brilliance of the German war effort (which defeated Russia,

for the first and last time in modern history), the effect of modern propaganda, the false hopes offered by technology and techniques of mobilization, and the inability of either side to score a decisive victory in the west. None of these explanations alone have ever proved wholly satisfactory to historians. However, the explanation of a German search for a wider role in a world of ruthless empire-building and exploitation, allied to modern technology, an institutionally and socially unstable German Reich and the personalities of the German Kaiser and Prussian General Staff have usually figured heavily.

The Great War brought together several trends in warfare which had been developing since the nineteenth century, such as the use of trenches, rifles, machine guns and naval weapons, with modern innovations such as gas, barbed wire, aerial bombardment of civilians and the tank. These latter arose in partial response to the failure of initial military plans in the west. It is widely acknowledged, for instance, that both France and Germany entered the war with sets of strategic and tactical plans in place, though the coherence and unity of these efforts has been questioned. German plans required, inter alia, the fast deployment of troops through **Belgium** into France, and the encirclement of Paris, whilst French plans envisaged a strike into Germany. The Germans anticipated this with a scheme to lure French forces into Alsace-Lorraine, where they would be decimated. That they were not, and the subsequent addition of British to French forces in the north to stop the German armies at Mons caused a 'race to the sea' between the powers, which ended in stalemate, and continued Anglo-French domination of the English Channel and Atlantic coast, are what prolonged the war. With neither the Allies nor the Central Powers able to defeat each other in the west, trench warfare spread across north-east France. This involved fixed, vast systems of trenches and underground complexes in which concealed fire was punctuated by massive engagements. These engagements usually delivered little except mass slaughter. This in turn spurred efforts to develop a technology-based path to victory.

The picture of the west is in contrast to the mobile war in the east. In 1914, for example, German and Austrian forces, aided by the general inefficiency and poor organization of nominally superior forces, scored great if devastating victories at Tannenberg and the Masurian Lakes, which prefigured their eventual defeat of Russia in 1917 and its removal from the war by the **Treaty of Brest-Litovsk** in 1918. This eastern aspect of the war has largely been forgotten; instead, the great engagements of the Marne, Mons, first and second Ypres (1914–15), **Verdun** (1916), the devastating Somme campaign of summer and autumn 1916 in which 'Europe committed suicide' and Britain alone suffered some half a million casualties, Arras and Passchendaele (1917), and the failed amphibious landing at Gallipoli (1915), have remained in the public imagination of the former belligerents.

Although styled a world war, and although it involved many colonial forces (most notably the Indian Army), World War I was largely confined to western Eurasia. The great navies of Britain and Germany largely avoided each other, with one great exception at the Battle of Jutland, and extra-European encounters were rare. German forces were engaged in South West Africa, western **Africa**, the Belgian Congo and on some Pacific islands, but casualties were slight and easily contained by British and French colonial forces.

The war did have major consequences on the various home fronts, however. For instance, the position of women in society was irrevocably changed, as men went to the front and women worked in factories and fields; economies were nationalized and subordinated to the state; inflation and family loss destroyed the base of the European aristocracy in Britain and Germany; and several older empires collapsed, to be replaced by republics or soviets, in Germany, **Hungary**, Russia and eastern Europe. The map of the **Middle East** was redrawn. The UK lost most of **Ireland** (with the independence of the Irish Republic) and ceded its dominant economic role in global affairs to the USA, which joined the war in 1917 and attempted to impose its own settlement, involving a **League of Nations** and a new economic order, at the **Paris Peace Conference** of 1919, which also gave rise to the **Treaty of Versailles**. The war left many questions unanswered, left Europeans with a stark choice of **liberalism**, **fascism** and **communism** as political systems, and produced a legacy of dislocation and bitterness which ran through the subsequent twenty-one years until the outbreak of **World War II**.

World War II (1939–1945)

A global conflict which began in September 1939 and lasted until August 1945. The principal protagonists were the Axis powers of **Germany**, **Italy** and **Japan**, on the one hand, along with their associated states, and the 'United Nations' of the **British Empire**, the **United States**, **France**, **China** and (after 1941) the **USSR**, on the other. The war ranged from the European battlefield through Eurasia, North Africa, the Pacific islands, South East Asia

and the North and South Atlantic, and saw the coordinated use of heavy aerial bombing, the **Holocaust** and the use of atomic weapons as well as the total mobilization of society. It also marked the effective collapse of the **League of Nations** and the world order which had emerged at the **Paris Peace Conference** of 1919.

The origins of the war lay in the expansionism of the National Socialist regime in Germany, and in the geo-strategy of the German leader, **Adolf Hitler**. Having come to power in 1933 determined to free Germany from the **Treaty of Versailles**, it was Hitler's intention to bring all German-speaking peoples together into one autarkic empire or *reich* (the third in German history) and then to acquire 'living space' at the same time as the destruction of world communism by the invasion and division of the **Soviet Union**. This plan required the destruction of European borders, guaranteed by Britain and France, amongst others, which had emerged after **World War I**. Between 1935 and 1939 Hitler was allowed to proceed with this plan because of a policy of 'appeasement' on the part of Britain and France, and the indifference of the United States. After 1939 the resolution of Britain and France to stop Hitler led to a world war in which at least 60 million people were killed (20 million in the USSR alone, a further 6 million in the **Holocaust** and over 34 million in other theatres). Hitler and the Nazis were accompanied in their desire for war by the Italian Fascists, led by **Benito Mussolini**, who eagerly joined their German partners after the success of the campaign against France in 1940. **Spain** and **Portugal**, however, remained outside the conflict. In a separate development, the determination of the Japanese Empire to attack the United States in 1941, and a German move to support the Japanese thereafter, mounted a global challenge to the liberal democratic tradition of the Atlantic countries and to the established European empires in general.

The immediate causes of the war lay in the Czech and Polish crises of 1938–9. **Czechoslovakia** had emerged from World War I as a stable democracy, which contained within its border peoples of Czech, Slovak, German and Jewish extraction, amongst others. Following the successful annexation of **Austria**, Hitler set his eyes on a similar incorporation of the German ethnic areas of the Czech lands. In the Munich conference, Britain, France and Italy agreed to the division of the Czechoslovak state, even though resistance could have led to a German Army coup against Hitler or a difficult winter war which Hitler was not guaranteed to win. This success led Hitler (and the Soviet Union, which joined in a perverse alliance with Hitler the following year) to a deepened contempt for the democracies and a determination to annex all of the remaining Czech lands and large parts of **Poland** in 1939. Britain and France could not allow such a step, and indicated a determination to guarantee the borders of Poland, but with the USSR equally determined to coordinate its own invasion of that state with the Germans, the guarantee could only be backed by the threat of war. Hitler interpreted this threat as a bluff, but it was one that was called in September 1939.

A 'phoney war' in which little seemed to happen from the British and French perspective then set in until 1940. In fact, the Polish campaign illustrated the relative weakness of the German horse-drawn army and their failure to completely perfect the techniques of blitzkrieg and manoeuvre that they had been attempting to develop since the **Spanish Civil War**. In Poland the Germans lost some 49,000 soldiers to death or wounds, and their Soviet counterparts lost an extra 8,000, but at the cost of almost a million Poles. Having absorbed Poland, war began in the west in earnest in 1940. During ferocious fighting, France was overwhelmed by May; the **Battle of Britain**, a contest for air supremacy in the west, began; and a rump French state was established at **Vichy**. At the same time, British and French armed forces were evacuated from Dunkirk in a defeat which became a 'famous victory' in part thanks to the rhetoric of the new prime minister, **Winston Churchill**. The following year saw campaigns in Greece and North Africa and the continuation of the city bombing of Britain known as the Blitz. It was also the year in which Hitler launched a campaign against the USSR, which almost succeeded, and the Japanese Empire, in December, attacked the US fleet at **Pearl Harbor**, in the Pacific. The year 1941 also saw the emergence in Germany of a plan to eliminate European Jews and also Roma, homosexuals and communists through the mechanism of mass industrial slaughter in specialized ways behind the lines. This programme, refined as a 'Final Solution' at the Wannsee conference under Reinhard Heydrich, and pursued by various elements of Hitler's state, came to be known as the Holocaust.

Reverses for Japan and Germany, hitherto dominant, began to appear by 1942, with **Stalingrad** and **El Alamein** halting German armies whilst the Battle of **Midway** marked the decline of Japan in the Pacific, despite victory at **Singapore** earlier in the year. From 1942 onwards Allied superiority in numbers, technology, the organization of the home front and economic capacity placed increasing

momentum behind the 'United Nations'. Following a series of hard-fought battles, Italy surrendered in 1943; D-Day, the allied invasion of Europe in Normandy, complemented the Anzio Landings in Italy in 1944; Soviet Operation 'Bagration' brought Marshal **Stalin**'s forces to Berlin; and Hitler committed suicide along with senior staff in 1945. In the meantime, fearing a Soviet invasion of Japan and the loss of hundreds of thousands of soldiers in an American invasion campaign, the United States deployed two atomic bombs in Japan which ended the military struggle in the East.

The war left a conflicted legacy. Although the USA and USSR continued to work together in the Nuremberg trials of remaining Nazi leaders and war criminals, in truth the **Cold War** had already begun in the struggle for what were soon to be 'decolonized peoples'. The war dealt fatal blows to the remaining colonial empires of Europe, and to British and French pretensions of world power, and Germany was divided for forty-five years between East and West and locked, apparently permanently, into European and Atlantic democratic structures. On the other hand, the war – the worst conflict in human history – elevated the **United Nations** and the **Universal Declaration of Human Rights**, as well as the **Bretton Woods** system, all of which proved more durable than the institutions established in the aftermath of World War I.

Wounded Knee, Battle of (1890) (USA)

Massacre in South Dakota marking the last major act of the **United States**' military suppression of **Native Americans**. The Lakota Sioux had adopted the millenarian 'Ghost Dance', which promised to reverse the depletion of the bison and white encroachment on to native lands. Concerned authorities shot and killed their leader **Sitting Bull** whilst arresting him (15 December 1890). Somehow, the Seventh Cavalry's attempted disarmament of a group comprised mostly of women and children also broke out into indiscriminate gunfire that killed between 150 and 200 people (29 December).

Wright brothers, Wilbur (1867–1912) and Orville (1871–1948)

American inventors credited with being the first to design and fly a powered aircraft in 1903. Their crucial invention consisted of a new and effective method of controlling a flying machine by means of a three-axis control. Their concern was with controlling the aircraft once in the air rather than with its power or wing designs.

Xi'an Incident (1936) (China)

Chiang Kai-shek, leader of the Kuomintang Party, was kidnapped by Zhang Xueliang while visiting troops in Xi'an, Shaanxi province, to discuss strategies against the Communists. Chiang was placed under house arrest and forced to give up his campaign against the **Communist Party of China** and lead a national war against the Japanese. Chiang finally agreed to Zhang's demands, which included a decision to end the civil war and form a United Front with the Communists against the Japanese.

XYZ Affair (1797–1798)

During the winter of 1797/8 an American delegation in Paris sought a negotiated settlement to a crisis in Franco-American relations. Negotiations broke down and the Americans were preparing to depart when they were approached by three French agents, designated X, Y and Z by the Americans, who demanded a 250,000-dollar bribe in order to reach an agreement. The Americans rebuffed the approach, negotiations broke down completely and a 'quasi-war' between the two countries, fought at sea, ensued.

Y

Yalta conference (1945)

A meeting held between 4 and 11 February 1945 at Yalta, in the Crimea. It was attended by the three major Allied leaders of World War II (Churchill, Stalin and **Roosevelt**) and their staffs, and discussed the settlement of post-war European affairs. At the meeting, Stalin promised to oversee free elections in **Poland** (a promise he subsequently broke) whilst arguing that **Romania**, **Bulgaria**, eastern Germany and parts of eastern Europe should become a Soviet sphere of influence in return for agreement on post-war **Germany**, participation in the war against **Japan** and reparations. The conclusions of Yalta were ratified at Potsdam in July by **Truman**, Attlee and **Stalin**, and have always been controversial.

Yamagata, Aritomo (1838–1922)

Meiji founder of the modern Japanese army and political system. He was involved in the Choshu domain's movement to overthrow the **Tokugawa** shogunate. After the Restoration he studied military science in Europe, modelling the Imperial Army on the Prussian Army when he became war minister in 1873. As prime minister, concerned about the encroachment of Russian military by the trans-Siberian route, he argued in the first Imperial Diet (1890) that **Korea** was a strategic buffer zone.

Yamamoto, Isoroku (1884–1943)

Yamamoto was Commander-in-Chief of the Japanese Navy until his death in action. A graduate of Imperial Japanese Naval Academy and an alumnus of the US Naval War College and Harvard University, he was opposed to war with the **USA**. One of **Japan**'s most talented naval strategists, he planned the **Pearl Harbor** attack (7 December 1941) and the ensuing six months of victories around the Pacific, culminating in the serious losses at **Midway** and **Guadalcanal** (June–August 1942) that destroyed the capabilities of the Japanese Navy.

Yan'an

Headquarters for the Chinese Communist Party in 1935 after the **Long March**, the formation of the United Front ended a period of instability with the National Revolutionary Army. Yan'an province developed following a Soviet model of land reforms, improving social services, lower taxation and political organization, which provided the basis for the Communist's growing popularity during the second **Sino-Japanese War**. This period provided the foundation for the Communist's success in the **Chinese Civil War**.

Yangtze floods (1931)

A flood in 1931 which killed more than 400,000 and affected more than 50 million people in **China**'s Yangtze and Huai river basins. The flood also brought about an epidemic of diseases that killed thousands after the flood. Due to improvements made to the river, the loss of life in subsequent floods has been significantly reduced.

Yankee (USA)

This mid-eighteenth-century word's etymology is unclear, albeit most plausibly Dutch, and its meaning is layered. Outside the **United States**, a Yankee may simply be an American; to Southern Americans, a Northerner; and to Northerners, a rural New Englander of English ancestry. A British then a **Confederate** pejorative during the **American Revolution** and **American Civil War** respectively, the label is conversely a source of patriotic pride. It has variously evoked parochialism, reform-minded morality and commercial or technological ingenuity.

yellow fever

Yellow fever is a mosquito-borne disease that had devastating effects on the geopolitics of tropical America during the early modern period. Europeans, especially non-immune soldiers and sailors confined in close quarters, were highly vulnerable to catching the disease. Mortality rates were very high, often leading to expeditionary forces losing 75 to 90 per cent of their troops. Its prevalence in the eighteenth-century Caribbean helps to explain why it was very difficult for white populations to be self-sustaining, thus encouraging large importations of African slaves. It also helps to explain why it was so hard for European armies and navies to attack reasonably well-defended large islands and continental colonies. Spanish America was the main beneficiary of the effects of the disease, as the European forces could not attack its colonies easily but the diseases played a significant role in the American and Haitian revolutions. Yellow fever only became treatable after 1914.

Yemen

– *see also* **Aden**.

Arab, Muslim republic in south-western Arabia with its capital at Sana'a. For much of its modern history the country was divided between the Shi'ite Zaidi imamate of the Mutawakilite dynasty in the north and British-ruled southern Arabia. The overthrow of the imamate and the protracted **Yemeni Civil War** (1962–70) resulted in the formation of the Yemen Arab Republic while British withdrawal from the south brought the Marxist People's Republic of South Yemen. The two states merged in 1990 with north Yemeni strongman Ali Abdullah Salih as president. Southern dissatisfaction resulted in a brief, unsuccessful civil war in 1993, but southern opposition continues to destabilize the country. In addition, a Zaidi-inspired tribal rebellion in the north and internal challenges from **al-Qaida** in the Arabian peninsula continue to disrupt the state. leading to full-scale civil war and intervention by **Saudi Arabia** and, more clandestinely, by **Iran**.

Yemeni Civil War (1962–1970)

The conflict between royalist supporters of the Shi'ite Zaidi imamate and Republican military officers proclaiming a Yemen Arab Republic. The war began on 26 September 1962 when Egyptian-trained Abdallah al-Sallal and other army officers overthrew Imam Muhammad al-Badr, who had succeeded his father, Imam Ahmed bin Yahya, just a week before. Muhammad al-Badr escaped to northern Yemen and organized tribal support with financial aid from **Saudi Arabia** while an Egyptian military force that arrived in early October reinforced the Republican effort. **Egypt**'s defeat in the 1967 **Arab–Israeli War** compelled its withdrawal from **Yemen** by the end of that year, and royalist forces seemed on the verge of victory. However, a stalemate ensued as many tribes, no longer alienated by the Egyptian presence, switched over to the Republican side. The war continued for another two years, but ended with a Republican victory in December 1970.

Yom Kippur War (1973)

Also known as the October War and the Ramadan War, and initiated by the surprise Egyptian and Syrian attacks on **Israel**, 6 October 1973, the Jewish religious holiday of Yom Kippur. It is deduced that **Egypt**'s President **Sadat**, who knew that he could not win a war with an **Israel** armed by the **United States**, had the more limited and realizable objectives of hopefully winning some eventual concessions from Israel, gaining the respect of the US, and breaking the Middle Eastern deadlock.

The joint Egyptian and Syrian attack was well planned and denied Israel the easy victory it had enjoyed in the Six Day War of 1967. **Iraq** and other Arab states sent supporting forces and reduced **oil** production. The Egyptian drive across the Suez Canal, having overwhelmed Israel's Bar-Lev defence line to attack the Israeli-held Sinai peninsula, and the Syrian drive towards the Golan Heights, continued for several days until Israeli forces recrossed the **Suez Canal**, 15–16 October. The US, which was anxious to contain the unexpected crisis, proved slow to supply additional armaments to Israel, while the Arab states launched an oil embargo against the US and increased oil prices. An initial Israeli–Egyptian ceasefire broke down and Israel moved to surround the Egyptian Third Army around Port Said (Bur Sa'id), 22–23 October 1973. The crisis escalated as the **Soviet Union** threatened to send troops to the **Middle East** and America responded by putting its armed forces worldwide on high 'defence condition', but a new ceasefire agreement was brokered on 24–25 October 1973. An Israeli–Egyptian agreement to consolidate the ceasefire was signed 11 November 1973, and the disengagement of Israeli and Egyptian forces became the subject of talks between Egypt, Israel, **Jordan**, the Soviet Union and the US in Geneva, 21–22 December 1973, with a disengagement agreement concluded between Egypt and Israel, 18 January 1974. Tension, however, remained live with a more than doubling of oil prices by Middle Eastern producers, 23 December 1973, for which the crisis engendered by the Yom Kippur War was one motive.

The war came to an end when American Secretary of State **Henry Kissinger** finally succeeded in negotiating an Israeli–Syrian ceasefire agreement, 31 May 1974. Although the superior military performance of the Arab armies compared with the **Six Day War** of 1967 had greatly boosted President **Sadat**'s domestic prestige, it had no direct lasting impact on the ground. On the other hand, it had significantly facilitated his deemed objectives of securing American respect, obtaining concessions from Israel and introducing movement into Arab–Israeli relations. Its true fruit was arguably the **Camp David Accords** between America, **Egypt** and **Israel**, 6–17 September 1978, and the Egyptian–Israeli peace treaty, 26 March 1979, which implemented them. Egypt thereby recognized Israel and Israel evacuated the occupied Sinai peninsula.

Yorktown Campaign (1781) (USA)

During the summer of 1781 General **Charles Cornwallis** led his army, the largest British force in the Southern colonies, into Virginia from North Carolina seeking supplies. In August Cornwallis withdrew his force of 7,200 men to Yorktown on a peninsula between the York and James Rivers where he hoped the Royal Navy could give him supplies. In a combined land and naval operation, French and American rebel forces prevented the resupply effort and laid siege to Cornwallis at Yorktown. Cornwallis was compelled to surrender on 19 October 1781.

Young Ottomans

– see also **Ottomanism**.

Officially organized as a group in 1865, the Young Ottomans were Ottoman intellectuals whose chief goals were the development of Ottoman patriotism and a more liberal, constitutional order within the empire. Key figures of the movement included Ibrahim Sinasi, Ali Suavi and Namik Kemal. An intellectual movement largely targeting educated, Ottoman speakers, their immediate, popular significance was limited. Nonetheless, their publications, including *Basiret, Ulum, Inkilab* and, especially, *Hurriyet*, won an important readership among educated Ottomans, particularly within the expanding Ottoman bureaucracy.

Young Ottoman thought was varied and contradictory, but most of it stemmed from efforts to adapt European intellectual currents to the needs of Ottoman society. Many of the leading figures spent a considerable amount of their careers in exile in **Europe** and were very much affected by the liberal currents there. Like many Muslim intellectuals of the late nineteenth century, they worked to rethink Islamic tradition in ways that made it more conducive to modernization, and embraced interpretations of **Islam** that seemed to coincide with contemporary European practice. They were also deeply critical of what they saw as a facile secularism and lack of respect for Islamic

tradition within the **Tanzimat** reforms. Instead, they argued that Islam, if properly understood, supported women's rights, science and, especially, democratic institutions. A large proportion of their efforts was spent demonstrating the *Islamic* basis of their liberalism; arguing, for example, that there was a Qur'anic basis for such concepts as 'parliament' and 'democracy'.

The Young Ottomans believed that over-reliance on authoritarian control and a lack of popular participation undermined the goals of Tanzimat reformers, and their ideas became increasingly influential as the empire lurched from crisis to crisis. By the beginning of the 1870s, key members of the movement were returning from exile. The future sultan, **Abdülhamid II**, entered into negotiations with the Young Ottomans as part of his rise to power in 1876. Their influence was particularly felt on the development of the Ottoman Constitution, which was promulgated the same year. The constitution implemented many of the Young Ottomans' chief goals, particularly the establishment of an elected parliament. In the crisis which followed the **Russo-Turkish War** of 1877–8, however, Abdülhamid prorogued the parliament and most of the liberal reforms envisioned by the Young Ottomans were abandoned. Ali Suavi died during a coup attempt in 1878. Namık Kemal was forced into internal exile. Others returned to Europe or abandoned their political activities. Nonetheless, if, in the short term, Young Ottoman successes were limited, the movement's long-term influence on Ottoman intellectuals was significant and Young Ottoman writings would be revisited by a new generation of Ottoman reformers at the beginning of the twentieth century.

Young Plan (1929)

The Young Plan of 1929 was the final attempt by the Allies to reform the post-**World War I** German **reparations** system before the **Great Depression** struck. The impossibly high demands of the **Versailles Treaty** for reparations had already been sharply reduced by the **Dawes Act**, 1924. The Young Plan proposed further substantial reductions, but became irrelevant when dollar flows to **Germany** collapsed after 1929. The Lausanne conference, 1932, in effect recognized the impossibility of further payments.

Young Turks

The popular name given to the group of young army officers, students and nationalist officials who sought a reformed and renewed Ottoman Empire at the turn of the twentieth century, of which the nucleus was the Committee of Union and Progress formed by a group of exiles in Paris. Amongst the Young Turks were **Enver Pasha**, Hasan Cemal, Talat Pasha and, in an as yet minor role, **Mustafa Kemal**, later **Atatürk**. The Young Turks were particularly active in Macedonia, which they thought would be the next province to escape from Ottoman control, and they became dominant in the empire with the Young Turk constitutional revolution of 1908. Despite growing power and election victory in 1912, however, they remained unable to control the government until, stimulated by news of the impending surrender of the city of Edirne to the Bulgarians in January 1913, they assassinated the minister of war and took effective control of the empire until its defeat in 1918.

Yrigoyen, Hipólito (1850–1933)

Leader of the Radical Civic Union in **Argentina**, 1916–30, he was president of Argentina in 1916–22 and again in 1928–30. His presidencies were marked by economic crisis at both ends, with massive export-led expansion in between, and by his suppression of demonstrations and strikes. However, he also developed a reputation as a social reformer who aided the position of the working class. He was instrumental in the achievement of universal male suffrage in 1912. He was deposed by a coup led by General Uriburu and died under house arrest in Buenos Aires.

Yucatán peninsula

Made up of the south-eastern Mexican states of Yucatán, Campeche and Quintana Roo, northern Tabasco, north-eastern Chiapas and northern parts of **Guatemala** and **Belize**, the peninsula remains a centre of Maya culture. The Caste War that began in 1847 resulted in henequen production in the north-west replacing sugar production in the centre and east as the new cash crop. Tourism, which is central to the region's economy, is presently threatened by the spread of drug-related violence.

Yugoslavia

Proclaimed, 1918, as the Triune Kingdom of the Serbs, Croats and Slovenes, with the monarch of **Serbia** as king. It recognized the aspirations of southern (Yugo-)Slav nationalists by bringing into one state the Slovenes, the Croats and Serbs of **Austria–Hungary**, and the Serbs and Macedonians of Serbia proper, together with the ethnically identical but hitherto independent Montenegrins. Disrupted from the beginning by tensions between the dominant Orthodox Serbs and the Roman Catholic Croats, it was renamed Yugoslavia in 1929. Attacked by **Germany** and **Hungary**, 1941, it divided into a nominally independent **Croatia**, a Hungarian Vojvodina, a Bulgarian-occupied Macedonia, an Italian Slovenia and Montenegro, an Italian–Albanian Kosovo and a rump Serbia. Liberated, 1945, with a major contribution from **Tito**'s communist Partisans, it became a communist federation, 1945–91, but was determinedly independent of the **Soviet Union** after 1948. In 1991–2 it dissolved into its five constituent republics, except for **Serbia** and Montenegro (Crna Gora) whose federation lasted until 2006, although the name Yugoslavia was dropped in 2002.

Z

Zaghlul, Sa'ad (Sa'd Zaghlul Pasha ibn Ibrahim) (1857–1927)

Egyptian nationalist leader who foreshadowed the political and social **Free Officers** revolution of 1952 and the policies of Colonel **Nasser**. Of Egyptian peasant stock, he attended **Al-Azhar University** in Cairo, and the Egyptian School of Law prior to practising as an advocate. A judge in the Court of Appeal, 1892, he married a daughter of the then prime minister, 1895. Minister of education, 1906–10, he was active in the formation of the People's Party (Hizb al-Ummah), which was seen approvingly by the British consul general, the Earl of Cromer, as advocating a policy of 'cooperation with Europeans in the introduction of western civilization into the country'. As minister of justice, 1910–12, he resigned following a disagreement with the khedive. Elected to the unicameral Legislative Assembly, 1912, and its vice president, 1913. He adopted a nationalist position critical of government until the Assembly's dissolution by the British, who made **Egypt** a protectorate on the outbreak of World War I, in 1914. He formed activist groups throughout the country during the war years, when Egyptian resentment at the clear British intention of making Egypt a formal colony and at the inflationary and other consequences of the war was running high, and, unlike many other politicians who were seen as collaborators with the British, he was seen as a true nationalist.

Together with Isma'il Sidqi (Ismail Sedky) and Hamid al-Basil, Zaghlul organized the **Wafd** Party, 13 November 1918, as a permanent 'delegation' of the Egyptian people, and demanded, initially unsuccessfully, to be heard at the forthcoming peace conference. The ensuing rioting instigated by his nationalist activist groups caused him and three other leaders to be arrested and deported, March 1919. Their release by the new British high commissioner, General Edmund Allenby, eased the unrest and Zaghlul was allowed to attend the peace conference to make the Egyptian case to the Allies. Although the result was negligible, his attendance gave him hero status in Egypt, and ensured that he

would be the sole negotiator with the British colonial secretary, Lord Milner, in the 1920 negotiations on the Anglo-Egyptian relationship. He secured Milner's informal agreement to a proposal for a treaty to replace the protectorate. Fearing, however, that any agreement would compromise his standing in Egypt as an anti-British nationalist, he refused his endorsement and undermined all attempts by the prime minister, his rival, to negotiate the treaty. His instigation of disorder to prevent the formation of any alternative government led to his arrest by Allenby and deportation, with **Mustafa an-Nahhas**, to the Seychelles. Following the unilateral British declaration of a new treaty and grant of limited independence to Egypt, February 1922, Zaghlul was released to fight the 1924 elections, becoming prime minister of a Wafd government. Unable to control the violence he had initiated, however, including the assassination of the British commander-in-chief of the Egyptian Army, he was effectively forced to resign by Allenby. He was president of the Chamber until his death.

Zaibatsu

Business conglomerates which dominated the Japanese process of industrial development before **World War II**. Through favourable tax policies and subsidies from the government, Mitsui, Mitsubishi, Sumitomo and Yasuda, in particular, consolidated their privileged position in trade, banking, railways, textiles, mining, sugar and strategic industries. Under the Allied occupation, *zaibatsu* were broken up to enhance economic competition within the post-war democratic market economy. However, a strong connection between bureaucrats and business enterprises has remained.

Zaire

– *see* **Congo, Democratic Republic of**.

Zambia

This former British colony in southern Africa was a flourishing eighteenth- and nineteenth-century Arab and Portuguese slave trading base. From 1890 the **British South Africa Company** exerted control through local chiefs and in 1911 the country became Northern Rhodesia. The discovery of copper in the 1920s encouraged white immigration. In 1952 the country was absorbed into a Central African Federation but there were growing demands for British withdrawal from the United National Independence Party (UNIP) led by **Kenneth Kaunda** (1924–). Zambia gained independence in 1964 under Kaunda. His government nationalized the mining industry and in 1968 banned opposition parties. As economic problems mounted, Kaunda legalized opposition and in 1991 the Movement for Multiparty Democracy under Frederick Chiluba (1943–2011) defeated UNIP. He followed a programme of privatization and marketization. Western-oriented policies continued under Presidents Levy Mwanawasa (1948–2008), Rupiah Banda (1937–), Michael Sata (1937–2014) and Edgar Lungu (1956–). The population is overwhelmingly Christian. Agriculture and copper mining are the main economic activities.

ZANU (Zimbabwe African National Union)

Political movement established in Rhodesia in 1963 by the Reverend Ndabaningi Sithole (1920–2000) to gain black majority rule, subsequently led by **Robert Mugabe**. Outlawed in 1964, ZANU fought a guerrilla war until 1980 when Mugabe headed the first post-independence government. ZANU merged with the Zimbabwe African People's Union in 1987 to create ZANU-PF, the country's sole legal party. In 2008 ZANU-PF formed a power-sharing government with the Movement for Democratic Change.

Zanzibar

Semi-autonomous part of **Tanzania** which has come under Arab, Persian and Portuguese influence and was an important eighteenth- and nineteenth-century slave trading centre. The island became a British protectorate in 1890, gaining independence in 1963. In 1964 left-wing rebels overthrew the minority Arab ruling elite, establishing a republic. An act of union was signed with Tanganyika establishing the United Republic of Tanzania. Elements of the opposition Civic United Front presently advocate independence from Tanzania.

Zapata, Emiliano (1879–1919)

Mexican revolutionary hero. Born in Aneneculco, Morelos, Zapata demanded agrarian reform in the

Mexican Revolution. When President Francisco Madero did not redistribute **ejidos**, Zapata revolted. He later joined the constitutionalists to oust **Victoriano Huerta** and with **Pancho Villa** tried to engender a populist revolution. Venustiano Carranza contrived Zapata's assassination, but the 1917 constitution included his demands for land reform. Zapata remains a folklore hero who represents the rights, especially lands, of rural peoples.

Zeppelin

A type of airship or dirigible ('steerable') employed between 1900 and 1937 in Europe, and then on transatlantic routes. Zeppelins were named after their sponsor and inventor, Graf Ferdinand von Zeppelin, who based his 'rigid' aluminium-framed balloons, which were filled with hydrogen gas, on aircraft employed by French and American militaries as communication and reconnaissance devices after 1863. Zeppelins carried transport vehicles beneath the balloon and could be piloted by engines based upon propeller technology. The first true Zeppelin flew in 1900 at Bodensee, beside Lake Constance, and represented the first widespread form of commercial aircraft. Thirty-four specially developed versions were employed experimentally to bomb London between May 1915 and 1916. After **World War I** Zeppelins heralded a new era of luxurious commercial travel in the air until a series of horrible accidents related to the high flammability of their hydrogen–oxygen mix led to their displacement by fixed-wing aeroplanes. Improvements in technology, the rising cost of fuel, and survival as advertising vehicles led to a renewal of interest in Zeppelin technology in the twenty-first century.

Zhou Enlai (1898–1976)

Chinese Communist leader. Zhou was second only to **Mao Zedong** in the **Communist Party of China**. Born in Jiangsu province, he was elected to the politburo of the Chinese Communist Party in 1927. After 1949 he was foreign minister and premier of the State Council. He brought President **Nixon** and **Mao** together for their 1972 meeting that marked the beginning of rapprochement between the **USA** and **China**. In China, he was able to curb the worst excesses of the **Cultural Revolution**.

Zhou–Tanaka Communiqué (1972)

This was signed on 29 September 1972 and normalized relations between **China** and **Japan**. The communiqué was the result of a meeting between Chinese leader **Mao Zedong** and Japanese prime minister Kakuei Tanaka. Japan recognized that **Taiwan** was part of China, and expressed regret for damage done to the Chinese during the second **Sino-Japanese War**. The Chinese renounced any claims for war reparations from Japan and formal diplomatic relations were established.

Zia ul-Haq, Muhammad (1924–1988)

Appointed **Pakistan**'s chief of army staff in 1976 by the then prime minister, **Zulfiqar Ali Bhutto**. He staged a coup in 1977, overthrew Bhutto's government and subsequently imposed martial law in Pakistan, serving as chief martial law administrator and from 1978 president as well. Zia ul-Haq attempted to legitimate his regime through both limited elections and an Islamization process that impinged on women's and minority rights in particular.

Zia-ur-Rahman (1936–1981)

A hero of the Bangladesh Liberation War and president of **Bangladesh**. A major in the Pakistan Army, in 1971 he spearheaded a military revolt and declared the independence of Bangladesh. After a period of political unrest, he assumed the presidency in 1977. A charismatic and popular leader, he focused on developing the Bangladeshi economy and worked to forge international alliances. He was assassinated as part of a military coup.

Zimbabwe

Formerly the British colony of Southern Rhodesia administered by the **British South Africa Company**, the country became self-governing under white minority control in 1923. In 1965, reluctant to work towards majority African rule, the government made an illegal declaration of independence under **Ian Smith** (1919–2007). Two major African nationalist groups, the Zimbabwe African People's Union (ZAPU) (formed 1962) and the Zimbabwe African National Union (formed 1963) opposed the regime, conducting a guerrilla struggle known as the Second Chimurenga (war of independence). Following independence in 1979, **ZANU** leader **Robert Mugabe** (1924–) conducted initially cautious policies as prime minister. In 1987, ZAPU merged with ZANU to form ZANU-PF. In the same year Mugabe became executive president and became more active in his land redistribution policy. As economic conditions worsened, unemployment reaching 70 per cent at one point, Mugabe and ZANU-PF continued to win successive

much criticized legislative and presidential elections against a weak and intimidated opposition. The economy is based on agriculture and mining and the population is predominantly Christian, with small Muslim and Hindu minorities.

Zionism

– see also **state formation**.

The political movement founded by **Theodor Herzl** in the 1890s to establish a Jewish homeland, normally in Palestine, the 'promised land' of the Old Testament from which the Jews had been ejected by the Romans for persistent rebellion, AD 70. Zionism was a concept borrowed from the emerging European nationalist programmes of the time and thus had no precedent in the actual tradition which had given the Jewish people their lasting identity for millennia. This is not to say that political Zionism had no roots. **Napoleon** had wondered about establishing a Jewish state in **Palestine** and the British Jewish prime minister, **Disraeli**, had written *Tancred*, a Zionist novel. More specifically, Jewish groups in eastern Europe and the **Russian Empire** were trying to settle agricultural emigrants in then Ottoman Palestine in the latter part of the nineteenth century, and after the Russian pogroms of 1881 Leo Pinsker had written *Auto-Emanzipation*, a pamphlet appealing to western European Jews to lend those attempts their support.

On the other hand, the Jewish Colonisation Association, founded by the French Baron Maurice de Hirsch, aimed to settle Jews from the Russian Empire and **Romania** in **Argentina** and elsewhere in **Latin America**. The Haskala (Enlightenment) movement of the late eighteenth century had urged Jews to assimilate into western secular culture and in the early nineteenth century it was Christian millennarians rather than Jews who dreamed of a Jewish return to Palestine. Moreover, the linkage of nationality with territory was problematic for all peoples with a substantial diaspora and not just the Jews, and many favoured an alternative definition of nationality whereby members of a group would enjoy 'cultural autonomy' wherever they happened to live. Jewish Zionists were thus opposed by Jewish *Bundists* (covenanters). Nevertheless, although for Herzl personally the territory to be acquired by the Jewish people did not have to have historic Jewish links, the Basel programme of the first Zionist Congress, 1897, was specific that 'Zionism strives to create for the Jewish people a home in Palestine secured by public law.'

It was in the eighteen years following the publication of *Der Judenstaat* that the classical tradition of Zionist symbols, images and historical myths was essentially invented. The modern Hebrew language, which had only been invented in 1880 as a language for everyday use as distinct from a sacred tongue, it having passed out of such use in the days of the Babylonian captivity or even earlier, was developed, and *Hatikvah* (*The Hope*) with words by N. N. Imber, 1878, was adopted as the Jewish, and now Israeli, National Anthem by the first Zionist Congress, 1897. After Herzl's death, the Zionist Austro-German leadership moved from Vienna to Cologne and then to Berlin, although support was concentrated in the Russian Empire. The failure of the 1905 Revolution there stimulated emigration and by 1914 the number of Jews in Palestine had reached 90,000, with financial support in particular from the French Jewish Baron Edmond de Rothschild. Nevertheless, it remained a minority movement within the Jewish community.

The Zionists' opportunity came, as for many other nationalist agitators, with **World War I**. Two London-based Russian Jews, **Chaim Weizmann** and Nahum Sokolow, secured the **Balfour Declaration** from the then British foreign minister, A. J. Balfour, on 2 November 1917: a letter to the Zionist leader Lord Rothschild declaring that the British government would grant a home to the Jews in Palestine. The declaration had been deliberately vague so as to attract Jewish support during the war and to pre-empt a possible parallel German offer, whilst postponing any consideration of how such a homeland could be created in a country already populated by Arabs. It was assumed in any event that the number of immigrants would be comparatively small and Zionism had the added appeal to the British of being a means of keeping the French from being neighbours of the **Suez Canal**.

The **mandate** awarded over Palestine to Britain by the **League of Nations** after the war declared equally evasively that the immigration of Jews was to be permitted although the rights of the Arabs were to be respected. Nevertheless, it is generally agreed that, despite the Balfour Declaration, the Zionist movement declined sharply in popularity among Jews almost everywhere in the 1920s, perhaps because of the difficulty of integrating World War I experience into Zionism, and more certainly because of the dissolution of the Russian Pale of Settlement after 1917 and the rapid upward social mobility achieved by many immigrant Jews in **Britain** and the **United States** during the 1920s. The number of Jews in Palestine was nonetheless slowly rising. An estimated 108,000 in 1925 had reached 238,000, 20 per cent of Palestine's population, by 1933, and the immigrants made no secret of their ambition to create a Jewish national state. The resulting Arab riots of 1929 stimulated a British white paper of October 1930 concluding that Jewish immigration must effectively stop, and Zionism thereafter readily saw the British as the enemy. Immigration, however, continued, stimulated by the growth of European, and particularly German, **anti-Semitism** during the 1930s, provoking further Arab revolts in 1936–9 and a British royal commission under Lord Peel, which recommended, July 1937, that Palestine be partitioned into an Arab state, a Jewish state, and a British mandate for **Jerusalem** and Bethlehem with a corridor to the sea. A partition commission under Sir John Woodhead concluded, however, in 1938 that communal interpenetration made partition impracticable, and a further white paper of 1939 promised the end of Jewish immigration once another 75,000 Jews had been admitted over a five-year period.

The forces unleashed by **World War II** swamped all such deliberations. Within Palestine, two new Zionist para-military organizations were formed, Irgun Zvai Leumi and the Haganah, directed against British and Arabs alike. For many Zionists, however, the British remained the real enemy and the Stern Gang, acting for Haganah, assassinated Lord Moyne, the British Minister Resident in the **Middle East**, in November 1944. Nevertheless, the Labour Party, in office in Britain 1945–51, had traditionally been deeply committed to the Zionist cause and **Ben-Gurion**'s Zionist socialist party, Poale Zion, was affiliated to the Labour Party in Britain itself. On the other hand, Ernest Bevin, foreign secretary from 1945, was anxious for a settlement acceptable to both Arabs and Jews and had contempt for those political pressures in the United States which urged unlimited and immediate mass immigration.

An Anglo-American committee of inquiry report proposed, on 1 May 1946, the issue of 100,000 Jewish immigration certificates immediately and continued immigration thereafter, but rejected both partition and the definition of Palestine as either a Jewish or an Arab state. The blowing up by the Zionist Irgun, commanded by **Menachem Begin**, Israeli prime minister (1977–83), of the British headquarters in Jerusalem, the King David Hotel, on 22 July 1946, and US President **Truman**'s call, probably for domestic electoral reasons, for much more immigration than previously agreed, led the British to conclude that the Palestinian problem was insoluble, and to decide on 20 September 1947 to surrender the mandate and withdraw all troops by 1 August 1948. Their final withdrawal on 14 May 1948 was followed by Arab–Jewish war, the declaration by the Jews of the state of **Israel**, and the creation of 800,000 Palestinian Arab refugees. Zionism had triumphed at a still incalculable price.

Zululand

Also known as Kwazulu, the name given to the north-eastern part of Natal, **South Africa**. Technically independent until 1887, when it became a British protectorate and was annexed to Natal in 1897. The homeland of the **Zulus**, it was given a high degree of autonomy under the **apartheid** regime when it was designated a 'homeland' in an attempt to weaken support for the **ANC** with whom the Zulus were often in conflict.

Zulus

Warrior, Bantu-speaking people who became a powerful kingdom in south-east Africa under **Dingiswayo** (c. 1780–c. 1817) and King **Shaka Zulu** (c. 1787–1828). Shaka reorganized their military system and weaponry under his rule from 1816, establishing domination over a large part of Natal. His successor, Dingale (c. 1800–40), challenged the **Boers** on the **Great Trek** but was defeated at Blood River (December 1838). **Cetewayo**, a nephew of Shaka, was crowned king in 1873 and resisted British demands to establish a protectorate. Part of an invading British Army was annihilated at Isandhlwana on 22 January 1879, one of the most crushing defeats of a European power by native forces in the history of imperialism, giving the Zulus a reputation for military prowess which has persisted. Finally defeated at Ulundi in July 1879, Cetewayo was captured and **Zululand** made a British protectorate and annexed by Natal in 1897. A Zulu uprising against a poll tax in 1906 was ruthlessly suppressed and political representation only surfaced briefly in the 1920s through the cultural association, **Inkatha**, though soon forced underground. Under the **apartheid** regime Zulu identity was encouraged with the designation of

Zululand as a 'homeland' under the leadership of Chief **Buthelezi** as a rival to the **African National Congress**. The Inkatha Freedom Party participated in the first multiracial elections in April 1994, gaining approximately 10 per cent of the vote, mainly in Zululand, Buthelezi serving in President **Mandela**'s first government.

Zulu War (1878–1879)

The **Zulus** under **Cetewayo** ignored a British demand in December 1878 for the establishment of a British protectorate, largely originating from the High Commissioner for South Africa, Sir Bartle Frere, who saw Zulus as a threat to a South African confederation. Lord Chelmsford invaded **Zululand** in January 1879 but after initial successes divided his forces into separate columns to converge on the Zulu capital at Ulundi. One force was wiped out at Isandhlwana on 22 January 1879, though a heroic defence by 140 men at Rorke's Drift against 4,000 Zulus allowed Chelmsford to extricate his forces. A second invasion by Chelmsford in May 1879 led to a comprehensive defeat of the Zulus at Ulundi in July 1879 and the capture of Cetewayo by Chelmsford's successor, General Wolseley. Cetewayo was deposed and Zululand annexed as a British protectorate. There was widespread admiration for the courage and discipline of the Zulu forces, subsequently recognized in a memorial to the Zulu dead at Ulundi and commemoration of their prowess in film and literature.

Zwangendaba Kaziguda Jele Gumbi (c. 1785–1848)

King of the Ngoni people from *circa* 1815 until his death. After being driven north by the expansions of the **Zulus** during the *mfecane* in southern Africa, Zwangendaba led the Ngoni on a thousand-mile migration that lasted twenty years. Settling around **Tanzania, Mozambique, Zimbabwe** and **Malawi**, the Ngoni broke into several groups following Zwangendaba's death. During their migration, Zwangendaba used similar tactics as the Zulu King **Shaka** to bring his people together, including rigid military and social structures.